Reprints of Economic Classics

OFFICIAL CIRCULARS
OF
PUBLIC DOCUMENTS AND INFORMATION

Volumes VII-X

OFFICIAL CIRCULARS

OF

PUBLIC DOCUMENTS AND INFORMATION

DIRECTED BY THE

POOR LAW COMMISSIONERS TO BE PRINTED, CHIEFLY
FOR THE USE OF BOARDS OF GUARDIANS AND
THEIR OFFICERS

TEN VOLUMES IN TWO
Volumes VII - X

[1840 - 1851]

REPRINTS OF ECONOMIC CLASSICS

Augustus M. Kelley · Publishers
NEW YORK 1970

First Published 1840 - 1851

(London: Knight & Co., *90, Fleet Street,* Publishers
by Authority to The Poor Law Board, 1840-1851)

Reprinted 1970 by

AUGUSTUS M. KELLEY · PUBLISHERS

REPRINTS OF ECONOMIC CLASSICS

New York New York 10001

. . . .

S B N 678 00581 8
Vol II 678 04010 9

L C N 68 56565

. . . .

PRINTED IN THE UNITED STATES OF AMERICA
by SENTRY PRESS, NEW YORK, N. Y. 10019

OFFICIAL CIRCULARS

OF

PUBLIC DOCUMENTS AND INFORMATION;

DIRECTED BY THE

POOR LAW COMMISSIONERS AND THE POOR LAW BOARD TO BE PRINTED, CHIEFLY FOR THE USE OF THE BOARDS OF GUARDIANS AND THEIR OFFICERS.

VOLS. VII.—X.

LONDON:

KNIGHT & Co., 90, FLEET STREET,

Publishers by Authority to the Poor Law Board.

GENERAL INDEX

TO

VOLS. VII.–X.

OF THE

OFFICIAL CIRCULARS.

INDEX.

NOTE.—The numerals, VII., VIII., etc., refer to the No. of the Volume; and the Figures, 1, 2, etc., to the pages. The Nos. with a * affixed refer to pages in Vol. VII., where corresponding Nos. occur in the Volume.

B.

C.

INDEX.

INDEX.

STATUTES—continued.

Table of Statutes cited:—

STATUTES—continued.

Table of Statutes cited:—

STATUTES—continued.

Table of Statutes cited:—

STATUTES—continued.

Table of Statutes cited:—

INDEX.

VOLUME VII
[1847-1848]

VOLUME VII

AN

OFFICIAL CIRCULAR

OF PUBLIC DOCUMENTS AND INFORMATION:

DIRECTED BY THE POOR LAW COMMISSIONERS TO BE PRINTED, CHIEFLY FOR THE USE OF THE MEMBERS AND PERMANENT OFFICERS OF BOARDS OF GUARDIANS, UNDER THE POOR LAW AMENDMENT ACT.

No. 1.] CIRCULAR ISSUED JANUARY 1ST, 1847. [N. S.

THE Poor Law Commissioners directed that the following documents be printed and circulated for the information of Guardians and Officers of the several Unions, viz.

(Signed) By order of the Board,

EDWIN CHADWICK, *Secretary.*

I.—REMOVAL OF PAUPERS.

1. CIRCULAR LETTER TO BOARDS OF GUARDIANS DIRECTING ATTENTION TO THE 9 & 10 VIC. c. 66.

Poor Law Commission Office,
Somerset House,
September 17th, 1846.

SIR,—I am directed by the Poor Law Commissioners to call the attention of the guardians to the provisions of the new statute relating to the removal of the poor, (9 and 10 Vic. c. 66,) which received the royal assent on the 26th of August last, and came immediately into operation.

The statute relates to the removal of paupers, which depends upon their settlement; and does not, therefore, directly concern the guardians, who are engaged exclusively in the administration of relief. But indirectly the new provisions will materially affect the discharge of the functions of the guardians in the relief of the poor.

The guardians will perceive that the first four clauses prohibit the removal of paupers from the place of their residence under certain circumstances.

The first clause prevents the removal of every person from the parish in which such person has resided for the space of five years next before the application for the warrant of removal.

But in the computation of this period of five years, it is provided, that certain periods shall be for all purposes excluded. These periods are as follow:—

The time during which such person
shall be a *prisoner* in a prison;
shall be serving Her Majesty as a *soldier*, *marine*, or *sailor*;

or reside as an *in-pensioner* in *Greenwich* or *Chelsea* hospitals;

or shall be confined in a *lunatic asylum*, or house duly licensed, or hospital registered for the reception of lunatics;

or as a patient in a *hospital;*

or during which any such person shall receive *relief* from *any* parish;

or shall be wholly or in part maintained by *any* rate or subscription raised in a parish in which such person does not reside—not being a *boná fide* charitable gift.

There is a proviso to prevent the application of the Act to the removal of lunatics; and another to prevent the separation, in cases of removal, of husband and parent from a wife and children.

In reference to this clause it is incumbent upon the guardians to observe that the administration of relief to paupers, whether resident or non-resident, can have no important effect upon their removal hereafter, inasmuch as the time during which relief is so given is excluded in the computation of time.

By the operation of this statute, many persons now receiving non-resident relief, or who might hereafter receive non-resident relief, will become irremovable in the place in which they reside. Non-resident relief is given because the pauper, on becoming chargeable to the place where he resides, might be removed to the place of his settlement. In every case, therefore, in which a pauper becomes irremovable under this statute, no reason for continuing or for granting such non-resident relief will exist. The obligation to relieve rests upon the place where the pauper lives; and as he cannot be removed from that place, the ground in respect of which non-resident relief was originally given, or might have been granted, will wholly fail. On the other hand, paupers who have not resided in a place long enough to become irremovable, will remain liable to removal as before, and it will be necessary that the guardians should preserve the evidence of all payments made on account of any other parish or union; such evidence may be required hereafter to prevent the time during which relief was received from being reckoned in the time necessary to make the person irremovable.

The second clause prevents the removal of every widow resident with her husband at the time of his death, for twelve calendar months after his decease, provided she continues so long a widow. In this case, upon the same grounds as those above stated, the charge of the maintenance of the widow will be exclusively imposed for a year upon the place where she resided at the time of her husband's death. Consequently so long as she is in the same place, the place of her settlement, if different from the place of her residence, will, during that period, be relieved from that charge. The provision, therefore, has an important bearing upon the relief of non-resident poor.

The third clause prevents the removal of children, step-children, and illegitimate children from the parish in which they are residing with their parents, or reputed fathers, in every case where the parent, or reputed father, cannot be removed. This clause will, probably, not much affect the guardians, in regard to the execution of their duties.

By the fourth clause, the power of removing paupers, in cases where the relief is made necessary by sickness or accident, is taken away, unless the justices granting the warrant state in such warrant that they are satisfied that the sickness or accident will produce permanent disability.

The object of the clause is to prevent removals in cases of temporary sickness or accident. It will materially interfere, therefore, with the granting of suspended orders of removal; and will consequently remove the inducement for the allowance of non-resident relief in many such cases as those which have heretofore occurred. The paupers will have to be maintained by the parish where they are sick.

This provision will, probably, be found to have some bearing upon those cases of considerable practical difficulty, which arise in the relief of casualties, and the charging of the cost of such relief.

The Commissioners deem it right to call the attention of the guardians to the sixth section, which provides, that "if any officer of any parish or union do, contrary to law, with intent to cause any poor person to become chargeable to any parish to which such person was not then chargeable, convey any poor person out of the parish for which such officer acts, or cause or procure any poor person to be so conveyed, or give directly or indirectly any money, relief, or assistance, or afford or procure to be afforded any facility for such conveyance, or make any offer or promise, or use any threat to induce any poor person to depart from such parish; and if in consequence of such conveyance or departure, any poor person become chargeable to any parish to which he was not then chargeable, such officer, on conviction thereof before any two justices, shall forfeit and pay, for every such offence, any sum not exceeding five pounds, nor less than forty shillings."

The benefit of this clause, as calculated to repress much misconduct on the part of parochial and union officers in their endeavours to shift the burthen of charges of relief, is obvious. The Commissioners, therefore, request the guardians to take the earliest opportunity of communicating to all their officers the terms and effect of this enactment, and of impressing upon them the risk they will run, if they violate the provisions herein contained.

The guardians will perceive that it is desirable to call the attention of the master and other officers of the workhouse to the duty imposed on those officers by the seventh section, as to receiving paupers who may be brought to the workhouse, under warrants of removal directed to overseers; the section providing, that the delivery of any such pauper at the workhouse of the parish, or of any union to which such parish belongs, to any officer of such workhouse, is to be deemed a delivery of such pauper to the overseers of such parish.

The Commissioners recommend the guardians to give directions to the officers of the workhouse, especially the master and the porter, that when a pauper is brought to the workhouse with a warrant of removal, they should take the earliest possible opportunity of communicating the fact of his delivery at the workhouse to the overseers to whom the warrant is addressed.

I am, Sir, your obedient servant,
W. G. LUMLEY, *Assistant Secretary.*

---

2. CIRCULAR LETTER TO BOARDS OF GUARDIANS COMMUNICATING THE OPINION OF THE ATTORNEY-GENERAL AND THE SOLICITOR-GENERAL ON CERTAIN POINTS IN THE APPLICATION OF THE 9 & 10 VIC. c. 66.

Poor Law Commission Office,
Somerset House,
October 20th, 1846.

SIR,—I am directed by the Poor Law Commissioners to state that in consequence of various inquiries made of them as to the construction of the late Removal Act, 9 and 10 Vic. c. 66, they have deemed it right to consult the Attorney-General and the Solicitor-General upon certain points which appeared to be of most importance in the application of the statute.

The Commissioners think it may assist the guardians if they communicate to them the opinions which the Commissioners have obtained in answer to the questions which they submitted, and they have accordingly directed me to inform the guardians that the counsel above-mentioned are of opinion:—

1.—"That the proviso to the 1st section of the 9 and 10 Vic. c. 66, which sets forth the exceptions to the principal enactments that are to be excluded in the computation of time, is *not retrospective* in its operation, so as to apply to cases where the five years' residence was complete before the statute.

2.—"That an *interval* between the completion of the five years' residence and the application for the warrant of removal filled up by one of the exceptions contained in the proviso, *will not prevent* the operation of the statute in restraining the removal of the pauper who had resided for the specified time.

3.—"That orders of removal obtained previous to the passing of the Act, but not then executed by the removal of the paupers, *cannot* now be executed in cases where the 1st or 2nd section would have prevented them from being granted if the applications were made subsequently to the passing of the Act.

4.—"That the 2nd section does not apply to the cases of widows whose husbands *died before* the passing of the Act.

5.—"That the 4th section does apply to persons who became chargeable before the passing of the Act, and continued to do so till the application for the warrant.

6.—"That the statute applies *equally* to the removal of persons born in Scotland, Ireland, or the Channel Islands, as to persons having settlements in England, so as to override *pro tanto* the provisions of the 8 and 9 Vic. c. 117."

The Commissioners presume that the guardians will have no difficulty in applying these opinions to the parts of the statute to which they relate. They will see that according to the view taken by the high legal authorities above referred to, as to the effect of the first proviso, so far as it relates to the *time before the passing of the Act*, the simple fact of the actual residence of the pauper is alone to be considered, and consequently that no time during which the party may have been in the receipt of relief is to be omitted from the calculation of the term of residence, while any absence during that period, such as that caused by an imprisonment, or a residence in an hospital, is to be treated as an interruption of the continuous residence to which the statute applies.

With reference to the second question, I am to observe that although in terms it is confined to an interval between the completion of the residence and the application for the warrant, the Commissioners consider that the principle of the construction must equally apply to intervals in the time during which the period of residence is comprised, so that for example a residence of three years in a parish may be united with a subsequent residence of two years in the same parish, though in the interval the party may have been out of the parish in prison for several months, or serving Her Majesty as a soldier for several years; this observation is, however, to be qualified by the supposition that the absence is one which is protected by the proviso.

As some inquiries have been made upon the point, the Commissioners wish me to state that in the application of this statute no difference exists whether the cause arise between two parishes in the *same* union, or in *different* unions.

The Commissioners take this opportunity of impressing upon the guardians that though this statute does not create any *settlement* in regard to the parties rendered by it irremovable from a parish, such parties will be, in reference to the subject of relief, altogether in the same situation as settled paupers, and any difference in the treatment of the two classes of paupers settled, and paupers simply irremovable, with reference to the nature, quantity, or quality, of relief administered to them, cannot be too strongly censured as not being warranted by law, and as being at variance with every principle of fairness.

I am also to desire the guardians strictly to caution their officers against any attempt to procure the transfer from one parish to another of the parties whom this statute has rendered irremovable, by threats, or promises, or other inducements. The penalty imposed by the statute on such conduct has already been brought under the notice of the guardians by the Commissioners, in their letter of the 17th ultimo.

I remain, Sir,

Your most obedient servant,

W. G. LUMLEY, *Assistant Secretary.*

---

3. CIRCULAR LETTER TO BOARDS OF GUARDIANS RELATIVE TO THE RELIEF OF POOR PERSONS BECOME IRREMOVABLE BY THE OPERATION OF THE 9 & 10 VIC. C. 66.

Poor Law Commission Office,
Somerset House,
December 4th, 1846.

SIR,—The attention of the Poor Law Commissioners has been directed to certain cases in which it is alleged that relief has been either wholly refused or inadequately supplied by boards of guardians to poor persons, who, through the operation of the late statute relating to the removal of the poor, have now become irremovable from parishes in which they were resident, though settled elsewhere.

The Commissioners believe that this conduct has, in part, resulted from an erroneous supposition that poor persons, so circumstanced, are not intitled to relief in the parishes where they reside.

The Commissioners desire to impress upon the guardians, that a long course of authorities, consisting of legal decisions, and the opinions of the ablest text writers, upon this subject, has established the rule, that the poor are to be relieved, as their necessities require, in and by the parish where they are resident.

Indeed, the proposition that the poor who happen to be destitute in any particular place, are not to be relieved there by the officers who have the administration of the relief, until it is ascertained that they are settled there, or are casual poor, or that some other parish is under a legal liability to repay the relief, is so contrary to all established principles upon the subject, that the Commissioners have only thus adverted to it, because they are informed that such a doctrine has recently been circulated, and may have influenced some of the boards of guardians in their course of action.

The Commissioners have already, in their Circular Letter of the 20th of October last, pointed out, that no difference ought to be made in the treatment of the two classes of paupers settled, and paupers simply irremovable, with reference to the nature, quantity, or quality, of relief administered to them.

The Commissioners admit, indeed, that the cases of the non-settled poor may, for the most part, require to be carefully considered by the boards of guardians, who, by the operation of this statute, are called upon to relieve them, because it may be found that the relief heretofore supplied by a distant authority has been inapplicable, either in kind or quantity, to the party requiring it, or that the case has not been sufficiently investigated.

If, therefore, the guardians direct a careful inquiry to be made into the circumstances of the parties, and the actual necessities of the cases, with a view simply of satisfying themselves, as to the proper relief to be administered; and on receiving the result of such inquiry, proceed to administer the relief as they would do under similar circumstances, in respect to a settled pauper in their union, no objection can be made to their proceedings. But if any difference be made for the purpose of compelling the paupers, now irremovable, to seek relief in other parishes, it is clear that the course will be generally adopted by unions and parishes, as a matter of self-defence, and that great suffering and hardship to the poor must ensue.

There can be no doubt that such a course of proceeding is at variance with the spirit of the recent statute, which assumes that the irremovable poor, so long as their residence remains unchanged, will be relieved in the same manner, and on the same terms, as the settled poor.

I am desired to request the guardians to point out to the relieving officers the effect of these observations, and to warn them that the Commissioners will consider any neglect of the poor who may be resident within their respective districts, although not settled therein, equally culpable with the neglect of the settled poor, and will not hesitate to treat any refusal of relief to the irremovable poor, on the ground of their settlement elsewhere, as a gross violation of their duty.

The Commissioners wish to advert to one other point, namely,—the continuance of non-resident relief. In the observations which they have made in their Circular Letter of the 17th September last upon this subject, they have not advised the guardians to discontinue the relief in cases where the non-resident paupers are removable. They desire it to be understood, that they, by no means, recommended an indiscriminate withdrawal of such relief. They believe that the boards of guardians may find it desirable, in many cases in which the statute does not apply, to continue that relief; and the Commissioners do not consider that it would be unlawful for them to adopt this course, although it may not be advisable now to allow it, *for the first time*, even in cases where it would not be unlawful.

I have the honor to be, Sir,
Your obedient servant,
W. G. LUMLEY,
Assistant Secretary.

5

II.—POOR REMOVAL ACT.

1. THE ACT APPLICABLE TO PARISHES IN THE SAME UNION.

October 20th, 1846.

Mr. ———— *Bicester Union*—Inquired whether the provisions of the late Removal Act apply to parishes in the same union, or only to those in other unions; the practice of the guardians of the Bicester Union being to relieve paupers who live out of their parishes, in the places where they reside, and to charge the cost of such relief to the parishes to which those paupers respectively belong.

Ans.—The provisions of the late Act, 9 and 10 Vic. c. 66, apply equally to parishes in the same union as to parishes situate in different unions. Where, therefore, it would be improper, as between parishes in different unions, to grant non-resident relief to a pauper on the ground of the irremovability of such pauper, by the operation of the late statute, and the consequent release of the parish of the settlement from further liability to relieve, while the irremovability continues, it would be equally improper, as between parishes in the same union, to charge the relief to the parish in which the pauper does not reside: in other words, to the parish whereto no removal could be made.

2. RESIDENCE: HOW CONSTITUTED.

October 28th, 1846.

Vestry Clerk of Parish of St. George, Hanover Square—Requested the Commissioners' opinion on the following points, with reference to section 1 of the late Removal Act; namely,—1st. Whether the five years' residence must be consecutive to prevent removal. 2ndly. Whether the five years' residence must be the five years immediately preceding the date of the application for the order of removal. 3rdly. Whether, as the time during which the pauper has been in the receipt of parochial relief is not to be computed in the five years' residence, there must be five consecutive years' residence without receiving relief, &c., to entitle such pauper to the benefit of the clause conferring irremovability. 4thly. In cases where orders of removal have been made and executed, previous to the passing of the Act, and the paupers have been accepted and relieved by the parishes to which they were removed, but have returned to reside in the parish from which they were removed within the five years preceding the passing of the Act, are such paupers irremovable therefrom?

In answer, the Commissioners forwarded a copy of their Circular, communicating the opinions of the Attorney-General and Solicitor-General, upon some of the principal points which have arisen in the construction of the late Removal Act, and especially as to the meaning of the first clause; and stated that it resulted from those opinions, that in a case where the five years' residence was complete at the time the Act passed, and continues, irremovability attaches, notwithstanding the person was in receipt of relief during the whole, or any portion, of that time; for as the first proviso to the first section has not (according to those legal authorities alluded to) a retrospective operation, the time during which the poor person may have been in the receipt of relief prior to that date, is *not* to be omitted from the calculation of the term of residence. The Commissioners apprehended that in such a case, the residence must have been actually consecutive, and next before the application for the warrant of removal. An absence from the parish which would interrupt the continuity of the five years' residence, would defeat the operation of the statute. 2nd and 3rd. In a case to which the proviso does apply; that is, to a residence occurring since the passing of the Act, the residence (of five years) must be (actually or constructively) consecutive, and next before the application for the warrant of removal. It will be seen, from the Circular, that the Commissioners are advised by the Attorney-General and Solicitor-General, that, notwithstanding the existence of an interval between the completion of the five years' residence, and the application for the warrant of removal, if such interval be filled up by one of the exceptions contained in the proviso (as, for instance, the receipt of relief during that interval,) the pauper will still be irremovable. The result of this, as the Commissioners understand, is, that the words "next before," in the statute, do not (in a case to which the proviso is applicable) mean that the five years should be one unbroken period, occurring actually before the application for the warrant; but that a five years' residence, made up of broken or detached periods, the intervals between the periods being filled up by the receipt of relief, or any other of the exceptions named in the proviso, will be constructively continuous residence next before the application in the sense of the statute. 4th. The point involved in your fourth inquiry, is, as the Commissioners understand, whether the removal of a person, under an order of justices, operates as an interruption of the residence in the parish from which the removal takes place. The Commissioners are not prepared to say that this is necessarily the result, or effect, in all cases. Generally, it will occur that, where a pauper is removed from a parish, by an order, he changes his home and abode, and the residence is consequently broken. But there may be cases in which the pauper removed does not relinquish his home or domicile in the removing parish; for instance, the pauper may not continue in the parish of the settlement, but may return to his abode on the same day in which the order is executed, either with, or without, the sanction of the parish authorities. The Commissioners are disposed to think that, in a case of this description, if the residence occurring before and subsequently to the execution of the order should amount together to a period of five years, such residence, if it occurred prior to the passing of the late Act, would, notwithstanding the fact of removal, and the receipt of relief, during the second period, from the parish of the settlement, render that pauper irremovable. Where, however, it shall clearly appear, from the facts of the case, that the residence in the removing parish was determined upon the execution of the order of removal, there will appear to be no doubt that, on the return of the pauper, the residence subsequent to the return would not be added to the previous residence, so as to complete the period of five years, and render such pauper irremovable.

3. RESIDENCE—TEMPORARY INTERRUPTION OF BY REMOVAL UNDER AN ORDER.

November 7th, 1846.

Clerk of Henstead Union—E. D. who resided with her husband (now deceased) in the parish of Tasburgh, in the Depwade Union, nearly all her life, was, about two and a half years since, removed with her husband, by warrant of removal, to the parish of Bracon Ash, in the Henstead Union, and the man remained there twenty-four days, but the wife returned immediately to Tasburgh, and was joined by her husband after he left the Depwade Workhouse. They continued to reside at Tasburgh, and on her husband's death the widow applied for and received relief from Bracon Ash up to the passing of the Act of 9 and 10 Vic. c. 66, when it was discontinued, but she still remains at Tasburgh. Inquired whether the twenty-four days' residence of the husband in the Depwade workhouse was such an interruption of the widow's residence in Tasburgh as to render her removable to Bracon Ash.

Ans.—The only case now in question being that of the widow, the Commissioners think that her going to Bracon Ash under the order of removal and her immediate return, did not break the continuity of her residence in Tasburgh, and, consequently, that she is irremovable therefrom.

4. REMOVABILITY—INFIRMITY OF AGE.

November 7th, 1846.

Clerk of Henstead Union—Inquired whether a pauper of the age of seventy, resident for many years in one parish, during which he has been relieved by another parish, to which he belongs, and whose only disability is the infirmity of old age, is irremoveable under section 1 of the Removal Act; or whether his infirmity is such a sickness as produces permanent disability, so as to bring him within sec. 4 of the same act.

Ans.—Presuming the pauper, in the case put by you, still resides in the parish wherein he had resided for five years before the passing of the Act 9 and 10 Vic., c. 66, the Commissioners think he is now irremovable under section 1 of that Act. The Commissioners do not think that the infirmity of old age is a sickness to which the 4th section of the Act applies.

5. REMOVABILITY OF WIFE DESERTED BY HER HUSBAND.

Nov. 9, 1846.

Chairman of the Dulverton Union—Inquired whether a married woman, with a family, who has been deserted by her husband can be removed from the parish in which she has resided during the five years preceding the passing of the Removal Act.

Ans.—The Commissioners think that in the case referred to in your letter, as the husband is not in the parish in which his wife resides, he cannot be said to be removable from it, and consequently his wife and children cannot be removed from such parish by virtue of the 1st sec. of the 9th and 10th Vic. c. 66.

6. RESIDENCE INTERRUPTED BY A TEMPORARY ABSENCE IN AN INFIRMARY.

Nov. 11, 1846.

Clerk of Cockermouth Union—J. G., who had been resident, with his family, in the township of Papcastle for upwards of five years preceding the month of May last, became at that time chargeable to the township, on account of illness, and was sent to the Cumberland Infirmary in Carlisle, where he remained for several weeks, his family continuing to reside in the township of Papcastle. Subsequently an order was obtained for the removal of the man and his family to the township of Cockermouth, which order was afterwards abandoned. Inquired, whether the pauper is now removable from Papcastle to Cockermouth.

Ans.—The question in this case is, whether the abode in the infirmary necessarily broke the residence contemplated by the statute, 9 and 10 Vic. c. 66. There is no doubt that an abiding in an infirmary might, under certain circumstances, be such an interruption. The statute evidently contemplates such a case by the provision contained in the first proviso, but it is not necessarily an interruption. The Commissioners think that where a man quits his home in consequence of an accident, or sickness, and goes to an hospital for his cure, leaving his wife and family in the place of his former residence, and returns to it after a limited absence, it would not be held that the continuity of the residence had been broken. Consequently in the present case the Commissioners think that J. G. is now irremovable from the township of Papcastle, but not that he has become settled there.

7. THE DUTY OF BOARDS OF GUARDIANS TO CARRY THE ACT INTO EFFECT.

November 12*th*, 1846.

Clerk of Camelford Union—Inquired whether the guardians would be justified in neglecting to act on the statute 9 and 10 Vic. c. 66, in all cases where their acknowledged paupers have resided out of the Camelford Union for five years; or, in carrying out its provisions to the fullest extent in all cases of acknowledged paupers in the several parishes within the union.

Ans.—The Commissioners certainly consider the guardians of the Camelford Union would not be justified in neglecting to act to the fullest extent on the provisions of the above-named statute, in any case to which those provisions apply; whether the two parishes concerned in any such case be both within the union, or not. It is incumbent upon the guardians to administer and to charge relief, according to the law as it is expressed by the legislature; and they cannot properly dispense with, or disregard, the enactments of the statute in question, in consideration of any opinion they may entertain of its inexpediency, or in contemplation of its being altered at any future time. Nor are the guardians at liberty to pass any resolution, or give any direction, relative to the charging of relief, otherwise than in conformity with the law, which would prevent the auditor from investigating the legality of the charges in the accounts of the guardians, the union officers, or the overseers, and disallowing them where they are not made in conformity with the law.

8. REMOVABILITY OF WIFE DESERTED BY HER HUSBAND.

November 12*th*, 1846.

Mr. ———, *Sudbury Union*—H. C. deserted his wife and family five years ago, leaving them chargeable to the parish of Belchamp Otten, in which he is settled. His wife and family reside in the parish of Cavendish, where they lived during the five years immediatety preceding the passing of the Removal Act of last session. Inquired whether the woman and her family are chargeable to Cavendish parish, or whether they can be removed to Belchamp Otten.

Ans.—The wife and children of H. C. are not, under the circumstances mentioned by you, removable from the parish of Cavendish. The first section of the Act 9 and 10 Vic., c. 66, contains a proviso to the following effect: "Provided always that whenever any person shall have a wife or children having no other settlement than his or her own, such wife and children shall be removable, whenever he or she is removable, and shall not be removable whenever he or she is not removable." By this proviso, therefore, the woman and children cannot be removed, unless her husband be removable from the parish in which they are residing. But as he is absent from the parish, it does not appear that he is removable, consequently they cannot be removed; and their maintenance must be charged to the parish from which they are irremovable.

9. RESIDENCE—IRREMOVABILITY OF WIDOW.

November 14*th*, 1846.

Clerk of Plomesgate Union—A man and his wife lived together for two years in a parish in which they were not settled, and the man having died, the widow continued to live in the same parish for four years previous to the passing of the late Removal Act, and she still resides there. Inquired whether she is removable to the parish of her husband's settlement.

Ans.—The Commissioners think that the woman having resided above five years in the parish, is irremovable therefrom; the fact of her having been a married woman for a portion of the time, makes no difference in this respect.

10. REMOVABILITY—INTERRUPTION OF RESIDENCE.

November 14*th*, 1846.

Clerk of Radford Union—In October, 1845, J. J. and his wife became chargeable to the parish of Radford, where they had resided nearly twenty years, and the man was removed, under an order of justices, to the parish of Battle, in which he was settled, and admitted into the Battle Union Workhouse, wherein he subsequently died. His wife, who had absconded, in order that she might not be removed with him, afterwards gave up her residence in Radford, and went to reside at Collingham, near Newark, where she remained about ten days, and then returned to lodge with a daughter in Radford, to which parish she is now chargeable. Inquired whether the pauper is removable from Radford to the parish of her settlement.

Ans.—Under the circumstances mentioned by you, the Commissioners are of opinion, that the woman is removable to the parish of her settlement. If an application for a warrant for her removal were now made, the Commissioners think she could not, according to your statement of the case, establish that for five years next before such application, she had resided in Radford.

11. IRREMOVABILITY OF CHILD—RESIDENCE—RELIEF.

Nov. 14th, 1846.

——— Inquired, 1, whether residence under the late Removal Act in the case of a child begins to run from the date of the child's birth, or merely from the date of his or her attaining the age of sixteen years. Cases continually occur of orphans under sixteen years of age who have resided five years and upwards in one parish, although not with any of the relations named in sec. 3 of the Act. 2. Whether lodgers who reside in more than one house in a parish during the five years, are irremovable from that parish, under the provisions of the Removal Act. 3. On the 26th of August, when the Act passed, A. B. had lived five years, all but one month, in the parish of *C.*, where he is still residing, having of course now accomplished a five years' residence, but for the last six or seven months he has been, as he still is, in the receipt of relief. Inquired, whether A. B. is removable, under the 1st sec. of the Act.

Ans.—In reference to your first and second questions, whether residence under the Poor Removal Act begins from the date of a child's birth, or merely from the date of its attaining the age of sixteen years, I am to state that the Commissioners think a child falls within the term *person* in the 1st section; and if such child resides in a place for five years, whether that period commences at birth, or any other time, the child will become irremovable from the parish, subject to the last proviso of the section adverted to, namely, the removability of the parents. With respect to your second question, the Commissioners see nothing in the Act to confine the residence of a person to one house, or tenement, in the parish. It appears to the Commissioners to be sufficient if the residence be anywhere in the parish at large. As regards the case to which your fourth question relates, the pauper had not, it appears, on the passing of the Act completed a five years' residence, and the time which has elapsed since cannot be taken into account, because during that period he has been in receipt of relief. Consequently five years' residence has not been completed hitherto, and the pauper is removable to his settlement.

12. RESIDENCE — TEMPORARY INTERRUPTION BY REMOVAL UNDER AN ORDER.

November 21st, 1846.

Clerk of Cranbrook Union—In the year 1844, R. E., was, with his wife and family, removed under an order of justices, from the parish of Cranbrook to the parish of Hawkhurst; they returned to the former parish on the same day that they were removed. R. E. died in August last, having resided in Cranbrook upwards of five years, and his family still live there, and receive relief at the cost of the parish of Hawkhurst. Inquired whether the relief should be charged to Cranbrook or Hawkhurst.

Ans.—It appears from your statement of the case that, in point of fact, the widow's late husband resided five years in Cranbrook previous to his death, which was before the passing of the Act 9 and 10 Vic. c. 66. The Commissioners presume that his widow resided with him during that time; and, if so, she is now irremovable from Cranbrook, and her relief must be charged to that parish, according to the construction of the Attorney-General and Solicitor-General upon the statute.

13. DITTO.

December 5th, 1846.

Clerk of Cranbrook Union—Requested the Commissioners' reconsideration of the case of the widow of R. E., with reference to the fact of the man and his family having been actually removed from Cranbrook parish by an order of removal in the year 1844; the guardians being of opinion, as no time of absence is defined by the Removal Act, which would break the continuity of residence, that the removal, if even for one hour, under an order, and, therefore, against the will of the man, must be considered as destroying a residence of five years, next preceding the act.

Ans.—The statute, 9 and 10 Vic., c. 66, does not enact that an absence from the parish shall defeat the irremovability. It renders a person irremovable, who has resided in a parish for five years; and, unless a change of residence is effected by an absence from the parish (which, certainly, in numerous instances, would not be the case,) it cannot be laid down, as the Commissioners think, that any absence, whether voluntary, or involuntary, prevents the party from becoming irremovable. At the same time an absence for a day may be accompanied with a change of residence; and, then, the continuity, required by the Statute, would be broken. In the case, as described in your previous letter of the 11th ult., it was stated, that R. E. had lived at Cranbrook for upwards of five years before his death; and his widow had continued there since his death. It is true that *he* had been removed from Hawkhurst, but had returned the same day to Cranbrook. The Commissioners, in forming an opinion on the case, certainly assumed that he returned to the same home; and they conceived it to be difficult to say that, where a party had not slept out of the parish, he had resided out of it, having no home or abode elsewhere. If, however, in point of fact, he did give up his home and his furniture in Cranbrook, and returned afterwards to a different house, and obtained another home in Cranbrook after his return, the case might possibly be different, and there might then appear to be such a change of residence as would have broken the required continuity. Nevertheless, the Commissioners feel that this latter case is one of much difficulty, and they express their opinion upon it with hesitation. The question, moreover, is one to be decided by the justices, to whom an application may be made for an order of removal in the case.

14. DITTO.

November 23rd, 1846.

Clerk of Downham Union—E. S. who resided with her husband in the parish of Crimplesham for upwards of six years, and up to the time of his death, (in the year 1845,) was placed under an order of removal to the parish of Southery, in March, 1846, but the order was not executed in consequence of the latter parish admitting the pauper's settlement therein, and she therefore continued to reside at Crimplesham. Inquired whether the service of the order of removal and the admission of the parish of Southery that E. S. was settled therein, render her removable to that parish, under the Removal Act of last session. There are also in the union two other cases in which the paupers have, during the five years, been removed to the parishes of their settlement, under orders of justices, but returned to the parish from whence they were removed the same day; being afterwards relieved by the parishes to which they were removed. Inquired whether these paupers are irremovable.

Ans.—The Commissioners are of opinion, that in neither E. S.'s case, nor in the other cases to which you advert, has the residence for five years been broken; and that, consequently, the paupers are not removable from the parishes where they reside.

15. REMOVABILITY.

Nov. 25th, 1846.

Clerk of Stokesley Union—Requested the Commissioners' opinion upon the following cases with reference to the Removal Act of last session (9 and 10 Vic. c. 66);—namely, 1. H. S. a pauper having four children, and settled in Faceby, but resident at Whorlton, both in the Stokesley Union, was deserted by her husband about twelve months ago, and was then removed from the latter to the former place, under an order of justices, but she returned the same day, with her family, to her residence at Whorlton, where she had resided for more than five consecutive years prior to her removal. 2. E. B., a married woman, who has been separated from her husband for upwards of twelve years, and whose settlement is in Great Ayton, has resided at Stokesley ever since her separation, except for three or four weeks that she lived with her husband at Great Ayton, during which time she had never given up her residence at Stokesley, but had kept her furniture there. Her husband has lived at Great Ayton ever since his separation from his wife. 3. M. S., who is settled in Great Busby, but has resided at Great Ayton, for upwards of five years, was removed under an order of justices from the latter to the former place about three years ago, but returned to Great Ayton the same day. She has been relieved by Great Busby continuously for more than five years. 4. H. R., who is settled in Kildale, has a bastard child, eight years old, which has been brought up by its grandmother, at Great Ayton, for upwards of five years, during which time its mother has been in service, in another parish, in the receipt of one shilling per week, from the parish of Kildale, for the child's maintenance 5. H. F., belonging to the parish of Marton, in the Stokesley union, was transported for seven years, but returned about four years ago, to his family, who were, and had been from the time of his transportation, residing in the parish of Stainton, in the Stockton Union, where they still live. 6. J. C., an orphan, aged five years, who is settled in Seames, but has resided in Stokesley with his mother, (lately deceased,) ever since his birth, was admitted into the workhouse at Stokesley on the 31st of August last, at the cost of Seamer. 7. J. G., settled in Sexham, in this union, has been in the Stokesley workhouse for some years past, at the cost of Sexham, but his wife and family have resided at Hutton, also in this union, for more than five years successively. 8. R. P., an orphan, seven years old, born, and brought up by an aunt, at Stokesley, but settled and relieved by the parish of Leven, in the Beverley Union, has been in the habit of going to reside, for three or four months in each year, with another aunt in the Helmsley Union. 9. H. B., with two children, settled in and relieved by Whorlton, in this union, has resided with her father, at Kipwick, in the Thirsk Union, for more than five years. About a year ago her relief was discontinued, and she and her children were admitted into the Stokesley Union workhouse, where she remained for a few weeks, at the cost of Whorlton, and then returned to her father at Kipwick.

Ans. In the first case, that of H. S. and family, the Commissioners consider that she is, under the circumstances stated, irremovable from Whorlton, her removal from Whorlton to Faceby, by order of justices, did not interrupt the residence in Whorlton; and it appears that she has resided for five years successively in Whorlton. The case, therefore, falls within the principal enactment of sec. 1. of 9th and 10th Vic. c. 66; and although her husband, not having continued to reside, she will be removable if he return to the parish, yet at present, as he is not there, he is not removable from it, and she is not, therefore, liable to removal on this ground. In the second case, of E. B., it is to be observed that it is not stated at what period she went to live with her husband at Great Ayton. The Commissioners are, however, disposed to think that, on the supposition that this occurred within the last five years, E. B.'s residence in Stokesley was thereby interrupted. It is stated, indeed, that she did not give up her house in Stokesley, but kept her furniture therein, and that she returned to such house, having remained with her husband during three or four weeks only. Nevertheless, the Commissioners cannot but think that if the wife went to live with her husband, and did, in fact, live with him, his residence at the time must be taken to be her residence. The Commissioners think, as the facts are stated, however, that E. B. is irremovable from Stokesley, with reference to the last proviso to the 1st section of the statute, inasmuch as her husband does not appear to be removable, and, consequently, she is not so. In the third case, that of M. S., it appears that she has resided for the space of five years and upwards at Great Ayton, unless her removal to Great Busby, by order of justices, about three years since, interrupted such residence. The Commissioners think that, as the pauper returned the same day to Great Ayton, the residence in that parish was not broken by the mere fact of the removal. Then, if the pauper (as the Commissioners understand was the case,) resided in Great Ayton five years before the passing of 9th and 10th Vic. c. 66, the circumstance of her having received relief during the whole, or any portion, of such five years, from the parish of her settlement, would, according to the interpretation put by the Attorney-General and Solicitor-General, on the 1st proviso of the 1st sect. be wholly immaterial, so far as the question of irremovability is concerned, inasmuch as the proviso not being retrospective in its operation, the time would be reckoned notwithstanding the receipt of relief. In the fourth case, of H. R.'s illegitimate child, such child appears to be now irremovable from Great Ayton in consequence of the five years' residence. The case is not, however, one of those contemplated by the 3rd sec. of the statute, the grandmother not being one of the relatives therein mentioned. In the case of T. F., (No. 5,) it appears, from the statement, that he has not resided continuously, for the last five years, at Stainton, in which parish he is now resident. He is removable from Stainton; and his wife and family, by the operation of the last proviso of section one, are removable with him, notwithstanding that they have resided five years in Stainton. In the case of J. C., (No. 6,) it appears that he has resided at Stokesley from his birth, about seven years since; that on the 31st August last, he was admitted into the workhouse, in the parish of Stokesley, at the cost of the parish of Seamer. Under these circumstances, the Commissioners consider that J. C. is irremovable from Stokesley. The pauper has been in the receipt of relief since 31st of August last; that period, therefore, according to the 1st proviso, is to be wholly excluded in the computation of the period of residence. That period being so excluded, that is to say, being regarded as if it had not occurred, it results that the pauper has not been constructively resident in Seamer, since the 31st of August last (see sec. 56, 7th and 8th Vic. c. 101.) There was, therefore, an actual residence in Stokesley for five years, up to the 31st of August last, and the interval between that period and the present time, during which the pauper has been in receipt of relief, does not, according to the opinion of the Attorney-General and the Solicitor-General, break the continuity of that residence. The Commissioners observe that, as at the time of admission, being after the passing of this Act, J. C. was resident in Stokesley, and irremovable therefrom, the guardians had no authority to charge the relief to Seamer. In the case of J. G., (No. 7,) the Commissioners presume that the question refers to his wife and children. The Commissioners have to point out, therefore, that the last proviso to the 1st section applies to them, and they are now irremovable from Hutton, because the husband and father is not removable. He must be taken to reside in the place of his settlement, to which he is now chargeable, and consequently, no order of removal can be made; or, in the parish where the Union workhouse is situate, and as he is not chargeable thereto, no order of removal can be obtained. In the case of R. T., (No. 8,) the Commissioners are only able to say, upon the fact communicated, that there was no continuous residence in Stokesley, such as is necessary to create irremovability under the 1st section. In the case of H. B., (No. 9,) the Commissioners are disposed to think that the continuity of the pauper's residence in Kipwick was broken when she went into the workhouse at Stokesley, and remained there a few weeks with her two children. It does not appear that she had any home, or a house, of her own at Kipwick, but that her father's house was her home, while she lived with him; consequently when she left him she changed her residence. Nevertheless, the Commissioners cannot express any confident opinion on this case.

---

16. RESIDENCE: REMOVABILITY.

November 26th, 1846.

Clerk of Stroud Union—Requested the Commissioners' opinion on the following points, with reference to the removal act; namely,—1st. Whether the five years' residence must be the five consecutive years immediately preceding the passing of the Act; or, whether three years' residence in parish A., three years' residence in parish B., and then two years' residence in the former parish, make a pauper irremovable therefrom.—2ndly. Whether a pauper who had resided three years in parish A., and was then removed to parish B., by order of justices, but returned on the same day to the parish from whence he was removed, and resided there for two more years before the passing of the act, is irremovable therefrom.

Ans.—1st. The five years' residence, previous to the passing of the Act, must, in order to render a pauper irremovable, have been continuous. A residence of three years in a parish, interrupted by a residence for any time elsewhere, and followed by a residence of two years in the same parish, will not confer the irremovability provided for by the statute. In the second case stated in your letter, the departure of the pauper from the parish under the order of removal, does not appear to have interrupted the continuous five years' residence in that parish, and, therefore, the pauper is irremovable.

---

17. RESIDENCE: TEMPORARY INTERRUPTION OF.

Nov. 30th, 1846.

Clerk of Pateley Bridge Union—Inquired, whether a residence of a few weeks, or a few days, out of any township, during the five years preceding the passing of the Removal Act, will render the person, who may have so resided for this short time, removable or not; and whether the removal of any person to his legal settlement, under an order of justices, within the same period, will render such person removable; if he have returned immediately after his removal to the place of his former residence; also whether a man and his family are removable from the township where the family have resided for five years, the man having resided there only occasionally during twelve months of that time.

Ans.—If a party actually reside out of any parish, though for a few days during the five years, the party will be removable therefrom; but there must be an actual change of residence,—a giving up of the home in one parish,—and seeking another in a different parish. A removal under an order may, therefore, be a breaking of the five years' residence, or not, according to circumstances. If the pauper, though removed, immediately returns to his former home, which he had retained during his absence, the Commissioners think the continuity of the residence is not broken. With regard to the further question in your letter, I am to state that the wife and child of a man are not removable when he is not removable; and if, in the case put by you, the man is not in the township in which his wife and family reside, they cannot be removed from such township. See the last proviso to the first section of the 9th and 10th Vic. c. 66.

18. DITTO.

Dec. 1, 1846.

Clerk of Bedale Union—A. A. legally settled in the parish of Burrill, in the Leyburn Union, has resided for many years in the parish of Crakehall, in the Bedale Union, but has received relief from the former parish until recently. During part of the years from Midsummer to Martinmas, (1844 and 1846,) she left her cottage at Crakehall, and went to reside at Northallerton and elsewhere, and her cottage during part of those periods was occupied by another person. Inquired, whether these absences from the parish of Crakehall, during a part of the five years next preceding the passing of the Removal Act of last session, render A. A. removable from that parish to the parish of Burrill.

Ans.—Looking to the facts of the case, as represented by you, namely, that A. A. went to reside at Northallerton, and remained there from Midsummer to Martinmas, 1844, and that in the course of the present year she left Crakehall for a period of nearly seven months, it seems to the Commissioners that she is removable from Crakehall, as the continuous residence of five years, which would have rendered her irremovable, has been broken by her residence out of that parish.

19. RESIDENCE: TEMPORARY INTERRUPTION OF BY REMOVAL UNDER AN ORDER.

Dec. 1*st*, 1846.

Mr. ———— *Pontefract Union*—A person who resided a number of years in the township of Ferrybridge, was two or three years since removed to his legal place of settlement; but at the expiration of a few weeks or months returned to that place, where he still resides. The officers of the parish to which he was removed, now refuse to relieve him, on the ground that he has resided five years in the township of Ferrybridge. Inquired, whether the person alluded to is irremovable from that township, and whether the time during which he resided there previous to his removal can be added to the time of his residence since his return, so as to complete the five years' residence required by the first section of the Removal Act to render a pauper irremovable; or whether there must be a five years' residence subsequent to the execution of the order of removal.

Ans.—The question in the case submitted to the Commissioners in your letter depends upon whether, when the pauper alluded to was removed from the township of Ferrybridge, he actually changed his residence, that is, whether he gave up his home in the township from which he was removed, and returned afterwards to another home. If so, the five years' residence, to which the first sec. of the late Removal Act applies, was broken, and the pauper is now removable from the township of Ferrybridge. If the pauper did not give up his home but retained it while away, and returned to it after the short interval mentioned in your letter, there does not appear to have been an interruption of the residence in his case, and the Commissioners are of opinion that the pauper is irremovable under the section above referred to.

20. RESIDENCE: INTERRUPTION OF.

Dec. 1, 1846.

Clerk of Shardlow Union—W. W. belonging to parish A., resided in parish B., for ten years up to the month of July, 1844, when he deserted his wife and family, and went to a distant part of the country, and did not return to parish B. until April, 1845. During the time he was absent four of his children were admitted into the workhouse at the cost of parish A., but his wife refused to accompany them, and she, with one child, remained in parish B. Inquired, whether the pauper and his family are removable from parish B. to parish A.

Ans.—The Commissioners are of opinion, upon the facts stated in your letters, that W.W. has not resided for the last five years in the parish of B., and that he is, therefore, removable therefrom to his place of settlement.

21. RESIDENCE: TEMPORARY INTERRUPTION OF—BY REMOVAL UNDER ORDERS.

Dec. 4*th*, 1846.

Clerk of Cirencester Union—Some time prior to the passing of the late Removal Act, certain paupers who had resided in the Cirencester union for upwards of five years, were removed, under orders of removal, to a parish in a distant union, but afterwards returned, and henceforth continued to receive an allowance of relief from the union to which they had been removed up to the passing of the Act. Inquired, whether the circumstances of the removal (if the five years' residence were otherwise complete) would destroy the irremovability, and whether in determining a residence in future under the Removal Act the term of five years must be completed from the pauper's return to the union from whence he has been removed.

Ans.—The circumstance of the removal of a pauper does not, in the opinion of the Commissioners, conclude the question of the continuity of such pauper's residence in the removing parish, since it appears to the Commissioners that the question depends, in each case, upon the fact whether, upon the removal, a change of residence took place. If, indeed, the home of a pauper be broken up on his removal, the Commissioners think there will be, in general, evidence of a change of residence; whereas, if the former home be retained, and the pauper returns to it, it will be found, generally, that there has not been a change of residence.

22. RESIDENCE—IRREMOVABILITY.

December 4th, 1846.

Mr. ———— *Chepstow Union*—T. E. and his wife and family, came to reside in the parish of Alvington, in the Chepstow Union, in September, 1840, and in a few weeks became chargeable, and were afterwards relieved by the parish of Brynwyn, in the Abergavenny Union, (in which he was settled,) and continued to receive relief from that parish until his death, in July, 1846. His widow E. E. and her children, were then allowed weekly relief by Brynwyn, which was continued up to the 11th November last, when the Abergavenny Union discontinued it; and the family were ordered relief by the guardians of the Chepstow Union, at the cost of the parish of Alvington, under the impression that the five years' residence of the family in that parish, had rendered them irremovable therefrom. Inquired whether E. E. and her family are removable from Alvington to Brynwyn.

Ans.—E. E. under the circumstances mentioned in your letter, appears to the Commissioners not to be removable from the parish of Alvington, in which she resided for five years previous to the 26th of August last, (the date of the passing of the 9 and 10 Vic., c. 66,) and in which she continues to reside. She must, accordingly, be relieved at the cost of Alvington, so long as she resides therein.

23. RELIEF TO IRREMOVABLE PAUPERS NOT CHARGEABLE TO SETTLEMENT PARISHES.

December 5th, 1846.

Clerk of Tendring Union—Referred the Commissioners to the cases of Rex *v.* St. Giles in the Fields, Rex *v.* Saxmundham, and other cases, and inquired whether, considering the imperfect wording of the Act 9 and 10 Vic., c. 66, an order could not be made upon the settlement parishes of irremovable paupers, to maintain such paupers in the parishes where they reside.

Ans.—The Commissioners are of opinion, that there is no authority for charging the relief of a pauper, irremovable by virtue of the new statute, upon the parish in which such pauper is settled, but does not reside. It is true that some old cases are to be found, which supported orders by justices upon parishes for the maintenance of children under the age of nurture. The Commissioners believe that those orders were framed upon the equity of the Statutes 43rd Elizth. c. 2, 3rd Wm. 3. c. 11, sec. 11, and the 9th Geo. 1, c. 7, which enabled justices to make orders for relief of paupers. They can find no other authority for them. And the 4th and 5th Wm. 4, c. 76, sec. 54, now prevents justices from making any order for the relief of the poor, except in particular cases of urgency, and where there are no guardians or select vestry. Now, various authorities establish that the poor are to be maintained by the parish in which they reside; see 2 Nol. c. 34, Clypton St. Mary, *v.* Roristock, sett. cases 49, K., *v.* Chadderton, 2 East, 27; and, upon this ground, the relief given to a pauper, by the parish in which he resides, has always been considered as affording no evidence against the parish so relieving, of any settlement therein. Then, if the parish is bound to relieve the pauper residing in it, how can it be reimbursed that relief? No statute gives any power to justices, or to any one else, to make any order for such reimbursement, except the provision in the 4th and 5th Wm. 4, c. 76, sec. 84, which only applies to cases where a settlement has come in question, and has been adjudged, or admitted, between the parishes; and that must be, as the Commissioners think, after an order of removal has been obtained. In that case, indeed, relief given after the notice of chargeability has been served, may be recovered. If it could have been shown that any order could have been made upon a parish, to reimburse the parish of the residence, the ordinary order of removal would have been superseded. In a late case, Queen *v.* Justices of Radnorshire, 10 Jur., 785 and 15 L. I. R., (n. s.) m. c. 151, where a parish had been compelled to pay the charges for the relief of a lunatic, on an order which was quashed, the Court of Q. B. refused to grant a *mandamus* to the treasurer of the county to reimburse the parish, and the chief justice compared it to the case of an application by a parish to be reimbursed for the relief of casual poor, against the parish of the settlement, and said there was no authority for such application. Now, paupers irremovable under the present law, are in the same condition in this respect as casual poor. The Commissioners have, therefore, come to the conclusion, that no justices' order, or other authority, can be obtained against the parish of settlement, in favour of the place in which the pauper resides, but from which he is now irremovable.

---

24. RESIDENCE—WHETHER INTERRUPTED BY TEMPORARY ABSENCE.

December 7th, 1846.

Mr. ———— *Woodstock Union*—A pauper, belonging to the parish of Middle Aston, has resided in the parish of Steeple Aston for nine or ten years next before the passing of the Act 9 and 10 Vic., c. 66; but during the five years next before the passing of the Act, left Steeple Aston, for the purpose of visiting a relative, at a distance, and was absent several weeks, during the whole of which time he retained and paid for his lodgings in Steeple Aston, where he kept his bed and part of his clothes. Inquired to which parish the relief granted to the pauper should be charged.

Ans.—If the pauper, to whom you refer, changed his residence when he quitted the parish of Steeple Aston, he is now removable to the parish of his settlement, though he must be maintained by the parish where he now resides, until such removal; but if he did not change his residence, he would not be removable, and must continue to be relieved at the cost of the parish in which he lives. Upon the facts, as stated in your letter, the Commissioners are disposed to consider, that there was no change of residence in this case.

---

25. DITTO.

December 8th, 1846.

Clerk of Stourbridge Union—A pauper living in the parish of A. for more than five years, was about four years ago removed by an order of justices to the parish of B., in which parish she remained about a week, but returned to the parish of A. and was relieved there by the parish of B. till within the last month, when the relief was stopped. She then applied to the parish of A. and received relief therefrom. Inquired whether the pauper can be removed to the parish of B.

Ans.—The statute 9 and 10 Vic. c. 66, does not enact that an absence from the parish of the pauper's residence shall defeat his irremovability. The act renders a person irremovable, who has resided in a parish for five years, and the Commissioners think that such residence will not be necessarily interrupted by every absence from the parish, whether voluntary or involuntary, whether long or short, but that the question to be considered in each case is, whether a change of residence is effected by such absence. It appears to the Commissioners that an absence for a week, therefore, might readily occur, without a change of residence; while, on the other hand, an absence for a day might be accompanied by such a change of residence as would break the continuity which the statute requires. The Commissioners desire to observe, that they do not consider the mere fact of the pauper's absence from the parish having occurred in consequence of her removal under an order of justices, to be of itself conclusive as to her residence having been changed or interrupted. If she did not give up her home in the parish from which she was removed, but retained it, and returned to it after her removal, the Commissioners think that, notwithstanding her removal under the justices' order, and her absence for a week, she did not in fact break off her residence in the parish. If, however, she did give up her home on leaving the parish, and commenced a new residence therein on her return, it appears to the Commissioners that the case would be different.

26. RESIDENCE—WHETHER INTERRUPTED BY TEMPORARY STAY IN WORKHOUSE.

December 10th, 1846.

Clerk of Billericay Union—R. B. has had a house in Great Burstead for fifteen years, in which his wife and family have constantly resided, and for the first ten years he lived wholly with them; but during the remaining five years he has been residing with his family part of each year, and the remaining part he has been in the union workhouse (situated locally in Great Burstead,) at the cost of Brentwood, in which parish he is settled. He now applies for an order for the workhouse, which has been granted him; but the guardian of Brentwood objects to the pauper's relief being charged to that parish, as he considers his residence in Great Burstead has rendered him irremovable therefrom. Inquired whether the pauper's occasional residence in the workhouse during the last five years prevents the operation of the statute.

Ans.—The answer to this question depends upon the consideration, whether or not the pauper is now irremovable from Great Burstead. If he be irremovable, that parish would be clearly liable for the relief. If otherwise, that parish would only be liable for the relief, until they caused the pauper to be removed to his settlement. The Commissioners do not collect from the statement that the pauper, prior to his recent application for relief, had, in construction of law, resided in the parish of Great Burstead for the period of five years without interruption. It is true that the pauper had, with his family, occupied a house in Great Burstead for the period of fifteen years, and that during the last five years of such period he was either living with his family at his own house, or he was in the union workhouse, which is situate in Great Burstead. It seems too, from the statement, that he was relieved in the workhouse for an average period of five months in each year, returning to his own home on each occasion of his discharge from the workhouse. This relief was charged to the parish of settlement, Brentwood. The 56th sec. of 7 and 8 Vic. c. 101, enacts, "that for the purposes of relief, settlement, and removal of poor persons, and the burial of the poor, the workhouse of any union or parish, &c., &c., shall be considered as situated in the parish to which each poor person respectively to be relieved, removed, or buried, or otherwise concerned in any such purpose, is or has been chargeable." Now the effect of that section upon the present case appears to the Commissioners to be this. The pauper while in the workhouse was, in contemplation of law, resident in Brentwood for the purposes of relief and removal; while such constructive residence lasted he was not residing in the parish of Great Burstead, and consequently the continuity of the residence in the latter was broken. The Commissioners do not wish to be understood as expressing the above opinion confidently; and they still feel some doubt, whether, notwithstanding the constructive residence in Brentwood, the pauper might not also be considered to be resident in Great Burstead, from the circumstance that he retained his house there during the whole period in which his wife and family resided, and to which home he was in the habit of returning. Upon the whole, however, the Commissioners do not see any sufficient authority for holding that, for the purposes of 9th and 10th Vic. c. 66, a person can be regarded as having an actual place of residence, and a constructive place of residence, at one and the same time.

27. IRREMOVABILITY OF THE WIFE OF A PERSON WHO IS TRANSPORTED.

December 26th, 1846.

Chairman of Rhayader Union—About seven years ago, a parishioner of Llandewi, in the Knighton Union, was transported, upon which his wife removed into the parish of Nantmel, in the Rhayader Union, where she continued to reside until a few weeks ago, and received relief from the former parish, which has now been discontinued in consequence of the passing of the 9 & 10 Vict., cap. 66, and she has become chargeable to the parish of Nantmel. Inquired whether she is removable therefrom to the parish of Llandewi.

Ans.—As the husband of the woman referred to, is not removable from Nantmel, by the operation of the third proviso to section 1 of the 9 & 10 Vict., cap. 66, the woman herself is not removable, and consequently must be relieved at the charge of that parish.

LONDON:
Printed by order of the Poor Law Commissioners, by BLACKBURN and PARDON, 6, Hatton Garden, and Published by CHARLES KNIGHT and Co., 22, Ludgate Street, Publishers to the Poor Law Commissioners.

AN

OFFICIAL CIRCULAR

OF PUBLIC DOCUMENTS AND INFORMATION:

DIRECTED BY THE POOR LAW COMMISSIONERS TO BE PRINTED, CHIEFLY FOR THE USE OF THE MEMBERS AND PERMANENT OFFICERS OF BOARDS OF GUARDIANS UNDER THE POOR LAW AMENDMENT ACT.

No. 2.] CIRCULAR ISSUED FEBRUARY 1, 1847. [N.S.

Poor Law Commission Office,
Somerset House,
February 1, 1847.

THE Poor Law Commissioners directed that the following documents be printed and circulated for the information of Guardians and Officers of the several Unions, viz.

(Signed) By order of the Board,
EDWIN CHADWICK, *Secretary.*

I.—REMOVAL OF NUISANCES.

1. CIRCULAR LETTER TO BOARDS OF GUARDIANS, DIRECTING ATTENTION TO THE 9 AND 10 VIC., c. 96.

Poor Law Commission Office, Somerset House,
October 8*th*, 1846.

SIR—I am directed by the Poor Law Commissioners to bring under the notice of the guardians the provisions of the Act passed in the last session of parliament for the more speedy removal of certain nuisances, 9 and 10 Vic. c. 96, conferring certain powers upon the guardians, in respect of such matters.

The statute in section 1, after reciting that it is highly expedient for the purpose of preserving the health of divers of Her Majesty's subjects that better provision should be made for the removal of certain nuisances likely to promote or increase disease, empowers any town council, or other like body having jurisdiction within any corporate town, borough, city, or place, or any trustees or commissioners, or other like officers acting under the provisions of any act of parliament for the drainage, paving, or cleansing, or managing, or directing the police in any such place, or for any of the above purposes, *or in case* there shall be *no such town council* or other like body, *or no such trustees* or commissioners having jurisdiction, or acting as aforesaid, in any town, borough, city, or place, the guardians of the poor, (upon receipt of a certificate in writing, to the effect therein set out, signed by two duly qualified medical practitioners, *of the filthy and unwholesome condition of any dwelling-house, or other building, or of the accumulation of any offensive or noxious matter, refuse, dung, or offal, or of the existence of any foul or offensive drain, privy, or cesspool,*)

To lay a complaint before any two justices of the peace—who are to summon the owner or occupier of the premises before them.

And it requires the justices, upon proof to their satisfaction, of the existence of the nuisance,

Forthwith to make an order in writing, to the effect therein described, for the cleansing, whitewashing, or purifying of any such dwelling-house, or other building, or for the removal or abatement of the nuisance within a period, and in the manner therein prescribed;—

Which order, or a copy thereof, shall be forthwith served upon the owner or occupier, or if there be no such owner or occupier, or if the owner or occupier cannot be served, a true copy thereof shall be forthwith affixed upon some part of the premises.

If the nuisance be not removed, the persons who made the complaint, and who shall be authorised by the justices so to do, by themselves, their servants, and others, may enter the premises, to cleanse them, or to remove or abate the nuisance, described in the order.

Any person wilfully obstructing any person acting under the authority and in pursuance of the order, will be liable to a penalty not exceeding £10, nor less than £2.

Section 2, enables the persons who make the complaint, to recover the costs and expenses which they incur, from the owner or occupier, by summary proceedings before two justices, unless the justices think fit to excuse the party charged, on the ground of poverty or other special circumstances.

The term *guardians*, used in the first section, as explained by an interpretation clause, (sec. 17,) is to signify the guardians, directors, wardens, governors, or other like officers, having the management of the poor for any *union*, parish, township, hamlet, or place, *where the matter* requiring the cognizance of any such officers as aforesaid, respectively, *may arise.*

The above provisions, therefore, authorise the guardians of any union or parish where there is no town council, nor public trustees, or commissioners, to take the steps for the removal of the nuisances referred to. The guardians, adverting to the object of the legislature and the purport of the act, may properly cause inquiries to be forthwith made by the relieving officers, or others, as to the condition of those parts of the union where they have reason to expect that the nuisances and unwholesome dwellings and premises, to which the statute applies, are to be found; and if any cases of serious extent, calculated to produce injurious or mischievous consequences, are found, and the guardians cannot by urgent remonstrance with the proper parties, procure the removal of the nuisance or the cleansing of the premises, they will act most advisedly by proceeding forthwith under the powers and authorities of this act, bearing in mind the limitation which exists as to the places where they are empowered to interfere.

A provision somewhat similar to the present, restricted however to the metropolis and its neighbourhood—will be found in the 2nd and 3rd Vic. c. 71, § 41, (the metropolitan police act;) but it only authorised the guardians to cleanse the premises at the *cost of the occupier*, and as the occupiers of such premises are seldom in such a condition as to enable them to pay the costs of such cleansing, the provision has proved inoperative.

Although it is provided that the guardians shall recover the costs and expenses which they may incur, from the owner or occupier who may not be excused as above mentioned, yet to avoid any question as to the charge of those costs, it is enacted in section 13, that—

"*All expense* reasonably and properly incurred in carrying into effect any of the provisions of the act relating to the cleansing of houses, or the removal of nuisances, *and not recovered from the owners or occupiers*, shall be retained or defrayed out of the rates or monies raised or *contributed* for the relief of the poor of the parish, or extra-parochial place, maintaining its own poor, in which the same shall have been incurred."

The statute then requires two justices to order the treasurer of the guardians, or other officer of the union or parish, or the overseer of the parish in which any such expense has been so incurred, to pay the sums expressed in any such order, out of any monies which may come into his hands by virtue of his office; and this order may be enforced summarily by distress under a warrant of two justices.

It will thus be seen that all the expenses which may be reasonably and properly incurred in this matter, whether by the guardians or the other parties entitled to take the steps under the act, if not recovered from the owner and occupiers, are to be paid out of the poor rates of the parish in which they were incurred, which will be of course that in which the nuisance existed.

The Commissioners trust that no apprehension of casting a charge upon the parish will operate to induce the guardians to abstain from proceeding under the act in cases of urgency. The improvement of the sanitary condition of the poorer classes tends so greatly to remove many of the causes of destitution and pauperism, that the money judiciously expended on such an object, now sanctioned by the legislature in the cases to which the statute applies, will be found to be most profitably laid out even in reference to the more direct object of the duties of the guardians.

I am to notice that the statute having used the term *owner*, which has no technical meaning, proceeds in section 14, to define the term as signifying "the person receiving the rents of any property from the occupier thereof on his own account, or as trustee or agent for any other person."

Where an owner occupies his own property he falls under the term *occupier*, and may be proceeded against as such.

I am, Sir, your obedient servant,

W. G. LUMLEY, *Assistant Secretary.*

To the Clerk to the Guardians.

2. POWER OF GUARDIANS TO APPOINT INSPECTOR OF NUISANCES UNDER.

Dec. 7th, 1846.

Clerk of Hinckley Union—A short time since the guardians adopted the provisions of the Nuisances Removal Act, and appointed their clerk to act as inspector of nuisances, with directions to visit, inspect, and report upon all cases of nuisance that came within his knowledge, and to act on behalf of the guardians in carrying out the provisions of the act. The performance of these duties has been found to be attended with expenses for horse hire, tolls, assistance, &c. Inquired whether these expenses should be paid out of the poor rates, and charged to the establishment, or upon what other fund should they be charged.

Ans.—The Commissioners are not acquainted with any authority which the board of guardians have to appoint an inspector of nuisances, or to direct a person to ride round the district to search for nuisances. The Commissioners are, therefore, not aware of any lawful authority for the guardians charging the expenses referred to on any fund under their control. The Commissioners, in the circular which they have issued, having reference to the act relating to the removal of nuisances, advised the guardians as to what they thought the proper course for carrying out the provisions of the statute in regard to enquiries, which, if observed, would not have involved any expense.

3. FEE TO MEDICAL MEN FOR CERTIFICATES.

October 24th, 1846.

Clerk of Louth Union—Inquired whether any, and what, fee may be given to medical practitioners, for furnishing certificates, under the 9 & 10 Vic. c. 96, by order of the board of guardians; and if the medical practitioner is a medical officer of the union, and is directed by the board to give such certificate, whether he will be entitled to any and what fee.

Ans.—The 9 and 10 Vic. c. 96, is wholly silent on the subject of remuneration to the medical practitioners. If they originate the matter, which they apparently can do under the statute, they cannot claim any remuneration for their trouble. If the medical men are employed by the guardians, or by any other body, to make the examination, and to give the certificate, they will be entitled to a reasonable compensation. The Commissioners cannot state what should be the amount of such compensation. The Commissioners cannot require the medical officer of the union to give any such certificate by reason of any duty imposed upon such officer.

4. WHETHER THE ACT APPLIES TO OTHER PLACES THAN CORPORATE TOWNS.

November 10th, 1846.

Clerk of Sedbergh Union—Application has been made to the guardians to take proceedings under the 9 and 10 Vic. c. 96, for the removal of certain nuisances existing in the town of Sedbergh. Inquired whether they can safely do so under the provisions of that statute, as there is some doubt whether it applies to any place besides corporate towns, &c.

Ans.—The first section enacts, that any town council, or other like body, having jurisdiction within any corporate town, borough, city, or place, or any trustees or commissioners for drainage, &c., in any town, borough, city, or place, or in case there shall be no such town council, or other like body, or no such trustees or commissioners in any town, borough, city, or place, the guardians of the poor may take the proceedings therein specified. The Act does not in this clause express what guardians of the poor are to take the proceedings, but the Interpretation clause, (sec. 17) defines guardians of the poor to mean the guardians, &c., for any union, parish, township, hamlet, or place where the matter requiring their cognizance may arise. Although, therefore, it might at first be thought that the provisions of the act were confined to corporate and other large towns, the Commissioners think that a wide and general interpretation must be given to the word "place" in this section, and that consequently the guardians may act in rural places, such as hamlets and villages, as well as in populous towns. The term "corporate," which occurs in the first part of the clause, 1, referring to the town council, is omitted in the two subsequent clauses, probably for the sake of avoiding any limitation upon the nature of the places to which the statute is to apply.

5. POWER OF GUARDIANS TO ACT UNDER.

November 2nd, 1846.

Clerk of Loughborough Union—The guardians have received a certificate from two duly qualified medical practitioners of the existence of a nuisance in certain premises described in the certificate, and situate in the parish of Loughborough; but the guardians hesitate to institute any legal proceedings in the matter until they have the Commissioners' opinion as to whether they have any power to interfere in the parish of *Loughborough*, inasmuch as there is in that parish a board of surveyors, appointed under the Highway Act, (5 and 6 Wm. 4, c. 50,) whose duty it may be considered to be to drain, pave, and cleanse the parish; and, also, a board of inspectors for watching and lighting, under the provision of the 3d and 4th Wm. 4, c. 90, who have the managing, or directing, of the police. Inquired, whether either of the bodies abovementioned are to be considered like bodies to those particularly enumerated in the first section of the 9 and 10 Vic. c. 96.

Ans.—The 9 and 10 Vic. c. 96, sec. 1, enables any trustees or commissioners, or *other like officers*, acting under the provisions of any act of parliament, for the drainage, paving, cleansing, or managing, or directing the police in any town, borough, city, or place, or for any of the above purposes, to take the proceedings under the act. The board of guardians may act if there be no such town council, or like body, or no such trustees or commissioners; the words *or other like officers*, being here omitted. The Commissioners are disposed to think, that the trustees and commissioners, or other like officers, referred to in the former part of the clause, are intended to be such as are appointed under some local act for the purposes specified in any particular place; and that no power is given to such boards as the board of surveyors, or the board of inspectors, who derive their authority from general public statutes. But upon reference to that part of the clause which gives authority to the boards of guardians to act, it will be seen that where there are no town council, or trustees, or commissioners, they may act. Now, as neither the board of surveyors, nor the board of inspectors, are either trustees or commissioners, it appears, that the existence of such boards will not prevent the guardians from acting in carrying into effect the provisions of this salutary statute.

6. PROCEEDINGS UNDER.

November 2nd, 1846.

Mr. ——— ——— *Barnstaple Union*—Requested the Commissioners' opinion upon the following points, with reference to the act, 9 and 10 Vic. c. 96, for the Removal of Nuisances;—namely, 1. If a nuisance be reported to the guardians, and two medical practitioners give a certificate of the existence of such nuisance, whereupon a summons is issued, but the complaint is dismissed by the justices, on the ground that no nuisance exists, it having been removed or abated *after* the medical practitioners' certificate was given, though before the hearing of the case, is the defendant liable to the preliminary expenses "reasonably and properly incurred," as well as the expenses of the hearing? 2. If the defendant is not liable to such preliminary expences, can the guardians charge them to the parish where the nuisance existed under the 13th sec.? 3. Must a board of guardians take proceedings under the second sec. of the Act, and the defendant be excused on the "ground of poverty, or other special circumstances," before they can proceed against him under the 13th sec.? 4. Is it only on the ground of the defendant being "excused" that the complainant is enabled to proceed under the 13th sec.? 5. If the defendant escapes on the ground of non-liability, can the board of guardians charge the parish under the 13th sec.? 6. Can the board of guardians "retain" out of monies in their hands, the "reasonably and properly incurred expenses in carrying into effect the provisions of the Act," without obtaining an order for that purpose from two justices?

Ans.—On the best consideration which the Commissioners can give to the statute, they think the following to be the proper answers to your inquiries. 1st. The second section of the 9 and 10 Vic. c. 96, enables the complainants to recover from the owner, the costs and expenses incurred by them *in obtaining* such order, or in removing any nuisance, and otherwise carrying such order into effect. As these words contemplate the existence of an order, if no order be obtained, the costs incurred in the preliminary proceedings cannot be recovered against the owner or occupier. 2. If the order be not granted, because the owner or occupier after service of the summons removes the nuisance, the Commissioners think that, nevertheless, the preliminary costs may be treated as an expense reasonably and properly incurred in carrying into effect the provisions of the Act, and consequently, that such costs as cannot be recovered from the owner or occupier may be paid out of the poor rates. 3. The Commissioners are disposed to think that the complainants must, where an order has been obtained for the removal of the nuisance, take steps for the recovery of the costs and expenses, under the second section, and if the party be *excused*, or if the order for costs cannot be rendered available, the poor-rate will be liable, and it will also be available under the circumstances detailed in the second question. 4th. If the person charged proves not to be liable, so that no order is made, the Commissioners are disposed to think that the proceedings cannot be treated as taken under the Act, and therefore that the preliminary costs cannot be charged upon the poor rate. As, however, the facts of the nuisance, and the name of the occupier, can seldom be matters of doubt, the Commissioners think that this opinion, if correct, need not prove any serious obstacle. 5th. The Commissioners think that the order of justices is not a necessary requisite to enable the guardians to retain the expenses lawfully incurred under the act out of monies in their hands.

II.—POOR REMOVAL ACT.

1. Removability of daughter with her bastard child, who has not herself resided for five years in the parish, but who is living with her father, who has resided there for ten years.

Oct. 21st, 1846.

Chairman of Lampeter Union—M. J., a young woman with a bastard child, now residing with her father in the parish of Llanfihangel, (where he has lived for the last ten years,) has applied for relief to the parish of Ros y corn, in which her father is settled. She has not gained a settlement herself, nor has she resided for five years together in one parish. Inquired whether she can be removed to Ros y corn, her father's settlement?

Ans.—In the case of M. J., it appears that she has not resided for five years together in any parish, and has not gained any settlement of her own; but her father, with whom she is residing, is not removable; and the question arises, whether the last proviso to the first clause of the act does not apply. The Commissioners do not feel that they can express any confident opinion as to the proper interpretation of the proviso. If the word *children* therein used simply denotes the object of the relation, the woman, in this case, is irremovable, inasmuch as her father cannot be removed. If it signifies persons under 21, which is the common understanding of the term when used generally, she may be removed. But, in a case of doubt like the present, the Commissioners cannot advise the guardians to procure the removal.

---

2. Residence—not interrupted by a pauper becoming an inmate of a union workhouse.

Nov. 23rd, 1846.

Clerk of Shepton Mallet Union—A. G. and his family were admitted into the union workhouse situate in the parish of Shepton Mallet, in the month of October last, at the cost of that parish to which he belongs, though he has resided in the parish of Stoke Lane nearly the whole of his life, and during the last seven years without interruption, except for two weeks in the month of March, 1844, when he and his wife and child were inmates of the union workhouse; but after his discharge he returned to his residence in Stoke Lane, which he had retained possession of. Inquired whether the maintenance of the pauper and his family is to be charged to Stoke Lane or to Shepton Mallet.

Ans.—With reference to the case of A. G., the Commissioners think that the continuous residence in Stoke Lane was not broken by the admission of the pauper into the workhouse in 1844, and, consequently, that the pauper and his family were not removable from the parish in October last. That being the case, their relief ought to be charged to that parish, and not to Shepton Mallet.

3. RESIDENCE—IRREMOVABILITY OF ORPHAN CHILDREN.

January 1st, 1847.

Clerk of Derby Union—T. M. and J. M., aged respectively eight and six years, both orphans, born in the parish of A., but belonging to the parish of B. in the Derby Union, lost their father in or about the year 1840, and their mother in August, 1844, when they were placed under the care of a relative, who also lives in parish A.; and they have continued to reside with such relative, receiving relief from parish B. until last week, when it was discontinued, and the children were thrown upon parish A.—Inquired whether the children are removable, under the proviso in section 1 of 9 & 10 Vict., cap. 96, to the parish of their settlement, as it appears to the guardians that the children have no residence but in parish A., but must be considered as mere lodgers since the death of their mother in 1844.

Ans.—The Commissioners see nothing in the statute 9 & 10 Vict. c. 66, to prevent a lodger from becoming irremovable from a parish, by a residence of five years therein. The character of the residence required by the Act is quite unqualified. In the present case, the Commissioners are of opinion that the residence of the orphans in the parish of A. has rendered them irremovable therefrom.

4. RESIDENCE—IRREMOVABILITY OF WIDOW.

December 29th, 1846.

Clerk of Prescot Union—A. C., who became a widow in the year 1843, was then residing in the township of Prescot, where she has continued with her family ever since. Her husband having been settled in Rainhill township, she has been relieved by that township down to the present time. The pauper has resided continuously in Prescot for the last ten years; namely, seven years with her husband, and three years as a widow. Inquired whether she is irremovable from that parish; or, whether the five years' residence required by the Removal Act, must be computed as commencing only at the time of her husband's death.

Ans.—The Commissioners consider that the question submitted to them as to the removability of A. C. from the township of Prescot is quite free from doubt, and that having resided five years in Prescot, she is irremovable therefrom, although during part of that time she was a married woman.

5. IRREMOVABILITY OF A PERSON WHO HAS BEEN FOR FIVE YEARS ON BOARD THE DREADNOUGHT HOSPITAL SHIP.

January 4th, 1847.

Clerk of Axbridge Union—G. P. has been living on board the Dreadnought, hospital ship, in the river Thames, for upwards of five years, and though an invalid, he has been acting in the capacity of a paid nurse; but his wife and family have resided on shore at Greenwich. He has, until very recently, been in the receipt of relief from the Axbridge Union, but it having been discontinued, he applied to the relieving officer of the parish in which his family reside, for relief, the officers of which intend to apply for an order for his removal to his settlement in the Axbridge Union. Inquired whether G. P. and his family are irremovable from the parish where they now reside.

Ans. — Presuming the Dreadnought hospital ship has been stationary in the same parish for five years, the Commissioners are of opinion that G. P. is not removable from that parish, and as he cannot be removed, so his wife and child cannot be removed. See the third proviso to the first section of the statute 9 & 10 Vic., c. 66.

6. REMOVABILITY OF BASTARD CHILD.

January 1st, 1847.

Clerk of Stokesley Union—M. W., an illegitimate child, legally settled in Danby Wiske, in the Northallerton Union, was born at Carlton, in the Stokesley Union, about eleven years back, and resided there, until about two years and a half ago, with her mother's half brother, who then went to be a hired servant in the township of Facely for one year, and the child lived with him there during that period; at the expiration of which they went back to Carlton, and have remained there until the present time. The mother is living in another township. Inquired whether the child is removable to Danby Wiske.

Ans.—As M. W. has not resided in the place of her present residence for the five years last past, and is not now residing with her putative father; the Commissioners are of opinion that she is removable to the place of her settlement.

7. REMOVABILITY OF A BASTARD CHILD.

December 30th, 1846.

Clerk of Machynlleth Union—M. D., a single woman, gave birth to a bastard child about seven months ago, and the child has been ever since resident with a nurse in the parish of Towyn, in which the mother has also resided for upwards of five years, her settlement, however, being in the parish of Yallyllyn. Inquired, whether the child, as well as the mother, is irremovable from the parish of Towyn.

Ans.—The Commissioners are of opinion that the illegitimate child of M. D. is removable from Towyn to the parish of the settlement of the mother.

8. RESIDENCE—TEMPORARY INTERRUPTION OF.

Clerk of Lancaster Union.—E. A., a widow with six children, whose husband died about four years ago, has resided in the township of Heysham upwards of five years. Shortly after her husband's death, she and her children were removed, by an order of justices, to the township of Middleton in this union, and as the removal took place in the evening, the pauper and her children remained at the overseer's house in Middleton until the following day, when they returned to Heysham, and occupied the same cottage from which they had been removed on the preceding day, where they have resided ever since and have been allowed relief by Middleton, which relief has now been stopped. The following objections to the irremovability of the pauper and her children are made by the township of Heysham:—1st, That part of the five years' residence having been while the pauper was a married woman, is not such a residence as is intended by the 1st sec. of the Poor Removal Act. 2nd, That the execution of the order of removal acts was an interruption of the residence, which consequently has not been of five years' duration.

Ans.—With regard to the first objection raised against the widow's irremovability from Heysham, viz., that for part of the period of five years her residence in that parish had been in the character of a married woman, the Commissioners desire to observe that they cannot regard this objection as a valid one. The substantive enactment, 1st sec. of the 9 & 10 Vict., c. 66, refers to residence simply, and not to any character or relation of the resident. The second objection, founded on the removal of the widow under an order of justices, appears to the Commissioners to be open to some doubt; but under the circumstances of the particular case, they are disposed to consider that there was not such an interruption of the widow's residence in Heysham as would defeat her irremovability. The 9 & 10 Vict. c. 66, renders a person who has resided in a parish for five years, irremovable therefrom; but it does not enact that an absence from the parish during that period shall enable such person to be removed. It appears to the Commissioners that the question to be determined in every case is, whether the absence was of such a character as to effect a change of residence. In the present instance it does not seem that a change of residence was effected, inasmuch as the widow, as the Commissioners understand, did not give up her house, which was her home, in Heysham, when she was removed to Middleton, but retained it during her absence, and returned to it again, on coming back to Heysham. The Commissioners do not think that the mere fact of the widow's temporary absence, having occurred in consequence of an order of justices, would of itself make any difference in the case.

9. RESIDENCE — REMOVABILITY AFFECTED BY RECEIPT OF RELIEF.

December 8th, 1846.

Overseers of Birstwith Parish, Yorkshire—1. D. B. has been residing for two years in the township of Birstwith, but has been in the receipt of relief from the township of Hampsthwaite. If she resides three years longer in the former township, will she have a claim thereon by such residence? 2. W. T. has been in the receipt of relief for about five years, from the township of Birstwith, but has resided for the last two years in Pately, and previously, for about fifty years, in the township of Beverly. To which township does he belong?

Ans.—1. With reference to the case of D. B., the Commissioners direct your attention to the proviso to the 1st sec. of the 9 & 10 Vict. c. 66, which provides that the time "during which any such person shall receive relief from any parish shall for all purposes be excluded in the computation of time hereinbefore mentioned. Consequently, although D. B. may continue to receive relief in Birstwith, from Hampsthwaite or elsewhere, the time during which she may receive such relief will not be taken into account in reckoning the period of her residence in Birstwith, in reference to the question of her irremovability. 2. W. T. still belongs to the township in which he has his settlement, irrespective of the recent statute. He must be relieved, if destitute, in the place where he resides; but may be forthwith removed to the place of his settlement, his residence in Pately not having been long enough to render him irremovable under the 1st section of the act.

10. RESIDENCE—INTERRUPTION OF.

November 3rd, 1846.

——— 1. An old man has lived habitually, during the last twenty years, in the parish of Aylsham, but has, during that period, repeatedly received relief from a parish in the Walsingham Union, of the workhouse of which union he has also often been an inmate for periods of several weeks together, having been in it in fact for seven weeks during last spring. Would this residence in the Walsingham Union workhouse render the pauper removable from the parish of Aylsham, by destroying the continuity of his residence in that parish? 2. Three or four months ago, a family was removed by order of justices from a parish in the Walsingham to a parish in the Aylsham Union, by the overseers of which last parish they were duly acknowledged and relieved. Almost immediately afterwards this family of its own accord returned to the Walsingham Union, where they have, undoubtedly, resided more than five years, and where they now are. Was the residence of these paupers in the Walsingham Union broken, by their removal? 3. Supposing continuous residence to be needful, would the five years' residence be incomplete owing to a man's having gone for seven weeks this year, and for twelve weeks last year, to work in another parish some miles from his residence, to which however he returned every Saturday night?

Ans.—If, upon quitting the Aylsham Union, the pauper entirely gave up his home therein, so that when in the Walsingham Union workhouse, he had no other home, the Commissioners think that the continuous residence was broken, and that the pauper is removable. The second case requires a little more detail. The Commissioners think that the mere removal of a pauper, under an order of removal, from a parish in which he is residing, to another parish from which he returns, does not necessarily break the continuity of the residence. It is of importance to know the facts, what occurred upon the removal, and the length of time during which the pauper was absent, and what took place upon the return; so that it may be seen whether there was a change of home. The third case is of a person who, having a residence in a parish, went to work, during the working days of a week, out of it, his absence being only for the purpose of this work. It is not stated by you whether he had a family or not, but it seems that the place to which he returned every Saturday was in point of fact his home. It, therefore, appears to the Commissioners that in this case the residence was not interrupted. The Commissioners, in expressing their opinions, are aware that the questions arise upon absences previous to the passing of the Act.

11. RESIDENCE—IRREMOVABILITY OF DAUGHTER RESIDING WITH HER PARENTS.

December 17th, 1846.

Clerk of Pershore Union—E. L., aged twenty, has resided all her life with her parents, who are non-resident paupers, and irremovable from the parish in which they live. Inquired, whether the daughter is irremovable as well as the parents; or, whether the five years' residence must be in her own right, and commence from the date when she attained the age of sixteen.

Ans.—The Commissioners consider that a person who resides for five years in any parish, whether above, or under, the age of sixteen years, will be irremovable, unless brought within any of the exceptions in the provisoes to section 1 of the Poor Removal Act. In the present case the Commissioners entertain no doubt that E. L. is, under the circumstances mentioned by you, irremovable from the parish in which she resides, as well as her parents.

12. REMOVABILITY—RESIDENCE IN PREMISES SITUATE IN ONE DIVISION, BUT BELONGING TO ANOTHER DIVISION OF A PARISH.

December 9th, 1846.

Clerk of Ludlow Union—The parish of Leintwardine is, for parochial purposes, divided into two portions, viz., the north and south sides, which are quite distinct and separate in all respects, excepting that they have one church in common. In the church yard there is an almshouse, containing four rooms, two of which are considered to be the property of the north side, and two the property of the south side of the parish. For six or eight years the two rooms, the property of the south side of the parish, have been occupied by a pauper named A. B., who, on account of such residence, is now attempted to be handed over to the north side of the parish, the authorities of which protest against such movement, because, although the church is situated in the northern portion of the parish, all rights connected with the almshouse are vested 'in the south side. Requested the Commissioners' opinion on this case.

Ans.—The question raised in your letter, as to the removability of A. B., does not turn upon the property in the almshouse you describe, but upon its situation. If the whole of the almshouse be situated in the northern part of the parish of Leintwardine, the residence of the inmates, with reference to the application of the 9 & 10 Vic. c. 66, must be deemed to be in such northern part.

---

13. RESIDENCE — INTERRUPTION OF BY THE PAUPER BECOMING AN INMATE OF A WORKHOUSE.

December 14th, 1846.

Clerk of Howden Union—Inquired, whether a non-resident pauper who may have been during any portion of the five years previous to the passing of the Poor Removal Act, maintained in the union workhouse at the cost of his parish, is rendered removable thereby from the parish in which he resided, notwithstanding that the pauper may not have given up the occupancy of his dwelling-house, and may, after being discharged from the workhouse, have returned to and continued to reside therein. And whether there is any difference if such residence in the workhouse should have been prior or subsequent to the passing of the statute 7 & 8 Vic. c. 101, sec. 56.

Ans.—The point is not altogether free from doubt, because it may be urged that the pauper did not reside in the workhouse, but that his residence was in the parish where he retained his house and possibly his furniture. Assuming that there was a residence in the workhouse, which upon the whole would probably be held by the justices, then the Act 7 & 8 Vic. c. 101, s. 56, appears to establish that it must be considered to be a residence in the parish to which the pauper, while in the house, was chargeable, and this constructive residence would apply to cases of residence prior and subsequent to the Poor Removal Act. It appears, therefore, to the Commissioners, that a residence in the workhouse under the circumstances supposed, being, in construction of law, a residence in the parish of the chargeability, would be an interruption of the five years' residence in the parish in which the pauper previously lived, and still retained his dwelling-house, so as to prevent the operation of the 1st section of the Act last mentioned.

---

14. REMOVABILITY OF A SINGLE WOMAN IN A STATE OF PREGNANCY.

January 1st, 1847.

Clerk of Newton Abbot Union — Inquired whether, in reference to the Act of 9 & 10 Vic. c. 66, the pregnancy of a single woman is such an ailment as renders her irremovable from the parish where she happens to be, when she thereby becomes chargeable.

Ans.—The Commissioners are of opinion that the pregnancy of a woman would certainly not, of itself, produce a permanent disability, so as to justify the granting of a warrant for the removal of such person, under section 4 of 9 & 10 Vic. c. 66.

---

15. RESIDENCE—INTERRUPTION OF.

Dec. 9th, 1846.

Clerk of Machynlleth Union— J. W. whose place of settlement is supposed to be Llanbrynmair, in the Machynlleth Union, resided in the parish of Newtown from March 1834 to January 1838, and in the parish of Llanidloes from the last-mentioned date to February 1842, at which time he returned to Newtown, and has continued to reside there without interruption down to the present time. Inquired whether he is removable from Newtown; or whether a portion of the time during which he resided in Newtown on the first occasion, can be added to his present residence in that place, in order to make up the five years' residence required by the Poor Removal Act, to render a person irremovable.

Ans.—J. W.'s residence in Newtown was interrupted by his residence in Llanidloes; and no portion of the period of his former residence in Newtown, can be added to that of his later residence in the same place, so as to make up the five years required by the 9th and 10th Vict. c. 66, consequently when he was recently removed from Newtown, he had not resided there long enough to have become irremovable; and his removal, therefore, in that respect, was not improper.

---

16. RESIDENCE—REMOVABILITY OF WIDOW.

Dec. 4th, 1846.

Clerk of Hinckley Union—A man named F., who had resided with his wife in Shamford, for upwards of five years, prior to the year 1846, removed, at the commencement of that year, to the parish of Great Claybrook, to which they belonged; and after living there a few months the husband died, and the widow then returned to Shamford, where she now resides, and is chargeable thereto. Inquired whether the widow is removable from Shamford to Great Claybrook.

Ans.—The question of the removability of the widow F., depends upon the date of the death of her husband. The Commissioners assume that the death occurred before the 26th August, 1846, and if this assumption be correct, the Commissioners are advised by the law officers of the Crown, that the second section of the Poor Removal Act does not apply to widows who became such before the passing of that act, and consequently the provisions of that section do not prevent the widow F. from being now removed from the parish of Shamford to her place of settlement; and as her residence and that of her late husband was interrupted by their removal to Great Claybrook, she is not, in the opinion of the Commissioners, irremovable by the operation of the first section.

17. RESIDENCE—INTERRUPTIONS OF.

December 22nd, 1846.

——————, *Launceston Union*—G. P., a pauper, legally settled in the parish of St. Giles, has resided for upwards of six years in the parish of Preworthy, and during the whole of that time she has received relief from the former parish; but in each year she has gone to Devonport to visit a sister, with whom she has remained from a month to six weeks on each occasion. Inquired whether these different periods of absence should be deducted from the gross amount of residence: and whether, if the residue amount to five clear years, the pauper is irremovable from Preworthy. Inquired also whether, in calculating the five years' residence, provided the pauper has rented a house or lodgings during that time, periods of temporary absence are to be deducted from the residence; or whether the residence must be continuous and uninterrupted. And in cases where the pauper has been uninterruptedly in the receipt of relief from one parish, but has resided in another, whether temporary absence from the place of residence, in any one or more years, would destroy the irremovability.

Ans. In cases where it is sought to establish an irremovability by five years' residence, it is sufficient to show that the party has had his home in the parish for the space of five years, and the fact of an occasional absence from the parish for a temporary purpose or object, where there was no change of home, will not, in the opinion of the Commissioners, defeat the claim of irremovability. The object of the party in leaving his home must therefore be considered in each case. The fact of the receipt or non-receipt of relief will make no difference in the matter, except in those cases where the five years' residence was not complete at the passing of the act.

18. REMOVABILITY OF WIDOW AND HER CHILDREN.

Dec. 16, 1846.

Clerk of Lymington Union—In the month of March last, S. C., residing in the parish of Fawley, in the New Forest Union, became chargeable to that parish in consequence of illness; upon which, an order was obtained for the removal of the pauper and his family to the parish of Boldre, in the Lymington Union, being the place of his settlement. The pauper's state of health rendered it necessary that the execution of the order of removal should be suspended, which was accordingly done; and in the beginning of the month of November last, he died in the parish of Fawley, the order not having been executed. A few days after the burial of S. C., the relieving officer and assistant overseer of Fawley removed his widow and children to the parish of Boldre, and demanded a sum of £24 for expenses incurred in consequence of the suspension of the order of removal, together with £1 for his own expenses in conveying the widow and children from Fawley to Boldre. The sum of £24 demanded as costs under the order, includes the burial expenses of the pauper and relief to his widow and children after his decease, but the amount of such expenses or relief is not separately given in the account furnished. Inquired, 1st, Whether the widow and children of S. C. were, with reference to the act of 9 & 10 Vict. c. 66, legally removable to the parish of Boldre immediately after his death, he having died subsequently to the passing of that act in the parish of Fawley? 2nd. If the widow and children were not so legally removable, whether the relief given to them subsequently to the death of the husband can be recovered from the parish of Boldre? 3rd, Whether in reference to the 7 and 8 Vict. c. 101, sec. 31, the burial expenses of the pauper ought to be borne by the parish of Boldre, the place of settlement, or by the parish of Fawley, the place of death, the parish of Boldre not being under the control of the guardians of the New Forest Union, by whom these expenses were paid. And, 4th, If the widow and children of S. C. were removable immediately after his death, whether the expense of conveying them to Boldre is legally chargeable to that parish?

Ans.—1st, The widow and her children were not legally removed from Fawley, their removal being restrained by the 2nd section of the new statute (9 & 10 Vict. c. 66.) 2nd, The relief given to the widow and her children, they being irremovable from Fawley for twelve months after the death of the husband, cannot be recovered from Boldre, the parish of the husband's settlement. 3rd, The Commissioners are not prepared to say that the expenses of the burial of the husband ought not to have been included in the order. They were expenses incurred by the parish of Fawley by reason of the suspension of the order of removal. 4th, Your fourth question is answered by the answer given to the first question.

19. Residence—temporary interruption of.

December 16th, 1846.

Clerk of Alnwick Union—About two years ago, G. P. and his wife and family, became chargeable to the parish of Alnwick, and an order was obtained for their removal to the township of Longhoughton, as the place of their settlement. They were accordingly taken to Longhoughton under the order, where they remained only a few hours, and then returned to their house in the parish of Alnwick, where they now are. A few weeks ago, the guardians revised the list of paupers for this union, and finding that G. P. and his family had resided for upwards of five years before the 26th August last, in the parish of Alnwick, transferred the future relief from Longhoughton to Alnwick; but at a meeting of the board, held on the 28th ult., this was objected to on the part of the parish of Alnwick, on the ground that the removal from Longhoughton had broken the five years' residence in that parish, and the board concurring in this view, re-transferred the cost of the relief of the paupers to the parish of Longhoughton, though they still reside in the parish of Alnwick. Inquired, whether the guardians have acted correctly in charging the relief granted to the above paupers to the parish of Longhoughton.

Ans. — The Commissioners think that the course pursued by the guardians in the first instance, in transferring G. P.'s relief from Longhoughton to Alnwick, was correct; and that consequently, the re-transfer of the charge from Alnwick to Longhoughton was wrong. The Commissioners do not think that G. P.'s continuous residence in Alnwick was broken by his removal to Longhoughton, under the circumstances stated in your letter.

20. Resolution to relieve without reference to the statute.

January 1st, 1847.

Vice-Chairman of Patrington Union—Communicated the following resolution, passed by the board of guardians, with reference to the 9 & 10 Vict., c. 66, namely,—"That the paupers resident in the parishes situate in this union, although the said paupers have settlements in other parishes situate in this union, relief shall be granted and charged as heretofore, without reference to the Act 9 & 10 Vict. c. 69, and that the same shall be continued to the end of the next quarter, provided the Poor Law Commissioners do not object to it." He submitted for the consideration of the Commissioners, that the administration of relief to the poor is not altered by the Act 9 & 10 Vict. c. 66; at least, that it is still subject to the direction and control of the Commissioners; that, looking at the difficulties which present themselves under this Act, it would be impolitic for the Commissioners to withhold their sanction to the resolution of the guardians.

Ans.—Although the control of the administration of relief is still preserved to the Poor Law Commissioners, to the same extent as it was given by the Poor Law Amendment Act, they have no power to interfere with the liabilities and responsibilities of parishes in regard to the cost of relief; therefore, if the statute lately passed has in any manner altered it, and the Commissioners readily believe that it has done so in many places, neither they nor the board of guardians can, by any rule, order, or resolution, prevent the operation of the statute, in favour of, or against any particular parishes. The auditor will be bound to see that the provisions of the statute are properly attended to in the charges for relief in the union accounts, and to disallow all charges which are at variance with those provisions. The Commissioners, therefore, are not empowered to sanction the resolution in question; and they must add that, so far as it is proposed thereby to disregard the late statute, the resolution is illegal.

---

21. RESIDENCE—IRREMOVABILITY OF A SON WHO IS ABOVE 16, AND RESIDES WITH HIS PARENTS.

January 2nd, 1846.

Clerk of Stow-on-the-Wold Union—G. P., a settled parishioner of Upper Slaughter, has resided, with his wife and family, at Lower Slaughter, for a period of seven years, not having left his residence there within the five years preceding the passing of the Poor Removal Act, and still continues to reside there, thus becoming irremovable as concerns himself, and wife and children, unless the eldest of such children be removable under the third section of the Act, he having attained the age of sixteen years on the 14th August, 1846, twelve days before the passing of the Act. It is to be observed, that this boy of sixteen has lived as part of his father's family at Lower Slaughter, during all the time of his father's seven years' residence there. He has now become chargeable. Inquired whether the relief granted to him is chargeable to the parish of Upper Slaughter, or to that of Lower Slaughter.

Ans.—The Commissioners direct the attention of the board of guardians to the third proviso to the first section of the Act 9 & 10 Vict. c. 66, which renders a child, without regard to age, who has no settlement different from that of his parent, irremovable where his parent is irremovable. In the present case, therefore, the boy in question, though of the age of sixteen years, is not removable from the parish of Lower Slaughter because his father is not removable therefrom; consequently his relief whilst residing there must be charged to that parish.

III.—INSTRUCTIONS TO THE ASSISTANT POOR LAW COMMISSIONERS.

Poor Law Commission Office, Somerset House, 13th January, 1847.

SIR,

1. The attention of the Poor Law Commissioners has been recently directed to the Instructions to the Assistant Poor Law Commissioners which were issued in the year 1841, and are inserted in their Seventh Annual Report (pp. 55 and 181, ed. 8vo.) At the time when these Instructions were issued, the number of the Assistant Commissioners was greater and the size of their districts less, than at present. On this account they are, in several respects, unsuited to the existing state of things; and the Commissioners have therefore decided to revoke those instructions, and to issue, for the guidance of the Assistant Commissioners, the instructions which are subjoined.

2. The Poor Law Amendment Act contemplates the Assistant Commissioners as acting singly, and under the general instructions and control of the Commissioners. The powers of inquiry, of summoning witnesses, and examining them on oath, of requiring the production of papers, and of attending at local boards, which the Act confers on an Assistant Commissioner (s. 12 and 21,) may however be exercised by him on his own discretion, and without any specific authority or direction from the Commissioners.

3. The Commissioners have divided the whole of England into nine districts, each containing on an average about seventy unions and parishes under a board of guardians, and have assigned one of such districts to each of the Assistant Commissioners. Each Assistant Commissioner is legally competent to act in any part of England, but (unless he is specially instructed by the Commissioners) his duties are confined to the superintendence of the administration of the Poor Laws in the district assigned to him.

4. The Commissioners regard the ordinary duties to be thus exercised by an Assistant Commissioner as falling, for the most part, under the four following heads:—

1. To visit every union or parish in his district; to attend the meeting of the board of guardians; to inspect the workhouse; and to examine into the manner in which relief is administered, and the duties of the paid officers of the union or parish are discharged.

2. To report to the Commissioners any matter which, after any such visit and examination, may appear to him to deserve their notice, or to require their interference in respect to the administration of the law in the union or parish.

3. When required by the Commissioners, to ascertain the average expenditure of the several parishes or union under s. 28 of the Poor Law Amendment Act.

4. To make special inquiries into cases of alleged maltreatment of paupers, and into charges preferred against union and parish officers, either when he may be instructed by the Commissioners so to do, or when such an inquiry may appear to himself to be desirable.

5. Notwithstanding the large number of unions in a district, the Commissioners are desirous that the Assistant Commissioner should attend a meeting of each board of guardians once at least in every year, and that he should, if possible, visit and inspect each workhouse once in every six months.

6. The Assistant Commissioner will transmit to the Commissioners a weekly diary of his proceedings.

7. The Commissioners further desire that, after visiting each union, and inspecting the workhouse, the Assistant Commissioner will forward to them a report upon it, in the form of answers to the annexed queries:—

Report on Union, after a Visit on the day of 184

1. Date of last previous visit.

2. Is the workhouse generally adequate to the wants of the union, in respect of size and internal arrangements?

3. Is the provision for the sick and for infectious cases sufficient? Are the receiving wards in a proper state?

4. Is the workhouse school well managed?

5. Are there vagrant wards in the workhouse, and are they sufficient? Are the arrangements for setting the vagrants to work effective, and is the resolution of the guardians under 5 & 6 Vict., c. 57, s. 5, duly observed?

6. Does the visiting committee regularly inspect the workhouse? Do any of their answers to the queries in the workhouse regulations suggest the propriety of any interference on the part of the Commissioners?

7. Has the maximum number of inmates of the workhouse, fixed by the Commissioners, been constantly observed since your last visit?

8. Are the proper extracts from the Poor Law Amendment Act, and the Regulations of the Commissioners, hung up in the workhouse?

9. Have all appointments of new officers, and changes in salaries and districts, since your last visit been reported to the Commissioners?

10. Is there any officer whose appointment has been sanctioned provisionally? If so, state your opinion of his fitness.

11. Have you any reason to believe that any of the books or forms prescribed by the Poor Law Commissioners are not properly kept?

12. Have you observed any illegal practice, or any departure from the regulations of the Commissioners?

13. Has any marked change taken place in the state of the workhouse, the number of the inmates, or the general condition of the union, since your last visit?

14. Observations not falling under any of the preceding heads.

(Signed) *Assistant Commissioner.*

Dated the day of 184

8. It will not be necessary for the Assistant Commissioner to make a report in the above form more than once in six months, although he may visit a union several times during that period.

9. The Assistant Commissioner, on going through the workhouse, ought to receive readily any complaint which may be made to him by any of the inmates; and if he has reason to suspect that any of the officers have behaved in a harsh or unbecoming manner towards the inmates, it is proper that he should question the inmates on the subject, and, if necessary, in the absence of the officers of the establishment.

10. The Assistant Commissioner will be furnished by the clerk of each union in his district with a weekly return, comprising the several particulars specified in Form A., attached to the general order of the 21st of April, 1842. By this return his attention will be directed periodically to any sudden increase in the amount of the relief, to any special minute of the guardians, to any deficiency of funds in the hands of the treasurer, and to some other peculiar circumstances which may render it expedient for him to visit the union, or take some other step in reference to the matter.

11. With respect to the taking of averages, the Commissioners have already prepared a statement of the law on the most material points: this statement was issued separately on the 21st August, 1844.

12. On the subject of the inquiries which the Assistant Commissioner may be called on to institute as to alleged maltreatment or neglect of paupers, and as to alleged malversations and misconduct of paid officers, it is to be observed that the Poor Law Amendment Act confers on him powers specially intended for this purpose, viz., a power of summoning witnesses for any distance less than 10 miles from the place of their abode,

and a power of examining them upon oath (s. 12, 13;) and a provision is made by the same Act for the payment from the poor rates of the reasonable expenses of witnesses so summoned (s. 14;) no such power has been conferred by the Legislature upon the board of guardians, or any other of the local functionaries, with respect to alleged abuses in the administration of the Poor Laws.

13. In cases in which the Assistant Commissioner inquires into the conduct of a paid officer of a board of guardians, it is in general desirable that such inquiry should be held in the presence of the board of guardians or of some of its members, and also of the officer himself. Questions may properly be put to the officer relating to the matter charged, inasmuch as every paid officer is presumed to accept his office on the implied condition of explaining his conduct to his official superiors in regard to any imputation which may be made upon it on apparently reasonable grounds. The witnesses should be examined by the Assistant Commissioner, who will of course put any proper question to a witness which may be suggested by any person present, and which may seem to tend to elicit the truth; the Assistant Commissioner may, however, if he should think fit, permit any witnesses to be examined by a party whose conduct is in question. Applications have sometimes been made to the Commissioners to permit solicitors or counsel to attend at an inquiry held by an Assistant Commissioner. The Commissioners do not wish to lay down any rule on this point, and in case of any such application being made, they will leave the Assistant Commissioner to exercise his discretion thereon, according to the circumstances of the case.

14. The Assistant Commissioner should bear in mind that although he may admit any persons to any inquiry he may hold, so far as he has the control of the room in which it takes place, he has no power analogous to that of a judge or police magistrate to keep order in a court of justice. On this account, as well as from the nature of the subjects of his inquiries, he may sometimes find it necessary not to admit all persons indiscriminately to the inquiry.

15. It is convenient that all notes of the evidence of witnesses taken at such an inquiry should be written in the first person, and should in general be signed by the witness after having been read over to him.

16. In reporting to the Commissioners the result of any such investigation, the Assistant Commissioner will first set out the charges preferred against the officer, or the other subject of inquiry; he will then state the substance and effect of the evidence taken by him, and will in general subjoin his opinion as to its result, together with any measure which he may wish to recommend to the Commissioners in reference to it.

17. If any witnesses have been summoned whose expenses are to be charged to the union, under s. 14 of the Act, he will transmit to the Commissioners a list of such witnesses, with a statement of the distance travelled by them from their homes, and of the number of days of their attendance; and similar information should be supplied in respect of witnesses who may attend without summonses.

18. The collection and diffusion of useful information as to the management of workhouses, the administration of out-door relief, the state of pauperism in general, and the welfare of the industrious classes, is an important function of the Poor Law Commissioners, and can only be accomplished by the co-operation of their Assistant Commissioners.

19. The Assistant Commissioner will find it a beneficial part of his duties to transplant into a union the arrangements and modes of management which, either of his own personal knowledge, or by means of information communicated to him from the Commissioners, he may know to have been introduced into other unions with successful results.

20. Before they close these instructions, the Commissioners will remark, that the ordinary and detailed management of the workhouse, and superintendence of the union officers, is vested in the guardians, and, therefore, that the guardians are primarily responsible for any abuses or irregularities in the administration of the law which may occur within their union. If, however, any illegal or reprehensible practice should habitually prevail in the union, with respect either to the state or management of the workhouse, the administration of out-door relief, the keeping of the union books, or the conduct of the paid officers, it ought not to escape the observation of the Assistant Commissioner, who will not fail to report it without delay, to the Commissioners.

Signed by Order of the Board,
W. G. LUMLEY, *Assistant Secretary.*

To

Assistant Poor Law Commissioner.

The following are the Instructions to the Assistant Commissioners on the subject of the taking of Averages, referred to in the above Letter.

Poor Law Commission Office, Somerset House,
21st August, 1844.

There are two sets of books from which the account of the expenditure is to be framed; those kept by the Clerk to the guardians, and those kept by the Parish Officers.

I. To begin with the former of these sets;—It seems desirable that the information should be derived from the *Ledger* in which the various charges are ultimately made against each Parish. From the *Debtor* side of the *Ledger* in the account of each Parish should be selected:—

1. All charges for relief and clothing, whether in-door or out-door, whether given absolutely or by way of loan, or on the understanding of repayment, or subsequent recovery, and all advances to pensioners.
2. All charges for funerals.
3. All such charges for expences in administering relief, and all remuneration to any superintendent of labour, or other officer employed in the administration of relief, as shall not have been included in the common charges according to the averages.
4. All charges for medical relief, and all midwifery and surgical fees charged to the Parish, and not included in the common charges according to the averages.
5. All expences incurred in apprenticing pauper children.

It may be observed that No. 1 should include the maintenance of paupers when on their journey under an order of removal, but not the costs of their conveyance, supposing that any charge in connection with the removal finds its place in the Union accounts at all.

The cost of Emigration should be omitted.

From the above sums on the *Debtor* side of the *Ledger* should be deducted:—

1. Payments made, whether to any officer of the guardians, or to the Overseers, under any order in bastardy.
2. Payments under orders of maintenance made on relatives of paupers.
3. Re-payments of loans to paupers.
4. Re-payments of relief advanced to pensioners or their families.
5. Re-payments to the guardians from other Parishes or Unions, so far as they are in respect of relief and maintenance, or in respect of any other charge which, according to the above directions, could properly be included.
6. The net proceeds of any work done by paupers employed in out-door labour.

The Commissioners have deemed it right to omit from the calculation the establishment or common charges of the Union, since they think that neither the words nor the spirit of the 28th section of the Poor Law Amendment Act require their insertion. They may have been disproportionately large in one Parish, and disproportionately small in another, on account of some circumstances which existed previous to the three years now under consideration, and which will have raised or lowered the rate of contribution to the Union fund during this latter period. The object of declaring new averages is to alter the scale of contribution which the insertion of these common charges would have the effect of perpetuating.

II. From the accounts of the Overseers, or the abstract of those accounts contained in Form B 12, should be selected:—

1. All charges incurred directly in the relief of the Poor in cases of sudden and urgent necessity, or by the direction of the board of guardians.
2. All costs of conveyance of paupers to the Workhouse of the Union.
3. All medical expences paid by the Overseers.
4. All payments to other Parishes and Unions for relief to paupers under order of removal, whether suspended or not suspended.
5. All payments for lunatic paupers maintained in any lunatic asylum or licensed house.

Due deductions must also be made in respect of any such repayments to the Overseers, as have been already pointed out in reference to the Union accounts, or in respect of any payment made by the guardians, and charged in their accounts to the Parish.

Charges connected with the collection of the *Rate*, whether included in the Union or Parish account, or with the defence of appeals against the rate, or with orders of removal other than the actual maintenance of the paupers, the Commissioners think should not be included in the calculation of the average expenditure. The two former are rather reductions of the net receipts, than money expended in connection with relief, and the latter cannot be deemed relief to the poor within the words of the Statute, and have no connection with the future amount of pauperism, or probable demand on the stock and establishment of the Union.

The salary of an Assistant Overseer, or of a Collector acting as Assistant Overseer, is a more doubtful matter. The Commissioners think, that if such an officer acts only as Collector, his salary must be admitted on the principle stated in the last paragraph, and at any rate the share which an Assistant Overseer can have in the administration of the actual relief to the poor, in a Union constituted by the Commissioners, is so small, that the Commissioners think that no part of his salary need be included in the calculation. When the Parish under consideration has not been included in any such Union, and the Assistant Overseer has taken an active and principal share in the relief of the poor, so that his salary has thus been a remuneration for duties immediately connected with the administration of relief, a proportion at least of such salary should be charged in the expenditure which is to be made the basis of the averages. It is right to add, that charges disallowed by the Auditor or Justices are not to be considered as representing money expended.

If it be shown, to the satisfaction of the Assistant Commissioner, that payments have in any particular Parish been made from the Highway Rate, or from any private rate or other fund, for the purpose of diminishing the cost of the relief of the poor chargeable to the ordinary Poor Rate, and that the averages will be thereby affected so as to produce injustice to the other Parishes in which no such fraudulent or irregular payments have been made, he should examine strictly into the particulars of each such case, and cause the Parish officers to explain fully the mode in which such payments have been made. Should it then appear that the payments in question are such in their character, and have been so made, as to come within the terms of the 28th section, as a part of the expense incurred by such Parish for the relief of the poor, they should be included in the calculation of the averages of the Parishes to which they relate. But if it appear that the payments in question cannot be deemed to be within the words of that Section, it will be proper for the Assistant Commissioner to report specially the case to the Commissioners, and for the latter to determine whether fresh averages should then be taken, since, by such a course, the fraud upon the other Parishes would be successful.

The Commissioners do not think it necessary to comment in detail on the various other charges in the Overseers' account, which should be omitted in the calculation of the averages; —the principles to be kept in view, in any doubtful case, seem to be—

1. That the charge to be included should be in immediate connection with relief.
2. That it should be a charge upon the Parish, as an individual member of the Union, made on some principle distinct from that of the average expenditure proposed to be revised.

Doubtful cases will present themselves; but the Commissioners believe that, in almost all such cases, the principle just referred to will be a sufficient guide, and they request that, in any particular instance of difficulty, the facts may be reported to their board, and, if necessary, their instructions waited for.

It remains to add, that, in order to prevent misunderstanding, a supplementary memorandum should accompany the declaration of the averages, showing the total average expenditure, including the establishment charges. This memorandum the Commissioners would wish to be made in the following form:—

	£ s. d.
In-maintenance—out-door relief, and other charges connected with relief, paid by the guardians.	
Charges connected with relief paid by the overseers .	
Total . .	£
Average of common charges, including salaries of officers, and other establishment charges	
Average of repayments of Workhouse loans and the interest thereon	
Total expenditure connected with relief of the Poor .	£

Printed by Order of the Poor Law Commissioners, by BLACKBURN AND PARDON, 6, Hatton Garden, and Published by CHARLES KNIGHT and Co., 22, Ludgate Street, Publishers to the Poor Law Commissioners.

AN

OFFICIAL CIRCULAR

OF PUBLIC DOCUMENTS AND INFORMATION:

DIRECTED BY THE POOR LAW COMMISSIONERS TO BE PRINTED, CHIEFLY FOR THE USE OF THE MEMBERS AND PERMANENT OFFICERS OF BOARDS OF GUARDIANS, UNDER THE POOR LAW AMENDMENT ACT.

Nos. 3 & 4.] CIRCULAR ISSUED MARCH 17TH, 1847. [N. S.

Poor Law Commission Office,
Somerset House,
March 17, 1847.

THE Poor Law Commissioners have directed that the following Order and Circular relating thereto be printed and circulated, for the information of Guardians and Officers of the several Unions.

By Order of the Board,
EDWIN CHADWICK, *Secretary.*

To the GUARDIANS OF THE POOR of the several Unions named in the Schedule F., hereunto annexed;—

To the CHURCHWARDENS and OVERSEERS OF THE POOR of the several Parishes and Places comprised within the said Unions;—

To the Clerk or Clerks to the Justices of the Petty Sessions held for the Division or Divisions in which the Parishes comprised within the said Unions are situate;—

And to all others whom it may concern.

WE, THE POOR LAW COMMISSIONERS, in pursuance of the authorities vested in us by an Act of Parliament passed in the 5th year of the reign of King William IV., intituled "*An Act for the Amendment and better Administration of the Laws relating to the Poor in England and Wales,*" DO HEREBY, from the 1st day of May, 1847, RESCIND all such Orders, and all such parts of any Orders, heretofore issued by the Poor Law Commissioners to the several Unions named in the Schedule F. hereunto annexed, as relate to the keeping, examining, closing, auditing, allowing, and publishing of the accounts of the said Unions, and of the parishes therein, and of the officers thereof, or to the keeping of any books of account relating to such Unions or parishes by any officer thereof, other than a chaplain or medical officer, or to the accounting of any such officer to the auditor, or to any other party, so far as this present Order applies to the keeping of the same or similar books, and to the accounting of such officers.

AND we do hereby, nevertheless, Order, that until the 25th day of March, 1848, the Guardians of any such Union, and the officers thereof, and the Overseers of the parishes therein, may keep their accounts and books of account in the Forms now used by them respectively.

AND subject thereto, in every case in which the Poor Law Commissioners shall not assent to a departure from any of the regulations contained in this Order, and in reference to such of the officers in the said Unions to whom this Order shall be applicable not yet appointed, as shall from time to time be appointed hereafter, WE DO, from the said 1st day of May, 1847, ORDER AND DIRECT as follows:—

KEEPING OF ACCOUNTS.

SEPARATE PAROCHIAL ACCOUNTS.

Overseers.

Art. 1.—The Overseers of every parish in the Union shall (except so far as such books are kept under their direction by any Collector) punctually enter and accurately keep the following books according to the forms and directions in the Schedule A. hereunto annexed:—

1. *A Rate Book.*—In this book shall be inserted the particulars of the assessment and collection of the Poor Rate of the parish, as set forth in the *Form* numbered 1; and in addition to the declaration required by the Act passed in the 7th year of the reign of King William the Fourth, intituled "An Act to regulate Parochial Assessments," such overseers shall, before any rate is presented to the Justices for their allowance, sign a declaration, in words at length, of the total amount of the rate so presented for allowance, according to the form or to the effect set forth in the said *Form* numbered 1.

2. *A Book of Receipts and Payments.*—On one side of this book shall be entered according to the *Form* numbered 2, an account of all monies received by the overseers, by virtue of their office, on behalf of the parish, from (1) the Poor Rate,

And, with the proper dates, under some one of the following heads:—

(2.) The rents and profits of lands or tenements

belonging to the parish, and applicable in aid of the Poor Rate.

(3.) The income or profits of other property belonging to the parish, and applicable in like manner.

(4.) Payments by the relations of paupers.

(5.) Payments by the fathers or mothers of bastard children.

(6.) Payments which may be made to the Parish on account of loans under the provisions of the first-mentioned Act.

(7.) Repayments made under orders of removal.

(8.) Relief in kind by overseers repaid under the authority of the Guardians.

(9.) Payments made by order of magistrates, or of any Court, or in consequence of any civil or penal procedings.

(10.) Proceeds of the sale of lists of claimants or lists of voters.

(11.) Payments made to the overseers on behalf of the parish from other sources, such payments to be specified in detail.

And on the other side of such Book, the overseers shall enter, in like manner, with the proper dates, an account of all monies paid and expended by them, by virtue of their office, on behalf of the parish, in respect of any of the following matters:—

(1.) Payments to the Treasurer of the Union under the authority of the Board of Guardians.

(2.) The contribution on behalf of the parish to the county, borough, hundred, police, or other rate, payable out of the Poor Rate, when paid by the overseers to the High Constable or County or Borough Treasurer.

(3.) Constables' expenses.

(4.) Costs of any proceedings before justices.

(5.) Costs of any proceedings at law or in equity.

(6 and 7.) Cost of removing paupers, distinguishing,—1st, Travelling expenses and cost of conveyances; 2d, Relief and maintenance of the paupers.

(8.) Relief in kind or medical relief administered by the overseers to poor persons in cases of sudden and urgent necessity, or sudden and dangerous illness.

(9.) Repairs or outgoings which may have been lawfully defrayed by the overseers in respect of lands or tenements belonging to the parish.

(10.) Payments of principal and interest made by the overseers in respect of money borrowed and lawfully charged on the Poor Rate.

(11.) Collector's or assistant overseer's salary or poundage.

(12.) Expenses allowed by revising barrister or other competent authority in respect of parliamentary or municipal voters.

(13.) Cost of preparing lists of jurymen.

(14.) Other charges authorized or required to be paid under any Act of Parliament by the overseers, and other expenses which may be lawfully defrayed by the overseers, such charges and expenses to be specified in detail.

And at the foot of every such account, the overseers shall insert, before each Audit, a "*Memorandum*" in respect of each rate made and allowed by justices during the half year, containing the particulars of the amount of the rate allowed, and the amount not received.

Art. 2.—The overseers of every Parish shall make out, in the *Form* numbered 3, *a Balance Sheet of the Receipts and Payments* for every half year, according to the said Receipt and Payment Book; and the overseers shall deliver such Balance Sheet to the auditor, at the audit of their accounts, to be by him examined, signed, and delivered to the Clerk of the Guardians as herein-after directed.

Art. 3.—In every case in which there are more than thirty rate-payers on the Rate Book, and in which there is no collector, the overseers shall, and in other cases the overseers may, use the following Receipt Check Books:—

1. *A Rate Receipt Check Book*, the leaves of which shall contain the *Form* numbered 4. The receipts and notes thereof shall be numbered consecutively with numbers corresponding with those in the Rate Book, and whenever the amount paid shall not require a stamped receipt, the receipt shall be detached from the said book, and issued to the rate-payer of such parish, as and when he shall pay such rate, and the note shall be retained in the said book.
2. *A General Receipt Check Book*, the leaves of which shall respectively contain the *Form* numbered 5, to be used for any payments made on account of such parish other than in respect of rates; the receipt, when the amount paid shall not require a stamped receipt, shall be detached and issued to the person who shall make such payment, and the note shall be retained in the said book.

If the amount paid by any one person for rates, or in aid of the poor rate, require a stamped receipt, the receipt directed to be given shall be retained, and a stamped receipt substituted; and a memorandum shall be made on the note of the receipt so retained that a stamped receipt has been given.

No receipt shall be detached from either of the said books until the payment of the money, in respect of which such receipt is to be given, shall have been actually made.

Art. 4.—The overseers of every Parish shall, whenever they are required so to do by the Auditor for the time being, or by the Poor Law Commissioners, accurately and truly make out a *Terrier* of the lands and tenements, and an *Inventory* of stock, monies, goods, and effects belonging to such Parish, or given or applicable in aid of the poor rates thereof, according to the *Forms* numbered 6 and 7.

Collector.

Art. 5.—Every collector already appointed or to be hereafter appointed by any Board of Guardians or other persons, under any Order of the Poor Law Commissioners, or under the provisions of any Act of Parliament, shall enter up so much of any books or Forms of the overseers relating to the collection of the Poor Rate, or the relief of the poor herein prescribed, as he may be directed to enter up by the overseers for the time being, and shall enter in the Rate Book all such particulars of every assessment as he is directed by such overseers to enter therein; and every such collector shall attend before the Auditor at the same time as the overseers of the parish for which he acts.

Provided that the signature of any such Collector to any book presented to the Auditor shall not be taken to stand for or supply the place of the signature of any overseer which may be otherwise required by this our Order.

Art. 6.—Every such collector shall in all cases fill up and use, as is herein-before directed in the case of overseers of Parishes in which there are more than thirty rate-payers on the Rate Book, a *Rate Receipt Check Book*, in the form herein-before prescribed; and when he shall receive the amount due for poor rate on behalf of any parish or its officers, he shall, at the time of receiving the same, and not before, give to the person paying such money a proper receipt, as directed in this Order in the case of overseers, and shall insert in such receipt the true date of the receipt.

Art. 7.—It shall be the duty of every collector, before he shall proceed to collect any rate, to prepare receipts in the aforesaid form, numbered both on the receipt and the note thereof with the same number consecutively throughout the book, and properly to fill in the same respectively with the names of the several rate-payers, and the sum to be collected from each; and to submit such Receipt Check Book, so numbered and filled up, to the overseers of the Parish for which such rate is to be collected, before he proceeds to collect the rate; and such overseers shall cause the correctness of the numbering, and the correspondence of the sums, and of the names filled in, with the Rate Book to which they relate, to be ascertained; and on the leaf next after the last of the receipts so made out in respect of any one rate, the said overseers shall certify the fact that such Receipt Check Book has been examined and ascertained to be correct, and shall state in words at length the number of receipts filled up for the rate then to be collected. If upon the closing of any rate there shall remain in the Rate Receipt Check Book any receipts made out for such rate unused, the collector to whom such book shall belong shall enter upon each of such receipts the reason of its not having been used, and date and sign such entry.

Art. 8.—Every such collector shall every week pay over all monies collected by him, or in his hands, belonging to any parish, to the banker whom the overseers of such parish may direct, to be placed to the account of one or more of them; or, in the absence of any such direction, to one of the said overseers in person, provided that as often as at any time in the course of any week the sum or sums of money in the hands of such collector belonging to any parish or parishes shall together exceed fifty pounds, such collector shall forthwith pay over such sum or sums as is herein-before directed.

Art. 9.—Every such collector shall keep a book to be called the *Collecting and Deposit Book*, according to the *Form* numbered 8, in which shall be entered accurately, and under their true dates, all sums received and paid over by him as such collector, and also the number of every receipt given by him out of the said Rate Receipt Check Book.

Art. 10.—Every such collector shall make out a *Monthly Statement*, containing the several particulars set forth in the *Form* numbered 9, and such statement shall be made up to the last day of each calendar month inclusive, excepting in the case of the month of March, when it shall be made up to the 25th, and in that of the month of September, when it shall be made up to the 29th; so that any receipts or payments on the remaining days of those months respectively shall be included in the next monthly statement; and he shall forthwith deliver a copy of such statement, signed by himself, to one or more of the overseers of the parish to which such statement relates, and every collector appointed by a Board of Guardians shall also deliver, or cause to be delivered, a copy so signed to the Board of Guardians at their next ordinary meeting. Provided that the Board of Guardians or the overseers of the parish may, if they think fit, require a statement containing the several particulars set forth in the said Form, numbered 9, to be made out and delivered to them respectively every week or fortnight; and the Clerk to the Guardians shall preserve the copies forwarded to the Board of Guardians, and shall produce the same to the Auditor at the next audit.

The collector shall attend any of the ordinary meetings of the Board of Guardians, if thereunto required by them.

Art. 11.—Every collector shall, at each audit, produce to the Auditor a statement, in the *Form* numbered 10, showing the name of every person rated to the relief of the poor, from whom nothing shall have been received on account of the rates made during the preceding half-year, and the other particulars set forth in such Form.

Art. 12.—In every case in which there shall be more than one collector employed in the collection of any one rate, the provisions herein-before made shall apply to the portion of such rate assigned to each collector as if such portion were one entire rate.

GENERAL ACCOUNTS OF THE UNION.

Clerk's Books.

Art. 13.—The Clerk to the Board of Guardians shall enter in the Minute Book of the Guardians a statement of the books and accounts examined by him, and of all orders drawn on the Treasurer, and monies paid or received, and all minutes relating to the allocation or division of charges, or any other pecuniary transaction of the Board of Guardians on behalf of the Union, or of any parish therein; and shall insert marginal notes of reference to the folios of the respective ledgers in which the items relating to any of such orders, payments, receipts, or other transactions are entered.

Art. 14.—The clerk shall punctually enter, and accurately keep, the following Books of Account, according to the Forms and directions in the Schedule B. hereunto annexed:—

1. *A General Ledger*, in the *Form* numbered 11, in which items of the various transactions of receipt or payment of monies by the Guardians, on behalf of the Union, or any parish therein, contained in the Minute Book, shall be entered and posted up under the following heads of account, and such additional heads as may be or may from time to time become necessary;

In-Maintenance.	Building Account.
Out-Relief.	Workhouse Loan Account.
Non-resident Poor Account.	Provisions Account.
Relief by way of Loan.	Clothing Account.
Lunatic Asylum Account.	Parish Property Account.
Extra Medical Fees.	Invoice Account, or if the Board of Guardians so direct, Tradesmen's Accounts.
Emigration Expenses.	Non-settled Poor Account.
Emigration Loan Account.	Treasurer's Account.
Vaccination Fees.	General Balance.
Registration Fees.	
County Rate.	
Common Charges.	

With the respective dates of such transactions, and references to the folios of the Minute Book, in which the entries relating to such transactions are contained, and to the folios of the corresponding credits and debits respectively.

He shall keep an account in such ledger, or in a separate ledger, to be called *The Parochial Ledger*, with every parish in the Union, in the *Form* numbered 12, and containing the particulars set forth therein.

He shall keep another account in such ledger, or in a separate ledger of the same form, to be called *The Non-settled Poor Ledger*, with every other Union and parish chargeable with relief to non-settled poor; and every such account shall be debited with the amounts to be charged against, and credited with the amounts discharged by such Union and parish.

2. *The Relief Order Book*, in which shall be entered the names of all the paupers to whom relief is ordered or allowed, together with the relief ordered or allowed in each case, and the other particulars set forth in the *Form* numbered 13.

3. *The Order Check Book.* This book shall be kept according to the *Form* numbered 14, the leaves of which shall contain all orders given by the Guardians for provisions, stores, repairs, and for other articles or work, and notes of such orders, and forms of the invoices to accompany commodities supplied, or to be delivered when work is done; such orders, when signed by the clerk, together with the form of invoice, shall be detached from the said book, and issued to the tradesmen or other persons dealt with or employed; and such notes, certified by the clerk's initials, shall be retained in the said book.

4. *The Pauper Classification Book*, in which, at the end of every half-year, shall be entered, in the *Form* numbered 15, in the columns appropriated for that purpose, the number of persons of each class relieved during the half-year, and the other particulars set forth therein.

WORKHOUSE ACCOUNTS.

Master's Books.

Art. 15.—The master of every workhouse of the Union shall punctually enter up and accurately keep the following books and accounts, according to the Forms and directions in the Schedule C. hereunto annexed.

1. *An Inventory.* In this book shall be entered, in the *Form* numbered 20, a list of all the fixtures, furniture, utensils, bedding, house linen, and other effects in the workhouse, and the stock and other like property belonging to the Union, in the workhouse, not included in the Provisions and Clothing Books, and every particular relating to the use, sale, or disposal thereof; and such book shall be completed from time to time by the entry of articles purchased or otherwise obtained, and of articles condemned as worn out, sold, or otherwise disposed of by the direction of the Board of Guardians.

2. *The Admission and Discharge Book.* In this book shall be kept, in the *Form* numbered 21, an account of every pauper admitted into, and of every pauper discharged from the workhouse, and such account shall be balanced weekly, or daily if the Board of Guardians so direct.

3. *The In-door Relief List*, in which shall be entered, for each parish of the Union, in the *Form* numbered 22, the names of the paupers chargeable thereto, with the number of days in each week, and in the half-year, during which each such pauper has been in the workhouse, and the other particulars set forth in the said form.

4. *The Abstract of the In-door Relief List*, in which shall be entered, in the *Form* numbered 23, the aggregate number of days in each week, and in the half-year, passed in the workhouse by the paupers of each parish, and the total number of such days for all the parishes in the Union, for each week and for the half-year.

5. *A Day Book*, in the *Form* numbered 24, on the one side of which shall be entered the amount of the

invoices of all goods delivered at the workhouse, together with the several particulars relating thereto, in the said *Form* set forth, and on the other side a true account, with the proper dates, of all sums of money received and of all sums of money expended by the master.

The invoices shall be entered and numbered in the order in which they are received, and shall be filed and preserved in the same order.

6. *The Daily Provisions Consumption Account.* In this account shall be entered, in the *Form* numbered 25, the number of paupers of the several classes at each meal in the workhouse, and the quantities of the principal articles of provisions daily consumed by them.

7. *The Weekly Provisions Consumption Account.* In this account shall be entered, in the *Form* numbered 26, the quantities of the principal articles of provisions consumed by the paupers in the workhouse; and also the quantities taken from the stores for the officers and servants of the workhouse in each week.

8. *The Provisions Receipt and Consumption Account.* In this account shall be entered, in the *Form* numbered 27, the quantities of the several articles of provisions and necessaries received and consumed weekly, and the quantities on hand at the commencement and end of every week, and the other particulars in such Form set forth.

9. *A Quarterly Summary of Provisions Received and Consumed.* This Summary shall be made up in the *Form* numbered 28, from the said Provisions Receipt and Consumption Account, and shall be completed quarterly.

10. *A Quarterly Balance of the Provisions Account.* In this account shall be entered, in the *Form* numbered 29, the total quantities and values of the several articles of provisions received and consumed in the quarter; and also the quantities and values of the several articles in store at the beginning and end of the quarter, and the other particulars in such Form set forth.

11. *The Clothing Materials Receipt and Conversion Account.* In this account shall be entered, in the *Form* numbered 30, a statement of all the articles of clothing materials and of bed and house linen (not made up,) from time to time received into the workhouse, and the several particulars of their conversion, and the other particulars in such Form set forth.

12. *The Clothing Receipt and Expenditure Account.* In this account shall be entered, in the *Form* numbered 31, on the one side the several articles of clothing received from tradesmen or made up in the house, and, on the other side the several articles given out, together with the numbers marked thereon.

The articles shall, as far as practicable, before they are given out, be numbered in suits, so that all the articles of a suit shall bear the same number.

The numbers shall begin with No. 1, and follow each other consecutively; but whenever any article shall have been condemned or cut up for use in mending other articles, its number may be marked on a new article of the same description.

The last two accounts, namely, *The Clothing Materials Receipt and Conversion Account,* and *The Clothing Receipt and Expenditure Account,* shall be made up, balanced, and compared with the stock in store at the end of every half year, when the accounts of the Union are closed, as herein-after mentioned, and at such other times as the Board of Guardians may require.

13. *The Clothing Register Book.* In this book shall be entered, in the *Form* numbered 32, under the number marked on the suit of clothes given out to each pauper admitted into the workhouse, the name of the pauper, together with the dates of his or her admission and discharge; and a ticket bearing such number shall be attached to the pauper's own clothes.

In addition to the number marked on the clothes, the master shall insert in the said book a number to indicate the size of the suit.

Art. 16.—So much of this Order as relates to the duties of the master of the workhouse shall be applicable to and be binding upon the matron of any workhouse not having a master; and also to and upon the matron or other person having the charge of any workhouse during the temporary absence of the master.

Out-door Relief.

Relieving Officer's Books.

Art. 17.—The relieving officer of every district in the Union shall punctually enter up and accurately keep the following books and accounts, according to the Forms and directions in the Schedule D. hereunto annexed:—

1. *The Application and Report Book.* In this book shall be entered, in the *Form* numbered 33, the applications made from time to time through the Relieving Officer for relief, and such of the particulars therein set forth as, on making the requisite examination into the circumstances of the case, he shall collect, as well as the medical relief or relief in kind, (if any,) already given by the relieving officer at his discretion, or reported to him to have been given by an overseer of the poor.

A note of the decision or direction of the Board of Guardians shall be inserted at the Board, and authenticated by the initials of the Chairman or clerk, in the column contained in the Form for this purpose.

2. *The Out-door Relief List.* In this book shall be entered, in the *Form* numbered 34, the sums of relief in money, and the value of relief in kind, given by the relieving officer to or for each pauper relieved by him in each week. The entries shall include only relief given to the pauper himself, or to some person properly authorised to receive it, and shall be made

after the relief has been actually so given, and not before or otherwise. In this book shall also be entered, in the proper columns, the number of individuals of any of the several classes relieved in each case, and the other particulars in such form set forth. The relieving officer shall enter up this book every week, and shall complete the same at the end of every half year, taking care that no pauper appear in such Relief List more than once in the half year.

3. *The Abstract of the Out-door Relief List.* In this book shall be entered, in the *Form* numbered 35, the names of the several parishes of the Union, and opposite to the names of such parishes, the amount of relief charged against them weekly in the Out-door Relief List. And such entries shall be made on the days of the ordinary meetings of the Boards of Guardians, and the Book shall remain in the custody of the clerk.

4. *The Receipt and Expenditure Book.* In this book the relieving officer shall keep, in the *Form* numbered 36, an account of all monies received and disbursed by him, and of all tickets or orders for relief in kind issued by him, and also of all articles received and given out by him for the relief of the out-door poor of each parish in his district; and he shall balance such account weekly. In this book the relieving officer shall also enter, at the end of every quarter's account, *a Summary of Receipts and Expenditure* for the quarter, in the *Form* numbered 37.

EXAMINATION AND CLOSING OF ACCOUNTS.

Art. 18.—On the day of every ordinary meeting of the Board of Guardians, or on the day next before it, unless such day shall be Sunday, and then on the previous Saturday, the clerk shall examine the Master's Day Book, and shall compare the entries of invoices with the invoices themselves, and shall see that all the goods supplied are carried by the master to the proper accounts, and shall certify the correctness of the same by his initials. He shall also compare the entries of payments, in the receipt and payment account therein, with the vouchers, and ascertain that the master has debited this account with all sums received by him, and shall insert his initials at the foot of such account. And he shall inspect the other books required to be kept by the master by this Order, so as to ascertain that they are properly kept.

The clerk shall also examine the weekly accounts in each relieving officer's Out-door Relief List, Abstract of the Out-door Relief List, and Receipt and Expenditure Book, so as to ascertain the accuracy of the entries therein, and shall certify the correctness of the same by his initials.

And the master and relieving officer shall respectively, under the direction of the Board of Guardians, present their books and accounts to the clerk for his examination on such day as aforesaid.

Art. 19.—The overseers of every parish, and every collector acting for any parish, shall make up and balance to the 25th day of March and the 29th day of September in each year, all such books as they are required, by the Act passed in the 8th year of the reign of Her Majesty Queen Victoria, intituled "*An Act for the Amendment of the Laws relating to the Poor in England*," to deposit for the inspection of the rate-payers at some house within the parish seven days at least before the audit.

Art. 20.—All the accounts of the Union and of the officers of the union shall be closed at the end of every half-year, that is to say, up to the 25th day of March and the 29th day of September in each year, or the end of the week nearest thereto. And the several officers keeping such accounts shall forthwith lay, or cause to be laid, their respective accounts so closed before the Board of Guardians.

Art. 21.—The master of the workhouse shall, at the end of every half-year, allow each relieving officer to inspect the In-door Relief List for the half-year last expired.

And each of the relieving officers shall, within fourteen days after the end of the half-year, inspect the names entered in such In-door Relief List, and shall affix a mark in red ink against the name of every pauper who shall have been entered in the Out-door Relief List in the course of the said half-year.

Art. 22.—The clerk or medical officer in possession of the District Medical Relief Books shall, at the end of every half-year, allow each of the relieving officers to inspect such books; and each of the relieving officers shall, within fourteen days after the end of the half-year, inspect the names in such books, and shall affix a mark in red ink against the name of every pauper who shall not have received any other relief during the last half-year than medical relief.

Art. 23.—The Clerk shall, under the direction of the Board of Guardians, prepare from the accounts of the Union,—1. A Statistical Statement showing the number of paupers of all classes actually relieved in the course of the last half-year, and the other particulars, according to the *Form* and directions in the said Schedule B. numbered 16; and—2. A Financial Statement showing the accounts of the Union for the last half-year in the *Form* in the said Schedule B. numbered 17; which statements the clerk shall submit to the auditor at the time of his auditing the Union accounts.

The auditor, if satisfied of the correctness of such statements, shall sign the same; and after they have been signed by the auditor, the clerk shall transmit them to the Poor Law Commissioners, and shall make a duplicate of the Financial Statement, which shall also be signed by the auditor, and shall be preserved by the clerk for the use of the Board of Guardians.

Art. 24.—The clerk shall, as soon as he shall receive notice from the auditor of the day or days appointed by him for the auditing of the half-yearly accounts of the Union, and the several parishes comprised therein, cause the following notice to be affixed on the external gate or door of every workhouse in the Union, or at some other place or places where Union notices are usually affixed, and shall continue the same so affixed until the audit is completed:—

"_______________Union.

"Notice is hereby given, that the Half-yearly Statement of the Accounts of this Union, together with the *Relief Order Book* and the *Ledgers*, will, on the day of be deposited at ; and such statement and books will be open to be inspected, examined, and copied by any owner of property or rate-payer in the said Union, at any reasonable hour in the day time, when the Board of Guardians is not sitting, until the day of ; and that on the last-mentioned day, at the hour of the accounts of the Union will be audited by the auditor of the district comprising this Union, at when and where every such owner or rate-payer in the Union, who may have any objection to any matter contained in the above-mentioned accounts, may attend, and prefer his objection, and the same will be heard by the auditor.

"Dated

"Clerk to the Board of Guardians."

Art. 25.—The clerk shall, three clear days before the day appointed for auditing the Union accounts, deposit the said Half-yearly Statement of the Accounts of the Union, together with the Relief Order Book and Ledgers, in the Board Room of the Guardians of the Union, or such other place as the Board of Guardians may appoint, and shall permit the said Statement, Book, and Ledgers to be inspected, examined, and copied by any rate-payer or owner of property in the Union, in the presence of the clerk or some other person approved of by the Board of Guardians, at any reasonable hour in the day time, when the Board of Guardians shall not be sitting, after the said Statement, Book, and Ledgers shall be so deposited, and previous to the day appointed for the auditing thereof.

Art. 26.—In case the auditing of any of the said Union or parish accounts shall be adjourned for any longer period than from day to day, the clerk, on receiving from the auditor notice thereof, shall affix, in manner aforesaid, notice of the time and place of such adjournment, and of the accounts remaining to be audited, as often as such adjournment shall be made.

Art. 27.—Within fourteen days after the 25th day of March and the 29th day of September in every year, the clerk, without waiting for the completion of the said statements or for the audit, shall transmit to the Poor Law Commissioners the following particulars for the half-year just ended as computed by him at the time:—

1. Total amount of out-door relief for the whole Union in the half-year just ended.
2. Cost of in-maintenance of paupers in one sum for the whole Union in the half-year just ended.
3. Amount of the cost of maintenance of workhouse establishment, salaries, and all other common charges distributed according to the averages for the time being.
4. Amount of any salaries paid by the Guardians not charged according to the averages.
5. Amount of principal of loans repaid, and the interest thereon.

Art. 28.—Within fourteen days after the conclusion of the audit of the accounts of the half-year ending the 25th day of March in every year, the clerk shall make up in duplicate, from the Balance Sheets of the Receipts and Payments of the Overseers, an Abstract of the separate Accounts of each parish, for the year ending on such 25th day of March, according to the *Form* and directions given in the said Schedule B. numbered 18; and one copy of such yearly Abstract shall be signed by the clerk, and transmitted to the Poor Law Commissioners, and the other copy, signed also by the clerk, shall be laid before the Board of Guardians, and preserved with the papers belonging to the Union.

Art. 29.—Every master of a workhouse shall, within seven days after the end of each half-year, insert in the proper columns, according to the *Form* in Schedule B. numbered 19, called *the Parochial List and Statement of Account*, for every parish in the Union, or, with the consent of the Board of Guardians, in a separate list containing similar columns, to be called the *Parochial List of In-door Poor*, the name of every pauper chargeable to every such parish during the previous half-year, together with the number of days each pauper has been maintained in the workhouse; and every relieving officer shall, within fourteen days after the end of each half-year, enter in the proper columns of the said *Parochial List* for every parish in his district, or, with the consent of the Board of Guardians, in a separate list containing similar columns, to be called the *Parochial List of Out-door Poor*, the name of every pauper contained in the Out-door Relief Lists for the previous half-year, together with the amounts of relief in money and in kind charged as given to each pauper.

Such Parochial Lists, when filled up by the master and relieving officers respectively, shall be delivered by them to the clerk, who shall examine the entries made therein, and shall certify to the accuracy thereof by his signature. The clerk shall also make out, in the form given at the foot of such Parochial List, a complete statement of the account of each parish with the Union, and shall sign the same.

Art. 30.—The relieving officers of the Union shall, within thirty days after the end of each half-year, under the direction of the Board of Guardians, or of the clerk, deliver a copy of each of such Lists and Statement for every parish in his district to the overseers thereof, who shall lay the same before the next vestry meeting, and preserve the same with the parish papers.

Art. 31.—The Guardians may, if they think fit, pay to each officer who has not been removed or suspended from his or her office, and who is entitled to receive from them payment of any salary, whether by way of annual stipend, poundage, or other emolument, on account of such salary, the amount which may be due at the expiration of every quarter, provided the accounts of such officer shall have been presented by him or her to the Board of Guardians duly made up. The Guardians may, however, if they think fit, defer the payment of the salary of any officer until his or her accounts shall have been allowed by the auditor.

AUDITING OF ACCOUNTS.

Art. 32.—Every auditor shall audit the accounts of all the Unions in his district, and of the parishes comprised therein, once in every half-year; that is to say, as soon as may be after the 25th day of March and the 29th day of September, respectively. Provided always, that if the auditor shall see fit, in any special case, with the consent of the Poor Law Commissioners, to hold an extraordinary audit, either of the whole or of any portion of the accounts of any Union or parish, in addition to the ordinary audit, at any time between such two days, it shall be the duty of any person who would be or would have been accountable at the ordinary audit to account at such special audit in like form and manner as at such ordinary audit, so far as the same shall be applicable to such special audit; and the surcharge, allowance, disallowance, or decision of the auditor on any item, or other matter, at such special audit, shall, so far as regards the provisions and regulations which may be contained in any Order of the Poor Law Commissioners, have the same effect as if the same were made or given at the ordinary audit of the accounts of such Union or parish.

Art. 33.—The auditor shall give to the clerk to the Guardians fourteen days' notice in writing of the time and place, on and at which he intends to commence the audit of the accounts of the Union, and of the parishes therein.

Art. 34.—The officers of the Union, and of the parishes in the Union, who by law are bound to account to such auditor, shall attend at the time and place appointed by him for the audit of their accounts, and shall submit to the auditor all books, documents, bills, and vouchers containing or relating to their accounts; and the same shall at the time of the audit be open to the inspection of any owner of property or rate-payer interested in such accounts, but to such extent and in such manner only as will not in the judgment of the said auditor interfere with the audit.

Art. 35.—In auditing the accounts, the auditor shall see that they have been kept and are presented in proper form; that the particular items of receipt and expenditure are stated in detail, and that the payments are supported by adequate vouchers and authority; and he shall ascertain whether all sums received, or which ought to have been received, are brought into account; and he shall examine whether the expenditure is in all cases such as might lawfully be made; and he shall reduce such payments and charges as are exorbitant, and disallow and strike out such as are contrary to the Orders, Rules, and Regulations of the Poor Law Commissioners, or are not otherwise authorised by law.

Art. 36.—The auditor shall examine and collate the several books and papers of account of the several accounting parties; and shall ascertain that the several entries correspond with and balance each other, where such balance may be required.

Art. 37.—The auditor shall compute the said accounts so as to verify the arithmetical accuracy thereof, and the balance due to or from the officers rendering the same at the time of the audit; and he shall state the balance in words at length, and certify the same by his signature or initials, and add the date of the audit.

Art. 38.—The auditor shall, at each audit, compare the Balance Sheet herein-before directed to be delivered to him by the overseers of every parish with the entries in the Book of Receipts and Payments of the overseers; and having certified by his signature or initials at the foot of such Balance Sheet that it is in conformity with the said book, shall deliver such Balance Sheet to the clerk to the Board of Guairdians, who shall preserve it, together with the other Balance Sheets of the same half-year, with the books and papers of the Guardians.

Art. 39.—The auditor shall receive any objection made by a rate-payer or any person aggrieved against the accounts undergoing audit, or any item or charge therein, or any vouchers or authority for the same, and shall examine into the merits of such objection, and make a decision respecting the same.

Art. 40.—If the auditor shall doubt the correctness of any account, or any item or charge in any account, he shall require the officer rendering the account, or any other person holding or accountable for any money, books, deeds, or chattels, relating to the Poor Rates or the relief of the poor, to appear before him, and shall call upon such person to produce any accounts, books, or papers which he may lawfully require; and he shall examine such officer or person, and accounts, books, and papers as may appear or be produced before him, respecting such account, item, or charge.

Art. 41.—If the auditor find that any money, goods, or chattels belonging to the Union, or any parish therein, have been purloined, embezzled, wasted, or misapplied, or that any deficiency or loss has been incurred by the negligence or misconduct of any officer or other person accounting, and shall surcharge such officer or person with such amount or value in his account, he shall submit a statement of such amount or value to the Board of Guardians as soon as he conveniently can do so.

Art. 42.—The auditor having audited the several accounts in the ledger, shall sign a certificate at the foot of the Balance Sheet therein, to the following effect:—

"I have examined the several accounts of which the foregoing is the Balance Sheet, and I have compared the several payments credited to the Treasurer with the vouchers, and I hereby certify that the entries appear to be correct and legal. And that [when the balance in the Treasurer's Book does not agree with the balance in the Ledger,] subject to the explanation below [the difference to be explained at the foot of the certificate,] the balance of the Treasurer's Account, viz., £ , agrees with the balance which by his own book appears to have been in his hands at the time of closing such account.

"Dated (Signed)

"Auditor."

And in the other books the auditor shall make a note or mark of his having audited the same.

Art. 43.—The auditor shall, at the close of each audit of the accounts of the Unions in his district, transmit to the Poor Law Commissioners a statement, in the *Form* numbered 38, Schedule E. of the books directed by this Order to be kept by the Union officers, showing which, if any, is not kept at all, or is imperfectly kept.

Art. 44.—The auditor shall, at the close of the audit of the accounts of the Unions in his district, next after the 25th day of March, in every year, transmit to the Poor Law Commissioners a statement, in the *Form* numbered 39, Schedule E, setting forth the name of each Union officer and collector of Poor Rates in his district required to give a bond, and whether such bond, together with any certificate or proof that each of the sureties named therein is living, and is not bankrupt or insolvent, was produced to him at such audit; and also, in the column headed "Observations," stating any defects in such securities.

And the auditor shall, at the close of such audit of the accounts of each Union, report to the Board of Guardians thereof the fact of such bonds and certificates having been produced to him, together with any defects in such securities.

Art. 45.—The personal representatives of an officer accountable under this Order dying before the half-yearly audit of his accounts, shall, so far as they may be by law required, account, in conformity with the provisions herein contained, in the place of such deceased officer; and all regulations affecting the accounts of such officer shall, so far as is otherwise lawful, affect the accounts of the personal representatives of such officer.

Art. 46.—If any person, being clerk to a Board of Guardians, master of the workhouse, or collector appointed by the Guardians, or relieving officer, accountable under this Order, shall resign his office or be removed therefrom before the audit of his accounts, such person shall lay before the Board of Guardians, at a time to be fixed by them, a true and complete account of all monies, matters, and things committed to the charge of, or collected, received, held or distributed by such person on behalf of the Union, or any parish therein, in such form as he would have had to produce them before the auditor at the end of the current half-year, if he had so long continued in office; and shall deliver over all balances, books, papers, matters, and things in his hands, to the Board of Guardians, or to the person whom they may appoint to receive the same, subject always to the liability of such person to account to the auditor at an audit, and without prejudice to the power of the auditor to allow or disallow the account of such person or any charge therein, or to surcharge him in respect of any charge to which he might be liable.

Art. 47.—Every person voluntarily undertaking to fulfil either wholly or in part the duties of any officer affected by this Order, shall, so far as relates to the accounts prescribed by this Order to be kept or presented by any such officer, keep and present such accounts in the same form and manner as any such officer is by this Order directed to keep and present such accounts.

Art. 48.—The clerk shall, at all reasonable times, at the request of any owner of property or rate-payer in the Union, permit him to inspect the Statements of the Union or Parish Accounts for the twelve months prior to the last audit.

AND, in reference to the PURCHASE AND CUSTODY OF BOOKS AND PAPERS for the accounts, WE DO HEREBY ORDER AND DIRECT, as follows:—

Art. 49.—The proper Books and Papers of Account for the clerk, the master of the workhouse, the medical officers, and the relieving officers, shall be purchased by the Board of Guardians at the common charge of the parishes in the Union.

Art. 50.—The Union Books and Papers of Account in current use shall remain in the custody of the proper officers accounting, and shall be produced and exhibited at the ordinary meetings of the Guardians, and whenever else the Board of Guardians may require their production, as well as on other lawful occasions.

Art. 51.—The Union Books and Papers, containing the accounts which are closed, shall be deposited for safe custody with such persons, and at such place or places, as the Board of Guardians may from time to time direct.

AND, in reference to the MEANING OF CERTAIN WORDS used in this Order, WE DO HEREBY ORDER AND DECLARE, as follows:—

Art. 52.—Whenever the word "Overseers" is used in this Order, it shall be taken to mean and include Overseers of the Poor and Churchwardens so far as they are authorised or required by law to act in the management or relief of the poor, or in the collection or distribution of the Poor Rate in any parish, and to apply to the majority of the whole body of churchwardens and overseers, or of the overseers only, as the case may be.

Art. 53.—The term "Collector," in the construing of this Order, shall be taken to include any person appointed under any Act of Parliament, or any Order of the Poor Law Commissioners, to collect the rates for the relief of the poor in any parish or parishes, whether such person shall be designated Collector of Poor Rates, or Assistant Overseer, or be called by any other name whatever.

Art. 54.—Whenever the word "Parish" is used in this Order, it shall be taken to signify any place separately maintaining its own poor.

Art. 55.—Whenever the word "Union" is used in this Order, it shall be taken to include not only a Union of parishes formed under the provisions of an Act passed in the fifth year of the reign of His late Majesty King William the Fourth, entitled, "An Act for the Amendment and better Administration of the Laws relating to the Poor in England and Wales," but also any Union of parishes incorporated or united for the relief or maintenance of the poor under any Local Act of Parliament.

Art. 56.—Whenever the word "Guardians" is used in this Order, it shall be taken to include not only Guardians appointed or entitled to act under the provisions of the said last-mentioned Act, but also any Governors, Directors, Managers, or Acting Guardians entitled to act in the ordering of relief to the poor from the Poor Rates under any Local Act of Parliament.

Art. 57.—Whenever the word "Chairman" is used in this Order, it shall be taken to mean any person acting as Chairman for the time being.

Art. 58.—Whenever the words "Board of Guardians" are used in this Order, they shall be taken to mean not only a Board of Guardians competent to act under the provisions of the said Act of the fifth year of His late Majesty, but also a meeting of such Guardians, or such a number of any Guardians as are competent to order relief to the poor from the Poor Rates under any Local Act of Parliament.

Art. 59.—Whenever in this Order any Article is referred to by its number, the Article of this Order bearing the number referred to shall be taken to be signified thereby.

SCHEDULE (A.)

Containing the Forms of the Parish Accounts to be kept by the *Overseers and Collectors.*

FORM 1. (a)—*The Rate Book.*

Form of heading to the "Rate."

An Assessment for the Relief of the Poor of the Parish of , in the County of , and for other purposes chargeable thereon, according to Law, made this day of , in the year of our Lord One thousand eight hundred and , after the rate of in the pound.

	ARREARS.		RATE.								COLLECTION.							
														Uncollected at balancing this Book.				
															Irrecoverable at balancing the Book.			
																Otherwise not recoverable.		
Number.	Due, or if excused.	If excused write the word "excused."	Name of Occupier.	Name of Owner.	Description of Property rated.	Name or situation of Property.	Estimated Extent.	Gross Estimated Rental.	Rateable Value.	Rate at — in the Pound.	Recoverable Arrears of former Rates.	Total amount to be collected.	Amount actually collected.	Recoverable Arrear at balancing the Book.	Amount legally excused.	Amount.	Causes.	
1.	2.	3.	4.	5.	6.	7.	8.	9.	10.	11.	12.	13.	14.	15.	16.	17.	18.	
	l. s. d.						A. R. P.	l. s. d.	l. s. d.	l. s. d.	l. s. d.	l. s. d.	l. s. d.	l. s. d.	l. s. d.	l. s. d.		

Form of Declaration at the foot of the "Rate."

We, do declare the several particulars specified in the respective columns of the above Rate to be true and correct so far as we have been able to ascertain them, to which end we have used our best endeavours.

We do also declare that the above Rate amounts in the whole to the sum of pounds shillings and pence.

———, *Overseer.*
———, *Overseer.*
———, *Churchwarden.*
———, *Churchwarden.*

(a) See Art. 1.

FORM 2. (a)—*Overseers' Book of Receipts and Payments.*

______ Union. Parish of ______

The Overseers' Account for the Half-year ending the day of 18 .

RECEIPTS.			PAYMENTS.		
Dates.	Items.	Totals.	Dates.	Items.	Totals.
	Memorandum.				
	Rate on £ at per £1 . .				
	Amount of Rates legally excused	.. .. ..			
	Ditto ditto not recoverable . .	.. .. ..			
	Amount to be accounted for . .	.. .. ..			

We declare the entries in the above Account and Memorandum to be true, just, and complete; and in verification thereof, we have hereunto subscribed our names this day of , 18

______ } *Overseers.*

______ } *Churchwardens.*

I find the Balance of this Account to be pounds, shillings, and pence, against (or in favour of, as the case may be) the Overseers.

Dated ______ ______ *Auditor.*

NOTE.—This Account, as well as the Rate Books and other Accounts of the Overseers, must be made up and balanced seven clear days at least before the day fixed for the Audit. See 7 and 8 Vict., c. 101, s. 33.

(a) See Art. 1.

______ *Union.* *Parish of* ______

FORM 3. (a)—*Balance Sheet of the Overseers' Receipts and Payments for the Half Year ended* 184

RECEIVED.	£	s.	d.	PAID.	£	s.	d.
Balance (if any) against the Overseers at the end of the last Half Year, when the same has not been paid to the Treasurer of the Union				Balance (if any) in favour of the Overseers at the end of the last Half Year, and paid to them .			
1. From Poor Rates				1. Contributions and other Monies paid to the Treasurer of the Union upon Orders of the Guardians			
Received in aid of the Poor Rate:—				*Separate Expenditure:—*			
2. From Rents of Parish Property . . .				2. County, Borough, Hundred, or Police Rate paid by Overseers			
3. From Income of Funds of Parish . . .				3. Constables' Expenses			
4. From Relatives of Paupers				4. Costs of Proceedings before Justices . . .			
5. From Fathers and Mothers of Bastards . .				5. Costs of other Proceedings at Law or in Equity			
6. From Repayments of Loans to Paupers . .				6. Conveyance and Travelling Expenses in removing Paupers under Orders of Removal . .			
7. From Payments under Orders of Removal .				7. Maintenance of the Paupers during Removal .			
8. Value of Relief in kind by Overseers, repaid by Relieving Officer				8. Value of Relief in Kind in cases of necessity .			
9. From Fines, &c., paid under Convictions or Orders of Justices				9. Repairs of Parish Property where lawfully made			
10. From Lists of Claimants and of Voters sold .				10. Repayment of Money and Interest duly charged on the Poor Rates			
11. Other Receipts, viz. :— (£ s. d.)				11. Collector's or Assistant Overseer's Poundage or Salary			
				12. Expenses of Parliamentary or Municipal Registration allowed by the Revising Barrister or other competent Authority			
				13. Cost of Jury Lists			
				14. Other Payments, viz. :— (£ s. d.)			
Total received				Total expended			
Balance (if any) in favour of the Overseers at the end of this Half-year				Balance (if any) against the Overseers at the end of this Half-year			

I hereby certify that this Balance Sheet is correct. ______ *Auditor.*

(a) See Art. 2.

FORM 4. (a)—*The Rate Receipt Check Book.*

This part is to be retained by the Overseers.

Parish of
of ______ 18 the day
Mr.
Rate £
Arrear £

£ ______

______ UNION.
Parish of the day of 18
Received of the Sum of in respect of the Poor Rate of the above Parish, viz. :—

	£	s.	d.
Rate made on £ Assessment, at in the Pound . . .			
Arrear of former Rate			
Total			

(Signed) ______

(a) See Art. 3, No. 1, and Art. 6.

FORM 5. (b)—*The General Receipt Check Book.*

This part is to be retained by the Overseers.

_______________ UNION.
Parish of
the day of
Mr.
For

£ ______

_______________ UNION.
Parish of the day of 18
Received of
the sum of
on behalf of the above Parish, in respect of

£ ______

(Signed) _______________

(b) See Art. 3. No. 2.

FORM 6. (a)—*Terrier of Lands and Tenements belonging to the Parish of* ________ *in the* ________ *Union.*

Name of the Estate.	Tenure of the Estate.	Name of the Parish or Place where situate.	Name of Tenant or Occupier.	Yearly Rent.	Present Application of original Rents.	Date of Original Gift or Conveyance, and Trusts thereof.	Incumbrances on the Estate.	Remarks.	Signature of Overseers and Date of signing.

FORM 7. (a)—*Inventory of Stock, Monies, and Effects belonging to the Parish of* ________ *in the* ________ *Union.*

Amount of principal Fund.	Nature of Security in which invested.	Amount of Yearly Income.	Present Application of Income.	Date of Original Gift or Assignment, and Trust thereof.	Trustees in whose Names now standing.	Remarks.	Signature of Overseers and Date of Signing.

(a) See Art. 4.

FORM 8. (a)—*The Collecting and Deposit Book.*

________ UNION. Parish of ________

RECEIPTS.											DEPOSITS.				
From Rates.					From other Sources.										
Date.	No. of Receipt.	Amount.			Date.	On what Account, and from whom received.	Amount.				Date.	With whom deposited.	Amount.		
		l.	s.	d.			l.	s.	d.				l.	s.	d.

(a) See Arts. 8 and 9.

FORM 9. (b)—*The Collector's Monthly Statement.*

_______________ UNION.

Parish of Month of 18

Drs.				The Rate-payers in account with the Collector.				Cr.
	£	s.	d.		£	s.	d.	
Amount of Rate allowed on the day of Recoverable arrears, as per last month's statement				Amount of Rates collected since last month's statement Arrears legally excused Ditto irrecoverable Ditto recoverable				
Total				Total				

Dr.				The Collector in account with the Overseers.				Crs.
Balance (if any) in the Collector's hands, at the end of last month Amount of Rates collected since Other sums than Rates collected since, (viz.)				Amount deposited with_______________ Balance (if any) in the Collector's hands				
Total				Total				

Monies due in aid of the Poor Rates, but not yet collected.

		s.	d.

Dated 18 _______________ Collector.

(b) See Art. 10.

FORM 10. (a)—*The Collector's Unpaid Rates Statement,*

Showing the Parties rated to the relief of the Poor, from whom nothing has been received on account of the Rates made during the Half Year ended_______________.

_______________ UNION. Parish of_______________

Date of the Rate.	Number in Rate Book.	Name of the Person assessed.	Rateable Value.	At what Rate per £1.	Amount of Rates.	Reason why not paid.
			£ s. d.		£ s. d.	

Dated_______________ _______________Collector.

If the Collector should be provided with a list of persons legally excused, with the numbers placed against their names, it will be sufficient for him to fill up the last four columns of this Form, by inserting the total amount excused from each rate, and the total amount of the corresponding rateable value; and it will not be necessary to insert the numbers or the names of the persons excused.

(a) See Art. 11.

SCHEDULE (B.)

Containing the General Accounts of the Union, to be kept by the *Clerk to the Board of Guardians.*

FORM 11. (a)—*The General Ledger.*

_______________ UNION. _______________ UNION.

Fo.	Dr.					CONTRA					Cr. Fo.
Date.	Folio of Minute Book.	Folio of corresponding Credit.	Corresponding *Credit* and Items.	(1)	Totals.	Date.	Folio of Minute Book.	Folio of corresponding Debit.	Corresponding *Debit* and Items.	(2)	Totals.
			To	£ s. d.	£ s. d.				By	£ s. d.	£ s. d.

(1) When to any account any sum is debited, part of which is credited to one account, and the remainder to another or others, the several sums so credited are to be written in this column, and their total in the next column. The several accounts to which such parts are credited to be written against them respectively, together with the requisite explanation in the column for "Corresponding Credit and Items."

(2) When to any account any sum is credited, part of which is debited to one account, and the remainder to another or others, the several sums so debited are to be written in this column, and their total in the next column. The several accounts to which such parts are debited to be written against them respectively, together with the requisite explanation in the column for "Corresponding Debit and Items."

(a) See Art. 14.

FORM 12. (a)—*Parochial Ledger Account.*

______ UNION. Parish of ______ Half Year ending ______

Fo.—— Dr.						Cr. Fo.——					
Date.	Folio of Minute Book.	Folio of Corresponding *Credit.*		l. s. d.	Totals. l. s. d.	Date.	Folio of Minute Book.	Folio of Corresponding *Debit.*		l. s. d.	Totals. l. s. d.
			To Balance against the Parish brought forward	.. .. ..					By Balance in favour of the Parish brought forward	.. .. ..	
			Separate Charges.						1. Treasurer of the Union		
			1. In-Maintenance	.. .. ..					" "		
			2. Out-Relief, as per Out-door Relief List						" "		
			" to Non-resident Paupers not in ditto						" "		
			3. " by way of Loan..........	.. .. ..					2. Income from Parish Property, viz.—		
			4. Maintenance of Lunatics in Asylums	.. .. ..							
			5. Extra Medical Fees or Payments....	.. .. ..							
			6. Emigration Expenses	.. .. ..					3. Other Receipts or Credits, viz.—		
			7. Vaccination Fees	.. .. ..							
			8. Registration Fees	.. .. ..							
			9. County Rates, First Quarter........								
			" Second Quarter......								
			10. Instalment of Emigration Loan, when entered into by the Guardians								
			Interest								
			11. Other separate Charges, (viz.)—								
			Common Charges.								
			12. Instalment of Workhouse Loan....								
			Interest								
			13. Salaries of Officers, and other common Charges, Share of	.. .. ..							
			Balance in favour of the Parish....	.. .. ..					Balance against the Parish		

In the columns headed "Totals" are to be entered the totals of the several classes of receipts and expenditure which are designated by the several numbers above, and these totals shall be transferred to the half-yearly "Statement of Account," Form 18, under their proper headings. In the other money columns are to be entered the several sums comprised in these totals, which are separately transferred to this account from the General Ledger Accounts. (a) See Art. 14.

FORM 13. (a)—*The Relief Order Book.*

______ UNION. Quarter ending 18

Name of Applicant.	Parish to which chargeable.	Where resident if not in the foregoing Parish.	Relief ordered or allowed by the Board of Guardians. Amount in Money.		In Kind. Quantity and Description.	Value.		For what time ordered or allowed.	Other Orders of the Board (if any.)
			s.	d.		s.	d.		

Dated this Day of 18 ,} being for the Week of Quarter. ______ *Clerk.*

FORM 14. (b)—*The Order Check Book.*

No. 184
Mr.

(*Signature.*

No. Union.
Mr. 184
Please to *

(*Signature.*)

The Particulars and Price of the Goods or Work to be inserted, and the Invoice or Account returned when the Order is executed.

No. 184
The Guardians of the Union,
Drs. To

Date.	Articles supplied or Work done.	l.	s.	d.
	Total......£			

Exd. and Entd. ______ *Master.*
______ 184 .
Correct, ______ *Clerk.*

* Insert in these spaces the name of the Tradesman, the goods to be supplied, and the place at which they are to be delivered, or the work is to be done, as the case may be.

NOTE.—This Order, with the Invoice or Account in blank, is to be detached from the note thereof, and sent to the Tradesman; the Order is to be kept by the Tradesman, and the Invoice or Account returned when the Order is executed.

(a) See Art. 14. (b) See Arts. 14 and 16.

Pauper Classification Book.

Parish of ______________ ______________ UNION. FORM 15. (a)—Statement of the Numbers of the several Classes of Paupers relieved in the half year ended ______________

IN-DOOR. Numbers of the several classes of Paupers in the Workhouse, (not including Classes 14, 15, 16, and 17.)

	1. Able-bodied and their Children. Adults. Married Couples. Males.	2. Able-bodied, Adults, Married Couples, Females.	3. Able-bodied, Adults, Other Males.	4. Able-bodied, Adults, Other Females.	5. Children under 16 of Able-bodied Inmates. Illegitimate Children.	6. Children under 16 of Able-bodied Inmates. Other Children.	7. Not able-bodied. Adults. Married Couples. Males.	8. Not able-bodied, Adults, Married Couples, Females.	9. Not able-bodied, Adults, Other Males.	10. Not able-bodied, Adults, Other Females.	11. Not able-bodied, Children under 16. Of Parents not Able-bodied being Inmates. Illegitimate Children.	12. Of Parents not Able-bodied being Inmates. Other Children.	13. Orphans or other Children relieved without Parents.	14. Lunatics, Insane Persons, and Idiots. Males.	15. Lunatics, &c. Females.	16. Lunatics, &c. Children under 16.	Summary of the preceding Columns. Adults. Males.	Summary, Adults, Females.	Summary, Children under 16.	Summary, Total.	17. Vagrants relieved in the Workhouse.	A. Total relieved in the Workhouse.
1. Persons relieved in the Half Year, as shown by the In-door and Out-door Relief Lists.																						
2. Non-resident Paupers not in the Relief Lists, including Lunatics in Asylums, Licensed Houses, and Registered Hospitals, and other Paupers in Hospitals.																						
3. Persons having received Medical Relief only, not included in the previous classes.*																						
Total............																						
The actual Number of each Class relieved on the 1st of———†.																						

OUT-DOOR. Numbers of the several Classes of Paupers relieved out of the Workhouse (not including Classes 22, 23, 24, and 25.)

	1. Able-bodied, or the Families of Able-bodied. Adult Males (married or single) relieved in Cases of Sudden and urgent Necessity.	2. Adult Males (married or single) relieved in Cases of their own Sickness, Accident, or Infirmity.	3. Adult Males relieved on account of Sickness, Accident, or Infirmity of any of the Family, or of a Funeral.	4. Adult males (married or single) relieved on account of Want of Work, or other similar Causes.	5. Families of Adult Males, in Columns 1, 2, 3, and 4, resident with the Father. Wife.	6. Families of Adult Males, &c. Children under 16.	7. Widows.	8. Children under 16 dependent on Widows.	9. Single Women without Children.	10. Illegitimate Children and their Mothers. Mothers.	11. Illegitimate Children and their Mothers. Children.	12. Families relieved on account of Parent being in Gaol, &c. Wives.	13. Families relieved on account of Parent being in Gaol, &c. Children.	14. Families of Soldiers, Sailors, and Marines relieved. Wives.	15. Families of Soldiers, Sailors, and Marines relieved. Children.	16. Resident Families of other non-resident Males relieved. Wives.	17. Resident Families of other non-resident Males relieved. Children.	18. Not Able-Bodied. Males.	19. Not Able-Bodied. Females.	20. Children under 16 relieved with Parents.	21. Orphans or other Children under 16 relieved without Parents.	22. Lunatics, Insane Persons and Idiots. Males.	23. Lunatics, &c. Females.	24. Lunatics, &c. Children under 16.	Summary of the preceding columns of Out-door Paupers. Adults. Males.	Summary, Adults, Females.	Summary, Children under 16.	Summary, Total.	25. Vagrants relieved out of the Workhouse.	B. Total relieved out of the Workhouse.	C. Gross Total, being the Sum of Columns A and B.
1. Persons relieved in the Half Year, as shown by the In-door and Out-door Relief Lists.																															
2. Non-resident Paupers not in the Relief Lists, including Lunatics in Asylums, Licensed Houses, and Registered Hospitals, and other Paupers in Hospitals.																															
3. Persons having received Medical Relief only, not included in the previous classes.*																															
Total............																															
The actual Number of each Class relieved on the 1st of———†.																															‡

* For the mode of ascertaining the number of persons having received Medical Relief only, see Art. 22 of this Order.

† The Clerk is to insert on this line the number of each class of paupers actually relieved on the *first day of January*, in the Statement for the first Half Year, and on the *first day of July* in the Statement for the second Half Year.

(a) See Art. 14.

‡ Gross Total relieved in the Half Year ....

Deduct—

1st. The number of paupers whose names appear both in the In-door and Out-door Relief Lists § ....

2nd. The number of paupers entered in the Relief Lists originally, but whose relief has since been transferred to the Non-settled Poor Account ....¶

Net Total of Paupers Relieved in the Half Year ....

§ For the mode of ascertaining the numbers to be deducted on account of entries in both the In-door and Out-door Relief Lists, see Article 21 of this Order.

¶ With regard to paupers transferred from the Relief List to the Account of Non-settled Poor, the Clerk shall call upon each Relieving Officer to give him information of any such cases which appear in his Relief List for the Half Year.

[*Statistical Statement.*] ______________ UNION. FORM 16 (a)—*Statement* (b) *of the Numbers of the several Classes.*

IN-DOOR.

PARISHES.	Numbers of the several classes of Paupers in the Workhouse (not including Classes 14, 15, 16, and 17.)													Lunatics, Insane Persons, and Idiots.			Summary of the preceding Columns.					
	Able-bodied and their Children.						Not Able-bodied.															
	Adults.				Children under 16 of Able-bodied Inmates.		Adults.				Children under 16.						Adults.					
	Married Couples.						Married Couples.				Of Parents not Able-bodied being Inmates.											
	Males.	Females.	Other Males.	Other Females.	Illegitimate Children.	Other Children.	Males.	Females.	Other Males.	Other Females.	Illegitimate Children.	Other Children.	Orphans or other Children relieved without Parents.	Males.	Females.	Children under 16.	Males.	Females.	Children under 16.	Total.	Vagrants relieved in the Workhouse.	Total relieved in the Workhouse.
	1	2	3	4	5	6	7	8	9	10	11	12	13	14	15	16					17	A
Total																						
As compared with the corresponding Half Year of last Year.... Increase																						
As compared with the corresponding Half Year of last Year.... Decrease																						
The No. of each class relieved on the 1st of —																						

FIRST QUARTER.							
NAME OF WORKHOUSES.	Classes of Paupers in each Workhouse.	No. of In-door Paupers in each at the Commencement of the Quarter.	No. of Births in the Quarter in each.	No. admitted during the Quarter in each.	No. discharged during the Quarter in each.	No. of deaths during the Quarter in each.	No. of In-door Paupers at the end of the Quarter in each.

SECOND QUARTER.							
NAME OF WORKHOUSES.	Classes of Paupers in each Workhouse.	No. of In-door Paupers in each at the Commencement of the Quarter.	No. of Births in the Quarter in each.	No. admitted during the Quarter in each.	No. discharged during the Quarter in each.	No. of deaths during the Quarter in each.	No. of In-door Paupers at the end of the Quarter in each.

(a) See Art 23.

(b) This Statement is made up from the *Pauper Classification Book*; it will not be necessary to make a duplicate of it.

*of Paupers relieved in the Half-Year ended*____________________

OUT-DOOR.

Numbers of the several Classes of Paupers relieved out of the Workhouse (not including Classes 22, 23, 24, and 25.) — Able-bodied, or the Families of Able-bodied: Adult Males (married or single) relieved in Cases of Sudden and urgent Necessity.	Adult Males (married or single) relieved in Cases of their own Sickness, Accident, or Infirmity.	Adult Males relieved on account of Sickness, Accident, or Infirmity of any of the Family, or of a Funeral.	Adult males (married or single) relieved on account of Want of Work, or other Causes.	Families of Adult Males, in Columns 1, 2, 3, and 4, resident with the Father: Wife.	Children under 16.	Widows.	Children under 16 dependent on Widows.	Single Women without Children.	Illegitimate Children and their Mothers: Mothers.	Children.	Families relieved on account of Parent being in Gaol, &c.: Wives.	Children.	Families of Soldiers, Sailors, and Marines relieved: Wives.	Children.	Resident Families of other non-resident Males relieved: Wives.	Children.	Not Able-Bodied: Males.	Females.	Children under 16 relieved with Parents.	Orphans or other Children under 16 relieved without Parents.	Lunatics, Insane Persons, and Idiots: Males.	Females.	Children under 16.	Summary of the preceding columns of Out-door Paupers: Adults: Males.	Females.	Children under 16.	Total.	Vagrants relieved out of the Workhouse.	Total relieved out of the Workhouse.	Gross Total, being the Sum of Columns A and B.	Deduct Persons relieved, both In-door and Out-door, and included twice in Column C.; also Persons whose Relief has been transferred to the Non-settled Poor-Accounts.	Net Total of Persons relieved.
1	2	3	4	5	6	7	8	9	10	11	12	13	14	15	16	17	18	19	20	21	22	23	24					25	B	C	*	†

Number of different Cases attended by the Medical Officers in each District and in the Workhouse in the Half Year.

Name of the Medical Officer.	District or Workhouse.	Number of Cases.
	Total........	

____________________ *Clerk.*

____________________ *Auditor.*

* This column is to contain the total numbers to be deducted from the gross total for each Parish, according to the *Pauper Classification Book.*

† This column is to contain the net total for each Parish, according to the *Pauper Classification Book.*

[Financial Statement.] ____________ Union. Form 17. (a)—*Statement of Account, showing the Receipts, Expenditure, and Balances, for the Half Year ended* ____________ 18

PARISHES.	RECEIPTS.								EXPENDITURE.																	
										Separate Charges.													Common Charges.			
											Out-Relief.															
	Balance in favour of each Parish at the Commencement of this Half Year.	Contributions paid during this Half Year. 1	Dividends or Parish Property Produce, credited to the Parishes. 2	Other Receipts, specifying them. 3 (1)	(2)	(3)	Balance against each Parish at the End of this Half Year.	Total.	Balance against each Parish at the Commencement of this Half Year.	In-Maintenance. 1	Out-Relief in Money, and in Kind, including Relief to Non-resident Poor.* 2	Relief by way of Loan. 3	Maintenance of Lunatics in Asylums or Licensed Houses. 4	Extra Medical Fees or Payments charged to the Parishes. 5	Emigration Expenses. 6	Vaccination Fees. 7	Registration Fees. 8	County Rates. 9	Emigration Loans and Interest Repaid. 10	Other separate Charges, specifying them. 11 (1)	(2)	(3)	Workhouse Loan and Interest Repaid.† 12	Salaries of Officers and other Common Charges, apportioned according to the existing averages.¶ 13	Balance in favour of each Parish at the end of the Half Year.	Total.
Total............			..					...																		
Expenditure of corresponding Half of last Year	..	..		..	..	..	..	..	..																..	..
As compared with the corresponding half of last year. Increase of Expenditure	..	..	..	..	..	..	..	..	..																..	..
As compared with the corresponding half of last year. Decrease of Expenditure	..	..	..	..	..	..	..	..	..																..	..

Total Receipts (exclusive of Balances) £————

Total Expenditure (exclusive of Balances) £————

* Non-resident relief which passes through the hands of the Relieving Officer in the ordinary course will be included in this Column from the Relief List. Non-resident relief, which does not pass through his hands, must be added by the Clerk to the amount of the Relief List before the Sum is entered here.

† Apportioned according to the averages in force at the Time the Money was borrowed.

Name of Officer.	Office.	Half-Year's Salary.			Totals. § l.	s.	d.

¶

Principal Particulars of the "other Common Charges."	l.	s.	d.

§ The totals of the salaries to the Medical Officers, and the totals of the salaries to the other Officers, are to be carried out separately; and the total cost of the Maintenance of the Workhouse Establishment for each quarter and for the half year, as shown by the Provisions Receipt and Consumption Account (see Form No. 27) is to be entered after the other salaries.

(a) See Art. 23.

____________ Clerk.

____________ Auditor.

____________ UNION. FORM 18. (a)

[Abs]tract of the Separate Accounts of the Parishes in the Union for the Year ended the 25th day of March, 18

RECEIPTS.

County of	PARISHES.	In aid of the Poor Rates.												Total of Receipts in aid of Poor Rates.	Total Receipts from Poor Rates and Payments in aid thereof.	Balance due last Year from Parish Officers and not paid to the Treasurer of the Union.	Total.	Balance due to Parish Officers at the End of this Year.	Total.
		From Poor Rate.	From Rents of Parish Property.	From Income of Funds of Parish.	From Relations of Paupers.	From Fathers and Mothers of Illegitimate Children.	From Repayments of Loans to Paupers.	From Payments under Orders of Removal.	Value of Relief in Kind repaid by Relieving Officer.	From Fines, Penalties, and Forfeitures, paid under Convictions or Orders of Justices.	From Lists of Claimants and of Voters sold.	Other Receipts.							
		1	2	3	4	5	6	7	8	9	10	11							

EXPENDITURE.

Contributions to the Union and other Sums paid on account of the Parish to the Credit of the Guardians with the Treasurer.	Separate Expenditure.														Total of Payments to Union, and Separate Expenditure.	Balance due last Year to Parish Officers.	Total.	Balance due from Parish Officers at the End of this Year.	Total.
	County, Borough, Hundred, or Police Rates, paid by Overseers.	Constables' Expenses.	Costs of Proceedings before Justices.	Other Costs of Proceedings at Law or in Equity.	Cost of Conveyance and Travelling Expenses in Removals.	Maintenance of the Paupers during Removal.	Value of Relief in Kind in Cases of Necessity.	Repairs of Parish Property where lawfully made.	Repayment of Money & Interest duly charged on the Rates.	Collector's or Assistant Overseer's Poundage or Salary.	Expenses allowed by Revising Barrister or other competent Authority, in respect of Parliamentary or Municipal Registration.	Cost of Jury Lists.	Other Payments.	Total of Separate Expenditure.					
1	2	3	4	5	6	7	8	9	10	11	12	13	14						

A true Abstract from the Balance Sheets of the Receipts and Payments of the several Parishes in the Union, made this day of

(a) See Art. 28. ____________ *Clerk to the Guardians.*

FORM 19. (a)—*The Parochial List and Statement of Account.*

____________ UNION. Parish of ____________

List of Paupers whose Relief is charged against the Parish, together with a Statement of the Amounts respectively credited and debited to the Parish, in the Union Accounts for the Half Year ending ____________ 18

IN-DOOR POOR.		OUT-DOOR POOR.								
Names of the Paupers.	No. of Days' Maintenance.	Names of the Paupers.	If not in the above Parish, where resident.	Cause of requiring Relief.	Amount given to each Pauper during the Half Year.					
					In Money.			In Kind.		
					l.	*s.*	*d.*	*l.*	*s.*	*d.*

____________ Master. ____________ Relieving Officer.

Dr.

	l.	*s.*	*d*
Balance against the Parish, brought forward			
Separate Charges.			
In-Maintenance			
Out-Relief, as per Out-door Relief Lists................			
,, to Non-resident Paupers, not in ditto.........			
,, by way of Loan..			
Maintenance of Lunatics in Asylums			
Extra Medical Fees or Payments			
Emigration Expenses			
Vaccination Fees			
Registration Fees			
County Rates, First Quarter.......			
,, Second Quarter..			
Instalment of Emigration Loan when entered into by the Guardians			
Interest			
Other Separate Charges (viz.)			
Common Charges.			
Instalment of Workhouse Loan, apportioned according to the averages in force at the time the money was borrowed			
Interest, apportioned in like manner			
Salaries of Officers and other common charges, apportioned according to the existing averages, share of			
Balance in favour of the Parish			

Cr.

	l.	*s.*	*d.*
Balance in favour of the Parish, brought forward			
Contributions and other Monies paid to the Treasurer of the Union upon Orders of the Guardians			
Income from Parish Property (viz.)			
Other Receipts or Credits (viz.)			
Balance against the Parish			

(a) See Arts. 30 and 31. ____________ *Clerk.*

SCHEDULE (C.)

Containing the Forms of the Workhouse Accounts to be kept by *the Master of the Workhouse.*

UNION. ____________

FORM 20. (a)—*The Inventory Book.*

Date of Entry.	(*)						Articles transferred, condemned, or disposed of.		
	Fixtures.	Furniture.	Utensils.	Bedding. †	House Linen. †	Other Effects.	Date.	Notes of Articles transferred to other Parts of the House.	Notes of Articles condemned or disposed of.

* A separate page is to be devoted to each office, room, or apartment, and in this space is to be inserted the name of the office, room, or apartment to which the page is appropriated.

† Under the head "Bedding" are to entered mattresses, beds, blankets, sheets, and rugs; and under "House Linen" are to be entered table cloths and towels.

A blank space should be left at the end of each apartment or division for the inser ion of new articles.

Notes of articles transferred to other parts of the house, condemned, or disposed of, should be made as soon as the same takes place, and the new purchases should be punctually entered so as to represent the exact state of the house in reference to the articles to be entered in this book at all

______________ UNION.

FORM 21. (a)—*The Admission and Discharge-Book.*

ADMITTED.																				DISCHARGED.																
Day of the Month.	Day of the Week.	Next Meal after Admission.	Name.	Class for Diet.*									Number affixed to the Paupers' Clothes.	Parish to which charged	By whose Order admitted.	Date of the Order of Admission.	If born in the House, Name of Parent.	Cause of seeking Relief.	Observations on Condition at the Time of Admission, & any other General Remarks	Date.	Day of the Week.	Last Meal before Discharge	Name.	Class for Diet. *									Parish to which charged	How discharged; and if by Order, by whose Order.	In case of Death, say "Dead."	Observations on general Character and Behaviour in the Workhouse.
				1	2	3	4	5	6	7		9												1	2	3		5	6	7	8	9				

When a Pauper is admitted before breakfast the Master is to enter in the column for "next meal after admission" the letter B; when before dinner the letter D; and when before supper the letter S. And when a Pauper is discharged after breakfast the Master is to enter in the column for "last meal before discharge" the letter B; when after dinner the letter D; and when after supper the letter S.

* The columns "Class for Diet," are to be filled up by the figure 1. The Classes for Diet are,—1. Able-bodied Men; 2. Old and Infirm Men; 3. Boys from 9 to 13 or 16, according to the Dietary Order; 4. Boys from 2 to 9; 5. Able-bodied Women; 6. Old and Infirm Women; 7. Girls from 9 to 13 or 16, according to the Dietary Order; 8. Girls from 2 to 9; 9. Infants.

FORM 22. (a)—*In-door Relief List for the Parish of*______________.

______________ UNION. Half Year ending______________.

Able-bodied and their Families (exclusive of Vagrants.)						Not able-bodied and their Families (exclusive of Vagrants).							Lunatics, Insane Persons, and Idiots.			Calling of Pauper.	When born.	Of what Religious Persuasion.	Name of Pauper.	Number of Days in the House in each Week.																											Totals for the Half Year.
Adults.				Children under 16 of Able-bodied Inmates		Adults.				Children under 16.																																				
Married Couples.						Married Couples.				Of Parents (not able-bodied) being Inmates																																				
Males.	Females.	Other Males.	Other Females.	Illegitimate.	Other Children.	Males.	Females.	Other Males.	Other Females.	Illegitimate.	Other Children.	Orphans or other Children relieved without their Parents.	Males.	Females.	Children under 16.					1st Week.	2d Week.	3d Week.	4th Week.	5th Week.	6th Week.	7th Week.	8th Week.	9th Week.	10th Week.	11th Week.	12th Week.	13th Week.	14th Week.	15th Week.	16th Week.	17th Week.	18th Week.	19th Week.	20th Week.	21st Week.	22nd Week.	23rd Week.	24th Week.	25th Week.	26th Week.	27th Week.	
1	2	3	4	5	6	7	8	9	10	11	12	13	14	15	16																															
																Totals of each Class			Total Days for each Week																											
																			Number of Vagrants Total....																											

1. The columns for the classification of the Paupers are to be filled by inserting the figure 1 in the proper column opposite each name, and leaving all the rest blank.
2. Whenever, in this Relief List, two or more persons of the same name occur, the Master of the Workhouse shall annex to the name of each of such persons a number in brackets, to distinguish him from other persons of the same name.
3. No Pauper is to be entered as a "vagrant" who is relieved for more than 24 hours, or who is regularly admitted into the Workhouse.
4. The number of each class of paupers actually relieved on the *First of January*, and on the *First of July*, respectively in each year, is to be shown at the beginning of this Book, a portion of the Book being set apart and ruled for this purpose.

(a) See Art. 15.

FORM 23. (a)

______________ UNION.

ABSTRACT of the IN-DOOR RELIEF LISTS for the Half Year ending______________18

Folio of the In-door Relief List.	Parishes.	1st Week.	2nd Week.	3rd Week.	4th Week.	5th Week.	6th Week.	7th Week.	8th Week.	9th Week.	10th Week.	11th Week.	12th Week.	13th Week.	14th Week.	15th Week.	16th Week.	17th Week.	18th Week.	19th Week.	20th Week.	21st Week.	22nd Week.	23rd Week.	24th Week.	25th Week.	26th Week.	27th Week.	Total Days for the Half Year.
	Total Days for each Week																												

The aggregate number of days in each week passed in the Workhouse by the total number of Paupers of each parish must be taken from the columns of total days for the several weeks in the In-door Relief Lists.

A few sheets of this Abstract (according to the extent of the Union) are to be bound up at the end of the Book containing the In-door Relief Lists.

______________ UNION.

FORM 24. (a)—*The Master's Day Book.*

INVOICES.					
Date.	No. of Invoice.	Account to be charged.	Name and Trade.	Amount.	Clerk's Initials.

RECEIPTS.					PAYMENTS.				
Date.	Name and Particulars.				Date.	Name and Particulars.			

(a) See Art. 15.

_______________ UNION. FORM 25. (a)—*Daily Provisions Consumption Account for* _______ *the* _______ *day of* _______ 18 .

BREAKFAST.

CLASS.	Total Numbers.	Deduct. Sick. *	Deduct. Absent.	Net Numbers.	Prepared Provisions. (1) oz. each.	lb.	oz.	Pints each.		each.	
1											
2											
3											
4											
5											
†											
6											
7											
8											
9											
Totals (2)											
Quantities of the several principal Articles in their unprepared state taken from the Stores to supply the above Meals (3).											

DINNER.

CLASS.	Total Numbers.	Deduct. Sick. *	Deduct. Absent.	Net Numbers.	Prepared Provisions. oz. each.	lb.	oz.	each.		each.	
1											
2											
3											
4											
5											
6											
7											
8											
9											
Totals											

SUPPER.

CLASS.	Total Numbers.	Deduct. Sick. *	Deduct. Absent.	Net Numbers.	Prepared Provisions. oz. each.	lb.	oz.	each.		each.	
1											
2											
3											
4											
5											
6											
7											
8											
9											
Totals											

(1) The names of the articles prescribed in the Dietary are to be inserted.
(2) The total quantities on this line represent the quantities of the several articles of prepared provisions required for each meal.
(3) The quantities of the several principal articles in their unprepared state, necessary to supply the quantities of prepared provisions so required, are to be entered under the quantities of prepared provisions for each meal, and carried to the "*Weekly Provisions Consumption Account* (Form 26.) In the case of meat, the weight of bone and meat are to be shown separately, but the weight of bone may be added to the meat in the Weekly Account, (Form 26.)
* Those only of the Sick who have not the ordinary diet are to be deducted.
† On this line are to be placed such of Class 5 as have larger allowances than the Diet Table gives, on account of their being employed as nurses or in the household work.
(a) See Art. 15.

_______________ UNION. FORM 26. (a)—*Weekly Provisions Consumption Account. The* _______ *Week of the Quarter ending* _______ 18

Date.	Day of the Week.	Meal.	Consumed by the Paupers. lb.	oz.	lb.	oz.					Taken from the Stores for the Officers and Servants of the Workhouse (1).						Number of Paupers in the House during the Day.	Number of Members of the Establishment.
		Breakfast..........															}	
		Dinner																
		Supper																
		Breakfast..........															}	
		Dinner																
		Supper																
		Breakfast..........															}	
		Dinner																
		Supper																
		Breakfast..........															}	
		Dinner																
		Supper																
		Breakfast..........															}	
		Dinner																
		Supper																
		Breakfast..........															}	
		Dinner																
		Supper																
		Breakfast..........															}	
		Dinner																
		Supper																
Sick as per Medical Relief Book																		
Totals to be carried to the "*Provisions Receipt and Consumption Account,*" (Form 27.)																	(2)	

(1) The quantities of the articles taken from the stores for the Officers and Servants of the Workhouse are to be entered at the time when they are taken.
(2) This total should agree with the total number of days in the Abstract of the In-door Relief List for the corresponding week.

FORM 27. (a)—*Provision Receipt and Consumption Account for the* ________ *Week of Quarter ending* ________

________ UNION.

ARTICLES.	Stock brought forward.	New Stock.	No. of Invoice.	Totals of Stock brought forward, and new Stock.	Consumed. By the Paupers.	Consumed. By the Officers and Servants of the Workhouse.	Remaining in Store.	Totals consumed and remaining in Store.	Required for next Week.

The "New Stock" of the several Articles, and the quantities "Consumed" "by the Paupers," and "by the Officers and Servants of the Workhouse" respectively, are to be carried to the "Summary of Provisions Received and Provisions Consumed." (Form 28.

(a) See Art. 15.)

FORM 28. (a)—*Summary of Provisions Received and Provisions Consumed in the Quarter ending* ________

________ UNION.

	*														
Received 1st week	lb. oz.	lb. oz.													
" 2nd															
" 3rd															
" 4th															
" 5th															
" 6th															
" 7th															
" 8th															
" 9th															
" 10th															
" 11th															
" 12th															
" 13th															
Totals received															
Consumed by the Paupers 1st week															
" 2nd "															
" 3rd "															
" 4th "															
" 5th "															
" 6th "															
" 7th "															
" 8th "															
" 9th "															
" 10th "															
" 11th "															
" 12th "															
" 13th "															
Totals consumed by the Paupers															
Consumed by the Officers and Servants of the Workhouse 1st week															
" 2nd "															
" 3rd "															
" 4th "															
" 5th "															
" 6th "															
" 7th "															
" 8th "															
" 9th "															
" 10th "															
" 11th "															
" 12th "															
" 13th "															
Totals consumed by the Officers and Servants of the Workhouse........															

* The names of the Articles are to be placed at the head of the several Columns.

The "Totals received," the "Totals consumed by the Paupers," and the "Totals consumed by the Officers and Servants of the Workhouse," are to be carried to the "Balance of the Provisions Account for the Quarter." (Form 29.)

(a) See Art. 15.

______________ UNION. FORM 29. (a) *Balance of the Provisions Account for the Quarter ending* ______________.

Articles.	Stock brought forward.	Price.		Cost of Stock brought forward.			New Stock.	Price.		Cost of New Stock.			Total Cost of New Stock, and Stock brought forward.			Consumed. By the Paupers.				Consumed. By the Officers and Servants of the Workhouse.				Stock remaining in Store.	Cost of Stock remaining in Store.			Total Cost of Articles Consumed and in Store.		
																Quantities.	Cost.			Quantities.	Cost.			Quantities						
		s.	d.	l.	s.	d.		s.	d.	l.	s.	d.	l.	s.	d.		l.	s.	d.		l.	s.	d.		l.	s.	d.	l.	s.	d.

(a) See Art. 15.

______________ UNION. FORM 30. (a)—*Clothing Materials and Receipt and Conversion Account.*

RECEIVED. (*)				CONVERTED. (*)			Folio of Clothing Receipt and Expenditure Book, or of Inventory Book.
Date.	Of whom.	No. of Invoice.	Quantity.	Date.	Into what.	Quantity used.	

* A separate Account is to be kept of each article, and the name of the article is to be entered at the head of the page.
The entries are to be made in the true order of time according as the articles are received and converted; and the account is to be made up and balanced every half-year.
Sheets, bedding, and house linen are to be entered in the Inventory, Form 20, and charged by the Clerk in the Ledger to the Common Charges Account.
The articles of clothing into which the materials are converted are to be carried to the Clothing Receipt and Expenditure Account, Form 31, in their proper columns.
(a) See Art. 15.

______________ UNION. FORM 31. (a)—*Clothing Receipt and Expenditure Account.*

RECEIVED.

Date.	From whom or whence received.	Men's and Boys' Clothing. Coats and Jackets.	Waistcoats.	Trousers.	Shirts.	Shoes.	Stockings.	Hats.	Handkerchiefs.	Women's and Girls' Clothing. Gowns and Frocks.	Under Petticoats.	Upper Petticoats.	Shifts.	Aprons.	Handkerchiefs.	Shoes.	Stockings.	Caps.	Bonnets.

GIVEN OUT.

Date.	Men's and Boys' Clothing. Number of the Suit.	Coats and Jackets.	Waistcoats.	Trousers.	Shirts.	Shoes.	Stockings.	Hats.	Handkerchiefs.	Date.	Women's and Girls' Clothing. Number of the suit.	Gowns and Frocks.	Under Petticoats.	Upper Petticoats.	Shifts.	Aprons.	Handkerchiefs.	Shoes.	Stockings.	Caps.	Bonnets.

In the several Columns is to be entered, according to the circumstances of the case, the number of the articles received and given out.
The Entries are to be made in the true order of time, according as the articles are received and converted, and the Account is to be made up and balanced every half year.
(a) See Art. 15.

_______________ UNION.

FORM 32. (a)—*Clothing Register Book.*

MALES.									FEMALES.								
No.* . [Size .]			No. . [Size .]			No. . [Size .]			No. . [Size .]			No. . [Size .]			No. . [Size .]		
Date of Admission.	Names.	Date of Discharge.	Date of Admission.	Names.	Date of Discharge.	Date of Admission.	Names.	Date of Discharge.	Date of Admission.	Names.	Date of Discharge.	Date of Admission.	Names.	Date of Discharge.	Date of Admission.	Names.	Date of Discharge.

* By the No. here is intended the Number given by the Master to each suit.

(a) See Art. 15.

SCHEDULE (D.)

Containing the Forms of the Accounts of Out-Relief and Out-door Paupers to be kept by *the Relieving Officer.*

_______________ UNION.

FORM 33. (a)—*The Application and the Report Book for the Quarter ending* _______________ 18 . Parish of _______________

Names of Applicants, their Wives and Children under 16, dependent on them.	Age.	Residence, where, or with whom.	Calling.	If Adult, whether Single, Married, Widow, or Widower. If Child, whether Orphan, Deserted, or Illegitimate.	If ordinarily Able-bodied.	If partially or wholly Disabled, and the Description of Disability.	IF RECEIVING		Present Cause of seeking Relief, or nature of Application.	OBSERVATIONS and Names of Relations liable by Law to relieve the Applicant, distinguishing those apparently capable of assisting the Applicant.	Present Weekly Earnings, or other Income of Applicants, and Family dependent on them.	Quantity and Description of Relief in Kind.		Value.	Date when given.	Relief ordered by Guardians.				Other Orders of the Board (if any.)	Week when Order made.	Initials of Chairman or Clerk.	Observations.
							Medical Relief.	Regular or Temporary Relief, and any other, and what Relief from Clubs, Charitable Institutions, Government Pensions, or otherwise; such Relief, Pension, Allowance, or Contribution to be described, and the Amount stated.				Reported as given by Overseers.	Given by Relieving Officer.			Money.	Kind.		For what time allowed, or nature of the Order made.				
																	Quantity and Description.	Value.					
														s. d.		s. d.		s. d.					

Instructions to the Relieving Officer for filling up the Application and Report Book.

1. The names of individuals comprised in families seeking relief must be inserted in the List in succession, thus:—
John Smith, Father, Rachael Smith his Wife, } Children {Anne, Jane;
with the requisite particulars of each member of each family placed opposite his name in the proper column.

2. If the age be not exactly known, it must be given as correctly as may be.

3. In setting down the calling of the applicant for relief, the name of the particular branch of labour which he has exercised must be inserted, thus :—" Agricultural labourer," "Thatcher," &c. In like manner, the callings of the relations of the applicant who may be liable to contribute to his or her maintenance should be stated. In the cases of children the parents' calling must be inserted.

4. Care must be taken to inquire closely into the causes of the applications for relief, and to insert a correct statement of them.

5. In specifying the causes of the applications for relief by able-bodied labourers, where the application is founded on the loss of work, name the particular sort of work.

6. In specifying the causes of the applications for relief of children who become chargeable from the neglect or inability of their parents to provide for them, specify the nature of the inability or other cause; as, " Father's insanity ;" " Father's inability to obtain work ;" " Father absent from home ;" " Father imprisoned."

7. In cases of applications arising from infirmity of mind or body, designate the nature and extent of the infirmity; as a " Lunatic," or " Idiot," or " Deaf and Dumb," or " Crippled in the hand or foot," or " Helpless from old age."

(a) See Art. 18.

FORM 34. (a)—*Out-*

_______________ UNION.

Parish of _______________ Half Year ending _______________

STATISTICAL PORTION.

Able-bodied, or the Families of able-bodied.																	Not able-bodied.								Name of the Pauper.	If not residing in the Parish to which the Relief is charged, where resident.		1st Week, ending	2nd Week, ending	3rd Week, ending	4th Week, ending
Adult Males, (married or single) relieved in Cases of sudden and urgent Necessity.	Adult Males (married or single) relieved in Cases of their own Sickness, Accident, or Infirmity.	Adult Males relieved on account of Sickness, Accident, or Infirmity of any of the Family, or of a Funeral.	Adult Males (married or Single) relieved on account of Want of Work, or other Causes.	Families of Adult Males, in Columns 1, 2, 3, & 4, resident with the Father.		Widows.	Children under 16, dependent on Widows.	Single Women without Children.	Illegitimate Children and their Mothers.		Families relieved on account of Parent being in Gaol, &c.		Families of Soldiers, Sailors, and Marines relieved.		Resident Families of other non-resident Males relieved.		Males.	Females.	Children under 16 relieved with Parents.	Orphans or other Children under 16 relieved without their Parents.	Lunatics, Insane Persons, and Idiots.			Vagrants relieved out of the Workhouse.							
				Wife.	Children under 16.				Mothers.	Children.	Wives.	Children.	Wives.	Children.	Wives.	Children.					Males.	Females.	Children under 16.								
1	2	3	4	5	6	7	8	9	10	11	12	13	14	15	16	17	18	19	20	21	22	23	24	25				s. d.	s. d.	s. d.	s. d.
																											In Money ..				
																											In Kind				
																											In Money ..				
																											In Kind				
																											In Money ..				
																											In Kind				
																											In Money ..				
																											In Kind				
																											In Money ..				
																											In Kind				
																											In Money ..				
																											In Kind				
																											In Money ..				
																											In Kind				
																											In Money ..				
																											In Kind				
																											In Money ..				
																											In Kind				
																											In Money ..				
																											In Kind				
																											In Money ..				
																											In Kind				
																											In Money ..				
																											In Kind				
																											In Money ..				
																											In Kind				
																											In Money ..				
																											In Kind				
																											Weekly Totals				
																											Clerk's Initials	Correct.	Correct.	Correct.	Correct.

Instructions as to

1. If an able-bodied man, being head of the family, is sick or temporarily disabled, he is to be entered in column 2; if out of work, in column 4; and in either case the whole family dependent on him are to be entered as chargeable in columns 5 and 6.

2. If the relief is given on account of the sickness of a wife or child, or specially for a wife or child only, and the head of the family, are to be inserted in the list; the man in the case of such sickness in column 3, and in any other case in column 4, the wife or child in column 5 or 6. If the relief is given on account of the funeral of any member of a family, the surviving head of the family only is to be entered as the person relieved; if there be no surviving head of the family, then the person buried must be considered as the pauper. Relief given to women and their children dependent on them is to be entered in the proper column in the same manner.

3. Non-resident as well as resident paupers, when paid through the Relieving Officer, are to be entered in the account for the Parish to which they belong, but non-settled paupers residing in the Union, and relieved by the Relieving Officer, whose relief is to be repaid by other Unions, are to be entered in separate accounts to be opened in the Out-Relief List for the Unions to which such paupers belong.

4. The column 4, in Unions where the Prohibitory Order is in force, will contain the special cases of relief to adult males or their families in which out-door relief is given under Article VI. of that Order, not being within the exceptions of the Order.

(a) See Art. 17.

door Relief List.

_______________ Relieving Officer.

MONEY PORTION.

5th Week, ending .	6th Week, ending .	7th Week, ending .	8th Week, ending .	9th Week, ending .	10th Week, ending .	11th Week, ending .	12th Week. ending .	13th Week. ending .	Totals for the First Quarter. In Money.	Totals for the First Quarter. In kind.	1st Week, ending .	2nd Week, ending .	3rd Week, ending .	4th Week, ending .	5th Week, ending .	6th Week, ending .	7th Week, ending .	8th Week, ending .	9th Week, ending .	10th Week, ending .	11th Week, ending .	12th Week, ending .	13th Week, ending .		Totals for the Second Quarter. In Money.	Totals for the Second Quarter. In Kind.	Totals for the Half Year.
s. d.	s. d.	s. d.	s. d.	s. d.	s. d.	s. d.	s. d.	s. d.	s. d.	s. d.	s. d.	s. d.	s. d.	s. d.	s. d.	s. d.	s. d.	s. d.	s. d.	s. d.	s. d.	s. d.	s. d.		s. d.	s. d.	£ s. d.
																											b
									£ s. (a) d.																£ s. (a) d.		
Cor-rect.	Cor-rect.	Cor-rect.	Cor-rect.	Cor-rect.	Cor-rect.	Cor-rect.	Cor-rect.	Cor-rect.	Correct.		Cor-rect.	Cor-rect.	Cor-rect.	Cor-rect.	Cor-rect.	Cor-rect.	Cor-rect.	Cor-rect.	Cor-rect.	Cor-rect.	Cor-rect.	Cor-rect.	Cor-rect.	Cor-rect.	Correct.		Correct

filling up this Form.

5. The same person is on no account to be entered twice in the half year, either in the money or statistical portion of this Relief List.
6. In the column headed "Name of the Pauper," the name of the head of the family alone is to be inserted.
7. The number of each class of Paupers actually relieved on the *first of January* and on the *first of July* is to be shown at the beginning of the Out-door Relief List, a portion of the List being set apart and ruled for that purpose. By persons in the receipt of relief on these particular days is meant not only persons to whom relief is actually given on either of these days, but persons whose allowance is for any period which includes either of these days.
8. The totals marked (*a*), being the quarterly totals of the relief in money and kind, will answer to the cross-castings of the previous thirteen "Weekly Totals." The final total marked (*b*) will be the amount of the two quarterly totals; the column of totals for the half year being obtained by cross-casting for each pauper the quarterly totals in money and kind respectively. This final total is to be credited to the Out-Relief Account, and debited to the several Parishes in the Parochial Ledger.
9. Where relief in kind is administered through the medium of Tickets, all relief out of the cash in the Relieving Officer's hands, whether in money or articles of necessity, is to be entered as Money.

______ UNION. FORM 35. (a)—*Abstract of the Out-door Relief List.*

Names of Parishes.	1st Week	2nd Week	3rd Week	4th Week	5th Week	6th Week	7th Week	8th Week	9th Week	10th Week	11th Week	12th Week	13th Week	14th Week	15th Week	16th Week	17th Week	18th Week	19th Week	20th Week	21st Week	22nd Week	23rd Week	24th Week	25th Week	26th Week		Totals.
	l. s. d.	l. s. d.	l. s. d.	l. s. d.	l. s. d.	l. s. d.	l. s. d.	l. s. d.	l. s. d.	l. s. d.	l. s. d.	l. s. d.	l. s. d.	l. s. d.	l. s. d.	l. s. d.	l. s. d.	l. s. d.	l. s. d.	l. s. d.	l. s. d.	l. s. d.	l. s. d.	l. s. d.	l. s. d.	l. s. d.	l. s. d.	l. s. d.
Totals.																												
Clerk's Initials																												

______ UNION. FORM 36. (a)—*The Relieving Officer's Receipt and Expenditure Book.*

______ DISTRICT. ______ Week of the Quarter ending ______ 18 .

______ Relieving Officer, in account with the Board of Guardians of the ______ Union.

Dr.							*Cr.*						
Date.	Money received, and Tickets issued.						Parishes and Unions charged.						
		l.	s.	d.	l.	s.	d.		l.	s.	d.	l.	s.	d.

(a) See Art. 17.

FORM 37. (a)—*Summary of Receipts and Expenditure for the Quarter ended* ______ 184 .

(To be entered immediately after the Account for the last Week of every Quarter in the Relieving Officer's Receipt and Expenditure Book.)

Dr.	Money.			Kind.			*Cr.* Parishes and Unions charged.	Money.			Kind.		
	l.	s.	d.	l.	s.	d.		l.	s.	d.	l.	s.	d.
Balance brought forward							Parishes in Relieving Officer's District, as per Out-Relief List, viz.—						
							" "						
							" "						
							" "						
							" "						
As per Receipt and Expenditure Book—1st week							Totals (1)..........						
" " 2nd "													
" " 3rd "							Unions charged with Relief to Non-settled Poor, as per Out-Relief List, viz.—						
" " 4th "							" "						
" " 5th "							" "						
" " 6th "							" "						
" " 7th "													
" " 8th "													
" " 9th "							Totals (2)..........						
" " 10th "													
" " 11th "													
" " 12th "							Sums of Totals (1) and (2) respectively..					(B)	
" " 13th "							Balance in hand at the end of the Quarter						
		(A)			(B)				(A)				

(a) See Art. 17.

The totals marked (A) and (B) respectively must correspond. The totals of the expenditure in money in respect of the relief of the settled and non-settled poor, with the balance in hand (if any), will give the total marked (A), and those of the relief in kind will give the total marked (B), on the credit side of this account.

SCHEDULE (E).

FORM 38. (a)—*Statement of the Auditor in reference to the Books of the several Unions in the* ________ *District for the Half Year ended* ________, 18

		SCHEDULE (B). CLERK.						SCHEDULE (C). MASTER OF WORKHOUSE.													SCHEDULE (D). RELIEVING OFFICER.					
Names of Unions.	Name of Officer omitting to keep any Book, or keeping it imperfectly.	Minute Book.	General Ledger.	Parochial Ledger.	Relief Order Book.	Order Check Book.	Pauper Classification Book.	Inventory.	Admission and Discharge Book.	In-door Relief List.	Abstract of In-door Relief List.	Master's Day Book.	Daily Provisions Consumption Account.	Weekly Provisions Consumption Account.	Provisions Receipt and Consumption Account.	Quarterly Summary of Provisions Received and Consumed.	Quarterly Balance of Provisions Account.	Clothing Materials Receipt and Conversion Book.	Clothing Receipt and Expenditure Book.	Clothing Register Book.	Application and Report Book.	Out-Relief List.	Abstract of Out-Relief List.	Receipt and Expenditure Book.	Quarterly Summary of Receipts and Expenditure.	Observations.
			11	12	13	14	16	20	21	22	23	24	25	26	27	28	29	30	31	32	33	34	35	36	37	

Dated ________, 18 ________, *Auditor.*

Under the name of any Book contained in this Schedule which is not kept at all, or is imperfectly kept, the Auditor is to write, opposite to the name of the officer ordered to keep such book, in the former case "not kept," and in the latter the word "imperfectly." If there be no defect the Auditor must state that fact in the Column for Observations.

(a) See Art. 43.

FORM 39. (a)—Statement of the Auditor of the ________ District in reference to the Officers' Bonds required to be produced to him at the Audit next after the 25th day of March, 18

Names of Unions.	Name of every Officer required to give a Bond.	Office.	Whether the Bond was produced.	Whether any Certificate or Proof, that each Surety is living, and is not Bankrupt or Insolvent, was produced.	Observations.

Dated ________, 18

(a) See Art. 44. ________ *Auditor.*

SCHEDULE (F.)

Containing the Names of the Unions to which the annexed Order applies.

Aberaeron.
Abergavenny.
Aberystwith.
Abingdon.
Albans, St.
Alcester.
Alderbury.
Alnwick.
Alresford.
Alton.
Altrincham.
Amersham.
Amesbury.
Ampthill.
Andover.
Anglesey.
Asaph, St.
Ashbourne.
Ashby-de-la-Zouch.
Ashford, East
Ashford, West.
Ashton-under-Lyne.
Aston.
Atcham.
Atherstone.
Auckland.
Austell, St.
Axbridge.
Axminster.
Aylesbury.
Aylsham.
Bakewell.
Bala.
Banbury.
Bangor and Beaumaris.
Barnet.
Barnstaple.
Barrow-on-Soar.
Basford.
Basingstoke.
Bath.
Battle.
Beaminster.
Bedale.
Bedford.
Bedminster.
Belford.
Bellingham.
Belper.
Berkhampstead.
Berwick-upon-Tweed.
Beverley.
Bicester.
Bideford.
Biggleswade.
Billericay.
Billesdon.
Bingham.
Bishop Stortford.
Blaby.
Blackburn.
Blandford.
Blean.
Blofield.
Blything.
Bodmin.
Bolton.
Bootle.
Bosmere and Claydon.
Boston.
Boughton, Great
Bourn.
Brackley.
Bradfield.
Bradford (Wilts.)
Bradford (York.)
Braintree.
Brampton.
Brecknock.
Brentford.
Bridge.
Bridgend and Cowbridge.
Bridgwater.
Bridgnorth.
Bridlington.
Bridport.
Brixworth.
Bromley.
Bromsgrove.
Bromyard.
Buckingham.
Builth.
Buntingford.
Burnley.
Burton-upon-Trent.
Bury.
Caistor.
Calne.
Cambridge.
Camelford.
Cardiff.
Cardigan.
Carlisle.
Carmarthen.
Carnarvon.
Castle Ward.
Catherington.
Caxton and Arrington.
Cerne.
Chailey.
Chapel-en-le-Frith.
Chard.
Cheadle.
Chelmsford.
Cheltenham.
Chepstow.
Chertsey.
Chesterfield.
Chester-le-Street.
Chesterton.
Chippenham.
Chipping Norton.
Chipping Sodbury.
Chorley.
Chorlton.
Christchurch.
Church Stretton.
Cirencester.
Cleobury Mortimer.
Clifton.
Clitheroe.
Clun.
Clutton.
Cockermouth.
Colchester.
Columb, St., Major
Congleton.
Conway.
Cookham.
Corwen.
Cosford.
Cranbrook.
Crediton.
Crickhowel.
Cricklade & Wootton Basset.
Croydon.
Cuckfield.
Darlington.
Dartford.
Daventry.
Depwade.
Derby.
Devizes.
Dewsbury.
Docking.
Dolgelly.
Doncaster.
Dorchester.
Dore.
Dorking.
Dover.
Downham.
Drayton.
Driffield.
Droitwich.
Droxford.
Dudley.
Dulverton.
Dunmow.
Durham.
Dursley.
Easington.
Easingwold.
Eastbourne.
East Grinstead.
Easthampstead.
East Retford.
Eastry.
East Ward.
Ecclesall Bierlow.
Edmonton.
Elham.
Ellesmere.
Ely.
Epping.
Epsom.
Erpingham.
Eton
Evesham.
Faith, St.
Falmouth.
Fareham.
Faringdon.
Farnham.
Faversham.
Festiniog.
Flegg, East and West.
Foleshill.
Fordingbridge.
Forehoe.
Freebridge Lynn.
Frome.
Fulham.
Fylde.
Gainsborough.
Garstang.
Gateshead.
Germans, St.
Glanford Brigg.
Glendale.
Glossop.
Gloucester.
Godstone.
Goole.
Grantham.
Gravesend and Milton.
Greenwich.
Guildford.
Guiltcross.
Guisborough.
Hackney.
Hailsham.
Halifax.
Halstead.
Haltwhistle.
Hambledon.
Hardingstone.
Hartismere.
Hartley Wintney.
Haslingden.
Hastings.
Hatfield
Havant.
Haverfordwest.
Hay.
Hayfield.
Headington.
Helmsley Blackmoor.
Helston.
Hemel Hempstead.
Hendon.
Henley.
Henstead.
Hereford.
Hertford.
Hexham.
Highworth and Swindon.
Hinckley.
Hitchin.
Holbeach.
Holborn.
Hollingbourn.
Holsworthy.
Holywell.
Honiton.
Hoo.
Horncastle.
Horsham.
Houghton-le-Spring.
Howden.
Hoxne.
Huddersfield.
Hungerford.

Huntingdon.
Hursley.
Ipswich.
Ives, St.
Keighley.
Kendal.
Kettering.
Keynsham.
Kidderminster.
Kingsbridge.
Kingsclere.
King's Lynn.
King's Norton.
Kingston-upon-Thames.
Kingston.
Knighton.
Lampeter.
Lancaster.
Lanchester.
Langport.
Launceston.
Ledbury.
Leek.
Leicester.
Leigh.
Leighton Buzzard.
Leominster.
Lewes.
Lewisham.
Lexden and Winstree.
Leyburn.
Lichfield.
Lincoln.
Linton.
Liskeard.
Llandilo Fawr.
Llandovery.
Llanelly.
Llanfyllin.
Llanrwst.
Loddon and Clavering.
London, City of.
London, East.
London, West.
Longtown.
Loughborough.
Louth.
Ludlow.
Luton.
Lutterworth.
Lymington.
Macclesfield.
Machynlleth.
Madeley.
Maidstone.
Maldon.
Malling.
Malmsbury.
Malton.
Manchester.
Mansfield.
Market Bosworth.
Market Harboro'.
Marlborough.
Martley.
Medway.
Melksham.
Melton Mowbray.
Mere.
Meriden.
Merthyr Tydvil.
Midhurst.
Mildenhall.
Milton.
Mitford and Launditch.
Monmouth.
Morpeth.
Mutford and Lothingland.
Nantwitch.
Narberth.
Neath.
Neot's, St.
Newark.
Newbury.
Newcastle-in-Emlyn.
Newcastle-under-Lyne.
Newcastle-upon-Tyne.
Newent.
New Forest.
Newhaven.
Newmarket.
Newport (Monmouth.)
Newport (Salop.)
Newport Pagnell.
Newton Abbot.
Newtown and Llanidloes.
Northallerton.
Northampton.
North Aylesford.
Northleach.
Northwich.
North Witchford.
Nottingham.
Nuneaton.
Oakham.
Okehampton.
Olave's, St.
Ongar.
Ormskirk.
Orsett.
Oundle.
Pateley Bridge.
Patrington.
Pembroke.
Penkridge.
Penrith.
Penzance.
Pershore.
Peterborough.
Petersfield.
Petworth.
Pewsey.
Pickering.
Plomesgate.
Plympton, St. Mary.
Pocklington.
Pont-y-pool.
Poole.
Poplar.
Portsea Island.
Potterspury.
Prescot.
Presteigne.
Preston.
Pwllheli.
Radford.
Reading.
Redruth.
Reeth.
Reigate.
Rhayader.
Richmond (Surrey.)
Richmond (Yorkshire.)
Ringwood.
Risbridge.
Rochdale.
Rochford.
Romford.
Romney Marsh.
Romsey.
Ross.
Rothbury.
Rotherham.
Royston.
Rugby.
Runcorn.
Ruthin.
Rye.
Saffron Walden.
Salford.
Samford.
Saviour's, St.
Scarborough.
Sculcoates.
Sedbergh.
Sedgefield.
Seisdon.
Selby.
Settle.
Sevenoaks.
Shaftesbury.
Shardlow.
Sheffield.
Sheppey.
Shepton Mallett.
Sherborne.
Shiffnal.
Shipston-upon-Stour.
Skipton.
Skirlaugh.
Sleaford.
Solihull.
Southam.
South Molton.
South Shields.
South Stoneham.
Southwell.
Spalding.
Spilsby.
Stafford.
Staines.
Stamford.
Stepney.
Steyning.
Stockbridge.
Stockport.
Stockton.
Stokesley.
Stone.
Stourbridge.
Stow.
Stow-on-the-Wold
Strand.
Stratford-upon-Avon.
Stratton.
Stroud.
Sturminster.
Sudbury.
Sunderland.
Swaffham.
Swansea.
Tamworth.
Taunton.
Tavistock.
Teesdale.
Tenbury.
Tendring.
Tenterden.
Tetbury.
Tewkesbury.
Thakeham.
Thame.
Thanet, Isle of
Thetford.
Thingoe.
Thirsk.
Thomas, St.
Thornebury.
Thorne.
Thrapston.
Ticehurst.
Tisbury.
Tiverton.
Todmorden.
Tonbridge.
Torrington.
Totnes.
Towcester.
Tregaron.
Truro.
Tunstead and Happing.
Tynemouth.
Uckfield.
Ulverstone.
Uppingham.
Upton-upon-Severn.
Uttoxeter.
Uxbridge.
Wakefield.
Wallingford.
Walsal.
Walsingham.
Wandsworth and Clapham.
Wangford.
Wantage.
Ware.
Wareham and Purbeck.
Warminster.
Warrington.
Warwick.
Watford.
Wayland.
Weardale.
Wellingborough.
Wellington (Salop)
Wellington (Somerset.)
Wells.
Welwyn.
Wem.
Weobly.
Westbourne.
West Bromwich.
Westbury-upon-Severn.
Westbury and Whorwelsdown.
West Derby.
West Firle.
West Ham.
West Hampnett.
West Ward.
Weymouth.
Wheatenhurst.
Whitby.
Whitchurch.
Whitechapel.
Whitehaven.
Wigan.
Wigton.
Williton.
Wilton.
Wimborne and Cranborne.
Wincanton.
Winchcombe.
Winchester, New.
Windsor.
Winslow.
Wirrall.
Wisbeach.
Witham.
Witney.
Woburn.
Wokingham.
Wolstanton and Burslem.
Wolverhampton.
Woodbridge.
Woodstock.
Worcester.
Worksop.
Wortley.
Wrexham.
Wycombe.
Yeovil.
York.

Given under our Hands and Seal of Office, this Seventeenth day of March, in the year One thousand eight hundred and forty-seven.

(Signed) GEO. NICHOLLS.
G. C. LEWIS.
EDMUND W. HEAD.

POOR-LAW COMMISSION OFFICE,
SOMERSET HOUSE,

The Clerk to the Board of Guardians. 17*th March*, 1847.

SIR,—The Poor Law Commissioners' Order, relating to accounts, now rescinded, was issued generally, in 1836. During the period which has elapsed since the issuing of that Order, experience has shown that the books and forms prescribed by it are susceptible of being rendered, in some respects, more complete. A change, moreover, has become necessary in consequence of the alteration in the periods of the Audit of Accounts, effected under the authority of the Act of 7 and 8 Vic. c.101.

The Commissioners have accordingly framed the Order sent with this letter, and have issued it as a general rule to the Unions throughout the country.

It will be observed, that until the 25th of March, 1848, the adoption of the Books and Forms prescribed by this order will be discretionary with the Board of Guardians, and the officers of Unions and parishes, and thus will be avoided much of the inconvenience, which otherwise might be occasioned by the sudden introduction of an entirely new set of books and forms.

The Commissioners will now proceed to point out the chief alterations which this Order effects, and explain such of its provisions as seem to require explanation.

ART. 1-4—relate to the books and accounts of Overseers.

The Rate Book.—(Form 1.)—The form of this book differs from that prescribed by the Commissioners in their General Order, dated 22nd April, 1842, relating to the duties of Overseers, and the present Form supersedes the one referred to. The arrears of rates in column No. 2, which are not excused, are, according to this Form, to be carried to column 12, headed "recoverable arrears of former rates;" and the sums in that column, and the amount of the new rate as stated in column 11, being added together, will constitute the "amount actually to be collected," to be entered in column 13.

The Overseers' Book of Receipts and Payments—(Form 2)—is to contain an account of all sums received and paid by the overseers on behalf of the parish; these, as the law now stands, will be found to come under some of the heads of receipts or payments set forth in Art. 1; and also in the *Balance Sheet*, Form 3. Every transaction, excepting receipts from poor rate, should be entered under its true date. Monies received from the poor rate cannot be entered in this manner, but the total amount received on account of each rate during the half year, should be entered in one sum. In the *memorandum* at the foot of the account for the half year, should be entered in respect of each rate,—1. the total amount of the rate; 2. the amount legally excused in such rate; 3. the amount not recoverable; and 4. the sum remaining to be accounted for.

The attention of the overseers is particularly directed to section 33, of the Act 7 and 8 Vic. c. 101, which requires that the rate-books and other accounts of the parish, should be made up and balanced seven clear days at least before the day fixed for the audit of accounts, and that the books so made up should be forthwith deposited for inspection at the house of some one of the overseers, or other officers, or of the collector or assistant overseer, or at same other house within the parish. The non-observance of these requisitions may subject the overseers to certain penalties.

The Balance Sheet of the Overseers' Receipts and Payments—(Form 3)—is a modification of the overseers' present "Quarterly Statement," and is to contain the total amount of each class of the overseers' receipts and payments for the half-year, arranged in the order, and under the heads indicated in the Form. This balance sheet will furnish the Clerk of the Board of Guardians with the materials for preparing the Yearly *Abstract of the separate accounts of the Parishes*—(Form 18)—the headings of which correspond, in all respects, with the items in the "Balance Sheet." (See Art. 28.)

It will be seen, by reference to Art. 19, that the overseers' books are to be made up and balanced to the 25th of March, and the 29th of September, in each year.

ART. 3.—*The Rate Receipt Check-Book, and General Receipt Check-Book.*—(Forms 4 and 5.)—It will be observed that the overseers are not bound to use these books when there are less than thirty rate-payers on the Rate-Book. Collectors, however, being paid Officers, are, in all cases, bound, by Art. 6, to keep the former of these books.

ART. 4.—*The Terrier and Inventory*—(Forms 6 and 7)—which, under the former Order, all overseers were required to make out at the end of the Michaelmas quarter of every year, are now to be made out when the overseers are required to do so by the auditor, or by the Commissioners.

ART. 5-12—contain provisions in regard to collectors. It will be noticed that, according to Art. 53, the term collector includes both the assistant overseers and collectors, whether appointed under any Act of Parliament, or any order of the Commissioners.

ART. 6.—In parishes where the number of the rate-payers is large, it will be convenient if the collector leaves a note, properly dated, of the demand for Poor Rate at the house of every rate-payer who may not pay the rate when first demanded.

It is obviously undesirable that a collector of poor rates should hold money in his hands for a longer time than is absolutely necessary; and the Commissioners have, therefore, by Art. 8, required that every collector shall pay over weekly, all monies in his hands belonging to the parish, to the overseers' banker, or to one of the overseers themselves; and that, whenever, in the course of any week, the sum of money in his hands shall exceed £50, he shall pay over the sum forthwith. The "*Collecting and Deposit Book*" (Form 8) is prescribed for the purpose of showing the amount in the collector's hands at any time.

The Collector's Monthly Statement—(Form 9)—which will be made up from the materials contained in the "Collecting and Deposit Book" is, in pursuance of Art. 10, to be delivered by every collector to one or more of the overseers, and by every collector appointed under an order of the Commissioners it is also to be delivered to the Board of Guardians. The object of this statement is to inform the overseers and the Board of Guardians of the state of the collector's account at the close of each month. The Commissioners request the particular attention of overseers and Boards of Guardians to the necessity of superintending the proceedings of persons employed in collecting the poor rates: full opportunity for doing so will be given by the *statement* now prescribed, and proper vigilance, on the part of the local authorities, may prevent loss.

The Collector's Unpaid Rates Statement.—(Form 10.)—Under section 32, of the 7 and 8 Vic. c. 101, the overseers are liable for any money which may be lost through their neglect; and the auditor is empowered to surcharge them therewith. The object of this statement is to enable the auditor to ascertain whether any, and what amount of poor rates may have been so lost; and, also, whether any poor rates remain uncollected, which are recoverable, and which ought to have been collected. It is necessary for overseers to bear this in mind, as by section 61 of 7 and 8 Vic. c. 101, every collector or assistant overseer is bound to obey the majority of the overseers of the parish for which he acts in all matters relating to the collection of the rates; and it must, at the same time, be remembered that the responsibility of the overseers for the payment of contributions and other matters, is not diminished by the appointment of a collector or assistant overseer whom they themselves have the power of controlling.

ART. 13 and 14 relate to the accounts to be kept by the clerk.

The Minute Book.—It will be observed, that Art. 13 requires the clerk to set forth in the Minutes, in addition to the proceedings of the Board, a statement of the books and accounts examined by him.

The General Ledger.—(Form 11.)—The principle upon which the Ledgers are to be kept, is the same as that exemplified in the Commissioners, former Order. Several additional accounts have, however, become necessary since the issuing of that Order. With regard to the "Invoice Account," or "Tradesmen's Accounts," the Commissioners recommend that the Invoices entered in the Master's *Day Book* (Form 24) should be posted, either to the credit of an "Invoice Account," or, if the Board of Guardians so direct, to the credit of separate "Tradesmen's Accounts," and to the debit of the "Provisions Account," the "Common Charges Account," or such other proper accounts as each case may require.

The Parochial Ledger—(Form 12)—is intended to contain the accounts of the several parishes with the Union, to the debit of which accounts are to be posted the portions of the several classes of expenditure chargeable to such parishes; and to the credit of which are to be posted the contributions paid by the overseers to the treasurer of the Union, and any other sums to the credit of which the parishes may be entitled, such, for example, as balances struck by the auditors, and paid over to the treasurer in pursuance of 7 and 8 Vic. c. 101, sec. 32. The Parochial Ledger will be adopted in such Unions only as contain a sufficient number of parishes to make it desirable to do so. In small Unions it will, probably, be found most convenient to open accounts with the several parishes in the General Ledger, as has been the custom under the former Order.

It will be observed, that the several items in the "Parochial Ledger" are to be printed and numbered in precisely the same order as they appear in the "*Financial Statement,*"—(Form 17.) This will greatly facilitate the making up of the statement, and will materially contribute to the accuracy of this branch of the accounts.

The Non-settled Poor Ledger.—The Commissioners think that it may be found convenient in Unions, in which there are accounts for relief to non-settled poor against many other Unions, to keep such accounts in a separate ledger, so that the account against each of such Unions for several years may appear at one view, and also be separated from the General Accounts of the Union advancing the relief.

With regard to the necessity for keeping the Parochial Ledger, and the Ledger for Non-settled Poor in separate books, the clerk will take the directions of the Board of Guardians. No extra trouble will be imposed upon him by the mere separation of the books.

The Relief Order Book—(Form 13)—is substituted for the present "Abstract of the Application and Report Book," and is to contain entries of those cases in which the Board of Guardians order relief to be given, or allow relief provisionally given by the relieving officers. It will not be necessary that minutes of any orders for relief entered in this book should be entered also in the ordinary Minute Book, but minutes may be made therein referring to the particulars recorded in this book: care should be taken that the entries in this book correspond with those in the *Application and Report Book*—(Form 33)—on which it is a check, the latter being ordinarily in the custody of the relieving officer.

The Order Check Book.—(Form 14.)—This book is to be used in every case in which orders are given by the Board of Guardians, for articles to be supplied, or for work or repairs to be done.

The Pauper Classification Book.—(Form 15.)—This book is to be made up from the Statistical portion of the In-door and Out-door Relief Lists, the Non-resident Poor Accounts, and the Medical Relief Books. The numbers of paupers belonging to each parish of the several classes relieved in the half-year being brought together in this book, will constitute the materials for making up the *Statistical Statement* (Form 16) which the clerk, by Art. 23, is required to transmit to the Commissioners.—See Articles 21 and 22, and the Notes at the foot of the Form. No fresh labour is imposed on the clerk by keeping this book, the particulars being substantially the same as those contained in the "Quarterly Abstract;" on the contrary, a saving of labour is effected, inasmuch as this book and the Statistical Statement, will have to be made up only half yearly. This book, moreover, renders unnecessary any copy or duplicate of the Statistical Statement. The "Pauper Description Book" is discontinued.

ART. 15—prescribes the accounts to be kept by the master of the workhouse.

1. *The Inventory Book.*—(Form 20.)—It will be observed, that bedding and house linen which, under the former Order were entered in the Clothing Accounts, are to be entered in this book in addition to fixtures, furniture, utensils, and other effects.

2. *The Admission and Discharge Book.*—(Form 21.)—This book, as revised, is so arranged as to show the numbers in the workhouse at each meal, of the several classes into which the paupers are distributed in the "Daily Provisions Consumption Account."—(Form 25.) —It will show also the number attached to the pauper's own clothes when they are put aside upon his admission, and also marked on the clothes given out to such pauper. Under the same number his name will be found in the "Clothing Register Book."—(Form 32.)

3. *The In-door Relief List*—(Form 22)—as revised, is adapted to the half-yearly accounts. The present mode of indicating in the "In-door Relief List" the classes to which the paupers belong having been found inconvenient in making up the statistical portion of the former "Abstract"—(Form 11 B)—the Commissioners have inserted in the present Form the several columns of the "Statistical Statement," which will now be substituted for that portion of the Abstract.

The entries in these columns being made by the master, the several totals may be transferred by the clerk to the "Pauper Classification Book," with far greater readiness than can now be done, when he has to abstract and classify the individuals entered in the Relief Lists.

4. *The Abstract of the In-door Relief List*—(Form 23)—has merely been adapted to the half-yearly accounts.

5. *The Master's Day Book.*—(Form 24.)—This book is provided in order that the master may record all the invoices of goods supplied, and of work done at the workhouse. It also furnishes a cash account in which the master is to enter all his receipts and payments. By Art. 18 the clerk is required to examine the entries in this book, and to see that all the goods supplied are carried by the master to the proper accounts in his books. It will be the clerk's own duty to carry them to the proper accounts in the ledger.

6. *The Daily Provisions Consumption Account*—(Form 25) is introduced to facilitate the ascertaining of the quantities of the several principal articles of cooked or prepared provisions required according to the Diet Table, for each meal; and also to record these quantities, together with the quantities of the articles in the form in which they are received into the house, that is, in their raw or unprepared state. It is essential that the master should record the actual consumption of the raw provisions taken out of store and not returned thereto, rather than, as is sometimes the case at present, enter as the quantities consumed a mere weekly estimate or calculation made with reference to the Diet Table.

7. *The Weekly Provisions Consumption Account.*—(Form 26.)—This account is prescribed for the purpose of collecting together, in weekly totals, the quantities in their raw or unprepared state, of the several articles which appear by the "Daily" Account to have been used during each week. The weekly entry for such of the sick as *have not the ordinary house diet*, will be checked by the diet and the amount of extras, every article of which for the week should be entered opposite each name in the *Workhouse Medical Relief Book*. The blank columns in that book may be used for the entry of the articles of an ordinary kind not mentioned in the printed headings.

8. *The Provisions Receipt and Consumption Account*—(Form 27)—as revised, differs from the form now in use principally in being divested of the money columns. A considerable saving of time and labour to the master will be effected, by requiring the calculations of the money value of the quantities of the several articles entered in this account to be made quarterly instead of weekly.

In order, however, to effect this alteration, it was necessary to introduce the *Quarterly Summary of Provisions Received and Provisions Consumed*—(Form 28)—so as to enable the master to ascertain the quarterly totals of provisions received, provisions consumed by the officers and servants of the workhouse, and provisions consumed by the paupers.

10. *Quarterly Balance of the Provisions Account.*—(Form 29.)—This Form is similar to that of the "Provisions Receipt and Consumption Account," excepting that money columns are added for the purpose of introducing the calculations referred to in the notice of that account. Should this account not balance on the first trial, it will at once be seen, by comparing the columns of totals, in reference to which article, the error has arisen: and by tracing backwards the entries relating to that article the error will readily be detected.

With regard to the Provisions Accounts generally, it may appear at first sight, that the Forms now prescribed are more complicated than those in use. In fact, however, all the steps prescribed in these Forms have heretofore been necessarily taken by the master, if his accounts have been properly kept, although he may not have preserved a permanent record of them; and the keeping of these accounts ought, therefore, to entail no additional labour on him.

11. *The Clothing Materials Receipt and Conversion Account.*—(Form 30.)—This book, in its modified form, will be in the nature of a *Dr.* and *Cr.* account of every article of materials for clothing and bed and house linen. The Account will be debited with the several articles of materials supplied to the workhouse from time to time, and credited with the quantities of such materials from time to time converted into clothing or bed and house linen.

12. *The Clothing Receipt and Expenditure Account.*—(Form 31.)—The number of articles of clothing of each description purchased, or made up in the house, is to be entered in the proper column of this Account, when purchased or made up, in the same manner as the number of articles is entered in the present "Clothing Receipt Book." In reference to the expenditure of clothing a different system to that hitherto pursued is introduced. It will be seen, that clothing is to be numbered in suits before it is given out. A suit for a man will probably consist of one coat, one waistcoat, one pair of trowsers, two

shirts, a pair of shoes, two pairs of stockings, one hat, and two handkerchiefs, all of which will bear the same number. When a suit is given out, the number marked thereon is to be entered in the column appropriated for that purpose, and the number of articles of each description comprised in the suit, is also to be entered in the proper columns. This account being balanced at the end of the half-year, will shew the numbers of the several new articles remaining in store.

13. *The Clothing Register Book.*—(Form 32.)—At the head of the several columns of this book, numbers will be inserted beginning with Number 1, and following each other consecutively; and when a suit of clothes is given out, the name of the person to whom it is given, with the date of his admission, will be entered under the number marked on the suit. In addition to this number, another number, indicating the size of the suit, is to be inserted in the space set apart for it. When the person to whom the suit was given out is discharged, the date of his discharge is to be entered, and such entry will show that the suit is available for any other person whom it may fit; and the name of the other person to whom the same suit is given out, will be entered under the previous name. When any article of a suit is worn out, another article of the same size and description is to take its number, and be substituted for it. This article will, of course, be entered in the Clothing Receipt and Expenditure Account in the manner already explained.

The Commissioners have not come to the determination of adopting this system, without first ascertaining that it was not only practicable, but perfectly simple, and that it had been in use in some workhouses for several years. The Commissioners have learnt that Mr. CHARLES KNIGHT will be prepared to supply the stamps and ink necessary for impressing the numbers on the clothes, at a trifling cost. The number should on no account be stamped on a conspicuous part of the garment, but it should be so placed, as not to be visible when the garment is worn.

The principle on which the charge for clothing is to be distributed, like that on which the charge for provisions is distributed, is the collective number of days during which the paupers of each parish have been maintained in the workhouse. It is difficult, however, to estimate accurately the wear and tear of clothes, some of which last a longer and some a shorter time.

The Commissioners believe that the most common, although not the most accurate plan is, to charge against the parishes whose paupers have been received into the workhouse during the quarter, the cost of all *new* clothing given out of store (*not all new clothing purchased*) in the course of that quarter. Thus, the balance of the clothing account carried on represents the value of the new clothing in store, and what has been given out (though the master is of course bound to account for it, to preserve it, and to use it,) is charged when it is given out *once for all.* The Commissioners believe that it is a general rule that if the cost of clothing exceeds a halfpenny a day, inquiry should be made into this department of the accounts.

It will be for the Guardians to approximate as nearly as possible to the principle of the Poor-Law Amendment Act, that each parish should bear the cost of the relief afforded to the poor chargeable to it in the workhouse, and the Commissioners do not prescribe the adoption of any one particular method of arriving at the result: but what they do prescribe is uniformity in the mode in which the facts are recorded, and the books are to be kept, so that it may always be possible to obtain the necessary data for ascertaining how far the charge made is a proper charge.

ART. 17—prescribes the books and accounts to be kept by the relieving officers.

1. *The Application and Report Book.*—(Form 33.)—The form of this book has been revised, but not materially altered. The notes at the foot of the Form contain full instructions as to the manner in which the book should be kept.

2. *The Out-door Relief List.*—(Form 34.)—This book, like the "In-door Relief List," has been adapted to the half-yearly accounts, and it will be seen that the relief in money and kind are required to be entered in the same columns. The several columns in the "Paupers' Classification Book," and the "Statistical Statement," which relate to the out-door poor, have been inserted in this list in the same manner as those which relate to the in-door poor, have been inserted in the "In-door Relief List," and for a similar reason.

3. *The Abstract of the Out-door Relief List*—(Form 35)—has also been adapted to the half-yearly accounts. It is no longer to be bound up with the "Out-door Relief List," but is to be made up at the meetings of the Board of Guardians, and left in the custody of the clerk, in order that he may possess a duplicate of the out-door relief account against each parish, in the event of the "Out-door Relief List" itself being lost or destroyed. A case has actually occurred, in which great embarrassment has arisen from an accidental loss of this description.

4. *The Relieving Officers' Receipt and Expenditure Book* (Form 36) *and the Summary thereof.*—(Form 37.)—The weekly accounts in money and in kind will no longer be entered separately in the "Receipt and Expenditure Book," as will appear by the "Out-door Relief List" from which they are posted. The relief in money and in kind which are carried out separately in the Out-door Relief List, at the end of each quarter, will be entered separately in the quarterly *Summary* and in this the relieving officer's money account, and account of relief in kind will be balanced separately.

With regard to relief to *Non-Resident* and *Non-Settled* poor it should be observed of *Non-Resident* relief that it is of two kinds—namely, that which is paid through the relieving officer of the Board allowing it, and that which is paid by an order on the treasurer or other means as prescribed by the Commissioners. In the first case the pauper's name will appear in the "Out-door Relief List," as a matter of course, and will be charged by the relieving officer to the parish in the same manner as relief to a resident pauper. In the second case, the relieving officer will have nothing to do with the matter, and the relief will ultimately be a credit to the treasurer, and a debit to the parish against which it is charged in the "Parochial Ledger."

Non-Settled Relief so far as it appears in the accounts of the Union, by the officers of which it is advanced, will be entered in a separate account, in the "Out-door Relief List," by the relieving officer who pays it, and will not be carried into any account against a particular parish. Accounts should be opened in the Out-door Relief List for the several Unions to which the non-settled poor in the relieving officer's district belong; and the relief of such poor should be entered in such accounts in the same manner as the relief to the settled poor is entered under their several parishes.

ART. 18.—By the former Order, the clerk was required to examine previously to the hour appointed for the Guardians to assemble, all the master's entries in his "Weekly In-door Relief List," and "Abstract thereof, and in his Provisions Accounts, and also the relieving officers' entries in their Out-door Relief Lists, and abstracts thereof, and in their "Receipt and Expenditure Books." It has been found scarcely practicable in many Unions, to make so extensive an examination effectively in so limited a time. All that the clerk is now required to do in reference to the master's accounts, is to see that he has made the proper entries in the "Day Book," and has given credit in the proper books and accounts for all the goods supplied at the workhouse. The examination of the relieving officers' accounts, the Commissioners have considered indispensable. The examination, however, both of the master's and the relieving officers' accounts, may now be made on the day, or on the day before the day of the Guardians' meeting.

ART. 23.—The clerk will perceive by this article, that the money portion of the former "Abstract" (Form 11 B), is now separated from the statistical portion, and forms a separate statement, (*Financial Statement*, Form 17.) Some additional columns have been inserted, in order to render this statement more complete. The statistical portion of that "Abstract" also forms a separate statement, (*Statistical Statement*, Form 16,) in regard to which the Commissioners refer to the observations already made, in relation to the "Pauper Classification Book."

ART. 27.—The attention of the clerks is particularly directed to this article, which requires them to furnish to the Commissioners the half-yearly totals of certain heads of expenditure within fourteen days after the 25th day of March and the 29th day of September, without waiting for the completion of the above mentioned statements, or for the audit. The Commissioners' object is, that the materials for estimating the amount of the relief in the preceding half-year, may be accessible without waiting for the completion of the audit.

ART. 28.—It will be observed, that instead of the four Quarterly Abstracts of the separate parish accounts, an annual *Abstract* (Form 18) only will now be required, which will be made up from the overseer's half-yeaarly "Balance Sheets."

ART. 29 and 30.—*The Parochial List and Statement of Account* (Form 19.)—Instead of the extracts from the Quarterly Abstracts which have hitherto been furnished to the parish officers, and instead also of the lists of the paupers relieved, affixed to church doors, and other places, the clerk is required by Art. 29, to make out half-yearly, a separate account for each parish, from the Parochial Ledger Account; the master is to make a list for each parish, of the poor persons relieved in the workhouse, and the relieving officer a list of those who shall have received out-door relief. By Article 30, each relieving officer is required to deliver these lists and statements to the overseers within 30 days after the end of each half-year, to be by them laid before the next vestry meeting.

ART. 31—authorizes the Board of Guardians to pay the Union Officers' Salaries at the end of each quarter, without waiting for the audit, provided they shall first produce their books, made up to the satisfaction of the Board of Guardians.

ART. 32—which relates to the audit of Accounts, contains a provision empowering any auditor, with the consent of the Commissioners, to hold a special audit of the accounts of any Union or parish in the interval between the ordinary audits, which in all respects will have the same legal effect as an ordinary audit. The Commissioners believe that circumstances may arise, which would render a special audit necessary.

ART. 43.—The Commissioners have hitherto felt, that some more effective mode is required of ascertaining whether the books and accounts prescribed are properly kept, and they have therefore, in this article, called upon the auditor to make a return to them on the subject, in the form numbered 38, at the close of each audit.

ART. 44.—The Commissioners have by this article prescribed a *Statement* (Form 39) relating to the Officers' Bonds, to be made by the Auditor to the Commissioners, annually, at the close of the audit of the accounts for the half year ending 25th of March.

The Commissioners have requested Mr. CHARLES KNIGHT, their Publisher, to prepare for use the books and forms prescribed by the Order; and they understand that the same will be ready for sale forthwith. The Commissioners think it right, however, to state that it will be open to any other publisher to publish these books and forms.

I am, Sir,

Your most obedient Servant,

W. G. LUMLEY,

Assistant Secretary.

LONDON:
Printed by order of the Poor Law Commissioners, by BLACKBURN and PARDON, 6, Hatton Garden, and Published by CHARLES KNIGHT and Co., 22, Ludgate Street, Publishers to the Poor Law Commissioners.

AN

OFFICIAL CIRCULAR

OF PUBLIC DOCUMENTS AND INFORMATION:

DIRECTED BY THE POOR LAW COMMISSIONERS TO BE PRINTED, CHIEFLY FOR THE USE OF THE MEMBERS AND PERMANENT OFFICERS OF BOARDS OF GUARDIANS, UNDER THE POOR LAW AMENDMENT ACT.

No. 5.] CIRCULAR ISSUED MAY 1ST, 1847. [N. S.

Poor Law Commission Office,
Somerset House,
May 1, 1847.

THE Poor Law Commissioners have directed that their Thirteenth Annual Report be printed and circulated, for the information of Guardians and Officers of the several Unions.

By Order of the Board,
EDWIN CHADWICK, *Secretary.*

TO THE RIGHT HON. SIR GEORGE GREY, BART.,
Her Majesty's Principal Secretary of State for the Home Department.

Poor Law Commission Office, Somerset House,
May 1, 1847.

Poor Rate Expenditure.

SIR,

1. We commence the report of our proceedings for the last year, by laying before you the account of the receipt and expenditure of the moneys levied as poor's rate, in England and Wales, for the parochial year ending at Lady-day, 1846, together with a comparative statement of the several items of the same amount for that and the preceding year.

An Account of the Receipt and Expenditure of the Poor's Rate, for the year ended Lady-day, 1846.

Receipt.	£.
Amount of money levied by assessment . .	6,809,318
Received from other sources in aid of poor rate .	187,620
Total receipt .	£6,996,938
Expenditure.	
For relief to the poor	4,962,026
Law charges, parochial and Union . . .	83,285
Expenses before magistrates, and constables' expenses (parochial and Union) . . .	52,266
Payments under the Parochial Assessments Act (for surveys, valuations, &c.) and loans repaid under the same	21,169
Expenses under the Vaccination Act . .	27,486
Expenses under the Act for Registering Births, Deaths, and Marriages	54,901
Payments for county and borough rate, and for county and local police forces . . .	1,297,505
Cost of voters, burgesses, and jury lists . .	21,609
Expenses of parish property	15,858
Money expended for all other purposes . .	218,745
Total expenditure	£6,754,850

Comparative Statement of Receipt and Expenditure for Poor Rates, &c., in England and Wales, during the Years ended at Lady-day, 1845 and 1846, respectively.

	RECEIPT.			EXPENDITURE.											
Years ended Lady-day.	Amount of Money levied by Assessment.	Received from all other Sources in aid of Poor Rate.	Total Amount of Money received for Relief of the Poor, &c.	Amount expended for Relief, &c., of the Poor.	Law charges.	Expenses before Magistrates, Constables' Expenses, &c.	Expenses under the Vaccination Act, Fees to Vaccinators, &c.	Payments under the Registration Act, Fees to Registrars, &c.	Payments under the Parochial Assessments' Act (Surveys, Valuations, &c.)	Payments towards County or Borough Rate.	Payments towards County and Local Police Forces.	Cost of Voters, Burgess, and Jury Lists.	Expenses of Parish Property.	Money expended for all other Purposes.	Total Parochial Rates, &c., expended.
	£.	£.	£.	£.	£.	£.	£.	£.	£.	£.	£.	£.	£.	£.	£.
1845	6,791,006	218,505	7,009,511	5,039,703	95,397	57,988	25,905	57,388	22,877	1,046,412	233,550	20,153	14,752	243,277	6,857,402
1846	6,809,318	187,620	6,996,938	4,962,026	83,285	52,266	27,486	54,901	21,169	1,067,692	229,813	21,609	15,858	218,745	6,754,850
Increase	18,312	...	...	...	...	...	1,581	...	...	21,280	...	1,456	1,106	...	...
Decrease	...	30,885	12,573	77,677	12,112	5,722	...	2,487	1,708	...	3,737	...	...	24,532	102,552

2. From the comparative statement, it will be seen that the amount received as poor rate in the two parochial years, 1845 and 1846, scarcely varied; but that in the expenditure for the relief of the poor there was, in 1846, as compared with the previous year, a diminution of 77,677*l*. In the law charges, likewise, there was a diminution of 12,112*l*. The payments towards the county and borough rate increased by 21,280*l*.; but in the total expenditure from the poor rate there was a decrease of 102,552*l*.

3. The following is a statement of the expenditure for the relief of the poor in the four last parochial years; whence it appears that the expenditure in the year 1846 was less than in either of the three preceding years.

Years ending at Lady-day.	Expenditure for the Relief of the Poor.
1843	£5,208,027
1844	4,976,093
1845	5,039,703
1846	4,962,026

4. Although there was a general diminution in the expenditure for the relief of the poor throughout England in the parochial year 1846, amounting, as compared with the previous year, to 2·2 per cent., yet its rate varied in different parts of the country. In some counties it exceeded 10 per cent., while in others there was a slight increase. Some of these differences will appear from the following table:—

Counties.	Years ended Lady-day.		Decrease per cent. in 1846 compared with 1845.	Increase per cent. in 1846 compared with 1845.
	1845.	1846.		
	£	£		
Salop	60,657	49,779	17·9	...
Westmoreland	18,225	15,469	15·1	...
York, West Riding	186,321	163,364	12·3	...
Chester	76,124	68,794	9·6	...
Durham	75,824	70,243	7·4	...
Stafford	98,266	91,198	7·2	...
Brecon	21,354	19,817	7·2	...
Berks	92,615	94,032	...	1·5
Montgomery	24,892	25,450	...	2·2
Middlesex	285,945	293,886	...	2·8
Pembroke	21,294	22,106	...	3·8
Lancaster	211,694	220,062	...	4·0
Carnarvon	26,577	27,640	...	4·0
Flint	19,711	20,491	...	4·0

5. The diminished expenditure in Shropshire, Durham, Staffordshire, and Brecknockshire, may probably be attributed to the improvement in the iron and coal trades, which occurred during this period. The diminution in the expenditure of the West Riding of York has been progressive in the three years ending at Lady-day, 1846.

	Years ending at Lady-day.		
	1844	1845	1846
York, West Riding	208,805*l*.	186,321*l*.	163,364*l*.

The expenditure for Lancashire, on the other hand, has decreased in 1845, as compared with 1844; and has increased in 1846, as compared with 1845.

	Years ending at Lady-day.		
	1844	1845	1846
Lancashire	231,648*l*.	211,694*l*.	220,062*l*.

This increase in the latter year is, however, confined to a few Unions, and is mainly owing to an extraordinary outlay in the Manchester Union for a new pauper school.

6. The following table exhibits the principal items of the Poor Law Expenditure in the Unions and parishes, acting under the regulations of the Commissioners, from which the accounts are transmitted to us in a prescribed form:—

Comparative Statement of the Amount of Money expended under the following heads in 588 Unions and single Parishes in England and Wales, under the Poor Law Amendment Act, during the Years ended Lady day, 1845 and 1846, respectively.

Years ended Lady-day.	In-maintenance.	Out-relief.	Establishment Charges and Salaries.	Workhouse Loans Repaid.	Other Charges connected with Relief to the Poor.	Total Expenditure for the Relief and Maintenance of the Poor.
	£	£	£	£	£	£
1845	714,523	2,767,903	750,372	177,603	6,572	4,416,973
1846	682,857	2,716,188	737,740	173,273	9,826	4,319,884
Increase	...	...	...	...	3,254	...
Decrease	31,666	51,715	12,632	4,330	...	97,089

Number of Paupers relieved.

7. It will be observed that (with the trifling exception of the miscellaneous item) there is a decrease in each branch of this expenditure for the year 1846, as compared with the preceding year. A similar diminution, as appears from the subjoined table, took place in the number of paupers relieved in the quarter ending at Lady-day, 1846, as compared with the corresponding quarter of the previous year.

Comparative Statement of the Number of In-door and Out-door Paupers relieved in England and Wales, during the Quarters ended Lady-day, 1845 and 1846, respectively.

Quarters ended Lady-day.	Number of Paupers Relieved.			Rate per Cent. of Total Number of Paupers on Population in 1841.
	In-door.	Out-door.	Total.	
1845	215,325	1,255,645	1,470,970	9·2
1846	198,762	1,131,795	1,330,557	8·4
Decrease.	16,563	123,850	140,413	0·9

Population in 1841 ... ... 15,906,741.

NOTE.—An Estimate is made of the number of Paupers relieved in places not in Union, and included in the above Totals.

8. Confining ourselves to the able-bodied poor, we find (as is shown in the subjoined table) that the number relieved in the workhouse, during the Lady-day quarter of 1846, was less, by five per cent., than that relieved in the corresponding quarter of 1845. In the number of able-bodied persons receiving out-door relief, the diminution was still greater, being equal to $12\frac{1}{10}$ per cent.

Comparative Statement of the number of Able-bodied Paupers relieved in England and Wales, during each of the Quarters ended Lady-day, 1845 and 1846.

Quarters ended Lady-day.	In-door. On Account of temporary Sickness or Accident.	In-door. All other Causes including Vagrants.	In-door. Total In-door.	Out-door. On Account of temporary Sickness or Accident.	Out-door. All other Causes including Vagrants.	Out-door. Total Out-door.	Total In-door and Out-door.
1845	11,407	76,216	87,623	167,277	165,196	332,473	420,096
1846	11,229	71,991	83,220	143,479	148,864	292,343	375,563
Decrease per cent.	1·6	5·5	5·0	14·2	9·9	12·1	10·6

NOTE.—An Estimate is made for places not in Union under the Poor Law Amendment Act. The above results are obtained from the Union Quarterly Abstracts.

Failure of Potato Crop.

9. We are not, at present, able to state the complete amount of the Poor Law expenditure for the year ending at last Lady-day; but we entertain no doubt, from the partial accounts which we have received, that it has considerably exceeded the amount for the preceding year. During the summer and autumn of 1846, the employment of the working classes throughout England, both in the agricultural and manufacturing districts, was indeed sufficiently constant, and the rates of wages not below the average. There was, however, in England, as in Ireland, a general failure of the potato crop of 1846; and the destruction of this important article of food, by contributing to raise the prices of grain and other provisions, materially influenced the condition of the poor. The extent to which the prices of grain and pulse have, by a concurrence of various causes, been raised during the last winter, may be perceived by a comparison of the recent averages as declared in the *Gazette.*

	Average Prices for the six weeks ending April 3, 1847. s. d.	Average Prices for the same period in 1846. s. d.
Wheat	75 6	54 11
Barley	52 10	29 10
Oats	31 8	21 11
Rye	56 3	33 9
Beans	52 5	34 9
Peas	56 10	34 0
Total	325 6	209 2

Therefore, whereas, in the spring of 1846, a quarter of the six principal sorts of grain and pulse could be purchased for 10*l.* 9*s.* 2*d.*, the same articles could not be procured in the present spring for less than 16*l.* 5*s.* 6*d.* The contract price of potatoes for Lambeth Workhouse for the half year ending last Michaelmas, was 5*l.* 10*s.* per ton; for the half-year ending next Michaelmas, 10*l.* per ton. Butchers' meat and bacon have likewise somewhat risen in price since the spring of 1846.

10. The effects of the potato blight were, however, felt by the poorer classes, not merely through its indirect influence on the prices of food, but also, more immediately, by the destruction of the crop planted by the labourer in places where the allotment system prevails. We have found that this direct dependence of the agricultural labourer upon his own crop of potatoes is most prevalent in Wiltshire, Somersetshire, and Devonshire; and in several unions in those counties, the failure of the potatoes has, during the past winter, been represented to us as a cause of peculiar distress among the agricultural labourers, and as a ground for giving them temporary out-door relief.

11. To the causes already enumerated as contributing to produce distress among the working classes, may be added the long-continued and severe cold of last winter—a circumstance which exercises a most important influence upon the employment of the agricultural labourers.

Workhouses of many Unions full during the winter.

12. In consequence of the state of things which we have described, the workhouses of many Unions became full during the winter; and in these Unions, where the prohibitory order had been issued, we either permitted out-door relief to the able-bodied in cases reported under Art. 6 of that order, or issued an order authorizing generally out-door relief to this class of poor, subject to an out-door labour test. The following is a list of the chief part of the Unions in which the workhouse was thus filled during the winter:—

Axbridge.
Basford.
Bradford (Wilts).
Bridgewater.
Calne.
Canterbury.
Caxton and Arrington.
Cheltenham.
Chipping Norton.
Chipping Sodbury
Chorlton.
Clifton.
Henley.
Hereford.
Hinckley.
Holborn.
Hoxne.
Kensington.
Kettering.
Leicester.
Manchester
Melksham.
Newbury.
Newmarket.
Nottingham.
St. George in the East.
St. George the Martyr (Southwark).
Shepton Mallet.
Thame.
Wellington (Somerset).
Wells.
West Derby.
Whitechapel.
Wigan.
Wincanton.
Winchcomb.
Wokingham.
Woodbridge.
Worcester.

Amongst these Unions, several, such as Canterbury, Chorlton, Holborn, Kensington, Manchester, West

Derby, &c., are under no limitation with respect to out-door relief. In Worcester, the insufficiency of the workhouse was slight, while in Caxton and Arrington, and Newmarket, the necessity for out-door relief recurs every winter. In Hinckley the difficulty was only partial, owing to a dispute between the stocking-weavers and masters about wages. In Clifton and Chipping Sodbury, the workhouse was crowded through the want of employment of the hatters.

Alteration of Dietaries in consequence of failure of Potato Crop.

13. We may here mention, with reference to the failure of the potato crop, that it became necessary for us, in numerous Unions, to sanction an alteration in the workhouse dietary by the substitution of some other article for potatoes. The substitutes have, for the most part, been bread, or boiled rice; in other cases, turnips, carrots, parsnips, cabbage, peas, or hominy, have been used. We have, likewise, at the desire of the Board of Trade, instructed our Assistant-Commissioners to obtain information upon certain particulars respecting the failure of the potatoes. From the reports which have been sent in, and which have been transmitted to the Board of Trade, it appears that the failure of the potatoes has extended generally over the country, but that the early sorts of the potato have failed the least.

Other causes of increase of Expenditure.—Influx of Irish poor.

14. Other causes also have contributed to increase the expenditure for the relief of the poor since last autumn in the manufacturing districts and the large towns. Owing to the high price of cotton, and the diminished demand for manufactures, the hours of work have been shortened, or the work has been even temporarily suspended in some factories in the Lancashire district. Moreover, the severity of the distress in Ireland has produced an influx of Irish, in a state of extreme destitution, into several towns on the western coast of England. Liverpool, as being the port nearest to Dublin, and with which the principal steam communication is carried on, received the largest number of this class of immigrants. The numbers having begun to increase in December, advanced rapidly in January and February last, and still more rapidly in March and April. From the 13th of January to the 20th of April, during which period an accurate account of Irish immigrants was kept, there arrived at Liverpool 133,069 persons from Ireland. The Select Vestry adopted prompt and efficient measures for meeting the increased number of applications;* and it will be seen from the annexed Report of our Assistant Commissioner, Mr. Austin, that these measures were attended with considerable success in preventing imposition, and in providing for the destitute. The precautions taken by the vestry against the spread of fever and disease, from the crowded dwellings of the Irish, are on a large and expensive scale; but not, it is to be feared, beyond the necessity of the case.

15. It has not been thought advisable by the local authorities to make any attempt to pass the Irish immigrants back to Ireland under the 8 and 9 Vict. c. 117. Some have remained chargeable on the rates of Liverpool, others have proceeded further into the interior of the country, but several thousands have emigrated to Canada, or the United States. Many have reached Manchester, and the other manufacturing towns of Lancashire, as well as of the West Riding and Cheshire; and we have received statements from several Boards of Guardians on the subject of a provision for the increased number of Irish vagrants. Large numbers of Irish have also landed at Newport and Chepstow, and have thence moved on to Cheltenham, and other towns in the midland counties. A considerable number of Irish poor (estimated at about 1000 within a week) have recently been landed in London by steamers from Cork and Dublin. In addition to these, some Irish have reached the metropolis from Bristol and Newport.

16. The Removals Act of last session (to the operation of which we shall advert more particularly hereafter), has likewise increased the amount of relief to the Irish in the large towns, especially in the metropolis. By the operation of this Act, Irish and Scotch, who have been resident five years in an English parish, become irremovable from that parish; and thus many Irish, who had been resident for that period, became applicants for relief, although previously to the passing of that Act, they had been deterred from applying by the fear of being passed back to their own country. The expectations of benefit under this Act formed by the resident Irish in the metropolis appear to have been excessive, and led to their applying, in large numbers, to several London parishes and Unions at the beginning of the winter. The pressure was, however, only temporary, for the applications have been generally met by an offer of the workhouse or out-door labour, and the offers were in few cases accepted.

17. Owing to the combined operation of the causes above stated, (namely, the general failure of the potato crop throughout England, the high prices of corn and other articles of food, the length and severity of the winter, the diminution of manufacturing prosperity, the large immigration of destitute Irish into England, and, in some degree, the operation of the Removals Act,) the pressure upon the poor rates has been considerably increased since last autumn, and the Poor Law expenditure for the year ending Lady-day, 1847, will, when ascertained, doubtless prove to have been greater than that for the preceding year. We have, however, the satisfaction of being able to

* The Reports of Mr. Austin, and other correspondence and documents on this subject, have been printed for the Houses of Parliament (House of Lords, Sess. Paper, Nos. 24 and 28. House of Commons, No. 193.)

state, that the Boards of Guardians and other local authorities have found no serious difficulty in overcoming the obstacles against which they have had to contend, and that the system of relief has been efficient and orderly. Indeed, we are not aware, that, at any time since we have held our present offices, the administration of the Poor Law has been in a more regular and satisfactory state than during the period since last autumn, or has been conducted with a more willing co-operation on the part of the local authorities.

District Asylums for relief of Casual Poor.

18. In our last Annual Report, par. 24—7, we described the measures which we had adopted for the formation of district asylums for the relief of the casual poor of the Metropolis; we likewise adverted to the appointment of a Select Committee of the House of Commons, in last session, to inquire into the manner in which the discretion of the Commissioners had been exercised; and we added that we had abstained from taking active steps for carrying the provisions of the Act into effect, until it appeared whether any alteration of the law was likely to result from the recommendations of the Committee.

19. After the date of our Report, the Select Committee completed their examination of witnesses; but they merely reported the evidence, without expressing any opinion upon the question referred to them (12th June, 1846).

20. Sir William Somerville subsequently addressed to us a letter, dated the 3rd of September, referring to the subject of district asylums, and conveying to us your opinion that further proceedings with respect to them should be suspended, until an opportunity had been afforded to the Legislature for considering the evidence reported by this Committee.

21. Before we adopted any step for suspending the proceedings of the District Boards of Management, we thought it right to take the opinion of counsel, as to our powers over the Boards which had been called into existence. We accordingly submitted to Mr. Tomlinson this question:—

"Whether the Poor Law Commissioners have any power, under the Act 7 and 8 Victoria, c. 101, either separately or in connexion with the previous Poor Law Acts, to issue an order for the purpose of suspending the monthly meetings of the respective Asylum District Boards indefinitely, either in the cases where the Boards have continued to hold their monthly meetings, or where they have not done so?"

In answer to this question Mr. Tomlinson stated as follows:—

"I am of opinion that the Poor Law Commissioners have no power under the Act 7 and 8 Vict. c. 101, either separately, or in connexion with the previous Poor Law Acts, to issue an order for the purpose of suspending the monthly meetings of the respective Asylum District Boards indefinitely, after such Boards have been once duly constituted, either in the cases where the Boards have continued to hold their monthly meetings, or where they have not done so. The 43rd section gives the Commissioners the same powers for regulating the proceedings of any District Board, as they have with respect to the proceedings of Boards of Guardians. The power of *regulating* does not imply the power of *suspending indefinitely*, which is in effect a power to nullify the constitution of the Board. The Legislature treats these Boards as a permanent institution. By the same section, the Commissioners can only add any parish to the district, or take any parish from the district, with the consent of a majority of the Board. No power is given to the Commissioners to dissolve such district or such board, directly or indirectly. In the parallel case of Boards of Guardians, an express power to dissolve the Union is given by the 32nd section of 4th and 5th Wm. 4, c. 76, but only with the consent of a majority of two-thirds of the guardians, and the necessity of such consent to a dissolution is not taken away by the 66th section of 7 and 8 Victoria, c. 101. These provisions, and the obvious intent to give permanent constitutions to the newly constituted relieving districts, in effect limit the general power to suspend, alter, or rescind the Commissioners' rules given by the 15th section of the first Act, at least after Boards have been once fully constituted. If this construction is not put upon the Acts, the Commissioners might evade all the limitations of their powers of adding to, taking from, or dissolving unions, by rescinding the orders constituting such Unions, and issuing new orders constituting new Unions, with entirely new classifications of districts."

22. After the receipt of this opinion, the Commissioners addressed a letter to the several Boards of Management (dated the 21st of September,) stating it to be advisable that these Boards should not take any further step in pursuance of their powers, beyond what was rendered absolutely necessary by the engagements into which they had entered, until an opportunity should have been afforded to the Legislature, in the next session of Parliament, of considering the evidence reported to the House of Commons by the Committee. In the same letter the Commissioners announced their intention, with a view to enable the Boards of Management to act on this advice, of issuing an order, modifying that part of their orders constituting the respective District Asylums, which required the Boards of Management to hold their meetings at certain stated periods.

23. The Commissioners subsequently issued orders to the several Boards of Management, providing that, until the Commissioners should otherwise direct, it should not be necessary for the Board to hold a meeting once in every month, as required by the previous orders. Since that time no steps have been taken by any of the Boards of Management, except by that of the North-Eastern Metropolitan District,

which having previously entered into a contract for the purchase of a site, and having obtained a loan of 3500*l.* from the Public Works' Loan Board, have been in treaty for the purchase of a site and buildings.

24. Having described the course which has been pursued with respect to the asylums for the houseless poor in the metropolis, we proceed to give some further explanations which are rendered necessary by the present state of this question.

25. It appears from the proceedings of the Select Committee on District Asylums, that the Poor Law Commissioners are believed to have introduced a lax system of administration too favourable to the relief of casual and wandering poor; in particular, there seems to be an impression that the letters of instruction and proceedings of the Commissioners in 1837, 1838, and 1839, relative to the casual poor of the metropolis, recommended the indiscriminate relief of this class of poor, without setting the able-bodied mendicants and trampers to work; and that, in consequence of this interference, the vagrancy of the metropolis has been greatly increased.

26. The belief, to which we have just referred, appears to have arisen from a misunderstanding either of the real state of the law respecting casual and wandering poor, or of the precise nature of the steps taken by the Commissioners with regard to this difficult subject.

27. In our last Annual Report, we stated our view of the law relating to the relief of casual poor, and we showed that a wanderer, becoming destitute in a parish, though not settled in it, was entitled to relief. We there made the following remarks on this question:—

The laws relating to the relief of the poor confer a right to relief irrespective of settlement. All destitute persons have a right to be relieved at the cost of the parish in which they are. This right in the first instance is absolute; but if a person so relieved has a settlement in another parish, the officers of the parish to which he has become chargeable can, if they think fit, remove him to the place of his settlement. According, therefore, to the established law, a wandering poor person who applies for relief in a parish, metropolitan or rural, although he has not acquired any settlement in it, must, if he be destitute there, receive parochial relief. It is doubtless desirable, as far as possible, to avoid all encouragement of habitual mendicancy and vagrancy, by affording undue facilities for obtaining relief to persons leading a life of this sort, which is always accompanied with laziness and vice, and almost always with crime. But a wandering mendicant, if he become destitute and applies for relief, has as good a legal right to it as any other poor person in a similar condition.*

28. With respect to the proceedings of the Commissioners for enforcing the legal relief of the casual poor of the metropolis, the Commissioners (as we showed in our last Annual Report, par. 29) confined themselves, in their letter to the Commissioners of Police of Sept. 6, 1837, to a statement of the law, and the obligation of the officers under it. In the same letter they likewise pointed out the necessity of punishing vagrants properly so called.*

29. The same views were afterwards expressed by the Commissioners, in a circular letter to the Metropolitan Boards of Guardians, dated December 12, 1838, in which especial stress was laid on the performance of work by the persons receiving relief. One passage of this letter is as follows:—

"These arrangements contemplate the performance of work proportioned to the bodily ability of the applicant in a part of the workhouse appropriated to that use, previously to the administration of relief in kind to the casual poor, in all cases excepting those of sudden or pressing emergency, to which succour must be administered without delay, independently of all ordinary considerations.

"The Commissioners conceive these arrangements, when generally adopted, will promote the success of the exertions of the police for the suppression of habitual mendicancy, inasmuch as the difficulties and hazard attending the profession of a common beggar would be greatly augmented thereby." (Fifth Annual Report, Appendix A., No. 10.)

The whole tenor of this letter will show that the Commissioners were desirous to secure relief for the destitute, and to exact work from such as might be able to perform it; a distinction is drawn throughout between the really destitute poor and those who may be habitual vagrants or common beggars.

30. In the Circular Letter of 1839, the propriety of imposing a task of work is also impressed upon the Guardians, as will be seen by the following extracts:—

"The Commissioners request the Board of Guardians to warn their officers, that no consideration of past service will be deemed by the Commissioners a sufficient reason for their hesitating to remove any officer who, after this period, shall have neglected his primary duty in relieving any case of urgent casual destitution brought under his notice, by affording such relief within the workhouse, *in all cases in which there is ability to labour*, or in which relief within the workhouse is desirable, such as cases of houseless destitution and casualty, or by affording such relief as may be appropriate in other cases in articles of absolute necessity.

"The necessary arrangements having been made, the Commissioners hope the Board of Guardians will not hesitate to issue to the rate-payers of their parish or union, tickets entitling all wayfarers to be received into the workhouse, and there provided with necessary relief and assistance, and at the same time set to work proportioned to their bodily strength." (Sixth Annual Report, Appendix A., No. 6.)

31. It is apparent from these extracts that the letters of 1837-38 and 1839 did not recommend indiscriminate relief of vagrants, without setting the able-bodied to work, but that they distinctly inculcated the necessity of providing such work, and kept this principle in view throughout. It is right, however, to add, with reference to the letters in question, that when those of 1837 and 1838 were issued, only

* Twelfth Ann. Rep., p. 17, ed. 8vo.

* Concerning the large amount of vagrancy, and its increase, before 1834, see the Report of Mr. Codd, Appendix E to the Report of the Commissioners of Poor Law Inquiry, p. 36.

one of the present Commissioners was a member of the Commission, and he was absent on duty in Dublin in the latter year; whilst, as regards that of 1839, only one other of the Commissioners, now members of the Board, was then acting in England.

32. The expediency of enforcing a task of work from casual poor and trampers admitted into a workhouse was always recognised by the Commissioners; but the difficulty consisted in its practical application. As persons of this class usually applied for admittance at a late hour in the evening, and departed at an early hour in the following morning, they thereby obtained a supper, a night's lodging, and a breakfast, without the possibility of being required to work. The Commissioners, aware of this difficulty, on the 15th of February, 1841, addressed a circular letter to the Boards of Guardians throughout the country, intended to ascertain their views with respect to a remedy for this evil. The following are the most important passages of this letter:—

"There is a class of paupers who contrive to enjoy the physical comforts of the workhouse, *without performing the labour or submitting to the discipline* which are in general the necessary conditions for obtaining those advantages.

"Those paupers do not, as a class, possess or deserve the compassion of the public; and even if it were desirable to relax the discipline of the workhouse, and to convert it into an almshouse or lodging-house for paupers, they are probably the last class of persons to whom it would be thought expedient to extend this supposed indulgence at the expense of the frugal and industrious part of the community.

"These are the mendicant vagrants, who are known to be generally persons of dissolute character, to lead habitually a life of laziness and imposture, and not unfrequently to resort to intimidation and pilfering.

"Vagrants of this sort usually apply for admission into the workhouse at a late hour in the day, obtain a supper and a night's lodging, and leave the workhouse at an early hour in the following morning, *without performing any work in return for the relief which they have received.* In this manner, wandering beggars convert the workhouse into a lodging house or inn, where they take up their quarters at the end of the day's tramp, and are maintained at the public cost without any inconvenience to themselves, or any interruption to their ordinary mode of life. * * * *

"For the purpose of diminishing the evils of mendicant vagrancy, the Commissioners have recommended the establishment of a ward for vagrants in the workhouse, and the admission of vagrants by tickets distributed among the ratepayers. This system has been introduced into many Unions.

"The Commissioners have likewise advised that every vagrant should, as far as possible, *be required to perform some work in return for the relief which he obtains.* The Commissioners have also, in a few instances, sanctioned a difference in diet between vagrants and other able-bodied inmates.

"The restrictions on vagrants relieved in workhouses, which the present law permits, have, however, not proved sufficient to prevent a great pressure on the workhouses by paupers of this class; and the Commissioners entertain no doubt that the indisposition to give immediate relief to non-settled poor (which indisposition, notwithstanding their repeated admonitions on the subject, still continues to a considerable extent) arises, in great measure, from the consciousness of the Guardians and their officers that the law does not enable them to provide for vagrants such a mode of relief as is suited to the circumstances of their case."

After stating that the Commissioners had recommended to Her Majesty's Government a clause making the cost of casual poor a charge upon the common fund of a Union, the letter proceeds thus:—

"It appears, however, to the Commissioners, that some further provision is needed, which should enable the Guardians to prevent vagrants, relieved in a workhouse, *from avoiding the labour and restraint to which all other able-bodied inmates of a workhouse are subjected.*

"The Commissioners are desirous of making some recommendations to Her Majesty's Government on this matter, with reference to the Bill now before Parliament; but before they make any such recommendation, they request to be informed of the opinion of the Guardians upon the two following points:—

"1. Whether it would be reasonable to confer on the Guardians, a power of detaining an able-bodied vagrant for six hours, during working time, on the day following the day of his or her admission therein?

"2. Whether such a power of detention would be effectual in preventing the abuse of workhouse relief by vagrants which takes place under the existing law?"

33. This letter, together with an abstract of the answers to it made by the Boards of Guardians (which were generally favourable to the power of detention for a limited time), was presented to the House of Commons in the session of 1841 (Parl. Paper, No. 149), and the Commissioners afterwards submitted to Sir James Graham a clause for giving effect to the suggestion. The clause was embodied in the Poor Law Bill introduced by Her Majesty's Government in 1842, and formed part of the Act of 5 and 6 Vict., c. 57. It stands thus in the statute referred to:—

"Be it enacted, that it shall be lawful for the Guardians of any parish or Union, subject always to the powers of the Poor Law Commissioners, *to prescribe a task of work to be done by any person relieved in any workhouse,* in return for the food and lodging afforded to such person; but it shall not be lawful to detain any person against his will, for the performance of such task of work, for any time exceeding four hours, from the hour of breakfast in the morning succeeding the admission of such person into the workhouse." —S. 5.

34. The clause which we have just recited contains the only power under the existing law for detaining casual poor in a workhouse in order to set them to work. The Commissioners have never ceased, since it was passed, to urge its adoption upon the Boards of Guardians; and in so doing, they have met with considerable reluctance to make the exertions and arrangements requisite for giving employment to the very troublesome class of paupers in question.

35. In our Eighth Annual Report, dated May, 1842, we spoke of the difficulty attending the relief of this class of paupers, in the following terms:—

"In giving advice and instruction on this subject, we had to avoid two opposite sets of evils. In the first place, we ran a risk of encouraging mendicancy and imposture, and on the other, if we neglected to recognise a sufficient right to relief on the part of any person becoming destitute in a parish where he had no settlement, and where he did not come with the intention of residing, we should have encouraged some of those abusive practices by which overseers endeavoured indirectly to shift these casual burdens on the neighbouring district, and professed to consider some claim to settlement as a condition precedent to the right of relief."

We also pointed out in the same Report (which

was presented before the passing of the Act of 5 and 6 Vict.) the fact that the nature of the present workhouse buildings was, in many instances, ill calculated for the reception of these paupers, and that there was no effectual power to detain them, or to require work in the morning from them.

36. The evils of a lax administration of relief to trampers and casual poor, were again illustrated, in the Commissioners' Report of 1844,* by statistics showing the decrease which had invariably followed the exaction of a task of work, and we pointed out the evils attendant on the relief of such paupers in the vagrant wards of each separate metropolitan workhouse. These conclusions were not adopted without sufficient evidence, but were the result of repeated correspondence with the Boards of Guardians, and inquiry into the whole subject through our Assistant Commissioner.

37. The practical difficulties which attend the relief of casual and wandering poor, not only in the metropolitan parishes but generally throughout the country, are very great. That it is not easy to make provision in workhouses for setting this class of poor to work, may be inferred from the fact, that the parish of Marylebone, which resisted the establishment of separate District Asylums, has made no attempt to exact any labour from the able-bodied tramps admitted into the vagrant ward of its workhouse. The same is likewise the case in the workhouse of St. Pancras.†

38. The vagrant wards in Marylebone workhouse were established early in last year, just at the time of the appointment of the Select Committee of the House of Commons to inquire into the subject. Some extension of the provision for this class was made in the workhouse of St. George, Hanover-square, at a more recent period. Other metropolitan workhouses are still without vagrant wards: in several the wards are situated in the basement; and in many, though above ground, they are very far from suitable to their purpose, for want of space, ventilation, and light. This difference in the means of relief possessed by the metropolitan workhouses is still a source of complaint, on the ground of the inequality it causes in the incidence of the burden, and the undue annoyance as well as expense brought by the default of others upon the parishes which endeavour to make proper provision for this class of poor. The unsuitableness of the accommodation is still alleged as tending to the origination and propagation of disease; and the large number of offenders committed to metropolitan prisons, chiefly as we have ascertained from this department of the workhouses, has been noticed during the last year in the Report of the Visiting Justices for the House of Correction in Middlesex, and by the Inspectors of Prisons with reference to the gaol at Brixton. We are not aware of any powers vested in us, by the exercise of which the evils of unequal burden, insalubrious accommodation, and want of proper means of dealing with the insubordinate, can, under existing circumstances, be remedied.

39. We have endeavoured to ascertain what is the actual extent of the accommodation for vagrants in the workhouses of all the Unions and parishes included in the Metropolitan Asylum Districts; for it might have appeared that the existing accommodation was, on the whole, adequate, and that the difficulty of the case might be got rid of by making arrangements for a proper distribution of the applicants for relief among the several workhouses proportionally. But, apart from all considerations of the practicability of making such distribution (which is very doubtful), and of the unfitness of the existing accommodation, our inquiries have led us to conclude that the accommodation, such as it is, is not sufficient.

40. According to the statements contained in the Returns made to us on this point, the number of persons that might be lodged for the night in these wards is 1538. But, taking into account merely the superficial dimensions of the wards, it appears to us that not more than 1416 persons could be accommodated; and if we consider also the height of the wards, and allow only 216 cubic feet of space for each person, that is, a space of 8 feet long, by 3 feet in width and 9 feet in height, 1140 would be all that could be lodged in all the wards. In considering the Asylum Districts, when we addressed ourselves to the duty of forming them in 1845, we were disposed to acquiesce in Mr. Hall's estimate of the probable number of persons for whom it would be necessary to provide, namely, 1600. Assuming that this estimate was not incorrect—assuming, also, that no space is lost in the existing wards (which is to assume that they are all of proper shape, and of the same height)—still the extent of accommodation, allowing 216 cubic feet for each individual, falls short by about one-third of the number to be accommodated. There are reasons, moreover, for concluding that the estimate of 1600 as the maximum is not high enough; for the average number of poor persons of this class lodged nightly in the wards of the London workhouses in February last was 690; while the voluntary asylums were lodging at the same time, on the average, 1120 persons nightly, making together 1810 persons; so that, after all the vagrant wards in the workhouses had been filled, there would have been, but for the voluntary asylums, nearly 700 persons unrelieved on the average. If the maximum number for whom relief was required on any one night had been ascertained, of course the relative deficiency of accommodation would have been shown to be greater.

* Tenth Ann. Rep., p. 10, ed. 8vo.

† See Report on the Relief of the Poor in St. Marylebone and St. Pancras, pp. 13, 16.

41. The evidence taken by the District Asylum Committee, and the experience of the last year, have only served to strengthen our conviction of the expediency of a separate set of establishments for this class of poor in the metropolis. We believe that the District Asylums might be so regulated and managed as to be more effectual than any other establishments for the relief of real destitution, with the least possible encouragement to mendicancy and imposture. It is not improbable that a change might be advantageously made in the law of vagrancy; but any such change in the direction of increased severity is scarcely consistent with the present tendency of legislation; and it would imply that a discretion far wider than is now given in deciding who is really destitute, and who is an habitual tramper or impostor, should be conferred on the magistrates. Such a discretion must be exercised on presumption rather than on proof; and the decisions, if they are to have any effect, must carry with them the sanction of some more effective punishment in the shape of labour than is now imposed in most of the prisons.

42. The question respecting the relief of casual poor in the Metropolis must be considered at present as in an unsettled state; and we will therefore confine ourselves to the expression of our conviction on the following points:—

First. We believe that the system of relief now carried on in the vagrant wards of workhouses in the Metropolis ought not to be allowed to continue.

Secondly. We believe that the nature of those buildings, the other occupations of the officers, and the number of establishments, is such as to make impossible the general enforcement of a proper task of work, the efficient superintendence over the vagrants, or the easy recognition of such as may be habitual trampers; and that, on the other hand, to stop the relief administered to this class, without providing some substitute for the present system, would lead to the risk of withholding relief from really destitute wanderers.

Thirdly. We believe that the Asylum Districts, contemplated by 7th and 8th Vict., c. 101 (the constitution of which is in legal existence), would enable material improvement to be made in the system pursued, and would facilitate rather than impede any further amendment in the law relating to vagrancy in the metropolis.

43. With regard to the casual poor, and trampers relieved in the workhouses throughout the country at large, the following statement will show their number for the weeks ending respectively December the 20th, 1845, and December the 19th, 1846:—

Summary of Returns, from 603 Unions and Places under Local Acts in England and Wales, of the Number of Vagrants and Trampers relieved in Workhouses on each night of the Week ending 20th December, 1845, and also on each night of the corresponding week of last Year, namely, the Week ended the 19th December, 1846.

I. Week ended 20th December, 1845.

Days.	Males.				Females.				Total Males and Females.
	Under 16 years of Age.	From 16 to 60 years of Age.	Above 60 years of Age.	Total.	Under 16 years of Age	From 16 to 60 years of Age.	Above 60 years of Age.	Total.	
Sun. Dec. 14, 1845	121	1,128	37	1,309	77	242	13	343	1,721
Mon. 15th ,,	122	1,163	26	1,327	86	290	12	397	1,796
Tues. 16th ,,	100	1,178	41	1,363	85	300	13	419	1,910
Wed. 17th ,,	124	1,161	36	1,419	83	286	10	386	1,897
Thurs. 18th ,,	122	1,201	36	1,384	90	306	11	414	1,859
Friday, 19th ,,	125	1,192	37	1,371	80	267	13	366	1,788
Saturd. 20th ,,	99	1,017	26	1,189	61	188	13	270	1,563

II. Week ending 19th December, 1846.

Days.	Males.				Females.				Total Males and Females.
	Under 16 years of Age.	From 16 to 60 years of Age.	Above 60 years of Age.	Total.	Under 16 years of Age.	From 16 to 60 years of Age.	Above 60 years of Age.	Total.	
Sun. Dec. 13, 1846	194	1,314	40	1,548	141	355	21	517	2,096
Mon. 14th ,,	234	1,364	38	1,636	154	393	24	571	2,240
Tues. 15th ,,	223	1,361	42	1,626	161	381	24	566	2,224
Wed. 16th ,,	220	1,436	46	1,702	166	379	22	567	2,304
Thurs. 17th ,,	216	1,368	29	1,613	153	373	20	547	2,198
Friday, 18th ,,	271	1,454	49	1,774	163	405	26	594	2,397
Satur. 19th ,,	211	1,325	49	1,585	136	311	25	473	2,106

Average Number relieved on each night of the week ended .... 20th Dec. 1845 ... 1,791
,, ,, ,, 19th ,, 1846 ... 2,224

From this return (which includes the entire kingdom, with the exception of about 30 unions or parishes), it will be seen that the total number of this class of poor admitted into the workhouses, in any one night, is not large; the highest amount being less than 2400. It likewise appears that the number admitted was somewhat larger in December, 1846, than in December, 1845, which, on account of the causes above adverted to in this Report, was naturally to be expected.

Pauper Apprenticeship.

44. In our last Annual Report, (par. 44), we adverted to some modifications of our order of 31st December, 1844, respecting pauper apprenticeship, which we had been induced to make; we have received no further representations respecting the general operation of the order in question, and we have every reason to believe that it is upon the whole working satisfactorily.

Revised Order of Accounts.

45. The forms prescribed for keeping the Parish and Union accounts, and the regulations for closing and auditing those accounts, have been for some time before the Commissioners. In our last Annual Report we stated our intention of issuing a revised order of

accounts, with as little delay as might be compatible with the importance of its provisions. This order has now been issued, and we believe it will be found calculated to ensure greater regularity on the part of the officers, and to afford additional securities against fraud and peculation of every kind.

46. Many Boards of Guardians had a stock of books in hand, which were not used, and some loss to the public would have ensued from bringing the order into compulsory operation at once; we have therefore so framed it, as to allow of the old books and forms being used until the 25th of March, 1848, after which date its provisions will become imperative.

47. We will state briefly a few of the points to which our attention has been directed in framing the amended order.

48. In the first place, we have now prescribed a particular form of accounts for the persons acting as collectors, or assistant overseers, whom we consider as the paid servants of the annual overseers for the time being; but we have made the latter responsible for checking the rate receipt check-book entrusted to the collector. We have required every collector to pay over the moneys collected by him weekly, or so often as the amount in his hand, on account of any parish or parishes, shall exceed 50*l*. We have also directed him to lay a monthly settlement of his receipt and collection before the overseers, and when he is appointed by the Guardians, before the Board of Guardians.

49. With reference to the provision accounts, we have made the forms more minute than those previously in use, so as to show the quantity of provisions taken out of the store for each meal. We were aware of the objections which exist to occupying too much of the time of the master of the workhouse with the details of books; on the other hand, we had to bear in mind, the quantity of stores which passes through the hands of such an officer, and the extreme difficulty of tracing back to its source any error or falsification in the account of such minute articles. Upon the whole, we are satisfied that a diligent and punctual master may keep the forms now prescribed with very little more labour than was necessary to fill up those contained in the former order, if the quantities in the latter were properly entered, and were not (as was too often the case) a mere estimate framed from the dietary. The only efficient check on an officer, like a master of a workhouse, consists in requiring the entry at the time of all minute particulars, so that subsequent falsification or alteration of the accounts shall be rendered impossible.

50. The clothing accounts, also, have been made more precise, and more easily intelligible, with a view to the taking of stock by the Guardians.

51. We have often regretted the impossibility of arriving at an exact statement of the number of persons chargeable at one time throughout England; and we adverted to this inaccuracy in our last Annual Report. The Quarterly Abstract (Form B. 11), as prescribed by the former order of accounts, was necessarily more or less incorrect. This incorrectness arose from several sources.—In the first place, many persons appeared in the abstracts of more than one Union, having been chargeable during the quarter to more than one in succession; in the second place, the same person might appear twice in the same abstract—once, as classed amongst paupers receiving out-door relief, and again, as admitted into the workhouse. We have no doubt that, from these sources of error, and from other causes, the number of paupers has been somewhat exaggerated in all our returns. We have endeavoured to obviate these difficulties in our present order; and, whilst we have separated the statistical portion of the abstract from that part which gives the pecuniary result of the accounts, we have required the clerk to deduct such classes of persons as appear twice in the gross number of paupers. We have also required that a statement should be given of the actual number of persons chargeable on the 1st of January and 1st of July in every year.

52. With reference to the audit of accounts we have inserted a provision in our order to the following effect:—

"Provided always, that if the Auditor shall see fit, in any special case, with the consent of the Poor Law Commissioners, to hold an extraordinary audit, either of the whole or of any portion of the accounts of any Union or Parish, in addition to the ordinary audit, at any time between such two days, it shall be the duty of any person who would be, or who would have been accountable at the ordinary audit, to account at such special audit, in like form and manner as at such ordinary audit, so far as the same shall be applicable to such special audit; and the surcharge, allowance, disallowance, or decision of the auditor on any item, or other matter, at such special audit, shall, so far as regards the provisions and regulations which may be contained in any order of the Poor Law Commissioners, have the same effect as if the same were made or given at the ordinary audit of the accounts of such Union or Parish."

The object of this direction is to enable an auditor to examine the accounts of any officer suspected of peculation, and to strike a balance against a defaulter or an officer who is about to be dismissed, at any time, with the same legal consequences as if the balance were struck at the regular half-yearly audit. Without some such provision, the Guardians must have waited for the next audit until they could obtain the authoritative judgment of the auditor on any illegal items of account. It will be necessary that these extraordinary services, when required by the Commissioners, should be paid for as something not included in the auditor's salary.

53. We have required, in Article 43, that the auditor shall, at the close of each audit of the accounts of the Unions in his district, transmit to the Poor Law Commissioners a statement of the books directed by their orders to be kept by the Union officers, showing which, if any, are not kept at all, or are imperfectly kept.

54. We have moreover taken such precaution as we have thought practicable for ensuring the validity

of the bonds and the solvency of the sureties of officers giving security to the Guardians, by providing—

"That the auditor shall, at the close of the audit of the accounts of the Unions, in his district next after the 25th March in every year, transmit to the Poor Law Commissioners a statement setting forth the name of each Union officer and collector of poor rates in his district required to give a bond, and whether such bond, together with any certificate or proof that each of the sureties named therein is living, and is not bankrupt or insolvent, was produced to him at such audit; and also a statement of any defects in such securities: he is also required to report to the Board of Guardians the fact of such bonds and certificates having been produced to him, together with any defects in such securities."

55. The order itself, and the instructional letter which accompanied it, will be found in the Appendix to this Report.

District Auditors.

56. In our Report of last year we explained the steps which we had taken for the appointment of district auditors, in pursuance of the statute 7 and 8 Vic. c. 101. We also stated our conviction that the operation of the audit by this class of officers was likely to be extremely beneficial; we anticipated that illegal practices would be checked, and irregularities in the accounts more strictly investigated (par. 36-40). We have not been deceived in these expectations. Every audit under the present system tends to show more clearly to the overseers that the lawfulness of payments out of the poor-rates must be considered by them before the money of the rate-payers is expended. The Union officers feel that any error or laxness in the accounts which their duty requires them to keep, will probably lead to a disallowance or surcharge against themselves, if not to more serious consequences.

57. The auditors are bound by the statute to report to the Poor Law Commissioners any disallowance or surcharge. On receiving such report, we usually cause a letter to be addressed to the Clerk to the Guardians of the Union, to ask whether the sum so disallowed or charged has been paid over to the treasurer of the Union, in accordance with the provisions of the Act of Parliament. If this is not done within a given time, it becomes the auditor's duty to proceed to the recovery of the money. For the most part, the sums certified to be due by the auditor are paid without hesitation: several cases have occurred in which proceedings before justices under the statute have been instituted by the auditors: a few of these have failed, mainly on technical objections, whilst, on the other hand, the recovery from guardians or overseers of money unlawfully expended has often been enforced.

58. In our last Report, we stated the nature of certain legal questions which had arisen respecting the appointment of district auditors, and we adverted especially to the case of the Winslow Union, in which our order for the appointment of a district auditor was resisted without success. In two other cases, legal proceedings, which involve the right of the Poor Law Commissioners to direct the appointment of a district auditor in places under a local Act, are now pending. The two places in question are Bristol and Hull. The Board of Governors of the former incorporation took part in the election of the district auditor, and thus conformed to the order in the first instance; in the latter case, the Board of Guardians refused to take any steps under the order. Rules *nisi* were, in both these cases, granted by the Court of Queen's Bench in Hilary Term last, and we believe that the decision of the Court is likely to be given in the present term.

Appeals against Decisions of Auditors.

59. An important portion of our duty, in connexion with the audit, has been to receive applications in the nature of an appeal under section 33 of 7 and 8 Vic., c. 101. We have considered that, as the object of the provision was remedial, the Auditor might be called upon to state his reasons even after the conclusion of the audit, and we have accordingly received applications from parties who had neglected, at the time of the audit, to require that the reasons for the allowance or disallowance of any item should be stated in the book by the Auditor. Several such appeals have been made to us in a formal shape. In many of them, the party complaining has been satisfied with the expression of our opinion, without wishing us to issue a formal order. In ten cases, however, such orders have been issued, of which seven went to establish the lawfulness of the reasons assigned by the Auditor, and three decided against those reasons. None of these orders have yet been removed into the Court of Queen's Bench; a course which it is competent for any party to take who is dissatisfied with our decision.

60. We are advised that, in these appeals, we are only competent to consider the lawfulness or unlawfulness of the reasons assigned by the Auditor, and that we cannot go into equitable considerations, or make allowance for the good intentions of the officers against whom any surcharge or disallowance may be recorded. We have had, in some cases, reason to regret the hardship which is thus necessarily brought on individuals by the introduction of a system of greater strictness; but we are satisfied if a discretion had been left to the Commissioners, the result would have been great uncertainty on the part of the Auditors and the officers themselves; each individual case would have presented some exceptional features in the eye of the person or body expending the money, and each person or body would have calculated on the probability of the equity being strong enough in the particular instance to secure a favourable decision from the Poor Law Commissioners. As it is, these cases of hardships will gradually cease. The Auditors, each acting over a large surface of country, will make known the principles on which

their audit will be conducted; and the chance of success on appeal to the Commissioners will be a matter capable of being ascertained with more certainty, in proportion as more decisions are given with reference to similar cases.

Salaries of District Auditors.

61. In the present spring, a deputation of the District Auditors have made a representation to us of the inadequacy of their present salaries. These gentlemen stated that, independently of the great expense of their travelling and living at inns (all of which is included in their salary), the correspondence arising out of the audits occupied much of the time which remained after they returned home from the actual business of the audit; the duty, too, of personally conducting proceedings for recovering, before justices, balances, &c., which are not discharged, supplementary as it is to the audit, breaks in materially on the time which they might be supposed capable of devoting to some other occupation. They further urged, that, as their salary will now be paid, the income-tax will be deducted from the whole, although a large portion of such salary is in reality the repayment for expenses actually out of pocket. We are of opinion that these representations are entitled to consideration. At the same time, we think that any increase might fairly be accompanied with the condition that, in the event of further service being required of them, they should hold themselves in readiness to audit the accounts of the surveyors of the highways, and perhaps of some other local officers, without additional remuneration. In fact, such duties might be performed without casting on the Auditors, or on the public, any additional travelling expenses; one half yearly visit to the spot would suffice for the audit of the parish and Union accounts, as well as for those of the highways. In our Report of last year, we spoke of the district auditors as persons whose services might be easily made available in this manner.

Parliamentary Grant for Payment of Salaries of Officers.

62. In the last Session of Parliament, the House of Commons voted a grant of 61,500*l.* for the payment of a moiety of the salaries of medical officers, exclusive of extra fees payable under the Commissioners' order, and the whole of the salaries of workhouse schoolmasters and schoolmistresses, and district Auditors. This grant was for the salaries of the half-year ended the 31st of March last.

63. By a circular letter, dated the 7th of November last, the Commissioners explained to the Board of Guardians the nature of the arrangements which her Majesty's Government had sanctioned for the distribution of the grant. Under these arrangements, the sum payable to each Union in respect of the salaries of the medical officers, and the schoolmasters and schoolmistresses, will be paid over once in each year by the Paymaster of the Civil Service to the treasurer of the Union. The treasurer will place the amount, so paid over to him, to the credit of the establishment account of the Union. On this account, the Board of Guardians will draw cheques for the salaries in question, in the same manner as those for the other paid officers of the Union.

64. For the half-year ended the 31st of March last, the salaries, as existing on the 1st of October last, have been taken as the standard of the payments to the Union treasurers. In order to enable the Commissioners to ascertain the amount actually paid by the Board of Guardians, in each case, to each of the officers entitled to the grant, the Commissioners require the clerk of the Board to furnish them at the close of each quarter, with a statement, in duplicate, authenticated by the signature of the Chairman, setting forth, in the case of the medical officers, the name of the officer, the name of his district, the date of his appointment, the amount per annum of his salary exclusive of fees, and the amount of his salary for the preceding quarter; and in regard to the schoolmaster and schoolmistress, their names, the date of their appointments, the amount per annum of their salaries, and the sums payable to them in respect of the preceding quarter. Copies of these quarterly statements will be sent to the Auditors to be compared with the vouchers for the salaries actually paid to the officers; and from the statements thus examined by the Auditors, the Commissioners will be able to prepare annually an estimate for the use of her Majesty's Treasury, and to guard against the application of an undue proportion of the grant in any case.

65. According to the principle sanctioned by Her Majesty's Government, it is necessary, in order that any parish or Union should participate in the grant for the officers' salaries, that the salaries should have been previously approved by the Commissioners; and the Commissioners, therefore, on the 7th of November last, addressed a circular letter to all parishes and other places governed under local Acts of Parliament, whose officers' salaries are not, as is the case in Unions, submitted for the approval of the Commissioners, informing the local authorities that if they desired to receive a share of the grant for their officers, the salaries of those officers must, in the first instance, be reported to the Commissioners for their approbation.

66. While the medical officers, schoolmasters, and schoolmistresses are to be paid by the Paymaster of the Civil Service, through the Union treasurers, it has been deemed the most convenient course to pay the salaries of the district auditors through the Commissioners. The limited number (50) of the auditors, and the fact that their salaries are made up of small fixed payments in respect of several hundreds of Unions, rendered the former plan almost imprac-

ticable; moreover, it would not have provided that satisfactory accounting which the latter course will secure.

67. The salaries of the auditors were fixed in every case by an order under the seal of the Commissioners, and the several Unions were directed by the order to pay their respective contributions towards the salary; and the Commissioners have, therefore, by a general order dated the 10th of February last, suspended so much of all such orders as related to the payment of the salaries of auditors. They have also, by a circular letter dated the 18th of February last, required the auditors to furnish them with a statement in regard to the audit of the accounts of the Unions in their respective districts, for the half-year ended the 29th of September last, showing the names of the Unions in the district, the date when the audit was completed; if the audit of the accounts of any Union had not been completed, the cause thereof; if any Union had paid the salary in respect of the audit, the amount so paid, and the name of a banker in London to whom the salary might be paid by the Commissioners. A return of these particulars enabled the Commissioners to pay the salaries which accrued to the auditors in respect of the last-mentioned audit; and a similar return will be called for half-yearly.

68. By a letter dated the 7th of November last, we called the attention of our Assistant Commissioners to the grant made for the repayment of the salaries of the Poor Law medical officers, and the schoolmasters and schoolmistresses of workhouses. In the same letter, we stated further that it was the intention of Her Majesty's Government, in proposing these votes, to contribute to an improvement in the character of the workhouse schools, and in the supply of medical relief to the poor; and we instructed the Assistant Commissioners to report with respect to those Unions, in their respective districts, in which the schools are least effective, and the medical relief least satisfactory, in order that the Commissioners might take steps for improving both those branches of the Union management. By a later letter, dated the 17th of December, we communicated to our Assistant Commissioners, the intention of Her Majesty's Government to appoint separate inspectors of the workhouse schools, under the control of the Committee of Council for Education, as well as your wish that no expectation should be held out that the salaries of the workhouse schoolmasters and mistresses would be repaid after the current half-year, without some inquiry into their efficiency. We have lately received several reports from our Assistant Commissioners, containing detailed accounts of the state of the arrangements for the medical relief and workhouse instruction in the different Unions, and we are gradually taking measures for removing the defects pointed out. With respect, however, to the teachers in the workhouse schools, we abstain from establishing any general principle, or interfering on a large scale, until the inspection of the officers appointed by the Committee of Council shall have been completed.

Medical Relief.

69. Upon the subject of medical relief, we have nothing material to add to the explanations in our Annual Reports since 1842. The expenditure under this head has been nearly stationary in the two last parochial years, as appears from the following Table:

Total Expenditure for Medical Relief.

Years ending Lady-day.	Amount of Medical Relief.
1838	£136,775
1839	148,652
1840	151,781
1841	154,054
1842	152,006
1843	160,726
1844	166,257
1845	174,330
1846	175,269

Vaccination.

70. With respect to vaccination during the past year, we have to report that, as in previous years, we called for returns of the numbers vaccinated by the public vaccinators from the clerks of the several Boards of Guardians, and in the Appendix to this Report, we have inserted a summary of the returns received from 539 Unions and parishes. The following table shows the numbers vaccinated during the past two years in 580 and 539 Unions respectively, and the ratio of persons vaccinated to the number of births in each year.

	Number of Unions, &c.	No. of Persons Vaccinated.	No. of Persons successfully Vaccinated.	No. of Registered Births.	Ratio of Persons Vaccinated to the No. of Births.	Ratio of Persons successfully Vaccinated to the No. of Births.
1845	580	362,087	347,765	486,632	100 in 134	100 in 140
1846	539	271,219	258,165	483,480	100 in 178	100 in 187

It will be observed that the number vaccinated by the public vaccinators during last year is less in proportion to the births than in the previous year; but we have no reason to suppose that the diminution has been caused by any want of zeal on the part of the vaccinators.

71. The Boards of Guardians, generally, are alive to the importance of carrying out the provisions of the Vaccination Extension Act to the fullest extent. A few Boards, however, still manifest great indifference on the subject; we more particularly refer to the Board of Guardians of the Todmorden Union, and of the parish of St. George the Martyr, Southwark. On a former occasion,* we felt it our duty to report that the Guardians of the Todmorden Union had not carried the provisions of the Vaccination Act into effect, and we regret that, up to the present time (so far as we are aware,) no steps whatever have

* Eleventh Ann. Rep. p. 27, 8vo.

been taken by them in the matter. The Guardians of the parish of St. George the Martyr, Southwark, in July, 1844, passed a resolution that all cases for vaccination, in connexion with the parish, be performed at the workhouse, in Mint-street, on and after the 29th of September then next ensuing, and that the vaccinators in their respective districts appoint the particular day and hours of attendance for such purpose. On being made acquainted with that resolution we addressed a letter to the Board of Guardians objecting to the arrangement, and we stated that it would put an end to the general vaccination of the residents of the parish, many of whom, not being actually paupers, would feel unwilling to take their children to the workhouse, under the impression that by so doing they were placing themselves in the position of paupers. That we were correct in apprehending the almost entire cessation of vaccination by the public vaccinators of the parish from the altered arrangement is proved by the returns of the number of persons vaccinated, since received from the parish. In the year ended 29th September, 1844, at which date vaccination was first restricted to the workhouse, the number of persons vaccinated was 1079, and in 1845 the number fell to 42, and in 1846 it was only 44. We have endeavoured to prevail upon the Guardians to alter their resolution of July, 1844, but we regret to state without effect; we are, however, still in communication with them on the subject, and hope to induce them to revert to the original arrangement, under which the public vaccinators were permitted to vaccinate at their own residences.

72. The fees paid to the public vaccinators during the year ended 25th March, 1846, amounted to 27,486*l.*, being an increase of 1581*l.* upon the amount paid to them in the previous year.

Proceedings as to new Workhouse for Kensington.

73. During the last year, some proceedings have taken place with respect to the building of a workhouse in the parish of Kensington, which are sufficiently important to require an explanation in this Report.

74. The parish of Kensington is under a separate Board of Guardians, and its workhouse stands on land belonging to the Trustees of the Camden Charity, but held under them by the Guardians at a rent of 315*l.* a-year. This workhouse was found insufficient in size and accommodation; and it became necessary for the Guardians to decide whether they would alter and enlarge the existing workhouse, or purchase a freehold site, and build a new workhouse upon it. The Guardians, with our concurrence and approbation, preferred the latter course; and having received from them the written consent required by the Act of Parliament, we issued an order, dated the 21st of March last, authorising them to purchase a site for a sum not exceeding 4000*l.*, and to build upon it a workhouse, of a size sufficient to hold four hundred persons, at a cost not exceeding 9000*l.*

75. A short time afterwards, Mr. Stephen Bird, a parishioner of Kensington, applied to the Court of Queen's Bench for a writ of certiorari to bring up this order, on the ground that the consent of a majority of the owners and ratepayers had not been obtained to the measure. The Court held this objection to be invalid, and discharged the rule with costs against the party making the application. (Trinity Term, 11 June, 1846.)*

76. Subsequently, on the 21st of July, we received a deputation from the parish of Kensington, who laid before us in writing several objections to the plan of a new workhouse proposed by the Guardians. The chief of these objections were its unnecessary expense, the insalubrity and inconvenience of the site, and the insufficiency of the drainage. These objections were transmitted by us to the Board of Guardians, and the Board of Guardians afterwards sent us an answer, (dated the 12th of August,) in which the objections to their plan were considered in detail, and which was accompanied by the reports of surveyors and medical men. This answer (a copy of which we communicated to the complaining parties) was considered by us as satisfactory, and we accordingly declined to rescind our order. Other objections to the proceedings of the Guardians were afterwards raised, (particularly with reference to an alleged difficulty as to a right of way to the site for the new workhouse;) but they were not considered by us to be such as to render it advisable that we should overrule the discretion of the Guardians, or to induce us to alter our opinion of the matter.

77. In consequence of the plan selected by the Guardians requiring a larger outlay than was estimated by their architect, it became necessary for the Commissioners to authorise them to expend a larger sum upon the building of the workhouse, and we therefore, on their application, issued, on the 1st of April last, an order, enlarging the previous limit of expenditure by 4000*l.*

78. We are informed that the recent annual election of Guardians in the parish of Kensington has been favourable to the building of a new workhouse, and that the course pursued by the late Board of Guardians appears to have been in accordance with the general opinion of the ratepayers.

Inquiries as to St. Marylebone and St. Pancras.

79. In consequence of the verdicts of Coroners' juries, we instituted in last winter inquiries into the management of outdoor relief in the parishes of St. Marylebone and St. Pancras, and subsequent proceedings have taken place; on the whole of which we have made to you a separate Report, dated the 9th of April last, and presented to both Houses of Parliament. We had previously made an investigation by means of our Assistant Commissioner, Mr. Hall, into the management of the workhouse of St. Pancras; and in consequence of the irregularities in the disci-

* See 16 Law Journal, Rep. 29.

pline and punishment of pauper inmates which that Report disclosed, we issued our workhouse regulations to that parish, in an order dated the 9th of December, 1846.

Removals Act.

80. The principal legislative measure of last Session affecting the Poor Law is the Act relating to the Removal of the Poor, 9 and 10 Vict., c. 66, which received the Royal assent on the 26th of August last. The object of this Act was, without altering the grounds of acquiring a settlement, to diminish the frequency of removals, by rendering the poor irremovable from a parish under certain defined circumstances. The principal classes of poor thus rendered irremovable may be described in general terms as follows:—

1. Persons who have been resident in a parish for five years.
2. Widows for twelve calendar months after the death of the husband.
3. Persons receiving relief on account of temporary sickness or accident.

81. We addressed a circular letter to the Boards of Guardians, dated the 17th of September, giving an outline of the provisions of the Act, and calling the attention of the Guardians to some of its consequences. Soon afterwards, however, we found that doubts were entertained in many quarters with respect to the construction of parts of the Act, and we accordingly submitted to the Attorney and Solicitor General six questions arising out of it. Having received their opinion, we communicated the substance of it to the Boards of Guardians, by a letter dated the 20th of October. The most important of the questions submitted to the Crown lawyers related to the construction of the proviso annexed to the first clause of the Act. By this proviso, it was declared (amongst other things), that the time during which a person is in the receipt of relief shall not reckon as a portion of the five years rendering him irremovable: it was certain that this provision applied to a residence *subsequent* to the passing of the Act, but there was a doubt whether it applied to a residence *anterior to* the passing of the Act. The Attorney and Solicitor General were of opinion that the proviso did *not* apply to a residence anterior to the passing of the Act. We believe that the Bill, as originally framed and introduced into Parliament, would have had a different effect, and would have extended this exception to a residence which had occurred *before* the passing of the Act. But the Bill was altered in its passage through Parliament into the form in which it now stands; and the distinction which the Act, as it passed, draws between the two periods of residence may unquestionably be defended on this ground, that whereas the residence which had already taken place, could not have been influenced by any motive originating in the Act itself, parishes might, *after* the passing of the Act, give non-resident relief for the purpose of rendering their own settled paupers irremovable from other parishes.

82. As soon as the Act began to be put in force, we found that a disposition existed to make a distinction between the relief of the settled poor of a Union and the non-settled poor, resident in it, who had become irremovable under its operation. In many cases, these non-settled poor were aged persons, who had been receiving relief from other Unions, and who, in consequence of the construction put upon the Act by the Attorney and Solicitor General, had become irremovable from the parishes where they had resided five years. The relief of this class of poor having been stopped by the Unions in which they were settled, the Unions in which they were resident showed in many cases a disposition either to refuse them relief altogether, or to give them insufficient relief, or merely to offer them relief in the workhouse. In order to counteract this disposition, we issued a circular letter to the Boards of Guardians, dated the 4th of December, in which we pointed out the impropriety of making a distinction between the relief of the settled and the non-settled but irremovable poor. Afterwards we addressed a similar letter to the Boards of Guardians, inquiring whether they made any such distinction (dated the 18th of January); and out of 500 Unions from which we received answers to this inquiry, only nine stated that they made such distinction. We likewise addressed a letter to our Assistant Commissioners, dated the 17th of February, requesting them, if they had observed such a distinction in any Unions, or any cases of hardship arising under the Removal Act, to report them to us. The answers which have been made to us show that, in general, no such perversion of the Act has come to the knowledge of the Assistant Commissioners. We have received a few complaints with regard to single cases of hardship under the Act, arising from the stoppage of relief, at the moment of the change of chargeability. We have heard likewise of some cases in which the change of law has led to the discharge of labourers who had been employed, not because their services were wanted, but in order to keep them off the poor-rates.

83. These, however, and other similar inconveniences, were the temporary consequences of the adjustment necessary in order to carry the Act into effect; and could scarcely fail to arise under any alteration creating an extensive transfer of pauper chargeability from one to another set of parishes. The difficulty of the adjustment was likewise aggravated by the doubts which existed as to the interpretation of the Act. Now that the adjustment has been effected, and that the construction of the Act recommended by the Crown lawyers has been almost universally adopted, the practice of the Boards of Guardians is, as we believe, tolerably uniform. In accordance with our recommendations, they relieve the settled and non-settled, but irremovable, poor in the same manner.

and they continue the relief to their non-resident poor who have not become irremovable.

84. Many persons who were liable to removal before the passing of this Act, and who were deterred from applying for relief by the fear of removal, have since last autumn become applicants for relief, and in numerous cases have been relieved. This description particularly applies to the Irish, who had been resident for some years in the metropolis and other large towns. With these exceptions, the principal effect of the Act has been to transfer the cost of the relief of the poor from the parishes of their settlement to the parishes of their residence, and not to create any new burden.

Law relating to Pauper Lunatics.

85. The Act 9 and 10 Vict., c. 5, which contained some amendments of the statute of the previous year relating to County Lunatic Asylums, removed one of the difficulties which existed in regard to the removal of pauper lunatics, in cases where the lunatic was not such as to require confinement in an asylum, or one likely to be cured by the medical treatment therein. Under the previous statute it was considered by the Justices that they had no discretion, but were bound to issue an order in every case which was brought before them. The 1st section of the new statute declares that it shall not be incumbent upon the Justices and the other parties who are competent to act in this matter, in all cases to issue the order; and it requires such Justices and parties to satisfy themselves as to the propriety of confining the lunatic in an asylum before they sign the order, except, indeed, a medical certificate be obtained from the medical officer of the Union, in which case this discretion is removed.

Sanitary Act.

86. The Sanitary Act (9 and 10 Vict., c. 96) for the removal of nuisances, conferred certain powers upon Boards of Guardians, to enable them to procure the removal of such private nuisances as are of a nature calculated to injure health. We thought it advisable to issue a circular letter to all Boards of Guardians to point out the nature of its provisions, and the powers and authorities which the statute conferred upon them; and we urged upon the Guardians the exercise of these powers. A difficulty was suggested as to the proper construction of the statute, with reference to the places in which the Boards of Guardians could act; and we were consulted, on several occasions, as to the extent of its operation in rural districts. We expressed our opinion, that the Act had a general operation in all parts of England and Wales; and we are glad to learn, from a communication lately made to us by your direction, that the law officers of the Crown have given the same opinion. We believe that many Boards of Guardians have acted upon the statute with beneficial result.

British Guarantee Society.

87. We deem it right to notice an Act, passed during the last session, to incorporate a society, under the name of *The British Guarantee Society*, for the purpose of providing security for persons in offices of trust. In that Act an express provision is contained to enable the Boards of Guardians to take the security of this society in lieu of the security required to be given by the officers of such Guardians; but in such form, and subject to such rules and regulations, as the Poor Law Commissioners shall require, approve, or direct. We have under our consideration at the present time, the proper form of policy to be issued by the society in reference to the officers of Unions and Parishes.

Emigration.

88. We have to state, with reference to the emigration of poor persons, that very little took place last year under our orders. Indeed, the amount of parochial emigration was much less than in any previous year, and scarcely to an extent worthy of notice. Mr. Buchanan reports (in Parliamentary Paper, Session 1847) that the number of such emigrants who went out under our superintendence, and landed in Canada, was 79; a few proceeded to Australia, under the regulations of the Colonial Land and Emigration Commissioners.

89. Our attention having been called to the Instructions to the Assistant Commissioners which had been prepared and issued in the year 1841, when the number of the Assistant Commissioners was greater than at present (see the Seventh Annual Report, p. 55), we revised them with reference to the existing state of things, and re-issued the revised Instructions at the beginning of this year. A copy of these Instructions is inserted in the Appendix.

90. By the sudden death of Colonel Wade, in November last, we were deprived of his valuable services in the inspection of the Welsh district; and we have appointed in his place Mr. Aneurin Owen, a gentleman who was recommended for employment in that part of the country by his previous official experience in Wales under the Tithe Commission, as well as by his knowledge of the Welsh language.

[*The portion of the Report which relates to "Proceedings in Ireland," is omitted.*]

We have the honour to be, &c. &c

(Signed) George Nicholls.
George Cornewall Lewis.
Edmund W. Head
L. S. E. T. B. Twisleton.

LONDON:
Printed by order of the Poor Law Commissioners, by Blackburn and Pardon, 6, Hatton Garden, and Published by Charles Knight and Co., 22, Ludgate Street, Publishers to the Poor Law Commissioners.

AN

OFFICIAL CIRCULAR

OF PUBLIC DOCUMENTS AND INFORMATION:

DIRECTED BY THE POOR LAW COMMISSIONERS TO BE PRINTED, CHIEFLY FOR THE USE OF THE MEMBERS AND PERMANENT OFFICERS OF BOARDS OF GUARDIANS, UNDER THE POOR LAW AMENDMENT ACT.

No. 6.] CIRCULAR ISSUED JUNE 1st, 1847. [N. S.

Poor Law Commission Office,
Somerset House,
June 1, 1847.

THE Poor Law Commissioners have directed that the following information be printed and circulated for the information of Guardians and Officers of the several Unions.

By Order of the Board,
EDWIN CHADWICK, *Secretary.*

I.—ACCOUNTS.

1. DISALLOWANCE OF SALARY TO TOWNSHIP SOLICITOR.

March 15*th*, 1847.

Overseers of ———.—The district auditor has disallowed a sum of £50, paid by them to Mr. S. their legal adviser, for professional services, under an arrangement made with him in 1845, to pay him a fixed sum per annum for such services. Requested that the auditor might be instructed to allow the item in their accounts.

Ans.—The Commissioners are not cognizant of any legal authority which supports such an arrangement as that entered into with Mr. S. The law does not empower the township officers, or the vestry, to appoint a solicitor to the township at a fixed salary, and the solicitor can only charge for the services he actually renders.

---

2. WHETHER AUDITOR CAN BE REQUIRED TO STATE HIS REASONS FOR A DISALLOWANCE SUBSEQUENT TO THE AUDIT.

February 26th, 1847.

Mr. T. K. Roberts, District Auditor—He has received a requisition calling upon him to state his reasons for disallowing, in October last, certain items in the accounts of the late overseers of one of the townships in the ——— Union. Inquired whether he can be required to give his written reasons for such disallowance subsequent to the audit.

Ans.—The Commissioners consider the district auditor should state his reasons for any disallowance, &c., whenever he may be required to do so at any reasonable time after the audit. The Commissioners are strongly induced to come to this conclusion, by the consideration that disallowances or surcharges may be made against parties not present at the audit. At the same time, the Commissioners think it right to observe that they do not consider the district auditor bound to go to the parish, or place, where the books of account may be, in order to state his reasons. The party requiring such statement should send or bring the books to him.

II.—AUDITORS' SALARIES.

1. GENERAL ORDER SUSPENDING SO MUCH OF FORMER ORDERS AS DIRECTED THE PAYMENT OF AUDITORS' SALARIES.

To the guardians of the poor of the several unions, incorporations, and parishes and places named in the schedule hereunto annexed;—

To the churchwardens and overseers of the said several parishes and of the parishes and places comprised within the said unions;—

To the clerk or clerks to the justices of the petty sessions held for the division or divisions in which the said unions, incorporations, and parishes are situate;—

And to all others whom it may concern.

Whereas, by several Orders, the dates whereof are set forth in the first column of the schedule hereunto annexed, the Poor Law Commissioners, under the authority of the statute passed in the eighth year of the reign of her Majesty, intituled "*An Act for the further amendment of the Laws relating to the Poor in England*," did combine the several unions, incorporations of parishes, and parishes and places, also set forth in the third column of the said schedule, into the several districts for the audit of accounts in the said Orders specified, and did fix the salaries to be paid to the several auditors to be appointed under the same respectively; and did order the guardians of the poor of the several unions, incorporations, and parishes to pay the said salaries in certain proportions and at certain periods as therein fully set forth.

And whereas a sum of money hath been granted by Parliament to be applied in the payment of the salaries of such auditors, for the half year ending the thirty-first day of March next, and similar grants may hereafter be made; and it is accordingly expedient that so much of the said orders as requires the guardians of the said several unions, incorporations, and parishes to contribute to the payment of the salaries of the said auditors should be suspended as hereinafter mentioned.

Now, therefore, we, the Poor Law Commissioners, acting under the authority of an Act passed in the fifth year of the reign of his late Majesty, King William the Fourth, intituled, "*An Act for the Amendment and better Administration of the Laws relating to the Poor in England and Wales*," do hereby henceforth, and until the Poor Law Commissioners shall otherwise order, suspend so much of the said several Orders set forth in the said schedule as directs the guardians aforesaid to contribute to the payment of the salaries of the several auditors for the time being appointed under the same.

SCHEDULE to which this Order refers.

[*The schedule consists of the dates of the Orders, combining unions, incorporations of parishes, and parishes and places into audit districts; the names of such districts; and the names of the unions, incorporations, and parishes and places comprised in each district.*]

Given under our hands and seal of office, this tenth day of February, in the year one thousand eight hundred and forty-seven.

(Signed) GEO. NICHOLLS.
G. C. LEWIS.
L.S. EDMUND W. HEAD.

---

2. CIRCULAR TO AUDITORS RESPECTING THE PAYMENTS OF THEIR SALARIES.

Poor Law Commission Office,
Somerset House,
February 18th, 1847.

SIR,—I am directed by the Poor Law Commissioners to inform you, that the amount voted in the last session of Parliament to pay the salaries of district auditors for the half year ending the 31st of March next, will be placed in the hands of the Commissioners for payment; and the Commissioners, therefore, in order to be able to pay the salary due to you in respect of the last half-yearly audit of the accounts of the unions in your district, wish to be furnished with the several particulars mentioned in the enclosed form.

A copy of an Order which the Commissioners have issued for suspending so much of the Order under which you were appointed as relates to the payment of your salary by the guardians, is sent to you herewith.

I have, &c.

EDWIN CHADWICK, *Secretary.*

To

District Auditor.

FORM referred to in the above Circular.

________________ *Audit District.*

STATEMENT in reference to the audit of the accounts of the unions in the above district for the half year ended the 29th of September, 1846.

Names of the Unions, &c., in the above District.	Date when the Audit was completed.	If the Audit of the Accounts of any Union has not been completed state the cause thereof.	If any Union has paid the Salary in respect of the above Audit insert the amount so paid.			The name of a Banker in London to whom the Salary may be paid by the Poor Law Commissioners.
			£	s.	d.	

The salary now due to me in respect of the above mentioned audit amounts to £ „ „

________________ *District Auditor.*

Date ________________

To

The Poor Law Commissioners,
&c. &c. &c.

3. CIRCULAR TO BOARDS OF GUARDIANS RESPECTING THE PAYMENT OF AUDITORS' SALARIES.

Poor Law Commission Office,
Somerset House,
May 10th, 1847.

SIR,—I am directed by the Poor Law Commissioners to inform you that they have paid out of the Parliamentary grant, the salaries of the district auditors in respect of the audit of the accounts for the half year ended the 29th of September last. In some instances the salaries, in respect of this audit, had been previously paid by the unions, and the Commissioners have requested the auditors, in those instances, to refund the amounts to the union treasurers.

I am, &c.

EDWIN CHADWICK, *Secretary.*

To

The Clerk to the Board of Guardians.

III.—ASSESSED TAXES.

ASSESSING A WORKHOUSE MASTER IN RESPECT OF THE WINDOWS OF HIS APARTMENTS.

February 18th, 1847.

Clerk of Windsor Union—The master of the workhouse occupies apartments in the workhouse which have six windows; some of these, it is stated, are wider than allowed for single windows, and are, therefore, charged to the assessed taxes as three windows each. Inquired as to the obligation to pay the charge.

Ans.—The Commissioners have communicated with the Commissioners of Stamps and Taxes on this subject, and learn from a letter which they have received from Mr. Pressley, the secretary to that department, that it is found upon inquiry that there are fourteen windows in the apartments solely occupied by the master, and of these four are chargeable as double windows, being considerably more than four feet nine inches in breadth, and three feet six inches in height; and that the assessment consequently being made upon eighteen windows is correct. Mr. Pressley adds, that the Commissioners of Stamps and Taxes entertain no doubt that the windows in question are liable to be charged as double windows; but that it is open to the master of the workhouse to appeal against the assessment to the Commissioners of the district, and if he should be dissatisfied with their decision he may demand a case upon the point for the opinion of the judges.

IV.—BREAD—HIGH PRICE OF.—CIRCULAR.

Poor Law Commission Office,
Somerset House,
May 21st, 1847.

SIR,—The Poor Law Commissioners presume that the attention of the guardians has been already directed to everything which can promote economy in the consumption of grain, with reference to the diet of the paupers in the workhouse, and to the out-relief afforded in the shape of bread.

The high price of wheat and other grain at the present moment, and the fear that such prices may not diminish before harvest, make it expedient that in this matter every precaution should be used which is consistent with the health and proper sustenance of the persons relieved by the guardians; on these two points, however, no risk should be incurred; and wherever doubt exists the medical officers should be consulted.

Subject to such precautions the Commissioners think it will be expedient to supply, in the administration of relief, bread somewhat inferior in description to the finer quality of the same article; and in unions, where the habits of the labouring classes admit of it, as in Wales and the north of England, oat-cake, or stirabout, may be occasionally substituted for bread.

The Commissioners will be willing to make any alteration of the dietary which may be necessary for enabling the guardians to act upon the suggestions contained in this letter.

I am, Sir, your obedient servant,
W. G. LUMLEY, *Assistant Secretary.*

To
The Clerk to the Guardians.

[*The following is a copy of a paper received by the Poor Law Commissioners from the chairman of the Atherstone Union.*]

BREAD.

A Method of saving one-third of wheaten flour, and about 23 *per cent. in price, in the manufacture of bread.*

Hominy is produced from Indian corn. It is the corn coarsely ground or kibbled, and is thus distinguished from Indian meal flour, which is finely ground. It is sold by provision merchants, at from £20 to £22 per ton, or about 22*s.* a cwt., if with the addition of carriage (£1 per hundred miles), the cost, as nearly as can be calculated, would be 2¾*d.* a lb.

Hominy has the quality of imbibing from five to seven times its weight in water, which Indian meal flour does not; and this constitutes the important distinction between the two.

The proportion of hominy and seconds wheaten flour for good bread is 1½ lbs. of hominy to a stone (14 lbs.) of flour.

The hominy must be soaked sixteen or eighteen hours in cold water before it is cooked.

TO MAKE HOMINY BREAD.

The hominy having been properly soaked, drain off the water, and add of fresh water seven and a half pints for each pound and a half of hominy as weighed before soaking; let this simmer for four hours (if boiled rapidly it will become hard and never swell), the hominy will then be fit for stirabout or bread. For bread, mix it gradually with the flour, making the dough in the ordinary way, and adding yeast in rather more than the usual proportion.

This bread will keep moist and good for a longer time than if made entirely of wheaten flour.

COST.

Of 14 lbs. of seconds flour, 3*s.*, making 16 lbs. of bread.

Of 14 lbs. of seconds flour (3*s.*) and 1½ lbs. of hominy (4¼⅛*d.*), 3*s.* 4¼⅛*d.*, making 23½ lbs. of bread.

The cost of bread made of seconds flour is, therefore, nine farthings per pound, and of flour with hominy, seven farthings per pound, which is a saving of nearly twenty-three per cent. upon the hominy bread; and as the hominy has swelled to 7½ lbs. and the flour to 16 lbs., the bread is formed of as nearly as possible two-thirds wheaten flour, and one-third hominy flour.

May, 1847.

V.—BURIALS—CHARGING EXPENSES OF.

May 14th, 1847.

Clerk of Wigan Union—R. S., a single woman, belonging to the township of Aspull, in the Wigan Union, was admitted into the workhouse at Hindley about six months ago, where she was delivered of a bastard child. On her recovery she left the workhouse with her child, and went to reside in Wigan, where the child died, after a residence there of between two and three months. The mother, being unable to bury the child, obtained a coffin, and the means of doing so, from the relieving officer of Wigan. Inquired whether the relief thus granted to R. S. should be charged to Aspull or to Wigan; and whether midwifery expenses are payable by the township in which the birth occurs, or by that in which the mother is settled, if both townships be in the same union.

Ans.—The question as to the charging of the cost of the funeral expenses incurred in the burial of the bastard child of R. S. depends solely upon the 7 & 8 Vict. c. 101, s. 31, which cannot be affected by any resolution or agreement of the townships in the Wigan Union. By the provision in question the expenses referred to are to be charged to the township to which the deceased was chargeable, or that in which the death occurred. In the present instance the child was not chargeable at all, neither was its mother at the time of the death of the child. The Commissioners understand the words in the 31st section, "to which such person may have been chargeable," to refer to the chargeability existing at the time of the decease; and it follows, therefore, that the expenses in this case cannot be charged to any township, on the ground of chargeability. It consequently remains that the expenses should be charged to the township in which the death occurred. There is no ground for charging the expenses to the township of the settlement. The expenses of the delivery of the mother in child-birth must be borne by the township to which the mother, at the time, was chargeable. If that be the township of the settlement, those expenses will follow the other charges. If it be the township of the residence, they will be chargeable to that township.

VI.—EXTRA-PAROCHIAL PLACES—Relief to the Poor in.

May 13th, 1847.

Clerk of Bellingham Union—The parish of Bellingham comprises six townships, and within its boundary, but not in, or forming part of any of the townships, is a large tract of undivided moor-land, called Hareshaw Common. Encroachments have been made on the common and cottages built thereon, some of which are occupied by paupers. Inquired—1. Whether the townships in which such paupers were last settled are now liable to relieve them; and, if so, whether they can be removed to such townships. 2. Whether paupers who have resided on the common for the last five years, and who have been receiving relief from other townships than those in the parish of Bellingham, ought still to continue chargeable to such townships.

Ans.—The paupers who reside in the extra-parochial place referred to have no claim for relief upon the Bellingham Union, nor upon any parish whatever. So long as they continue to reside in the extra-parochial place, no parish is liable to relieve them, and the guardians of the union have no authority to interfere. Moreover, the parish of the settlement, if the paupers have any, is not liable to maintain them, unless they can be removed, and no removal can take place from an extra-parochial place.

VII.—ELECTION OF GUARDIANS.

1. Validity of Nomination, Parish Imperfectly Named.

March 31st, 1847.

Clerk of Wimborne and Cranborne Union—Inquired as to the validity of a nomination for the office of guardian, stated to be for the parish of "Wimborne," there being parishes in the union called "Wimborne Minster" and "Wimborne St Giles."

Ans.—If there be no parish which, in ordinary parlance, is termed Wimborne alone, the nomination is void for uncertainty; but if any parish is generally known as Wimborne, though strictly it should bear another name, the Commissioners think that you might treat it as a valid nomination for that parish.

2. Validity of Nomination Paper having no Date.

March 23rd, 1847.

Clerk of Leeds Township—Stated that he has received a paper nominating a person for the office of guardian for the township, without any date attached to it. Inquired whether the nomination is valid.

Ans.—The case of Beenlen *v.* Hockin, 16 L. J. R. n. s. C. P. 49, appears to show conclusively that the nomination paper for the election of guardians is bad in the case submitted in your letter. The Commissioners think, however, that you may inform the nominator of the defect in the nomination.

3. Qualification of Person Nominated.

April 1st, 1847.

Clerk of Lichfield Union—One of the persons nominated for the office of guardian for the parish of Shenstone, appears upon the rate-book as rated for a "house and land, five acres, thirty-four perches, and garden twenty perches," at a gross estimated rental of £26. 5*s*. 1*d*., and rateable value of £21. 16*s*. The qualification of a guardian of the Lichfield Union is "to be rated in respect of hereditaments of the annual value of £25." It has been ascertained that the person so nominated ceased to occupy between four and five acres of the land above referred to on the 25th of March last.—Inquired whether he is not now disqualified to act as guardian of the Lichfield Union.

Ans.—The Commissioners assume that the annual value of the property upon which the candidate was rated, was of the amount of £25, and that this rate still continues. They think, by analogy to the case of Bushell *v.* Luckett, 15 L. I. R. n. s. C. P. 88, the party continues to be rated upon it, though he has ceased to occupy a portion of the property. When a new rate is made, he will become disqualified in respect of this property.

---

4. OWNERS' CLAIMS TO VOTE.

Feb. 19th, 1847.

Mr. ——, Northampton Union—Requested the Commissioners' opinion on the following questions, with reference to the election of guardians; namely—1. Whether, where there are several tenants' names inserted in an owner's claim to vote, the rent paid by each should be stated separately. 2. Whether proxies' names should be sent in before the 1st of February, or whether it would be sufficient to send in the appointment and the name of the proxy within fourteen days of an election. 3. Whether, where a proxy's claim to vote has been sent in before the 1st of February, it is necessary that it should be again sent in fourteen days before an election. 4. Whether service of an owner's statement on a Sunday is valid. 5. Whether, where a statement has been sent in purporting to be signed by an owner or his proxy, but which has been signed without the knowledge of either, the vote of such owner or proxy will be valid. 6. Whether the "gross estimated rental," or the "rateable value," is to be taken as the guide in computing the number of votes to which each voter is entitled; and if the former should have been taken as the basis of the calculation in any union, would the votes so calculated be lost on objection, or be allowed on being reduced to their proper number.

Ans.—1. The Commissioners are disposed to consider, that, according to the language of the statute, the rent paid by each tenant should be stated separately, and not in the aggregate; at the same time, as the owner's right to vote depends upon the aggregate amount of the property, and not upon the number of tenants, in point of principle, there does not appear to be any sufficient ground for the severance. 2. They consider that proxies' names need not be sent in before the 1st of February, but if sent in fourteen days before the voting or acting of such proxies, it will suffice. 3. It is not necessary to send in a proxy's claim a second time, until the lapse of two years after its being made. 4. The Commissioners think that a claim sent in on a Sunday is valid. (See Rawlins *v.* the Overseers of West Derby, 10 Jur. 268.) 5. The statement of the owner is required by 7 & 8 Vict. c. 101, to be signed by him. If he gave no authority to another to sign the statement, it seems clear that the provision of the statute has not been complied with. The 4 & 5 Wm. 4, c. 76, s. 40, makes a similar provision in regard to the appointment of a proxy. 6. The statute 7 & 8 Vict. c. 101, s. 14, provides expressly that the scale of votes shall be calculated upon the *rateable value* at which the property is rated. It is the duty of the clerk to assign the number of votes to each voter; and if he makes an error, the vote is not lost, but the number of votes given at the election is to be reduced or increased according to the nature of the error.

---

5. CLAIMS TO VOTE.

March 4th, 1847.

Clerk of Lancaster Union—Several claims to vote in the election of guardians have been made, under section 15 of the 7 & 8 Vict. c. 101, but no objection against any of such claims has been made. Inquired whether it is necessary to give notice of a day to be appointed for the revision of such claims, and for the purpose of signing the register-book; or whether the entries of the claims therein should be alone considered as conclusive evidence of the claimants' right to vote; also whether he (the clerk) should strike out defective claims to vote, although no objections have been made to them.

Ans.—If there be no objections to the claims to vote under the 15th section of the 7 & 8 Vict. 101, the Commissioners think it is not necessary for you to attend to revise the book in which such claims are entered. It is no part of the duty of the clerk to the guardians to examine the claims in any case where there is no opposition; and, where there is an opposition, he must confine his attention to the particular subjects of objection.

---

6. QUALIFICATION OF VOTERS.

April 9th, 1847.

Mr. ————, Petersfield Union—Inquired whether persons occupying houses, whose names appear in the rate-book, but who pay their rates to the owners of the houses, and not to the collector, are entitled to vote on the election of guardians: and, whether, if such persons have not occupied their dwellings for the whole of the last twelve months, and have paid only one rate, they are entitled to vote.

Ans.—As regards your first inquiry, the Commissioners are not prepared, without more precise information, to express an opinion, whether or not the occupiers in the case stated are, or are not, qualified to vote as rate-payers in the election of guardians. They would observe, however, that the 4 & 5 Wm. 4, c. 76, s. 40, provides, "that no person shall be deemed a rate-payer, or be entitled to vote, or do any other act, matter, or thing, as such, under the provisions of this Act, unless he shall have been rated to the relief of the poor for the whole year immediately preceding his so voting, or otherwise acting as such rate-payer, and shall have paid the parochial rates and assessments made and assessed on him, for the period of one whole year, as well as those due from him at the time of so voting, or acting, except such as shall have been made, or become due, within six months immediately preceding such voting or acting." You will perceive from this provision that a person must be both rated to the poor-rate and must pay the rate. As regards the payment, the Commissioners do not understand that it is necessary that a person should pay the rate by his own hand; it is sufficient if he do this by his agent. The Commissioners apprehend, however, that it must appear that the person who actually pays the rate is the agent for this purpose of the person who is assessed, and from whom the rate is due. A payment of the rate by the landlord may be good, therefore, if it be done with the tenant's knowledge and acquiescence. It is immaterial how long a person may have occupied the premises, if in point of fact he has been rated for one year prior to the time of voting, and paid the poor-rate assessed for the requisite period of one year.

---

7. QUALIFICATION OF VOTERS.

Feb. 27th, 1847.

Clerk of Patrington Union—1st. As to two persons in partnership rated at £313 a year, inquired in what manner, whether jointly or singly, and to what extent, they are entitled to vote in the election of guardians; 2nd. Whether mortgagees in the receipt of rents; and, 3rd. Whether trustees or executors in the receipt of rents are entitled to vote as owners at such election.

Ans.—1st. The Commissioners think that the property which you state is rated at £313 a year will, under the 14th sect. of the Act, 7 & 8 Vict. c. 101, give six votes; and the partners who occupy the property will be entitled to vote in proportion to their interest therein, so that if such interest be equal, such partner will be entitled to three votes. 2nd. The term "owner," by the interpretation clause (109) of the Poor Law Amendment Act, includes a mortgagee in possession. 3rd. A trustee, or executor, cannot vote as owner, unless he receives the rack-rent of the property, in respect of which the claim is made on his own account. (See the clause above referred to.)

---

8. WHETHER CLERK SHOULD MAKE RETURN OF GUARDIANS PROTESTED AGAINST.

April 21st, 1847.

Clerk of Wakefield Union—Stated that he has been served with a protest against the return of the guardians elected for the township of ——— ; and requested the Commissioners' instructions as to how he is to act.

Ans.—It is your duty to exercise your own judgment upon the whole of the case, and make such a return as you believe to be correct. The parties who shall feel dissatisfied with your decision may appeal to the Commissioners, in conformity with sec. 8 of the 5 & 6 Vict. c. 57.

VIII.—GUARDIANS.

1. POWER OF, TO ORDER HOUSES OF POOR PERSONS TO BE WHITEWASHED AND FUMIGATED.

May 22nd, 1847.

Clerk of Bolton Union—Forwarded the following extract from the minutes of the board of guardians: "Ordered, that the several relieving officers be instructed to see that the dwelling-houses of paupers, sick of fever, in their respective districts, are properly whitewashed and fumigated; and that they furnish to such paupers, at the cost of the township in which they reside, a sufficient quantity of chloride of lime, and other materials, for that purpose. Ordered also, that, with the view of preventing the spread of fever, the surveyors of highways of the several townships in this union be recommended to suppress all nuisances within their respective districts; and, if needful for that purpose, to take the necessary proceedings under the Act for the suppression of nuisances; and that they be recommended to advise, and, as far as practicable, to enforce the general whitewashing of all dwelling-houses."

Ans.—The Commissioners entertain no doubt of the advantage of the object which the guardians have in view; but the Commissioners must, in the first place, point out that the guardians have no control over the surveyors of the highways.

With regard to the relieving officers, the Commissioners are of opinion that the guardians may properly cause the dwelling-house of any pauper actually sick of fever to be whitewashed and fumigated, and may supply to such pauper chloride of lime, and other materials, for that purpose; such a course, in fact, constituting a portion of the means essential for the recovery of the sick person, assuming that the steps are taken under the advice and direction of the medical officers in attendance. The Commissioners, however, are of opinion that the guardians cannot lawfully supply materials for the whitewashing, or fumigating, of houses at the cost of the townships in which the paupers live, by way of prevention merely. The Commissioners themselves have no authority to supply to the guardians the powers which may be wanting in these matters. If the houses are brought under the operation of 9 & 10 Vict. c. 96, the guardians will doubtless think it right that the proceedings therein pointed out should be carried into execution, where the guardians can act in the suppression of nuisances. They may also call the attention of the town council of Bolton to the matter in reference to the statute cited. The Commissioners are not aware of any power which the surveyors of highways have under the Act referred to.

2. WHETHER GUARDIAN WHO HAS CEASED TO BE QUALIFIED CAN CONTINUE TO ACT.

December 16th, 1846.

Clerk of Wandsworth and Clapham Union—One of the elected guardians of the parish of Clapham now resides at a considerable distance from the union, and no longer attends the meetings of the board, nor is he an owner or occupier of property within the union. Inquired whether he can vote in the election of officers, or otherwise take part in the proceedings of the board.

Ans.—If the party referred to has ceased to be rated to the poor-rate, for property of sufficient value, in any parish or parishes of the union, he has become disqualified to act as a guardian of such union, and ought not, in the Commissioners' opinion, to vote on any appointment of an officer, or other matter before the board. But, according to the provisions of 5 & 6 Vict. c. 57, s. 13, his vote would not vitiate any proceedings in which he may have taken part.

3. WHETHER A SUPERINTENDENT REGISTRAR IS ELIGIBLE FOR THE OFFICE OF GUARDIAN.

May 11th, 1847.

Chairman of —— Union—Inquired whether a superintendent registrar of births, &c., is eligible for the office of guardian.

Ans.—The Commissioners do not find that a superintendent registrar is disqualified from acting as a guardian, where he is not a clerk to a board of guardians. But a registrar is prevented from so acting by a regulation of the registrar-general applicable to his office.

4. ELIGIBILITY OF SURVEYOR OF HIGHWAYS FOR THE OFFICE OF GUARDIAN.

March 26th, 1847.

Clerk of Williton Union—Inquired whether an overseer of the poor, who is also a surveyor of highways, appointed under the 5 & 6 Wm. 4, c. 50, with a salary payable out of the highway-rates, is thereby disqualified from acting as guardian for the same parish for which he is appointed surveyor.

Ans.—The 5 & 6 Vict. c. 57, s. 14, renders "any paid officer engaged in the administration of the laws for the relief of the poor incapable of serving as a guardian." The words "paid officer" are limited by the words which immediately follow. They do not include any person holding an office in a parish distinct from the administration of relief, and receiving his salary from a different fund. To bring the case within the prohibition, the office, for performing which the emolument is received, must be one connected with the administration of relief. A person, therefore, who is surveyor of the highways, under the 5 & 6 Wm. 4, c. 50, with a salary payable out of the highway-rate of the parish for which he is also overseer of the poor, is undoubtedly a paid officer of the parish. But it is not as an officer connected with the administration of relief that he is paid, and sec. 14 of the 5 & 6 Vict. c. 57, does not therefore apply.

IX.—LAW BILLS—REFUSAL OF AUDITOR TO ALLOW, UNLESS TAXED.

Feb. 25th, 1847.

Messrs. ———.—Stated that the district auditor has refused to pass any of their bills, for professional business done for parishes in the ——— Union, unless they are taxed by the deputy clerk of the peace for the county.—Inquired whether such bills must be taxed; and, if so, upon what principle; and by whom the expense of the taxation is to be paid.

Ans.—The Commissioners desire to refer you to the 7 & 8 Vict. c. 101, s. 39, wherein you will perceive the provision which induces the auditor to require law bills to be taxed. If such bills be not taxed, he must, in accordance with that section, exercise his own judgment upon the bills; a course which he may think it more advisable, as a general rule, to avoid. The Commissioners entirely agree in the propriety of the taxation of all solicitors' bills, and the generality of the practice entirely removes all invidious remark. The Commissioners cannot give any direction as to the principle of the taxation, though they presume this would be the ordinary case of taxation between solicitor and client. The cost of the taxation, so far as the overseers require it for their indemnity, must be borne by them, though probably some measure may be adopted by which that cost may be rendered as little burthensome as possible.

X.—LUNATIC PAUPERS.

1. WHO MAY AUTHORISE THE ADMISSION OF LUNATIC PAUPERS INTO LICENSED HOUSES, ETC.

March 17th, 1847.

Mr. S. Millard, Whitchurch, Herefordshire—On the 14th Sept., 1846, S. H., a pauper lunatic, belonging to the parish of Ragland, in the Monmouth Union, was brought to his house, under the 8 & 9 Vict. c. 100, s. 48, accompanied by a certificate signed by a surgeon, who is not the medical officer of the union, and an order and statement signed by a justice of the peace, and an overseer of the parish of Ragland. The Commissioners in Lunacy have certified that the order, statement, and medical certificate are correct. He has sent in his account for the care, maintenance, and clothing of the pauper to the Monmouth Union, amounting to £6. 10*s.*, being at the rate of 10*s.* per week, and he understands that the board of guardians have disallowed the account. The pauper has been discharged cured.

Clerk of Monmouth Union—(To whom the above letter was referred for his observations.) The guardians conceive that where proceedings are taken to remove paupers to an asylum from parishes in union, it should be done by, or under, the direction of the relieving officer, and not the overseer. Some of the magistrates' clerks in the neighbourhood are, however, of opinion that overseers have still a concurrent duty to perform in cases of pauper lunatics with the relieving officers, and have caused the former to sign the statement and remove the paupers to the asylum. S. H. having been removed to the asylum by the overseer before the relieving officer knew anything of the case, the board of guardians objected to allow the expenses of the removal, and when the asylum account was laid before them they hesitated in paying it on the same ground, and, also, because it contained a charge of 10*s.* 6*d.* for a certificate from a surgeon residing at Monmouth.

Ans.—(To Mr. Millard and the Clerk of the Union)—The Commissioners collect from the explanation which the guardians have given upon the subject of Mr. Millard's application to the Commissioners, that the proceedings in S. H.'s case were not taken by the guardians or their officers. The guardians are, therefore, under no legal obligation to discharge Mr. Millard's claims. The Commissioners are not, however, prepared to say, that the guardians, if they saw fit, could not adopt the act of the overseer in sending the pauper to the licensed house, and pay the cost of the maintenance during the period of confinement. The Commissioners infer from your letter of the 24th ultimo, that the guardians of the Monmouth Union are not prepared to interfere in this way. Mr. Millard's claim will therefore, probably, be against the parties who procured the admission of the lunatic. According to Mr. Millard's statement, these were, a justice of the peace and the overseer of the parish in which S. H. was resident. Upon referring to s. 48 of 8 & 9 Vict. c. 100, the Commissioners think it is not clear from the terms of that section, that the overseer of a parish in a union, has not equal power with the relieving officer of such union to procure the admission of an insane person into a licensed house. If he has this power, it appears to follow, that any payment which he may be required by law to make in respect of the lunatic's maintenance, could be inserted in his accounts, and allowed by the auditor.

Clerk of Monmouth Union—Refers to the above correspondence, and states—The guardians think that s. 48 of the 8 & 9 Vict. c. 100, is merely directory and monitory to the keeper of the asylum. That s. 48 of the 8 & 9 Vict. c. 126, is mandatory. That s. 51 of the same statute is similar, though not verbatim, to s. 48 of c. 100. In cases of sickness or other cause the clergyman, &c., may act; but he should specify in his order the reason why he supersedes the justice of the peace; and if the distinction of his parish being in union or not, runs through the whole of the mandatory section, viz. 48 of c. 126, the owner of the asylum should be very careful in his examination of the order before he accepts the patient. He has the liberty of refusing, and is subject to serious inconvenience (independent of the penalty on a misdemeanour) if he makes a mistake.

Ans.—The Poor Law Commissioners had occasion to consult the Commissioners in Lunacy on this point. The opinion expressed by the Commissioners in Lunacy was in substance as follows: That the power of officiating clergymen, and relieving officers, or overseers, to make orders for the admission of insane paupers into licensed houses, existed prior to the Act 8 & 9 Vict. c. 100, and that this statute has made no substantial alteration with respect thereto. That those parties may now, as before, in all cases, make orders for the reception of pauper lunatics into hospitals or licensed houses, without a preliminary order of justices. That the case is different with regard to county asylums, as to which the power of directing admission rests primarily with the justices of the county; the Act 8 & 9 Vict. c. 126, extending the power, in special cases, to officiating clergymen, together with the relieving officer or overseers. According to this construction the intervention of the justices in the case supposed is not necessary. Then, having regard to the terms of s. 48 of 7 & 8 Vict. c. 100, the Commissioners, as they intimated in their letter to Mr. Millard, are not prepared to say that in the case of a parish in a union, an order signed by the officiating clergyman and the overseer of the parish, is not a valid order, a sufficient authority to the keeper of the licensed house to receive the patient, and a justification for the payment of the costs of the maintenance out of the poor-rates.

---

2. DITTO.

March 18th, 1847.

Mr. Kell, District Auditor—A man named C—, who belongs to the parish of Battle, in the Battle Union, but resides in the parish of St. Leonard's, in the Hastings Union, lately became insane and made two attempts upon his life. The relieving officer of the Hastings Union gave notice to the relieving officer of the Battle Union of C.'s insanity, and the board of guardians of the Battle Union directed the overseers of the parish of Battle to cause the lunatic to be removed to St. Luke's Hospital, London. One of the overseers of Battle parish proceeded, in consequence, to Hastings, and obtained the signature of the mother of the lunatic to a petition of the mother, as the nearest relative of the lunatic, to the governors of St. Luke's, to receive him into that hospital. The overseer also obtained a surgeon's certificate of C.'s insanity, together with a certificate from the officiating clergyman of the parish of St. Leonard's, and of the overseer of the same parish. The lunatic has been received into the hospital on a deposit of £4 being paid by the overseer of Battle parish, and an agreement signed by him and two sureties, in a penalty of £100, for the future removal of the lunatic from the hospital. By the payment of the £4 to the hospital the patient will be kept there, without any further charge, for one year. No doubt this is the least expense to the parish, as, instead of paying 12*s*. or 14*s*. a week to a lunatic asylum, the pauper is maintained at St. Luke's for a whole year for £4, and the board of guardians may be of opinion that they are merely giving relief to the pauper by assisting the nearest relation to get him into the hospital. Requested the opinion of the Commissioners, whether, in case of persons residing in a parish in union becoming insane, it is competent for the board of guardians of another union, to a parish in which the pauper may belong, to interfere by this mode of relief; and whether in such a case, or in the case of a resident pauper, it is not necessary that the provisions of the Lunacy Acts should be strictly observed; and whether the Act of 8 & 9 Vic. c. 126, does not require the proceedings directed by the sec. 48 of that Act to be taken, the Act of cap. 100, sec. 48, not going to the same extent, though the forms in the schedule are similar. Inquired also whether the overseers of a parish in union have any jurisdiction or authority to act in the cases of pauper lunatics, or whether it is the business of the relieving officers only; and whether the expenses incurred by the overseer, in the case in question, may, under the circumstances, be allowed by him as auditor. Those expenses, it is understood, consist of correspondence with St. Luke's Hospital, expenses to Hastings to visit pauper, and procure examination and certificate, fee to surgeon for examination, expenses of conveyance of lunatic and officer to St. Luke's, and of officer back, and the deposit of £4 paid at St. Luke's. And, further, whether such expenses, if they may be allowed, should be inserted in the accounts of the overseers of the parish, or in the out-relief book of the relieving officer. The lunatic was, for some time previous to the proceedings taken for his removal to St. Luke's, receiving non-resident relief from the parish of Battle, to which he belonged. The lunatic was not prevented, on account of his health or any other cause, from being taken before a justice.

Ans.—The Commissioners think in C.'s case, though the removal to St. Luke's Hospital has been effected without the intervention of a magistrate, it was not an authorised proceeding. It appears that he was residing in the parish of St. Leonard's, and was sent to the lunatic hospital with what is termed a certificate, but it was doubtless an order signed by the officiating clergyman of that parish, with the overseer thereof, and a medical certificate, therefore the proceedings are regular so far as the admission of the pauper is concerned under the 8 & 9 Vic., c. 100, s. 48, according to its terms; although, in fact, the proceedings took effect at the instance of the overseer of another parish, and the guardians of another union. Now the 8 & 9 Vic., c. 126, s. 48, contains a power under which pauper lunatics are required to be sent to asylums, or licensed houses, or hospitals, and, accordingly, the interposition of a justice would be necessary, in such a case as this, if the proceedings had been compulsory, or it had been desired to send the lunatic to a county asylum. But the Commissioners do not see that this provision supersedes the other, and prevents the board of guardians or other persons from resorting to the course of proceeding authorised by the former Act in what may be considered as spontaneous proceedings on their part. It is certainly competent for a board of guardians to relieve an insane pauper by procuring such party to be maintained in a licensed house or hospital of their own accord, and the latter statute only compels them to have the lunatic removed to and maintained in the asylum or such other place, by the order of the justices or officiating clergyman as therein pointed out when they neglect to act spontaneously. It would, therefore, have been perfectly lawful, as the Commissioners think, for the guardians of the Battle Union to have proceeded without the order of the justices if the pauper had been resident in their own union. Then, assuming that this was a case in which non-resident relief might have been granted by the guardians of that union, it seems to the Commissioners that the guardians were justified in sending an agent on their behalf to the parish in which the pauper was resident, and procuring the steps to be taken which are requisite under the above-cited section of the statute applicable to lunatic hospitals, and in paying the expenses of the removal to St. Luke's. No doubt some question may exist as to whether, under sec. 48 of the 8 & 9 Vict., c. 100, the order should have been signed by the overseers of St. Leonard's, from which parish the pauper was sent, or by the overseer of Battle, at whose cost the pauper was sent; but the former appears to be according to the language of the statute, and this point need hardly be raised before you. If the form of order required by the statute was not adopted, but something equivalent, a question may be raised as to whether there has been a violation of the statute; but, in the absence of all improper motives, such formal defect is probably not necessarily a matter which you would inquire into, as it is more properly one for the consideration of the Commissioners in Lunacy in their inspection of the orders and certificates at that hospital. Then, as regards the sum deposited or paid to the authorities of St. Luke's, on the admission of C., pursuant to the regulations of the establishment, the Commissioners are disposed to think, that, viewed as non-resident relief, its payment by the guardians of the Battle Union might not be unlawful. But, as regards this and the expenses of the removal, the opinion of the Commissioners must be considered as given on an imperfect knowledge of the facts, and without prejudice to any decision which they may hereafter be called upon to give in the case if applied to under s. 36 of 7 & 8 Vic. c. 101. As regards the case of the lunatic pauper of the parish of Bexhill, who was removed to St. Luke's under like circumstances, but previously to the recent Acts, 8 & 9 Vic. c. 100 and 126, the Commissioners do not see any impropriety in the course taken. The statutes which at that time regulated the admission of pauper lunatics into asylums or licensed houses were 9 Geo. 4, c. 40, and 2 & 3 Wm. 4, c. 107. No proceeding under the former of these was lawful without the intervention or order of a justice. Under the latter, however, insane persons could, apparently, be admitted upon the order of the officiating clergyman and one of the overseers of the parish to which such insane persons belonged (s. 29). This, as the Commissioners understand, was the course pursued in the case in question, and the Commissioners do not think the expenses resulting therefrom would be an unlawful charge on the poor-rates. The Commissioners have communicated with the Commissioners in Lunacy on the points involved in this case, who coincide in the view herein expressed.

---

3. WHETHER AN ORDER ADJUDICATING THE SETTLEMENT OF LUNATIC PAUPER, CAN BE APPEALED AGAINST.

April 21*st*, 1847.

Clerk of Atcham Union—A pauper lunatic residing in the union of A—, was sent, under an order of a justice, at the instance of the relieving officer, to the county lunatic asylum. An inquiry as to the pauper's settlement was made subsequently, and an order adjudicating the settlement to be in a neighbouring parish (not in union) was duly executed by two justices for the coun y, not being visitors of the asylum. The order was served on the overseers of the parish of the alleged settlement, and on the visitors of the asylum, but no order of maintenance has yet been made. Inquired, 1, whether the parish of the alleged settlement has any right of appeal against the order of adjudication; and if so, on whom should the notices be served? 2. The order having been served on the visitors of the asylum, is the A. Union any longer liable for the maintenance of the pauper?

Ans.—1. The Commissioners do not find, on reference to the statute 8 & 9 Vic., c. 126, that a parish has any right of appeal against an order of justices adjudicating the settlement of an insane person to be in such parish, unless that order be followed by another made in pursuance of sec. 62, directing that parish to reimburse the treasurer of the union or parish from which the lunatic was sent to the asylum, the costs incurred thereby, as well as to pay for the future care and maintenance of the lunatic. The Commissioners do not see that the parish of the settlement is, in fact, aggrieved until an order of maintenance is made. But, assuming it to be aggrieved, the statute apparently does not give the right of appeal against an order merely adjudicating the settlement, not followed, as before stated, by an order of maintenance. 2. The Commissioners think that the liability of the parish from which, or at the instance of the officers of which, the lunatic is sent to the asylum, ceases upon an adjudication of justices that the insane person is settled elsewhere (see sec. 57.)

---

4. LIABILITY OF HUSBAND TO CONTRIBUTE TO THE MAINTENANCE OF HIS WIFE, WHO IS CONFINED IN A LUNATIC ASYLUM.

May 21st, 1847.

Clerk of Bodmin Union—The wife of W. S., whose earnings average 15*s*. a week, and who derives an income of £2. 10*s*. a year from property, is an inmate of a lunatic asylum. W. S., refusing to contribute anything towards his wife's maintenance, was summoned before the magistrates, who were of opinion that he was able to contribute 4*s*. a week towards that object; but they knew of no authority under which they could make an order to enforce the payment of any contribution. Requested the Commissioners' advice in the matter.

Ans.—The justices are not empowered to make an order on the husband to contribute to the support of his wife, and to fix the amount of his liability. The case is not within 43rd Elizabeth c. 2, s. 7, which authorises justices to make orders upon persons for the support of their relations. The only question is whether the case is within the provisions of the Vagrant Act, 5 George 4, c. 83, s. 3, which enacts that every person wilfully refusing to maintain his wife shall be deemed to be an idle and disorderly person. The Commissioners think it difficult to contend that where a man's wife has been taken away from him and sent to a lunatic asylum, he can be brought within this enactment, because he refuses to pay the cost of her maintenance in the asylum.

---

5. AS TO CHARGING THE EXPENSE OF THE REMOVAL OF A PAUPER LUNATIC TO AN ASYLUM, AND OF HIS MAINTENANCE THEREIN.

May 7th, 1847.

Clerk of Aberystwyth Union—J. W., a lunatic pauper belonging to Uwchgarreg in the Machynlleth Union, was farmed out, more than five years ago, to his sister, who resided in Isayndre, in the Aberystwyth Union, and to whom the former township paid for the lunatic's maintenance, &c., 2*s* 6*d*. a week, until within the last two or three months, when the payment was discontinued, on the ground that the Act of 9 and 10 Vict. c. 66, had rendered the lunatic irremovable from Isayndre. The lunatic having recently become dangerous, the board of guardians of the Aberystwyth Union have determined to send him to an asylum; but before doing so, they wished to know which of the two townships would be liable to the expense of his removal, and of his maintenance in the asylum.

Ans.—This case should be dealt with under the 8 & 9 Vict. c. 126, without reference to the recent Poor Removal Act (9 & 10 Vict. c. 66.) Under the former Act the lunatic pauper will be sent to the asylum at the cost of the township from which he shall be so sent to the asylum. When there, the township from which he shall be so sent may obtain an order upon the township of the pauper's settlement, to reimburse them for the cost of the removal, and to provide for his future maintenance. See ss. 57, 58, and 62.

---

6. WHETHER THE CHARGEABILITY OF A LUNATIC PAUPER IS AFFECTED BY THE POOR REMOVAL ACT.

Clerk of Lutterworth Union—J. H., who is settled in the parish of Catthorpe, in the Lutterworth Union, but who resided for upwards of five years prior to the passing of the Poor Removal Act in the parish of Burbage, in the Hinckley Union, has been removed to a lunatic asylum at the cost of the latter parish; but the guardians of the Hinckley Union wish the guardians of the Lutterworth Union to pay for the pauper's maintenance in the asylum, though the latter are advised that he was irremovable from Burbage at the time he was sent to the asylum. Inquired which of the above parishes is liable for the pauper's support.

Ans.—The case of J. H. is not affected by the Poor Removal Act. It appears, from your letter, that J. H. has been removed to the lunatic asylum under the provisions of the Act 8 & 9 Vict. cap. 126, which renders the parish from which a pauper lunatic is removed liable for the cost of such pauper's maintenance in the first instance; but enables it to obtain an order from the parish of the settlement for reimbursement. If, therefore, such an order be obtained by the parish of Burbage, from which the pauper in question was removed to the asylum, the parish of Catthorpe, in which he is settled, will be liable to pay the expenses of his maintenance.

7. DITTO.

May 7th, 1847.

Mr. ——, Bradford Union, Yorkshire—In the year 1845, J. M., an insane pauper, was removed, under an order of justices, from the township of D., to a lunatic asylum, and his maintenance directed to be charged to the township of P., in which he was legally settled. That township paid the cost of his support in the asylum up to the time of the passing of the 9 and 10 Vic., c. 66, which it is believed will throw the burthen of his maintenance on the township of D., where the lunatic's wife and children now reside, and where he resided for upwards of five years prior to his removal to the asylum. Inquired to which of the above townships J. M. is now chargeable.

Ans.—The charge of the lunatic in the asylum is made under the authority of the order of justices made in conformity with the provisions of the 8 & 9 Vic., c. 126, upon the place of the settlement. That is not affected by the late statute (the 9 & 10 Vic., c. 66), and must continue to be obeyed. But the charge of the wife and children falls upon the township in which they reside, unless they can be removed. However, no such removal can, accordingly to the statement in your letter, take place; firstly, because the wife and family are stated to have resided more than five years in the township of D., and, secondly, because they cannot, by the third proviso to sec. 1, be removed; inasmuch as the pauper J. M. (the husband and father) is not removable.

XI.—OVERSEERS—CANNOT PAY LAW CHARGES NOT INCURRED WITHIN THEIR YEAR OF OFFICE.

January 9th, 1847.

Clerk of Tamworth Union—Inquired whether the auditor is justified in striking out of the accounts of overseers any legal bill which has not become due within their year of office; and if so, in what way such bills are to be paid. There are several accounts (particularly law accounts in cases of settlements, &c.), owing by various parishes in this union for business transacted from time to time over the last few years. These bills have been delivered; but the overseers for the time being, not knowing that it was necessary that they should be paid within the year of their office, and the persons to whom they are owing not knowing that it was requisite that they should insist upon the payment within the years in which they were incurred, they have been permitted, from time to time, to stand over: and now, when payment is proposed by the parishes, the auditor expresses his intention to disallow them: the consequence is, the bills remain unpaid. The present question arises out of bills delivered by Mr. A. B., a solicitor in this union, against the parish of Kingsbury, for business commencing in May, 1844, and ending towards the latter end of 1845, and other businesses ending early this year. The bills are for conducting appeals.

Ans.—The Commissioners having had several other cases of a similar nature before them, have deliberated on the subject, with the view of considering if anything can be done in the matter to assist those parties who are presumed to be placed in difficulties, or under embarrassment, in consequence of the practice which has much prevailed in many places with reference to the bills of attorneys engaged for parishes. No principle is better established in law than that all parochial charges should be brought into their accounts within the year of office of the overseers. The Commissioners need only refer to the well-known authorities, Tawney's case, Salk 531, 1 Bott. 81, and Rex *v.* Goodcheap, 6 T. R. 159; Rex *v.* Chapelwardens of Bradford, 12 East, 556; Rex *v.* Churchwardens of Dursley, 5 A. & E. 15; Chesterton *v.* Farlar, 1 Curtis Ecclesiastical Rep. 345, 367, 371; Ellis and Gough *v.* Griffin, 2 Curtis, 677. The Commissioners consider that the neglect of this principle cannot be alleged by professional men, who in no case can justify an ignorance of the law, as a ground for the passing of items of expenditure in accounts which are not legal. And as regards the officers themselves, however it may be a matter of regret that they should be induced to pay charges which, not having been incurred by them, are not therefore legally due from them, and cannot be paid out of the fund entrusted to them; the disallowance is a consequence to which the law has subjected them in this as in many other cases. The law provides for the repayment to overseers of advances by their predecessors in respect of moneys allowed in their accounts out of the arrears of rates transferred by the latter to their successors, 17 Geo. 2, c. 38, s. 11; but the Commissioners are not aware of any other authority to sanction reimbursement of the past overseers, and certainly of none for the payment of debts previously incurred, but not charged in the rates by any provision of law. Indeed, they believe that the proposition is not disputed, but that it is thought that the Commissioners can interpose, by some means, to prevent the present district auditors from performing their duties in a manner strictly conformable with the law. The Commissioners have no authority to do so. They have, on the other hand, only power in cases of appeal under the 36th section of the 7 & 8 Vict. c. 101, to control the decision of the auditor where he does not proceed according to law. It has been sometimes urged, with reference to the bills of attorneys in the cases of appeals, that the proceedings may, and frequently do, run over the years of office of several overseers, and that it is inconvenient to send in the bill until the work has been completed. This excuse, however, does not prevail in all cases; as, for instance, in the bill of Mr. A.B., which begins in May, 1844, and ends in February, 1845. But, however this may be, the objection is met by the judgment of the Court of Common Pleas, in the case of an action by an attorney against vestrymen of a parish for the costs of an indictment defended by the surveyor of the highways under the direction of the vestry. The vestrymen were sued in a year subsequent to that in which the business was done, and were held not liable. The court, in their judgment, point out that the bill, which had run over several years, should have been presented yearly, that the parish might determine, from time to time, whether they would sustain the expense of further proceedings, and that every inhabitant might be assessed in due proportion, and the burthens might be thrown on those who inhabited the parish at the time, and who ought to sustain it. The Commissioners, therefore, return Mr. A. B.'s bill, for the payment of which they can point out no other way than a private and personal subscription.

XII.—PAUPER.—CHARGEABILITY OF, HAVING HELD AN OFFICE IN THE WORKHOUSE AFTER HIS ADMISSION.

Feb. 18th, 1847.

Clerk of Alton Union—J. P. was admitted into the union workhouse, in November, 1836, at the cost of the parish of Binstead; and being of good character, was shortly after appointed overlooker of the bone-crushing mill, with a salary, and board, &c., and his appointment was sanctioned by the Commissioners. He held this appointment until the Commissioners' order prohibiting bone-crushing in workhouses was issued, when he was appointed overlooker of the oakum pickers; but he has now resigned the latter appointment in consequence of his advanced age, and has again become a pauper. Inquired whether the cost of his relief should be charged to the parish of Binstead, or to the parish of Alton, in which the workhouse is situate.

Ans.—As J. P. was residing in the parish of Alton when he applied for relief, that parish is certainly primarily liable. The charge must also continue to be borne by that parish, if, as the Commissioners conclude, the pauper is now irremovable from that parish by operation of 9 & 10 Vict. c. 66. The Commissioners understand that J. P.'s residence in the workhouse from June, 1837, to the 5th inst., was in character of an officer of the workhouse, and not in that of a pauper, and that the cost of his maintenance or rations was charged not to Binstead, as relief, but in the same manner as the maintenance of other officers of the workhouse: if so, the residence constructing a residence in the parish of Binstead, by operation of sec. 56, of 7 & 8 Vict. c. 101. The Commissioners also collect from the statement that the residence in Alton was uninterrupted.

XIII.—RATING—OF MILL SITUATE ON RIVER IN TWO TOWNSHIPS.

Dec. 7th, 1846.

Clerk of Todmorden Union—The townships of Todmorden and Walsden, and Stansfield, are divided by the river Calder, the boundary line being the centre of the stream. A mill, which has been erected on the river for about thirty years, stands partly in each township; but the head-quoit, dam, and water-wheel being wholly in Todmorden and Walsden, the water power has hitherto been wholly assessed to the poor-rate for that township. A question, however, has now been raised, whether so much of the water-power as is required for working the machinery in that part of the mill situate in Stansfield ought not to be rated to the poor-rate of that township. Requested the Commissioners' opinion on the subject.

Ans.—The Commissioners are disposed to think that, in rating that part of the mill in question, which stands in the township of Stansfield, the correct rule will be to leave out of consideration the water-power, which is stated to be situated in a different township. The case appears to the Commissioners to be analogous to that of the stations on a line of railway; which, though they tend to increase the value of the entire property, *i. e.*, to augment the profits derived from the use of the railway, in all the parishes on the line, are nevertheless rateable solely in the parish in which they are actually situate. R. *v.* Great Western Railway Company, 6 Adol. & Ell. N. S. 179. The Commissioners also think that an analogy may be found in the case of a coal mine extending into two parishes, the pit, engines, and fixed machinery being situate in one of such parishes; in which case it has been held that, though the occupiers of the mine are rateable in both parishes for the coals actually found or gotten in each parish, yet the shaft and machinery were correctly rated in that parish in which they were situated. (R. *v.* Foleshill, 2 Adol. & Ell. 593.)

XIV.—REGISTRATION—PAYMENT OF FEES IN EXTRA-PAROCHIAL PLACES.

May 18th, 1847.

Clerk of Worcester Union—There is an extra-parochial place, called Blockhouse, situate in the Worcester Union, which has been included in the superintendent registrar's district.—Inquired whether the fees for registering births and deaths occurring in such extra-parochial place can be charged to the parishes comprising the Worcester Union; and if so, to what account should they be charged.

Ans.—The Commissioners are of opinion that the fees for registering births and deaths in the place adverted to, must be charged to the common account of the union. The Act 6 & 7 Wm. 4, c. 86, s. 29, requires that the guardians should pay the fees to the registrars out of their funds, and that the amount should only be charged to the account of the parishes in which the births or deaths have occurred. But, as in the case of the extra-parochial place in question, there is on account, the Commissioners consider, that, though the guardians must, in the first instance, pay the charge, they cannot apply to any fund for reimbursement.

XV.—REMOVAL ACT—WHETHER IT AFFECTS THE ADMINISTRATION OF CHARITABLE TRUSTS.

Jan. 11th, 1847.

The Rev. F. Whalley, Old Hutton, Kendal Union—The rents of a small farm in the township of Old Hutton, are distributed half-yearly amongst poor people belonging to that township, who are not in the receipt of parochial relief. The trustees are the minister, the chapel wardens, and the overseer, and they have distributed the money amongst the deserving poor, whether resident in the township or not. Some of the rate-payers, however, now think that no portion of the money should be given to poor persons who have resided out of the township for five years. Inquired—1st. Whether there is anything in the Poor Removal Act which can affect the discretion of the trustees of charities of the kind above adverted to. 2nd. Whether the administration of a portion of the charity fund to poor persons who have resided out of the township for upwards of five years, would entitle them to be removed thereto, in the event of their requiring parochial aid. 3rd. Whether the trustees would be justified in allowing individuals who do not belong to the township, but have resided in it for five years, to become recipients of any portion of the funds.

Ans.—1st. The Commissioners are not aware of anything in the recent Poor Removal Act, 9 & 10 Vict. c. 66, which at all affects the trusts of charities. The Commissioners consider that, whatever course was lawfully pursued in relation to such trusts, previous to the passing of that Act, may be lawfully pursued now; and the trustees may proceed to distribute the funds of the endowment in the same manner as they were legally authorised in doing before the statute. 2nd. So far as the statute applies to your second inquiry, the Commissioners would observe that the first proviso to the first section prevents the operation of any gift of money, being a *bonâ fide* charitable gift, upon the removability of the person to whom it is given. 3rd. Your third question depends upon the terms of the particular trust, and the Commissioners are not able to express any opinion upon it, as they do not know what those terms are precisely. They can only state that, if the objects of the charity must be "settled" inhabitants, the persons who have resided for five years in the parish do not thereby gain a settlement, and consequently are not, by reason of such residence alone, within the trust.

XVI.—RELIEF—To step-children.

May 20th, 1847.

Clerk of Bedminster Union—A widow, aged thirty-three, with five children, aged fourteen, twelve, six, four, and two, chargeable to the parish of Pertbury, in this union, has married a youth aged nineteen, belonging to the same parish. The youth has appeared before the board of guardians and stated, as is the fact, that he is unable to maintain the children. Inquired whether the relief should be afforded to him, or to the children, out of the workhouse.

Ans.—If the husband applies for relief to be granted to himself, the prohibitory order will apply to him; and, therefore, if able-bodied, the guardians can only afford him relief in the workhouse. If, however, the husband makes no application, and the relief is supplied to the children of his wife, the circumstance will not bring him or his wife within the provisions of the order.

XVII.—WORKHOUSE — Admission into of dead body found in river.

Feb. 16th, 1847.

Clerk of Ashton-under-Lyne Union— A policeman called at the union workhouse, and desired the master to send four men, with suitable things, to convey to the workhouse the body of a man which had been in a river in the neighbourhood. The master refused to comply with this request, and likewise told the policeman that he would not allow the body to be brought into the workhouse without receiving an order from the clerk to the guardians, or from the guardians themselves, directing him to receive the body. The policeman left the workhouse, but afterwards returned unobserved by any one therein, and watching an opportunity when the gates were opened, rushed in with four men, who were carrying the body, and directed it to be placed under the master's window, where he left it, having acted, as it appears, under the orders of the deputy-constable. Inquired whether the deputy-constable, or any other officer, has the power of demanding that a dead body, under such circumstances, shall be received into the workhouse.

Ans.—The Commissioners are not aware of any authority in law, which justifies the constable, or any private individual, in bringing a dead body to a workhouse. That building is provided for the reception of the poor who are admitted therein, according to the regulations of the Commissioners, or where no such regulations have been issued, according to the regulations of the board of guardians. By the term "poor" the Commissioners understand living persons. It may, doubtless, be convenient where there is proper accommodation in a workhouse, that unknown corpses found in any parish should be deposited therein, until they are identified, or until an inquest can be held; but this is clearly optional with the board of guardians. In the present instance it appears to the Commissioners that the proceedings were most improper, and if there be any authority to which the constable in question is amenable, the Commissioners think that the guardians should prefer a formal complaint of the misconduct. The constable should have retained the custody of the corpse until the holding of the inquest, when the coroner would have directed the burial of it, and the guardians might, and doubtless, if there were no relatives in a condition of life to undertake it, would, have authorised a proper burial, unless prevented by the finding of the jury.

LONDON:

Printed by order of the Poor Law Commissioners, by Blackburn and Pardon, 6, Hatton Garden, and Published by Charles Knight and Co., 22, Ludgate Street, Publishers to the Poor Law Commissioners.

AN

OFFICIAL CIRCULAR

OF PUBLIC DOCUMENTS AND INFORMATION:

DIRECTED BY THE POOR LAW COMMISSIONERS TO BE PRINTED, CHIEFLY FOR THE USE OF THE MEMBERS AND PERMANENT OFFICERS OF BOARDS OF GUARDIANS, UNDER THE POOR LAW AMENDMENT ACT.

Nos. 7 & 8.] CIRCULAR ISSUED JULY 26, 1847. [N. S.

Poor Law Commission Office, Somerset House, July 26, 1847.

The Poor Law Commissioners have directed that the following General Order be printed and circulated for the information of Guardians and Officers of the several Unions.

By Order of the Board, EDWIN CHADWICK, *Secretary*.

GENERAL CONSOLIDATED ORDER.

To the Guardians of the Poor of the several Unions named in the Schedule hereunto annexed:—

To the Churchwardens and Overseers of the several Parishes and Places comprised within the said Unions;—

To the Clerk or Clerks to the Justices of the Petty Sessions held for the Division or Divisions in which the Parishes and Places comprised within the said Unions are situate;—

And to all others whom it may concern.

We, the Poor Law Commissioners, in pursuance of the authorities vested in Us by an Act passed in the fifth year of the reign of His late Majesty King William the Fourth, intituled "*An Act for the Amendment and better Administration of the Laws relating to the Poor in England and Wales,*" and by all other Acts amending the same, do hereby rescind every Order, whether General or Special, heretofore issued by the Poor Law Commissioners to the Unions named in the Schedule hereunto annexed, which relates to the several subjects herein provided for, except so far as the same may have related to the apprenticeship of any poor person not yet completed, or may have required or authorized the appointment of any officer, or the giving of any security, or the making of any contract not yet executed, or the making of any orders by the Guardians for contributions and payments not yet obeyed, or may have defined the salaries of any officers, or have prescribed the districts within which the duties of any officer shall be performed, or may have provided for the class of paupers or their number to be received into any particular Workhouse, or may have provided for the election of Guardians in any case where such election shall not have been completed when this Order shall come into force, and except the Order regulating the mode of election of Guardians, bearing date the Sixth day of March One thousand eight hundred and forty-six, and addressed to the Guardians of the Poor of the Nottingham Union.

And We do hereby Order, Direct, and Declare, with respect to each of the said Unions, as follows:—

ELECTION OF GUARDIANS.

Article 1. The Overseers of every Parish in the Union shall, before the Twenty-sixth day of March in every year, distinguish in the rate-book the name of every rate-payer in their parish who has been rated to the relief of the poor for the whole year immediately preceding the said day, and has paid the poor-rates made and assessed upon him for the period of one whole year, except those which have been made or become due within the six months immediately preceding the said day.

Art. 2. The Clerk shall at every future annual election of Guardians perform the duties hereby imposed upon him, and all other duties suitable to his office which it may be requisite for him to perform in conducting and completing such election; and in case the office of Clerk shall be vacant at the time when any duty relative to such election is imposed on the Clerk by this order, or in case the Clerk, from illness or other sufficient cause, shall be unable to discharge such duties, the Guardians shall appoint some person to perform such of the said duties as then remain to be performed, and the person so appointed shall perform such duties.

Art. 3. The Guardians shall, before or during every such election, appoint a competent number of persons to assist the Clerk in conducting and completing the election in conformity with this Order; but if the Guardians do not make such appointment within the requisite time, the Clerk shall take such measures for securing the necessary assistance as he may deem advisable.

Art. 4. The persons appointed under Article 3 shall obey all the directions relative to the conduct of the election, which may be given by the Clerk for the execution of this Order.

Art. 5. The Overseers of every Parish in the Union, and every Officer having the custody of the poor-rate books of any such Parish, shall attend the Clerk at such times as he shall require their attendance, until the completion of the election of Guardians, and shall, if required by him, produce to him such rate-books, and the registers of owners and proxies, together with the statements of owners, and appointments and statements of proxies, and all books and papers relating to such rates in their possession or power.

Provided that, where any register of owners shall have been prepared in any Parish containing a population exceeding two thousand persons, it shall not be necessary to produce the statements of owners.

Art. 6. The Clerk shall prepare and sign a notice, which may be in the Form marked (A.) hereunto annexed, and which shall contain the following particulars:—

1st. The number of Guardians to be elected for each Parish in the Union.

2d. The qualification of Guardians.

3d. The persons by whom, and the places where, the Nomination Papers in respect of each Parish are to be received, and the last day on which they are to be sent.

4th. The mode of voting in case of a contest, and the days on which the Voting Papers will be delivered and collected.

5th. The time and place for the examination and casting up of the votes.

And the Clerk shall cause such notice to be published on or before the Fifteenth day of March, in the following manner:—

1st. A printed copy of such notice shall be affixed on the principal external gate or door of every Workhouse in the Union, and shall from time to time be renewed, if necessary, until the Ninth day of April.

2d. Printed copies of such notice shall likewise be affixed on such places in each of the Parishes of the Union as are ordinarily made use of for affixing thereon notices of parochial business.

Provided that whenever the day appointed in this Order for the performance of any act relating to or connected with the Election of Guardians shall be a Sunday or Good Friday, such Act shall be performed on the day next following, and each subsequent proceeding shall be postponed one day.

Art. 7. Any person entitled to vote in any Parish, may nominate for the office of Guardian thereof, himself, or any other person or number of persons (not exceeding the number of Guardians to be elected for such Parish,) provided that the person or persons so nominated be legally qualified to be elected for that office.

Art. 8. Every nomination shall be in writing in the Form marked (B.) hereunto annexed, and be signed by one person only, as the party nominating, and shall be sent after the Fourteenth and on or before the Twenty-sixth day of March, to the Clerk, or to such person or persons as may have been appointed to receive the same, and the Clerk, or such person or persons, shall, on the receipt thereof, mark thereon the date of its receipt, and also a number according to the order of its receipt; provided that no nomination sent before the Fifteenth or after the said Twenty-sixth day of March shall be valid.

Art. 9. If the number of the persons nominated for the office of Guardian for any Parish shall be the same as, or less than, the number of Guardians to be elected for such Parish, such persons, if duly qualified, shall be deemed to be the elected Guardians for such Parish for the ensuing year, and shall be certified as such by the Clerk under his hand as herein-after provided in Art. 22.

Art. 10. But if the number of the duly qualified persons nominated for the office of Guardian for any Parish shall exceed the number of Guardians to be elected therein, the Clerk shall cause Voting Papers, in the Form marked (C.) hereunto annexed, to be prepared and filled up, and shall insert therein the names of all the persons nominated in the order in which the

Nomination Papers were received, but it shall not be necessary to insert more than once the name of any person nominated.

Art. 11. The Clerk shall on the Fifth day of April cause one of such Voting Papers to be delivered by the persons appointed for that purpose, to the address in such Parish of each rate-payer, owner, and proxy qualified to vote therein.

Art. 12. If the Clerk consider that any person nominated is not duly qualified to be a Guardian, he shall state in the Voting Paper the fact that such person has been nominated, but that he considers such person not to be duly qualified.

Art. 13. If any person put in nomination for the office of Guardian in any Parish shall tender to the Officer conducting the election his refusal, in writing, to serve such office, and if in consequence of such refusal the number of persons nominated for the office of Guardian for such Parish shall be the same as, or less than, the number of Guardians to be elected for such Parish, all or so many of the remaining Candidates as shall be duly qualified shall be deemed to be the elected Guardians for such Parish for the ensuing year, and shall be certified as such by the Clerk under his hand, as herein-after provided in Art. 22.

Art. 14. Each Voter shall write his initials in the Voting Paper delivered to him against the name or names of the person or persons (not exceeding the number of Guardians to be elected in the Parish) for whom he intends to vote, and shall sign such Voting Paper; and when any person votes as a proxy, he shall in like manner write his own initials and sign his own name, and state also, in writing, the name of the person for whom he is proxy.

Art. 15. Provided that, if any voter cannot write, he shall affix his mark at the foot of the Voting Paper in the presence of a witness, who shall attest the affixing thereof, and shall write the name of the Voter against such mark, as well as the initials of such Voter against the name of every Candidate for whom the voter intends to vote.

Art. 16. If the initials of the Voter be written against the names of more persons than are to be elected Guardians for the parish, or if the Voter do not sign or affix his mark to the Voting Paper, or if his mark be not duly attested, or his name be not duly written by the witness, or if a proxy do not sign his own name, and state in writing the name of the person for whom he is proxy, such Voter shall be omitted in the calculation of votes.

Art. 17. The Clerk shall cause the Voting Papers to be collected on the Seventh day of April, by the persons appointed or employed for that purpose, in such manner as he shall direct.

Art. 18. No Voting Paper shall be received or admitted, unless the same have been delivered at the address in each Parish of the Voter, and collected by the persons appointed or employed for that purpose, except as is provided in Article 19.

Art. 19. Provided that every person qualified to vote, who shall not on the Fifth day of April have received a Voting Paper, shall, on application before the Eighth day of April to the Clerk at his office, be entitled to receive a Voting Paper, and to fill up the same in the presence of the Clerk, and then and there to deliver the same to him.

Art. 20. Provided also, that in case any Voting Paper duly delivered shall not have been collected through the default of the Clerk, or the persons employed for that purpose, the Voter in person may deliver the same to the Clerk before twelve o'clock at noon on the Eighth day of April.

Art. 21. The Clerk shall, on the Ninth day of April, and on as many days immediately succeeding as may be necessary, attend at the Board Room of the Guardians of the Union, and ascertain the validity of the votes, by an examination of the rate-books, and the registers of owners and proxies, and such other documents as he may think necessary, and by examining such persons as he may see fit; and he shall cast up such of the votes as he shall find to be valid, and to have been duly given, collected, or received, and ascertain the number of such votes for each Candidate.

Art. 22. The Candidates, to the number of Guardians to be elected for the Parish, who being duly qualified, shall have obtained the greatest number of votes, shall be deemed to be the elected Guardians for the Parish, and shall be certified as such by the Clerk under his hand.

Art. 23. The Clerk, when he shall have ascertained that any Candidate is duly elected as Guardian, shall notify the fact of his having been so elected, by delivering or sending, or causing to be delivered or sent, to him a notice in the Form (D.) hereunto annexed.

Art. 24. The Clerk shall make a list containing the names of the Candidates, together with (in case of a contest) the number of votes given for each, and the names of the elected Guardians, in the Form marked (E.) hereunto annexed, and shall sign and certify the same, and shall deliver such list, together with all the Nomination and Voting Papers which he shall have received, to the Guardians of the Union, at their next meeting, who shall preserve the same for a period of not less than two years.

Art. 25. The Clerk shall cause copies of such list to be printed, and shall deliver or send, or cause to be delivered or sent, one or more of such copies to the Overseers of each Parish.

Art. 26. The Overseers shall affix, or cause to be affixed, copies of such list, at the usual places for affixing in each Parish notices of parochial business.

Art. 27. In case of the decease, necessary absence, refusal, or disqualification to act, during the proceedings of the election, of the Clerk or any other person appointed or employed to act in respect of such election, the delivery of the nominations, Voting Papers, or other documents to the successor of, the

Clerk or person so dying, absenting himself, refusing or disqualified to act, shall, notwithstanding the terms of any notice issued, be as valid and effectual as if they had been delivered to such Clerk or person.

MEETINGS OF THE GUARDIANS.

Art. 28. The Guardians shall upon the day of the week, and at the time of day, and at the place already appointed for holding the ordinary meetings, hold an ordinary meeting once at least in every week or fortnight for the execution of their duties; and may, when they think fit, change the period, time, and place of such ordinary meeting, with the consent of the Commissioners previously obtained.

Art. 29. The Guardians shall at the first meeting after the Fifteenth Day of April, elect out of the whole number of Guardians a Chairman and a Vice-Chairman, who, provided they be Guardians at the time, shall continue respectively to act as such Chairman and Vice-Chairman for the Year next ensuing.

Art. 30. The Guardians at any time may elect two Vice-Chairmen, and if such Vice-Chairmen be appointed at the same time, the Guardians shall determine their precedence; according to which precedence one of the said Vice-Chairmen shall thenceforth preside and act as in the case when only one Vice-Chairman is elected.

Art. 31. If a Chairman or a Vice-Chairman cease to be a Guardian, or refuse, or become incapable, to act as Chairman, or Vice-Chairman, before the expiration of the term of office, the Guardians shall, within one month after the occurrence of the vacancy, refusal, or incapacity, elect some other Guardian to be Chairman or Vice-Chairman, as the case may be.

Art. 32. Whereas no act of any meeting of the Guardians will be valid unless three Guardians be present and concur therein; if three Guardians be not present at any meeting, the Clerk shall make an entry of that fact in the minute book, and the time for holding such meeting shall be deemed to have expired as soon as the said entry shall have been made. But one hour at least shall be allowed to elapse from the time fixed for the commencement of the meeting, before such entry shall be made.

Art. 33. If three or four or more Guardians be present at any ordinary meeting, such three, or the majority of such four or more Guardians, may adjourn the same, to the day of the next ordinary meeting, or to some other day previous to the next ordinary meeting.

Art. 34. An extraordinary meeting of the Guardians may be summoned to be held at any time, upon the requisition of any two Guardians, addressed to the Clerk. Every such requisition shall be made in writing, in the Form (F.) hereunto annexed, and no business, other than the business specified in the said requisition, shall be transacted at such extraordinary meeting.

Art. 35. Notice of every change in the period, time, or place of holding any meeting, and notice of the adjournment of any meeting, and notice of every extraordinary meeting, shall be given in writing to every Guardian. Every such notice shall be respectively in the Forms (G.), (H.), and (I.) hereunto annexed, and shall be given or sent by the Clerk to every Guardian, or left at his place of abode two days, if practicable, before the day appointed for the meeting to which it relates.

Art. 36. If any case of emergency arise, requiring that a meeting of the Guardians should immediately take place, they, or any three of them, may meet at the ordinary place of meeting, and take such case into consideration, and may make an order thereon.

PROCEEDINGS OF THE GUARDIANS.

Art. 37. At every meeting the Chairman, or in his absence, a Vice-Chairman shall preside: but if at the commencement of any meeting the Chairman and Vice-Chairman or Vice-Chairmen be absent, the Guardians present shall elect one of themselves to preside at such meeting as Chairman thereof, until the Chairman or a Vice-Chairman take the chair.

Art. 38. Every question at any meeting consisting of more than three Guardians shall be determined by a majority of the votes of the Guardians present thereat, and voting on the question, and when there shall be an equal number of votes on any question, such question shall be deemed to have been lost.

Art. 39. No resolution agreed to or adopted by the Guardians shall be rescinded or altered by them, unless some Guardian shall have given to the Board seven days' notice of a motion to rescind or alter such resolution, which notice shall be forthwith entered on the minutes by the Clerk. Provided always, that this regulation shall not extend to any resolution which immediately concerns the allowance of relief to any person, or the punishment of any pauper, or to any resolution which the Commissioners may request the Guardians to re-consider or amend, or to any question of emergency.

Art. 40. The Guardians may, from time to time, (as occasion may require,) appoint a Committee to consider and report on any special subject, and such Committee may meet at such times and places as to them may seem convenient; but no act or decision of any such Committee shall of itself be deemed to be the act of the Guardians.

Art. 41. At every ordinary meeting of the Guardians, the business shall, as far as may be convenient, be conducted in the following order:

Firstly.—The minutes of the last ordinary meeting, and of any other meeting which may have been held since such ordinary meeting, shall be read to the Guardians; and, in order that such minutes may be recognised as a record of the acts of the Guardians at their last meeting, they shall be signed by the Chairman presiding at the meeting at which such minutes are read, and an entry of the same having been so read shall be made in the minutes of the day when read.

Secondly.—The Guardians shall dispose of such business as may arise out of the minutes so read, and shall give the necessary directions theron.

Thirdly.—They shall proceed to give the necessary directions respecting all applications for relief made since the last ordinary meeting, and also respecting the amount and nature of relief to be given and continued to the paupers then in the receipt of relief, until the next ordinary meeting, or for such other time as such relief may be deemed to be necessary.

Fourthly.—They shall hear and consider any application for relief which may be then made, and determine thereon.

Fifthly.—They shall read the report of the state of the Workhouse or Workhouses, examine all books and accounts relative to the relief of the paupers of the Union, and give all needful directions concerning the management and discipline of the said Workhouse or Workhouses and the providing of furniture and stores and other articles.

Sixthly.—They shall examine the Treasurer's account, and shall, when necessary, make orders on the Overseers or other proper authorities of the several Parishes in the Union, for providing such sums as may be lawfully required by the Guardians on account of the respective Parishes.

Seventhly.—They shall transact any such business as may not fall within any of the above classes.

Art. 42. When the Guardians have allowed relief in the Workhouse to any applicant, a written or printed order for his admission therein, signed by the Clerk, shall be forthwith delivered to the applicant, or to any person on his behalf.

Art. 43. When the Guardians have allowed outdoor relief, in money or kind, to any applicant, the particulars of such relief shall be entered, by the proper Relieving Officer, in a ticket according to Form (K.) hereunto annexed, and such ticket shall be delivered by him to the applicant, or to some person on his behalf.

Contracts of the Guardians.

Art. 44. All contracts to be entered into on behalf of the Union relating to the maintenance, clothing, lodging, employment, or relief of the poor, or for any other purpose relating to or connected with the general management of the poor, shall be made and entered into by the Guardians.

Art. 45. The Guardians shall require tenders to be made in some sealed paper for the supply of all provisions, fuel, clothing, furniture, or other goods, or materials, the consumption of which may be estimated, one month with another, to exceed ten pounds per month, and of all provisions, fuel, clothing, furniture, or other goods, or materials, the cost of which may be reasonably estimated to exceed fifty pounds in a single sum, and shall purchase the same upon contracts to be entered after the receipt of such tenders.

Art. 46. Any work or repairs to be executed in the Workhouse, or the premises connected with the Workhouse, or any fixtures to be put up therein, which may respectively be reasonably estimated to exceed the cost of fifty pounds in one sum, shall be contracted for by the Guardians, on sealed tenders, in the manner prescribed in Articles 45 and 47.

Art. 47. Notice of the nature and conditions of the contract to be entered into, of the estimated amount of the articles required, of the last day on which tenders will be received, and the day on which the tenders will be opened, shall be given in some newspaper circulating in the Union, not less than ten days previous to the last day on which such tenders are to be received; and no tender shall be opened by the Clerk, or any Guardian, or other person, prior to the day specified in such notice, or otherwise than at a meeting of the said Guardians.

Art. 48. When any tender is accepted, the party making the tender shall, in pursuance of these regulations, enter into a contract, in writing, with the Guardians, containing the terms, conditions, and stipulations mutually agreed upon, and whenever the Guardians deem it advisable, the party contracting shall find one or more surety or sureties, who shall enter into a bond conditioned for the due performance of the contract, or shall otherwise secure the same.

Art. 49. Provided always, that if from the peculiar nature of any provisions, fuel, clothing, furniture, goods, materials, or fixtures to be supplied, or of any work or repairs to be executed, it shall appear to the Guardians desirable that a specific person or persons be employed to supply or execute the same, without requiring sealed tenders as herein-before directed, it shall be lawful for such Guardians, with the consent of the Commissioners first obtained, to enter into a contract with the said person or persons, and to require such sureties and securities as are specified in Art. 48.

Art. 50. Every contract to be hereafter made by any Guardians shall contain a stipulation requiring the contractor to send in his bill or account of the sum due to him for goods or work, on or before some day to be named in the contract.

Art. 51. The Guardians shall fix some day or days, not being more than twenty-one days after the end of each quarter, for the attendance of contractors and tradesmen, or their authorized agents, and the Clerk shall notify such day to every contractor or tradesman to whom money may be due, or to his agent, or he shall, under the direction of the Guardians, cause the same to be advertised in some newspaper.

APPRENTICESHIP OF PAUPER CHILDREN.

PARTIES.

Art. 52. No child under the age of nine years, and no child (other than a deaf and dumb child) who cannot read and write his own name, shall be bound apprentice by the Guardians.

Art. 53. No child shall be so bound to a person who is not a housekeeper, or assessed to the poor-rate in his own name.

Or who is a journeyman, or a person not carrying on trade or business on his own account;

Or who is under the age of twenty-one;

Or who is a married woman.

THE PREMIUM.

Art. 54. No premium, other than clothing for the apprentice, shall be given upon the binding of any person above the age of sixteen years, unless such person be maimed, deformed, or suffering from some permanent bodily infirmity, such as may render him unfit for certain trades or sorts of work.

Art. 55. Where any premium is given it shall in part consist of clothes supplied to the apprentice at the commencement of the binding, and in part of money, one moiety whereof shall be paid to the master at the binding, and the residue at the termination of the first year of the binding.

TERM.

Art. 56. No apprentice shall be bound by the Guardians for more than eight years.

CONSENT.

Art. 57. No person above fourteen years of age shall be so bound without his consent.

And no child under the age of sixteen years shall be so bound without the consent of the father of such child, or if the father be dead, or be disqualified to give such consent, as hereinafter provided, or if such child be a bastard, without the consent of the mother, if living, of such child.

Provided, that where such parent is transported beyond the seas, or is in custody of the law, having been convicted of some felony, or for the space of six calendar months before the time of executing the indenture has deserted such child, or for such space of time has been in the service of Her Majesty, or of the East India Company, in any place out of the United Kingdom, such parent, if the father, shall be deemed to be disqualified as herein-before stated, and if it be the mother, no such consent shall be required.

PLACE OF SERVICE.

Art. 58. No child shall be bound to a master whose place of business, whereat the child is to work and live, is distant more than thirty miles from the place in which the child is residing at the time of the proposed binding, or at the time of his being sent on trial to such master;

Unless in any particular case the Commissioners shall, on application to them, otherwise permit.

PRELIMINARIES TO THE BINDING.

Art. 59. If the child whom it is proposed to bind apprentice, be in the Workhouse, and under the age of fourteen years, the Guardians shall require a certificate in writing from the Medical Officer of the Workhouse as to the fitness in regard to bodily health and strength of such child to be bound apprentice to the proposed trade, and shall also ascertain from the Master of the Workhouse the capacity of the child for such binding in other respects.

Art. 60. If the child be not in the Workhouse, but in the Union by the Guardians of which it is proposed that he shall be bound, the Relieving Officer of the district in which the child is residing shall examine into the circumstances of the case, the condition of the child, and of his parents, if any, and the residence of the proposed master, the nature of his trade, the number of other apprentices, if any, then bound to him, and generally as to the fitness of the particular binding, and shall report the result of his enquiry to the Guardians.

Art. 61. If in any case within Article 60, the Guardians think proper to proceed with the binding, they shall, when the child is under the age of fourteen years, direct the Relieving Officer to take the child to the Medical Officer of the district, to be examined as to his fitness in respect of bodily health and strength for the proposed trade or business; and such Medical Officer shall certify in writing according to his judgment in the matter, which certificate shall be produced by the said Relieving Officer to the next meeting of the Guardians.

Art. 62. If the child be not residing within the Union, the Guardians who propose to bind him shall not proceed to do so unless they receive such a report as is required in Article 60 from the Relieving Officer of the district in which such child is residing, and a certificate from some medical man practising in the neighbourhood of the child's residence to the effect required in Article 61.

Art. 63. When it is proposed to give a premium other than clothing upon the binding of any person above the age of sixteen years, the guardians shall require a certificate in writing from some medical practitioner, certifying that the person is maimed, deformed, or disabled, to the extent specified in such Article, and shall cause a copy of such certificate to be entered on their minutes before they proceed to execute the indenture.

Art. 64. When such certificate, as is required by Articles 59, 61, 62, and 63, is received, or in case from the age of the child no such certificate is required, the Guardians shall direct that the child and the proposed master, or some person on his behalf, and in case the child be under the age of sixteen, that the parent or person in whose custody such child shall be then living, attend some meeting of the Board to be then appointed.

Art. 65. At such meeting, if such parties appear,

the Guardians shall examine into the circumstances of the case; and if, after making all due inquiries, and hearing the objections (if any be made) on the part of the relatives or friends of such child, they deem it proper that the binding be effected, they may forthwith cause the indenture to be prepared, and, if the master be present, to be executed, but if he be not present they shall cause the same to be transmitted to him for execution; and when executed by him, and returned to the Guardians, the same shall be executed by the latter, and shall be signed by the child, as provided in Article 67.

Art. 66. If the proposed master reside out of the Union, but in some other Union or Parish under a Board of Guardians, whether formed under the provisions of the first-recited Act, or of the Act of the twenty-second year of the reign of King George the Third, intituled "*An Act for the better Relief and Employment of the Poor,*" or of any local Act, the Guardians shall, before proceeding to effect the binding, communicate in writing the proposal to the Guardians of such other Union or Parish, and request to be informed whether such binding is open to any objection, and if no objection be reported by such Guardians within the space of one calendar month, or, if the objection does not appear to the Guardians proposing to bind the child to be sufficient to prevent the binding, the same may be proceeded with; and when the indenture shall have been executed, the Clerk to the Guardians who executed the same shall send notice thereof in writing to the Guardians of the Union or Parish wherein the said apprentice is to reside.

INDENTURE.

Art. 67. The indenture shall be executed in duplicate, by the master and the Guardians, and shall not be valid unless signed by the proposed apprentice with his name, or if deaf and dumb with his mark in the presence of the said Guardians; and the consent of the parent, where requisite, shall be testified by such parent signing with his name or mark, to be properly attested, at the foot of the said indenture; and where such consent is dispensed with under Article 57, the cause of such dispensation shall be stated at the foot of the indenture by the clerk.

Art. 68. The name of the place or places at which the apprentice is to work and live shall be inserted in the indenture.

Art. 69. One part of such indenture, when executed, shall be kept by the Guardians; the other shall be delivered to the master.

DUTIES OF THE MASTER OF A PAUPER APPRENTICE.

Art. 70. And We do hereby prescribe the duties of the master to whom such poor child may be apprenticed, and the terms and conditions to be inserted in the said indenture, to be as follows:

No. 1. The master shall teach the child the trade, business, or employment set forth in the indenture, unless the Guardians authorise the substitution of another trade, business, or employment.

No. 2. He shall maintain the said child with proper food and nourishment.

No. 3. He shall provide a proper lodging for the said child.

No. 4. He shall supply the said child with proper clothing during the term of the binding, together with the necessary provision of linen.

No. 5. He shall, in case the said child be affected with any disease or sickness, or meet with any accident, procure, at his own cost, adequate medical or surgical assistance, from some duly qualified medical man, for such child.

No. 6. He shall, once at least on every Sunday, cause the child to attend some place of Divine worship, if there be any such within a reasonable distance, according to the religious persuasion in which the child has been brought up, so, however, that no child shall be required by the master to attend any place of worship to which his parents or surviving parent may object, nor when he shall be above the age of sixteen, any place to which he may himself object.

No. 7. Where such parents or parent or next of kin desire it, he shall allow the said child to attend any Sunday or other school which shall be situated within the same parish, or within two miles distance from his residence, on every Sunday, and, if there be no such school which such child can attend, he shall, at some reasonable hour on every Sunday, allow any minister of the religious persuasion of the child to have access to such child for the purpose of imparting religious instruction.

No. 8. Where the apprentice continues bound after the age of seventeen years the master shall, in every case where the Guardians require him so to do, pay to such apprentice, for and in respect of every week that he duly and properly serves the said master, as a remuneration, a sum to be inserted in the indenture, or to be agreed upon by the Guardians and the said master when that time arrives, or, if they cannot agree, to be settled by some person to be then chosen by the said master and such Guardians, and, until such sum be agreed upon or settled, not less than one fourth of the amount then commonly paid as wages to journeymen in the said trade, business, or employment.

No. 9. The master shall, himself or by his agent, produce the apprentice to the Guardians by whom such apprentice was bound at their ordinary meeting next preceding the end of the first year of the binding, and before the receipt of the remainder of the premium, if any be due, and shall in like manner produce the said apprentice at some one of their ordinary meetings, to be held at or about the middle of the term, and whenever afterwards required to do so by the said Guardians: Provided, that if the apprentice reside out of the Union by the Guardians whereof he was bound, the apprentice shall be produced, as hereinbefore directed, to the Guardians of the Union or Parish, as described in Article 66, in which the apprentice may be residing.

No. 10. The master shall not cause the said apprentice to work or live more than ten miles from the place or places mentioned in the indenture, according to Article 68, without the leave of the Guardians so binding him, to be given under their common seal: Provided, that such Guardians may in such licence so to be given under their common seal, by express words to that effect, if they think fit, authorise the master, at any time during the residue of the term of the apprenticeship, to change the place of the abode or service of the apprentice, without any further application to them or their successors.

Art. 71. These duties of the master set forth in Article 70 shall be enforced by covenants and conditions to be inserted in the indenture to be executed by him.

Art. 72. The master shall also covenant, under a penalty to be specified in the covenant, not to assign or cancel the indenture, without the consent of the Guardians, under their common seal, previously obtained, and to pay to the said Guardians all costs and expences that they may incur in consequence of the said apprentice not being supplied with medical or surgical assistance by the master, in case the same shall be at any time requisite.

Art. 73. The indenture shall be made subject to the following provisoes:

No. 1. That if the master take the benefit of any Act for the relief of insolvent debtors or be discharged under any such Act, such indenture shall forthwith become of no further force or effect.

No. 2. That if, on a conviction for a breach of any one of the aforesaid covenants and conditions before a Justice of the Peace, the Guardians who may be parties to the said indenture declare by a resolution that the indenture is determined, and transmit a copy of such resolution, under the hand of their clerk, by the post or otherwise, to the said master, such indenture shall, except in respect of all rights and liabilities then accrued, forthwith become of no further force or effect.

Art. 74. Nothing contained in this Order shall apply to the apprenticing of poor children to the sea service.

MODE OF OBTAINING MEDICAL RELIEF BY PERMANENT PAUPERS.

Art. 75. The Guardians shall, once at least in every year, cause to be prepared by the Clerk or Relieving Officers a list of all such aged and infirm persons, and persons permanently sick or disabled as may be actually receiving relief from such Guardians, and residing within the district of each Medical Officer of the Union, and shall from time to time furnish to each District Medical Officer a copy of the list aforesaid.

Art. 76. Every person whose name is inserted in such list shall receive a ticket in the Form (L.) hereunto annexed, and shall be entitled on the exhibition of such ticket to the Medical Officer of his district to obtain such advice, attendance, and medicines, as his case may require, in the same manner as if he had received an order from the Guardians, and such ticket shall remain in force for the time specified therein, unless such person shall cease to be in the receipt of relief before the expiration of such time.

RELIEF OF NON-SETTLED AND NON-RESIDENT POOR.

Art. 77. If any Board of Guardians undertake to administer relief allowed to a non-settled pauper living within the Union for which they act, on behalf of the Officers, or of the Board of Guardians, of the Parish or Union in which such pauper is deemed to be settled, every such undertaking shall be made in conformity with the rules and regulations of the Commissioners in force at the time.

Art. 78. No money shall be transmitted to any Guardians or to any Officer of a Parish or Union, to be applied to the relief of any non-resident pauper, except in conformity with the provisions of this Order.

Art. 79. No money shall be paid on account of any non-resident pauper to the Guardians or to the Officer of any Union or Parish in which the relief is administered by a Board of Guardians, except in one of the three following ways:

No. 1. By post-office order payable to the Treasurer of the Union or Parish to the account of which the money is to be paid, or to the banker of such Treasurer.

No. 2. By cheque or order payable to the Treasurer of such Parish or Union, or to his order.

No. 3. By cheque payable to bearer (where the same may lawfully be drawn), and crossed as payable through the Treasurer of such Parish or Union, or his banker, or through the agent of such Treasurer or banker; and every such cheque shall be so crossed by the Clerk before it is signed by the presiding Chairman.

Art. 80. Every account for relief duly administered to non-resident poor shall be discharged by the Guardians, within two calendar months from the receipt of such account, by the transmission of the amount due, in one of the modes prescribed in Art. 79.

ORDERS FOR CONTRIBUTIONS AND PAYMENTS.

Art. 81. The Clerk shall, four weeks at least before the Twenty-fifth day of March and the Twenty-ninth day of September respectively in each year, refer to and ascertain the cost to each Parish in the Union for the maintenance of the poor, and other separate charges, as well as for the common charges incurred in the half of the last year corresponding to the half year next coming, and shall estimate and, as near as may be, divide amongst the Parishes any extraordinary charges to which the Union may be liable in the coming half year, and he shall also estimate the probable balance due to or from the Parish at the end of the current half year, and shall then prepare the orders on the several Parishes for the sums which, upon such computation, it shall appear necessary for them to contribute to the expenses of the Union for the coming half year; and the orders so prepared shall be laid before the Guardians for their consideration, three weeks at least before the expiration of the current half year.

Art. 82. The Guardians shall make orders on the Overseers or other proper authorities of every Parish of the Union, from time to time, for the payment to the Guardians of all such sums as may be required by them for the relief of the Poor of the Parish, and for the contribution of the Parish to the common fund of the Union, and for any other expences chargeable by the Guardians on the Parish; and in such orders the contributions shall be directed to be paid in one sum or by instalments, on days specified, as to the Guardians may seem fit.

Art. 83. Every such order shall be made according to the Form (M.) hereunto annexed. It shall be signed by the presiding Chairman of the meeting, and two other Guardians present thereat, and shall be countersigned by the Clerk.

Art. 84. The Guardians shall pay every sum greater than Five Pounds by an order, which shall be drawn upon the Treasurer of the Union, and shall be signed by the presiding Chairman and two other Guardians at a meeting, and shall be countersigned by the Clerk.

Art. 85. The Guardians shall examine at their Board, or shall cause to be examined by some Committee or Guardian authorised by them for the purpose, every bill exceeding in amount one pound (except the salaries of officers) brought against the Union; and when any such bill has been allowed by the Board, or by such Committee or Guardian, a note of the allowance thereof shall be made on the face of the bill before the amount is paid.

CUSTODY OF BONDS.

Art. 86. The Guardians shall provide for the safe custody of all bonds given in pursuance of the Regulations of the Commissioners, so always that no bond given by any person shall remain in the custody of such person himself.

Art. 87. The Guardians shall, at the audit next after the Twenty-fifty day of March in every year, cause every person having the custody of bonds given by any officer of the Union to produce such bonds to the Auditor for his inspection.

GOVERNMENT OF THE WORKHOUSE.

ADMISSION OF PAUPERS.

Art. 88. Every pauper who shall be admitted into the Workhouse, either upon his first or any subsequent admission, shall be admitted in some one of the following modes only; that is to say:—

By a written or printed order of the Board of Guardians, signed by their Clerk according to Art. 42.

By a provisional written or printed order, signed by a Relieving Officer or an Overseer.

By the Master of the Workhouse, (or during his absence, or inability to act, by the Matron,) without any order, in any case of sudden or urgent necessity.

Provided that the Master may admit any pauper delivered at the Workhouse under an order of removal to a parish in the Union.

Art. 89. No pauper shall be admitted under any written or printed order as mentioned in Art. 88, if the same bear date more than six days before the pauper presents it at the Workhouse.

Art. 90. If a pauper be admitted otherwise than by an order of the Board of Guardians, the admission of such pauper shall be brought before the Board of Guardians at their next ordinary meeting, who shall decide on the propriety of the pauper's continuing in the Workhouse or otherwise, and make an order accordingly.

Art. 91. As soon as the pauper is admitted, he shall be placed in some room to be appropriated to the reception of paupers on admission, and shall then be examined by the Medical Officer.

Art. 92. If the Medical Officer upon such examination pronounce the pauper to be labouring under any disease of body or mind, the pauper shall be placed in the sick ward, or in such other ward as the Medical Officer shall direct.

Art. 93. If the Medical Officer pronounce the pauper to be free from any such disease, the pauper shall be placed in the part of the Workhouse assigned to the class to which he may belong.

Art. 94. No pauper shall be detained in a receiving ward for a longer time than is necessary for carrying into effect the regulations in Arts. 91, 92, and 93, if there be room in the proper ward for his reception.

Art. 95. Before being removed from the receiving ward, the pauper shall be thoroughly cleansed, and shall be clothed in a workhouse dress, and the clothes which he wore at the time of his admission shall be purified, and deposited in a place appropriated for that purpose, with the pauper's name affixed thereto. Such clothes shall be restored to the pauper when he leaves the Workhouse.

Art. 96. Every pauper shall, upon his admission into the Workhouse, be searched by or under the inspection of the proper officer, and all articles prohibited by any Act of Parliament, or by this Order, which may be found upon his person, shall be taken from him, and, so far as may be proper, restored to him at his departure from the Workhouse.

Art. 97. Provided always, that the regulations respecting the admission, clothing, and searching of paupers shall not apply to any casual poor way-farer, unless the Guardians shall so direct, or unless he is compelled to remain in the Workhouse from illness or other sufficient cause, in which case he shall be admitted regularly as an inmate.

CLASSIFICATION OF THE PAUPERS.

Art. 98. The paupers, so far as the Workhouse admits thereof, shall be classed as follows :—

Class 1. Men infirm through age or any other cause.

Class 2. Able-bodied men, and youths above the age of fifteen years.

Class 3. Boys above the age of seven years, and under that of fifteen.

Class 4. Women infirm through age or any other cause.

Class 5. Able-bodied women, and girls above the age of fifteen years.

Class 6. Girls above the age of seven years, and under that of fifteen.

Class 7. Children under seven years of age.

To each class shall be assigned that ward or separate building and yard which may be best fitted for the reception of such class, and each class of paupers shall remain therein, without communication with those of any other class.

Art. 99. Provided,

Firstly.—That the Guardians shall from time to time, after consulting the Medical Officer, make such arrangements as they may deem necessary with regard to persons labouring under any disease of body or mind.

Secondly.—The Guardians shall, so far as circumstances will permit, further subdivide any of the classes enumerated in Art. 98, with reference to the moral character, or behaviour, or the previous habits of the inmates, or to such other grounds as may seem expedient.

Thirdly.—That nothing in this order shall compel the Guardians to separate any married couple, being both paupers of the first and fourth classes respectively, provided the Guardians shall set apart for the exclusive use of every such couple a sleeping apartment separate from that of the other paupers.

Fourthly.—That any paupers of the fifth and sixth classes may be employed constantly or occasionally in any of the female sick wards, or in the care of infants, or as assistants in the household work; and the Master and Matron shall make such arrangements as may enable the paupers of the fifth and sixth classes to be employed in the household work, without communication with the paupers of the second and third classes.

Fifthly.—That any pauper of the fourth class, whom the Master may deem fit to perform any of the duties of a nurse or assistant to the Matron, may be so employed in the sick wards, or those of the fourth, fifth, sixth, or seventh classes, and any pauper of the first class, who may by the Master be deemed fit, may be placed in the ward of the third class, to aid in the management, and superintend the behaviour, of the paupers of such class, or may be employed in the male sick ward.

Sixthly.—That the Guardians, for a special reason to be entered on their minutes, may place any boy or girl between the ages of ten and sixteen years, in a male or female ward respectively, different from that to which he or she properly belongs, unless the Commissioners shall otherwise direct.

Seventhly.—That the paupers of the seventh class may be placed in such of the wards appropriated to the female paupers as shall be deemed expedient, and the mothers of such paupers shall be permitted to have access to them at all reasonable times.

Eighthly.—That the Master (subject to any directions given or regulations made by the Guardians) shall allow the father or mother of any child in the same workhouse, who may be desirous of seeing such child, to have an interview with such child at some one time in each day, in a room in the said Workhouse to be appointed for that purpose. And the Guardians shall make arrangements for permitting the members of the same family who may be in different Workhouses of the Union to have occasional interviews with each other, at such times, and in such manner, as may best suit the discipline of the several Workhouses.

Ninthly.—That casual poor way-farers admitted by the Master or Matron, shall be kept in a separate ward of the Workhouse, and shall be dieted and set to work in such manner and under such regulations as the Guardians by any resolution now in force, or to be made hereafter, may direct.

Art. 100. The Guardians shall not admit into the Workhouse, or any ward of the same, or retain therein, a larger number or a different class of paupers than that heretofore or hereafter from time to time to be fixed by the Commissioners ; and in case such number shall at any time be exceeded, the fact of such excess shall be forthwith reported to the Commissioners by the Clerk.

Art. 101. No pauper of unsound mind, who may be dangerous, or who may have been reported as such by the Medical Officer, or who may require habitual or frequent restraint, shall be detained in the Workhouse for any period exceeding fourteen days, and the Guardians shall cause the proper steps to be taken for the removal of every such pauper to some asylum or licensed house as soon as may be practicable.

DISCIPLINE AND DIET OF THE PAUPERS.

Art. 102. All the paupers in the Workhouse, except the sick and insane, and the paupers of the first, fourth, and seventh classes, shall rise, be set to work, leave off work, and go to bed at the times mentioned in the Form (N.) hereunto annexed, and shall be allowed such intervals for their meals as are therein stated, and these several times shall be notified by the ringing of a bell; provided always, that the Guardians may, with the consent of the Commissioners, make such alterations in any of the said times or intervals, as the Guardians may think fit.

Art. 103. Half an hour after the bell shall have been rung for rising, the names of the paupers shall be called over by the Master and Matron respectively, in the several wards provided for the second, third, fifth, and sixth classes, when every pauper, belonging to the respective wards, shall be present, and shall answer to his name, and be inspected by the Master and Matron respectively, provided that the paupers of the third and sixth class may be called over and inspected by the Schoolmaster and Schoolmistress.

Art. 104. The meals shall be taken by all the paupers, except the sick, the children, persons of unsound mind, casual poor way-farers, women suckling their children, and the paupers of the first and fourth classes, in the dining-hall or day-room, and in no other place whatever, and during the time of meals order and decorum shall be maintained.

Art. 105. No pauper of the second, third, fifth, or sixth classes shall go to, or remain in his sleeping-room, either in the time hereby appointed for work, or in the intervals allowed for meals, except by permission of the Master or Matron.

Art. 106. The Master and Matron shall (subject to the directions of the Guardians) fix the hours of rising and going to bed, for the paupers of the first, fourth, and seventh classes, and determine the occupation and employment of which they may be capable; and the meals for such paupers shall be provided at such times and in such manner as the Guardians may from time to time direct.

Art. 107. The paupers shall be dieted with the food and in the manner set forth in the Dietary Table which may be prescribed for the use of the Workhouse, and no pauper shall have or consume any liquor, or any food or provision other than is allowed in the said Dietary Table, except on Christmas Day or by the direction in writing of the Medical Officer, as provided in Article 108.

Art. 108. Provided,

First.—That the Medical Officer may direct in writing such diet for any individual pauper as he may deem necessary, and the Master shall obey such direction until the next ordinary meeting of the Guardians, when he shall report the same in writing to the Guardians.

Secondly.—That if the Medical Officer at any time certify that he deems a temporary change in the diet essential to the health of the paupers in the Workhouse, or of any class or classes thereof, the Guardians shall cause a copy of such certificate to be entered on the minutes of their proceedings, and may forthwith order, by a resolution, the said diet to be temporarily changed, according to the recommendation of the Medical Officer, and shall forthwith transmit a copy of such certificate and resolution to the Commissioners.

Thirdly.—That the Medical Officer shall be consulted by the Matron as to the nature of the food of the infants, and of their mothers when suckling, and the time at which such infants should be weaned.

Fourthly.—That the Guardians may, without any direction of the Medical Officer, make such allowance of food as may be necessary to paupers employed as nurses or in the household work; but they shall not allow to such paupers any fermented or spirituous liquors on account of the performance of such work, unless in pursuance of a written recommendation of the Medical Officer.

Art. 109. If any pauper require the Master or Matron to weigh the allowance of provisions served out at any meal, the Master or Matron shall forthwith weigh such allowance in the presence of the pauper complaining, and of two other persons.

Art. 110. The clothing to be worn by the paupers in the Workhouse shall be made of such materials as the Board of Guardians may determine.

Art. 111. More than two paupers, any one of whom is above the age of seven years, shall not be allowed to occupy the same bed, unless in the case of a mother and infant children.

Art. 112. The paupers of the several classes shall be kept employed according to their capacity and ability; and no pauper shall receive any compensation for his labour.

Art. 113. No pauper in the Workhouse shall be employed or set to work in pounding, grinding, or otherwise breaking bones, or in preparing bone dust.

Art. 114. The boys and girls who are inmates of the Workhouse shall, for three of the working hours, at least, every day, be instructed in reading, writing, arithmetic, and the principles of the Christian Religion, and such other instruction shall be imparted to them as may fit them for service, and train them to habits of usefulness, industry, and virtue.

Art. 115. Any pauper may quit the Workhouse upon giving to the Master, or (during his absence or inability to act) to the Matron, a reasonable notice of his wish to do so; and in the event of any able-bodied pauper, having a family, so quitting the house, the whole of such family shall be sent with him, unless the Guardians shall, for any special reason, otherwise direct; and such directions shall be in conformity with the Regulations of the Commissioners with respect to relief in force at the time.

Art. 116. Provided, nevertheless, that the Guardians may, by any general or special direction, authorize the Master to allow a pauper, without giving any such notice as is required in Art. 115, to quit the Workhouse, and to return after a temporary absence only; and every such allowance shall be reported by the Master to the Guardians at their next ordinary meeting.

Art. 117. Provided also, that nothing herein contained shall prevent the Master from allowing the paupers of each sex under the age of fifteen, subject to such restrictions as the Guardians may impose, to quit the Workhouse, under the care and guidance of himself, or the Matron, Schoolmaster, Schoolmistress, Porter, or some one of the assistants and servants of the Workhouse, for the purpose of exercise.

Art. 118. Any person may visit any pauper in the Workhouse by permission of the Master, or (in his absence) of the Matron, subject to such conditions and restrictions as the Guardians may prescribe; such interview shall take place in a room separate from the other inmates of the Workhouse, and in the presence of the Master, Matron, or Porter, except where a sick pauper is visited.

Art. 119. No written or printed paper of an improper tendency, or which may be likely to produce insubordination, shall be allowed to circulate, or be read aloud, among the inmates of the Workhouse.

Art. 120. No pauper shall play at cards, or at any game of chance, in the Workhouse; and the Master may take from any pauper, and keep until his departure from the Workhouse, any cards, dice, or other articles applicable to games of chance, which may be in his possession.

Art. 121. No pauper shall smoke in any room of the Workhouse, except by the special direction of the Medical Officer, or shall have any matches or other articles of a highly combustible nature in his possession, and the Master may take from any person any articles of such a nature.

Art. 122. Any licensed minister of the religious persuasion of an inmate of the Workhouse, who may at any time in the day, on the request of any inmate, enter the Workhouse for the purpose of affording religious assistance to him, or for the purpose of instructing his child or children in the principles of his religion, shall give such assistance or instruction, so as not to interfere with the good order and discipline of the other inmates of the Workhouse, and such religious assistance or instruction shall be strictly confined to inmates who are of the religious persuasion of such minister, and to the children of such inmates, except in the cases in which the Guardians may lawfully permit religious assistance and instruction to be given to any paupers who are Protestant dissenters, by licensed ministers who are Protestant dissenters.

Art. 123. No work, except the necessary household work and cooking, shall be performed by the paupers on Sunday, Good Friday, and Christmas Day.

Art. 124. Prayers shall be read before breakfast and after supper every day, and Divine Service shall be performed every Sunday, Good Friday, and Christmas Day in the Workhouse (unless the Guardians, with the consent of the Commissioners, otherwise direct), and at such prayers and Divine Service all the paupers shall attend, except the sick, persons of unsound mind, the young children, and such as are too infirm to do so; provided that those paupers who may object so to attend, on account of their professing religious principles differing from those of the Established Church, shall also be exempt from such attendance.

Art. 125. The Guardians may authorize any inmates of the Workhouse, being members of the Established Church, to attend Public Worship at a parish church or chapel, on every Sunday, Good Friday, and Christmas Day, under the control and inspection of the Master or Porter, or other officer.

Art. 126. The Guardians may also authorize any inmates of the Workhouse, being dissenters from the Established Church, to attend Public Worship at any dissenting chapel in the neighbourhood of the Workhouse, on every Sunday, Good Friday, and Christmas Day.

PUNISHMENTS FOR MISBEHAVIOUR OF THE PAUPERS.

Art. 127. Any pauper, being an inmate of the workhouse, who shall neglect to observe such of the regulations in this order as are applicable to him as such inmate;—

Or who shall make any noise when silence is ordered to be kept;

Or shall use obscene or profane language;

Or shall by word or deed insult or revile any person;

Or shall threaten to strike or to assault any person;

Or shall not duly cleanse his person;

Or shall refuse or neglect to work, after having been required to do so;

Or shall pretend sickness;

Or shall play at cards or other game of chance;

Or shall refuse to go into his proper ward or yard, or shall enter or attempt to enter, without permission, the ward or yard appropriated to any class of paupers other than that to which he belongs;

Or shall climb over any fence or boundary wall surrounding any portion of the Workhouse premises, or shall attempt to leave the Workhouse otherwise than through the ordinary entrance;

Or shall misbehave in going to, at, or returning from Public Worship out of the Workhouse, or at Divine Service or Prayers in the Workhouse;

Or having received temporary leave of absence, and wearing the Workhouse clothes, shall return to the Workhouse after the appointed time of absence, without reasonable cause for the delay;

Or shall wilfully disobey any lawful order of any officer of the Workhouse;

Shall be deemed DISORDERLY.

Art. 128. Any pauper, being an inmate of the Workhouse, who shall, within seven days, repeat any one, or commit more than one, of the offences specified in Art. 127;

Or who shall by word or deed insult or revile the Master or Matron, or any other officer of the Workhouse, or any of the Guardians;

Or shall wilfully disobey any lawful order of the Master or Matron after such order shall have been repeated;

Or shall unlawfully strike or otherwise unlawfully assault any person;

Or shall wilfully or mischievously damage or soil any property whatsoever belonging to the Guardians;

Or shall wilfully waste or spoil any provisions, stock, tools, or materials for work, belonging to the Guardians;

Or shall be drunk;

Or shall act or write indecently or obscenely;

Or shall wilfully disturb other persons at Public Worship out of the Workhouse, or at Divine Service or Prayers in the Workhouse;

Shall be deemed REFRACTORY.

Art. 129. The Master may, with or without the direction of the Guardians, punish any disorderly pauper by substituting, during a time not greater than forty-eight hours, for his dinner, as prescribed by the Dietary, a meal consisting of eight ounces of bread, or one pound of cooked potatoes or boiled rice, and also by withholding from him, during the same period, all butter, cheese, tea, sugar, or broth, which such pauper would otherwise receive, at any meal during the time aforesaid.

Art. 130. The Guardians may, by a special direction to be entered on their minutes, order any refractory pauper to be punished by confinement in a separate room, with or without an alteration of diet, similar in kind and duration to that prescribed in Article 129 for disorderly paupers; but no pauper shall be so confined for a longer period than twenty-four hours, or, if it be deemed right that such pauper should be carried before a Justice of the Peace, and if such period of twenty-four hours should be insufficient for that purpose, then for such further time as may be necessary for such purpose.

Art. 131. If any offence, whereby a pauper becomes refractory under Art. 128, be accompanied by any of the following circumstances of aggravation; (that is to say,) if such pauper

Persist in using violence against any person;

Or persist in creating a noise or disturbance, so as to annoy other inmates;

Or endeavour to excite other paupers to acts of insubordination;

Or persist in acting indecently or obscenely in the presence of any other inmate;

Or persist in mischievously breaking or damaging any goods or property of the Guardians;

the Master may, without any direction of the Guardians, immediately place such refractory pauper in confinement for any time not exceeding twelve hours; which confinement shall, however, be reckoned as part of any punishment afterwards imposed by the Guardians for the same offence.

Art. 132. Every refractory pauper shall be deemed to be also disorderly, and may be punished as such; but no pauper who may have been punished for any offence as disorderly, shall afterwards be punished for the same offence as refractory, and no pauper who may have been punished for any offence as refractory, shall afterwards be punished for the same offence as disorderly.

Art. 133. No pauper shall be punished by confinement or alteration in diet for any offence not committed in the Workhouse since his last admission, except in such cases as are expressly specified in Articles 127 and 128.

Art. 134. No pauper who may have been under medical care, or who may have been entered in the medical weekly return as sick or infirm, at any time in the course of the seven days next preceding the punishment, or who may be reasonably supposed to be under twelve, or above sixty years of age, or who may be pronounced by the Medical Officer to be pregnant, or who may be suckling a child, shall be punished by alteration of diet, or by confinement, unless the Medical Officer shall have previously certified in writing that no injury to the health of such pauper is reasonably to be apprehended from the proposed punishment; and any modification diminishing such punishment which the Medical Officer may suggest, shall be adopted by the Master.

Art. 135. No pauper shall be confined between eight o'clock in the evening, and six o'clock in the morning, without being furnished with a bed and bedding suitable to the season, and with the other proper conveniences.

Art. 136. No child under twelve years of age shall be punished by confinement in a dark room, or during the night.

Art. 137. No corporal punishment shall be inflicted on any male child, except by the Schoolmaster or Master.

Art. 138. No corporal punishment shall be inflicted on any female child.

Art. 139. No corporal punishment shall be inflicted on any male child, except with a rod or other instrument, such as may have been approved of by the Guardians or the Visiting Committee.

Art. 140. No corporal punishment shall be inflicted on any male child until two hours shall have elapsed from the commission of the offence for which such punishment is inflicted.

Art. 141. Whenever any male child is punished by corporal correction, the Master and Schoolmaster shall (if possible) be both present.

Art. 142. No male child shall be punished by flogging whose age may be reasonably supposed to exceed fourteen years.

Art. 143. The Master shall keep a book to be furnished him by the Guardians, in the Form (O.) hereunto annexed, in which he shall duly enter,

Firstly, All cases of refractory or disorderly paupers, whether children or adults, reported to the Guardians for their decision thereon.

Secondly, All cases of paupers, whether children or adults, who may have been punished without the direction of the Guardians, with the particulars of their respective offences and punishments.

Art. 144. The person who punishes any child with corporal correction shall forthwith report to the Master the particulars of the offence and punishment; and the Master shall enter the same in the book specified in Art. 143.

Art. 145. Such book shall be laid on the table at every ordinary meeting of the Guardians; and every entry made in such book since the last ordinary meeting shall be read to the Board by the Clerk.

The Guardians shall thereupon, in the first place, give direction as to the confinement or other punishment of any refractory or disorderly pauper reported for their decision, and such direction shall be entered on the minutes of the proceedings of the day, and a copy thereof shall be inserted by the Clerk in the book specified in Art. 143.

The Guardians, in the second place, shall take into their consideration the cases in which punishments are reported to have been already inflicted by the Master or other officer, and shall require the Master to bring before them any pauper so punished, who may have signified a wish to see the Guardians. If the Guardians in any case are of opinion that the officer has acted illegally or improperly, such opinion shall be entered on the minutes, and shall be communicated to the Master, and a copy of the minute of such opinion shall be forwarded to the Commissioners by the Clerk.

Art. 146. If any pauper above the age of fourteen years unlawfully introduce or attempt to introduce any spirituous or fermented liquor into the Workhouse, or abscond from the Workhouse with clothes belonging to the Guardians, the Master may cause such pauper to be forthwith taken before a Justice of the Peace, to be dealt with according to law. And whether he do so or not, he shall report every such case to the Guardians at their next ordinary meeting.

Art. 147. The Master shall cause a legible copy of Arts. 127, 128, 129, 130, and 131 to be kept suspended in the dining-hall of the Workhouse, or in the room in which the inmates usually eat their meals, and also in the Board-room of the Guardians.

VISITING COMMITTEE.

Art. 148. The Guardians shall appoint one or more *Visiting Committees* from their own body; and each of such committees shall carefully examine the Workhouse or Workhouses of the Union once in every week at the least, inspect the last reports of the Chaplain and Medical Officer, examine the stores, afford, so far as is practicable, to the inmates an opportunity of making any complaints, and investigate any complaints that may be made to them.

Art. 149. The Visiting Committee shall from time to time write such answers as the facts may warrant to the following queries, which are to be printed in a book, entitled the VISITORS' BOOK, to be provided by the Guardians, and kept in every Workhouse for that purpose, and to be submitted regularly to the Guardians at their ordinary meetings:—

Q. 1. Is the Workhouse, with its wards, offices, yards, and appurtenances, clean and well ventilated in every part?—and is the bedding in proper order?—if not, state the defect or omission.

Q. 2. Do the inmates of the Workhouse, of all classes, appear clean in their persons, and decent and orderly in their behaviour; and is their clothing regularly changed?

Q. 3. Are the inmates of each sex employed and kept at work as directed by the Guardians, and is such work unobjectionable in its nature?—if any improvement can be suggested in their employment, state the same.

Q. 4. Are the infirm of each sex properly attended to, according to their several conditions?

Q. 5. Are the boys and girls in the school properly instructed as required by the regulations of the Commissioners, and is their industrial training properly attended to?

Q. 6. Are the young children properly nursed and taken care of, and do they appear in a clean and healthy state?—Is there any child not vaccinated?

Q. 7. Is regular attendance given by the Medical Officer?—Are the inmates of the Sick wards properly tended?—Are the nurses efficient?—Is there any infectious disease in the workhouse?

Q. 8. Is there any dangerous lunatic or idiot in the Workhouse?

Q. 9. Is Divine Service regularly performed?—Are prayers regularly read?

Q. 10. Is the established dietary duly observed?—and are the prescribed hours of meals regularly adhered to?

Q. 11. Are the provisions and other supplies of the qualities contracted for?

Q. 12. Is the classification properly observed according to Arts. 98 and 99?

Q. 13. Is any complaint made by any pauper against any officer, or in respect of the provisions or accommodations?—if so, state the name of the complainant, and the subject of the complaint.

Q. 14. Does the present number of inmates in the Workhouse exceed that fixed by the Poor Law Commissioners?

REPAIRS AND ALTERATIONS OF THE WORKHOUSE.

Art. 150. The Guardians shall once at least in every year, and as often as may be necessary for cleanliness, cause all the rooms, wards, offices, and privies belonging to the Workhouse to be limewashed.

Art. 151. The Guardians shall cause the Workhouse and all its furniture and appurtenances to be kept in good and substantial repair; and shall, from time to time, remedy, without delay, any such defect in the repair of the house, its drainage, warmth, or ventilation, or in the furniture or fixtures thereof, as may tend to injure the health of the inmates.

GOVERNMENT OF THE WORKHOUSE BY THE GUARDIANS.

Art. 152. We do declare, that, subject to the rules and regulations herein contained, the guidance, government, and control of every Workhouse, and of the officers, servants, assistants, and paupers within such Workhouse, shall be exercised by the Guardians of the Union.

APPOINTMENT OF OFFICERS.

Art. 153. The Guardians shall, whenever it may be requisite, or whenever a vacancy may occur, appoint fit persons to hold the under-mentioned offices, and to perform the duties respectively assigned to them; namely,

1. Clerk to the Guardians.
2. Treasurer of the Union.
3. Chaplain.
4. Medical Officer for the Workhouse.
5. District Medical Officer.
6. Master of the Workhouse.
7. Matron of the Workhouse.
8. Schoolmaster.
9. Schoolmistress.
10. Porter.
11. Nurse.
12. Relieving Officer.
13. Superintendent of Out-door Labour.

And also such assistants as the Guardians, with the consent of the Commissioners, may deem necessary for the efficient performance of the duties of any of the said offices.

Art. 154. The officers so appointed to or holding any of the said offices, as well as all persons temporarily discharging the duties of such offices, shall respectively perform such duties as may be required of them by the Rules and Regulations of the Commissioners, in force at the time, together with all such other duties, conformable with the nature of their respective offices, as the Guardians may lawfully require them to perform.

Provided always, that every regulation applying to any officer holding his office under this Order, shall apply to any officer of the like denomination appointed by the Guardians, although such officer may have been appointed before this Order shall have come into force.

MODE OF APPOINTMENT.

Art. 155. Every officer and assistant, to be appointed under this Order, shall be appointed by a majority of the Guardians present at a meeting of the Board, consisting of more than three Guardians, or by three Guardians if no more be present. Every such appointment shall, as soon as the same has been made, be reported to the Commissioners by the Clerk.

Art. 156. No appointment to any of the offices specified in Art. 153, shall be made under this Order, unless a notice that the question of making such appointment will be brought before the Board has been given and entered on the minutes, at one of the two ordinary meetings of the Board next preceding the meeting at which the appointment is made, or unless an advertisement, giving notice of the consideration of such appointment, shall have appeared in some public paper by the direction of the Guardians at least seven days before the day on which such appointment is made: Provided that no such notice or advertisement shall be necessary for the appointment of an assistant or temporary substitute.

Art. 157. The Guardians shall not, by advertisement, or other public notice, printed or written, invite tenders for the supply of medicines, or for the medical attendance on the paupers of the Union, unless such advertisement or notice shall specify the district or place for which such supply of medicines and such attendance is required, together with the amount of salary or other remuneration.

Art. 158. The Guardians may from time to time divide the union into districts for general and medical relief, with the consent of the Commissioners; and on any change in the division of the Union into districts for general and medical relief, or in the assignment of Relieving Officers and Medical Officers to such districts, the Clerk shall report every such change to the Commissioners for their approbation.

Art. 159. The guardians shall not assign to any Medical Officer a district which exceeds in extent the area of fifteen thousand statute acres, or which contains a population exceeding the number of fifteen thousand persons, according to the then last enumeration of the population published by authority of Parliament.

Art. 160. Provided that if it be impracticable, consistently with the proper attendance on the sick poor, for the Guardians to divide the Union into districts containing respectively an area and population less than is specified in Art. 159, then and in such case the Guardians shall cause a special minute to be made and entered on the usual record of their proceedings, stating the reasons which, in their opinion, make it necessary to form a district exceeding the said limits, and shall transmit a copy of such minute to the Commissioners for their consideration, and if the Commissioners signify their approval thereof to such Guardians, then and in such case, but not otherwise, such Guardians may proceed to assign the said district to a Medical Officer.

Art. 161. Provided also, that the limit of fifteen thousand statute acres, prescribed in Art. 159, shall not apply to any medical district situate wholly or in part within the principality of Wales; but no medical district situate wholly or in part within that principality shall be assigned to any Medical Officer residing more than seven miles from any part of any parish included within such district, unless such district shall have been specially sanctioned by the Commissioners in the same manner as is directed in Art. 160.

QUALIFICATIONS OF OFFICERS.

Art. 162. No person shall hold the office of Clerk, Treasurer, Master, or Relieving Officer under this Order who has not reached the age of twenty-one years.

Art. 163. No person shall hold the office of Master of a Workhouse, or Matron of a Workhouse having no Master, unless he or she be able to keep accounts.

Art. 164. No person shall hold the office of Relieving Officer unless he be able to keep accounts, and unless he reside in the district for which he may be appointed to act, devote his whole time to the performance of the duties of his office, and abstain from following any trade or profession, and from entering into any other service.

Art. 165. No person shall hold the office of nurse who is not able to read written directions upon medicines.

Art. 166. Provided always, that the Guardians may with the consent of the Commissioners previously obtained, but not otherwise, dispense with any of the conditions specified in Articles 162, 163, 164, & 165.

Art. 167. No person shall be appointed to the office of Master, Matron, Schoolmaster, Schoolmistress, Porter, or Relieving Officer, under this Order, who does not agree to give one month's notice previous to resigning the office, or to forfeit one month's amount of salary, to be deducted as liquidated damages from the amount of salary due at the time of such resignation.

Art. 168. No person shall hold the office of Medical Officer under this Order unless he possess one of the four following qualifications; that is to say,—

1. A diploma or degree as surgeon from a Royal College or University in England, Scotland, or Ireland, together with a degree in medicine from an University in England, legally authorized to grant such degree, or together with a diploma or licence of the Royal College of Physicians of London.
2. A diploma or degree as surgeon from a Royal College or University in England, Scotland, or Ireland, together with a certificate to practise as an apothecary from the Society of Apothecaries of London.
3. A diploma or degree as surgeon from a Royal College or University in England, Scotland, or Ireland, such person having been in actual practice as an apothecary on the first day of August, one thousand eight hundred and fifteen.
4. A warrant or commission as surgeon or assistant-surgeon in Her Majesty's Navy, or as surgeon or assistant-surgeon or apothecary in Her Majesty's Army, or as surgeon or assistant-surgeon in the service of the Honourable East India Company, dated previous to the first day of August, One thousand eight hundred and twenty-six.

Art. 169. Provided always, that if it be impracticable, consistently with the proper attendance on the sick poor, for the Guardians to procure a person residing within the district in which he is to act, and duly qualified in one of the four modes recited in Art. 168, to attend on the poor in such district, or that the only person resident within such district, and so qualified, shall have been dismissed from Office by the Commissioners, or shall be unfit or incompetent to hold the office of Medical Officer, then and in such case the Guardians shall cause a special minute to be made and entered on the usual record of their proceedings stating the reasons which, in their opinion, make it necessary to employ a person not qualified as required by Art. 168, and shall forthwith transmit a copy of such minute to the Commissioners for their consideration; and the Commissioners may permit the employment by such Guardians of any person duly licensed to practise as a medical man, although such person be not qualified in one of the four modes required by Art. 168.

Art. 170. Provided also, that the Guardians may, with the consent of the Commissioners, continue in office any Medical Officer duly licensed to practise as a medical man already employed by any such Guardians, although such Medical Officer may not be qualified in one of the four modes required by Art. 168.

Art. 171. No person shall hold the office of Chaplain under this Order without the consent of the Bishop of the diocese to his appointment, signified in writing.

REMUNERATION OF THE OFFICERS.

Art. 172. The Guardians shall pay to the several officers and assistants appointed to or holding any office or employment under this Order, such salaries or remuneration as the Commissioners may from time to time direct or approve.

Provided that the Guardians, with the approval of the Commissioners, may pay to any officer or person employed by such Guardians a reasonable compensation on account of extraordinary services, or other unforeseen circumstances connected with the duties of such officer or person or the necessities of the Union.

Art. 173. The salary of every officer, or assistant, appointed to, or holding any office or employment under this Order, shall be payable up to the day on which he ceases to hold such office or employment, and no longer.

Art. 174. If no remuneration or salary be expressly assigned to the Treasurer, the profit arising from the use of money from time to time left in his hands shall be deemed to be the payment of his services.

Art. 175. An officer who may be suspended, and who may, without the previous removal of such suspension, be dismissed by the Commissioners, shall not be entitled to any salary from the date of such suspension.

Art. 176. The Guardians shall not pay to any officer bound to account, to be hereafter appointed, who may have been removed, or who may be under suspension from his office, any salary claimed by such officer until his accounts shall have been audited by the Auditor.

Art. 177. No salary of any District Medical Officer shall include the remuneration for operations and services of the following classes performed by such Medical Officer in that capacity for any out-door pauper, but such operations and services shall be paid for by the Guardians, according to the rates specified in this Article.

	£	s.	d.
1. Treatment of Compound Fractures of the Thigh 2. Treatment of Compound Fractures or Compound Dislocations of the Leg 3. Amputation of Leg, Arm, Foot, or Hand 4. The Operation for Strangulated Hernia	5	0	0
5. Treatment of Simple Fractures or Simple Dislocations of the Thigh or Leg	3	0	0
6. Amputation of a Finger or Toe	2	0	0
7. Treatment of Dislocations or Fractures of the Arm	1	0	0

The above rates shall include the payment for the supply of all kinds of apparatus and splints.

Art. 178. Provided that except in cases of sudden accident immediately threatening life, no Medical Officer shall be entitled to receive such remuneration for any amputation, unless he shall have obtained at his own cost the advice of some member of the Royal College of Surgeons of London, or some fellow or licentiate of the Royal College of Physicians of London, before performing such amputation, and unless he shall also produce to the Guardians a certificate from such member of the Royal College of Surgeons, or such fellow or licentiate, stating that in his opinion it was right and proper that such amputation should be then performed.

Art. 179. Provided also, that if in any case the patient has not survived the operation more than thirty-six hours, and has not required and received several attendances after the operation by the Medical Officer who has performed the same, such Medical Officer shall be entitled only to one half of the payments respectively prescribed above.

Art. 180. Provided also, that if several of the fees specified in Art. 177, become payable with respect to the same person at the same time, and in consequence of the same cause or injury, the Medical Officer shall be entitled only to one of such fees, and if they be unequal, to the highest.

Art. 181. In any surgical case, not provided for in Art. 177, which has presented peculiar difficulty, or required and received long attendance from the District Medical Officer, the Guardians may make to the said Medical Officer such reasonable extra allowance as they may think fit, and the Commissioners may approve.

Art. 182. In cases in which any Medical Officer, either for the Workhouse or a district, shall be called on by order of a person legally qualified to make such order, to attend any woman in or immediately after childbirth, or shall, under circumstances of difficulty or danger, without any order, visit any such woman actually receiving relief, or whom the Guardians may subsequently decide to have been in a destitute condition, such Medical Officer shall be paid for his attendance and medicines by a sum of not less than ten shillings, nor more than twenty shillings, according as the Guardians may agree with such Officer.

Art. 183. Provided that in any special case in which great difficulty may have occurred in the delivery, or long subsequent attendance in respect of some puerperal malady or affection may have been requisite, any District Medical Officer shall receive the sum of two pounds.

SECURITY OF THE OFFICERS.

Art. 184. Every Treasurer, Master, Matron of a Workhouse in which there is no Master, Collector, or Relieving Officer, every person hereafter appointed as Clerk, and every other officer whom the Guardians shall require so to do, shall respectively give a bond conditioned for the due and faithful performance of the duties of the office, with two sufficient sureties, not, in the case of any security to be hereafter entered into, being officers of the same Union; and every officer who shall have entered into any such security shall give immediate notice to the Guardians of the death, insolvency, or bankruptcy of either of such sureties, and shall, when required by the Guardians, produce a certificate, signed by two householders, that his sureties are alive, and believed by them to be solvent, and such officer shall supply a fresh surety, in the place of any such surety who may die, or become bankrupt or insolvent.

Art. 185. Provided that the Guardians may, if they think fit, take the security of any society or company expressly authorized by statute to guarantee or secure the faithful discharge of the duties of such officers.

Art. 186. Provided also, that the Guardians may, with the consent of the Commissioners, dispense with such security in the case of any banking firm acting as Treasurer, or in the case of a Treasurer, being a banker or partner of such firm.

CONTINUANCE IN OFFICE AND SUSPENSION OF OFFICERS.—SUPPLY OF VACANCIES.

Art. 187. Every officer appointed to or holding any office under this Order, other than a Medical Officer, shall continue to hold the same until he die, or resign, or be removed by the Commissioners, or be proved to be insane, to the satisfaction of the Commissioners.

Art. 188. Provided always, that every porter, nurse, assistant, or servant may be dismissed by the Guardians without the consent of the Commissioners; but every such dismissal, and the grounds thereof, shall be reported to the Commissioners.

Art. 189. If any Master and Matron hereafter appointed be husband and wife, and one of them should be dismissed by Order of the Commissioners, or should otherwise vacate his or her office, or should die, the other survivor shall, at the expiration of the then current quarter, cease to hold his or her office of Master or Matron, as the case may be.

Art. 190. No officer of a Workhouse who may have been dismissed by any Order of the Commissioners, shall, after such dismissal, remain upon the Workhouse premises, or enter therein for the purpose of interfering in the management of such Workhouse, unless the Commissioners have consented to his subsequent appointment to an office in such Workhouse, under the provisions of the said first-recited Act, or to his temporary employment therein.

Art. 191. Every Medical Officer duly appointed shall, unless the period for which he is appointed be entered on the Minutes of the Guardians at the time of making such appointment, or be acknowledged in writing by such Medical Officer, continue in office until he may die or resign, or become legally disqualified to hold such office, or be removed therefrom by the Commissioners.

Art. 192. The Guardians may, at their discretion, suspend from the discharge of his or her duties any Master, Matron, Schoolmaster, Schoolmistress, Medical Officer, Relieving Officer, or Superintendent of Out-door Labour; and the Guardians shall, in case of every such suspension, forthwith report the same, together with the cause thereof, to the Commissioners; and if the Commissioners remove the suspension of such officer by the Guardians, he or she shall forthwith resume the performance of his or her duties.

Art. 193. If any officer, or assistant, appointed to or holding any office or employment under this Order, be at any time prevented by sickness or accident, or other sufficient reason, from the performance of his duties, the Guardians may appoint a fit person to act as his temporary substitute, and may pay him a reasonable compensation for his services; and every such appointment shall be reported to the Commissioners as soon as the same shall have been made.

Art. 194. The Vice-Chairman, or some Guardian to be appointed by the Guardians, may perform any of the duties assigned to the Clerk until any vacancy in the office shall have been filled, or until a substitute be appointed in the case of the sickness, accident, or absence of the Clerk.

Art. 195. When any officer may die, resign, or become legally disqualified to perform the duties of his office, the Guardians shall, as soon as conveniently may be after such death, resignation, or disqualification, give notice thereof to the Commissioners, and proceed to make a new appointment to the office so vacant in the manner prescribed by the above regulations.

Art. 196. If any officer give notice of an intended resignation to take effect on a future day, the Guardians may elect a successor to such officer, in conformity with the above regulations, at any time subsequent to such notice.

Art. 197. In the case of any Medical Officer who holds his office for a specified term, the Guardians may provide for the continuance of such officer, or appoint his successor, within the three calendar months next before the expiration of such term.

PERSONAL DISCHARGE OF DUTIES.

Art. 198. In every case not otherwise provided for by this order, every officer shall perform his duties in person, and shall not intrust the same to a deputy, except with the special permission of the Commissioners on the application of the Guardians.

Art. 199. Every Medical Officer shall be bound to visit and attend personally, as far as may be practicable, the poor persons intrusted to his care, and shall be responsible for the attendance on them.

Art. 200. Every Medical Officer shall, as soon as may be after his appointment, name to the Guardians some legally qualified medical practitioner to whom application for medicines or attendance may be made, in the case of his absence from home, or other hindrance to his personal attendance, and who will supply the same at the cost of such Medical Officer, and the name and residence of every Medical Practitioner so named shall be forwarded by the Clerk to each Relieving Officer, and to the Overseers of every Parish in the District of such Medical Officer.

DUTIES OF THE OFFICERS.

Art. 201. And We do hereby define and specify the duties of the several Officers appointed to or holding their offices under this Order, and direct the execution thereof, to be as follows:—

DUTIES OF THE CLERK.

Art. 202. The following shall be the duties of the Clerk:—

No. 1. To attend all meetings of the Boards of Guardians, and to keep punctually minutes of the proceedings at every meeting, to enter the said minutes in a book, and to submit the same so entered to the presiding Chairman at the succeeding meeting for his signature.

No. 2. To keep, check, and examine all accounts, books of accounts, minutes, books, and other documents as required of him by the Regulations of the Commissioners, or relating to the business of the Guardians, and from time to time to produce all such books and documents, together with the necessary vouchers, and the bonds of any Officers, with any certificates relating thereto, which may be in his custody, to the Auditor of the Union, at the place of audit and at the time and in such manner as may be required by the Regulations of the Commissioners.

No. 3. To peruse and conduct the correspondence of the Guardians according to their directions, and to preserve the same, as well as all Orders of the Commissioners, and letters received, together with copies of all letters sent, and all letters, books, papers, and documents belonging to the Union, or intrusted to him by the Guardians, and to make all necessary copies thereof.

No. 4. To prepare all written contracts and agreements to be entered into by any parties with the Guardians, and to see that the same are duly executed, and to prepare all bonds or other securities to be given by any of the Officers of the Union, and to see that the same are duly executed by such Officers and their sureties.

No. 5. To receive all requisitions of Guardians for extraordinary meetings, and to summon such meetings accordingly; and to make, sign, and send all notices required to be given to the Guardians by this or any other Order of the Commissioners.

No. 6. To countersign all Orders legally made by the Guardians on Overseers, for the payment of money, and all Orders legally drawn by the Guardians upon the Treasurer.

No. 7. To ascertain, before every ordinary meeting of the Board, the balance due to or from the Union, in account with the Treasurer, and to enter the same in the minute book.

No. 8. At the first meeting of the Guardians in each quarter, to lay before the Guardians, or some Committee appointed by them, the non-settled poor account, and the non-resident poor account, posted in his ledger to the end of the preceding quarter, and to take the directions of the Guardians respecting the remittance of cheques or post office orders to the Guardians of any other Union or Parish, or the transmission of accounts due from other Unions or Parishes, and requests for payment.

No. 9. Within fourteen days from the close of each quarter, to transmit by post all accounts of relief administered in the course of the preceding quarter to non-settled poor to the Guardians of the Unions and Parishes on account of which such relief was given; and to state in every account so transmitted the names and classes of the several paupers to whom the relief in question has been administered.

No. 10. To communicate to the several officers and persons engaged in the administration of relief within the Union, all orders and directions of the Commissioners, or of the Guardians; and so far as may be, to give the instructions requisite for the prompt and correct execution of all such Orders and Directions, and to report to the Guardians any neglect or failure therein which may come to his knowledge.

No. 11. To conduct all applications by or on behalf of the Guardians to any Justice or Justices at their Special, Petty, or General Sessions, and if he be an attorney or solicitor, to perform and execute all legal business connected with the Union, except prosecutions at the assizes, actions at law, suits in equity, or parliamentary business, without charge for anything beyond disbursements.

No. 12. To prepare and transmit all reports, answers, or returns, as to any question or matter connected with or relating to the administration of the laws for the relief of the Poor in the Union, or to any other business of the Union, which are required by the regulations of the Commissioners, or which the Commissioners, or any Assistant Commissioner, may lawfully require from him.

No. 13. To conduct duly and impartially, and in strict conformity with the Regulations in force at the time, the annual or any other election of Guardians.

No. 14. To observe and execute all lawful orders and directions of the Guardians applicable to his office.

DUTIES OF THE TREASURER OF THE UNION.

Art. 203. The following shall be the duties of the Treasurer of the Union :—

No. 1. To receive all monies tendered to be paid to the Guardians, and to place the same to their credit.

No. 2. To pay out of any monies for the time being in his hands belonging to the Guardians, all orders for money which shall be drawn upon him, in conformity with Art. 84, when the same shall be presented at the house or usual place of business of the Treasurer, and within the usual hours of business.

No. 3. To keep an account, under the proper dates, of all monies received and paid by him as such Treasurer, to balance the same at Lady Day and Michaelmas in every year, and to render an account of such monies to the Guardians, when required by them to do so.

No. 4. Whenever there are not funds belonging to the Guardians in his hands as Treasurer of the Union, to report in writing the fact of such deficiency to the Commissioners.

No. 5. To submit a proper account, together with the bonds of any officers which may be in his custody, to the Auditor at the place of audit, and at the time and in such manner as may be required by the regulations of the Commissioners.

No. 6. To receive the monies payable to him as Treasurer of the Union, under any Act of Parliament or other authority of law.

Art. 204. Provided that the regulations in Art. 203 shall not be applicable to cases in which the Governor and Company of the Bank of England may act as Treasurer of the Union or Bankers to the Guardians.

Duties of a Medical Officer.

Art. 205. The following shall be the duties of every Medical Officer appointed by the Guardians, whether he be the Medical Officer for a Workhouse or for a District:—

No. 1. To give to the Guardians, when required, any reasonable information respecting the case of any pauper who is or has been under his care; to make any such written report relative to any sickness prevalent among the paupers under his care, as the Guardians or the Commissioners may require of him; and to attend any meeting of the Board of Guardians when requested by them to do so.

No. 2. To give a certificate respecting children whom it is proposed to apprentice, in conformity with Articles 59 and 61.

No. 3. To give a certificate under his hand in every case to the Guardians, or the Relieving Officer, or the pauper on whom he is attending, of the sickness of such pauper or other cause of his attendance, when required to do so.

No. 4. In keeping the books prescribed by this Order, to employ, so far as is practicable, the terms used or recommended in the regulations and statistical nosology issued by the Registrar General; and also to show when the visit or attendance made or given to any pauper was made or given by any person employed by himself.

Duties of a District Medical Officer.

Art. 206. The following shall be the duties of a District Medical Officer:—

No. 1. To attend duly and punctually upon all poor persons requiring medical attendance within the District of the Union assigned to him, and according to his agreement to supply the requisite medicines to such persons, whenever he may be lawfully required to furnish such attendance or medicines by a written or printed order of the Guardians, or of a Relieving Officer of the Union, or of an Overseer.

No. 2. On the exhibition to him of a ticket, according to Art. 76, and on application made on behalf of the party to whom such ticket was given, to afford such medical attendance and medicines as he would be bound to supply if he had received in each case an order from the Guardians to afford such attendance and medicines.

No. 3. To inform the Relieving Officer of any poor person whom he may attend without an order.

No. 4. To make a return to the Guardians at each ordinary meeting, in a book prepared according to the Form marked (P.) hereunto annexed, and to insert therein the date of every attendance, and the other particulars required by such Form, in conformity with Art. 205, No. 4.

Provided, however, that the Medical Officer may, with the consent of the Guardians, but not otherwise, make the entries which he is directed to make in such book on detached sheets of paper, according to the same Form, and cause the same to be laid before the Guardians at every ordinary meeting, instead of such book; and the Guardians shall, in that case, cause such sheets to be bound up at the end of the year.

Duties of the Medical Officer for the Workhouse.

Art. 207. The following shall be the duties of the Medical Officer for the Workhouse:—

No. 1. To attend at the Workhouse at the periods fixed by the Guardians, and also when sent for by the Master or Matron.

No. 2. To attend duly and punctually upon all poor persons in the Workhouse requiring medical attendance, and according to his agreement to supply the requisite medicines to such persons.

No. 3. To examine the state of the paupers on their admission into the Workhouse, and to give the requisite directions to the Master according to Articles 91 and 92.

No. 4. To give directions and make suggestions as to the diet, classification, and treatment of the sick paupers, and paupers of unsound mind, and to report to the Guardians any pauper of unsound mind, and to report to the Guardians any pauper of unsound mind in the Workhouse whom he may deem to be dangerous, or fit to be sent to a Lunatic Asylum.

No. 5. To give all necessary instructions as to the diet or treatment of children and women suckling children, and to vaccinate such of the children as may require vaccination.

No. 6. To report in writing to the Guardians any defect in the diet, drainage, ventilation, warmth, or other arrangements of the Workhouse, or any excess in the number of any class of inmates, which he may deem to be detrimental to the health of the inmates.

No. 7. To report in writing to the Guardians any defect which he may observe in the arrangements of the infirmary, and in the performance of their duties by the nurses of the sick.

No. 8. To make a return to the Guardians, at each

ordinary meeting, in a book prepared according to the Form (Q.) hereunto annexed, and to insert therein the date of every attendance, in conformity with Art. 205, and the other particulars required by such Form to be inserted by the Medical Officer, and to enter in such return the death of every pauper who shall die in the Workhouse, together with the apparent cause thereof.

No. 9. To enter in the commencement of such Book, according to the Form marked (R.) hereunto annexed, the proper dietary for the sick paupers in the house in so many different scales as he shall deem expedient.

DUTIES OF THE MASTER.

Art. 208. The following shall be the duties of the Master:—

No. 1. To admit paupers into the Workhouse, in obedience to the orders specified in Art. 88, and also every person applying for admission who may appear to him to require relief through any sudden or urgent necessity, and to cause every pauper, upon admission, to be examined by the Medical Officer, as is directed in Art. 91.

No. 2. To cause every male pauper above the age of seven years, upon admission, to be searched, cleansed, and clothed, and to be placed in the proper ward.

No. 3. To enforce industry, order, punctuality, and cleanliness, and the observance of all regulations for the government of the workhouse by the paupers, and by the several officers, assistants, and servants therein.

No. 4. To read prayers to the paupers before breakfast and after supper every day, or cause prayers to be read, according to Art. 124.

No. 5. To cause the paupers to be inspected, and their names called over, in conformity with Art. 103, in order that it may be seen that each individual is clean and in a proper state.

No. 6. To provide for and enforce the employment of the able-bodied adult paupers, during the hours of labour; to assist in training the youths in such employment as will best fit them for gaining their own living; to keep the partially disabled paupers occupied to the extent of their ability; and to allow none who are capable of employment to be idle at any time.

No. 7. To visit the sleeping wards of the male paupers at eleven o'clock in the forenoon of every day, and see that such wards have been all duly cleansed and are properly ventilated.

No. 8. To see that the meals of the paupers are duly provided, dressed, and served, according to the directions in Articles 104 and 107, and to superintend the distribution of the food.

No. 9. To say, or cause to be said, grace before and after meals.

No. 10. To visit all the wards of the male paupers before nine o'clock every night in winter, and ten o'clock in summer, and see that all the male paupers are in bed, and that all fires and lights therein are extinguished, except so far as may be necessary for the sick.

No. 11. To receive from the Porter the keys of the Workhouse at nine o'clock every night, and to deliver them to him again at six o'clock every morning, or at such hours as shall from time to time be fixed by the Guardians.

No. 12. To see that the male paupers are properly clothed, and that their clothes are kept in proper repair.

No. 13. To cause the birth of every child born in the Workhouse to be registered by the Registrar of Births and Deaths within the space of one week after such child shall have been born; and also to enter such birth in a register kept according to Form (S.) hereunto annexed.

No. 14. To send for the Medical Officer in case any pauper is taken ill or becomes insane, and to take care that all sick and insane paupers are duly visited by the Medical Officer, and are provided with such medicines and attendance, diet and other necessaries, as the Medical Officer or the Guardians direct, and to apprise the nearest relation in the Workhouse of the sickness of any pauper, and, in the case of dangerous sickness, to send for the Chaplain, and any relative or friend of the pauper, resident within a reasonable distance, whom the pauper may desire to see.

No. 15. To take care that no pauper at the approach of death shall be left unattended either during the day or the night.

No. 16. To give immediate information of the death of any pauper in the Workhouse to the Medical Officer, and to the nearest relations of the deceased who may be known to him, and who may reside within a reasonable distance; and if the body be not removed within a reasonable time, to provide for the interment thereof.

No. 17. When requisite, to cause the death of every pauper dying in the Workhouse to be duly registered by the Registrar of Births and Deaths within five days after the day of such death; and also to enter such death in a register kept according to Form (T.) hereunto annexed.

No. 18. To deliver an inventory of the clothes and any other property of any pauper who may have died in the Workhouse, to the Guardians at their next ordinary meeting.

No. 19. To keep such portion of the Workhouse Medical Relief Book prescribed in this Order as is assigned to him in the Form marked (Q.,) and to keep all books or accounts which he is, or hereafter may be, by any Order of the Commissioners, directed and required to keep, to allow the same to be constantly open to the inspection of any of the Guardians of the Union, and to submit the same to the Guardians at their ordinary meetings.

No. 20. To submit to the Guardians, at every ordinary meeting, an estimate of such provisions and other articles as are required for the use of the Workhouse, and to receive and execute the directions of the Guardians thereupon.

No. 21. To receive all provisions and other articles purchased or procured for the use of the Workhouse, and before placing them in store to examine and compare them with the bills of parcels or invoices severally relating thereto; and after having proved the accuracy of such bills or invoices, to authenticate the same with his signature, and submit them to the Guardians at their next ordinary meeting.

No. 22. To receive and take charge of all provisions, clothing, linen, and other articles belonging to the Workhouse, or confided to his care by the Guardians, and issue the same to the Matron or other persons as may be required.

No. 23. To report to the Guardians from time to time the names of such children as the Schoolmaster may recommend as fit to be put out to service, or other employment, and to take the necessary steps for carrying into effect the directions of the Guardians thereon.

No. 24. To take care that the wards, rooms, larder, kitchen, and all other offices of the Workhouse, and all the utensils and furniture thereof, be kept clean and in good order; and as often as any defect in the same, or in the state of the Workhouse, shall occur, to report the same in writing to the Guardians at their next ordinary meeting.

No. 25. To submit to the Guardians, at every ordinary meeting, a report of the number of the inmates in the Workhouse according to the Form (U.) hereto annexed.

No. 26. To bring before the Visiting Committee or the Guardians any pauper inmate desirous of making a complaint or application to the Guardians.

No. 27. To report forthwith to the Medical Officer and to the Guardians, in writing, all cases in which any restraint or compulsion may have been used towards any pauper inmate of unsound mind in the Workhouse.

No. 28. To keep a book, in which he shall enter all his written reports to the Guardians or to the Medical Officer, and to lay the same before the Guardians at every ordinary meeting.

No. 29. To inform the Visiting Committee and the Guardians of the state of the Workhouse in every department, and to report in writing to the Guardians any negligence or other misconduct on the part of any of the subordinate officers or servants of the establishment; and generally to observe and fulfil all lawful orders and directions of the Guardians suitable to his office.

Art. 209. The Master shall not, except in case of necessity, purchase or procure any articles for the use of the Workhouse, nor order any alterations or repairs of any part of the premises, or of the furniture or other articles belonging thereto, nor pay any monies on account of the Workhouse, or of the Union, without the authority of the Guardians, nor apply any Articles belonging to the Guardians to purposes other than those authorized or approved of by such Guardians.

DUTIES OF THE MATRON.

Art. 210. The following shall be the duties of the Matron:—

No. 1. In the absence of the Master, or during his inability to act, to act as his substitute in the admission of paupers into the Workhouse, according to Articles 88 and 208, Nos. 1 and 2, and to cause every pauper upon such admission to be examined by the Medical Officer, as is directed in Art. 91.

No. 2. To cause the pauper children under the age of seven years, and the female paupers, to be searched, cleansed, and clothed upon their admission, and to be placed in their proper wards.

No. 3. To provide for and enforce the employment of the able-bodied female paupers during the hours of labour, and to keep the partially disabled female paupers occupied to the extent of their ability, and to assist the Schoolmistress in training up the children so as best to fit them for service.

No. 4. To call over the names of the paupers as is directed in Art. 103, to inspect their persons, and see that each individual is clean.

No. 5. To visit the sleeping wards of the female paupers at eleven o'clock of the forenoon of every day, and to see that such wards have been duly cleansed and are properly ventilated.

No. 6. To visit all the wards of the females and children every night before nine o'clock, and to ascertain that all the paupers in such wards are in bed, and all fires and lights not necessary for the sick or for women suckling their children therein extinguished.

No. 7. To pay particular attention to the moral conduct and orderly behaviour of the females and children, and to see that they are clean and decent in their dress and persons.

No. 8. To superintend and give the necessary directions for making and mending the linen and clothing supplied to the male paupers, and all the clothing supplied to the female paupers and children, and to take care that all such clothing be properly numbered and marked on the inside with the name of the Union.

No. 9. To see that every pauper in the Workhouse has clean linen and stockings once a week, and that all the beds and bedding be kept in a clean and wholesome state.

No. 10. To take charge of the linen and stockings for the use of the paupers, and the other linen in use in the Workhouse, and to apply the same to such purposes as shall be authorized or approved of by the Guardians, and to no other.

No. 11. To superintend and give the necessary directions concerning the washing, drying, and getting up of the linen, stockings, and blankets, and to see that the same be not dried in the sleeping wards, or in the sick wards.

No. 12. To take proper care of the children and sick paupers, and to provide proper diet for the same, and for women suckling infants, and to furnish them with such changes of clothes and linen as may be necessary.

No. 13. To assist the Master in the general management and superintendence of the Workhouse, and especially in—

Enforcing the observance of good order, cleanliness, punctuality, industry, and decency of demeanour among the paupers:—

Cleansing and ventilating the sleeping wards and the dining-hall, and all other parts of the premises;—

Placing in store and taking charge of the provisions, clothing, linen, and other articles belonging to the Union.

No. 14. When requested by the Porter in pursuance of Art. 214, No. 5, to search any female entering or leaving the Workhouse under the circumstances described in that Article.

No. 15. To report to the Master any negligence or other misconduct on the part of any of the female officers, or servants of the establishment, or any case in which restraint or compulsion may have been used towards any female inmate of unsound mind.

No. 16. And generally to observe and fulfil all lawful orders and directions of the Guardians suitable to her office.

DUTIES OF THE CHAPLAIN.

Art. 211. The following shall be the duties of the Chaplain:—

No. 1. To read prayers and preach a sermon to the paupers and other inmates of the Workhouse on every Sunday, and on Good Friday and Christmas Day, unless the Guardians, with the consent of the Commissioners, may otherwise direct.

No. 2. To examine the children, and to catechise such as belong to the Church of England, at least once in every month, and to make a record of the same, and state the dates of his attendance, the general progress and condition of the children, and the moral and religious state of the inmates generally, in a book to be kept for that purpose, to be laid before the Guardians at their next ordinary meting, and to be termed "THE CHAPLAIN'S REPORT."

No. 3. To visit the sick paupers, and to administer religious consolation to them in the Workhouse, at such periods as the Guardians may appoint, and when applied to for that purpose by the Master or Matron.

DUTIES OF THE SCHOOLMASTER AND SCHOOLMISTRESS.

Art. 212. The following shall be the duties of the Schoolmaster and Schoolmistress for the Workhouse, or either of them:—

No. 1. To instruct the boys and girls according to the directions in Art. 114.

No. 2. To regulate the discipline and arrangements of the school, and the industrial and moral training of the children, subject to the direction of the Guardians.

No. 3. To accompany the children when they quit the Workhouse for exercise, or for attendance at public worship, unless the Guardians shall otherwise direct.

No. 4. To keep the children clean in their persons, and orderly and decorous in their conduct.

No. 5. To assist the Master and Matron respectively in maintaining due subordination in the Workhouse.

DUTIES OF A NURSE.

Art. 213. The following shall be the duties of a Nurse for the Workhouse:—

No. 1. To attend upon the sick in the sick and lying-in wards, and to administer to them all medicines and medical applications, according to the directions of the Medical Officer.

No. 2. To inform the Medical Officer of any defects which may be observed in the arrangements of the sick or lying-in ward.

No. 3. To take care that a light is kept at night in the sick ward.

DUTIES OF THE PORTER.

Art. 214. The following shall be the duties of the Porter of the Workhouse:—

No. 1. To keep the gate, and to prevent any person not being an officer of the Workhouse, or of the Union, an Assistant Poor Law Commissioner, or any person authorised by law, or by the Commissioners, or Guardians, from entering into or going out of the house without the leave of the Master or Matron.

No. 2. To keep a book in which he shall enter the name and business of every officer or other person who shall go into the Workhouse, and the name of every officer or other person who shall go out thereof, together with the time of such officer's or person's going in or out.

No. 3. To receive all paupers who apply or present themselves for admission in conformity with Art. 88, and if the Master and Matron be both absent, to place such paupers in the receiving ward until the Master or Matron return.

No. 4. To examine all parcels and goods before they are received into the Workhouse, and prevent the admission of any spirituous or fermented liquors, or other articles contrary to any of the regulations contained in this order, or otherwise contrary to law.

No. 5. To search any male pauper entering or leaving the Workhouse whom he may suspect of having possession of any spirits or other prohibited articles, and to require any other person entering the Workhouse whom he may suspect of having possession of any such spirits or prohibited articles, to satisfy him to the contrary before he permit such person to be admitted, and in the case of any female, to cause the Matron to be called for the purpose of searching her, if necessary.

No. 6. To examine all parcels taken by any pauper out of the Workhouse, and to prevent the undue removal of any article from the premises.

No. 7. To lock all the outer doors, and take the keys to the Master, at nine o'clock every night, and to receive them back from him every morning at six o'clock, or at such hours as shall from time to time be fixed by the Guardians; and if any application for admission to the Workhouse be made after the keys shall have been so taken to the Master, to apprise the Master forthwith of such application.

No. 8. To assist the Master and Matron in preserving order, and in enforcing obedience and due subordination in the Workhouse.

No. 9. To inform the Master of all things affecting the security and order of the Workhouse, and to obey all lawful directions of the Master or Matron, and of the Guardians, suitable to his office.

Duties of a Relieving Officer.

Art. 215. The following shall be the duties of a Relieving Officer:—

No. 1. To attend all ordinary meetings of the Guardians, and to attend all other meetings when summoned by the Clerk.

No. 2. To receive all applications for relief made to him within his district, or relating to any parish situated within his district, and forthwith to examine into the circumstances of every case by visiting the house of the applicant (if situated within his district), and by making all necessary inquiries into the state of health, the ability to work, the condition and family, and the means of such applicant, and to report the result of such inquiries in the prescribed form to the Guardians at their next ordinary meeting, and also to visit from time to time as requisite all paupers receiving relief, and to report concerning the same as the Guardians may direct.

No. 3. In any case of sickness or accident requiring relief by medical attendance to procure such attendance by giving an order on the District Medical Officer, in the Form (V.) hereunto annexed, or by such other means as the urgency of the case may require.

No. 4. To ascertain from time to time from the District Medical Officer the names of any poor persons whom such Medical Officer may have attended or supplied with medicines, without having received an order from himself to that effect.

No. 5. In every case of a poor person receiving medical relief, as soon as may be, and from time to time afterwards, to visit the house of such person, and until the next ordinary meeting of the Guardians, to supply such relief (not being in money) as the case on his own view, or on the certificate of the District Medical Officer, may seem to require.

No. 6. In every case of sudden or urgent necessity, to afford such relief to the destitute person as may be requisite, either by giving such person an order of admission into the Workhouse, and conveying him thereto if necessary, or by affording him relief out of the Workhouse, provided that the same be not given in money, whether such destitute person be settled in any Parish comprised in the Union or not.

No. 7. To report to the Guardians at their next ordinary meeting all cases reported to him by an Overseer in conformity with Art. 218, and to obey the directions of the Guardians with reference to the relief administered in such cases.

No. 8. To perform the duties with respect to pauper apprentices prescribed by Arts. 60, 61, and 62.

No. 9. To give all reasonable aid and assistance at the request of any other Relieving Officer of the Union, by examining into the case of any applicant for relief, or administering relief to any pauper whose name has been entered on the books of such other Relieving Officer, and who may be within his own district.

No. 10. Duly and punctually to supply the weekly allowances of all paupers belonging to his district, or being within the same, and to pay or administer the relief of all paupers within his district to the amount and in the manner in which he may have been lawfully ordered by the Guardians to pay or administer the same.

No. 11. To visit, relieve, and otherwise attend to non-settled poor, being within his district, according to the directions of the Guardians, whose officer he is, and in no other way, subject always to the obligation imposed on him in cases of sudden or urgent necessity.

No. 12. To set apart one or more pages in his outdoor relief list, in which he shall duly and punctually enter up the payments made by authority of his own Board of Guardians to non-settled poor, and to take credit for such payments in his receipt and expenditure book.

No. 13. To present his weekly accounts to the Clerk for his inspection and authentication before every ordinary meeting of the Guardians, and to the Guardians, at such meeting, for their approval.

No. 14. To submit to the Auditor of the Union all his books, accounts, and vouchers, at the place of audit, and at such time, and in such manner, as may be required by the Regulations of the Commissioners.

No. 15. To assist the Clerk in conducting and completing the annual or other election of Guardians, according to the Regulations of the Commissioners.

No. 16. To observe and execute all lawful orders and directions of the Guardians applicable to his office.

Art. 216. The Relieving Officer shall in no case take credit in his accounts, or enter as paid or given by way of relief, any money or other articles which have not been paid or given previously to the taking of such credit, or the making of such entry; and he shall not take credit in such accounts for any money paid to any tradesman or other person without producing, at the next ordinary meeting of the Guardians, a bill from such tradesman or person with voucher of payment.

DUTIES OF A SUPERINTENDENT OF OUT-DOOR LABOUR.

Art. 217. The duties of a Superintendent of Out-door Labour shall be to superintend any able-bodied paupers not inmates of the Workhouse who may be set to work by the Guardians, to take care that they perform the work respectively assigned to them, and to report truly to the Guardians respecting the performance of such work.

RECEIPT AND PAYMENT OF MONEY BY OFFICERS.

Art. 218. No Clerk, Relieving Officer, Master, or other officer appointed to or holding any office under this Order, shall, directly or indirectly, receive or bargain to receive any gratuity, per-centage, or allowance of any kind with reference to any contract with the Guardians, or in respect of any payment made or to be made for goods supplied or work executed according to the order of such Guardians or on their behalf.

Art. 219. No Clerk shall directly or indirectly cause to be paid to himself, or shall pay away on his own account or for his own benefit, any cheque drawn by the Guardians, and made payable to any person other than himself.

Art. 220. Every Clerk receiving any cheque or money from the Guardians on account of any other party, shall transmit the same within fourteen days to the proper persons, and shall produce the receipt or acknowledgment for the same at the next ordinary meeting after the same has come to his hands.

Art. 221. Every officer of the Union who may receive money on behalf of the Guardians thereof, shall forthwith pay the same into the hands of the Treasurer of the Union, to the credit of the Guardians, notwithstanding that any salary or balance may be due from the Union to such officer.

Art. 222. No Relieving Officer, or other officer of any Guardians, nor any Assistant Overseer or Collector, shall receive money for the relief of any non-settled pauper on behalf of any officer, or of the Guardians, of any other Parish or Union, or shall constitute himself in any way the agent of any officer or Guardians of such other Parish or Union, except as is provided in this Order.

Art. 223. If any money be transmitted to any officer, contrary to the provisions of this Order, such officer shall forthwith pay such money into the hands of the Treasurer of the Union whose officer he is, and shall report to the Guardians at their next meeting the fact that such money has been so received and paid, and shall make a true entry accordingly in his accounts.

EXPLANATION OF TERMS.

Art. 224. Whenever the word "Parish" is used in this Order, it shall be taken to include any place maintaining its own poor, whether parochial or extra-parochial.

Art. 225. Whenever the word "Overseer" is used in this Order, it shall be taken to include any person acting, or legally bound to act in the discharge of any of the duties usually performed by Overseers of the Poor, so far as such duties are referred to in this Order.

Art. 226. Whenever the word "Commissioners" is used in this Order, it shall be taken to mean the Poor Law Commissioners.

Art. 227. Whenever the word "medicines" is used in this Order, it shall be taken to include all medical and surgical appliances; whenever the words "medical attendance" are used in this Order, they shall be taken to include surgical attendance; and whenever the words "medical relief" are used in this Order, they shall be taken to include relief by surgical as well as medical attendance.

Art. 228. Whenever the words "Medical Officer" are used in this Order, they shall be taken to include any person duly licensed as a medical man, who may have contracted or agreed with any Guardians for the supply of medicines, or for medical attendance.

Art. 229. Whenever the words Clerk, Master, or Matron are used in this Order, they shall be taken to mean the Clerk to the Guardians, and the Master or Matron of the Workhouse respectively.

Art. 230. The term "non-resident poor" in this Order shall be taken to mean all paupers in receipt of relief allowed on account of any Union in relation to which the term is used, but not residing therein.

Art. 231. The term "non-settled poor" in this Order shall be taken to mean all paupers residing in the Union in relation to which the term is used, but to whom relief is allowed on account of some Parish or Union other than that in which they reside.

Art. 232. Whenever in describing any person or party, matter or thing, the word importing the singular number or the masculine gender only is used in this Order, the same shall be taken to include, and shall be applied to, several persons or parties as well as one person or party, and females as well as males, and several matters or things as well as one matter or thing, respectively, unless there be something in the subject or context repugnant to such construction.

Art. 233. Whenever in this Order any Article is referred to by its number, the Article of this Order bearing that number shall be taken to be signified thereby.

FORM (A.)

Election of Guardians of the Poor.

____________________ UNION.

I, Clerk to the Guardians of the Poor of the Union, with reference to the ensuing Election of Guardians of the Poor for the several Parishes in the said Union, do hereby give notice—

1. That the number of Guardians of the Poor to be elected for the Parishes in the said Union is as follows :—
   For the Parish of One Guardian.
   For the Parish of Two Guardians.

2.—That any person not otherwise disqualified by law who shall be rated to the Poor-rate in any Parish in the Union, in respect of hereditaments of the annual rental of pounds, is qualified to be nominated for the Office of Guardian at the said Election, by any person then qualified to vote.

3.—Nominations of Guardians must be made according to the form below, which is the form prescribed by the Poor Law Commissioners. Such nominations must be sent, on or before the day of *March*, to me or to Mr. at for the Parish of , or to Mr. at for the Parish of , who alone are authorised to receive the same. Nominations sent after that day, or sent to any other person, will be invalid.

4.—That I shall, if more than the above-mentioned number of Guardians be nominated for any Parish, cause Voting Papers to be delivered on the day of , at the address in such Parish of each Rate-payer, Owner, and Proxy qualified to vote; and that on the day of I shall cause such Voting Papers to be collected.

5.—That on the day of I shall attend at the Board Room of this Union at the hour of and that I shall on that day, and, if necessary, the following days, proceed to ascertain the number of votes given for each candidate.

6.—That any person put in nomination for the Office of Guardian may, at any time during the proceedings in the Election, tender to me in writing his refusal to serve the Office, and the Election, so far as regards that person, will be no further proceeded with.

Form of Nomination Paper.

Parish of____________________ }
____________________ UNION. } This day of 184 .

Names of Persons nominated to be Guardians.	Residence of the Persons nominated.	Quality or Calling of Persons nominated.

I, being* duly qualified to vote in the Parish aforesaid, nominate the above to be Guardian (*or* Guardians) for the said Parish.

____________________ Signature } of Nominator.
____________________ Address }

* *Note.*—Only one person is empowered to sign this paper, and after the word *being* he must insert (*a rate-payer*) or (*owner of property*) according to his qualification.

Given under my hand, this day of 184 .

____________________ Clerk to Guardians to the Poor of the Union.

FORM (B.)

Nomination Paper.

Parish of ______________ }
______________ UNION. }

This day of 184 .

Names of Persons nominated to be Guardians.	Residence of the Persons nominated.	Quality or Calling of Persons nominated.

I, being* duly qualified to vote in the Parish aforesaid, nominate the above to be Guardian (*or* Guardians) for the said Parish.

______________ Signature } of Nominator.
______________ Address }

* *Note.*—Only one Person is empowered to sign this Paper, and after the word *being* he must insert (*a rate-payer*) or (*owner of property*,) according to his qualification.

FORM (C.)

Voting Paper.

______________ UNION. Voting Paper for the Parish of

No. of Voting Paper.	Name and Address of Voter.	Number of Votes.	
		As Owner.	As Rate-payer.

Directions to the Voters.

The Voter is entitled to vote for ______________ Guardian (*or* Guardians,) and no more.

The Voter must write his initials against the name of every person for whom he votes, and must sign this Paper.

If the Voter cannot write, he must affix his mark, but such mark must be attested, and the name of the Voter filled in, by a witness, and such witness must write the initials of the Voter against the name of every person for whom the Voter intends to vote.

If a Proxy vote, he must in like manner write his own initials, sign his own name, and state in writing the name of the person for whom he is Proxy: thus—*John Smith* for *Richard Williams.*

This Paper must be carefully preserved by the Voter, as no second Paper will be given. When it is filled up, it must be kept ready for delivery to Mr. , who will call for the same on the day of . No other person is authorised to receive the Voting Paper.

If the Voting Paper be not ready for the person appointed to collect it when called for, the Vote will be lost. It will also be lost if more than name be returned in the List, with the initials of the Voter placed against such name , or if the Voting Paper be not signed by the Voter, or if the mark of the Voter be not attested when attestation is required.

Initials of the Voter against the Name of the Person for whom he intends to vote.	Names of the Persons nominated as Guardians.	Residence of the Persons nominated.	Quality or Calling of the Persons nominated.	Names of the Nominators.	Address of the Nominators.	Opinion of the Clerk as to Disqualification.

I vote for the Persons in the above List, against whose Names my initials are placed.

(Signed) ______________

(*Place for the mark*) ______________ Voter's Name ______________

Witness to the mark ______________

or ______________ for ______________

FORM (D.)

Notice to Guardians elected.

______________ UNION.

Parish of ______________

Sir,—I do hereby give you notice, and declare, that you have been duly elected a Guardian of the Poor for the Parish of in the Union, and that the next meeting of the Board of Guardians of the said Union will be held at on next, at the hour of

Signed this day of

______________ Clerk to the Guardians of the Poor of the Union.

To Mr. ______________ of

FORM (E.)

__________ UNION.

I do hereby certify, that the Election of Guardians of the Poor for the several Parishes in the Union was conducted in conformity with the Order of the Poor Law Commissioners, and that the Entries contained in the Schedule hereunder written are true.

Parishes (arranged alphabetically.)	Names of Persons nominated as Guardians.	Residence.	Quality or Calling.	No. of Votes given for each Candidate.	Names of the Guardians elected.	Names of the Guardians qualified to act in the Parishes where no Guardian has been elected.

Given under my hand this day of

__________ Clerk to the Guardians of the Poor of the Union.

FORM (F.)

To the Clerk of the Guardians of the Union.

REQUISITION FOR AN EXTRAORDINARY MEETING OF GUARDIANS.

We the undersigned, being two of the Guardians of the Poor of the Union, do hereby require an Extraordinary Meeting of the Guardians of the said Union to be summoned, to be holden at on the day of 18 , at o'clock in the forenoon, to take into consideration [*set out the business.*]

__________ } Guardians.
____

FORM (G.)

Notice of Change of Period, Time, or Place of Meeting.

A.B. Guardian of the Poor of the Union. __________ day of __________ 184

Sir,—You are hereby informed, that the next Ordinary Meeting of the Guardians of the Poor of the Union will take place at on day the day of 18 , at o'clock in the noon, for the transaction of business; and that the ordinary Meetings of the said Guardians will henceforth be held [*weekly or fortnightly, as the case may be.*] at the same place, on the same day of the week, and at the same hour.

__________ Signature of Clerk to the Guardians.

FORM (H.)

Notice of an Adjourned Meeting of Guardians.

To *A.B.* Guardian of the Poor of the Union. __________ day of __________ 184

Sir,—This is to give you notice, that an adjourned Meeting of the Guardians of the Poor of the Union will be held at on the day of 18 , which meeting you are hereby requested to attend.

__________ Signature of Clerk to the Guardians.

FORM (I.)

Notice of an Extraordinary Meeting of Guardians.

To *A. B.* Guardian of the Poor of the Union. __________ day of __________ 184

Sir,—I am directed by *C. D.* and *E. F.*, two of the Guardians of the Poor of the Union, to summon an Extraordinary Meeting of the Guardians of the Poor of the said Union, at on the day of 18 , at o'clock in the forenoon, to take into consideration [*set out the business,*] which meeting you are hereby requested to attend.

__________ Signature of Clerk to the Guardians.

FORM (K.)

Out-Relief Ticket.

__________ UNION.

Weekly Relief ordered the day of 184

Name.	Money.	Loaves, lb. each.	For what Period.
	Other Articles.		

__________ Signature of Relieving Officer.

FORM (L.)

Ticket for Permanent Medical List.

_______________ UNION.

Date_______________

Good until the_______________day of_______________184

Name of Pauper_______________

Residence of Pauper_______________

Name of Medical Officer_______________

Residence_______________

Usual hour at which he is at home_______________

FORM (M.)

Order for Contributions.

To *A.B.* and *C.D.*, Overseers (*or**) of the Parish of

You are hereby ordered and directed to pay to *F.G.*, of on behalf of the Guardians of the Poor of the Union, on the day of [*or* in the following manner, that is to say,] at the sum of Pounds Shillings and Pence, from the Poor Rates of the Parish of towards the relief of the Poor thereof and to the contribution of the Parish to the common fund of the Union, and such other expenses as are chargeable by the said Guardians on the said Parish, and to take the receipt of the said *F.G.*, indorsed upon this paper, for the said sum of

Given under our hands, at a meeting of the Guardians of the Poor of the said Union, held on the day of 18

(Signed) *X.Y.* Presiding Chairman.

W.X. } Guardians.
U.V. }

_______________Countersignature of the Clerk to the Guardians.

* Here insert the names of any parties in the Parish authorised to make the Poor Rate in place of the Overseers.

FORM (N.)

	Time of Rising.	Interval for Breakfast.	Time for Work.	Interval for Dinner.	Time for Work.	Interval for Supper.	Time for going to Bed.
From 25th March to 29th Sept.	¼ before 6	From ½ past 6 to 7	From 7 to 12	From 12 to 1	From 1 to 6	From 6 to 7	8 o'clock.
From 29th Sept. to 25th March.	¼ before 7	From ½ past 7 to 8	From 8 to 12	From 12 to 1	From 1 to 6	From 6 to 7	8 o'clock.

FORM (O.)

Workhouse Punishment Book.

No. of the Case.	Name.	Offence.	Date of Offence.	Punishment inflicted by Master or other Officer.	Opinion of the Guardians thereon.	Punishment ordered by Board of Guardians.	Date of Punishment.	Initials of Clerk.	Observations.

FORM (P.)

District Medical Relief Book.

Week ending day of 184 .

Name.	Age.	Residence.	Parish to which chargeable.	Nature of Disease.	Days when attended, or when Medicines were furnished.*							Necessaries ordered to be given to the Patient.	Present State or Termination of the Case.	Observations.
					S.	M.	T.	W.	Th.	F.	Sat.			

* Attendances at the Patient's own house are to be denoted by the letter (H.) Attendances at the Surgery or Medical Officer's residence, by the letter (S.) Medicine supplied without seeing the patient by the letter (M.) Any attendance given by a substitute or other person, instead of the Medical Officer, is to be entered in *red* ink.

FORM (Q.)

Workhouse Medical Relief Book.

(A.) To be filled up by the Medical Officer.

Initials of Medical Officer in attendance on every Case.	Name of the Sick Pauper.	When admitted to Sick Ward.	When discharged.	Nature of Disease.	Days when attended.							Males. The No.* of the Dietary on which placed.							Females. The No.* of the Dietary on which placed.							Extras. What ordered.	Extras. When ordered.	Extras. When discontinued.	State or Termination of the Case, and in the event of Death, the apparent Cause thereof.
					S.	M.	T.	W.	Th.	F.	Sat.	S.	M.	T.	W.	Th.	F.	Sat.	S.	M.	T.	W.	Th.	F.	Sat.				
					Total No. each Day																								Total Quantity consumed

(B.) To be filled up by the Master of the Workhouse, with the Articles actually given.

Quantity of Provisions consumed.											Extras provided.									Remarks.
Bread.	Meat.	Bacon.	Cheese.	Rice.	Oatmeal.	Milk.					Ale.	Porter.	Wine.	Brandy.	Gin.					
lbs.	lbs.	lbs.	lbs.	lbs.	lbs.	pts.					pts.	pts.	pts.	pts.	pts.					

* The Dietaries for the Sick are to be numbered thus:—No. 1. House Diet. No. 2. Full Diet. No. 3. Low Diet. No. 4. Fever Diet.

As regards the sick Paupers on Diet No. 1. (House Diet) the extras only should be entered in this Book, since their ordinary Diet will appear in the "Daily Provisions Consumption Account," for which see Form 26 of the General Order of the Commissioners, bearing date the 17th day of March, 1847.

The Number of the Paupers on each description of the Dietaries and according to the several Sexes is to be carried by the Master at the close of each week to a Summary at the end of the book, to be prepared in the following form:—

WEEKLY SUMMARY.

No. of the Dietary.	Description of Classes in the Diet Table.	Number of Patients each Day. S.	M.	T.	W.	Th.	F.	Sat.	Collective Number of Days.
1	House Diet.—Males								
1	House Diet.—Females								
2	Full Diet.—Males								
2	Full Diet.—Females								
3	Low Diet.—Males								
3	Low Diet.—Females								
4	Fever Diet.—Males								
4	Fever Diet.—Females								
	Total Number of sick Paupers........								

FORM (R.)

DIETARY FOR SICK PAUPERS.

No. 1.	House Diet, being the ordinary diet for the paupers in the house.									
No. 2.		BREAKFAST.		DINNER.					SUPPER.	
2	Full Diet									
		ounces.	pints.	ounces.	pints.	ounces.	ounces.	pints.	ounces.	pints.
2	Males									
2	Females									
		BREAKFAST.		DINNER.					SUPPER.	
3	Low Diet									
		ounces.	pints.	ounces.	pints.	ounces.	ounces.	pints.	ounces.	pints.
3	Males									
3	Females									
		BREAKFAST.		DINNER.					SUPPER.	
4	Fever Diet									
		ounces.	pints.	ounces.	pints.	ounces.	ounces.	pints.	ounces.	pints.
4	Males									
4	Females									

N.B.—Sugar, Arrow Root, Sago, Butter, Milk, Wine, Spirits, Porter, and Beer, are in all cases to be treated as extras, to be expressly ordered when required, and the quantity is to be then specified in the proper column of this book.

* If thought proper by the Medical Officer any additional number of dietaries may be introduced, and numbered consecutively.

FORM (S.)

____________ UNION. *Register of Births in* ____________ *Workhouse.*

Date of Birth.	Whether Male or Female.	Name of Parents, or Mother.	To what Parish chargeable.	When baptized.	In what Name baptized.	Remarks.

FORM (T.)

____________ UNION. *Register of Deaths in* ____________ *Workhouse.*

Date of Death.	Name.	Age.	To what Parish chargeable.

FORM (U.)

____________ Union Workhouse.

Week ending 184 .

WARDS.	Beds therein.	Number of Occupants each Night. S.	M.	T.	W.	Th.	F.	Sat.	Total.	Observations.
Able-bodied Men										
Old Men										
Boys										
Male Infirmary										
—— Infectious										
—— Receiving										
Total ...										
Able-bodied Women...										
Old Women..............										
Girls										
Female Infirmary										
Lying-in Ward										
Female Infectious......										
—— Receiving										
Total......										

The foregoing is a true statement.

____________ Master.

____________ Matron.

FORM (V.)—*The Medical Relief Order Check Book.*

No.________

To________________, Medical Officer.

Name,____________________________
Age,____________________________
Residence,________________________
Nature of Case,____________________

Forwarded by ____________________ at________o'clock in the_______ of the_______day of____ 184 .

________________Relieving Officer.

No.

To__________, Medical Officer,__________ Union.

Sir,

You are hereby requested to visit and undertake the treatment of the under-mentioned case.

Name,____________________________
Age,____________________________
Residence,________________________
Nature of Case,*____________________

Forwarded by____________________at________o'clock in the________of the_____day of________184

________________Relieving Officer.

* This is to be filled up so as to distiuguish—
1. Midwifery Cases.
2. Fractures and Accidents.
3. Cases of urgency, which require immediate attention.

SCHEDULE, *containing the Names of the Unions to which the annexed Order applies.*

Aberaeron.
Abergavenny.
Aberystwith.
Abingdon.
Albans, St.
Alcester.
Alderbury.
Alnwick.
Alresford.
Alton.
Altrincham.
Amersham.
Amesbury.
Ampthill.
Andover.
Anglesea.
Asaph, St.
Ashbourne.
Ashby de la Zouch.
Ashford, East.
Ashford, West.
Ashton-under-
Aston. [Lyne.
Atcham.
Atherstone.
Auckland.
Austell, St.
Axbridge.
Axminster.
Aylesbury.
Aylsham.
Bakewell.
Bala.
Banbury.
Bangor and Beau-
Barnet. [maris.
Barnstaple.
Barrow-upon-Soar.
Basford.
Basingstoke.
Bath.
Battle.
Beaminster.
Bedale.
Bedford.
Bedminster.
Belford.
Bellingham.
Belper.
Berkhampstead.
Berwick-upon-
Beverley. [Tweed.
Bicester.
Bideford.
Biggleswade.
Billericay.
Billesdon.
Bingham.
Bishop Stortford.
Blaby.
Blackburn.
Blandford.
Blean.
Blofield.
Blything.
Bodmin.
Bolton.
Bootle. [Claydon.
Bosmere and
Boston.
Broughton, Great.
Bourn.

Brackley.
Bradfield.
Bradford (Wilts.)
Bradford (Yorks.)
Braintree.
Brampton.
Brecknock.
Brentford.
Bridge. [bridge.
Bridgend and Cow-
Bridgwater.
Bridgnorth.
Bridlington.
Bridport.
Brixworth.
Bromley.
Bromsgrove.
Bromyard.
Buckingham.
Builth.
Buntingford.
Burnley.
Burton-upon-Trent
Bury.
Caistor.
Calne.
Cambridge.
Camelford.
Cardiff.
Cardigan.
Carlisle.
Carmarthen.
Carnarvon.
Castle Ward.
Catherington.
Caxton and Arring-
Cerne. [ton.
Chailey.
Chapel-en-le-Frith.
Chard.
Cheadle.
Clelmsford.
Cheltenham.
Chepstow.
Chertsey.
Chesterfield.
Chester-le-Street.
Chesterton.
Chippenham.
Chipping Norton.
Chipping Sodbury.
Chorley.
Chorlton.
Christchurch.
Church Stretton.
Cirencester.
Cleobury Mortimer
Clifton.
Clitheroe.
Clun.
Clutton.
Cockermouth.
Colchester.
Columb St. Major.
Congleton.
Conway.
Cookham.
Corwen.
Cosford.
Cranbrook.
Crediton.
Crickhowel.

Cricklade and
Wootton Bassett.
Croydon.
Cuckfield.
Darlington.
Dartford.
Daventry.
Depwade.
Derby.
Devizes.
Dewsbury.
Docking.
Dolgelly.
Doncaster.
Dorchester.
Dore.
Dorking.
Dover.
Downham.
Drayton.
Driffield.
Droitwich.
Droxford.
Dudley.
Dulverton.
Dunmow.
Durham.
Dursley.
Easington.
Easingwold.
Eastbourne.
East Grinstead.
Easthampstead.
East Retford.
Eastry.
East Ward.
Ecclesall Bierlow.
Edmonton.
Elham.
Ellesmere.
Ely.
Epping.
Epsom.
Erpingham.
Eton.
Evesham.
Faith, St.
Falmouth.
Fareham.
Faringdon.
Farnham.
Faversham.
Festiniog.
Foleshill.
Fordingbridge.
Freebridge Lynn.
Frome.
Fulham.
Fylde.
Gainsborough.
Garstang.
Gateshead.
Germans, St.
Glanford Brigg.
Glendale.
Glossop.
Gloucester.
Godstone.
Goole.
Grantham. [ton.
Gravesend and Mil-
Greenwich.

Guildford.
Guiltcross.
Guisborough.
Hackney.
Hailsham.
Halifax.
Halstead.
Haltwhistle.
Hambledon.
Hardingstone.
Hartismere.
Hartley Wintney.
Haslingden.
Hastings.
Hatfield.
Havant.
Haverfordwest.
Hay.
Hayfield.
Headington. [moor
Helmsley Black-
Helston.
Hemel Hempstead
Hendon.
Henley.
Henstead.
Hereford.
Hertford.
Hexham. [Swindon.
Highworth and
Hinckley.
Hitchin.
Holbeach.
Holborn.
Hollingbourn.
Holmsworthy.
Holywell.
Honiton.
Hoo.
Horncastle.
Horsham.
Houghton-le-
Howden. [Spring.
Hoxne.
Huddersfield.
Hungerford.
Huntingdon.
Hursley.
Ipswich.
Ives, St.
Keighley.
Kendal.
Kettering.
Kenysham.
Kidderminster.
Kingsbridge.
Kingsclere.
King's Lynn.
King's Norton.
Kingston-upon-
Knighton. [Thames
Lampeter.
Lancaster.
Lanchester.
Langport.
Launceston.
Ledbury.
Leek.
Leicester.
Leigh.
Leighton Buzzard.
Leominster.

Lewes.
Lewisham.
Lexden and Wins-
Leyburn. [tree.
Lichfield.
Lincoln.
Linton.
Liskeard.
Llandilo Fawr.
Llandovery.
Llanelly.
Llanfyllin.
Llanrwst. [ing.
Loddon and Claver-
London, City of.
London, East.
London, West.
Longtown.
Loughborough.
Louth.
Ludlow.
Luton.
Lutterworth.
Lymington.
Macclesfield.
Machynlleth.
Madeley.
Maidstone.
Maldon.
Malling.
Malmsbury.
Malton.
Manchester.
Mansfield.
Market Bosworth.
Market Harboro'
Marlborough.
Martley.
Medway.
Melksham.
Melton Mowbray.
Mere.
Meriden.
Merthyr Tydvil.
Midhurst.
Mildenhall.
Milton.
Miftord and Laun-
Monmouth. [ditch.
Morpeth.
Nantwich.
Narberth.
Neath.
Neot's, St.
Newark.
Newbury. [Emlyn.
Newcastle-in-
Newcastle-under-
Lyne.
Newcastle-upon-
Newent. [Tyne.
New Forest.
Newhaven.
Newmarket.
Newport (Monmouth.)
Newport (Salop.)
Newport Pagnell.
Newton Abbot.
Newtown and
Llanidloes.
Northallerton.

Northampton.
North Aylesford.
Northleach.
Northwich.
North Witchford.
Nottingham.
Nuneaton.
Oakham.
Okehampton.
Olave's, St.
Ongar.
Ormskirk.
Orsett.
Oundle.
Pateley Bridge.
Patrington.
Pembroke.
Penkridge.
Penrith.
Penzance.
Pershore.
Peterborough.
Petersfield.
Petworth.
Pewsey.
Pickering.
Plomesgate.
Plympton St. Mary.
Pocklington.
Pont-y-pool.
Poole.
Poplar.
Portsea Island.
Potterspury.
Prescot.
Presteigne.
Preston.
Pwllheli.
Radford.
Reading.
Redruth.
Reeth.
Reigate.
Rhayader.
Richmond (Surrey.)
Richmond (York-
Ringwood. [shire.)
Risbridge.
Rochdale.
Rochford.
Romford.
Romney Marsh.
Romsey.
Ross.
Rothbury.
Rotherham.
Royston.
Rugby.
Runcorn.
Ruthin.
Rye.
Saffron Walden.
Salford.
Saviour's, St.
Scarborough.
Sculcoates.
Sedbergh.
Sedgefield.
Seisdon.
Selby.
Settle.
Sevenoaks.

Shaftesbury.
Shardlow.
Sheffield.
Sheppy.
Shepton Mallett.
Sherborne,
Shiffnal.
Shipston-upon-
Skipton. [Stour.
Skirlaugh.
Sleaford.
Solihull.
Southam.
South Molton.
South Shields.
South Stoneham.
Southwell.
Spalding.
Spilsby.
Stafford.
Staines.
Stamford.
Stepney.
Steyning.
Stockbridge.
Stockport.
Stockton.
Stokesley.
Stone.
Stourbridge.
Stow.
Stow-on-the-Wold.
Strand.
Stratford-upon-
Stratton. [Avon.
Stroud.
Sturminster.
Sudbury.
Sunderland.
Swaffham.
Swansea.
Tamworth.
Taunton.
Tavistock.
Teesdale.
Tenbury.
Tendring.
Tenterden.
Tetbury.
Tewkesbury.
Thakeham.
Thame.
Thanet, Isle of
Thetford.
Thingoe.
Thirsk.
Thomas, St.
Thornbury.
Thorne.
Thrapston.
Ticehurst.
Tisbury.
Tiverton.
Todmorden.
Tonbridge.
Torrington.
Totnes.
Towcester.
Tregaron.
Truro.
Tynemouth.
Uckfield.

Ulverstone.
Uppingham.
Upton-upon-Severn
Uttoxeter.
Uxbridge.
Wakefield.
Wallingford.
Walsal.
Walsingham.
Wandsworth and
Clapham.
Wangford.
Wantage.
Ware.
Wareham and Pur-
Warminster. [beck.
Warrington.
Warwick.
Watford.
Wayland.
Weardale.
Wellingborough.
Wellington (Salop.)
Wellington (Somer-
Wells. [set.)
Welwyn.
Wem.
Weobly.
Westbourne.
West Bromwich.
Westbury-upon-
Severn.
Westbury and
Whorwelsdown.
West Derby.
West Firle.
West Ham.
West Hampnett.
West Ward.
Weymouth.
Wheatenhurst.
Whitby.
Whitchurch.
Whitechapel.
Whitehaven.
Wigan.
Wigton.
Williton.
Wilton. [Cranborne
Wimborne and
Wincanton.
Winchcombe.
Winchester, New.
Windsor.
Winslow.
Wirrall.
Wisbeach.
Witham.
Witney.
Woburn.
Wokingham.
Wolstanton and
Burslem.
Wolverhampton.
Woodbridge.
Woodstock.
Worcester.
Worksop.
Wortley.
Wrexham.
Wycombe.
eovil. York.

Given under our Hands and Seal of Office, this Twenty-fourth day of July, in the year One thousand eight hundred and forty-seven.

(Signed) GEO. NICHOLLS.
GEORGE CORNEWALL LEWIS.
EDMUND W. HEAD.

L. S.

AN

OFFICIAL CIRCULAR

OF PUBLIC DOCUMENTS AND INFORMATION:

DIRECTED BY THE POOR LAW COMMISSIONERS TO BE PRINTED, CHIEFLY FOR THE USE OF THE MEMBERS AND PERMANENT OFFICERS OF BOARDS OF GUARDIANS UNDER THE POOR LAW AMENDMENT ACT.

No. 9.] CIRCULAR ISSUED SEPTEMBER 1, 1847. [N.S.

Poor Law Commission Office,
Somerset House,
September 1st, 1847.

THE Poor Law Commissioners directed that the following documents be printed and circulated for the information of Guardians and Officers of the several Unions, viz.

(Signed) By order of the Board,
EDWIN CHADWICK, *Secretary.*

I.—ACCOUNTS — OUT-RELIEF OUT OF THE WORKHOUSE STORES, HOW TO BE BROUGHT INTO ACCOUNT—NEW GENERAL ORDER.

Aug. 6th, 1847.

Clerk of Hatfield Union—It has been the practice of the guardians from the formation of the union, to give the greater part of the out-door relief allowed by them, in *kind;* and the whole of such relief is taken from the workhouse stores, in order that the applicants for relief may be supplied with the various articles at contract prices. The guardians would be unwilling to depart from this plan, but they observe that the Forms in the new Order of Accounts are inapplicable to such a plan of relief, and they wish, therefore, to have the Commissioners' instructions on the subject.

Ans.—Though the Forms as set forth in the new Order of Accounts are framed to meet the common ordinary supply of relief, and, therefore, the master's books apply to the supply of provisions to the in-door poor, there is nothing to prevent the introduction of other matters into the books, where provisions are supplied to other parties. The Commissioners see no objection to the master inserting the quantity of provisions given out of the workhouse stores during every week for out-door relief in Form 26, after the entry for the sick, and in such case the total to be carried to the "Provisions Receipt and Consumption Account" (Form 27) will consist of the quantities consumed in the house, and that consumed in out-door relief; or, if it be considered more convenient, an intermediate total, showing the quantity of provisions consumed in the house, as in the old forms, might be made. To that must then be added the amount expended in out-door relief, and the gross total will then go on, through Forms 27 and 28, the value of the whole amount when carried to the ledger will, as heretofore, be distributed between in-maintenance and out-door relief, according to the separate amounts.

II.—BURIAL.

1. COST OF THE BURIAL OF A PERSON DYING IN AN INFIRMARY.

April 21st, 1847.

Clerk of Atcham Union—The Salop Infirmary is situate in the parish of St. Mary, in the borough of Shrewsbury, which parish does not form a part of the Atcham Union. The infirmary is supported by voluntary contributions, each subscriber having the right of sending one or more patients annually, according to the amount of the subscription paid. The Atcham Union does not subscribe to the infirmary. A poor person, residing in the Atcham Union, but not in receipt of relief, was received into the infirmary on the recommendation of a subscriber. After a few weeks' residence in the infirmary, the patient died, and application was made by the officers of the institution to the clerk of the Atcham Union for an undertaking to pay the expenses of the funeral in St. Mary's. Requested the Commissioners' advice upon the subject.

Ans.—There is no legal liability upon the Atcham Union to pay the expense in question; on the contrary, the trustees of the infirmary were bound to bury the deceased at their own cost, and not the parish of St. Mary, in which the infirmary is situated. This was decided by the case of Q. *v.* Stewart, 10 A. & E. 773.

2. MAXIMUM SUMS FIXED BY GUARDIANS FOR THE EXPENSES OF PAUPER FUNERALS.

June 15th, 1847.

——— *Union*—A representation having been made to the Commissioners of the inconvenience that resulted from a resolution passed by the board of guardians of the ——— Union, fixing the maximum sum to be allowed for the expenses of a pauper funeral at 27*s.*, (as in cases where the paupers were buried in other parishes than those in which death occurred, double fees were charged,) the Commissioners stated, in reply thereto, that they did not think it right for the guardians to fix a maximum sum for the expenses of pauper funerals, if thereby they could not discharge the fees legally payable on the interment of such paupers.

III.—CONSTABLES—WHETHER THE CHARGES OF SUPERINTENDING CONSTABLE ARE PAYABLE OUT OF THE POOR-RATES.

March 11th, 1847.

Clerk to Magistrates, Amersham—The district auditor has refused to allow a bill incurred by J. L., a superintending constable, (appointed under the 5 & 6 Vic. c. 109) in endeavouring to find out, at the instance of Mr. G., a person who had stolen a sheep belonging to him. J. L. was appointed superintending constable for the hundred of A., and the several parishes in the hundred of B., at a salary of £75 per annum. Inquired whether the bill can be lawfully paid out of the poor-rates.

Ans.—The Commissioners observe that J. L. is a superintending constable, appointed under the 23rd sec. of the 5th and 6th Vic. c. 109. That section provides that a superintending constable "shall have all the powers and immunities of a parish constable under this Act;" but these terms do not confer upon him the rights of a parish constable with respect to remuneration. Indeed, the section afterwards expressly directs that he shall receive a salary out of the county rates. On the other hand, the 17th section provides, in terms, for the payment of fees and allowances to "any constable appointed under this Act;" and it appears impossible to say that a superintending constable, appointed under the 23rd section, does not come within that description. The Commissioners have had occasion to consult counsel on a similar question relating to such parish constables as are paid by salary under sections 18 and 20 of the Act; and they have been advised that fees and allowances may be paid under the 17th section to such constables, where the salary is not fixed to be in lieu of all fees and allowances. The Commissioners presume that the like opinion would apply to the case of superintending constables. But under the 17th section, fees and allowances can only be granted "for the service of summonses and execution of warrants, and for the performance of such other occasional duties which may be required of the said constables." As there was no service of a summons or execution of a warrant in the present case, nor any performance of a duty required of the constable by the justices, (J. L. having been apparently employed by Mr. G. himself,) the Commissioners do not see on what ground any claim for compensation from the poor-rates, under the 17th section, can be sustained. It appears to the Commissioners that the transaction was altogether a private one; and that, consequently, the party who employed J. L. is probably responsible for payment.

IV.—EDUCATION OF POOR CHILDREN—THE EDUCATION OF OUT-DOOR POOR CHILDREN CANNOT BE PROVIDED FOR FROM THE POOR-RATES.

February 3rd, 1847.

Overseers of Thurgoland, Wortley Union—It has been customary for the overseers of Thurgoland to pay one guinea quarterly to a schoolmaster in the township for the education of six poor children. As the district auditor objects to allow the charge in the overseers accounts, requested the Commissioners' instructions for their guidance in future.

Ans.—The Commissioners are not aware of any provision in the law which authorises a charge on the poor-rates for the purpose of providing education for the children of the out-door poor. When pauper children are maintained in a workhouse, the board of guardians may make due arrangements for their instruction, and the Commissioners, by section 15 of the Poor Law Amendment Act, are expressly empowered to issue regulations for the education of such children. But as regards the out-door poor, however desirable an object it may be to extend the advantages of education to them, this cannot lawfully be done at the expense of the poor-rates.

V.—ELECTION OF GUARDIANS.

1. GENERAL ORDER RELATING TO THE PAYMENT OF THE EXPENSES OF.

To the Guardians of the Poor of the several Unions named in the Schedules hereunto annexed;—

To the Churchwardens and Overseers of the Poor of the several Parishes comprised in the said several Unions;—

To the Clerk or Clerks to the Justices of the Petty Sessions held for the Division or Divisions in which the said several Unions are situate;—

And to all others whom it may concern.

We, the Poor Law Commissioners, do hereby, under the authority of an Act passed in the fifth year of the reign of His late Majesty King William the Fourth, intituled "*An Act for the Amendment and better Administration of the Laws relating to the Poor in England and Wales*," rescind all such of the provisions contained in any Order or Orders under the Hands and Seal of the Poor Law Commissioners as direct the payment of expenses to be incurred in the Election of Guardians of the Poor for the several Parishes comprised in the several Unions named in the Schedules hereunto annexed.

And whereas by a General Order under the Hands and Seal of the Poor Law Commissioners, bearing even date herewith, addressed to the Guardians of the Poor of the said several Unions, the said Commissioners have (amongst other things) prescribed the manner of conducting the future Election of Guardians of the Poor for the several Parishes comprised in the said Unions; and it is expedient that provision should be made for the payment of the expenses to be incurred in such Elections.

Now, therefore, We, the said Poor Law Commissioners, do hereby Order and Direct in regard thereto, with reference to each of the said Unions named in the said Schedules as follows:—That the expenses of every future Election of Guardians of the Poor of the several Parishes comprised in the said Unions shall be defrayed by the Guardians of the said Unions in the manner herein-after set forth; that is to say,

Article 1.—The cost of providing the several Forms marked (A.,) (D.,) and (E.,) contained in the said Order, being the Notice of Election, the Notice to the Guardians elected, and the Certificate of the Election, shall be defrayed out of the common fund of the Union.

Article 2.—The cost of providing the Form marked (C.,) contained in the said Order, being the Voting Paper, shall be defrayed out of the funds in the possession of the said Guardians belonging to the respective Parishes to which the Voting Papers shall relate.

Article 3.—The compensation which shall be paid to the Clerk, or to the person appointed under the authority of the said recited Order to act as such in the performance of the duties thereby prescribed, shall include the remuneration of the persons who may have been appointed or employed to assist him in conducting and completing the Election, and shall, in respect of the several Unions named in the following Schedule marked A., be such sum, not exceeding *Ten Pounds*, as the Guardians shall determine, and shall, in respect of the several Unions named in the following Schedule marked B., be such sum, not exceeding *Fifteen Pounds*, as the Guardians shall determine, and such sums respectively shall be defrayed out of the common fund of the Unions.

Article 4.—And in the case of every contested Election One Farthing per Head on the population of the Parish in which the contest shall have taken place, if the population shall be more than five hundred, and One Halfpenny per head on the population of the Parish in which the contest shall have taken place, if the population be not more than five hundred, shall be paid to the said Clerk or other person as aforesaid in addition to such compensation, and shall be defrayed out of the funds in the possession of the said Guardians belonging to such Parish. And for the purpose of ascertaining the last-mentioned sums, the population of the Parish shall be taken to be as stated in the Census which at the time of such Election shall have been last made under the authority of any Act of Parliament.

And We do hereby Declare, that whenever the word "Parish" is used in this Order, it shall be taken to signify any Place in the Union separately maintaining its own Poor.

Schedule A. *containing the Names of the Unions in which the sum is not to exceed Ten Pounds.*

- Aberaeron.
- Abergavenny.
- Aberystwith.
- Albans, St.
- Alcester.
- Alderbury.
- Alresford.
- Alton.
- Amersham.
- Amesbury.
- Ampthill.
- Asaph, St.
- Ashby-de-la-Zouch.
- Ashford, East.
- Ashford, West.
- Ashton-under-Lyne.
- Aston.
- Atherstone.
- Austell, St.
- Axminister.
- Bala.
- Bangor & Beaumaris.
- Barnet.
- Barrow-upon-Soar.
- Bath.
- Battle.
- Beaminster.
- Bedale.
- Bedminster.
- Berkhampstead.
- Berwick upon-Tweed.
- Bideford.
- Biggleswade.
- Billericay.
- Bishop's Stortford.
- Blaby.
- Blackburn.
- Blean.
- Bodmin.
- Bolton.
- Bootle.
- Boston.
- Brackley.
- Bradfield.
- Bradford (Wilts.)
- Bradford (York.)
- Braintree.
- Brampton.
- Brentford.
- Bridge.
- Bridgnorth.
- Bridport.
- Bromley.
- Bromsgrove.
- Buckingham.
- Buntingford.
- Burnley.
- Bury.
- Calne.
- Cambridge.
- Camelford.
- Cardigan.
- Carlisle.
- Carmarthen.
- Carnarvon.
- Catherington.
- Caxton & Arrington.
- Cerne.
- Chailey.
- Chapel-en-le-Frith.
- Cheadle
- Cheltenham.
- Chertsey.
- Chester-le-Street.
- Chippenham.
- Chipping Sodbury.
- Chorley.
- Chorlton.
- Christchurch.
- Church Stretton.
- Cleobury Mortimer.
- Clifton.
- Clun.
- Clutton.
- Colchester.
- Columb, St. Major.
- Conway.
- Cookham.
- Corwen.
- Cosford.
- Cranbrook.
- Crediton.
- Crickhowel.
- Cricklade and Wootton Bassett.
- Croydon.
- Cuckfield.
- Dartford.
- Daventry.
- Derby.
- Devizes.
- Dewsbury.
- Dolgelly.
- Dore.
- Dorking.
- Dover.
- Drayton.
- Droitwich.
- Droxford.
- Dudley.
- Dulverton.
- Dunmow.
- Durham.
- Dursley.
- Easington.
- Easingwold.
- Eastbourne.
- East Grinstead.
- Easthampstead.
- Eastry.
- East Ward.
- Ecclesall Bierlow.
- Edmonton.
- Elham.
- Ellesmere.
- Ely.
- Epping.
- Epsom.
- Eton.
- Evesham.
- Faith, St.
- Falmouth.
- Fareham.
- Farnham.
- Faversham.
- Festiniog.
- Foleshill.
- Fordingbridge.
- Frome.
- Fulham.
- Fylde.
- Garstang.
- Gateshead.
- German's, St.
- Glossop.
- Godstone.
- Goole.
- Gravesend & Milton.
- Greenwich.
- Guildford.
- Guiltcross.
- Guisborough.
- Hackney.
- Hailsham.
- Halifax.
- Halstead.
- Haltwhistle.
- Hambledon.
- Hardingstone.
- Hartley Wintney.
- Haslingden.
- Hastings.
- Hatfield.
- Havant.
- Hay.
- Hayfield.
- Headington.
- Helston.
- Hemel Hempstead.
- Hendon.
- Henley.
- Hertford.
- Highworth & Swindon
- Hinckley.
- Hitchin.
- Holbeach.
- Holborn.
- Hollingbourn.
- Holsworthy.
- Holywell.
- Honiton.
- Hoo.
- Horsham.
- Houghton-le-Spring.
- Hoxne.
- Hungerford.
- Hursley.
- Ipswich.
- Ives, St.
- Keighley.
- Kettering.
- Keynsham.
- Kidderminster.
- Kingsbridge.
- Kingsclere.

King's Lynn.
King's Norton.
Kingston-on-Thames.
Kington.
Knighton.
Lampeter.
Lancaster.
Lanchester.
Langport.
Launceston.
Ledbury.
Leek.
Leicester.
Leigh.
Leighton Buzzard.
Leominster.
Lewes.
Lewisham.
Lichfield.
Linton.
Liskeard.
Llandilo Fawr.
Llandovery.
Llanelly.
Llanfyllin.
Llanrwst.
London, East.
London, West.
Longtown.
Loughborough.
Luton.
Lymington.
Machynlleth.
Madeley.
Maidstone.
Malling.
Malmsbury.
Manchester.
Mansfield.
Market Bosworth.
Marlborough.
Martley.
Medway.
Melksham.
Mere.
Meriden.
Merthyr-Tidvil.
Midhurst.
Mildenhall.
Milton.
Neath.
Neot's, St.
Newbury.
Newcastle-in-Emlyn.
Newcastle-under-Lyne.
Newcastle-upon-Tyne
Newent.
New Forest.
Newhaven.
Newmarket.
Newport (Salop.)
Newtown & Llanidloes.
Northampton.
North Aylesford.
Northleach.
North Witchford.
Nuneaton.
Oakham.
Okehampton.
Olave's, St.
Ongar.
Ormskirk.
Orsett.
Pateley Bridge.
Patrington.
Pembroke.
Penkridge.
Penzance,
Petersfield.
Petworth.
Pewsey.
Pickering.
Plympton St. Mary.
Pont-y-Pool.
Poole.
Poplar.
Portsea Island.
Potterspury.
Prescot.
Priesteigne.
Preston.
Radford.
Reading.
Redruth.
Reeth.
Reigate.
Rhayader.
Richmond (Surrey.)
Ringwood.
Risbridge.
Rochdale.
Rochford.
Romford.
Romney Marsh.
Romsey.
Ross.
Rotherham.
Royston.
Ruthin.
Rye.
Salford.
Saviour's, St.
Sculcoates.
Sedbergh.
Sedgefield.
Seisdon.
Selby.
Sevenoaks.
Shaftesbury.
Sheffield.
Sheppey.
Shepton Mallett.
Sherborne.
Shiffnal.
Solihull.
Southam,
South Molton.
South Shields.
South Stoneham.
Spalding.
Stafford.
Staines.
Stepney.
Steyning.
Stockbridge.
Stockport.
Stokesley.
Stone.
Stourbridge.
Stow-on-the-Wold.
Strand.
Stratton.
Stroud.
Sturminster.
Sunderland.
Swansea.
Tamworth.
Tavistock.
Tenbury
Tenterden.
Tetbury.
Tewkesbury.
Thakenham.
Thanet, Isle of.
Thornbury.
Thorne.
Thrapston.
Ticehurst.
Tisbury.
Tiverton.
Todmorden.
Tonbridge.
Torrington.
Totnes.
Towcester.
Tregaron.
Truro.
Tynemouth.
Uckfield.
Ulverstone.
Upton-upon-Severn.
Uttoxeter.
Uxbridge.
Wakefield.
Wallingford.
Walsal.
Wandsworth & Clapham.
Wangford.
Ware.
Wareham & Purbeck.
Warminster.
Warrington.
Watford.
Wayland.
Weardale.
Wellingborough.
Wellington (Salop.)
Wellington (Somerset.)
Wells.
Welwyn.
Wem.
Weobly.
Westbourne.
West Bromwich.
Westbury-on-Severn.
Westbury & Whorwelsdon.
West Derby.
West Firle.
West Ham.
West Ward.
Weymouth.
Wheatenhurst.
Whitby.
Whitchurch.
Whitechapel.
Whitehaven.
Wigan.
Wilton.
Wimborne & Cranborne.
Winchcombe.
Windsor.
Winslow.
Wisbeach.
Witham.
Woburn.
Wokingham.
Wolstanton & Burslem.
Wolverhampton.
Worcester.
Worksop.
Wortley.

SCHEDULE B. *containing the Names of Unions in which the sum is not to exceed Fifteen Pounds.*

Abingdon.
Alnwick.
Altrincham.
Andover.
Anglesey.
Ashbourne.
Atcham.
Auckland.
Axbridge.
Aylesbury.
Aylsham.
Bakewell.
Banbury.
Barnstaple.
Basford.
Basingstoke.
Bedford.
Belford.
Bellingham.
Belper.
Beverley.
Bicester.
Billesdon.
Bingham.
Blandford.
Blofield.
Blything.
Bosmere & Claydon.
Boughton, Great.
Bourn.
Brecknock.
Bridgend & Cowbridge.
Bridgwater.
Bridlington.
Brixworth.
Bromyard.
Builth.
Burton-upon-Trent.
Caistor.
Cardiff.
Castle Ward.
Chard.
Chelmsford.
Chepstow.
Chesterfield.
Chesterton.
Chipping Norton.
Cirencester.
Clitheroe.

Cockermouth.	Henstead.	Mitford & Launditch.	Runcorn.	Thetford.
Congleton.	Hereford.	Monmouth.	Saffron Walden.	Thingoe.
Darlington.	Hexham.	Morpeth.	Scarborough.	Thirsk.
Depwade.	Horncastle.	Nantwich.	Settle.	Thomas, St.
Docking.	Howden.	Narberth.	Shardlow.	Uppingham.
Doncaster.	Huddersfield.	Newark.	Shipton-upon-Stour.	Walsingham.
Dorchester.	Huntingdon.	Newport (Monmouth)	Skipton.	Wantage.
Downham.	Kendal.	Newport Pagnell.	Skirlaugh.	Warwick.
Driffield.	Lexden & Winstree.	Newton Abbot.	Sleaford.	West Hampnet.
East Retford.	Leyburn.	Northallerton.	Southwell.	Wigton.
Erpingham.	Lincoln.	Northwich.	Spilsby.	Williton.
Faringdon.	Loddon & Clavering.	Oundle.	Stamford.	Wincanton.
Freebridge Lynn.	London, City of.	Penrith.	Stockton.	Winchester, New.
Gainsborough.	Louth.	Pershore.	Stow.	Wirrall.
Glanford Brigg.	Ludlow.	Peterborough.	Stratford-on-Avon.	Witney.
Glendale.	Lutterworth.	Plomesgate.	Sudbury.	Woodbridge.
Gloucester.	Macclesfield.	Pocklington.	Swaffham.	Woodstock.
Grantham.	Maldon.	Pwllheli.	Taunton.	Wrexham.
Hartismere.	Malton.	Richmond (York.)	Teesdale.	Wycombe.
Haverfordwest.	Market Harborough.	Rothbury.	Tendring.	Yeovil.
Helmsley Blackmoor.	Melton Mowbray.	Rugby.	Thame.	York.

Given under our Hands and Seal of Office, this twenty-fourth day of July, in the year One thousand eight hundred and forty-seven.

---

2. THE CLERK OF ONE UNION NOT ELIGIBLE FOR THE OFFICE OF GUARDIAN OF ANOTHER UNION.

April 1st, 1847.

Clerk of ——— *Union*—Mr. B., the clerk of an adjoining union, has been nominated a guardian for two parishes (A. & B.) in this union. In parish A. he has nominated himself and four other persons; and there, a contest will probably take place; in parish B. he is the only person nominated. With regard to parish A., Mr. B.'s name appears for the first time on the poor-rate in May, 1846; and he has, consequently, not been rated for a whole year. Inquired whether it will be proper to omit Mr. B.'s name from the voting papers in the event of a contest, or from the return of the guardians elected, where he is the only person nominated.

Ans.—The Commissioners consider that the clerk of a Poor Law Union, being a paid officer engaged in the administration of the laws for the relief of the poor, is disqualified from serving as a guardian, not only in the union of which he is an officer, but in any other union; (see section 14, of 5 & 6 Vic. c. 57.) It will be seen from the terms of the section, that the prohibition is general. The Commissioners are not aware of the capacity in which Mr. B. was nominated, whether as rate-payer or owner. If in the former, it would seem from your statement that the nomination cannot be sustained, on the ground that Mr. B. is not a rate-payer within the meaning of sec. 40, of 4th and 5th Will. c. 76, he not having been rated for the period of one year prior to his nominating or acting as rate-payer. The case would of course be different as regards the validity of the nomination (so far as the four persons are concerned, whose names are associated with Mr. B.) if Mr. B. nominated himself as owner, and if he be legally entitled to vote as an owner in parish A. with reference to 4th and 5th Will. 4, c. 76, sec. 40, and 7th and 8th Vic. c. 101, sec. 15. In the case of parish B., for which Mr. B. is alone nominated as a guardian, you will, in the opinion of the Commissioners, be warranted in omitting his name from the return (Form E.) on the ground mentioned in the former part of this letter; as a prohibition from serving the office of guardian implies, in the opinion of the Commissioners, a legal incapacity to be elected to that office.

---

3. REGISTER OF OWNERS' CLAIMS TO VOTE.

April 10th, 1847.

Clerk of Wimborne and Cranborne Union—In the year 1843, numerous claims to vote as owners were sent to the overseers of Wimborne Minster, by whom they were duly registered; and the votes were subsequently allowed in the election of guardians in the parish. None of these claims describe the nature of the interest or estate which the party had, as required by the 7 & 8 Vict. c. 101, sect. 15, and there has not since been any revision of the register, no objection having been made to any of the claims.

Ans.—The Commissioners are not prepared to say, that the clerk, as returning officer, is absolutely concluded by the register of owners, so as to be prevented from going into the question of the validity of the claims sent in by owners, when the votes given at the election of guardians are under consideration. The statute, however, having provided a means by which the names of persons making claims which cannot be supported, are to be expunged from the register, by enabling persons interested in the matter to object to such claims, it appears to the Commissioners that, where no such objection is, in fact, made, the intention was, that the persons entered in the book, under the provisions of the statute, by the overseers, should be treated by the returning officer as the persons entitled to vote as owners in the parish, at the time when they were registered.

---

4. VALIDITY OF VOTING PAPER.

April 8th, 1847.

Clerk of Wimborne and Cranborne Union—Inquired whether a voting paper, which is signed by the voter himself, but to which the voter's initials opposite the candidates' names, are added by another person, is valid; and also, whether it is sufficient if a voting paper is signed by the wife or a daughter of a voter in his name and with his sanction.

Ans.—It is not only necessary that the voter should sign the voting paper, but that he should place his initials against the names of the candidates for whom he votes. (See Article 14 of the Order of Election.) If the initials be placed by some other person on behalf of the voter, (the case not being one in which the voter is unable to write,) it will not be a compliance with the article cited, and the vote will be bad. Where a voter is able to write, it will not be sufficient that the voting paper be signed by the wife or daughter of the voter, though this be done with the sanction of the latter.

5.—REFUSALS TO SERVE THE OFFICE OF GUARDIAN.

March 31st, 1847.

Clerk of Wolstanton and Burslem Union—Two nomination papers have been duly received for the parish of B.; they contain the names of ten persons, who are proposed as guardians, eight only being the number required for the parish. With respect to two of the gentlemen nominated, he had received the following communications:—1. "J** T** declines being nominated as a guardian for the ensuing year." 2. "Should my name appear on any of the nomination papers for the new board of guardians, I will thank you to write 'objects to serve,' as it is not my intention to be a guardian for this year at least. I am, &c. G** B**." Inquired whether these communications may be considered to be refusals to serve.

Ans.—The Commissioners think the communications in question may be regarded as refusals to serve the office of guardian within the meaning of section 9 of 5 & 6 Vict. c. 57. The letter signed "G** B**" appears to be a refusal *in terms* to serve the office of guardian. The letter or note of Mr. T** is certainly not a very formal document, nor does it contain an express refusal to serve the office of guardian. But it states, that "he declines to be nominated as guardian for the ensuing year;" and the Commissioners, having regard to the obvious intention of the writer, think this is tantamount to a declaration, that he declines the execution of the office. The Commissioners are of opinion, upon the whole, that you would be warranted in regarding Messrs. J. T** and G** B** as no longer candidates for the parish of Burslem, and in returning the remaining eight, if duly qualified, as elected.

VI.—EMIGRATION TO SOUTH AUSTRALIA.

(CIRCULAR)

Government Emigration Office,
9, *Park St. Westminster,*
May, 1847.

REGULATIONS to be observed in the selection of LABOURERS for a PASSAGE (including Provisions and Medical Attendance during the Voyage,) to SOUTH AUSTRALIA; and also the CONDITIONS on which the Passage, when granted, must be understood to be accepted.

Trade or Calling.

1. The Emigrants must chiefly be Agricultural Labourers, Shepherds, Miners, and Female Domestic Servants. *A few* country mechanics may also be accepted, such as Blacksmiths, Wheelwrights, Carpenters, &c. &c.

2. All the Adults must be capable of Labour, and must be really Working Labourers or mechanics of the above description, and going out with the intention of settling in the Colony.

3. Persons who are intending to buy Land in the Colony, or invest a small capital in Trade, are not eligible for a free passage, nor are their families, the free passage being designed to benefit labourers or mechanics as above, who have not the means of paying their own passage.

4. Reduced Tradesmen and persons resident in a Workhouse, or in the habitual receipt of parish relief, are not considered eligible for a free passage.

Description of Family, and Age.

5. The Emigrants must consist principally of married couples, not above forty years of age at their last birth-day; but for every child above fourteen an excess of one year will be allowed in the age of the parents, if they are still hale and capable of labour. The Candidates most acceptable are young couples who have no children.

6. No family can be taken which includes three children under seven, or four under ten years of age. The separation of parents from children under eighteen, will in no case be allowed.

7. Single women, under eighteen, without their parents, are not admissible unless they are emigrating under the immediate care of some near married relatives, or are under engagement as domestic servants to ladies going out as cabin passengers in the same ship.

8. Single men cannot be allowed, except in a number not exceeding that of the single women in the same ship. If named by a person who has deposited Money in this Country for the purchase of Land, they can only be accepted, if eligible in other respects, in case the same party has named an equal number of single women who conform to Regulation 7.

9. All Emigrants, Adults as well as Children, must have been vaccinated, or have had the Small Pox.

10. The Commissioners are occasionally able to allow Relatives of Emigrants accepted for free passages, although those relatives may be themselves ineligible under the Regulations to be conveyed at the public expense, an option of proceeding in the same vessel on paying the expense of their passages; but this must entirely depend on the space available in the Ship and on the Commissioners' discretion.

Character.

11. Good Character is indispensable, and decisive certificates will be required both to this point, and also to competence in the professed trade or calling of the proposed Emigrant.

Form of Application.

12. All applications must be made in the form hereunto annexed, which must be duly filled up and attested, as explained in the form itself, and then forwarded to this Office, with Baptismal and Marriage Certificates.

13. Should it be found that the signatures attached to the certificates are not genuine, or that any other deception is attempted, the application will be rejected; or should any Emigrant, on personal examination at the Port of Embarkation, be discovered to have made any mis-statement whatever with regard to age, calling, health, &c., such person will not be allowed to proceed in the ship.

14. The nomination of Labourers for a free passage by Land Purchasers, will be subject to the approval of the Commissioners, whose answer must be received before the Emigrants are led to make any preparation.

Proceedings subsequent to Application and Approval.

15. If approved of, the Emigrant will be so informed, and will receive a passage as soon as the arrangements of the Commissioners will admit. But due notice will be given to them of the Ship by which they are to sail, and of the time appointed for sailing; and, unless they receive such notice, they must, on no account, withdraw from their employment, or make any preparation for departure. Those who fail to attend to this warning, will do so at their own risk, and will have no claim whatever on the Commissioners.

16. The expense of reaching the Port of embarkation must be paid by the Emigrants.

17. Before the Embarkation Order, entitling them to a Passage, is issued, 1*l.* must be paid for every person above fourteen, and 10*s.* for every child above one and under fourteen, which will be retained to meet the expense of Bedding and Mess Utensils, which will be supplied for them.

18. If any Emigrants fail to attend at the appointed time and place for embarkation, they will never again be allowed a free passage, and will forfeit any money that may have been paid, unless they give to the Commissioners timely notice and a satisfactory reason of their inability to proceed.

19. Provisions and Cooking Utensils will be found. The Emigrants will also be provided with new Mattresses, Bolsters, Blankets, and Counterpanes, and with Canvas Bags intended to contain one Month's Linen, &c.; likewise with a Knife and Fork, two Spoons, a metal Plate, and a Drinking Mug, the whole of which articles may be kept by the Emigrants after arrival in the Colony. But they must bring their own Sheets and Towels, and also a supply of Soap.

20. The Emigrants must bring their own Clothing, which will be inspected at the Port

No. 11.   Register No.__________

FORM OF APPLICATION.

Form to be filled up by Persons desirous of obtaining a Passage to SOUTH AUSTRALIA, then to be *separated* from the other page and returned as a *letter, pre-paid*, and directed to "S. WALCOTT, ESQ. *No. 9, Park Street, Westminster*," or to the Commissioners' Agent from whom it was received.

The same Form will do for a Man, his Wife, and Children under Fourteen. Every Person above Fourteen must have a separate Form

The Names of the Parents and of all their Children under Fourteen Years of age, are to be written in this Column.	Age of each Person at last Birth-day.	Day and Year when each Person born. *N.B. The Extract of the Register of Birth, or the Certificate of Baptism for each Person, must be sent with this Form.*	State whether Vaccinated or had the Small Pox.	Can the Applicants read and write? Say "Yes," or "No," opposite each name. Read.	Write

Trade or Calling of Applicant ....

Place of Residence ....

Married, or Single. If married, the Certificate of Marriage must be inclosed ....

Name and Address of some late Employer, and the time the Applicant worked for him

Name and Address of the Minister of the Parish in which the Applicant resides. ......

Has Applicant been in the receipt of Parish Relief, and if so, for how long? ....

Has Applicant been out before to any Colony, and if so, to which? ....

I do hereby declare, that all of the above statements are true; that I have carefully read, or have heard read, the Regulations for the selection of Emigrant Labourers, attached to this paper, and that in applying for a Passage to the Colony, I am really and truly acting in accordance with the spirit of those Regulations, which I understand to be this:—That the privilege of a Passage, if granted, will be allowed me in the expectation that I go to the Colony as one willing and intending to work there for Wages. And I further declare, that I have neither paid, nor agreed to pay, for the purpose of obtaining a passage, any fee or gratuity whatever, to, or for the use of, the party through whom this Application is made. I also engage to conform, during the Voyage, to such Regulations as may be established for the good government and welfare of all on board; and I further pledge myself not to leave the Ship until she reaches her destination.

Signed by the Applicant.

It is particularly requested that no one will sign these Certificates unless thoroughly convinced of the truth of their statements.

Certificate to be signed by Two respectable Householders.—N.B. This is not to be signed by Publicans or Dealers in Beer or Spirits.

WE certify, that we are well acquainted with the above-named Applicant, and have known__________ to have worked as an__________ for a period of __________ years, and that we believe the above statements to be strictly true;—further, that we believe the Applicant to be honest, sober, industrious, and of general good character, and not likely to become a burthen to the Colony.

Signature.   Signature.
Place of abode.   Place of abode.

*** *Fill up the Blanks in this Certificate*

Certificate of a Physician or Surgeon.—I certify, that I have examined the above-named Applicant, and his Wife and Children, and that none of them are seriously mutilated nor deformed in Person, nor, in my opinion, afflicted with any disease calculated to shorten life, or to impair physical or mental energy. I certify also that they have all had the small pox or have been vaccinated, and are entirely free from every disease usually considered infectious or contagious.

Signature.   Place of residence.

Certificate of the Magistrate or Clergyman of the Parish in which the Applicant resides.

I certify to the best of my belief, that the above Certificates are authentic, and that the Persons whose Signatures are affixed to them, viz.—the two Householders and the Surgeon or Physician, are worthy of credit.

Signature of the Magistrate.   Place of residence.
Signature of the Clergyman.   Place of residence.
Signature of the Roman Catholic Priest.   Place of residence.

Declaration of Agent.—Should the above party have been selected by one of the Commissioners' Agents, the following declaration must be signed by such Agent:

I do hereby declare that I have carefully inquired as to the validity of the above Statements, and that I am perfectly satisfied of their correctness; also that I have made all other inquiries and examinations named in my instructions, and that I believe the above parties to be in all respects desirable Emigrants. And I further declare, that I have neither received, nor agreed to receive, from or in respect of the Emigrants above described, any fee or gratuity whatever, on account of their obtaining a Passage through my Agency.   Agent for

1. No fee or gratuity whatever is to be given to any Officer or Agent of the Commissioners on any pretence whatsoever.
2. *If this Paper contains any false Statements or false Signatures, the Applicant will thereby forfeit the Deposit paid, and also all claim to a Free Passage.*
3. *This Paper must be kept clean, and will be returned unless filled up exactly according to the Directions given above. No erasures or mutilations must be made.*
4. *** Until the Commissioners have duly notified their approval of the Applicants they are not to consider that a free passage can be granted to them; and until the Applicants are called upon by Notice from the Secretary to pay their Deposit, they are on no account to quit their employment, or make any preparations for departure. Applicants who fail to attend to this warning will do so at their own risk, and will have no claim whatever on the Commissioners.

Government Emigration Office,
9, Park Street, Westminster.

By Order of the Board,
STEPHEN WALCOTT, *Secretary.*

by an Officer of the Commissioners; and all parties are particularly desired to observe that they will not be allowed to embark unless they provide themselves with a sufficient supply for their health during the voyage. The lowest quantity that can be admitted for each Person is as follows:—

FOR MALES.	FOR FEMALES.
Six Shirts	Six Shifts.
Six pairs Stockings	Two Flannel Petticoats
Two ditto Shoes	Six pairs Stockings
Two complete suits of exterior Clothing.	Two ditto Shoes
	Two Gowns.

As a general rule, it may be stated that the more abundant the stock of Clothing, the better for health and comfort during the passage. The usual length of the voyage to the Australian Colonies is about four months, and at whatever season of the year it may be made, the Emigrants have to pass through very hot and very cold weather, and should therefore be prepared for both.

21. It is desirable that Emigrants should take out with them the necessary Tools of their Trades; bulky Agricultural Implements, however, cannot be admitted, on account of their inconvenient size and weight; neither can Furniture be received on board; Mattresses especially, and Feather Beds, are strictly prohibited.

22. The whole quantity of Baggage for each Emigrant must not measure more than twenty cubic or solid feet, nor exceed half a ton weight. It must be divided into two or three boxes, of not more than 2½ or 3 feet long, by about 20 inches wide and 18 inches high. People should not crowd the Ship with Boxes only half filled, and must pack their effects close. Large packages and extra baggage will not be taken unless paid for, and only in case there be room in the Ship.

23. Only the luggage really belonging to each family of passengers is intended to be taken under the foregoing allowance. If any one should attempt to impose on the Commissioners by letting the baggage of other persons, not members of his family, go under his name, he will forfeit his passage, and not be suffered to proceed.

24. The Emigrants will be at perfect liberty to engage themselves to any one willing to employ them, and to make their own bargain for wages in the Colony. No repayment is required from them for the passage out. The only return expected is a strict observance, on board, of the Regulations framed with a view to their health and comfort during the voyage, and general good conduct and industrious habits in the Colony.

25. Letters and Applications should be addressed, Post-paid, to Stephen Walcott, Esquire, Secretary to the Board of Emigration, No. 9, Park Street, Westminster.

By Order of the Board,
STEPHEN WALCOTT, *Secretary*.

VII.—FEVER.

CHLORIDE OF ZINC.—DISINFECTING AGENT. (CIRCULAR.)

Poor Law Commission Office,
Somerset House,
July 6th, 1847.

SIR,—I am directed by the Poor Law Commissioners to state that they have received from the Secretary of State for the Home Department a copy of a Report from the Surgeon of Her Majesty's Ship Vengeance, to the Director General of the Medical Department of the Navy, together with other papers, on the subject of the salutary effect of Chloride of Zinc, when used as a disinfecting agent.

In consequence of the prevalence of fever at present in some parts of the country, it appears very desirable that the properties of this article, as described in the papers in question, should be made generally known. The Commissioners, therefore, in accordance with the suggestion of the Secretary of State, transmit herewith, for the information of the Guardians, copies of the papers referred to, and they request that the Guardians will draw the attention of their Medical Officers to the same, with the view to the use of Chloride of Zinc being adopted under their directions in the Fever Wards, and other parts of the Workhouses, and in the dwellings of Pauper Patients attacked by fever, and that the Guardians will for this purpose provide such a supply of the article as may be necessary.

The Commissioners are informed that it may be procured at the Office of the Proprietors of the Patent, No. 53, King William-street, London-bridge.

The Commissioners request that in any case in which Chloride of Zinc is used they may receive from time to time Reports as to its efficacy.

I am, Sir, your most obedient servant,
W. G. LUMLEY, *Assistant Secretary*.

To
The Clerk to the Board of Guardians.

Admiralty, June 22nd, 1847.

SIR,—I had the honour some time ago to call your attention to the salutary and extraordinary effect produced by the use of the Chloride of Zinc as a disinfecting agent, and also its singular and beneficial properties in immediately, on its application, destroying and decomposing the noxious smells arising from the putrefaction of animal and vegetable substances, and also its instant destruction of the smell of Bilge Water arising in the Holds of Ships. I now beg leave to solicit your attention to the Copy of a Letter herewith enclosed from the Surgeon of Her Majesty's Ship Vengeance, just returned to Portsmouth, after carrying large bodies of Troops; and at a period like the present, when contagious fever is spreading far and wide in Ireland and in some of our own towns, from the immigration of the destitute Irish, I cannot but think that its use would be attended with the greatest advantage, and most materially to the preservation of life and the subduing of the contagion or infection.

Having, as you will easily suppose, paid more than common attention to the case of the unfortunate Eclair, I have no hesitation in saying that it was by the use of the Chloride of Zinc in that Ship that the fever was finally overcome.

The Chloride has been in general use in the Navy for more than a year.

I have, &c.
W. BURNETT, M.D.,
Director General Medical Department.
Right Honourable Sir George Grey.

H.M.S. Vengeance, Portsmouth,
June 13th, 1847.

SIR,—Having used the Chloride of Zinc rather extensively on board H.M.S. Vengeance, whilst employed in the conveyance of Troops, I think proper to report to you the result thereof. We carried the 1st Battalion of the 42nd Regiment, consisting of about 700 men, women, and children, from Malta to Bermuda—"Measles" had prevailed epidemically in the regiment previously to their embarkation, but we received none on board labouring under the disease; yet, after being ten days at sea, several cases occurred simultaneously among the soldiers, and, on the 1st of April, having been then a month at sea, the disease appeared among our own people, ten cases occurring on that day; and from that day to the 15th of the month, when we arrived at Bermuda, fresh cases were almost of daily occurrence, either among our own people or the troops. On getting rid of the troops, which we did at Bermuda, my attention was of course specially directed to every means whereby the contagion could be destroyed. Cleanliness and ventilation were duly attended to, and every part of the ship where the sick had been, after being cleaned and aired, was sponged well over with the Solution of Chloride of Zinc several times. Than the result nothing could be better; the disease totally ceased, no fresh case occurring after. On our passage from Halifax, with the 60th Regiment on board, the weather was so bad, and the ship working so much, that it was quite impossible to open any of the lower deck ports, on which deck the whole of the people lived, troops as well as our own people, for eight days; the air throughout the deck was exceedingly vitiated with every mixture of noxious smell, but the free use of the Chloride of Zinc tended, in a most surprising manner, to do away with the bad smell; so much so, that the surgeon of the regiment came to me to get some to use in the part of the ship where the ladies of the officers were. The effect of the Chloride of Zinc is most obvious in correcting all bad and offensive effluvia; and, from the sudden and surprising manner in which the measles disappeared after its use, it is not, I think, too much to say, that it must have been very instrumental in decomposing the miasm, or state of atmosphere in the ship, which tended to the generation of the disease.

It has struck me, Sir, and I hope you will not deem the observation out of place, that it might be most beneficially used in the Fever Hospitals in Ireland, at the present time, and more especially in the houses of the better classes of the people there, where fever so much prevails.

It strikes me, in such cases, the best way to use it would be:—after washing and airing rooms where fever had been, to sponge the boards well over with the solution, and allow the moisture to dissipate itself with free ventilation.

I have the honour to be, &c. &c.
(*Signed*) B. VERLING, *Surgeon.*
To SIR W. BURNETT, K.C.H., &c. &c. &c.

SIR WILLIAM BURNETT'S PATENT

for the Preservation of Timber, Canvas, Cotton, Woollen, and of all Animal and Vegetable Substances, from Rot, Mildew, Moth, and Premature Decay, is to be applied to

The Preservation of Animal Matter.

The Disinfection of Hospitals, &c., and of Putrescent Substances, or

The Purification of Bilge Water,

in the following manner:—

Dissecting Room.

Immerse the subject in a Solution made in the proportion of one pint of the Patent Solution with five gallons of water. Let it remain about two hours in the dilute Solution; after which time it will be purified. As the dissection proceeds, the parts should be sponged over with the same.

Hospitals, Poor Law Union Houses, &c. &c.

For the purpose of purifying the atmosphere, add one pint of the Patent Solution to five gallons of water. With this dilute fluid, moisten a piece of flannel-cloth attached to a long rod, and wave it through the air of the apartment for ten minutes at a time,—in addition to which, the floor should be mopped or sprinkled over with the same at least once a day. In fever wards, when a patient dies of fever, the body should be sponged over with the dilute Solution, and the clothes and bedding should be immersed and kept in the same (in a spacious tub) for forty-eight hours, before being washed. The floor should be well mopped over with the Solution. Flannel moistened with it as before recommended, should be waved through the room, and a small quantity of the same dilute Solution should be put into the close-stools and bed-pans. The water-closets should also be cleansed with it, and a couple of gallons occasionally thrown down each. This being carefully attended to in all Hospitals, Union Workhouses, Prisons, &c. &c., will most effectually prevent the emission of any noxious smell from cess-pools, &c.

For the Purification of Bilge-Water, &c. on board Ships.

The Patent Solution should be mixed with water in the proportion of one pint of the former to two gallons and a half of the latter. It should be well stirred with a clean stick, and it will be ready for use in a few minutes. The quantity to be used at a time is twenty gallons for each hundred tons of the ship's measurement.

It should be poured into the air-holes of the ship, so that it may find its way by the limber-holes into the well; and it should be thrown by a small engine into places where it may be inconvenient to introduce it by other means. A portion may also be poured down the ship's pumps, the boxes being previously removed to allow of its free passage below.

The Solution should be allowed to remain in the ship twenty-four hours. At the expiration of that time, the ship should be pumped as dry as possible, the well thoroughly cleansed and washed with the Solution, and the operation repeated as occasion may require.

VIII.—GUARDIANS.

1. ELECTION OF VICE-CHAIRMAN, IN THE PLACE OF ONE ABSENT.

July 24th, 1847.

Clerk of ——— Union—One of the vice chairmen of the board of guardians has absented himself from the board, and from his home for some weeks past, and it is believed that he will not return. He has not made any communication to the board on the subject. The guardians have elected another guardian to the office of vice-chairman in his place.

Ans.—Unless the vice-chairman alluded to has ceased to be qualified for the office of guardian, or has resigned his office, the board cannot fill up his place as vice-chairman; but if he do not attend the meeting of the guardians, and the other vice-chairman is not present, the board of guardians may elect any other person to be their chairman for the occasion.

2. QUALIFICATION OF AN EX-OFFICIO GUARDIAN.

May 1st, 1847.

———, *Woodbridge Union*—He is a county magistrate residing in the Woodbridge petty sessional division; but he does not pay poor-rates in any parish in the Woodbridge Union. Inquired whether he is entitled to act as an ex-officio guardian of the board of guardians of that union.

Ans.—The material question is, whether you reside within the union itself; if you do so, and also act for the county in which the union, or any part of the union, is situated, you are qualified to act as an ex-officio guardian of the union. (See sec. 38, 4th and 5th Wm. 4, c. 76, and sec. 24 of 7th and 8th Vic. c. 101. The assessment to the poor-rates is not material in regard to the qualification of an ex-officio guardian.

IX.—MEDICAL ORDER—MEDICAL AND SURGICAL APPLIANCES—LINSEED POULTICES.

June 11th, 1847.

To the Clerk of Wrexham Union—The obligation of the medical officer to furnish "medical and surgical appliances" depends upon the terms of his agreement with the guardians. Assuming the medical officer to be under this obligation, according to such agreement, the Commissioners are disposed to consider that any ingredient kept by druggists, and not forming part of the ordinary consumption of the workhouse, nor included in the common domestic stores, should, strictly speaking, be furnished by the medical officer; and linseed meal is probably of this description. The Commissioners, however, see no objection to the guardians providing the meal in question.

X.—PAUPER—POWER OF GUARDIANS OF ONE UNION TO SEND A PAUPER TO THE WORKHOUSE OF ANOTHER UNION.

July 3rd, 1847.

Clerk of ——— *Union*—Inquired whether the guardians can send a pauper to be maintained in the workhouse of a neighbouring union against his will, the guardians being desirous of making use of better-regulated workhouses than their own.

Ans.—The guardians may offer relief to any person applying for it, on such terms as they may think proper; but the terms must be lawful, or such as can be carried into effect. Now the master of the workhouse in the other union referred to, cannot, in conformity with the order of the Commissioners, admit any pauper into that workhouse upon the order of the guardians of the ——— Union. The relief, therefore, in the manner contemplated cannot be given, or, in other words, the relief is, in point of law, refused by the guardians of the union. The Commissioners are also advised that the guardians of one union cannot contract with the guardians of another union, for the maintenance of the poor of the former in the workhouse of the latter.

XI.—POOR-RATE—COSTS OF PROCEEDINGS FOR THE RECOVERY OF.

June 28th, 1847.

Mr. ———, *Witney Union*—The overseers of the township of ——— have lately been obliged to take proceedings before the justices for the recovery of poor-rate from several of the rate-payers; and the justices have issued distress warrants for the amount of the rate due, but have refused to include therein the costs of the summons, &c., or to issue a separate distress warrant for such costs under the 18 Geo. 3, c. 19, unless indemnified by the overseers against any proceedings. Inquired what course the overseers should adopt under the circumstances; and whether the vestry can empower the overseers to give an indemnity to the justices, which would be binding on the rate-payers.

Ans.—The Commissioners think the justices can only order payment of the costs of such summonses under the statute 18 Geo. 3, cap. 19, and they consider that the case of Skingley *v.* Surridge, 11 Mees. and W. 516, supports justices in this view. The Commissioners do not apprehend that the vestry can authorise an indemnity, but the overseers might apply to the Court of Queen's Bench for a mandamus to the justices, and if the court grant the writ the justices will be indemnified under the 6 and 7 Vic. cap. 67, sec. 3. The costs of such proceedings would properly be borne by the poor-rates.

XII.—RELIEF ON LOAN—RECOVERY OF IN COUNTY COURTS.

July 12th, 1847.

Clerk of Garstang Union—Inquired whether the guardians can take proceedings in the county court, under the 9 and 10 Vic. c. 95, for the recovery of relief granted to poor persons on loan.

Ans.—The Commissioners have referred to the 58th section of the 9 and 10 Vic. c. 95, which defines the jurisdiction of the county courts, and they find that it applies to all pleas of personal actions. The Commissioners entertain great doubts whether the relief which is granted under the Poor Law Amendment Act, is so granted as to warrant a personal action for its recovery; and, if not, the case does not appear to fall within this enactment. They see no objection, however, to the guardians taking the judgment of the court itself, in some case where the recovery of the relief would be proper.

XIII.—REMOVALS—REFUSAL OF PAUPERS TO BE SWORN TO THEIR SETTLEMENTS.

Aug. 23rd, 1847.

Clerk of Bury Union—The board of guardians lately gave directions for proceedings to be taken for the removal of two Irish paupers from the Bury Union, who, upon being taken before the justices, refused to be sworn to their settlement. Inquired what power the guardians, or the justices, have to punish parties who thus refuse to be sworn to their settlements.

Ans.—It appears to the Commissioners that this is purely a question of jurisdiction in the justices over the parties before them. If those parties have been summoned before the justices as witnesses according to the 70th section of the 7th & 8th Vict. c. 101, and when there refuse to give evidence, the justices may, in conformity with that provision, commit them to prison. But if the parties have not been summoned, the Commissioners are not aware of any proceedings which can be taken against them for refusing to be sworn as to their settlements.

XIV.—REMOVAL ACT.

1. (9 & 10 VICT. c. 66)—INTERRUPTION OF RESIDENCE BY A CONFINEMENT IN A LUNATIC ASYLUM.

April 29th, 1847.

Overseers of Saint Sampson, York Union—A pauper, who, with his wife and children, belongs to the parish of Saint Sampson, has resided for the last six years in the parish of Minster Yard. The pauper, in March, 1841, and whilst residing in the latter parish, was removed to a lunatic asylum, where he remained till January, 1844; and then returned to his family, who continued to occupy the residence from which he was so removed. In March, 1845, the pauper was again removed to a lunatic asylum, and on being discharged therefrom in February, 1847, returned to his family to the same residence. Inquired whether, under the circumstances, the pauper is removable from the parish of Minster Yard.

Ans.—The Commissioners are disposed to think that, in the case of the pauper referred to, it would be held that the time during which the pauper was an inmate of the lunatic asylum, was a breach of his continuous residence in the township of Minster Yard, and, consequently, that he is now removable from that township to his settlement in the parish of Saint Sampson; if so, his wife and children would be removable with him, although they may have resided for five years continuously in Minster Yard.

---

2. REMOVAL ACTS, 10 AND 11 VICT. c. 110—SCOTCH POOR REMOVAL ACT, 10 AND 11 VICT. c. 33—(CIRCULAR.)

Poor Law Commission Office,
Somerset House,
August 26th, 1847.

SIR,—I am directed by the Poor Law Commissioners to state that in consequence of various communications which they have received, relative to the statute 10 & 11 Vict. c. 110,* passed in the last session of Parliament on the subject of the removal of paupers, they have deemed it advisable to communicate their views as to the construction of the statute and the best mode of carrying it into effect.

§ 1. The Act came into operation on the 23rd day of July last, and after reciting the 1st section of the Act of the 9 & 10 Vict. c. 66, and stating that the effect of the recited enactment had been to increase unduly the amount of expenditure for the relief of the poor in particular parishes, it enacts that all the expenditure which shall be incurred by any parish, township, or place, forming part of a union for the maintenance, relief, or burial of any person or persons who shall have been at any time within one year before the passing of the 9 & 10 Vict. c. 66, (*i.e.* the 26th August, 1846,) in the receipt of relief from some other parish, township, or place, by right of settlement or reputed settlement therein, and who by the above recited enactment are, or may be, exempted from the liability to be removed from the parish, township, or place, in which such

* This Act is as follows:—
An Act to amend the Laws relating to the Removal of the Poor, until the First Day of *October* One thousand eight hundred and forty-eight.
(10 & 11 Vict. c. 110, passed 23rd *July*, 1847.)
WHEREAS by an Act passed in the last Session of Parliament, intituled *An Act to amend the Laws relating to the Removal of the Poor*, it was, amongst other things, enacted as follows, "that from and after the passing of this Act no person shall be removed, nor shall any Warrant be granted for the Removal of any Person, from any parish in which such Person shall have resided for Five Years next before the Application for the Warrant; provided always, that the Time during which such Person shall be a Prisoner in a Prison, or shall be serving Her Majesty as a Soldier, Marine, or Sailor, or reside as an In-Pensioner in *Greenwich* or *Chelsea* Hospitals, or shall be confined in a Lunatic Asylum or House duly licensed or Hospital registered for the Reception of Lunatics, or as a Patient in a Hospital, or during which any such Person shall receive Relief from any Parish, or shall be wholly or in part maintained by any Rate of Subscription raised in a Parish in which such Person does not reside, not being a *bonâ fide* charitable Gift, shall for all Purposes be excluded in the Computation of Time herein-before mentioned, and that the Removal of a Pauper Lunatic to a Lunatic Asylum under the Provisions of any Act relating to the Maintenance and Care of Pauper Lunatics shall not be deemed a Removal within the Meaning of this Act; provided always, that whenever any Person shall have a Wife or Children having no other Settlement than his or her own, such Wife and Children shall be removable when he or she is removable, and shall not be removable when he or she is not removable:" And whereas the Effect of the above-recited Enactment has been to increase unduly the Amount of Expenditure for Relief of the Poor in particular Parishes; Be it therefore enacted by the Queen's most Excellent Majesty, by and with the Advice and Consent of the Lords Spiritual and Temporal, and Commons, in this present Parliament assembled, and by the Authority of the same, That all the Expenditure which shall be incurred by any Parish, Township, or Place forming Part of a Union for the Maintenance, Relief, or Burial of any Person or Persons who shall have been at any Time within One Year before the passing of the above-recited Enactment in the Receipt of Relief from some other Parish, Township, or Place, by Right of Settlement or reputed Settlement therein, and who by the above-recited Enactment are or may be exempted from the Liability to be removed from the Parish, Township, or Place in which such Person or Persons shall be residing, shall from and after the passing of this Act, so long as such Person or Persons shall continue to be so exempted, be charged to the common or general Fund of such Union in the same Manner as the Cost of building or providing Workhouses in Unions and other Union Expences are directed to be charged by an Act passed in the Fifth Year of the Reign of His late Majesty King *William* the Fourth, intituled *An Act for the Amendment and better Administration of the Laws relating to the Poor in* England *and* Wales.

II. And be it enacted, That this Act shall continue in force until the First Day of *October* in the Year One thousand eight hundred and forty-eight.

III. And be it enacted, That this Act may be amended or repealed by any Act to be passed in this Session of Parliament.

person or persons shall be residing, shall, from and after the passing of this Act, so long as such person or persons shall continue to be so exempted, be charged to the common or general fund of such union, in the same manner as the cost of building or providing workhouses in unions, and other union expenses are directed to be charged by the 4 & 5 Wm. 4, c. 76.

§ 2. By the 2nd section of the statute its operation is limited to the 1st day of October, 1848.

§ 3. The effect of the enactment appears to the Commissioners to be that the cost of the relief of those paupers in unions who, in the year prior to the passing of the 9 & 10 Vict. c. 66, were relieved in a particular manner, and have been, or may be, rendered irremovable by the 1st section of that statute, is henceforth, so long as they continue irremovable by reason of that section, to be borne by the common fund of the union, and, consequently, to be charged to the parishes in the union according to the current averages.

§ 4. According to this view, therefore, those paupers only are within the enactment who have received relief in the manner referred to, at some time in the period within the year, before August 26th, 1846, and the Act does not apply to paupers so relieved prior to the commencement of that period, or subsequently to its termination, but who were not in the receipt of such relief at any time in that interval. The relief must have been received by right of settlement, or reputed settlement, from some parish other than that in which the pauper is residing at the time when the expenditure to be transferred to the union is incurred. Therefore the relief to Irish or Scotch paupers is not within the Act.

§ 5. The enactment is limited so as to apply only to cases of irremovability under the 1st section of the 9 & 10 Vict. c. 66, and, consequently, does not affect the relief given to those paupers who by reason of widowhood, childhood, or temporary sickness, or accident, have been rendered irremovable only by the other sections of that statute. Neither, therefore, does it apply to cases where the parish officers have from any cause other than the operation of the 1st section of that Act abstained from obtaining orders of removal.

§ 6. The exemption from removal need not have been complete at the time of the passing of the former Act, or of this Act, as such an exemption completed hereafter, is included in the latter, as one existing at its date.

§ 7. It is certainly, often doubtful whether a pauper is, or is not, irremovable under section 1 of the 9 & 10 Vict. c. 66; but the difficulty of determining the fact, in single cases, does not suspend the operation of this statute. As the guardians must decide, one way or the other, they must ascertain, as far as they are able, the true state of the facts, and determine, to the best of their judgment, whether the exemption does or does not exist.

§ 8. Although the decision must affect the interests of the guardians, the Commissioners do not doubt that they will fairly and impartially exercise their judgment upon it. But if the decision should not be satisfactory, either to the parish which may be interested or to any of the guardians, it will be competent for any party, so interested, to bring the matter before the auditor for the purpose of being properly adjusted in the accounts, and his decision will be open to the same appeal as in other cases.

§ 9. The Act took effect upon the day of its date, so as to apply to all future charges, but has no retrospective operation, and, therefore, does not apply to any charges incurred before it was passed. On the other hand it applies to all charges incurred since the day of its passing, (*i.e.*, the 23rd July last,) and the guardians cannot postpone its operation until the end of the current quarter, or until any other period. Neither have the guardians any discretion as to the adoption of the statute.

§ 10. Several communications have been made, with reference to the mode in which the accounts of this relief are to be kept. But it appears to the Commissioners that little difficulty will arise in this respect.

It will be seen that the statute requires that the *expenditure which shall be incurred by any parish* shall be charged to the common fund. No disturbance, therefore, need be caused in the present mode of dealing with the relief.

Assuming that the cost of every irremovable pauper is, as it ought to be, charged to the parish in which he is irremovable, every such pauper being within the provision of this new statute, will continue to be treated as a pauper of the parish to which he is chargeable. His relief must still be entered by the relieving officer or master of the workhouse to that parish, but at the closing and balancing of the accounts the guardians must transfer to the Common Charges Account the amount of the expenditure entered on account of any such pauper.

It is desirable, however, that the particulars of the relief so transferred should appear on the minutes of the board of guardians, and the Commissioners recommend that the account of that relief, and the particulars thereof, should be prepared by the clerk or by a committee of guardians a short time previous to the end of each quarter or each half year. Such account, which should contain not only the sums but also the names of the paupers, should be submitted to the board of guardians, and according as the same is adopted, modified, or rejected, should be entered on the minutes.

The process with reference to the accounts will therefore be as follows:

The parish will be *debited* with the amount of all relief as heretofore, and will be *credited* with the amount from which it is to be relieved under this statute. The Common Charges Account will be *debited* with the collective amount of the relief thus credited and transferred, distributed under the heads of the several parishes to which it is to be transferred, and will be *credited* by the shares due from all the parishes in the union, (according to their averages,) on that account increased by this expenditure.

§ 11. In addition to the above remarks upon the statute 10 & 11 Vict. c. 110, the Commissioners desire me to state that another statute of the last session, 10 & 11 Vict. c. 33,* makes an alteration of the law relating to the removal of poor persons from England and Scotland. The first section enables any guardian, relieving officer, or overseer of any parish or union in England, to take and convey before two justices of the peace, without summons or warrant, every poor person who shall become chargeable to some parish in England, and who he may have reason to believe is liable to be removed from England under the 8 & 9 Vict. c. 117, and the justices before whom any such person shall be so brought, shall hear and examine and proceed in the same manner in all respects as if such person had been brought before them under and in the manner directed by that Act.

By section 3, every such person shall, in the execution of the Act in that behalf, have and exercise all the rights, privileges, powers, and immunities with which a constable is by law invested.

This statute relieves the guardians from a difficulty in regard to the process under the 8 & 9 Vict. c. 117, which rendered that statute in many cases unavailing.

I am, Sir, your obedient servant,
W. G. LUMLEY,
Assistant Secretary.

To
The Clerk to the Guardians.

* This Act is as follows:—
An Act to amend the Laws relating to the Removal of poor Persons from *England* and *Scotland*.

(10 & 11 Vict. c. 33, passed 21st *June*, 1847.)

WHEREAS an Act was passed in the Ninth Year of the Reign of Her Majesty, for the Removal from *England* of poor Persons who, though born in *Scotland*, *Ireland*, or the Islands of *Man*, *Scilly*, *Jersey*, or *Guernsey*, and not settled in *England*, are chargeable to some Parish in *England*, [8 & 9 Vict. c. 117;] and by another Act passed in the same Year Provision was made for the Removal from *Scotland* of poor Persons who, though born in *England*, *Ireland*, or the *Isle of Man*, and not settled in *Scotland*, receive Relief from some Parish or Combination in *Scotland*, [8 & 9 Vict. c. 83, s. 77;] And whereas it is expedient that the certain Provisions of the said Acts should be amended: Be it enacted by the Queen's most Excellent Majesty, by and with the Advice and Consent of the Lords Spiritual and Temporal, and Commons, in this present Parliament assembled, and by the Authority of the same, That it shall be lawful for any Guardian, Relieving Officer, or Overseer of any Parish or Union in *England* to take and convey before Two Justices of the Peace, without Summons or Warrant, every poor Person who shall become chargeable to any Parish in *England*, and who he may have Reason to believe is liable to be removed from *England* under the first-recited Act; and the Justices before whom any such Person shall be so brought shall hear and examine and proceed in the same Manner in all respects as if such Person had been brought before them under and in the Manner directed by that Act.

II. And be it enacted, That it shall be lawful for any Inspector of the Poor, or other Officer appointed by the Parochial Board of any Parish or Combination in *Scotland*, to take and convey before the Sheriff or any Two Justices of the Peace of the County in which the Parish or Combination for which such Inspector or Officer acts, or any Portion thereof is situated, without previous Complaint or Warrant in that Behalf, every poor Person who shall be in the Course of receiving Parochial Relief in any Parish or Combination in *Scotland*, and who he may have Reason to believe is liable to be removed from *Scotland* under the secondly-recited Act; and the Sheriff or Justices before whom any such Person shall be so brought shall make such Examination, and proceed in the same Manner in all respects as if such Person had been brought before him or them under and in the Manner directed by that Act.

III. And be it enacted, That every Person who by this Act is authorized to take and convey any poor Person before any Sheriff or Justices shall, in the Execution of this Act, in that Behalf have and exercise all the Rights, Privileges, Powers, and Immunities with which a Constable is by Law invested.

IV. And be it enacted, That in the Construction of this Act the Singular Number or Masculine Gender shall, except when the Context excludes such Construction, be understood to include and shall be applied to several Persons, Matters, or Things, as well as to one Person, Matter, or Thing, and to Females as well as Males respectively; and that the Words "Justices of the Peace" shall be understood to include and extend to a Justice of the Peace or Magistrate of a County, County of a City, or County of a Town, or of any City or Town Corporate.

V. And be it enacted, That this Act may be amended or repealed by any Act to be passed in this Session of Parliament.

LONDON:

Printed by order of the Poor Law Commissioners, by BLACKBURN and PARDON, 6, Hatton Garden, and Published by CHARLES KNIGHT and Co., 22, Ludgate Street, Publishers to the Poor Law Commissioners.

AN

OFFICIAL CIRCULAR

OF PUBLIC DOCUMENTS AND INFORMATION:

DIRECTED BY THE POOR LAW COMMISSIONERS TO BE PRINTED, CHIEFLY FOR THE USE OF THE MEMBERS AND PERMANENT OFFICERS OF BOARDS OF GUARDIANS, UNDER THE POOR LAW AMENDMENT ACT.

No. 10.] 1 October, 1847. [N.S.

Poor Law Commission Office,
Somerset House, Oct. 1, 1847.

The Poor Law Commissioners directed that the following documents be printed and circulated for the information of Guardians and Officers of the several Unions, viz.:—

(Signed) By order of the Board,
Edwin Chadwick, *Secretary.*

I.—ACCOUNTS—Application of Penalties for Gaming and Drunkenness.

March 20th, 1846.

Relieving Officer of Haslingden Union—Inquired whether penalties for gaming in public-houses, and fines for tippling and drunkenness, should go to the credit of the poor-rates.

Ans.—In convictions under 12 Geo. 2, c. 28, and 13 Geo. 2, c. 19, sec. 9, for gaming, the penalties or forfeitures inflicted are to be applied, one-third to the informer, and two-thirds to the use of the poor of the parish where the offence was committed. There are, however, other cases, as in the convictions under the 42nd Geo. 3, c. 119, in which the penalty goes to the crown, the informer, and the parties apprehending, in the proportion of one-third to each. Penalties inflicted on persons convicted of drunkenness, under 4 Jac. 1, c. 5, s. 4, and 21 Jac. 1, c. 7, ss. 1 and 3, are for the use of the poor of the parish where the offence is committed. By the words "to the use of the poor of the parish," in the statutes cited, the Commissioners are disposed to think it is meant that the money should go in aid of the poor-rates.

II.—AUDITORS—Circular.

Poor Law Commission Office,
Somerset House, July 2nd, 1847.

Sir,

On the 22nd of March last, the Poor Law Commissioners forwarded to you a copy of a General Order issued by them, with reference to the keeping and examining of the accounts of unions and parishes. The Commissioners had deferred the transmission of any general instructions addressed to district auditors until the provisions of this Order were in force, and could be referred to, as operating on the several officers of the unions and parishes, and regulating the audit of their accounts. They now think it right to address to you some observations on the important duties which are discharged by district auditors.

The Commissioners entertain no doubt that you have made yourself fully acquainted with the several provisions relating to your functions, which are contained in the 7 & 8 Vic. c. 101. The Order of Accounts lately issued will be found to contain the regulations which are binding on the persons accounting at the audit. The Articles numbered 32—44 relate more especially to the audit itself, and the mode of conducting it; and, therefore, more immediately concern your own duties, whilst the other portions of the Order show what is required of others.

You will observe, that until the 25th of March, 1848, it is optional with the guardians and overseers whether they keep the accounts and books in the forms prescribed by the Order: but after that day the Order, in all its parts, operates upon them compulsorily. Such of the provisions of the Order, however, as relate to the duties of the auditor, and also to the accounting of officers and the closing and examining of accounts, have already come into operation.

The Commissioners do not know that any good end would be obtained by their reciting, in a letter, the various provisions in the Order, which relate more particularly to the audit, or that they could set them out more clearly than is already done in the regulations themselves. They may add, however, with regard to the time of audit prescribed in Article 32, that they rely on the endeavours of the auditors to let as little delay intervene between the closing of the half year and the audit of accounts for that half year as circumstances will allow; because, although the 31st Article is so framed as to prevent any inconvenience to the officers from the retention of their salaries until the audit is concluded,—at least in all cases in which the guardians are satisfied that there is no apparent reason to mistrust the accounts of the persons to whom such salaries are due,—it is manifestly, for many reasons, desirable that the accounts should be audited as soon as possible after they have been closed.

With reference to the place of audit, (of which fourteen days' notice is required to be given,) in one or two instances complaints have been received by the Commissioners that the audit was not held at the workhouse. As a general rule, the Commissioners are of opinion that it is expedient that the audit should be held in the board-room, and they believe that such an arrangement will, for the most part, suit the convenience of all parties better than any other. It is desirable that, in fixing the day of the audit, you should so arrange as to avoid taking the accounts of the union on a day which would interfere with one of the meetings of the guardians, as in such case it might become necessary for that day to adjourn the audit elsewhere. Special cases may also occur in which the situation of the workhouse or board-room may make another place preferable. Whenever any deviation from the previous course of proceeding occurs in this respect, the Commissioners wish to be informed of the fact, and the cause which renders such a deviation necessary. Whenever you may find it requisite to adjourn the audit of any particular account, you will do well, as far as lies in your power, to cause notice of the time and place of such adjournment to be communicated to all parties interested in the matter.

The Commissioners wish particularly to draw your attention to Article 32 of the Order, in which provision is made for special audits in the intervals of the regular half-yearly audits, whenever the peculiar circumstances of any union or parish may require such a course to be taken. You will see that no obligation of holding a special audit is, by this article, imposed on the auditor, although, when it is held with the consent of the Commissioners, the proceedings at such audit are made to carry legal consequences equivalent to those at a general audit.

The Commissioners do not now propose to dwell on the legal character of the duties performed by you as a district auditor. They will, however, mention that you have to consider the lawfulness of the items contained in the accounts submitted to you, and that lawfulness will in many instances depend on the regulations with reference to relief and other matters issued by the Poor Law Commissioners. In some of these regulations, a discretion in certain peculiar cases is expressly reserved to the Poor Law Commissioners, and where this is done, or where such a discretion is expressly given by Act of Parliament, the fact whether the Commissioners have or have not sanctioned a particular charge becomes most material, and must be clearly ascertained by you. When, however, no such discretion is given by statute, nor reserved in the regulations, it is for you as auditor to decide as to the legality of an item, according to the best of your judgment on the facts before you. In such cases the sanction of the Commissioners could not, if given, make that lawful which was in itself unlawful, and on appeal from your decision their power is limited by law to the deciding upon the lawfulness of the reasons for such decision. These reasons, you, when required, are bound to state in the book of accounts, and they must show distinctly the grounds on which you have allowed or disallowed any item objected to. The Commissioners think that the omission or neglect of the party interested to require that such reasons should be stated at the time of the audit, will not necessarily prevent you from stating them in the book at some subsequent time, and as this step is a condition preceding the application for redress of a supposed wrong, they think you ought not to refuse to set forth the reasons whenever you may be called on to do so.

You are aware that, when the reasons are thus stated, the party objecting to your decision may either remove such decision directly into the Queen's Bench, or may appeal to the Poor Law Commissioners. It is, therefore, of importance that you should state your reasons with precision, absolutely, and without any reservation. Though it is necessary that your reasons should be stated so as to be clearly understood, it is not desirable that they should be set forth with prolixity or diffuseness. As every item of disallowance, or surcharge, may be the subject of future discussion, your reasons, if assigned at all, should be stated separately and completely with reference to every such item, and in such a manner that each item may be capable of being fully and conclusively discussed if appealed against alone. Moreover, you must decide all matters of fact yourself, as your allowance or disallowance must be absolute and conclusive. You may adjourn your audit from time to time, but cannot leave any item open and undecided until some future time after your audit is once concluded. Every certificate should be confined to the subject matter of the particular account under examination, and such certificate should be made at the time of the audit and not *afterwards*. You have no power, the Commissioners believe, to re-open a former audit and to reinvestigate accounts previously closed and audited.

You should, in case of any disallowance or surcharge, state in express terms that you have disallowed or surcharged the particular item or items, and not simply include such item or items in the general balance found by you, and in a certificate formed on such balance. And it will be well that, in your certificate, you should set forth accurately the particular individual against whom you may make your certificate.

The legal character of the audit entrusted to you, may often oblige you to disallow charges incurred without any intention to violate the law, and in ignorance of the necessity which exists for a statutory authority of some kind to support all expenditure from the poor-rate. The Commissioners are extremely anxious that, so far as is compatible with the discharge of your duty, your powers should be exercised with all possible consideration for the officers who may submit their accounts to you, and that care should be taken by you to avoid all expressions of severity, and to soften by your manner any impression of harshness which the exercise of functions of this nature must occasionally carry with it.

Your duty is confined to the audit of the accounts, and, when necessary, the recovery of balances, and though the Commissioners see no objection to your giving advice to the accounting officers, they consider that you will do well to use great caution in expressing your opinion publicly, as to the accounts which may have been laid before you. Whenever you may form an opinion that the general conduct of a parish or a union, in regard to their proceedings, is open to animadversion, the Commissioners will be desirous to receive a report from you on the subject.

The statute 7 & 8 Vic. c. 101, sec. 32, has imposed upon you the duty of enforcing the payment of the moneys which you certify to be due, and it frequently may be necessary for you to resort to legal proceedings. The Commissioners are aware of the difficulties which necessarily attend all proceedings of this nature: but such difficulties arise from the strictness of proof, and the accuracy required in the proceeding, which is often considered to be of a penal character, though it is, in fact, a recovery of money from an agent or trustee who has improperly expended it.

You are entitled, in such cases, to the ordinary legal assistance of an attorney; but the employment before the justices of counsel, who must generally be retained specially, requires much deliberation, and can rarely be justified.

Where you have instituted any proceedings, the Commissioners are of opinion that you should use your utmost endeavours that not only the sum due be recovered, but also that the parish or union should be indemnified in respect to the costs which you incur, since these will, if not recovered from the party proceeded against, fall upon such parish or union: thus, notwithstanding the success of your application, loss may be sustained by the parish or union in behalf of which you recover the sum lawfully due to it.

Although the position of the Commissioners, as being liable to be called upon to review your decision in any case, renders it improper in them to give you advice as to the course to be pursued by you in any particular instance, they will nevertheless be always ready to express their views generally as to any points which may arise in reference to the performance of your duties.

I am, &c.

W. G. LUMLEY, *Assistant Secretary.*

To District Auditor.

III.—BASTARDY — GUARDIANS CANNOT INTERFERE IN CAUSING AN APPLICATION TO BE MADE FOR AN ORDER IN.

January 14th, 1846.

Clerk of Reigate Union — A female pauper, who has been in the workhouse for several years, is now pregnant, and has declared the late schoolmaster to be the father of her child. The guardians, considering it their duty to prevent the parish of the pauper's settlement from being burdened with the maintenance of the child, were about to inform her that it would be her duty to take the necessary steps for procuring an order of filiation upon the reputed father, but were met with the difficulty of the enactment in the 7th section of the 7 and 8 Vic. c. 101, which declares that "no officer of any union shall in any way interfere, as such officer, in causing any application to be made for an order," &c. Inquired whether this restriction applies to the guardians, and prevents them from urging paupers maintained in the workhouse to take steps for affiliating their bastard children.

Ans.—The Commissioners are advised that the words "officer of any parish or union," contained in the 7th section of the 7 & 8 Vic. c. 101, extend to and include guardians of the poor. The section renders it unlawful for "any such officer to conduct any application to make or enforce the order of petty sessions, or in any way to interfere as such officer in causing such application to be made." It appears to the Commissioners that, in advising, or urging, the mother of an illegitimate child, in any case, to make application to the justices for an order, the guardians are, in the words of the statute, "causing such application to be made."

IV.—BURIAL OF PAUPERS.

July 9th, 1846.

Clerk of West Derby Union—Submitted the following opinion with regard to the construction of the Act 7 & 8 Vic. c. 101, as it respects the burial of paupers, and requested to be informed whether his views thereon were correct—sec. 31. The guardians may bury the body of any poor person dying within the union, and charge the expense thereof to the township to which such person was chargeable; if such person was not chargeable, the expense to be charged to the township in which the death occurred; if the place of death cannot be ascertained, (as in the case of a body being found on the sea-shore,) the expense of burial must be charged to the township in which the body was found. In all cases where the guardians do bury, they *may*, if they please, and *must*, if requested by the person dying, or by his next of kin, bury such person in the churchyard or burial-ground of the township to which he was chargeable: or, they *may* (if not otherwise requested as aforesaid) bury such person in the churchyard, or other consecrated burial-ground belonging to the township in which the death occurred. It would appear, therefore, that where the burial takes place in the township to which the deceased was chargeable, it is competent for the guardians to inter in any churchyard or burial-ground in such township whether such a burial-ground be consecrated or not; but if such interment do not take place in the township to which the deceased was chargeable, the body must be buried in some churchyard or other consecrated burial-ground in or belonging to the township in which the death may have occurred. By sec. 56, it is enacted, that for the purpose of the burial of the poor the workhouse of the union shall be considered as situate in the township to which any person dying in such workhouse has been chargeable.

Ans.—The Commissioners do not entirely concur in the views which you take of the effect of the 31st sec. of the 7 & 8 Vic. c. 101. 1. The guardians, where they act under the section, may bury the body in the churchyard or burial-ground of the parish to which the person was chargeable. They may do this in compliance with the request of the deceased or of his relatives, or for any other cause. But such request, or the existence of any sufficient cause, does not, as the Commissioners think, make it compulsory on the guardians so to bury the body in the parish to which the deceased was chargeable. 2. In case the guardians act under the power now referred to of burying in the churchyard or burial-ground of the parish to which the deceased was chargeable, you appear to consider that the terms of the provision allow of a burial in unconsecrated ground. This place of burial is described as the churchyard or burial-ground *of* the parish, not as a churchyard or burial-ground *in* the parish. If any burial-ground *of* the parish or township, be unconsecrated, the provision allows of the guardians burying the body there; but it does not justify the burial in any unconsecrated burial-ground *in* the parish, such ground not belonging to the parish. It is the provision in the words which follow that allows of burial in unconsecrated ground, namely, where the deceased, or the husband, wife, or next of kin, have desired that the body should not be buried in the churchyard or consecrated burial-ground of the parish where the death occurred. Generally, the effect of the whole provision, so far as your opinion is involved, appears to the Commissioners to be as follows:—1. As a general rule, all bodies buried by guardians are to be buried in the churchyard or in a consecrated burial-ground, and this in the parish, or township, of the death. 2. But the burial in such churchyard or consecrated burial-ground, may be dispensed with by the desire of the deceased, or husband, wife, or next of kin. 3. If the burial in the churchyard or consecrated burial-ground be dispensed with in compliance with such desire, the guardians may apparently authorise the burial anywhere, *i.e.*, in unconsecrated ground, or in ground out of the parish of the death. 4. Also the guardians may authoritatively direct the burial to take place in the parish where the deceased was chargeable. But this is a departure from the general law, and is in this clause made the exception. It is only authorised when the deceased or his relatives have desired it, or the guardians see particular cause for it. This case may arise as in case 2, when there is an objection of the deceased or his friends to burial in the churchyard or consecrated burial-ground of the parish. And if there be any burial-ground of the parish or township (*i.e.*, belonging to the township) which is not consecrated, the guardians may bury the body in such burial-ground.

V.—ELECTION OF GUARDIANS—WHETHER GUARDIAN CAN BE ELECTED FOR A SECOND PARISH—INSPECTION OF VOTING PAPERS.

April 16th, 1846.

Mr. ————, *Brentford Union*—Inquired, 1st, whether a person who has been elected a guardian for one parish in a union can become a candidate for the same office for another parish in the same union; and, 2ndly, whether persons, who are candidates for the office of guardian, or those who have been already elected to that office, can claim to see the voting papers after the clerk has made his return of the guardians elected.

Ans.—1. The Commissioners are not aware of anything to prevent a person being nominated and elected guardian for two, or more, parishes in the same union. The Commissioners think, in the case put, the law does not impose any obligation on the person nominated to decline to serve, if elected, so as to put an end to the contest. It is entirely in the discretion of the candidate whether he will give the notice contemplated by sec. 10 of 5 & 6 Vic. c. 57. 2. No candidate, or elected guardian, can claim, as of right, to see and examine the voting papers. Before the clerk makes his return in the form (E.) prescribed in the Order of Election, the voting papers are in his custody, as the returning officer, and he is certainly under no obligation to allow an inspection of such papers to any one, however interested in the result of the election. After the return is made, the voting papers will be in the possession of the board of guardians, pursuant to Article 24 of the Order, and it will then be for the guardians to determine what examination shall be permitted or allowed.

VI.—GUARDIANS.

1. REFRESHMENTS TO, AT THEIR MEETINGS, FROM WORKHOUSE STORES.

Oct. 12th, 1846.

Clerk of Carnarvon Union—The meetings of the guardians are held at the union workhouse, about a mile from the town of Carnarvon, and some of the guardians who attend come a distance of from twelve to fifteen miles, direct from home. Inquired whether the master of the workhouse may supply the guardians with a basin of soup, and a piece of bread each, in order to insure the attendance of the guardians till the termination of the proceedings of the board.

Ans.—The Commissioners are well aware of the value of the public services of the guardians of unions, and of the time and attention which they devote to the discharge of their official duties. The Commissioners would readily concur in any arrangement which could be properly made, either for promoting the comfort and convenience of the guardians, or for diminishing the claims made upon the time which they might otherwise devote for the transaction of their private affairs; but the proposition alluded to in your letter is not one to which the Commissioners' concurrence could give any validity, since the law itself has not placed the matter within their discretion, so as to render any expense which might be incurred for such a purpose legally payable out of the poor-rates.

2. VOTING AT MEETINGS OF GUARDIANS.

October 29th, 1846.

Chairman of ———— *Union* — A guardian having moved a resolution at the board, an amendment to it was proposed, and carried by a majority of 15 to 4; an amendment to such amendment was then moved, and carried by a majority of 11 to 2, and the chairman thereupon decided that the first amendment was lost. Inquired, whether the chairman should not have again submitted the first amendment to the board, after the guardians had divided on the second.

Ans.—The Commissioners have a difficulty in expressing an opinion on the question submitted to them by you, without being informed of the terms of the motion and of the two amendments. The Commissioners understand, from your statement, that the second amendment was not proposed until the first amendment had been put to the vote and carried. If this was the case, they think that it was too late to propose the motion as an amendment, and that the question ought to have been put as a substantive motion, instead of an amendment upon a motion which had been carried.

VII.—JUSTICES—JURISDICTION OF.

April 13th, 1846.

Clerk of Newport Union, Salop—The Newport Union is situate partly in the county of Salop and partly in the county of Stafford, and a petty sessional district, called the Newport division of the hundred of Bradford, is held at Newport, the magistrates acting for which are also magistrates for the county of Stafford. The parishes of Adbaston and High Offley, which are in the Pirehill division of the county of Stafford, being in arrear with their contributions to the union funds, an application was made to the justices acting for the Newport division, for a summons against the overseers of those parishes, under the 2 & 3 Vic. c. 84, sec. 1, but it is doubted whether the case can be tried at Newport; inasmuch as the business of the Pirehill division is always transacted at Stafford, where, it is contended, the application must be made. Inquired whether the Newport justices can act in this case; and, if not, whether proceedings can be taken against the overseers under the 7 & 8 Vic. c. 101, s. 63, and how the penalty imposed by that Act is to be recovered.

Ans.—The 28th Geo. 3, c. 49, provides, that "it shall and may be lawful for any justice or justices of the peace acting as such for any two or more counties, being adjoining counties, to act as a justice or justices of the peace in all matters and things whatsoever concerning, or in anywise relating to, any or either of the said counties; and that all act and acts of such justice or justices of the peace, and the act and acts of any constable or other officer in obedience thereto shall be as valid, good, and effectual in the law, to all intents and purposes whatsoever, as if such act or acts of the said justice or justices had been done in the county or counties to which such act or acts particularly relate." It appears to the Commissioners that the effect of this provision, in regard to the case put, is to enable the justices, acting both for Salop and Stafford, to summon the overseers of the parishes of Adbaston and High Offley (situate in the latter county) to attend a special sessions at Newport, to answer the complaint of the chairman of the Newport Union of nonpayment of the contribution order. The question, however, being one of jurisdiction, it is for the justices to satisfy themselves as to the power to entertain the matter if that course be taken. If the justices should entertain doubts upon the point, the safe course will be to summon the overseers of the parishes in question to attend a special sessions to be convened at the ordinary place at which special sessions are held for the division, or district including those parishes; though this course may not be so convenient as the former. The Commissioners are disposed to think that, in a proceeding under the 63rd section of 7 & 8 Vic. c. 101, the overseers of Adbaston and High Offley might be summoned to attend a petty sessions held at Newport, composed of justices having jurisdiction in Salop and Stafford. The 63rd section is silent as to the mode of recovering the penalty imposed by it; but the Commissioners apprehend that the mode of recovering penalties under the 4 & 5 Wm. 4, c. 76, is applicable here. As the 7 & 8 Vic. c. 101, (see section 74,) is to be construed as one Act with the 4 & 5 Wm. 4, c. 76; and section 99 of the latter Act points out the particular mode in which such penalties inflicted or authorised to be imposed by such Act are to be recovered.

VIII.—LOANS—COLLECTION OF REPAYMENTS OF.

September 15th, 1846.

Clerk of Braintree Union—Inquired who should be directed to collect the repayments on account of loans advanced by the board of guardians.

Ans.—The Commissioners advise the guardians to instruct the relieving officer of the district to collect the loans in question. The relieving officer must, of course, debit himself with the payments so made to him, in his receipt and payment book, and he should pay over the sums so received, at once, to the treasurer of the union, on account of the guardians, taking credit in his book for such payment.

IX.—MIGRATION—OF FAMILIES CHARGEABLE IN UNIONS, TO THE MANUFACTURING DISTRICTS.

March 16th, 1846.

Clerk of Towcester Union—Messrs. ———, a manufacturing firm, near Stockport, had made application to the guardians recommending that families (particularly widows, with two or three children turned thirteen years of age,) who were chargeable, or otherwise, should remove to the manufacturing districts, where they would improve their condition. The writers offered employment to ten or twenty young females, and a few boys. Inquired the Commissioners' views as to the effects of such migrations.

Ans.—It is not advisable for the board of guardians to take any active steps in effecting the removal of families according to the proposals of Messrs. ———. In all probability, there may be amongst the persons chargeable to the union, several to whom the proposed migration would be advantageous, but the Commissioners think that any agreement between such persons and Messrs. ———, should be left to their private mutual understanding. The Commissioners, at the same time, wish to add, that there can be no objection to Messrs. ———, or other persons, having access to persons destitute, to whom they may wish to offer employment.

X.—OVERSEERS.

1. CUSTODY OF RATE-BOOKS.

October 31st, 1846.

Mr. ———, *Shepton Mallet*—Inquired whether overseers are bound to allow surveyors of highways to have the poor-rate book to enable them to make a highway rate, which must be made out in accordance with the poor-rate.

Ans.—The overseers are not obliged to part with the custody of the poor-rate books for the purpose stated by you, but the surveyor of highways is entitled himself, at all reasonable times, to inspect the poor-rates, or assessments, and to make a copy, or take extracts therefrom; or he may grant authority to some person to do this on his behalf. (See 5 & 6 Wm. 4, c. 50, s. 28.)

---

2. LIABILITY OF OVERSEERS TO PENALTY FOR DOING WORK IN THE UNION WORKHOUSE.

October 8th, 1846.

Overseer of Shepton Mallet—Inquired whether he was liable to be sued for a penalty, for doing any work in his business of a plumber and glazier, at the Shepton Mallet union workhouse, under the orders of the board of guardians.

Ans.—It was decided, in Barber *v.* Waite, 1 A. and E. 514, that an overseer, who was a plumber, glazier, and painter, was *not* liable to the penalties imposed by the 55 Geo. 3, c. 137, for doing some repairs to the workhouse, such as mending the windows, painting, and repairing the lead-work, though he supplied the glass, paint, lead, &c., necessary to the execution of the repairs. The Commissioners will not undertake to say, however, that this case precisely coincides with your own.

NAMES of COUNTIES.	Population in 1841.	LUNATICS.			IDIOTS.			Grand Total Lunatics and Idiots.	WHERE In County Lunatic Asylums and Hospitals.			In Licensed House.			In Union Workhouse.		
		M.	F.	Total.	M.	F.	Total		M.	F.	Total	M.	F.	Total	M.	F.	Total
ENGLAND:																	
Bedford	112,379	38	41	79	33	33	66	145	41	34	75	...	5	5	19	20	39
Berks	190,367	63	84	147	75	84	159	306	7	7	14	58	74	132	42	45	87
Buckingham	138,255	41	50	91	37	40	77	168	5	8	13	30	31	61	15	24	40
Cambridge	171,848	42	52	94	38	34	72	166	10	15	25	20	28	48	16	14	30
Chester	367,019	61	91	152	63	82	145	297	56	82	138	3	6	9	28	38	66
Cornwall	340,728	65	99	164	70	82	152	316	61	72	133	...	...	...	43	76	119
Cumberland	177,912	52	50	102	42	44	86	188	3	1	4	36	35	71	42	46	88
Derby	242,786	47	43	90	57	61	118	208	3	3	6	29	24	53	39	41	80
Devon	531,880	131	185	316	128	124	252	568	118	144	262	8	11	19	54	71	125
Dorset	167,874	68	86	154	35	40	75	229	55	71	126	8	6	14	13	19	32
Durham	325,997	56	68	124	62	62	124	248	...	2	2	55	54	109	40	40	80
Essex	320,818	66	114	180	80	77	157	337	3	4	7	59	91	150	40	37	77
Gloucester	394,828	147	203	305	114	144	258	608	115	140	255	19	26	45	83	135	218
Hereford	110,675	27	36	63	48	42	90	153	...	...	...	23	20	43	5	5	10
Hertford	176,173	44	67	111	67	77	144	255	37	47	84	8	10	18	33	37	70
Huntingdon	55,573	18	28	46	16	19	35	81	13	17	30	4	9	13	11	4	15
Kent	549,694	158	241	399	111	108	219	618	136	173	309	27	51	78	63	75	138
Lancaster	1,709,959	439	478	917	249	269	518	1,435	303	280	583	75	116	191	209	245	454
Leicester	220,232	68	90	158	59	63	122	280	54	60	114	3	9	12	34	45	79
Lincoln	356,347	95	107	202	86	85	171	373	46	47	93	20	26	46	67	64	131
Middlesex	1,574,465	616	940	1,556	180	202	382	1,938	353	467	820	298	452	750	127	204	331
Monmouth	150,222	41	54	95	23	25	48	143	7	6	13	29	34	63	10	22	32
Norfolk	405,123	139	153	292	119	140	259	551	103	97	200	29	27	56	67	73	140
Northampton	197,197	66	77	143	73	77	150	293	57	62	119	3	3	6	33	33	66
Northumberland	265,988	78	105	183	60	74	134	317	1	4	5	56	73	129	54	58	112
Nottingham	270,719	103	130	233	58	75	133	366	94	95	189	...	2	2	42	80	122
Oxford	159,476	54	73	127	67	60	127	254	42	56	98	7	5	12	35	40	75
Rutland	23,150	9	8	17	6	5	11	28	5	7	12	1	...	1	5	3	8
Salop	242,703	55	76	131	52	66	118	249	40	46	86	12	14	26	29	41	70
Somerset	454,446	115	172	287	149	174	323	610	7	15	22	95	113	208	72	87	159
Southampton	339,160	115	1.1	286	115	120	235	521	2	1	3	97	117	214	70	94	164
Stafford	442,348	109	116	225	117	135	252	477	103	79	182	31	36	67	66	96	162
Suffolk	314,722	98	163	261	77	75	152	413	90	138	228	7	19	26	44	34	78
Surrey	577,775	224	316	540	105	122	227	767	175	207	382	59	109	168	70	96	166
Sussex	278,608	65	94	159	88	103	191	350	2	1	3	66	72	138	45	54	99
Warwick	388,987	121	152	373	81	89	170	443	18	21	39	63	80	143	77	86	163
Westmorland	56,469	14	28	42	12	20	32	74	...	1	1	9	13	22	10	19	29
Wilts	243,332	94	108	202	68	94	162	364	...	...	...	88	93	181	35	57	92
Worcester	336,108	70	94	164	72	95	167	331	9	11	20	51	51	102	39	64	103
York, East Riding	221,847	57	76	133	40	42	82	215	7	14	21	46	51	97	24	28	52
,, North Riding	180.527	40	39	79	32	35	67	146	11	5	16	26	24	50	21	24	45
,, West Riding	879,492	221	247	468	175	162	337	805	151	170	321	29	19	48	117	127	244
TOTALS	14,664,208	4,230	5,605	9,835	3,239	3,560	6,799	16,634	2,343	2,710	5,053	1,587	2,039	3,626	1,988	2,502	4,490
WALES:																	
Anglesey	38,105	5	13	18	16	20	36	54	...	...	...	1	...	1	...	...	...
Brecon	55,399	14	13	27	22	25	47	74	1	...	1	7	4	11	5	2	7
Cardigan	75,136	21	39	60	28	34	62	122	1	1	2	2	4	6	...	...	...
Carmarthen	110,404	26	44	70	43	43	86	156	...	...	...	7	10	17	6	5	11
Carnarvon	86,728	24	20	44	35	55	90	134	...	...	...	5	1	6	3	2	5
Denbigh	68,483	3	11	14	36	32	68	82	...	...	...	5	8	13	5	7	12
Flint	64,355	8	11	19	20	22	42	61	3	1	4	4	8	12	9	8	17
Glamorgan	178,041	46	43	89	35	51	86	175	1	...	1	30	19	49	10	13	23
Merioneth	50,696	9	11	20	36	31	67	87	1	1	2	1	...	1	1	3	4
Montgomery	75,230	17	17	34	45	57	102	136	9	6	15	1	...	1	7	7	14
Pembroke	78,563	15	19	34	24	27	51	85	10	9	19	...	...	...	2	2	4
Radnor	19,554	4	5	9	11	12	23	32	1	...	1	3	2	5	...	...	...
TOTALS	900,694	192	246	438	351	409	760	1,198	27	18	45	66	56	122	48	49	97
TOTALS of Unions and Places under Local Acts in England and Wales	15,564,902	4,422	5,851	10,273	3,590	3,969	7,559	17,832	2.370	2,728	5,098	1,653	2,095	3,748	2,036	2,551	4,587
TOTALS of Unions under Gilbert's Act	196,948	40	39	79	25	16	41	120	27	17	44	4	9	13	22	22	44
TOTALS of Parishes and Townships not in Union or under Local Act	144,891	37	40	77	22	14	36	113	...	...	...	...	...	...	...	...	...
TOTALS for England & Wales	15,906,741	4,499	5,930	10,429	3,637	3,999	7,636	18,065	2,397	2,745	5,142	1,657	2,104	3,761	2,058	2,573	4,631

MAINTAINED. With their Friends, or elsewhere. M.	F.	Total.	AGES. 0 to 5.	5 to 10.	10 to 20.	20 to 80.	30 to 40.	40 to 50.	50 to 60.	60 to 70.	70 and upwards.	Dangerous to Themselves and Others.	Of Dirty Habits.	NAMES of COUNTIES.
														ENGLAND:
11	15	26	...	...	9	25	28	31	27	20	5	45	23	Bedford.
31	42	73	...	...	26	72	60	63	51	23	11	92	49	Berks.
28	26	54	...	...	9	24	42	37	28	18	10	43	26	Buckingham.
34	29	63	1	...	17	32	36	38	23	15	4	46	27	Cambridge.
37	47	84	...	1	15	64	75	67	43	23	9	74	33	Chester.
31	33	64	...	1	18	59	65	65	49	39	20	89	52	Cornwall.
13	12	25	...	1	6	44	48	49	19	18	3	38	16	Cumberland.
33	36	69	...	...	12	46	51	40	32	17	10	45	26	Derby.
79	83	162	...	4	26	107	121	128	89	67	26	141	95	Devon.
27	30	57	...	1	4	42	46	44	46	26	20	73	29	Dorset.
23	34	57	...	...	10	52	69	49	36	20	12	93	37	Durham.
44	59	103	...	...	35	75	75	54	58	31	9	76	55	Essex.
44	46	90	...	4	36	115	139	131	95	60	28	196	88	Gloucester.
47	53	100	...	1	12	34	28	26	31	14	7	30	34	Hereford.
33	50	83	...	...	18	63	52	42	46	29	5	64	27	Hertford.
6	17	23	...	1	7	14	18	19	11	9	2	17	9	Huntingdon.
43	50	93	...	2	25	96	154	142	104	59	36	165	88	Kent.
101	106	207	1	5	67	304	362	346	205	108	37	464	151	Lancaster.
36	39	75	1	...	14	45	67	58	48	27	20	65	33	Leicester.
48	55	103	...	1	16	84	66	91	58	34	23	92	55	Lincoln.
18	19	37	...	2	72	363	448	463	335	173	82	591	356	Middlesex.
18	17	35	...	...	9	29	21	33	23	20	8	46	18	Monmouth.
59	96	155	...	1	32	108	125	114	81	64	26	159	95	Norfolk.
46	56	102	...	1	12	60	52	68	53	31	16	59	52	Northampton.
27	44	71	...	...	16	55	82	78	45	26	15	78	44	Northumberland.
25	28	53	...	3	18	66	89	80	56	40	14	111	62	Nottingham.
37	32	69	...	1	18	53	46	56	44	29	7	37	22	Oxford.
4	3	7	...	...	1	...	6	7	6	6	2	5	2	Rutland.
26	41	67	...	...	4	56	58	74	31	17	9	61	21	Salop.
90	131	221	...	5	34	143	140	122	95	44	27	165	119	Somerset.
61	79	140	...	...	24	95	102	115	98	65	22	128	78	Southampton.
26	40	66	...	1	20	109	96	112	75	51	13	101	63	Stafford.
34	47	81	...	1	27	83	85	87	69	41	20	136	102	Suffolk.
25	26	51	...	2	24	146	192	172	140	61	30	191	126	Surrey.
40	70	110	1	...	25	76	83	73	52	26	14	63	61	Sussex.
44	54	98	...	3	27	95	110	79	72	35	22	132	97	Warwick.
7	15	22	...	1	4	10	19	13	12	11	4	2	7	Westmorland.
39	52	91	...	1	19	70	67	61	77	52	17	106	71	Wilts.
43	63	106	...	...	19	55	80	71	44	40	22	94	41	Worcester.
20	25	45	...	...	3	39	58	47	33	27	8	71	40	York, East Riding.
14	21	35	...	...	9	22	37	27	23	17	11	43	20	,, North Riding.
99	93	192	...	3	49	122	199	198	133	82	19	265	160	,, West Riding.
1,551	1,914	3,465	4	47	848	3,252	3,797	3,670	2,696	1,615	705	4,592	2,610	.........TOTALS.
														WALES:
20	33	53	...	...	1	13	16	10	7	6	1	1	6	Anglesey.
23	32	55	...	...	7	17	14	12	10	11	3	11	21	Brecon.
46	68	114	...	2	4	17	30	25	24	14	6	7	7	Cardigan.
56	72	128	...	1	5	21	39	47	17	21	5	12	17	Carmarthen.
51	72	123	...	...	8	15	24	28	26	25	8	7	36	Carnarvon.
29	28	57	...	...	6	15	19	20	9	9	4	8	7	Denbigh.
12	16	28	...	...	5	24	12	5	4	5	6	11	8	Flint.
40	62	102	...	...	9	37	38	32	25	20	14	31	25	Glamorgan.
42	38	80	...	...	2	13	23	9	25	12	3	4	23	Merioneth.
45	61	106	...	...	10	26	24	20	23	25	8	8	25	Montgomery.
27	35	62	...	...	...	23	14	20	11	11	6	5	13	Pembroke.
11	15	26	...	...	6	4	6	8	7	...	1	4	10	Radnor.
402	532	934	...	3	63	225	259	236	188	159	65	109	198	.........TOTALS.
1,953	2,446	4,399	4	50	911	3,477	4,056	3,906	2,884	1,774	770	4,701	2,808	TOTALS of Unions and Places under Local Acts in England & Wales.
12	7	19	...	1	5	27	31	21	19	10	6	32	22	TOTALS of Unions under Gilbert's Act.
...	...	...	...	...	...	...	...	...	...	...	...	...	...	TOTALS of Parishes and Townships not in Union or under Local Act.
1,965	2,453	4,418	4	51	916	3,504	4,087	3,927	2,903	1,784	776	4,733	2,830	TOTALS for England & Wales

3. ONE OVERSEER ACCOUNTABLE FOR THE OTHER IN PAYING OVER CONTRIBUTIONS TO THE UNION FUND.

March 9th, 1846.

Overseer of ———, ————.—Inquired how far he was responsible for the other overseer who had served the office, and collected nearly all the rates for the second half of the year, and paid over only a portion of the amount to the guardians. He himself had served the office the first half year, but the guardians had applied to him for the money which the other overseer ought to have paid.

Ans.—The guardians of the union can only look to the overseers generally for the payment of the money required as contribution from the parish. They cannot regard any private arrangement by which one of the overseers performs the duties of the office and collects the rates for the first six months, and the other overseer for the remaining six months. The overseers are appointed for a year, and their duties and responsibilities extend over that year, and are not confined or limited by an arrangement entered into for the purpose of convenience. If your co-overseer misapplies the moneys which have come to his hands during the time he has performed the active duties of the office, he will be liable to make good such amount to the parish, as well as to be proceeded against criminally, but you will not be answerable for your colleague's default, nor liable to pay over to your successors, money which has not in fact come to your hands, unless indeed you should be liable to be charged with any deficiency or loss incurred by negligence or misconduct within the meaning of sec. 32 of the 7 and 8 Vic. c. 101.

4. COLLECTION OF POOR-RATE—RIGHT OF OVERSEER TO VISIT WORKHOUSE.

March 28th, 1846.

Overseer of ————, *Dover Union*—Inquired —1. Whose duty it is to appoint the time and place for persons to pay their rates, who omitted to pay the collector when he called upon them. 2. Is it the duty of the assistant overseer to lay before the overseers a list of defaulters, previously to their being summoned? 3. Can an overseer visit a pauper in the union workhouse without an order?

Ans.—1. The law has not made it the duty of any person to appoint a time for the rate-payer to call and pay his rate. The collector may, however, make any arrangement on this head, which he thinks proper. 2. By the terms of the Order of the Commissioners, dated April 4, 1839, the collector is required to furnish to the overseers a list of all defaulters. 3. The overseers cannot, as a matter of right, visit a pauper in the workhouse. Doubtless, if he have any reasonable ground for doing so, the guardians would not refuse to allow him to be admitted.

XII.—PAUPER—PARTIALLY DISABLED, REFUSING TO ENTER THE WORKHOUSE WITH HIS FAMILY, WHO ARE DESTITUTE.

July 18th, 1846.

Clerk of Church Stretton Union—E. C., who is partially disabled, is not fully employed, and neglects to supply his family with necessaries. The guardians have several times offered to him an order for the workhouse, which he has always declined, and they have, consequently, been obliged to afford temporary out-relief in order to save the family from starvation. Inquired whether E. C., by refusing to avail himself of an order for admission into the workhouse, (his family being in want of the necessaries of life at the time,) is guilty of neglecting or refusing to maintain them, so as to render him punishable under the Vagrant Act; and, if not, what proceedings should the guardians take in the matter.

Ans.—The Commissioners do not think that a partially disabled person, such as E. C. appears to be, can be brought within the provision of the Vagrant Act because he refuses to come into the workhouse; but it is competent to the guardians to refuse relief to him otherwise than in the workhouse.

XIII.—POOR-RATES—CHARGES ON, OF COSTS OF PROSECUTION FOR CONCEALMENT OF BIRTH.

June 10th, 1846.

Clerk of Parish of Bermondsey—The guardians have passed a resolution authorising the prosecution of a woman for concealing the birth of her bastard child, the case not being sufficiently strong to justify an indictment being preferred against her for child-murder. Inquired whether the guardians would be justified in paying the costs of this prosecution out of the poor-rates, as murder and concealment of birth are not amongst the crimes enumerated in section 59 of 7 & 8 Vic. c. 101.

Ans.—The Commissioners are of opinion that there is no ground to justify the guardians in paying the costs of the prosecution of the woman out of the poor-rates. The case is not one in which the 59th sec. of the 7 & 8 Vic. c. 101, appears to apply, or in which any authority is conferred, as far as the Commissioners perceive, by any other statute, for charging the poor-rates with such costs.

XIV.—RATING.

1. Right of shooting, whether assessable to the poor-rate.

July 24th, 1846.

Mr. ———, *Garstang Union*—Inquired whether a right of shooting over land, on which game has been preserved, and which has been let for the purpose of shooting, is assessable to the poor-rate; and, if so, whether the proprietor of the land, or the person to whom the right of shooting has been let, is the party liable to pay the rate.

Ans.—A mere right or privilege of shooting over land, is not in itself rateable to the poor-rate. The parties using the right or privilege, although paying a rent or consideration for it, are not, unless also in possession of the soil, occupiers upon whom the poor-rate can be levied. If in the case submitted, the moor, or ground in question, over which the right of shooting extends, has been let, it will be rateable not as waste ground, but as a shooting ground. The lessee, if the occupier, would, in this case, be rateable. If indeed the moor be not let, but the right of shooting is let, still the moor is rateable if in the occupation of the proprietor, and the rent paid for the shooting will afford a criterion for ascertaining the value of the land itself.

2. Cottage property—application by guardians for an act to make owners liable to the poor-rate.

March 2nd, 1846.

Clerk of Hitchin Union—The amount of excused rates on cottage property within the union being very considerable, attempts have been made to enforce the payment from the occupiers, or to collect it from the owners, which have but partially succeeded, such difficulties have been met with, that it is impracticable to carry out the measure effectually. Extreme measures to compel payment from the cottagers generally, drive the occupiers to seek assistance from the poor-rate. Inquired whether, with the approval of the majority of the guardians, there should be any objection to the union, as a body, applying for an Act of Parliament, to make the payment of all rates within the union upon properties assessed under £10, compulsory on the owners.

Ans.—As a question of rating, the Commissioners do not in any way disapprove of the proposal, that an Act of Parliament should be obtained with the object specified. They desire, however, to inform the guardians, that unless a special provision were made in such Act of Parliament, directing that the expenses incurred in obtaining the bill should be made a charge upon the poor-rate, no part of such expenses could legally be paid from the rates. The guardians, therefore, would not be justified in incurring any liability *as guardians of the union*, in respect of such expenses, inasmuch as it would be doubtful whether, or not, the legislature would allow the expenses, or any portion thereof, to be borne by the poor-rate. Upon the whole, the Commissioners doubt whether the forms of the proceedings in Parliament would enable the guardians of the union to carry their proposals into execution.

3. Exemption of chief-rents, etc.

March 27, 1846.

Mr. ———, *Valuator*—There is a chief-rent charged on the lands in the parish of West Pennard, which has not been heretofore assessed. Inquired whether such property is exempt, or, in making a new valuation of the parish, if he is to charge the same.

Ans.—Quit-rents, chief-rents, &c., being incorporeal hereditaments, are not rateable *as such* to the poor-rate. They are, in fact, included in the rent which the occupier of the lands pays for the value of his occupation, and the occupier being rated to the poor-rate for such occupation; if the owner of the chief or other rent were also assessed, a double rate would, in effect, be imposed for the same property or thing, and this the law does not authorise.

XV.—RELATIVES—Costs of procuring an order of maintenance.

August 31*st*, 1846.

The Overseers of ——— ———.—Inquired whether the cost of procuring an order against A. B. for the maintenance of his son can be defrayed out of the poor-rates.

Ans.—The Commissioners think that, if proceedings be taken for obtaining an order upon A. B. for the maintenance of his son, the costs which may not be recovered from him may be paid out of the poor-rates of the parish.

XVI.—RELIEF—Power of guardians to continue to relieve the wife in the workhouse where the husband offers to take her out, she refusing to live with him on account of his cruelty.

July 22nd, 1846.

Clerk of Maldon Union—J. C. is now in the workhouse with her children, where she has been for some time past. Her husband, who has only just returned from prison, has offered to take his wife and children out of the house, but admits that he has no home to take them to; and his conduct is so cruel to his wife, (on account of which he has been repeatedly imprisoned,) that she refuses to live with him. The man has sold all his goods, and talks of going to a distant part of the country in search of a harvest job. Inquired what course the guardians should adopt in this case.

Ans.—The Commissioners consider that the guardians need not, and, under any circumstances, the Commissioners think they should not, compel the woman and her children to leave the workhouse. If, as stated, she refuses to go to her husband, the guardians may allow her to remain in the house. It does not appear from your letter that the man applies for relief. It would seem clear, however, that the man and his family are destitute. Under the circumstances, therefore, the Commissioners think that the best course will be for the guardians to give the man an order for the workhouse, and nothing else, whether he accepts it or not. If the woman chooses, however, to leave the workhouse, it may be right perhaps to consider whether the husband ought not to be bound to keep the peace towards her.

XVII.—REMOVAL.

1. Of an Irish pauper of weak mind.

July 16th, 1846.

Clerk of Tamworth Union—An Irishman lately arrived in Tamworth, and, being in a state of destitution, he was admitted into the union workhouse, where he still remains. He is weak in mind, and does not seem to know anything save his name, and that he is from Ireland. The guardians, therefore, feel a difficulty in removing the man to Liverpool, to be thence passed to Ireland, and request the advice of the Commissioners with respect to the case.

Ans.—If the man is not competent to be examined, the guardians cannot proceed, under the statute 8 & 9 Vic. c. 117, as they will not have evidence to justify the justices in making an order for his removal; and without such an order the guardians are not justified in sending the pauper to Ireland. There is, therefore, no alternative but that the guardians of the Tamworth Union should continue to relieve him so long as he remains destitute. The Commissioners presume that the pauper is not so far a lunatic as to fall within the provisions of the 8 & 9 Vic. c. 126.

2. Removability of the pauper inmates of a lunatic asylum.

January 4th, 1847.

Clerk of Tunstead and Happing Incorporation—Inquired whether the charges made by the county of Norfolk Lunatic Asylum for paupers maintained and clothed therein belonging to the hundreds, are still to be defrayed by the particular parish to which each pauper belongs, and by which the cost of their maintenance has hitherto been paid; or whether the operation of the Act of 9 & 10 Vic. c. 66, will render the parish of Thorpe, wherein the asylum is situate, liable to the expense of the support of all such paupers who have resided in the asylum for more than five years.

Ans.—The Commissioners presume that the orders under which the guardians have hitherto paid the charges in question to the Lunatic Asylum, have been made under the Acts relating to lunatic asylums. Such orders are made upon the parishes in which the paupers are settled, or from which they had been sent to the asylum, and are not at all affected by the statute adverted to, which applies to the removal of poor persons. That statute will not, therefore, interfere with the previous practice of the guardians in regard to charging the costs of the maintenance of the paupers in the asylum referred to.

3. Proof of chargeability on removal.

March 16th, 1846.

Clerk of Cardigan Union—Inquired whether the production of the application and report book by the relieving officers at petty sessions, was sufficient proof of the order of relief to a pauper, in the case of an order of removal, or should the clerk attend with the chairman's book.

Ans.—What is to be proved with a view to an order of removal is not the order of the guardians to give relief, (which alone is shown in the application and report book,) but the actual chargeability and receipt of relief by the pauper at the charge of the particular parish. It appears to the Commissioners, that the certificate under sec. 69 of the 7 and 8 Vic. c. 101, removes all difficulty in the matter.

XVIII.—TAXATION — Of law bills by the clerk of the peace.

January 7th, 1846.

Messrs. ———, *Leicester Union*—The auditor has required that their bill, for business done for one of the parishes, should be taxed before the clerk of the peace. The parish for which the business has been done is in the county of Northampton, and the office where it was transacted is in the county of Leicester. The parish is about eighteen or twenty miles from Leicester, and about twenty-four from Northampton, and their residence is in Leicester. The overseers of the parish attend more frequently at Leicester than at Northampton, and it would be more convenient for all parties if the bill were taxed by the clerk of the peace for Leicester. Inquired whether such taxation can take place at Leicester.

Ans.—By the 39th section of the 7 & 8 Vic. c. 101, it is the duty of the clerk of the peace for the county, in which the parish is situate for which the business was done, to tax the costs claimed by the attorney for the performance of such business, if he be required to do so. You state that, in the case to which your question applies, the parish for which the business was done is in the county of Northampton, but the office at which it was transacted is situate in the county of Leicester. The clerk of the peace for the former county is, therefore, the proper person to be applied to, for the mere circumstance of the business having been performed in Leicester, cannot enable the clerk of the peace for that county to take cognisance of the matter, under the provision in the Act above referred to.

XIX.—TREASURER.

1. His obligation to attend as a witness before justices.

April 22nd, 1847.

Mr. ———.—Inquired whether it is the duty of the treasurer of the ——— Union, to attend before the justices, on a proceeding against overseers to enforce the payment of a balance, without being subpœned, and without being paid any remuneration for his attendance; and if he is entitled to any remuneration, at what rate should he be remunerated.

Ans.—The treasurer of a union is not under any obligation to attend before the justices, as a witness, by any regulation of the Commissioners, or otherwise, as far as they are aware. He appears to the Commissioners to be entirely in the same situation as other parties, and should have been summoned by the justices, in conformity with the 70th section of the 7 & 8 Vic. c. 101, which provides that the reasonable expenses of the witness are to be paid. The Commissioners cannot say what they may be; whatever is customary in similar proceedings should be paid or tendered in the present instance.

2. Whether treasurer can act as guardian.

April 16th, 1847.

Mr. J. B., ——— *Union*—Stated that, having been elected a guardian for one of the parishes in the union, he attended the first meeting of the board, and was appointed one of the vice-chairmen, but the validity of his election as guardian was objected to, on the ground of his being treasurer of the union. Inquired, whether the fact of his being treasurer to the union, receiving no salary for discharging the office, disqualifies him from acting as a guardian and vice-chairman of the board.

Ans.—The Commissioners have always felt the question to be one of some difficulty. They do not see how it can be assumed that no profit is derived from the office of treasurer of a union, though no salary be paid to him. Indeed, the case of Delane *v.* Hillcoat, 9 B. and C. 310, appears to be an authority as to the opinion of the courts of law upon a similar point, that a profit may be derivable from such an office. The Act 5 & 6 Vic. c. 57, sec. 14, provides that no *paid* officer, engaged in the administration of the laws for the relief of the poor, shall be capable of serving as a guardian, and from subsequent language it appears to the Commissioners, that the legislature have contemplated that an officer may be paid, though he have not a fixed salary or emolument. The impression upon the minds of the Commissioners is, that the treasurer of a union, though receiving no salary, is disqualified from serving as a guardian, but in a matter of doubt of this nature they must leave you to act upon your own judgment.

XX.—VAGRANTS.

1. Distinctive clothing for, when they destroy their own clothes.

March 26th, 1846.

Clerk of the ——— *Union* — Vagrants who obtained a night's lodging and provisions in the workhouse, destroyed their own clothes in order to compel the union to provide them with other and better clothing; the guardians were desirous of providing clothing of an inferior quality to that worn by their own poor, to be of a distinctive colour, and on which should be printed, or stamped, the initials of the union and the word "vagrant," and that every vagrant who should, during temporary lodging in the workhouse, destroy his own clothes, should be supplied with the marked clothing. Inquired whether such regulation would be legal and expedient.

Ans.—The proposal in question is not at variance with any order or regulation issued by the Commissioners. It is quite open to the guardians—indeed, it seems requisite—that they should provide clothing to be given to those casual poor persons, who, having destroyed their own clothes, would, if not relieved by the guardians, be destitute of decent and necessary covering; but such clothing need not be of the same quality or colour as that ordinarily supplied to the inmates of the workhouse. It is also open to the guardians to direct that their property (the clothing being their property until it is given as out-door relief) should be marked in such a manner as may enable the guardians, and the master of the workhouse to identify it. The Commissioners think the guardians would hardly be justified in doing more than this, and that the word "vagrant" ought not to be stamped on the clothing. Clothing can be properly given as relief only to destitute persons, and that relief ought not to be given in such a way as to inflict a punishment: to stamp the word "vagrant" on the clothing, would seem to partake of a punishment. If vagrants destroy their clothes in the workhouse, they will commit an offence punishable under the provisions of the Act 5 and 6 Vic. c. 57, s. 5.

---

2. PUNISHMENT OF VAGRANTS FOR REFUSING TO WORK.

Oct. 28th, 1846.

Clerk of ——— Union—Requested the Commissioners' sanction to a resolution come to by the guardians, that vagrants admitted into the workhouse for the night shall be set to work to pick oakum for two hours, prior to having any breakfast; and in case of refusal to work, the master to be empowered to detain the person so refusing for two hours, and then to discharge him or her without any breakfast.

Ans.—The statute (5 & 6 Vic. c. 57) which authorises the setting to work of occasional poor persons relieved in the workhouse, declares that the task of work which shall be prescribed, shall be performed in return for the food and lodging afforded to such person. It appears to the Commissioners that, according to the language of the Act, the guardians would not be justified in withholding food from a pauper, even though such pauper should neglect or refuse to perform the task of work prescribed. The pauper relieved with a night's lodging in the workhouse will require food in the morning, especially after detention (as proposed by the guardians) for two hours in the workhouse. The Commissioners have no objection to the guardians requiring a portion of the task of work allotted to vagrants, to be performed before breakfast. But notwithstanding the pauper may refuse to perform the work, or any portion of it, the Commissioners think that he should be allowed his breakfast at the usual hour. The Commissioners certainly think that the master of the workhouse ought not to have the discretionary power to discharge the pauper without his breakfast. Moreover, had the master such power, there could be no satisfactory check on his expenditure. The resolution of the guardians, as reported in your letter, appears to contemplate that the only punishment for neglect, or refusal to work, shall rest in the hands of the master, who is to be at liberty to detain the pauper for two hours, and then to discharge him without any breakfast. The Commissioners think such a resolution would not be in accordance with the statute, and they therefore suggest that the master be directed to require the pauper to perform the task of work prescribed; and if he refuse to do it, that the master be directed to take proceedings under the Vagrant Act against him, as an idle and disorderly person, liable to be imprisoned in the house of correction with hard labour for a month.

---

3. VAGRANTS ON WHOM MONEY IS FOUND AFTER ADMISSION INTO THE WORKHOUSE.

June 9th, 1847.

Clerk of Williton Union—An Irish tramper, who asserted that he was destitute, having applied for relief, received an order for admission into the union workhouse. Upon entering the house he was searched, and the sum of seven shillings and two-pence halfpenny was found secreted about his person. When he left, on the following morning, the money was returned to him by the master, who conceived that he had no power to keep any part of it. Inquired whether the master would be justified in searching every pauper admitted into the workhouse; and in refusing to allow any one to remain upon whom he found sufficient money to pay for lodging and necessaries for the night; or whether he could appropriate a part of the money so found in payment of the cost of the maintenance of the pauper whilst in the workhouse, and return him the balance on leaving.

Ans.—The guardians, in the opinion of the Commissioners, would be justified in refusing admission to the workhouse to any vagrant, unless he consented to be searched; and if money sufficient to pay for food and lodging is found upon him, he would be liable to be proceeded against under the Vagrant Act; but the money should be returned to him. If a justice order a search to be made, and a conviction take place, then the money found in the possession of the vagrant may, under the Vagrant Act, be kept to pay the expenses of the prosecution, and applied to the maintenance of the offender during the time for which he is committed.

XXI.—WORKHOUSE.

1. As to subordinate officers leaving.

Oct. 16th, 1846.

Workhouse Master, ——— *Union*—Inquired whether the subordinate officers of the workhouse have a right to leave the house without the consent of the master or matron.

Ans.—The general workhouse rules do not impose on the subordinate officers the obligation to obtain the sanction of the master or matron to their leaving the workhouse; and such sanction, if given, would not avail the officer, if, by reason of his absence from the workhouse, there should be any default of duty. But whilst the officers are thus individually responsible, it would be the duty of the master, in case of any neglect, to bring the same under the notice of the guardians. The Commissioners think it proper, as a general rule, that any subordinate officer, about to leave the workhouse, should inform the master of his intention to do so.

---

2. Construction of sec. 23 of 10 & 11 Vic. c. 109, as to the separation of aged married couples in workhouse.

Aug. 11th, 1847.

Clerk of ——— *Union*—Requested to be informed of the interpretation, which the Commissioners put upon the clause, in the 10 & 11 Vic. c. 109, which provides that married persons, who are respectively above the age of sixty years, shall not be compelled to live separate and apart from each other in the workhouse; and what is the legal meaning of the word separation; also, whether the guardians would be safe if they obtain from this class of paupers their consent, to be bound by the ordinary rules of the workhouse, either verbally or in writing; and, whether the parties should be allowed free access to each other during the whole twenty-four hours; or only be allowed to sleep together, and be employed in the ordinary work of their respective classes, during the day.

Ans.—There is nothing, apparently, to prevent the guardians obtaining from the class of persons to whom the section applies, on application for admission into the workhouse, the consent of such persons to be bound by the general rules, with respect to classification, in force in the workhouse, and a verbal assent would seem to be all that is required. The guardians might simply notify to such persons, what course must be followed if they elect to go into the workhouse, leaving it to the parties to object, (if they think fit) to enter the workhouse on those conditions, or enabling them, subsequently, to quit the workhouse if they are unwilling, any longer, to abide by those conditions. But, the Commissioners think that it would be advisable in all cases that the question as to the willingness of the parties, to be separated when in the workhouse, should be specifically put to the applicants, and that their answer should be noticed on the minutes. The Commissioners are not aware of any peculiar legal signification attaching to the word, "separation." On referring to 23rd sec. of 10 & 11 Vic. c. 109, it will be seen that the words therein contained are, "such two persons shall not be compelled to live separate and apart from each other in the workhouse." The Commissioners think that these words must be understood to express the general course of life, so that, besides sleeping together, the parties are to have full opportunities of intercourse, and of passing their time in each other's company. But, nevertheless, this must be subject to the rules in the workhouse, which regulate the order and discipline, thereof, so that where either of the parties is required to work during the day, the proper classification is to be observed, in regard to each party in connexion with the performance of such work. It will be seen that there is nothing in the workhouse regulations, which requires persons of the description in question to take their meals in the common room or hall, and the Commissioners, therefore, think that the guardians should not prevent such persons from taking their meals together, where they desire it. The Commissioners direct the attention of the guardians to the provision contained in the General Consolidated Order, Art. 99, No. 3, which applies to the providing of a separate sleeping apartment for married couples, who may be considered as "infirm through age or other cause." This provision will apply to cases where the guardians deem it right to admit couples to live together in the workhouse.

---

3. INMATES OF WORKHOUSES RECEIVING MONEY BY POST OFFICE ORDERS.

October 1*st*, 1846.

Clerk of Hatfield Union—Inquired what course the master of the workhouse ought to pursue in a case where a pauper inmate receives a post office order for money.

Ans.—The master has no authority to interfere in the matter; he may, however, receive the money on the order for the pauper, or may allow the pauper to receive it himself. But he cannot take the money from the pauper. The guardians, so long as the pauper ceases to be destitute, can cease to relieve him, or they may give him relief by way of loan. If the guardians can prove that the pauper becomes wilfully chargeable, being able wholly, or in part, to maintain himself, he may be punished under the Vagrant Act.

---

4. REFUSAL OF MOTHER OF BASTARD TO TAKE HER CHILD ON QUITTING WORKHOUSE.

October 24*th*, 1846.

Clerk of ———— *Union*—Inquired whether the master of the workhouse can legally refuse to allow the mother of a bastard child to quit the house unless she takes her child with her.

Ans.—The Commissioners consider that the master of a workhouse would not be justified in forcibly detaining in a workhouse any person who might desire to quit the workhouse after giving reasonable notice to that effect. In the case referred to, the Commissioners would advise, that the child should be sent out of the workhouse with the mother; and, if she thereupon leave the child, the authorities at the workhouse should instantly receive it back again, and proceedings should then be taken against the mother, under the provisions of the Vagrant Act, 5 Geo. 4, c. 83, and under the Act 7 & 8 Vic. c. 101, sec. 6.

---

5. WHETHER A PERSON OF WEAK INTELLECT CAN BE DETAINED IN WORKHOUSE AGAINST HIS WILL.

July 1*st*, 1846.

Clerk of Torrington Union—A pauper named S. B. was sent to the Plympton Lunatic Asylum, where he remained about four years, and was, about two years ago, discharged cured. Since his return to his parish, he has shown no disposition whatever to injure either person or property, and he can always obtain employment as a labourer whenever he is disposed to work; but his propensity is to lead a rambling, vagrant life, committing petty thefts, sleeping in haylofts and outhouses; and, as he is an inveterate smoker, it is feared he will accidentally fire some premises. Inquired, whether the guardians would be justified in detaining the man in the workhouse against his will, if he can be induced to enter it, as he is considered a person of weak intellect, and incapable of taking care of himself.

Ans.—Under the circumstances of the case, the Commissioners could not advise the guardians to detain the party referred to against his will in the workhouse. The Commissioners have stated, in the letter which accompanied the Workhouse Rules, (Art. 23,) that "it is desirable (although this precaution is not legally necessary) that persons of weak intellect should not be permitted to leave the workhouse, except on application, and, if possible, in the company of some relation, or other person likely to take care of them." But, according to the strict provision of the law, an order of magistrates, under the statutes of 8 & 9 Vic. cc. 100 and 126, or the statutes which relate to insane prisoners, or persons whose insanity render them dangerous, would be required to justify the permanent detention of persons of unsound mind against their will, and that only in an asylum or licensed house.

Published by Order of the Poor Law Board, by CHARLES KNIGHT, 90, Fleet Street.

AN

OFFICIAL CIRCULAR

OF PUBLIC DOCUMENTS AND INFORMATION:
DIRECTED BY THE POOR LAW COMMISSIONERS TO BE PRINTED, CHIEFLY FOR THE USE OF THE MEMBERS AND PERMANENT OFFICERS OF BOARDS OF GUARDIANS, UNDER THE POOR LAW AMENDMENT ACT.

No. 11.] JANUARY, 1848. [N.S.

CONTENTS.

I.—ACCOUNTS ORDER.

1. FINANCIAL STATEMENT (FORM No. 17.)

CIRCULAR.

Poor Law Commission Office,
Somerset House,
6th Nov. 1847.

SIR,—I am directed by the Poor Law Commissioners to state, that questions have recently been put to them by clerks to boards of guardians with reference to the preparation of the Financial Statement, in the Form (No. 17) prescribed in the General Order of Accounts so far as regards the mode of entering the relief of those paupers who, by the operation of the recent statute 10 & 11 Vic. c. 110, are rendered chargeable to the common fund of the union; and the Commissioners, therefore, deem it advisable to communicate to you the following instructions, as to the course to be taken in the matter.

In their circular letter of the 26th August last, the Commissioners explained their views, as to the mode of dealing with the relief in question in the union ledger, in the following terms:

> "The parish will be debited with the amount of all relief, as heretofore, and will be credited with the amount from which it is to be relieved under this statute. The common charges account will be debited with the collective amount of the relief, thus credited and transferred, distributed under the heads of the several parishes to which it is transferred, and will be credited by the shares due from all the parishes in the union, (according to their averages,) on that account increased by this expenditure."

The Financial Statement is intended to contain all the sums, entered in the column, for totals in the parochial ledger accounts; the statute 10 & 11 Vic. c. 110, will, therefore, render it necessary to enter in one of the columns provided for "other receipts," the amounts credited to the several parishes, on account of the relief to irremovable poor originally charged against them. The column in which these amounts are entered may be headed thus: "Relief to Irremovable Poor transferred to the common charges."

The total amounts of "in-maintenance," and "out-relief," appearing in the parochial ledger accounts, will be entered in the columns for "in-maintenance" and "out-relief" respectively, in the Financial Statement, and will include the relief to irremovable poor; this relief having, in the first instance, been charged against the parishes, together with the relief to their settled poor, and afterwards transferred to the common charges account in the ledger, in the manner explained in the circular letter quoted above.

Although the amount of the relief, so transferred, will appear under the head of "receipts," and will be entered in the column, charges account, on the side of "expenditure," the total should be inserted in the subsidiary table at the foot of the statement, among the "principal particulars of the other common charges."

It is desirable that the irremovable poor should be distinguished in the parochial list and statement of accounts, Form 19, from the poor whose relief is not transferred to the "common charges account;" and the best way of doing this appears to be by placing them at the bottom of the list, and writing above their names the words, "irremovable and chargeable to the union."

No alteration, however, seems to be requisite in regard to the preparation of the statistical statement, Form 16, which must still show the number of paupers relieved on account of the several parishes, although the relief of some of them may be reimbursed by the union.

The Commissioners think it right to observe, that the course which they have pointed out above, in regard to the preparation of the Financial Statement, appears to them to be, on the whole, the most proper and convenient under the peculiar circumstances of the case; though they are quite aware that it will have the effect of exhibiting the same relief twice over, and thus of presenting an apparently greater expenditure by the union than will in fact have been incurred. The Commissioners remark, however, that the statute above referred to, is a temporary one, and was passed after the issue of their General Order of Accounts.

In preparing any statement for the use of the guardians or of the several parishes in the union, it will be necessary to point out, in a clear manner, the fact of the repayment of the relief in question, and its amount.

I am, Sir, your obedient Servant,
W. G. LUMLEY, *Assistant Secretary.*

To

The Clerk to the Guardians.

---

2. EXPLANATIONS ON FORM No. 36.

Dec. 8th, 1847.

Clerk of Southwell Union—Inquiring as to the proper mode of filling up the several columns of the Relieving Officer's Receipt and Expenditure Book, Form 36 of the General Accounts Order.

Ans.—The Form No. 36 of the General Order of Accounts, is to show the receipt and expenditure of the relieving officer. The first column of the Form is for the date, the second is for the matters received by the relieving officer, such as the cheques paid to him by the guardians, the money which may come to him from other sources, and the tickets which the guardians may place at his disposal for the paupers. The third column is for the money payments, and the fourth for the value of the tickets or relief in kind supplied to him by the guardians. On the opposite side he will carry out what he has expended, by charging the amount to the proper parishes and unions. But, he is not to show, on this account, to whom he has paid the money which has been supplied to him. The relieving officer should be debited weekly with all bread which he receives, and the value carried out against him, in the money columns, whether the guardians pay the contractor weekly or quarterly.

II.—ACCOUNTS.

1. OF OVERSEERS—CIRCULAR TO DISTRICT AUDITORS.

Poor Law Commission Office,
Somerset House,
17th August, 1847.

SIR,—I am directed by the Poor Law Commissioners to inform you that their attention has been called to the existence of a practice, in regard to the accounts of overseers of the poor, which they think it right to bring under your notice.

The Commissioners have received a communication, which leads them to believe that, when items have been disallowed in the accounts of overseers, it has, sometimes, been attempted, and not unsuccessfully, to make up for the loss, by collecting the poor-rate from parties who have been legally excused from payment.

The Commissioners do not doubt that, your

attention having been now directed to this circumstance, you will take care to guard against its occurrence in your district, so far as you may be able to do so, and, when any ground for suspicion may exist, that you will call upon the overseers to make a declaration on the subject.

I am, Sir, &c.

W. G. LUMLEY, *Assistant Secretary.*

To

District Auditor.

2. DETAILED ACCOUNTS OF PAYMENTS BY OVERSEERS TO CONSTABLES TO BE PRODUCED TO THE AUDITORS.

Nov. 30th, 1847.

Clerk to the Magistrates of ——— The overseers of the ——— Union complain of the disallowance by the auditor of payments made by them to the constables for duties performed under 5 & 6 Vic. c. 109. The reason assigned by the auditor for the disallowances is, that the whole of the items composing the sum allowed to the constable should be stated in detail. The clerk to the justices is not aware of any law which requires this to be done.

Ans.—The Commissioners consider that the only correct mode of proceeding, in regard to such fees as those adverted to, is, for the justices in the one case, and the clerk to the justices in the other, to set out the different items in detail for which the fees are charged. It is impossible otherwise for the overseers and the auditor to know whether the fees are charged according to law, and for services lawfully chargeable to the poor-rates. The Commissioners have recently been advised by counsel, in reference to orders of justices made under the Parish Constables Act, (sec. 17, 5 & 6 Vic. c. 109,) that the justices are bound to specify in the order, or in a schedule to it, the particular fees allowed, and cannot order payment of a gross sum as the aggregate of fees not specified.

III.—BREAD CONTRACTOR — OBLIGATION OF, TO CARRY WEIGHTS TO WEIGH BREAD IN HIS DISTRICT.

July 8th, 1846.

Mr. ———, *Chard Union*—Inquired, whether a baker, who contracts to supply a union with bread, is liable to a penalty for omitting to carry weights to weigh the bread on delivering it to the several parishes in his district.

Ans.—Where bread is conveyed, or carried out, for sale in and from a cart, or other carriage, by any baker of bread, his journeyman, or servant, it is certainly necessary that such baker, journeyman, or servant, (as the case may be,) should be provided with, and carry in the cart or carriage, a correct beam and scale, with proper weights: neglect to do so subjects him to a penalty of £5, (6 & 7 Wm. 4, c. 37, sec. 7.) The case of a baker contracting to supply the union with bread, which is to be delivered in the several parishes of his district, does not appear to be an exception to this rule.

IV.—BURIAL—COST OF, PERSONS DYING IN PRISONS.

Dec. 22nd, 1847.

Clerk of Worcester Union—Referred to the case of Reg. *v.* Stewart, cited at page 130, No. 9, N. S., of the Official Circular, and inquired whether the decision given in that case applied to the burial of persons dying in city and county prisons as well as to the burial of persons dying in infirmaries; and, whether boards of guardians have any discretionary power either in assenting, or refusing, to bury persons dying in such places as above referred to.

Ans.—The Board are of opinion that the case of Reg. *v.* Stewart, 12 A. & E. 773, applies equally to the case of persons dying in city or county prisons, or in hospitals. The Board consider that the guardians, notwithstanding the 31st sec. of the Act 7 & 8 Vic. c. 101, have a discretion, whether or not they will undertake, and defray the cost of the interment in such cases. The 31st sec. of the statute adverted to, would probably enable the guardians to undertake the interment (if the prison were within any parish in the union, not otherwise) but certainly does not compel them to do so. The *legal obligation* to bury in the cases put by you would seem, on the authority of Reg. *v.* Stewart, to rest upon the persons having charge or control of the prison, in which the death occurs.

V.—CHAIRMAN—HIS DUTY IN REGARD TO AN ILLEGAL MOTION.

Oct. 8th, 1847.

Chairman of ——— *Union*—Inquired if he should be authorised to refuse putting a motion directing the Chairman and two guardians to sign cheques for payment of officers' salaries, or any other current expenses, supposing that there is not sufficient funds belonging to the guardians in the hands of the treasurer of the union, the clerk being directed by the board to keep back the cheques until a sufficient amount of the unpaid calls was paid to liquidate the balances; say for the space of fourteen days, if so long required.

Ans.—The Commissioners are of opinion that there is nothing actually illegal in the motion that the cheques be drawn under the circumstances above mentioned, and consequently the chairman would not be justified in refusing to put the question; but, when the cheques are drawn, the chairman cannot be compelled to sign them. With reference to the question as to the clerk's detaining the cheques drawn by the guardians, the Commissioners refer you to Art. 220 of the Consolidated Order lately issued by them, which directs that every clerk receiving any cheque or money from the guardians on account of any other party shall transmit the same, within fourteen days, to the proper persons, and shall produce the receipt or acknowledgment for the same at the next ordinary meeting after such receipt has come to his hands. If, therefore, the clerk be directed to keep the cheque longer than fourteen days, the motion so directing the clerk would become illegal: at any rate, the practice of leaving cheques in the clerk's hands is most objectionable, although a motion proposing it be not absolutely illegal.

Oct. 19th, 1847.

On receiving a further communication from the chairman, pointing out the limitation of his inquiry respecting the retention of the cheques in the clerk's hands, to the space of fourteen days, if so long required, the Commissioners replied—

Ans.—Assuming the resolution as to the detention of the cheques were limited in the manner pointed out in your communication, there would certainly be no actual illegality in it; but the Commissioners cannot but consider any such direction of the guardians to their officer to be highly inexpedient, as affording a justification for his doing what he should not do under any circumstances, namely, withholding the cheques from the parties who ought, indeed, to receive them immediately upon their being issued. The proper course in the emergency would have been for the guardians to take instant steps for placing a proper balance in their treasurer's hands, and postpone the issue of the cheques until such balance had been so placed.

VI.—CHARGEABILITY.

June 28th, 1847.

Clerk of Thirsk Union—J. D., a pauper inmate of the union workhouse, chargeable to the township of Knayton, under the 9 and 10 Vic. c. 66, but settled in the township of Thornton-le-Moor, left the house, to visit a friend at Pickhill, and applied for re-admission, three days afterwards, when she was again admitted, and the cost of her maintenance charged by the master to Knayton, to which that township objects, on the ground that her residence therein was broken by her visit to Pickhill. Inquired, to which of the above townships the cost of the pauper's maintenance should be charged.

Ans.—The Commissioners are of opinion, that if the pauper discharged herself, or was discharged absolutely, from the workhouse, her chargeability to the parish of Knayton ceased, on her leaving the workhouse, and a new chargeability accrued to the parish, where she afterwards became destitute, and from which she came to the workhouse. This, however, does not appear to have been the parish of her settlement.

VII.—CONSTABLE—APPOINTMENT OF PORTER AS.

September 26th, 1846.

Clerk of —— Union — The guardians are desirous of having the porter at the —— Workhouse sworn before justices as a resident constable, with a view to check any insubordination which may occur in the house; and an application has been made to the justices for this purpose, but they are advised that they have no power to make such an appointment, and that a special constable can be appointed only upon oath made before them that a breach of the peace is immediately apprehended. Requested the Commissioners' opinion upon the subject.

Ans.—The justices do not, in the opinion of the Commissioners, possess the power of swearing in the porter as a special constable, as the statute under which special constables are appointed (1 and 2 Wm. 4, c. 41) only contemplates the interference of the justices in this way—where tumult or felony has taken place, or may be reasonably apprehended in any parish or township, and the justices may consider that the ordinary officers appointed for preserving the peace and protection of property are not sufficient for that purpose. If, however, the porter has the requisite qualification, he might probably be appointed a constable of the parish in which the workhouse in question stands, pursuant to the provisions of the Parish Constables Act, 5 and 6 Vic. c. 109. It should be observed, however, that if he be so appointed he will be obliged to perform all the duties of a parish constable whenever occasion arises, and therefore he may be rather distracted from the performance of his duties as porter, than aided in that office by his appointment as constable. The appointment, therefore, in this form appears objectionable, and it will probably be found, too, in the present case, that the porter has not the qualification for the office of constable prescribed by the Act last referred to, *i.e.*, that he is not rated to the relief of "the poor, or to the county rate, or any tenements of the net yearly value of four pounds or upwards."

VIII.—DESERTION—OF BASTARD CHILD, BY A MARRIED WOMAN WHOSE HUSBAND IS IN GAOL.

July 1st, 1846.

Clerk of Fareham Union—E. S., previous to the passing of the Poor Law Amendment Act, was delivered of a bastard child, and subsequent to the passing of that Act was married to the putative father. The husband having been committed to prison for uttering base coin, the woman and her child were received into the workhouse, but she subsequently left, and abandoned her child, which had, in consequence, been re-admitted into the workhouse. Inquired whether the guardians can prosecute the woman under the Vagrant, or any other Act.

Ans.—The Commissioners think the case which you have submitted to them is not without difficulty. The 7 & 8 Vic. c. 101, sec. 6, makes provision for the punishment of mothers for neglecting or deserting their bastard children; the words of the latter part of that section, appear to embrace the case of E. S., but the Commissioners think it may be contended that those words should be qualified by reference to the former part of the section; and that to bring the case within the enactment, the woman must be able to maintain the children. If this construction of the statute be correct, it would follow that the case of a married woman, who has no property in law, is not within the clause. It may be well to take the opinion of the justice who has jurisdiction in the matter, as to the liability of the pauper in question to the penalties of the Act.

IX.—JUSTICES' CLERKS—ALLOWANCES OF FEES TO, FOR CONVENING SPECIAL SESSIONS.

June 20th, 1846.
Sept. 22nd, 1846.

Messrs. ———, ——— *Union*—The district auditor has refused to allow their fees, as justices' clerks, for notices of convening more than four special sessions, during the year, for hearing appeals under the Parochial Assessments Act. Requested the Commissioners' directions to the district auditor to allow the expenses of as many special sessions as the justices may consider proper to be convened.

Ans.—The statute 6 and 7 Wm. 4, c. 96, makes no provision for the case; and, in the absence of such provision, the Commissioners very much doubt whether there are any sufficient grounds for holding the overseers of parishes legally liable to the clerk to the justices for the notices in question. Even if it be urged that such notices are for the benefit of the rate-payers of a parish generally, still, as regards the overseers, the notices are not issued on any application from them, but entirely independently of those officers; nor is the issuing of the notice any advantage or benefit to them as overseers. The Commissioners certainly consider it but reasonable that the labour of the clerk to the justices in this particular should be requited, and they would have been glad, therefore, if they had been able to return a decided answer favourable to their claims. But they are bound to say that, as at present advised, they think the case one in which the law does not make a specific provision for payment, and one in which it is very doubtful whether an inference can be safely drawn in favour of such payment out of the poor-rates. The Commissioners must be understood to express the opinion which is conveyed in this letter without prejudice to any consideration of the subject which they may be called upon to give in pursuance of section 36 of 7 and 8 Vic. c. 101.

Messrs. ———: The 6 and 7 Wm. 4, c. 96, after requiring the justices to hold, four times at least in every year, special sessions for hearing appeals against rates, enacts, that the justices shall cause public notices of such special sessions to be affixed to, or near, the door of the parish church, twenty-eight days at least before the holding of the same. The 26 Geo. 2, c. 14, authorises and requires the justices in quarter sessions to make and settle a table of the fees which shall be taken by the clerks to justices of the peace; such table to be afterwards confirmed by the judges of assize as therein mentioned.

Under the last-mentioned Act, a table of fees to be taken by the clerks to the justices of the peace acting in and for the county of ——, was made in the year 1841, and confirmed by the judges on the 14th of March, 1842, (since the passing of the 6 and 7 Wm. 4, c. 96) in which fees for precepts and notices of every kind are set down. The justices consider that the statutes and law bearing on the subject established in their clerks a legal claim to fees for convening any number of special sessions that may be ordered by the justices; that the liability for such fees clearly falls upon the subject matter of the proceedings, namely, the poor-rate; and that the overseers, as the legal assessors and disbursers of that rate, although not personally setting the proceedings in motion, nor personally benefited thereby, are the proper parties to be called upon to make the requisite payments. Requested that the Commissioners will give such directions as may insure to the justices and their legal officers that indemnity against expense in the performance of their public duties, which they feel assured the legislature intended to give them.

Ans.—The Commissioners do not perceive that the case is one in which the law enables them to give any such directions as those suggested; and, consequently, any such directions would be wholly nugatory if given. Upon a subject upon which the Commissioners are not empowered to give any authoritative direction, they can only, when applied to for their opinion, express what they deem to be the law of the case. Accordingly, in their former communication (no appeal having been directly brought before them in pursuance of section 36 of 7 and 8 Vic. c. 101,) the Commissioners confined themselves to a statement of the principal considerations which led them to the conclusion that the poor-rates were not legally liable to the payment of the fees claimed by you for carrying into effect (as the agents of the justices) the 6th section of the 6 and 7 Wm. 4, c. 96. A further consideration of the subject, with reference to the several arguments urged in your letter, has not altered this conclusion. The Commissioners feel bound here to repeat, "that the case appears to them one in which the law does not make any specific provision for payment, and one in which it is very doubtful whether an inference can be safely drawn in favour of such payment out of the poor-rates." In your last communication, the Act 26 Geo. 2, c. 14, is referred to as apparently conferring an authority for the payments now in question out of the poor-rates. The Commissioners wish it to be understood that they have not questioned the power of the quarter sessions to include in any table of fees, settled under the 26 Geo. 2, c. 14, a fee for the particular duty performed by the clerk to the justices in carrying into effect section 6 of the 6 and 7 Wm. 4, c. 96. But, admitting the existence of such power, the question still remains whether the fees are lawfully demandable, as against the overseers. The Commissioners do not understand that the table of fees professed to indicate the parties by whom the fees are to be paid; but merely specifies the amount of the fee which may be claimed by the clerk in the particular case of the person who may be liable for the payment. Though the clerk to the justices may be justified and protected by the table, in receiving the fee fixed by the table, it does not therefore follow that he has any legal claim upon the overseers in such case; or that, as between the overseers and the ratepayers, the former could justify the payment out of the poor-rates. In conclusion, the Commissioners have only to express their regret that they are unable to return an answer in accordance with the views which the justices entertain on this subject.

X.—LUNATICS—IN WORKHOUSES—CIRCULAR.

Poor Law Commission Office,
Somerset House,
11th Sept. 1847.

SIR,—The Poor Law Commissioners have received a communication from the Commissioners in Lunacy, in which they state, that it would, in their opinion, be extremely convenient and useful, if a separate list of the names of all the lunatics, insane persons, and idiots were kept in each workhouse, and periodically revised and approved by the medical officer of the house.

The Poor Law Commissioners concur in the expediency of such a list being kept in the workhouse, and they request that the guardians will direct the master to prepare such a list in the accompanying Form, the list to be revised and approved by the medical officer; to be altered from time to time as any changes in the number of lunatics and idiots maintained in the workhouse occur; and to be laid before the board of guardians at their weekly meetings.

I am, Sir, your most obedient Servant,
W. G. LUMLEY, *Assistant Secretary.*

To

The Clerk to the Board of Guardians.

List of Lunatics and Idiots in the Workhouse.

No.	Name.	Parish to which chargeable.	Whether Lunatic or Idiot.	Observations.

XI.—MEDICAL PRACTITIONER—MEANING OF "DULY QUALIFIED" IN THE REMOVAL OF NUISANCES ACT.

September 7th, 1847.

Clerk of Congleton Union—At a recent hearing of a case under the Nuisances Removal Act, the certificate required by the Act to be delivered to the justices previous to the issuing of a summons was objected to, on the ground that one of the medical practitioners who had signed it was not a licentiate of the Apothecaries' Company, but only a member of the Royal College of Surgeons, and this fact having been admitted, the summons was dismissed. It was contended that the fact of the medical man being a member of the College of Surgeons was a sufficient qualification.

Ans.—The term used in the Act in question, 9 & 10 Vic. c. 96, "duly qualified medical practitioner," is very vague, and has not any definite legal meaning. The Commissioners believe the law has assigned qualifications to apothecaries and physicians, and to surgeons within a limited district. The Commissioners are disposed to think, therefore, that the Legislature must have referred to the persons who are so qualified, rather than to persons who have no qualification recognised by the law.

XII.—OVERSEERS—THEIR DUTY IN REGARD TO THE RELIEF OF CASUAL POOR.

Oct 18th, 1847.

Relieving Officer of ——— Union—Frequent applications for temporary or casual relief, or a night's lodging, are made by trampers or vagrants, which the assistant overseer refers to the relieving officer, to arrive at whose residence they must go through the city, where, from fatigue, they often apply for and get the relief they require. The magistrates of the city threaten both the assistant overseer and the relieving officer with prosecution if these things occur. Inquired, whether the assistant overseer, or overseer of a parish, should refer all or any cases to the relieving officer of a parish, when this officer is absent, or does not reside in the parish. Or, whether the law does not give the overseers and their assistant the same discretion to relieve a casual, as it does a settled pauper.

Ans.—The Commissioners are not informed of the powers conferred on the assistant overseer by his warrant of appointment; but, assuming him to have the same powers as an overseer of the poor in regard to giving relief, then it will be observed that the only cases in which an overseer of a parish in an union can give relief, are those provided for by the 54th section of the Poor Law Amendment Act, *i.e.* cases of sudden and urgent necessity. Where application is made to the assistant overseer for relief by a vagrant, or person casually in the parish, and the case is not sudden and urgent in its nature, the assistant overseer does right in referring the applicant to the relieving officer of the district, he being alone empowered, the board not being then assembled, to give relief in such a case. It does not make any difference as regards the duties and powers of the overseers and assistant overseer in the matter, whether the applicant be a settled pauper, or whether he is only casually in the parish; in either case, the duty of the overseers, or the assistant overseer, as the case may be, is to administer relief at once in articles of necessity, if the case be really sudden and urgent; and if it be not, to refer the applicant to the relieving officer. The Commissioners do not see how the assistant overseer can prevent the parties passing through the city, if the way to the relieving officer's residence lies in that direction; neither are they aware that he exposes himself to any penal proceedings in consequence of their so doing.

XIII. — PAUPERS—UNCLAIMED CLOTHES OF THOSE WHO HAVE DIED IN THE WORKHOUSE.

Oct. 11th, 1847.

Clerk of Totnes Union—Inquired whether the Commissioners will sanction the sale, by the guardians, of a quantity of unclaimed clothes which belonged to paupers who have died in the union workhouse.

Ans.—The Commissioners do not see that there would be any objection to the sale of the articles of clothing referred to in your letter, in the way proposed by the guardians. Before that is done, however, the Commissioners think it would be a proper precaution to have a separate value placed on the clothing which belonged to each deceased pauper, so that, in case any inquiry or claim in this respect should be made hereafter by the pauper's relations or next of kin, the guardians would be enabled to give a satisfactory explanation. The Commissioners apprehend that the effects left by a deceased person are by law applicable in the first instance to the payment of the expenses of his decent interment. The case where a person is buried at the charge of the poor-rates appears to be no exception to this rule. The guardians might therefore lawfully apply the produce of the sale of the clothing to defray the costs of the interment in each case. If there should be any surplus, this object having been provided for, it would be best to retain such surplus, until such a period had elapsed, as (having regard to the statute of limitations) would prevent any claim being effectively made. At least if the money, as probably must be the case, be placed into the hands of the treasurer to the general account of the parish, the guardians must be prepared to pay over such surplus to any party who shall hereafter be in a condition to make a valid legal demand for it.

XIV.—POOR LAW BOARD—CIRCULAR.

Somerset House,
Dec. 18th, 1847.

SIR,—I am directed to state that Her Majesty having been pleased, under the late statute 10 & 11 Vic. c. 109,* to appoint Commissioners for administering the laws for the relief of the poor in England, and the notice of the issue of such

* The statute (10 and 11 Vic. c. 109) is as follows:—

AN ACT FOR THE ADMINISTRATION OF THE LAWS FOR THE RELIEF OF THE POOR IN ENGLAND. 23rd JULY, 1847.

Appointment of Commissioners—Whereas an Act was passed in the Fifth Year of the Reign of His late Majesty, intituled *An Act for the Amendment and better Administration of the Laws relating to the Poor in* England *and* Wales; and divers Acts have since been passed for the Amendment of the said Act, or otherwise relating to the Laws for the Relief of the Poor in *England*: And whereas the Administration of the Laws for the Relief of the Poor in *England* is subject to the Direction and Control of the Poor Law Commissioners, whose Commission will expire at the End of the Session of Parliament next after the Thirty-first Day of *July* in this Year, and it is expedient to make further Provision for the Administration of the said Laws: Be it enacted by the Queen's most Excellent Majesty, by and with the Advice and Consent of the Lords Spiritual and Temporal, and Commons, in this present Parliament assembled, and by the Authority of the same, That it shall be lawful for Her Majesty, by any Letters Patent, or by any Commission or Commissions to be issued under the Great Seal of *Great Britain*, from Time to Time to nominate, constitute, and appoint during Pleasure such Person or Persons as Her Majesty shall think fit to be and who shall accordingly be and be styled "Commissioners for administering the Laws for Relief of the Poor in *England*;" and whenever in this Act the Word Commissioners shall be used without Addition it shall be taken to mean the said Commissioners for administering the Laws for Relief of the Poor in *England*.

Commissioners ex-officio—II. And be it enacted, That the Lord President of the Council, the Lord Privy Seal, Her Majesty's Principal Secretary of State for the Home Department, and the Chancellor of the Exchequer for the Time being shall be, by virtue of their respective Offices, Commissioners for administering the Laws for Relief of the Poor in *England*, with the Person or Persons nominated in any such Letters Patent or Commission as aforesaid, and shall have the same Powers as if they were expressly nominated in such Commission.

When Commissioners shall enter on their Office—III. And be it enacted, That Notice of the Issue of every such Commission shall be published in the *London Gazette*; and the Commissioners first appointed under this Act shall enter on their Office, and all the Powers by this Act vested in them shall take effect, on the Day after the first Publication of such Notice in the *London Gazette*.

Who shall preside at Meetings of the Commissioners—IV. And be it enacted, That the Commissioner first named in any such Letters Patent or Commission for the Time being shall be and be styled the "President;" and whenever in the Absence of the President Two or more of the Commissioners shall meet for the Execution of any Powers vested in them by this Act, the Commissioner next in order of Nomination in the said Commission or this Act, of those who shall be present, shall for that Turn preside; and if the Commissioners present at any Meeting shall be equally divided in opinion upon any Question before them, the President, or in his Absence the Commissioner presiding at that Meeting, shall have a Second or casting Vote.

Seal of the Commissioners—V. And be it enacted, That the Commissioners shall cause a Seal to be made for their Use, and such Seal shall have the same Force and Effect as the Seal of the Poor Law Commissioners now has in *England*, and Documents purporting to be sealed or stamped therewith shall be received in Evidence in like Manner and with the like Effect as Documents sealed or stamped with the Seal of the Poor Law Commissioners are now received in Evidence.

Appointment of Secretaries, Clerks, &c.—VI. And be it enacted, That the Commissioners shall from Time to Time, by Order under their seal, appoint Two Secretaries, and may, by a like Order under their Seal, remove any Secretary so appointed, and shall also from Time to Time appoint so many Clerks, Messengers, and Servants as shall be allowed by the Lord High Treasurer or the Commissioners of Her Majesty's Treasury; and all the Persons so appointed shall hold their Offices during the Pleasure of the Commissioners.

Who are competent to act in execution of Act—VII. And be it enacted, That any Two of the said Commissioners or the said President alone, except as herein-after provided, shall be competent to act in the Execution of any Powers vested in the Commissioners by this Act: provided that no Act of the Commissioners which is required to be under their Seal, or which, if done by the Poor Law Commissioners, must have been done under their Hands and Seal, shall be of any Validity unless it shall purport to be signed by at least Two of the Commissioners, or by the President, and if signed by the President alone, countersigned by one of the Secretaries to the Commissioners; and during any Vacancy among the Commissioners, the surviving or continuing Commissioners or Commissioner may continue to act with the same Powers and in the same Manner respectively as before such Vacancy.

Salaries—VIII. And be it enacted, That there shall be paid to the President and to the said Secretaries, Clerks, Messengers, and Servants, such Salaries as shall be from Time to Time regulated by the Lord High Treasurer or the Commissioners of Her Majesty's Treasury, but no Commissioner, other than the said President, shall be entitled to have any Salary or Remuneration for acting in the Execution of this Act

President and One Secretary may sit in the House of Commons—IX. And be it enacted, That the Office of President shall not be deemed such an Office as shall render the Person holding such Office incapable of being elected, or of sitting or voting as a Member of the Commons House of Parliament, or as shall avoid his Election if returned, or render him liable to any Penalty for sitting or voting in Parliament; and that One only of the said Secretaries shall at the same Time be capable of sitting and voting in the Commons House of Parliament.

commission having been published in the London Gazette, on the 17th day of December instant, all the powers and duties of the Poor Law Commissioners, appointed under 4 & 5 Wm. 4, c. 76,

Transfer of Powers and Duties of the Poor Law Commissioners—X. And be it enacted, That on the Day on which the Commissioners first appointed under this Act shall enter on their Office, all the Powers and Duties of the Poor Law Commissioners with respect to the Administration or Control of the Administration of Relief to the Poor throughout *England*, and all other Powers and Duties now vested in them, shall be transferred to and vested in the Commissioners, and shall be thenceforth exercised by them, and by the Commissioners appointed from Time to Time in and by any new Commission or Letters Patent under the Provisions of this Act, and all Provisions in any Act relating to the Administration of Relief to the Poor in *England*, or to the Powers or Duties of the Poor Law Commissioners, shall be construed as if in the said several Acts, the Commissioners had been named instead of the Poor Law Commissioners, subject nevertheless to any Amendments made by this Act, either as to the Substance or Manner of exercising any of the Powers of the said Poor Law Commissioners; and at the same Time all Powers and Authorities vested by any Act in the Poor Law Commissioners appointed under the first-recited Act, or any Act passed for the Amendment thereof, shall cease, and all Secretaries, Assistant Secretaries, Clerks, Messengers, and Officers appointed and employed by the said Poor Law Commissioners in the Business of their Office shall cease to hold their several Offices and Employments.

Power to summon Witnesses—XI. And be it enacted, That the Commissioners, by Summons under their Seal, may require the Attendance of all Persons upon any Matter connected with the Execution of any of the Powers by Law vested in them at such Time and Place as shall be set forth in the Summons, and may make Inquiry and require Returns, and require and enforce the Production upon Oath of Books, Contracts, Agreements, Accounts, Maps, Plans, Surveys, Valuations, and Writings, or Copies thereof respectively, in anywise relating to any such Matter, the Commissioners or any One of them may upon such Matters administer Oaths, and examine upon Oath all Persons so brought before them or him, and, when they or he shall think fit, instead of requiring such Oath as aforesaid, may require any such Person to make and subscribe a Declaration of the Truth of the Matters respecting which he shall have been or shall be so examined: Provided always, that no Person shall be required, in obedience to any such Order, to go more than Ten Miles from the Place of his Abode: Provided also, that nothing herein contained shall empower the Commissioners to require the Production of the Title, or of any Paper or Deed relating to the Title of any Lands, Tenements, or Hereditaments, not being the Property of any Parish or Union.

Repeal of certain Enactments as to the Records of the Commissioners. 5 & 6 Vic. c. 57.—XII. And be it enacted, That so much of the said Act of the Fifth Year of the Reign of His late Majesty, or of an Act passed in the Sixth Year of the Reign of Her Majesty, intituled *An Act to continue until the Thirty-first Day of* July *One thousand eight hundred and forty-seven, and to the End of the then next Session of Parliament, the Poor Law Commission, and for the further Amendment of the Laws relating to the Poor in* England, or of any other Act as would require any Minute of the Opinion of each of the Commissioners to be made in the Record of their Proceedings in Cases of final Difference of Opinion upon any Order or Proceeding, or as would require any Record or general Report of the Proceedings of the Commissioners to be submitted to one of Her Majesty's Principal Secretaries of State, shall be repealed.

Annual Report to Her Majesty to be laid before Parliament—XIII. And be it enacted, That the Commissioners shall once in every Year submit to Her Majesty a general Report of their Proceedings, and every such general Report shall be laid before both Houses of Parliament within Six Weeks after the Date thereof if Parliament be then sitting, or if Parliament be not then sitting, within Six Weeks after the next Meeting of Parliament.

How Rules are to be made—XIV. And be it enacted, That from and after the Day on which the Commissioners first appointed under this Act shall enter on their Office the Power vested in the Poor Law Commissioners to make Rules, Orders, and Regulations, and from Time to Time to vary or rescind the same, shall be vested in the Commissioners constituted under this Act, to be exercised by them in the Manner herein-after specified, and the Commissioners shall make all such Rules, Orders, and Regulations under their Seal, except such as are intended only for their own Guidance or Procedure, or for the Guidance or Procedure of any Persons appointed or employed by them for the Business of their Office, and shall make all General Rules under their Seal, and under the Hands of Three or more of the Commissioners, of whom the President shall be One.

Definition of General Rules—XV. And be it enacted, That every Rule, Order, or Regulation of the Commissioners which at the Time of issuing the same shall be directed to and affect more than One Union, shall be deemed a General Rule, and every Rule. Order, and Regulation made to vary or rescind a General Rule, whether it be directed to or affect One or more than One Union, shall also be deemed a General Rule.

Repeal of Part of 4 & 5 W. 4, c. 76, as to making General Rules—XVI. And be it enacted, That from and after the Day on which the Commissioners first appointed under this Act shall enter on their Office so much of the said Act of the Fifth Year of the Reign of His late Majesty as relates to the making of General Rules by the Poor Law Commissioners, or to the Time or Manner when or how any such General Rule shall operate or take effect, or to the Disallowance of any such General Rule, or any Part thereof, shall be repealed.

Disallowance of General Rules by the Queen in Council—XVII. And be it enacted, That if Her Majesty shall be pleased at any Time, by the Advice of Her Privy Council, to disallow any such General Rule, or any part thereof, the same, so far as it shall have been so disallowed, shall cease to be of any Force or Validity, except as to all things lawfully done under the same before such Disallowance, which shall be and continue to be valid.

Confirmation of existing Rules—XVIII. Provided always, and be it declared and enacted, That all lawful Rules, Orders, and Regulations of the Poor Law Commissioners made before the Day on which the Commissioners first appointed under this Act shall enter on their Office shall continue in full Force and Effect until rescinded or varied under the Authority of this Act.

Appointment of Inspectors—XIX. And be it enacted, That the Commissioners shall from Time to Time, by Order under their Seal, appoint so many fit Persons as shall be allowed by the Lord High Treasurer or Commissioners of Her Majesty's Treasury, to be Inspectors, to assist in the Execution of this Act and of other Acts now or which shall be hereafter in force for the Relief of the Poor in *England*, and may from Time to Time assign to the Inspectors so appointed, or any of them, such Duties in the Execution of this Act as they think fit; and the Commissioners, by Order under their Seal, may remove all or any of the said Inspectors, and appoint others in their Stead; and there shall be paid to every such Inspector such Salary as shall be from Time to Time regulated by the Lord High Treasurer or the Commissioners of Her Majesty's Treasury.

Duties of Inspectors—XX. And be it enacted, That the said Inspectors, and each of them, shall be entitled to visit and inspect every Workhouse or Place wherein any poor Person in receipt of Relief shall be lodged, and to attend every Board of Guardians and every parochial and other local Meeting held for the Relief of the Poor, and to take Part in the Proceedings, but not to vote at such Board or Meeting.

Inspectors may summon Witnesses—XXI. And be it enacted, That the said Inspectors may summon before them such Persons as they may think necessary for the Purpose of being examined before them upon any Matter concerning the Administration of the Laws relating to the Relief of the Poor, or any other Matter placed by Law under the Control or Regulation of the Commissioners, or for the Purpose of producing and verifying upon Oath any Books, Contracts, Agreements, Accounts, Writings, or Copies of the same, in anywise relating with respect to the administration or control of the administration of relief to the poor throughout England, and all other powers and duties vested in them, have, by virtue of sec. 10 of the first mentioned statute, been transferred to and vested in the Commissioners so now constituted and appointed by Her Majesty, and such powers and duties are henceforth to be exercised by them and their successors, and all provisions in any Act relating to the administration of relief

to such Matter, and not relating to or involving any Question of Title to any Lands, Tenements, or Hereditaments not being the Property of any Parish or Union, and may examine any Person whom they shall so summon, or who shall voluntarily come before them to be examined upon any such Matter upon Oath, which each of the said Inspectors shall be empowered to administer, or instead of administering an Oath, the Inspector may require the Party examined to make and subscribe a Declaration of the Truth of the Matter respecting which he shall have been or shall be so examined; and all Summonses made by any such Inspector for any such Purpose as aforesaid shall be obeyed by all Persons as if such Summons had been the Summons and Order of the Commissioners, and the Nonobservance thereof shall be punishable in like Manner; and that the Costs and Expences of such Person so summoned shall be paid in such Cases and in such Manner as the Costs and Expences of Persons summoned under the authority of the first-recited Act are now payable: Provided always, that no Person shall be required in obedience to any such Summons, to go or travel more than Ten Miles from his Place of Abode.

Special Inquiries—XXII. And be it enacted, That so much of the said Act of the Sixth Year of the Reign of Her Majesty as relates to the Appointment of any Assistant Commissioner or of any Person for the Purpose of conducting any special Inquiry as an Assistant Commissioner shall be repealed; and that, whenever it may seem fitting to the Commissioners, they, with the Consent of the Lord High Treasurer or the Commissioners of Her Majesty's Treasury for the Time being, may appoint some fit Person to Act as an Inspector for the Purpose of conducting any special Inquiry for a Period not exceeding Thirty Days, and the said Commissioners may delegate to every Person so appointed for the Purpose of conducting such Inquiry all such of the powers of the said Commissioners as they may deem necessary or expedient for summoning Witnesses and conducting such Inquiry.

Persons being married, above 60 *Years of Age, not compelled to live apart in Workhouses*—XXIII. Provided always, and be it enacted, That when any Two Persons, being Husband and Wife, both of whom shall be above the age of sixty years, shall be received into any Workhouse, in pursuance of the Provisions of the said recited Act or of this Act, or of any Rule, Order, or Regulation of the Commissioners appointed by Authority of this Act, such Two Persons shall not be compelled to live separate and apart from each other in such Workhouse.

For ensuring the due Visitation of Workhouses—XXIV. And be it enacted, that in all Cases where Boards of Guardians neglect to appoint a Visiting Committee for the Purpose of visiting the Workhouse of the Union, or when Three Months shall have elapsed during which such Committee shall have neglected to visit such Workhouse, the Poor Law Commissioners shall be required to appoint a Visitor, not being one of the Guardians, at a Salary to be fixed by them, to be paid out of the general Fund of the Union: Provided always, that the Appointment of any such paid Visitor shall cease at the Expiration of Three Calendar Months next after the Appointment of any Visiting Committee by the Guardians, subject nevertheless to his Re-appointment in case of any Repetition of such Neglect of the Guardians or Visiting Committee as aforesaid.

For Confirmation of the Proceedings of Boards of Guardians—XXV. And be it enacted, That in any civil or criminal Proceeding it shall not be necessary to prove the sending of the original Order of the Poor Law Commissioners, or of the Commissioners, constituting any Board of Guardians, in any Case in which any Persons professing to form a Board in obedience to such Order shall have taken upon themselves to act, and shall have continued for Three Years to act, in the Execution of the Laws for the Relief of the Poor; and in no Proceeding shall it be lawful to question the Qualification or Validity of the Election of any Person as a Guardian after the End of Twelve Months next following the Election, or the Time when the alleged Disqualification or Want of Qualification of the Person against whom such Proceeding shall be directed shall have arisen.

Penalties for giving false Evidence, or refusing to give Evidence—XXVI. And be it declared and enacted, That every Person who upon any Examination under the Authority of this Act shall wilfully give false Evidence, or wilfully make or subscribe a false Declaration, shall, on being convicted thereof, suffer the Pains and Penalties of Perjury, and every Person who shall refuse or wilfully neglect to attend in obedience to any Summons of the Commissioners, or any Inspector, or to give Evidence, or who shall wilfully alter, suppress, conceal, destroy, or refuse to produce any Books, Contracts, Agreements, Accounts, Maps, Plans, Surveys, Valuations, or Writings, or Copies of the same, which may be required to be produced for the Purposes of this Act, to any Person authorized by this Act to require the Production thereof, shall be deemed guilty of a Misdemeanor.

Confirmation of Proceedings under recited Acts—XXVII. And be it enacted, That, save when varied or repealed by this Act, and subject to the Provisions herein contained, all the Powers and Provisions of the recited Acts and of all other Acts relating to the Relief of the Poor in *England*, and every Thing lawfully done under the same, or in pursuance thereof, and all lawful Acts and Proceedings of the Poor Law Commissioners, and their Assistant Commissioners, and any Officers acting under them, or in virtue of the said Acts, or any of them, or under their Authority, or by any other Person acting in the Administration of the Laws for the Relief of the Poor in *England*, on or before the Day when the Commissioners first appointed under this Act shall enter on their Office, shall be as valid as if this Act had not been passed; and every Suit or other Proceeding civil or criminal, begun before the last-mentioned Day in the Name and under the Authority of the Poor Law Commissioners, shall have the same Force and Effect, if continued in their Names under the Sanction of the Commissioners as if the Poor Law Commissioners had continued to act in execution of the said Acts of Parliament; and nothing herein contained shall in any way take away or interfere with any Right of Action or of Defence to the same, or any Liability to be sued or prosecuted for any Penalty, for or against any Person under the said Acts, or any of them, according to the respective Provisions thereof, which shall have accrued wholly or in part before the last-mentioned Day.

Commission to continue for Five Years—XXVIII. Provided always, and be it enacted, That no Commissioner constituted under this Act, nor any Inspector, Secretary, or other Officer or Person to be appointed and employed by the Commissioners in the Business of their Office under this Act, shall continue to hold his respective Office under this Act, or exercise any of the Powers given by this Act, for a longer Period than Five Years next after the Day of the passing of this Act, and thenceforth until the End of the then next Session of Parliament; and from and after the Expiration of the said Period of Five Years, and of the then next Session of Parliament, so much of this Act as enables Her Majesty to appoint any Commissioner shall cease to operate or to have any Effect whatever.

Interpretation of Act—XXIX. And be it enacted, That this Act shall be construed in the same Manner as the said Act of the Fifth Year of the Reign of His late Majesty and the said Act of the Sixth Year of the Reign of Her Majesty, and the several Acts passed for the Amendment of the said Acts or either of them, and as One Act with the same, and with the Acts and Provisions thereby directed to be construed as One Act, unless where otherwise directed by this Act.

Act may be amended, &c.—XXX. And be it enacted, That this Act may be amended or repealed by any Act to be passed in this Session of Parliament.

to the poor in England, or to the powers or duties of the Poor Law Commissioners, are to be construed as if in the several Acts the present Commissioners had been named instead of the Poor Law Commissioners, subject, nevertheless, to any amendments made by 10 & 11 Vic. c. 109, either as to the substance or manner of exercising any of the powers of the Poor Law Commissioners.

By the 18th sec. it is declared that all lawful rules, orders, and regulations of the Poor Law Commissioners made before the day on which the Commissioners first appointed under that Act shall enter on their office, (*i.e.* before the 18th day of December,) shall continue in full force and effect, until rescinded or varied under the authority of that Act.

By the 27th sec., it is enacted, that save when varied or repealed by that Act, and subject to the provisions therein contained, all the powers and provisions of the therein-recited Acts, (*i.e.*, the 4 & 5 Wm. 4, c. 76, and the Acts since passed for amendment of the said Act, or otherwise relating to the laws for the relief of the poor in England,) and of other Acts relating to the relief of the poor in England, and every thing lawfully done under the same, or in pursuance thereof, and all lawful acts and proceedings of the Poor Law Commissioners and their Assistant Commissioners, and any officers acting under them, or in virtue of the said Acts, or any of them, or under their authority, or by any other person acting in the administration of the laws for the relief of the poor in England, on or before the day when the Commissioners first appointed under 10 & 11 Vic. c. 109, shall enter on their office, (*i.e.* the said 18th day of December instant,) shall be as valid as if that Act had not been passed.

By virtue of the provisions contained in the 10th clause of the new Act, the Assistant Commissioners appointed under the authority of the 4 & 5 Wm. 4, c. 76, have ceased to hold their offices. But the 19th sec. of the said Act empowers the present Commissioners to appoint, by Order under their Seal, fit persons to be inspectors to assist in the execution of that Act, and of other Acts now or which shall be hereafter in force for the relief of the poor, and may assign to such inspectors such duties in the execution of that Act as they may think fit; and I am to inform you that the Commissioners have appointed the same gentleman to be an inspector under that Act as was in charge of your union as an Assistant Poor Law Commissioner when they entered upon their office, and have assigned to him the same duties as those heretofore exercised by the Assistant Poor Law Commissioners, and have placed him in charge of your union.

I am further to state that all correspondence between the board of guardians or their officers and the Commissioners, is to be continued in like manner as heretofore with the Poor Law Commissioners, and the same style of address may be used in the correspondence.*

All communications, inquiries, and returns, which have been required from the guardians or their officers by the Poor Law Commissioners, in the course of correspondence, or by virtue of their orders, are to be made and transmitted to the present Commissioners, and whenever the sanction, approval, or order of the Poor Law Commissioners would have been required to any act of the guardians or their officers, application must now be made to the present Commissioners for the same.

In conclusion, I am to assure the guardians that the present Commissioners will be at all times ready to receive communications and to render their advice and assistance to the guardians and their officers, in respect to their duties in the administration of the poor law.

I am, Sir, your obedient Servant,

W. G. LUMLEY, *Assistant Secretary.*

To

The Clerk to the Guardians.

XV.—SANITARY—REPORT OF THE GUARDIANS OF AXMINSTER UNION.

Union Office, Axminster,
23rd December, 1847.

GENTLEMEN—I transmit you herewith, at the request of the board of guardians, copy report of the sanitary committee appointed by this board, in reference to the several parishes of the union.

I am, &c.

CHAS. BOND, *Clerk.*

The Poor Law Commissioners.

AXMINSTER UNION.—DECEMBER, 1847.

Report of the Sanitary Committee appointed at the Meeting of the Board of Guardians, held the 12th November, 1847.

The committee proceeded to examine and to

* It will be more correct to style the Board, as "The Poor Law Board," and to address them, as "My Lords and Gentlemen."

condense the reports, sent in by the guardians, of the sanitary condition of their respective parishes, pursuant to the resolution of the board of guardians adopted at the said meeting on the 12th ult., as follows :—

DEVON PARISHES.

1. *Axminster.*—The guardians and medical officer of the parish of Axminster report, that, in the greater part of the gardens and yards of the houses occupied by the labouring classes, they found heaps of dung and rubbish, &c., in general very close to the back-doors. In several places they found cesspools, of a very offensive character; and one particularly so, near Castle Hill, a locality seldom free from disease. The few privies that are in existence are, in general, without drains. In several places there is only one privy, common to four or five houses. There are nine houses in Anchor Road, a locality also much subject to disease, without any privy at all. The houses at Millbrook are also without privies, and there is a vast accumulation of filthy matter behind them. The guardians particularly remark upon the bad state of the drain and ditch opposite the grounds in the occupation of Mr. Sanford, at Smallbridge, which they attribute to the neglect of the surveyors of the highways.

The condition of the greater part of the tenements occupied by the poorer classes has been already in some degree improved by whitewashing, and others are now undergoing the same process; but in some there is a great want of proper accommodation, and consequently of cleanliness. In one there are only two small bed-rooms for nine persons; and in another only one bed-room for the accommodation of the same number of individuals.

The guardians add, that the occupiers of the several premises referred to "expressed their willingness to remove the nuisances complained of immediately, and gave it as their opinion that all the drains of houses in the town of Axminster should be immediately made to communicate with the common sewer, which is not the case in many instances at present."

2. *Axmouth.* — The guardian and medical officer of this parish have merely sent in to the committee a list of nuisances existing in the parish, such as offensive dunghills, drains, and pigstyes, forty-seven in number, and state that several dwelling-houses require both ventilation and whitewashing.

3. *Colyton.* — The guardians of this parish report that they found numerous existing nuisances, but do not enter into particulars, merely stating that many of the nuisances had already been removed, and that effectual means were being taken for the removal of the remainder.

4. *Coombpyne.*—The report from this parish is similar to that from the parish of Axmouth.

5. *Dalwood.* — The guardian and medical officer of this parish report, that, after a careful inspection of all the cottages of the poor, they found a great want of cleanliness and accommodation both within and without, and that the inmates generally were destitute of the means of much improving their condition. They complain that "the farmers on whose estates the greater part of the cottages are situated, do not seem disposed to exert themselves in the matter;" and the guardian and medical officer suggest, that a quantity of lime be provided and given out to the poor, who, they thought, would then whitewash their cottages themselves, under the superintendence of a mason to be paid for his trouble.

6. *Kilmington.* — In the report from this parish no particulars are given. The guardian and medical officer, in the first place, report, that having carefully inspected the cottages of the poor, they found them "in as cleanly a state as could be reasonably expected," and then strongly urge the removal of all nuisances both within and without, and further the well lime-washing all the walls. They add, moreover, that many of the houses have no privies attached to them, and that the old poor-house is in a very bad state of repair, which latter evil they understood would shortly be remedied.

7. *Membury* (Southern District.) — The guardian and medical officer of this parish report that the cottages of the poor are generally in a very bad condition, as regards cleanliness and accommodation. They consist generally of two rooms only, on the ground floor, one being a small pantry, or wood house. That the upper rooms are, for the most part, very indifferent, and that the nuisances on the outside of many of them are of a very noxious character. They particularly press upon the attention of the board, that, in Membury Street, close to the church, there are some houses and premises in such a dreadful state, that, in case of any epidemic in this place, the pernicious effluvia from this place would, no doubt, prove highly prejudicial. That this property belongs to an individual (named in the report) whose obstinacy and parsimony induce him to oppose

everything like remedy; that the cottages in general greatly require whitewashing.

Membury (Northern District.)—The guardian and medical officer report that matters are not quite so bad in this district as in the southern. "There are, however, a few dunghills and cesspools which require to be removed, and that the ventilation in three or four of the cottages is very defective, but that, upon the whole, taking into consideration the one with the other, the northern district of Membury appears to be in a tolerably clean state, the worst houses belonging to the individual above alluded to, some of which are too well ventilated."

N.B. In a supplementary report from the parish of Membury the guardian states, that, on a second visit to the cottages of the poor, he found many of the nuisances complained of either removed or in progress of removal, and many of the ceilings whitewashed; and further, that the individual so much complained of in the first report had partially improved the condition of his premises, but that much still remained to be done.

8. *Musbury.* — The guardian of Musbury states, that, in conjunction with the medical officer, he had inspected generally the condition of the parish, and found but few nuisances of any kind, for the removal of which, however, with one exception, effectual steps were being taken; the exception alluded to being the stagnant pool and ditch containing a collection of offensive matter at the lower corner of the village, on the road leading to Whiteford, which taint the atmosphere, and endanger the health of the inhabitants.

9. *Seaton and Beer.* — The guardians and medical officer of this parish have merely sent in a list of nuisances, about one hundred in number; chiefly defective drains of the most dangerous and offensive character, dunghills, and pigstyes, many of which discharge themselves into, or are near to, the public street. Among these are specially to be noticed a row of houses in Seaton, two out of four of which are not occupied, on account of the very offensive state of the drains; another open drain, which, receiving the whole drainage of Seaton, is most unhealthy and offensive, even to those passing it, and another drain from a cottage privy, that empties itself into a well of water. In the village of Beer, the pigstyes seem generally to require removal; several very offensive drains discharge themselves into the street, one of which renders the water that supplies the neighbourhood unwholesome.

N.B. In a supplementary report made by the guardians of the parish of Seaton and Beer, they state that many of the nuisances enumerated in the list above referred to have, at their suggestion, been removed, or are in progress of removal, but that others remained still in the same offensive condition, and the guardians pointed out about eighteen cases which, in their opinion, required to be immediately dealt with as the law directs.

10. *Shute.*—In the report from this parish, the guardians and medical officer dwell particularly upon the filthy condition of portions of the hamlet of Whiteford; there appears to be great want of privies, and many of those in existence are in a very offensive state. In one instance the privy is attached to the house, having a door that opens into it, and which has already been known to generate typhus fever. Where there are no privies, the consequences are obvious; but it appears quite unaccountable, that, in one particular case, where there appears to be a tolerably good privy attached to the house, many of the family never use it, but make nuisanees on the road around the house. There is a very serious case of a large collection of filth close to the back doors of three cottages, which is very offensive, and requires to be immediately removed. Another large collection of very offensive matter is caused by the stoppage of a drain, which passes under two of the cottages. All the drains in this hamlet would seem, by this report, to require cleansing, and the guardians and medical officer specially recommend that a stream of water which runs down a lane at the upper part of Whiteford, should be brought by an open gutter to the Porch House, near the public house, as it would then carry off the filth there accumulated, and greatly tend to purify the air in that immediate neighbourhood. The guardian and medical officer are of opinion that, if the existing nuisances were removed, the cottages whitewashed, and proper privies attached to them, so as to prevent the public roads from being made a substitute for them, the principal sources of danger from miasma would be effectually removed.

11. *Stockland* — The medical officer of this parish, at the request of the guardian, reports very favourably of its sanitary condition in general. "He found but few nuisances calling for any interference, and those rather private than public annoyances, and in every instance

he found a willingness on the part of the inhabitants to remove such nuisances before a second visit;" the cases being chiefly dunghills, and filthy heaps of refuse, in close contact with the dwellings of the cottagers.

12. *Uplyme.* — The guardian and medical officer of this parish do not report as now existing many of the nuisances so much complained of in other parishes; they state that, although "as a rural district, its general ventilation is much more perfect than it could be in a locality densely populated, yet still the poverty of many of its poor is of a character so extreme as to leave some apparently not in possession of many of the common necessaries of life." In many of the wretched hovels visited on this occasion, wherein there are only two apartments, "the room above for sleeping in, is accessible only by means of a bad imitation of a ladder, most insecure to mount upon, and in some the upper rooms are so broken and rotten, that it is with the utmost risk they can be entered on." Some of these rooms are represented to be almost totally destitute of all necessary furniture and accommodation; others as having windows which cannot be opened, "rendering the supposition of the visitation of any severe epidemic amongst the poor people a melancholy reflection."

The guardian suggests, "that facilities for purifying the apartments of the poor, and changing the impure air therein, might be rendered available by causing the windows to be made capable of being opened;" and they further recommend that the cottages should be white-washed, and privies attached to them, of which convenience many of them are now destitute.

DORSET PARISHES.

13. *Charmouth.* —The medical officer of this parish reports, "the poor to be, comparatively speaking, well off and cleanly;" he states, that part of the village of Charmouth which is situated upon a declivity, is well drained, with one or two exceptions, the exceptions for the most part depending on the want of a common sewer. Towards the higher part of the village, the drainage is in some cases defective and bad. In one instance, a drain, common to several houses and one privy, "passes either under or over a stream of water which passes through and supplies the place;" in another, the common drain from several privies being obstructed, the contents escape, and "lie stagnant and exposed to the open air." Measures, however, are stated to be in contemplation for the early removal of these inconveniences.

14. *Chardstock.*—The guardians of this parish report, that, out of above one hundred and forty cottages which they personally examined, nearly all require white-washing; of this entire number, seventy-nine had no privies; forty had privies of some kind, twelve of which were common to several houses; they found dung-heaps and open cess-pools, in many places close to the doors, and on examining the interior of the cottages, observed that some families lived "huddled together on the ground floor, having no upstair room, and in one of them eight sleep in one small room, and that very imperfectly ventilated." Referring to the street of Alston, a small hamlet in this parish, the guardians state it to be in a most filthy condition throughout, owing to the cattle being allowed to stand there for a long time together: in one place there is a large dung-heap close to the road; in another, a green stagnant pool, in which cattle are suffered to drink. Added to which, the drains on the sides of the road are in a most neglected condition. From the general state of the poor in this parish, the guardians express apprehension, that should cholera, or any other epidemic, visit them, the loss of life would, in all probability, be frightful, as, in many cases, three sleep in one bed; and, in some instances, even more.

15. *Hawkchurch.* — The guardian reports, that he had examined the whole of the cottages in this parish, and found them generally in a state of cleanliness and decency; but that in many instances they required white-washing; that, he met with no nuisances, with the exception of two or three drains required to be cleansed and their course altered, which he directed to be immediately done—at the same time ordered the necessary white-washing to be at once completed.

16. *Lyme Regis.* — The guardians and medical officer of this parish state in their report, that the general condition of the dwellings of the poor is unhealthy and bad, chiefly owing to the defective state of the drains; the insufficient supply of water, (which in most cases has to be brought from a distance,) the want of privies, and, in certain localities, the accumulation of offensive matter in dung-heaps, cess-pools, pigstyes, &c. They refer to one case especially—a large open drain near Sherborne-lane—as a subject of general complaint, and to the constant sickness of the inhabitants in that quarter, as a decisive proof of its baneful influence; they are

of opinion that the immediate white-washing of all habitations of the lower orders is advisable, and close their remarks by saying, that although the attention of the local authorities is now directed towards some of the most prominent nuisances, which are already in course of removal, they entertain little, if any, very material improvement in the sanitary state of the poor, until the law imposes greater stringency in compelling the owners of houses to construct drains far more efficient than those existing at the present time.

17. *Thorncombe.* — The guardians and medical officer of this parish state, in the first place, that, where nuisances exist, " they have given strict orders that the inmates of the adjacent houses take immediate steps to remove them to as great a distance as possible, from their own thresholds, and from the public thoroughfares adjoining." They next require the opinion of the board as to the most desirable and convenient method of efficient draining and white-washing, and, " as to what share (if any) of the necessary expense will fall upon the parish;" and conclude by stating, that " as the parish lies high, on the side of a hill, is less exposed to malaria from stagnant and accumulating vegetable matter than many other places, and that the pauper population is now remarkably free from disease, more healthy, in fact, than it has been for many years past at this season of the year."

The committee refrain from making any lengthened remarks on the foregoing reports—they speak for themselves; it is difficult to conceive anything more wretched than the condition of certain classes of the poor in many of the parishes of this union, and quite as difficult to separate from it the grossest vice and immorality; the subject demands the most serious and immediate attention of the different parochial authorities, who, although they may not have it in their power to apply at once an effectual remedy to the entire of the existing evils, may, nevertheless, greatly mitigate them, by vigilant superintendence, by precept and example, by a judicious application of parochial aid, and by attracting towards them the attention of those amongst their fellow-parishioners whom Providence has exempted from similar privation and distress; and who, having to give, give bountifully, as many of them doubtless will do, in aid of suffering humanity, and to rescue their respective parishes from reproach and shame. The exterior nuisances, spread about the district, admit of a legal remedy, and this the Committee strongly recommend should be immediately applied, without partiality, favour, or affection.

Domestic cleanliness, perfect ventilation, and the removal of all filthy deposits likely to generate or to increase the virulence of pestilential miasma, are the best and surest, perhaps the only palliatives or preventives which the parochial authorities have it in their power to apply against the expected visitation of Asiatic cholera; but there is one which the committee think might be found, in certain cases, eminently useful. namely, the establishment of reception rooms, or isolated buildings, for the temporary accommodation of tramps and vagrants, as was practised in Axminster, in the year 1832, and which was supposed to have been the principal means of keeping that town free from cholera, whilst it existed in other places in its immediate neighbourhood.

C. A. MAC ALESTER, *Chairman.*

Answer of the Poor Law Board, dated January 15th, 1848.

The Poor Law Board, in acknowledging the receipt of the report of the sanitary committee appointed by the guardians of the Axminster Union, cannot refrain from expressing their warm approbation of the spirit with which its members, in their respective localities, appear to have carried on their investigations, and their earnest hope that the useful example set by the Axminster Union will be very generally followed by the other unions.

The sanitary condition of the dwellings of the labouring classes is of paramount importance, not only in the religious and moral considerations so properly alluded to by the general committee at the close of their report, but also on account of the sickness and death, and consequent pauperism, resulting from deficiencies in this respect.

As is truly observed in the report, the local authorities, in the present state of the law upon this subject, have less power of effective interference than might be desired; but with regard to the powers now vested in the guardians, of which those of the Axminster union will, doubtless, be ready to avail themselves to the utmost, the Board would refer to the Circular Letter of the late Poor Law Commissioners of Oct. 1846, on the Nuisances' Removal Act, a copy of which is inserted in their last Annual Report, p. 159, and in the Official Circular, No. 6, of 1st June, 1847. The Board heartily concur in the trust there expressed, "that no apprehension of casting a charge upon the parish will operate to induce the guardians to abstain from proceeding under the act in cases of urgency." And in their opinion that, "the improvement of the sanitary condition of the poorer classes tends so greatly to remove many of the causes of destitution and pauperism, that the money judiciously expended on such an object, now sanctioned by the legislature in the cases to which the statute applies, will be found to be most profitably laid out even in reference to the more direct object of the duties of the guardians."

On a few points in the detailed parochial reports, the Board would make the following observations :—

With regard to the suggestion made in that from *Dalwood*, as to the whitewashing of the cottages of the labourers, the Board would invite the perusal of the accompanying extract from an answer returned by the late Commissioners to an application from Bolton :—

"The Commissioners are of opinion that the guardians may properly cause the dwelling-house of any pauper actually sick of fever to be whitewashed and fumigated, and may supply to such pauper chloride of lime, and other materials, for that purpose; such a course, in fact, constituting a portion of the means essential for the recovery of the sick person, assuming that the steps are taken under the advice and direction of the medical officers in attendance. The Commissioners, however, are of opinion that the guardians cannot lawfully supply materials for the whitewashing, or fumigating of houses at the cost of the townships in which the paupers live, by way of prevention merely. The Commissioners themselves have no authority to supply to the guardians the powers which may be wanting in these matters. If the houses are brought under the operation of 9 & 10 Vic. c. 96, the guardians will doubtless think it right that the proceedings therein pointed out should be carried into execution, where the guardians can act in the suppression of nuisances. They may also call the attention of the town council of Bolton to the matter in reference to the statute cited. The Commissioners are not aware of any power which the surveyors of highways have under the act referred to."

With regard to the state of a part of *Membury* street, they would remark that it is for the guardians to consider how far they are likely to be able to satisfy the justices that this case is one which, if the evil complained of continues, they ought to deal with under the Nuisances' Removal Act.

With respect to the nuisances made by the inhabitants of one house in *Shute*, on the road, the guardians would do well to ascertain whether the case is provided for by the General Turnpike Act, or the General Highways Act, and, if so, to draw the attention, either of the trustees of the roads, or of the surveyor of highways, to this practice.

With reference to the recommendations in the *Uplyme* report, as to improving the ventilation in certain cottages therein, the Board are bound to state that they are not aware of any steps which can be taken, unless proceedings can be had under the act already referred to. If the opening of the windows be requisite for the purpose of purifying the dwellings, which are represented as being in an unwholesome state, it may be a question whether the case is not within the statute. The Board observe that though the language of the first sections of the 9 & 10 Vic. c. 96 is joint, and couples the term "*filthy and unwholesome*," the form of the certificate given in the schedule is in the disjunctive, namely, "filthy *or* unwholesome;" it may therefore be fairly contended that the statute extends to dwellings which, though not filthy, are nevertheless unwholesome.

The Board will be glad to learn whether the guardians deem it advisable to take proceedings in any one of these cases; and if so, the result.

In conclusion, the Board entirely concur in the opinion expressed by the Axminster committee that ventilation, cleanliness, and the removal of filthy deposits, are most important for the preservation of health, and for preventing the occurrence of disease; and the Board consider that the union and parochial authorities will confer great benefit upon the working classes, and upon the district generally, by exerting their influence to the utmost both as individuals, and in their official capacity, in effecting these objects; and where necessary, by calling in the aid of the law, and the several provisions of the Nuisances' Removal Act.

At the same time, the Board, adverting to the phrase as to "*the judicious application of parochial aid*," must caution the guardians not to encourage the parochial authorities in applying that aid, either by way of relief or otherwise, in any manner, however beneficial they may deem it, which may not be supported by the sanction of the law, as they will thus expose themselves to loss, through the auditors' disallowance of such charges.

London: Published by Order of the Poor Law Board by CHARLES KNIGHT & Co., 90, Fleet Street.

AN

OFFICIAL CIRCULAR

OF PUBLIC DOCUMENTS AND INFORMATION:

DIRECTED BY THE POOR LAW COMMISSIONERS TO BE PRINTED, CHIEFLY FOR THE USE OF THE MEMBERS AND PERMANENT OFFICERS OF BOARDS OF GUARDIANS, UNDER THE POOR LAW AMENDMENT ACT.

No. 12.] FEBRUARY, 1848. [N.S.

CONTENTS.

I.—ACCOUNTS ORDER.

1. CLOTHING ACCOUNTS AND RELIEF LISTS.

Mr. Hotson, the district auditor, has communicated to the Board the following replies to questions submitted to him by workhouse masters in reference to the clothing accounts, and the mode of entering in the relief lists the number of paupers relieved on the 1st of January and 1st of July in each year:—

Clothing Accounts.—It appears to me, judging from the following portions of your letter, that you labour under misapprehensions respecting the system of clothing accounts. You say: 1. That without an 'old stock account,' no master of a house can tell what he may have in store, or be able to give an account of such when required. 2. That the Clothing Register Book does not answer the purpose for want of columns for each article, and because it is not shown how some articles belonging to a suit which may be worn out before the others are to be accounted for, supplied, or exchanged. 3. That this book cannot be properly kept, because there is a continual wearing out of one article before another, and that by the very same classes. I will endeavour briefly to give you such an explanation as will answer these objections. In the Clothing Register Book, Form 32, you will have as many numbers (for males and females) as you have suits at any time, and as many sizes as you may require. Suits No. 1, No. 2, No. 3, &c., will be permanently kept up, and you will keep up as many suits as may be necessary, by substituting new articles for those worn out, whether they be two or three, or all the articles of a suit, and these articles you will mark with the number marked on the articles for which they are substituted; but the substitutions will not appear in this book, which will contain only the names of the paupers wearing the several suits, with the dates of their admission and discharge; the absence of a date of discharge against the last name showing that the suit is still in wear, and *vice versa;* a date of discharge against the last name will show that the suit is in store and available. Thus this book will show, not only what suits are in store, but what are the sizes of those suits, and when the master gets accustomed to a set of sizes, he will know by glancing at a pauper admitted what size will suit such pauper. By the article in the order relating to this book (Form 32) a ticket bearing the number of a suit given to a pauper is required to be attached to the pauper's own clothes, and I would suggest that the same ticket be attached to the suit itself when in store, and further that this ticket should bear a subsidiary number indicating the size of the suit. It will be very easy to make from this book a summary of the articles in wear and in store for the purpose of your half-yearly valuation, or at any time it may be required. The new articles given out by way of substitution, as above explained, or by way of increasing the number of suits, will be entered in the Clothing Receipt and Expenditure Book, (Form 31) and every substitution will indicate an article worn out, or cut up for mending others, and by looking through the column for 'number of the suit,' you may see when the article worn out was given out, and therefore how long it has lasted, and by a further reference to Form 32, by whom it has been worn, and how long by each person; and when we see who have worn the suit, we shall know why the article in question has worn so short a time, or the contrary. Thus it appears that much more is indicated by the plain and simple entries in Forms 31 and 32 than meets the eye of a stranger to the system. I have now only to point out how you may adapt this system to the arrangements you generally make in favour of the old people, and for the purpose of preventing the idle from destroying new clothes, or absconding with them, which appear to me well worth continuing. Under the above system it cannot but happen that some suits will, upon the whole, be much better than others, and *vice versa*, and I see no objection to your transferring an old man from an indifferent suit to a good one, provided you enter in the column for 'date of discharge' in Form 32, the words 'transferred to No. —' together with the date; the indifferent suit will then be ready for an inmate to whom it may not be prudent to give a good suit. This will, I think, afford you sufficient latitude for the purpose.

As to the number of paupers relieved on the 1st of January and 1st July in each year.—The note (4) at the foot of Form 22 upon which the question asked in your letter arises, refers to the numbers of the several classes of paupers charged to each parish, and a memorandum of the numbers in question should be made at the beginning of the book containing Form 22 for the purpose of furnishing the materials for filling up the line set apart for them in Form 15 at the foot of the statement for each parish, and for the corresponding portion of Form 16.

The memorandum in question may be in the following Form:—

Numbers relieved on the first of ———

Parishes.	Classes as in Form 22.																Summary as in Forms 15 and 16.
	1	2	3	4	5	6	7	8	9	10	11	12	13	14	15	16	
Diss .																	
Harleston																	*
Harston				1			1			2							
Thorpe .																	
Totals																	†

* These numbers are to be inserted in Form 15, by the clerk.

† These in Form 16.

---

2. PROVISIONS ACCOUNTS: FORMS NOS. 25 & 26.

Nov. 18th, 1847.

Clerk of Wellington Union, Salop—A doubt has arisen as to the articles of food required to be entered in the master's Daily and Weekly Provisions Consumption Accounts, Forms 25 & 26, in the General Accounts Order. The articles entered by the master of the Wellington Workhouse comprise flour, oatmeal, cheese, butter, beef, mutton, and potatoes, which he contends are all that he is bound to insert. There are several other important articles consumed, but they can only be inserted by converting one column into two, which the master objects to do. Inquired, whether any other than the principal articles consumed should be brought into the above accounts.

Ans.—All articles consumed at the respective meals of the inmates of the workhouse are to be brought into the accounts in question, and not merely such as the master may think to be the principal or most important. If the master's book has not columns enough, more columns should be introduced. The books are intended to disclose the actual consumption of provisions in the workhouse, and if any articles are omitted the accounts will not be correct. See note No. 1, to the Form 25 of the General Accounts Order.

II.—DIETARY.

1. GENERAL ORDER RELATING TO.

To the guardians of the poor of the several unions named in the schedule hereunto annexed :—

To the clerk or clerks to the justices of the petty sessions held for the division or divisions in which the said unions are situate :—

And to all others whom it may concern.

Whereas the Poor Law Commissioners have, by various orders under their hands and seals, issued to the several unions named in the schedule hereunto annexed, the dates whereof are set forth in the said schedule, ordered and directed that the paupers of the respective classes and sexes who might then or thereafter be received and maintained in every workhouse of the said respective unions should, during the period of their residence therein, be fed, dieted, and maintained with the food and in the manner described in the table or tables set forth in each order respectively.

Now, we, the Commissioners for administering the Laws for Relief of the Poor in England, do hereby confirm all the said orders now in force in the said several unions; and do order and direct, that the same shall continue to be acted upon and obeyed in the unions to which the same have been respectively directed until the said Commissioners shall, with reference to any one or more of such unions, by their order, otherwise direct.

Provided, however, that if the guardians of any union shall at any time or times deem it expedient that a change should be made either temporarily or permanently, in the nature or quantity of the food specified in the order last issued to such union, or in the manner therein described, and shall send a complete and accurate statement of the proposed alteration, in writing, signed by the presiding chairman of the meeting of the board whereat the resolution for making such alteration was adopted, to the said Commissioners, and the said Commissioners shall sanction and approve of such alteration, the guardians may, when the same shall have been so sanctioned and approved of, but not before, cause the same to be adopted and used in the workhouse or workhouses of the said union, as the case may be, without any further order of the said Commissioners in that behalf.

Provided, also, that nothing herein contained shall be taken to rescind or alter any provision or regulation of the Poor Law Commissioners contained in their General Order bearing date the twenty-fourth day of July, one thousand eight hundred and forty-seven, and addressed to the said several unions herein referred to, which applies to the subject of the diet of the paupers in the workhouse or workhouses of such unions.

SCHEDULE above referred to.

Names of the Unions.	Dates of the Dietary Orders.
Aberaeron . .	19th June, 1839
Abergavenny .	5th March, 1844
Aberystwith . .	16th June, 1846
Abingdon . .	13th January, 1846
Albans, St. . .	20th January, 1836
Alcester . .	24th January, 1839
Alderbury . .	16th April, 1841
Alnwick . .	24th January, 1840
Alresford . .	18th March, 1836
Alton . . .	5th March, 1846
Altrincham . .	24th August, 1843
Amersham . .	5th November, 1840
Amesbury . .	17th October, 1837
Ampthill . .	17th November, 1845
Andover . . .	22nd November, 1847
Asaph, St. . .	21st May, 1846
Ashbourne . .	6th August, 1846
Ashby-de-la-Zouch .	8th May, 1839
Ashford, East . .	27th April, 1837
Ashford, West . .	25th February, 1837
Ashton-under-Lyne .	2nd March, 1847
Aston . . .	31st March, 1847
Atcham . . .	4th August, 1846
Atherstone . .	17th July, 1838
Austell, St. . .	18th November, 1837
Axbridge . . .	24th September, 1846
Axminster . .	25th September, 1844
Aylesbury . .	2nd July, 1841
Aylsham . . .	2nd October, 1845
Bakewell . . .	31st December, 1846
Banbury . . .	28th June, 1839
Bangor and Beaumaris	28th October, 1846
Barnet . . .	4th January, 1836
Barnstaple . .	28th November, 1846

Names of the Unions.	Dates of the Dietary Orders.
Barrow-upon-Soar	18th May, 1844
Basford	2nd October, 1846
Basingstoke	25th November, 1843
Bath	18th November, 1841
Battle	14th October, 1847
Beaminster	17th November, 1846
Bedaie	19th July, 1841
Bedford	24th April, 1847
Bedminster	16th February, 1847
Belford	17th May, 1844
Bellingham	25th November, 1847
Belper	28th May, 1847
Berkhampstead	15th April, 1844
Berwick-upon-Tweed	11th October, 1837
Beverley	23rd September, 1840
Bicester	7th June, 1847
Bideford	28th August, 1838
Biggleswade	12th July, 1836
Billericay	9th January, 1846
Billesdon	18th May, 1847
Bingham	18th May, 1847
Bishop Stortford	29th June, 1847
Blaby	3rd May, 1845
Blandford	9th February, 1837
Blean	14th February, 1837
Blofield	14th July, 1845
Blything	21st January, 1836
Bodmin	10th August, 1846
Bootle	11th March, 1843
Bosmere and Claydon	2nd March, 1846
Boston	15th October, 1845
Bourn	12th December, 1837
Brackley	16th May, 1837
Bradfield	25th August, 1847
Bradford (Wilts.)	31st October, 1843
Braintree	8th April, 1847
Brampton	24th February, 1847
Brecknock	2nd March, 1846
Brentford	21st January, 1840
Bridge	30th October, 1835
Bridgend and Cowbridge	1st June, 1847
Bridgwater	9th April, 1847
Bridgnorth	18th May, 1847
Bridlington	23rd June, 1837
Bridport	31st December, 1846
Brixworth	13th February, 1847
Bromley	17th February, 1838
Bromsgrove	14th November, 1846
Bromyard	12th February, 1846
Buckingham	2nd January, 1839
Buntingford	9th December, 1845
Burton-upon-Trent	14th April, 1847
Caistor	11th March, 1840
Calne	14th April, 1836
Cambridge	6th July, 1847
Cardiff	5th January, 1837
Carmarthen	25th May, 1842
Carnarvon	2nd October, 1846
Castle Ward	20th November, 1845
Catherington	24th April, 1838
Caxton and Arrington	6th July, 1837
Cerne	27th September, 1847
Chailey	1st October, 1836
Chapel-en-le-Frith	29th November, 1841
Chard	18th February, 1847
Cheadle	9th January, 1838
Chelmsford	18th June, 1847
Cheltenham	16th December, 1846
Chepstow	21st December, 1846
Chertsey	1st August, 1846
Chesterfield	22nd March, 1847
Chester-le-Street	27th November, 1837
Chesterton	5th April, 1838
Chippenham	21st October, 1847
Chipping Norton	5th February, 1847
Chipping Sodbury	4th December, 1846
Chorlton	14th February, 1848
Christchurch	12th November, 1847
Church Stretton	4th December, 1845
Cirencester	8th February, 1847
Cleobury Mortimer	22nd September, 1847
Clifton	14th January, 1848
Clun	17th December, 1836
Clutton	18th January, 1841
Cockermouth	12th December, 1845
Colchester	10th April, 1838
Columb, St. Major	9th August, 1845
Cookham	23rd December, 1837
Corwen	29th November, 1842
Cosford	19th April, 1843
Cranbrook	4th December, 1835
Crediton	21st January, 1846
Crickhowel	8th September, 1846
Cricklade and Wootton Bassett	15th May, 1837
Croydon	15th March, 1847
Cuckfield	23rd June, 1843
Darlington	20th July, 1837
Dartford	10th June, 1836
Daventry	10th August, 1843
Depwade	28th April, 1843

Names of the Unions.	Dates of the Dietary Orders.	Names of the Unions.	Dates of the Dietary Orders.
Derby . . .	11th December, 1843	Glendale . .	11th June, 1841
Devizes . . .	7th September, 1847	Gloucester . .	28th May, 1847
Dewsbury . .	14th May, 1842	Godstone . .	7th January, 1836
Docking . . .	15th September, 1843	Goole . . .	6th February, 1841
Doncaster . .	31st July, 1846	Grantham . .	24th November, 1846
Dorchester . .	24th June, 1847	Gravesend and Milton	23rd August, 1836
Dore . . .	24th May, 1839	Greenwich . .	7th February, 1837
Dorkin . . .	15th October, 1845	Guildford . .	7th September, 1836
Dover . . .	3rd March, 1846	Guiltcross . .	4th April, 1837
Downham . .	1st February, 1847	Guisborough . .	20th September, 1841
Drayton . .	9th August, 1847		
Driffield . .	7th August, 1840	Hackney . . .	24th December, 1842
Droitwich . .	24th December, 1845	Hailsham . .	5th January, 1837
Droxford . .	14th September, 1842	Halifax . .	13th March, 1847
Dudley . . .	6th June, 1837	Halstead . .	8th February, 1843
Dunmow . .	27th June, 1847	Haltwhistle . .	4th August, 1847
Dursley . . .	15th June, 1842	Hambledon . .	29th July, 1837
		Hardingstone . .	4th May, 1841
Easingwold . .	9th August, 1843	Hartismere . .	10th July, 1840
Eastbourne . .	22nd August, 1836	Hartley Wintney .	24th May, 1836
East Grinstead .	1st August, 1839	Hastings . .	4th January, 1847
Easthampstead .	15th May, 1837	Hatfield . . .	10th November, 1847
East Retford . .	5th March, 1847	Havant . . .	6th July, 1838
Eastry . . .	11th February, 1837	Haverfordwest . .	21st October, 1846
Ecclesall Bierlow .	20th August, 1841	Hay . . .	18th March, 1846
Edmonton . .	26th September, 1846	Hayfield . . .	4th May, 1847
Elham . . .	3rd December, 1835	Headington . .	7th June, 1847
Ellesmere . .	23rd September, 1839	Helmsley Blackmoor	29th October, 1847
Ely . . .	20th August, 1836	Helston . . .	30th January, 1847
Epping . . .	27th May, 1837	Hendon . . .	20th January, 1836
Epsom . . .	5th November, 1840	Henley . . .	28th May, 1845
Erpingham . .	15th August, 1845	Henstead . .	29th July, 1837
Eton . . .	21st April, 1847	Hereford . .	29th May, 1838
Evesham . .	15th February, 1847	Hertford . .	15th January, 1836
		Hexham . . .	12th October, 1838
Faith, St. . .	21st January, 1846	Highworth and Swindon	25th January, 1836
Falmouth . .	3rd February, 1848		
Fareham . . .	7th January, 1847	Hinckley . .	29th June, 1847
Faringdon . .	27th January, 1846	Hitchin . . .	21st January, 1836
Farnham . .	7th April, 1847	Holbeach . .	14th January, 1847
Faversham . .	18th June, 1842	Holborn . . .	8th July, 1842
Festiniog . .	12th January, 1846	Hollingbourn . .	29th May, 1847
Foleshill . .	3rd June, 1844	Holywell . .	29th March, 1847
Fordingbridge . .	6th March, 1847	Honiton . . .	2nd March, 1839
Freebridge Lynn .	3rd April, 1846	Hoo . . .	11th November, 1836
Frome . . .	7th December, 1846	Horncastle . .	27th April, 1838
Fulham . . .	23rd February, 1847	Horsham . .	5th August, 1847
		Howden . . .	24th April, 1844
Gainsborough . .	10th January, 1844	Hoxne . . .	30th April, 1845
Gateshead . .	24th July, 1841	Hungerford . .	4th September, 1847
Germans, St. . .	9th February, 1846	Huntingdon . .	29th June, 1837
Glanford Brigg .	13th January, 1847	Hursley . .	21st December, 1835

Names of the Unions	Dates of the Dietary Orders.	Names of the Unions.	Dates of the Dietary Orders.
Ipswich . .	9th February, 1837	Marlborough . .	14th December, 1846
Ives, St. . .	22nd February, 1845	Martley . .	15th September, 1847
		Medway . . .	7th August, 1840
Kendal . . .	24th December, 1847	Melksham . .	18th December, 1846
Kettering . .	14th July, 1840	Melton Mowbray .	30th December, 1846
Keynsham . .	7th December, 1846	Mere . . .	17th December, 1846
Kidderminster . .	13th January, 1846	Meriden . . .	31st March, 1838
Kingsbridge . .	27th March, 1847	Midhurst . .	16th January, 1843
Kingsclere . .	9th February, 1847	Mildenhall . .	17th December, 1835
King's Lynn . .	17th November, 1847	Milton . . .	28th October, 1843
King's Norton .	26th November, 1846	Mitford and Launditch	11th February, 1847
Kington . .	19th February, 1846	Monmouth . .	11th December, 1846
		Morpeth . .	15th April, 1839
Lanchester . .	16th April, 1847		
Langport . .	20th October, 1836	Nantwich . .	23rd November, 1847
Launceston . .	14th December, 1837	Narberth . .	11th March, 1846
Ledbury . . .	2nd October, 1847	Neath . . .	1st April, 1843
Leek . . .	10th September, 1839	Neots, St. . .	16th July, 1847
Leicester . .	29th June, 1847	Newark . . .	11th January, 1843
Leighton Buzzard .	15th June, 1846	Newbury . .	14th February, 1845
Leominster . .	2nd March, 1847	Newcastle-under-Lyme	4th March, 1845
Lewes . . .	16th January, 1847	Newcastle-upon-Tyne	15th October, 1841
Lewisham . .	13th December, 1841	Newent . .	7th June, 1839
Lexden and Winstree	30th September, 1837	New Forest . .	23rd February, 1837
Leyburn . .	6th March, 1847	Newhaven . .	7th June, 1839
Lichfield . . .	11th February, 1847	Newmarket . .	28th January, 1840
Lincoln . . .	16th February, 1847	Newport (Monmouth)	19th January, 1847
Linton . . .	21st January, 1836	Newport (Salop) .	22nd May, 1837
Liskeard . . .	20th October, 1842	Newport Pagnell .	29th December, 1845
Llandovery . .	3rd September, 1846	Newton Abbot .	12th February, 1846
Llanelly . . .	7th March, 1840	Newtown and Llanidloes	16th September, 1843
Llanfyllin . .	29th March, 1843		
London, East . .	2nd September, 1847	Northallerton . .	11th April, 1845
Longtown . .	17th December, 1846	Northampton . .	23rd August, 1837
Loughborough .	7th May, 1845	North Aylesford .	7th March, 1836
Louth . . .	10th February, 1847	Northleach . .	22nd November, 1847
Ludlow . . .	10th November, 1841	Northwich . .	29th April, 1846
Luton . . .	9th November, 1846	North Witchford .	25th August, 1836
Lutterworth . .	12th January, 1846	Nuneaton . .	16th January, 1845
Lymington . .	6th January, 1848		
		Oakham . .	20th March, 1847
Macclesfield . .	13th March, 1847	Okehampton . .	23rd August, 1838
Madeley . .	10th October, 1836	Ongar . . .	21st April, 1847
Maidstone . .	7th March, 1837	Orsett . . .	3rd August, 1839
Maldon . . .	19th January, 1841	Oundle . . .	11th August, 1836
Malling . . .	14th April, 1837		
Malmsbury . .	17th December, 1847	Patrington . .	8th April, 1839
Malton . . .	8th June, 1841	Pembroke . .	26th March, 1847
Manchester . .	3rd August, 1841	Penkridge . .	23rd August, 1847
Mansfield . .	15th December, 1846	Penzance . .	21st November, 1846
Market Bosworth .	6th May, 1847	Pershore . . .	26th August, 1845
Market Harborough .	20th March, 1847	Peterborough . .	24th February, 1846

Names of the Unions.	Dates of the Dietary Orders.	Names of the Unions.	Dates of the Dietary Orders.
Petersfield . .	13th March, 1841	Southam . .	10th February, 1847
Petworth . .	25th March, 1836	South Molton .	22nd October, 1846
Pewsey . . .	7th September, 1847	South Shields . .	3rd August, 1839
Pickering . .	8th November, 1843	South Stoneham .	13th June, 1840
Plomesgate . .	19th January, 1848	Southwell . .	18th February, 1847
Plympton, St. Mary .	5th August, 1843	Spalding . . .	14th December, 1846
Pont-y-pool . .	14th December, 1846	Spilsby . . .	14th February, 1842
Poole . . .	17th January, 1842	Stafford . . .	23rd January, 1847
Poplar . . .	29th November, 1837	Staines . . .	7th April, 1847
Portsea Island . .	13th December, 1837	Stamford . .	9th April, 1846
Potterspury . .	12th December, 1846	Stepney . .	23rd June, 1842
Prescott . . .	2nd March, 1847	Steyning . .	21st January, 1845
		Stockbridge . .	16th October, 1847
Radford . . .	6th December, 1838	Stockport . .	5th February, 1846
Redruth . . .	5th October, 1841	Stockton . .	13th May, 1847
Reeth . . .	11th September, 1847	Stokesley . .	11th June, 1839
Reigate . . .	25th November, 1836	Stone . . .	21st September, 1847
Richmond (Surrey) .	22nd August, 1836	Stourbridge . .	21st April, 1847
Richmond (Yorkshire)	10th June, 1842	Stow . . .	11th June, 1845
Ringwood . .	9th March, 1842	Stow-on-the-Wold .	8th July, 1847
Risbridge . .	30th July, 1838	Strand . . .	4th June, 1836
Rochford . .	7th May, 1847	Stratford-upon-Avon	3rd April, 1846
Romford . .	6th May, 1845	Stroud . . .	4th July, 1843
Romney Marsh .	1st February, 1838	Sturminster . .	23rd December, 1845
Ross . . .	2nd December, 1846	Sudbury . .	3rd February, 1848
Rothbury . .	15th July, 1841	Sunderland . .	2nd February, 1847
Rotherham . .	3rd February, 1847	Swaffham . .	7th May, 1840
Royston . .	4th February, 1837	Swansea . .	21st January, 1846
Rugby . . .	10th May, 1847		
Rye . . .	4th September, 1845	Tamworth . .	16th May, 1846
		Taunton . .	24th December, 1846
Saffron Walden .	12th November, 1840	Tavistock . .	4th December, 1845
Saviour's, St. .	26th June, 1837	Teesdale . .	5th April, 1842
Scarborough . .	5th March, 1846	Tenbury . .	13th March, 1846
Sculcoates . .	29th December, 1845	Tendring . .	31st October, 1839
Sedberg . . .	8th October, 1847	Tenterden . .	16th February, 1846
Sedgefield . .	22nd August, 1837	Tetbury . .	6th December, 1836
Seisdon . .	26th March, 1847	Tewkesbury . .	29th June, 1847
Selby . . .	27th September, 1844	Thakeham . .	17th March, 1836
Sevenoaks . .	28th March, 1839	Thame . . .	3rd May, 1847
Shaftesbury . .	31st August, 1839	Thanet, Isle of .	15th January, 1836
Shardlow . .	24th October, 1846	Thetford . .	5th January, 1847
Sheffield . .	20th February, 1847	Thingoe . . .	19th September, 1839
Sheppey . .	7th January, 1846	Thirsk . . .	23rd March, 1847
Shepton Mallett .	24th November, 1847	Thomas, St. . .	24th February, 1846
Sherborne . .	7th December, 1838	Thornbury . .	9th February, 1847
Shiffnal . .	16th November, 1840	Thorne . . .	6th April, 1839
Shipston-upon-Stour	25th April, 1837	Thrapston . .	20th June, 1846
Skipton . . .	28th October, 1846	Ticehurst . .	12th February, 1845
Skirlaugh . .	22nd September, 1847	Tisbury . . .	3rd September, 1847
Sleaford . . .	24th June, 1842	Tiverton . . .	11th May, 1836
Solihull . . .	22nd December, 1838	Tonbridge . .	2nd March, 1836

Names of the Unions.	Dates of the Dietary Orders.
Torrington . .	14th February, 1848
Totness . . .	11th February, 1837
Towcester . .	18th July, 1840
Truro . . .	1st April, 1843
Tynemouth . .	15th November, 1841
Uckfield . . .	17th December, 1835
Ulverstone . .	5th March, 1847
Uppingham . .	22nd April, 1846
Upon-upon-Severn .	7th December, 1838
Uttoxeter . .	17th March, 1847
Uxbridge . .	31st December, 1841
Wallingford . .	13th November, 1846
Walsall . . .	9th February, 1838
Walsingham . .	18th May, 1837
Wandsworth and Clapham	31st January, 1839
Wangford . .	11th March, 1846
Wantage . .	3rd August, 1836
Ware . . .	22nd October, 1846
Wareham and Purbeck	13th September, 1841
Warminster . .	11th December, 1847
Warrington . .	4th November, 1846
Warwick . .	31st May, 1839
Watford . .	12th January, 1847
Wayland . .	9th August, 1839
Weardale . .	3rd July, 1840
Wellingborough .	30th June, 1837
Wellington (Salop) .	3rd November, 1836
Wellington (Somerset)	1st April, 1847
Wells . . .	26th March, 1847
Wem . . .	9th March, 1847
Weobly . . .	30th December, 1846
Westbourne . .	6th December, 1836
West Bromwich .	13th September, 1837
Westbury-upon-Severn	11th May, 1847
Westbury and Whorwelsdown	1st October, 1847
West Firle . .	29th June, 1836
West Ham . .	27th January, 1847
West Hampnett .	25th August, 1836
West Ward . .	1st July, 1847
Weymouth . .	6th May, 1847
Wheatenhurst . .	1st February, 1847
Whitby . . .	24th May, 1842
Whitchurch . .	17th December, 1847
White hapel . .	3rd July, 1847
Whitehaven . .	22nd May, 1846
Wigton . .	13th September, 1841
	24th November, 1846

Names of the Unions.	Dates of the Dietary Orders.
Wilton . . .	17th November, 1846
Wimborne and Cranborne	11th July, 1840
Wincanton . .	31st October, 1846
Winchcombe . .	4th September, 1847
Winchester, New .	5th June, 1841
Windsor . .	1st December, 1846
Winslow . .	23rd May, 1840
Wirrall . . .	14th November, 1846
Witham . , .	23rd March, 1836
Witney . . .	19th May, 1847
Woburn . . .	18th November, 1847
Wokingham . .	3rd February, 1838
Wolstanton and Burslem	7th June, 1847
Wolverhampton .	22nd October, 1847
Woodbridge . .	8th April, 1843
Woodstock . .	2nd March, 1847
Worcester . .	3rd March, 1841
Worksop . . .	15th August, 1842
Wrexham . .	17th February, 1847
Wycomb . .	26th October, 1844
Yeovil . . .	13th February, 1847
York . . .	9th January, 1838

Given under our hands and seal of office, this sixteenth day of February, in the year one thousand eight hundred and forty-eight.

CHAS. BULLER, Jun.
President.

G. GREY.
C. WOOD.

2. CIRCULAR ACCOMPANYING THE ABOVE ORDER.

Poor Law Board,
Somerset House,
17th February, 1848.

SIR,—I am directed by the Poor Law Board to state, that they have had under their consideration the mode which has heretofore been pursued for effecting alterations in the dietaries in the different workhouses, which had been prescribed by the Poor Law Commissioners.

As those dietaries had been prescribed by an Order under seal, the only legal mode by which any alteration could be made in them, except under the particular circumstances specified in the General Consolidated Order, was by the issuing of another Order, under the seal of the Poor

Law Board. This process was necessarily attended with considerable delay and some trouble, and it has therefore appeared to the Board to be advisable to make a change in this respect, and they propose to give a power to the guardians to alter the dietary as occasion may arise, without the necessity of a formal order of the Poor Law Board, under their seal.

The Board do not however propose that the alteration shall be made without their sanction, and have accordingly provided in the Order which they have issued, that, before any alteration can take effect, a copy of the proposal shall be transmitted to them for their approval; and when they shall, by letter, have approved of it, the alteration shall thenceforth be adopted, without the necessity of a formal Order. The guardians will however observe, that until the approval has taken place, the proposed change in the dietary must not be adopted.

The Board further desire, in order to assist them in their decision as to any proposed alteration, that, the opinion of the medical officer of the workhouse upon its propriety, with reference to the health of the inmates, should be forwarded by the guardians.

The Board believe that the schedule contains the last Order which has been issued to the respective unions to fix the dietary. If there be any error in this respect, the guardians will send up a reference to the Order which is actually in force, and the Board will give their directions upon the subject.

There are several applications now before the Board, which have been delayed until this Order has been issued. In these cases it will be necessary that the proceedings pointed out in the order should be pursued, and the Board think it advisable that the guardians who have applied for and expect an order, should at once take those steps, and transmit the requisite documents to the office.

In conclusion, I beg to refer the guardians to the 16th sec. of the 10 and 11 Vic. cap. 109, which repeals the provision contained in the 16th sec. of the Poor Law Amendment Act, requiring a General Rule to remain for forty days with one of the Secretaries of State before it comes into operation. The present Order will come into operation fourteen days after the transmission of the same to the Unions to which it is addressed.

I am, Sir, your obedient Servant,

W. G. LUMLEY, *Assistant Secretary.*

To

The Clerk to the Guardians.

III.—ELECTION OF GUARDIANS.

CIRCULAR.

Poor Law Board,
Somerset House,
26th Feb. 1848.

SIR,—I am directed by the Poor Law Board to call your attention to the proviso in Article 6 of the General Consolidated Order of July, 1847, which is as follows:—

> "Provided that, whenever the day appointed in this Order for the performance of any act relating to or connected with the election of guardians shall be a Sunday or Good Friday, such act shall be performed on the day next following, and each subsequent proceeding shall be postponed one day."

By Article 8 of the above-mentioned Order, it is directed that the last day for receiving nominations shall be the 26th day of March; but as that day in the present year falls upon a Sunday, the last day for receiving nominations at the approaching annual election of guardians will be Monday, the 27th of March.

The delivery of the voting papers under Article 11, will take place on the 6th of April; and the collection of those papers under Article 17 will be made on the eighth of the same month.

Following the same rule of postponement, the opportunity of obtaining voting papers under Article 19 will be extended to the 8th of April, and the proceeding provided for in Article 20 would be delayed until the 9th; but as that day will fall upon a Sunday a further postponement will become necessary, and the 10th of April will, accordingly, be the day on which parties whose voting papers may have not been collected may deliver them to the clerk.

Under these circumstances, it seems requisite that the examination and computation of the votes under Article 21, should take place on the 11th of April, so as to allow a due interval between the proceedings respectively provided for by Articles 20 and 21. And this view appears to the Board to be in strict accordance with the terms of the proviso in Article 6 of the Order. But as there may be some doubt as to the correct construction of the Order in this respect, the Clerk will do well to open the examination of the votes on the 10th, and either adjourn the same to the next day, or formally revise on the 11th what he may have done on the 10th, and sign the certificate on the 11th, if the examination of the votes be then concluded.

The Board have deemed it advisable to issue the foregoing instructions, partly because they have already received several inquiries on the subject, and partly because their attention has been directed to some publications in which the notification of dates, in reference to the proceedings adverted to, appears to be in some respects inaccurate.

I am, Sir, your obedient Servant,
W. G. LUMLEY, *Assistant Secretary.*

IV. — RELIEF — ENGAGEMENTS TO REPAY NON-RESIDENT RELIEF, HOW AFFECTED BY THE POOR REMOVAL ACT, 9 AND 10 VIC. c. 66.

May 3rd, 1847.

Clerk of Warminster Union—Before the passing of the Poor Removal Act (9 & 10 Vic. c. 66) the board of guardians had entered into engagements with other unions to repay the relief which they might grant to the non-resident paupers belonging to the Warminster Union; and the guardians of other unions had entered into similar engagements with the Warminster board. On the 6th October, 1846, the Warminster board addressed a letter to the several unions to which they had given such engagements withdrawing the same; and intimating that the relief which might be given to any non-settled poor residing in the Warminster Union would be charged to the parishes in which they resided. Accounts of the non-resident relief granted by the Warminster board up to the 6th October, 1846, were forwarded, amongst others, to the Wincanton Union. The Wincanton board object to repay any relief advanced to the non-resident paupers of that union subsequent to the close of the September quarter, 1846, alleging that the Poor Removal Act rendered all engagements to repay non-resident relief nugatory. The Wincanton board, however, on the 14th October, 1846, wrote to the Warminster board withdrawing their engagement to repay non-resident relief. Requested the Commissioners' opinion as to whether the course adopted by the Warminster board, as detailed above, or that pursued by the Wincanton board is the correct course.

Ans.—The Commissioners cannot say that the guardians of the Wincanton Union can be compelled by law to pay to the guardians of the Warminster Union the sum which is in question. The Commissioners are disposed to think that the alteration of the law in regard to irremovable paupers destroyed the consideration in those cases upon which the engagement of guardians to repay non-resident relief was founded; and thereby, in point of law, dissolved the engagement itself in respect of such non-resident paupers. Therefore, if the relief in the cases referred to was supplied in the first instance by the guardians of the Warminster Union, and they were to be reimbursed by the guardians of any other union on the ground of the liability of the latter to maintain the paupers if removed to them, the consideration having failed, the liability to make such reimbursement has ceased. But if the guardians of the Warminster Union have been requested to administer the relief as the agents of any other union, the Commissioners think it would be held that such agency continued until it was determined by the latter; and the former, therefore, are entitled to be repaid the amount which they expended upon the paupers of the union on whose behalf they acted. In the former case, if the relief be not repaid, the amount must be charged to the parishes in which the paupers resided. But, in the latter case, if the guardians cannot recover the amount, it appears that the charge would be one which must be borne by the union at large, the guardians having, in their corporate capacity, undertaken the charge. With regard to paupers still removable, the undertaking of the union remained binding upon the other until it was actually revoked.

V.—REMOVAL ACT—CONSTRUCTION OF 10 & 11 VIC. c. 110.

September 10th, 1847.

Clerk of Rye Union—Inquired, 1. Whether the relief granted on account of sickness or accident not producing permanent disability, to a non-settled pauper, who is rendered irremovable by the operation of the 1st sec. of the Poor Removal Act, 10 & 11 Vic. c. 110, and who occasionally had non-resident relief, between the 26th August, 1845, and 26th August, 1846, can now be charged to the common fund of the union. 2. Whether the relief granted on the death of the husband to a non-resident widow, irremovable under the 1st sec. of the Poor Removal Act, 9 & 10 Vic. c. 66, and whose husband was relieved between the 26th August, 1845, and 26th August, 1846, can now be charged to the common fund of the union. And, 3. Whether the mode of charging midwifery, surgical, and vaccination fees paid to medical officers should be governed by the same rule as the relief in any case legally chargeable to the common fund of the union.

Ans.—1. If, in the case first put, the non-settled pauper be irremovable under sec. 1 of 9 & 10 Vic. cap. 66, and if, during the time specified, namely, between 26th August, 1845, and 26th August, 1846, he received relief from some other parish in the union, by right of settlement, or reputed settlement, in such parish, the relief now given to such person, though made necessary by sickness or accident, not producing permanent disability, must be charged to the common fund of the union. In this case, the person being irremovable with reference to the 1st sec. of 9 & 10 Vic. c. 66, it makes no difference as regards the operation of the 10 & 11 Vic. c. 110; that the case likewise falls within some other section of the 9 & 10 Vic. c. 66, than the first. 2. In the second case, the Commissioners understand the widow to have become so since the passing of the 9 & 10 Vic. c. 66, and to be now irremovable by reason of the operation of the first section of that Act. If this be so, the only material question, in determining whether the common fund be liable for her present relief is, whether or not she can, under the circumstances stated, be regarded as having been in receipt of relief during the year preceding the passing of the 9 & 10 Vic. c. 66. This appears to the Commissioners to be entirely a question of fact, and is to be determined by a consideration of what actually occurred. If the relief were given to her husband on her account solely, or even partly on her account, so that she can be regarded as having been wholly or partially maintained by such relief, it appears to be right to treat her as having been in the receipt of relief within the meaning of 10 & 11 Vic. c. 110, so as to warrant the charging the present relief to the common fund. But if no part of the relief advanced to the husband were given on her account, or, in fact, applied in her support, either because she maintained herself independently of her husband, or was absent from her husband at the time the relief was advanced, or for any other cause, it does not appear that she could be regarded as having been in the receipt of relief within the meaning of 10 and 11 Vic. c. 110, and her relief would not, therefore, be chargeable to the common fund. 3. The Commissioners consider that the special fees to medical officers, enumerated in your third inquiry, (with the exception of vaccination fees,) are relief, and with reference to the question of charging such fees, dependent upon the same considerations as apply to other relief; so that such fees would be chargeable to the common fund, under the recent statute, where the other relief to the paupers could be so charged. Vaccination, or surgical or medical assistance incident to the vaccination, is, by the 4 & 5 Vic. c. 32, expressly declared not to be parochial relief to the person vaccinated; and it is only the cost of relief, maintenance, or burial, of a pauper that, by reason of 10 & 11 Vic. c. 110, is to be charged to the common fund. The charging of vaccination fees is, therefore, not affected by that statute.

VI.—WORKHOUSE SCHOOLMASTER.

LEAVE OF ABSENCE.

March 1st, 1847.

Mr. ——,—Inquired whether it was necessary for the workhouse schoolmaster to apply to the guardians for permission to leave the workhouse for an hour or two after his duties with the children are over, or would the consent of the master of the workhouse for that purpose be sufficient.

Ans.—It is competent to the schoolmaster of a union workhouse to leave the workhouse temporarily when his attendance on duty is not required, without the leave of the master or the guardians; but it is not competent to him to absent himself from the performance of his duties at the workhouse, without the consent of the board of guardians.

VII.—WORKHOUSE—TABLES FOR CALCULATING THE TOTAL QUANTITIES OF PROVISIONS REQUIRED FOR EACH MEAL IN WORKHOUSE; AND LOSS IN COOKING, ETC.

Windsor Union Workhouse,
February 14th, 1848.

My Lords and Gentlemen,—I have taken the liberty of transmitting to you a complete set of tables for the calculation of the quantities of provisions consumed in union workhouses, also tables to compute the loss in cooking, cutting, weighing, &c., of all provisions and necessaries, adapted to the new form of Provisions Accounts, recently prescribed by the Poor Law Commissioners.

If the Poor Law Board would publish the tables they would be found very useful to the masters, clerks, and auditors of Unions, as saving much time and trouble.

I have, &c.,
WM. NICHOLLS, Jun

TABLE FOR CALCULATING THE QUANTITY OF PROVISIONS CONSUMED BY ANY NUMBER OF PERSONS ACCORDING TO THE WORKHOUSE DIETARY, AND ALSO THE LOSS INCURRED IN COOKING, CUTTING, AND WEIGHING PROVISIONS.

For Tea, Sugar, Butter, Cheese, &c., &c. — OUNCES EACH.

No. of Persons.	¼ lbs	¼ ozs	½ lbs	½ ozs	¾ lbs	¾ ozs	1 lbs	1 ozs	1¼ lbs	1¼ ozs	1½ lbs	1½ ozs	1¾ lbs	1¾ ozs
2		½		1		1½		2		2½		3		3½
3		¾		1½		2¼		3		3¾		4½		5¼
4		1		2		3		4		5		6		7
5		1¼		2½		3¾		5		6¼		7½		8¾
6		1½		3		4½		6		7½		9		10½
7		1¾		3½		5¼		7		8¾		10½		12¼
8		2		4		6		8		10		12		14
9		2¼		4½		6¾		9		11¼		13½		15¾
10		2½		5		7½		10		12½		15	1	1½
11		2¾		5½		8¼		11		13¾	1	0½	1	3¼
12		3		6		9		12		15	1	2	1	5
13		3¼		6½		9¾		13	1	0¼	1	3½	1	6¾
14		3½		7		10½		14	1	1½	1	5	1	8½
15		3¾		7½		11¼		15	1	2¾	1	6½	1	10¼
16		4		8		12	1	0	1	4	1	8	1	12
17		4¼		8½		12¾	1	1	1	5¼	1	9½	1	13¾
18		4½		9		13½	1	2	1	6½	1	11	1	15½
19		4¾		9½		14¼	1	3	1	7¾	1	12½	2	1¼
20		5		10		15	1	4	1	9	1	14	2	3
21		5¼		10½		15¾	1	5	1	10¼	1	15½	2	4¾
22		5½		11	1	0½	1	6	1	11½	2	1	2	6½
23		5¾		11½	1	1¼	1	7	1	12¾	2	2½	2	8¼
24		6		12	1	2	1	8	1	14	2	4	2	10
25		6¼		12½	1	2¾	1	9	1	15¼	2	5½	2	11¾
26		6½		13	1	3½	1	10	2	0½	2	7	2	13¼
27		6¾		13½	1	4¼	1	11	2	1¾	2	8½	2	15¼
28		7		14	1	5	1	12	2	3	2	10	3	1

For Beer, Soup, Porridge, Broth, &c., &c. — PINTS EACH.

No. of Persons.	½ pts	1 pts	1½ pts	2 pts	2½ pts	3 pts
2	1	2	3	4	5	6
3	1½	3	4½	6	7½	9
4	2	4	6	8	10	12
5	2½	5	7½	10	12½	15
6	3	6	9	12	15	18
7	3½	7	10½	14	17½	21
8	4	8	12	16	20	24
9	4½	9	13½	18	22½	27
10	5	10	15	20	25	30
11	5½	11	16½	22	27½	33
12	6	12	18	24	30	36
13	6½	13	19½	26	32½	39
14	7	14	21	28	35	42
15	7½	15	22½	30	37½	45
16	8	16	24	32	40	48
17	8½	17	25½	34	42½	51
18	9	18	27	36	45	54
19	9½	19	28½	38	47½	57
20	10	20	30	40	50	60
21	10½	21	31½	42	52½	63
22	11	22	33	44	55	66
23	11½	23	34½	46	57½	69
24	12	24	36	48	60	72
25	12½	25	37½	50	62½	75
26	13	26	39	52	65	78
27	13½	27	40½	54	67½	81
28	14	28	42	56	70	84

Loss in Cooking, Cutting, Weighing, &c. — OUNCES IN THE POUND.

No. of lbs.	¼ lbs	¼ ozs	½ lbs	½ ozs	¾ lbs	¾ ozs	1 lbs	1 ozs	2 lbs	2 ozs	3 lbs	3 ozs	4 lbs	4 ozs	5 lbs	5 oz.	6 lbs	6 oz.
2		½		1		1½		2		4		6		8		10		12
3		¾		1½		2¼		3		6		9		12		15	1	2
4		1		2		3		4		8		12	1	0	1	4	1	8
5		1¼		2½		3¾		5		10		15	1	4	1	9	1	14
6		1½		3		4½		6		12	1	2	1	8	1	14	2	4
7		1¾		3½		5¼		7		14	1	5	1	12	2	3	2	10
8		2		4		6		8	1	0	1	8	2	0	2	8	3	0
9		2¼		4½		6¾		9	1	2	1	11	2	4	2	13	3	6
10		2½		5		7½		10	1	4	1	14	2	8	3	2	3	12
11		2¾		5½		8¼		11	1	6	2	1	2	12	3	7	4	2
12		3		6		9		12	1	8	2	4	3	0	3	12	4	8
13		3¼		6½		9¾		13	1	10	2	7	3	4	4	1	4	14
14		3½		7		10½		14	1	12	2	10	3	8	4	6	5	4
15		3¾		7½		11¼		15	1	14	2	13	3	12	4	11	5	10
16		4		8		12	1	0	2	0	3	0	4	0	5	0	6	0
17		4¼		8½		12¾	1	1	2	2	3	3	4	4	5	5	6	6
18		4½		9		13½	1	2	2	4	3	6	4	8	5	10	6	12
19		4¾		9½		14¼	1	3	2	6	3	9	4	12	5	15	7	2
20		5		10		15	1	4	2	8	3	12	5	0	6	4	7	8
21		5¼		10½		15¾	1	5	2	10	3	15	5	4	6	9	7	14
22		5½		11	1	0½	1	6	2	12	4	2	5	8	6	14	8	4
23		5¾		11½	1	1¼	1	7	2	14	4	5	5	12	7	3	8	10
24		6		12	1	2	1	8	3	0	4	8	6	0	7	8	9	0
25		6¼		12½	1	2¾	1	9	3	2	4	11	6	4	7	13	9	6
26		6½		13	1	3½	1	10	3	4	4	14	6	8	8	2	9	12
27		6¾		13½	1	4¼	1	11	3	6	5	1	6	12	8	7	10	2
28		7		14	1	5	1	12	3	8	5	4	7	0	8	12	10	8

29		7¼		14½	1	5¾	1	13	2	4¼	2	11½	3	2¾
30		7½		15	1	6½	1	14	2	5½	2	13	3	4½
31		7¾		15½	1	7¼	1	15	2	6¾	2	14½	3	6¼
32		8	1	0	1	8	2	0	2	8	3	0	3	8
33		8¼	1	0½	1	8¾	2	1	2	9¼	3	1½	3	9¾
34		8½	1	1	1	9½	2	2	2	10½	3	3	3	11½
35		8¾	1	1½	1	10¼	2	3	2	11¾	3	4½	3	13¼
36		9	1	2	1	11	2	4	2	13	3	6	3	15
37		9¼	1	2½	1	11¾	2	5	2	14¼	3	7½	4	0¾
38		9½	1	3	1	12½	2	6	2	15½	3	9	4	2½
39		9¾	1	3½	1	13¼	2	7	3	0¾	3	10½	4	4¼
40		10	1	4	1	14	2	8	3	2	3	12	4	6
41		10¼	1	4½	1	14¾	2	9	3	3¼	3	13½	4	7¾
42		10½	1	5	1	15½	2	10	3	4½	3	15	4	9½
43		10¾	1	5½	2	0¼	2	11	3	5¾	4	0½	4	11¼
44		11	1	6	2	1	2	12	3	7	4	2	4	13
45		11¼	1	6½	2	1¾	2	13	3	8¼	4	3½	4	14¾
46		11½	1	7	2	2½	2	14	3	9½	4	5	5	0½
47		11¾	1	7½	2	3¼	2	15	3	10¾	4	6½	5	2¼
48		12	1	8	2	4	3	0	3	12	4	8	5	4
49		12¼	1	8½	2	4¾	3	1	3	13¼	4	9½	5	5¾
50		12½	1	9	2	5½	3	2	3	14½	4	11	5	7½
51		12¾	1	9½	2	6¼	3	3	3	15¾	4	12½	5	9¼
52		13	1	10	2	7	3	4	4	1	4	14	5	11
53		13¼	1	10½	2	7¾	3	5	4	2¼	4	15½	5	12¾
54		13½	1	11	2	8½	3	6	4	3½	5	1	5	14½
55		13¾	1	11½	2	9¼	3	7	4	4¾	5	2½	6	0¼
56		14	1	12	2	10	3	8	4	6	5	4	6	2
57		14¼	1	12½	2	10¾	3	9	4	7¼	5	5½	6	3¾
58		14½	1	13	2	11½	3	10	4	8½	5	7	6	5½
59		14¾	1	13½	2	12¼	3	11	4	9¾	5	8½	6	7¼
60		15	1	14	2	13	3	12	4	11	5	10	6	9
61		15¼	1	14½	2	13¾	3	13	4	12¼	5	11½	6	10¾
62		15½	1	15	2	14½	3	14	4	13½	5	13	6	12½
63		15¾	1	15½	2	15¼	3	15	4	14¾	5	14½	6	14¼
64	1	0	2	0	3	0	4	0	5	0	6	0	7	0
65	1	0¼	2	0½	3	0¾	4	1	5	1¼	6	1½	7	1¾

Example.—To ascertain the quantity of butter required for 59 persons, to each of whom ½ oz. is allowed, find 59 in the first column, and opposite to that number in the column headed "½ oz." will appear the quantity, 1 lb. 13½ oz.

14½	29	43½	58	72½	87
15	30	45	60	75	90
15½	31	46½	62	77½	93
16	32	48	64	80	96
16½	33	49½	66	82½	99
17	34	51	68	85	102
17½	35	52½	70	87½	105
18	36	54	72	90	108
18½	37	55½	74	92½	111
19	38	57	76	95	114
19½	39	58½	78	97½	117
20	40	60	80	100	120
20½	41	61½	82	102½	123
21	42	63	84	105	126
21½	43	64½	86	107½	129
22	44	66	88	110	132
22½	45	67½	90	112½	135
23	46	69	92	115	138
23½	47	70½	94	117½	141
24	48	72	96	120	144
24½	49	73½	98	122½	147
25	50	75	100	125	150
25½	51	76½	102	127½	153
26	52	78	104	130	156
26½	53	79½	106	132½	159
27	54	81	108	135	162
27½	55	82½	110	137½	165
28	56	84	112	140	168
28½	57	85½	114	142½	171
29	58	87	116	145	174
29½	59	88½	118	147½	177
30	60	90	120	150	180
30½	61	91½	122	152½	183
31	62	93	124	155	186
31½	63	94½	126	157½	189
32	64	96	128	160	192
32½	65	97½	130	162½	195

Example.—In ascertaining the quantity of soup required for 59 persons, each of whom is allowed "1½ pints," find 59 in the first column, opposite to which in column headed 1½ pt. will appear the quantity, 88½.

	7¼		14½	1	5¾	1	13	3	10	5	7	7	4	9	1	10	14	29
	7½		15	1	6½	1	14	3	12	5	10	7	8	9	6	11	4	30
	7¾		15½	1	7¼	1	15	3	14	5	13	7	12	9	11	11	10	31
	8	1	0	1	8	2	0	4	0	6	0	8	0	10	0	12	0	32
	8¼	1	0½	1	8¾	2	1	4	2	6	3	8	4	10	5	12	6	33
	8½	1	1	1	9½	2	2	4	4	6	6	8	8	10	10	12	12	34
	8¾	1	1½	1	10¼	2	3	4	6	6	9	8	12	10	15	13	2	35
	9	1	2	1	11	2	4	4	8	6	12	9	0	11	4	13	8	36
	9¼	1	2½	1	11¾	2	5	4	10	6	15	9	4	11	9	13	14	37
	9½	1	3	1	12½	2	6	4	12	7	2	9	8	11	14	14	4	38
	9¾	1	3½	1	13¼	2	7	4	14	7	5	9	12	12	3	14	10	39
	10	1	4	1	14	2	8	5	0	7	8	10	0	12	8	15	0	40
	10¼	1	4½	1	14¾	2	9	5	2	7	11	10	4	12	13	15	6	41
	10½	1	5	1	15½	2	10	5	4	7	14	10	8	13	2	15	12	42
	10¾	1	5½	2	0¼	2	11	5	6	8	1	10	12	13	7	16	2	43
	11	1	6	2	1	2	12	5	8	8	4	11	0	13	12	16	8	44
	11¼	1	6½	2	1¾	2	13	5	10	8	7	11	4	14	1	16	14	45
	11½	1	7	2	2½	2	14	5	12	8	10	11	8	14	6	17	4	46
	11¾	1	7½	2	3¼	2	15	5	14	8	13	11	12	14	11	17	10	47
	12	1	8	2	4	3	0	6	0	9	0	12	0	15	0	18	0	48
	12¼	1	8½	2	4¾	3	1	6	2	9	3	12	4	15	5	18	6	49
	12½	1	9	2	5½	3	2	6	4	9	6	12	8	15	10	18	12	50
	12¾	1	9½	2	6¼	3	3	6	6	9	9	12	12	15	15	19	2	51
	13	1	10	2	7	3	4	6	8	9	12	13	0	16	4	19	8	52
	13¼	1	10½	2	7¾	3	5	6	10	9	15	13	4	16	9	19	14	53
	13½	1	11	2	8½	3	6	6	12	10	2	13	8	16	14	20	4	54
	13¾	1	11½	2	9¼	3	7	6	14	10	5	13	12	17	3	20	10	55
	14	1	12	2	10	3	8	7	0	10	8	14	0	17	8	21	0	56
	14¼	1	12½	2	10¾	3	9	7	2	10	11	14	4	17	13	21	6	57
	14½	1	13	2	11½	3	10	7	4	10	14	14	8	18	2	21	12	58
	14¾	1	13½	2	12¼	3	11	7	6	11	1	14	12	18	7	22	2	59
	15	1	14	2	13	3	12	7	8	11	4	15	0	18	12	22	8	60
	15¼	1	14½	2	13¾	3	13	7	10	11	7	15	4	19	1	22	14	61
	15½	1	15	2	14½	3	14	7	12	11	10	15	8	19	6	23	4	62
	15¾	1	15½	2	15¼	3	15	7	14	11	13	15	12	19	11	23	10	63
1	0	2	0	3	0	4	0	8	0	12	0	16	0	20	0	24	0	64
1	0¼	2	0½	3	0¾	4	1	8	2	12	3	16	4	20	5	24	6	65

Example.—If the loss on bread be ¾ of an ounce in the pound, (which is believed to be about the quantity,) and the total quantity used be 59 lbs., the column headed ¾, opposite to that number in the last column, will show the total loss to be 2 lb. 12¼ oz.

No. of Persons.	For Tea, Sugar, Butter, Cheese, &c., &c. — OUNCES EACH. ¼		½		¾		1		1¼		1½		1¾	
	lbs	ozs	lbs	ozs	lbs	ozs	lbs	ozs	lbs	ozs	lbs	ozs	lbs	ozs
66	1	0½	2	1	3	1½	4	2	5	2½	6	3	7	3½
67	1	0¾	2	1½	3	2¼	4	3	5	3¾	6	4½	7	5¼
68	1	1	2	2	3	3	4	4	5	5	6	6	7	7
69	1	1¼	2	2½	3	3¾	4	5	5	6¼	6	7½	7	8¾
70	1	1½	2	3	3	4½	4	6	5	7½	6	9	7	10½
71	1	1¾	2	3½	3	5¼	4	7	5	8¾	6	10½	7	12¼
72	1	2	2	4	3	6	4	8	5	10	6	12	7	14
73	1	2¼	2	4½	3	6¾	4	9	5	11¼	6	13½	7	15¾
74	1	2½	2	5	3	7½	4	10	5	12½	6	15	8	1½
75	1	2¾	2	5½	3	8¼	4	11	5	13¾	7	0½	8	3¼
76	1	3	2	6	3	9	4	12	5	15	7	2	8	5
77	1	3¼	2	6½	3	9¾	4	13	6	0¼	7	3½	8	6¾
78	1	3½	2	7	3	10½	4	14	6	1½	7	5	8	8½
79	1	3¾	2	7½	3	11¼	4	15	6	2¾	7	6½	8	10¼
80	1	4	2	8	3	12	5	0	6	4	7	8	8	12
81	1	4¼	2	8½	3	12¾	5	1	6	5¼	7	9½	8	13¾
82	1	4½	2	9	3	13½	5	2	6	6½	7	11	8	15½
83	1	4¾	2	9½	3	14¼	5	3	6	7¾	7	12½	9	1¼
84	1	5	2	10	3	15	5	4	6	9	7	14	9	3
85	1	5¼	2	10½	3	15¾	5	5	6	10¼	7	15½	9	4¾
86	1	5½	2	11	4	0½	5	6	6	11½	8	1	9	6½
87	1	5¾	2	11½	4	1¼	5	7	6	12¾	8	2½	9	8¼
88	1	6	2	12	4	2	5	8	6	14	8	4	9	10
89	1	6¼	2	12½	4	2¾	5	9	6	15¼	8	5½	9	11¾
90	1	6½	2	13	4	3½	5	10	7	0½	8	7	9	13½
91	1	6¾	2	13½	4	4¼	5	11	7	1¾	8	8½	9	15¼
92	1	7	2	14	4	5	5	12	7	3	8	10	10	1
93	1	7¼	2	14½	4	5¾	5	13	7	4¼	8	11½	10	2¾
94	1	7½	2	15	4	6½	5	14	7	5½	8	13	10	4½
95	1	7¾	2	15½	4	7¼	5	15	7	6¾	8	14½	10	6¼
96	1	8	3	0	4	8	6	0	7	8	9	0	10	8
97	1	8¼	3	0½	4	8¾	6	1	7	9¼	9	1½	10	9¾
98	1	8½	3	1	4	9½	6	2	7	10½	9	3	10	11½
99	1	8¾	3	1½	4	10¼	6	3	7	11¾	9	4½	10	13¼
100	1	9	3	2	4	11	6	4	7	13	9	6	10	15

No. of Persons.	For Beer, Soup, Porridge, Broth, &c., &c. — PINTS EACH. ½	1	1½	2	2½	3
	pts	pts	pts	pts	pts	pts
66	33	66	99	132	165	198
67	33½	67	100½	134	167½	201
68	34	68	102	136	170	204
69	34½	69	103½	138	172½	207
70	35	70	105	140	175	210
71	35½	71	106½	142	177½	213
72	36	72	108	144	180	216
73	36½	73	109½	146	182½	219
74	37	74	111	148	185	222
75	37½	75	112½	150	187½	225
76	38	76	114	152	190	228
77	38½	77	115½	154	192½	231
78	39	78	117	156	195	234
79	39½	79	118½	158	197½	237
80	40	80	120	160	200	240
81	40½	81	121½	162	202½	243
82	41	82	123	164	205	246
83	41½	83	124½	166	207½	249
84	42	84	126	168	210	252
85	42½	85	127½	170	212½	255
86	43	86	129	172	215	258
87	43½	87	130½	174	217½	261
88	44	88	132	176	220	264
89	44½	89	133½	178	222½	267
90	45	90	135	180	225	270
91	45½	91	136½	182	227½	273
92	46	92	138	184	230	276
93	46½	93	139½	186	232½	279
94	47	94	141	188	235	282
95	47½	95	142½	190	237½	285
96	48	96	144	192	240	288
97	48½	97	145½	194	242½	291
98	49	98	147	196	245	294
99	49½	99	148½	198	247½	297
100	50	100	150	200	250	300

Loss in Cooking, Cutting, Weighing, &c. — OUNCES IN THE POUND. ¼		½		¾		1		2		3		4		5		6		No. of lbs.
lbs	ozs	lbs	ozs	lbs	ozs	lbs	ozs	lbs	ozs	lbs	ozs	lbs	ozs	lbs	ozs	lbs	ozs	
1	0½	2	1	3	1½	4	2	8	4	12	6	16	8	20	10	24	12	66
1	0¾	2	1½	3	2¼	4	3	8	6	12	9	16	12	20	15	25	2	67
1	1	2	2	3	3	4	4	8	8	12	12	17	0	21	4	25	8	68
1	1¼	2	2½	3	3¾	4	5	8	10	12	15	17	4	21	9	25	14	69
1	1½	2	3	3	4½	4	6	8	12	13	2	17	8	21	14	26	4	70
1	1¾	2	3½	3	5¼	4	7	8	14	13	5	17	12	22	3	26	10	71
1	2	2	4	3	6	4	8	9	0	13	8	18	0	22	8	27	0	72
1	2¼	2	4½	3	6¾	4	9	9	2	13	11	18	4	22	13	27	6	73
1	2½	2	5	3	7½	4	10	9	4	13	14	18	8	23	2	27	12	74
1	2¾	2	5½	3	8¼	4	11	9	6	14	1	18	12	23	7	28	2	75
1	3	2	6	3	9	4	12	9	8	14	4	19	0	23	12	28	8	76
1	3¼	2	6½	3	9¾	4	13	9	10	14	7	19	4	24	1	28	14	77
1	3½	2	7	3	10½	4	14	9	12	14	10	19	8	24	6	29	4	78
1	3¾	2	7½	3	11¼	4	15	9	14	14	13	19	12	24	11	29	10	79
1	4	2	8	3	12	5	0	10	0	15	0	20	0	25	0	30	0	80
1	4¼	2	8½	3	12¾	5	1	10	2	15	3	20	4	25	5	30	6	81
1	4½	2	9	3	13½	5	2	10	4	15	6	20	8	25	10	30	12	82
1	4¾	2	9½	3	14¼	5	3	10	6	15	9	20	12	25	15	31	2	83
1	5	2	10	3	15	5	4	10	8	15	12	21	0	26	4	31	8	84
1	5¼	2	10½	3	15¾	5	5	10	10	15	15	21	4	26	9	31	14	85
1	5½	2	11	4	0½	5	6	10	12	16	2	21	8	26	14	32	4	86
1	5¾	2	11½	4	1¼	5	7	10	14	16	5	21	12	27	3	32	10	87
1	6	2	12	4	2	5	8	11	0	16	8	22	0	27	8	33	0	88
1	6¼	2	12½	4	2¾	5	9	11	2	16	11	22	4	27	13	33	6	89
1	6½	2	13	4	3½	5	10	11	4	16	14	22	8	28	2	33	12	90
1	6¾	2	13½	4	4¼	5	11	11	6	17	1	22	12	28	7	34	2	91
1	7	2	14	4	5	5	12	11	8	17	4	23	0	28	12	34	8	92
1	7¼	2	14½	4	5¾	5	13	11	10	17	7	23	4	29	1	34	14	93
1	7½	2	15	4	6½	5	14	11	12	17	10	23	8	29	6	35	4	94
1	7¾	2	15½	4	7¼	5	15	11	14	17	13	23	12	29	11	35	10	95
1	8	3	0	4	8	6	0	12	0	18	0	24	0	30	0	36	0	96
1	8¼	3	0½	4	8¾	6	1	12	2	18	3	24	4	30	5	36	6	97
1	8½	3	1	4	9½	6	2	12	4	18	6	24	8	30	10	36	12	98
1	8¾	3	1½	4	10¼	6	3	12	6	18	9	24	12	30	15	37	2	99
1	9	3	2	4	11	6	4	12	8	18	10	25	0	31	4	37	8	100

A TABLE FOR ASCERTAINING THE QUANTITY OF PROVISIONS ANY NUMBER OF PERSONS MAY CONSUME, AT A GIVEN NUMBER OF OUNCES EACH.

No. of Persons.	2		3		4		5		6		7		8		9		10		11		12		13		14		15		No. of Persons.
	lbs	ozs	lbs	ozs	lbs	ozs	lbs	ozs	lbs	ozs	lbs	ozs	lbs	ozs	lbs	ozs	lbs	ozs	lbs	ozs	lbs	ozs	lbs	ozs	lbs	ozs	lbs	ozs	
1		2		3		4		5		6		7		8		9		10		11		12		13		14		15	1
2		4		6		8		10		12		14	1	0	1	2	1	4	1	6	1	8	1	10	1	12	1	14	2
3		6		9		12		15	1	2	1	5	1	8	1	11	1	14	2	1	2	4	2	7	2	10	2	13	3
4		8		12	1	0	1	4	1	8	1	12	2	0	2	4	2	8	2	12	3	0	3	4	3	8	3	12	4
5		10		15	1	4	1	9	1	14	2	3	2	8	2	13	3	2	3	7	3	12	4	1	4	6	4	11	5
6		12	1	2	1	8	1	14	2	4	2	10	3	0	3	6	3	12	4	2	4	8	4	14	5	4	5	10	6
7		14	1	5	1	12	2	3	2	10	3	1	3	8	3	15	4	6	4	13	5	4	5	11	6	2	6	9	7
8	1	0	1	8	2	0	2	8	3	0	3	8	4	0	4	8	5	0	5	8	6	0	6	8	7	0	7	8	8
9	1	2	1	11	2	4	2	13	3	6	3	15	4	8	4	1	5	10	6	3	6	12	7	5	7	14	8	7	9
10	1	4	1	14	2	8	3	2	3	12	4	6	5	0	5	10	6	4	6	14	7	8	8	2	8	12	9	6	10
11	1	6	2	1	2	12	3	7	4	2	4	13	5	8	6	3	6	14	7	9	8	4	8	15	9	10	10	5	11
12	1	8	2	4	3	0	3	12	4	8	5	4	6	0	6	12	7	8	8	4	9	0	9	12	10	8	11	4	12
13	1	10	2	7	3	4	4	1	4	14	5	11	6	8	7	5	8	2	8	15	9	12	10	9	11	6	12	3	13
14	1	12	2	10	3	8	4	6	5	4	6	2	7	0	7	14	8	12	9	10	10	8	11	6	12	4	13	2	14
15	1	14	2	13	3	12	4	11	5	10	6	9	7	8	8	7	9	6	10	5	11	4	12	3	13	2	14	1	15
16	2	0	3	0	4	0	5	0	6	0	7	0	8	0	9	0	10	0	11	0	12	0	13	0	14	0	15	0	16
17	2	2	3	3	4	4	5	5	6	6	7	7	8	8	9	9	10	10	11	11	12	12	13	13	14	14	15	15	17
18	2	4	3	6	4	8	5	10	6	12	7	14	9	0	10	2	11	4	12	6	13	8	14	10	15	12	16	14	18
19	2	6	3	9	4	12	5	15	7	2	8	5	9	8	10	11	11	14	13	1	14	4	15	7	16	10	17	13	19
20	2	8	3	12	5	0	6	4	7	8	8	12	10	0	11	4	12	8	13	12	15	0	16	4	17	8	18	12	20
21	2	10	3	15	5	4	6	9	7	14	9	3	10	8	11	13	13	2	14	7	15	12	17	1	18	6	19	11	21
22	2	12	4	2	5	8	6	14	8	4	9	10	11	0	12	6	13	12	15	2	16	8	17	14	19	4	20	10	22
23	2	14	4	5	5	12	7	3	8	10	10	1	11	8	12	15	14	6	15	13	17	4	18	11	20	2	21	9	23
24	3	0	4	8	6	0	7	8	9	0	10	8	12	0	13	8	15	0	16	8	18	0	19	8	21	0	22	8	24
25	3	2	4	11	6	4	7	13	9	6	10	15	12	8	14	1	15	10	17	3	18	12	20	5	21	14	23	7	25
26	3	4	4	14	6	8	8	2	9	12	11	6	13	0	14	10	16	4	17	14	19	8	21	2	22	12	24	6	26
27	3	6	5	1	6	12	8	7	10	2	11	13	13	8	15	3	16	14	18	9	20	4	21	15	23	10	25	5	27
28	3	8	5	4	7	0	8	12	10	8	12	4	14	0	15	12	17	8	19	4	21	0	22	12	24	8	26	4	28
29	3	10	5	7	7	4	9	1	10	14	12	11	14	8	16	5	18	2	19	15	21	12	23	9	25	4	27	3	29
30	3	12	5	10	7	8	9	6	11	4	13	2	15	0	16	14	18	12	20	10	22	8	24	6	26	6	28	2	30
31	3	14	5	13	7	12	9	11	11	10	13	9	15	8	17	7	19	6	21	5	23	4	25	3	27	2	29	1	31
32	4	0	6	0	8	0	10	0	12	0	14	0	16	8	18	0	20	0	22	0	24	0	26	0	28	0	30	0	32
33	4	2	6	3	8	4	10	5	12	6	14	7	16	8	18	9	20	10	22	11	24	12	26	13	28	14	30	15	33
34	4	4	6	6	8	8	10	10	12	12	14	14	17	0	19	2	21	4	23	6	25	8	27	10	29	12	31	14	34
35	4	6	6	9	8	12	10	15	13	2	15	5	17	8	19	11	21	14	24	1	26	4	28	7	30	10	32	13	35
36	4	8	6	12	9	0	11	4	13	8	15	12	18	0	20	4	22	8	24	12	27	0	29	4	31	8	33	12	36
37	4	10	6	15	9	4	11	9	13	14	16	3	18	8	20	13	23	8	25	7	27	12	30	1	32	6	34	11	37
38	4	12	7	2	9	8	11	14	14	4	16	10	19	0	21	6	23	12	26	2	28	8	30	14	33	4	35	10	38
39	4	14	7	5	9	12	12	3	14	10	17	1	19	8	21	15	24	6	26	13	29	4	31	11	34	2	36	9	39
40	5	0	7	8	10	0	12	8	15	0	17	8	20	0	22	8	25	0	27	8	30	0	32	8	35	0	37	3	40
41	5	2	7	11	10	4	12	13	15	6	17	15	20	8	23	1	25	10	28	3	30	12	33	5	35	14	38	7	41
42	5	4	7	14	10	8	13	2	15	12	18	6	21	0	23	10	26	4	28	14	31	8	34	2	36	12	39	6	42
43	5	6	8	1	10	12	13	7	16	2	18	13	21	8	24	3	26	14	29	9	32	4	34	15	37	10	40	5	43
44	5	8	8	4	11	0	13	12	16	8	19	4	22	0	24	12	27	8	30	4	33	0	35	12	38	8	41	4	44
45	5	10	8	7	11	4	14	1	16	14	19	11	22	8	25	5	28	2	30	15	33	12	36	9	39	6	42	3	45
46	5	12	8	10	11	8	14	6	17	4	20	2	23	0	25	14	28	12	31	10	34	8	37	6	40	4	43	2	46
47	5	14	8	13	11	12	14	11	17	10	20	9	23	8	26	7	29	6	32	5	35	4	38	3	41	2	44	1	47
48	6	0	9	0	12	0	15	0	18	0	21	0	24	0	27	0	30	0	33	0	36	0	39	0	42	0	45	0	48
49	6	2	9	3	12	4	15	5	18	6	21	7	24	8	27	9	30	10	33	11	36	12	39	13	42	14	45	15	49
50	6	4	9	6	12	8	15	10	18	12	21	14	25	0	28	2	31	4	34	6	37	8	40	10	43	12	46	14	50
51	6	6	9	9	12	12	15	15	19	2	22	5	25	8	28	11	31	14	35	1	38	4	41	7	44	10	47	13	51
52	6	8	9	12	13	0	16	4	19	8	22	12	26	0	29	4	32	8	35	12	39	0	42	4	45	8	48	12	52

OUNCES EACH.

No. of Persons.	2		3		4		5		6		7		8		9		10		11		12		13		14		15		No. of Persons.
	lbs	ozs	lbs	ozs	lbs	ozs	lbs	ozs	lbs	ozs	lbs	ozs	lbs	ozs	lbs	ozs	lbs	ozs	lbs	ozs	lbs	ozs	lbs	ozs	lbs	ozs	lbs	ozs	
53	6	10	9	15	13	4	16	9	19	14	23	2	26	8	29	13	33	2	36	7	39	12	43	1	46	6	49	11	53
54	6	12	10	2	13	8	16	14	20	4	23	10	27	0	30	6	33	12	37	2	40	8	43	14	47	4	50	10	54
55	6	14	10	5	13	12	17	3	20	10	24	1	27	8	30	15	34	6	37	13	41	4	44	11	48	2	51	9	55
56	7	0	10	8	14	0	17	8	21	0	24	8	28	0	31	8	35	0	38	8	42	0	45	8	49	0	52	8	56
57	7	2	10	11	14	4	17	13	21	6	24	15	28	8	32	1	35	10	39	3	42	12	46	5	49	14	53	7	57
58	7	4	10	14	14	8	18	2	21	12	25	6	29	0	32	10	36	4	39	14	43	8	47	2	50	12	54	6	58
59	7	6	11	1	14	12	18	7	22	2	25	13	29	8	33	3	36	14	40	9	44	4	47	15	51	10	55	5	59
60	7	8	11	4	15	0	18	12	22	8	26	4	30	0	33	12	37	8	41	4	45	0	48	12	52	8	56	4	60
61	7	10	11	7	15	4	19	1	22	14	26	11	30	8	34	5	38	2	41	15	45	12	49	9	53	6	57	3	61
62	7	12	11	10	15	8	19	6	23	4	27	2	31	0	34	14	38	12	42	10	46	8	50	6	54	4	58	2	62
63	7	14	11	13	15	12	19	11	23	10	27	9	31	8	35	7	39	6	43	5	47	4	51	3	55	2	59	1	63
64	8	0	12	0	16	0	20	0	24	0	28	0	32	0	36	0	40	0	44	0	48	0	52	0	56	0	60	0	64
65	8	2	12	3	16	4	20	5	24	6	28	7	32	8	36	9	40	10	44	11	48	12	52	13	56	14	60	15	65
66	8	4	12	6	16	8	20	10	24	12	28	14	33	0	37	2	41	4	45	6	49	8	53	10	57	12	61	14	66
67	8	6	12	9	16	12	20	15	25	2	29	5	33	8	37	11	41	14	46	1	50	4	54	7	58	10	62	13	67
68	8	8	12	12	17	0	21	4	25	8	29	12	34	0	38	4	42	8	46	12	51	0	55	4	59	8	63	12	69
69	8	10	12	15	17	4	21	9	25	14	30	3	34	8	38	13	43	2	47	7	51	12	56	1	60	6	64	11	69
70	8	12	13	2	17	8	21	14	26	4	30	10	35	0	39	6	43	12	48	2	52	8	56	14	61	4	65	10	70
71	8	14	13	5	17	12	22	3	26	10	31	1	35	8	39	15	44	6	48	13	53	4	57	11	62	2	66	9	71
72	9	0	13	8	18	0	22	8	27	0	31	8	36	0	40	8	45	0	49	8	54	0	58	8	63	0	67	8	72
73	9	2	13	11	18	4	22	15	27	6	31	15	36	8	41	1	45	10	50	3	54	12	59	5	63	14	58	7	73
74	9	4	13	14	18	8	23	2	27	12	32	6	37	0	41	10	46	4	50	14	55	8	60	2	64	12	69	6	74
75	9	6	14	1	18	12	23	7	28	2	32	13	37	8	42	3	46	14	51	9	56	4	60	15	65	10	70	5	75
76	9	8	14	4	19	0	23	12	28	8	33	4	38	0	42	12	47	8	52	4	57	0	61	12	66	8	71	4	76
77	9	10	14	7	19	4	24	1	28	14	33	11	38	8	43	5	48	2	52	15	57	12	62	9	67	6	72	3	77
78	9	12	14	10	19	8	24	6	29	4	34	2	39	0	43	14	48	12	53	10	58	8	63	6	68	4	73	2	78
79	9	14	14	13	19	12	24	11	29	10	34	9	39	8	44	7	49	6	54	5	59	4	64	3	69	2	74	1	79
80	10	0	15	0	20	0	25	0	30	0	35	0	40	0	45	0	50	0	55	0	60	0	65	0	70	0	75	0	80
81	10	2	15	3	20	4	25	5	30	6	35	7	40	8	45	9	50	10	55	11	60	12	65	13	70	14	75	15	81
82	10	4	15	6	20	8	25	10	30	12	35	14	41	0	46	2	51	4	56	6	61	8	66	10	71	12	76	14	82
83	10	6	15	9	20	12	25	15	31	2	36	5	41	8	46	11	51	14	57	1	62	4	67	7	72	10	77	13	83
84	10	8	15	12	21	0	26	4	31	8	36	12	42	0	47	4	52	8	57	12	63	0	68	4	73	8	78	12	84
85	10	10	15	15	21	4	26	9	31	14	37	3	42	8	47	13	53	2	58	7	63	12	69	1	74	6	79	11	85
86	10	12	16	2	21	8	26	14	32	4	37	10	43	0	48	6	53	12	59	2	64	8	69	14	75	4	80	10	86
87	10	14	16	5	21	12	27	3	32	10	38	1	43	8	48	15	54	6	59	13	65	4	70	11	76	2	81	9	87
88	11	0	16	8	22	0	27	8	33	0	38	8	44	0	49	8	55	0	60	8	66	0	71	8	77	0	82	8	88
89	11	2	16	11	22	4	27	13	33	6	38	15	44	8	50	1	55	10	61	3	66	12	72	5	77	14	83	7	89
90	11	4	16	14	22	8	28	2	33	12	39	6	45	0	50	10	56	4	61	14	67	8	73	2	78	12	84	6	90
91	11	6	17	1	22	12	28	7	34	2	39	13	45	8	51	3	56	14	62	9	68	4	73	15	79	10	85	5	91
92	11	8	17	4	23	0	28	12	34	8	40	4	46	0	51	12	57	8	63	4	69	0	74	12	80	8	86	4	92
93	11	10	17	7	23	4	29	1	34	14	40	11	46	8	52	5	58	2	63	15	69	12	75	9	81	6	87	3	93
94	11	12	17	10	23	8	29	6	35	4	41	2	47	0	52	14	58	12	64	10	70	8	76	6	82	4	88	2	94
95	11	14	17	13	23	12	29	11	35	10	41	9	47	8	53	7	59	6	65	5	71	4	77	3	83	2	89	1	95
96	12	0	18	0	24	0	30	0	36	0	42	0	48	0	54	0	60	0	66	0	72	0	78	0	84	0	90	0	96
97	12	2	18	3	24	4	30	5	36	6	42	7	48	8	54	9	60	10	66	11	72	12	78	13	84	14	90	15	97
98	12	4	18	6	24	8	30	10	36	12	42	14	49	0	55	2	61	4	67	6	73	8	79	10	85	12	91	14	98
99	12	6	18	9	24	12	30	15	37	2	43	5	49	8	55	11	61	14	68	1	74	4	80	7	86	10	92	13	99
100	12	8	18	12	25	0	31	4	37	8	43	12	50	0	56	4	62	8	68	12	75	0	81	4	87	8	93	12	100
150	18	12	28	2	37	8	46	14	56	4	65	10	75	0	84	6	93	12	103	2	112	8	121	14	131	4	140	10	150
200	25	0	37	8	50	0	62	8	75	0	87	8	100	0	112	8	125	0	137	8	150	0	162	8	175	0	187	8	200
250	31	4	46	14	62	8	78	2	93	12	109	6	125	0	140	10	156	4	171	14	187	8	203	2	218	12	234	6	250
300	37	8	56	4	75	0	93	12	112	8	131	4	150	0	168	12	187	8	206	4	225	0	243	12	262	8	281	4	300
350	43	12	65	10	87	8	109	6	131	4	153	2	175	0	196	14	218	12	240	10	262	8	284	6	306	4	328	2	350
400	50	0	75	0	100	0	125	0	150	0	175	0	200	0	225	0	250	0	275	0	300	0	325	0	350	0	375	0	400

AN

OFFICIAL CIRCULAR

OF PUBLIC DOCUMENTS AND INFORMATION

DIRECTED BY THE POOR LAW BOARD TO BE PRINTED, CHIEFLY FOR THE USE OF THE BOARDS OF GUARDIANS AND THEIR OFFICERS.

No. 13.] MARCH, 1848. [N.S.

CONTENTS.

I.—ACCOUNTS.

1. CIRCULAR RESPECTING THE GENERAL ACCOUNTS ORDER.

Poor Law Board,
Somerset House, March 6th, 1848.

SIR,

I am directed by the Poor Law Board to direct the attention of the guardians to the provisions of the General Order issued by the Poor Law Commissioners on the 17th March, 1847, for regulating the keeping accounts in unions.

Although the guardians, for a time, had a discretion as to the adoption of the books of account and forms prescribed by this Order, that discretion will cease on the 25th instant, and it will be thenceforth obligatory upon them and their officers to conform strictly to such books and forms.

The Board think it right to refer to the Letter of the Commissioners which accompanied the Order, but do not feel it necessary, on the present occasion, to enter on a discussion of its provisions. They will, however, observe, that in the case of any particular union where it shall be deemed expedient, the Board have a power to authorize a departure from the forms prescribed by the Order. But no such departure will be lawful except with the express sanction of the Board; and this restriction applies to additions to the forms and books of account as well as to omissions.

The Board attach so much importance to general uniformity in the mode of keeping the accounts, which apply to officers acting under the same rules and regulations, and bound to account to auditors of extensive districts, whose examination of the accounts may be much embarrassed by even minute variations, that the Board will not readily sanction any departure from the prescribed forms where no necessary or substantial demand for such departure can be established.

In certain unions, however, some of the books of account may not be at present requisite, but as the arrangements in those unions change, the different provisions of the Order will become applicable.

The Annual Poor Rate Return will in future be prepared in this office from the Half-yearly Financial Statement, (Form 17 of the Order,) and the Yearly Abstract, (Form 18;) and the Board wish that the clerk, in making out those documents, will, where the union extends into more than one county, arrange the several parishes in the union in their respective counties, according to alphabetical order, so as to enable a total to be readily made for the parishes in each such county, as well as a total for the whole union. Such an arrangement will much facilitate the calculation of the expenditure for the several counties throughout England and Wales.

It will be observed that the clerk, by Article 27 of the Order, is required, within fourteen days after the 25th of March and the 29th of September in every year, to transmit to the Board a statement of the amount expended under the several heads therein specified, in addition to, and without waiting for, the half-yearly statements, (Forms 16 and 17.) The Board are very desirous that there may be no failure on the part of the clerk in this respect, or in the transmission of the statements last mentioned, immediately after the audit of the accounts shall have been completed.

The attention of the relieving officers should be called to Articles 21 and 22, whereby they are required within fourteen days after the end of the half-year to affix a mark against the name of every pauper entered in the *In-door Relief List*, who shall have been entered in the *Out-door Relief List* in the course of the half-year; and also in the District Medical Relief Books against the name of every pauper who shall not have received any other relief during the half-year than medical relief. The relieving officers will be careful that no pauper appear in the relief list more than once in the half-year. Strict attention to the provisions of the Order in this respect is essential to insuring an accurate return of the number of in-door and out-door paupers relieved during the half-year.

I am, Sir, &c.,

EBRINGTON, *Secretary*.

To the Clerk to the Guardians.

II. AUDITOR — DUTIES OF, IN REGARD TO BALANCES IN THE HANDS OF RELIEVING OFFICERS AT THE AUDIT.

———, 1848.

Chairman of ——— *Union*—Objected to the proceedings of the auditor in certifying as due from the relieving officers of the union, the balances stated by the officers themselves as well the sums disallowed by the auditor in their respective accounts.

Ans.—Whatever sum the district auditor certifies as due from any person accounting, must be paid over by such person under the provisions of the 32nd sec. of the 7 & 8 Vic. c. 101, within seven days, to the treasurer of the union. The question arises, however, as to what the district auditor is authorized to certify as being "due," with reference to the balances in the hands of the officers accounting at the audit. Where the officer continues in office after the accounts are finally made up, the Board are disposed to consider that the amount which may happen, at the time to which the balance relates, to be in his hands, and which has been paid to him for current expenses, or can be reasonably deemed applicable thereto, may properly be regarded as not being "due" from him at that time, and, consequently, may be excluded by the auditor in certifying the amount to be paid over to the union treasurer. Undoubtedly, under ordinary circumstances, the sum thus remaining in his hands applicable for current expenses will be the entire amount of the balance shown by his accounts, exclusive of any surcharges or disallowances. There may, however, be cases in which the auditor may find it right to include in the sum which he certifies as "due," more than the mere amount of the items surcharged or disallowed, (items which must, of course, in all cases, be paid over to the treasurer,) as he may find that the officer has in his hands, out of the money advanced to him on account, during the preceding half-year, a larger sum than can reasonably be deemed necessary for the current expenses incident to his office. The Board think that the auditor should require such surplus, together with the items surcharged or disallowed. (if any,) to be paid over to the treasurer.

III. — BASTARDY—ENFORCEMENT OF ORDER ON PUTATIVE FATHER OF A BASTARD CHILD, THE MOTHER BEING DEAD.

29*th April*, 1847.

Clerk to Richmond (Yorkshire) Union—About two years ago, A. B. (who was an orphan) became the mother of an illegitimate child. The mother went to service soon after her confinement, and the child was put out to nurse; the father, by an order of sessions, paying 1*s.* 9*d.* per week, and the mother, out of her wages, contributing 1*s.* 3*d.* per week towards the maintenance of the child. About two months ago, the mother of the child died, and the child has since been removed to the workhouse. Inquired whether the guardians have power to compel the father to continue to pay the 1*s.* 9*d.* per week towards the maintenance of the child. The 7th clause of the 7 & 8 Vic. c. 101, enables the guardians to enforce an order on the death of the mother, provided the child ceases to be chargeable to the parish; but does not seem to give the power to receive a less sum than will maintain the child. If this be the case, the father, in this instance, would escape payment altogether.

Ans.—The enforcement of the order by the guardians can only be made upon the condition that the illegitimate child cease to be chargeable to the parish or union. (See concluding part of sec. 7 of 7 and 8 Vic. c. 101.) So, likewise, such enforcement cannot take place until some person has been appointed by the justices to have the custody of the child under sec. 5; because the payments for the maintenance of the child, in pursuance of the application of the guardians, are to be made to the person to be appointed from time to time by the justices, to have the custody of the child. To enable the enforcement of the order, it does not appear that the amount of the payment fixed by the order need be sufficient for the actual maintenance of the child, if, in fact, it be sufficient to induce a person to take upon himself the charge or custody of the child. Undoubtedly, if the smallness of the weekly payment or other considerations operate to prevent any person taking the custody of the child, the liability of the putative father cannot (the mother being dead) be enforced, either on the application of the guardians or otherwise.

IV.—CONTRIBUTION ORDERS—COUNTY-RATE.

March 6*th*, 1848.

Clerk of Droitwich Union—The form of contribution order, prescribed by the General Consolidated Order, does not appear to contemplate that any explanation is to be given to the overseers, as to how much of the sum thereby called for is required for county, police, or other rates, although such rates are included by estimation in it. Inquired whether any, and what steps, should be taken to enable the overseers to fill up, in their balance sheets, (Form 3 of the General Accounts Order,) the sums paid for county-rates. The yearly Abstract of the Parochial Accounts (Form 18 of the last-mentioned Order) contains a column headed "county, borough, hundred, or police rates, paid by overseers," which, it is presumed, should be filled up from the balance-sheets, (Form 8;) but which cannot, of course, be done, if such rates are not distinguished in the balance-sheets.

Ans.—Where these payments are not made directly by the overseers to the county treasurer, but by the guardians out of the contributions furnished by the parishes to the union, the overseers will not be required to make any entry in their accounts of the payment. On the other hand, if the guardians do not pay the county-rate, but it is paid by the overseers, then the latter will enter the payment so made in their own accounts; but no entry in this case will appear in the accounts of the guardians. Form 18, to which you refer, will, with regard to the entries to be made in it, correspond with the account, or balance-sheet of the overseers, Form 3. If no payments appear in Form 3, as made in respect of the county-rate, none will be entered in Form 18.

V.—MEDICAL OFFICER—MEDICAL RELIEF BY WAY OF LOAN.

Dec. 13*th*, 1847.

Medical Officer of ——— *Union*—He had sent to the guardians accounts amounting to £30 for attending upon persons to whom they had given orders for relief by way of loan. The guardians refused to lay the claim on the ground that he was required to attend upon all poor persons requiring medical relief, or assistance, without regard to the terms on which such relief might be given by the guardians. No written contract had been entered into between himself and the guardians; but the following minute was made by them of his appointment, viz., "resolved, that Mr. M. be appointed as medical officer for the third medical officer's district of this union, at a salary of £35 per annum, exclusive of charges for fractures, &c. under the order of the Poor Law Commissioners, and 10*s.* 6*d.* for every case of midwifery attended by him, the same to be attended under an order of the board of guardians, or the relieving officer of the union." He submits that parties to whom relief is given by way of loan are not paupers, as the granting of relief in that form implies a decision on the part of the guardians, that such parties are capable of repaying the relief, and that they are, therefore, not within his contract. Requested the opinion of the Commissioners on the subject.

Ans.—The Commissioners do not see upon what grounds you can claim to be specially remunerated for the class of cases referred to in your letter. The Commissioners find that you were appointed by the guardians as medical officer of the third district of the union, at a salary of £35 a year, exclusive of the surgical and midwifery fees. It is undoubtedly most desirable that specific contracts should be entered into by the guardians of unions with their medical officers: but, although no such contract has been entered into in your own case, your salary, according to the terms of your appointment, appears to cover all the pauper cases you may be lawfully required to attend, with the exception of the surgical and midwifery cases, for which special fees are provided. It rests with the guardians to determine what persons are destitute and in need of relief, and to decide whether they will grant relief, either medical or general. When they have resolved to grant relief in any instance, they may determine to grant it upon loan: but the condition thus annexed to the grant is not intended for the benefit of the party who may actually supply the relief, except in so far as it may operate as a test to prevent undue applications. If the medical officer were to receive the benefit of the loan in cases of medical relief, the same right might equally be claimed by the contractors for bread and other articles supplied to those paupers to whom ordinary relief may be afforded on loan. The Commissioners cannot assume that the guardians have, in any case, given orders for medical relief improperly.

The Commissioners addressed a letter also to the guardians, advising them to enter into specific contracts with their medical officers, so that all misunderstanding between both parties as to their respective rights and obligations might be as far as possible avoided.

VI.—MEDICAL RELIEF—TO A NON-SETTLED PAUPER.

September 1st, 1846.

Clerk of Bourn Union—A pauper, named W. J., belonging to the Stamford Union, resides in the Bourn Union, by the guardians of which he has been relieved, and his relief repaid by the Stamford guardians, who refuse, however, to repay the fee of £1, allowed by the General Medical Order, for the medical officer's attendance on a fractured collar bone, until the Commissioners' opinion is taken as to their liability to do so.

Clerk of Stamford Union—By the contracts entered into by the Stamford Union, and also, it is believed, by the Bourn Union, the medical officers are "duly to attend to and take care of all poor persons requiring medicine, or surgical relief, whether permanently or casually resident within the district." There does not appear to be anything in the Medical Order, or in the Non-resident and Non-settled Relief Order, to vary the form in which relief is given in each union; and the guardians, although they repaid the relief given to the pauper, requested that the Commissioners' opinion might be taken as to the repayment of the surgical fee.

Ans.—The main point on which, as it appears to the Commissioners, depends the liability of the Stamford guardians to repay, and the right of the Bourn guardians to recover, the cost of the medical relief afforded to W. J., does not seem to have been adverted to by either board. That point really is, whether the Stamford guardians originally authorised the guardians of the Bourn Union to charge the medical relief to them. As this was the case of an accident, it is manifest that no such previous authority could be given, and therefore it is difficult to bring the case, so far as relates to this item, within the application of the order regulating non-resident relief, or to show any obligation on the guardians of the Stamford Union to pay the fee.

VII.—POOR-RATE—EXCUSAL FROM PAYMENT OF: POWER OF JUSTICES.

Dec. 2nd, 1847.

King's Lynn Union—The court of guardians of the parish of ——— is constituted under a local act, and the collectors of poor-rates of the different wards in that parish render an account to the court of all persons who have refused, or neglected, to pay the amount of their rates, after having been repeatedly called upon to do so. Each case is then inquired into, and those persons whom the court deem unable to pay are excused from payment, and those who are considered able to pay are summoned before the justices. Inquired, whether the justices have the power to excuse any of the persons, so summoned, from payment of their rates.

Ans.—The Commissioners do not find, on reference to the local act, that it contains any provision as to the excusal of poor persons from payment of poor-rates. The Commissioners, therefore, apprehend that the general statute, 54 Geo. 3, c. 170, sec. 11, applies. That statute gives power to the justices to excuse poor persons from payment of the rate, but requires the consent of the churchwardens and overseers, or other persons having the ordinary management, control, or direction of the poor of the parish, to such excusal. It is clear, therefore, that, unless this consent be given, the justices, upon proceedings taken by the proper authorities, with a view to enforce payment of the rate, have no power to withhold their warrant simply on the ground of the alleged poverty of the parties.

VIII.—RATING—OF SCHOOL-HOUSE.

March 3rd, 1848.

The Rev. ————. He is master of the free-school in the town of ———, of which the mayor and corporation are trustees, and which is endowed with the sum of £21 10*s.* 6*d.* per annum, for the purpose of educating, free of expense, six poor boys, who are nominated by the trustees. In addition to these boys, he is allowed to take private pupils into the school on his own terms, the endowment being so small, the school could not otherwise be carried on. The school is kept in a detached building provided for it, rent free. There is no residence connected with the building, which is used for no other purpose than as a school-house. The building has never until lately been assessed to the poor-rate. Inquired whether it was liable to be so assessed.

Ans.—The circumstance of property being devised and occupied for a charitable purpose does not exempt it from liability to the poor-rate, if any emolument be derived from the occupation in any personal or private respect. The Board, indeed, find this difference between the circumstances of the present case, and those which existed in Rex *v.* Catt, 6 T. R. 332—there the master of the endowed school had a residence and a garden for his occupation, and was held rateable for the same, though the school appears to have been simply a free school. There is, on the other hand, other circumstances in the present case, that you are at liberty to take private pupils in the school upon your own terms; and the Board collect from your statement, that this privilege is exercised; the occupation must, in consequence, be considered as beneficial to you, and if so, rateability attaches to it, though the question of amount is still open. Indeed, the case of Q. *v.* Sterry, 12 Adol. & Ellis, 24, appears to be a strong recent authority in support of the rate.

IX.—RELIEF.

1. PROCEEDINGS FOR THE RECOVERY OF RELIEF BY WAY OF LOAN.

October 19th, 1846.

Clerk of Buntingford Union—Inquired, how the guardians are to act in the recovery of loans granted to paupers, inasmuch as the Poor Law Amendment Act seems to throw on an individual guardian the duty of taking the money and giving a receipt for it, and which duty no guardian could be compelled to perform.

Ans.—The proceedings indicated in the 59th section of the 4 & 5 Wm. c. 76, are to be taken "upon the application of the overseers, or *guardians*, of the parish, or union, providing the relief." The Commissioners think, therefore, that where the relief has been advanced on loan by the guardians, the application should be made under the direction of the guardians; *i.e.*, of the guardians as a board, as to which, see the 5 & 6 Vic. c. 57, section 17. The amount ordered by the justices to be repaid out of the party's wages, is to be paid "to such overseers, or *guardians*." It appears to the Commissioners, that, under this provision, it may be paid to any person authorised by the board of guardians to receive it on their behalf. But the enactment proceeds to declare, that "the payment to and receipt of any such overseer, or *guardian*, shall be a good discharge," &c. Having regard to these expressions, which refer to a single guardian, the Commissioners apprehend that the board of guardians might authorise some one of their own body to receive the amount; and if, on his producing the justices' order to the master, or employer, he fails to obtain payment, the further proceedings pointed out in the section may be resorted to. But if payment were made to the relieving officer, or the treasurer, or other person authorised as above, the Commissioners presume that the guardians would be satisfied.

2. RELIEF TO FAMILY OF SEAMAN—RECOVERY OF.

Dec. 13*th*, 1847.

Clerk of Rye Union—The wife and children of a seaman, who is now on board a vessel, which has gone to a port in the Mediterranean, have recently become chargeable to the parish of Rye, in consequence of the owners of the vessel having discontinued the payment to them of a portion of his wages, and the guardians have passed a resolution, declaring the relief to be given on loan; but they entertain some doubt as to their power to carry out the resolution, as they fear that not only the 32nd section of the 59 Geo. 3, c. 12, is repealed by the 12th section of the 7 & 8 Vic. c. 112, but that the latter Act prevents justices attaching the wages of seamen, under the 59th section of the 4 & 5 Wm. 4, c. 76. Requested the Commissioners' opinion, as to whether the relief is recoverable under the last-mentioned Act; and, if not, whether the guardians can take proceedings for its recovery under the County Courts Act.

Ans.—As at present advised, the Commissioners are disposed to think that the 12th section of 7 & 8 Vic. c. 112, (the terms of which are very comprehensive,) would prevent the recovery of relief granted to the family of a seaman in his absence, either by the proceeding contemplated by sec. 32 of 59 Geo. 3, c. 12, which applies to the recovery of relief not given on loan, or by the proceeding under 59th sec. 4 & 5 Wm. 4, c. 76, which is applicable to the recovery of relief given on loan by the guardians. The 12th sec. of 7 & 8 Vic. c. 112, provides, that no assignment which may have been made of wages, nor any attachment or incumbrance thereon, nor any attachment to be issued from any court whatever, shall prevent the payment of wages to any seaman by the master or owner. The order of the justices, made under sec. 32 of 59 Geo. 3, c. 12, and that made under 59th section of 4 & 5 Wm. 4, c. 76, is certainly an attachment, or incumbrance, on the wages of the person to whom, or on whose account, or to whose family, the relief was given. The Commissioners entertain great doubt whether any remedy for the recovery of relief given on loan, in cases such as you describe, exists in the County Court. But the guardians may, if an opportunity occur, obtain the judgment of the judge of that court without much risk or cost.

3. RELIEF TO A PERSON AGED TWENTY-TWO, LIVING WITH HER FATHER.

Feb. 18*th*, 1848.

Clerk of Malling Union—A. S., a pregnant single woman, aged twenty-two years, lately working at a mill in an adjoining parish, where she also resided, is now, in consequence of the stoppage of the mill, residing with her father, an able-bodied labourer, with a wife and two other children, and has applied to the guardians for admission into the workhouse, her father being unable to support her. The father himself does not apply for any relief. The guardians have refused to grant her an order for the workhouse, on the ground that she is a part of her father's family, who is liable to maintain her; and that if unable to do so, he is the proper party to apply for relief, which he refuses to do. There is, however, a difference of opinion among the guardians, some of them thinking that, under the 56th section of the 4 & 5 Wm. 4, cap. 76, A. S. being above the age of sixteen, is entitled to make an application for relief on her own account, leaving the parish to their remedy (if there be any) under the 59th Geo. 3, cap. 12. Requested the Poor Law Board's opinion on the case.

Ans.—As the pauper is above the age of sixteen, she is to be regarded for the purposes of relief as not forming part of her father's family; and her application should, therefore, be dealt with as an independent application, and as made on her own account, (sec. 56, 4 & 5 Wm. 4, cap. 76.) The Board do not, however, see any sufficient reason to regard the provision above-cited as interfering with the liability created by 43 Eliz. cap. 2, sec. 7, and 59 Geo. 3, cap. 12, sec. 26, upon parents to maintain their children, or as in any way altering the conditions or circumstances under which the liability could be enforced. On the contrary, it will be seen that the concluding proviso to the 56th sec. expressly preserves the statutory liabilities of parents in respect of the support of their children. There is nothing in the language of 43 Eliz. cap. 2, sec. 7, and 59 Geo. 3, cap. 12, sec. 26, to limit the liability of the parent to the case where the child is actually resident with the parent. However, the question will arise in each case, whether the parent has the requisite ability to maintain, for the statutes make that a necessary condition to the making of the order by the justices. If, therefore, in such a case as you have put, the father is practicably unable to support his child of the age of sixteen years, the Board do not see what remedy the parish could have against him; for the same question would arise in a proceeding against the father under the Vagrant Act, 5 Geo. 4, cap. 83, sec. 3; the ability to maintain on the part of the head of the family being in like nanner necessary to be shown in order to constitute the omission to maintain an offence.

---

4. RELIEF TO AN ABLE-BODIED MAN FROM THE WANT OF A DWELLING.

Feb. 22nd, 1848.

Clerk of Wells Union—A few weeks ago a strong able-bodied man, having a settlement in a parish in the union, with his wife and three children, made application to the guardians for relief. He had been for some years working in the iron-works, which are now stopped. His own parish was prepared to give him employment, but no suitable dwelling could be found for him; and he was also without any article of furniture or tools. He was, therefore, received into the workhouse, which he is willing to leave, if means can be granted him to go in search of work.

Ans.—The Board feel some difficulty in advising the guardians how to act in this case. Undoubtedly, the guardians can, in the exercise of their discretion, order the discharge from the workhouse of any poor person whom they may think able to maintain himself; but, beyond the offer of shelter in the workhouse, it does not seem to fall within the scope of either the guardians' powers or duties to provide residences for the poor, or to supply them with the means of purchasing furniture or work-tools; these not being articles required for the relief of actual destitution. When work, which a pauper can readily accept, is offered at adequate wages, the Board think that it would be proper, in most cases, for the guardians to direct the discharge of the pauper to whom the employment is offered, after due notice of their intention to do so. But if, as in the present case, it is admitted that the man cannot procure a house, either in his own parish or elsewhere, the Board would not advise that he be ejected from the workhouse against his will, so long as such inability to procure shelter for himself and family exists.

---

5. RELIEF TO CHILDREN DESERTED BY THEIR FATHERS.

Feb. 24th, 1848.

Clerk of Droitwich Union—Inquired whether, in cases where children between seven and sixteen years of age, who have been deserted by their parents, apply for relief, out-door relief can legally be granted without subsequently obtaining the sanction of the Poor Law Board, in the manner prescribed by Art. 6 of the Prohibitory Order.

Ans.—The Board see nothing to prevent the guardians giving out-door relief in cases such as those described by you; and consider that it is not necessary that the Board's sanction, under Article 6 of the Prohibitory Order, should be applied for. It is true that relief to children under the age of sixteen is, constructively, relief to the father; but, in the cases put, the children, being deserted by their father, apply for relief on their own account, and, not being able-bodied persons, do not come within Article 1 of the Order, and the cases can, therefore, be dealt with irrespective of that article. It is a different question how far it may be desirable that the guardians should afford out-door relief in cases of this description.

---

6. REPAYMENT OF COST OF RELIEF.

May 14th, 1846.

Clerk of Walsall Union—A few weeks ago T. T. and family were removed, by order of justices, from Bagworth to Wednesbury, and, on appeal at the last sessions, the order was confirmed, subject to a case, which has not, however, been yet submitted to the Court of Queen's Bench. Since the hearing of the case at the sessions, the pauper has left the appellant parish, which is in the West Bromwich Union, and has come to reside in the Walsall Union, where he has become chargeable in consequence of illness. The overseers of Wednesbury are advised not to receive the pauper again unless he is removed there under an order of justices, which cannot be done without bringing the clerk of the peace for Leicester, and the person who executed the order for his removal from Bagworth, before the justices as witnesses, at a cost of several pounds. The overseers of Wednesbury are willing to repay to Walsall the cost of the pauper's relief up to the time of the decision on the case by the Court of Queen's Bench, if they can legally do so; and, if that court should confirm the order of sessions, the overseers of Walsall would readily accede to this proposal. Inquired, whether the overseers of Wednesbury can legally repay the relief as above proposed, and the officers of Walsall accept it.

Ans.—In the absence of an order of removal, the relief given to the pauper, at the charge of Walsall, could only be repaid by Wednesbury as being non-resident relief. In the present state of the law, overseers have no authority to grant non-resident relief in any case; and, consequently, the overseers of Wednesbury could not lawfully make such repayment as that adverted to in your letter. Whether the repayment could be made by the guardians of the West Bromwich Union, is a different question, and depends upon the further question, whether the pauper is, or is not, settled in the parish of Wednesbury. If he is not settled in that parish, the guardians cannot grant him non-resident relief at its expense; if he is so settled, they can, if not prevented by the Commissioners' regulations. The Commissioners understand from your letter that the question of his settlement is yet pending; and, while it remains undecided, the Commissioners do not think that the guardians of the West Bromwich Union could properly repay the relief adverted to, although, perhaps, they might enter into some conditional arrangements on the subject with the guardians of the Walsall Union.

X.—REMOVAL.

1. REFUSAL OF PAUPER TO BE SWORN FOR THE PURPOSES OF AN ORDER FOR HIS REMOVAL TO IRELAND.

March 6th, 1848.

Clerk of Ashton-under-Lyne—An Irishman, who was taken before the magistrates, for the purpose of obtaining the necessary order to remove him to Ireland, obstinately refused to be sworn, and was in consequence ordered into custody. The magistrates doubted, however, whether they had the power to commit the man, and wished that the opinion of the Poor Law Board might be obtained on this point.

Ans.—The only course which can be pursued under the circumstances appears, to the Poor Law Board, to be that authorised by sec. 70 of the 7 & 8 Vic. cap. 101; under which, in connexion with the provisions of the 8 & 9 Vic. cap. 117, the party may be summoned before the magistrates as a witness in the case.

2. REMOVAL OF AN IRISHWOMAN AND HER CHILDREN, THE HUSBAND BEING IN PRISON.

27th January, 1848.

Clerk of Cheadle Union—An Irishwoman and her two children were recently received into the union workhouse, in consequence of her husband having been committed to prison on a charge of felony. The guardians directed that orders for the removal of the family to Ireland should be applied for. Upon the application being made, one of the magistrates objected to signing the order, contending that, as the husband is not in the parish in which his wife resides, the family is, by the operation of the 3rd proviso to sec. 1 of the 9 & 10 Vic. cap. 66, rendered irremoveable. Inquired, 1. Whether the proviso in question applies at all to the case of an Irish family not having a residence in any parish in England. 2. Whether the proviso is to be construed to refer to those cases where the husband is rendered irremovable by a five years' residence, or from sickness; and not to cases where he is irremovable by being in prison or from having deserted his family.

Ans.—The Poor Law Commissioners were advised by the Attorney-General and the Solicitor-General, that the Statute 9 & 10 Vic. cap. 66, applies equally to the removal of persons born in Scotland, Ireland, or the Channel Islands, as to persons having settlements in England; and, consequently, operates to prevent the removal of the former in those cases in which the latter, by reason of the statute, would be irremovable. The Board apprehend that, as regards the case submitted, the effect of the last proviso to the 1st section of the Statute last cited, is to prevent the removal of the wife and family to Ireland, the husband not being, in fact, removeable. The Board construe the third proviso literally, and it will be noticed that the language of the proviso is quite unrestricted, and would, in terms, include every case in which the husband, from whatever cause, was not capable of being removed, whether physically from not being in the parish at the time, or by reason of the five years' residence, or from sickness not producing permanent disability. But, independently of the operation of 9 & 10 Vic. cap. 66, in restraining the removal in this case, the Poor Law Board entertain strong doubts whether the enactment of 8 & 9 Vic. cap. 117, which applies to the removal of poor persons to Ireland, would of itself warrant the justices in making an order for the removal of the wife and family without the husband. The justices will, doubtless, observe that this is a question of jurisdiction, and, therefore, they must decide for themselves, whether they have the legal power to remove the parties in question, and that, if they have the power to make the order, it is clearly in their discretion whether they will do so or not.

3. EVIDENCE OF IRREMOVEABILITY IN ORDER TO CHARGE THE UNION UNDER 10 & 11 VIC c. 110.

Sept. 10th, 1847.

Clerk of Wrexham Union—The guardians, after the passing of the Act 9 & 10 Vic. c. 110, came to a resolution that the necessary evidence of the irremoveability of a pauper in order to transfer the cost of his maintenance to the common fund of the union, was a certificate from the clerk to the justices, that an order for the removal of such pauper had been refused, on the ground of irremoveability, under the 9 & 10 Vic. c. 66. Inquired, whether the Commissioners think such a certificate necessary; and if not, what other evidence the guardians should require, as they do not consider themselves competent to determine questions of settlement; also, whether in the case of a reference to the auditor, it will be incumbent on the objector to prove that a pauper had been improperly charged to the union, instead of to a parish; or, whether the guardians must, first, justify the manner in which they have charged such relief.

Ans.—The Commissioners cannot admit that it is necessary for the guardians, in all cases, to have a certificate from the clerk to the justices of the kind referred to. In most cases the guardians can readily learn whether the paupers have resided the specified time in the particular parish, so as to have become irremoveable. The guardian of the parish, the relieving officer, the overseer, or the guardians themselves, may by inquiry ascertain this fact; and a reference to the union accounts will show whether the pauper was in the receipt of the relief, in the manner stated, in the Act 10 & 11 Vic. c. 110. It is not at all necessary for them to inquire into any question of settlement. It is possible, that in some particular case the guardians may deem it necessary to apply for the certificate of the clerk to the justices, and may act upon it, where it establishes the irremoveability of the pauper. But if the certificate should not establish that point, the parish will not be concluded by the certificate, if they can show that the pauper is in fact exempt from the liability to removal. The Commissioners cannot state what the auditor may hold in regard to the objection by the ratepayers to the charge to the parish. But he would probably hear the objection stated, and require the objector to make out at least a *primâ facie* case.

4. Removal Acts — (9 & 10 Vic. c. 66, and 10 & 11 Vic. c. 110,) construction of.

Nov. 12th, 1847.

Clerk of Witney Union—A pauper, now seventeen years of age, has resided in the parish of Witney for seven years last past, and during the year between August, 1845, and August, 1846, he formed part of his father's family, and lived under his roof: his father received relief for him during that year, which relief was charged to the parish of Witney, and afterwards repaid by Hailey, the parish of settlement. Inquired whether such relief can, with reference to the Acts of 10 & 11 Vic. c. 110, and 9 & 10 Vic. c. 66, be charged to the common fund of the union; or, as the pauper is settled in Hailey, he can be removed there, notwithstanding his residence with his father in Witney during the last five years, and his having received relief as one of his father's family during the year preceding August, 1846.

Ans—The Commissioners do not think the fact of a child under sixteen years of age, living with its parents for five years in any place, prevents it from becoming irremoveable by reason of such residence. In the case adverted to by you the child is not therefore removeable to Hailey. The question as to charging the relief in such case to the common fund of the union, depends upon whether the child was relieved at the cost of the parish of its settlement, during the year previous to August, 1846. The relief in the case to which you refer, it appears, was actually given to the father of the pauper, but on account of the child, and was ultimately charged to the parish of the settlement. The Commissioners, therefore, think that the child must be considered to have been relieved at the cost of the parish of its settlement; and, consequently, that the relief now given is chargeable to the common fund of the union.

XI. — SCHOOLMASTERS AND SCHOOLMISTRESSES OF WORKHOUSES — Application of Parliamentary Grant in Payment of their Salaries: Circular.

Poor Law Board,
Somerset House,
31st March, 1848.

Sir,—The Poor Law Board desire to bring under the consideration of the board of guardians the subject of the grant voted by Parliament for the salaries of the teachers of workhouse schools.

When the question of this grant was first submitted to Parliament in the early part of 1846, it was stated by Sir Robert Peel, on the part of Her Majesty's Government, that the grant should be employed as a means for the improvement of this class of schools; and the Poor Law Board feel it to be their duty to do whatever lies in their power to secure the fulfilment of this object.

The whole of the salaries of the schoolmasters and schoolmistresses of workhouses became charged on this fund from the 1st of October, 1846; since which time masters and mistresses have, in several instances, been appointed where no such officers existed previously; and in other cases inefficient officers have been superseded by persons who had been trained and fitted for their duties. No comprehensive effort has, however, hitherto been made to introduce any system for raising the general standard of the qualifications of this class of officers.

The proper education and training of children in the workhouses is essential to the improvement of their condition, as well as highly important with reference to the social condition of the working classes generally; and the increasing of the efficiency of workhouse schools must, therefore, always be an object of much solicitude with this Board.

The subject of the workhouse schools has also occupied the attention of the Lords of the Committee of Council on Education, as well as the Lords Commissioners of Her Majesty's Treasury.

From the Lords of the Committee of Council on Education, the Board have received a communication, of which the following is an extract:—

"That during the year 1848 the inspectors of schools be instructed to examine the qualifications of the teachers of workhouse schools.

"That the board of guardians be, during this year, informed what are the qualifications of these teachers, and the certificate and salary which, in the year 1849, would thus be awarded to them if their qualifications remained unchanged.

"That in the year 1849 every teacher be again examined for a certificate; and that the salaries granted in that year be, in each case, determined by the certificate attained by the teacher, and the extent of his duties as follows:—

"To a schoolmaster holding a certificate of permission, granted for one year, a salary of from 5*l.* to 15*l.* be granted.—

"—A certificate of probation granted for one year, a salary of from 15*l.* to 30*l.*—

"—A certificate of competency, a salary of from 30*l.* to 40*l.*—

"A certificate of efficiency, a salary of from 40*l.* to 50*l.* and upwards.

"That salaries of two-thirds these sums be granted to schoolmistresses holding these certificates respectively.

"That, as certain of the masters now holding office may be unable to obtain certificates entitling them to their present salaries, the Poor-Law Commissioners be recommended to permit the guardians to provide, for one year, the difference between the grant awarded and the salary voted, from the rates of the Union.

"That the certificates be determined by the Committee of Council on Education, on the Report and examination papers submitted by Her Majesty's Inspectors of Schools; and that the decision be communicated from time to time to the Poor Law Commission, who will inform the Lords of the Treasury.

"That it be recommended to the Poor Law Commission to issue regulations to every board of guardians, requiring, as conditions of these grants, that convenient and respectably furnished apartments be provided for the teachers in workhouses; that they be supplied with rations, the same in kind and quantity as the master of the workhouse; that they be subjected to no menial offices; that they have proper assistance in the management of the children when not in school, so that they may have time for exercise, and for the education of their pupil teachers, and otherwise defining their duties and privileges; and that the Secretary be directed to communicate with the Poor Law Commission on these subjects.

"Their Lordships had further under consideration the expediency of encouraging teachers, who obtain certificates of competency and efficiency, by permitting, under the Minutes of August and December, 1846, certain of their scholars to be apprenticed to them, and by allowing them the annual gratuities granted in those Minutes, for the instruction of their apprentices; and their Lordships resolved—

"That one-half the above stipends of pupil teachers, and the entire gratuities to the teacher for the successful education of apprentices, be granted to teachers of workhouse schools, holding certificates of competency or efficiency, on condition that the stipend of the pupil teacher be reserved by the Committee of Council to form a fund, which shall be given to him on his leaving the workhouse, if he successfully complete his apprenticeship, in order to provide for his further education in any training school which he may enter with their Lordships' approbation."

From the Lords Commissioners of Her Majesty's Treasury, the Board have also received a communication in reference to this matter, of which the following is an extract:—

"If any parishes, not under your control and superintendence, desire to participate in the Grant of Parliament, such benefit should not be extended in any cases until the amount of the salaries proposed to be paid to the schoolmasters and schoolmistresses, and the medical officers, shall have been reported to you, and your approval of such salaries shall have been first obtained.

"Nor should any sum be paid out of the Grant to any person employed in unions or parishes for instructing paupers who shall not have been duly appointed to the office of schoolmaster or schoolmistress, and the amount of their salaries been sanctioned by you.

"My Lords consider the proper education of the poor in the several unions and parishes to be of such vital importance, that if any of the unions or parishes should neglect to appoint competent persons to the offices of schoolmasters and schoolmistresses, or should fail in allowing those who reside in the workhouse the same quality and amount of rations as are allowed to the master and matron, their Lordships will feel themselves justified, upon representation being made to them of any such neglect or default, to withhold the benefit of the Grant of Parliament from any union or parish so acting.

"My Lords also consider it very desirable, to ensure orderly conduct amongst the children in the workhouses, that in all cases where it is practicable, the schoolmasters and schoolmistresses should reside in the workhouses."

The plan thus laid down by the Lords of the Committee of Council on Education, and approved by the Lords Commissioners of Her Majesty's Treasury, will form the basis on which the Grant will, after the present year, be distributed; and the Board entertain an earnest hope that such a distribution of the Grant will gradually lead to the appointment to the office of teacher, such persons only as are competent and have received suitable training for the office, and that the workhouse schools will thus be ultimately placed on an efficient and satisfactory footing.

During the present year, and until the 1st of April, 1849, the salaries of the schoolmasters and schoolmistresses will be paid in the same manner as heretofore. After that period, the payment of these salaries will be proportioned according to the scale laid down by the Committee of Council on Education, and subject to the certificates of the school inspectors.

In like manner, wherever those inspectors shall recommend that any workhouse school be furnished with books and the necessary school apparatus, the guardians will, it is expected, promptly attend to such recommendation: but if in any case the guardians fail to do this, and decline to provide the books and apparatus which are necessary, the Board will feel it to be their duty to advise the withholding of the Grant, leaving the entire salary of the teachers to be defrayed out of the funds of the Union.

I am, Sir, your obedient Servant,

GEO. NICHOLLS,
Secretary.

To

The Clerk to the Board of Guardians.

XII.—VACCINATION.

1. CHARGE FOR VACCINATION OF CHILDREN IN WORKHOUSE BY THE WORKHOUSE MEDICAL OFFICER.

April 17th, 1847.

Medical Officer, ——— *Union*—He is medical officer and vaccinator of a district in the union, which includes the union workhouse. Inquired whether he is precluded from charging for such cases as he may vaccinate in the workhouse, there being no provision to that effect in his contract.

Ans.—As by Art. 78, No. 5, of the General Workhouse Rules, it is made the duty of the medical officer of the workhouse to vaccinate such of the children in the workhouse as may require vaccination, in the absence of any express contract providing for a specific payment to the medical officer for vaccination in the workhouse, he cannot claim payment from the guardians under his general vaccination contract for the vaccination of such children, inasmuch as, when he vaccinated them, he was acting in his character of medical officer, and not in that of public vaccinator.

2. REFUSAL OF PARENTS TO ALLOW THEIR CHILDREN TO BE VACCINATED.

Aug. 7th, 1847.

Chairman of ——— *Union*—The medical officers of the ——— Union, with a view to carry out the directions of the Commissioners relating to vaccination, agreed to attend every week at certain places named in each of their districts, and notices were affixed at conspicuous places in each district, requesting parents to bring their children to be vaccinated. The small number of children vaccinated showed, however, that vaccination was neglected to a large extent in the union. Requested the Commissioners' advice upon the subject.

Ans.—The Commissioners regret to learn the apathy displayed by the residents of ———

union, on the subject of vaccination; but they are unable to suggest any other course for adoption by the guardians than that of addressing a circular letter to the clergy and principal inhabitants of the several parishes in the union, requesting their co-operation with the public vaccinators in the extension of vaccination. The guardians might also individually, as occasion offered, impress upon the poor of their respective parishes, the necessity of getting their children vaccinated, and the danger which may arise, not only to themselves, but to the community at large, should small pox make its appearance whilst their children are unprotected from its attack by vaccination.

---

3. POWER OF MEDICAL OFFICER TO VACCINATE CHILDREN IN WORKHOUSE WHEN THE PARENTS OBJECT TO HIS DOING SO.

10*th March*, 1848.

Clerk of North Aylesford Union—The medical officer having reported to the board that there are in the union workhouse four children, belonging to two women, (who are also in the workhouse,) requiring vaccination, but that the mothers refuse to allow him to vaccinate them. Inquired whether the medical officer has the power of vaccinating children in the workhouse notwithstanding the parents of such children may object to his doing so.

Ans.—If the parents choose to remain in the workhouse and to keep their children there, parents and children must conform to the regulations established for the management of the workhouse. By Article 207, No. 5, of the General Consolidated Order, it is made the duty of the medical officer to vaccinate such of the children in the workhouse as require it. If he and the guardians think that the children of the two women referred to in your letter require vaccination, the Board are of opinion that he should vaccinate them forthwith.

---

4. VACCINATORS—THEIR QUALIFICATIONS.

Feb. 22*nd*, 1848.

Clerk of Oldham Union—Inquired whether the guardians can appoint as vaccinators for any of the districts in the union, medical practitioners not qualified in the modes prescribed in the Orders of the Poor Law Board, the words of the statute, 3 & 4 Vic. cap. 29, being "medical officers of the union," or "with any legally qualified medical practitioner for," &c. The interpretation clause, sec. 9, says, the Act shall be interpreted as in the Act 4 & 5 Wm. 4, cap. 76; and it is, therefore, assumed that the Board have, by their order with reference to medical officers, defined the meaning of the words "legally qualified," in the statute first referred to.

Ans.—The 3 & 4 Vic. cap. 29, requires that the guardians should contract with a medical officer of the union, or a legally qualified medical practitioner. The Poor Law Commissioners have prescribed the qualifications for the medical officer of the union; but have not professed to define the precise meaning of the terms "legally qualified medical practitioner." They certainly do not consider that the person to be appointed as a vaccinator need be qualified in the same manner as the medical officer of the union. If vaccination be a surgical operation, any practitioner who is legally qualified to practice surgery, may be contracted with by the guardians, under the statute. If it be a medical operation, falling within the office of an apothecary, the party must be qualified to practise as an apothecary, in his general practice. This is the view taken by the Poor Law Board of this subject.

XIII.—VAGRANTS

1. REFUSAL TO WORK.

Sept. 16*th*, 1847.

Clerk of South Stoneham Union—It is customary for vagrants to apply for admission into the workhouse of the South Stoneham Union too late in the evening to perform any kind of work, and they are supplied with supper and a night's lodging therein; but they refuse, on the following morning, to perform the task of work prescribed by the guardians, under sec. 5 of the 5 & 6 Vic. c. 57, and are quite willing to leave the workhouse without any breakfast.—Inquired whether such vagrants can be taken before the justices, and punished under the 5 Geo. 4, c. 83, for such refusal to work; or whether, if the master detains them four hours beyond the breakfast, without any food, they can be further punished.

Ans.—The Commissioners think that, if a person relieved in a workhouse by supper and lodging, refuse, on the following morning, to perform (when thereunto required) a task of work, the case falls within the 5th sec. of 5 & 6 Vic. c. 57, and that the person is, for such refusal, punishable under 5 Geo. 4, c. 83. It makes no difference, in the opinion of the Commissioners, as regards constituting the offence, that the person, in the case supposed, may be willing to leave the workhouse without breakfast; as the statute makes the offence to consist simply in the refusal to perform a task of work "in return for food and lodging afforded." Where supper has been given to a pauper, and the pauper has also passed the night in the workhouse, food and lodging have certainly been afforded. It is not necessary that the pauper should also have received breakfast; though the period of detention, for the purpose of "working," is reckoned from the hour of breakfast in the morning. The master can, as it seems to the Commissioners, detain a person so admitted, so relieved, and so refusing to work, for the period of four hours from the breakfast hour, with the view of taking him, or causing him to be taken, before a justice of the peace. The period of "four hours" is the limit to which a person may be detained for the purpose of working. But, for the purpose of punishment, the limit seems to be such time as may be necessary to cause the offender to be taken before a justice of the peace. By the 6th section of 5th Geo. 4, c. 83, (which provision, having regard to the terms of sec. 5 of 5 & 6 Vic. c. 57, must be taken to be incorporated with the latter statute,) it is rendered lawful for any person to apprehend any person found offending against the Act as an idle and disorderly person, or a rogue and a vagabond, and forthwith to take and convey such person before some justice of the peace, or to deliver him to a constable, or peace officer, for that purpose. The word "forthwith," by judicial interpretation, is taken to mean within the earliest practicable period.

---

2. DIET OF VAGRANTS IN WORKHOUSE.

Feb. 11th, 1848.

Clerk of Tiverton Union—The guardians, in consequence of the very great increase of vagrants and trampers admitted into the union workhouse, think it is necessary that the diet for this class of paupers should be altered, but the guardians wish first to obtain the opinion of the Board on the subject.

Ans.—It is not usual to provide the same diet for tramps as for the other inmates of a workhouse; but it is in the discretion of the guardians to make such alteration in the diet of tramps whilst they remain in the vagrant wards, as the guardians may deem fit, provided that any such alteration is reported to the Board, and receives its sanction. The Board would also recommend the guardians to enforce the task of work, which they may prescribe for this class of persons, under the provisions of 5 & 6 Vic. c. 57, sec. 5, and to take the proceedings therein pointed out in case of refusal to perform it. The guardians might take a further course that would be likely to have a beneficial effect on the health and habits of the tramps themselves, as well as to prevent their spreading disease amongst others, by causing such persons to be put into a bath and to be well washed on their first admission into the workhouse.

Feb. 19th, 1848.

The Clerk transmitted the following copy of an order made by the guardians on the 8th instant:—"Ordered, that all vagrants or tramps that may be admitted into the workhouse be furnished, on their admission, with the usual supper, according to the dietary; and, in the morning, should they refuse to labour, no breakfast to be allowed."

Ans.—With reference to the provision in the order, that if the vagrants "refuse to labour, no breakfast to be allowed," the Board direct attention to the provisions of the Act already referred to, (5 & 6 Vic. cap. 57, sec. 5,) wherein the allowance of food is not made conditional on the performance of the work, but that, in return for food already given, the guardians may exact a certain task of work; and that, in case of refusal to perform such work, a remedy is provided in taking proceedings under the Vagrant Act. The breakfast, therefore, could not properly be made conditional upon the performance of a task of work, except where food has already been given to the vagrant for supper. Where it has, the work can be legally exacted from the vagrant before breakfast, and it is desirable a portion of the work should be so. It does not appear from the order, that the guardians contemplate making any difference between the diet of vagrants and the other inmates, except in so far as breakfast is made contingent on the previous performance of work.

---

3. CHARGING THE COST OF THE MAINTENANCE OF VAGRANTS.

March 6th, 1848.

Clerk of Northleach Union—Requested the Board's instructions as to the manner in which the maintenance of vagrants should be charged in the accounts of the master of the workhouse.

Ans.—The charge of the relief of vagrants generally falls upon one particular parish, which not only suffers from the disproportionate burden thus cast upon it, but, where they are numerous, is additionally taxed for the benefit of the other parishes, by means of the present mode of distributing this charge. It is obvious that the cost of relieving vagrants must be much smaller per head than that of relieving the regular inmates of the workhouse. Not only are the bedding and meals allowed them in most unions inferior in quality to that which the other inmates receive, but the meals they on the average take are fewer. They generally arrive in the evening, frequently too late for supper, are supplied with a night's lodging and a breakfast the next morning, and leave before dinner. The cost per head of thus relieving them cannot, on the average, exceed one-half of that of ordinary inmates per diem; and yet each of these vagrants is charged in the accounts as one inmate for a whole day. The result is, that the average charge per head of maintenance in the workhouse is lowered below its real cost, to the gain of the other parishes; while that of the vagrants is as unduly raised above it, to the detriment of the particular parish upon which the law has in effect imposed the whole burden of relieving them. As there is not anything in the provisions of the law generally, nor in the order of the Poor Law Commissioners regulating the accounts, to prevent the guardians from establishing a separate charge in respect of those paupers who are received, fed, and treated as vagrants, from that which is fixed in respect of the regular inmates of the workhouse, by reference either to the time to be charged, or to the amount to be charged—and as the justice of doing so cannot be doubted, the Board would strongly recommend to the guardians the adoption of this course. There is, practically, no difficulty found in keeping a separate book for vagrants; that is, (according to the Note to Form 22 of General Accounts Order,) "Paupers who have not been relieved more than twenty-four hours, nor regularly admitted into the workhouse." This course is adopted in many unions. The name of the vagrant, the parish chargeable, and the amount of food given, are entered in each case; and the cost, at the end of the quarter, is calculated and charged, per head, accordingly. As regards the Weekly Provisions Book, the quantity of food given to vagrants is brought forward as a total from the Vagrant Book, in the same manner as the quantity of food given to the sick is brought from the Medical Relief Book.

4. TASK OF WORK PRESCRIBED FOR VAGRANTS.

March 14th, 1848.

Clerk of Bridgwater Union—Transmitted the following resolution of the guardians for the Poor Law Board's approval—"That the master of the workhouse do set every adult person not suffering under any temporary or permanent infirmity of body, being an occasional poor person, who shall be relieved in the said workhouse, in return for the food and lodging afforded to such person, to perform the following task of work: that is to say, every able-bodied man shall be required to crush one hundred weight of stone, fit for gravel-walks, or to pump for three hours; and that the women shall be required to make their beds, and clean the room, or any other household work; provided no such person shall be detained against his or her will for the performance of such task of work, for any time exceeding four hours, from the hour of breakfast in the morning next after admission; and provided also, that such amount of work shall not be required from any person to whose age, strength, or capacity, it shall appear not to be suited."

Ans.—The Board observe that it is proposed that the women of this description, (casual poor,) when relieved, shall be required to make their beds and clean the room, or any other household work. This class of casual poor may very properly be required to clean out the tramp or vagrant wards, after the men have quitted them; but they should on no account be permitted to mix with the other inmates of the workhouse, or to do any work in any other part of the house, than that which is appropriated for their own use, and for the use of the male tramps. In addition to cleaning out the vagrant wards, the Board recommend that the female casual poor be required to pick a given weight of junk into oakum, which, at Bridgwater, might be done with some profit to the union. If the guardians adopt this recommendation, it will be necessary that they should pass an amended resolution, prescribing oakum-picking as a task of work for the female casual poor, and at the same time making the resolution more definite as regards the part of the premises where they are to do the household work.

XIV.—WORKHOUSE.

1. INMATES OF WORKHOUSE CANNOT BE COMPELLED TO ATTEND A PLACE OF WORSHIP OUT OF IT.

Feb. 12th, 1848.

Clerk of ——— Union — Inquired whether the guardians have the power, by Art. 125 of the General Consolidated Order, of ordering the paupers belonging to the Established Church to attend public worship in the parish church, or dissenters in a place of dissenting worship, and of punishing any who may refuse so to attend, there being no regular chaplain or chapel for the workhouse.

Ans.—The article above referred to only authorises the guardians to permit the absence of the paupers from the workhouse for the purpose of attending public worship; it does not confer on the guardians any power to order such attendance, so as to subject to punishment any pauper refusing to attend.

---

2. PAUPERS REFUSING TO LEAVE THE WORKHOUSE TO TAKE EMPLOYMENT OFFERED TO THEM.

Feb. 22nd, 1848.

Clerk of Barnstaple Union—There are in the union workhouse three able-bodied young men, with their wives and children, who have been offered work out-of-doors at stone-breaking, at such wages, as would, in the opinion of the guardians, enable them to earn enough for the support of themselves and their families, but who refuse to quit the workhouse. Inquired whether the guardians have power to turn those parties out of the house; and, if not, what steps should the guardians take in regard to them.

Ans.—The Board are of opinion that, if any pauper be offered work at competent wages for the support of himself and family, and refuses to accept such offer, remaining at the same time chargeable to his parish, he would be liable to be dealt with under the 3rd sec. of the Vagrant Act. That section provides, "That any person, being able wholly, or in part, to maintain himself or herself, or his or her family, by work, or other means, and wilfully refusing or neglecting so to do, by which refusal or neglect, such person, or any of his or her family, shall have become chargeable, &c., shall be deemed an idle and disorderly person." The law has invested the guardians with full power to withhold relief if they are satisfied that any applicant is of ability and has the means to maintain himself and those dependent on him, "or uses an ordinary or daily trade of life to get his living by," (see sec. 1, 43 Eliz., c. 2.) They might, therefore, discharge a pauper from the workhouse to whom suitable employment might be offered, but refused by him. Such a course of proceeding, however, ought not to be taken without due inquiry and precaution, as it might expose the guardians to serious responsibility, if the decision should turn out to be erroneous, and any ill consequences should ensue from the discharge of the pauper and his family from the workhouse.

---

3. AN INMATE NOT ACTING ON HIS NOTICE TO QUIT WORKHOUSE: POWER OF MASTER.

March 13th, 1848.

Clerk of Luton Union—An inmate of the union workhouse, immediately after his breakfast on a Thursday, gave notice to the master of his intention to leave; whereupon the master gave to him his clothes, for the purpose of changing them for the workhouse clothes: but the pauper appeared at dinner without having changed his clothes, and said that he had changed his mind, and should not go out till Saturday. The guardians, apprehending some inconvenience if steps be not taken to discourage conduct of this kind, inquired whether the master would have been justified, in this case, in insisting on the pauper changing his clothes and leaving the workhouse, and, if necessary, causing him to be turned out; or, would the pauper's disobedience of an order of the master to change his clothes and leave the workhouse, be deemed a wilful disobedience of a lawful order of an officer of the workhouse, under Art. 127 of the Consolidated General Order.

Ans.—The pauper, in this case, does not appear to have committed any offence against the regulations of the workhouse. Article 115 of the General Consolidated Order provides that a pauper may quit the workhouse upon giving reasonable notice of his wish to do so; but it is not compulsory on him to leave in accordance with such notice, after having given it. The Board consider that the refusal of the pauper to exchange the workhouse dress for his own clothes, when required by the master, was not a disobedience of a lawful order of an officer of the workhouse, within the meaning of Art. 127. The Board are farther of opinion that the master would not have been justified in turning the pauper out of the workhouse. Still it might have been desirable, with a view to prevent the recurrence of such a practice, for the guardians to have discharged the pauper from the workhouse at their next meeting after the notice to leave, as they might reasonably presume he would not have thought of doing so unless he expected to be able to maintain himself out of the workhouse; the master would in that case have, of course, the power of re-admitting him before another meeting of the guardians, if he, in his discretion, should deem the pauper's case, by that time, had become one of urgent necessity.

---

4. PERSONS WHO OBTAIN FREQUENT ADMISSION INTO A WORKHOUSE AND QUIT IT WITHOUT ANY PROSPECT OF EMPLOYMENT, HOW TO BE DEALT WITH.

31 *March*, 1848.

Clerk of ——— *Union*—There are many able-bodied men, most of them unmarried, and of a bad character, who are continually applying for admission to the workhouse in the evening, and leaving again the next day after dinner; and thus going in and out of the workhouse three, and sometimes four times a week. They seldom do any work, being such characters as few will employ; and they are consequently in a state of destitution at the time they apply for admission into the workhouse. They leave the house without any prospect of work, and it is believed that they often do so with a view solely of giving trouble and annoyance to the officers of the house. In this way they proceed week after week, and they often induce others to leave the house with them, in the same manner, who would otherwise remain quiet until they saw a fair prospect of work. It often happens, also, that men obtain an order for the workhouse on the Saturday afternoon, merely for the purpose of obtaining the Sunday's breakfast and dinner (meat,) leaving the house on the Sunday afternoon. The guardians are desirous of putting an end to these practices, and wish the advice of the Poor Law Board on the matter.

Ans.—The Board are of opinion that in any case of this kind the men should not be taken again into the workhouse without a strict application of the rules for the admission of paupers, which require them to be placed in the probationary ward, and washed, cleansed, and dressed in the workhouse dress. The Board also desire to point out that the workhouse master is only authorised to admit applicants without an order, in cases of urgent necessity; and unless the applicant should exhibit visible signs of being in such necessity, the master would not be justified in readmitting him without a fresh order. The master of the workhouse should bring before the guardians the case of any inmate who has been in the habit of frequently going in and out of the workhouse in the way described; and the guardians should inform such inmate, that if he choose to discharge himself again he would not be readmitted without the order of the board at their next meeting. This warning should also be repeated to the man by the workhouse master on his leaving the workhouse. In any case of real urgency, such as illness, the workhouse master would take care to admit the applicant at once.

5. AGED FEMALES LEAVING WORKHOUSE FOR EXERCISE AND RECREATION.

March 9*th*, 1848.

Clerk of Malton Union—Transmitted the following resolution, passed by the guardians:—"Resolved, that the workhouse master be empowered at his discretion to allow any of the aged female inmates to leave the workhouse for the purpose of exercise and recreation."

Ans.—The Poor Law Board refer the guardians to Article 116 of the Consolidated General Order, which contains the regulations for the allowance of temporary leave of absence to paupers in the workhouse. If the guardians are satisfied, on certificate of the medical officer, or otherwise, that exercise out of the workhouse is necessary for the health of any aged female inmate, the case would come within the provisions of that Article, and the guardians might give directions to the master of the workhouse accordingly. But the permission as a general rule for all the aged females to go out of the workhouse without restriction appears to the Board inconsistent with the maintenance of proper order and regularity, and liable to the objections that it would occasion risk of the introduction of infection into the workhouse, and would give the opportunity of bringing in forbidden articles, or of disposing clandestinely of food or other property of the union. Unless, therefore, under proper regulations and restrictions which might prevent such evils, the Board cannot approve of the arrangement proposed in the resolution of the guardians.

London: Printed by Order of the Poor Law Board, by S. Blackburn, 90½ Holborn Hill, and Published by CHARLES KNIGHT, 90, Fleet Street.

AN

OFFICIAL CIRCULAR

OF PUBLIC DOCUMENTS AND INFORMATION:

DIRECTED BY THE POOR LAW BOARD TO BE PRINTED, CHIEFLY FOR THE USE OF THE BOARDS OF GUARDIANS AND THEIR OFFICERS.

Nos. 14 & 15.] APRIL & MAY, 1848. [N.S.

CONTENTS.

I.—ACCOUNTS.

1. FORM OF RATE-BOOK, &c.

29*th Feb.*, 1848.

Assistant Overseers of ———.—Inquired if they would be at liberty to insert a column in the Rate Book for the purpose of assessing owners under 59 Geo. 3, c. 12, instead of occupiers; and another column between those numbered 13 and 14, as a column of reference to be headed "date when paid." Under Art 7 of the Accounts Order every collector is required before proceeding to the collection of any rate to fill up a receipt in the receipt check-book for each rate-payer, including a statement of the amount of rate owing. In a case when at the time of laying the rate a house is unoccupied, and becomes occupied before the expiration of the rate, the tenant being liable to a proportion only of the rate—or, when a house is occupied by one person during the first part of the rate and by another person during the remaining part (in which case each party would be liable to pay his own proportion)—inquired what course the collectors ought to pursue, there being only one receipt check-book, and that already filled up. Inquired also in respect of the receipt check-book, and the notes or counterparts to be retained by the collector, if it would be sufficient in the first instance to number them consecutively, and at the time of receiving the rate to insert the other particulars required by the Order of Accounts.

Ans.—Before assenting to a deviation in the Parish of ——— from the form of the Rate Book prescribed in the General Order of Accounts, the Board wish to be informed more particularly of the grounds on which the overseers consider the additional columns desirable. The Board presume that in the parish of ——— the owners are rated instead of the occupiers, in accordance with the provisions of the 59 Geo. 3, c. 12. If a house be unoccupied at the time when a poor-rate is made in the parish, the Board apprehend there will be some practical difficulty in subsequently including it in such rate, should it become occupied before a new rate is imposed. The provisions of the 17 Geo. 2, c. 38, sec. 12, with reference to such a case, do not appear capable of being very readily carried out. With regard, however, to the receipts to be given for any sums that may be paid by in-coming tenants under such circumstances, the Board think the proper course will be that such additional receipts as may be requisite should be prepared and certified as nearly as possible in the manner pointed out in Art. 7 of the General Order for Accounts. The Board are disposed to consider, that where the tenant of a house included in the poor-rate quits his occupation during the currency of such rate, and another tenant succeeds him, the adjustment of the proportionate payments under the 17 Geo. 2, c. 38, sec. 12, is a matter which rests between the two tenants themselves; and that the overseers will be justified in looking to the tenant actually assessed in the rate, as the party liable to them for the payment of the entire sum. If, however, separate payments be in point of fact made in any such case, the Board think that the requisite receipts should be prepared and certified as suggested above with regard to the case of unoccupied houses. Although, perhaps, it is somewhat doubtful whether the terms of the 7th Article of the General Order for Accounts, require that the names and sums (as well as the numbers) should be entered in the notes or counterparts of the rate receipts, at the same time when the receipts themselves are filled up and certified, the Board at all events consider it highly desirable that this should be done, unless some sufficient reason can be shown for the adoption of a different practice in any instance.

20*th March*, 1848.

Assistant Overseers of ———.—One of the additional columns which it is desired may be introduced into the Rate Book is rendered necessary on account of a large number of cottage owners in the township being rated under the 59 Geo. 3, c. 12, and the other on account of there being two collectors employed in the township, in order that the "date of payment" as respects each of them may be shown separately.

Ans.—The Board will not object to a subdivision of the fourteenth column of the Rate Book for the purpose of showing the "Date of payment," but they do not think it desirable to introduce an entirely distinct column, or to disturb the order of the numbers of the columns as they stand in the prescribed form. With regard to the assessment of owners under the 59 Geo. 3, c. 12, the Board do not perceive any necessity for an additional column to meet such cases. It appears to the Board that the names of the owners so assessed should be entered in column No. 5, and if it be thought advisable to distinguish them from the other owners, such distinction may be marked in any way that may be found most convenient. In these cases, however, the name of the occupier should also be entered in the appropriate column, as the Act (sec. 20) clearly contemplates that the occupier should be continued rated and expressly provides for a distraint upon his goods.

---

2. RELIEF ORDER BOOK AND APPLICATION AND REPORT BOOK.

6th March, 1848.

Clerk of Rye Union.—Submitted certain questions respecting the Relief Order Book and the Application and Report Book.

Ans.—First, you inquire whose duty it is to enter the names, &c., in the *Relief Order Book.* The Board think that on reference to the order of accounts, and the schedules annexed to it, there can be little doubt that this book is to be kept by the clerk. It is, as noticed in the letter which accompanied the order, a substitution for the Abstract of the Application and Report Book, which was always kept by the clerk. As to the entry of the order of the guardians in the *Application and Report Book,* the Board think that the Chairman, or clerk, who, according to Art. 17, No. 1, of the order is to authenticate it by his initials, may properly enter the Order of the Board as heretofore was done. They also think that the value of the relief in kind ordered by the guardians and entered in that book may be readily computed at the time when it is ordered to be given. This form as well as the Relief Order Book doubtless contemplates an estimate of the value of the relief in kind. The relieving officer will show in his Out-Relief List, and his Receipt and Expenditure Book, the actual cost of this relief. It will not be necessary that the name of every applicant for relief should be repeated weekly in the Application and Report Book. The order for relief will be given in numerous instances for a definite period, and the case need not be mentioned again until this period has elapsed, and then the application must be renewed. In strictness, a new entry should be made in the book on an application being made for the continuance of relief; but the Board consider that it will be competent for the relieving officer to bring the case forward and obtain an order for further relief without entering full details of the case afresh. The Board see nothing in the present order to alter the existing course of proceeding with reference to the reading of the Application and Report Book. The general practice is for the chairman to read it, but whatever course has been pursued by the guardians of the Rye Union may be still continued.

---

3. ORDER CHECK-BOOK—NUMBERING INVOICES.

16th March, 1848.

Clerk of Tendring Union.—In the Order Checkbook prescribed by the Accounts Order, all the invoices and counterfoils are to bear consecutive numbers as they are made and detached from the book. The master is to enter and number the invoices in the order in which they are received, and to file and preserve them in the same order. It may, however, happen that invoice No. 10, for example, may not be returned to the master until some days after invoice No. 20, although both may have been issued on the same day. Inquired whether it was intended that the master should give another number to the invoices as he receives and enters them under the head "No. of Invoice;" or, whether the number which the invoice bore when issued by the Board is the number to be entered under the head "No. of Invoice."

Ans.—It is the duty of the clerk to number all orders given by the guardians for certain articles or work required by the guardians; and also to fill in the like numbers on the corresponding invoices, but as it is likewise required of the master of the workhouse to number the invoices as they are received, the Board are of opinion that this should be done by a different number, and would suggest that such number should be affixed on the back of the invoice. The object of this latter process is to secure a record of the order in which the invoices are returned.

---

4. ENTRY OF RELIEF IN OUT-DOOR RELIEF LIST.

2nd May, 1848.

Clerk of ——— *Union.*—1st, A. B., a single woman, is in service in the parish of L———, in this union, and has a child residing in the parish of M———, also in this union, receiving parish relief. Should the child's name be inserted in the Out-door Relief Book for the relief given to such child, or should that of its mother be inserted? The mother is quite unable to support the child, and the union has no workhouse. 2nd, Is it competent for the clerk to order books and stationery, and also printing to be done for the use of the union, without waiting for a meeting of the board of guardians to obtain authority, when the delay may be attended with inconvenience.

Ans.—1st, The relief should be entered in the Out-Door Relief List, according as it is given. If it be given for the child of A. B. to the persons who have the custody of the child, the relief should be entered in the name of the child; and, consequently, be charged to the parish where such child resides. If the relief be given to the mother, then the name of the mother should be entered, and against the parish where the mother lives. But the Board think it would be most correct to charge the relief to the parish where the child resides. 2nd, The Board could hardly advise the clerk to the guardians to order any such articles as are specified in your second question, without the authority of the guardians first obtained, as without that authority he would render himself liable for the payment; nor do they see what sudden necessity can arise for ordering these articles in the interval between the meetings of the guardians, if reasonable precaution be used by the clerk to ascertain beforehand whether the supply of books, stationery, &c., required for the union, will last during that time. Of course, in the case of a sudden loss by fire, or other accident, the guardians would not be likely to refuse to confirm the clerk's unauthorized orders.

5. RELIEF LIST, HOW TO BE FILLED UP.

1848.

Clerk of Aston Union.—1. A pauper, who had been receiving relief from the union for several weeks, in consequence of sickness, is now dead, and the guardians have granted a continuance of the relief to the widow and her child. The relief up to the husband's death was entered in the relief list in his name, and his wife and child were entered in the statistical portion, as required by Article 17 of the Order of Accounts. Inquired whether the relief to the widow is to be entered in the relief list, as a new case; and also how the statistical portion of the list is to be filled up, so that the same individuals may not appear as twice relieved. 2. In the case of an able-bodied man whose wife is sick, inquired whether he or she is to be entered in the list under the head "Name of pauper," the relief being given virtually to the woman during such sickness only. 3. Also, in the case of an outfit for children under 16 years, inquired, whether the father or children are to be inserted under the head "Name of pauper," and in which columns of the statistical portion of the list they should be entered.

Ans.—1. The Board consider that the widow must be entered in the proper columns for a widow and child, namely, Nos. 7 and 8. 2. In regard to the able-bodied husband of the sick wife, as the relief is given to him, though for the necessity of his wife, his name alone must be entered in the column headed "Name of the pauper," and numbers must be entered in columns 3 and 5 for himself and his wife. 3. Where an outfit is given to a child under 16, the relief is given to the father, if the child be resident with him, and his name must be entered in the list; and for the same reason, the case must be entered in column No. 4, and a number must also be entered in column 6 for the number of all the children in respect of whom an outfit is provided.

6. CHARGING OF FUNERAL EXPENSES AND PAYMENTS PER CASE TO MEDICAL OFFICERS.

1848.

Clerk of Witham Union.—Inquired in what account in the ledger under the General Order of Accounts, the funerals of in-door paupers are to be charged. Heretofore the funerals of out-door paupers have been included in the out-relief lists, and it is proposed to continue that practice. But the funerals of in-door paupers have been charged to an account called "Funeral Account." In the list of accounts required to be kept under the Order, no such account as "Funeral Account" appears. The medical officers in this union are paid at per case. Inquired whether such payments should be charged to out-relief or be included in the common charges. The former has been the course hitherto adopted, but if the medical officers were paid by salaries instead of fees, such salaries would undoubtedly be spread over the whole union, each parish paying according to the amount of its average, and not according to the number of cases.

Ans.—The cost incurred in the burial of paupers dying in the union workhouse will properly follow the cost of the relief supplied to such paupers when living, and should consequently be entered in the accounts under the head of in-maintenance. 2nd, The payments per case to medical union officers being clearly relief to the particular paupers, should be charged to the respective parishes on whose account it is given, in the same way as ordinary relief to the paupers would be charged. This course cannot, however, be adopted where the medical officers are paid by a fixed salary; in that case the salary being charged upon the common fund, the parishes would contribute in proportion to their averages.

7. VOUCHERS FOR PAYMENTS CHARGED IN THE GUARDIANS' ACCOUNTS.

11th May, 1848.

District Auditor.—The only vouchers presented at the audit of the accounts of ——— for sums paid to contractors and others, for goods delivered, and to the several officers for salaries, have hitherto been merely the counterparts of checks on the treasurer. The auditor not considering that these were sufficient securities to the guardians, stated to the clerk that he could not in future take upon himself the responsibility of passing any payments made by the guardians unless a proper and sufficient voucher was produced.

Ans.—The Board consider that the course adopted by the auditor in this matter is the correct one.

8. RECEIPTS FOR OFFICERS' SALARIES—STAMPS.

Clerk of ——— *Union.*—The auditor having from time to time hesitated to receive unstamped receipts from the officers of this union for their respective salaries, inquired whether it is usual to insist upon stamped receipts being given.

Ans.—The Board see no reason why the officers of the union should not give stamped receipts for their salaries. The guardians have a right to expect legal discharges in respect of payments made by them, and an unstamped receipt where the amount requires a stamp is not a legal discharge.

II.—ASSISTANT OVERSEER—EMPLOYMENT OF IN REMOVING POOR PERSONS.

28th March, 1848.

Overseers of ——— *Bolton Union.*—The assistant overseer of the township of ——— in the Bolton Union, has, since his appointment, in addition to the collection of the poor rate, attended to the removal of paupers, and the passing of Irish poor to Ireland. Inquired whether the Poor Law Board approved of these duties being performed by this officer.

Ans.—The assistant overseer appointed by the guardians of the Bolton Union, for the township of ——— under the order of the Poor Law Commissioners, of the 1st April, 1845, is required, by a previous order of the Commissioners, dated November 12th, 1838, to assist the overseers in all the duties of their office, and not merely in the collection of the poor-rates. With regard, however, to the removal of Irish paupers, the Board desire to point out that it forms no part of the duties of the overseers to take proceedings for such removals. Under the 2nd sec. of the 8 & 9 Vic. c. 117, the complaint is to be laid before the justices by the guardians of the union, where the parish or township is within a union; and it is only where there are no guardians that the overseers are authorised to act. The later Statute, 10 & 11 Vic. c. 33, appears to the Board to make no difference in this respect; although it enables "any guardian, relieving officer, or overseer," to take the pauper before the justices without a summons or warrant, it requires the justices to proceed in all respects as under the former Act, that is to say, upon the complaint of the guardians.

III.—BURIAL FEES.—POWER OF RELIEVING OFFICER.

1st March, 1848.

Clerk of ——— *Union.*—The fees taken at funerals in the parish of ——— are of two kinds; one description consists of the offerings of sums of money placed by the friends of the deceased on the altar, at the close of the service in the church, and the other is the fixed sum of ten shillings and eight-pence, which is expected to be paid when no offerings are presented. By the section 31st of the 7 & 8 Vic. c. 101, "in all cases of burials under the direction of the guardians," the fee or fees "payable by the custom of the place of burial, shall be paid out of the poor-rates for the burial of each such body, to the person or persons who by such custom may be entitled to receive any fee." It is presumed that in the intervals between the fortnightly meetings of the guardians, the direction of the relieving officer to bury under this section would be tantamount to a direction by the guardians themselves. Inquired whether, in case of the parties having the custody of the dead body of a pauper being unable to make offerings or pay the fee of ten shillings and eight-pence, the relieving officer is bound to order its burial; and whether the vicar can refuse to cause a grave to be opened in the churchyard, or to read the burial service, in a case where there are no offerings made, and the fee is not paid; and also, whether he can demand of the guardians the amount of the deficiency where the offerings fall short of the fee of ten shillings and eight-pence.

Ans.—The burial of the poor in accordance with the provisions of sec. 31 of the 7 & 8 Vic. c. 101, is a matter altogether distinct from the administration of relief, and one in which the relieving officer of a union is not, as such, empowered either by the terms of that enactment, or by the regulations of the General Consolidated Order, to exercise any authority or discretion. But the Board are nevertheless disposed to consider that the guardians might lawfully, by an express resolution, give the relieving officer a general authority to deal, on their behalf, with the class of cases in question, in the intervals of their meetings, provided that such resolution be so definitely expressed as to allow the relieving officer no further discretion than that of deciding whether any given case comes within its terms. The Board are inclined to think that a direction given by the relieving officer, for a burial in accordance with such a resolution, would, after adoption at their next meeting, be tantamount to a direction by the guardians themselves. The Board fully recognise the inconvenience that may result, should the relieving officer be wholly unable to act in the matter without the previous instructions of the guardians in each individual case; but, at the same time, they cannot advise the guardians with the view of avoiding such inconveniences, to adopt any course which is not in conformity with the law. They conceive, however, that the course above suggested would be in conformity with the statute. It will be observed that, in one of the clauses of the 31st sec., it is contemplated that the direction for the burial may be given by "the guardians, or any of their officers duly authorised." With regard to the amount of the fee or fees that may be lawfully demanded on the burial of a pauper in the parish of ———, the Board are not in a position to express a specific opinion; they can do no more than refer the guardians to that provision of the statute which requires, in such cases, the payment of the customary fees. What may be the amount of the customary fees in ——— is a question of fact which the Board cannot undertake to decide. The Board think it right to add that, according to the ecclesiastical law of this country, they believe the vicar of the parish is not justified in refusing interment, (supposing the case one in which a right of sepulture within the parish may lawfully be claimed,) on the grounds of non-payment of the fees. He is bound to perform his duty in burying the corpse entitled to burial in the parish, before he can demand his rightful dues.

IV.—CHARGEABILITY.

1. THE OBLIGATION OF PARISH IN WHICH A PAUPER HAS LAST SLEPT.

20*th March,* 1848.

The Rev. ———, *Horncastle Union.*—W. S., a man whose settlement is disputed, but who certainly did not belong to Horncastle, married in April, 1847, E. E., of Belchford, (a parish in the Horncastle Union,) a single woman with two illegitimate children, one aged three years, and the other an infant of two months, of which she had been confined in the union workhouse, where she was at the cost of Belchford. After the marriage, W. S. and his wife went to lodge with his brother in Horncastle, and they were both shortly after apprehended on a charge of larceny and sent to Spilsby for trial. The infant accompanied its mother to gaol, and remained with her during her imprisonment; the eldest child was placed in the workhouse chargeable to Belchford, but was afterwards taken by its grandmother. In July, 1847, W. S. was sentenced to seven years' transportation, and the wife to six months' imprisonment. In January, 1848, at the expiration of her sentence, the wife was discharged from gaol, and returned straightway to her mother's house in Belchford, where her eldest child was staying. On the 8th of January she came over to Horncastle, and made application to the relieving officer of the district (who resides there) for pecuniary assistance. He offered her an order of admission into the workhouse, which she declined, and immediately returned to her mother's house, where she continued to reside until the 21st of January. Having by that time ascertained that no other kind of relief was to be obtained, she resolved to go into the workhouse, and with this intention set off for Horncastle in the afternoon of that day with her two children. She arrived at Horncastle rather late in the evening. On entering the town she stopped at the house of a friend, who gave her and the children some food, and then, as she found it was too late to take the necessary steps for procuring admission into the workhouse that night, she lodged for the night in a public house adjoining her friend's. Early next morning she called on the relieving officer, obtained from him an order for the workhouse, and went straight thither. When her admission into the workhouse was reported to the board, it was decided that she and her two children were to be charged to the parish of Horncastle, because they had slept in that parish on the night previous to their admission into the workhouse, no account being taken of their connexion with Belchford, or of the cause of their lodging for the night in Horncastle. It is the custom of this union to charge vagrants and trampers who have no fixed residence in the union and become chargeable to it, through illness or destitution, to the parish in which they stopped the night before making application for relief, and on this custom the decision of the board was grounded, but he contended that the case of E. S. did not fall under that rule, and requested the Board's opinion on the case.

Clerk of Horncastle Union.—It is the uniform practice of the guardians of this union to charge all relief to the parish in which the pauper slept the night before the order for relief was given. And in compliance with that rule the guardians directed the maintenance of E. S. and her children to be charged to the parish of Horncastle. The circumstances under which the order for the workhouse was given in this case led to some discussion, but the guardians did not think that they afforded any ground for departing from the rule above referred to.

Ans. to the guardians.—The Board can understand that such a rule as the guardians have prescribed to themselves may have much to recommend it on the score of convenience; but, though the rule be both simple and convenient, the guardians would not be warranted in acting upon it, unless it be supported by legal considerations. The Board entertain considerable doubt as to the legality of such a rule, at all events without qualification. The Board apprehend that the mere fact of a party having slept in a parish does not in itself create a legal liability on that parish to afford relief on the morrow. There may be indeed other circumstances connected with the case which may create such a liability. The pauper may be destitute in the parish in which he slept, and there may be reasonable evidence that the pauper would have made application for relief in that parish, if the union arrangements had not compelled him to make the application in a different parish. But where the destitution may have arisen since the sleeping in a different parish, the Board think it quite clear that the circumstance of the sleeping is not one which could conclude the question of chargeability to any particular parish The Board have thought it necessary to make these remarks upon the general rule or practice of the guardians described in your letter. With regard however to the case of E. S., the Board, on a careful consideration of the circumstances, are not able to concur in the decision of the guardians in charging the relief to the parish of Horncastle. They admit, however, that the case is peculiar, and cannot express more than a doubtful opinion. The pauper it seems had been residing at Belchford, and went from thence direct to Horncastle, for the sole purpose of making her application for relief, the union arrangements rendering such a course unavoidable in consequence of the relieving officer of the district in which Belchford is situate residing at Horncastle. The pauper does not appear to have remained in Horncastle any longer than was necessary under the circumstances for making the application. She arrived in the evening, at too late an hour to make, it would seem, on that night the necessary application to the proper officer. But this she did early on the following morning, when an order for her admission into the workhouse was given. It appears to the Board that all that occurred at Horncastle is to be regarded as forming part of the application, and that the delay in making it was unavoidable. The Board are aware that the general rule or principle, on which the chargeability is determined, is, that that parish is liable in which a pauper being destitute applies for and obtains relief. In unions, however, this rule is subject to the important exception, that where the union arrangements render it necessary that the application should be made in a different parish from that in which the party is when the necessity for the relief arises, the mere fact of making the application in the parish in which the workhouse is situate, or in which the relieving officer resides, does not release the parish of the residence from the liability to afford relief. The application, indeed, in such a case is to be regarded as having been constructively made in the parish where that necessity arose, which will be generally the parish wherein the pauper lives at the time when the application is made. Applying this principle to the circumstances of the present case, the Board think that Belchford was the parish liable for the cost of E. S.'s relief.

---

2. CHARGEABILITY OF A CHILD DESERTED BY ITS MOTHER.

11*th May*, 1848.

Clerk of Pembroke Union.—A bastard child having been deserted, in the parish of Lanrenny, in this union, was carried by the woman in whose house it was left to the relieving officer, who brought the case before the board of guardians. The guardians suspected there was some collusion between the mother and the woman, and refused immediately to give an order for the due care of the child. The woman then dropped the child on the floor of the board room, (the guardians being then assembled,) and decamped. Requested the opinion of the Poor Law Board as to what parish the child is chargeable.

Ans.—The child in question is chargeable to the parish of Lanrenny, where it was deserted by its mother, and where, therefore, it became destitute, so as to require relief. It appears to the Board, upon your statement of the case, that no fresh circumstance of destitution intervened between its desertion by its mother and its being left by the woman who took it to the meeting of the guardians; and that, consequently, there is nothing to affect the liability resting upon the parish of Lanrenny to provide for the relief of the child, which was deserted and destitute within it.

V.—COLLECTOR OF POOR-RATES.

1. APPOINTMENT OF.

29th April, 1848.

Mr. ———, *Darlington Union.*—The office of assistant overseer and collector of the poor-rates for the township of——— being now vacant, inquired whether in the event of the Commissioners issuing their Order to the guardians of the union to elect a paid collector of rates, they will be empowered to appoint such collector to perform the duties of assistant overseer, at such salary as they may fix; or, will it remain with the inhabitants in vestry to assign the duty and fix the salary of the officer.

Ans.—By the Order of the Poor Law Commissioners, dated Feb. 28th, 1837, the guardians were empowered to appoint the collector, and to require the same person to perform the duties of an assistant overseer. But the Poor Law Board think that the 7 & 8 Vic. c. 101, sec. 61, overrules this Order, so far as to give the power of appointing the officer to perform the duties of assistant overseer to the inhabitants of the township, who may consequently fix the proper amount of salary.

2. NO SUBSTITUTE FOR COLLECTOR CAN BE APPOINTED.

19th Feb., 1848.

Clerk of Wolverhampton Union.—Requested the sanction of the Poor Law Board to the appointment by the guardians of a substitute for the collector of the poor-rates for the parish of Bilston.

Ans.—The guardians have no authority to make the appointment in question. A collector is not an officer for whom they can, under Art. 193 of the Consolidated Order, appoint a substitute, the officers therein referred to being those only enumerated in Art. 153 of that Order; and the Order under which the collector for Bilston was appointed does not provide for the appointment of a deputy or a substitute.

VI.—CONTRACTOR.—WHETHER DISQUALIFIED FROM BEING APPOINTED COLLECTOR OF POOR-RATES.

22nd February, 1848.

Clerk of ——— *Union.*—The contractor for supplying the union workhouse with bread and flour is desirous of obtaining the appointment of collector of poor-rates, for a parish in the union, unless disqualified by reason of such contract. Inquired whether such was the case.

Ans.—The fact of a person being under contract to supply the union with provisions does not create any legal incapacity upon the part of such person to be elected to the office of collector. But how far such a contractor, if elected, could continue to perform his contract, without subjecting himself to penalties, is a different question. It will be seen that the penalties imposed by the 55 Geo. 3, c. 137, upon persons having the management of the poor, if concerned in contracts for the supply of goods and provisions, are by sec. 51 of 4 & 5 William 4, c. 76, expressly extended to officers appointed under the provisions of that Act. Now, although in the case of Reg. *v.* The Poor Law Commissioners, in *re* Cambridge Union, 2 P. and D. 223, it was held that a collector of poor-rates was not an officer whose appointment was contemplated by the 4th & 5th William 4, c. 76, still a subsequent Act, 2nd & 3rd Vic. c. 84, cured the defect, and gave the same force and validity to orders for the appointment of collectors, as if they had been warranted by the first-mentioned statute. Having regard to this, and seeing also that the 2nd & 3rd Vic. c. 84, is by 5th & 6th Vic. c. 57, directed to be construed as one act with 4th & 5th William 4, c. 76, the Board are disposed to consider that the penalties imposed by sec. 51 of the latter act would be held to extend to a collector of poor-rates. But, perhaps, this is rather a point upon which it would be for the contractor, if appointed, to assure himself. In any case, however, it would seem desirable that the contract should be determined at the earliest possible period.

VII.—CONTRIBUTION ORDERS.

1. PERIODS AT WHICH THEY SHOULD BE MADE.

29th April, 1848.

Clerk of Aylesbury Union.—Inquired whether the Poor Law Board have any objection to contribution orders for the purposes of the union being made quarterly instead of half-yearly, as mentioned in the General Consolidated Order.

Ans.—It is not required under the General Consolidated Order that the guardians should make orders for contribution half-yearly; on the contrary, it will be seen on reference to Art. 82 that such orders are to be made from time to time, as the guardians may find it necessary. It is true that Art. 81 requires the clerk to make an estimate every half-year of the probable charges of the ensuing half-year, and to prepare the orders for that period; but the guardians are not compelled to adopt such order. They may direct the contributions to be made for a shorter period, or they may issue half-yearly orders, requiring the payments under them to be made by quarterly instalments.

2. ESTIMATES FOR CONTRIBUTION ORDERS.

18th March, 1848.

Clerk of Market Bosworth Union.—He has in accordance with the Consolidated Order made an estimate of the contributions to be paid by the several parishes for the ensuing half-year. The guardians, however, consider this course inconvenient, as it prevents the taking of the balance due to or from the parishes at Lady-day into consideration, and the inconvenience will be the more as the overseers are now required to pay the balance in their hands at the Lady-day audit into the treasurer's, which, in some instances, are very considerable. The guardians require that estimates may be made as heretofore, separately for each quarter, which would allow of the Lady-day balance being taken into account.

Ans.—It appears to the Board that the guardians have misapprehended the provisions of the General Consolidated Order, which require that their clerk shall ascertain the cost to each parish in the union for the maintenance of the poor, and other charges; and shall make an estimate thereof in respect of the coming half-year, and then prepare the orders for contributions on the several parishes, to be laid before the guardians, who will themselves make their orders either for one quarter's demand, or otherwise, as they may think proper. The orders should be so made upon the several parishes irrespective of the balances which may be paid in to the treasurer of the union, or which may happen to be in his hands. But when the orders have been issued the guardians must give credit to the parishes in respect of the sums of money which they may have severally paid to the treasurer, in whatever manner they have been so paid.

3. HOW CONTRIBUTION ORDERS SHOULD BE ADDRESSED.

2nd March, 1848.

Clerk to Shepton Mallet Union.—Article 83 of the General Consolidated Order refers to a form marked M, (Contribution Order,) in which the initials of supposed overseers are placed. Inquired whether it is absolutely requisite that the names of the overseers of the parishes should be written on the Order, or the general address, "To the churchwardens and overseers of ———— :" as overseers leave office, and others are appointed in their stead within fourteen days after the 25th of March, the overseers in office when Orders are made may be replaced by their successors before the contribution is required to be paid to the treasurer.

Ans.—The General Consolidated Order certainly contemplates that the names of the overseers should be inserted in the Contribution Order. In this there can be no difficulty, because if the Orders are intended to apply to the overseers appointed after the 25th of March, the actual making of the orders may be delayed until such appointment has been made. On the other hand, if the Orders are intended to operate upon the existing parish officers, *i. e.*, if the funds needed are required to be raised by them before they go out of office, their names are doubtless well known, and there can be no difficulty in acting in strict compliance with form M, as required by the article referred to. The Board deem it necessary to state that they think it very doubtful whether, as regards an order of contribution made upon the existing overseers, the succeeding overseers could be proceeded against for any neglect to pay to the treasurers the money required by such Order.

4. SERVICE OF CONTRIBUTION ORDERS.

29th May, 1848.

Clerk of Eton Union.—Represented the inconvenience and expense caused by the necessity for addressing Contribution Orders to every churchwarden and overseer by name, and for serving such orders on each of the officers personally. From the formation of the union until Michaelmas last one order addressed quarterly to the overseers of each parish by name of office, and served by the relieving officers upon the acting overseer, was considered sufficient, and no practical inconvenience or expense ever resulted. When the orders were disobeyed the overseers alone were summoned and fined. But as it appeared from a note appended to Art. 202, No. 10, in the General Consolidated Order, that these orders must be addressed to each and all of the churchwardens and overseers by name, and served personally by the clerk, and that the guardians have no power to direct the service of the orders by the relieving officer, a considerable quarterly expense is caused to the rate-payers, as well as loss of time and trouble to the clerk.

Ans.—The Order of the Poor Law Commissioners to which you refer was framed as it now stands, upon advice which they had received that to proceed effectually against overseers for an omission to satisfy any order for contributions, it was necessary that all those answerable for making and collecting the poor-rate should have had notice of such order, and this was difficult of proof unless the order had been addressed to and served personally on all. The clerk, it is to be observed, as the officer of the guardians is to cause the orders to be served, but he can do so by a responsible agent. It is not a duty of the relieving officer to serve them, but in some instances his services might perhaps be made available for this purpose when visiting parishes in his district for other objects. At the same time, the Board think it right to observe, that where the guardians have reason to believe that their orders will not be disobeyed, and that there will be no necessity for them to resort to penal proceedings, they will be justified in causing the order to be served upon some one of the parish officers, who will be likely to attend to it. If it should so happen that it has not been obeyed, the guardians certainly will then be bound to make a fresh order, and cause it to be served upon all the officers of the parish in question.

VIII.—COUNTY-RATE.—INSTRUCTIONS FOR MAKING.

12*th April*, 1848.

The Chairman of County-Rate Committee for Cumberland.—The justices for the county of Cumberland in Quarter Sessions assembled, have appointed a committee of their number, in the terms of the Act of 8 & 9 Vic. c. 111, for the purposes of preparing fair and equal county-rates, and of altering and amending such rates as circumstances may require. Requested advice, 1st, As to what is the maximum deduction that ought to be made under the Parochial Assessments Act, from the gross estimated rental of houses and land, that is to say, farms where the the tenant pays all out-goings except repairs and insurance? 2nd, What is the maximum deduction to be made from houses and other buildings under the same circumstances? The committee are aware that buildings containing machinery are an exception, and require a variable and sometimes large allowance to maintain them in a situation to command the estimated rent. 3rd, The county-rate committee, having made an assessment according to 6 & 7 Wm. 4, c. 96, the same not being appealed against or being confirmed on appeal, and the overseers thereafter making a rate for the relief of the poor, differing therefrom, or unequal in principle—have the justices power to refuse the allowance?

Ans.—In answer to your first and second inquiries, the Board observe, that they are not in a position to express any opinion as to what should be the maximum deduction that should be allowed under the Parochial Assessments Act, 6 & 7 Wm. 4, c. 96, to form the gross estimated rental of houses and land, that is to say, farms where the tenant pays all out-goings except repairs and insurance; or, what such deduction should be in the case of houses and buildings under the same circumstances. The Board apprehend, indeed, that no general rate or scale of deduction can be properly laid down. The amount of deduction must depend upon the actual circumstances of the particular properties which are the subject of assessment; and the law seems to cast upon the overseers, (or, where a professional valuation is made, upon the valuer,) the duty of estimating the deductions from the gross estimated rental by references in each case to the state and condition of the property; as that state and condition vary, so ought the amount of the deductions, and what would be a reasonable allowance in this respect in some cases would not be so in others. It is possible that in practice a scale might be adopted in valuing a parish for the purposes of the Parochial Assessments Act, which, if applied to properties of the same description or character, would not produce an incorrect result, so far as the net or rateable value is concerned. But it is difficult to conceive that any general scale could be framed, which could be made generally applicable in revising the valuations of different parishes. It seems reasonable to suppose that the variations in the deductions in such case would be considerable. As between houses and land for instance, the amount of valuation would obviously be very great. With reference to the third inquiry, the Board are not prepared to say that a valuation or assessment made by the county-rate committee, in accordance with 6 & 7 Wm. 4, c. 96, would in law be conclusive on the overseers in making the poor-rate; neither could the justices lawfully refuse to allow a rate presented to them by the overseers on the ground that it differed from a valuation made by the county-rate committee, the allowance of a poor-rate being a ministerial act: see Reg. *v.* The Earl of Yarborough, 12 A. and E. 416. Still, as the county-rate is to be made upon the "full and fair annual value of property" in a parish, which words are declared by sec. 6 of 8 & 9 Vic. c. 111, to mean "the net annual value at which property is by law required to be assessed to the poor-rate," the Poor Law Board do not see how the overseers would be warranted in departing from a valuation made by the county-rate committee, unless, indeed, they were prepared to show that such valuation did not accord with the principles of the Parochial Assessments Act. If they did so depart without sufficient grounds from such a county-rate valuation in making the poor-rate, it is probable that on appeal such rate would be quashed by the sessions, and that the overseers themselves might be exposed to the liability of paying the costs incurred in defending it.

IX.—DESERTION.—COSTS OF PROCEEDINGS UNDER 7 & 8 VIC. C. 101, SEC. 59.

17th Jan., 1848.

Clerk of Bradford Union.—Forwarded a list of sums paid by the board of guardians under sec. 59 of the 7 & 8 Vic. c. 101, for the apprehension of parties for neglecting their families, and requested the approval of the Poor Law Board to the guardians charging the amount thereof to the townships to which the paupers were chargeable, or to the common fund of the union. Requested also to be informed whether the approval of the Board is necessary as to the mode of charging the costs of the proceedings mentioned in the first part of the sec. 59, or only to those legal proceedings which may be instituted by any auditor, referred to in the latter part of that section.

Ans.—The rule which the Poor Law Commissioners laid down as to charging these expenses was, to sanction their being placed to the common fund, as the apprehension and conviction of a pauper for the offence of desertion, being a criminal proceeding and intended to operate by way of example, concerns all the townships in the union, and is no special benefit to any one of them. This rule the Board adopt, and they will generally continue to act upon it. They cannot, however, give any general direction to the guardians as to the mode of charging the expenses referred to, as the consent of the Board must be obtained in each case as it arises. In the cases referred to in your letter, they approve of the expenses incurred being charged to the common fund of the union. The Board understand the 59th sec. of the 7 & 8 Vic. c. 101, to require that their consent should be given to the charging of all costs or expenses incurred under the authority of that sec. The words in the concluding part of the section, "in any of the cases aforesaid," are general, and (as the Board consider,) govern in grammatical construction the entire section.

X.—GUARDIANS.

1. MEDICAL OFICER CANNOT ACT AS AN EX-OFFICIO GUARDIAN.

12th April, 1848.

Medical Officer of ——— Union.—Had been a medical officer of the union for some years, and had recently been placed in the commission of the peace for the county in which the union is situate. Inquired whether he could still hold his appointment as medical officer.

Ans.—The mere fact of your being a justice of the peace for the county does not prevent your continuing to hold the office of medical officer of the ——— union. But the Board consider you to be prevented from serving as an ex-officio guardian, a medical officer being a paid officer engaged in the administration of the poor laws, within the 14th sec. of the 5 & 6 Vic. c. 57, which appears to the Board to apply to ex-officio as well as to elected guardians.

2. MEETING OF GUARDIANS IN CASE OF EMERGENCY.

24th May, 1848.

Clerk of East Stonehouse Parish.—Inquired whether, in a case of emergency, a meeting may be held under Art. 36 of the Consolidated Order, by three or more of the guardians of the parish without notice to the rest.

Ans.—The Board think a meeting may be held, under the circumstances mentioned, by three or more of the guardians, although the rest may not be summoned. A meeting in cases of emergency seems to be carefully distinguished in the Order, from an extraordinary meeting. It would undoubtedly be desirable, however, in any case of emergency, that as many of the guardians should be called together as could be summoned on the occasion without prejudicial delay; but the guardians or officers on the spot must be the judges of the urgency of the case, and of the course which it may be best to adopt under the particular circumstances.

---

3. DIVISION OF BUSINESS AT MEETINGS OF GUARDIANS.

26th April, 1848.

——— *Union.*—It has hitherto been the custom of the board of guardians for the chairman to take the books of one of the relieving officers, and the vice-chairman those of the other, and thus as it were making two boards. Requested to be informed whether this practise is in accordance with the regulations of the Poor Law Board.

Ans.—The regulations of the Poor Law Board contemplate all business being transacted by the guardians collectively, and the Board are strongly opposed to guardians conducting their business, as regards the administration of relief, in the manner adverted to by you. Besides its being of very questionable legality, it virtually throws the relief of each parish into the hands of the guardian of the parish and the relieving officer, and militates against the regularity and uniformity so desirable in the proceedings of the guardians. It is, moreover, of very little, if any advantage, in the saving of time.

XI.—ELECTION OF GUARDIANS.

1. NOMINATION.

28th March, 1848.

Clerk of Aston Union.—Inquired, whether he should admit the nomination of a person to be guardian or reject it on account of the nominator's name not appearing in the Rate Book, under the following circumstances. He has occupied the tenement for which he claims to vote eight or ten years, and until August last was rated to and paid every rate made for the relief of the poor. On the 9th July, 1846, the Aston Rates Act, 9 & 10 Vic. cap. 225, was passed, which by the 1st sec. enacts, that the owner of every tenement which may be assessed at any sum not exceeding the sum of £7, shall be assessed and pay the rates instead of the actual occupier thereof. On the 19th August, 1847, a poor-rate was granted which for the first time omitted the names of all occupiers of tenements under £7. The name of the present claimant was omitted, and the column for the occupier left blank, because his occupancy was only assessed at £6. 4*s*. The owner thereof compounded for the rate and paid the full amount of the composition to which he was liable, and there appears to be no arrears due from the tenement. Since this payment the occupier (the present claimant) has demanded from one of the overseers, and also from the collector of rates, in whose custody the Book was, to have his name inserted in the rate, but he has not paid or tendered any money on account of the rate, (the composition for which was previously paid by the owner.) It is contended that the overseers have improperly omitted his name from the Rate Book, and that in compliance with the general law it was their duty, in addition to inserting the landlord's name in the owner's column, also to insert the name of the occupier in the column appointed for that purpose, and not to have left it blank. It is further contended that the present claimant's name should have been inserted in the Rate Book when he demanded it as above stated. But the main point is the construction he puts upon the proviso to the 1st sec. of the said Act, in conjunction with the wording of the 4th sec., which declares the amount the owner is liable to pay where there is a composition. The 1st sec. provides that notwithstanding the rating of, or payment by any such owner under this Act, such rating or payment by the owner shall not affect or prejudice the right of any occupier to the enjoyment of any parochial franchise or privilege to which he might be or become entitled, in case such owner and occupier, or either of them, shall have paid the full amount payable in respect of the property for which such occupier claims to vote. It is urged that this proviso was inserted for the purpose of securing the occupier's former parochial privileges, in cases where the owner pays the full amount to which he is liable. And as the 4th sec. of the act declares that where there is a composition, the owner shall only be liable to pay the amount of such composition, which shall be entered in the Rate Book, and such owner rated accordingly. It is contended that, in the case in question, the owner has "paid the full amount payable in respect of the property for which such occupier claims to vote," and that, by reason thereof, the occupier is entitled to his vote, the proviso stating he shall be so entitled if the full amount payable is paid by either of them. It is further urged, that it would be unjust to deprive the occupier of his vote, seeing that the 6th sec. enacts that it shall be lawful for the owner to recover from the occupier any sum which he may have paid in respect of such premises for any rate or composition. The supporter of the above construction contends that the proviso to the first section of the act cannot mean anything else, and in proof that the Legislature does sanction votes of occupiers being taken where owners are rated and pay the rate, refers to the Wolverhampton Rates Act, 10 & 11 Vic., passed 8th June, 1847, which at sec. 4 enacts as follows: "And be it enacted that, notwithstanding the rating of or payment by any such owner under this Act, the occupier shall have the same right of voting in respect of all parochial matters as he would have had in case he had been rated and paid the rates in respect of the tenement."

Ans.—The question turns upon the right of the nominator, under the circumstances which you describe, to vote at the election of guardians. Under the 40th sec. of the 4 & 5 Wm. 4, c. 76, no person is entitled to vote as a rate-payer unless he has been rated to the relief of the poor for the whole year preceding, and has paid all the poor-rates (see 7 & 8 Vic. c. 101, sec. 16) due from him, except those made within six months. It appears from your statement, that the nominator in question was not rated to the poor-rate made in the parish of Ashton, on the 19th August last, and so far it is clear that he does not come within the terms of the enactment above-mentioned. With regard to the claim to vote which, notwithstanding this omission, he urges, under the provisions of the Local Act, 9 & 10 Vic. c. 225, the Board do not think that such claim can be sustained. In the first place, it appears to them that the overseers acted rightly in not rating the nominator, (though possibly his name should, nevertheless, have been entered in the proper column of the Rate Book,) inasmuch as the 1st sec. of the Local Act expressly directs that in such cases the owner shall be rated "instead of the actual occupier," and not in addition to or in conjunction with him. And the disqualification resulting from this omission does not seem to the Board to be removed by the proviso to that section, which merely preserves to the occupier the franchise which he might be or become entitled to, on the actual payment of the rate, either by himself or by the owner. But he does not become entitled to vote at the election of guardians on the mere payment of the rate; it is necessary, under the 4 & 5 Wm. 4, c. 76, that he should also be rated. It may be remarked that the language of the 4th sec. of the Wolverhampton Local Act, (which you cite,) differs materially from that of the proviso above referred to, with respect to this point. The principal difficulty in the case appears to arise upon the 13th sec. of the Aston Local Act, under which the occupier may claim to be rated; but the Board are disposed to consider that such claim can only be made where the rate has not been paid by the owner. The section provides that the occupier, on making the claim, shall be rated "instead of the owner," and that then, "upon payment or tender by him of such rate," he shall be entitled to the franchise: where the owner has already paid the rate, it is difficult to see how the occupier can be rated in his stead. It is stated in your letter that the nominator did not claim under this section until after the owner had paid the rate, nor did he make or tender any payment on account of such rate. With regard to the argument drawn from the 6th sec. of the Act, the Board may remark that that section seems to them to refer exclusively to the rights of the owner and occupier in their relations towards one another, and not in any way to overcome the difficulties already pointed out. On the whole, therefore, the Board, as at present advised, are of opinion that the nominator is not entitled to vote or nominate at the present election of guardians for the parish of Aston.

---

2. REFUSAL TO SERVE—NOMINATION BY OWNER —BY RATE-PAYER—ELIGIBILITY OF CHAPLAIN FOR THE OFFICE OF GUARDIAN.

31st March, 1848.

Clerk of Bradford (*York*) *Union.*—Inquired, 1st, Whether the following can be considered a sufficient refusal to serve the office of guardian to warrant him in excluding the party's name from the list of persons nominated,—

Bradford, March 25th, 1848.

SIR,—I request you to withdraw my name from the list of nominated guardians for Bradford.

By so doing you will oblige,

H—— R——.

To J. R. Wagstaff, Esq., Clerk.

2nd, Whether an owner of property as such can nominate guardians when (not having complied with the provisions of the 7 & 8 Vic. cap. 101) he is not entitled to vote in that capacity; and if not, 3rd, Whether a nomination by an owner of property will under such circumstances be valid, provided he was qualified to nominate as a rate-payer, though not so describing himself in the nomination paper. 4th, Whether a rate-payer who has not paid a rate made and signed by the overseers on the first of October last, and allowed by the magistrates on the same day, is entitled to nominate guardians, seeing that if he does not pay it prior to the tenth of April he will not be entitled to vote at the coming election; and 5th, Whether the chaplain of the Bradford Workhouse be disqualified for serving the office of guardian, he having had a nominal salary of £1 per annum fixed for his services.

Ans.—1st, The Board think that the notice in question may be regarded by you as a sufficient refusal on the part of the writer to serve the office of guardian, though it is not precisely in the terms of the Act. 2nd, A person cannot lawfully nominate as owner, if at the time of his purporting to perform that act he is not entitled to vote as owner. 3rd, If a nominator profess to nominate as owner, not being at the time entitled to do so, the defect will not be cured by his being entitled to vote as a rate-payer, as the latter is not the character in which he assumes to act. 4th, The Board consider that the non-payment of the rate in question would not disqualify a rate-payer from nominating. The effect upon his voting is another question, which possibly may never arise, as there may be no contest; or, if there be, he may pay the rate in the interval. But the six months not having expired at the time of the nomination, he is not then disqualified by the non-payment. 5th, The Board think the chaplain is clearly disqualified for the office of guardian under the 14th sec. of the 5 & 6 Vic. cap. 57.

3. REFUSAL TO SERVE.

14th April, 1848.

Clerk of Melton Mowbray Union.—The election of guardians for this union being virtually ended, in consequence of there being no contest in any parish, although the notices to the guardians elected are not yet delivered—inquired whether a refusal to serve the office, received on the 7th April, was too late.

Ans.—As there was no contest for any parish in the union, the election was concluded on the 27th of March, and consequently a refusal to serve, delivered on the 7th of April, came too late. The guardian must therefore serve the office, or resign it under the 11th sec. of the 5 & 6 Vic. c. 57. In case he wishes to resign the office it will be necessary that his resignation should be sent to the Poor Law Board for their acceptance under the provision cited.

4. RETURN OF CLERK—ELECTION OF CHAIRMAN AND VICE-CHAIRMAN.

27th March, 1848.

Clerk of Bath Union—Inquired, 1st, Whether, if upon the receipt of the nomination papers for a particular parish, he finds that no more persons are nominated than the requisite number, he is immediately, under Article 22 of the General Consolidation Order, to certify to them the fact of their election; and 2ndly, Whether, if no contest should arise in any parish in the union, the guardians can proceed forthwith to elect a chairman and vice-chairman; or, are they required, under the General Order, to wait until the first meeting after the 15th day of April; and if so, will the chairman and vice-chairman of the present year continue in office until their successors are appointed.

Ans.—Where it shall appear after the last day for nominating guardians (26th March) has past, that the number of persons duly nominated in any case does not exceed the number of guardians to be elected for the parish, it will be necessary under Article 23 of the Consolidated Order, that you should notify to such persons the fact of their election according to the form "D." It will not be necessary, however, that you should at that time make the certificate of the fact of election (Form E;) this may be deferred until the elections throughout the union, if any be pending, have been brought to a conclusion. With respect to the second inquiry, the Board think that the election of chairman and vice-chairman for the ensuing year cannot take place until the first meeting of guardians after the 15th April, according to Article 29 of the Order. The Board think, that the chairman and vice-chairman elected for the current year might continue to act in those capacities respectively, until the appointment of successors after the 15th of April next, provided their office of guardians has not been previously put an end to or determined. Their power to act as chairman and vice-chairman manifestly could not continue longer than the office in right or in virtue of which they were elected chairman and vice-chairman.

XII.—EMIGRATION.—FAMILY OF CONVICT.

22*nd Jan.*, 1848.

Clerk of Salisbury united Parishes.—An application has been made to the churchwardens and overseers of the united parishes of this city, by a pauper belonging to them, to be sent out to her husband, a convict in Van Diemen's Land, whose term of transportation expires in April next, and who will then proceed to Port Adelaide, where he intends to remain, provided he can have his family, which consists of three boys, of the ages of 16, 14, and 9, sent to him there. Requested the Board's advice on the subject.

Ans.—The Board have communicated with the Colonial Land Emigration Commissioners with reference to this case, who have acquainted them that the wife and children of a convict under the circumstances described could not be allowed a free passage, unless the convict should be recommended by the governor of the colony, both as deserving of the indulgence, and as capable of providing for the maintenance of his family.

XIII.—LAND.—HIRING OF, BY OVERSEERS, TO BE LET IN ALLOTMENTS.

24*th Jan.*, 1848.

Clerk to Malton Union.—Transmitted a resolution passed by the select vestry of the parish of Norton, in the Malton Union, whereby the overseers requested the sanction of the Poor Law Board to their renting eight acres of land, for the purpose of being let to labourers belonging to the parish, in small allotments of half a rood or more, according to the number of the family.

Ans.—The act 5 & 6 Wm. 4, cap. 69, sec. 4, has provided that all the powers given by the statutes (59 Geo. 3, cap. 12; 1 & 2 Wm. 4, cap. 42; 1 & 2 Wm. 4, cap. 59; and 2 & 3 Wm. 4, cap. 42) which authorize the taking of land or ground for allotments to the poor in parishes, are to be exercised under the Order, and subject to the rules of the Poor Law Commissioners, by the guardians of the poor of the union, and not by the overseers. The overseers of Norton cannot, therefore, hire the land in question for the purpose proposed. The Board would further observe, that the conditions imposed by the statutes mentioned upon these proceedings are such, that the Poor Law Commissioners have not been able to frame any Regulations upon the subject; and consequently have not advised boards of guardians to act upon the powers conferred upon them by the statute 5 & 6 Wm. 4, cap. 69.

XIV.—LUNATIC.

1. COST OF MAINTAINING THE WIFE OF AN ABLE-BODIED MAN, RECEIVING WAGES, IN A LUNATIC ASYLUM.

18*th Jan.*, 1848.

Clerk of Plympton St. Mary Union.—A woman who lately came to inhabit in one of the parishes of the union is a decided idiot, and the medical officer states that she must he removed to an asylum. Her husband also lives in the same parish in service, where he receives twenty guineas a year wages, with board and lodging. The man proposes to contribute his surplus wages towards his wife's support, but the whole amount is inadequate to defray the cost of keeping her in an asylum. Inquired whether the guardians can support the woman in the county lunatic asylum, receiving from the husband what his means may allow towards her support, and then procure an order of maintenance for the remainder of the cost on the parish to which she may belong, and in default of that not being ascertained, upon the county.

Ans.—It appears to be admitted that the husband's means are not equal to the burden of defraying the cost of his wife's maintenance in an asylum. But it also appears that at present the woman is not chargeable to any parish in the union. If she were, and it seems that regard being had to the condition of the husband and her state of mind, she must soon become so, the Board consider that proceedings should be taken by the relieving officer under sec. 48 of 8th and 9th Vic. c. 126, to procure an order for the woman's admission into an asylum. So if she be not chargeable, the case may be dealt with in a similar manner under sec. 49, which applies to insane persons not chargeable who are at large, and not properly taken care of by their relatives or friends. Whichever of these courses be taken, the parish from which the insane person is sent will be liable in the first instance for the cost of the maintenance, (secs. 49 & 57.) But if the parish of the settlement can be discovered, then an order may be made by justices under sec. 62, for the reimbursement of the parish first charged with the lunatic's maintenance. If the husband be able and willing to contribute towards lessening the cost to the parish liable for the maintenance, there is no objection to such a proceeding, and any money which may be obtained from him must be applied in reduction of the cost.

---

2. LUNATIC POSSESSED OF PROPERTY.

21*st Feb.*, 1848.

Clerk of Sculcoates Union.—A woman who is a lunatic has been brought into the workhouse of this union, upon whose person a sum of 9*l.* was found by the master. Inquired whether the guardians will be entitled to take possession of this money, and apply it to the payment of the cost of the pauper's maintenance.

Ans.—The Board are of opinion, that as the pauper is a lunatic, the workhouse master would be justified in taking charge of the money for her until proceedings can be taken, under the provisions of the 7th & 8th Vic. c. 101, sec. 27, by the overseers of the parish to which the pauper is chargeable, for an order of justices to enable the overseers to appropriate the money to the purpose of reimbursing the parish to the extent of the cost incurred by it in the care and maintenance of the pauper.

---

3. LUNATIC CONFINED IN A PRIVATE ASYLUM, BUT WHOSE FRIENDS ARE UNABLE TO PAY FOR HIS MAINTENANCE.

14*th March*, 1848.

Clerk of Brentford Union.—Mr. F. M———, on the 8th November, 1847, was admitted as a patient into a private lunatic asylum, on the application of his mother, and with the usual medical certificate, and he still remains there a dangerous lunatic. One of the authorities of the asylum has attended the board of guardians, and stated that he had applied to the lunatic's mother for the payment of his maintenance, &c., but had since ascertained that she was little better than a pauper, and could not pay the amount, and he therefore requested that the guardians would transfer him from their asylum to the county lunatic asylum at Hanwell, there to be placed to the account of the parish of I———, that being the parish in which the asylum is situate. If the guardians declined to adopt that course, it was stated that they would open the gates of the asylum and set the lunatic at large. Inquired 1st, Whether the authorities of a private lunatic asylum can discharge a dangerous lunatic without the consent of the commissioners in lunacy, 8 & 9 Vic. cap. 100, sec. 75. 2nd, Whether Mr. F. M——— can be deemed a pauper, and if so, is the parish of I——— bound to take charge of him. 3rd, If the authorities at the asylum should set Mr. F. M——— at large, what course should be adopted with regard to him, as from the nature of the lunacy and propensities of the lunatic, it is feared that he would commit some outrage.

Ans.—The Board, after communicating with the commissioners in lunacy, stated that notwithstanding the provision in the 8th & 9th Vic. c. 100, sec. 75, which imposes a restraint in certain cases upon the discharge of dangerous lunatics from a licensed house, the proprietor of such house is not legally prevented from discharging a lunatic, though he be dangerous, if the parties who placed him in the asylum, and agreed to pay for his support, do not fulfil such agreement. Upon this construction of the statute, as the proprietors of ——— lunatic asylum, (not being bound by any legal consideration to retain in their establishment Mr. F. M———, for whose maintenance they appear unable to obtain any remuneration,) have expressed their intention of setting him at large, notwithstanding that he is a dangerous lunatic, it becomes urgently necessary that some other arrangement should be made for his future care and safe custody. The statement appears to show that Mr. M——— is at present only living in the ——— asylum on sufferance, and that his condition is practically that of a pauper, though at the present moment he is not actually chargeable to any parish. It seems, therefore, a proper case for the interference of the authorities of the Brentford Union, in which the ——— asylum is situated. If the lunatic were discharged from the asylum, relief might be at once applied for on his behalf, in I——— parish, in which ——— asylum is situate. This application, if granted, would render him chargeable to the parish. The case could then be dealt with under sec. 48 of 8 & 9 Vic. c. 126, which applies to lunatics who are chargeable. Then, if the justices made an order for the confinement of the lunatic, the cost of the maintenance would primarily fall upon the parish of I———, under sec. 57, but that parish can afterwards take measures which will secure its reimbursement by procuring an order for that purpose on the parish of the settlement, or on the county if the settlement cannot be ascertained. But the case might also be dealt with differently. If the proprietors were to place Mr. M—— outside the doors of their establishment, the relieving officer, under sec. 49 of the statute above cited, might (treating him as a lunatic found wandering) take him before a justice to be dealt with as that sec. requires, and he might be sent to the county asylum. If this course be taken, however, it should be by previous arrangement with the guardians and their officers, so that until the relieving officer takes charge of him, he should be under the care of a responsible person or keeper. In this way Mr. F. M——— would be received either as a county patient at once, so that the parish of I———— would not incur any special liability under the 57th sec.; or, if as a parochial patient, with the same means of redress as above.

XV.—MEDICAL OFFICER.—PERSONAL DISCHARGE OF DUTIES.

4*th April*, 1848.

The Rev. ——— *Rochford Union.*—1st, Inquired in reference to the General Consolidated Order, whether Articles 198 and 199 of that Order, which relate to the personal discharge of duties by officers, are to be taken in connection with Art. 200. 2nd, A medical officer having appointed a substitute, inquired whether the medical officer will be allowed to send his apprentice or assistant to attend the sick poor, or to attend a woman in labour.

Ans.—Art. 200 of the General Consolidated Order is to be taken in connection with Art. 199; but the latter Art. certainly requires the medical officer to attend personally, as far as may be practicable, to the cases of the sick paupers whom he may be directed to visit. The Board are not prepared to say that in ordinary cases the medical officer may not employ, under his own superintendence, his assistant or apprentice to visit the sick paupers under his care; but they must distinctly point out that his doing so would not in any degree relieve him from any portion of the responsibility attaching to the discharge of the duties of his office. In the particular class of cases to which you advert, viz., of women in childbirth, the Board think it incumbent on the medical officer to be extremely cautious; and they would remark that in such cases, if he cannot attend himself, he should send his appointed substitute, rather than his assistant or apprentice.

XVI.—PARENTS.—LIABILITY TO MAINTAIN CHILDREN ABOVE THE AGE OF SIXTEEN.

13*th March*, 1848.

Clerk of Kingsclere Union.—Set forth several cases, in which the fathers of children above sixteen years of age had refused to maintain them, on the ground that the children having attained that age, they, the fathers, were not liable to maintain them.

Ans.—The 56th sec. of the 4 & 5 Wm. 4, c. 76, merely provides that relief given to children under sixteen years of age shall be considered as given to their parents; but it does not otherwise affect, in any way, the liabilities of parents in respect of their children's support. Indeed, the proviso to that section expressly guards against its being construed to interfere with the enactments of the 43 Eliz. c. 2, in this behalf. If, therefore, a parent neglects to maintain any of his children, who may be above the age of sixteen years, and may be unable to work, the provisions of the 43rd Eliz. c. 2, may be resorted to, supposing the parent to be of sufficient ability to maintain such child. Moreover, in such a case proceedings might be taken against the parent, under the 3rd sec. of the Vagrant Act, (5 Geo. 4, c. 83,) if the child, in consequence of the parents' neglect, becomes chargeable to the parish, assuming that such child is a part of the parents' family at the time, and be one whom such parent is, by the statute of Elizabeth, bound to maintain. If it be found, (as your letter appears to indicate,) that it is becoming a practice in the Kingsclere union for parents, able and liable to maintain their children, to take advantage of the exemption which they may erroneously suppose the 56th sec. of the 4th & 5th Wm. 4, c. 76, confers upon them, it is a question for the grave consideration of the guardians, whether it would not be advisable to take proceedings, either under the 43rd Eliz. c. 2, or under the 5 Geo. 4, c. 83, in some selected case or cases, with the view of making an example, and showing practically that the parent's liability for the support of his child, under the limitation already pointed out, is not limited in law to the age of sixteen years.

XVII.—PAUPERS. — REMOVAL AND RELIEF OF NON-SETTLED POOR.

11th May, 1848.

Clerk of Walsall Union.—Inquired, 1st, Whether it was the duty of the guardians to give notice to the overseers of the resident parishes, (and if so, in what form such notice should be,) that certain persons are being relieved by order of the guardians, and that such persons are not settled in such parish but removable therefrom by justice's orders. 2nd, Whether the guardians should exercise their discretion as to the desirableness of removing such persons from the parish, and if the question be decided in the affirmative, whether the guardians ought to make an order upon the overseers in writing directing them to take measures for such person's removal accordingly.

Ans.—1st, By the parochial lists made out in accordance with Art. 29 of the General Order of Accounts, the guardians of the Walsall Union will put the officers of every parish in the union in possession of the names of the paupers relieved by the guardians on account of such parish. In the meantime the guardians of any parish attending the meetings of the guardians will have full means of communicating from time to time information to the overseers of that parish of the fact of paupers having been relieved at its cost. Upon receiving such information the overseers may act as they see fit in regard to procuring orders of removal in any given case. 2nd, In respect of the power of the guardians to make order upon the overseers of any parish in the union to proceed to remove non-settled paupers resident therein, the Board are of opinion that the guardians in the present state of the law cannot make an order upon the overseers directing the removal of paupers to their settlement, which would be operative upon the overseers. The legal discretion as to applying for orders of removal appears still to rest in the overseers.

XVIII.—RELIEF.

1. DUTIES OF RELIEVING OFFICERS, GUARDIANS, ETC.

The Rev. J. E. L———.—1st, Is it the duty of the relieving officer, when a pauper receiving out-door relief is represented by a respectable inhabitant to be in a state of great destitution, neglect, and wretchedness, to visit such pauper at his own house? 2nd, Is it the duty of such officer to offer to admit such pauper into the workhouse, and if necessary to convey him there at the parish expense? 3rd, Is it his duty, if the offer of the house be declined, to give additional temporary relief, and to lay the case before the guardians at their next meeting, in order that increased relief may be given so long as necessity requires? 4th, Is the relieving officer acting right in replying to an ordinary application for relief in such terms as to deter the parties from applying to the guardians, and if such be the result of his behaviour, is he on that account liable to be censured by the guardians, and ought he so to be? 5th, Do the Commissioners require a book to be kept, and an annual or other return to be made to them of the attendance of guardians in each union at the meetings of the board, and have they any means of knowing the number who attend, or of controling the selection of persons unlikely to be regular? 6th, If the pauper has no friends, is it the duty of the relieving officer to see that he be kept clean at the parish expense? 7th, Is it the duty of the board of guardians to appoint a chaplain, and can they be compelled by the Commissioners to appoint one? 8th, Can a minister of religion, visiting the poor in the workhouse, require to see any pauper of his persuasion, for the purpose of spiritual advice and consolation, when practicable alone, and if not alone without the attendance of the master or matron?

Ans.—1st, It is undoubtedly the duty of a relieving officer, when a poor person residing within his district, (whether in the receipt of relief or not,) is represented to him to be in a state of great destitution, to visit such person at his own house, and to administer such relief upon his own responsibility, as the case may appear to him to require, either by giving an order for the workhouse or relief in kind, (but not in money,) and if necessary by providing means for the conveyance of the poor person to the workhouse. 2nd, Your second inquiry is answered by the reply to your first. 3rd, If the offer of the workhouse be declined, it will then be the duty of the relieving officer to relieve the destitute person in kind, until the next meeting of the board of guardians; when he will be required to report the case to the guardians, and take their directions upon it. 4th, If in any case it should be proved to the satisfaction of the Commissioners, that a relieving officer replied to an application from a destitute person for relief in such terms as to deter the applicant from applying to the board of guardians, the Commissioners would certainly feel themselves bound to take serious notice of the offence, according to the circumstances of the case. When an application for relief is made to a relieving officer, it is his duty to enter it in his application and report book, together with the particulars of the case; and the case at the next meeting of the guardians is then considered along with the others; and whatever lawful directions the guardians may then give, the relieving officer is bound to act upon. 5th, The minute book of the guardians will show the individual guardians present at each meeting of the board, but the Commissioners do not require any return to be made to them of the attendance of the guardians at each meeting, nor have the Commissioners any power to control the election of persons as guardians whose attendances are likely to be irregular. It is for the ratepayers themselves to elect persons in whom they have confidence to act as guardians, according to the provisions of the statutes and the Commissioners' regulations in that behalf; and as regards the attendance of the resident justices, who are constituted ex-officio guardians by the Poor Law Amendment Act, the Commissioners have no authority to interfere. 6th, It is not in general the duty of a relieving officer to see to the personal cleanliness of a pauper, but if a pauper has no friends, and if he be living in a state of filth, the relieving officer in that case should report the matter to the board of guardians, who would probably give an order for the removal of the pauper to the workhouse. If that cannot be done, and if he be in a helpless state, and incapable of attending to his personal cleanliness, they might direct the relieving officer to hire a person to attend upon him, and to keep him clean. 7th, The Commissioners are desirous that every workhouse should have a paid chaplain appointed by the board of guardians of the union, and by Article 60 of the General Workhouse Rules the guardians are authorized to appoint a chaplain among other officers. 9th, When a minister of religion is called upon to visit any poor person of his own persuasion in a workhouse, for the purpose of spiritual consolation, the Commissioners think that every facility should be afforded for permitting the interview between the parties to take place in a room by themselves. It may not, however, be practicable to allow this in all cases; but where the interview takes place in the presence of third parties, such third parties should, if possible, keep at a sufficient distance, so as not to permit of their overhearing what passes between the minister and the pauper, to whom he is administering spiritual advice and consolation.

2. DEFINITION OF THE TERM "ABLE-BODIED."

17th April, 1848.

Clerk of Stow-on-the-Wold Union.—Inquired the definition of the term "able-bodied persons, male or female," as used in the Order prohibiting out-door relief. The guardians consider that females unable to earn 6*d*. per day at field-work are not to be classed with this description of persons; as also young females just emancipated. It is, therefore, not unusual for the guardians, in the case of the former, to give occasionally a pair of shoes when applied for, to enable the party to labour in the fields, as they consider that she is not able out of such earnings to procure them for herself. In the latter case, when young females are just leaving home for service, at very low wages, and the parents are too poor to assist them, the guardians acting on this view of the subject sometimes afford assistance by giving clothing to the amount of from 7*s*. to 15*s*., in order to enable them to enter upon their situation. Inquired also, whether poor persons who have frequent ailments, who are ruptured, and are generally of weak constitution, but yet receive the usual amount of wages given to able-bodied labourers, and persons who are not of weak constitution, but who from their inaptitude to labour are employed at wages below the average amount given to able-bodied men, are to be regarded as able-bodied, within the meaning of the Prohibitory Order.

Ans.—With respect to the cases first mentioned in your letter, namely, females unable to earn 6*d*. a day at field-work, and young females just emancipated, the Board have to state that they see nothing to take these cases out of the description of "able-bodied," unless the parties are sick, have met with an accident, or are labouring under bodily or mental infirmity. If any such persons require relief, it must be given to them subject to the regulations of the Order prohibiting out-door relief to able-bodied paupers; but the Board would be prepared to consider the cases of any females of the above description to whom the guardians may think it necessary to give relief in clothing, on the particulars of each case being reported to the Board under Article 6 of that Order. The Board think that the second class of cases mentioned in your letter, namely, poor persons who have frequent ailments, who are ruptured, and are generally of weak constitutions, while they may be in the receipt of full wages, must be dealt with as able-bodied persons, as relief is not given by the statute of Elizabeth to such as have an ordinary and daily trade of life to get their living by. The last class of cases alluded to, namely, persons who are not of weak constitution, but who from their inaptitude to labour are employed at wages below the average amount given to able-bodied men, the Board think cannot be viewed in any other light than as able-bodied persons, and relief to them must, therefore, be given subject to the restrictions of the Prohibitory Order.

3. RELIEF TO A WIDOW WHO HAS AN ILLEGITIMATE CHILD.

6*th Jan.*, 1848.

Clerk of Bingham Union.—A widow, with two children dependent upon her, one aged fourteen, legitimate, and another aged three, illegitimate, born since the commencement of her widowhood, has applied to the guardians for out-relief, on account of sickness of the eldest child. Several of the guardians are of opinion that out-relief could be granted in this case, as being within the Exception 2, of Article 1 in the Prohibitory Order, of December, 1844, it being a case of sickness affecting the widow's family. Others of the guardians, thinking that her being a widow, and having an illegitimate child born since her widowhood, precludes her from receiving relief, except in the workhouse.

Ans.—The Poor Law Board are of opinion that the case of the widow in question falls within the second exception to Article 1 of the general Prohibitory Order. The fact of its not being within the 5th exception does not affect the case. It is of course in the discretion of the guardians to grant relief in the case, either in or out of the workhouse, as they may see fit.

4. RELIEF TO AN ILLEGITIMATE CHILD.

23*rd Feb.*, 1848.

Chairman of Llanelly Union.—By the 7 & 8 Vic. c. 101, sec. 6, every woman neglecting to maintain her bastard child, being able wholly or in part so to do, whereby such child becomes chargeable to any parish or union, shall be punished as an idle and disorderly person. A woman was brought before him by a relieving officer charged with this offence. She is in service, and willing as far as she is able to contribute towards the support of her child. He had decided that she was not liable under the statute, and refused to convict. The relieving officer is at a loss to know how he should act in regard to the maintenance of the child, there being no order of filiation. Requested instructions on the subject.

Ans. — It will devolve upon the guardians of the union and their officers to give them such relief as may be necessary, having due regard to the regulations in force in the union. As regards the nature of the relief, the Board apprehend that the guardians are not restrained from giving out-door relief, if that should appear to them, under the circumstances, to be the best mode of dealing with the case. The relief, as the Board understand, in the present instance is applied for on behalf of the child solely, the child not being resident with the mother. This fact takes the case out of the scope of Art. 1 of the Prohibitory Order, which, if the mother applied for relief on account of her child, such child being resident with her, would require that both mother and child be relieved in the union workhouse. It is of course open to the guardians to admit the child into the workhouse if that course seems to them upon the whole to be desirable. But as relief to the child is held by law to be relief to the mother, who is liable for its maintenance, the Board would direct your attention to the Art. 7 of the Prohibitory Order, so that with all the details of the case before the guardians they may judge how far that Article is available for the purpose.

5. RELIEF TO AN ABLE-BODIED WOMAN.—PROCEEDINGS UNDER VAGRANT ACT.

14*th March*, 1848.

The Rev. E. R., Launceston Union.—J. C., a widow, with five children, maintained by the parish of R——, in the Launceston Union, was, in the year 1845, delivered of a bastard child. Her three eldest children were placed in farm houses in the parish, and she, with the bastard and the two youngest legitimate children, were received into the union workhouse, where they have remained up to the present time at the charge of the parish of R——. The guardians of the parish have several times questioned the woman to ascertain if she would return to service in the parish, which she refuses to do. In consequence of these refusals, the parishioners at the vestry meeting determined to take some steps to compel the woman, who is able-bodied, to contribute towards the maintenance of herself and family. Accordingly, a respectable farmer of the parish, a married man with a family, with whom two of this woman's children have been living for several years, offered to take her as a servant, and to maintain her and her bastard child for her services. A place was also provided for the elder of her two legitimate children, now in the house, about eight years of age, in another farmhouse in the parish; and for the youngest, now about six years of age, a situation was provided, where due care would be taken of it, and the child sent daily to school. These places were selected that each of the children might be within twenty minutes' walk of the situation offered to the mother. The woman has refused these offers, but has applied to the guardians for out-door relief. To this the parish has great objection. It is considered that the safest plan to prevent a repetition of her former conduct is to place her in a respectable house, and under the supervision of a mistress. The guardians are of opinion that it is competent to the woman to refuse to leave the house, and they decline to interfere unless a sum of money as wages is offered to her. The parish contends that the guardians have no authority to dictate terms, and that any further remuneration than maintenance for herself and child must depend upon her future conduct. The woman and her three children are still in the workhouse. The opinion of the Commissioners is requested. 1st, Whether it be competent to an able-bodied pauper to refuse labour offered as a means to maintain, wholly or in part, herself and family, and to continue chargeable to a parish, unless such terms as she shall dictate be agreed to, and does she not by such refusal come within the operation of the 5th Geo. 4, c. 83, sec. 3. 2nd, Whether it be competent in a board of guardians, when labour has been offered by a parish as a means to remove the pauper and family from all chargeability on the union funds, to retain such pauper and family in the union-house at the charge of the parish.

Ans.—1st, If work be offered to an able-bodied widow which will enable her to maintain herself and her family, wholly or in part, and she refuses to maintain them, she is liable to be brought before the justices as an idle and disorderly person, under the 5th Geo. 4, c. 83. But the Board cannot undertake to say whether the justices would deem the offer of work, without wages, to create such an ability as to bring the woman within the statute referred to. 2nd, If the party be destitute, no matter from what cause, it is incumbent upon the guardians of the union to provide her with relief; and they can certainly insist upon her being relieved in the workhouse. Indeed, in the present instance, so long as the guardians of the Launceston Union are satisfied that the pauper requires relief, they are bound to give it to her in the workhouse, under the provisions of the General Prohibitory Order; and, unless they can lawfully refuse relief to her and her children altogether, they must retain them in the workhouse. The Board, however, desire to observe, that in that case it would be incumbent upon the guardians to keep the pauper in constant work while she remained an inmate, so that she may have an inducement to seek employment out of the workhouse.

18*th April,* 1848.

The Rev. E. R———.—It would appear that, *primâ facie,* J. C—— was within the operation of the statute 5th Geo. 4, c. 83. The maintenance of her child, which is offered to this woman, and which cannot be estimated at a less amount than five pounds a year, must be reckoned as wages. The labour market is open, and she is at liberty to make a better bargain if she can. The simple question is, can she, without exposing herself to the operation of the statute referred to, refuse this offer, and throw herself and family wholly on the parish funds. It is quite clear that as long as J. C—— is destitute she is under the direction and management of the guardians. But can she legally be said to be destitute when work is offered to her, (she being able-bodied,) and maintenance for her work. If not, can the guardians "lawfully" continue to treat this woman as a pauper within the protection of the Poor Law, or dictate the terms on which she is to be permitted to leave the workhouse.

Ans.—The Board think that on farther reference to their letter of the 14th you will perceive that they by no means intimate their decided opinion that J. C—— has committed any offence against the Vagrant Act. They entertain a doubt whether a party has the means of maintaining herself and her family by her work within the meaning of that statute, when in consideration of her own labour, without wages, she is relieved from the maintenance of her children. It is true that in this case a maintenance is offered to the woman for herself, but it is coupled with the condition of her leaving her children, one of whom, though illegitimate, is under the age of nurture. In regard to your second inquiry, namely, whether the guardians can legally relieve this family when service under the circumstances stated has been offered, the Board consider that if the family be actually destitute, an express obligation lies upon the guardians to relieve them. Destitution is a fact to be alone considered with reference to relief. The guardians cannot deliberate upon the cause of the destitution, or whether it may be avoided by the adoption of any particular line of conduct, if they are satisfied that the applicant is actually destitute. If the destitution be the consequence of any offence which is punishable, steps may be taken at the instance of the guardians to procure the proper punishment, when the urgent and immediate distress has been relieved. Cases continually occur where the refusal to accept work which has been offered affords to the guardians strong evidence to negative the fact of destitution, and in such cases they may refuse to continue the relief. In such cases the guardians have only to take care that they do not draw a wrong conclusion, and so produce consequences of a very serious character, either to the party against whom they propose to act or to some of the family. It follows from these observations, that as the law has vested the relief of the poor in the guardians, they are not bound in any particular case to refuse relief to a pauper who declines to avail himself of an offer made to him, which is the result of any arrangement in the parish to which he is chargeable. Being responsible for the relief of the destitute poor, the guardians cannot be controlled by any such arrangement. At the same time, it is equally incumbent upon the guardians to give due and ready attention to any representations made on behalf of the parish, which would show that in consequence of proper and reasonable offers of work the pauper need not be destitute. In any such cases they will give such directions as to amount and continuance of relief as may appear to them to be proper, and will direct their officers to watch the conduct and proceedings of the party so long as the relief continues, taking care to apply such tests of destitution as the law affords them.

---

6. RELIEF TO ABLE-BODIED PAUPERS.

11*th May*, 1848.

Clerk of ——— *Union.*—Requested the sanction of the Poor Law Board to the guardians departing from the Prohibitory Order by giving outdoor relief in bread for a period of two months to mechanics (with large families) out of work—the scarcity of work being only temporary.

Ans.—In the opinion of the Board, relief in the workhouse ought to be offered to able-bodied men requiring relief, so long as the workhouse is not inconveniently crowded; and when there is no longer suitable accommodation for that class in the workhouse, the out-door labour test ought to be resorted to in all cases in which it is applicable. The Board think that the workmen generally would be rather injured than benefited, if men who are in distress from being employed but one or two days in the week, were to have their earnings eked out by bread at the expense of the rate-payers; on the other hand, the surplus of labour would be somewhat diminished by the application of the workhouse test, and the out-door labour test. The Board cannot, therefore, consent to dispense generally with the provisions of the Prohibitory Order in the ——— Union, but they will be prepared to consider any special cases that may be reported to them by the guardians under Art. 6 of the Prohibitory Order. At the same time, the Board think it right to state that they cannot hold out any expectation that they will be able to sanction out-door relief in any case without work being required in return, unless some very special reasons for their doing so are put forth.

---

7. RELIEF TO A WAYFARER.—POWER OF AN INDIVIDUAL GUARDIAN.—DUTIES OF A RELIEVING OFFICER.

12*th May*, 1848.

A Guardian of ——— *Union.*—On Wednesday afternoon last, a young woman of about twenty years of age called on him, and informed him that having walked that day a distance of twenty-two miles on her way home, she had applied to the relieving officer for an order for the workhouse for a night's lodging, and that he had refused to grant her request. He had satisfied himself that the woman was destitute, had no connections in the town, and was a proper object for the shelter and protection which the workhouse is intended to afford to poor casual wayfarers; and he, therefore, addressed a note to the relieving officer, requesting him to furnish the woman with an order for the workhouse. About nine o'clock in the evening she again came to him, and told him that the relieving officer would not attend to the note, but had sent her away. He in consequence accompanied the woman to the workhouse, and obtained admission for her. At the next meeting of the guardians he brought the case before them, in order to take their opinion as to whether the relieving officer was justified in refusing to comply with the written recommendation which he had addressed to him. The chairman at the meeting stated that the guardians had nothing at all to do with the relieving officer in the discharge of his duties out of doors, and thus the question was disposed of without eliciting the sentiments of the guardians. 1st, Inquired whether the person in question was a proper object for admission into the workhouse for a night. 2nd, Whether the relieving officer was right in refusing to comply with his request. 3rd, Whether the chairman was right in stating that the guardians have nothing to do with the relieving officer in his duties out of doors.

Ans.—In answer to your first question, the Board must state, that the proper inquiry in a case of this kind is, whether a party applying for relief is or is not a destitute person who requires immediate relief. It is not the duty of the guardians or the overseers to provide shelter and protection for a night to any person who may think proper to apply to them for it. The officer to whom the application is made must judge from the circumstances which are brought to his knowledge respecting the individual who applies for relief, whether he be, or be not, in such a state of destitution as to require immediate relief from the officer. He is not necessarily bound to afford the shelter and protection of the workhouse to every poor casual wayfarer; though if the applicant be really destitute and require a lodging, he will generally do right in giving such applicant an order for admission into the workhouse. He should in this respect treat destitute wayfarers in the same manner as other paupers, leaving the master of the workhouse to deal with the applicant according to the rules of the workhouse, affecting the class to which the wayfarer belongs. In regard to the particular case which you have brought under the notice of the Board, the circumstances which you state lead to the inference that the party was destitute and required relief; but the relieving officer might possess a knowledge of facts which led him to come to a different conclusion. If you will supply the Board with the name of the relieving officer and of the female referred to, the Board will call upon him for an explanation. With reference to your second question, the Board think that the answer depends in the first place upon the knowledge which that officer possessed, or the opinion which he formed as to the real state of the applicant. If he knew, or had any strong ground for believing, that the woman was not really destitute, the Board are not able to say that he was wrong in refusing to comply with your request. In the second place, the answer depends upon the nature and form of your note to the relieving officer. If you merely communicated to the relieving officer your knowledge of the case, the result of your inquiries, and your belief as to the destitution of the party, the Board think that the relieving officer was bound to attend to the case, so as to enable him to determine whether it was a case which required his interference. His duty in this respect would have been the same, if the information, or note, had come from any other individual. But if your note assumed an authoritative tone, and was framed so as to be an order upon the relieving officer to give the relief, the Board must state that it could not be binding upon the relieving officer, inasmuch as the Poor Law Amendment Act, in sec. 38, has expressly enacted that no guardian shall act as such except as a member of the board. If, therefore, your note, although apparently a request, was intended to be an order upon the relieving officer, the Board are of opinion that the relieving officer was not legally bound to obey it, and was in this respect justified in refusing to comply with it. The third question arising out of the opinion expressed by the chairman at the board will be answered by the observations which have already been made. The Board desire to state in conclusion, that though a guardian cannot in that capacity alone, and away from the board, direct the relieving officer in discharge of his duties, or in any way interfere with him, he can nevertheless give him information or advice, and if the officer neglect it, and evil consequences ensue, the guardian may bring his conduct, and the circumstances of the case, before the guardians or the Poor Law Board, as may appear most desirable. If it shall appear that the officer acted wrongly, and wilfully neglected the information and advice properly tendered to him by one of the guardians of the union, his misconduct, whatever it may be, would be deemed more censurable and less excusable than if he had acted without the tender of any assistance.

---

8. RELIEF TO THE ILLEGITIMATE CHILD OF A SOLDIER'S WIFE.—MUTINY ACT.

22*nd May*, 1848.

Clerk of Farnham Union.—A private soldier married, since 1834, a woman having an illegitimate child, which has now become chargeable to a parish in this union. The man refuses to support the child, and refers to the 52nd section of the last Mutiny Act, 11 & 12 Vic. c. 10, which enacts that "No soldier shall be arrested by the warrant of any justice for not supporting, or for leaving chargeable to any parish, any wife or any child or children, legitimate or illegitimate." Inquired whether any means could be adopted for compelling the man to maintain the child.

Ans.—The Board are not prepared to point out any mode by which the soldier in this case could be compelled to maintain the illegitimate child of his wife, born before marriage. The provision 11 & 12 Vic. c. 11, sec. 52, to which you refer, would, the Board are disposed to consider, effectually protect the soldier from any proceeding under the Vagrant Act, for the desertion of, or neglect to maintain this child.

XIX.—RELIEVING OFFICER.

1. HIS DISCRETION IN THE ADMINISTRATION OF RELIEF.

15*th May*, 1848.

Relieving Officer, Huntingdon Union.—Inquired whether it is contrary to the rules and regulations of the Poor Law Board for a relieving officer to give relief partly in money, when the board of guardians make the order for relief discretionary.

Ans. to the Clerk.—The duty of the relieving officer in this respect is prescribed by Art. 215, No. 10, of the General Consolidated Order. He is to pay or administer the relief of all paupers within his district to the amount and in the manner in which he may have been lawfully ordered by the guardians to pay or administer the same. The Board are of opinion that it is not competent for the guardians to delegate their discretion to the relieving officer, and to allow him to give what amount of money he may think proper in any case. Such a direction would not be an ordering of relief by them. The guardians are bound to decide upon the information before them what amount of relief is likely to be necessary for the pauper before their next meeting, and to direct the relieving officer to pay so much of it in money as they may think requisite. If, in the interval, an urgent necessity for more relief should arise, the relieving officer will supply, in kind, whatever in his discretion he thinks necessary.

2. DUTY OF RELIEVING OFFICER AS TO APPLICATIONS FOR RELIEF.

29*th May*, 1848.

Chairman of the Board of Guardians, Bridgwater Union.—At the board of guardians, a question was raised with reference to the obligations of a relieving officer to bring under the consideration of the Board the application of every pauper seeking relief. It seemed to be the opinion of several guardians that if the pauper's case had been considered, and his application refused at a preceding meeting, the relieving officer was justified in exercising his own discretion, and, supposing the circumstances of the case remained unaltered, that he was not bound again to report the name of the pauper, upon his renewing his application, but on the contrary was entitled to reject it. Requested the opinion of the Poor Law Board on the subject.

Ans.—The Board consider that it is the duty of a relieving officer, under Art. 215, No. 6, of the Consolidated Order, to report every application made to him by or on behalf of a poor person for relief to the guardians, notwithstanding that they may on a previous occasion have refused relief to the party; and this though there may be no change in the circumstances of the particular case since the last application.

XX.—RELIGION.—AGE AT WHICH CHILDREN IN WORKHOUSE MAY DETERMINE WHAT PLACE OF WORSHIP THEY WILL ATTEND.

9*th March*, 1848.

Clerk of ———————.—Inquired at what age children in the workhouse, who have no parents or god-fathers surviving to prescribe their religious instructions, are to be considered by the guardians as competent to determine for themselves what place of worship they will attend in lieu of the usual services in the workhouse, or at the parish church.

Ans.—It appears to the Board to be the principle of the law and manners of this country, to assume that every one belongs to the national church, unless he expressly dissents from it, or unless the circumstances of his parentage or education lead to a presumption of dissent. In the case submitted to the Board by the guardians, none of the latter circumstances are alleged to exist; and the children must, therefore, be considered in the communion of the Church of England, until they expressly dissent from it. The law has fixed no period at which any one may do this, and the Board do not think it would be competent to them to lay down any precise limit of age. As a general rule, they are of opinion that it would be safe to treat any disposition to exercise at an early age a choice in respect of religion as a mere indication of that volatility which, if indulged, would lead to young people's having no religion at all. At the same time, if the disposition exhibits itself with steadiness and earnestness; if the guardians believe that the youth has formed convictions, however ill-grounded, and holds them with sincerity, the best plan will be to allow such youth to follow the bent of his feelings or convictions. Various circumstances in the character and conduct of the youth will have much more influence on a right decision respecting the course to be taken than the mere fact of age. The question as submitted to the Board and the guardians is one to which the Board can give no more precise answer than this very general intimation of what they deem the sound principle. But if the question be asked with reference to any particular case, they recommend that the guardians should lay a statement of the facts of that case before the inspector of the district, who will be ready to give any assistance in his power with reference to it, and if necessary will refer it to the Board for consideration.

XXI.—REMOVAL.

1. OF IRISH POOR.

24*th March*, 1848.

Assistant Overseer, Wrexham Abbot. — In consequence of the great influx of Irish paupers in this township, the overseers have caused to be removed several families by orders of justices to Liverpool, in order to be conveyed thence to Ireland. Requested to be informed whether the expenses of such removals are to be defrayed by the individual township, or out of the common fund of the union. The bills for the expenses have been laid before the board of guardians for the purpose of being discharged out of the common fund, but they refuse to take cognizance of the matter in consequence of the removals not having taken place under their direction.

Ans.—The overseers were not the proper parties to undertake the removal of the paupers referred to. Under the 2nd sec. of the 8 & 9 Vic. c. 117, the guardians alone (in the case of a parish in a union) are empowered to make application to the justices; who, after the matter complained of has been heard and examined into by them, may issue their warrant to remove the parties in question at the expense of the union. But no authority is given to the overseers of a parish to make the application, except where there may be no guardians. The Board are apprehensive that the overseers of Wrexham Abbot will themselves be liable to bear the expenses they have thus incurred, as they cannot lawfully charge the amount on the poor-rates.

5*th April*, 1848.

Assistant Overseer, Wrexham Abbot.—Referred the Board to the 10 & 11 Vic. c. 33, amending the 8 & 9 Vic. c. 117. By the former Act power seems to be given to overseers equally with guardians or relieving officers for the removal of Irish paupers. The guardians declined interfering in the removal of such paupers, whereupon the overseers who had been authorised by the vestry to do so undertook to remove them.

Ans.—The Board did not overlook the statute 10 & 11 Vic. c. 33, to which you allude. But that Act only empowers "any guardian, overseer, or relieving officer," to perform the particular act of taking the pauper to be removed before the justices, without a warrant or summons; and expressly provides, that when the pauper is so brought before the justices, they shall proceed in all respects as under the earlier Act, (8 & 9 Vic. c. 117,) which requires in the case of a parish within a union, that the complaint on which the justices are to act shall be made by the guardians of that union. The Board, therefore, do not think that the overseers are authorised to make the complaint, or that the 10 & 11 Vic. c. 33, makes any difference in this respect.

---

2. REMOVAL OF WIDOW.

25*th May*, 1848.

Clerk of Wolverhampton Union. — The idiot child of S. and C. C———, who resided at Bilston, in this union, being found to be removable to the Bridgnorth union, the child was admitted into the workhouse of that union. The parents were subsequently induced to receive back the child, with an allowance of five shillings weekly. The father soon after went into a hospital at Birmingham, and in the course of a few weeks died there, the mother and family having remained at Bilston. On the death of the father, the pay from the Bridgnorth union was stopped. Inquired, if the widow and family are, under the circumstances, irremovable for the first twelve months of the widowhood, under sec. 2 of 9 & 10 Vic. c. 66.

Ans.—It appears that the husband of the widow in question had his home in Bilston, where his wife and family were residing at the time of his death, but that he himself died in a hospital at Birmingham, where he had been previously staying for a few weeks. The question which arises upon this state of facts is not free from difficulty, and owing to the want of a clear definition of the term "residing," as employed in the 2nd sec. of the 9 & 10 Vic. c. 66, if the husband is to be considered as having been resident at Birmingham, where his death actually occurred, it is as clear that the widow, who was then at Bilston, was not residing in the parish with her husband at the time of his death, and the case therefore would not come within the enactment alluded to. But as the husband went to Birmingham, not in order to reside there permanently, but merely for the temporary purpose of staying at the hospital with a view to improving his health, as he did not intend to make the hospital his home, and as his home, in point of fact, continued in Bilston, where his wife and family remained, he may perhaps be properly considered, in law, as "residing" in Bilston at the time of his death, though that event, (owing to his temporary absence from his home under the circumstances mentioned,) happened to take place in Birmingham. If this latter view be adopted, it will follow that his wife was residing with him at the time of his decease, and that she is accordingly irremovable from Bilston under the 2nd of the Act adverted to. This is the view which the Board themselves are disposed to adopt; and they would suggest that, where there is so much doubt, it will be the better course for the parish of Bilston to abstain from endeavouring to effect the removal. It may be added, that it was doubtless the object of the legislature, in the enactment in question, to prevent a widow from being removed from her home at the moment of the loss of her husband, and that object would be defeated, if the death of her husband in a hospital, away from her home, were held to prevent the operation of the section.

3. EXPENSES OF REMOVAL.

1st May, 1846.

Clerk of Ludlow Union.—A pauper has been under suspended order of removal from Liverpool to Stoke St. Milborough, since 31st August, 1840. An application has been made by the overseers of the former to those of the latter parish for payment of 47*l.* 13*s.* 6*d.*, the amount of relief afforded to the pauper, and the cost of serving the order. The guardians are aware of the usual practice of leaving the cost of all expenses incurred under a suspended order unpaid until removal takes place, when the amount is embodied in the order, and directed by the magistrates to be paid by the overseers of the parish to which the pauper belongs to those of the removing parish. The guardians think it would be much fairer for the rate-payers, frequently changing occupancy, and to persons newly coming to reside in parishes, if it were ordered that the cost of all relief advanced under a suspended order of removal, (after a given time when appeal would be illegal,) should be paid annually, that is, before Lady Day, so that a person about to leave a parish should bear his fair proportion of the cost of relief so afforded during the time of his tenancy. In the present case the guardians will direct that the amount claimed by Liverpool, to the present time, shall be paid, if the Commissioners should not advise them that such a proceeding will be improper. In the next place, inquired who is the proper party to pay a claim made upon overseers for relief advanced under an order of removal, and also under a suspended order of removal—the overseers of a parish, or the relieving officer of the union, in which the parish is situate, the amount being firstly approved by the board of guardians.

Ans. — In the Commissioners' opinion, the guardians of the Ludlow Union cannot lawfully pay the amount claimed in the case to which you refer, so long as the pauper is living and unremoved. Nor do the Commissioners think that the overseers of Stoke St. Milborough could lawfully do so. The only authority under which the payment could be claimed, or made, is the 2nd sec. of the 35th Geo. 3, c. 101. That section enables the justices to order the churchwardens and overseers of the parish to which the pauper is directed to be removed, to pay the charges proved on oath to have been incurred by the suspension of the order, in case any removal shall take place, or in case of the pauper's death before the execution of the order. And it has been expressly held that the statute does not provide for the recovery of the charges in any other event than the death or removal of the pauper, (Reg. *v.* Chagford, 4 B. & A. 235). Unless, therefore, such death or removal takes place, there is no ground for a legal claim against the parish; and in the absence of any such ground, the officers acting on behalf of the parish would not be justified in discharging the claim out of the poor-rates. Where, however, there is a valid claim, the overseers of the parish, and not the guardians of the union, are the parties to discharge it.

XXII.—SURETIES.—DUTY OF GUARDIANS TO ENFORCE BOND GIVEN BY.

13*th Jan.*, 1848.

Clerk of Eton Union.—Inquired whether it is compulsory or optional on the part of the guardians to enforce a bond given by the sureties of an assistant overseer who is a defaulter.

Ans.—Having regard to the language of sec. 61 of 7 & 8 Vic. cap. 101, the Board are not prepared to say that the guardians cannot exercise a discretion as to putting a bond in suit against the sureties. As, however, the guardians act as trustees for the rate-payers, in cases of this kind, the Board think that the duty of the guardians would be best discharged in taking steps to protect the parish, by enforcing the security, wherever there may be reasonable grounds for concluding that the sureties are solvent.

XXIII.—VAGRANT ACT.—MOTHER NEGLECTING TO MAINTAIN HER BASTARD CHILD.

28*th Feb.*, 1848.

Clerk of Bromsgrove Union.—S. T———, a single woman, having neglected to maintain her child, aged 9, the child became and now is chargeable to the parish of Bromsgrove. The board of guardians ordered the woman to be prosecuted for such neglect; the justice, however, before whom the case was heard, dismissed the charge on the ground that the earnings, 4*s.* 6*d.* a-week, were not more than sufficient for her own support. The guardians fear that many single women with bastard children resident in the union may neglect or desert their children, if they learn that they may do so with impunity, and, therefore, request the advice of the Poor Law Board as to how they should act in this and similar cases in future.

Ans.—The ability of the party to maintain upon whom the obligation to do so rests, is certainly essential to make the omission to maintain an offence under sec. 3 of the Vagrant Act. But it will be observed that the statute does not require a full ability on the person to maintain; it is sufficient to bring the case within the provision, if there be an ability in part to maintain, by work or other means, and a neglect to do so. In the case to which your letter applied, the justices are reported to have dismissed the charge, on the ground that the earnings of the woman charged with the neglect were not more than sufficient for her own support. The Board can only observe, that they are not able to concur in the principle, or distinction, upon which the decision of the justices is stated to have been founded. The Board apprehend that a person's earnings, or means, are applicable (so far as they will go) as well to the maintenance of his family as to his own support, and that he cannot divest himself of his legal obligation to maintain one member of his family in part, by the reason or pretext that his means or earnings are not more than sufficient for the full support of another member. Though this is the view which the Board take upon the general question raised in this case, they are bound to add that it is a matter entirely for the decision of the justices in each case, whether or not the person charged is or is not able wholly or partially to maintain his family, and whether or not the circumstances of the case afford reasonable evidence of a wilful determination not to maintain the family by work or other means. The Board may add that apparently the woman has been guilty of another offence, namely, the desertion of the child, but this to some extent involves the question of intention and the ability of the party to maintain the child.

XXIV.—VAGRANTS.

1. RELIEF TO.

Clerk of Battle Union.—Inquired, 1st, whether a relieving officer is bound to give an order for the workhouse to able-bodied vagrants without families, when he does not consider them wholly destitute. 2nd, In cases where vagrants are provided with lodgings in parishes, other than that in which the union workhouse is situate, is the relieving officer obliged to give them food without exacting some kind of labour from them in return?

Ans.—1st, A relieving officer is not authorized to give relief of any kind either to a professed vagrant or any other poor person, without the special direction of the guardians, except in cases of sudden or urgent necessity, (see Art. 215, No. 6, General Consolidated Order,) and therefore unless the applicant exhibit signs of being in actual want, the relieving officer would not be justified in giving an order for the workhouse, but in any case of real urgency, such as illness, it would be his duty to give the order at once. 2nd, In a case of real urgency, the relieving officer should afford the required relief out of the workhouse in the manner most suitable to the circumstances of the case, but he cannot make the performance of a task by the vagrant a condition of his accepting the relief. If, however, the relief be given in the workhouse, the guardians having first prescribed a task of work to be done by casual poor persons in return for the relief afforded, may require the performance of such task of work; see 5 & 6 Vic. c. 57, s. 5.

---

2. BEDS FOR VAGRANTS.

15*th April*, 1848.

Stourbridge Union.—The following letter on the subject of beds for vagrants has been addressed by the Poor Law Board to the clerk of the guardians of this union, in reply to an inquiry as to whether the Board had any objection to the use of straw in the vagrant wards, which had been recommended instead of beds:—

"The Poor Law Board think it desirable that some better accommodation should be provided in the vagrant wards of the workhouse of the Stourbridge Union than straw, which harbours vermin, and is otherwise objectionable. The Board have had a plan of a vagrant bed submitted for their inspection, which they think would answer the purpose, and could be made at a small cost, and in the end would be found less expensive as well as more cleanly than straw. The following description of it is, therefore, forwarded for the information of the guardians. The bedstead consists of a strong frame, six feet long, and of any breadth that may be deemed convenient, raised sufficiently to allow the floor to be swept without moving the frame. This frame is divided into compartments of eighteen inches wide each, by wooden partitions about twelve inches high; on each of these compartments is placed a mattress, six feet by eighteen inches, made of stout canvass, painted with one or two coats of black paint, and stuffed with hay. One end of each compartment has, besides, a board slanting at an angle of forty-five degrees, moving on hinges, which raises the top of the mattress sufficiently to answer the purpose of a pillow, whilst at the same time the space under the board serves as a safe depository for any property the vagrant may have with him; in lieu of a rug, two dressed sheep-skins without the wool, and sewn together, are used to give sufficient warmth. The cost of the bed and covering, exclusive of carpenter's work, the Board are informed does not exceed 14*s*. when bought; or 11*s*. when made, or rather put together, by the workhouse inmates.

XXV.—VOTING.—IN VESTRIES.

6*th May*, 1848.

The Rev. ———, *Tendring Union.*—In consequence of the omission, in the Poor Rate Book, of a column for the insertion of the number of votes of each rated occupant, he did not know how the votes in a parish vestry were to be ascertained, or upon what authority the chairman was to rely. Requested to be informed what guide he was to adopt in the event of a poll being called for in vestry, to ascertain the votes.

Ans.—The Poor Law Board believe the Poor Law Commissioners did not include in the form of the Rate Book any column for the number of votes, partly because the Parochial Assessments Act (6 & 7 Wm. 4, c. 96) does not expressly require the insertion of that information, and partly because the rules laid down by the statutes, for the calculation of the votes may readily be applied on any occasion, according to the assessment. As respects the election of guardians, the rule given in the 7 & 8 Vic. c. 101, sec. 15, is so simple as to admit of easy application; and with regard to ordinary voting at vestries, the rule laid down by the Vestries' Act (58 Geo. 3, c. 69) must be applied, when requisite, in accordance with the information furnished by the Rate Book.

XXVI.—WORKHOUSE.

1. INMATES SMOKING IN.

11*th Feb.*, 1848.

Clerk of ——— *Union.*—The guardians some time since passed a resolution prohibiting inmates in the union workhouse from smoking in any room, yard, &c., and several able-bodied paupers having lately persisted in smoking in the yard, inquired whether the magistrates are empowered to commit inmates of the workhouse to gaol for a breach of such order; and also whether the master would be justified in punishing any pauper for a like offence.

Ans.—Article 121 of the General Consolidated Order expressly directs that "no pauper shall smoke in any room in the workhouse;" and as smoking in any room is prohibited by the above order, any pauper by persisting in doing so will clearly commit an offence within Article 127 of that order, and become punishable by the master under the provisions of Articles 129 and 130. The Board are of opinion that it is certainly competent to the justices to punish any pauper inmate of the workhouse who disobeys the order above referred to, under sec. 98 of the Poor Law Amendment Act; and they are, moreover, disposed to consider that smoking in the workhouse would be a misbehaviour in the workhouse, punishable under the 54 Geo. 3, c. 170, or 55 Geo. 3, c. 137, but the Board do not recommend that proceedings should be taken before the justices in such case unless there be an instance of gross insubordination. Though the Order of the Poor Law Commissioners does not expressly apply to smoking in the yards and other premises belonging to the workhouse, it is competent for the guardians to make an order to prevent the practice of smoking therein. If such order be disobeyed, and the pauper do not refrain from smoking in the yards when ordered to do so by the master or other officer of the workhouse, such pauper would be guilty of an offence within Art. 127 of the Consolidated Order.

---

2. ADMISSION INTO WORKHOUSE OF PERSONS UNDER INFECTIOUS DISORDERS.

3rd May, 1848.

Clerk of Swaffham Union.—On the 4th ult., W. G., who had previously been an inmate of the union workhouse, was confined in the gaol at Swaffham, although the term of his imprisonment had expired, and being ill of typhus fever was conveyed to the workhouse by the relieving officer at the request of the gaoler. On the 26th ult. two men, named P. H. and D. F., whose term of imprisonment was expired, were removed into the workhouse by the direction of the gaoler, whilst they were labouring under an attack of fever. One of them was reported by the medical officer to be in a delirious state when received in the house. Inquired whether the master of the workhouse is bound to admit persons who are either positively subject to typhus fever, small pox, or other contagious disorders, or who are in such a state of disease as might terminate in typhus, and become infectious.

Ans.—The Board observe that the answer to your inquiry appears to them to depend upon the nature and intensity of the disease, as well as upon the accommodation of the workhouse. If there are the means of separating persons labouring under infectious disease, without risk to the other inmates of the establishment, the Board think that the master should receive such persons into the house. If on the other hand there are no such means of accommodation, and the safety of the inmates would be endangered by the admission, the Board think that the master would not be bound to admit infected persons brought with the order of the relieving officer. In any such case, however, the master should instantly send for the relieving officer or overseer, to see that the case is properly attended to, by providing some temporary accommodation or lodging for the sick person, and such attendance as the urgency of the case may call for.

---

3. ABLE-BODIED PAUPERS LEAVING THE WORKHOUSE FOR IMPROPER PURPOSES, AND RETURNING AGAIN.

7th March, 1848.

Clerk of ——— *Union.*—Transmitted the following resolution passed by the board of guardians:—That the attention of the Poor Law Commissioners be called to the minute in the report of the visiting committee, relative to the practice of able-bodied paupers, to seven of whom that minute refers, chiefly men and women of notoriously bad character, leaving the house on the occasion of fairs, &c., and returning within a day or two; accompanied with an earnest request that the Commissioners would, as soon as possible, provide for such increased authority to boards of guardians as may enable them to apply an effectual remedy to check so great and growing an evil in workhouses in the neighbourhood of large towns. Also, that the clerk in writing to the Commissioners make it known to them that the three hours' notice which was originally intended to apply only to the final quitting of the house, is now used as an evasion of the rules of the workhouse, and as a means of visiting ——— when it suits the convenience of the parties.

Ans.—The Poor Law Board is fully aware of the growing evil to which the guardians of the ——— Union have directed their attention. The Board can, however, only observe that the remedy for the state of things complained of in the ——— Workhouse rests mainly with the guardians themselves. The guardians are not obliged to admit all applicants for relief into the workhouse as a matter of course. The discretion as to the nature and extent of the relief to be given is vested in the guardians, who should exercise that discretion (having always due regard to the condition of the applicants) in the way which to them appears most fitting in every case. The Poor Law Board is desirous of giving every support to the guardians of which the law will admit, in the discharge of their important duties. It may be difficult to lay down a rule applicable alike to all cases, but the guardians may restrain the re-admission of the disorderly characters, who go out of the workhouse in the way described, so as to check the evil of which the guardians complain.

4th April, 1848.

Chairman of same Union.—Jemima Legg, an able-bodied pauper, having discharged herself from the workhouse on the 7th March, with her two illegitimate children, (the youngest of whom is ten months old,) applied on the 15th of March to the relieving officer for an order of re-admission. The officer refused the order, and informed the woman that she must apply in person for an order to the board of guardians at their next meeting, which she accordingly did. The relieving officer, in refusing an order in this case, acted in accordance with the resolution of the guardians set forth above. The guardians directed that all paupers of this description should, upon giving notice of their intention to discharge themselves, be informed by the governor of the difficulties which would be placed in the way of their re-admission, and accordingly Jemima Legg was made fully aware that she would not again, as on many previous occasions, be received as a matter of course on her application to the relieving officer, but that she would have to submit her case to the consideration of the board of guardians. This woman is the mother of five illegitimate children, with the father of two of whom the board was by one of the guardians informed she still occasionally cohabited; and though from the time of her application to the relieving officer, to that of her appearance before the board, a full week had elapsed, there were no symptoms of her having been exposed to want, nor was her dress by any means such as to betoken great poverty. Under these circumstances, on a division of 16 to 8, it was decided to refuse relief to Jemima Legg, the minority protesting against the legality of such decision, and contending that the fact of her attendance before the board to renew the application, which she had made to the relieving officer, was sufficiently indicative of such a degree of destitution as made it compulsory upon the guardians to afford her relief in the workhouse. In the course of the meeting of the guardians, another pauper applied for admission into the workhouse, under circumstances exactly similar, and in consequence of almost all the members who voted in the majority in the first case having previously left the room, those present decided in favour of the application, and granted an order for the workhouse. Inquired whether the course which the guardians had taken in the case of Jemima Legg was right, and that the majority who voted on the case were correct in drawing from the Poor Law Board's letter of the 7th March the inference that they would uphold the guardians should they, in the application of the relief clauses of the Poor Law Act, discriminate between worthless and deserving paupers; or, whether the minority were correct in their opinion, that it is imperative upon a board of guardians in administering relief, to consider the mere fact of application as a proof of destitution, and to give an order for the workhouse without any regard to the character of the applicants, nor to repeated abuse of such orders previously given to them.

Ans.—With reference to the course adopted by the guardians of the ——— Union in relation to the case of Jemima Legg, at their meeting on the 22nd ultimo, the Board desire to observe, that the propriety of refusing all relief to Jemima Legg appears to them to depend upon the question of fact, whether she was or was not destitute at the time. If she was not destitute, the guardians of course acted quite rightly in refusing relief; but if, on the other hand, she was destitute, the Board are bound to point out that neither her general irregular conduct, nor alleged immorality, nor even the circumstances under which she might have previously quitted the workhouse, would have afforded a sufficient justification to the guardians for withholding relief if it was really necessary. With regard to the evidence of destitution, the Board can only remark that this must depend upon the particular circumstances of every case. The Board cannot acquiesce in the view adverted to in your letter, "that it is imperative upon a board of guardians, in administering relief, to consider the mere fact of application for it as a proof of destitution;" they consider it, on the contrary, to be the express duty of the guardians to inquire into the circumstances of every applicant that comes before them, so as to satisfy themselves, as far as they may be able to do so, whether the applicant is really destitute or not. Undoubtedly this may often be a difficult question to determine ; but the guardians will, of course, proceed upon the best information they can obtain, and act upon the best decision at which they may be able to arrive. The Board cannot undertake to express any opinion as to whether Jemima Legg, on the occasion adverted to, was or was not in a state of destitution, requiring immediate relief. The Board may suggest, however, that if she had been considered by the guardians to be destitute, and had received an order for admission into the workhouse, she should have been treated in all respects in accordance with the provisions of Arts. 91 to 96 of the General Consolidated Order. The Board think that a strict observance of those provisions, in cases of this kind, on every occasion of re-admission, may have a tendency to check the evil of which the case of Jemima Legg presents an illustration. The Board at the same time desire to refer you to the enclosed copy of the Official Circular, No. 25, which contains, at page 94, the opinion of the Poor Law Commissioners upon the subject matter of this correspondence.

XXVII.—RETURNS RELATING TO THE ADMINISTRATION OF THE POOR LAW, MADE TO PARLIAMENT DURING THE SESSION OF 1847.

Casual Poor.—A Return of the number of persons, (distinguishing men, women, and children,) relieved as casual poor in Liverpool, on each day from the 1st January, 1847, inclusive, distinguishing also the English, Scotch, and Irish; and with respect to the Irish, distinguishing those resident in Liverpool from those recently arrived. Also similar returns from Bristol, Glasgow, and the Ports on the Clyde. And also similar returns for the corresponding period of 1846. (H. of L., No. 24,) ordered to be printed, 15th February, 1847.

Further return of the number of persons, (distinguishing men, women, and children,) relieved as casual poor in Liverpool, on each day from the 1st January, 1847, inclusive, distinguishing also the English, Scotch, and Irish; and with respect to the Irish, distinguishing those resident in Liverpool from those recently arrived. Also similar returns from Bristol, Glasgow, and the Ports on the Clyde. And also similar returns for the corresponding period of 1846. (H. of L., No. 28,) ordered to be printed, 25th February, 1847.

Dudley Union—Cost of Christmas dinner —A copy "of the Correspondence which has passed between the Guardians of the Dudley Poor Law Union and the Poor Law Commissioners, respecting the disallowance of a sum of money paid for the last Christmas day dinner, given to the paupers by the guardians. (H. of C., No. 276,) moved for by Mr. Benbow, presented 24th February, 1847.

Emigration.—Return, showing the number of persons who have been aided in Emigration from England and Wales under the provisions of the Poor Law Amendment Act, distinguishing the number of such Emigrants, and the costs incurred by such Emigration in every year; and also the countries from which such Emigration proceeded. (H. of L., No. 113,) ordered to be printed, 27th April, 1847.

Gulson, Mr.—Weymouth Union.—A Return "of the names of the unions taken from the Assistant Poor Law Commissioners' district now held by Mr. Gulson, on his being appointed to it in November, 1846, and copies of all applications from Mr. Gulson, or any of his predecessors, or from any person connected with the Weymouth Union, for the removal of that union from Mr. Gulson's district; and of all correspondence of the Poor Law Commissioners, or portions of correspondence relative to the removal of the Weymouth Union from Mr. Gulson's district, on its restoration thereto." (Mr. Christie.)

Copies "of Correspondence of the Poor Law Commissioners, relative to the Exchange of districts between Mr. Gulson and Mr. Graves, in November, 1846. (H. of C., No. 263,) Sir William Somerville, presented 31st March, 1847.

Irish Poor—Liverpool.—Copies of, or extracts from, any Correspondence addressed to Her Majesty's Secretary of State for the Home Department, relative to the recent Immigration of destitute Irish into Liverpool. (H of C., No. 193,) moved for by Mr. Poulett Scrope, ordered to be printed, 16th March, 1847.

Keighley Union.—No. 1. A Return "of the number of times and dates thereof that the Bingley Poorhouse in the Keighley Union has been visited by Assistant Poor Law Commissioners since the 9th day of June, 1842."

No. 2. "The number of inmates in the said poorhouse on that day, and the number of inmates on each succeeding 1st day of January."

No. 3. "Also Copies of all Instructions which have been issued by the Poor Law Commissioners, and all communications which they have received relating to the said poorhouse, since the 9th day of June, 1842."

No. 4. "Also Copies of any Instructions which they have issued to the Auditor of the Keighley Union, authorizing him to prohibit the constable of Bingley from relieving destitute persons whom he may find in the night-time in a state of starvation; and, if no such instructions have been issued by them, whether the said auditor has acted upon his own responsibility in issuing such order." (H. of C., No. 54,) moved for by Mr. Ferrand, presented 9th February, 1847

Lunatic Paupers.—A Return of the number of pauper lunatics and idiots chargeable to parishes and townships in each of the unions in England and Wales, and also to parishes and townships not comprised in unions, on the 1st day of January, 1847 ; distinguishing those maintained in county lunatic asylums and hospitals, licensed houses, workhouses and elsewhere. (H. of C., No. 542,) moved for by Lord Seymour, presented 17th June, 1847.

Poor Law Commissioners.—Copies of letters from the Poor Law Commissioners to the Secretary of State respecting the transaction of the business of the Commission. (H. of C., No. 148,) moved for by Sir William Somerville, ordered to be printed, 5th March, 1847.

Poor Law Inquiry—Report, 1834.—Extract from first Report of Commissioners for inquiring into the practical operation of the poor laws (1834) as relates to the system of out-door relief, page 8 to 29. (H. of L., No. 25,) ordered to be reprinted, 15th February, 1847.

Poor Law Inquiry, 1833.—Copy of the letter addressed by the Chancellor of the Exchequer to the Commissioners for inquiring into the poor laws, dated 23rd February, 1833, and of the answer returned by the Commissioners. Presented in pursuance of an address of the House of Lords, dated 9th February, 1847; ordered to be printed, 5th March, 1847.

Poor Law Statistics.—Return "showing the population, the annual value of property rated to the poor's rate, the expenditure for the relief and maintenance of the poor, the rate in the pound on the value of rated property of such expenditure, the total number of paupers relieved, including casual poor, the proportion per cent. to the population of the persons relieved, and the rate per head of the expenditure on the total number of paupers relieved, according to the last Returns which have been laid before Parliament, in England and Wales, Scotland and Ireland, respectively. (H. of C. 144,) moved for by Mr. Brown; presented, 5th March, 1847.

Poor Removal Act.—Report from the Select Committee of the House of Lords on the operation of the Poor Removal Act of last session. (No. 369, H. of C.,) ordered to be printed, 10th May, 1847.

Relief.—Abstract of Returns showing in classes the number of paupers relieved in each of the workhouses of the unions in Oxfordshire, North Riding of Yorkshire, and in Liverpool, the Strand and Whitechapel unions, and Norwich, including both in-door and out-door relief, during the half years ending 25th March, 1844, and 29th September, 1844; and also showing the number of applicants for relief who were refused admission into the workhouse in the same period, in similar classes; also the population of each union according to the last census. (H. of C., No. 100,) moved for by Mr. Pusey, ordered to be printed, 23rd February, 1847.

St. Marylebone and St. Pancras.—Report of the Poor Law Commissioners upon the relief of the poor in the parishes of St. Marylebone and St. Pancras. Presented by command.

Unions—their Area and Population.—No. 1. Return of the names of unions and single parishes in England and Wales, under the Poor Law Amendment Act and under local acts, with the population according to the census of 1841, and the area in statute acres, so far as the same can be ascertained.

No. 2. Return of the names of unions and single parishes, under the Poor Law Amendment Act, and of incorporations and single parishes under local acts in England, arranged according to their largest contents in statute acres.

No. 3. Return of the names of unions and single parishes under the Poor Law Amendment Act, and of incorporations and single parishes under local acts in England and Wales, arranged according to their highest population in 1841. (H. of L., No. 77,) ordered to be printed, 15th April, 1847.

Ware Union—Resignation of Clerk.—Copies "of all letters to and from the Poor Law Commissioners, and their Assistant Commissioner, Mr. Hall, relative to the compulsory resignation of Mr. Palmer, late clerk and superintendent-registrar of the Ware union, received subsequently to those presented to the House of Commons in July, 1846. (In continuation of Parliamentary Paper, No. 524, Session 1846.)" (H. of C., No. 88,) moved for by Mr. Cowper, presented 12th February, 1847.

Warminster Union—Burial of a Pauper.—"Copies of all correspondence between the chairman of the board of guardians of the union of Warminster and the Poor Law Commissioners, relative to the refusal of the vicar of Warminster to bury Sarah Garrett, a pauper of that union."

"Copies of all correspondence between the chairman and vice-chairman of the said board; also between the said vicar and the Secretary of State for the Home Department on the same subject."

"Copies of all correspondence between the said Secretary of State and the diocesan of the said vicar, on the same subject." (H. of C., 694,) moved for by Mr. Bouverie, ordered to be printed, 20th July, 1847.

Weymouth Union.—"Copies of all reports made by Mr. Payne, District Auditor to the Poor Law Commissioners on the Weymouth Union."

A "Copy of the last Report by the Assistant Commissioner of the district on the Weymouth Union, with the date of the Report." (H. of C., No. 63,) moved for by Mr. Christie, presented 12th February, 1847.

Workhouses—Extent of Accommodation, &c.—Return of the number of workhouses in England and Wales, showing the number of inmates which they are calculated to receive, and of the population of each union in England and Wales by the last census. (H. of L., No. 78,) ordered to be printed, 15th April, 1847.

Workhouses—Married Couples in.—Return of the number of married couples above the age of sixty years each now in the several union workhouses in England and Wales, so far as the Returns have been received at the Poor Law Commission Office up to the 19th July, 1847. (H. of L., No. 305,) ordered to be printed, 19th July, 1847.

Workhouse Schools.—Copies or Extracts "of all Reports made by Assistant Commissioners to the Poor Law Commissioners on the subject of workhouse schools, since the 1st day of January, 1846." (H. of C., No. 514,) moved for by Mr. Ewart, presented 15th June, 1847.

Wycombe Union—Union Accounts—Conduct of Auditor and Clerk.—Return. Copies of all Correspondence and Communications relative to the Accounts of the Wycombe Union, which took place between the Poor Law Commissioners, their Assistant Commissioners, and the board of guardians of the union, their auditor, clerk, and officers, between the month of January, 1839, and the month of December, 1843.

And also Copies of all the Reports and other Communications in writing, whether addressed to the Board of Commissioners or their Secretary, by their Assistant Commissioners or others, in relation to the conduct of the auditor and clerk of the Wycombe Union for the above-mentioned period.

And of all written communications and letters from the Commissioners in relation thereto. (H. of L., No. 234,) ordered to be printed, 25th June, 1847.

London: Printed by Order of the Poor Law Board, by BLACKBURN & BURT, 90½, Holborn Hill, and Published by CHARLES KNIGHT, 90, Fleet Street.

AN

OFFICIAL CIRCULAR

OF PUBLIC DOCUMENTS AND INFORMATION:

DIRECTED BY THE POOR LAW BOARD TO BE PRINTED, CHIEFLY FOR THE USE OF THE BOARDS OF GUARDIANS AND THEIR OFFICERS.

No. 16.] JUNE, 1848. [N.S.

CONTENTS.

I.—BILLS.*

1. A BILL TO MAKE PROVISIONS FOR THE PAYMENT OF PARISH DEBTS, THE AUDIT OF PAROCHIAL AND UNION ACCOUNTS, AND THE ALLOWANCE OF CERTAIN CHARGES THEREIN.

22nd June, 1848.—12 Vic.

1. *Preamble—Parish debts may be discharged in the course of the year after they have been incurred.*

Whereas it is expedient to make some provisions as to the payment in certain cases of debts incurred by the overseers of the poor in parishes after their year of office has expired; Be it therefore enacted, by the Queen's most excellent Majesty, by and with the advice and consent of the Lords Spiritual and Temporal, and Commons, in this present Parliament assembled, and by the authority of the same, That, if the overseers of the poor in any parish shall lawfully, by virtue of their office, contract any debt on account of the parish, within *three* months prior to the termination of their year of office, and the same shall not have been discharged by them before their year of office shall have determined, such debt shall be payable by and recoverable from their immediate successors in office, and chargeable upon the poor-rate of the said parish, in like manner as the same would have been payable and chargeable by such first-mentioned overseers during their year of office; and if any such debt shall have been contracted during their year of office, but more than *three* months prior to its termination, the same shall be payable by and recoverable from their immediate successors in office, if the rate-payers of the parish in vestry assembled, and the Commissioners for administering the laws for relief of the poor in England shall consent, but not otherwise.

2. *Provision as to Bills for legal proceedings.*

Provided, nevertheless, and be it enacted, That where any proceedings have been commenced, or shall be hereafter carried on, for or on behalf of any parish, in a court of law regarding any matter affecting the poor-rates of such parish, it shall not be necessary that the bill of costs of the solicitor or attorney engaged therein shall be paid before the termination of the proceedings; but in any such case the amount of the bill, when duly

* These Bills were brought into the House of Commons by the President of the Poor Law Board and Lord Ebrington, one of the Secretaries of the Board, on the 22nd June, 1848.

taxed, if otherwise chargeable against the parish, shall be payable out of the poor-rates within the space of *one year* next following the termination of the proceedings, but not afterwards, unless the Commissioners aforesaid shall, where the amount is heavy, and the matter litigated one, in their judgment, of great interest to the parish, by order under their seal, authorise the payment of the costs and expenses attending any such proceedings, by annual instalments not exceeding *five*, to commence from their termination.

3. *Parties who have advanced money on behalf of unions and parishes to be reimbursed.*

And whereas in many cases sums of money expended by officers or other persons on behalf or for the benefit of unions and parishes, without legal authority, have not been allowed by the auditors, though the guardians of the unions and the rate-payers of the parishes interested have been willing and desirous that such sums should be paid out of the funds of those unions or parishes respectively, and great loss, in consequence of such sums not being allowed, has been sustained by individuals, and it is desirable that power should be given for the relief of such persons under certain circumstances; Be it therefore enacted, That if any person since the passing of the Act of the fifth year of the reign of his late majesty, intituled, "An Act for the Amendment and better Administration of the Laws relating to the Poor in England and Wales," and before the passing of this Act, have advanced or expended money on behalf and for the benefit of any union or parish without having had due legal authority for such advance or expenditure, and the same shall not have been allowed in the accounts of the union or of the parish on behalf of which it has been expended or advanced, and the major part of the guardians of such union or parish or the rate-payers of such parish in vestry assembled, as the case may be, shall express their consent to the reimbursement of such sum of money, out of the funds of the union or parish so interested, the Commissioners aforesaid may if they think fit, by their order authorize the reimbursement of such sum of money by the guardians of the union or parish, or the overseers of the parish, as the case may require, in such manner as the said Commissioners shall deem most advisable, so however that if the same be not repaid at once, it shall be repaid by equal annual instalments, not exceeding *five;* and all payments subsequently made in conformity with such order, but not otherwise, shall be allowed by the auditor in the accounts of the guardians overseers, or other officers who shall make the payment in obedience to such order: provided always, that nothing herein contained shall apply to authorize the repayment of any sum of money which has been paid on any other account than that of the relief of the poor, or in respect of some matter chargeable upon or connected with the poor-rate.

4. *Appeal against disallowances and surcharges may be determined by the Poor Law Board on the merits, and such disallowances and surcharges may be remitted where the payments were fair and reasonable.*

And be it enacted, That where any appeal shall be made to the said Commissioners against any allowance, disallowance, or surcharge made by any auditor in the accounts of any guardians, overseers, or their officers, it shall be lawful for the said Commissioners to decide the same according to the merits of the case; and if they shall find that any disallowance or surcharge shall have been or shall be lawfully made, but that the subject matter thereof was incurred under such circumstances as make it fair and equitable that the disallowance or surcharge should be remitted, they may, by an order under their seal, direct that the same shall be remitted upon payment of the costs, if any, which may have been incurred by the auditor or other competent authority in the enforcing of such disallowance or surcharge.

5. *Mode of certifying as to balances to officers.*

And whereas doubts exist as to the powers and duties of auditors in certifying the sums due from the overseers and other officers, and it is desirable to remove such doubts; Be it therefore enacted, That where any overseer or officer shall be continuing in office at the time when the accounts are audited; the auditor shall certify as due such sums of money only as shall be disallowed or surcharged by him in the accounts so audited; but where the term of office of such overseer or officer shall have expired at the time when the accounts are audited, he shall ascertain the balance which he shall find to be then due on the accounts so audited, together with the sums, if any, which he shall have disallowed or surcharged, and shall give credit for all sums which shall be proved before him to have been paid in respect of such balance to the succeeding overseers or officers, or otherwise lawfully applied on behalf of the parish or union interested therein before the date of this audit, and he shall certify, report, and recover in the manner provided by law the balance remaining due after such credit shall have been given.

6. *What shall be required to be proved by the auditor.*

And be it enacted, That in any proceedings to be taken by an auditor before justices to recover sums certified by him to be due, it shall be sufficient for him to state and prove that the audit was duly held, that the certificate was made in the proper book of account of the union or parish to which the same relates, and that the sum certified to be due had not been paid to the treasurer of the guardians of the union or of the parish, as the case may require, within *seven* days after the same had been so certified, nor within *three* clear days before the laying of the information, of which non-payment a certificate in writing, purporting to be signed by the treasurer, shall be sufficient proof on the part of the auditor; and if at the hearing of such information it shall be proved that the said sum had been paid to the treasurer subsequently to the date of such last-mentioned certificate, the costs incurred by such auditor shall be paid by the party against whom the information shall be laid, unless he prove that notice of such payment had been given to the auditor *twenty-four* hours at least prior to the laying of the information.

7. *Parishes may agree to share Costs of several Appeals involving the same common principle.*

And be it enacted, That where appeals are brought at the same time against the poor-rates of several parishes which may appear to involve some common principle, it shall be lawful for the overseers or other authorities therein, with the consent of the respective vestries of such parishes, to enter into an agreement, to be approved of by the said Commissioners, mutually to bear the costs which may be properly incurred in and about the trial of such appeals on the part of the several respondents, as well as costs of the appellants, if any, which may be awarded against the respondents, in such proportions as shall be fixed and determined with reference to the amount of interest of the several parishes in the question or otherwise, as shall appear just, and the said agreement shall continue binding upon the several parishes and their respective overseers in succession, until the several appeals shall have been finally determined: provided nevertheless, that the payments for the current costs and expenses may be called for from time to time pending the trials of the appeals.

8. *To enable out-door Relief to be granted in certain parishes where no such Relief can be lawfully given.*

And whereas in certain parishes and unions wherein the relief of the poor is administered by guardians or other competent authorities under the provisions of particular Statutes or local Acts applicable thereto, doubts have been entertained whether any poor person can be relieved by such guardians or other authorities out of the workhouses belonging to such parishes and unions respectively, and it is expedient to remove such doubts, and to give authority for such relief out of the workhouse; Be it enacted, That in all cases where the relief of the poor is administered in any parish or union under the provisions of any local Act, it shall be lawful for the guardians or other competent authority administering the relief to the poor in any such parish or union, if they think fit, to administer such relief in all respects in like manner and with the like powers and authorities as any board of guardians of a union formed under the provisions of the Act passed in the fifth year of the reign of his late majesty aforesaid is now or shall hereafter be authorized to do; and all relief heretofore granted by such guardians or other authority shall, if otherwise lawfully granted, be held lawful for all purposes, although the same shall have been granted out of the workhouse of such parish or union, as the case may be, and the cost and charges thereof shall not be disallowed by any auditor, justice, or other competent authority in that behalf, on the ground that the same was granted out of the workhouse: provided always, that the cost of all such relief so given, or to be given, shall be charged among the parishes in the same union, in like manner and in like proportion as the relief heretofore or hereafter to be given in the workhouse of such parish or union is now or shall hereafter be chargeable.

9. *Interpretation Clause.*

And be it enacted, That the several words used in this Act shall be construed in the manner prescribed by the said hereinbefore recited Act, and the Acts explaining and extending it.

---

2. A BILL TO AMEND THE LAW FOR THE FORMATION OF DISTRICTS FOR THE EDUCATION OF INFANT POOR.

1. *Preamble—Recital of* 7 & 8 *Vic. c.* 101 —

Any Pauper Child under Sixteen may be sent to the District School.

June 22nd, 1848.—12 Vic.

Whereas by an Act passed in the eighth year of the reign of her Majesty Queen Victoria, intituled, "An Act for the further Amendment of the Laws relating to the Poor in England," provisions are made for the combination of unions into districts for the management of infant poor not above the age of sixteen years, and by reason of certain restrictions therein contained, the provisions so made for such purpose have proved inoperative, and it is expedient that such of the restrictions as are hereinafter mentioned should be removed, and that the management should be extended to other children than those mentioned in the said Act; Be it therefore enacted, by the Queen's most excellent Majesty, by and with the advice and consent of the Lords Spiritual and Temporal, and Commons, in this present Parliament assembled, and by the authority of the same, That in every such district to be formed under the authority of the said Act for the management of infant poor, any poor child not above the age of *sixteen*, who shall be chargeable to any union or parish in such district, may be sent to the school of such district by the guardians or other authority lawfully empowered to relieve such child.

2. *Limitation on the area of the School District removed—Limitation as to the amount of the Expense to One-fifth of the average Expenditure removed.*

And be it enacted, That so much of the said Act as prevents the Commissioners therein mentioned from including in any such district any parish, any part of which would be more than fifteen miles from any other part of such district; and so much thereof as provides that the principal sum or sums to be raised for the purpose of providing any building or buildings for any school for any such district as aforesaid, and charged on any union, or on any parish not included in a union, shall in no case exceed one-fifth of the average annual amount of the aggregate expenditure relating to the relief of the poor within any such parish for *three* years ending the twenty-fifth day of March next preceding the raising of such money shall be repealed.

3. *Certain provisions in the 5 & 6 Vic. c. 57, relating to Guardians, extended to Members of District Boards formed under 7 & 8 Vic. c. 101.*

And be it enacted, That all the provisions contained in the statute passed in the sixth year of the reign of her Majesty, intituled, "An Act to continue until the Thirty-first day of July, One thousand eight hundred and Forty-seven, and to the End of the then next Session of Parliament, the Poor Law Commission; and for the further Amendment of the Laws relating to the Poor in England," in respect of the election, qualification, resignation, and the acts of guardians of a union, and in respect of the supply of vacancies in the board of guardians, shall apply to the members of the district boards formed or to be formed under the authority of the first-recited Act.

4. *Interpretation Clause.*

And be it enacted, That the several words in this Act shall be construed in the manner prescribed in the said first-recited Act.

---

3. A BILL TO AUTHORISE THE PAYMENT OF SUPERANNUATION ALLOWANCES TO OFFICERS ENGAGED IN THE ADMINISTRATION OF THE LAWS FOR THE RELIEF OF THE POOR.

June 22nd, 1848.—12 Vic.

1. *Preamble—Guardians may recommend Superannuation Allowances to certain Officers, and the Poor Law Board may order the payment.*

Whereas it is fitting that provision should be made to secure to officers of unions and parishes engaged in the administration of the laws for the relief of the poor some proper allowances when they shall become disabled from continuing in office by reason of old age, or bodily or mental infirmity; Be it therefore enacted, by the Queen's most excellent Majesty, by and with the advice and consent of the Lords Spiritual and Temporal, and Commons, in this present Parliament assembled, and by the authority of the same, That after the *passing of this Act*, if the guardians of any union or parish wherein the relief of the poor is administered by a board of guardians, upon the resignation of any officer, assistant or servant of such union or parish, being of the age of *sixty* years at the least, and having served the guardians of such union or parish for a period not less than *twenty* years, shall recommend in writing to the Commissioners for administering the laws for relief of the poor in England, that such officer, assistant or servant, shall receive a superannuation allowance by way of annuity during the remainder of the life of such officer, assistant or servant, such Commissioners may, by an order under their hands and seal, direct that such allowance shall be thenceforth paid by the guardians to such officer, assistant or servant, and such order shall have the same effect and consequences, and shall be enforceable in like manner as other orders of the said Commissioners; and the said allowance shall be payable to or on behalf of the person to whom it shall have been so ordered to be paid in like manner and out of the same fund as the salary was previously paid to such person.

2. *Scale of Allowance.*

And be it enacted, That the said guardians shall fix the amount of the allowance so to be given as aforesaid, according to the proportions following; (that is to say,) wherever the period of service shall have been *twenty* years and less than *twenty-five* years, the allowance shall not exceed *one-third* part of the previous salary of the officer, assistant or servant; where the period shall have been *twenty-five* years but less than *thirty-five* years, the allowance shall not exceed *one-half* of such salary; and where the period shall have been *thirty-five* years or more, the allowance shall not exceed *two-thirds* of such salary.

3. *Provision for Allowance where Officer is disabled by sickness or mental infirmity—In what cases the Allowance is to be suspended.*

And be it enacted, That where any officer, assistant or servant of the guardians of any union or parish, being under the age of *sixty* years, or having served for a less period than *twenty* years, shall have heretofore ceased, or shall hereafter cease, by reason of bodily or mental infirmity, to hold his office or to continue in his service, and a certificate under the hand of two medical practitioners (one of whom at least shall be at the time a medical officer of the said union or parish,) certifying that such person, by reason of some permanent sickness, disease or bodily infirmity, or from some permanent mental infirmity, is incapable of discharging the duties of the office or service, shall be laid before the said guardians, an allowance not exceeding *one-third* of the salary may be recommended by the said guardians, and ordered to be paid by the said Commissioners, as in the cases hereinbefore provided for: Provided always, That if any person so entitled to any such last-mentioned allowance shall, after the same shall have been granted, take any office or service of profit, the payment of the said allowance shall cease to be due and payable so long as such person shall hold such new office or service, unless the guardians of the union or parish charged with the payment thereof, with the consent of the Commissioners, shall otherwise direct; but upon the relinquishment of such office or service, the said allowance shall, with the consent of the said Commissioners, but not otherwise, become due and payable again from the time when such new office or service shall have been relinquished.

4. *What is to be deemed the salary.*

And be it enacted, That the salary upon which such allowance shall be computed shall be the average annual amount of the salary in money received, whether for the same or for different offices in the same union or parish, by the person to whom the allowance is to be paid during the *seven* years next preceding the time when the office or service shall have terminated; or if the total period of the service do not amount to *seven* years, then the computation shall be made upon the average annual amount of the salary received during the period of service.

5. *Interpretation Clause.*

And be it enacted, That the several words herein contained shall be construed in like manner as the same words are directed to be construed in the Act passed in the fifth year of the reign of his late Majesty, intituled, "An Act for the Amendment and better Administration of the Laws relating to the Poor in England and Wales," and of the several subsequent Acts amending or explaining the same.

[*A Bill, intituled, "A Bill to alter the Provisions relating to charges for the Relief of the Poor in Unions, and the mode of Payment thereof, and to provide for the Relief of the Poor in Extra-parochial Places," was also brought into the House of Commons by the President of the Poor Law Board, and will be communicated to the Boards of Guardians in a subsequent Number of the Official Circular.*]

II.—FOURTEENTH REPORT OF THE POOR LAW COMMISSIONERS.

TO THE RIGHT HONOURABLE SIR GEORGE GREY, BART., HER MAJESTY'S PRINCIPAL SECRETARY OF STATE FOR THE HOME DEPARTMENT.

Poor Law Commission Office,
Somerset House,
Dec. 17th, 1847.

Poor-rate Expenditure.

SIR,—1. As the constitution of this Commission is on the point of being changed, we feel it our duty to make a short Report to you, continuing the account of our proceedings from the Report, dated the 1st of May last, up to the present time.

2. The following is a summary of the expenditure and pauperism of the year ending Lady-day, 1847, so far as the returns for 592 unions already abstracted enable us to give it.

SUMMARY OF RETURNS received from 592 Unions in England and Wales, under the Poor Law Amendment Act, showing the Pauperism and Expenditure for the Relief of the Poor during the Year ended Lady-day, 1846 and 1847 respectively.

NUMBER OF PAUPERS RELIEVED.

Years ended Lady-day.	In-door.	Out-door.	Total.	Increase per Cent. in Number of Paupers relieved in 1847 compared with 1846.	Proportion per Cent. of the Number of Paupers relieved, to the Population in 1841.
1846	171,149	967,244	1,138,393	. .	8·4
1847	226,499	1,244,554	1,471,053	. .	10·8
Increase	55,350	277,310	332,660	29·2	2·5

Note.—The number of Paupers relievedi n unions under Local Acts, and other places not under the administration of the Poor Law Amendment Act, may be estimated at about 250,000. Population of the 592 unions in 1841—13,593,758.

EXPENDITURE FOR THE RELIEF AND MAINTENANCE OF THE POOR.

Years ended Lady-day.	In-Maintenance.	Out-Relief.	Establishment and Salaries.	Workhouse Loans Repaid.	Other Charges connected with Relief to the Poor.	Total Expenditure for Relief to the Poor.	Increase per Cent. in 1847 compared with 1846.	Rate per Head of Total Expenditure on Population in 1841.
	£.	£.	£.	£.	£.	£.	£.	s. d.
1846	687,179	2,741,378	741,937	173,438	9,833	4,353,765	..	6 4¾
1847	768,360	2,963,693	760,179	163,061	8,989	4,664,282	..	6 10½
Increase . . .	81,181	222,315	18,242	..	..	310,517	7·1	..
Decrease . . .	..	..	..	10,377	844	..	..	..

3. Several workhouses have been reported to us as being full, or on the point of becoming so. Those of the following unions are amongst the most recent:—

1. Ashton-under-Lyne.
2. Bethnal Green.
3. Bootle.
4. Calne.
5. Chorlton.
6. Foleshill.
7. Greenwich.
8. Hinckley.
9. Holborn.
10. Leicester.
11. Mansfield.
12. Nottingham.
13. Nuneaton.
14. Preston.
15. St. Albans.
16. Shepton Mallett.
17. Tavistock.
18. Truro.
19. Uxbridge.
20. Warrington.
21. West Derby.
22. Wigan.
23. Whitechapel.

We have, in every instance, directed the guardians to reduce the number in excess of the prescribed limit; and we have urged, to the utmost of our power, the adoption of a test of work in connexion with the relief of the able-bodied.

Issue of Consolidated Orders.

4. With reference to our own Orders, on the 24th July last, we issued a Consolidated Order, embodying, in one form, the contents of the following Orders:—

1. General Order for the Election of Guardians.
2. General Order regulating the Proceedings of Boards of Guardians.
3. General Order for Apprenticing Poor Children.
4. General Order prescribing Medical Regulations.
5. General Order relating to Non-resident Relief.
6. General Order prescribing Workhouse Regulations.
7. General Order prescribing Duties of Officers.

Some slight modifications were made in the regulations as they existed previously; and we have every reason to think, that the issuing of this Order has conduced to the convenience of the guardians and their officers, whilst it has brought before the public in one connected body the principal rules (not directly affecting relief) issued by this Commission. It is satisfactory to us to report, that the changes in the regulations, such as they are, have facilitated the working of the law.

5. This Consolidated Order had been some time in preparation, and it issued on the day after the Poor Law Administration Act had received the Royal Assent. The Order, as then framed, was adapted only to unions; and it was necessary again to modify it, so as to make it applicable to single parishes, in which the relief was administered by a board of guardians. We hesitated for some time to prepare and issue this Supplementary Order, because we were uncertain when it might be convenient for her Majesty's Government to bring into operation the provisions of the Poor Law Administration Act. Upon the whole, however, it has seemed desirable to us to place the regulations of unions and parishes, such as we have last referred to, on a uniform footing, before our Commission is finally superseded; and we have, therefore, as you are aware, now issued a Consolidated Order to the several parishes acting under boards of guardians. We have introduced into this Order such slight modifications as the nature of the case required, and as the experience obtained in the course of the last few months suggested to be expedient. Substantially, and for all practical purposes, the two Orders are the same.

Relief of casual Poor.

6. We have so lately had occasion to advert to the subject of casual poor in the parish of St. Marylebone, that we will not occupy your time further than by stating, that a variety of circumstances, such as the influx of Irish poor and the discharge of railroad labourers, will, we fear, create an increased demand for relief to those persons who ask for it as wanderers and wayfarers.

7. We adhere to the opinion which we have always expressed, namely, that to such persons, being able-bodied, and not affected by sickness, or apparently in urgent destitution, relief may properly be refused; or, if given, that it should always be afforded on the condition of work under proper superintendence. We have, in our last Report, set forth at length our views on the mode of meeting the claims of this class of paupers in the metropolis.

8. It is our duty, in connexion with this subject, to mention the fact that a Bill in Chancery has been filed against the North-West District Asylum Board, constituted under the 7 & 8 Vic. c. 101, in order to compel them to complete the purchase of a site for which they had agreed. The case has been heard before the Master of the Rolls, who has, we believe, decreed a specific performance of the contract.

District Auditors.

9. We see no reason to alter the opinion already expressed as to the probable efficiency of the District Auditors; although, as you, Sir, are aware, from the correspondence which has recently taken place, obstacles have in one or two instances presented themselves to enforcing by the justices, the disallowances made by the Auditor.

10. It is unnecessary for us to inform you that the proceedings which we had thought it our duty to institute, in order to enforce submission to the District Auditor on the part of the corporations of the poor of Hull and Bristol, stand over till next term.

Medical Relief.

11. On the subject of medical relief, we have felt especially anxious to introduce every possible amendment; and we have thought it our duty to issue orders raising the salary of one or more of the medical officers in the following unions:—

1. Bangor and Beaumaris.	7. Hinckley.
2. Boston.	8. Honiton.
3. Brampton.	9. Horncastle.
4. Calne.	10. Leek.
5. Cockermouth.	11. Lutterworth.
6. Haltwhistle.	12. Thorne.
	13. Whitechapel.

12. In the Calne Union, and in the Bangor and Beaumaris Union, the provisions of the General Order have, with your consent, been modified so as to allow of a plan, one feature of which is, that the guardians should find drugs, instead of contracting for drugs and attendance with the medical officers. In the Calne Union this was no new scheme; but we trust that its adoption in that of Bangor and Beaumaris will prove one of a series of steps to be hereafter taken by the guardians for improving the system of medical relief in the principality of Wales.

Apprenticeship Order.

13. We have no reason to think that our General Order as to apprenticeship works otherwise than beneficially,

Pauper Lunatics.

14. With reference to pauper lunatics, we have as far as possible urged upon the guardians the necessity of acting on the suggestions and

advice of such Commissioners in Lunacy as may have visited the union workhouses; and we have maintained a frequent communication on all important cases with the Board of Commissioners in Lunacy.

Workhouse Schools.

15. The influence of the parliamentary grant for the salaries of schoolmasters and schoolmistresses is beginning to be felt, and has enabled us to press upon the guardians with success, many improvements in the management of the schools, and in the instruction of the children educated in them.

Workhouse Infirmaries.

16. Our special attention has been directed to the defective condition of the infirmaries and sick wards in many workhouses, and we have great satisfaction in stating that, under the advice of our Assistant Commissioners, we believe great improvements in the accommodation and separation of these classes will be found to have been effected in the course of the summer just ended.

17. You, Sir, are aware of the lamentable increase of fever cases in many unions, especially in the north of England, and of the necessity which has existed for providing temporary accommodation for the reception of Irish poor, and others suffering under maladies of this description. The guardians have, for the most part, met the evil readily and cheerfully, so far as their means would allow. It is to be lamented that several medical men, as well as other officers and servants employed in attending upon the sick, have lost their lives in the course of such attendance; and we rejoice that Her Majesty's Government have consented to grant pecuniary assistance to the families of some of these persons.

Emigration, Parish Property, and Vaccination.

18. We feel it unnecessary to advert to the topics of emigration, parish property, and vaccination, which will be better discussed after the expiration of the year, and after the returns shall have been received which bear on these subjects.

Removal Act.

19. We have had, on many occasions, to advise boards of guardians and their officers upon cases arising on the late Removal Act; but we believe we may say, that the construction put upon the first clause by the Attorney and Solicitor-General is now generally acquiesced in. We regret to be obliged to state, that from several instances which have come to our knowledge, the penal clause of that Act is not sufficient for the prevention of illegal removals. There is difficulty in procuring convictions, in consequence of the necessity of proving an intention to impose a charge on a specific parish, which frequently does not exist, and where it does, can seldom be proved. We have strongly impressed upon boards of guardians, in several cases, the great impropriety of the adoption of any means, other than those provided by the law, for the removal of paupers from one parish or union to another.

10 & 11 *Vic. c.* 110.

20. Soon after the Statute 10 & 11 Vic. c. 110 (Mr. Bodkin's Act) came into operation, we addressed a letter to all boards of guardians, containing our views as to its effect and operation, and pointing out the course which we considered the guardians should pursue in regard to the charge for the maintenance of those paupers to which it applies. We have appended a copy of that letter to this Report.

21. The Statute referring to the mode of charging the contributions to the common fund, under 4 & 5 Wm. 4, c. 76, was not applicable to any of the remaining Gilbert's unions, because we have not hitherto issued any order under that Statute declaring the averages of the parishes in those unions. One of those unions has, however, applied to us to have the averages declared, so that they may avail themselves of the late Act; and we have directed our Assistant Commissioner of the district to make the necessary investigation upon the subject. From what we have hitherto learnt, we believe that this Act works satisfactorily.

British Guarantee Association.

22. In our last Report we stated, that we had under our consideration the proper form of policy to be issued by the British Guarantee Association, in reference to the officers of unions and parishes under the private Act incorporating that Society. We have since settled with the solicitor of that society the form, and have issued an Order to declare it. A copy of this order is appended.

St. Pancras.

23. In our Report to you of the 9th April last, upon the relief of the poor in the parishes of St. Marylebone and St. Pancras, we stated that we had addressed a requisition to the directors of the poor of those parishes to return to us copies of all resolutions of their boards, defining the duties of the paid officers employed in the administration of out-door relief, and that the directors had not

then made any return in conformity with this requisition. Considerable delay occurred on the part of the directors and the vestry of the parish of St. Pancras; and, in the beginning of the last month, we deemed it right to ascertain by examination on oath of the clerk to that board the cause of the delay, so that we might put ourselves in a position to take proceedings in the Court of Queen's Bench to enforce our requisition. Before any steps were taken, the board of directors and the vestry directed their clerk to transmit copies of their regulations to us, in conformity with our requisition, and he is stated to be now engaged in preparing the requisite copy for us.

Oldham Union.

24. In our Twelfth Annual Report, we stated that we had taken proceedings against the overseers of the several townships in the Oldham Union to enforce an order, which we had issued to them, to elect a returning officer to conduct the election of guardians for that union, and that we had obtained leave to issue a writ of mandamus to them: to this writ the overseers made a return, calling in question the validity of our Order. The case was argued last Trinity term, when the Court of Queen's Bench affirmed the validity of the Order, and directed a peremptory mandamus to issue. This writ was served upon the overseers in the course of the autumn, and was duly obeyed. The overseers of the several townships met, and appointed a gentleman as returning officer. The election followed, and was conducted with perfect regularity, and a board of guardians was duly returned. The guardians have since met, appointed the proper officers, and taken upon themselves the management of the relief of the poor throughout the union. Our Assistant Commissioner, Mr. Austin, attended the first meetings of the guardians, and afforded his advice and assistance to facilitate the commencement of the new system of relief in that populous union. We have much satisfaction in stating that, notwithstanding the pressure upon the manufacturing classes in that district, the proceedings have taken place without any opposition or disturbance, and, so far as we know, the relief is satisfactorily administered.

25. We have thus brought into active operation for the relief of the poor, the last of the unions which were formed in the manufacturing districts of Lancashire and the West Riding of Yorkshire in 1837, for registration purposes, of which an account will be found in the Third Annual Report, page 18.

We have the honour to be, Sir,
Your obedient humble servants,
GEO. NICHOLLS.
EDMUND W. HEAD.

III.—ACCOUNTS—OBJECTIONS TO THE GENERAL ACCOUNTS ORDER.

2nd May, 1848.

The Chairman of ——— *Union*—Having addressed a letter to the Poor Law Board, urging certain objections against the General Order of Accounts, the Board replied thereto as follows:—

The Board have given careful consideration to your objections, and readily express their acknowledgment as to the judicious manner in which they learn that the guardians of the ——— Union have heretofore carried into execution the provisions of the laws for the relief of the poor, and the care and attention which they have bestowed upon the subject. The Board are, therefore, most desirous to remove from the minds of the guardians of that union the impression which they have formed as to the general inexpediency of the Order referred to.

The Board wish to state in the first place, that this, being a General Order, has, in conformity with the provisions of the Statute, been laid before the Secretary of State for the Home Department, and before Parliament. It has obtained the acquiescence of the Privy Council and Parliament. It was adopted in some unions as soon as it came into operation, and in many others at Michaelmas last; and the Board have reason to believe that, in the far greater number of cases, it has been found, upon experience, to be of great practical benefit. In some instances, difficulties have arisen from a misapprehension of some of the details of the Order, which the Poor Law Commissioners and the present Board have been able to remove by explanation; and, in others, objections have been raised by officers, who anticipated an addition of labour from the adoption of the new accounts; but it has been shown them that, in truth, no such addition will follow their adoption. It should also be stated, that objections have been made in cases where, previously, there was much reason to fear that a loose practice in the mode of keeping accounts prevailed.

The Board believe that the Order was framed after a long and careful deliberation, not with any view of carrying out speculative theories, but upon an attentive consideration of numerous suggestions, and after consultation with many officers of unions, and persons practically acquainted with the working of poor law accounts; and to obviate complaints which had been made of the insufficiency of the former Order, to prevent fraud and waste on the part of the officers of unions and parishes.

Moreover, in regard to many unions, no order for keeping accounts had been issued, and, consequently, nothing obligatory in this particular, upon the officers of those unions, was in force. It being necessary to provide for those unions, the original Accounts Order was revised, and, in conformity with the opinion which had been often expressed in regard to the regulations of the Commissioners, was made a General Order, so as to be subjected to the control already alluded to.

Having made these general observations, the Board will now proceed to consider your objections in detail:—

Your *first objection* is as to the expense. Now, if the books of the officers in use under the former Order have been exhausted—and this is probably the case—the substitution of the new books for the former books will clearly create no additional expense; but, with reference to the books which are now introduced for the first time, it will be found, as regards the officers of the union who were required to keep books under the former Order, that, whereas the *clerk* was required to keep *six* books, he is now to keep only *five;* the *master*, who was to keep *ten* books, exclusive of the registers of births and deaths, is now required to keep *twelve;* the *relieving officer*, who was to keep *three* books, and is now required to keep the like number. As regards the union officers, there is, therefore, no increase in the *total* number of books which they are required to keep.

As regards the *overseers*, it will be seen that they were previously required to keep *seven* books —they are now required to keep *five*, but may be called upon to fill up *two* additional forms.

The collectors' books, indeed, are new; but they are officers whose accounts had not been previously regulated by the Commissioners in any way; though in practice there is no doubt that the collectors did keep books of accounts. The recent Order only prescribes that they shall keep one book, namely, the collecting and deposit book, (Form 8,) and it is a book which every prudent collector would keep in some form or other, even if not prescribed by the Order, and one which appears to be highly necessary to secure diligence and fidelity in that officer. The expense of providing the collectors' monthly statements, (Form 9,) and the unpaid rates statement, (Form 10,) is too trifling to require comment.

With regard to the receipts to be given by the collectors, the Board are unable to see anything in the Order which will increase the number of receipts which the collector is to give, assuming that he has been hitherto in the practice of giving a receipt to the ratepayer whenever he received the payment of the rate.

Your *second objection* is that the abstract has been changed from quarterly to half-yearly, and that, therefore, the account will be more complicated. It is to be observed with reference to this objection that the alteration is not entirely that of the Commissioners, but was rendered almost necessary by the provision of the statute 7 & 8 Vic. c. 101, which made the audit half-yearly, instead of quarterly, as under the 4 & 5 Wm. 4, c. 76. The abstracts which were required to be signed by the auditor after his audit could no longer be so signed quarterly; and although there might have been two quarterly abstracts prepared for each audit, it certainly seems a less complicated course to have one half-yearly abstract to be laid before the auditor. On reference to the statements which are now to be prepared in the place of the previous abstracts, the Board are not able to see any additional complexity—on the contrary, they consider that the Financial Statement, (Form 19,) is more simple than the abstract for which it is substituted, and furnishes a more explicit statement of the actual expenditure of the union. The Board will, however, be happy to learn from the guardians in reference to this point any specific difficulty which is felt by them, as the Board think they may probably be able to remove it by explanation.

Thirdly,—It is stated that the great increase of writing will cause additional assistance to be required by the officers. The Board would be glad to learn from the officers themselves the precise amount of increase in this respect which they contemplate. The Board do not think much more writing is imposed upon the master, or relieving officer, if those officers actually performed the work which was required to be done by the previous Order, and if there be a slight increase in regard to some of the books of the former officer, they believe that he will find advantages to compensate him in the greater facility which are now afforded to him in the keeping of those accounts of the workhouse expenditure, which seem indispensable in every well-regulated establishment.

As regards the clerk, it appears to the Board to be clear that his labours are diminished under this Order. As respects the number of weekly entries which the clerk is required to make, there is probably no material difference, though the *Relief Order Book* now prescribed, it may be observed, is more simple than *the abstract of the Application and Report Book*, but the accounts are to be closed half-yearly, and the statements are to be made half-yearly instead of quarterly, as heretofore, it is difficult to avoid the conclusion that the clerk's labour is, on the whole, considerably diminished. Under the former Order he had to apportion the expenditure, transfer the shares of the several parishes, and make up and balance the parochial ledger accounts four times a year. He will now do this only *twice*. He had to make in duplicate *four* abstracts from the union accounts containing a *financial* and *statistical* statement; now he will have to make only *two* statements during the year, and from the improvements in the books of the other officers the materials for framing these statements are more readily obtainable. The fact must not be overlooked, that the clerk's labour in examining the books of the officers has been lightened by the recent Order.

The *fourth* objection is undoubtedly the gravest, and one which the Board are ready fully to admit. You complain of the change of system whereby the payment of the poor-rates collected by the collector is required to be made to the overseers themselves and not to the treasurer of the union. The only answer which the Board can give to this objection is, that (as the Poor Law Commissioners were advised) the Orders which had been issued requiring the collectors to pay the rates to the Treasurer of the union could not, after the decision of the Court of Queen's Bench in the case of Queen *versus* the Poor Law Commissioners *in re* the Cambridge Union, (2 P. and D. 323,) be supported in this respect. The Poor Law Commissioners were advised that they had no authority to direct the guardians in effect, to take, by the officer whom they appointed, the monies raised from the poor-rates of the parishes, and cause the amount to be paid to the treasurer of the union. The poor-rates are, by law, to be raised by the overseers, who may have the assistance of a collector, but such collector must render to such overseers (or to their banker or the treasurer on their account) the money collected by him.

The Board feel strongly the great advantage of the payments being made in many instances to the treasurer of the union direct, but, without powers, which the Legislature have not yet given, such a mode of dealing with the parish funds cannot, they think, be supported in law. The case above cited, decided that the guardians could not derive from the Order of the Poor Law Commissioners the power to appoint a collector of poor-rates, and, indeed, prosecutions of officers appointed under similar orders, have lately failed in consequence of the peculiar position in which they were placed with reference to the guardians and the overseers.

Lastly, you object to the intricacy and unnecessary increase of checks. In the absence of a statement of the precise checks to which you refer, the Board feel a difficulty in dealing with the objection, and will not trouble you with general observations upon the necessity of some checks over officers having the collection and distribution of the large funds annually raised for the relief of the poor. The checks which may be termed new, as far as the present Order is concerned, apply to the collector and the master, but the Board are not convinced that they are not highly expedient. As to the collector's forms, the Board believe that their utility is self-evident.

In regard to the master, the increase is principally in the introduction of the Daily Provision Consumption Account (Form 25.) Now it was felt, that such an account had been long wanted by the master. Under the former system, when he was engaged upon urgent business, and obliged consequently to entrust the preparing of the meals to subordinate officers, or paupers acting as servants, there was no account which afforded him a check upon these persons. Again, there was no record in any account of the daily expenditure of provisions, whereby it could be ascertained whether more than the proper quantities were consumed, or whether the inmates had the quantities prescribed for them in the dietary. This new account is, therefore, necessary as a check for the purpose, as well of ensuring to the inmates their proper allowance of food, as of preventing carelessness, or waste in preparing their meals, whilst it is manifestly of great avail in tracing fraud or peculation. There are other checks in the Clothing Books which, as the Board conceive, will be found to be in no respect unnecessary.

The Board will not prolong this communication; they request the guardians of the —— union to give a trial to the Order, and let the experience of their officers be the test of its efficiency, with the recollection of what alone the law enables the Poor Law Board to do in this matter.

If in any respect after a due and proper trial it shall be found that any portion of the Order is really inapplicable, or produces an injurious effect, the Board will be ready to exercise in favour of this union, the power of dispensation which has been reserved to them. But they cannot do so until they are satisfied that a fair trial has been given, and that their interposition in this manner is necessary.

IV.—AUDITOR—His duty as to the recovery of balances.

March 25th, 1848.

———, *District Auditor*—It has been his custom, when he has made disallowances and surcharges in the accounts of overseers, to add or deduct items disallowed, to or from the balance, as the case might be and certify such balance to carry it to the next quarter's account, and not to compel the amount disallowed to be paid to the treasurer, as he did not see the reason why the sum disallowed should be paid over, any more than the rest of the balance in hand. In Mr. Lumley's notes to his edition of 7 & 8 Vic. c. 101, sec. 32, he says, that this provision in the statute is not intended to compel the balance to be paid by the officer accounting; and as the disallowance or surcharge is a part of that balance, it confuses the accounts to separate them, and he (the auditor) thought the payment of "the certified default within seven days," to the treasurer of the union, could only have been intended to apply to parties who were not otherwise holding balances. The disallowances in overseers' accounts were frequently not more than a few shillings, and there could be no reason for enforcing the payment of a small sum to the treasurer, when, at the same time, they were holding a large sum as a balance. Requested to be informed if it was the wish of the Poor Law Board, that in every case of disallowance or surcharge, he should order the sum to be paid over to the treasurer within seven days. He trusted, however, that he might be allowed a discretion in the matter, as he should take care to give no lenity where he had any doubt.

Ans.—With regard to the recovery of sums certified by a district auditor to be due, the 32nd section of the Act 7 & 8 Vic. cap. 101, leaves the auditor no discretion, nor have the Board any power to authorise him to exercise any discretion. The sums so certified must, according to the specific terms of the enactment, be paid over to the union treasurer; and if not so paid, it is the duty of the auditor to take the requisite proceedings to enforce payment; and, unless he does so, he will not carry out the express provision of the statute. The Board may add, that, no doubt, a question arises as to what the auditor should certify to be due. It may not always be right to treat the balances in the hands of parties continuing in office as moneys due; but the Board think that items disallowed, or surcharged, may fairly be so considered, and that the payment thereof, however small the amount, should be enforced by the auditor.

V.—OVERSEERS—Payment of balance in the hands of.

March 21st, 1848.

———, *Esq.*, *Cerne Union*—The overseers of the parish of ———, on going out of office on the 25th March, and making up their accounts, will have a balance in hand, probably, of from 40*l.* to 60*l.* They do not understand how this balance is to be disposed of, in consequence of the clerk of the union claiming whatever balance they may have in hand on quitting office, to be paid to the treasurer of the union, exclusive of any sum which may be payable under any Contribution Order which the guardians may make. The overseers wish to be allowed to pay over any such balance to their successors, to be appropriated by them in payment of the first Contribution Order made by the guardians after the 25th March. Requested the Board's advice.

Ans.—Some difficulty arises upon the construction of the several enactments which relate to the payment of the balance due from overseers on quitting office; but, on the whole, the Board are disposed to consider that if the overseers, having regard to the provisions of the 43 Eliz. c. 2, and 17 Geo. 2, c. 38, pay over to their successors, before their accounts are audited, the sum which they admit to be due from themselves, it will be competent to the auditor to take cognisance of such payment (if duly vouched,) and accordingly to exclude that sum in certifying the amount which he finds to be due at the time of the audit. The amount which the accounting overseers will be liable in such a case to pay over to the union treasurer, under the 7 & 8 Vic. c. 101, sec. 32, will only be the amount (if any) thus actually certified by the auditor. On reference to the General Order of Accounts of the Poor Law Commissioners, it will be seen that the overseers are to account in the "Receipt and

Payment Book" for the amount which they may receive from their predecessors in respect of the balance in the hands of the latter, not paid to the treasurer.

VI.–DIETARY–FOR THE SICK IN WORKHOUSES.

17th May, 1848.

J. Burton, Esq., M.D., Walsall Union—I have the honour to submit to your notice the following observations in reference to the extra sick diet in the Workhouse Medical Relief New Book, Forms Q and R of the Consolidated Order, which comes into use in this union after this day. 1st. Sugar, milk, and butter, are not extra diet in this workhouse, but are allowed to certain parties without medical order. They are, however, extras in the sick dietary under the new Order, and are in "every instance to be entered as such." 2nd. There is no space allowed in the column for extras ordered, sufficient to enter the items of such extras; nor will it be easy to specify the quantities, if entered seriatim, in such a manner as to enable the governor to show the totals in ounces, pints, &c. in the "Account of Provisions Consumed." 3rd. In several articles of sick dietary, as tea, coffee, gruel, arrow-root, sago, rice, and other puddings, the use of milk and sugar are indispensable to their being prepared in a manner to enable the sick to eat them, and the medical officer will, in those cases, find it convenient rather to take from the matron the account of what she has used of such articles, than himself to enter the specific several small quantities going to make up each particular dish, and, consequently, all check upon the quantities will be lost. 4th. Broth, an article of diet much in use, can only be entered in the account of provisions consumed in the shape of pounds of meat consumed. To illustrate the difficulty, suppose I order for a patient a sago pudding, consisting of sago, milk, sugar, perhaps an egg, in the present form under column, "what ordered," I must enter, "sago, one ounce; sugar, one ounce; milk, three quarters of a pint; egg, half; to make a pudding;" the same for rice-pudding, and, indeed, several compound articles for diet, consisting of, or including, small quantities of articles of extra diet. 5th. I propose to get rid of the difficulty, and, at the same time, to preserve the check upon the governor's account which the medical officer's ought to be, by entering on form of diet, No. 6, a pudding diet, in which the quantities are constant in regard to their several proportions; and thus, in this particular, the dietary entry, No. 6, will, by referring to the form for that number, show the exact quantity of each ingredient which ought to be summed up in the proper column of provisions consumed; and further, by entering a form or prescription for tea and coffee, in a state fit to be used, which, in like manner, shows for each pint of either infusion ordered, a constant and definite proportion of sugar in ounces. For broth, two prescriptions of different degrees of nutritive power, in which the meat required always bears in ounces or pounds, a definite proportion to the pints of "broth," or "weak broth," consumed by the sick. If this plan for the sick dietary of Walsall Workhouse meets your approval, I shall be glad to receive your signification to that effect, in order that at the next audit in this union, the accounts, if kept in a way differing ever so little from the prescribed manner in the Forms Q and R, may not be objected to by Mr. Simkiss the auditor. In the articles arrow-root, tapioca, and sago, I do not think a case can occur to call for their use whilst we have the potato farina: which, viewed in regard to its wholesomeness or economy, cannot be exceeded, if equalled, by any foreign starch, at any price. I can now buy potato starch at 4¼*d.* per lb., whilst Bermuda arrow-root is 1*s.* 10*d.*; and the rubbish sold under the name cannot be had under 1*s.* to 1*s.* 2*d.* per lb.: and I propose using the potato starch and rice as the whole material for a farinaceous dietary—abundant experience in my private practice justifies this step. The sick have usually had butter allowed, but now they cannot have it without a medical order, and as I do not consider it indispensable as an article in sick dietary, I do not feel justified in ordering it specially. The sick complain loudly of the privation, and I shall be glad to order it, if I am informed that the Board, in issuing the new books, did not contemplate the privation of the sick of their butter, but only wished the medical officer's entries to check the governor's account of provisions consumed in certain articles.

Ans.—1st. The sugar, milk, and butter which you describe as being allowed to certain inmates in the workhouse of the Walsall Union, without medical order, will not appear at all in the medical officer's books which refer exclusively to the sick. 2nd. You remark that the space allowed in Form 2 of the General Consolidated Order, in the columns for the "extras," is not sufficient to admit of the items being entered. The Board apprehend, however, that if the book supplied for use in the Walsall Workhouse be of the ordinary size, the columns in question will be sufficiently large for the entries, if made with the brevity which was contemplated by the framers of the Orders. 3 & 4. With regard to the mode of entering the "extras" in the book referred to, the Board would observe, that in the case of compound articles of diet, the medical officer need not specify the exact quantities of the several items of each such article in detail; but should make the entry in a general manner, (as a rice pudding, a cup of sago, a basin of broth,) leaving the master of the workhouse to set out the particular ingredients in the appropriate columns. 5. The Board desire to express their approval of the plan which you propose for checking the account kept by the workhouse master, by establishing a pudding dietary, which shall specify the proportionate quantities of the several ingredients of the puddings for the sick, and also by adopting some similar arrangement as respects the preparation of tea, coffee, broth, weak broth, and so forth. It appears to the Board that such a plan would be very beneficial, and would, in fact, be carrying out more in detail the views which the Poor Law Commissioners entertained, in requiring the formation of sick dietaries. 6. If the butter, which you state to have been usually allowed to the sick, has been given to them in accordance with the regular dietary in force in the Walsall Workhouse, the allowance may be then continued as heretofore; the medical officer will, of course, in some cases, have to prohibit it; but if he does not do so, he need take no notice of it; unless, indeed, he thinks proper to enter it as one of the subjects of the sick dietaries, according to Form R. As the Board cannot conceive butter being often necessary, or, indeed, in many cases at all a desirable ingredient in a dietary for the sick in other workhouses than that of Walsall, where the guardians appear to have accustomed the sick paupers to the use of it, the latter course would probably be adopted. The Board, in conclusion, desire to thank you for the information contained in your letter with regard to potato farina, and generally for the practical and useful remarks with which you have favoured the Board.

VII.—REMOVAL—Fee to Justices' Clerks for taking Examination for the Purposes of.

May 6th, 1848.

Assistant Overseer of ———, *Seisdon Union.*—The clerk to the justices at ——— has been applied to, to attend at a distance of six miles to take the examination of a sick pauper for the purposes of removal, and refuses to do so unless he is paid an extra fee. Inquired whether such extra fee can be legally paid.

Ans.—If the pauper, in consequence of illness or infirmity, be unable to be brought up to the petty sessions to be examined, the course to be pursued appears to be that pointed out by section 4 of 50 Geo. 3, cap. 49; which provides that in such a case the magistrate acting for the district in which the sick pauper may be, may take the examination at the residence of the said pauper, and report the same to any other magistrate of the district, who can then, jointly with him, make and suspend the order of removal. The Board observe that it would not be competent for the clerk to the justices to take the examination except in the presence of the justice. If the justice declines to take the examination without the presence and assistance of the clerk to the justices of the district, the Board are not prepared to say that such clerk cannot claim to be paid his expenses of his journey to the residence of the pauper by the person at whose instance the order of removal is applied for.

VIII.—VACCINATION—Circular as to the Extension of.

Poor Law Board,
Somerset House,
May 1st, 1848.

SIR,—In consequence of the small number of persons which, from the returns presented to this Board, appear to have been vaccinated in some of the unions during the year ending on the 29th of September, 1847, the Poor Law Board addressed communications to the guardians of the different unions, pointing out to them the great importance of the general practice of vaccination to the health and well-being of the community, and requesting to be informed how far the existing arrangements in the several districts are calculated to promote vaccination, or are capable of being made more efficient for the purpose.

The Board are satisfied, from the answers which they have received, that the boards of guardians and local authorities, as well as the public vaccinators have, in general, done all in their power to extend the practice of vaccination, and that the smallness of the number of children vaccinated is not, except in some few instances, attributable to any indifference or negligence on their part.

The Board, however, regret to find, that the benefits which result from vaccination do not appear to be generally known or appreciated, and that much misapprehension and prejudice on the subject exist in the minds of parents throughout the country, which prevent the efforts of the boards of guardians and public vaccinators from being as successful as they otherwise would be. The Board find that there is an impression on the part of too many parents, that the vaccination of their children makes them ill instead of protecting them against illness, and that the mere fact of allowing them to be vaccinated at the public expense exposes them to the imputation of being in the receipt of parish relief.

Nothing can be more erroneous than these impressions. Vaccination is perfectly harmless, and is never attended with the slightest risk to the health of the child; whilst on the other hand a child not vaccinated is constantly exposed to the liability of catching the small pox, which frequently disfigures and is always dangerous.

The children of parents in the middle and upper classes are invariably vaccinated, and deaths amongst them from small pox scarcely ever occur; whilst amongst the children of the labouring classes deaths from small pox are still very common, owing to the comparatively small number of their children who are vaccinated. In one parish, with a population of 1,751 persons, at the last census, since increased by a body of railway labourers at present employed in the neighbourhood, 50 deaths occurred, of which ten were caused by small pox.

It is altogether a misapprehension to suppose that parents accept, or can be supposed to accept, parish relief by allowing their children to be vaccinated by public vaccinators, as it is expressly enacted by the 4 & 5 Vic. cap. 32, that the vaccination of any person resident in any union or parish, or of any of his family, shall not be considered parochial relief, alms, or charitable allowance to such person.

It is for the advantage of the whole community, with a view to the ultimate extirpation of the small pox, that the practice of vaccination should be as widely adopted as possible, and the legislature has consequently afforded parents the opportunity of having their children vaccinated free of expense.

The Board approve on the whole of the arrangements in respect of vaccination, which have been made in the various districts; but they consider it very desirable to endeavour to remove the misapprehension unfortunately prevailing on the subject, and to diffuse still more widely the knowledge that parents are entitled to have their children gratuitously vaccinated, and that by availing themselves of it they alike benefit their children by protecting them against future illness, and the public, by guarding it against the spread of a dangerous disease.

It has been suggested to the Board, that it would tend greatly to disseminate information on the subject, if the registrars of births and deaths were to give persons attending to register a birth, a copy of a hand-bill, containing all the requisite information, and the suggestion having met with the approval of the registrar-general, the Board have caused the form of notification annexed to the Poor Law Commissioners' Circular of the 20th of August, 1840, to be slightly modified in accordance with what they believe to be the opinion of the medical profession generally, as to the period of life when vaccination should be performed. The Board having been applied to by some guardians for a form of notice on the subject, now forward one herewith for the convenience of the guardians, and request that they will cause a supply of notices to be printed and furnished to the registrar, who will be instructed by the registrar-general so to distribute them. Similar notices may also be posted, from time to time, in the several parishes of the union.

With a view of lessening the labour of the public vaccinator as much as possible, the Board are disposed to think, that the certificate which the vaccinators are now required to give of the successful vaccination of each child might be dispensed with without any inconvenience; the Board believe that such certificates are seldom preserved, and when preserved answer no practical purpose, as the cicatrix on the arm of the child is considered the best test of the success of the operation. It would still, however, be proper, though the certificates may be generally dispensed with, that they be granted when demanded by the parties whose children are vaccinated. The vaccinators should continue to keep the registers as heretofore.

I am, Sir, your obedient servant,

EBRINGTON, *Secretary.*

To ——— *The Clerk to the Board of Guardians,*
——————— *Union.*

GRATUITOUS VACCINATION.

IT is requested that parents of children, and all other persons, will take notice of the provisions made by the Act of the 3rd and 4th years of the reign of Queen Victoria, for the extension of vaccination with the cow pox, and the prevention of the spread of small pox; which latter disease, chiefly in consequence of the want of due care, and the proceedings of ignorant individuals, has occasioned annually, not only the deaths of many *thousand persons* in England and Wales, but has entailed suffering and permanent disfigurement, and occasionally loss of sight, to a much larger number of persons, who have been attacked by the disease, but have escaped death.

Cow pox is merely a mild form of small pox: vaccination with the cow pox is perfectly free from danger, and either prevents or mitigates an attack of small pox. In nearly all the instances in which small pox has attacked persons who have been vaccinated, the vaccination has been imperfectly performed, or the attack of small pox has been in a very mitigated form, nearly free from danger of disfigurement or danger to life. By vaccination being made universal, small pox would be entirely banished from the country. To secure the benefits of *vaccination*, it should be performed, and its progress watched, by a medical man.

For the extension of vaccination, it is provided under the authority of the Act, that the following duly authorised medical practitioners are appointed to vaccinate persons resident in this union, without charge to such persons:—

Names of the Medical Practitioners who are the Public Vaccinators.	Their Residences.	Days and Hours of Attendance for performing Vaccination thereat.
(Insert the Names.)	*(Insert the Residences.)*	*(Insert the Day or Days, and the fixed times of Attendance.)*

It is also appointed, that for the purpose of performing vaccination, the public Vaccinator will attend at the following stations, viz.—

Vaccination Stations.	Attendance given for performing Vaccination.
(Insert the names of the Places where Children will be Vaccinated.)	*(Insert the times fixed for the attendance of the Public Vaccinators.)*

The fact of the person having been vaccinated will be registered, and the party will be required to attend eight days thereafter to enable the vaccinator to ascertain whether the operation has been successful.

Every child should be taken to be vaccinated between the second and third month after its birth, unless it be delicate, or suffering from disease, when the operation should be deferred for a week or two; but during the prevalence of cases of small pox in any neighbourhood, all persons who have not been vaccinated, and had the cow pox or the small pox, should be vaccinated without delay, even infants a few days after birth.

Many parents have thought, that because small pox has not prevailed in their neighbourhood, they need not have their children vaccinated, all such persons are hereby cautioned of the danger of deferring vaccination until small pox has actually appeared, as they not only thereby endanger the lives of their own children, but the lives of the children of their neighbours.

It is also to be observed, that in consequence of the great number of deaths, and of the evils, including blindness, which have been occasioned by the inoculation of children with small pox, which has generally been done by ignorant persons, the Act of Parliament has made it an offence punishable with *one month's imprisonment* for any person by any means to produce the small pox; and further, that whilst it is an offence against the law to produce small pox by inoculation, *it is also an offence to endanger other persons by carrying about or exposing any person who may have caught the small pox*, whether naturally, or by inoculation. For any one to endanger the safety of the public by causing persons who have any infectious disease, and who are in a state to communicate it, to be exposed or carried about at the risk of infecting others, is, by the common law of this kingdom, illegal, and punishable by imprisonment.

It is the duty of all persons, therefore, not only to avoid committing the offence of creating small pox by inoculation or otherwise, but to give information to the magistrate or some other peace officer, of any persons who have been guilty of the offence, that effectual means may be taken for the protection of the public.

Though the fee for vaccination is paid out of the poor-rates, it is not to be considered, in any shape, as parochial relief; it is expressly enacted, by the Act passed in the 4th and 5th years of the reign of Queen Victoria, that the vaccination of any person resident in any union or parish, or of any of his family, shall not be considered to be parochial relief, alms, or charitable allowance to such person. By Order.

Clerk to the Guardians.

London: Printed by Order of the Poor Law Board, by S. BLACKBURN, 90½, Holborn Hill, and Published by CHARLES KNIGHT, 90, Fleet Street.

AN

OFFICIAL CIRCULAR

OF PUBLIC DOCUMENTS AND INFORMATION

DIRECTED BY THE POOR LAW BOARD TO BE PRINTED, CHIEFLY FOR THE USE OF THE BOARDS OF GUARDIANS AND THEIR OFFICERS.

No. 17.] JULY AND AUGUST, 1848. [N.S.

CONTENTS.

Aug. 10*th*, 1848.—12 Vic.

I.—A BILL

INTITULED AN ACT TO ALTER THE PROVISIONS RELATING TO THE CHARGES FOR THE RELIEF OF THE POOR IN UNIONS.

1. 4 & 5 Wm. 4. c. 76.—*Costs for Relief of Wandering Poor, &c. to be charged to the common Fund of Unions.*

Whereas by an Act passed in the fifth year of the reign of King William the Fourth, intituled, "An Act for the Amendment and better Administration of the Laws relating to the Poor in England and Wales," provision is made for the formation of unions for the relief of the poor, and for the charge for the relief of the poor belonging to the several parishes comprised therein; and it is expedient to alter the mode in which the relief of certain poor persons is now chargeable; be it therefore enacted, by the Queen's most excellent Majesty, by and with the advice and consent of the Lords Spiritual and Temporal, and Commons, in this present Parliament assembled, and by the authority of the same, that after the thirtieth day of *September* next until the thirtieth day of *September* in the year one thousand eight hundred and forty-nine, the cost of the relief to be given to any poor person chargeable or becoming chargeable in any union formed or to be formed under the provisions of the said Act, being a destitute wayfarer, or wanderer, or foundling, as well as the cost of the burial of the body of any such person dying within such union, shall be chargeable to the common fund of such union.

2. *Poor Persons meeting with accidents to be relieved by the Parishes of their abode or previous chargeability.*

And be it enacted, That where any poor person having a fixed place of abode in a parish in any such union, shall hereafter, by reason of accident or sudden bodily casualty occurring to him while in some other parish, require relief, the cost of all the relief given by lawful authority in that behalf, as well medical and surgical as otherwise, shall, if the poor person be at the time in receipt of relief, be paid in like manner and by the same party as any other relief shall be then payable; but if he be not then in receipt of relief, it shall be paid or reimbursed, as the case may require, by the parish in which such poor person shall then have his place of abode, unless by reason of any provision of the law he would, if otherwise chargeable, have been chargeable to the common fund of such union, in which case the payment or reimbursement shall be made by the guardians of the union comprising such parish, and shall be charged to the common fund of the union; and it shall be lawful for the guardians of any union, if they think proper, to pay for any medical or other assistance which shall be rendered to any poor person on the happening of such accident or casualty, although no order shall have been given for the same by them or any of their officers, or by the overseers, and to charge the same to some one parish in the union, or to the common fund of the union, according as such parish or union would have been liable for the ordinary relief of such poor person; provided that nothing herein contained shall exempt the guardians of the union or parish, or their officers, or the overseers of the parish in which such poor person shall require relief by reason of such accident or casualty, from their liability to supply the requisite relief to such poor person, whilst in such union or parish.

3. *Paupers rendered irremovable by the* 9 & 10 *Vic. c.* 66, *rendered chargeable to the Common Fund of the Union.*

And be it enacted, That after the *thirtieth day of September* next, until the *thirtieth day of September* in the year one thousand eight hundred and forty-nine, all the costs incurred in the relief, as well medical as otherwise, of any poor person, who, not being settled in the parish where he resides, shall, by reason of some provision of the Act passed in the tenth year of the reign of her Majesty, intituled, "An Act to amend the Laws relating to the Removal of the Poor," be or become exempted from the liability to be removed from the parish where he resides, shall, where the said parish shall be comprised in any such union as aforesaid, be charged to the common fund of such union, so long as such person shall continue to be so exempted; and the expenses of the burial of any such person so exempted at the time of his death, shall, if legally payable by the guardians of the union, likewise be charged to the said common fund.

4. *Guardians may assist in the Emigration of certain Poor, and charge the Cost upon the Common Fund of the Union, or Parish, in case of not being in Union.*

And be it enacted, That the guardians of any union or parish may, with the order of the said Commissioners, and in conformity with such regulations as they shall make, procure, or assist in procuring, the emigration of any poor person removable by virtue of the provisions of the said last-mentioned Act, and chargeable, or who would, if relieved, be chargeable upon the common fund of such union, or in the case of any parish not comprised in a union, who may, though not settled therein, be exempt from liability to remove therefrom, and such guardians shall, in the case of a union, charge the costs and expenses incurred in such emigration upon the common fund, and in the case of a parish not in a union upon the monies in their hands for the relief of the poor.

5. *Any question as to such Exemption may be referred to and decided by the Poor Law Board.*

And be it enacted, That where, in any such union, a question shall arise with reference to the charging of the cost of his relief, as to whether any pauper be so exempted as aforesaid, the guardians thereof, or the overseers of any parish therein, may submit such question to the Commissioners for administering the laws for the relief of the poor in England, who may thereupon, if they think proper, entertain such question, and, by an order under their seal, determine the same; but no such order shall be liable to be removed by writ of *certiorari* or otherwise, into the Court of Queen's Bench, after the expiration of the term next ensuing the time when the copy thereof shall have been sent to the guardians, nor shall the same be quashed for any defect of form therein; and every such order not rescinded or quashed shall be, in all courts and for all purposes, final and conclusive between the guardians and every parish in the union interested in the matter.

6. *Mode of charging the Relief herein provided for.*

And be it enacted, That the cost of all the relief which under the provisions of this Act shall be chargeable to the common fund of any union, shall be charged to the common fund of such union, in the same manner as union expenses are directed to be charged by the herein first-recited Act.

7. *Guardians may procure Partial Valuations.*

And be it enacted, That the guardians of any union may, on the application of the major part of the overseers of any parish comprised in it, or of any person assessed to the poor-rate in any such parish, cause a valuation to be made at any time of any property alleged to be rateable to the relief of the poor, being a part only of the rateable property of such parish, and may charge the expenses of such valuation to the overseers of such parish, or to such person so applying as aforesaid.

8. *Guardians may obtain Orders of maintenance, and recover Relief advanced by way of loan, in the County Court.*

And be it enacted, That the guardians of any union shall be entitled to obtain orders of maintenance upon the relations liable under any statute now in force to maintain any poor person whose relief would be chargeable to the common fund of the union, in like manner as the churchwardens and overseers of any parish can now obtain the same; and may expend, in respect of such person, out of such fund, any money for any purpose which the overseers of the parish to which such person, if chargeable, would have belonged, might have done; and all relief to be granted by the guardians to any pauper upon loan, and which shall be chargeable to the common fund of the union, may be recoverable in the county court, or other court for the recovery of small debts for the district wherein the union or the major part thereof shall be comprised, on the plaint of the said guardians, who may apply and be heard in such court by any officer appointed by them for such purpose, in manner prescribed by the statutes enabling them to appoint officers to act for them: Provided nevertheless, That the remedy already provided by law for the recovery of the relief granted on loan shall be in force, and applicable to the relief so chargeable to the common fund as aforesaid.

9. *Persons being chargeable upon the common Fund of a Union, and being convicted of any Offence, may be committed by a Justice to the Common Gaol, &c., the Expenses of which shall be charged upon the County, &c.*

And be it enacted, That if any person herein-before made chargeable upon the common fund of the union shall be convicted before any justice of any offence committed in any workhouse while maintained therein, or of deserting or running away from any workhouse, and carrying away clothes or other property therefrom, and be liable to be committed to any gaol or house of correction, the justice before whom such person shall be convicted may commit such person to the gaol or house of correction of the county or place containing the parish in which such person, if chargeable to the common fund by reason of being exempt from removal under the statute herein-before mentioned, shall have been residing, when admitted into the workhouse, or to that of the county or place comprising the major part of such union, in the case of any other person herein rendered chargeable on the said common fund, notwithstanding such workhouse may not be situated in such county or place, or that such justice may not be a justice of such county or place; and the charges of the conveyance of such person to such gaol or house of correction, and all other charges consequent upon such committal, shall be borne by such county or place in like manner as the charges of persons committed in the ordinary mode to the gaol thereof shall be borne.

10. *Interpretation of Act.*

And be it enacted, That the several words used in this Act shall be construed in the manner prescribed by the said first herein-recited Act, and the statutes explaining and extending it.

11. *Act may be Amended.*

And be it enacted, That this Act may be amended or repealed by any Act to be passed in this session of Parliament.

II.—BURIAL—AS TO PROVIDING GROUND FOR THE BURIAL OF PAUPERS.

March 8th, 1848.

Clerk of Congleton Union—The churchyard of the parish in which the union workhouse is situated is now more than full, and the vicar has given notice to the guardians that he cannot find room for the burial of persons who may die in the workhouse. There is, however, spare ground attached to the workhouse, and it has been suggested that a small portion of that ground should be set apart, and consecrated for the purposes of burial.

Ans.—By the law, as it now stands, in regard to deaths in the workhouse, the guardians are bound, where the pauper while living, or any of his relations after his death, express any wish to that effect, to bury him in the churchyard or burial-ground of the parish to which he was chargeable; and they have the power to do so, in any case, without the expression of any such wish. It appears to the Board to be desirable that, in rural unions, the guardians should, as a general rule, bury every pauper dying in the union workhouse in the parish to which he was chargeable. Such a course appears to be proper on the ground of feeling. There can be no reason why the pauper should not rest in the parish where, if he had not been a pauper, he would have been buried. By such a course, moreover, the practical inconveniences which result from overcrowding the burial-ground of the parish in which the union workhouse happens to be situated, would be avoided. But if this were adopted as the general practice, there would still be many cases in which poor persons dying in, and chargeable to the parish of the workhouse, could not be sent away from it to be buried in any other parish. With reference to such persons there would be no objection, in point of feeling or policy, to their being interred in a burying-ground belonging to the workhouse, or in the churchyard of the parish, probably enlarged for the purpose of the reception of such corpses. The former of these two plans would have this advantage, that though the bishop would probably require, on the consecration of the burying-ground, that it should be open to the use of the whole parish; yet, practically, very few bodies, except those of the inmates of the workhouse, would ever be buried there. The Board believe, that if such workhouse burying-grounds were resorted to only when it was considered improper to convey the poor person from the parish in which he died, no public feeling would be excited against such places. The second plan may, in some instances, be the more convenient; but there are many practical and legal difficulties in the way of adopting it. The Board do not consider it at all necessary that a workhouse burial-ground should be in the immediate vicinity of the workhouse. On the contrary, every consideration of health would seem to require that such ground should be removed to some distance from the workhouse, as well as from other human habitations. The Board submit these observations for the consideration of the guardians upon the general proposition.

III.—COUNTY-RATE—PROCEEDINGS TAKEN IN THE COUNTY OF DEVON, UNDER THE 8 & 9 VIC. C. 111, FOR MAKING A NEW COUNTY-RATE.

London, July 27th, 1848.

MY DEAR LORD EBRINGTON—You asked me some time since to give you a short statement of the course of proceeding pursued by the magistrates of Devon, in making a new county-rate, under the powers of the Act of the 8 & 9 Vic. c. 111. The county-rate for Devon, which was previously in force, was, as you aware, made a great many years since, under the Act 55 Geo. 3, c. 31, and was most unequal, not only from the change of value in different parishes consequent upon the lapse of years, but also from its having been originally assessed upon the faith of returns made by the parish officers, whose interest it was to have their parishes assessed as low as possible, and whose consciences were relieved in making capricious returns upon oath, by the multifarious modes in which the poor-rates were made.

It was to enable the magistrates to correct this evil in an inexpensive manner, that the Act of the 8 & 9 Vic. was passed, and I scarcely know how to describe the course pursued by the magistrates in making our new rate better, than by referring you to the provisions of the Act itself.

A committee was appointed by the sessions, as provided in the Act, and held their earlier meetings at Exeter, as a central place.

Our first step was to require returns from the clerks to the Commissioners of Property-tax, of the annual value of property in each parish. (Forms Nos. 1 and 2.)

We also required from the overseers of the poor a return of the gross and rateable value of the parish. (Forms 3 and 4.)

From what we termed town parishes, as distinguished from entirely rural parishes, we procured full copies of their existing poor-rates, in order that we might see the proportion of house property, which in any estimation of value we considered required a considerable extra deduction for repairs and insurance. (See Form 5.)

Having collected all the information in our power, we found that little or no reliance could be placed on the poor-rates, for notwithstanding a recent Act required them to be all made on a full estimate of the actual value, for the most part, parish officers had been inattentive to that part of their duty, and the rates had been made upon an arbitrary value, much below what the law required. We, therefore, turned to the property-tax, and this, coupled with our own knowledge of the parishes, enabled us to obtain pretty nearly the real value of each parish.

In entirely rural parishes, we deducted a small per centage from the Property-tax Assessment, because we considered that assessment did not make a sufficient allowance for landlords' burdens.

From town parishes we deducted a further sum, varying between certain limits, according as we considered the general *state of house property* of each parish required it.

Having thus made the assessment, we printed it, and sent a copy to every parish, with a circular letter, (see 6 and 7,) naming a day for hearing appeals. We fixed to meet in certain towns on the days named, and thus the parish officers had not far to travel. (See Letter 8.) This we found gave great satisfaction.

In many cases of appeal we lowered our assessment—in others we increased it.

We tested the accuracy of the assessment by examining the poor-rate, and having found the actual rent of one or two estates in the parish, we got at the proportion of rating to rent, and then by deducting from, or adding to, the remainder, a similar relative sum, we ascertained the actual value of all. Upon this principle we corrected our assessment: and having finally settled it, we reported it to the sessions, when it was ordered to be printed, and sent to each parish, (see 10 and 11,) and no further appeals having been made, or objections raised, the assessment was confirmed at the following quarter sessions.

The result was, the increase of the annual value of the rateable property in the county, to double what it stood previously.

We believe that we have obtained pretty nearly the fair value of all the parishes; and we have the great satisfaction of knowing that all parties are content, and think the assessment fairly made. The time occupied in the whole of these proceedings was less than a year, and the total cost was under £500, which, I think, you will agree with me, was exceedingly small, for so large a county as Devonshire.

I hope this letter will afford you the information which you wished to obtain, and am

Yours very truly,
J. T. B. DUCKWORTH.

The Viscount Ebrington,
&c. &c. &c.

No. 1.

Exeter, October 15th, 1845.

SIR,—I am directed by the Committee of Justices appointed for this county under the provisions of the Act 8 & 9 Vic. c. 111, for preparing a fair and equal county-rate, to request you will supply them from the Property-tax Assessments in your custody, with the information required by the form [2.] The object is to obtain the *total of each parish* under the three separate heads given in the form, which will appear by the total of the columns 5, 6, and 9, in the Property-tax Assessments, under Schedule A., for the past three years.

The Committee will, under the powers of the Act, order payment of your charges for the trouble this will occasion, on your informing me the amount, and I am directed to express their hope that you will return me the form accurately filled up without loss of time, as the Committee will meet again in about a week.

I am, Sir, your very obedient servant,
T. E. DRAKE,
Clerk to the Committee.

To the Clerk to the Commissioners,
for the Division of

No. 2.

DEVON.

A RETURN of the Parishes within the District of and of the Annual Value as stated in the Property-tax Assessment for such Parishes.

PARISH.	Total Rent or Annual Value returned by the Parties.			Total Amount at which rated to the Poor.			Total Value by determination of Commissioners.		

No. 3.

Exeter, November 25th, 1845.

SIR,—I am directed by the Committee of Magistrates appointed at the last sessions under the provisions of the Act 8 & 9 Vic. c 111, for preparing a fair and equal county-rate, to request you will fill up the annexed form with a statement of the total gross value, and the total rateable value, of all the rateable property in your parish; and that you will also state what deductions are made from the gross value as respects lands, and what as respects houses. I must beg the favour of your being accurate in this return, as the Committee may require it hereafter to be verified on your oath, and that you will transmit it to me immediately.

I am, Sir, your very obedient servant,
T. E. DRAKE,
Clerk to the Committee.

To the Overseers of the Poor,
Parish of

No. 4.

DEVON.

A RETURN of the Overseers of the Poor of the Parish of in the said County.

PARISH.	Gross Value as stated in the Poor-rate.	Rateable Value, as stated in the Poor-rate.	Proportion in which deductions are made from Lands and from Houses.

Castle of Exeter, January 5th, 1846.

GENTLEMEN,—I am directed by the County-rate Committee to request that you will, forthwith, make the return required by my circular letter, of the total gross and rateable value of the property in your parish. The Committee are unwilling to exercise their power of imposing penalties, but they will feel themselves under the imperative necessity of doing so, unless the return be sent to me, before the close of the sessions this week.

I am, Gentlemen,
your very obedient servant,
T. E. DRAKE,
Clerk to the Committee.

To the Overseers of the Poor.

No. 5.

Castle of Exeter, April 18th, 1846.

SIR,—I am directed by the Committee of Justices appointed under the provisions of the Act of Parliament, 8 & 9 Vic. cap. 111, for amending the Laws relating to the Assessing of County-rates, to request you will prepare and sent to me, for their information, a true copy of the last rate made for the relief of the poor of your parish.

The Committee will meet again in about a fortnight, and I shall thank you to supply me with a copy in time for their meeting. They will be ready to order a reasonable allowance out of the county-rate to be made to you for the trouble this will occasion.

I am, Sir, your very obedient servant,
T. E. DRAKE,
Clerk to the Committee.

To the Overseers of the Poor.

No. 6.

Castle of Exeter, July 11th, 1846.

SIR,—I am directed by the Committee appointed under the Act of Parliament passed in the last session, "for amending the Laws relating to the assessing of County-rates," to transmit to you the accompanying printed copy of a proposed county-rate which the Committee have prepared; and to request your attention to the provisions of the Act, which direct you to call a vestry-meeting of your parish within twenty-one days after the receipt hereof, and to submit the copy of the rate to such vestry-meeting; which copy is to be, at all reasonable times, open to the inspection and examination of any person rated to the relief of the poor, or liable to contribute to the county-rate in your parish, who may take extracts or copies therefrom without the payment of any fee for the same.

I am further directed by the Committee to apprise you, that any objections to the proposed rate, whether it be on account of the parish being rated on a sum *beyond* the full and fair annual value of the property liable to be assessed toward the county-rate, or on account of some other parish being rated on a sum *less* than the full and fair annual value of the property liable to be assessed towards the county-rate, or otherwise, may be forwarded to me, as well by you as by any other person affected by such rate, on or before the first day of September next.

The Committee will fix a time and place for taking such objections into consideration, and for hearing the parties making such objections, of which time and place due notice will be given to you.

I am, Sir, your most obedient servant,
T. E. DRAKE,
Clerk to the Committee.

To the Overseers of the Poor,
Parish of

No. 7.

DEVON.

NEW COUNTY-RATE,*

Proposed by the Committee appointed under the Act of 8 *&* 9 *Vic. c.* 111.

AXMINSTER HUNDRED.

	Annual Value.		Rate at one Farthing in the Pound.		
	£.		£.	s.	d.
Axminster	13,880	..	14	9	2
Uplyme	4,416	..	4	12	0
Musbury	4,062	..	4	4	7
Axmouth	4,781	..	4	19	7
Combpyne	924	..	0	19	3
Kilmington	2,950	..	3	1	5
Honiton	12,924	..	13	9	3
Combrawleigh	2,306	..	2	8	0
Luppitt (including Shapcombe Tything)	4,950	..	5	3	1
Upottery	5,354	..	5	11	6
Membury	4,969	..	5	3	6
Yarcombe	3,836	..	3	19	11
Stockland	6,587	..	6	17	2
Dalwood	2,280	..	2	7	6

No. 8.

Exeter, October 26th, 1846.

SIRS,—The proposed assessment on your parish in the new county-rate, now preparing by the Committee appointed for that purpose, having been objected to by the parish of

I am directed by the Committee to give you notice, that they intend to meet at

on the day of

next, at o'clock, for taking such objections into consideration, and for hearing all parties thereon.

The Committee will require you to attend and produce the existing poor-rate, and also all valuations, and other documents in your custody, or power, relating to the value of the property in your parish, and to examine you upon oath, touching the same.

I am also directed to request that you will inform me immediately, the name and address of every person by whom your parish has been surveyed and valued within the last fifteen years.

I am, Gentlemen, your obedient servant,

T. E. DRAKE,

Clerk to the Committee.

To the Overseers of the Poor,
Parish of

* The Paper, No. 7, contained the proposed new county-rate in all the hundreds in the county of Devon.

No. 9.

Exeter, December 7th, 1846.

SIR,—I am directed by the County-rate Committee to inform you that they have finally corrected the proposed new county-rate, and that it will be submitted to the court at the next quarter sessions. In that rate it is intended that your parish shall stand at the annual value of £ , instead of the sum stated in the printed copy of the proposed rate, which has been already sent to you.

I am, Sir, your very obedient servant,

T. E. DRAKE.

To the Overseers of the Poor.

No. 10.

Exeter, January 12th, 1847.

SIR,—I am directed to inclose to you a copy of a new County-rate [No. 11] finally corrected by the Committee appointed for the purpose, and submitted by them to the court at the last quarter sessions, and to add that such rate will be taken into consideration at the next quarter sessions.

I am, Sir, your most obedient servant,

T. E. DRAKE.

To the Overseers of the Poor.

No. 11.

DEVON.

NEW COUNTY-RATE,*

As finally Corrected and Approved by the Committee appointed under the Act of 8 *&* 9 *Vic. c.* 111, *and laid before the Court of General Quarter Sessions of Peace for the said County, at Epiphany Sessions,* 1847.

AXMINSTER UNION.

	Annual Value.		Rate at one Farthing in the Pound.		
	£.		£.	s.	d.
Axminster	13,558	..	14	2	6
Axmouth	4,780	..	4	19	7
Beer and Seaton	5,588	..	5	16	5
Colyton	11,075	..	11	10	9
Combpyne	924	..	0	19	3
Dalwood	2,551	..	2	13	2
Kilmington	2,950	..	3	1	6
Membury	4,969	..	5	3	6
Musbury	4,062	..	4	4	7
Shute	4,164	..	4	6	9
Stockland	6,587	..	6	17	2
Uplyme	4,416	..	4	12	0
	£65,624		£68	7	2

* The new county-rate was set forth in like manner for all the hundreds in the county.

Exeter, January 12th, 1847.

SIR,—The Committee on the county-rate have ordered the payment to you of £ for the copy of the poor-rate of your parish, supplied by you, and which I shall be ready to pay to any person you may direct, on their calling at my office.

I am, Sir, your very obedient servant,
T. E. DRAKE,
Clerk to the Committee.

IV.—EDUCATION.

1. IN UNION WORKHOUSE SCHOOL.

July 26th, 1848.

The Guardians of the ——— Union—Having directed the mistress of the union workhouse school not to teach writing or arithmetic to the children under her care, and passed a resolution to the effect, that they felt that the system of giving pauper children in the workhouse a better education than the children of poor people out of the workhouse, was subversive of the principle on which they had always conducted their duties, the Poor Law Board addressed the following letter on the subject to the chairman of the board of guardians:—

The Poor Law Board learn with regret from the reports of the inspector of the district, Mr. Graves, that the guardians of the —— union have directed the schoolmistress not to instruct the children in the workhouse school in writing and arithmetic. The Poor Law Board desire to point out to the guardians, that the law leaves them no discretion on this point. By the 114th Article of the Consolidated Order, which has the force of law, the schoolmistress is bound to give instruction in writing and arithmetic, and for wilful neglect of duty prescribed by the Order of the Poor Law Commissioners, she is not only liable to dismissal, but the law has rendered her subject to pecuniary penalties. The Poor Law Board trust, therefore, that the guardians will not continue to act in opposition to the law, and to the declared policy of the legislature. They request that the guardians will countermand any illegal orders which may deter the schoolmistress from the due performance of her duties. The Poor Law Board have carefully considered the resolution passed by the board of guardians on the 2nd November, 1846. If the species of education to be given to children in the workhouses were left to the discretion of the guardians, and were not regulated by positive law, the Poor Law Board would still be unable to concur with the guardians in the principle of that resolution. The object of the policy which prescribes that the condition of paupers in the workhouse should not be rendered more eligible than that of the poor who support themselves by their own labour, is to diminish pauperism, by promoting habits of industry and prudence, and by discouraging a reliance upon eleemosynary relief. This object would not be answered by lowering the education of children in a workhouse below the standard of that which is ordinarily given by the industrious poor to their own children; many would, not improbably, become voluntarily paupers, if they thought that they would not diminish their own comforts by ceasing to trust to their own resources, but few, indeed, would be induced to become paupers in the hope of procuring for their children such an education as the law provides for boys and girls in a workhouse school. The children of parents reduced to destitution by improvidence or crime, are not themselves to blame for their unfortunate position; placed in a workhouse, they are subject to many disadvantages which it requires the aid of a careful education to counteract. They have not, like the children of working men out of doors, a practical training in the pursuits of industry. They have less free play of the faculties and affections, less knowledge of natural objects, and less opportunity of becoming acquainted with the characters and ways of mankind; on the other hand, they may generally be said to be without the stimulus arising from good example, and to be more subject to demoralising and degrading associations. In order to give the child in a workhouse the best chance of becoming an independent and useful member of society, the great distance which separates his condition from that of a self-supporting labourer's child must be diminished by education. The guardians will find that obedience to law in this matter will be a wise economy in the end, for the well-trained child will be more unwilling to re-enter the workhouse which he has once quitted, and more able to provide for himself out of it. Such are some of the reasons which justify the regulation laid down in Article 114; but there are other reasons of great weight upon which the regulation may also be vindicated. The guardians are for some purposes placed in *loco parentis* to the children, many of them orphans and deserted, who are inmates of the workhouse; and they would ill-fulfil the duties of guardianship, if they were voluntarily to leave these children exposed to the evils, moral as well as physical, which experience proves to result from a defective education, united with early habits of pauperism.

---

2. EDUCATION OF ROMAN CATHOLIC CHILDREN IN WORKHOUSE.

Feb. 29th, 1848.

——————— complained as to the course pursued in the religious education of Roman Catholic children in the workhouse of the ——— Union.

Ans.—The Board are of opinion that the letter of the 4th and 5th Wm. 4, c. 76, sec. 19, would not be violated, if an orphan child of Roman Catholic parents were to be instructed according to the doctrines of the Church of England, provided neither the child itself, nor its godfather nor godmother, objected to such instruction. Nor would the letter of that Act be violated, if access to such orphan child in the workhouse were denied to a Roman Catholic priest, where the child did not require his attendance. The Board think, however, that the guardians would exercise their discretion wisely, if they permitted Roman Catholic orphan children to attend mass, and allowed the Roman Catholic priest to visit them at the workhouse, under such regulations as might be consistent with the order and discipline of the establishment. The Board are also of opinion that the chaplain would do well not at all to interfere with the religious instruction of Roman Catholic children, and that the schoolmistress in teaching them should not employ the Liturgy, or other formularies of the Church of England, but should strictly confine her religious lessons to the general principles of Christianity, so far as those principles are clearly accepted by Roman Catholics.

V.—NUISANCES—PROCEEDINGS FOR THE REMOVAL OF.

April 3rd, 1848.

Clerk of Luton Union—The guardians have taken proceedings, under the statute 9 & 10 Vic. cap. 96, against several owners of premises for the removal of nuisances, which were certified to them, at the request of the guardians, by two of their medical officers, one of whom has sent in a bill, amounting to £3. 3*s.* for his fees, for certificates and attendances before the justices. In some of the cases, the parties have removed the nuisances without an order of justices, and in others orders have been issued. Inquired whether the charges of the medical men for certificates and attendances upon the justices are recoverable under sections 2 and 13 of the said Act: whether in those cases in which the parties have been summoned, but have removed the nuisance without an order, the justices can order payment of the expenses incurred: and, if not, whether the guardians can charge such expenses, including the medical men's fees, in the accounts of the respective parishes.

Ans.—The Board, having consulted counsel in the matter, are advised that the public authorities alluded to in the 1st section of the 9 & 10 Vic. cap. 96, have power to originate proceedings under that section; and that where medical practitioners are employed by them to inquire into, and certify as to, a nuisance, such medical practitioners may lawfully claim remuneration for their certificate from the authorities so employing them; though, if they send such certificate of their own accord, or at the instance of any private individuals, they would have no such legal claim. The Board are further advised, that such medical practitioners could not claim remuneration for their attendance before the justices, without a special contract, (see Payne *v.* the Guardians of the Strand Union, 8 Q. B. Rep. 326;) but that (under the 13th section of the Act,) they might be paid such reasonable remuneration as might be made the subject of a proper agreement. With regard to the fund, or party chargeable with the expenses in question, the advice given to the Board is to the effect, that the party complained against is not liable to reimburse the expenses of the preliminary inquiry, the costs recoverable from him, under the 2nd section of the Act, being limited to those incurred in obtaining and executing the order, *i. e.* necessarily incurred in the proceeding pointed out by the 1st section, which follows the receipt of the certificate; but that the costs incurred by the public authorities in causing inquiries to be made and premises examined, or in taking proceedings under the Act, may, (provided they are reasonable and proper for effecting the general objects of the Act,) be defrayed out of the poor-rates under the 13th section, in the several cases where no application is made to the justices, or where no order is obtained on such application, or where an order is obtained, and the justices, nevertheless, in the exercise of their discretion, decline to make an order for costs under the 2nd section.

VI.—REMOVAL.

1. ACT OF 11 & 2 VIC. C. 31.

CIRCULAR.

Poor Law Board,
Somerset House,
July 26th, 1848.

SIR,—I am directed by the Poor Law Board to forward, for the perusal of the guardians, a copy of a very important statute, (the 11 & 12 Vic. c. 31,) passed on the 22nd instant, affecting the mode of procedure in obtaining orders of removal, and in appealing against such orders.

The Act comes into operation on the 1st day of August next, and the Board recommend that the guardians should forthwith direct the attention of the overseers of the parishes of the union to its provisions.

I am, Sir, &c.,
W. G. LUMLEY, *Assistant Secretary.*

To
The Clerk to the Board of Guardians.

The Act referred to above.
11 & 12 Vic. cap. 31.

AN ACT TO AMEND THE PROCEDURE IN RESPECT OF ORDERS FOR THE REMOVAL OF THE POOR IN ENGLAND AND WALES, AND APPEALS THEREFROM.

[*July* 22, 1848.]

1. *So much of* 4 *&* 5 *W.* 4, *c.* 76, *as provides that certain Notices shall be accompanied by a Copy of Examination, &c. repealed.*

Whereas the communication now by law required to be made, by the overseers or guardians of any parish seeking to enforce an order for the removal of a poor person to the overseers or guardians of the parish to which such poor person is intended to be removed, of a copy of the examination upon which such order has been made, has been found to produce much expensive and useless litigation upon points of mere form, so that few cases of appeals against such orders are now decided upon the merits: for remedy thereof be it enacted by the Queen's most excellent Majesty, by and with the advice and consent of the Lords Spiritual and Temporal, and Commons, in this present Parliament assembled, and by the authority of the same, That so much of an Act passed in the session of Parliament holden in the fourth and fifth years of the reign of his late Majesty King William the Fourth, intituled, "An Act for the Amendment and better Administration of the Laws relating to the Poor in England and Wales," as provides, in cases of orders of removal, that the notice thereby required to be sent by the overseers or guardians of the parish obtaining the order shall be accompanied by a copy of the examination upon which such order was made, shall be and the same is hereby repealed.

2. *Such Notice to be accompanied by a Statement of Grounds of Removal instead of Copy of Examination.*

And be it enacted, That instead thereof such notice shall be accompanied by a statement in writing under the hands of such overseers or such guardians, or any three or more of such guardians, setting forth the grounds of such removal, including the particulars of the settlement or settlements relied upon in support thereof: Provided always, That on the hearing of any appeal against any order of removal, it shall not be lawful for the respondents to go into, or give evidence of, any other grounds of removal than those set forth in such statement.

3. *Copy of Depositions to be furnished on Application.*

And be it enacted, That the clerk to the justices who shall make any order of removal shall keep the depositions upon which such order was made, and shall, within seven days, furnish a copy of such depositions to the overseers or guardians as aforesaid, of the parish to which the removal is by such order directed to be made, if such overseers or such guardians shall apply for such copy, and pay for the same at the rate of two-pence for every folio of seventy-two words; provided, that no omission or delay in furnishing such copy of the depositions shall be deemed or construed to be any ground of appeal against the order of removal; provided also, that on the trial of any appeal against an order of removal, no such order shall be quashed or set aside, either wholly or in part, on the ground that such depositions do not furnish sufficient evidence to support, or that any matter, therein contained or omitted, raises an objection to, the order or grounds of removal.

4. *As to the sufficiency of Statement of Grounds of Removal or Appeal. Power to amend Statement of Grounds of Removal or Appeal.*

And whereas a statement of the grounds of removal or of appeal is required to be communicated for the purpose of enabling the party receiving it to inquire into the subject of such statement, and, if need be, to prepare for trial: Be it therefore enacted, That upon the hearing of any appeal against an order of removal, no objection whatever on account of any defect in the form of setting forth any ground of removal or of appeal in any such statement shall be allowed, and no objection to the reception of legal evidence offered in support of a ground of removal or appeal alleged to be set forth in any such statement shall prevail, unless the court shall be of opinion that such alleged ground is so imperfectly or incorrectly set forth as to be insufficient to enable the party receiving the same to inquire into the subject of such statement, and to prepare for trial: Provided always, That in all cases where the court shall be of opinion that any such objection to such statement, or to the reception of evidence, ought to prevail, it shall be lawful for such court, if it shall so think fit, to cause any such statement of grounds of removal or appeal, to be forthwith amended by some officer of the court or otherwise, on such terms as to payment of costs to the other party, or postponing the trial to another day in the same sessions or to the next subsequent sessions, or both payment of costs and postponement, as to such court shall appear just and reasonable.

5. *Party making frivolous or vexatious Statement of Grounds of Removal or Appeal liable to pay costs.*

And be it enacted, That if either of the parties to the said appeal shall have included in the statement of grounds of removal or of appeal sent to the opposite party any ground or grounds of removal or of appeal which shall, in the opinion of the court determining the appeal, be frivolous and vexatious, such party shall be liable, at the discretion of the said court, to pay the whole or any part of the costs incurred by the other party in disputing any such ground or grounds, such costs to be recovered in the same manner as any penalties or forfeitures are recoverable under the said Act passed in the session of Parliament holden in the fourth and fifth years of the reign of his late Majesty King William the Fourth.

6. *Power for Court to amend Order of Removal on account of Omission or Mistake. Proviso.*

And be it enacted, That if upon the trial of any appeal against an order of removal, or upon the return to a writ of certiorari, any objection shall be made on account of any omission or mistake in the drawing up of such order, and it shall be shown to the satisfaction of the court that sufficient grounds were in proof before the magistrates making such order to have authorised the drawing up thereof free from the said omission or mistake, it shall be lawful for the court, upon such terms as to payment of costs as it shall think fit, to amend such order of removal, and to give judgment as if no such omission or mistake had existed: Provided always, That no objection on account of any omission or mistake in an order of removal brought up upon a return to a writ of certiorari shall be allowed, unless such omission or mistake shall have been specified in the rule for issuing such writ of certiorari.

7. *Decisions of Courts upon hearing of Appeals final.*

And be it enacted, That the decision of the court upon the hearing of any appeal against any order of removal, as well upon the sufficiency and effect of the statement of the grounds of removal and of appeal, and of the notice of chargeability, and of the copy or counterpart of the order of removal sent to the appellant parish, as upon the amending or refusing to amend the order of removal as aforesaid, or the statement of grounds of removal or appeal, shall be final, and shall not be liable to be reviewed in any court, by means of a writ of certiorari or mandamus, or otherwise.

8. *Abandonment of Orders of Removal. As to Payment of Costs on Abandonment.*

And be it enacted, That in any case in which an order shall have been made for the removal of any poor person, and a copy or counterpart thereof sent as by law required, it shall and may be lawful for the overseers or guardians of the parish who shall have obtained such order of removal, whether any notice of appeal against such order shall or shall not have been given, and whether any appeal shall have been entered or not, to abandon such order by notice in writing under the hands of such overseers or guardians, or any three or more of such guardians, to be sent by post or delivered to the overseers or guardians as aforesaid of the parish to which such person is by the said order directed to be removed; and thereupon the said order, and all proceedings consequent thereon, shall become and be null and void to all intents and purposes as if the same had not been made, and shall not be in any way given in evidence in case any other order of removal of the same person shall be obtained: Provided always, That in all cases of such abandonment the overseers or guardians of the parish so abandoning shall pay to the overseers or guardians of the parish to which such person is by the said order directed to be removed the costs which the said last-mentioned overseers or guardians shall have incurred by reason of such order, and of all subsequent proceedings thereon, which costs the proper officer of the court before whom any such appeal (if it had not been abandoned) might have been brought shall and he is hereby required, upon application, to tax and ascertain at any time, whether the court shall be sitting or not, upon production to him of such notice of abandonment, and upon proof to him that such reasonable notice of taxation, together a copy of the bill of costs, has been given to the overseers or guardians abandoning such order, as the distance between the parishes shall in his judgment require, and thereupon the sum allowed for costs, including the usual costs of taxation, which such officer is hereby empowered to charge and receive, shall be indorsed upon the said notice of abandonment, and the said notice so indorsed shall be filed among the records of the said court; and if the said costs so allowed be not paid within ten days after such costs shall have been lawfully demanded, the amount thereof may be recovered from such last-mentioned overseers or guardians in the same manner as any penalties or forfeitures are recoverable under the said Act passed in the session of Parliament holden in the fourth and fifth years of the reign of King William the Fourth.

9. *No Appeal if Notice be not given within a certain Time after Notice of Chargeability.*

And be it enacted, That no appeal shall be allowed against any order of removal if notice of such appeal be not given as required by law, within the space of twenty-one days after the notice of chargeability and statement of the grounds of removal shall have been sent by the overseers or guardians of the removing parish to the overseers or guardians of the parish to which such order shall be directed, unless within such period of twenty-one days a copy of the depositions shall have been applied for as aforesaid by the last-mentioned overseers or guardians, in which case a further period of fourteen days, after the sending of such copy, shall be allowed for the giving of such notice of appeal; but in such case no poor person shall be removed under such order of removal until the expiration of such further period of fourteen days.

10. *Service of suspended Orders of Removal and Orders consequent thereon.*

And be it enacted, That all the provisions which relate to the sending and service of copies of orders of removal shall apply to such orders when suspended, and to all orders consequent upon such suspension, and to all copies of charges arising thereon, and demands of payment of such charges.

11. 4 & 5 *Wm.* 4, *c.* 76, *and all Acts amending the same, to be construed with this Act.*

And be it enacted, That the said Act passed in the session of Parliament holden in the fourth and fifth years of the reign of his late Majesty King William the Fourth, intituled, "An Act for the Amendment and better Administration of the Laws relating to the Poor in England and Wales," and all Acts to amend and extend the same, and the present Act, shall (except so far as the provisions of any former Act are altered, amended, or repealed by any subsequent Act,) be construed as one Act.

12. *Commencement of Act.*

And be it enacted, That this Act shall commence and take effect on the first day of August one thousand eight hundred and forty-eight.

13. *Act may be amended, &c.*

And be it enacted, That this Act may be amended or repealed by any Act to be passed in this present session of Parliament.

---

2. REMOVAL OF IRISH POOR.

March 27th, 1848.

Clerk of Stafford Union—Inquired, 1st, Whether the costs incurred in the removal of Irish paupers, by warrant under the hands and seals of the justices of the borough of Stafford, should be paid by the union or the parishes within the borough to which the jurisdiction of the justices is limited. 2nd. Whether the 10 & 11 Vic. c. 33, empowers a relieving officer to apply to the justices of the peace for a warrant for the removal of such persons from the union workhouse to Ireland, without the sanction or authority of the board of guardians. 3rd. Whether an application made by the relieving officer for a warrant of removal without the concurrence of the board of guardians, would be considered as an application by the board of guardians, in the event of an appeal to the Court of Quarter Sessions, against the removal of such poor persons to Ireland. 4th. Whether the Act 8 & 9 Vic. c. 117, and the Act 10 & 11 Vic. c. 33, are compulsory, or only directory on the guardians as to the removal of Irish paupers.

Ans.—1st. The Board are of opinion that, under the second section of the 8 & 9 Vic. c. 117, which authorises the removal of the party "at the expense of such union, or parish," the costs lawfully incurred in the removal of an Irish pauper, chargeable to any parish within a union, should be charged upon the common fund of such union, and not to any particular parish or parishes therein. The Board apprehend that the alternative expression,—"or parish,"—refers exclusively to the case of a parish not within a union. But they do not mean to say the guardians are liable in respect of any unauthorised removal. 2nd. It appears to the Board, that the 1st section of the 10 & 11 Vic. c. 33, does not empower the relieving officer of a union to apply to the justices for a warrant of removal, without the previous sanction or authority of the board of guardians. That enactment merely enables "any guardian, relieving officer, or overseer," to take the Irish paupers before the justices "without summons or warrant," a summons being requisite under the previous statute, 8 & 9 Vic. c. 117; but it does not authorise the justices to act in such a case otherwise than in the mode prescribed by the last-mentioned statute; indeed, it expressly requires them to "hear and examine and proceed in the same manner in all respects as if such person had been brought before them under and in the manner directed by that Act." Now, that Act renders it necessary that the justices should proceed upon the complaint of the guardians of the union, and issue their warrant, if they think fit, after they have heard and examined into "the matter of such complaint." The Board, therefore, think that the proceedings must still originate under the direction of the guardians of the union, though the relieving officer may perform the particular act of taking the party before the justices, without previously obtaining either a summons or a warrant. 3rd. In answer to your 3rd inquiry, the Board must state their opinion that the application of the relieving officer, unauthorised by the guardians, would not be an application by them. According to the view which the Board take, the warrant was not legal. 4th. The Board consider that the statutes referred to do not place the guardians of a union under any obligation to remove their Irish paupers to Ireland; neither do they compel the justices before whom the paupers are brought to issue their warrant.

VII.—VAGRANCY.*

1. CIRCULAR, TRANSMITTING MINUTE OF THE POOR LAW BOARD AS TO VAGRANTS.

Poor Law Board,
Somerset House,
August 5th, 1848.

SIR,—I am directed by the Poor Law Board to request that you will lay before the board of guardians the enclosed minute on the subject of relief to vagrants.

I am, &c.,
GEO. NICHOLLS, *Secretary.*

The Clerk to the Board of Guardians.

2. MINUTE OF THE POOR LAW BOARD.

The Board have received representations from every part of England and Wales respecting the continual and rapid increase of vagrancy. After making due allowance for the influence of circumstances that have created temporary distress, it is impossible to come to any other conclusion than that the system, which has of late years been adopted in the relief of casual poor, has been the principal cause of the extension of vagrancy. It is not difficult to see that a regular provision of food and lodging, at the public expence, for every person who chooses to demand them at any place, must diminish the risks and privations of a vagrant life, and tempt a resort to it on the part of many who would otherwise have been deterred from adopting it. Experience has shown that the roughness of the lodging and coarseness of the fare provided, while they inflict undesirable hardship on the really meritorious and destitute wayfarer, do not counterbalance the inducement which the certainty of sustenance and shelter holds out to the dishonest vagrant. The task of work prescribed and found useful where it has been properly applied has, from its being only occasionally enforced, exercised no general influence as a test; and the laws against vagrancy and disorderly conduct have failed to produce the effect of repression. The Board are unable to suggest any additional test or punishment that shall prevent the abuse of relief indiscriminately extended to every stranger who may represent himself destitute. A sound and vigilant discrimination in respect of the objects of relief, and the steady refusal of aid to all who are not ascertained to be in a state of destitution, are obviously the most effectual remedies against the continued increase of vagrancy and mendicancy.

The power of exercising this discrimination is vested by law in the boards of guardians and their officers. On them rests the responsibility of exercising it effectually. The boards of guardians, as they represent those who suffer from the evil, must seek the remedy principally in their own vigilance and energy. They can expect little help from Parliament, when no material increase

* The above Minute and Circulars may be had of Mr. Charles Knight in a separate form.

of their present power appears to be requisite; nor can they be supplied by this Board with any rules of action that can relieve them from the obligation, or prescribe to them the precise mode of exercising that discretion which is and must be left entirely to the local authorities in each case. The guardians must, therefore, encounter the responsibilities of their position, and entrust the business of administering relief, to officers who shall possess sufficient discrimination to distinguish those whose urgent destitution gives them a claim to relief, from those who throw themselves habitually on public charity because it is extended to all who choose to ask it. It is equally the duty of those officers to relieve the destitute and to repel the impostor; and it would appear to require no more than ordinary intelligence and care to avoid erring seriously in either direction. The Poor Law Board cannot by general rules supply the place of that discrimination which will in every individual case be required from those who have to administer relief. But they think that, without prescribing any strict rules to be followed in every case, they can make their general experience serviceable by offering some suggestions as to the principles on which relief should be administered to the wandering poor.

There is, obviously, a wide distinction between those who are temporarily and unavoidably in distress, and the habitual tramp or vagrant who simulates destitution; and one of the worst results of the present undiscriminating treatment of all, who are commonly denominated "casuals," is, that some of the most fitting objects of public charity are subjected to the discomforts that were intended to repel the worthless. Among all the unfortunate there are none whose destitution is more unquestionable, and whose hard lot presents stronger claims to sympathy than the widow and orphan, deprived, at a distance from home, of their natural supporter, and the honest artisan or labourer who is seeking the employment of which accidental circumstances have suddenly deprived him. Yet under the present system such persons as these either share the discomforts, the filth, the turbulence, and demoralising fellowship of the thief, the mendicant, and the prostitute, who crowd the vagrant wards of the workhouses, or are compelled to brave the inclemency of the weather and the pains of hunger, by reason of their unconquerable aversion to such companionship.

It would not appear to be difficult to establish a system by which this deserving class of persons might be furnished with such evidences of their character and circumstances, as might afford a fair presumption of the truth of their plea of destitution. A wayfarer of this class might, at the place where the cause of destitution occurs, be enabled by those who are cognizant of it, to obtain a certificate from some proper authority, setting forth his name, the cause of destitution, and the object and destination of his journey. On his presenting this certificate at any workhouse, the master, on finding that it was satisfactory, that the applicant was on the road to his destination, and that he was without money or other means, might at once admit him, and supply him with the usual accommodation of the inmates. In this way, the honest but destitute wayfarer, possessed of such credentials, would obtain the advantage of being admitted into the workhouse without reference to the relieving officer, and also of receiving better accommodation than that at present afforded to him in the vagrant ward.

These certificates would doubtless be open to abuse from forgery and personation. But as they would be granted only for a particular route, and a necessarily limited period, the facilities for such abuse would be less than those which existed under a somewhat similar system in former times: and, with the agency of the present improved class of poor law officers, additional precautions might readily be devised. At any rate, this mode, however defective, would supply far better securities against imposture than the present system of indiscriminate relief.

With such means of distinguishing the class of wayfarers, who would be furnished with presumptive evidence of the truth of their plea of destitution, the Board are of opinion that a different course should be pursued with the other kinds of vagrants. It would be advisable that the masters of workhouses should be directed by the guardians to refuse admission to persons not having such certificate, without an order from the relieving officer or overseer. Of course, an exception must also be made in the case of persons labouring under sickness, or extreme feebleness from want of food. In such cases, where it might appear that any delay would be attended with serious consequences to life or health, the necessary relief when sought at the workhouse should be at once afforded therein. But with these exceptions, all applicants should be referred to the relieving officer, who should inquire and decide as to the necessity of relief, as well in the instance of vagrants as of other poor, and grant or refuse it according to the necessity of each case.

With respect to the applicants that will thus come before him, the relieving officer will have to exercise his judgment as to the truth of their assertions of destitution, and to ascertain by searching them whether they possess any means of supplying their own necessities. He will not be likely to err in judging from their appearance whether they are suffering from want of food. He will take care that women and children, the old and infirm, and those who, without absolutely serious disease, present an enfeebled or sickly appearance, are supplied with necessary food and shelter. As a general rule, he would be right in refusing relief to able-bodied and healthy men; though in inclement weather he might afford them shelter, if really destitute of the means of procuring it for themselves. His duties would necessarily make him acquainted with the persons of the habitual vagrants; and to these it would be his duty to refuse relief, except in case of evident and urgent necessity.

A plan, which has been adopted with success in some towns in different parts of England, is that of employing a trustworthy officer of the local police as assistant relieving officer for vagrants. As the habitual vagrant has generally rendered himself amenable to the law by criminal acts, he dreads being confronted with the police: and the effect of this arrangement, where it has been adopted, is said to have produced the speedy disappearance of the greater proportion of the usual applicants. In all cases it has greatly diminished the number of vagrants applying for relief; and the presence of an authority capable of enforcing order has checked their usual insolence and turbulence. If parliament should sanction the provisions contained in a bill now before it, whereby the relief of vagrancy is made an union charge, one of the great practical difficulties that have stood in the way of a general adoption of such an arrangement would be removed. Wherever there exists an efficient county or borough police, the Board would be glad to sanction such an arrangement, as well as to authorise the reception of vagrants in a building altogether apart from the workhouse.

Such are the general suggestions which the Board have to offer for the consideration of the guardians; and by the adoption of which they hope that the evil now so loudly complained of may be greatly mitigated. It is very desirable that, on a subject which may be said to have rather a general than a local bearing, there should be a certain uniformity of action throughout England. At the same time the Board will be happy to co-operate in any sound and practicable plan for attaining the same object, which may be deemed by those who have to administer the law to be best suited to their particular localities.

The Board cannot close this minute without again impressing on boards of guardians, the absolute necessity of discriminating by inquiry and investigation between real and simulated destitution. This is no principle of partial applicability or incomplete obligation. It is the undoubted principle of the law, which equally requires the grant of relief to the destitute, and prohibits the misapplication of the public fund to those who are not destitute.

It was found necessary by the late Poor Law Commissioners at one time to remind the various unions and their officers of the responsibility which would be incurred by refusing relief where it was required. The present state of things renders it necessary that this Board should now impress on them the grievous mischiefs that must arise, and the responsibilities that may be incurred, by a too ready distribution of relief to tramps and vagrants not entitled to it. Boards of guardians and their officers may, in their attempts to restore a more wise and just system, be subjected to some obloquy from prejudices that confound poverty with profligacy. They will, however, be supported by the consciousness of discharging their duty to those whose funds they have to administer, as well as to the deserving poor, and of resisting the extension of a most pernicious and formidable abuse. They may confidently reckon on the support of a public opinion, which the present state of things has aroused and enlightened; and those who are responsible to the Poor Law Board may feel assured that, while no instance of neglect or harshness to the poor will be tolerated, they may look to the Board for a candid construction of their acts and motives, and for a hearty and stedfast support of those who shall exert themselves to guard from the grasp of imposture that fund which should be sacred to the necessities of the poor.

CHARLES BULLER,
President.

Poor Law Board, Somerset House,
4th August, 1848.

3. CIRCULAR OF INSTRUCTIONS AS TO THE FORM AND MODE OF ISSUING CERTIFICATES TO VAGRANTS REQUIRING RELIEF.

Poor Law Board,
Somerset House,
August 7th, 1848.

SIR,—With reference to the minute of this Board, which I had the honour of forwarding to you on Saturday last, I am directed by the Poor Law Board to call your attention to the suggestion therein made for the adoption of a form of certificate, which should entitle the bearer to immediate relief in any union workhouse at which he might present it.

As it is of importance that a provision of this kind should be adopted without unnecessary delay, the Board are desirous of suggesting a plan which appears to them the best fitted for the purpose in view.

The certificate should be signed by some one person in each union, holding a position of recognised authority. For this reason this duty had better be intrusted to the clerk of the board of guardians. As, however, it is not desirable to throw on that officer any substantive addition to his present duties, his part in the issuing of these certificates need be little more than formal. He should give them on the recommendation of a relieving officer, whose ordinary business would naturally render him the fittest agent for ascertaining the truth of the statements made by the applicants for the documents. The clerk's labour would, in fact, consist of nothing more than the filling up and issuing blank certificates, which might run in the following form:—

————————*UNION,*

The bearer (*insert here the name,*) aged ,
whose occupation is that of a ,
is certified to me by ,
relieving officer of this union, as a person who has become destitute owing to (*insert here the cause of destitution,*) and who is now on his way to
in the county of
(*insert here the reason of going thither, as* "where he expects to get employment," *or* "where he has friends," *or the like*)

(*Signature*)

————————

Clerk to the Board of Guardians.

Date
The bearer leaves for
the

————————

These certificates should be written or printed on the top of a sheet of foolscap, on the blank portion of which every master of a workhouse at which the bearer is relieved should be instructed to enter the date of his arrival, together with the date of his departure, and his destination for the ensuing day. This entry should be in the following form:—

Received into workhouse,
the of 18
Left for (*name of place of day's destination*)
the of 18

————————

Master of Workhouse.

The union officers giving these papers, or receiving the bearers at the workhouses, must on no account give relief in the form of money. This would subject the officers to very serious penalties.

I have the honour to be, Sir,
Your obedient servant,
GEO. NICHOLLS,
Secretary.

The Clerk to the
Board of Guardians.

London: Printed by Order of the Poor Law Board, by S. Blackburn, 90½, Holborn Hill, and Published by CHARLES KNIGHT, 90, Fleet Street.

AN

OFFICIAL CIRCULAR

OF PUBLIC DOCUMENTS AND INFORMATION:

DIRECTED BY THE POOR LAW BOARD TO BE PRINTED, CHIEFLY FOR THE USE OF THE BOARDS OF GUARDIANS AND THEIR OFFICERS.

Nos. 18 & 19.] SEPTEMBER AND OCTOBER, 1848. [N.S.

CONTENTS.

I.—EDUCATION:

1. EDUCATION OF BOYS AND GIRLS TOGETHER IN WORKHOUSE SCHOOLS.

The Board have addressed the following Letter on this subject to J. C. Kay Shuttleworth, Esq., Secretary to the Committee of Council on Education:—

Poor Law Board,
Somerset House,
6th October, 1848.

SIR,—I am directed by the Poor Law Board to inform you that, in consequence of the opinions recorded in the Visitors' Book by some of the School Inspectors, that it would be advantageous that the boys and girls in workhouse schools should be educated together, the Board have given their best consideration to the subject, and have also consulted their Inspectors upon it.

The Board are sensible of the beneficial results likely to ensue from the association together of young persons of both sexes, and of the influence which the different nature and qualities of the one exercise over those of the other. The position of children in a workhouse is, however, to some extent, an anomalous one, and necessarily precludes that free and unrestricted intercourse which takes place amongst children differently situated.

The ordinary check and control on young people, which arises from their mixing together in the presence of older persons of both sexes, cannot exist in workhouses; and as no amount of care and vigilance, on the part of any person who might be directed to watch over them, could adequately supply this deficiency, it was from the first found necessary to direct that the boys and girls should be kept and educated separately.

The question which the Board has now to consider, therefore, is, whether it is safe and expedient to relax this regulation with the view of permitting young people of different sexes to be associated together for the purposes of education; and having given the subject their best attention, and obtained all the information thereon which they deem to be necessary, the Board have come to the conclusion that the existing regulations cannot be safely departed from, except to the extent hereafter mentioned.

The Board consider that schoolmistresses should not, in any case, be dispensed with in the workhouse schools, nor the general admixture of the two sexes allowed; but it may, in some cases, be advantageous that the boys and girls should receive instruction from the same teacher; and when the arrangements of the workhouse admit of it, the Board would not object to their being in the same schoolroom together for that purpose for two or three hours every day. On such occasions, however, the schoolmaster and schoolmistress should both be present, and use the greatest caution and vigilance to prevent the evil consequences which might possibly follow from allowing young people of such a description to mix unrestrainedly together. The Board consider that the boys and girls should on such occasions occupy separate forms or benches, and that they should enter and leave the schoolroom separately and in order, accompanied by their respective teachers.

The Poor Law Board therefore propose shortly so far to modify workhouse regulations at present in force, as to allow the guardians, with the Board's sanction, to make arrangements for the occasional association of pauper children of the third and sixth classes, for the purpose of instruction.

I have, &c.,
EBRINGTON,
Secretary.

---

2. THE EMPLOYMENT OF YOUTHS (INMATES OF WORKHOUSE) AS ASSISTANT TEACHERS IN WORKHOUSE SCHOOLS.

16*th June*, 1848.

Clerk of Eton Union.—The guardians of the Eton Union have passed a resolution that two of the boys in the workhouse school should be employed as pupil teachers for five years; and the Committee of Council on Education have expressed their approval of such resolution. Requested the sanction of the Poor Law Board to the same, and inquired whether the boys should be considered as officers of the union, and receive a stipulated payment to provide clothing during their pupilage out of the common fund of the union, or whether they must continue chargeable to their respective parishes.

Ans.—The Board are glad to see that the guardians of the Eton Union are desirous of rendering the means provided by the Council of Education available for some of the boys in the workhouse. They consider that the boys so selected must be appointed by the guardians as assistants to the schoolmaster, and to such extent must be regarded as officers of the workhouse, and that, consequently, the charge for their maintenance and other remuneration must, like that of other officers, be borne by the common fund of the union. It does not, however, appear necessary that any salary should be attached to their office. The guardians may, like any other masters, legally engage servants or officers on any terms they and such servants together agree upon. In these cases the agreement may be for the guardians to provide the boys with food, clothes, and lodging, only during such time as the guardians think fit to keep them, and with the power reserved of dismissing them from their office upon the commission of any offence against such rules as the guardians may lay down for their conduct, or upon a formal complaint from the schoolmaster of their negligence or inaptitude as assistants. It is obvious that it will be the schoolmaster's interest, though engaged originally only to take charge of paupers' children, to undertake the additional trouble of teaching these youthful assistants in consideration of the sum proposed to be allowed under the minutes of August and December last, out of the Parliamentary Grant, to each schoolmaster for every pupil teacher under his care. It will also be for the interest of the pupil teachers in workhouses, though originally paupers, and living much in the same manner as their former pauper school-fellows, to exert themselves to merit the continuance of their maintenance in office by diligence in learning their future profession, and by strict conformity to the regulations and conditions under which they have received their appointments from the guardians, not only for the sake of their prospects of employment as schoolmasters hereafter, but also for the sake of the allowances they will be entitled to receive as pupil teachers from the Parliamentary Grant, under the minutes before referred to. The Board conceive that, by the plan suggested in your letter, the intentions of the minutes of the Committee of Council, as regards pupil teachers, can practically be carried into effect. The Board, after they have advised with the Committee of Privy Council on this subject, will again communicate with you upon it.

29th August, 1848.

Further Ans.—The Board suggest to the guardians the adoption of the following arrangements, founded on the experience of the Norwood school, in reference to the pupil teachers proposed to be employed in the workhouse of the Eton Union:—1. With regard to lodging, the pupil teachers should continue in the boys' division, and be charged to assist in maintaining order. It is desirable that they should sleep in the same dormitory with the boys, in a recess partitioned off to about eight feet high, with a pane of glass in the side to enable them to exercise supervision over the boys. The recess would serve as their study, where they may daily prepare themselves for their examinations.—2. As to clothing, it is suggested that they should have a suit of strong blue cloth, instead of fustian, or whatever other material may be in use in the workhouse; and it should be made in a different pattern to distinguish them from the other boys. —3. With regard to their meals, it is unnecessary to say more than that they should sit at the ends of the tables at which the boys take their meals, and assist the master in keeping order. The Board rely on the discretion and good feeling of the guardians to deal satisfactorily with any further details in the arrangements to be made for this new class of inmates in the workhouse; but will, of course, be happy, at any time, to furnish them with additional suggestions and information upon any points with regard to which the guardians may find it necessary to communicate with the Board.

---

3. THE EMPLOYMENT OF ASSISTANT TEACHERS IN A WORKHOUSE SCHOOL.

The Poor Law Board received, on the 7th September, 1848, a letter from the Committee of Council on Education, stating that they would forego, in the case of J. H., who was proposed to be employed as a pupil teacher in the workhouse school of ———, the requirement of any indentures of apprenticeship, and would be satisfied with the resolution of the guardians, sanctioning the employment of J. H. accordingly: and also, that the Committee of Council would, on the fulfilment of the usual conditions of the engagement of pupil teachers, be ready to provide the ordinary annual gratuity as an addition to the master's salary, and to set apart one-half of the stipend usually paid the pupil teachers as a fund, which, at the close of the engagement, might be applied to complete J. H.'s education as a teacher.

The Poor Law Board, on the 21st September, addressed the following communication to the churchwardens and overseers of the incorporation:—The Board will readily give their sanction to the employment of the boy in question as a pupil teacher in the ——— workhouse school, and they suggest that the board of churchwardens and overseers should appoint him as an assistant to the schoolmaster. By such an appointment he will become an officer of the establishment, and the charge for his maintenance and clothing will be borne by the united parishes, in the same manner as the rations and allowances to the other workhouse officers are borne. In appointing the boy as an assistant to the schoolmaster, the churchwardens and overseers should provide him with food, clothes, and lodging, during such time as he remain in that capacity; and they should reserve the right to dismiss him upon the commission of any offence against any rules which they may lay down for his conduct, or upon any sufficient or well-founded complaint from the schoolmaster of his negligence or inaptitude as an assistant. It will be alike the schoolmaster's duty and interest to instruct J. H., and he will, in consideration of any additional labour which he may thereby incur, receive the sum proposed to be allowed under the minutes of the Committee of Council on Education of August and December, 1847, out of the parliamentary grant to each schoolmaster for every pupil teacher under his care. It will also be the interest of the boy to merit the confidence and goodwill of the churchwardens and overseers, by his assiduity and zeal in the discharge of his duties as a teacher, by qualifying himself for the profession of a schoolmaster. By a strict attention to the rules and regulations laid down for his guidance, and by diligence and good conduct, he will be entitled to the allowance of a pupil teacher in the first instance, and may ultimately receive an appointment as a schoolmaster. The Board suggested the adoption of arrangements in regard to the boy similar to those set forth in their letter to the guardians of Eton Union. See page 275.

---

4. SOME FACTS RESPECTING THE FARM-SCHOOL OF THE BRIDGENORTH UNION AT QUATT, SALOP.

This school is exclusively for the instruction of the pauper children of the union. They often amount to sixty in number: the object not being to get rid of them as soon as possible, but to give them such an industrial *training* as may remove habits of idleness and incapacity, which are productive of future pauperism, and to facilitate the means of a permanent and independent livelihood when they leave the school. For this purpose the children of out-door paupers are sometimes admitted.

A private dwelling-house has been taken for the establishment, in a rural village four miles from the workhouse, with about four acres of arable and half an acre of meadow land. About fifteen boys cultivate this land, and attend to the stable, cows, pigs, &c.: not quite so many girls are instructed and employed in household-work, sewing, baking, washing, and the dairy. The afternoons are wholly devoted to industrial labour, and the mornings chiefly to school instruction, in which the attainments of the children are very superior to those of most workhouse schools, where no industrial training exists.

The system of cultivation pursued and its produce are fully set forth in the following letter and balance-sheet, which were furnished by the master to H. M. Inspector of Workhouse Schools of the district, at his request, for the information of other unions. By the latter it appears that a net profit of above £65, resulted from the farm during last year. It is worthy of note, that this large produce is owing to the quantity of liquid manure applied to the land, and which is derived from the drains of the house, together with all refuse matter suitable for the purpose, collected in one large cesspool constructed to receive it, whence it is drawn out in pails as it is required.

Bridgenorth Union School, Quatt,
27th June, 1848.

SIR,—I beg to forward you an account of the rent and other expenses connected with the school-farm, in the copy of the ledger account annexed.

I am not able to state accurately the quantity or the value of some of the crops grown, as they are consumed by the cows; but the amount realized for butter and milk may be considered as its value.

The kinds of produce are, mangel-wurzel, carrots, cabbage, vetches or tares, Italian rye-grass, and potatoes. These last supply the school at a market price; and if there be any to spare, they are sold wherever I can find the best market.

I must not omit to tell you, sir, that I always endeavour, when practicable, to take a second crop off the same ground, which I am in general able to do, from the large amount of liquid manure I have at command; for instance, after early potatoes I get rape or white mustard, after the winter vetches I get swedes, and after the first-sown spring vetches, turnips. The cultivation of Italian rye-grass, too, is particularly worthy the attention of any one having plenty of liquid manure, as it may be cut three or four times during the season. I have had it more than two feet high this year, have cut it twice, and shall cut it twice more.

It may not be uninteresting to you to know that one of the boys grew on one perch of ground last year, mangel-wurzels weighing 6 cwt. 1 qr. 5 lbs., or more than 50 tons per acre. I believe, too, I may say the average weight per acre of the crops we grow are, as near as may be, as follows:—Cabbage, 50 tons; carrots, 20 to 24 tons; swedes, 30 tons; wurzels, 30 to 40; potatoes, 300 bushels of 90 lbs., or more than 12 tons.

We have four acres of ground cultivated by the spade, and nearly half an acre of an orchard; this last belonged to the house before the farm was established. The rent is £2 10*s*. per acre, to which is added the interest of the money expended in erecting the cow-house, shed, tank, enclosing and draining, and also the rates and other charges.

I have, &c

HENRY GARLAND.

J. C. Symons, Esq., H. M. Inspector,
&c. &c.

Dr. LEDGER ACCOUNT.—QUATT SCHOOL FARM. *Cr.*

		£.	s.	d.			£.	s.	d.
1847.	March quarter.				1847.	March quarter.			
	To cash for milk supplied to the school	9	16	1		By loss on cow had upon trial	0	5	0
	To cash for potatoes do. do.	4	2	11		By purchase of cow and calf	18	10	0
	To do. for butter sold . .	9	15	9		By cash for sow to brawn, and cow to bull . . .	0	5	0
	To cash per cheque from Treasurer, *for purchase of cow* .	18	0	0		By expense attending sale of cow . . . . , .	0	3	0
	To cash from sale of cow .	10	0	0		By purchase of hay, malt-dust, and grains	3	10	3
	To do. from sale of calf . .	3	0	0		By purchase of sow, bran, and vetches	5	12	9
	To do. do. do. . .	2	8	0		By purchase of straw-engine, pans, and seed potatoes .	3	1	11
						By expense attending sale of butter	0	1	6
						By balance paid to Treasurer .	25	13	4
		£57	2	9			£57	2	9

Dr. LEDGER ACCOUNT.—QUATT SCHOOL FARM. *Cr.*

		£.	s.	d.			£.	s.	d.
1847.	June quarter.				1847.	June quarter.			
	To cash from sale of butter .	11	18	10		By purchase of hay and grains	7	13	5
	To do. for milk supplied to school	10	1	9½		By do. of bran 18*s.* 9*d.*, linseed 8*d.*	0	19	5
	To sale of ass	0	17	6		By do. of embrocation, 1*s.* 0½*d.*, muslin 9*d.* . .	0	1	9½
						By do. of cabbage-plants 10*s.*, spades 5*s.* 6*d.* . .	0	15	6
						By do. of lucern-seed 3*s.* 8*d.*, currycomb and brush 2*s.*	0	5	8
						By do. of wurzel and swede seed 1*s.* 8*d.*	0	1	8
						By do. of two pairs boys' gloves 1*s.* 6*d.*	0	1	6
						By do. of pony of Mr. Warder	7	7	0
						By sow to brawn, and 2 cows to the bull	0	7	6
						By cash to hedger for 2 days' work	0	4	0
						By expense attending sale of butter	0	7	6
						By balance carried to September quarter	4	13	2
		£22	18	1½			£22	18	1½

Dr. LEDGER ACCOUNT.—QUATT SCHOOL FARM. *Cr.*

1847. September quarter.

	£.	s.	d.
To balance brought forward from June quarter	4	13	2
To cash from sale of butter	8	9	8½
To cash for milk supplied to the school	10	3	11½
To cash for potatoes supplied to the school	4	12	11
To cash from sale of sow and pigs	5	5	0
	£33	4	9

1847. September quarter.

	£.	s.	d.
By grains, sharps, malt-dust, and hay	1	5	10
By expense attending mowing grass 7*s.* 6*d*, two hay-rakes 2*s.* 4*d.*	0	9	10
By sulphate of iron 8*s.* 10*d.*, two lbs. tarred rope 1*s.*	0	9	10
By turnip-seed 8*d.*, rape-seed 2*s.* 4*d.*, bone-dust 3*s.* 3*d*	0	6	3
By a remove and shoeing pony 3*s.*, drench for cow 10*d.*	0	3	10
By spinach-seed 3*s.* 6*d.*, expense attending sale of butter 5*s.*	0	8	6
By cash a year's rent, including interest on money expended in the erection of building, rates, and rent-charge	18	13	0
By value of sixty-three perch of the orchard at 50*s.*	0	19	8¼
By balance carried to December quarter	10	7	11¾
	£33	4	9

Dr. LEDGER ACCOUNT.—QUATT SCHOOL FARM. *Cr.*

1847. December quarter.

	£.	s.	d.
To balance brought forward from September quarter	10	7	11¾
To cash from sale of butter	5	18	10
To cash for milk supplied to school	8	14	1
To cash for potatoes supplied to school	7	7	9
To cash for potatoes supplied to St. Leonard's	6	15	0
To cash from sale of calf to Mr. Walker	2	11	0
To cash from sale of 8 pigs to Mr. Smith	6	0	0
To cash from sale of fruit	1	2	6
	£48	17	1¾

1847. December quarter.

	£.	s.	d.
By purchase of Indian meal, as bills	2	1	6
By ditto of Italian rye-grass seed	0	11	0
By attendance of Ecob and Rushton on cow	1	6	6
By three drenches 2*s.* 6*d.*, lard 10*d.*, bran 4*s.*	0	7	4
By seed of Messrs. Dixon and Co., as bill	2	8	4
By castration of pigs 2*s.*, pig-trough 1*s.*	0	3	0
By one bush. winter vetches 9*s.*, rye 1*s.*	0	10	0
By grains 10*s.* 6*d.*, toll-gate 1*s.* 3*d.*, embrocation 1*s.* ½*d.*	0	12	9½
By blacksmith's bill 9*s.* 6*d.*	0	9	6
By sow to brawn 2*s.* 6*d.*, sale of butter 6*s.* 6*d.*	0	9	0
By balance paid to Treasurer	39	18	2¼
	£48	17	1¾

Market Drayton Union, 6th June, 1848.

SIR,—Having been engaged with the Board, and also the auditor, since you visited this workhouse, I now hasten to lay before you a return of the proceeds of the workhouse garden for the last year, agreeably to your request; at the same time I beg to observe that I have not charged that part of the produce used in the workhouse at the outside value, as I am personally interested in keeping down the cost of the in-maintenance of the paupers *more* than I am in showing a large profit on the garden. I also beg to observe that, if I had proper means of consuming the produce, I could make upwards of £10 a-year more than what is made.

Statement.

	A.	R.	P.	£.	s.	d.
Potatoes debited to in-maintenance and credited to establishment for the quarter ending September 29, 1847				4	8	3½
Ditto for the quarter ending Dec. 25, 1847				6	6	0¾
1700 lbs. of cabbage used, but not charged, estimated at half the price of potatoes				2	7	2½
Sold early cabbage . . .				14	6	8
Ditto turnip-tops, 30 cwt. at 4½*d* .				0	11	3
Ditto red-cabbage				0	10	8
Quantity of land	0	2	38½	28	10	1¾
Ditto . .	0	0	17	8	8	7
	0	3	15½	£36	18	8¾

The 17 p. is the land on which I grow onions, thyme, parsley, mint, sage, peas, French beans, carrots, parsnips, &c., the profits of which I have estimated at double that of the other part of the ground. I also beg to observe, that the wash is sold and taken off the premises, and have only the urine, night-soil, soap-suds, decayed vegetables, fine ashes, and the straw out of the beds, to manure with, and yet I have sometimes manure to sell.

I am, Sir,
Your humble and obedient servant,
WILLIAM CRUTCHLEY.

Jelinger Symons, Esq.,
H. M. Inspector of Workhouse Schools.

II.—RELIEF—DISTRIBUTION OF THE CHARGES OF, IN CERTAIN PLACES:

1. CIRCULAR TO BOARDS OF GUARDIANS RESPECTING A BILL FOR THE MORE EQUITABLE DISTRIBUTION OF THE CHARGES OF RELIEF IN CERTAIN PLACES.

Poor Law Board,
Somerset House,
25th Sept., 1848.

SIR,—I am directed by the Poor Law Board to transmit to you two copies of a Bill, introduced into the House of Commons by the President, "To provide for the more equitable Distribution of the Charge of the Relief of the Poor in certain Cities and Towns." The Bill was introduced shortly before the prorogation; and in moving for leave to bring it in, the President stated that his object at that time was, to have the Bill printed and circulated throughout the country, in order that he might be enabled during the recess to ascertain the feelings of those interested in the matter.

Whatever may be the validity of the arguments that are advanced in behalf of parochial chargeability for the general relief of the poor, they appear hardly to hold good in the case of towns comprising several parishes. The labour and property of every town must be regarded as the common stock of the whole town. The labourer does not ordinarily work in the parish in which he resides; but the fact more commonly is, that while the shops, factories, wharfs, counting-houses, and the better kind of dwelling-houses are in one part of the town, the poor reside in another part, which is often in another parish. The pauperism of the latter parish has to be maintained by its own poor inhabitants, while the bulk of the property of the town has little or no pauperism to maintain. This unequal distribution of a common burthen, seems to be inconsistent with justice and policy; and the object of the present Bill is, to apply a remedy, by enacting, that henceforth all the parishes in the cities and towns mentioned in the Schedule, shall, for the purpose of maintaining the poor therein, be treated as one parish.

The machinery provided by the Bill is by no means complex. It is based on a Schedule containing the names of all cities and towns consisting of more than one parish, and that are co-extensive with the limits of a union; and it is proposed to give the Poor Law Board power to declare such unions combined as one parish for all purposes of relieving the poor. The poor would be relieved for the whole union by an uniform charge, to which each parish would contribute in proportion to the value of the assessable property contained in it. The means of ascertaining that value, and making fresh valuations where necessary, are provided in the Bill.

As the general question of the laws of Settlement and Removal will, in all probability, come before Parliament next session, the Bill proposes no alteration in the law on that subject.

Your union not being co-extensive with the limits of a single town, is not included in the Schedule of this Bill. I am, however, directed by the Poor Law Board to desire that you will bring the Bill under the consideration of the guardians, not only with the view of obtaining their opinion on its provisions, but still more with that of eliciting their opinion with respect to the propriety of applying the same principle to towns comprising more than one parish, but not extending over the whole union in which they are situated.

For this purpose, it has been suggested that another Bill should be prepared, containing in its schedule the towns which are within the category last mentioned. This Bill would give the Poor Law Board power to declare the parishes in such towns to be united as one parish for all purposes of relief. The rating and administration of relief for the other parishes of the union, would not be in any respect interfered with; but the united parishes would thenceforth contribute in proportion to the rateable property of each. Thus, suppose a town to contain two parishes, C and D, both, (to simplify the illustration) of equal rateable value; C contains the poor part of the town, and now contributes £1,200 a-year; while D, which contains the residences of the wealthier inhabitants, contributes only £600. Under the plan suggested, instead of charging on each parish these respective amounts, the two amounts would be added together, making £1,800, and £900, the half of the total, would be charged on each. If D were twice as rich as C, D would be charged £1,200, and C £600. If D were only half as rich as C, D would be charged £600, and C £1,200.

The Board have no wish to proceed in this matter contrary to the wishes of the parties interested in such a change; and they will feel obliged by any expression of opinion on the subject, which your union, or any town in it, may favour them with.

I am, sir,
Your obedient servant,
GEO. NICHOLLS.

To
The Clerk to the Board of Guardians.

2.—A BILL TO PROVIDE FOR THE MORE EQUITABLE DISTRIBUTION OF THE CHARGE OF THE RELIEF OF THE POOR IN CERTAIN CITIES AND TOWNS.

31*st August*, 1848.—12 Vic.

1. *Preamble.—All the Parishes in certain Unions shall be combined for Relief of the Poor.—As to Liabilities.—Contributions in Arrear.*

Whereas, in many cities and towns comprising several parishes, the charge for the relief of the poor is unduly distributed among such parishes, and it is expedient to provide a mode whereby such charge may be imposed thereon with more equity than at present; Be it therefore enacted, by the Queen's most Excellent Majesty, by and with the advice and consent of the Lords Spiritual and Temporal, and Commons, in this present Parliament assembled, and by the authority of the same, that as and when the Commissioners for administering the laws for the relief of the poor in England and Wales shall, by their order, so direct, all the costs and charges for the relief of the poor in the several parishes contained in the unions named in the Schedule hereunto annexed, shall be borne by the common fund of such union, to which the several parishes therein shall contribute, in proportion to the annual rateable value of the lands, tenements, and hereditaments in such parishes respectively, assessable by the laws in force for the time being, to the relief of the poor, whether actually rated or not, and whether the rate levied shall be collected in full or upon any composition: Provided always, that nothing herein contained shall alter or affect the liability of any parish comprised in any such union in regard to any charge lawfully created in the said union, and secured upon the poor-rates of all or any of the parishes comprised therein, which shall have been created at any time previous to the issue of such order, but the same shall continue to be charged and payable in like manner as it would by law have been charged and payable if this Act had not been passed. Provided also, that nothing herein contained shall apply to any contribution which shall be in arrear from any parish in such union at the time when the said order shall have been sent; but the same shall be recoverable, and shall be applicable in the same manner as if this Act had not been passed.

2. *Mode of Ascertaining the Annual Rateable Value.*

And be it enacted, that the guardians of every such union, in making their order of contribution on the several parishes, shall take the annual rateable value of such property in every parish therein from the valuation upon which such parish was assessed to the county-rate; or where there is no county-rate, to the borough or ward-rate, or other rate in the nature of a county-rate, in the assessment made last, before one month next preceding the making of such order for contribution.

3. *If Union extend into several Counties, a Valuation may be obtained by the Poor Law Board.*

And be it enacted, that where any of the said unions shall extend into several counties, or shall comprise any borough or part of a borough not assessed to a county-rate, and also a parish which shall be so assessed, and a question shall be raised as to the fairness of the valuation of all or any of the parishes in such union upon which the orders of contribution shall be so made by the guardians, it shall be lawful for the guardians of such union, or for the major part of the overseers of the poor of any parish therein, at any time, and from time to time, to apply to the Commissioners aforesaid to investigate such question, and thereupon the said Commissioners shall entertain the said application, and, if they see sufficient reason, shall cause the valuation of the several parishes in the said union to be equalized, by means of a survey and valuation of the rateable property of all or any of such parishes, or otherwise as to them shall appear most expedient; and shall, if they think necessary, by order under their seal, declare the proper valuation of the several parishes in the said union, and shall order the costs and expenses which shall be incurred in the making of such survey and valuation to be paid by the several parishes in the said union, according to the proportions of rateable value established by such valuation, or by some one or more of the said parishes, as they shall think most equitable; and the valuation of the several parishes in any union so declared by the said Commissioners shall be used by the guardians thereof for the purposes of this Act until the said Commissioners shall, by their order, under seal, otherwise direct.

4. *Until such Valuation, previous Valuation to be used.*

And be it enacted, that while any such last-mentioned valuation shall be in course of being made, or until the question shall be determined by the Commissioners, the guardians shall make their orders for contributions upon the several parishes according to the valuation previously acted upon.

5. *No Order for Contribution to be deemed Void by reason of Error in the Calculation.*

And be it enacted, that no order of guardians for contribution, purporting to be made in accordance with this Act, shall be deemed to be void by reason of any error in the estimate of the rateable value of the property in any parish in the union upon which the contribution shall have been calculated, but every parish affected by such error shall be entitled to have the same set right in the making out and closing of the accounts of the union, or at the audit thereof.

6. *How the Poor to be described as Chargeable, and provision for Costs of Removal,*

And be it enacted, that where any parishes shall be so combined as aforesaid, by virtue of this Act, and of the order of the said Commissioners, and an order for the removal of any poor person whose relief shall be chargeable to the parishes so combined shall be applied for, such poor person shall, for the purpose of such order of removal, be deemed to be chargeable to the parish in which he shall be inhabiting at the time when he shall be so relieved, and the costs and expenses which shall be properly incurred in and about the procuring and executing of such order, and the defence thereof against any appeal, shall be paid by the guardians of the union, and charged, in like manner, as the cost of the relief prior to the removal was chargeable.

7. *Provision as to Appeal.*

And be it enacted, That where any order of removal shall have been made to any parish so combined in any such district, the churchwardens and overseers, or the overseers, as the case may be, of such parish, may appeal against such order, in like manner and with the like effect as if this Act were not passed; and if the consent of the guardians of the union, comprising such parish, to such appeal be obtained, or if the order of removal be quashed on such appeal, the costs and expenses properly incurred in and about such appeal shall be paid and charged in like manner as the relief of the poor person named in such order would have been payable and chargeable if no such appeal had been made, and the poor person had been removed.

8. *Interpretation of the word " Parish."*

And be it enacted, That the term " Parish" in this Act shall be construed to signify every place separately maintaining its own poor.

9. *Act may be repealed, &c.*

And be it enacted, That this Act may be repealed or amended by any Act to be passed in this Session of Parliament.

SCHEDULE.

List of Unions.

Cambridge.	Lewes.
Colchester.	Medway.
Derby.	Newcastle-upon-Tyne.
Gravesend.	Nottingham.
Ipswich.	Portsea.
King's Lynn.	Reading.
Leicester.	Worcester.

STATUTES:

1. CIRCULAR TO BOARDS OF GUARDIANS RESPECTING THE PARISH DEBTS AND AUDIT ACT (11 and 12 Vic. c. 91.) DISTRICTS' SCHOOLS (11 & 12 Vic. c. 82.) &c.

Poor Law Board,
Somerset House,
9th October, 1848.

SIR,—The Poor Law Board, in furtherance of the intention expressed in their letter of the 29th ultimo, desire to call the attention of the guardians to the provisions of the Statute 11 & 12 Vic. c. 91, relating to the payment of parochial debts and the audit of parochial and union accounts, to those of the 11 & 12 Vic., c. 82, for facilitating the formation of districts for the education of infant poor, and to some other Acts relating to the poor laws, passed in the last session of parliament.

The Act 11 & 12 Vic. c. 91, will be found to deal principally with two subjects, (1) the payment of debts by parish officers, (2) the audit of accounts and the proceedings of the auditor in respect thereof.

The guardians are aware of the difficulties which have occurred in regard to the payment of debts contracted by overseers a short time before the expiration of their year of office, but not discharged before the appointment of their successors. The carrying out of the strict rule of law, which required the overseers to discharge all their liabilities before their year of office expired, has been found to be often impracticable, and to produce when enforced harsh consequences to persons who have been compelled to fill the onerous office of overseer. This Act now provides a remedy. It enables debts contracted by overseers, within three months prior to the termination of their year of office, to be paid by and recovered from their immediate successors. It also provides that if any debt shall have been contracted before that time, and within the year of office, it shall be payable by such successors, if the rate-payers of the parish and the Poor Law Board consent.

Provision is made in sec. 2 for the payment of the costs of legal proceedings commenced on

---

The following are some of the Acts referred to in the above Circular Letter:—

11 & 12 VIC. c. 91.

An Act to make Provision for the Payment of Parish Debts, the Audit of Parochial and Union Accounts, and the Allowance of certain Charges therein.

31st August, 1848.

1. *If Overseers contract Debts within Three Months of Termination of their year of office, their immediate Successors shall discharge the same.*

Whereas it is expedient to make some provisions as to the payment in certain cases of debts incurred by the overseers of the poor in parishes after their year of office has expired: be it therefore enacted by the Queen's most excellent Majesty, by and with the advice and consent of the Lords Spiritual aud Temporal, and Commons, in this present Parliament assembled, and by the authority of the same, that if the overseers of the poor in any parish shall lawfully, by virtue of their office, contract any debt on account of the parish within three months prior to the termination of their year of office, and the same shall not have been discharged by them before their year of office shall have determined, such debt shall be payable by and recoverable from their immediate successors in office, and chargeable upon the poor-rate of the said parish, in like manner as the same would have been payable and chargeable by such first-mentioned overseers during their year of office; and if any such debt shall have been contracted during their year of office, but more than three months prior to its termination, the same shall be payable by and recoverable from their immediate successors in office, if the rate-payers of the parish in vestry assembled, and the Commissioners for administering the laws for relief of the poor in *England*, shall consent, but not otherwise.

2. *Provision for Payment of Bills of Costs for Legal Proceedings.*

Provided nevertheless, and be it enacted, that where any proceedings have been commenced or shall be hereafter carried on, for or on behalf of any parish, in a court of law,

behalf of parishes in certain cases. It will not be necessary that the costs be paid until the termination of the proceedings. They must however be paid within one year after the termination of the proceedings, unless the Poor Law Board authorize their being paid by annual instalments, not exceeding five.

As it appears that there are many outstanding claims of overseers and other officers, as well as of private individuals, in respect of money advanced or expended on behalf of parishes or unions, which have not been allowed in the accounts, it has been thought proper in sec. 3 to enable those claims to be discharged wherever the guardians of the union or parish, or the vestry of the parish, desirous of discharging them consent. The order of the Poor Law Board is however required to sanction the reimbursement, and the claim must be one which has accrued since the passing of the Poor Law Amendment Act (August, 1834) and before the passing of the present Act. The reimbursement must also be made forthwith or by equal annual instalments, not exceeding five.

The guardians will doubtless perceive that it is not proposed by this clause to refund any money wrongfully paid, and properly disallowed by auditors, and the Poor Law Board wish it to be understood that no proposal which would have that effect will receive their sanction. But they will be ready to entertain any case in which it can be shown that money has been really advanced for the benefit of the union or parish, but without that strict legal authority which the auditor in the discharge of his important duties deemed to be requisite.

The next seven clauses relate to the audit, and the proceedings of the auditor, and have been framed for the purpose of removing some difficulties which attended the audit itself, and facilitating the enforcing of the auditors' certificates.

In the first place, enlarged powers are given to the Poor Law Board in deciding appeals to them against the auditors' decisions. By the 7 & 8 Vic. c. 101, § 36, the Poor Law Commissioners could only decide as to the lawfulness of the reasons assigned by the auditor for his allowance, disallowance, or surcharge. By sec. 4 of this Act the Poor Law Board can now entertain the whole matter and decide it according to its merits. They are also empowered to remit any surcharge or disallowance lawfully made by an

---

regarding any matter affecting the poor-rates of such parish, it shall not be necessary that the bill of costs of the solicitor or attorney engaged therein shall be paid before the termination of the proceedings, but in any such case the amount of the bill, when duly taxed, if otherwise chargeable against the parish, shall be payable out of the poor rates within the space of one year next following the termination of the proceedings, but not afterwards, unless the Commissioners aforesaid shall by their order authorise the payment of the costs and expenses attending any such proceedings by annual instalments not exceeding five, to commence from such termination.

3. *Parties who have advanced money on behalf of Unions and Parishes to be reimbursed.*

And whereas in many cases sums of money expended by officers or other persons on behalf or for the benefit of unions and parishes, without legal authority, have not been allowed by the auditors, though the guardians of the unions and the rate-payers of the parishes interested have been willing and desirous that such sums should be paid out of the funds of those unions or parishes respectively, and great loss, in consequence of such sums not being allowed, has been sustained by individuals; and it is desirable that power should be given for the relief of such persons, under certain circumstances: be it therefore enacted, that if any person, since the passing of the Act of the fifth year of the reign of his late Majesty, intituled, *An Act for the Amendment and better Administration of the Laws relating to the Poor in* England *and* Wales, [4 & 5 *Wm.* 4. c. 76.] and before the passing of this Act, have advanced or expended money on behalf and for the benefit of any union or parish, without having had due legal authority for such advance or expenditure, and the same shall not have been allowed in the accounts of the union or of the parish on behalf of which it has been expended or advanced, and the major part of the guardians of such union or parish, or the rate-payers of such parish in vestry assembled, as the case may be, shall express their consent to the reimbursement of such sum of money out of the funds of the union or parish so interested, the Commissioners aforesaid may, if they think fit, by their order authorise the reimbursement of such sum of money by the guardians of the union or parish, or the overseers of the parish, as the case may require, in such manner as the said Commissioners shall deem most advisable, so however that if the same be not repaid at once it shall be repaid by equal annual instalments not exceeding five; and all payments subsequently made in conformity with such order, but not otherwise, shall be allowed by the auditor in the accounts of the guardians, overseers, or other officers who shall make the payment in obedience to such order: provided always, that nothing herein contained shall apply to authorise the repayment of any sum of money which has been paid on any other account than that of the relief of the poor, or in respect of some matter chargeable upon or connected with the poor-rate.

4. *Appeal against Disallowances and Surcharges may be determined by the Poor Law Board on the Merits, and such Disallowances, &c., may be remitted in certain Cases.*

And be it enacted, that where any appeal shall be made to the said Commissioners against any allowance, disallowance, or surcharge made by any auditor in the accounts of any guardians, overseers, or their officers, it shall be lawful for the said Commissioners to decide the same according to the merits of the case; and if they shall find that any disallowance or surcharge shall have been or shall be lawfully made, but that the subject matter thereof was incurred under such circumstances as make it fair and equitable that the disallowance or surcharge should be remitted, they may, by an order under their seal, direct that the same shall be remitted, upon payment of the costs, if any, which may have been incurred by the auditor or other competent authority in the enforcing of such disallowance or surcharge.

auditor, where they shall consider that such remission would be fair and equitable.

The 5th sec. describes in detail what monies the auditor is to certify to be due, and the manner in which he is to do so; and removes difficulties which have heretofore been experienced. It provides that where any overseer or officer shall be continuing in office at the time of the audit, the auditor shall certify as due such sums only as he shall disallow or surcharge in the accounts so audited. But where the term of office shall have expired the auditor shall ascertain the *balance then* due, together with the sums, if any, disallowed or surcharged, and shall give credit for all sums which shall be proved before him to have been paid in respect of such balance to the succeeding overseers or officers, or otherwise lawfully applied on behalf of the parish or union interested therein, and shall certify the balance remaining due after such credit shall have been given. Small sums disallowed by the auditor, amounting in the aggregate to less than forty shillings, may be paid over with the balance due instead of being paid to the Treasurer. It will be observed that forms of certificate to be used by the auditor are given in a Schedule to the Act.

Complaints have often been made that payments made to constables by overseers in obedience to orders of Justices have been disallowed in the accounts of such overseers, because the orders were not legal, or the fees were not such as were legal in amount. It has been thought undesirable that, having obeyed what appeared to be a due legal authority, the overseers should be exposed to loss in consequence. It is therefore now provided, that the order of a Justice or Justices, purporting to have been made under the 18 Geo. 3. c. 19, or the 5 & 6 Vic. c. 109, sec. 17, for the payment to a constable, shall be of itself a conclusive justification of the overseer before the auditor for the payment.

Sec. 7 provides, that the notice of the audit shall be published in a newspaper circulating in the union, but does not supersede the notice required to be given to officers accounting under the 7 & 8 Vic. c. 101, sec. 33.

The statute makes no provision for the payment of the expense of publishing this notice, and though perhaps the auditor who is required to publish the notice would in strictness be bound to do so at his own cost, yet as in fixing the amount of the salaries of the auditors no such expense was contemplated, the Board do not think it right that they should bear it. While their salaries are paid as at present by the Government, the Poor Law Board will undertake to pay this expense.

Sec. 8 requires notice to be given by the auditor to any person, (not being an accounting officer,) before he shall surcharge such person in respect of any improper payment which he may

5. *Mode of certifying as to Balances to officers.*

And whereas doubts exist as to the powers and duties of auditors in certifying the sums due from the overseers and other officers, and it is desirable to remove such doubts: be it therefore enacted, that where any overseer or officer shall be continuing in office at the time when the accounts are audited, the auditor shall certify as due such sums of money only as shall be disallowed or surcharged by him in the accounts so audited; but where the term of office of such overseer or officer shall have expired at the time when the accounts are audited, he shall ascertain the balance which he shall find to be then due on the accounts so audited, together with the sums (if any) which he shall have disallawed or surcharged, and shall give credit for all sums which shall be proved before him to have been paid in respect of such balance to the succeeding overseers or officers, or otherwise lawfully applied on behalf of the parish or union interested therein, before the date of his audit, and he shall certify, report, and recover, in the manner provided by law, the balance remaining due after such credit shall have been given; and every certificate made by any auditor, if made according to the forms set forth in the schedule hereunto annexed, or to the like effect, shall be deemed to be sufficient: provided always, that where the sum, or the aggregate of the sums, disallowed by the auditor in the account of any officer, shall not amount to forty shillings, the same may be paid over with the balance due from such officer, instead of being paid to the treasurer.

6. *Sums paid by overseers to constables, &c., by order of Justices under* 18 G. 3. c. 19, *or* 5 & 6 Vic. c. 109, *not to be disallowed by Auditors.*

And be it enacted, That where any money shall have been paid by an overseer to a constable, headborough, tithingman, or other peace officer, in obedience to any authority in writing purporting to be an order of a justice made according to the provision of the Act passed in the eighteenth year of the reign of his late Majesty *George* the Third, for the payment of the charges of constables in certain cases, or an order of justices in petty sessions assembled, purporting to be made in conformity with the provisions contained in the Act of the sixth year of the reign of Her present Majesty, for the appointment and payment of parish constables, it shall not be disallowed by any auditor or other authority competent to examine, allow, and disallow the accounts of overseers, on any ground whatsoever.

7. *Notice of Audit to be advertised.*

And be it enacted, that, in addition to the notices now required by law to be given by the auditor, he shall also give notice by advertisement in some newspaper circulating in the county wherein the union or the greater part of it, or, in the case of a parish not comprised in a union, wherein such parish shall be situated, a reasonable time prior to the holding of his audit; and the production of a copy of such newspaper shall in all courts and for all purposes be deemed sufficient evidence of the notice of the audit; and, except where a party, not being an officer bound to account to the auditor, shall be surcharged by such auditor, it shall not be necessary to prove that the audit of any accounts was adjourned, and that notice of any such adjourned audit was given.

have authorized, so that such person having received due notice may appear before the auditor and defend his act.

As the auditors have found much difficulty in enforcing their certificates before justices in conseqence of the technical proof required on various points, the 9th sec. removes the difficulty arising from this source, and sets forth clearly the only matters which the auditors shall be required to prove before the justices, and facilitates in some respects the proof. This enactment dispenses with the expensive proofs heretofore required from the auditor, the costs of which frequently fell upon the union or some parish in it.

The 10th sec. enables the auditor, with the consent of the Poor Law Board, to appoint a person to act temporarily as his deputy.

The 11th sec. enables parishes mutually to bear the costs of appeals brought at the same time against their respective poor rates, where such appeals appear to involve some common principle. The agreement for this purpose must be with the consent of the vestries and with the approval of the Poor Law Board.

The 12th sec. in no respect applies to boards of guardians formed under the Poor Law Amendment Act, but is confined to some few parishes and unions governed by local Acts; and the 13th and last sec. relates simply to the interpretation of words.

---

8. *As to Proceedings necessary to be taken against Persons now liable to be surcharged by Auditor, and to whom no Notice is required to be given.*

And be it enacted, that if an auditor shall see cause to surcharge any person now liable by law to be surcharged by him, and to whom no notice is now required by law to be given, with any sum of money in reference to any payment considered by him to have been illegally or improperly made, he shall, if the person be not present at such audit, cause notice in writing of his intention to make such surcharge to be given, by post or otherwise, to the person against whom he shall propose to make this surcharge, addressed to him at his last known place of abode, and shall adjourn the audit, so far as it shall relate to such particular matter, for a sufficient time to allow of such person appearing before him, and showing cause against such surcharge. and at such time the said auditor shall hear the party, if present, and determine according to the law and justice of the case.

9. *What shall be required to be proved by Auditors in order to recover Sums certified by them to be due.*

And be it enacted, That in any proceedings to be taken by an auditor, or by his attorney, before justices, to recover sums certified by him to be due, it shall be sufficient for him to produce a certificate of his appointment under the seal of the Poor Law Commissioners, or of the Commissioners aforesaid, and to state and prove that the audit was held, that the certificate was made in the book of account of the union or parish to which the same relates, and that the sum certified to be due had not been paid to the treasurer of the guardians of the union or of the parish, as the case may require, within seven days after the same had been so certified, nor within three clear days before the laying of the information, of which nonpayment a certificate in writing purporting to be signed by the treasurer, shall be sufficient proof on the part of the auditor; and if at the hearing of such information it shall be proved that the said sum had been paid to the treasurer subsequently to the date of such last-mentioned certificate, the costs incurred by such auditor shall be paid by the party against whom the information shall be laid, unless he prove that notice of such payment had been given to the auditor twenty-four hours at least prior to the laying of the information.

10. *Auditor may, upon Cause being shown, appoint a Deputy.*

And be it enacted, that the said Commissioners may at any time, upon sufficient cause being shown to them, authorize any person, selected by the auditor, to act temporarily as his deputy, and shall communicate to the several unions and places forming his district the name of the person so appointed to act as his deputy, and such person shall thereupon be empowered to act in all respects, and with the same authorities, and subject to the same duties and liabilities, as the auditor himself is entitled or subject to.

11. *Power for Parishes, with Consent of Vestries, mutually to bear the Costs of several Appeals involving the same common Principle.*

And be it enacted, that where appeals are brought at the same time against the poor rates of several parishes, which may appear to involve some common principle, it shall be lawful for the overseers or other authorities therein, with the consent of the respective vestries of such parishes, to enter into an agreement, to be approved of by the said Commissioners, mutually to bear the costs which may be properly incurred in and about the trial of such appeals on the part of the several respondents, as well as costs of the appellants, if any, which may be awarded against the respondents, in such proportions as shall be fixed and determined with reference to the amount of interest of the several parishes in the question, or otherwise, as shall appear just; and the said agreement shall continue binding upon the several parishes and their respective overseers in succession, until the several appeals shall have been finally determined.

12. *Power for Guardians of Parishes, &c., under Local Acts, to grant out-door Relief, in the same manner as in Unions formed under 4 & 5 Wm. 4, c. 76.*

And whereas in certain parishes and unions wherein the relief of the poor is administered by guardians or other competent authorities under the provisions of particular Statutes or local Acts applicable thereto, doubts have been entertained whether any poor person can be relieved by such guardians or other authorities out of the workhouses belonging to such parishes and unions respectively, and it is expedient to remove such doubts, and to give authority for such relief out of the workhouse: be it enacted, that in all cases where the relief of the poor is administered in any parish or union under the provisions of any local Act, it shall be lawful for the guardians or other competent authority administering the relief to the poor in any such parish or union, if they think fit, to administer such relief in all respects in like manner and with the like powers and authorities as any board of guardians of a union formed under the provisions of the Act passed in the fifth year of the reign of His late Majesty aforesaid, is now or shall hereafter be authorized to do: and all relief heretofore granted by such guardians or other authority, shall, if otherwise lawfully granted, be held lawful for all purposes, although the same shall have been granted out of the workhouse of such parish or union, as the case may be, and the costs and charges thereof shall not be disallowed by any auditor, justice, or other competent authority in that behalf, on the ground that the same was granted out of the workhouse: Provided

The Board believe that the guardians will find that this Statute, though dealing with minute details, is one of much practical use and value.

The Statute 11 & 12 Vic. c. 82, facilitates the formation of districts for establishing schools for poor children, by enabling the Poor Law Board to combine unions, and parishes not in union, with the consent of the guardians thereof, although situated beyond the limit of distance prescribed by the 7 & 8 Vic. c 101. It further enables the board of the district so combined, "to the formation whereof such consent has been obtained," to expend whatever may be requisite for erecting or providing adequate buildings, notwithstanding the limit of expense prescribed by the former Act. It also renders the various provisions which were enacted in the 5 & 6 Vic. c. 57, respecting guardians of unions, applicable to the members of the district board. This Statute will enable the guardians of certain unions to carry into effect what it is believed has been their wish in regard to the better education of pauper children.

The Board have to notice that the Statute for exempting stock in trade from rateability has been renewed for another year, and they would also draw attention to an Act, the 11 & 12 Vic. c. 111, which has explained a provision in the 1st sec. of the Poor Removal Act, 9 & 10 Vic. c. 66. The meaning of the third proviso to that sec. was open to much doubt. It has therefore been repealed, and it has been enacted that whenever

always, that the cost of all such relief so given or to be given shall be charged among the parishes in the same union in like manner and in like proportion as the relief heretofore or hereafter to be given in the workhouse of such parish or union is now or shall hereafter be chargeable.

13. *Interpretation of Act.*

And be it enacted, that the several words used in this Act shall be construed in the manner prescribed by the said herein-before recited Act, and the Acts explaining and extending it.

SCHEDULE to which this Act refers.

FORMS OF CERTIFICATES.

1.—*Against an accounting Officer.*

I do hereby certify, that in the account of A. B., the [*set out the name of the office*] of the parish of [*or* of the Union,] I have disallowed [*or* surcharged] the sum of £

As witness my hand, this day of 1848.

M. N., auditor of the district, which comprises the abovenamed parish or Union.

2.—*Against a Person not an accounting Officer.*

I do hereby certify, that in the accounts of the Union [*or* of the parish of] I have disallowed the sum of £ as a payment illegally made out of the funds of such union [*or* parish] and I find that *C. D.*, of authorized the making of such illegal payment, and I do hereby surcharge the said *C. D.* with the same.

As witness my hand this day of 1848.

M. N., auditor of the district which comprises the abovenamed union or parish,

11 & 12 VIC. c. 82.

An Act to amend the Law for the Formation of Districts for the Education of Infant Poor.

31st August, 1848.

1. ***Removal of Limitations on the Area of the School District, the Expense of Building, and the Amount of certain Expenditure in certain Cases.***

Whereas by an Act passed in the eighth year of the reign of Her Majesty Queen *Victoria* intituled *An Act for the further Amendment of the Laws relating to the Poor in England*, [7 & 8 Vic. c. 101,] provisions are made for the combination of unions into districts for the management of infant poor not above the age of sixteen years, and by reason of certain restrictions therein contained the provisions so made for such purpose have proved inoperative, and it is expedient that such of the restrictions as are hereinafter mentioned should, in certain cases, be removed: be it therefore enacted by the Queen's most Excellent Majesty, by and with the advice and consent of the Lords Spiritual and Temporal, and Commons, in this present Parliament assembled, and by the authority of the same, that so much of the said Act as prevents the Commissioners therein mentioned from including in any such district any parish, any part of which would be more than fifteen miles from any other part of such district, and so much thereof as provides that the principal sum or sums to be raised for the purpose of providing any building or buildings for any school for any such district as aforesaid, and charged on any union, or on any parish not included in a union, shall in no case exceed one-fifth of the average annual amount of the aggregate expenditure relating to the relief of the poor within any such parish for three years ending the twenty-fifth day of *March* next preceding the raising of such money, shall not apply to prevent the combination of any union, or any parish not in union, for the purposes aforesaid, nor the raising of any money for the purpose aforesaid, when the major part of the guardians of the several unions and parishes not in union proposed to be combined shall, previously thereto, consent, in writing, to such combination.

2. *Certain Provisions in 5 & 6 Vic. c. 57, relating to Guardians extended to Members of District Boards formed under 7 & 8 Vic. c. 101.*

And be it enacted, that all the provisions contained in the Statute passed in the sixth year of the reign of Her Majesty, intituled *An Act to continue until the Thirty-first day of July, One thousand eight hundred and forty-seven, and to the end of the then next Session of Parliament, the Poor Law Commission; and for the further Amendment of the Laws relating to the Poor in* England, in respect of the election, qualification, resignation, and the acts of guardians of a union, and in respect of the supply of vacancies in the board of guardians, shall apply to the members of the district boards formed or to be formed under the authority of the first-recited Act and of this Act.

3. *Interpretation of Act.*

And be it enacted, that the several words in this Act shall be constructed in the manner prescribed in the said first-recited Act.

11 & 12 VIC. C. 11.

An Act to amend an Act of the tenth year of Her present Majesty, for amending the Laws relating to the Removal of the Poor.

4th September, 1848.

1. *Repealing Proviso in 9 & 10 Vic. c. 66. in relation to Removal of Wives and Children, and substituting another proviso in lieu thereof.*

Whereas by an Act passed in the tenth year of the reign of Her Majesty, [9 & 10 Vic. c. 66.] intituled ***An Act to amend the Laws relating to the Removal of the Poor***, **after reciting that it was expedient that the laws relating to the removal**

any person should have a wife or children having no other settlement than his or her own, such wife and children should be removable from any parish from which he or she would be removable notwithstanding any provisions of the Act, and should not be removable from any parish from which he or she would not be removable by reason of any provision in the said Act. The object of the Act is to confine the operation of the proviso to the provisions of the Poor Removal Act; and to remove the difficulty that arose in the construction of that proviso in reference to cases in which the husband of the wife or parent of the children to be removed, was not in the same parish as such wife or children.

I am, Sir, your obedient servant,

W. G. LUMLEY,

Assistant Secretary.

To

The Clerk to the Guardians.

---

of the poor should be amended, it was enacted, that from and after the passing of that Act no person should be removed nor should any warrant be granted for the removal of any person from any parish in which such person should have resided for five years next before the application for the warrant: provided always, that the time during which such person should be a prisoner in a prison, or should be serving her Majesty as a soldier, marine, or sailor, or reside as an in-pensioner in *Greenwich* or *Chelsea* hospitals, or should be confined in a lunatic asylum, or house duly licensed or hospital registered for the reception of lunatics, or as a patient in a hospital, or during which any such person should receive relief from any parish, or should be wholly or in part maintained by any rate or subscription raised in a parish in which such person does not reside, not being a *bona fide* charitable gift, should for all purposes be excluded in the computation of time therein-before mentioned, and that the removal of a pauper lunatic to a lunatic asylum under the provisions of any act relating to the maintenance and care of pauper lunatics should not be deemed a removal within the meaning of that act: provided always, that whenever any person should have a wife or children having no other settlement than his or her own, such wife and children should be removable whenever he or she is removable, and should not be removable when he or she is not removable: and whereas by reason of the generality of the expressions used in the last proviso doubts are entertained as to the meaning thereof, and it is desirable to remove such doubts: be it therefore enacted by the Queen's most excellent majesty, by and with the advice and consent of the Lords Spiritual and Temporal, and Commons in this present Parliament assembled, and by the authority of the same, that the said last proviso be repealed, and that instead thereof the following be enacted: provided always, that whenever any person should have a wife or children having no other settlement than his or her own, such wife and children should be removable from any parish or place from which he or she would be removable, nothwithstanding any provisions of the said recited act, and should not be removable from any parish or place from which he or she would not be removable by reason of any provision in the said recited Act.

2. *Not to affect appeals of which Notice has been given.*

And be it enacted, that nothing herein contained shall affect any appeal of which notice shall have been given before the passing of this Act.

---

11 & 12 VIC. C. 114.

An Act to prevent District Auditors from taking proceedings in certain Cases.

2. CIRCULAR TO BOARDS OF GUARDIANS RESPECTING THE ACT, (11 & 12 VIC. C. 110,) TO ALTER THE PROVISIONS RELATING TO THE CHARGES FOR THE RELIEF OF THE POOR IN UNIONS.

Poor Law Board,
Somerset House,
29th Sept., 1848.

SIR,—The Poor Law Board desire to call the attention of the guardians to the provisions of the Act passed in the last session, the 11 & 12 Vic. c. 110, regulating the mode of charging the relief of certain poor in unions.

It will be seen that the Act deals mainly with two classes of paupers, namely, (1) destitute wayfarers, wanderers, and foundlings, and (2) paupers rendered irremoveable by the statutes 9 & 10 Vic. c. 66, and the 11 & 12 Vic. c. 111.

These two classes are to be relieved at the common charge of the union for the period of one year from the 30th instant. Such is the reasonable, and as the Poor Law Board consider, the legal construction of the words "30th of September next until the 30th of September, 1849," in the 1st and 3rd sections of the Act.

The Act makes this charge direct upon the union, while the statute of last year required that the several parishes should be charged in the first instance, and afterwards reimbursed by the union. This will materially simplify the accounts by preventing the two-fold entry of the relief to the irremovable poor, which necessarily occurred

---

4th *September*, 1848.

Nothing in any Act passed this Session as to payment of Parish Debts, &c., shall authorize Auditor to proceed to recover Sums certified by him to be due, &c.

Be it enacted by the Queen's most excellent Majesty, by and with the Advice and consent of the Lords Spiritual and Temporal, and Commons, in this present Parliament assembled, and by the authority of the same, that nothing contained in any Act passed in this present session of Parliament for making provision for the payment of parish debts, the audit of parochial and union accounts, and the allowance of certain charges therein, shall authorize any district auditor to proceed to recover any sum certified by him to be due in respect of which proceedings in any court or before any justice or justices shall have been taken and determined before the passing of this Act.

The following is the Act of 10 and 11 Vic. c. 110, referred to in the above Circular Letter:—

An Act to alter the Provisions relating to the Charges for the Relief of the Poor in Unions.

4th *September*, 1848.

1. *Costs for Relief of wandering Poor, &c., to be charged to the Common Fund of Unions.*

Whereas by an Act passed in the fifth year of the reign of King *William* the Fourth, intituled *An Act for the Amendment and better Administration of the Laws relating to the Poor in* England *and* Wales, [4 & 5 Wm. 4. c. 76.] provision is

under that Act, but the Board will, perhaps, find it expedient on a future occasion to give precise directions as to the alterations in the accounts of the union and its officers now rendered necessary.

As regards the first class, the guardians will perceive that the question as to what parish is liable for the relief of the vagrant poor will not hereafter arise, as the cost of that relief is no longer to be a charge upon any particular parish.

The second class it will be seen includes the several classes which are exempted from removal by the operation of the statute 9 & 10 Vic. c. 66, and not merely those exempted by reason of the five years' residence, to whom alone the 10 & 11 Vic. c. 110, (Mr. Bodkin's Act) applied.

The guardians are aware that many questions have arisen as to whether particular paupers have, or have not, become exempt from removal by reason of the 9 & 10 Vic. c. 66, on which the guardians could not of themselves obtain any judicial decision. They could, indeed, in such cases charge the relief in the manner they deemed most correct, but their decision was liable to be altered by the auditor, whose determination of the question was subject in its turn to be removed into the Court of Queen's Bench. If the case were so removed much expense and delay before the point at issue could be decided were inevitable. For the purpose of obviating this inconvenience, the legislature has now given an opportunity to the guardians and the parish interested in any question arising (with reference to the charging of relief) upon the statutes concerning exemption from removal, jointly to submit the same to the Poor Law Board. That Board, if they think fit to entertain it, are empowered to determine it by an order under their seal, which, if not rescinded, or taken into the Court of Queen's Bench in the ensuing term, and quashed there, will conclude the parties interested. The Board are not prepared at present to lay down any precise rule as to the course which they may deem it necessary to adopt in regard to these questions, but they think it right to state at once, that they will not generally be able to deal with any case in which the facts are not distinctly admitted by both parties.

The Poor Law Amendment Act of 1834 restricted the application of the poor-rates in furtherance of emigration to the cases of poor persons having settlements in the parish promoting it, but this restriction is now removed, and the guardians are, by sec. 5, empowered to assist in procuring the emigration of any poor

made for the formation of unions for the relief of the poor and for the charge for the relief of the poor belonging to the several parishes comprised therein; and it is expedient to alter the mode in which the relief of certain poor persons is now chargeable: be it therefore enacted by the Queen's most Excellent Majesty, by and with the advice and consent of the Lords Spiritual and Temporal, and Commons, in this present Parliament assembled, and by the authority of the same, that after the thirtieth day of *September* next until the thirtieth day of *September* in the year one thousand eight hundred and forty-nine, the cost of the relief to be given to any poor person chargeable or becoming chargeable in any union formed or to be formed under the provisions of the said act, being a destitute wayfarer or wanderer or foundling, as well as the cost of the burial of the body of any such person dying within such union, shall be chargeable to the common fund of such union.

2. ***Poor Persons having a fixed Place of Abode meeting with Accidents, &c., in some other Parish where they have no legal Settlement to be relieved by the Parishes of their Abode or previous Chargeability.***

And be it enacted, that where any poor person having a fixed place of abode in a parish in any such union shall hereafter, by reason of accident, bodily casualty, or sudden illness occurring while in some other parish, in which he has no legal settlement, require relief, the cost of all the relief given by lawful authority in that behalf, as well medical as otherwise shall, if the poor person be at the time in receipt of relief, be paid or reimbursed in like manner and by the same union or parish as any other relief shall be then payable, but if he be not then in receipt of relief, it shall be paid or reimbursed, as the case may require, by the parish in which such poor person shall then have his place of abode, unless by reason of any provision of the law he would if otherwise chargeable, have been chargeable to the common fund of such union, in which case the payment or reimbursement shall be made by the guardians of the union comprising such parish, and shall be charged to the common fund of the union; and it shall be lawful for the guardians of any union, if they think proper, to pay for any medical or other assistance which shall be rendered to any poor person on the happening of any accident, bodily casualty, or sudden illness, although no order shall have been given for the same by them or any of their officers, or by the overseers, and to charge the same to some one parish in the union, or to the common fund of the union, according as such parish or union would have been liable for the ordinary relief of such poor person; provided that nothing herein contained shall exempt the guardians of the union or parish, or their officers, or the overseers of the parish in which such poor person shall require relief by reason of such accident, bodily casualty, or sudden illness, from their liability to supply the requisite relief to such poor person whilst in such union or parish.

3. ***Paupers rendered irremovable by the 9 & 10 Vic. c. 66. rendered chargeable to the Common Fund of the Union.***

And be it enacted, that after the thirtieth day of *September* next until the thirtieth day of *September* in the year one thousand eight hundred and forty-nine, all the costs incurred in the relief, as well medical as otherwise, of any poor person, who, not being settled in the parish where he resides, shall, by reason of some provision of the act passed in the tenth year of the reign of Her Majesty, intituled *An Act to amend the Laws relating to the Removal of the Poor*, be or become exempted from the liability to be removed from the parish where he resides, shall, where the said parish shall be comprised in any such union as aforesaid, be charged to the common fund of such union, so long as such person shall continue to be so exempted; and the expenses of the burial of any such person so exempted at the time of his

persons irremovable under 9 & 10 Vic. c. 66, who either actually are, or would, if relieved, be chargeable upon the common fund.

The guardians are, by sec. 8, invested with the same powers to obtain orders of maintenance upon the relations of poor persons rendered chargeable to the common fund, and to expend money in respect of those poor persons, that overseers have by law in the case of poor persons chargeable to their parish.

The recovery of relief advanced by the guardians on loans, either on account of the common fund of the union, or of any of the parishes therein, is facilitated by the same section; as the guardians, while retaining the previous remedy given by the 4 & 5 Wm. 4, c. 76, are besides authorised to have recourse to the process of the county court for the recovery of such relief. The guardians can avail themselves of the powers conferred upon them by the 5 & 6 Vic. c. 57, for the appointment of the proper officer to conduct the proceedings in that court.

The statute 7 & 8 Vic. c. 101, contained a provision for the committal of persons guilty of offences in the workhouse to the prison of the county wherein the parish of their chargeability was situated. In regard to paupers now rendered chargeable upon the common fund, this enactment is inoperative; another provision has, therefore, been made for this purpose in sec. 9, whereby the committal of persons rendered irremovable under 9 & 10 Vic. c. 66, is required to be made to the gaol of the county containing the parish where they resided when admitted into the workhouse, and the committal of vagrants to the gaol of the county in which the greater part of the union is comprised.

Besides the temporary provisions in reference to the two classes of paupers mentioned, a permanent alteration has been made by sec. 2, in regard to the relief of paupers who meet with accidents, bodily casualties, or sudden illness under certain circumstances. Heretofore the charge of the relief given in consequence of such contingencies was borne by the parish wherein they arose, if the relief was obtained there. It is now provided, that where a pauper in receipt of relief meets with any accident, the charges incurred thereby shall be borne in the same manner as the previous relief was; but where the party was not at the time in receipt of relief, it is to be borne, not by the parish where the accident hap-

death shall, if legally payable by the guardians of the union, likewise be charged to the said common fund.

4. *Questions arising as to Cost of Relief, &c., may be referred to and decided by the Poor Law Board; whose Orders shall not be removable after a certain Time, nor be quashed for Want of Form.*

And be it enacted, that where in any such union a question shall arise between any parishes therein, or between the guardians and any parish or parishes therein, with reference to the charging of the cost of his relief, as to whether any pauper be so exempted as aforesaid, the parties may jointly submit such question to the Commissioners for administering the laws for the relief of the poor in *England*, who may thereupon, if they think proper, entertain such question, and by an order under their seal determine the same; but no such order shall be liable to be removed, by writ of certiorari or otherwise, into the Court of Queen's Bench, after the expiration of the term next ensuing the time when the copy thereof shall have been sent to the guardians, nor shall the same be quashed for any defect of form therein; and every such order not rescinded or quashed shall be in all courts and for all purposes final and conclusive between the guardians and every parish in the union interested in the matter.

5. *Guardians may assist in the Emigration of certain Poor, and charge the Cost upon the Common Fund of the Union, or Parish in case of not being in Union.*

And be it enacted, that the guardians of any union or parish may, with the order of the said commissioners, and in conformity with such regulations as they shall make, procure or assist in procuring the emigration of any poor person rendered irremovable by virtue of the provisions of the said last-mentioned act, and chargeable, or who would, if relieved, be chargeable upon the common fund of such union, or in the case of any parish not comprised in a union who may, though not settled therein, be irremovable as aforesaid therefrom, and such guardians shall in the case of a union charge the costs and expenses incurred in such emigration upon the common fund, and in the case of a parish not in a union upon the monies in their hands for the relief of the poor.

6. *Mode of charging the Relief herein provided for.*

And be it enacted, that the cost of all the relief which under the provisions of this Act shall be chargeable to the common fund of any union shall be charged to the common fund of such union, in the same manner as union expenses are directed to be charged by the herein first-recited Act.

7. *Guardians may cause a Valuation to be made at any Time of Property alleged to be rateable.*

And be it enacted, that the guardians of any union may, on the application of the major part of the overseers of any parish comprised in it, or of any person assessed to the poor rate in any such parish, cause a valuation to be made at any time of any property alleged to be rateable to the relief of the poor, being a part only of the rateable property of such parish, and may charge the expenses of such valuation to the overseers of such parish, or to such person so applying as aforesaid.

8. *Guardians may obtain Orders of Maintenance, and charge Expenses in like Manner as Churchwardens, &c., can. Relief advanced by way of Loan may be recovered in County Court, &c.*

And be it enacted, that the guardians of any union shall be entitled to obtain orders of maintenance upon the relations liable under any statute now in force to maintain any poor person whose relief would be chargeable to the common fund of the union, in like manner as the churchwardens and overseers of any parish can now obtain the same, and may expend in respect of such person, out of such fund, any money for any purpose which the overseers of the parish to which such person, if chargeable, would have belonged might have done; and all relief to be granted by the guardians to any pauper upon loan, and which shall be charge-

pens, (unless it be the parish of his settlement,) but by the parish or by the union wherein he has a fixed place of abode, according as any relief which he might have required under other circumstances would have fallen upon the parish, or upon the common fund.

The Board must, however, at the same time point out to the guardians that the responsibility of the officers charged with the relief of the poor in the place where the accident happens is in no degree diminished by the present Act. It will still be their duty to attend promptly and efficiently to all such cases, and the Board request the Guardians to warn the relieving officers as to their responsibilities in this respect.

The legislature has also, by the same section, removed a difficulty which boards of guardians have often felt in dealing with the claims of medical men and others who render assistance to poor persons on such occasions, without having received an order from any person authorised to give it. The Board feel satisfied that the guardians having been now empowered, at their discretion, to give remuneration for such services, will seldom feel a difficulty in awarding a fair and proper remuneration in such cases, without encouraging unnecessary interference on the part of interested persons, or unreasonable claims amounting to extortion or imposition.

Such are the provisions in the Act directly relating to relief, but there is one other, which will probably prove of much assistance to the guardians in the performance of their duty, remaining to be noticed.

Power is given to the officers of the union and the overseers not only to search all vagrant poor who apply for relief, but also to take any money which may be found upon them, and apply it in aid of the common fund. Moreover, to meet a case of imposition with which boards of guardians are familiar, every person applying for relief who does not, when required by the guardians, their officers, or the overseers, make complete and correct disclosure of the money or other property in his possession and under his immediate control, is declared to be "idle and disorderly" within the meaning of the Vagrant Act, and liable to be dealt with as such.

That Act, as is well known, renders the money and effects of idle and disorderly persons chargeable with the expenses of their apprehension and maintenance in gaol, and it is to be expected that

able to the common fund of the union, or to any parish therein may be recoverable in the county court or other court for the recovery of small debts for the district wherein the union or the major part thereof shall be comprised, on the plaint of the said guardians, who may apply and be heard in such court by any officer appointed by them for such purpose, in manner prescribed by the statutes enabling them to appoint officers to act for them: provided nevertheless, that the remedy already provided by law for the recovery of the relief granted on loan, shall be in force and applicable to the relief so chargeable to the common fund as aforesaid.

9. *Persons being chargeable upon the Common Fund of a Union, and being convicted of any Offence, may be committed by a Judge to the Common Gaol, &c., the Expenses of which shall be charged upon the county, &c.*

And be it enacted, that if any person hereinbefore made chargeable upon the common fund of the Union shall be convicted before any justice of any offence committed in any workhouse while maintained therein, or of deserting or running away from any workhouse, and carrying away clothes or other property therefrom, and be liable to be committed to any gaol or house of correction, the justice before whom such person shall be convicted may commit such person to the gaol or house of correction of the county or place containing the parish in which such person, if chargeable to the common fund by reason of being exempt from removal under the statute hereinbefore mentioned, shall have been residing when admitted into the workhouse, or to that of the county or place comprising the major part of such union, in the case of any other person herein rendered chargeable on the said common fund, notwithstanding such workhouse may not be situated in such county or place, or that such justice may not be a justice of such county or place; and the charges of the conveyance of such person to such gaol or house of correction, and all other charges consequent upon such committal, shall be borne by such county or place in like manner as the charges of persons committed in the ordinary mode to the gaol thereof shall be borne.

10. *Poor Persons may be searched on admisson to Workhouse. Persons in possession of Means applying for Relief punishable as idle and disorderly persons.*

And be it enacted, that upon application for relief by admission to the workhouse of any such union as aforesaid or otherwise by any poor person professing to be a destitute wanderer or wayfarer, the master, porter, or other officer of such workhouse, or the relieving officer of such union or overseer of any parish to whom such application for relief shall be made, may search such person, or cause him to be searched, and may take from such person any money which shall be found upon him, and shall deliver the same to the guardians, to be by them applied in aid of the common fund of the union; and every person who shall apply for relief at any workhouse, or to any relieving officer or overseer, having at the time of such application in his possession and under his immediate control any money or other property, of which, on inquiry made on the guardians or their officers, or by overseers, he shall not make correct and complete disclosure, shall be taken to be an idle and disorderly person within the meaning of the Act of the fifth year of the reign of his late majesty king *George* the Fourth for the punishment of idle and disorderly persons and rogues and vagabonds in *England*, and shall be punishable and dealt with in all respects and with the like proceedings as idle and disorderly persons under the said Act.

11. *Certificate of Chargeability in Form prescribed in Schedule to 7 & 8 Vic. c. 101. deemed sufficient Evidence.*

And be it enacted, that in any court and before any justice or justices, and for all purposes, a certificate of the chargeability of any person named therein in the form prescribed in the Schedule marked C. to the Act of the eighth year of the reign of her present Majesty for the

the cost of dealing with this class of offenders will be materially diminished by the exercise of these powers.

Much inconvenience had been caused by the state of the law concerning parish valuations, which practically prevented any valuation of a part of a parish only being made by competent authority for the purpose of the poor rate. This has been removed by sec. 7, which empowers guardians, on the application of the overseers, or of any party assessed to the poor rate of any parish, to cause, if they think fit, a valuation to be made of a part only of the rateable property therein.

The Board will communicate with the Guardians in a few days on the subject of the other measures passed in the last session, which affect the guardians in the discharge of their duties.

I am, &c.

W. G. LUMLEY,
Assistant Secretary.

To the Clerk of the Guardians.

3. CIRCULAR TO BOARDS OF GUARDIANS, RESPECTING THE ACT (11 & 12 Vic. c. 123,) FOR THE REMOVAL OF NUISANCES AND PREVENTION OF CONTAGIOUS AND EPIDEMIC DISEASES.

Poor Law Board,
Somerset House,
6th Oct., 1848.

SIR,—The Poor Law Board desire to call the attention of the guardians to the provisions of the statute the 11 & 12 Vic. c. 123, passed in the last session, to renew and amend the Act of the 10th year of Her Majesty, for the more speedy removal of certain nuisances, and the prevention of contagious and epidemic diseases.

The guardians will remember that the Poor Law Commissioners, by a Circular Letter, dated October 8, 1846, brought the provisions of the 9 & 10 Vic. c. 96, under the notice of the guardians.

The object of the statute is twofold. It provides (1) for the more speedy removal of certain nuisances; and (2) for the prevention of contagious and epidemic diseases, but the provisions for the latter object do not take effect till called into action by an order from the Privy Council.

The 1st sec. enacts, that upon the receipt (or as soon afterwards as can be) by certain bodies therein enumerated, or by any guardians of the poor, of a notice in a form set forth in a schedule to the Act, or to the like effect, signed by two or more inhabitant householders of the parish or place to which the notice relates, stating—

> That to the best of their knowledge and belief any dwelling-house or building in any city, town, borough, parish, or place, within or over which the jurisdiction or authority of such bodies or guardians extends, is in such a filthy and unwholesome condition as to be a nuisance to, or injurious to the health of, any person,

---

Amendment of the Laws for Relief of the Poor in *England*, and purporting to have been executed in the manner prescribed by that Act, shall be received within the space of twenty-one days from the date thereof as sufficient evidence of the chargeability of the person named therein unless the contrary be otherwise shown.

12. *Interpretation of Act.*

And be it enacted, that the several words used in this Act shall be construed in the manner prescribed by the said first herein-recited Act, and the Statutes explaining and extending it.

13. *Act may be amended, &c.*

And be it enacted, That this Act may be amended or repealed by any Act to be passed in this Session of Parliament.

The following is the Act 11 & 12 Vic. c. 123, referred to in the above Circular Letter:—

11 & 12 VIC. C. 123.

An Act to renew and amend an Act of the tenth year of Her present Majesty, for the more speedy removal of certain Nuisances, and the prevention of contagious and epidemic diseases.

4th September, 1848.

1. *In England and Ireland certain public Bodies upon Receipt of Notice in Writing from Two Householders, of the filthy condition of any Building, or of the existence of certain Nuisances, to cause examination to be made; and if upon such Examination, or a Medical Certificate, it appear that the Nuisance, &c., exists, public Body to make Complaint before a Justice, who shall summon the Owner or Occupier to appear before Two Justices; and who shall, upon proof, &c., order him to whitewash, &c., or remove the nuisance complained of; and if such Order be not complied with, the Owner or Occupier in default to be liable to Penalties, and public Body to enter the Premises, and do the Works ordered, or remove the Nuisance.*

Whereas an Act passed in the tenth year of Her Majesty's reign, [9 & 10 Vic. c. 96,] for the more speedy removal of certain nuisances, and to enable the Privy Council to make regulations for the prevention of contagious and epidemic diseases, will expire at the end of the present session of Parliament; and it is necessary that other provision should be made lieu thereof: Be it therefore enacted by the Queen's most excellent majesty, by and with the advice and consent of the Lords Spiritual and Temporal, and Commons, in this present Parliament assembled, and by the authority of the same, That in *England* and *Ireland*, upon receipt (or as soon afterwards as can be) by the town council, or by any trustees or commissioners for the drainage, paving, lighting, or cleansing, or managing or directing the police of any city, town, borough, or place, or by any other body of a like nature, or by any commissioners of sewers or guardians of the poor, or in *Ireland* by the officers of health of any parish, of a notice in writing in the form contained in the Schedule (A) to this Act annexed, or to the like effect,

Or that upon any premises within such jurisdiction or authority there is any foul and offensive ditch, gutter, drain, privy, cesspool or ash-pit, or any ditch, &c., kept or constructed so as to be a nuisance to, or injurious to the health of, any person,

Or that upon any such premises swine, or an accumulation of dung, manure, offal, filth, refuse, or other matter or thing are or is kept so as to be a nuisance to, or injurious to the health of, any person,

Or that upon any such premises (being a

signed by two or more inhabitant householders of the parish or place to which the notice relates, stating that, to the best of the knowledge and belief of the persons by whom such notice is signed, any dwelling-house or building in any city, town, borough, parish, or place within or over which the jurisdiction or authority of the town council, trustees, commissioners, guardians, officers of health, or other body to whom such notice is given extends, is in such a filthy and unwholesome condition as to be a nuisance to, or injurious to the health of any person, or that upon any premises within such jurisdiction or authority there is any foul and offensive ditch, gutter, drain, privy, cesspool, or ashpit, or any ditch, gutter, drain, privy, cesspool, or ashpit, kept or constructed so as to be a nuisance to or injurious to the health of any person, or that upon any such premises swine, or any accumulation of dung, manure, offal, filth, refuse, or other matter or thing, are or is kept so as to be a nuisance to or injurious to the health of any person, or that upon any such premises (being a building used wholly or in part as a dwelling-house,) or being premises underneath any such building, any cattle or animal are or is kept so as to be a nuisance to or injurious to the health of any person, such town council, trustees, commissioners, guardians, officers of health, or other body, or some committee thereof which may be temporarily or permanently appointed in this behalf by such town council, trustees, commissioners, guardians, officers of health, or other body, shall, after twenty-four hours' notice in writing, by delivering the same to some person on the premises referred to in such first-mentioned notice, or (if there be no person upon the premises who can be so served) by fixing the same upon some conspicuous part of such premises, (or in case of emergency without notice) by themselves, their servants or agents, with or without medical or other assistants, enter such premises, and examine the same with respect to the matters alleged in such first-mentioned notice, and do all such works, matters, and things as may be necessary for that purpose: and if upon such examination, or upon the certificate in writing of two legally-qualified medical practitioners, it appear that any dwelling-house or building so examined is in such a filthy and unwholesome condition as aforesaid, or that upon any premises so examined there is any such ditch, gutter, drain, privy, cesspool, ashpit, swine, cattle, or animal, or any such accumulation or other matter or thing as aforesaid, such town council, trustees, commissioners, guardians, officers of health, or other body, or such committee, shall make or cause to be made complaint before a justice, who shall thereupon issue a summons (which may be according to the form contained in the Schedule (B) to this Act annexed, or to the like effect,) requiring the owner or occupier of the premises examined to appear before two justices to answer such complaint; and such summons shall be served by delivering the same, or a true copy thereof, to some person upon the premises in respect whereof complaint is made, or (if there be no person upon the premises who can be so served) by fixing such summons or copy upon some conspicuous part of such premises; and if at the time and place appointed by such summons it be proved to the satisfaction of such justices that any dwelling-house or building in respect whereof complaint is made, is in such a filthy and unwholesome condition as aforesaid, or that any such cause or causes of complaint as aforesaid exists or exist, and (in case such owner or occupier do not appear) that such summons or copy was served as aforesaid, such justices shall make an order in writing under their hands and seals, (which order may be according to the form contained in the Schedule (C) to this Act annexed, or to the like effect, for cleansing, whitewashing, or purifying such dwelling-house or building, or for the removal or abatement of any such cause or causes of complaint, in such manner and within such time as shall be specified in such order (not being more than two clear days, exclusive of *Sunday*, after service of such order as herein-after directed;) and such order shall be forthwith served by delivering the same or a true copy thereof to some person upon the premises in respect whereof it is made, or (in case there be no person upon the premises who can be so served) by fixing such order or copy upon some conspicuous part of such premises; and if such order be not complied with, the owner or occupier against whom it is made shall be liable to a penalty not exceeding ten shillings for every day during the continuance of his default, and the town council, trustees, commissioners, guardians, officers of health, or other body mentioned therein, shall, by themselves, their servants or agents, or by such committee as aforesaid, their servants or agents, enter such last-mentioned premises, and cleanse, whitewash, or purify the same, or remove or abate the cause or causes of complaint in respect whereof the said order shall have been made, and do all such works, matters, and things as may be necessary for carrying such order into effect; and any dung, manure, offal, filth, or refuse, and any other matter or thing removed by any such town council, trustees, commissioners, guardians, officers of health, or other body as aforesaid, in pursuance of this enactment, may be destroyed or sold, and in case of sale, the proceeds arising therefrom shall be paid to or (as the case may require) be retained by the guardians of the poor, and shall be by them applied in aid of the rate for the relief of the poor of the parish, electoral division, or place in which such removal shall have been made.

2. *In Scotland, certain public Officers, upon receipt of Notice in Writing from Two Householders of the filthy Condition of any Building, or of the existence of certain Nuisances, to cause Examination to be made; and if upon such Examination or a Medical Certificate it appear that the Nuisance exists, public Body to make complaint before the Sheriff or a Justice, who shall order the Owner or Occupier to appear; and upon Proof, &c., whitewashing, &c., or Removal of the Nuisance complained of, to be ordered. If such last-mentioned Order be not complied with, Owner or Occupier in default to be liable to Penalties, and the public Officers to enter Premises, and do the Works ordered, or remove the Nuisance.*

And be it enacted, that in *Scotland*, upon or as soon as can be after notice in writing in the form contained in the Schedule (A) to this Act annexed, or to the like effect, signed by two or more of the inhabitant householders of the parish or place to which the notice relates, made to the procurator fiscal of any county, or the procurator fiscal or the dean of guild of any royal burgh, or the procurator fiscal of the justices of the peace of any county, or the commissioners of police, or trustees for paving, lighting, or cleansing any city, town, burgh, parish, or place, or the inspector of the poor of any parish, stating that any dwelling-house or building within any royal burgh, or in any city, town, burgh, parish, or place, within or over which the jurisdiction or authority of any such procurator fiscal, or of such dean of guild, or commissioners of police, or trustees for paving, lighting, or cleansing, or inspector of the poor, extends, is in such a filthy and unwholesome condition as to be a nuisance to or injurious to the health of any person, or

building used wholly or in part as a dwelling-house) or being premises underneath any such building, any cattle or animal are or is kept, so as to be a nuisance to, or injurious to the health of, any person,

Such bodies or guardians, or some committee thereof, appointed in this behalf by such bodies or guardians, shall, after twenty-four hours' notice in writing delivered to some person on the premises, or if there be no person there, affixed on some part of the premises (or in case of emergency without notice) by themselves, their servants or agents, with or without medical or other assistants, enter and examine the premises

---

that upon any premises within such jurisdiction or authority there is any foul and offensive drain, ditch, gutter, privy, cesspool, or ashpit, or any drain, ditch, gutter, privy, cesspool, or ashpit, kept or constructed so as to be a nuisance to or injurious to the health of any person, or that upon any such premises, swine, or any accumulation of dung, manure, offal, filth, refuse, or other matter or thing, are or is kept so as to be a nuisance to or injurious to the health of any person, or that upon any such premises (being a building used wholly or in part as a dwelling-house,) or being premises underneath any such building, any cattle or animal are or is kept so as to be a nuisance to or injurious to the health of any person, it shall be competent to any such procurator fiscal or dean of guild, or the proper officer of such commissioners of police or trustees, or such inspector of the poor respectively, after twenty-four hours from the giving notice in writing by service thereof upon some person on the premises referred to in such first-mentioned notice, or (if there be no person upon the premises who can be so served) by fixing the same upon some conspicuous part of such premises, or in case of emergency without notice, by himself or others acting under his authority, with or without medical or other assistants, to enter such premises, and examine the same with respect to the matters alleged in such first-mentioned notice, and do all such works, matters, and things as may be necessary for that purpose; and if upon such examination, or upon the certificate in writing of two legally-qualified medical practitioners, it appear that any dwelling-house or building so examined is in such a filthy and unwholesome condition as aforesaid, or that upon any premises so examined there is any such drain, ditch, gutter, privy, cesspool, ashpit, swine, cattle, or animal, or any such accumulation, or other matter or thing, as aforesaid, such procurator fiscal, dean of guild, officer, or inspector shall make or cause to be made complaint to the sheriff or magistrates or a justice, who shall thereupon order the owner or occupier of the premises examined to appear before such sheriff or magistrates or two justices to answer such complaint; and such order shall be served by delivering the same, or a true copy thereof, to some person upon the premises in respect whereof complaint is made, or (if there be no person upon the premises who can be so served) by fixing such order or copy upon some conspicuous part of such premises; and if at the time and place appointed by such order it be proved to the satisfaction of such sheriff or magistrates or justices that any dwelling house or building in respect whereof complaint is made is in such a filthy and unwholesome condition as aforesaid, or that any such cause or causes of complaint as aforesaid exists or exist, and (in case such owner or occupier do not appear) that such order or copy was served as aforesaid, such sheriff or magistrates or justices shall make an order in writing under their hands (which order may be according to the form contained in the Schedule (C) to this Act annexed, or to the like effect,) for cleansing, whitewashing, or purifying such dwelling house or building, or for the removal or abatement of any such cause or causes of complaint, in such manner and within such time as shall be specified in such order (not being more than two clear days, exclusive of *Sunday*, after service of such order,) and such last-mentioned order shall be forthwith served by delivering the same, or a true copy thereof, to some person upon the premises in respect whereof it is made, or, in case there be no person upon the premises who can be so served, by fixing such order or copy upon some conspicuous part of such premises; and if such order be not complied with the owner or occupier against whom it is made shall be liable to a penalty not exceeding ten shillings for every day during the continuance of his default, and the procurator fiscal or dean of guild or proper officer of the commissioners of police, or trustees or inspectors of the poor respectively, shall, by themselves or others acting under their authority, enter such last-mentioned premises, and cleanse, whitewash, or purify the same, or remove or abate the cause or causes of complaint in respect whereof the said last-mentioned order shall have been made, and do all such works, matters, and things as may be necessary for carrying such order into effect, and any dung, manure, offal, filth, or refuse, and any other offensive or noxious matter or thing removed in pursuance of this enactment, may be destroyed or sold, and in case of sale the proceeds arising therefrom shall be paid to or (as the case may require) be retained by the parochial board for the management of the poor, and shall be by them applied in aid of the funds for the relief of the poor of the parish or place in which such removal shall have been made.

3. *Recovery of Costs, &c., from Owner or Occupier of the Premises.*

And be it enacted, That whenever any such order as aforesaid for cleansing, whitewashing, or purifying any dwelling house or building, or for the removal or abatement of any such cause or causes of complaint as aforesaid, has been obtained, all costs and expenses reasonably incurred in obtaining such order, or in carrying the same into effect, shall be deemed to be money paid for the use and at the request of the owner or occupier of the premises in respect whereof such costs and expenses shall have been incurred, and may be recovered as such by the said town councils, trustees, commissioners, guardians, officers of health, or other body, or by the said procurators fiscal, deans of guild, commissioners of police, or trustees and inspectors of the poor respectively, as such, in any county court, civil bill court, or (in *Scotland*) before the sheriff or magistrates or justices of the peace; or such town council, magistrates, trustees, commissioners, guardians, officers of health, or other body, or procurators fiscal, deans of guild, or inspectors of the poor, may, if they shall think fit, recover such costs and expenses before two justices, or in *Scotland*, before the sheriff or magistrates or two justices, from the owner or occupier of the premises in respect of which such order is made; and any two justices, or, in *Scotland*, the sheriff or magistrates, or any two justices, upon the application of any such town council, magistrates, trustees, commissioners, guardians, officers of health, or other body, or procurator fiscal, dean of guild, or inspector of the poor, shall issue a summons, or, in *Scotland*, an order, requiring such owner or occupier to appear before them, or before him or them, at a time and place to be named therein; and at the time and place so named, upon proof to the satisfaction of such justices, or such sheriff or magistrates or justices, that any such costs and expenses have been so incurred as aforesaid, and (in case such owner or occupier do not appear) that a copy of such last-mentioned summons or order was served by delivering the same to some person on the premises in respect of which the costs and expenses were incurred, or, if there be no person upon the premises who can be so served, by fixing the same upon some conspicuous part of such

with reference to the matters alleged in the notice of the complainants, and do all that may be necessary for such purpose; and if upon such examination, or upon the certificate of two legally qualified medical practitioners, the existence of the nuisance appears, such body or guardians shall thereupon lay a complaint before a justice of the peace, who shall summon the owner or occupier to appear before two justices to answer such complaint.

Such justices are then required, if the existence of the nuisance is proved to their satisfaction, to make an order for cleansing, whitewashing, or purifying such dwelling-house or building, or for

---

premises, such justices, or such sheriff or magistrates or justices, unless they think fit to excuse the party summoned upon the ground of poverty or other special circumstances, shall, by order in writing, in *England* or *Ireland* under the hands and seals of such justices, or in *Scotland* under the hands of such sheriff or magistrates or justices, order him to pay the amount to the applicants, together with the costs attending such application and the proceedings thereon: and if the amount be not paid within seven days after demand, the same may, by warrant under the hands and seals of the same or any other two justices, or in *Scotland*, under the hands of the sheriff or magistrates or justices, by whom the last-mentioned order shall have been made, or any other two justices, be levied by distress and sale of the goods and chattels of the owner or occupier in default; and if no distress sufficient to satisfy the same can be found within the jurisdiction of the justices, or of the sheriff or magistrates or justices, by whom such warrant shall have been issued, and it so appear upon oath before two justices, or, in *Scotland* before the sheriff or magistrates or two justices. of any other county or jurisdiction in which any goods or chattels of the defaulter may be, such last-mentioned justices, or sheriff or magistrates or justices, shall indorse their or his signatures or signature upon the last-mentioned warrant. and thereupon to amount to be levied, or so much thereof as may be unsatisfied, shall be levied of the last-mentioned goods and chattels, in the same manner as if such warrant had been originally and properly issued by the justices, or by the sheriff or magistrates or justices, of such last-mentioned county or jurisdiction.

4. *Certain Expenses of this Act to be defrayed out of Poors' Rates, &c.*

And be it enacted, that all costs and expenses reasonably incurred as aforesaid in carrying into effect any of the provisions hereinbefore contained, and not recovered from any owner or occupier of the premises in respect of which such expenses shall have been incurred, shall, upon an order in writing, specifying the sum to be paid, under the hands and seals of two justices, or, in *Scotland*, under the hands of the sheriff or magistrates or two justices, (who are hereby required to make such order, upon proper application in this behalf,) be retained, paid, or defrayed by the treasurer of such guardians or parochial board, or by the overseers of the poor, or other proper officers or persons, out of the funds in their hands applicable to the relief of the poor, and shall be charged to the parish, electoral division, or place maintaining its own poor in which the premises in respect whereof such costs and expenses shall have been so incurred are situated, and in other places in *England* or *Ireland* out of any public rates or funds raised in such places, or applicable thereto under the authority of Parliament, or in case there be no such rates or funds as last aforesaid, then out of the funds for the relief of the poor of the parish, electoral division, or place nearest adjoining, or if there be two or more parishes or places nearest adjoining, out of the funds for the relief of the poor of such one of them as two justices shall, by order in writing under their hands and seals, appoint; and in case any such costs or expenses shall have been incurred on account or in respect of any parish in *Scotland* in which it shall happen that there is not at the time an assessment for the relief of the poor imposed or levied, then the same shall be paid or defrayed out of an assessment to be imposed and levied for that purpose, and to the extent necessary, under and in the manner provided by an Act of the ninth year of Her Majesty's reign, [8 & 9 Vic. c. 83,] for the amendment and better administration of the laws relating to the relief of the poor in *Scotland*, and if any such treasurer, overseers, or officers or persons, neglect or refuse to pay the sum specified in any order of justices, or of any sheriff or magistrates, made under this enactment, for the space of twenty-one days after the date of such order, the same may, by warrant under the hands and seals of the same or any other two justices, or, in *Scotland*, under the hands of the sheriff or magistrates or any two justices, by whom such order shall have been made, or any other two justices, be levied by distress and sale, together with the costs of such distress and sale, of the goods and chattels of the treasurer, overseers, or other officers or persons in default.

5. *Above Provisions not to apply to Districts and Places in which the Public Health Act is in force. Jurisdiction of Commissioners of Sewers not to be impaired.*

Provided always, and be it enacted, that nothing hereinbefore contained shall apply to any district parish, or place in which the Public Health Act, 1848, or any part thereof, shall be in force, unless and except in so far as the General Board of Health, by order in writing, sealed with the seal of such board, and signed by two or more members thereof, or (in case there be no such Board in existence) as one of Her Majesty's principal Secretaries of State, by order in writing under his hand, shall otherwise direct: provided also, that nothing in this Act shall be construed to impair, abridge, or take away any power, jurisdiction, or authority which may at any time be vested in any commissioners of sewers, or to take away or interfere with any course or proceeding which might be resorted to or adopted by such commissioners if this Act had not been passed.

6. *Surveyor of Highways required to cleanse open Ditches adjoining Highways, &c.* 5 & 6 *Wm.* 4. *c.* 50. 8 & 9 *Vic. c.* 41.

And whereas by an Act passed in the sixth year of the reign of King *William* the Fourth, for consolidating and amending the laws relating to highways in *England*, the surveyor and district surveyor or assistant surveyor therein mentioned, are empowered to scour, cleanse, and keep open all ditches, gutters, drains, or watercourses; and by an Act passed in the ninth year of Her Majesty's reign, for amending the laws concerning highways, bridges, and ferries in *Scotland*, the trustees or surveyors therein mentioned are empowered to cleanse the ditches made or to be made along the sides of any highway, in case of the neglect or refusal of the proprietor or occupier to cleanse such ditches when duly required so to do by such trustees or surveyors; and with a view to the more effectual removal of nuisances injurious to health, it is expedient that such surveyor, district surveyor, or assistant surveyor, trustees or surveyors, should not only be empowered but required to scour, cleanse, and keep clear, or cause to be scoured, cleansed, and kept clear, as far as may be practicable, all open ditches, gutters, drains, and watercourses upon, adjoining, or by or along the sides of any highway: be it therefore enacted, that the said surthe removal or abatement of the cause of complaint in such manner and within such time as shall be appointed.

This order is to be served in the same manner as the summons, and if not complied with, the owner or occupier against whom it is made will be liable to a penalty not exceeding ten shillings for each day of default, and the guardians or other body mentioned therein shall themselves or by their servants enter the premises and cleanse them, or remove the cause of complaint, and do all that may be necessary for carrying such order into effect.

Any dung, manure, or other thing which is removed, may be destroyed or sold, and if sold, the proceeds shall be paid to or retained by the guardians, and shall be applied by them in aid of the poor-rate of the place in which the removal shall have been made.

It should be mentioned, that the statute provides in sec. 16, that whosoever shall wilfully obstruct any person acting under the authority, or employed in the execution of the Act, shall be liable to a penalty not exceeding *five* pounds for each offence.

Sec. 3 provides, that the costs and expenses reasonably incurred in obtaining the order, or carrying it into effect, may be recovered from the owner or occupier of the premises in respect whereof they have been incurred as a debt in the county-court, or by summary process before two justices, unless such justices shall think fit to excuse such person upon the ground of poverty, or other special circumstances.

---

veyor, or district or assistant surveyor, trustees or surveyors, shall scour, cleanse, and keep clear, or cause to be scoured, cleansed, and kept clear, as far as may be practicable, all open ditches, gutters, drains, and watercourses upon, adjoining, or by or along the sides of any highway; and any sewage, drainage, soil, filth, or other matter or thing whatsoever which shall be removed by any such surveyor, district or assistant surveyor, trustees or surveyors, from any such ditch, gutter, drain, or watercourse, in scouring, cleansing, and keeping clear the same, shall be disposed of by such surveyor, assistant or district surveyor, trustees or surveyors, and the proceeds arising therefrom shall be applied towards the repair of the highway within the parish or place in which such removal shall have taken place; and the provisions herein-before contained with respect to ditches, gutters, drains, and watercourses upon, adjoining, or by or along the sides of highways, shall, in so far as the same relate to *England*, be deemed to be part of the said Act relating to highways in *England*, and in so far as the same relate to *Scotland* shall be deemed to be part of the said Act relating to highways in *Scotland*.

7. *Drainage into open Ditches from new Houses a Misdemeanor, &c.*

And be it enacted, that whosoever shall suffer any sewage, drainage, soil, filth, or any matter or thing of a noxious or offensive nature, to run or flow into, or to remain in any open ditch, gutter, drain, or watercourse, so as to be a nuisance to or injurious to the health of any person, from any dwelling house, building, or other premises which shall not have been occupied before the passing of this Act, or from any privy or water-closet which shall not have been constructed before that time, shall be deemed guilty of a misdemeanour; or in *Scotland* of an offence punishable by fine or imprisonment, and shall, in addition, be liable for every such offence, to a penalty not exceeding five pounds for every day during which the offence is continued.

8. *Notice to be given to General Board of Health, and in Ireland to Commissioners of Health, of Intention to build or open certain Hospitals, &c.*

And be it enacted, that whenever it is intended to build or open any hospital for the reception of patients afflicted with contagious or infectious diseases or disorders, the trustees, or other persons by whose authority such hospital is intended so to be built or opened as aforesaid, shall give notice of such intention to the said General Board of Health, or (in *Ireland*) to the Commissioners of Health herein-after mentioned; and no such hospital shall be built or opened as aforesaid until the said General Board of Health or Commissioners of Health, as the case may be, have approved thereof in writing; but nothing herein contained shall apply to the building or opening of any addition to a building which shall have been used as a hospital previously to such addition.

9. *Privy Council, &c., empowered to issue Orders for putting in force the Provisions of this Act relative to the Prevention of Epidemic Diseases, &c.*

And whereas it is expedient that when any part of the United Kingdom shall appear to be threatened with or affected by any formidable epidemic, endemic, or contagious disease, measures of precaution should be taken with promptitude, according to the exigency of the case: be it therefore enacted, that in *Great Britain* the Lords and others of Her Majesty's Most Honourable Privy Council, or any three or more of them, (the Lord President of the Council, or one of Her Majesty's principal Secretaries of State, being one,) and in *Ireland* the Lord Lieutenant or other chief governor or governors and Privy Council of *Ireland*, may, by Order or Orders to be by them from time to time made, direct that the provisions herein-after contained for the prevention of epidemic, endemic, and contagious diseases be put in force in *Great Britain* and *Ireland* respectively, or in such parts thereof, or in such places therein respectively as in such Order or Orders respectively may be expressed, and may from time to time, as to all or any of the parts or places to which any such Order or Orders may extend, and in like manner revoke or renew any such Order, and, subject to revocation and renewal as aforesaid, every such Order shall be in force for six calendar months, or for such shorter period as in such order shall be expressed.

10. *After Order by Privy Council, General Board of Health, &c., may issue Directions and Regulations.*

And be it enacted, that from time to time after the issuing of any such Order as last aforesaid, and whilst the same shall continue in force, the General Board of Health (in *Great Britain*), under the seal of the said Board, and the hands of two or more members thereof; and in *Ireland* the Commissioners of Health for the time being, under the hands of two or more of them, may issue such directions and regulations as the said Board or last-mentioned Commissioners (as the case may be) shall think fit for the prevention, as far as possible, or mitigation, of such epidemic,

The statute then enacts in sec. 4, that all costs and expenses reasonably incurred as aforesaid in carrying into effect any of these provisions, and not recovered from the owner or occupier of the premises in respect whereof they have been incurred, shall, upon an order of two justices, be retained, paid, or defrayed by the treasurer of the guardians or by the overseers of the poor out of the funds in their hands applicable to the relief of the poor, and shall be charged to the parish or place wherein the premises in respect whereof they have been incurred shall be situated. By the same section provision is made for the payment of these costs when incurred in extra-parochial places. This order, if not obeyed within twenty-one days, is to be enforced by a warrant of distress.

The guardians will perceive that this provision extends, as the similar one in the former Act did, to the expenses incurred by any party authorised to take proceedings, and consequently is not confined to expenses incurred by themselves.

By sec. 7, the drainage of filth, &c., from houses not occupied before the 4th of September, 1848, into open ditches, so as to occasion a nuisance to, or to be injurious to, the health of any person, will subject the occupier to a penalty of £5 per day during the continuance of the offence, and he may also be indicted for a misdemeanor.

There is a like provision with respect to drainage from water-closets or privies constructed after the 4th of September, 1848, and the penalties in that case will attach whether the privy or water-closet so constructed be attached to a house occupied before or after that day.

---

endemic, or contagious diseases, and from time to time, in like manner, revoke, renew, and alter any such directions or regulations, or substitute such new directions and regulations as to the said Board or last-mentioned Commissioners may appear expedient; and the said Board or last-mentioned Commissioners, as the case may be, may, by such directions and regulations, provide for the frequent and effectual cleansing of streets and public ways and places by the surveyors, district or assistant surveyors, of highways, trustees, county surveyors, and others by law intrusted with the care and management thereof, or by the owners and occupiers of houses and tenements adjoining thereto; and for the cleansing, purifying, ventilating, and disinfecting of houses, dwellings, churches, buildings, and places of assembly, by the owners or occupiers and persons having the care and ordering thereof, for the removal of nuisances, for the speedy interment of the dead, and generally for preventing or mitigating such epidemic, endemic, or contagious diseases, in such manner as the said Board or last-mentioned Commissioners, (as the case may be,) may seem expedient; and the said Board or last-mentioned Commissioners may, by any such directions and regulations, authorize and require the guardians of the poor in *England* and *Ireland*, and the parochial boards for the management of the poor in *Scotland*, by themselves or their officers, or any persons employed by them in the administration of the laws for the relief of the poor, or by officers specially appointed in this behalf to superintend and see to the execution of any such directions and regulations, and (where it shall appear that there may be default or delay in the execution thereof, by want or neglect of such surveyors, trustees, or others intrusted as aforesaid, or by reason of poverty of occupiers, or otherwise,) to execute or aid in executing the same within their respective unions and parishes and combinations, and in any extra-parochial places adjoining to or surrounded by the same in which the directions and regulations of the said Board or last-mentioned Commissioners shall not be executed by the inhabitants, and to provide for the dispensing of medicines, and for affording to persons afflicted by or threatened with such epidemic, endemic, or contagious diseases such medical aid as may be required, and to do and provide all such acts, matters, and things as may be necessary for superintending or aiding in the execution of such directions and regulations, or for executing the same, as the case may require; and the directions and regulations to be issued as aforesaid shall extend to all parts or places in which the provisions of this Act for the prevention of epidemic, endemic, or contagious diseases shall, for the time being, be put in force under such Orders as aforesaid, unless such directions and regulations shall be expressly confined to some of such parts or places, and then to such parts or places as in such directions and regulations shall be specified, and (subject to the power of revocation and alteration herein contained) shall continue in force so long as the said provisions of this Act shall be in force, under such Orders, in the parts or places to which such directions and regulations shall under this provision extend: provided always, that if at any time in *Ireland* there shall not be any Commissioners of Health the Lord Lieutenant or other Chief Governor or Governors of *Ireland*, by his or their warrants, may appoint so many persons as he or they may think fit, not being more in number than five, to act as Commissioners of Health in *Ireland*, without salary, fee, or reward, and may from time to time remove any of such Commissioners, and appoint any other person in his stead; and such Commissioners shall for all purposes be Commissioners of Health in *Ireland* within the meaning and for the purposes of this Act.

11. *One Medical Member of General Board of Health may be appointed. Treasury to pay Allowances appointed by Parliament.*

And be it enacted, that Her Majesty may, from time to time, during the continuance of any Order of Her Majesty's Privy Council or of any Members thereof as aforesaid by warrant under the Royal Sign Manual, appoint, in addition to the members for the time being of the General Board of Health, one fit person to be a medical member of such Board for the purposes of this Act; and Her Majesty may, at her pleasure, remove any person so appointed; and there shall be paid to the person or persons so appointed such allowance or allowances as shall be appointed by the Commissioners of Her Majesty's Treasury, out of the monies which may from time to time be appointed by Parliament for that purpose.

12. *Poor Law Commissioners, &c., may compel Guardians, &c., to execute Regulations and Directions of the General Board of Health, &c.*

And be it enacted that the Commissioners for administering the laws for the relief of the poor in *England* and *Ireland* respectively, and the Board of Supervision established under the said Act for the amendment and better

The statute requires each or any of the several bodies named in it to take proceedings upon receiving such a notice as has been described from competent parties. As, however, the guardians will have to pay the expenses of the proceedings wherever (as must frequently be the case) they are not recovered from the owner or the occupier, it will be most expedient for them to have the conduct of the whole matter. They will do well, therefore, to promote rather than to discourage applications being made to them under the statute.

It is also desirable that the guardians should be aware, that by the interpretation clause, sec. 22, the words "guardians of the poor" mean "the guardians, directors, wardens, governors, parochial board, or other like officers having the management of the poor for any union, parish or place, where the matter requiring the cognizance of any such officers arises;" and the word "*owner*" means "any person receiving the rents of the property in respect of which that word is used from the occupier of such property on his own account, or as trustee or agent for any other person, or who would receive the same if such property were let to a tenant."

The Board think it may be useful to advert briefly to the chief points of difference regarding the removal of nuisances, between the present Act and that which has just expired.

By the *present* Act a notice from two householders is sufficient to enable the guardians to

---

administration of the laws relating to the relief of the poor in *Scotland*, may require the officers and persons acting under them to inquire into, superintend, and report on the execution of the directions and regulations of the General Board of Health, or Commissioners of Health, as the case may be, under this Act, and shall have the same powers for enforcing and directing the execution of such directions and regulations by the said guardians and parochial boards respectively as they now or may hereafter have in relation to any matter concerning the administration of the laws for the relief of the poor.

13. *Power of Entry for the purpose of enforcing Regulations of the General Board of Health, &c.*

And be it enacted, that the said guardians and parochial boards acting in the execution of any such directions or regulations as aforesaid, or the officers or persons by them in this behalf authorised, at reasonable times in the daytime, may, and they are hereby empowered to enter and inspect any dwelling or place, if there be ground for believing that any person may have recently died of any such epidemic, endemic, or contagious disease in any such dwelling or place, or that there is any filth or other matter dangerous to health therein or thereupon, or that necessity may otherwise exist for executing, in relation to the premises, all or any of such directions and regulations as aforesaid.

14. *Expenses of Guardians, &c., to be paid out of Poor Rate, &c.*

And be it enacted, that the said guardians and parochial boards may appoint or employ, for the superintendence and execution of the said directions and regulations, officers or persons in aid of the officers or persons employed in the administration of the laws for the relief of the poor; and such guardians and parochial boards respectively shall defray the expenses incurred by them respectively in the superintendence and execution of such directions and regulations out of the funds of their respective unions, parishes, or combinations; and if any such expenses shall have been incurred on account or in respect of any extra-parochial place in *England* or *Ireland*, the same shall, upon an order in writing specifying the sum to be paid, under the hands and seals of two justices, who are hereby empowered to make such order, upon proper application in this behalf, be paid or defrayed out of any public rates or funds raised therein or applicable thereto under the authority of Parliament, or in case there be no such rates or funds as last aforesaid, then out of the funds of the union or parish for which the guardians by whom the expenses have been incurred act; and in case any such expenses shall have been incurred on account or in respect of any parish in *Scotland* in which it shall happen that there is not at the time an assessment for the relief of the poor imposed or levied, then the same shall be paid or defrayed out of an assessment to be imposed and levied for that purpose, and to the extent necessary, under and in the manner provided by the said Act [8 & 9 Vic. c. 83,] for the amendment and better administration of the laws relating to the relief of the poor in *Scotland.*

15 *Orders, Directions, and Regulations to be laid before Parliament and to be gazetted, &c.*

And be it enacted, that every order of Her Majesty's Privy Council, or of the Lord Lieutenant and Privy Council of *Ireland*, and every direction and regulation of the said general Board of Health or Commissioners of Health under this Act, shall, forthwith upon the issuing thereof, be laid before both Houses of Parliament, if Parliament be then sitting, and if not then, within fourteen days next after the commencement of the then next session of Parliament; and every such order of Her Majesty's Privy Council, or any members thereof, as aforesaid, shall be certified under the hand of the Clerk in Ordinary of Her Majesty's Privy Council, and shall be published in the *London Gazette*, and every such order of the Lord Lieutenant and Privy Council of *Ireland* shall be certified under the hand of one of the clerks of the Privy Council of *Ireland*, and shall be published in the *Dublin Gazette;* and every such direction and regulation as aforesaid, when issued in *Great Britain*, shall be published in the *London Gazette* and in the *Edinburgh Gazette;* and when issued in *Ireland*, in the *Dublin Gazette*, and such publication of any such order, direction, or regulation, shall be conclusive evidence of the order, direction, or regulation so published, to all intents and purposes.

16. *Penalties for obstructing Execution of this Act.*

And be it enacted, that whosoever shall wilfully obstruct any person acting under the authority, or employed in the execution of this Act, or who shall wilfully violate any direction or regulation issued by the General Board of Health, or such Commissioners of Health as aforesaid, under this Act, shall be liable for every such offence to a penalty not exceeding five pounds; and if the occupier of any premises prevent the owner thereof from obeying or carrying into effect the provisions of this Act, any justice, or in *Scotland* the sheriff, or any justice, to whom application is made in this behalf, shall, by order in writing, (which may be according to the Form contained

act; by the *late* Act a certificate, signed by two duly qualified medical practitioners, was needed, before the guardians could act. By the *present* Act it is made imperative on the guardians or other bodies to whom notice is given to proceed forthwith in the manner prescribed; by the *late* Act it was discretionary with the guardians and other bodies, whether they would take the proceedings for the abatement of the nuisance. By the *present* Act a penalty of ten shillings is imposed upon the owner or occupier who disobeys an order of justices for every day he makes default; by the *late* Act no such pecuniary penalty was imposed; by the *present* Act, to enable the guardians or other bodies to determine whether proceedings ought to be taken or not, an entry of the premises, for the purpose of examination, is authorised; by the *late* Act a right of entry only was given to enforce the order of justices when made. Under the *present* Act express powers are given for distraining a defaulter's goods wherever they may be found. The Act also authorises dung, &c., found on the premises to be destroyed or sold. These powers were not given by the *late* Act; the *present* Act distinctly assigns duties to the guardians and Poor-Law officers as well as to surveyors and others charged with the management of roads and surface cleansing. The provision for this purpose is new.

The former was a temporary Act; the present is permanent. The present, like the former Act, is applicable to the whole of the united kingdom. The only exception is in the cases of *"districts" formed* under the Public Health Act, where, in order to prevent conflicting jurisdiction, a dis-

in the Schedule (D) to this Act annexed, or to the like effect,) require such occupier to permit the execution of the works required to be executed, provided that such works appear to such sheriff or justice to be necessary for the purpose of obeying or carrying into effect the provisions of this Act; and if within a reasonable time after the making of such Order the occupier against whom it is made refuse to comply therewith, he shall be liable to a penalty not exceeding five pounds for every day afterwards during the continuance of such refusal.

17. *Recovery of Penalties in England or Ireland, and in Scotland. Application of Penalties.*

And be it enacted, that penalties imposed by this Act for offences committed in *England* or *Ireland* may be recovered by any person before any two justices, and may be levied by distress and sale of the goods and chattels of the offender, together with the costs of such distress and sale, by warrant under the hands and seals of the justices before whom the same shall be recovered, or any other two justices; and in case it shall appear to the satisfaction of such justices, before or after the issuing of such warrant, either by the confession of the offender or otherwise, that he hath not goods and chattels within their jurisdiction sufficient to satisfy the amount, they may commit him to any gaol or house of correction for any time not exceeding fourteen days, unless the amount be sooner paid, in the same manner as if a warrant of distress had issued and a return of Nulla Bona been made thereon; and penalties imposed by this Act for offences in *Scotland* may be recovered by the procurator fiscal of the court, or by any other person, before the sheriff or two justices, who may proceed in a summary way, and great warrant for bringing the parties complained upon immediately before him or them, and on proof on oath by one or more credible witness or witnesses, or other legal evidence, he or they may forthwith determine and give judgment, without any written pleadings or record of evidence, and grant warrant for the recovery of the penalties and expenses decerned for, and, failing payment within eight days after conviction, by poinding, and imprisonment for a period, at the discretion of the sheriff or justices, not exceeding fourteen days; and all penalties whatsoever recovered under this Act shall be paid to or (as the case may require) be retained by the guardians of the poor, or, in *Scotland*, the Parochial Board for the Management of the Poor, and shall be by them applied in aid of the rates or funds for the relief of the poor of the parish, electoral division, or place, in which the penalties may have been incurred.

18. *One or more of several joint Owners or Occupiers may be proceeded against alone.*

And be it enacted, that in case of any demand or complaint under this Act to which two or more owners or occupiers of premises may be jointly answerable, it shall be sufficient to proceed against any one or more of them, without in any manner proceeding against the others or other of them; but nothing herein contained shall prevent the parties so proceeded against from recovering contribution in any case in which they would now be entitled to contribution by law.

19. *Unnecessary to describe owner or occupier by Name in certain Cases.*

And be it enacted, that wherever in any proceeding under this Act, whether written or otherwise, it shall become necessary to mention or refer to the owner or occupier of any premises, it shall be sufficient to designate him as the "owner" or "occupier" of such premises, without name or further description.

20. *Proceedings not to be quashed for Want of Form.*

And be it enacted, that no order, nor any other proceeding, matter, or thing, done or transacted in or relating to the execution of this Act, shall be vacated, quashed, or set aside for want of form, or be removed or removable by certiorari, or by suspension or advocation, or other writ or process whatsoever, into any of the superior courts.

21. *Proceedings commenced under 9 & 10 Vic. c. 96, may be enforced, although that Act has expired.*

And be it enacted, that all proceedings whatsoever commenced or taken, or to be commenced or taken, under the said first-recited Act of the tenth year of Her Majesty's reign, and which shall not have been completed and enforced, whilst the last-mentioned Act continues in force, may be proceeded with and enforced under the provisions of that Act, although such provisions be no longer in force, in the same manner in all respects and to all intents and purposes as if the same continued to be in force, and as if the said last-mentioned Act had not expired.

22. *Interpretation of Terms.*

And be it enacted, that in this Act the following words and expressions shall have the meanings herein-after assigned to them, unless such meanings be repugnant to or inconsistent with the context; (that is to say,) the words "justice" and "justices" shall mean a justice or justices of the peace acting for the place where the matter or any part of the matter, as the case may be, requiring the cognizance of the "justice" or "justices" arises; the expression "two justices" shall mean two or more justices assembled and acting together, or one stipendary or police

cretion will be exercised by the General Board of Health as to how far the present Act shall be applied.

The guardians will observe that by the second part of the Act the Board of Health are charged with the duty of preparing regulations, which the union and parochial officers are required to enforce in the event of the country being afflicted or threatened with any formidable epidemic, endemic, or contagious disease.

The progressive advance of a formidable epidemic to the western part of Europe, has, in the opinion of Government, rendered necessary the enforcement of the Act. An Order in Council has accordingly been issued for putting it in force throughout the kingdom.

The guardians and the union and other local officers, must now, therefore, in compliance with these provisions, act upon all regulations which they may receive from the General Board of Health for such places as that Board may deem to require them; and on all questions regarding

magistrate acting in any police court for the place in which the matter or any part of the matter, as the case may be, requiring the cognizance of "two justices," arises; the word "sheriff" shall mean the sheriff of any county or place in *Scotland* where the matter requiring the cognizance of the "sheriff" arises, and shall include the sheriff's substitute; the word "magistrates" shall mean the magistrates of any royal burgh in *Scotland* where the matter requiring cognizance arises; the words "guardians of the poor" and the words "parochial board" shall mean the guardians, directors, wardens, governors, parochial board, or other like officers having the management of the poor for any union, parish, combination, or place where the matter requiring the cognizance of any such officers arises; the word "street" shall include every highway road, square, row, lane, mews, court, alley, and passage, whether a thoroughfare or not; the word "owner" shall mean any person receiving the rents of the property in respect of which that word is used from the occupier of such property, on his own account, or as trustee or agent for any other person, or who would receive the same if such property were let to a tenant; the word "person," and words applying to any person or individual, shall apply to and include corporations, whether aggregate or sole; and words and expressions importing the singular number shall include the plural number, and words importing the masculine gender shall include females.

23. *Mode of citing this Act.*

And be it enacted, that in citing this Act in other Acts of Parliament, and in legal instruments and other proceedings, it shall be sufficient to use the words "The Nuisances Removal and Diseases Prevention Act, 1848."

24. *Act may be amended, &c.*

And be it enacted, that this Act may be amended or repealed in this present session of Parliament.

SCHEDULES to which the foregoing Act refers.

SCHEDULE (A.)

Notice by Householders.

To the Town Council of the Borough of [*or* Guardians of the Poor of the Union *or* of the Parish of in the County of *or as the case may be; or, in Scotland*, to the Procurator Fiscal of the County of *or* to the Procurator Fiscal or Dean of Guild of the Burgh of *or* to the Procurator Fiscal of the Justices of the County of *or* to the Inspector of the Poor of the Parish of *or as the case may be.*]

WE, the undersigned inhabitants [*or, in Scotland*, householders] of [*insert the parish or place*,] and residing at in [*insert the parish or place before-mentioned*] aforesaid, do hereby give you notice, that to the best of our knowledge and belief a dwelling-house [*or* building] situate at No. in street in aforesaid [*or such other description as may be sufficient to identify the premises*] is in such a filthy and unwholesome condition as to be a nuisance to [*or* injurious to the health of] *A. B., or as the case may be*, [*or* that upon certain premises situate at [*inserting such a description as may be sufficient to identify the premises*] there is a foul and offensive drain, ditch, gutter, privy, cesspool, *or* ashpit, *or* a drain, &c., kept *or* constructed so as to be a nuisance to us, *or* to the occupiers of the premises adjoining the premises aforesaid, *or as the case may be, or* that upon certain premises situate at, &c., swine, *or* an accumulation of dung, manure, offal, filth, refuse, *or* matter, *or, as the case may be*, are *or* is kept so as to be injurious to our health, *or* to the health of *A. B., or* of the occupiers of the premises adjoining the premises aforesaid, *or* of persons living in the neighbourhood, *or* of the persons living in the premises aforesaid, *as the case may be, or* that upon certain premises, &c., swine, &c. are kept so as to be a nuisance to us, &c., *as the case may be.*] And we hereby require that you will cause such proceedings to be taken as are directed in this behalf by the "Nuisances Removal and Diseases Prevention Act, 1848."

Dated this day of one thousand eight hundred and

A. B.
C. D.

SCHEDULE (B.)

Summons to appear.

To the Owner [*or* Occupier] of a Dwelling-house [*or* Building, *or* of certain Premises,] situate at [*insert such a description as may be sufficient to identify the premises*].

County of [*or* Borough, &c. of *or* Metropolitan Police District, *or as the Case may be*] to wit. } WHEREAS complaint hath been made to the undersigned, one of Her Majesty's justices of the peace acting in and for the said county of *or* borough, &c., of], *or* one of the magistrates of the police courts of the metropolis holden at [*or as the case may be*], by the town council of the borough of [*or as the case may be*] that a certain dwelling-house [*or* building] situate at No. in the parish of [*or as the case may be*] in the county of [*or such other description as may be sufficient to identify the premises*] is in such a filthy and unwholesome condition as to be a nuisance to *or* injurious to the health of *A. B., or as the case may be*, [*or* that upon certain premises situate at [*inserting such a description as may be sufficient to identify the premises*], there is a foul and offensive drain, [ditch, gutter, privy, cesspool, *or* ashpit, *or* a drain, &c., kept or constructed so as to be a nuisance to *A.* B., *&c*, [*as the case may be*], *or* that swine [*or* an accumulation of dung, manure, offal, filth, refuse, or matter, *or as the case may be*,] are [*or* is] kept so as to be injurious to the health of *A. B*, *or* of the occupiers of the premises adjoining the premises aforesaid, *or* of persons living in the neighbourhood of the premises aforesaid, *or* of persons living in the premises aforesaid, *or* a nuisance to *A. B., &c., as the case may be.*] These are therefore to require you to appear before two of Her Majesty's justices of the peace [*or* one of the magistrates of the police courts of the metropolis, at the court holden at] on the day of next, at the hour of to answer the matter of the said complaint.

Given under my hand and seal, this day of in the year of our Lord one thousand eight hundred and

J. K. (L. S.)

the execution of this part of the Act, the guardians may communicate directly with the General Board of Health.

It must be stated to the guardians that on the subject matters of the present Act, and on the means for the prevention both of disease and of the destitution arising from sickness and premature mortality, the General Board of Health propose to communicate information specially adapted for the guidance of medical and other officers, by means of an *Official Circular,* which will be issued in the same form, and may be taken at the discretion of guardians, in the same manner as the Official Circular of the Poor Law Board.

While upon the subject of this Statute, which relates to the prevention of disease, the Board think it well to mention, though it does not immediately affect the guardians, that by sec. 67 of the Public Health Act, the churchwardens and overseers are required, from time to time, after the passing of that Act, to give public notice as to the provisions with respect to the occupation of cellars and underground rooms, and that these provisions are imperative whether the Public Health Act is in force within their parish or not.

In conclusion, the Board think it desirable to repeat the following observations of the late Commissioners, made in their Circular Letter of the 8th October, 1846:—

"The improvement of the sanitary condition of

SCHEDULE (C.)

Order for Removal of Nuisances, &c.

To the Owner [*or* Occupier] of the Dwelling House [*or* Building *or* Premises] situate at No. in Street, in the Parish of in the County of [*or such other description as may be sufficient to identify the Premises*], and to the Town Council of the Borough of [*or* to the Guardians of the Poor of the Union, *or* of the Parish of in the County of *or, in Scotland*, the Procurator Fiscal of the County of *or* the Procurator Fiscal *or* Dean of Guild of the Burgh of *or* the Procurator Fiscal of the Justices of the Peace of the county of *or* the Inspector of the Poor of the Parish of *as the case may be,*] and to their Servants or Agents, and to all whom it may concern.

County of [*or* Borough, *&c.* of *or* Metropolitan Police District, *or as the case may be*] to wit.

WHEREAS on the Day of last complaint was made before the undersigned [*or* before *J. K.*, esquire, one of Her Majesty's justices of the peace acting in and for the county of [or before the undersigned, or *J. K.*, esquire, one of the magistrates of the police courts of the metropolis, *or as the case may be*], by the town council of the borough of [*or* by the guardians of the poor o the union, *or* of the parish of in the county of *or, in Scotland*, by the procurator fiscal of the county of *or* by the procurator fiscal or dean of guild of the burgh of *or* by the procurator fiscal of the justices of the peace of the county of *or* by the inspector of the poor of the parish of *as the case may be*], that a dwelling house [*or* building] situate at No. in street in [*the parish or place before mentioned* aforesaid, [*or such other description as may be sufficient to identify the Premises*,] then was in such a filthy and unwholesome condition as to be a nuisance to [*or* injurious to the health of] *A. B., or, as the case may be*, [*or* that upon certain premises situate at [*inserting such a description as may be sufficient to identify the premises*] there then was a foul and offensive drain, [ditch, gutter, privy, cesspool, or ashpit, *or* a drain, *&c.*, kept *or* constructed so as to be a nuisance to *A. B. &c.*, as the case may be], *or* that upon certain premises, situate, *&c.*. swine, *or* an accumulation of dung, manure, offal, filth, *or* refuse, *or as the case may be*, are or is kept so as to be injurious to the health of *A. B., or* of the occupiers of the premises adjoining the premises first aforesaid, *or* of persons living in the neighbourhood of the premises first aforesaid, *or* of persons living in the premises first aforesaid, *or* so as to be a nuisance to *A. B., &c.*: and whereas the owner [*or* occupier] of the said dwelling house, building, or premises having this day appeared before us, two of Her Majesty's justices of the peace acting in and for the county [*or* borough] of [*or* before me, one of the magistrates of the police courts of the metropolis, *or, in Scotland*, before the sheriff or magistrates *or* two justices of the peace, *as the case may be,*] to answer the matter of the said complaint [*or in case the party charged do not appear*:] and whereas it hath this day been proved to our [*or* my] satisfaction, that a true copy of a summons requiring the owner [*or* occupier] of the said dwelling house [*or* building or premises] to appear this day before us [or me] has been duly served according to the Statute in such case made and provided, and it having been proved [or also proved *as the case may require,*] that the said dwelling house [*or* building] is in such a filthy and unwholesome condition as aforesaid [*or* that upon the premises aforesaid [*or* first aforesaid] there is a foul and offensive drain [privy, cesspool, *or* ashpit, *or* a drain, *&c.*, kept or constructed so as to be a nuisance to *A. B., &c., as the case may be,*] *or* that upon the premises aforesaid, or first aforesaid, an accumulation of dung, manure, offal, filth, *or* refuse, *or as the case may be*, is kept, *or* a pigsty exists, so as to be injurious to health as aforesaid, *or* so as to be a nuisance to *A. B., &c., as the case may be*]: We [*or* I] do hereby, in pursuance of the Statute in such case made and provided, order the said owner [*or* occupier] of the said dwelling house [*or* building *or* premises, *or* first-mentioned premises within hours from the service of this order [*or* a true copy thereof,] according to the Statute in such case made and provided, to cleanse [whitewash *or* purify] the said dwelling house] or to cleanse, cover, *or* fill up, *or as the case may require*, the said drain, [ditch, gutter, privy, cesspool, *or* ashpit, *or otherwise as the case may require,*] or remove the said pigsty *or* accumulation of dung, offal, fifth, refuse, *or* matter, *as the case may be*, so that the same shall not be injurious to health, *or* a nuisance as aforesaid]; and if this order be not complied with, then we [*or* I] authorize and require you the said town council [*or* guardians of the poor, *or, in Scotland*, the procurator fiscal of the county of *or* the procurator fiscal *or* dean of guild of the burgh of *or* the procurator of the justices of the peace of the county of *or* the inspector of the poor of the parish of *as the case may be*] to enter upon the said dwelling house, [*or* building, *or* premises, *or* first-mentioned premises,] and to do all such works, matters, and things, as may be necessary for carrying this order into effect, according to the Statute in such case made and provided.

And for your so doing this shall be your sufficient warrant.

Given under our hands and seals [*or* my hand and seal, *or, in Scotland*, our hands, *or* my hand], this day of one thousand eight hundred and

Signatures. { (L. S.)* (L. S.)*

* [*In Scotland without Seals.*]

the poorer classes tends so greatly to remove many of the causes of destitution and pauperism, that the money judiciously expended on such an object, now sanctioned by the legislature, in the cases to which the Statute applies, will be found to be most profitably laid out, even in reference to the more direct object of the duties of the guardians."

I am, &c.,
W. G. LUMLEY,
Assistant Secretary.

The Clerk to the Board of Guardians.

---

4. CIRCULAR TO THE POOR-LAW INSPECTORS ON THE ACT OF 11 & 12 VIC. C. 123, AS TO THE REMOVAL OF NUISANCES AND THE PREVENTION OF EPIDEMIC DISEASES.

Poor Law Board,
Somerset House,
6th October, 1848.

SIR,—I am directed by the Poor Law Board to call your attention to the fact, that an Order in Council has been issued for putting in force the provisions of the new Act, 11th & 12th Vic. c. 123, for the removal of nuisances, and the prevention of epidemic diseases. By that Act the General Board of Health are empowered, upon the issue of the Order in Council, to make regulations for the prevention of epidemic diseases, and by such regulations to authorise and require the guardians of the poor, by themselves or their officers, or any persons employed by them in the administration of the laws for the relief of the poor, or by officers specially appointed in this behalf, to superintend and see to the execution of any such regulations and directions.

For your information, a copy is enclosed of a Circular Letter directed to the board of guardians, calling their attention to the amended provisions contained in the new Act, and the extended powers given therein.

When this country was last visited by the Asiatic cholera (1832,) in most of the larger towns it was found to be necessary, in consequence of the insufficiency of the parochial local administrative machinery, to constitute new local administrative bodies, to act expressly for the purpose, as Boards of Health. But it has been deemed by the legislature, that the local administrative machinery, created since then, of boards of guardians, with regularly appointed medical officers, and relieving officers, having assigned duties in defined districts, with new houses, and well appointed wards for the reception of fever cases, will, in many cases, render unnecessary the creation of any new and separate local authority for the special emergency.

The Board are, however, aware of the heavy duties of the boards of guardians in many of the densely populated town districts, and that it would not be proper to call upon them to perform any additional or extraordinary services. Such cases have been provided for by the 14th sec. of the statute, which enacts that "the said guardians may appoint or employ for the superintendence and execution of the said regulations, officers (or persons in aid of the officers,) or persons employed in the administration of the laws for the relief of the poor."

The general Board of Health desire a house-to-house visitation to be made in the poor and badly conditioned districts, where the relieving officers are required to attend on cases of sickness, or where epidemic diseases most frequently prevail; (for it is in such places that the most severe visitations of cholera may be expected unless precautions be taken.) The regulations of the Board of Health will authorise the active

---

SCHEDULE (D.)

Order to permit Execution of Works by Owners.

County of [*or* Borough, *or* Burgh, *or* Metropolitan Police District, *or as the case may be*] to wit. } WHEREAS complaint hath been made to me, *E. F.*, esquire, one of Her Majesty's justices of the peace in and for the county [*or* borough, *&c.*] of [*or* one of the magistrates of the police courts of the metropolis, *or as the case may be, or, in Scotland,* to me, *G. H.*, sheriff, *or* one of Her Majesty's justices of the peace, *as the case may be*, of the county of], by *A. B.*, owner within the meaning of the "Nuisances Removal and Disease Prevention Act, 1848," of certain premises, to wit, a dwelling house [*or* building *or as the case may be*] situate [*insert such a description of the premises as may be sufficient to identify them,*] in the parish of in the said county [*or* borough *&c.*,] that *C. D.*, the occupier of the said premises, doth prevent the said *A. B.* from obeying and carrying into effect the provisions of the said Act, in this, to wit, that he the said *C. D.* doth prevent the said *A. B.* from [*here describe the works generally according to the circumstances; for instance, thus:* cleansing *or* whitewashing *or* purifying the said dwelling house, [*or* building,] *or* cleansing a foul and offensive drain [ditch, gutter, privy, cesspool, *or* ashpit] which exists upon the said premises, *or as the case may require*]: and whereas the said *C. D.* having been summoned to answer the said complaint, and not having shown sufficient cause against the same, and it appearing to me that the said works are necessary for the purpose of enabling the said *A. B.* to obey and carry into effect the provisions of the said Act, I do hereby order that the said *C. D.* do permit the said *A. B.* to execute the same in the manner required by the said Act.

Given under my hand and seal [*or, in Scotland,* under my hand] this day of in the year of our Lord one thousand eight hundred and

E. F. (L. S.)*

* [*In Scotland without seal.*]

lime-washing and complete cleansing of such places.

The attacks of cholera are preceded by premonitory symptoms, and if these symptoms are promptly attended to and properly treated, there is little danger of a fatal termination of the disease.

The Board of Health propose, after the first examinations have been made of the suspected districts for the purpose of directing preventive measures of cleansing, that there should be regular house-to-house visitations for ascertaining by inquiry the occurrence of the premonitory symptoms, and treating them at once.

The arrangements required for carrying out the contemplated regulations will, of course, vary with the state of the business of the boards of guardians and their officers; these officers you are requested to confer with, and suggest any orders which may appear to you necessary or advisable to be made under the 12th sec. of the Act, which you may refer to for this object.

Where the board of guardians may be prevented from acting as a body, a committee might be named, and might, under the authority of the 14th sec., associate with them some of the most respectable inhabitants that are willing to act. It is especially desirable that the clergyman of each parish should be associated with the special committee of guardians and other persons for carrying out the regulations of the general Board of Health, and fulfilling the objects of the Act.

In respect to the preventive measures of cleansing, it is to be observed that, by the 10th sec. of the Act, surveyors, district or assistant surveyors of highways, trustees, county surveyors, and others by law entrusted "with the care and management of streets and public ways and places," may, by the regulations of the general Board of Health, be required to give concurrent aid by the frequent and effectual cleansing of such ways and places. These officers will be required to assist the guardians and their officers, as will also, the owners, or occupiers, or the persons having the care of houses, dwellings, churches, buildings, and places of assembly.

It is to be observed that effectual cleansing operations, and all other preventive measures, will be as effective against the occurrence of typhus and the ordinary epidemics, as against cholera.

In respect to the medical service required, it is to be borne in mind as one effect observed during the former visitation of Asiatic cholera, that the ordinary epidemics merged in the new and extraordinary pestilence.

The medical assistance required in addition to local examinations, and the treatment of actual attacks, will be medicines for the relief of the premonitory symptoms of the disease. The requisite medicines should be dispensed at the houses of the medical officers, and also at such other places as the Board or Special Committee of Health may deem necessary. Packets should be made up to be carried about and given at the time of the occurrence of any premonitory symptoms. Other medical practitioners may be associated, under the authority of the Act, with the Poor Law medical officers, in cases where additional aid, counsel, or direction, appear requisite. In like manner, additional labourers may be employed in the cleansing operations.

It should be impressed on the guardians, that the arrangements under consideration ought to have precedence of all ordinary services; and the more so, as the other claims upon their time will certainly be diminished by the effectual execution of the above regulations, the efficacy of which has been proved by extensive experience. For measures of more permanent relief and complete prevention, you may take occasion to direct attention to the provisions of the Public Health Act.

You are requested to forward the arrangements described, and, in the course of your visits, to note any special local regulations that may be required for the towns, or parts of towns, within your district; and it is desirable that you should commence with those where the proportion of deaths and cases of sickness regularly recurring from epidemic disease have been most numerous, in proportion to other cases, as shewn by the mortuary registries, or the claims for relief on account of sickness.

I am, &c.,
GEO. NICHOLLS,
Secretary.

To ——
Poor Law Inspector.

5. NOTICE FROM BOARDS OF GUARDIANS IN REFERENCE TO THE ACT 11 & 12 VIC. C. 123.

The following Notice has been issued by several boards of guardians on this subject:—

REMOVAL OF NUISANCES.—NOTICE.—I am instructed by the board of guardians to make known throughout this union that the Act passed in the last sessions of parliament, to renew and amend an Act of the tenth year of Her present

Majesty, for the more speedy removal of certain nuisances, and the prevention of contagious and epidemic diseases, confers upon them the power, by themselves, their servants or agents, (upon receipt of a notice in writing, signed by two or more inhabitant householders of the parish or place to which the notice relates, stating that, to the best of the knowledge and belief of the persons by whom such notice is signed, any dwelling-house or building is in such a filthy and unwholesome condition as to be a nuisance to or injurious to the health of any person, or that upon any premises there is any foul and offensive ditch, gutter, drain, privy, cess-pool, or ashpit, or any ditch, gutter, drain, privy, cess-pool, or ashpit, kept or constructed so as to be a nuisance to or injurious to the health of any person, or that upon any such premises, swine, or any accumulation of dung, manure, offal, filth, refuse, or other matter or thing, are or is kept so as to be a nuisance to or injurious to the health of any person, or that upon any such premises, being a building used wholly or in part as a dwelling-house, or being premises underneath any such building, any cattle or animal are or is kept so as to be a nuisance to or injurious to the health of any person.)

To enter such premises and examine the same with respect to the matters alleged in such Notice, and, if necessary, to make a complaint before a justice, who shall thereupon summon the owner or occupier to appear before two justices.

And such justices are empowered,

To make an order for cleansing, whitewashing, or purifying such dwelling-house or building, or for the removal or abatement of any such cause or causes of complaint, in such manner and within such time as shall be specified in such Order.

If such Order be not complied with, the owner or occupier against whom it is made will be liable to a penalty not exceeding ten shillings for every day during the continuance of his default, and the guardians, by themselves or agents, are authorised to enter such premises, and cleanse, whitewash, or purify the same, or remove or abate the cause or causes of complaint in respect whereof the said Order was made.

The costs and expenses incurred by the guardians may be recovered from the owner or occupier of the premises in the County Court, or before two justices, by distress and sale of the goods and chattels of such owner or occupier.

Whosoever shall wilfully obstruct any person acting under the authority of the Act of Parliament, is made liable for every such offence to a penalty not exceeding five pounds.

All penalties imposed by the Act may be recovered by any person before any two justices, and may be levied by distress and sale of the goods and chattels of the offender.

It is expedient that all such dwelling-houses and premises as are before mentioned should forthwith be cleansed and whitewashed, and every nuisance, or cause of complaint, mentioned in the Act, removed.

The board of guardians therefore trust that all owners and occupiers of property within this union, will, without delay, in cases wherever it is required, do that which the law demands, for it cannot be too strongly impressed on the minds of owners and rate-payers, that the improvement of the sanitary condition of the poorer classes tends greatly to remove many causes of destitution and pauperism.

The board of guardians are, and will at all times be prepared, to put the Act in immediate operation in every case of neglect, upon receipt of a notice in writing, signed by any two inhabitant householders; and the board request the co-operation of the inhabitants generally throughout the union in the furtherance of so desirable an object.

(Signed) ____________________

Clerk to the Board of Guardians.

III.—VAGRANCY—SUPPRESSION OF, IN THE NEWTON ABBOT UNION.

The Poor Law Board, in acknowledging the receipt of the following report from the guardians of the Newton Abbot Union, expressed their belief that, if the circular which the guardians proposed to issue were generally acted upon, the great evil of vagrancy might be greatly mitigated.

Newton Abbot Union.—At a meeting of the visiting committee, held this day, Wednesday, August 16, 1848, the minute of the Poor Law Board on the subject of the suppression of vagrancy, dated August 4, 1848, having been submitted to the visiting committee by the direction of the board of guardians, in order that they might report it, the committee, therefore, submit the following as their opinion :—

The visiting committee having taken into consideration the best means of carrying out the minute of the Poor Law Board, contained in their Circular, dated 4th August last, relative to the " continual and rapid increase of vagrancy," and suggesting to the board of guardians certain rules and regulations to check the same, are of opinion that the board of guardians, as a body, can do but little to suppress the evil; for as long as the tender-hearted and benevolent individual exercises his deeds of charity indiscriminately, so long the lazy, the dissolute, and the dishonest, reap a bountiful harvest by day, and continue to fill our union-house by night.

Conceiving the above to be the sole support upon which vagrancy can exist, the committee are desirous of offering a suggestion to the Board, thinking it may at least tend to diminish the nuisance within the limits of this union.

The committee suggest that circulars, similar in import to the one annexed, should be sent to every parish within the union, to be distributed among the rate-payers, and posted in all public situations:—

Circular.—The board of guardians of the Newton Abbot Union have received a copy of a minute of the Poor Law Board, setting forth the vast increase of vagrancy throughout the country, and their desire that boards of guardians should co-operate with them in suppressing so great an evil, as well as to provide a more comfortable accommodation for "the really meritorious and destitute wayfarer."

Having taken these matters into their serious consideration, they are of opinion that, as a board of guardians, they can do but little to suppress this great and growing evil; but, if they are aided by the assistance and co-operation of all rate-payers and others within the union, much good may be effected.

The board of guardians conceive that, as long as the idle, the dissolute, and the dishonest wanderer can calculate upon alms from the benevolent by day, and obtain food and shelter in the nearest union by night, this iniquitous tax upon the charitable, as well as upon the honest rate-payer, will be perpetuated.

Acting upon these premises, the board of guardians emphatically, but respectfully, request from all persons in this parish, not to relieve, in money or kind, any tramp or travelling pauper that may solicit alms, but direct them at once to the relieving officer or overseer of the parish, who will have received from the board of guardians such instructions as will enable him to dispose of every case coming before him with proper humanity to the really destitute wayfarer, and disposing of the professional vagrant as the law directs, and in the towns (which are the principal resort of vagrants,) where an organized police exists, this board will be ready to make them such remuneration for carrying out their instructions as the Poor Law Board will allow. Finally, the board of guardians earnestly request that any vagrant using abusive or threatening language may be given into custody.

This Circular, if responded to by the public, (and the committee see no reason why it should not be,) will strike at the very root and existence of vagrancy.

As the districts attached to this union are exclusively rural, very few police are employed or required, so that the suggestion of the Poor Law Board to employ a member of that body as an assistant relieving officer for vagrants cannot be generally acted upon. The visiting committee, therefore, recommend that the Board do issue their instructions to every relieving officer and overseer, and request the magistrates at each petty sessions to issue their directions to the constables within their union, (together with a copy of the Board of Commissioners' minute,) to interrogate, and, if necessary, *search* every vagrant pauper brought before them, in order that they might form a sound and vigilant discrimination in respect of the objects of relief, and steadily refuse aid to all who are not ascertained to be in a state of destitution, and bestow it upon those whose urgent necessities give them a claim to relief; thus observing a just distinction between the destitute wayfarer and those who throw themselves habitually on public charity.

To the former class of paupers the relieving officer or overseer should be instructed to supply a certificate, as set forth in the minute of the Poor Law Board, and otherwise relieve, as the merits of the case may require; to the latter, after ascertaining them to be in a state of destitution, to supply them with needful food and lodging only.

The Committee depend mainly for the diminution of vagrancy in the limits of this union, upon the public *withholding alms* from travelling paupers, which will and must render vagrancy an unprofitable profession.

SAMUEL FOX,
Chairman.

London: Printed by Order of the Poor Law Board, by BLACKBURN and BURT, 90½, Holborn Hill, and Published by CHARLES KNIGHT, 90, Fleet Street.

AN

OFFICIAL CIRCULAR

OF PUBLIC DOCUMENTS AND INFORMATION

DIRECTED BY THE POOR LAW BOARD TO BE PRINTED, CHIEFLY FOR THE USE OF THE BOARDS OF GUARDIANS AND THEIR OFFICERS.

No. 20.] NOVEMBER AND DECEMBER, 1848. [N.S.

CONTENTS.

ACCOUNTS.

1. PAUPER CLASSIFICATION BOOK.

31*st Oct.*, 1848.

Clerk of Prescot Union.—The provision in the Accounts Order as to marking in the Medical Relief Books the names of those paupers who have not been in the receipt of any other than medical relief, does not afford all the information required for ascertaining the number, or making the classification correctly. Many cases are continued for several weeks together, or cease for a few weeks, and reappear several times during the half year as new cases; whilst there are no entries in the medical books to shew whether the patients are married, or single, parents or children, or to give any other information beyond names, ages, and nature of complaints: Inquired, first, whether it is intended that the medical cases should be classed and entered under the several heads in the Pauper Classification Book, in the same manner as outdoor relief cases; and secondly, if they are to be particularised, upon whom should the labour of the classification, &c., fall.

Ans.—First, the medical relief cases are required to be entered in the Pauper Classification

Book in the same manner, and with the same detail, as the other cases of relief; and secondly, the duty of filling up the Pauper Classification Book devolves upon yourself as clerk of the union, under the express provisions of Art. 14, No. 4, of the General Accounts Order. With regard to the source from which you are to obtain the information necessary to enable you to enter the requisite particulars of the medical relief cases in the Pauper Classification Book, the Board desire to point out, that, where the medical relief has been granted in consequence of an application to one of the relieving officers, you will find the particulars in question in his Application and Report Book; to which the Board presume that the information contained in the District Medical Relief Book, duly marked in accordance with the directions of Art. 22 of the order, will readily enable you to refer. Where, however, the medical relief is ordered by the guardians upon an application made to them, without the intervention of the relieving officer, the clerk will not be able to avail himself of the Application and Report Book, as in the cases above mentioned; and it will, therefore, apparently be necessary that when entering the order of the guardians in the Relief Order Book, he should take a memorandum of the particulars which he will afterwards require for his own information. The cases of this class are not distinctly provided for in the accounts order; but the Board apprehend that they are too few in number to need any special provision.

2. EXAMINATION OF THE WORKHOUSE MASTER'S ACCOUNTS.

12*th August*, 1848.

Clerk of ——— *Union.*—It being the wish of the guardians that the arithmetical accuracy of all the books kept by the master should be ascertained, requested the opinion of the Board on whom the duty of ascertaining such accuracy devolved.

Ans.—The arithmetical examination of the master's books is not a duty the performance of which is required from the clerk, but it is incumbent upon the district auditor to ascertain that the accounts and books of the master are correctly cast up and balanced.

3. CLOTHING AND PROVISIONS ACCOUNTS.

26*th Aug.* 1848.

Clerk of ——— *Union.*—Stated several difficulties which presented themselves in regard to the Clothing and Provisions Accounts prescribed by the General Order of Accounts.

Ans.—With reference to the "Clothing Register," prescribed by the General Order of Accounts, the Board believe the book was not ordered to be kept until the Poor Law Commissioners were satisfied that a book somewhat similar had been used with great advantage in some workhouses of considerable extent; and they see no reason to doubt that the system of clothing accounts prescribed by the order, including the book in question, is well suited, if carried out, to answer all the practical purposes of such accounts in the unions generally; and is, moreover, susceptible of being easily adapted to the exceptive cases referred to in your letter. The Board consider it necessary that a sufficient number of suits to clothe all the paupers who may be in the house at any time, should be kept up. The number of suits available, will therefore, exceed the greatest number of paupers likely to be in the house together. There will of course be as many numbers as suits; and no number will be cancelled unless the stock of clothing should be deemed more than sufficient; in which case, it might be thought unnecessary to replace a suit which may be worn out, or otherwise disposed of. It is left to the guardians with the experience of the master, to determine what articles shall generally constitute a suit, though the Poor Law Commissioners have, in their circular letter accompanying the order, given a general notion on the point. The suits for the same class of paupers will generally consist of the same description, and number of the different articles which are necessary to form a suit. The sizes of the suits are distinguished by subsidiary numbers. Whatever may be the description and number of the articles which the guardians may determine shall, as a general rule, constitute a suit, there will occasionally be cases of exception. It will not, however, be difficult with a little care to prevent the exceptive cases from embarrassing the master, or throwing his account into confusion. The case which you suppose, where an extra number of shirts are required, might be met by allotting to a certain number of suits, more than the regular number of shirts; such suits might distinguished by an index in the Clothing Register Book, showing, against the numbers marked on the suits, the articles of which they consist; or, where extra linen is required for the sick ward, it might be provided and entered in the inventory book, as linen belonging rather to the ward, than to any particular suit or suits. The Board are assured that a correct summary and an approximate valuation of the second-hand clothing may conveniently be made from the clothing register book at any time. The summary being for a temporary purpose, and the form of it being immaterial, it was unnecessary for the Poor Law Commissioners to prescribe any form or book in which it should be kept. The summary is to enable "the guardians to approximate as nearly as possible to the principle of the Poor Law Amendment Act, that each parish should bear the cost of the relief afforded to the poor chargeable to it in the workhouse." (See the circular letter above referred to.) The Register Book shows at all times the stock of second-hand clothing, and the Board therefore think that any other "old stock account" is unnecessary. As to the consecutive order of the numbers, the Board believe that every experienced master will so apportion the book as to prevent any material disturbance of the consecutive order. Under the most unfavourable circumstances any inconvenience which would otherwise arise from such disturbance may be obviated by an index as suggested. With regard to the provisions accounts the Board have briefly to remark:—1st, That from Notes 1 & 2 at the foot of Form 25, it is clear that none but the articles mentioned in the Diet Table, are to be inserted in the portion of this form allotted to "prepared provisions." 2nd, That in the portion of Form 25, allotted to provisions "in their unprepared state," the "principal articles" only are required to be entered. (See Note 3.) By the principal articles the Board understand those articles the requisite quantities of which can conveniently be regulated by weight or measurement according to the prescribed quantities of "prepared provisions." The remaining articles, not entered in Forms 25 & 26, are to be entered in Forms 27, 28, & 29; which are to contain all articles ("provisions" and "necessaries") received and consumed, and in the store. (See Art. 15). 3rd, That the waste in the cooking and the cutting into rations appears by the difference between the quantities of "prepared provisions" and the quantities of the articles in their unprepared state, entered daily in Form 25. 4th, That the loss in weights by keeping may be entered in Form 26, in the same manner as the bone in meat is entered.

---

4. TRUSSES, &C., HOW CHARGED.

18th August, 1848.

Clerk of Bath Union. — Inquired whether trusses, wooden legs, and articles of a similar description, furnished to in-door and out-door paupers, should be charged in the relieving officer's accounts as out-relief, or to the extra medical fees account.

Ans. — The articles in question cannot be charged to the extra medical fees account, as suggested by you; but as regards any such articles supplied to workhouse inmates, they should be charged to the in-maintenance account, and to the out-door relief account when furnished to out-door poor.

---

5. LOSS SUSTAINED BY THE DEFAULT OF RELIEVING OFFICER, HOW CHARGED.

9th August, 1848.

Clerk of ——— Union.—Proceedings were taken by the guardians to recover from the surety of the relieving officer of a district of the union the sum of £60. 5*s.* 8½*d.*, the amount of his defalcations. The guardians subsequently accepted of £30. in discharge of the claim. Inquired how the balance should be entered in the ledger, so that the account might be closed.

Ans.—The loss sustained in the present case should be borne by the union at large, as the relieving officer, although appointed for a particular district, was the officer of the board of guardians; and, accordingly, it appears to the Poor Law Board that the sum in question—viz., £30. 5*s.* 8½*d.*—should be distributed in the union accounts according to the averages.

AUDITORS' DUTIES—CONSTRUCTION OF 11 & 12 VIC. C. 91.

19th Sept., 1848.

Mr. ———, District Auditor—Requested advice on the following points, arising on the construction of the Act of 11 & 12 Vic. c. 91. 1. As to sec. 5, Whether the certificate of a balance found to be wholly omitted in the accounts of the continuing overseers at the approaching audit, and whether any and what memorandum of having audited the accounts (in addition to a certificate, if any, of allowance on surcharge,) is to be entered. 2. As to the Lady-day audit, the certificate set forth in the schedule under which recovery is to be effected, does not seem to apply to a balance found. Can any other, and what form of certificate be used? 3. Does the last proviso of this section enable overseers to pay to their successors their balances, irrespective of sums disallowed, leaving disallowances amounting to more than forty shillings, only payable to the treasurer? Would not this be irreconcileable with the treasurer's certificate, required by the 9th sec.? 4. Sec. 6. Whether this sec. will affect disallowances made before the passing of the Act, upon which proceedings have not terminated? 5. Sec. 7. In this district, it would be difficult to select in either of the counties comprised in it, any one paper which would circulate properly, the notice of audit. There being more than one paper circulating extensively in each of the counties, would insertion in one paper only in each county fulfil the intentions of the Act? 6. Sec. 9. Will not the limited proof herein prescribed, be sufficient in any proceedings to be taken after the passing of the Act, although founded on a previous certificate, unless they come within the Restriction Act? 7. What persons ought to be held answerable for illegal payments in the union accounts? The authority to pay is by minutes, signed only by the chairman; the payment is made by cheque. Does the Act enable the auditor to surcharge either the chairman signing the minutes, or the parties signing the cheque?

Ans.—1. The Board do not perceive that there is anything in the statute referred to, which interferes with the requisitions of the General Order of Accounts. The auditor, therefore, will still be required at every audit, to sign the memorandum at the foot of the overseers' half-yearly account of receipts and payments, specifying the amount of the balance appearing as the result of that account; and at the foot of the half-yearly balance-sheet, certifying its correctness. The Board are not aware that any further memorandum or certificate will be required from the auditor at the Michaelmas audit, unless there be a surcharge or disallowance. 2. Any balance that may be found by the auditor to be due from the outgoing overseers at Lady-day, after proceeding in the manner pointed out in the 5th sec. of the 11 & 12 Vic. c. 91, will be a sum to be certified by him as due under the 32nd sec. of the 7 & 8 Vic. c. 101. If, in such a case, there be any balance due, beyond surcharges and disallowances, the forms of certificate appended to the former Act will clearly not suffice, as they only apply to cases in which the auditor has made a disallowance or surcharge. 3. The balance which the outgoing overseers in any case admit to be due on their accounts, may (as appears from the terms of the 5th sec.,) be paid over by them to their successors, before the Lady-day audit takes place. If, however, it be not so paid, the Board think that, where there is no disallowance, or the disallowances amount to more than forty shillings, the sum certified by the auditor to be due from the outgoing overseers, should be paid to the union treasurer, under the 32nd sec. of the 7 & 8 Vic. c. 101. 4. With regard to proceedings actually commenced before the passing of the 11 & 12 Vic. c. 91, for the recovery of sums due, the Board may observe generally, that sec. 6. appears to be entirely prospective. The Board, however, would prefer to answer your inquiry on this point with reference to the circumstances of the particular case or cases on which it arises. 5. The Board think it will suffice to insert the advertisement of an audit for any particular union, in one newspaper only, provided such newspaper circulates within that union. 6. It appears to the Board, that the short form of information and proof, provided in the 9th sec. of the recent Act, may be adopted in proceedings that may be commenced subsequently to its passing, founded on a certificate made before the passing. 7. In reply to your last inquiry, the Board desire to point out, that the recent Act makes no alteration as to the liability of parties to be surcharged, which liability depends upon the 32nd sec. of the 7 & 8 Vic. c. 101. Under that enactment, the auditor is required to certify any money found by him to be due from any person, and to recover the same from all or any of the persons making or authorizing the the illegal payment. In deciding for himself in any case, who it was that authorized an illegal payment, the auditor will, no doubt, bear in mind that, while there may be a question whether all the guardians who passed the resolutions for the payment, would come within the reach of the statute, there is no doubt that those guardians who signed the cheque, thereby authorized the payment, and that consequently the auditor would be justified in certifying against them.

BURIAL.

1. Burial of Poor Persons Dying in a Hospital.

7th June, 1848.

Clerk of Guardians of ——— Parish.—The general hospital is situated in the parish of B., and is supported by voluntary contributions only. It is not incorporated nor endowed. Patients are received into it on the recommendation of subscribers, and it is open to cases of fever, accidents, and other urgent cases, whether the same occur in the parish of B. or elsewhere. There are no funds specially appropriated to defray the expenses of the funerals of such patients as may die therein. Inquired whether the expenses of interment should be borne by the parish from which the patient is brought into the hospital, or by the parish of B., in which the hospital is situate, or by the funds of the hospital itself.

Ans.—There is clearly no legal obligation cast upon the guardians of the unions or parishes from which the poor persons may have been brought into the hospital to provide for the interment of the bodies. Section 31 of 7 & 8 Vic. c. 101, gives power to the guardians of unions and overseers of parishes to bury in certain cases, but their power of interference in this way is limited to the case where the body is within the union or parish respectively for which such guardians or overseers act. Then, as between the guardians of the parish of B., in which the deaths occur, and the necessity for burial arises, and the authorities of the hospital, the Board are not able to say that the guardians could be compelled to provide for the interment of the bodies. The Board direct attention to the case of Reg *v.* Steward, 12 A. & E., 773. From that decision it appears that the principles of the common law would cast the legal obligations, in such a case as the present, upon the authorities of the hospital. It was observed by Lord Denman, "that the individual under whose roof a poor person dies, is bound to convey the body, decently covered, to the place of burial; he cannot keep him unburied, nor do anything which prevents Christian burial." The Board do not understand that the statute 7 & 8 Vic. c. 101, in giving a general power to the guardians to bury at the cost of the poor-rates the bodies of poor persons which may be within their union or parish, and whether, dying in any workhouse or otherwise, has relieved the authorities of a hospital, or the occupier of any house in which the death occurs, from the common law obligation which in Reg. *v.* Steward was declared to exist. Whether the guardians of the parish of B. (assuming their power) should interfere to relieve the authorities of the hospital from this obligation in any case, is a point upon which the Board do not feel themselves at present sufficiently informed to express an opinion.

---

2. Burial fees.

15th July, 1848.

Clerk of ——— Union.—J. R. was an acknowledged pauper of the parish of A., and resided there until within a few days of his death, when he came into the workhouse at B., and was there maintained as a pauper of A. up to his death, and pursuant to the ordinary practice of the Board was in accordance with his wish, and that of his friends, buried at A. The clergyman demanded, and has received, an extra fee on the burial, as in the case of a stranger, and the guardians consider that the deceased having been resident in A. up to within a day or two of his death, and then received, as a pauper of that parish, into the union workhouse, which, for parochial purposes, is within the manor of A. the extra fee ought not to have been charged.

Ans.—It appears to the Board that the clergyman, in making his claim, has overlooked the operation of secs. 31 & 56, of the 7 & 8 Vic. cap. 101, in such a case; the former of these secs. gives power to the guardians to direct the burial to take place in the churchyard of the parish to which the pauper is chargeable, and the latter renders the workhouse for the purpose (*inter alia*) of burial, constructively situate in the parish of the chargeability. In this case, therefore, it is to be considered that the pauper in construction of law died in the parish of A. so as (the guardians having directed the burial) to give the same right to interment in the churchyard of that parish, as though the death had actually occurred there. The Board are advised that where burial in the churchyard of a parish can be enforced as a right, the law does not entitle the incumbent to extra fees for performing the ceremony. Such a claim they are led to believe can only exist in the cases of persons who neither actually nor constructively die in the parish. In these cases, as the right of burial cannot be enforced, it may be that the incumbent, as the condition for allowing the interment and performing the ceremony, may be entitled to claim a fee.

---

3. The cost of burial treated as relief by way of loan.

24th Oct., 1848.

Clerk of St. Alban's Union.—A parent applied to the relieving officer to bury his child, and stated, that if not buried by the parish, the body must remain unburied. The relieving officer thereupon took on himself the funeral, and paid the carpenter for the coffin, and the minister and clerk for the burial fees, telling the parent that such payments would be considered as a relief to him by way of loan. Inquired whether such payments can be legally treated as relief by way of loan to such parent.

Ans.—As the facts of the case are set forth,

the Board understand that the proceedings for the burial of the child were taken under the 31 sec. of the 7 and 8 Vic. cap. 101. No relief was directly afforded to the parent in consideration of his necessities, occasioned by the death of his child; but the relieving officer (as the agent of the guardians of the union) took upon himself the entire charge of the burial, and paid the carpenter for the coffin, and the minister and clerk the usual burial fees, without apparently having previously satisfied himself as to the exact necessity, or circumstances of the parent. The guardians, by this act of their officer, certainly took upon themselves the discharge of an obligation, which must, otherwise, have been performed by the parent; but the Board are not prepared to say that the costs of burial so undertaken by the guardians under sec. 31 of the recited Act is necessarily relief. The Board are disposed to think that the cost of the burial in the present case, could not be legally treated as relief given by way of loan, so as to be recoverable from the parent.

Clerk of same Union.—Inquired in what manner the cost of the burial of poor persons dying out of the workhouse, should be paid by the relieving officer so that it may be treated as relief.

Ans.—There are two ways in which the guardians may provide for the burial of poor persons, dying out of the workhouse, viz., by giving directions for the burial, and taking the charge of the expenses on themselves, under the 31st sec. of the 7 and 8 Vic. cap. 101; or by affording relief to the person who may be bound by law to inter the body, for the purpose of enabling him to discharge that obligation. It appears to the Board that funeral expenses incurred by the guardians under the special provisions of the Act just mentioned, cannot be regarded in strictness as relief; and consequently cannot be recovered as such from any person or persons. But where the guardians grant assistance to a destitute person, to enable such person to inter a body for whose burial he is liable, but unable to provide, the Board see nothing to prevent the guardians affording such relief by way of loan, in the same manner, and to the same extent as they might any other relief.

CLERK—PRODUCTION OF UNION BOOKS AT A MEETING OF MAGISTRATES.

15*th Aug.*, 1848.

Clerk of ——— *Union.*—Inquired whether he, as clerk, is bound to produce the books of the union at any meeting of magistrates, when requested so to do by another union.

Ans.—It will be incumbent upon you to attend in such cases before the magistrates, if you are subpœnaed; and, though there may be some doubt whether the provisions contained in the Act 7 & 8 Vic. cap. 101. sec. 70. applies to orders of removal, the Board think that if any order of justices be served upon you in pursuance of that enactment, you should obey it.

CHARGEABILITY.—11 & 12 VIC. c. 110.

1*st Nov.*, 1848.

Clerk of Louth Union. — Inquired whether paupers who have become "chargeable in respect of relief made necessary by sickness or accident," not "producing permanent disability," and who are consequently irremovable under the 4th sec. of the 9 & 10 Vic. c. 66, are to be charged to the common fund of the union under the 3rd sec. of 11 & 12 Vic. c. 110, upon the statement of the relieving officers that such paupers have not, as far as can be ascertained, a settlement in the parish where they fell sick, or where the accident occurred. Also, requested the Board to lay down some rule for the guidance of the guardians in such cases.

Ans.—If the paupers in question became chargeable simply in consequence of sickness or accident, and that sickness or accident is not of a character to cause a permanent disability, they are exempt from removal under the 4th sec. of 9 & 10 Vic. c. 66. This opinion proceeds upon the assumption that such persons have no settlement in the respective parishes of their residence, nor where the sickness or accident occurred. If they have such settlement, they are not subject to removal under an order of justices; indeed the question of their removability does not in fact arise. The Board observe that the inability of a parish in which a pauper may be to procure legal evidence, in support of an order of removal, does not in any way show that the pauper's legal settlement is in that parish. It is quite possible that the pauper may not be settled therein, although the parish may be without the means of proving that a settlement exists elsewhere. The Board do not see that they can lay down any rule to be observed by the guardians in such cases as those to which your communication applies. They can only express their opinion generally that the guardians should use such means of information as they may possess, with a view to ascertain the fact of the pauper's being settled in the parish of his residence. If no legal evidence of such settlement be procurable, then they would be warranted in regarding him as settled elsewhere, and in applying the provisions of the 9 & 10 Vic. c. 66, accordingly. It is certainly competent to the guardians to rely upon the information which the relieving officers may be able to give in cases of this kind if they think fit. The cost of the relief given in the cases adverted to by you appears to the Board to be chargeable to the common fund of the union.

EMIGRATION OF A SOLDIER'S WIFE.

1*st August*, 1848.

Clerk of Penrith Union.—Can the guardians legally advance money to a female pauper, in order that she may join her husband, who is a soldier, now in America?

Ans.—The Poor Law Board cannot sanction any expenditure from the poor-rate for the purpose referred to, as it would interfere with the regulations of the military service, which only permit a limited number of females to accompany each regiment, and without an Order of the Board the expenditure could not legally be incurred by the guardians. The Board believe that much distress has in some cases been occasioned to the wives and families of soldiers serving abroad who have been sent out to join their husbands without due authority.

GUARDIAN.—WHETHER INTITLED TO TAKE COPIES OF MINUTES.

11*th Oct.*, 1848.

———, *Esq., a Guardian*—Inquired whether he, as a guardian, has the right of taking copies of the Minutes of the proceedings of the board of guardians without their consent previously obtained.

Ans.—The books, in which are recorded the proceedings of the guardians, are the property of the guardians collectively as a Board, and therefore no individual guardian possesses, by virtue of his office, any right to take copies of, or make extracts from those documents without the permission of the board of guardians.

LUNATICS.

1. LUNATIC PAUPERS.—DUTY OF RELIEVING OFFICER.

28*th Oct.*, 1848.

Clerks of Magistrates of ———.—Represented that a relieving officer of the ——— Union, who had been requested to sign the certificate prescribed by the Act, 8 & 9 Vic. c. 126, in regard to a wandering pauper lunatic, had refused to do so, stating that he had nothing to do with lunatics. The Poor Law Board, after communicating with the relieving officer himself on the subject, wrote to him as follows:—

Where you receive information of a lunatic person being found wandering, who has been detained either by the police or by any private individual, it would be the safest and most expedient course for you to adopt, if you have the opportunity, to cause the lunatic to be brought before a justice, in conformity with the 49th sec. of the 8 & 9 Vic. cap. 126. The justice will then decide upon the circumstances of the case, whether the lunatic found wandering is in such a condition as to give the justices jurisdiction to make an order for his removal under the above cited statute. If, however, you should meet with an insane person under such care as not to be considered within the meaning of the statute, a wandering lunatic, nor likely to become so, you will not be required to interfere, nor justified in interferring with the case, unless he be a pauper.

2. LUNATIC POSSESSED OF PROPERTY.

6*th Sept.*, 1848.

Clerk of ——— *Union.*—G. W. a dangerous lunatic, but not chargeable to any parish, was taken up on complaint of the parish officers of G., and sent by the justices to the lunatic asylum at Lincoln, at the charge of that parish. The lunatic being possessed of real and personal property to the amount of £50 per annum, the justices subsequently, under the 49th sec. of the Act 8 & 9 Vic. c. 126, made an order on the lunatic's wife, as his nearest relative, to pay the sum of £13. 11*s.* for the removal, examinations, and deposit on account of maintenance of the lunatic; which amount the wife objects to pay, stating that her income is not sufficient to allow of such payment, and also of the further weekly charge of about 12*s.*, for maintenance and clothing at the asylum, unless she has recourse to the principal fund; but she would be able and willing to spare 7*s.* a week towards such maintenance. The justices, however, holding that the estate, and not the income, of the lunatic is to be taken into account, intend to enforce the order, and direct the parish officers to seize and sell the household furniture, &c., of the lunatic, and out of the proceeds defray the expenses incurred. Inquired whether, under the 49th sec. of the Act, the income of the lunatic should be the guide of the justices in making their order; or, whether the effects of the lunatic (beyond the residue of income, after deducting a reasonable sum for the maintenance of his family) can be seized and sold for the purpose of paying such expences; and also whether any power of appeal is given against an order of this nature under the 62nd or 80th secs. of the Act, or there are any other means available for disputing its legality.

Ans.—The Board are of opinion that the "estate" of the lunatic referred to in the 49th sec. of the 8 & 9 Vic. c. 126, does not mean "income" merely, but property of all kinds. At the same time the Act seems to require that the surplus estate only shall be applied to the lunatic's support; and consequently the principal fund could not be taken for that purpose beyond such an amount as would still leave, after providing for all liabilities to which the estate may be subject, sufficient income for the maintenance of the lunatic's family. If, in the present case, the income is not more than enough for the support of the family, the Board apprehend that the order of the justices cannot be upheld or enforced. The Board may add, that, assuming the order in the present case to be properly made on the wife, the justices cannot call upon her to pay any deposit money. She can only be required to repay the costs already incurred in respect of the lunatic, and to provide the necessary weekly payment for his future maintenance. It is to be observed, moreover, that the 49th sec. of the Act does not apply to a merely dangerous lunatic, but to one wandering abroad or not properly taken care of by his relatives. The Board see no reason to suppose that the justices' order is not open to appeal, under the 80th sec. of the statute; and, indeed, if it be not lawfully made it may be otherwise resisted.

3. MEDICAL PRACTITIONER'S CERTIFICATE IN THE CASE OF A PAUPER LUNATIC.

15th Nov., 1848.

G. S., Esq.—Is a medical man, and his son is a medical officer of an union workhouse. He, the father, occasionally attends the workhouse for his son when he is prevented from doing so himself. Inquired,—1. Whether he, the father, is in consequence legally incapacitated from giving the necessary certificate in the case of a pauper lunatic belonging to the union, located in the workhouse, or in a district of the union. 2. The union is composed of the workhouse and two districts, a medical officer being appointed to each, is either of the district medical officers legally competent to give the required certificate in the case of a pauper lunatic located in the workhouse, or in either of the districts. 3. If a medical officer of a union give the certificate in question for the purpose of the admission of a pauper into a lunatic asylum and the proprietor of the asylum receives the pauper under such an authority, does the proprietor thereby commit a misdemeanor?

Ans.—1. It does not appear to the Board that the law disqualifies you for signing the requisite certificate in the case of a pauper lunatic belonging to a union of which your son is a medical officer, but in which you yourself hold no appointment, though you occasionally attend at the union workhouse professionally for your son. The Board think, however, that under the circumstances you would do well to abstain as much as possible from signing such certificates in respect of inmates of the workhouse. 2. The Board are of opinion that the prohibition contained in the 48th sec. of the 8 & 9 Vic. c. 100, applies generally to all the medical officers of a union, and is not confined to the medical officer of the particular district in which the lunatic resides. 3. The Board think that the proprietor of a licensed house, who should knowingly receive a pauper into his house under a certificate from a medical officer of the union only, would be guilty of a misdemeanor under the 48th sec. of the 8 & 9 Vic. c. 100. The Board may add that, in reference to proceedings under the 48th sec. of the 8 & 9 Vic. c. 126, express provision is made by the 9 & 10 Vic. c. 84, sec. 1, for obtaining the certificate of the medical officer of the union in certain cases.

MEDICAL OFFICER.

1. CERTIFICATE OF LUNACY BY SUBSTITUTE FOR,

July 14th, 1848.

Clerk of Huntingdon Union—Inquired whether a medical man who had been named as a substitute for a district medical officer was disqualified from signing the certificate of lunacy required under the 48th sec. of 8 & 9 Vic. c. 126.

Ans.—The substitute for the medical officer appointed under the authority of Art. 200 of the General Consolidated Order is so clearly identified with the medical officer, that the Board think that whatever ground exists for the prohibition of the medical officer in the 48th sec. of the 7 & 8 Vic. c. 126, must be considered to extend to the substitute. Without, therefore, expressing an opinion that the substitute is actually disqualified by law from giving the certificate, the Board think that the spirit of the statute requires that he should abstain from giving it.

---

2. CLAIM OF FEE FOR SETTING A FRACTURED THIGH.

30*th Aug.*, 1848.

Mr. ———, *District Medical Officer*—Received an order from the churchwarden of *A.* to attend a vagrant who had fallen and fractured her thigh; after the limb was set, as she had no home, the churchwarden had her conveyed to the union workhouse. On her arrival there, the medical officer of the workhouse found the splints displaced, and reset the limb. Evidence could be produced that the limb was properly set in the first instance. Inquired whether he was entitled to the fee payable under the Poor Law Commissioners' Order, which was also claimed by the medical officer of the workhouse.

Ans.—The fee prescribed by Art. 177, of the order of the Poor Law Commissioners, is for the "treatment" of a fracture; that is to say, not only for setting the limb, but also for attendance on the case, from the time the accident happens until the patient recovers. The Board, therefore, consider that you are not entitled in this case to the fee prescribed by Art. 177, but the guardians may if they think fit, having first obtained the approval of this Board, make you a reasonable compensation for the services which you rendered in setting the limb of the vagrant in question. The medical officer of the workhouse, who subsequently took charge of the case, is not entitled to a fee for resetting the limb, as Art. 177 does not apply to in-door paupers.

---

3. PROVIDING BOTTLES FOR MEDICINE.

22*nd September*, 1848.

Mr. ——— *Medical Officer.*—Inquired whether under any circumstances, it is the duty of a medical officer to provide bottles for the medicines supplied to pauper patients.

Ans.—Art. 206, No. 1, of the General Consolidated Order of the Poor Law Commissioners, prescribes as part of the duties of the medical officer that he shall supply the requisite medicines to his pauper patients. The Board are of opinion that he cannot be held to do this unless he supplies the medicines in such a state as to admit of their being conveyed to the patients; and if the latter are unable to send a bottle or vessel, in which liquid medicine may be put, the providing a bottle for the purpose rests with the medical officer, unless there is some special provision on the subject in his contract. The bottles ought, if furnished by the medical officer in any case, to be preserved and restored to him by the pauper patients.

MEDICAL RELIEF.

1. TO DOMESTIC SERVANTS.

22*nd June*, 1848.

Mr.———, *Medical Officer*—Inquired whether he is bound to afford medical relief to the hired yearly servant of a small farmer residing in the district, or whether the farmer is bound to pay for medical attendance on his sick servant, or whether the servant to whom no wages are due can be required to pay.

Ans.—As a general rule, yearly hired domestic servants, who fall sick while in their master's service, can scarcely be considered as destitute persons within the scope of the poor laws, so as to entitle them to be attended by the medical officer of the district. Still, the law does not (as the Board are advised) compel the master, in the absence of express contract, to provide medical or surgical assistance to any servant of his who may require it. Cases may certainly occur in which, if there be no wages, or the wages be insufficient, or are not immediately recoverable, a domestic servant may be practically a destitute person as regards the means of providing the medical aid necessary. In any clear case of this kind the Board apprehend that the guardians, or the relieving officer, if satisfied of the want of means on the part of the servant, might require the medical officer to attend the party. In such a case as that referred to by you, the sick person would not be liable to the medical officer, unless the sick person required the attendance, or in some way or other became responsible by way of contract to him. The Board feel that the practice of requiring union medical officers to attend domestic servants in sickness, is, unless considerable caution be exercised, susceptible of great abuse, from the facility with which a collusive understanding may be entered into between master and servant, to the detriment of the rate-payers, and they do not doubt that the guardians and their officers will recognize the propriety of very narrowly investigating the circumstances of any case of this description, in which their interference may be requested.

---

2. Ditto.

19*th June*, 1848.

Mr. ———, *Medical Officer.*— Having been required, by an order from an overseer of the parish of ——— to attend E. P., a hired domestic servant living in the family of a respectable tradesman, the medical officer visited the sick person accordingly, but informed her master that he should not continue to attend her as a pauper, but would look to him (the master) to pay his charges. Inquired, whether, as medical officer, he is legally justified in refusing to attend on domestic servants when sick.

Ans.—The Board consider that you are bound, by Art. 206, No. 1 of the General Consolidated Order, to attend any case which the overseer shall require you by a written or printed order to attend, if it be one in which the overseer is lawfully authorised to give relief, namely, a case of sudden and urgent necessity. Such a case may certainly exist under some circumstances where the alleged pauper is in service, inasmuch as the law does not compel the master (in the absence of contract) to provide medical or surgical assistance to any servant of his who may require it. Consequently, there are cases in which such assistance may be required from the parish or union; and if in any particular instance of this kind there be urgency and suddenness, the overseer is justified in giving relief, and in calling upon the medical officer to render the necessary assistance. Generally, however, there is not such urgency and suddenness in the cases of domestic servants, in actual service, as will authorise the overseers to interfere, and order relief; and if these circumstances should be wanting in any case in which the overseer may give an order, you will not be bound by virtue of your office to attend to it.

NUISANCES REMOVAL ACT, 1848.

6*th Dec.*, 1848.

Clerk of Epping Union.—Inquired whether the directions and regulations of the General Board of Health supersede the provisions of the "Removal of Nuisances Act, 1848," and enable the guardians to enter upon, and cleanse, &c., premises without obtaining an order upon summons as directed by the 1st sec. of the Act, and if the guardians have such a power, how can they recover or reimburse themselves the expenses.

Ans.—The Board consider that the regulations issued by the Board of Health to the Epping Union, do not supersede the provision contained in the first part of the Removal of Nuisances Act, *i.e.* they do not prevent the proceedings for the abatement of the nuisance being taken in conformity with sec. 1 of that Act; where, therefore, the guardians receive the notice, or complaint of two householders, it is proper that all the subsequent proceedings should be taken in conformity with sec. 1, *i.e.* the guardians should obtain the order of the justices upon previous summons to enter upon the premises, and remove the cause of nuisance. The Board think it the more desirable, that, wherever it is practicable, the proceedings should be taken under the 1st sec., as if the justices direct the removal of the nuisance, it will enable them to charge the costs attending the proceedings upon the owner or occupier, (as the case may be,) of the premises on which the nuisance exists; whereas, if the proceedings be taken by the guardians under the regulations of the Board of Health, the attendant expenses must be borne by the common fund of the union, and no provision is contained in the statute for reimbursement from any party.

---

2. Ditto.

14*th Dec.*, 1848.

Clerk of Wem Union—Inquired with regard to the Act for the removal of nuisances. 1st. Whether the guardians are obliged to act upon every notice they may receive, whether informal or not? 2nd. Whose duty is it to consider and judge of the insufficiency of the notice? 3rd. In cases of the justices dismissing the application through a defect in the notice, whether the party giving such notice is liable to pay the costs incurred? 4th. In sec. 20 of 11 & 12 Vic. cap. 123, providing that proceedings shall not be quashed for want of form, it is enacted, "That no order, nor any other proceeding," &c. Would this apply to a defective notice served by householders, or only to such of the proceedings as take place in the magistrates' office?

Ans.—1. It appears to the Board that the terms of the 1st sec. of the 11 & 12 Vic. cap. 123 are imperative; and that, on the receipt of a proper notice, the guardians are bound to proceed, the word "shall" being the expression used in the statute. If, however, the notice given to the guardians be informal, the propriety of acting upon it will be a question to be decided according to the circumstances of the particular case; but if the informality be slight, and the document be found really to contain a substantial notice of the nuisance, the guardians will probably not deem it their duty to decline to proceed. 2. The guardians must themselves judge, in the first place, as to the sufficiency of the notice; and in doing so it is, of course, open to them to consult their clerk upon it. If they consider the notice insufficient in any case, it would be well that they should refer the parties to the form given in the statute. 3. If the justices should dismiss the complaint, on the ground of the insufficiency of the notice, the guardians will have to bear whatever costs they may have incurred. The Board are not aware of any authority for charging the householders who give the notice, or any other parties, besides the guardians, with the amount. 4. The Board are of opinion that the 20th sec. of the 11 & 12 Vic. cap. 123 appears to be unrestricted in its terms, and to be applicable to the notices given by householders under the 1st sec.

3. DITTO.

20th Dec., 1848.

Clerk of ——— *Union.*—A notice, under the Nuisances Removal Act, was received, that a slaughter-house, in the town of ———, was in a filthy and unwholesome condition; and the occupier was served with the proper notice to abate the nuisance. On the premises being inspected by a committee of the guardians, it appeared that they had been very recently whitewashed, and indeed made as cleanly as the nature of them would admit; still there was a strong offensive smell; and from the situation of the premises, the committee were of opinion that nothing short of a discontinuance of the building as a slaughter-house would abate the nuisance. But, on applying for a summons for that purpose, the justice's clerk stated that the Act gave them no power beyond making an order to whitewash and cleanse the building; and, as that had already been done in this case, they would not interfere until it again became so filthy and unwholesome as to require fresh whitewashing. Requested the Board's opinion on the subject.

Ans.—The Board do not think that the powers given to the justices by the 1st sec. of the 11 & 12 Vic. cap. 123., extend to enable the justices to order the discontinuance of the use of the building you refer to as a slaughter-house. Apparently, all that the justices can do in the matter, is to require the cleansing of the building, and the removal of any refuse or offal which may have been allowed to accumulate on the premises, and which would be prejudicial to the health of the neighbourhood.

4. DITTO.

22nd Dec., 1848.

Clerk of ——— *Union.*—Forwarded resolution of the guardians, wherein they referred to the Circular Letter of the Poor Law Board, dated the 6th November last, respecting the mode of charging the expenses of carrying out the regulations of the General Board of Health, and objected to such expenses being charged to the common fund of the union, on the ground that they had been incurred in reference to the city of ——— only.

Ans.—It is not, as the guardians appear to suppose, the Poor Law Board who have directed that the expenses incurred in carring into effect the regulations of the General Board of Health should be charged to the common fund of the union; but it is the provision of the statute (14th sec. of the 11 & 12 Vic. cap. 123) which requires this mode of charging the expenses to be adopted. The guardians will see, therefore, that this Board have no power to make the alteration requested by the resolution. The object of the regulations being to prevent the spread of epidemic diseases, the Board cannot but consider that the whole of the parishes comprised in the ——— union are interested in those regulations being carried out, as well as the parishes within the city itself.

PAUPERS—APPROPRIATION OF THE CLOTHES OF PAUPERS DYING IN WORKHOUSE.

31st July, 1848.

Clerk of ——— *Union.*—It has been the general custom in this union to sell the clothes of paupers dying in the workhouse, and crediting the several parishes to which they were respectively chargeable with the amount realised; there have, however, been frequent applications from the relatives of paupers thus circumstanced to be permitted to have such clothes delivered to them, and on some occasions the guardians have assented to the application. These have now become so frequent, that the guardians wish to be informed of the proper course for them to pursue in the future appropriation of the clothes of pauper inmates dying in the house.

Ans.—The Board consider that the strict rule of law applicable to the subject is, that the guardians who bury the dead body of the pauper are entitled to obtain reimbursement of the costs of the burial out of the property left by the deceased; and inasmuch as they must charge these expenses to the parish to which the pauper was chargeable, they are under an obligation to obtain this reimbursement for the parish. The guardians have, however, no legal authority to retain any surplus which may remain in any case after paying these expenses, but such surplus should be paid over to the party entitled to it. In strictness, no one can be so entitled who is not an administrator or executor; but the guardians may, doubtless, in some cases, find themselves justified in distributing the surplus to the relatives of the deceased, without requiring legal proof of title.

POOR-RATE. — LIABILITY OF AN OUTGOING TENANT. 18*th Dec.*, 1848.

Mr. ——— *Stocton-on-Tees Union.*—Inquired whether the whole of a poor-rate, made on the 11th Nov., should be demanded from a tenant who quitted his holding on the 23rd of that month.

Ans.—A rate for the relief of the poor is due immediately after publication, and where a person is in actual occupation of the premises at the time the rate is made, the Board believe that in strictness the overseers could demand, and enforce payment from such occupier of the full amount of the rate as assessed. The 12th sec. of the 17th Geo. 2. cap. 38, applies to cases where persons come to occupy in the parish, subsequent to the making of the last rate, and contemplates that the outgoing and incoming tenants shall be charged with the rate in proportion to the time they respectively occupy the premises: these proportions, if there be any dispute, are to be settled by the justices; but the statute certainly raises some difficulty as to the parties who, in the first instance, are to affect the apportionment; *i.e.* whether this is to be matter of arrangement between the two occupiers, or is to be done by the overseers. The Board believe that a practice prevails for the overseers to make such an apportionment in their claim for the rate due in respect of the premises. Where there is an immediate successor in the occupation there will probably be no difficulty in this, but where no person succeeds to the occupation of the premises, and the full rate shall not have been obtained from the outgoing tenant, the result would be that the parish would lose a portion of the rate.

RATING.

1. OF FEVER HOSPITAL.

Dec. 16*th*, 1847.

Clerk of York Union—The overseers of Gate Fulford have rated the board of guardians to the poor-rates for a building erected by the guardians in a field situate in that township as a fever hospital for the use of the sick poor in the union. The guardians object to pay the rate, on the ground that the building is not rateable. But it has been agreed upon by the overseers and the board, that the opinion of the Commissioners shall be taken and abided by, as to whether the building is legally liable to be rated or not.

Ans.—The Commissioners do not see that this case is distinguishable in principle from Reg. *v.* The Guardians of the Wallingford Union, 2 P & D. 226, which established the liability of a workhouse used in common by several parishes in a union for the relief of their poor, to be assessed to the poor-rate of that parish in which the building was situate. The building used as a fever hospital, like the workhouse in the case cited, is used or occupied by the guardians of the York Union for the maintenance or relief of the sick poor of the entire union; and it is noticed that all the parishes in the union contributed to the erection of the building, and are charged in common with the expenses of upholding it. The Commissioners admit that they find some difficulty in reconciling the recent decision of Reg. *v.* St. George the Martyr, Southwark, (Bethlem Hospital, Law Journal report, vol. 16, N. S. M. C. page 129,) with Reg. *v.* the Guardians of the Wallingford Union; so far at least as some of the grounds are concerned, upon which the exemption was put in the former case. It is observed in the judgment, "the appellants (the trustees of the hospital) possess and use the premises in the exercise of a public duty, and have no beneficial occupation or emolument resulting from it in any personal or private respect." This description would appear to be equally applicable to the guardians of a union in regard to their occupation of a workhouse. Still, until Reg. *v.* the Guardians of the Wallingford Union is overruled, the Commissioners are not able to advise that a building occupied by the guardians in the nature of a workhouse, for the use or advantage of the sick poor of a union generally, is not liable to the poor-rate.

---

2. POLICE STATION.

2*nd Dec.*, 1848.

Assistant Overseer of ———.—About seven years ago, a house in the town was converted into a police station, lock-up cells, and some rooms in it were appropriated for the residence of the police serjeant. The rent of the house is paid by the county treasurer. The officer has paid poor-rates in respect of the rooms occupied by him until recently: but he now refuses to do so on the ground that his occupation of those rooms constitutes part of his wages. Inquired whether the whole or any part of the premises in question are rateable.

Ans.—If, as the Board understand, the premises in question are rented and held by the county justices for a public purpose, viz., for the purpose of a temporary gaol or lock-up house, then they are of opinion that the police serjeant in charge of the premises, and who, as it appears, resides therein as the servant of the justices, is not rateable, provided that the accommodation which he possesses is not greater than is reasonably necessary for the discharge of his duty. The Board would direct your attention to the case of Reg. *v.* Shepherd, 1 A. & E. n.s. 170.

3. RENT CHARGE: PROPERTY-TAX.

29th Dec., 1848.

The Rev. ——— ———.—Inquired whether the property-tax is an outgoing which may be deducted in order to ascertain the rateable value of a rent-charge.

Ans.—The property-tax is not an outgoing which may be deducted in ascertaining the rateable value of a rent-charge, The 6 & 7 Wm. 4, c. 96, sec. 1, only authorizes the deduction of tenants' rates and taxes; and the property-tax does not come within the definition of tenants' taxes as the term is employed in that section.

RELIEF.

1. TO MINERS IN WORK.

16th Aug., 1848.

The Rev. ——— ——— *Helston Union.*—When a miner first goes to work at a mine, it is the practice not to pay his wages for six or eight weeks. In some mines there is an advance made on account, called "subsist," at the end of a fortnight or three weeks; but this is not the general practice. At present the miners, from various causes, are in a very depressed state, and a large portion of the children of the miners are, in consequence, nearly destitute of clothing, the wages in many cases being barely sufficient, if sufficient, to provide the absolute necessaries of life. Under these circumstances the Helston board of guardians have felt it their duty to advance some temporary relief to the miner's family, till he could receive his pay at the mine. Requested the Board to relax their regulations in order to render such relief legal.

Ans.—The Board do not see that the case of a miner differs materially from that of any other labourer, except that it has become a practice in the Mining Districts of Cornwall to delay payments of any portion of his earnings for a certain period after he has entered upon any new undertaking. If a miner be of provident habits, and honest in his dealings, he can surely obtain credit for necessaries during the first weeks of his engagement, and the Board understand that the majority of the miners do thus obtain credit, and maintain their families independently of the parish, until the time arrives for their earnings to be paid. If it be admitted that they cannot do so, and that during the interval they are to be supported at the expense of their parish, it will of course be the means of making all the mining population paupers, as little inducement would then remain for a miner to keep up his credit. The Board have been informed that in the mining unions in which the guardians have a good workhouse, as at Redruth and Penzance, the practice of allowing "subsistence money" by the adventurers prevails to a much larger extent than in unions where there is a more lax system of relief; and the Board are led to believe that this allowance of subsistence money, which is in fact the legitimate remedy for the evil to which you refer, has been on the increase for the last few years, in consequence of the Poor Law Commissioners having refused, except in extreme cases, to relax their rules in regard to the allowance of out-door relief to the families of able-bodied men employed at the mines in Cornwall. The Board must, therefore, decline to consent to any relaxation of the rules which prohibit out-door relief to able-bodied paupers in the Helston Union, except on the condition of work being required in return for such relief.

2. TO ABLE-BODIED PERSONS TO DEFRAY EXPENSES OF TRAVELLING, &C.

27th Sept., 1848.

Clerk of Teesdale Union. — Requested the Board's sanction to the payment of certain sums advanced by the guardians on loan to several able-bodied weavers, to provide for the travelling expenses of themselves and their families in going to Millbridge in Yorkshire, where they were offered employment.

Ans.—The Board are not aware of any provision in law which would authorise the payment out of the poor-rates of travelling expenses under the circumstances of the present case. The

Board have the power, under Art. 6 of the prohibitory order, to sanction, in certain instances, payments which are at variance with the provisions of the order; but this they can only do where those payments are otherwise not unlawful. In the case under consideration the Board apprehend, that even if their sanction were given, it would not render the payments legal, nor ensure their allowance by the auditor.

RELIEVING OFFICER.—HIS DUTIES IN REGARD TO PERSONS REQUIRING RELIEF.

4th Nov., 1848.

Relieving Officer of ——— *Parish.*—Requested advice on certain points affecting his duties in regard to which his conduct had been impugned by members of the board of guardians. The Board replied as follows.

Ans.—The duties of a relieving officer must be exercised discreetly. He is not to run after every rumoured case of distress, nor is he bound to attend to every application made to him on behalf of persons reported to be destitute, unless he have reason to believe that such persons are unable to make application for themselves. A relieving officer is not bound to attach more weight to information given by a guardian, than to information afforded by any other person of equal credit; although a guardian may generally be presumed to be best informed on the subject of relief. But it is where applications are made by persons for themselves, or their natural relatives for them, or by persons brought by circumstances into some relation with them, as for instance fellow-lodgers, or close neighbours, that responsibility attaches to a relieving officer. It would be his duty to investigate, and to report upon cases so brought under his notice; and cases might, however, occur in which he would be deemed censurable or negligent if he refused to attend to information about others, brought to him by persons not so situated. It is impossible to lay down precise rules for the guidance of a relieving officer under every variety of circumstances that may arise. All the Board can do is, to inform him that he must be discreet, as well as attentive, and that a good relieving officer neither makes cases for relief, nor neglects any when brought under his notice.

TREASURER—CANCELLING BOND GIVEN FOR.

8th July, 1848.

Mr. ———The treasurer of the union, for whom he with another was security, resigned his office at Lady-day last. Subsequent to the auditing of the union accounts, he applied to the clerk of the guardians to deliver up the bond, when he declined to do so. Requested the Board's advice on the subject.

Ans.—The Board are advised that, by the strict rule of law, a surety cannot insist upon his bond being cancelled and given up to him, when the principal resigns the office in respect of which that bond was given. And, as a general rule, the Board consider it would not be prudent for parties to cancel bonds where the person, as a guarantee for whose good conduct they were entered into, may only recently have quitted office. It rests, however, in the present case, entirely with the guardians to determine whether the bond could be properly given up at present.

VAGRANTS.

1. ADMISSION OF, INTO A WORKHOUSE ON AN ASSISTANT OVERSEER'S ORDER.

9th Nov., 1848.

Clerk of ——— *Union.*—Represented that the exertions of the guardians for the discouragement of vagrancy are, to a great extent, frustrated by the proceedings of the assistant overseer of the parish of ———, in that he persists in giving orders for the indiscriminate admission into the workhouse of vagrants whose cases are neither sudden nor urgent.

Ans.—With respect to the general question raised as to what steps, (if any,) it is open to the guardians to take, for preventing such improper interference by this officer in the relief of vagrants, the Board observe, that the workhouse is only provided for the reception of paupers. The guardians of a union, or, in their absence, the master of the workhouse, must determine what applicants for relief are paupers (*i. e.* persons actually destitute) who should be admitted therein. It is true that the master is, by the effect of Art. 88, of the General Consolidated Order, relieved from the consequences of improperly admitting persons, who are not paupers, when they produce an order from an overseer, or assistant overseer, but the Board do not think that the terms of the order conclude him, or prevent the exercise of his judgment as to the fact of the applicant being a pauper. If, therefore, the master in the fulfilment of this duty take upon himself the responsibility of deciding in any case, and being satisfied that the party is not really destitute, the Board are of opinion that the master may properly refuse admission to him, although he produce an order from an overseer, or an assistant overseer. Of course, in refusing to admit a person producing such an order, the master must be prepared to justify his conduct should any question afterwards arise upon it.

2. Cost of conveying vagrants to workhouse.

7th Dec., 1848.

Clerk of Axminster Union.—The overseers of some of the parishes of the union occasionally send vagrants and wayfarers, found in their parishes, to the union workhouse in some hired vehicle. These vagrants and wayfarers probably remain one night only in the workhouse, the cost of their maintenance being charged to the union fund. The guardians are desirous of knowing whether the cost of their conveyance from the parish to the workhouse be properly a parochial or a union charge.

Ans.—The Board are disposed to consider that the cost of conveying a pauper to the union workhouse, in any case where a conveyance is required, must be regarded as a portion of the relief necessary in the case; and, consequently, in reference to wanderers and wayfarers, such cost should ultimately be charged with the other relief afforded to the common fund of the union.

WORKHOUSE.

1. Admission into of part of family.

21st Aug., 1848.

Clerk of ——— *Union.*—The relieving officer issued an order for the admission of a man and his wife and four children; the wife being able to maintain herself and three of the children, the man and the remaining child sought admission into the workhouse, which the master refused, in consequence of the wife and the other three children not presenting themselves for admission at the same time.

Ans.—The Board are of opinion that if the man and his child were really destitute when they presented themselves at the workhouse, the workhouse master did not act rightly in refusing to admit them, merely because they were not accompanied by the wife and remaining children.

2. Discharge of paupers from workhouse.

24th Nov., 1848.

Clerk of ——— *Union.*—An able-bodied pauper, relieved with his family in the workhouse, gave the master notice of his intention to leave; but the master, finding the pauper did not intend to take his family with him, and conceiving that the pauper could not leave without his family, refused to deliver up his clothes; notwithstanding which the pauper left, wearing the union dress, and leaving his family behind. Inquired, 1st, Whether the master had authority in the case stated to retain the pauper's clothes, or to prevent the pauper leaving the house without taking his family with him. 2nd. Whether the master, of his own authority, would have been justified in expelling the pauper's family from the house when the pauper himself left it.

Ans.—1. The master of the workhouse had no authority to prevent the pauper referred to from going out of the union workhouse, and was not justified in retaining his clothes. 2. By Art. 115 of the General Consolidated Order, the master could have sent the family of the pauper out of the workhouse with him, without waiting for the directions of the guardians to do so.

3. Allowance of beer and wine to the aged inmates of workhouse.

21st Aug., 1848.

Clerk of ——— *Union.*—The district auditor has inserted in one of the books of the workhouse master, a memorandum objecting to the practice of charging extras; viz. beer, wine, &c., without previously obtaining direct authority from the medical officer, who would be expected to enter in the book the name of each person under his care, whom he might consider required any extras, together with the quantities of such extras to be given. The guardians are of opinion that the aged and infirm ought to receive the indulgence referred to, and wish the Poor Law Board to consent to their medical officer giving a general order in favour of the aged and infirm, and that it should not be necessary for the master to obtain the authority of the medical officer weekly in each case.

Ans.—The Board have communicated with the district auditor on the subject of the memorandum alluded to, and they learn from him that his object in making the entry was to prevent the continuance of the practice, adopted by the workhouse master, of charging large quantities of beer and other extras in the weekly consumption account, without being able to point out by reference to the workhouse medical return, the names of the particular individuals to whom such extras have been authorized to be allowed. It is stated by the auditor, that "the medical officer has hitherto, at the commencement of each quarter, issued a general order, upon which the master has considered that he was authorized in giving beer, or porter, to the aged and infirm." With reference to this statement of the district auditor, the Board consider that the medical officer certainly cannot order beer and wine, as extras, to any of the workhouse inmates, whether aged or infirm, or otherwise, merely as comforts. He can only prescribe them as medicines, or as things specifically required for health. If the medical officer is of opinion that any persons from extreme age, or chronic disease, require to have any such extras as those referred to above, the Board would not object to the medical officer giving a general direction quarterly, or for any other convenient period, in respect of the particular paupers whom he may name; but if he were enabled to give a general order for the supply of these or any other articles to an entire class of the inmates, (such as the aged and infirm,) he would have the power of establishing a dietary for the workhouse, and thus supersede both this Board and the guardians.

---

4. PROVIDING COMMUNION PLATE FOR WORKHOUSE CHAPEL.

7th Aug., 1848.

Clerk of ——— *Union.*—Inquired whether the guardians should provide communion plate for the use of the workhouse chapel out of the union funds.

Ans.—Where the guardians may think it necessary the Board see no objection to communion plate being provided for the workhouse chapel; and if it be provided by the guardians, the cost must certainly be borne by the common fund of the union, as in the case of any other furniture required for the chapel or workhouse.

---

5. FURNITURE FOR OFFICERS' APARTMENTS IN WORKHOUSE.

26th Sept., 1848.

Clerk of Ludlow Union.—Inquired whether it is the duty of the guardians to find furniture for the rooms usually occupied by the master and matron, the schoolmistress and the porter, in the union workhouse.

Ans.—In some unions the guardians furnish the apartments of the workhouse officers, and in others they do not, leaving it to the officers to provide their own furniture. The Board, however, think it desirable that in every instance the substantial or indispensable articles of furniture should be provided by the guardians, and remain the property of the union like the ordinary furniture of the workhouse.

---

6. RIGHT OF GUARDIANS AS TO VISITATION OF WORKHOUSE.

7th Dec., 1848.

Mr. ———, *a Guardian.*—Gave an order to a person to visit his relatives who were inmates in the ——— union workhouse on a Sunday, as it would not be convenient for him to visit them on a Saturday nor on a Monday, the regular visiting days; but the workhouse master refused admission to him. Inquired whether the master was warranted in his refusal; and also whether a guardian was at liberty himself to visit the workhouse, and inspect the several rooms, without being accompanied by the master or matron, and if he could take with him a friend to view the establishment.

Ans.—The master of a union workhouse is bound by such conditions and restrictions as the board of guardians may prescribe for visiting paupers in the workhouse in compliance with the provisions of Art. 118 of the General Consolidated Order. As, therefore, the day on which you gave the order to the person in question was not one of the days fixed by the guardians for visiting the workhouse, it was for the master to decide whether the occasion was one on which the rule could be departed from, even when the person applying for admittance had an order from an individual guardian. It is customary to permit those who are desirous of seeing a workhouse to do so, but it is, in the opinion of the Poor Law Board, right that on such occasions the master or the matron should be in attendance on the visitor, whether a guardian or not. The board of guardians or the visiting committee, on an official inspection, may dispense with such attendance, and circumstances may render it expedient that they should inspect the wards unaccompanied by any officer of the establishment; the case of an individual guardian having no official authority is, however, different.

London: Printed by Order of the Poor Law Board, by BLACKBURN & BURT, 90½, Holborn Hill, and Published by CHARLES KNIGHT, 90, Fleet Street.

VOLUME VIII
[1849]

VOLUME VIII

AN

OFFICIAL CIRCULAR

OF PUBLIC DOCUMENTS AND INFORMATION

DIRECTED BY THE POOR LAW BOARD TO BE PRINTED, CHIEFLY FOR THE USE OF THE BOARDS OF GUARDIANS AND THEIR OFFICERS.

No. 21.] JANUARY, 1849. [N.S.

CONTENTS.

REPORT.

TO THE QUEEN'S MOST EXCELLENT MAJESTY.

Poor Law Board, Somerset House, December 30, 1848.

MAY IT PLEASE YOUR MAJESTY,

1. The Poor Law Commission, as constituted under the Act 10 and 11 Vic. cap. 109, came into operation on the 17th of December, 1847, and the period having arrived when the Report of the proceedings of the Commission, which is required by that Act, must be made, we now beg to submit the following to your Majesty.

2. Our Report will necessarily be less complete than it would have been if it had been prepared by Mr. Buller, the late President of the Board, for whose untimely decease we cannot refrain from expressing our deep and sincere regret. He devoted himself with unwearied assiduity to the duties of his office, and we feel that the country has sustained a severe loss in being thus early

and unexpectedly deprived of the services of one of so much ability in the administration of this department, and whose estimable qualities conciliated general goodwill and regard.

3. The first important matter to be stated, is the general amount of the relief of the poor, as exhibited under the heads of expenditure and pauperism, during the year ended on the 25th March, 1848. The preceedings of the present Board do not precisely correspond with the term to which this statement applies, it being made up to Lady-day, and consequently including only the first quarter of the year, to the exclusion of the other three quarters.

4. The following are the statements of pauperism and expenditure during the last parochial year. Tables containing other information connected with the relief of the poor are inserted in the Appendix.

COMPARATIVE STATEMENT of the Total Number of Paupers of all classes, relieved in the 592 Unions in England and Wales, during each of the Quarters ended at Lady-day 1847 and 1848.

Quarters ended Lady-day.	NUMBER OF PAUPERS RELIEVED.			
	In-door.	Out-door.	Total.	Proportion per Cent. of the Number of Paupers Relieved to the Population of 1841.
1847	226,579	1,244,554	1,471,133	10·8
1848	265,140	1,361,061	1,626,201	11·8
Increase	38,561	116,507	155,068	1·1

The population of the 592 Unions, in 1841, was 13,784,703.

COMPARATIVE STATEMENT of the Number of Able-bodied Paupers Relieved in 592 Unions in England and Wales, during each of the quarters ended Lady-day, 1847 and 1848.

Quarters ended Lady-day.	IN-DOOR			OUT-DOOR.			Total In-door and Out-door.
	On Account of Temporary Sickness or Accident.	All other Causes, including Vagrants.	Total In-door.	On Account of Temporary Sickness or Accident.	All other Causes including Vagrants.	Total Out-door	
1847	11,524	93,782	105,306	172,972	202,306	375,278	480,584
1848	13,072	122,012	135,084	176,242	266,119	442,361	577,445
Increase	1,548	28,230	29,778	3,270	63,813	67,083	96,861

Note.—Some of the Unions having made their return for Lady-day last on the new Form of Abstract, thereby rendering it impossible to make an exact comparison of pauperism, the return for the previous Lady-day quarter has, in those cases, been repeated as an approximation.

COMPARATIVE STATEMENT of the Amount of Money Expended for the Relief of the Poor in 592 Unions in England and Wales, during the Years ended at Lady-day, 1847 and 1848.

Years ended Lady-day.	EXPENDITURE FOR THE RELIEF AND MAINTENANCE OF THE POOR.							
	In Maintenance.	Out Relief.	Establishment and Salaries.	Workhouse Loans Repaid.	Other Charges connected with Relief to the Poor.	Total Expenditure for Relief to the Poor.	Increase per Cent. in 1847 compared with 1848.	Rate per Head of Total Expenditure on the Population of 1841.
	£	£	£	£	£	£		s. d.
1847	769,690	2,973,994	762,420	163,017	8,989	4,678,110	. .	6 9½
1848	955,700	3,339,248	970,988	160,161	9,876	5,435,973	. .	7 10¼
Increase	186,010	365,254	208,568	. .	887	757,863	16·2	. .
Decrease	. .	. .	. .	2,856	. .	. .	. .	. .

Note.—The above expenditure only applies to 592 Unions under the Poor Law Amendment Act, and does not include 531 parishes under Local Acts, Gilbert's Acts, and the 43rd of Elizabeth.

5. The total expenditure for the relief of the poor in England and Wales, as shown by the Annual Poor Rate Return received from the Clerks to the guardians and overseers of the poor, in continuation of the Parliamentary series, is as follows, viz. :—

Expenditure for the year ended Lady-day, 1847, in the 592 Unions	£4,678,110		
Ditto, ditto, in the 531 parishes under Local and Gilbert's Acts, etc.	620,677		
		£5,298,787	
Expenditure for the year ended Lady-day, 1848, in the 592 Unions	£5,435,973		
Ditto, ditto, in the 531 parishes under Local and Gilbert's Acts, etc.	744,792		
		£6,180,765	
Increase in 1848, compared with 1847		£881,978	or nearly 17 per cent.

6. From the above statements it appears that there has been a large increase, both in the expenditure and the numbers relieved, in the year 1847-8, over the year 1846-7. This increase has been mainly caused by the general depression which existed in the manufacturing districts, and by the influx of poor persons from Ireland, in a state of destitution.

7. It became in some cases necessary to provide for the pressure of the unemployed labourers in unions where the General Prohibitory Order is in force. In such cases, the Board issued the order which provides that a task of work should be required in return for the relief afforded, where the guardians are allowed to make exceptions from the Prohibitory Order, in consequence of the workhouse being full; and a similar order was issued to certain unions and parishes to which the General Prohibitory Order had not been applied. In some instances, the order was issued on the application of the Guardians, in others the Board deemed it right to issue it without such application. The order has been found generally to afford valuable assistance to the guardians, as a test of real destitution, and as a precaution against the injurious consequences of maintaining out of the poor-rates, able-bodied labourers and their families in a state of idleness.

8. The existence of the order, has induced many boards of guardians to endeavour to provide means of supplying employment to labourers who require relief on account of their being out work, by purchasing or hiring some portions of land contiguous to the workhouse for cultivation. To a certain extent this has, in a few instances, been sanctioned; but the Board have not been prepared to assent, as a general proposition, to the guardians engaging in any considerable undertakings of a farming character, which appear to the Board to be open to serious objection.

9. Immediately after the constitution of the present Board, the late Assistant Commissioners were appointed Inspectors, under the provisions of the 10 and 11 Vic. cap. 109, their powers and duties remaining unaltered. The number of Assistant Commissioners had been limited to nine, by the 5 and 6 Vic. cap. 56; but that number having been found insufficient for the proper fulfilment of the onerous and important duties required from them, the limit was removed by the 10 and 11 Vic. cap. 109. The present number of Inspectors is thirteen.

10. Certain alterations have been made in a few of the unions, of which the following are the particulars :—

The former Helmsley Blackmoor Union, in the North Riding of Yorkshire, contained 45 townships, which were divided by a range of hills into two distinct portions, so that Helmsley was the principle town of one, and Kirkby Moorside of the other. The communication between the two places was found to be inconvenient for the purposes of the union, and a proposal for the division of the union into two had been laid before the Poor Law Commissioners. The Board having received a report from their Inspector, Mr. Hawley, recommending the division, acceded to the proposal, and directed the separation of the Kirkby Moorside portion from the Helmsley Blackmoor Union, and forming the townships contained in that portion into a new union termed the Kirkby Moorside Union, which came into operation at Lady-day last.

11. It has also been deemed advisable to separate those parts of the Bradford Union, in the West Riding of Yorkshire, which formed the rural part of it, from the town portion, so as to leave four townships, comprising the whole of that populous place, in the Bradford Union; while the other townships have been formed into a union by themselves, termed the North Bierley Union. This took effect at Michaelmas last, and it is hoped that the new arrangement will work satisfactorily.

12. The populous parish of Hampstead has also been separated from the Edmonton Union,

of which it had previously formed a part, to the great inconvenience of the parishioners; and on its separation a board of guardians were elected for the administration of the relief of the poor of the parish on the 31st May last, and they have administered the relief accordingly from that time.

13. The condition of the Abergavenny Union, in Monmouthshire, having been brought under the consideration of the Board, it was found that the rapid and great increase of the population in the whole of the union, but especially in the two parishes of Bedwelty and Aberystruth, where the coal and iron mines of this district are situated, taken in connection with the physical nature of the different parts of the union, rendered it desirable that those parishes should be separated from the rest of the union. The Board are accordingly taking steps for the formation of those two parishes into a distinct union.

14. The attention of the Board was early and most urgently called to the state of the vagrant poor, and the alarming increase in their numbers. The subject has for a long time occupied a good deal of public attention, the evil being general, and no part of the country being exempt from the infliction. The Poor Law Commissioners, in their Reports, adverted to it on several occasions, and various suggestions have, from time to time, been made, by them and by other parties, for its repression.

15. The late President devoted much consideration to this question, and collected a large mass of information upon it from various quarters. At his suggestion Mr. Boase was employed to make a minute and detailed investigation into the state of vagrancy in different unions along the main lines of traffic in the country. Mr. Boase drew up an interesting and valuable Report, containing the practical results of his inquiry; and his Report, with a full Selection from other communications on the subject, has been already laid before Parliament.

16. As the great increase of the vagrant poor, appeared to be in some degree attributable to a want of vigilance and careful discrimination, in the administration of relief to that class, on the part of the boards of guardians and their officers; and as, owing to this laxity, the numbers of applicants had been swelled by the intrusion of unworthy objects, and direct encouragement was thus given to mendicancy, a Minute, prepared by Mr. Buller, was communicated to the boards of guardians and their officers, calling attention to the necessity of repressing this growing evil, and the importance of exercising greater vigilance and discrimination in the administration of relief to this class.

17. The Minute at the same time contained cautions equally strong against the neglect of real destitution, whenever it was ascertained to exist. This Minute will be found in the Appendix. It was intended only to convey advice, and general recommendations of a line of conduct to be pursued by guardians and union officers; but not any authoritative direction, and consequently it was not the subject of an order of the Board. It is yet too early to form a conclusion as to its general effect in repressing the evil of vagrancy, but a considerably diminution in the numbers of the vagrant poor who were in the habit of applying for relief, took place shortly after the Minute had been circulated, and as soon as its tenour had become known. The subject is one which will continue to occupy the attention of the Board.

18. In the Act of the last Session (11 & 12 Vic. cap. 110) there is a provision affecting this class of poor, which had been recommended by the Poor Law Commissioners, and which had been called for by most of the unions. It makes the relief of all destitute wayfarers, wanderers, and foundlings, a charge upon the common fund of the union, instead of upon some particular parish. The provision, which is only temporary, appears to give general satisfaction.

19. Another provision contained in the same Act, enables this class of applicants to be searched by the officers from whom they seek relief, and any money or other property which may be found upon them, to be taken and applied towards defraying the cost of the relief afforded.

20. The Board have been actively engaged, in conjunction with the Committee of Council on Education, in endeavouring to improve the education of the children in the several workhouses, and to raise the standard of qualification of the schoolmasters and schoolmistresses. With the view of effecting these objects, the Board have adopted a proposal for the examination, by inspectors appointed by the Committee of Council, of the schoolmasters and schoolmistresses in the several workhouses, and to the appropriation according to certain scales of efficiency thus ascertained, of the grant voted by parliament for the repayment of the salaries of those officers; so that larger sums will be granted to the boards of guardians who possess efficient schoolmasters and schoolmistresses, than to those whose officers possess inferior qualifications.

21. Although the terms upon which these officers have been appointed, under the regulations prescribed by the Poor Law Commissioners, do not warrant their dismissal where they fail to obtain a proper certificate, if in other respects they are unobjectionable; yet the Board do not doubt that when sufficient time has elapsed to enable the requisite arrangements to be made, with a due regard to existing engagements, the officers who prove to be unsuited for the education of this class of poor children, will be withdrawn from their appointments, and a better class of teachers be established.

22. The Board are also engaged, with the assistance of the Committee of Council, in procuring for the several unions, at the cheapest cost, a supply of the most eligible and useful school books and school apparatus, to be used in the workhouse schools; and they are glad to state that their applications to the publishers and proprietors of the several works have been readily acceded to.

23. In connection with the subject of education, the Board have the satisfaction of stating, that in many unions the boards of guardians have applied themselves with much energy to the industrial training of the children in the workhouse schools, and have taken active measures for their instruction in useful occupations so far as the limited resources of a single union would allow. The Board have been desirous of rendering every assistance in their power to the guardians in this respect, although it is believed that a really effective system of education and industrial training can only be established in unions having a considerable population, or where several unions are combined for the purpose. By the statute 7 & 8 Vic. c. 101, unions and parishes might be combined by the Poor Law Commissioners into school districts, provided they were situated within certain limited distances. This limitation practically prevented the formation of any school districts in the country; but the limitation was removed by the Act of 11 & 12 Vic. c. 32, which enables such districts to be formed beyond those limits, with the consent of the guardians of the several unions proposed to be combined. Two unions, in Hampshire and Surrey, are about to avail themselves of these facilities.

24. The general order which the Poor Law Commissioners issued in March, 1847, for the keeping of the union and parochial accounts, and which is described at length in their 13th annual report, came into full operation on the 25th of March last. In some instances objections were raised, on the ground of its interfering with the books and forms of accounts then in use, and of its being considered in some respects complicated. The Board in a few instances sanctioned its suspension until the books in use should be disposed of, and gave such explanations as for the most part removed the objections which had been raised. Any change in a general form of accounts is a matter of considerable difficulty, and one which cannot be dealt with without causing much trouble to all the persons who are required to keep the accounts; but it is obvious that clear and accurate accounts must be kept, as well for the protection of the ratepayers and the poor, as of the officers themselves; and the accounts must, moreover, be uniform in their arrangement, in order to afford the means of comparison. The Board have reason to believe, that as the present forms come to be better understood, the objections to them will disappear.

25. Some difficulty has long been felt in regard to the payment of debts incurred by overseers who quit their office without having liquidated the obligations which they have contracted on behalf of their parish. Even with the utmost care and vigilance on the part of those officers, this cannot always be avoided; and where they are, as is not unfrequently the case, persons unused to strict and regular habits of business, it is manifest that there must be frequent failures in this respect. The rule of law which requires the accounts and dealings of each year to be concluded by the annual officer at the close of his term of office, is nevertheless of great practical benefit.

26. In the Act of last session, introduced by the late President (11 & 12 Vic. c. 91,) a precise rule has been laid down, which it is hoped will deal with such claims in a satisfactory manner, indemnifying the parish officer from personal loss, affording a due security to the contractor or tradesman of the parish, and at the same time preserving parishes from the unjust pressure often heretofore caused by the outstanding claims of former years.

27. In the same Act a provision is made, by which *bonâ fide* debts incurred previous to the Act, on behalf of unions or parishes, and for their benefit, but without strict legal authority, may be adopted by such unions or parishes, and be now discharged with their consent, to be given after due notice, and with the approval of this Board. The Board have deemed it incumbent

upon them carefully to investigate all the applications made under this provision, so as to guard against any fraudulent or improper use of it.

28. The audit of the accounts, both in unions and parishes, though much improved by the establishment of district auditors under the 7 & 8 Vic. c. 101, was found to be impeded by various difficulties of a technical nature. The auditors could only enforce their certificates by expensive proceedings before justices, where objections wholly beside the merits were frequently raised, and were too often successful. Several provisions for the removal of those difficulties are contained in the Act just referred to.

29. Another important provision is contained in this Act, by which the same powers of relief are given to boards of guardians who have the management of the relief of the poor under the provisions of a local Act, as are possessed by guardians of unions formed under the Poor Law Amendment Act.

30. The dietaries established in the different workhouses had all been fixed by orders under the seal of the Poor Law Commissioners, and no change in them could be sanctioned except by an order under seal. This had become a subject of much inconvenience, especially as under the failure of the potato crop, frequent changes of the articles prescribed in the dietaries became necessary; and the application for the requisite order, and the issuing thereof, caused delay where expedition was often required. The Board therefore determined to dispense with the issuing of orders for sanctioning changes in the dietaries, whilst at the same time they prescribed arrangements by which the proper control of the Board is preserved, so as to prevent changes being made without their sanction. A general order on this subject was issued, which will be found in the Appendix.

31. The vaccination of the poor appeared to have decreased during the last year or two, not from any default on the part of the boards of guardians or their officers, to provide the proper means of supplying it to applicants, but from the neglect on the part of the poor to avail themselves of the aid offered to them through the provisions of the law. The Board deemed it necessary, therefore, to address a circular letter to boards of guardians, recommending the publication and general circulation of notices, pointing out the benefits and advantages of vaccination, and stating how and where it might be obtained gratuitously. This has been attended with much benefit, the returns showing that the number of persons vaccinated during the present year, far surpasses the average of previous years.

32. The Commissioners in Lunacy, in their visits to the several workhouses, in conformity with the provisions of the 8 & 9 Vic. c. 100, have found it necessary, on various occasions, to make special reports to this Board upon the condition of the inmates who are afflicted with insanity in some of the workhouses. These reports, when received by the Board, have been duly considered, and the immediate attention of the guardians called to the subject, where it appeared that they could remedy the matter complained of. In some instances, a difficulty has been felt in dealing with these unfortunate objects, as the nature of their maladies required, from the want of proper asylums, or other adequate accommodation in the county where the union or parish is situate. But for the most part the recommendations of those Commissioners have been promptly carried out, on the Board communicating with the proper authorities.

33. The provisions of the statute 11 & 12 Vic. c. 110, which contains the enactments relating to the union charges, were communicated to the guardians in a circular dated the 29th September, 1848, and in like manner the provisions which were enacted to provide for the payment of certain outstanding claims against unions and parishes, and for facilitating the proceedings of the audit, were communicated to the respective Boards. These letters will be found in the Appendix.

34. The emigration of poor persons under the sanction of this Board has greatly increased during the present year. There has been a very general movement on the subject of emigration, which has had its influence among the working classes in the mining and agricultural districts, while the rapidly improving condition of the Australian colonies, and the spirit of enterprise excited by the mineral treasures lately discovered there, have tended to increase the number of emigrants from this country to those colonies.

35. The emigration of a certain class of the labouring poor to the Australian colonies is carried on under the arrangements made by the Colonial Land and Emigration Commissioners, but this advantage can only be extended to parties possessing the qualifications which the Commissioners feel it necessary to require. Many others, however, have been enabled by other means to proceed to Australia, who could not be admitted by

the Commissioners as free emigrants; and hence it will be found that, while the emigration to British North America has not been less than in former years, there has been a very great increase in the emigration to Australia. The total amount of emigration at the cost of the poor-rates, has very much surpassed the average of late years.

36. Upon the application of the Colonial Land and Emigration Commissioners, the Board in the course of the spring sanctioned the emigration to Australia, under the management of your Majesty's Government, of a few young unmarried women of good character, of the ages of 16 and upwards, who were selected from different workhouses in the Metropolis and elsewhere. The Board have, subsequently, in conjunction with those Commissioners, expressed their readiness to assent to the emigration of female orphans of good character, and of a younger age, namely, from 12 to 16 years; and the terms under which this may be effected will appear from the letter addressed to certain of the unions, which is printed in the Appendix. The Board have every reason to expect that young females of this age will find employment in respectable situations immediately on their arrival in the colony.

37. Heretofore the emigration at the cost of the poor-rate has been entirely a parochial charge, being confined to the emigration of the settled poor. When the class of irremovable poor was created by the Poor Removal Act, the parishes where they resided were not able to forward their emigration, and the parishes of their settlement had no inducement to do so. By the Act of the last Session, whereby the irremovable poor are rendered a charge upon the common fund of the Union, a provision is made for enabling the guardians to provide for the emigration of such poor at the cost of the common fund, subject to the order of this Board. In several unions the guardians have already availed themselves of this power.

38. There is, however, an inconvenience in the present state of the law on this subject. No expense whatever can be incurred by any parish for the emigration of a poor person, without a parish meeting, and the express order of this Board. Where any considerable expense is to be incurred such precaution is doubtless proper, but where a small sum is to be advanced towards assisting one or two persons to emigrate, it seems to be scarcely necessary that such a proceeding should take place. The delay which it occasions often leads to disappointment in the case of poor persons who prepare to depart by particular vessels, but are prevented because the proper parish meeting has not been held, or has not been held with the proper legal formality.

39. The subject of the settlement and removal of the poor has occupied much of the attention of the Board. The change introduced by the Poor Removal Act of 1846 produced considerable disturbance in the charges for the relief of the poor in many places, but the temporary Act of the 10 & 11 Vic. c. 110, which threw the relief of a certain class of the irremovable poor upon the common fund of the Union, removed much of the dissatisfaction which had been the result of the previous Act.

40. The late President of this Board introduced a Bill, which received the sanction of Parliament, to continue this temporary Act in operation for another year, with an extension of its application to all the poor who were rendered irremovable by the late statute. The charge for the relief of all this class of poor is now borne by the common fund of the Union wherein they reside. There is also an important difference in the mode in which the charge is imposed. By the statute 10 & 11 Vic. c. 110, the parish which was charged with the cost of the relief in question, was to be reimbursed by the common fund; under the present statute, the 11 & 12 Vic. c. 110, the charge is to be made direct upon the common fund. The latter Act contains several provisions to assist the guardians in carrying this enactment into force; one of which, while it confers a new jurisdiction upon this Board, will, we believe, be found a great convenience to the union authorities—we refer to the authority which is conferred upon this Board to determine questions which arise as to the irremovability of poor persons. We do not presume to claim great or undue weight for the judgments which we may form upon such questions, so far as they involve legal construction or the application of principles of law, but we are enabled to give immediate answers to questions which require to be promptly disposed of, as they relate to the charge of certain current expenses; and our jurisdiction in this matter is free from the legal technicalities which attend proceedings in courts of law, and no charge is entailed on the parties appealing to us.

41. The Board have already received many applications under this statute, and have deemed it requisite to lay down a general rule, that a distinct statement of the facts of the case be drawn up by the clerk to the guardians, signed

by the chairman, on behalf of the union, and by the guardian or overseers, on behalf of the parish, and then submitted to the Board. When the parties require an order to be issued, we shall be prepared to do so, and an appeal will lie to the Court of Queen's Bench upon it, on the behalf of the party objecting to our judgment.

42. The Court of Queen's Bench has pronounced several decisions upon the construction of the Poor Removal Act of 1846. One of them is of great importance, being at variance with the opinion given by the Law Officers of the Crown, in the autumn of that year, and communicated by the Poor Law Commissioners to boards of guardians and their officers, as to the effect of the proviso to the 1st section of the Act. The Court has decided that the proviso in question has a retrospective as well as a prospective operation.

43. With the view of obtaining a minute and detailed account of the operation of the law of settlement in the agricultural districts, five gentleman were selected, and directed to proceed to the districts severally assigned to them, and to make a careful local investigation, embracing the whole subject of the operation of the Law of Settlement and Removal of the Poor.

They were directed to inquire into the practical effect of the law :—

"1. On the labouring classes ; their industrial habits and ability ; the free use and circulation of their labour, and the rate of wages ; their command of places of residence, and articles of consumption ; and on the comfort and condition of themselves and families.

"2. On the employers of labour ; on the state and progress of agriculture, manufactures, and other industrial arts, and the application of capital to them.

"3. On the continuance of pauperism and vagrancy.

"4. In increasing the burden of taxation, local and general."

They were instructed that "the inquiry should be prosecuted in districts differing widely as regards the size of parishes, the number and density of the population, and the nature of their employment."

They were also to "ascertain the opinions of persons conversant with, or effected by the Law of Settlement and Removal, as to the nature of any change which may appear to them to be desirable, and the reasons for which they recommend such change."

Those gentleman entered upon the inquiry in the month of April, and from three of them able reports have been received, and the Board are in daily expectation of receiving reports from the other two.

44. In the meantime, and pending this inquiry, at the close of the last Session, the late President introduced a Bill to provide for the more equitable distribution of the charge of relief in certain cities and towns, the proposal being to consolidate the parishes in those cities and towns in respect of the relief of the poor, and thus to equalize the burthen over the whole district. The Bill thus introduced has since been forwarded to the several unions throughout the country, for the purpose of eliciting the opinions of the parties interested in the subject, and many communications in reference to it have since been received.

45. The Act of last Session (11 & 12 Vic. cap. 31,) prepared by Mr. Baines, the Member for Hull, has been of great practical value. Its object was to put an end to the inconvenience which had arisen from those provisions in the Poor Law Amendment Act of 1834, which required the copies of the examinations upon which orders of removal were made, to be sent to the parishes to which paupers were to be removed, and which required the appellants against such orders to forward statements of the grounds of appeal.

46. The strictness of construction, and the technical niceties which had been applied by the courts of law to these proceedings, had greatly impeded the due administration of justice in such cases, and it was found that few appeals against orders of removal were decided upon their real merits.

47. The Act has prevented the recurrence of this evil, by enabling all proper amendments to be made where there is any inaccuracy in statement or defect in matter of form, at the same time that the distinct communication of the grounds upon which the parties proceed, either in removing the pauper, or in opposing that removal, is still required.

48. Immediately after the passing of the Act of last session, for the Removal of Nuisances and the prevention of Contagious Diseases, the Board caused a letter to be prepared, with the concurrence of the Board of Health, and sent to all the boards of guardians throughout the country, pointing out the provisions which the Act contained for the removal of nuisances and matters calculate to generate disease ; and preparing the guardians for the directions which would after-

wards be issued by the Board of Health, to whom, in consequence of the progress towards this country of a formidable epidemic, an order in council had been issued previous to the date of our letter, in conformity with the provisions contained in the latter part of the statute. The Board also addressed a special communication to the Poor Law Inspectors upon the same subject, with a view to their communicating with the several boards of guardians, and affording their advice and assistance on the occasion.

49. When the Board of Health subsequently issued their directions and regulations to all the boards of guardians, this Board undertook to forward to the different boards of guardians copies thereof, together with the notifications of advice and admonition which the Board of Health had prepared; and we have sent to the medical officers of the unions where the cholera has since appeared, from time to time, forms of returns to be filled up by them and transmitted to the Board of Health, detailing the minute particulars of the cases, and the mode of treatment adopted in each instance.

50. The Board has been in frequent communication with the guardians and other parties as to the proper mode of proceeding under the provisions of this statute, which in the present state of the public health require earnest attention; and information has been received from all parts of the country, showing that the Act is being zealously carried into effect, and that the urgency of the present occasion is sensibly felt, and actively met, by the guardians and their officers, upon whom the law has cast the obligation of carrying out its provisions. A separate account has been directed to be kept of the expense incurred under this head.

Signed, by Order of the Board,
GEO. NICHOLLS,
Secretary.

EMIGRATION OF YOUNG FEMALES TO AUSTRALIA.—CICULAR LETTER FROM THE POOR LAW BOARD TO THE BOARDS OF GUARDIANS

Poor Law Board,
Somerset House,
30th Nov., 1848.

SIR,—The Poor Law Board have received a communication from the Colonial Land and Emigration Commissioners, proposing to facilitate the emigration, to a limited extent, to Australia, of young females from the English workhouses, provided they be sent out as soon as they are fit for work, and have obtained sufficient education.

The enclosed extracts from the letter will explain to the guardians the terms on which it is proposed that the emigration should be conducted, and the Board request that the guardians will take the subject into their consideration, and inform them whether the guardians would be desirous of promoting the emigration of any young females in accordance with the arrangement therein suggested.

A set of forms is sent herewith, which will further show the conditions required to be fulfilled, and the course that must be pursued, in case the emigration is proceeded with.

I am, &c.
W. G. LUMLEY,
To *Assistant Secretary.*
The Clerk to the Board of Guardians.

EXTRACT FROM A LETTER DATED AUGUST 1, 1848, AND ADDRESSED BY THE COLONIAL LAND AND EMIGRATION COMMISSIONERS TO THE POOR LAW BOARD.

"The Emigration Commissioners would propose to admit as candidates for passages to Australia girls belonging to the sixth class of paupers (as defined in the workhouse rules of the Poor Law Commissioners) who may have lost their parents and have completed their thirteenth year. Such candidates should be capable of labour, and must have been vaccinated or have had the small-pox, and be free from all disease usually considered infectious or contagious. They should also have a sufficient knowledge of reading, writing, and arithmetic, and the principles of the Christian religion, and have a good character in respect of industry and general behaviour.

"If, as the Emigration Commissioners are led to suppose, the parishes would be willing to provide for persons answering these conditions, the cost of outfit, and the expense of the journey to the port of embarkation, and would contribute the sum of 5*l.* towards the passage of each person embarked, the Emigration Commissioners would be prepared to defray the other expenses attending their conveyance to the colony, out of funds applicable to emigration, under the management of the Board.

"The Secretary of State will instruct the Governors of New South Wales and South Australia to effect such preliminary arrangements as may be necessary for the reception of these young girls, and for placing them with respectable and trustworthy families on their quitting the protection of Government; and also to make such provision by local enactment as may be necessary for their apprenticeship.

"It may be here worth while to give the following extract of a report recently received from the surgeon superintendent of the "China," on the disposal of the emigrants by that ship, which shows the demand then existing in South Australia for the services of young girls:—'All the little girls from 12 to 15 years were immediately engaged at from 12*l.* to 13*l.* per annum as nurse girls.'"

EMIGRATION OF YOUNG FEMALES TO AUSTRALIA.—APPLICATION OF CANDIDATE TO THE BOARD OF GUARDIANS.

I, the undersigned, being desirous of emigrating to Australia under the direction of Her Majesty's Colonial Land and Emigration Commissioners, do make application to the Guardians of the poor of the Union [or Parish] to recommend me to the Poor Law Board as a fit candidate for emigration.

And I do hereby declare that the following statements written with my own hand are, to the best of my belief, true:—

Where born?

Answer—

Day and year when born?

Answer—

Place of residence, and the name of the person with whom resided up to the time of entering the workhouse?

Answer—

How long an inmate of the workhouse?

Answer—

Date of last admission into the workhouse?

Answer—

If father be living, his name, address and occupation?

Answer—

If father be not living, the name and address of mother, if living?

Answer—

If neither parent be living, the name and address of a near relative or friend with whom the candidate may have been chiefly brought up, and who could be communicated with on the subject of the proposed emigration?

Answer—

Dated

Witness

Signature of Candidate.

I, the undersigned,* of the above candidate do hereby certify that her proposed emigration to Australia is with my assent and concurrence.

Dated

Signature or Mark.

Witness

Address.

EMIGRATION OF YOUNG FEMALES TO AUSTRALIA.—RECOMMENDATION OF BOARD OF GUARDIANS TO THE POOR LAW BOARD.

We, the guardians of the poor, of the Union [or Parish] having received the accompanying application of and believing the statements therein contained to be true, do hereby recommend the said to the Poor Law Board as a fit person to emigrate to Australia under the direction of Her Majesty's Colonial Land and Emigration Commissioners.

And we hereby undertake to pay into the hands of the said commissioners the sum of £ in aid of the emigration of the said [†the Parish of to which she is chargeable having resolved to raise out of the poor-rates a sum not exceeding for that purpose.

And we also hereby certify in reference to the said that she possesses a sufficient knowledge of reading, writing, and arithmetic, and the principles of the Christian religion; and bears a good character in respect of industry and general behaviour.

Dated

[*U. S.*]

Chairman of the Board of Guardians.

Clerk to the Board of Guardians.

I certify that I have examined the above-named applicant, and that she is not mutilated nor deformed in person, nor in my opinion afflicted with any disease calculated to shorten life or to impair physical or mental energy. I certify also that she has had the small-pox or been vaccinated, and is entirely free from every disease usually considered infectious or contagious.

Dated

Medical Officer of the Union [*or Parish.*]

---

* Insert father, mother, or near relative, stating the relationship.

† To be struck out where the pauper is irremovable. See 11 & 12 Vic. c. 110, s. 5.

No. 1.

STATEMENT showing the Amount of Money Expended for In-Maintenance and Out-Relief for each of the *Years*, and the Total Number of In-door and Out-door Paupers Relieved in England and Wales, for each of the *Quarters* ended at Lady-day, 1840 to 1848 inclusive; together with the estimated Population for each year, the rate per head of such Expenditure, and the ratio per cent. of the number of Paupers Relieved on the Population, and the average price of Wheat per quarter, in each year.

Years ended Lady-day.	EXPENDITURE.					Average Price of Wheat per Quarter in each Year.*		Rate per Head of Expenditure for In-Maintenance and Out-Relief on the Population.		Population for each Year, estimated according to the Ratio of Increase.	Number of Paupers of all Classes Relieved (including Children.)					Ratio per Cent. of Total Number of Paupers Relieved to Population.
	In-Maintenance.	Proportion per Cent. to Total.	Out-Relief.	Proportion per Cent. to Total.	Total In-Maintenance and Out-Relief.						In-door.	Proportion per Cent. to Total.	Out-door.	Proportion per Cent. to Total.	Total In-door and Out-door.†	
	£.		£.		£.	s.	d.	s.	d.							
1840	808,151	22	2,931,263	78	3,739,414	68	6	4	9¾	15,562,000	169,232	14	1,030,297	86	1,199,529	7·7
1841	890,883	23	2,990,330	77	3,886,213	65	3	4	11¼	15,770,000	192,106	15	1,106,942	85	1,299,048	8·2
1842	934,158	23	3,090,884	77	4,025,042	64	0	5	0½	15,981,000	222,642	16	1,204,545	84	1,427,187	8·9
1843	958,057	22	3,321,508	78	4,279,565	54	4	5	3½	16,194,000	238,560	15	1,300,930	85	1,539,490	9·5
1844	833,856	21	3,223,618	79	4,057,474	51	5	4	11¼	16,410,000	230,818	16	1,246,743	84	1,477,561	9·0
1845	844,816	21	3,272,629	79	4,117,445	49	2	4	11½	16,629,000	215,325	15	1,255,645	85	1,470,970	8·8
1846	804,101	20	3,207,819	80	4,011,920	53	3	4	9¼	16,851,000	200,270	15	1,131,819	85	1,332,089	7·9
1847	899,095	21	3,467,960	79	4,367,055	59	0	5	1½	17,076,000	265,037	15	1,456,313	85	1,721,350	10·1
1848	1,102,822	22	3,853,297	78	4,956,119	64	6	5	8¾	17,304,000	305,956	16	1,570,585	84	1,876,541	10·8

* The average price of wheat per quarter was obtained from the Comptroller of Corn Returns.

† These numbers are for the quarter ended Lady-day in each year.

Note.—The above expenditure is for In-Maintenance and Out-Relief *only*, and does not include salaries to paid officers and other establishment charges, or workhouse loans repaid. An estimate is made for places not under the Poor Law Amendment Act.

The information, as regards Pauperism and Expenditure, was extracted from the Quarterly Abstracts received from the Clerks to the Guardians of the several Unions.

COMPARATIVE STATEMENT of the Number of Adult Able-bodied Paupers relieved in England and Wales during each of the Quarters ended Lady-day, 1842 to 1848 inclusive, distinguishing those Relieved on account of temporary Sickness or Accident.

Quarters ended Lady-day.	IN-DOOR.			OUT-DOOR.			Total Number of Able-bodied Relieved, In-door and Out-door.
	On Account of Temporary Sickness or Accident.	All other Causes, including Vagrants.	Total In-door.	On Account of Temporary Sickness or Accident.	All other Causes, including Vagrants.	Total Out-door.	
1842	10,922	74,249	85,171	134,641	192,078	326,719	411,890
1843	10,888	88,308	99,196	146,704	220,685	367,389	466,585
1844	11,458	86,327	97,785	158,280	175,419	333,699	431,484
1845	11,407	76,216	87,623	167,277	165,196	332,473	420,096
1846	11,258	74,413	85,671	144,394	152,352	296,746	382,417
1847	13,485	109,739	123,224	202,403	236,728	439,131	562,355
1848	15,084	140,795	155,879	203,373	307,086	510,459	666,338

Note.—The above results were obtained from the Union Quarterly Abstracts, and an estimate is made for those places not under the Poor Law Amendment Act.

No. 2.—SUMMARY OF RETURNS of the Amount Levied, &c., and Expended for the Relief and

COUNTIES.	RECEIPT.			EXPENDITURE.					
	Amount of Money levied by Assessment.	Received from all other Sources in aid of Poor Rate.	Total Amount of Money received for the Relief, &c., of the Poor.	Amount of Money Expended in the Relief, &c., of the Poor.	Amount of Money Expended in Law Charges (Parochial and Union.)	Expenses of Proceedings before Magistrates, and Constables' Expenses, Union and Parochial), not included in preceding Column.	Amount of Fees paid to the Vaccinators under the Vaccination Extension Act.	Payments on Account of the Registration Act: viz. Fees to Clergymen and Registrars, Outlay for Register Offices, Books, and Forms.
	s.	£. s.	£. s.	£. s.	£. s.	£. s.	£. s.	£. s.
ENGLAND.								
Bedford	62,320 9	308 4	62,628 13	49,998 0	374 6	426 3	113 9	384 14
Berks	113,137 13	1,125 2	114,262 15	92,957 0	386 13	1,341 3	312 14	633 7
Buckingham	117,621 8	3,402 3	121,023 11	94,236 1	829 11	1,435 12	973 4	538 1
Cambridge	125,116 15	1,191 10	126,308 5	91,540 10	1,017 3	1,377 1	153 2	595 17
Chester	118,057 10	3,003 16	121,061 6	96,327 2	1,578 7	1,311 13	644 8	1,478 12
Cornwall	122,468 7	1,780 1	124,248 8	97,868 17	3,481 19	1,125 12	659 19	932 13
Cumberland	56,120 8	834 8	56,954 16	43,900 13	366 7	215 6	299 17	614 16
Derby	77,153 11	1,475 7	78,628 18	61,349 14	553 18	1,181 11	368 8	886 4
Devon	268,323 2	2,460 3	270,783 5	229,409 10	3,604 10	2,648 3	294 19	1,572 8
Dorset	122,395 19	685 4	123,081 3	102,355 11	1,470 9	1,441 18	144 11	547 2
Durham	106,780 7	1,085 0	107,865 7	75,869 15	1,593 5	671 7	423 0	1,256 17
Essex	243,201 4	2,247 13	245,448 17	197,649 0	2,226 1	1,747 6	458 4	1,165 1
Gloucester	240,854 17	6,960 14	247,815 11	175,989 8	2,203 17	1,274 10	421 5	1,360 1
Hereford	66,557 4	536 10	67,093 14	54,720 9	686 10	702 13	99 11	326 2
Hertford	98,928 13	654 13	99,583 6	76,598 15	389 7	439 16	198 1	596 4
Huntingdon	39,541 6	564 15	40,106 1	31,813 1	399 9	489 6	42 13	201 11
Kent	293,623 9	6,472 8	300,095 17	225,543 18	2,040 18	3,643 15	1,090 16	1,831 0
Lancaster	617,969 9	10,984 2	628,953 11	575,812 0	3,952 15	4,145 9	2,847 12	7,869 8
Leicester	125,495 5	771 11	126,266 16	104,193 0	1,189 15	768 6	245 13	738 0
Lincoln	187,725 11	2,719 14	190,445 5	143,219 10	1,990 0	2,298 0	678 0	1,284 13
Middlesex	840,763 11	37,505 12	878,269 3	608,632 3	5,129 12	1,766 9	1,722 12	5,634 18
Monmouth	51,211 8	2,692 11	53,903 19	36,907 3	310 2	469 15	362 15	525 12
Norfolk	259,904 11	5,060 1	264,964 12	220,902 19	1,708 17	1,496 17	314 16	1,262 8
Northampton	133,094 12	1,285 9	134,380 1	106,684 16	594 5	847 17	150 14	711 6
Northumberland	97,435 5	1,094 10	98,529 15	86,032 2	955 0	558 16	422 14	1,057 12
Nottingham	108,702 15	2,056 0	110,758 15	86,954 18	850 11	1,007 17	354 5	814 4
Oxford	107,613 0	774 9	108,387 9	94,762 19	696 2	1,411 4	102 4	553 9
Rutland	10,648 7	99 5	10,747 12	8,582 15	94 10	105 11	26 8	76 0
Salop	85,121 9	846 2	85,967 11	62,052 13	1,220 9	477 6	243 5	649 14
Somerset	260,484 2	1,585 2	262,069 4	204,787 10	2,612 13	2,610 2	670 19	1,206 13
Southampton	222,461 18	1,602 0	224,063 18	167,087 2	1,737 1	819 17	428 8	1,189 1
Stafford	162,848 13	2,173 1	165,021 14	120,475 14	2,133 8	943 11	956 6	1,983 0
Suffolk	209,190 0	3,322 9	212,512 9	165,594 18	812 0	872 7	353 5	1,055 12
Surrey	344,385 8	17,330 19	361,716 7	256,742 1	3,966 4	2,107 1	972 14	2,215 6
Sussex	193,002 8	3,972 4	196,974 12	164,946 6	1,875 7	1,349 0	346 18	1,065 1
Warwick	171,555 17	4,481 2	176,036 19	127,288 7	1,163 16	1,435 15	520 16	1,408 11
Westmorland	19,475 12	735 8	20,211 0	15,992 8	204 15	135 15	72 19	183 18
Wilts	197,519 0	1,472 11	198,991 11	156,245 14	1,166 11	1,068 4	542 0	896 3
Worcester	111,604 9	1,355 15	112,960 4	83,067 2	828 2	441 13	497 16	902 5
York, East Riding	103,630 13	1,452 9	105,083 2	81,314 16	1,039 11	445 11	232 4	810 15
,, North Riding	70,024 13	1,434 7	71,459 0	62,208 13	1,041 7	512 0	235 0	663 10
,, West Riding	445,224 5	10,754 11	455,978 16	314,017 14	7,916 11	4,972 19	1,254 12	4,256 3
Totals of England	7,409,294 3	152,348 15	7,561,642 18	5,852,632 7	68,391 17	54,539 17	20,376 16	53,933 12
WALES.								
Anglesey	23,661 8	580 6	24,241 14	20,526 12	209 8	251 15	19 2	175 13
Brecon	26,005 9	925 14	26,931 3	20,910 10	145 14	285 2	83 5	232 15
Cardigan	25,193 7	153 9	25,346 16	20,254 4	193 7	149 18	103 16	188 13
Carmarthen	46,936 16	265 5	47,202 1	33,222 2	585 0	331 19	176 2	329 15
Carnarvon	36,409 9	988 11	37,398 0	31,978 10	1,287 4	462 13	8 16	271 11
Denbigh	43,341 17	212 11	43,554 8	34,604 3	255 14	379 6	172 5	277 16
Flint	30,274 6	136 2	30,460 8	23,963 3	595 16	505 2	98 8	285 1
Glamorgan	68,018 5	420 1	68,438 6	54,355 1	508 8	551 4	559 16	677 9
Merioneth	19,042 6	194 0	19,236 6	16,852 14	298 9	165 17	42 6	102 17
Montgomery	38,819 12	221 4	39,040 16	29,918 7	357 19	233 2	33 16	168 14
Pembroke	36,596 16	2,134 13	38,731 9	29,652 12	374 3	310 12	269 1	261 4
Radnor	13,835 17	33 15	13,869 12	11,894 5	235 12	98 13	21 10	77 7
Totals of Wales	408,135 8	6,315 11	414,450 19	328,132 3	5,046 14	3,725 3	1,588 3	3,048 15
Totals of England and Wales	7,817,429 11	158,664 6	7.976,093 17	6,180,764 10	73.438 11	58,265 0	21,964 19	56,982 7

Maintenance of the Poor, and for other purposes, during the year ended 25th March, 1848.

EXPENDITURE.

Payments under the Parochial Assessments Act (for Surveys, Valuations, &c.,) and Loans repaid under the same.	Payments for or towards the County or Borough Rate.	Payments for or towards the County and Local Police Forces (if any, and if not paid out of the County or Borough Rate, and included therewith in the preceding Column.)	Costs of Voters', Burgess, and Jury Lists.	Expenses of Parish Property.	Money Expended for all other Purposes.	Total Parochial Rates, &c., Expended.	Medical Relief.	COUNTIES.
£. s.	£. s.	£. s.	£. s.	£. s.	£. s.	£. s.	£. s.	ENGLAND.
151 16	8,090 18	154 3	202 7	34 0	452 13	60,382 9	1,826 17	Bedford.
257 0	14,433 8	219 5	177 0	83 16	1,537 17	112,339 3	3,921 4	Berks.
358 16	16,077 5	10 0	338 19	30 1	1,515 10	115,467 0	3,123 16	Buckingham.
173 10	19,596 9	1,606 4	336 14	75 4	2,236 9	118,708 3	3,486 2	Cambridge.
34 0	12,764 11	3,189 11	428 17	143 19	5,635 7	123,536 7	3,372 2	Chester.
110 0	9,823 17	52 0	306 6	526 16	6,494 7	121,382 6	2,532 8	Cornwall
131 10	8,263 16	..	140 18	67 6	1,633 3	55,633 12	1,274 14	Cumberland.
265 3	9,093 13	56 18	304 11	42 11	3,178 8	77,280 19	1,651 19	Derby.
347 16	24,076 5	17 10	548 18	158 1	5,259 15	267,937 15	6,040 12	Devon.
..	12,759 2	..	378 18	86 4	1,174 11	120,358 6	4,150 10	Dorset.
..	16,221 9	3,317 7	357 13	27 16	3,599 17	103,338 6	2,106 10	Durham.
279 16	26,429 16	5,053 4	231 10	145 13	4,837 5	240,222 16	7,937 15	Essex.
1,107 10	44,908 17	3,744 3	725 14	286 1	6,413 12	238,434 8	4,854 10	Gloucester.
17 10	8,741 0	404 7	184 19	61 2	1,101 16	67,045 19	2,312 6	Hereford.
382 13	16,651 7	595 17	298 19	149 8	1,342 7	97,642 14	4,387 2	Hertford.
..	5,023 2	7 0	49 16	22 14	495 9	38,544 1	1,218 18	Huntingdon.
695 18	42,492 10	6,575 6	882 2	439 0	10,912 6	296,147 9	8,219 14	Kent.
394 1	173,978 18	2,188 1	2,182 12	827 19	26,917 1	801,115 16	15,852 3	Lancaster.
169 11	16,563 16	646 19	313 17	92 5	2,506 3	127,427 5	2,780 8	Leicester.
167 2	29,930 16	52 0	899 9	217 8	4,151 7	184,888 5	4,284 15	Lincoln.
195 6	104,615 15	137,679 5	4,333 4	3,312 1	28,971 1	901,992 6	16,066 10	Middlesex.
217 16	8,427 7	450 17	128 14	91 7	1,539 5	49,430 13	1,348 13	Monmouth.
740 7	25,027 3	1,548 17	791 5	117 16	4,851 10	258,762 15	7,120 12	Norfolk.
402 10	21,310 17	222 3	371 17	140 9	1,778 12	133,215 6	3,228 0	Northampton.
..	7,996 8	189 15	87 4	177 6	2,911 16	100,388 16	3,014 18	Northumberland.
20 0	17,545 16	1,533 4	413 15	86 16	3,038 12	112,619 18	2,693 4	Nottingham.
35 4	10,829 13	6 16	240 10	42 1	1,075 15	109,755 17	2,990 18	Oxford.
..	1,514 19	125 17	37 17	17 7	118 3	10,699 7	346 12	Rutland.
373 8	11,471 1	4,163 19	144 2	13 13	2,351 12	83,161 2	2,863 4	Salop.
308 11	28,631 19	256 8	820 19	312 15	3,943 17	246,162 6	6,759 10	Somerset.
894 17	34,469 6	3,064 11	471 14	174 11	2,998 11	213,334 19	7,156 5	Southampton.
499 16	29,533 16	7,969 0	565 14	18 3	3,763 17	168,842 5	3,753 17	Stafford.
186 17	34,337 16	237 10	273 5	160 14	4,625 4	208,509 8	6,108 7	Suffolk.
1,695 0	37,944 6	40,976 18	1,461 12	194 2	18,123 16	366,399 0	8,046 5	Surrey.
1,498 1	15,905 8	1,242 12	554 12	1,186 12	5,290 13	195,260 10	7,250 4	Sussex.
214 14	36,431 12	1,320 6	505 8	604 2	3,896 7	174,789 14	3,263 1	Warwick.
..	2,677 16	..	58 11	69 2	532 16	19,928 0	568 3	Westmorland.
190 19	20,332 3	3,026 9	316 13	171 9	1,914 11	185,870 16	5,124 16	Wilts.
191 19	20,737 15	1,491 12	486 18	139 6	2,262 8	111,046 16	3,388 13	Worcester.
206 0	17,715 7	61 7	280 7	196 3	1,936 19	104,239 0	1,822 11	York, East Riding.
164 1	8,247 15	..	125 11	117 3	1,458 12	74,773 12	1,997 17	,, North Riding.
1,021 18	80,496 16	424 19	1,569 16	526 14	14,404 1	430,862 3	9,546 13	,, West Riding.
14,100 16	1,092,121 9	233,882 0	23,329 7	11,386 6	203,183 1	7,627,877 8	189,862 18	Totals of England.
								WALES.
..	1,569 6	1 13	21 1	15 0	767 0	23,556 10	293 15	Anglesey.
..	7,107 19	..	42 18	..	958 8	29,766 11	690 1	Brecon.
..	3,734 6	446 3	24 18	3 10	672 19	25,771 14	418 12	Cardigan.
14 3	11,568 3	1,892 13	61 9	12 11	1,058 11	49,252 8	807 9	Carmarthen.
..	3,506 19	6 2	90 14	27 1	1,505 4	39,144 14	1,168 3	Carnarvon.
..	7,256 2	38 8	140 8	1 19	1,058 4	44,184 5	631 0	Denbigh.
..	3,890 16	32 10	125 12	2 1	1,126 10	30,624 19	481 16	Flint.
..	10,188 7	1,216 17	256 18	57 11	1,770 17	70,142 8	1,114 10	Glamorgan.
..	1,686 19	1 2	36 6	2 6	627 5	19,816 1	495 12	Merioneth.
..	5,817 11	168 13	104 3	0 6	1,140 12	37,943 3	956 4	Montgomery.
..	3,462 5	65 19	58 14	26 7	730 16	35,211 13	789 13	Pembroke.
..	1,713 10	..	36 16	3 16	112 3	14,193 12	247 4	Radnor.
14 3	61,502 3	3,870 0	999 17	152 8	11,528 9	419,607 18	8,093 19	Totals of Wales.
14,114 19	1,153,623 12	237,752 0	24,329 4	11,538 14	214,711 10	8,047,485 6	197,953 17	Totals of England and Wales.

No. 3.

STATEMENT showing the Total Amount of Money levied for Poor Rates in England and Wales, in each year, from the earliest period for which authentic Parliamentary Returns have been received, to the year 1848, inclusive; also the Total Amount Expended under the following heads, for the same periods, showing also the Increase or Decrease in each year on the Expenditure for the Relief of the Poor, compared with the preceding year; with the average price of Wheat per quarter in each year.

Years ended Lady-day.	Total Amount of Money Levied for Poor Rates.	EXPENDITURE. Amount of Money Expended in the Relief, &c., of the Poor.	Total Amount Expended in Law Charges, Parochial and Union	Expenses of Proceedings before Magistrates, and Constables' Expenses, not included in previous column.	Amount of Fees Paid to the Vaccinators, under the Vaccination Extension Act.	Payments on Account of the Registration Act, Fees to Clergymen, &c.	Payments under the Parochial Assessments' Act (for Surveys, Valuations, &c.,) and Loans repaid under the same.	Payments for, or towards the County Rate, or Borough Rate.	Payments for or towards the County and Local Police Forces, (if any, and if not paid out of the County or Boro' Rate, and included therewith in previous columns.)	Costs of Voters', Burgess, and Jury List.	Expenses of Parish Property.	Money Expended for all other purposes.	Total Parochial Rates, &c., Expended.	Rate per Cent. of Increase or Decrease on Expenditure for Relief, &c., to the Poor, in each Year, compared with the preceding. Increase.	Decrease.	* Average Price of Wheat per quarter s.	d.	Medical Relief, included in column "Relief, &c., to the Poor."	Years ended Lady-day.
	£.	£.	£.	£.	£.	£.	£.	£.	£.	£.	£.	£.	£.			s.	d.	£.	
1803	5,348,205	4,077,891	190,072	..	..	..	..	273,490	..	..	..	760,615	5,302,068	..	..	64	8	..	1803
1813	8,646,841	6,656,106	324,957	..	..	..	..	547,042	..	..	..	1,313,305	8,841,410	..	..	108	9	..	1813
1814	8,388,974	6,294,581	332,663	..	..	..	..	524,689	..	..	..	1,356,128	8,508,061	..	5	73	11	..	1814
1815	7,457,676	5,413,846	324,596	..	..	..	..	572,544	..	..	..	1,189,862	7,505,848	..	14	64	4	..	1815
1816	6,937,425	5,724,839	..	..	..	..	..	559,090	..	..	..	654,981	6,938,910	6	..	75	10	..	1816
1817	8,128,418	6,910,925	..	..	..	..	..	590,080	..	..	..	620,640	8,121,645	21	..	94	9	..	1817
†1818	9,320,440	7,870,801	..	..	..	..	..	657,776	..	..	..	774,556	9,303,133	14	..	84	1	..	1818
1819	8,932,185	7,516,704	..	..	..	..	..	663,555	..	..	..	745,350	8,925,609	..	4	73	0	..	1819
1820	8,719,655	7,330,254	..	..	..	..	..	678,723	..	..	..	663,935	8,672,912	..	3	65	7	..	1820
1821	8,411,893	6,959,251	..	..	..	..	..	652,816	..	..	..	723,052	8,335,119	..	5	54	5	..	1821
1822	7,761,441	6,358,704	..	..	..	..	..	595,316	..	..	..	741,217	7,695,237	..	9	43	3	..	1822
1823	6,898,153	5,772,962	..	..	..	..	..	579,006	..	..	..	569,224	6,291,192	..	9	51	9	..	1823
1824	6,836,505	5,736,900	..	..	..	..	..	599,395	..	..	..	538,203	6,874,498	..	..	62	0	..	1824
1825	6,972,323	5,786,989	..	..	..	..	..	663,644	..	..	..	548,555	6,999,188	1	..	66	6	..	1825
1826	6,965,051	5,928,502	..	..	..	..	..	743,111	..	..	..	503,034	7,174,647	2	..	58	9	..	1826
1827	7,784,352	6,441,088	..	..	..	..	..	762,187	..	..	..	600,191	7,803,466	9	..	56	9	..	1827
1828	7,715,055	6,298,000	..	..	..	..	..	721,308	..	..	..	651,125	7,670,433	..	2	60	5	..	1828
1829	7,642,171	6,332,410	..	..	..	..	..	714,308	..	..	..	566,021	7,612,739	1	..	66	3	..	1829
1830	8,111,422	6,829,042	..	..	..	..	..	726,800	..	..	..	605,439	8,161,281	8	..	62	10	..	1830
1831	8,279,218	6,798,889	..	..	..	..	..	772,966	..	..	..	767,232	8,339,087	..	..	67	8	..	1831
1832	8,622,920	7,036,969	..	..	..	..	..	799,414	..	..	..	874,079	8,683,462	4	..	63	4	..	1832
1833	8,606,501	6,790,800	254,412	..	..	..	..	745,270	..	..	..	949,400	8,739,882	..	4	57	3	..	1833
‡1834	8,338,079	6,317,255	258,604	..	..	..	..	691,548	..	..	..	1,021,941	8,289,348	..	7	51	11	..	1834
1835	7,373,867	5,526,418	202,527	..	..	..	..	705,711	..	..	..	935,362	7,370,018	..	13	44	2	..	1835
1836	6,354,538	4,717,630	172,432	..	..	..	..	699,845	..	..	..	823,213	6,413,120	..	15	39	5	..	1836
§1837	5,294,566	4,044,741	126,951	..	..	..	..	604,203	..	..	..	637,043	5,412,938	..	14	52	6	..	1837
1838	5,186,389	4,123,604	93,982	..	..	35,662	25,680	681,842	..	..	..	507,929	5,468,699	2	..	55	3	..	1838
1839	5,613,939	4,406,907	63,412	..	..	52,306	56,846	741,407	..	..	..	493,703	5,814,581	7	..	69	4	148,652	1839
1840	6,014,605	4,576,965	67,020	..	..	51,228	49,963	855,552	..	..	..	466,698	6,067,426	3	..	68	6	151,781	1840
1841	6,351,828	4,760,929	69,942	..	11,664	53,728	43,157	1,026,035	..	..	..	527,717	6,493,172	4	..	65	3	154,054	1841
1842	6,552,890	4,911,498	68,051	..	33,744	52,379	40,178	1,003,651	227,067	..	..	‖ 375,203	6,711,771	3	..	64	0	153,481	1842
1843	7,085,595	5,208,027	84,730	..	16,425	53,896	30,420	1,051,878	243,738	..	..	346,007	7,035,121	6	..	54	4	160,726	1843
1844	6,847,205	4,976,093	105,304	..	16,980	56,094	30,083	1,111,236	245,221	..	..	359,106	6,990,117	..	..	51	5	166,257	1844
1845	6,791,006	5,039,703	95,397	57,988	25,905	57,388	22,877	1,046,412	233,550	20,153	14,752	243,277	6,857,402	1	..	49	2	174,330	1845
1846	6,800,623	4,954,204	83,298	52,240	27,447	54,821	21,162	1,067,692	229,813	21,556	15,820	218,532	6,746,585	..	2	53	3	175,190	1846
1847	6,964,825	5,298,787	76,385	51,565	18,115	59,328	17,289	1,076,954	257,816	25,041	12,322	201,055	7,094,657	7	..	59	0	179,526	1847
1848	7,817,430	6,180,764	73,439	58,265	21,965	56,982	14,115	1,153,624	237,752	24,329	11,539	214,711	8,047,485	17	..	64	6	197,954	1848

* The average price of wheat per quarter was obtained from the Comptroller of Corn Returns.
† In this year the expenditure for the relief of the poor was at the maximum.
‡ The Poor Law Amendment Act received the Royal Assent on the 14th August, 1834.
§ The expenditure for relief to the poor was at the minimum in this year.
‖ This amount includes the sum of £57,111, the expense incurred under the Act for taking the Census of 1841.

NOTE.—The Returns for the year 1803 were obtained under an Act of the 43rd Geo. 3, and those for 1813, 1814, and 1815, under the Act of 55th Geo. 3. For the years 1816 to 1834, inclusive, the Returns were made in pursuance of orders of the House of Commons; and from the latter period to the present time, they have been called for by the Commissioners, under the Poor Law Amendment Act, forming an unbroken Parliamentary series, from the year 1813 to the present time.

No. 4.

TABLE, showing the estimated Population, the Amount of Money Levied for Poor Rates, and the Amount Expended for the Relief and Maintenance of the Poor in England and Wales, for the Years ended at Lady-day, 1834 to 1848, both inclusive; with the Rate per Head of the Amount Levied and Expended for Relief to the Poor on the estimated Population, the Rate in the £. of Expenditure for Relief to the Poor on Annual Value of Rateable Property in 1847, and the Average Price of Wheat per Quarter in each Year.

Years ended at Lady-day.	Population estimated according to the ratio of Increase which prevailed between 1831 and 1841.	Amount of Money Levied for Poor Rates.	Total Expended in Relief and Maintenance of the Poor.	Rate per Head of Amount Levied and Expended in Relief to the Poor on the Estimated Population. Levy.	Relief to the Poor.	Rate in the £. of Expenditure for Relief to the Poor, in each Year, calculated on the Annual Value of Rateable Property in 1847.	* Average Price of Wheat per Quarter.
		£.	£.	s. d.	s. d.	s. d.	s. d.
†1834	14,372,000	8,338,079	6,317,255	11 7¼	8 9½	1 10½	51 11
1835	14,564,000	7,373,807	5,526,418	10 1½	7 7	1 7¾	44 2
1836	14,758,000	6,354,538	4,717,630	8 7½	6 4¾	1 4¾	39 5
1837	14,955,000	5,294,566	4,044,741	7 0¾	5 5	1 2½	52 6
1838	15,155,000	5,186,389	4,123,604	6 10¼	5 5¼	1 2¾	55 3
1839	15,357,000	5,613,939	4,406,907	7 3¾	5 8¾	1 3¾	69 4
1840	15,562,000	6,014,605	4,576,965	7 8¾	5 10½	1 4¼	68 6
1841	15,770,000	6,351,828	4,760,929	8 0¾	6 0½	1 5	65 3
1842	15,981,000	6,552,890	4,911,498	8 2½	6 1¾	1 5½	64 0
1843	16,194,000	7,085,595	5,208,027	8 9	6 5¼	1 6½	54 4
1844	16,410,000	6,847,205	4,976,093	8 4¼	6 0¾	1 5¾	51 5
1845	16,629,000	6,791,006	5,039,703	8 2	6 0¾	1 6	49 2
1846	16,851,000	6,800,623	4,954,204	8 0¾	5 10½	1 5¾	53 3
1847	17,076,000	6,964,825	5,298,787	8 2	6 2½	1 7	59 0
1848	17,304,000	7,817,430	6,180,764	9 0½	7 1¾	1 10	64 6

Seven Years in which the Price of Wheat was Highest.

Years ended at Lady-Day.	Population estimated according to the ratio of increase between 1831 and 1841.	Amount of Money Levied for Poor Rates.	Expended in Relief and Maintenance of the Poor.	Rate per Head of Amount Levied and Expended in Relief to the Poor, on the estimated Population. Levy.	Relief to Poor.	Average Price of Wheat per Quarter.
		£.	£.	s. d.	s. d.	s. d.
1839	15,357,000	5,613,939	4,406,907	7 3¾	5 8¾	69 4
1840	15,562,000	6,014,605	4,576,965	7 8¾	5 10½	68 6
1841	15,770,000	6,351,828	4,760,929	8 0¾	6 0½	65 3
1848	17,304,000	7,817,430	6,180,764	9 0½	7 1¾	64 6
1842	15,981,000	6,552,890	4,911,498	8 2½	6 1¾	64 0
1847	17,076,000	6,964,825	5,298,787	8 2	6 2½	59 0
1838	15,155,000	5,186,389	4,123,604	6 10¼	5 5¼	55 3
Totals	112,205,000	44,501,906	34,259,454	7 11¼	6 1¼	63 8

Seven Years in which the Price of Wheat was Lowest.

Years ended at Lady-Day.	Population estimated according to the ratio of increase between 1831 and 1841.	Amount of Money Levied for Poor Rates.	Expended in Relief and maintenance of the Poor.	Rate per Head of Amount Levied and Expended in Relief to the Poor, on the estimated Population. Levy.	Relief to Poor	Average Price of Wheat per Quarter.
	£.	£.	£.	s. d.	s. d.	s. d.
1836	14,758,000	6,354,538	4,717,630	8 7½	6 4¾	39 5
1835	14,564,000	7,373,807	5,526,418	10 1½	7 7	44 2
1845	16,629,000	6,791,006	5,039,703	8 2	6 0¾	49 2
1844	16,410,000	6,847,205	4,976,093	8 4¼	6 0¾	51 5
1837	14,955,000	5,294,566	4,044,741	7 0¾	5 5	52 6
1846	16,851,000	6,800,623	4,954,204	8 0¾	5 10½	53 3
1843	16,194,000	7,085,595	5,208,027	8 9	6 5¼	54 4
Totals	110,361,000	46,547,340	34,466,816	8 3½	6 3	49 2

Expended in relief to the poor in the 7 years when the price of wheat was lowest	£34,466,816
" " in the 7 years when the price of wheat was highest	34,259,454
More expended in the 7 years when wheat was lowest	207,362
	s. d.
Rate per head of such expenditure on estimated population of 7 years when wheat was lowest	6 3
" " " 7 highest years	6 1¼
More per head when wheat was lowest	0 1½

* The average price of wheat per quarter was obtained from the Comptroller of Corn Returns.

† The year 1834 was the last parochial year prior to the passing of the Poor Law Amendment Act.

Note.—The annual value of rateable property in 1847 was £67,320,587.

The annual value of Real Property assessed to the Property and Income Tax, in 1843, was £85,302,735. *See* Paper No. 165, Sess. 1845, House of Commons.

The Rate in the £. of the amount levied in 1847-8, calculated on the Property Tax Valuation, is 1*s.* 10*d.*, and that of the Expenditure for the Relief of the Poor for the same period 1*s.* 5½*d.*

No 5. VACCINATION EXTENSION ACT.—ABSTRACT of RETURNS from 627 Unions and Parishes in England and Wales, of the Number of Persons Vaccinated in such Unions and Parishes, in the Year ended 29th September, 1848.

COUNTIES.	Number of Unions, &c.	Number of Vaccinators.	Year ended 29th September, 1848. Number and Ages of Persons Vaccinated. Under One Year.	Above One Year.	Total.	Number of such cases which on inspection proved to have been successfully Vaccinated. Under One Year.	Above One Year.	Total.	Number of Registered Births in the Unions, etc., during the Year.
ENGLAND.									
Bedford	6	29	706	1,868	2,574	670	1,769	2,439	4,194
Berks	12	51	1,350	2,346	3,696	1,317	2,302	3,619	5,738
Buckingham	7	35	804	3,235	4,039	788	3,193	3,981	4,333
Cambridge	9	47	1,541	4,767	6,308	1,476	4,573	6,049	6,414
Chester	10	54	4,911	3,557	8,468	4,657	3,368	8,025	12,156
Cornwall	13	70	2,668	6,392	9,060	2,547	6,176	8,723	10,858
Cumberland	9	41	2,860	2,472	5,332	2,622	2,377	4,999	5,603
Derby	9	46	2,809	3,532	6,341	2,683	3,413	6,096	7,984
Devon	20	168	3,402	8,052	11,454	3,256	7,647	10,903	16,019
Dorset	12	48	585	1,774	2,359	548	1,724	2,272	4,295
Durham	14	61	6,214	3,782	9,996	6,034	3,683	9,717	14,041
Essex	17	119	3,171	6,548	9,719	3,038	6,238	9,276	10,362
Gloucester	17	58	3,573	4,593	8,166	3,310	4,327	7,637	11,155
Hereford	8	27	725	3,381	4,106	697	3,227	3,924	3,422
Hertford	13	59	1,436	3,838	5,274	1,338	3,725	5,063	5,564
Huntingdon	3	14	259	917	1,176	245	841	1,086	2,074
Kent	28	117	6,990	11,317	18,307	6,650	10,712	17,362	18,565
Lancaster	26	163	29,824	14,343	44,167	28,837	13,841	42,678	70,487
Leicester	11	49	2,014	1,843	3,857	1,961	1,806	3,767	7,181
Lincoln	14	105	3,530	6,491	10,021	3,454	6,385	9,839	12,352
Middlesex	32	169	18,075	8,661	26,736	17,212	8,133	25,345	54,719
Monmouth	5	23	1,870	2,857	4,727	1,812	2,777	4,589	4,848
Norfolk	22	108	2,871	5,689	8,560	2,796	5,474	8,270	13,021
Northampton	12	49	1,197	1,977	3,174	1,167	1,907	3,074	6,056
Northumberland	12	74	5,536	1,586	7,122	5,408	1,532	6,940	9,814
Nottingham	9	55	2,540	2,848	5,388	2,477	2,800	5,277	8,276
Oxford	9	40	644	3,020	3,664	627	2,896	3,523	4,538
Rutland	2	8	156	427	583	155	425	580	754
Salop	14	54	1,189	2,271	3,460	1,102	2,165	3,267	5,043
Somerset	17	110	4,338	8,695	13,033	3,963	8,289	12,252	12,590
Southampton	27	98	2,841	7,256	10,097	2,692	6,992	9,684	11,976
Stafford	16	98	7,838	5,544	13,382	7,583	5,328	12,911	17,576
Suffolk	17	88	1,911	8,078	9,989	1,870	8,003	9,873	10,393
Surrey	20	121	6,843	5,379	12,222	6,699	5,272	11,971	20,099
Sussex	22	100	1,761	6,476	8,237	1,719	6,301	8,020	8,384
Warwick	13	58	4,068	3,675	7,743	3,896	3,573	7,469	14,646
Westmorland	3	15	683	362	1,045	670	356	1,026	1,747
Wilts	18	75	2,180	9,739	11,919	2,120	9,491	11,611	7,229
Worcester	12	69	6,220	3,802	10,022	5,950	3,638	9,588	12,474
York, East Riding	10	55	2,237	2,006	4,243	2,154	1,937	4,091	7,852
,, North Riding	15	60	1,877	2,015	3,892	1,775	1,953	3,728	5,549
,, West Riding	20	132	10,795	8,612	19,407	10,384	8,343	18,727	35,846
Total	585	3,020	167,042	196,023	363,065	160,359	188,912	349,271	504,227
WALES.									
Anglesey	1	5	227	451	678	219	438	657	1,174
Brecknock	4	12	703	948	1,651	685	922	1,607	1,614
Cardigan	5	10	312	877	1,189	278	749	1,027	2,254
Carmarthen	5	17	759	1,634	2,393	744	1,588	2,332	3,458
Carnarvon	4	12	238	1,417	1,655	224	1,347	1,571	2,858
Denbigh	3	15	1,259	1,098	2,357	1,223	1,085	2,308	2,104
Flint	2	9	461	911	1,372	428	857	1,285	1,588
Glamorgan	5	24	3,437	2,825	6,262	3,158	2,667	5,825	6,927
Merioneth	4	10	282	991	1,273	272	958	1,230	1,300
Montgomery	3	10	1,359	2,602	3,961	1,294	2,334	3,628	1,558
Pembroke	3	12	567	2,486	3,053	545	2,452	2,997	2,419
Radnor	3	4	182	1,038	1,220	182	1,038	1,220	565
Total	42	140	9,786	17,278	27,064	9,252	16,435	25,687	27,819
Total of England and Wales	627	3,160	176,828	213,301	390,129	169,611	205,347	374,958	532,046

COMPARATIVE STATEMENT of the Numbers Vaccinated in the Years 1847 and 1848.

Years.	Number of Persons Vaccinated.	Number of Persons successfully Vaccinated.
1847	267,895	247,762
1848	390,129	374,958
Increase in 1848	122,234	127,196

London: Printed by Order of the Poor Law Board, by BLACKBURN & BURT, 90½, Holborn Hill, and Published by CHARLES KNIGHT, 90, Fleet Street.

AN

OFFICIAL CIRCULAR

OF PUBLIC DOCUMENTS AND INFORMATION:

DIRECTED BY THE POOR LAW BOARD TO BE PRINTED, CHIEFLY FOR THE USE OF THE BOARDS OF GUARDIANS AND THEIR OFFICERS.

No. 22.] FEBRUARY, 1849. [N.S.

CONTENTS.

I.—EDUCATION:

BOOKS AND MAPS FOR THE USE OF WORKHOUSE SCHOOLS. CIRCULAR.

Poor Law Board,
Somerset House,
25th January, 1849.

SIR,—The Committee of Council on Education had observed that, while by the aid of various associations,* the managers of schools had been enabled to procure a sufficient supply of books for religious instruction, other lesson and text books were often not found in elementary schools, or only to a limited extent. The Committee of Council accordingly selected such lesson and text books and maps as appeared to them best suited for this class of schools, and made arrangements for supplying the same to schools under inspection, at greatly reduced prices. A list of the books and maps so selected, with a brief description and the price of each, is given on the other side.

The Poor Law Board, desirous of promoting the introduction of suitable books into workhouse schools, have succeeded in making arrangements with the several publishers to supply, for the use of those schools, the books and maps in question, on the same terms as they are furnished to their lordships for the use of other schools. It will be observed that the reduction in the prices varies from 32 to 55 per cent. on the charge at which the books are sold to the public, and averages upwards of 43 per cent.

The books comprised in Schedule I. of the list are for the use of the scholars; and those in Schedule II. are for the teachers and assistant teachers.

Whenever the board of guardians require a supply of the books or maps named in the list, you will fill up one of the forms of application sent to you herewith, and forward it to this office. The Board will then direct their publisher, Mr. Charles Knight, whom they have appointed agent for the purpose, to furnish the books or maps required. The Board have authorized Mr. Knight to add to the prices, specified in the list, a commission of 10 per cent., to cover all expenses of packing, porterage, &c., and to enable him to include the books, &c., in his quarterly accounts with the unions.

In order to ensure the application of the books and maps to the object for which alone they are supplied, the name of the union must be written or stamped on each as soon as received.

It is desirable, that in every case the application should be made at least a fortnight before the books or maps are required, as some delay will necessarily occur in procuring them from the publishers, after the application has been examined and approved by this Board.

I am, Sir, your obedient servant,
GEO. NICHOLLS,
Secretary.

To
The Clerk to the Guardians.

* The aid of such Associations not being available for workhouse schools, any books which may be required for religious instruction, (in the selection of which the chaplain of the workhouse should be consulted,) can be obtained of Mr. Knight, with a proportionate reduction from the retail price.

SCHEDULE I.

Lesson Books for Workhouse Schools.

			Size of Paper on which it is printed.	No. of Sheets in Book.	No. Pages in Book	Size of Type in which it is printed.	No. and size of separate Maps or Plates if any.	No. of Woodcuts printed in same pages with type.	Description of Binding.	Price per Copy at which it is sold retail to the Public.	Price per Copy at which it is offered for use of Workhouse Schools.
Reading Lesson Books.											
Educational Books—											
The First Book	Society for Promoting Christian Knowledge	These Books are in use chiefly in Church of England Schools connected with the National Society.	Double Pott	1¼	48	Pica	. . .	12	Printd. Wrapr.	0 0 2	0 0 1¼
The Second book			do.	5	160	Small Pica	. . .	13	Cloth Limp	0 0 8	0 0 5¼
The Third Book			Demy	8	192	do.	. . .	. . .	Sheep	0 1 4	0 0 10
Reading Series—											
No. 1	do.	do.	do.	1⅔	60	Pica	. . .	. . .	Cloth Limp	0 0 3	0 0 2
No. 2	do.	do.	do.	1	36	L. Primer	. . .	. . .	do.	0 0 1½	0 0 1¼
Moral and Intellectual Series—											
No. 1, Daily Lesson Book	Compiled by some of the Chief Officers of the British and Foreign School Society.	These Books are in general use in Schools of the British and Foreign School Society.	Demy	1	46	Various	None	3	Union	0 0 3	0 0 1¾
No. 2, do.			Extra size eql. to Demy	3⅓	120	do.	1	None	do.	0 1 0	0 0 7½
No. 3, do.			Royal	5⅓	192	do.	None	do.	do.	0 1 6	0 0 11
No. 4, do.			do.	9	324	do.	do.	23	do.	0 2 6	0 1 6
Sequel to No. 1, or No. 1, in Sheets	do.	. . . .	Demy	15	30	do.	do.	None	Folio Sheets	0 3 0	0 1 9½
Sequel to do. No. 2	do.	. . . .	Extra size eql. to Demy	3⅔	128	L. Prim. & Brev.	do.	do.	Union	0 0 8	0 0 5
The Reading Lesson Books											
The First	Compiled and published under the authority of the Commissioners of National Education in Ireland.	These Reading Lesson Books were compiled for the National Schools, established under the Board of Education in Ireland, but they are also extensively in use among all classes of Schools in England, Wales, and Scotland.	Printing Demy	1	36	Pica	do.	do.	Printd. Wrapr.	0 0 2	0 0 1
The Second			do.	5	178	Small Pica	do.	do.	Cloth	0 0 7	0 0 4
The Third			do.	12	288	do.	do.	do.	do.	0 1 2	0 0 8
The Fourth			do.	15	358	do.	do.	do.	do.	0 1 4	0 0 9
The Fifth			do.	17½	420	L. Primer	do.	76	do.	0 1 8	0 0 11
Sequel to Second			do.	6½	232	Small Pica	do.	14	do.	0 0 9	0 0 5
Supplement to Fourth	do.		do.	18½	444	do.	do.	None	do.	0 1 8	0 0 11
Reading Book for the use of Female Schools	do.		do.	17½	420	L. Primer	do.	do.	do.	0 1 8	0 0 10
First Reading Book	By the Rev. J. M. Mc Culloch, LL.D.	Dr. Mc Culloch's Series of Reading Lessons is in very general use in efficient Middle Class Schools, and the best Parochial and other Elementary Schools in the North of England and Scotland. As their character has become known in the Midland and Southern Counties of England, they have had a constantly increasing sale	L. Demy & third	½	24	Pica & Min.	do.	do.	Printd. Wrapr.	0 0 1½	0 0 0¾
Second do.			do.	1	48	S. Pica & Bo.	do.	do.	do.	0 0 3	0 0 1¼
Third do.	do.		do.	3	144	Various	do.	do.	Sprnkd. Sheep	0 0 10	0 0 5¼
Series of Lessons in Prose and Verse	do.		Demy & third	7 5/16	234	do.	do.	do.	do.	0 2 0	0 0 11¼
Course of Elementary Reading	do.		do.	11¾	376	do.	do.	do.	Colord. Sheep, Lettered	0 3 0	0 1 5¾
Rural Spelling Book	By C. W. Johnson, F.R.S.	. . . .	Demy 12mo.	7	166	do.	. . .	38	Embossed Cloth Lettered	0 1 6	0 0 8
The New Series of School Books—											
The Child's First Book	Compiled for the Scottish School	This new Series has been compiled under the super-	Double Pott	¼	12	Dle. Pic. etc.	. . .	. . .	Stitched	0 0 1	0 0 0½
No. 1, Primer			Demy & third	¼	12	S. Pica, etc.	. . .	. . .	Printd. Wrapr.	0 0 1½	0 0 0¼

No. 2, Second Lessons	Book Association	intendence of the chief	Demy	1	36	L. Prim. etc.	. . .	. . .	Printd. Wrapr.	0	0	3	0	0	1½
No. 3, Third do.	do.	members of the Scottish Schoolmasters' Associa-	Demy & third	2¼	108	do.	. . .	. . .	½ bound flush, Printed Cover	0	0	6	0	0	3
Manual of English Pronunciation, or Sequel to Third Lessons	do.	tion, and may be regarded as the work of the most intelligent members of that	do.	1	48	do.	. . .	. . .	Printd. Wrapr.	0	0	4	0	0	2
Sheet Lessons	do.	body. The use of these	Extra Dle. Fcp.	15	30	Dle.Eng.etc.	. . .	. . .	Not bound	0	3	0	0	1	5
No. 4, Readings in Prose and Verse	do.	books is becoming more general in the Parochial	Demy & third	3	144	S. Pica, etc.	. . .	. . .	Cloth sewed on Tape	0	0	10	0	0	5
No. 5, First Collection of instructive Extracts	do.	and Private Schools of Scotland.	Extra Dle. Fcp.	7½	240	L. Prim. and Min.	. . .	. . .	do.	0	1	6	0	0	9
No. 6, Second Collection of instructive Extracts	do.	do.	do.	9¾	312	Do. & Min.	. . .	. . .	do.	0	2	0	0	1	0½
Reprints of Vocabularies from Nos. 5 and 6	do.	do.	do.	1½& 4 pp.	52	Bourgeois	. . .	. . .	Printd. Wrapr.	0	0	6	0	0	3
The Juvenile Reader.	By Neil Leitch.	A Reading Lesson Book for the First or Second Class of an Elementary School used in Scotland.	do.	6¾	216	Long Primer	. . .	15	Colored Sheep and Titled	0	1	6	0	0	9
Reading disentangled, being a series of elementary Reading Lessons on Sheets	By the Author of "Peep of Day."	In very general use for the instruction of very young children in reading in all Classes of Elementary Schools.	Fcp. broadside	37	37	Various	. . .	168	In Sheets Japand. Frame Mill board	0 0 0	6 12 12	0 0 0	0 0 0	4 7 7	0 0 6
Grammar and Etymology.															
Manual of English Grammar	By Rev. J. M. McCulloch, LL.D.	A grammar for an Elementary School of the highest class, but not adapted to a humble School. A proper Manual for Pupil Teachers and for Teachers.	Demy & third	3¾	180	Various	None	None	Sprinkled Sheep	0	1	6	0	0	6¼
An English Grammar for the use of Schools	By the Commissioners of National Education in Ireland.	. . . .	Printing Demy	5	178	Brevier	do.	do.	Cloth	0	0	8	0	0	4
Rudiments of English Grammar	By A. Reid, A.M.	Extensively used by the Scholars of Elementary Schools in Scotland.	L. Demy & third	2¾	46	Various	do.	do.	Cloth Limp	0	0	6	0	0	2
An attempt to simplify English Grammar	By Professor R. Sullivan.	Suitable for the Scholars of Elementary Schools.	Printing Demy	5 18mo	180	Brevier and Nonpl.	. . .	. . .	Colored Cloth, stmpd & lettrd	0	1	0	0	0	6
A System of English Grammar	By C. W. Connon	do.	Crown & third	5¼	168	Bourg. and Minion	None	None	Cloth lettered	0	2	6	0	1	2½
An English Grammar	By Allen and Cornwell.	do.	Demy 18mo.	4½	162	L. Prim. & Brev.	. . .	. . .	Cloth	0	1	9	0	1	0½
Grammar for beginners.	By Dr. Cornwell	do.	do.	2	72	do.	. . .	. . .	do.	0	1	0	0	0	7
An Initiatory Grammar of the English Language	By J. Millen.	Suitable for the Scholars of Elementary Schools.	Demy & third	2⅝	126	Bourg. and Brev.	None	None	Sprinkled Sheep	0	1	0	0	0	5¾
Principles of English Grammar	No. 8 of the Scottish School Book Association.	. . . .	do.	2½& 8pp.	128	L. Prim. etc.	. . .	. . .	Cloth sewed on Tape	0	0	9	0	0	4½
The Young Child's Grammar	do.	. . . .	Demy	1	36	Bourgeois	. . .	. . .	Printd. Wrapr.	0	0	3	0	0	1½
Outlines of Etymology	By Rev. A. Wilson	Suitable for the Scholars of Elementary Schools. Published by the Society for Promoting Christian Knowledge.	do.	⅔	24	Long Primer	. . .	. . .	Paper Wrappr.	0	0	1½	0	0	1
The Pupil's Guide to English Etymology	B. G. Manson	Suitable for the Scholars of Elementary Schools.	do.	3¾	132	Brevier	. . .	. . .	Half-bound, Printed Cover	0	1	0	0	0	6

			Size of Paper on which it is printed.	No. of Sheets in Book.	No. of Pages in Book.	Size of Type in which it is printed.	No. and size of separate Maps or Plates, if any.	No. of Woodcuts printed in same pages with type.	Description of Binding.	Price per Copy at which it is sold retail to the Public.	Price per Copy at which it is offered for use of Workhouse Schools.
Arithmetic.											
The Intellectual Calculator	By J. T. Crossley, and W. Martin.	These Authors have long been among the most useful Officers of the British and Foreign School Society, and the book is generally adopted both in British and in other Schools.	Demy	4	146	Various	1	None	Red Sheep	0 1 8	0 1 0
First Book of Arithmetic	By the Commissioners of National Education in Ireland.	. . . .	Prtng. Demy	4½	148	Brevier	None	do.	Cloth	0 0 8	0 0 4
A treatise on Arithmetic		. . . .	do.	17	408	Long Primer	do.	do.	do.	0 2 6	0 0 11
Elements of Book-keeping		. . . .	do.	5¼	126	do.	do.	do.	do.	0 0 10	0 0 5
Exercises in Arithmetic for Elementary Schools	Thomas Tate, Mathematical Master in the Battersea Training School.	Exercises to accompany the Tables, and adapted to the method of Pestalozzi.	do.	7& 4 pp.	172	Brevier	. . .	. . .	do.	0 1 6	0 1 0
Lessons on Arithmetic for Junior Classes	By James Trotter	Extensively in use in Parochial Schools in Scotland.	L. Demy & third	1	48	Various	None	None	Printed Wrapper	0 0 6	0 0 1½
Concise System of Practical Arithmetic	Melrose's, revised by A. Ingram and J. Trotter.	Extensively used in Parochial Schools and in Middle Schools in Scotland.	Demy & third	$4\frac{5}{12}$	212	do.	do.	do.	Sprinkled Sheep	0 1 6	0 0 7½
System of Practical Arithmetic	No. 11 of the Scottish School Book Association.	. . . .	do.	2¼	108	Bourgeois, etc.	. . .	. . .	Cloth sd. on Tape	0 0 9	0 0 4½
Key to do.	do.	. . . .	Demy board	. . .	1	Brevier	. . .	. . .	Not bound	0 0 2	0 0 0¾
First Lessons in Practical Arithmetic	do.	. . . .	Demy	1	36	Long Primer	. . .	. . .	Printed Wrapper	0 0 3	0 0 1½
Key to do.	do.	. . . .	Demy board	. . .	1	Bourgeois	. . .	. . .	Not bound	0 0 2	0 0 0¾
Geography.											
Geography Generalized	By Professor Sullivan	A book which should be read in all Elementary Schools in connexion with the study of the Maps.	Foolscap	81 sheets 8vo.	288	Bourg. and Brev.	1 Fcp. 4to.	27	Coloured cl. stamped and lettered.	0 2 0	0 1 3
A School Geography	By Dr. Cornwell	Written by a Master of the Normal School of the British and Foreign School Society, in the Borough Road, and extensively used in British and other Schools	Royal	9	318	Various	. . .	. . .	Cloth	0 3 6	0 2 1
Compendium of Geography	By the Commissioners of National Education in Ireland.	. . . .	Printing Demy	5½	196	Brevier	None	None	do.	0 1 0	0 0 5
An Introduction to Geography and History	By Professor Sullivan	. . . .	Demy	4 18mo.	144	Bourg. and Min.	1 Fcp. 4to.	18	Coloured cl. sd. & leterd.	0 1 0	0 0 6
Rudiments of Modern Geography	By A. Reid, A.M.	The first three very brief; for use with Maps.	L. Demy & third	2½	120	Various	in. 1in. 13 by 7¾	3	Sprinkled Sheep	0 1 0	0 0 5½
Outlines of Sacred Geography	do.	. . . .	do.	1	48	S. Pica & Bourg.	None	1	Printed Wrapper	0 0 6	0 0 1½
The Young Child's Geography	No. 9 of the Scottish Scl. Bk. Association.	. . . .	Demy	1	36	Long Primer	. . .	. . .	do.	0 0 3	0 0 1½

Outlines of Modern Geography	No. 10, do.	. . . .	Extra Dble. Foolscap	3¾	120	S. Pica and Min.	. . .	. . .	½ bd. flush paper sides	0 1 0	0 0 6
English History.											
A plain and short History of England	By the Bishop of Peterborough.	. . . .	Demy	7½	262	Long Primer	1	. . .	Half-bd. in Roan lettd.	0 2 6	0 1 6
A School History of England	J. W. Parker	. . . .	Demy 12mo.	27	648	Bourgeois	. . .	1	Blue Sheep	0 6 0	0 3 3
Mensuration.											
A Treatise on Mensuration	By the Commissioners of National Education in Ireland.	. . . .	Printing Demy	11½	276	Long Primer	None	174 Diagrams	Cloth	0 1 6	0 0 8
Vocal Music.											
Wilhelm's Method of Teaching Singing adapted to English use	By John Hullah	An excellent Manual, which has had a most extensive circulation.	Royal 8vo.	12¼	196	Pica, L. Primer, Min., and Music	. . .	. . .	do.	0 5 0	0 3 0
Set of Singing Tablets, for Elementary Schools	do.	. . . .	Demy Sheet	51 sheets pr. set on 32 bds.	. . .	Music	. . .	. . .	Mounted on Millboard, with Tapes, in a box.	1 11 6	1 2 0

SCHEDULE II.

Text Books for the Masters and Mistresses of Workhouse Schools, and for Assistant Teachers.

			Size of Paper on which it is printed.	No. of Sheets in Book.	No. of Pages in Book.	Size of Type in which it is printed.	No. and size of separate Maps or Plates, if any.	No. of Woodcuts printed in same pages with type.	Description of Binding.	Price per Copy at which it is sold retail to the Public.	Price per Copy at which it is offered for use of Workhouse Schools.
Reading and Composition.											
An Introduction to the Art of Reading	By the Commissioners of National Education in Ireland.	. . . .	Printing Demy	10½	252	Small Pica	None	None	Cloth	0 1 6	0 0 8
The Young Composer, Part I.	By Dr. Cornwell	. . . .	Royal 18mo.	3½	126	Various	. . .	. . .	do.	0 1 6	0 0 10½
The Spelling Book superseded	By Prof. R. Sullivan.	A useful book for lessons on dictation, to teach Children correct Orthography and punctuation, and thus to take the first step towards English composition.	Large Demy	6 8vo.	212	Bour. & Min.	. . .	. . .	Coloured cl. stamped and lettered	0 1 4	0 0 8
Abbott's Reader	. . . .	. . . .	Large Dbl. Pott	8¼	264	Long Primer	. . .	. . .	Cloth	0 3 0	0 1 4

			Size of Paper on which it is printed.	No. of Sheets in Book.	No. of Pages in Book.	Size of Type in which it is printed.	No. and size of separate Maps or Plates, if any.	No. of Woodcuts printed in same pages with type.	Description of Binding.	Price per Copy at which it is sold retail to the Public.	Price per Copy at which it is offered for use of Workhouse Schools.
Writing.											
Manual of Malhauser's Method	. . . .	Published under the sanction of the Committee of Council on Education.	Crown 8vo.	4½	72	LongPrimer	40 pp. Wrtg. Md ls.	58	. . Cloth . .	0 2 6	0 1 6
Writing Models, 1st Set	. . . .	. . . .	do.	40 cd. bd.		. . . .	. . .	. . .	Printed Packet .	0 2 6	0 1 6
Do. 2nd Set	. . . .	. . . .	do.	8 do.		. . . .	. . .	. . .	. . . do. . . .	0 1 0	0 0 5
Do. 3rd Set	. . . .	. . . .	do.	8 do.		. . . .	. . .	. . .	. . . do. . . .	0 1 0	0 0 5
Do. 4th Set	. . . .	. . . .	do.	8 do.		. . . .	. . .	. . .	. . . do. . . .	0 1 0	0 0 5
Grammar and Etymology.											
Manual of English Grammar	By the Rev. J. M. Mc Culloch, LL.D.	A proper Text Book for Pupil Teachers, and Manual for Schoolmasters and Schoolmistresses in superior Elementary Schools.	Dmy & third	3¾	180	Various	. . .	. . .	Sprinkled Sheep .	0 1 6	0 0 6¼
English Grammar . .	R. G. Latham, M.D.	. . . .	Demy12mo.	9¾	234	LongPrimer	. . .	. . .	Cloth, Paper Label	0 4 6	0 2 8
Rudiments of English Grammar	By A. Reid, A.M. .	. . . .	Large Demy and third	$\frac{23}{24}$	46	Various	. . .	. . .	Cloth, Limp .	0 0 6	0 0 2
Dictionary of the English Language	. . . do. . . .	. . . .	do.	17⅝	564	Minion & Nonpareil	. . .	. . .	Mock Russia, Marbled&Lettered	0 6 6	0 2 7
Ditto	By Prof. R. Sullivan.	. . . .	Large Demy	20 12mo.	480	Nonpareil	. . .	. . .	Coloured Cloth, Stamped&Lettered	0 3 6	0 1 10
Key to Exercises in the English Grammar	By the Commissioners of National Education in Ireland.	. . . .	Ptng. Demy	1	36	Brevier	None	None	Printed Wrapper	0 0 3	0 0 1
Arithmetic.											
Complete Treatise on Practical Arithmetic and Bookkeeping	(Hutton's, revised by Ingram & Trotter)	Much used in superior Parochial and Middle Class Schools in Scotland. Good	Crn. & thd.	$7\frac{13}{16}$	250	Brevier & Minion	. . .	. . .	Sprinkled Sheep	0 2 6	0 1 2½
Complete System of Practical Arithmetic	No. 14 of the Scottish School Book Association.	Practical Manuals for Schoolmasters, and good Text Books for Pupil Teachers	Extra Dble. Foolscap	5	160	Bourgeois	. . .	39	Cloth sd. on Tape	0 2 0	0 1 0
Key to do.	No. 15 do.	. . . . . .	do.	6s. 4p.	196	do. .	. . .	. . .	. . . do. . . .	0 4 0	0 1 10
Key to the First Book of Arithmetic	By the Commissioners of National Education in Ireland.	. . . . do.	Ptng. Demy	5	180	Brevier	None	None	. . Cloth . .	0 0 8	0 0 4
Key to the Elements of Book-keeping	. . . do. . . .	. . . . do.	do.	5	118	do.	do.	do.	. . . do. . . .	0 0 10	0 0 5
Treatise on Arithmetic	By Dr. J. Thomson	. . . . do.	Demy	12	288	Various	. . .	. . .	Roan Lettered .	0 3 6	0 1 4
Arithmetic, Theoretical and Practical	By W. Marr, (Chambers & Co.)	. . . . do.	Dble. Fcap	8	256	Brevier	. . .	. . .	Cloth Lettered .	0 2 0	0 1 1¾
The Principles and Practice of Arithmetic	By J. Hind . . .	Used in Public Schools in England.	Demy 12mo.	11½	276	Bourgeois	. . .	11	. . Boards . .	0 4 6	0 2 8
Husbandry.											
Agricultural Class Book	By the Commissioners of National Education in Ireland.	. . . .	Printing Demy	13½	318	Small Pica	. . .	21	. . Cloth . .	0 1 8	0 0 9

Domestic Economy.											
Useful Hints for Labourers, First Series	J. W. Parker	Useful to Schoolmasters and Pupil Teachers in the preparation of Lessons on Household Economy and Domestic Arts.	S. D. Pott 8vo.	5	152	Brevier	. . .	. . .	Cloth	0 1 6	0 0 10½
Second Series	do.		Dl. Fcp. 8vo.	5	152	do.	. . .	. . .	do.	0 1 6	0 0 10½
The Useful Arts employed in the production of food	do.		do.	6	192	do.	. . .	54	do.	0 2 6	0 1 5
Ditto on the construction of dwelling houses	do.	. . . . . .	do.	6¾	216	do.	. . .	47	do.	0 2 6	0 1 5
Ditto, clothing	do.	. . . . . .	do.	6¼	200	do.	. . .	76	do.	0 2 6	0 1 5
Instructions in Household matters	By a Lady	Useful to Schoolmistresses for Oral Lessons.	do.	4	124	LongPrimer	. . .	7	do.	0 1 6	0 0 10½
Geography.											
Complete System of Modern Geography	No. 12 of the Scottish School Book Association.	Extensively in use in Parochial and Middle Class Schools in Scotland.	Ex. D. Fcap.	10½	336	Various	1 steel engrv. 8vo.	. . .	Coloured Sheep, Titled on sides	0 3 6	0 1 9
Key to do.	No. 13, do.	. . . . . .	do.	5½	176	do.	. . .	. . .	Cloth sd. on Tape	0 2 6	0 1 3
Complete System of Modern Geography, with 9 Maps	. . . . . .	. . . . . .	do.	10½	336	do.	1 steel engrv. 8vo.	9 Mps 4to.	Coloured Sheep, Titled on sides	0 5 0	0 2 4
System of Geography	By T. Ewing	Extensively in use in Parochial and Middle Class Schools in Scotland.	Dem. & thd.	$11\frac{15}{16}$	382	do.	. . .	. . .	Mock Russia, Lettered	0 4 6	0 2 3
Compendium of Modern Geography	By the Rev. A. Stewart.	do.	do.	$6\frac{23}{24}$	334	do.	9	2	do.	0 3 6	0 1 6½
Recreations in Physical Geography	By Miss R. M. Zornlin	Two works containing useful general information, suitable for use as Text Books, from which Pupil Teachers may prepare Oral Lessons to Classes, or to two or more Classes collectively.	D. Fcp. 8vo.	13¼	424	Brevier	6	44	do.	0 6 0	0 3 2
The World of Waters	do.		do.	11¼	360	do.	. . .	35	do.	0 6 0	0 2 6
The Bible Atlas	By W. Murphy	A neat, small, but carefully prepared Atlas of Palestine, etc. A useful assistant to the reading of Pupil Teachers and Schoolmasters.	Demy	$1\frac{13}{16}$	58	do.	24	. . .	Cloth, Lettered	0 2 6	0 1 0
A New General Atlas	Of the Scottish School Book Association.	. . . . . .	Rl. Drawing	. . .	. . .	. . .	29 col outlines	. . .	Half-bound, Calf Back, Cloth sides & titled on side	0 10 6	0 6 6
Selected Atlas	do.	. . . . . .	do.	. . .	. . .	. . .	11 do.	. . .	¼ Bound, Paper Title	0 3 6	0 2 3
Epitome of Geographical Knowledge	By the Commissioners of National Education in Ireland.	. . . . . .	Printing Demy	25	600	Bourgeois	None	None	Cloth	0 3 0	0 1 3
English History.											
Historical Series—No. 1, The History of England	By the Society for Promoting Christian Knowledge.	. . . . . .	Demy	$5\frac{5}{6}$	140	LongPrimer	. . .	. . .	Cloth Boards	0 1 0	0 0 8
Goldsmith's History of England	Improved By R. Simpson.	. . . . . .	Dem. & thd.	14⅜	460	L. Prim. & Min.	. . .	. . .	Mock Russia. Lettered	0 3 6	0 1 10½
History & present state of the British empire	In W. and R. Chambers' Educational Series.	. . . . . .	Dle. Fcap.	9	288	LongPrimer	1	. . .	Cloth, Lettered	0 2 0	0 1 1¾

		Size of Paper on which it is printed.	No. of Sheets in Book.	No. of Pages in Book.	Size of Type in which it is printed.	No. and size of separate Maps or Plates, if any.	No. of Woodcuts printed in same pages with type.	Description of Binding.	Price per Copy at which it is sold retail to the Public.	Price per Copy at which it is offered for use of Workhouse Schools.
History of Scotland.										
History of Scotland	Tytler, adapted by the Rev. J. Tytler, D.D.&A. Reid, M.A.	Demy	14¾	252	Bourgeois	None	2	Purple roan	0 3 6	0 2 0
History of Scotland, 2 vols.	By Sir W. Scott	Crown 8vo.	34¾	1116	Long Primer	Ryl. 4to. colored	. .	Coloured Sheep, lettered on back	0 10 0	0 6 0
Preservation of Health.										
The House I live in	Parker	S. D. Pott 8vo.	7	224	Long Primer	. .	25	Cloth	0 2 6	0 1 2
On the Preservation of Health	By T. Hodgkin, M.D.	Royal 16mo.	31 half sheets	408	do.	. .	. .	Cloth	0 6 0	0 3 4
Principles of Teaching.										
Principles of Teaching, or the Normal School Manual	By Henry Dunn, Secretary of the British and Foreign School Society.	Royal	7⅔	276	do.	One	None	In Extra Boards	0 3 6	0 2 1
Account of the Sessional School	By John Wood.	Demy & third	10¼	328	S. Pica & Brev.	. .	. .	Full Cloth	0 5 0	0 2 10
Educational tour in Germany, France, Holland, and parts of Great Britain and Ireland	By Horace Mann.	Royal 16mo.	2½ Doubl Royal 12mo. equal to 17½ sheets 12mo.	240	do.	. .	. .	Cloth Boards	0 3 0	0 1 8½
Suggestive hints towards improving secular instruction, and making it bear upon practical life	By Rev. Richard Dawes.	Royal	5½	190	L. Prim. & Brev.	None	. .	Cloth	0 2 0	0 1 2
Hints on an improved and self-paying system of National Education, suggested from the working of a Village School in Hampshire	do.	do.	1⅔	60	do.	do.	. .	Sewed in Wrapper	0 0 8	0 0 4½
The Training System.	By David Stow.	Foolscap 8vo.	17⅛	548	L. Prim. & Brev.	3	12 pp.	Cloth	0 6 0	0 3 6
Mensuration.										
Appendix to the Mensuration (the Treatise is in schedule I.)	By the Commissioners of National Education in Ireland.	Printing Demy	5¼	124	Long Primer	None	58	do.	0 1 0	0 0 5

NAME OF MAP.	Name of Publisher or Society by whom issued.	Size of Map.	Description of Mounting.	Price per Map at which it is sold Retail to the Public.	Price per Map at which offered for the use of Workhouse Schools.
		ft. in. ft. in.		£ s. d.	£ s. d.
Map of the World . . .	Society for Promoting Christian Knowledge.	6 6 by 3 4	On canvas and roller .	0 12 0	0 8 6
England	. . do. . .	. do. .	Do.	0 6 0	0 3 6
Scotland	. . do. . .	. do. .	Do.	0 6 0	0 3 6
Ireland	. . do. . .	. do. .	Do.	0 6 0	0 3 6
British Isles	. . do. . .	. do. .	Do.	0 2 8	0 1 9
Palestine	. . do. . .	3 7 by 5 2	Do.	0 2 8	0 1 9
Countries mentioned in Old Test.	. . do. . .	. do. .	On canvas & roller, varn.	0 8 0	0 5 0
Countries mentioned in New Test.	. . do. . .	. do. .	Do.	0 8 0	0 5 0
Europe	. . do. . .	5 3 by 4 4	Do.	0 12 0	0 8 6
Asia	. . do. . .	. do. .	Do.	0 12 0	0 8 6
Africa	. . do. . .	. do. .	Do.	0 12 0	0 8 6
North America	. . do. . .	. do. .	Do.	0 8 0	0 5 6
South America	. . do. . .	. do. .	Do.	0 8 0	0 5 6
World	Smith and Sons, for the Irish Education Board.	6 8 by 3 6	On canvas and roller .	1 1 0	0 10 6
England.		4 4 by 5 8	Do.	0 16 0	0 8 0
Scotland	. . do. . .	. do. .	Do.	0 16 0	0 8 0
Ireland	. . do. . .	. do. .	Do.	0 16 0	0 8 0
British Isles	. . do. . .	7 0 by 8 0	Do.	1 10 0	0 15 0
Palestine	. . do. . .	4 4 by 5 8	Do.	0 16 0	0 8 0
Scripture World	. . do. . .	5 8 by 4 4	Do.	0 16 0	0 8 0
Europe	. . do. . .	. do. .	Do.	0 16 0	0 8 0
Asia	. . do. . .	. do. .	Do.	0 16 0	0 8 0
Africa	. . do. . .	4 4 by 5 8	Do.	0 16 0	0 8 0
America	. . do. . .	. do. .	Do.	0 16 0	0 8 0
World	Messrs. Chambers .	5 8 by 4 10	Cloth and rollers . .	1 1 0	0 12 0
England	. . do. . .	. do. .	Do.	0 14 0	0 8 0
Scotland	. . do. . .	. do. .	Do.	0 14 0	0 8 0
Ireland	. . do. . .	. do. .	Do.	0 14 0	0 8 0
Palestine	. . do. . .	. do. .	Do.	0 14 0	0 8 0
Europe	. . do. . .	. do. .	Do.	0 14 0	0 8 0
Asia	. . do. . .	. do. .	Do.	0 14 0	0 8 0
Africa	. . do. . .	. do. .	Do.	0 14 0	0 8 0
North America	. . do. . .	. do. .	Do.	0 14 0	0 8 0
South America	. . do. . .	. do. .	Do.	0 14 0	0 8 0
Chart of the World . . .	Scottish School Book Association .	5 2 by 4 6	Mounted on roller . .	1 0 0	0 12 6
Map of Central & Southn. Europe		. do. .	Do.	1 0 0	0 12 6
General Map of Europe . .	. . do. . .	3 0 by 2 5	Do.	0 7 6	0 4 3
Scotland	. . do. . .	. do. .	Do.	0 6 6	0 4 3
England	. . do. . .	. do. .	Do.	0 6 6	0 4 3
Ireland	. . do. . .	. do. .	Do.	0 6 6	0 4 3
Palestine	. . do. . .	. do. .	Do.	0 6 6	0 4 3
Hindostan	. . do. . .	. do. .	Do.	0 6 6	0 4 3
United States	. . do. . .	. do. .	Do.	0 6 6	0 4 3
Asia	. . do. . .	. do. .	Do.	0 6 6	0 4 3
Africa	. . do. . .	. do. .	Do.	0 6 6	0 4 3
North America	. . do. . .	. do. .	Do.	0 6 6	0 4 3
South America	. . do. . .	. do. .	Do.	0 6 6	0 4 3
Eastern Hemisphere . . .	Messrs. W. and A. K. Johnston .	4 2 by 3 6	Coloured, and mounted on cloth and rollers . .	0 10 0	0 5 6
Do. do.	. . do. . .	. do. .	Coloured, on cloth and rollers, and varnished. .	0 12 0	0 6 0
Western do.	. . do. . .	. do. .	Coloured, and mounted on cloth and rollers . .	0 10 0	0 5 6
Do. do.	. . do. . .	. do. .	Coloured, on cloth and rollers, and varnished .	0 12 0	0 6 0
Europe	. . do. . .	. do. .	Do. do. . . .	0 10 0	0 5 6
Do.	. . do. . .	. do. .	Do. do. varnished	0 12 0	0 6 0
Asia	. . do. . .	. do. .	Do. do. . . .	0 10 0	0 5 6
Do.	. . do. . .	. do. .	Do. do. varnished	0 12 0	0 6 0
Africa	. . do. . .	. do. .	Do. do. . . .	0 10 0	0 5 6
Do.	. . do. . .	. do. .	Do. do. varnished	0 12 0	0 6 0
America	. . do. . .	. do. .	Do. do. . . .	0 10 0	0 5 6
Do.	. . do. . .	. do. .	Do. do. varnished	0 12 0	0 6 0
England	. . do. . .	. do. .	Do. do. . . .	0 10 0	0 5 6
Do.	. . do. . .	. do. .	Do. do. varnished	0 12 0	0 6 0
Scotland	. . do. . .	. do. .	Do. do. . . .	0 10 0	0 5 6
Do.	. . do. . .	. do. .	Do. do. varnished	0 12 0	0 6 0

NAME OF MAP.	Name of Publisher or Society by whom issued.	Size of Map. ft. in. ft. in.	Description of Mounting.	Price per Map at which it is sold Retail to the Public.	Price per Map at which offered for the use of Workhouse Schools.
Ireland	Messrs. W. & A. K. Johnston . .	4 2 by 3 6	Coloured, and mounted on cloth and rollers	0 10 0	0 5 6
Do.	. . do. . . .	. do. .	Do. do. varnished	0 12 0	0 6 0
Palestine	. . do. . . .	. do. .	Do. do. . . .	0 10 0	0 5 6
Do.	. . do. . . .	. do. .	Do. do. varnished	0 12 0	0 6 0
The above 10 Maps in Wood Case, £3. 10s.					
SCHOOL AND FAMILY MAPS.					
Eastern Hemisphere . . .	. . do. . .	0 33 by 0 27	Coloured, and mounted on cloth and rollers . .	0 6 0	0 3 8
Do. do. . . .	. . do. . .	. do. .	Coloured, on cloth and rollers, varnished	0 7 0	0 4 0
Western do. . . .	. . do. . .	. do. .	Do. do. . . .	0 6 0	0 3 8
Do. do. . . .	. . do. . .	. do. .	Do. do. varnished	0 7 0	0 4 0
Europe	. . do. . .	. do. .	Do. do. . .	0 6 0	0 3 8
Do.	. . do. . .	. do. .	Do. do. varnished	0 7 0	0 4 0
Asia	. . do. . .	. do. .	Do. do. . . .	0 6 0	0 3 8
Do.	. . do. . .	. do. .	Do. do. varnished	0 7 0	0 4 0
Africa	. . do. . .	. do. .	Do. do. . . .	0 6 0	0 3 8
Do.	. . do. . .	. do. .	Do. do. varnished	0 7 0	0 4 0
America	. . do. . .	. do. .	Do. do. . . .	0 6 0	0 3 8
Do.	. . do. . .	. do. .	Do. do. varnished	0 7 0	0 4 0
England	. . do. . .	. do. .	Do. do. . . .	0 6 0	0 3 8
Do.	. . do. . .	. do. .	Do. do. varnished	0 7 0	0 4 0
Scotland	. . do. . .	. do. .	Coloured, and mounted on cloth and rollers . .	0 6 0	0 3 8
Do.	. . do. . .	. do. .	Coloured, on cloth and rollers, varnished . .	0 7 0	0 4 0
Ireland	. . do. . .	. do. .	Do. do. . .	0 6 0	0 3 8
Do.	. . do. . .	. do. .	Do. do. varnished	0 7 0	0 4 0
Palestine	. . do. . .	. do. .	Do. do. . . .	0 6 0	0 3 8
Do.	. . do. . .	. do. .	Do. do. varnished	0 7 0	0 4 0
Single Maps	. . do. . .	. do. .	In Sheets, coloured . .	0 4 0	0 2 6
Illustrations of Natural Philosophy	. . do. . .	4 2 by 3 6	Coloured, and mounted on cloth and rollers . .	0 10 0	0 5 6
Do. do. .	. . do. . .	. do. .	Coloured, on cloth & rollers, varnished	0 12 0	0 6 0
Map, illustrative of Geographical Terms, with Glossary . .	. . do. . .	0 33 by 0 27	Coloured, and mounted on cloth and rollers	0 6 0	0 3 8
Do. do. do.	. . do. . .	. do. .	Coloured on cloth and rollers, varnished	0 7 0	0 4 0
Do. do. do. .	. . do. . .	. do. .	Do in sheets . .	0 4 0	0 2 6
Map of the World (Mercator's) .	Mr. Varty . .	2 8 by 4 2	Do. and mounted on cloth and roller . .	0 12 0	0 7 6
Do. Globular .	. . do. . .	. do. .	Do.	0 10 0	0 6 4
England	. . do. . .	2 8 by 2 2	Do.	0 6 0	0 3 9
British Isles	. . do. . .	4 3 by 3 4	Do.	0 14 0	0 8 9
Scotland	. . do. . .	2 8 by 2 2	Do.	0 6 0	0 3 9
Ireland	. . do. . .	. do. .	Do.	0 6 0	0 3 9
Europe	. . do. . .	. do. .	Do.	0 6 0	0 3 9
Asia	. . do. . .	. do. .	Do.	0 6 0	0 3 9
Africa	. . do. . .	. do. .	Do.	0 6 0	0 3 9
America	. . do. . .	. do. .	Do.	0 6 0	0 3 9
Australia and New Zealand .	. . do. . .	. do. .	Do.	0 6 0	0 3 9
Palestine (Palmer's), with Jewish and Roman Divisions . .	. . do. . .	3 3 by 2 2	Do.	0 12 0	0 7 6
Do. Old Testament .	. . do. . .	2 8 by 2 2	Do.	0 6 0	0 3 9
Do. do. . .	. . do. . .	2 2 by 1 8	Do.	0 4 0	0 2 6
Do. New Testament .	. . do. . .	2 8 by 2 2	Do.	0 6 0	0 3 9
Do. do. . .	. . do. . .	2 2 by 1 8	Do.	0 4 0	0 2 6
Do. prior to the Conquest by the Israelites .	. . do. . .	2 8 by 2 2	Do.	0 6 0	0 3 9
Do. after the Conquest .	. . do. . .	. do. .	Do.	0 6 0	0 3 9
Plan of Jerusalem . . .	. . do. . .	. do. .	Do.	0 6 0	0 3 9
Map of the Journeyings of the Children of Israel . . .	. . do. . .	. do. .	Do.	0 6 0	0 3 9
Voyages and Travels of the Apostle Paul	. . do. . .	. do. .	Do.	0 6 0	0 3 9

Workhouse Schools.—Application for supply of books, etc.

__________________________________ *Union.*

__________________________________ *Workhouse.*

____________________________ 184

MY LORDS AND GENTLEMEN,

The board of guardians direct me to request that you will authorize Mr. Charles Knight to supply, for the use of the workhouse school of this union, the books and maps specified in the following schedule, and they hereby authorize me to declare that such books and maps shall be devoted solely to the use of the said school, and that the name of the union shall be written or stamped in each book, as soon as it is received.

The average number of children in the school during the last half-year was { Boys __________ Girls __________

The number of assistant teachers, if any, at present employed in the school is ______________

I have the honour to be,

MY LORDS AND GENTLEMEN,

Your obedient Servant,

The Poor Law Board. *Clerk to the Guardians.*

BOOKS.

Number required.	TITLE OF BOOK.	Name of Publisher or Society by whom issued.	Price per Copy to Workhouse Schools.*			Price per Dozen Copies to Workhouse Schools.			Total.
	Reading Lesson Series.		£	s.	d.	£	s.	d.	£ s. d.
	The First Book	S. P. C. K.	.	.	1¼	.	1	3	
	The Second do.	,,	.	.	5¼	.	5	3	
	The Third do.	,,	.	.	10	.	10	0	
	No. 1. Reading Series	,,	.	.	2	.	2	0	
	No. 2, do.	,,	.	.	1¼	.	1	3	
	No. 1, Daily Lesson Book	B. & F. S. S.	.	.	1¾	.	1	9	
	No. 2, do.	,,	.	.	7½	.	7	6	
	No. 3, do.	,,	.	.	11	.	11	0	
	No. 4, do.	,,	.	1	6	.	18	0	
	Sequel to do. No. 1	,,	.	1	9½	1	1	6	
	Sequel to do. No. 2	,,	.	.	5	.	5	0	
	The First Book	Irish Board.	.	.	1	.	1	0	
	The Second do.	,,	.	.	4	.	4	0	
	The Third do.	,,	.	.	8	.	8	0	
	The Fourth do.	,,	.	.	9	.	9	0	
	The Fifth do.	,,	.	.	11	.	11	0	
	Sequel to the Second Book	,,	.	.	5	.	5	0	
	Supplement to the Fourth Book	,,	.	.	11	.	11	0	
	Reading Book for the use of Female Schools	,,	.	.	10	.	10	0	
	First Reading Book . . (M'Culloch)	Oliver and Boyd.	.	.	0¾	.	.	9	
	Second do. . . do.	,,	.	.	1¼	.	1	3	
	Third do. . . do.	,,	.	.	5¼	.	5	3	
	Series of Lessons in Prose and Verse, do.	,,	.	.	11¼	.	11	3	
	Course of Elementary Reading do.	,,	.	1	5¾	.	17	9	
	Rural Spelling Book . . (Johnson)	Ridgway.	.	.	8	.	8	0	
	The Child's First Book	S. S. B. A.	.	.	0½	.	.	6	
			Amount carried forward . .						

* The prices charged being upon an average 43¾ per cent. below the retail price, arising out of special arrangements made by the Poor Law Board with the publishers of the same, Mr. Knight is authorized to add to these prices a commission of ten per cent. to cover all expenses of packing, porterage, etc., and to enable him to include these books in his quarterly accounts with the unions.

Number required.	TITLE OF BOOK.	Name of Publisher or Society by whom issued.	Price per Copy to Workhouse Schools.			Price per Dozen Copies to Workhouse Schools.			Total.
			Amount brought forward . .						
	Reading Lesson Series continued.		£	s.	d.	£	s.	d.	
	No. 1, Primer	S. S. B. A.	.	.	0¾	.	.	9	
	No. 2, Second Lessons	,,	.	.	1½	.	1	6	
	No. 3, Third do.	,,	.	.	3	.	3	0	
	Sequel to Third Lessons	,,	.	.	2	.	2	0	
	Sheet Lessons (per set, 15 sheets in set)	,,	.	1	5	.	17	0	
	No. 4, Readings in Prose and Verse	,,	.	.	5	.	5	0	
	No. 5, First Collection of Instructive Extracts	,,	.	.	9	.	9	0	
	No. 6, Second do. do.	,,	.	1	0½	.	12	6	
	Reprint of Vocabularies, from Nos. 5 and 6	,,	.	.	3	.	3	0	
	The Juvenile Reader . . (Leitch)	Leitch.	.	.	9	.	9	0	
	Reading Disentangled, being a series of elementary Reading Lessons on sheets	Varty.	.	4	0	2	8	0	
	Do. in Varty's Registered Serial Tablet Frame	,,	.	7	0	4	4	0	
	Do. mounted on Millboards	,,	.	7	6	4	10	0	
	An Introduction to the Art of Reading (Irish Board)	Irish Board.	.	.	8	.	8	0	
	Reading and Composition.								
	The Young Composer, part I. (Cornwell)	Cornwell.	.	.	10½	.	10	6	
	Abbott's Reader	Parker.	.	1	4	.	16	0	
	The Spelling Book Superseded (Sullivan)	Sullivan.	.	.	8	.	8	0	
	Grammar and Etymology.								
	Grammar for Beginners . (Cornwell)	Cornwell.	.	.	7	.	7	0	
	Manual of English Grammar (M'Culloch)	Oliver and Boyd.	.	.	6¼	.	6	3	
	English Grammar . . (Latham)	Taylor and Walton.	.	2	8	1	12	0	
	do (Allen and Cornwell)	Cornwell.	.	1	0½	.	12	6	
	Rudiments of English Grammar . (Reid)	Oliver and Boyd.	.	.	2	.	2	0	
	An English Grammar . (Irish Board)	Irish Board.	.	.	4	.	4	0	
	Key to Exercises in the English Grammar, do	,,	.	.	1	.	1	0	
	An Attempt to Simplify English Grammar (Sullivan)	Sullivan.	.	.	6	.	6	0	
	A System of English Grammar (Connon)	Oliver and Boyd.	.	1	2½	.	14	6	
	An Initiatory Grammar of the English Language . . . . (Millen)	,,	.	.	5¾	.	5	9	
	Principles of English Grammar (No. 8)	S. S. B. A.	.	.	4½	.	4	6	
	The Young Child's Grammar	,,	.	.	1½	.	1	6	
	Outlines of Etymology	S. P. C. K.	.	.	1	.	1	0	
	The Pupil's Guide to English Etymology (Manson)	M'Phail.	.	.	6	.	6	0	
	Dictionary of the English Language (Reid)	Oliver and Boyd.	.	2	7	1	11	0	
	Do. do.	Sullivan.	.	1	10	1	2	0	
	Writing.								
	Manual of Mulhauser's Method	Parker.	.	1	6	.	18	0	
	Writing Models, First Set	,,	.	1	6	.	18	0	
	Do. Second Set	,,	.	.	5	.	5	0	
	Do. Third Set	,,	.	.	5	.	5	0	
	Do. Fourth Set	,,	.	.	5	.	5	0	
	Arithmetic.								
	The Intellectual Calculator (Crossley and Martin)	B. and F. S. S.	.	1	0	.	12	0	
	First Book of Arithmetic (Irish Board)	Irish Board.	.	.	4	.	4	0	
	A Treatise on Arithmetic do.	,,	.	.	11	.	11	0	
	Elements of Book-keeping . (Colenso)	,,	.	.	5	.	5	0	
	Exercises in Arithmetic for Elementary Schools . . . . . . (Tate)	Parker.	.	1	0	.	12	0	
	Lessons on Arithmetic for Junior Classes (Trotter)	Oliver and Boyd.	.	.	1½	.	1	6	
	Concise System of Practical Arithmetic. (Melrose, revised by Ingram & Trotter)	,,	.	.	7¼	.	7	3	
	System of Practical Arithmetic	S. S. B. A.	.	.	4½	.	4	6	
	Key to do.	,,	.	.	0¾	.	.	9	
	First Lessons in Practical Arithmetic	,,	.	.	1½	.	1	6	
			Amount carried forward . .						

Number required.	TITLE OF BOOK.	Name of Publisher or Society by whom issued.	Price per Copy to Workhouse Schools. £	s.	d.	Price per Dozen Copies to Workhouse Schools. £	s.	d.	Total.
	Arithmetic continued.		Amount brought forward . .						
	Key to First Lessons in Practical Arithmetic	S. S. B. A.	.	.	$0\frac{3}{4}$	.	.	9	
	Complete Treatise on Practical Arithmetic and Book-keeping. (Hutton, revised by Ingram and Trotter)	Oliver and Boyd	.	1	$2\frac{1}{2}$	.	14	6	
	Complete System of Practical Arithmetic	S. S. B. A.	.	1	0	.	12	0	
	Key to do. . . . . . (No. 15)	. „ .	.	1	10	1	2	0	
	Key to the First Book of Arithmetic .	Irish Board.	.	.	4	.	4	0	
	Key to the Elements of Book-keeping .	. „ .	.	.	5	.	5	0	
	Treatise on Arithmetic . (Thompson)	Simms and M'Intyre	.	1	4	.	16	0	
	Arithmetic, Theoretical and Practical (Chambers)	Chambers.	.	1	$1\frac{3}{4}$	.	13	9	
	The Principles and Practice of Arithmetic (Hind)	Deighton.	.	2	8	1	12	0	
	Geography.								
	Geography Generalized . (Sullivan)	Sullivan.	.	1	3	.	15	0	
	A School Geography . . (Cornwell)	Cornwell.	.	2	1	1	5	0	
	Compendium of Geography . . .	Irish Board.	.	.	5	.	5	0	
	Rudiments of Modern Geography (Reid)	Oliver and Boyd.	.	.	$5\frac{1}{4}$	.	5	3	
	Outlines of Sacred Geography . do.	. „ .	.	.	$1\frac{1}{2}$	.	1	6	
	The Young Child's Geography (No. 9)	S. S. B. A.	.	.	$1\frac{1}{2}$	.	1	6	
	Outlines of Modern Geography (No. 10)	. „ .	.	.	6	.	6	0	
	Complete System of Modern Geography (12)	. „ .	.	1	9	1	1	0	
	Do. with 9 Maps	. „ .	.	2	4	1	8	0	
	Key to do. . . . . . . (No. 13)	. „ .	.	1	3	.	15	0	
	New General Atlas	. „ .	.	6	6	3	18	0	
	Selected Atlas	. „ .	.	2	3	1	7	0	
	System of Geography . . (Ewing)	Oliver and Boyd.	.	2	3	1	7	0	
	Compendium of Mdn. Geography (Stewart)	. „ .	.	1	$6\frac{1}{2}$	.	18	6	
	Recreations in Physical Geography (Zornlin)	Parker.	.	3	2	1	18	0	
	The World of Waters . . do.	. „ .	.	2	6	1	10	0	
	The Bible Atlas . . (Murphy)	Oliver and Boyd.	.	1	0	.	12	0	
	Epitome of Geographical Knowledge (Irish Board)	Irish Board.	.	1	3	.	15	0	
	An Introduction to Geography and History . . . . . (Sullivan)	Sullivan.	.	.	6	.	6	0	
	English History.								
	A plain and short History of England (Bishop of Peterboro'.)	Rivington.	.	1	6	.	18	0	
	A School History of England (S. P. C. K.)	Parker.	.	3	3	1	19	0	
	No. 1, History of England . .	S. P. C. K.	.	.	8	.	8	0	
	Goldsmith's History of England (Simpson)	Oliver and Boyd.	.	1	$10\frac{1}{2}$	1	2	6	
	History and Present State of the British Empire	Chambers.	.	1	$1\frac{3}{4}$	.	13	9	
	History of Scotland.								
	History of Scotland, 2 vols. . (Scott)	Cadell.	.	6	0	3	12	0	
	History of Scotland . . (Tytler)	Black.	.	2	0	1	4	0	
	Husbandry.								
	Agricultural Class Book	Irish Board.	.	.	9	.	9	0	
	Domestic Economy.								
	Useful Hints to Labourers First Series .	Parker.	.	.	$10\frac{1}{2}$	.	10	6	
	Do. Second Series	. „ .	.	.	$10\frac{1}{2}$	.	10	6	
	The useful Arts employed in the production of Food	. „ .	.	1	5	.	17	0	
	Do. on the construction of Dwelling Houses	. „ .	.	1	5	.	17	0	
	Do. do Clothing . .	. „ .	.	1	5	.	17	0	
	Instructions in Household Matters (A Lady)	. „ .	.	.	$10\frac{1}{2}$	.	10	6	
	Mensuration.								
	A Treatise on Mensuration . . .	Irish Board.	.	.	8	.	8	0	
	Appendix to the Mensuration . . .	. „ .	.	.	5	.	5	0	
			Amount carried forward . .						

Number required.	TITLE OF BOOK.	Name of Publisher or Society by whom issued.	Price per Copy to Workhouse Schools.	Price per Dozen Copies to Workhouse Schools.	Total.
			Amount brought forward . .		
	Preservation of Health.		£ s. d.	£ s. d.	
____	The House I Live in . . (Girtin)	Parker.	. 1 2	. 14 0	____
____	On the Preservation of Health (Hodgkins)	Simpkin & Marshall	. 3 4	2 0 0	____
	Principles of Teaching.				
____	Principles of Teaching, or the Normal School Manual . . . (Dunn)	B. and F. S. S.	. 2 1	1 5 0	____
____	Account of Sessional School . (Wood)	Oliver and Boyd.	. 2 10	1 14 0	____
____	Educational Tour . . . (Mann)	Simpkin & Marshall	. 1 8½	1 0 6	____
____	Suggestive Hints towards improving Secular Instruction . (Rev. R. Dawes)	Groombridge.	. 1 2	. 14 0	____
____	Hints on an improved and self-paying system of National Education . do.	„	. . 4½	. 4 6	____
____	The Training System . . (Stow)	Blackie.	. 3 6	2 2 0	____
	Vocal Music.				
____	Wilhem's Method of Teaching Singing (Hullah)	Parker.	. 3 0	1 16 0	____
____	Box of Singing Tables for Elementary Schools . . . . (Hullah)	The Government.	1 2 0	13 4 0	____

MAPS.

Number required.	TITLE OF MAP.	Name of Publisher.	Size of Map.	Description.	Price per Map to Workhouse Schools.	Total.
			Ft. In. Ft. In.			
____	Map of the World	S. P. C. K.	6 : 6 × 3 : 4	On Canvas & Roller	0 8 6	____
____	„ England	„	„ „	„	0 3 6	____
____	„ Scotland	„	„ „	„	0 3 6	____
____	„ Ireland	„	„ „	„	0 3 6	____
____	„ British Isles . . .	„	„ „	„	0 1 9	____
____	„ Palestine	„	3 : 7 × 2 : 5	„	0 1 9	____
____	„ Countries mentioned in the Old Testament	„	„ „	„ Varnished	0 5 0	____
____	„ „ „ New Testament.	„	„ „	„	0 5 0	____
____	„ Europe	„	5 : 3 × 4 : 4	„	0 8 6	____
____	„ Asia	„	„ „	„	0 8 6	____
____	„ Africa	„	„ „	„	0 8 6	____
____	„ North America . . .	„	„ „	„	0 5 6	____
____	„ South America . . .	„	„ „	„	0 5 6	____
____	„ World	Smith & Sons for Irish Commissioners . .	6 : 8 × 3 : 6	On Canvas & Roller	0 10 6	____
____	„ England	„	4 : 4 × 5 : 8	„	0 8 0	____
____	„ Scotland	„	„ „	„	0 8 0	____
____	„ Ireland	„	„ „	„	0 8 0	____
____	„ British Isles . . .	„	7 : 0 × 8 : 0	„	0 15 0	____
____	„ Palestine	„	4 : 4 × 5 : 8	„	0 8 0	____
____	„ Scripture World . .	„	5 : 8 × 4 : 4	„	0 8 0	____
____	„ Europe	„	„ „	„	0 8 0	____
____	„ Asia	„	„ „	„	0 8 0	____
____	„ Africa	„	4 : 4 × 5 : 8	„	0 8 0	____
____	„ America	„	„ „	„	0 8 0	____
____	„ World	Messrs. Chambers	5 : 8 × 4 : 10	Cloth and Roller	0 12 0	____
____	„ England	„	„ „	„	0 8 0	____
____	„ Scotland	„	„ „	„	0 8 0	____
____	„ Ireland	„	„ „	„	0 8 0	____
____	„ Palestine	„	„ „	„	0 8 0	____
____	„ Europe	„	„ „	„	0 8 0	____
____	„ Asia	„	„ „	„	0 8 0	____
				Amount carried forward .		____

Number required.	TITLE OF MAP.	Name of Publisher.	Size of Map.	Description.	Price per Map to Workhouse Schools.	Total.
			Ft. In. Ft. In.	Amount brought forward .		
	,, Africa	Messrs. Chambers	5 : 8 × 4 : 10	Cloth and Roller.	0 8 0	
	,, North America . . .	,,	,, ,,	,,	0 8 0	
	,, South America . . .	,,	,, ,,	,,	0 8 0	
	Chart of the World . . .	Messrs. White S. S. B. Assn.	5 : 2 × 4 : 6	Mounted on Roller	0 12 6	
	Map of Central and Southern Europe	,,	,, ,,	,,	0 12 6	
	General Map of Europe . .	,,	3 : 0 × 2 : 5	,,	0 4 3	
	Map of Scotland	,,	,, ,,	,,	0 4 3	
	,, England	,,	,, ,,	,,	0 4 3	
	,, Ireland	,,	,, ,,	,,	0 4 3	
	,, Palestine	,,	,, ,,	,,	0 4 3	
	,, Hindostan	,,	,, ,,	,,	0 4 3	
	,, United States . . ,	,,	,, ,,	,,	0 4 3	
	,, Asia	,,	,, ,,	,,	0 4 3	
	,, Africa	,,	,, ,,	,,	0 4 3	
	,, North America . . .	,,	,, ,,	,,	0 4 3	
	,, South America . . .	,,	,, ,,	,,	0 4 3	
	Eastern Hemisphere . . .	Messrs. W. & A. K. Johnston .	4 : 2 × 3 : 6	Coloured, and Mounted on Cloth & Roller	0 5 6	
	Do. do. . . .	,,	,, ,,	Coloured, on Cloth & Roller & Varnished	0 6 0	
	Western do. . . .	,,	,, ,,	Coloured, and Mounted on Cloth & Roller	0 5 6	
	Do. do. . . .	,,	,, ,,	Coloured, on Cloth & Roller and Varnished	0 6 0	
	Europe	,,	,, ,,	Coloured, and Mounted on Cloth & Roller	0 5 6	
	Do.	,,	,, ,,	Coloured, on Cloth & Roller Varnished	0 6 0	
	Asia	,,	,, ,,	,, . .	0 5 6	
	Do.	,,	,, ,,	. Varnished	0 6 0	
	Africa	,,	,, ,,	,, , .	0 5 6	
	Do.	,,	,, ,,	. Varnished	0 6 0	
	America	,,	,, ,,	,, . .	0 5 6	
	Do.	,,	,, ,,	. Varnished	0 6 0	
	England	,,	,, ,,	,, . .	0 5 6	
	Do.	,,	,, ,,	. Varnished	0 6 0	
	Scotland	,,	,, ,,	,, . .	0 5 6	
	Do.	,,	,, ,,	. Varnished	0 6 0	
	Ireland	,,	,, ,,	,, . .	0 5 6	
	Do.	,,	,, ,,	. Varnished	0 6 0	
	Palestine	,,	,, ,,	,, . .	0 5 6	
	Do.	,,	,, ,,	. Varnished	0 6 0	
	(The above 10 Maps in Wood Case)	,,	,, ,,	. . .	3 10 0	
	School and Family Maps.					
	Eastern Hemisphere . . .	,,	0 : 33 ×0 : 27	,, . .	0 3 8	
	Do. Do.	,,	,, ,,	. Varnished	0 4 0	
	Western do.	,,	,, ,,	,, . .	0 3 8	
	Do. do.	,,	,, ,,	. Varnished	0 4 0	
	Europe	,,	,, ,,	,, . .	0 3 8	
	Do.	,,	,, ,,	. Varnished	0 4 0	
	Asia	,,	,, ,,	,, . .	0 3 8	
	Do.	,,	,, ,,	. Varnished	0 4 0	
	Africa	,,	,, ,,	,, . .	0 3 8	
	Do.	,,	,, ,,	. Varnished	0 4 0	
	America	,,	,, ,,	,, . .	0 3 8	
	Do.	,,	,, ,,	. Varnished	0 4 0	
	England	,,	,, ,,	,, . .	0 3 8	
	Do.	,,	,, ,,	. Varnished	0 4 0	
				Amount carried forward		

Number required.	TITLE OF MAP.	Name of Publisher.	Size of Map.	Description.	Price per Map to Workhouse Schools.	Total.
			Ft. In. Ft. In.	Amount brought forward .		
	Scotland	Messrs. W. & A.K. Johnston .	0 : 33 × 0 : 27	Coloured, on Cloth & Roller	0 3 8	
	Do.	. " .	" "	. Varnished	0 4 0	
	Ireland	. " .	" "	" . .	0 3 8	
	Do.	. " .	" "	. Varnished	0 4 0	
	Palestine	. " .	" "	" . .	0 3 8	
	Do.	. " .	" "	. Varnished	0 4 0	
	Single Maps	. " .	" "	In Sheets Coloured	0 2 6	
	Illustrations of Natural Philosophy	. " .	4 : 2 × 3 : 6	Coloured, and Mounted on Cloth & Roller	0 5 6	
	Do. do. do. .	. " .	" "	Coloured, on Cloth & Roller Varnished	0 6 0	
	Map Illustrative of Geographical Terms, with Glossary .	. " .	0 : 33 × 0 : 27	Coloured, and Mounted on Cloth & Roller	0 3 8	
	Do. do. do. .	. " .	" "	Coloured, on Cloth & Roller Varnished	0 4 0	
	Do. do. do. .	. " .	" "	Coloured in Sheet	0 2 6	
	Map of the World (Mercator's) .	Varty	2 : 8 × 4 : 2	On Canvas & Roller	0 7 6	
	" " Globular . .	. " .	" "	. " .	0 6 4	
	" England	. " .	2 : 8 × 2 : 2	. " .	0 3 9	
	" British Isles . . .	. " .	4 : 3 × 3 : 4	. " .	0 8 9	
	" Scotland	. " .	2 : 8 × 2 : 2	. " .	0 3 9	
	" Ireland	. " .	" "	. " .	0 3 9	
	" Europe	. " .	" "	. " .	0 3 9	
	" Asia	. " .	" "	. " .	0 3 9	
	" Africa	. " .	" "	. " .	0 3 9	
	" America	. " .	" "	. " .	0 3 9	
	" Australia and New Zealand	. " .	" "	. " .	0 3 9	
	" Palestine (Palmer's) . .	. " .	3 : 3 × 2 : 2	. " .	0 7 6	
	" " Old Testament .	. " .	2 : 8 × 2 : 2	. " .	0 3 9	
	" " do. do. . .	. " .	2 : 2 × 1 : 8	. " .	0 2 6	
	" " New Testament .	. " .	2 : 8 × 2 : 2	. " .	0 3 9	
	" " do. do. . .	. " .	2 : 2 × 1 : 8	. " .	0 2 6	
	" " prior to Conquest by the Israelites .	. " .	2 : 8 × 2 : 2	. " .	0 3 9	
	" " after the Conquest by the Israelites .	. " .	" "	. " .	0 3 9	
	Plan of Jerusalem	. " .	" "	. " .	0 3 9	
	Map of the Journeyings of the Children of Israel . .	. " .	" "	. " .	0 3 9	
	Map of the Voyages and Travels of the Apostle Paul . .	. " .	" "	. " .	0 3 9	
				TOTAL . .		

London: Printed by Order of the Poor Law Board, by BLACKBURN & BURT, 90½, Holborn Hill, and Published by CHARLES KNIGHT, 90, Fleet Street.

AN

OFFICIAL CIRCULAR

OF PUBLIC DOCUMENTS AND INFORMATION:

DIRECTED BY THE POOR LAW BOARD TO BE PRINTED, CHIEFLY FOR THE USE OF THE BOARDS OF GUARDIANS AND THEIR OFFICERS.

No. 23.] MARCH, 1849. [N.S.

CONTENTS.

THE Board took into consideration the judgment of the Court of Queen's Bench, in the case of Reg. *v.* The Inhabitants of Christchurch, (3 New Sessions Cases, 320,) by which it was decided that the first proviso to the 1st sec. of the 9 & 10 Vic. c. 66, has a retrospective as well as prospective operation; and having referred to the Circular which was issued by the Poor Law Commissioners on the 20th October, 1846, communicating the opinion of the law officers of the crown to a contrary effect, the Board directed that the following communications should be printed and circulated for the information of the boards of guardians:—

I.—COMMUNICATIONS RELATING TO THE DECISION OF THE COURT OF QUEEN'S BENCH, IN REG. v. THE INHABITANTS OF CHRISTCHURCH.

1. Effect of the decision itself.

15th Feb., 1849.

Clerk of the Tamworth Union.—The guardians, having referred to the decision in Reg. *v.* Christchurch, and to the Poor Law Commissioners' Circular of the 20th Oct., 1846, request the Board's advice upon the subject.

Ans.—The Poor Law Commissioners, in their Circular of the 20th October, 1846, did not, as appears to be supposed by the guardians of the Tamworth Union, give any directions; they merely communicated to the guardians for their information, the opinion of the law officers of the crown upon certain important questions that were raised upon the construction of the statute 9 & 10 Vic. c. 66.

The Poor Law Board regret that the opinion so expressed by the law officers, as to the meaning and application of the proviso to the first section of that statute, was not a correct interpretation of the law; but as the recent decision of the Court of Queen's Bench, in the case of Reg. *v.* The Inhabitants of Christchurch (3 New Sess. Cases, 320,) has now determined the proper meaning of the Act, the course to be pursued by the guardians will henceforth be free from doubt.

It is remarked in your letter, that " on reference to that case (Reg. *v.* Christchurch) it will at once be seen that the Court of Queen's Bench have decided contrary to the opinion given by the Attorney and Solicitor-General; and that therefore it must follow that persons who had received relief during the five years prior to the passing of the Act (9 & 10 Vic. c. 66,) are still removable."

The Board must observe that the guardians have not taken quite a correct view of the effect of the decision. The Court has only decided that the proviso to the 1st section has a retrospective as well as a prospective operation; in other words, that the time of relief occurring before, as well as that occurring after the passing of the statute in question, is to be excluded from the calculation of the period of the five years.

If, after making these deductions, and taking into consideration the entire period of the pauper's residence in the parish, there remain in all a term of five years clear of relief, then the party will, as the Poor Law Board consider, be irremovable from the parish of his residence.

With regard to the time from which the transfer of the relief from the common fund to the parishes of chargeability respectively should be made, the Board desire to inform the guardians that the accounts, which have been closed and audited, cannot now be re-opened for the purpose of altering the charge of any relief which, under a mistaken impression as to the effect of the 1st proviso to sec. 1 of the 9 & 10 Vic. c. 66, may have been erroneously entered in the union ledger.

But with respect to future relief, as well as relief afforded since the close of the last audited accounts, it will be necessary for the guardians to place the charge to the debit of the parish of the pauper's residence. This parish, in the case of out-door relief, will be that where the pauper is actually residing; and, in the case of in-door relief, will be that where the pauper was resident when the admission into the workhouse took place. It will of course be open to the parish so charged to resort to the ordinary remedy, viz., an order of removal.

11th Dec., 1848.

Clerk of the Hastings Union.—Inquiring, with reference to the decision in Reg. *v.* Christchurch, " whether, to constitute a case of irremovability under relief, the whole term of residence in the parish may be computed."

Ans.—In ascertaining whether a person be irremovable under sec. 1 of the 9 and 10 Vic. c. 66, the inquiry need not be limited to the last five years, but may include the whole period or term of the pauper's residence in the parish, provided nothing has occurred at any time to interrupt the continuity of the residence. The time during which a pauper has been in receipt of relief must, whether prior to the 26th Aug., 1846, or since, according to the recent case of Reg. *v.* Inhabitants of Christchurch, be excluded in computing the residence of five years. But though such interval or time of relief cannot be reckoned, still it does not break the continuity of the residence, and therefore the period of five years required by sec. 1 of the Act may be made up of detached periods, that is, the time which a person spent in the parish before he received relief may be added to the time so spent after he ceased to receive relief, the time of relief being simply omitted from the calculation.

29th Dec., 1848.

Clerk of the Richmond Union, Yorkshire.—With reference to the decision in Reg. *v.* Christchurch, the guardians feel a difficulty, in regard to cases "where paupers have resided continuously for a period exceeding five years in any parish, during which they have at various periods (some of them within the last five years) been in receipt of relief, but where, after deducting such periods of relief, there still remains a clear period of five years' residence, consisting of the intervals of time during which they had no relief." The guardians inquire whether such paupers are removable, or irremovable.

Ans.—If, after deducting the time during which relief has been given to a pauper in the parish of his residence, there remain a term of five years during which he had so resided, without relief, he will then be irremovable, whether the time of the relief be next before the application for the warrant, or whether it may have occurred at intervals during the entire term of the residence. If, however, after making such deduction, a period of five years does not remain, the pauper will not be irremovable under the section in question from the parish of the residence.

11th January, 1849.

Clerk of the Carnarvon Union.—States the following case for the opinion of the Board, as to the mode of computing the period of the pauper's residence, with reference to the decision in Reg. *v.* Christchurch:—*A.* came to reside in the parish of B. in 1838, and his residence there has remained unbroken up to the present time, either by change of abode, or by removal under order of justices; but for a short period in each year of such residence he has received relief.

Ans.—The residence for the period of five years must certainly be continuous; but the Board do not consider that the fact of a person having received relief at any time would, in itself, operate as an interruption of the residence. If, therefore, in any case, after deducting the several portions of time during which relief has been given, there still remains a period of five years, the pauper would be irremovable.

---

2. CONSEQUENCES OF THE DECISION.

12th January, 1849.

Clerk of the Blything Union.—Referring to the decision in Reg. *v.* Christchurch, and requesting the Board's advice as to the course to be adopted, in order that the parishes which have been wrongly charged on account of paupers supposed to be irremovable may be effectually relieved.

Ans.—It is a matter of regret to the Board that the Poor Law Commissioners were erroneously advised as to the legal construction of the 1st proviso to the 1st section of the Poor Removal Act; but the error, so far as it applies to charges for relief in accounts closed and audited, is now they think irremediable. For the future, however, it may be easily corrected; and the Board advise the guardians that, in dealing with the cases of such paupers as are now decided to be removable, they should adopt the following course, where the relief has been charged to the common fund of the union upon the ground of the presumed irremovability of the pauper, whom the decision in question may now show to be removable; the charge of such relief, so far as it relates to accounts already closed and audited, cannot be altered or transferred, but from the date of the last audited accounts it will be proper for the guardians to transfer any charge for relief, erroneously placed to the common fund, in the case of any pauper now shown to be removable by reason of such decision.

In distributing, therefore, the charge of relief in cases to which the decision applies, the guardians, when they have ascertained that any such pauper is now removable, will merely have to transfer the relief given since the date of the last audited account to the parish of the pauper's residence, and to place all future relief to the debit of that parish, leaving such parish to its ordinary remedy, namely, the obtaining an order of removal.

2nd February, 1849.

Clerk of the Hereford Union.—Referring to the decisions in Reg. *v.* Christchurch, and Reg. *v.* Halifax; requesting advice as to the course to be adopted in consequence; and inquiring whether the Board are about to issue any general rules or regulations on the subject.

Ans.—It is not the intention of the Board at present to issue any general rules on the subject of the decision in Reg. *v.* Christchurch; but with reference to the request of the guardians of the Hereford Union, the Board desire to offer the following observations for their guidance as to the mode of dealing with cases affected by that decision; namely, with regard to the past, the accounts which have been closed and audited cannot now be re-opened for the purpose of altering the charge of any relief, which, under a mistaken impression as to the effect of the 1st proviso to section 1 of the 9 & 10 Vic. cap. 66, may have been erroneously entered in the union ledger.

But with respect to future relief, as well as relief afforded since the close of the last audited accounts, it will be necessary for the guardians to inquire carefully into the several cases to which the decision may apply; and when they have ascertained that the pauper, in any such case, is not only removable, so far as that decision is concerned, but is not irremovable on any other ground, it will be their duty to transfer the charge for relief given since the close of the last audited accounts, and to place the charge for future relief to the debit of the parish of the pauper's residence. This parish, in the case of out-door relief will be that where the pauper is actually residing; and, in the case of in-door relief, will be that where the pauper was resident when the admission into the workhouse took place. It will of course be open to the parish, so charged, to resort to the ordinary remedy, viz., an order of removal.

With relation to non-resident paupers, it will rest with the guardians to reconsider any case in which they may have discontinued relief, but in which a fresh application may now be made to them in consequence of the decision alluded to.

28th December, 1848.

Clerk of the York Union.—The guardians have received notice from one of the parishes in the Union, that it has determined to remove all paupers whose cases come within the decision in Reg. *v.* Christchurch, unless the relief be charged to the parishes to which they belong.

Ans.—The Board are of opinion that the only proper course open to the guardians of the York Union is for them to charge the cost of the relief to the parishes wherein the paupers reside, unless the parishes of the settlement consent to waive orders of removal, and to be charged with the relief given, in the case of all such non-resident paupers. In such cases, if the General Prohibitory Order does not interfere, the guardians are authorised to grant non-resident relief to the paupers who, by reason of the decision referred to, are now removable.

12th January, 1849.

Clerk of the Stokesley Union.—The guardians having received intimation from different unions that it is intended to remove paupers affected by the decision in Reg. *v.* Christchurch, wish to be informed how they should act in reference to such cases.

Ans.—In the cases of non-resident paupers to which the recent decision of the Court of Queen's Bench in the case of Reg. *v.* Christchurch applies, the guardians of the Stokesley Union, where the paupers are actually removed by order of Justices, will only have to relieve such paupers when so brought within the union. In other cases it will rest with the guardians to make a careful examination of the facts, and if there be nothing in the General Prohibitory Order to prevent it, and if the parishes interested do not object thereto, the guardians, if they think proper, may grant non-resident relief. It will be necessary in making this examination, that the guardians should ascertain with reference to the several provisions of the 9 & 10 Vic. c. 66, whether the paupers are not irremovable on some other ground than that of a five years' residence.

8th February, 1849.

Clerk of the Camelford Union.—Inquiring whether the guardians can proceed to cause the removal of all paupers residing in the union, but belonging to parishes in other unions, whose relief is now charged to the common fund, but as it now appears from Reg. *v.* Christchurch erroneously so.

Ans.—The guardians have, of themselves, no power to obtain orders of removal; the proceedings necessary to be taken, to effect such a course, must be at the instance of the overseers of the several parishes to which the paupers are chargeable. Those paupers, whom the recent decision above referred to affects, will be no longer chargeable to the union common fund, unless, indeed, they should be found to be irremovable upon some other ground. As, therefore, their relief is no longer chargeable to the common fund, it follows that they will become chargeable to the parishes in which they respectively reside, and the decision will rest with the overseers of such parishes, whether or not they will obtain orders of removal in any case where the paupers may be removable.

20th February, 1849.

Clerk of the Dolgelly Union—States that, in consequence of the decisions in Reg. *v.* Christchurch, and Reg. *v.* Harrow on the Hill, several paupers in that union have become removable; and the guardians wish to know whether they are not right in considering that such paupers should become chargeable to the parishes wherein they respectively reside, before orders for their removal can be obtained.

Ans.—The course which it appears that the guardians propose to adopt is correct. The guardians may direct their relieving officers to enter the paupers in question as chargeable to the respective parishes of the residence; and the several guardians of those parishes, being present at the general meeting of the guardians of the Dolgelly Union, as they must be presumed to be, will then learn the course pursued in respect to this matter, as in other cases which come under the consideration of the guardians.

---

3. PARTICULAR CASES AND OPINIONS.

13*th Jan.*, 1849.

Vice-Chairman of the Great Boughton Union.—Requested the Board's opinion, with reference to the decision in Reg. *v.* Christchurch, as to the removability of the paupers in the following cases:—1st, "A pauper had resided from thirty to forty years in the the township of *A.*, within this union, his legal settlement being in the township *B.*; whether *B.* is in this union or not I cannot take upon myself to say at this moment, but I apprehend that it is not material. For several years (upwards of five) of the first part of his residence in *A.*, he received no relief from any parish, but after ten or a dozen years' residence in *A.* he applied for relief to *B.*, which accepted and relieved him, and continued to relieve him until October, 1846, when *B.* refused to relieve him any longer, and he was transferred to *A.* 2nd, A pauper with his family has resided for the last 15 or 16 years in the parish of *C.* within this union, the place of his legal settlement being the parish of *D.* in the Wrexham Union. During these years he has been several times relieved by *D.*, sometimes for a year or perhaps nearly two years continuously; whenever he required assistance he was invariably relieved by *D.*, up to October, 1846, after which time the cost of whatever relief he received was charged to *C.* But it appeared that the various periods, during which he received no relief whatever, when added together amounted to a clear five years and upwards."

Ans.—The Board think it possible that the guardians of the Great Boughton Union may be under some misapprehension as to the effect of the decision of the Court of Queen's Bench, in Reg. *v.* Christchurch. The court in that case have only decided that the relief to paupers granted previous to the passing of the 9 & 10 Vic. c. 66, is to be treated in the same manner as relief granted subsequently to the Act, namely, as a ground of excluding the time of such relief from the calculation of the time of residence. If, after deducting all the periods during which relief of the pauper has been given, there still remain the term of five years' residence in the same parish without interruption, the pauper is irremovable. If a period less than five years remain, and there be no other ground of irremovability under the statute referred to, the pauper will be removable, and the cost of his relief will not be chargeable upon the common fund. Applying this principle to both the cases stated, it will be perceived that the paupers therein referred to are irremovable. The years without relief need not be consecutive, provided there be no interruption by residence out of the parish.

23*rd Jan.*, 1849.

Clerk of the Presteigne Union.—Stating the case of Sarah Roe, settled in a parish of the Presteigne Union, but resident in a parish of the Bromyard Union, where she had been receiving non-resident relief until August, 1846, when such relief was discontinued, as she was deemed to be irremovable in accordance with the construction put by the law officers of the crown on the proviso to sec. 1. of the 9 & 10 Vic. c. 66. On becoming acquainted with the decision in Reg. *v.* Christchurch, the Bromyard guardians have inquired of the Presteigne guardians, whether they will renew the non-resident relief to Sarah Roe, or receive her without an order of removal.

Ans.—In Reg. *v.* Christchurch, the Court of Queen's Bench decided (contrary to the opinion of the Attorney-General, and Solicitor-General) that the 1st proviso to the 1st sec. of the 9 & 10 Vic. cap. 66, has a retrospective as well as prospective effect, so as to require the deduction of the time of relief in estimating the period of residence, whether the relief has been afforded before or after the passing of the Act. (See the report of the decision in 3 N. S. C. 320.) If, on applying the rule laid down in this decision to the particular case of Sarah Roe, it be found that she has not resided in the parish of her present abode for five years, after deducting the time or times during which she has been receiving relief therein, she is not, as far as this point is concerned, irremovable; and, consequently, it is open to the guardians of the Presteigne Union to allow her non-resident relief, if they are not restrained by the General Prohibitory Order from doing so, and if the parish to which she would be chargeable, if removed, do not object. If, however, she has resided in the parish for five years, after making the requisite deduction, or if she is irremovable on any other ground, the guardians would not be justified in granting non-resident relief.

1st February, 1849.

Clerk of the Melksham Union.—Submitting for the Board's opinion as to the pauper's removability, a case of which the facts are as follows:—The place of legal settlement of the pauper Joseph Bennett is in the parish of North Bradley, within the Westbury Union. The pauper has resided in the parish of Trowbridge, in the Melksham Union, for about the last fifty years uninterruptedly, and for about the first twenty years of such residence did not receive relief from any parish; after which he occasionally received relief from the parish of North Bradley, and for the five years and upwards, immediately preceding the passing of the Act 9 & 10 Vic. cap. 66, the pauper constantly received relief from the parish of North Bradley, during all which time he resided in Trowbridge. Upon the passing of that Act, the parish of North Bradley refused any longer to acknowledge the pauper, and the parish of Trowbridge has continued to relieve him to the present time.

Ans.—The Board consider the pauper to be irremovable. According to the facts of the case, as set forth in such statement, there has been a residence of five years in the parish of Trowbridge during which time the pauper was not in receipt of relief; and it is immaterial to the question, that the whole time subsequently to the completion of a five years' residence has been a period of relief. This is determined by the cases of Reg. *v.* Harrow on the Hill, 3 N. S. C., 232; Reg. *v.* Croydon, 12 Law Times, 147; and by the language of the Court of Queen's Bench, in that of Reg. *v.* Christchurch.

5th February, 1849.

Clerk of the Poole Union.—Makes the following inquiries, with reference to Reg. *v.* Christchurch:—1st. "Whether all persons now resident in our union but who did not reside here five years previous to August, 1846, after deducting the time such parties have been in the receipt of relief, are now removable." 2nd. "In the case of a party whose examination was taken as far back as 1845, but who, in consequence of continued illness was unable to be removed, and is now relieved under a suspended order, whether, if the pauper had completed five years' residence (exclusive of the time he received relief) before August, 1846, the removing parish is not bound to maintain him and his family."

Ans.—1st. It may be that the parties referred to in this case have completed a residence of five years without receiving relief since the passing of the 9 & 10 Vic. c. 66, which period of five years was commenced previous to that date, and if so they will still be irremovable. They may also be irremovable under the statute on some other ground than that of residence. But if neither contingency have happened the parties will then be removable. 2nd. In this case the Board understand that there had been a residence for five years without relief, before the application for the order of removal was made. If so, they think that the party is irremovable, though the order itself has been suspended. If, however, the term of five years' residence was not completed until after the application, the party in question would be removable.

8th March, 1849.

Clerk of the Llanfyllin Union.—Requesting the Board's opinion on the following cases, with reference to the decision in Reg. *v.* Christchurch:—1st. "Whether a pauper who has resided in the parish of *A.* for twenty years, but belonging to the parish of *B.*, and has been for five successive years, during any part of the twenty years, without receiving relief from *B.*, is removable or irremovable."—2nd. "Whether, according to the decision of Lord Denman, it is necessary that before a pauper, resident in *A.*, can be removed to *B.*, he must have received relief from *B.* within the last five years, previous to the passing of 9 & 10 Vic. cap. 66."—3rd. "Whether a pauper belonging to *A.*, but residing in *B.* for five years previous to the passing of the Act above-mentioned, and receiving no relief from the parish of *A.* until after the passing of the Act, is irremovable."

Ans.—1st. If the pauper referred to continues to reside in the parish of *A.* he is not removable therefrom.—2nd. It is not necessary to the removal of a pauper that he should have been in receipt of relief before the passing of the 9 & 10 Vic. cap. 66. The Court of Queen's Bench decided in the case above cited, that relief given before that statute was to be treated in the same manner as relief administered subsequently to it, so that the time during which relief has been received by a pauper, whenever it occurred, is to be excluded from the computation of a five years' residence.—3rd. In this case the pauper referred to is irremovable from the parish of *B.*, though the relief was received by him from the parish *A.* after the passing of the statute.

II. — COMMUNICATIONS ON VARIOUS POINTS CONNECTED WITH THE ACTS 9 & 10 VIC. c. 66, and 11 & 12 VIC. c. 110.

1. Computation of period of residence.

23*rd Dec.*, 1848.

Chairman of the Warrington Union.—There is a difference of opinion among the guardians, as to the charging of relief to persons who have resided five years in some township in the union; some of the guardians being of opinion that all such paupers are chargeable to the union, since the 30th September last; others, that where they have had no relief within the year previous to August, 1846, they are to be charged as heretofore to the respective townships of their residence.

Ans.—The law undoubtedly requires that the relief of poor persons rendered irremovable by any provision of the 9 & 10 Vic. c. 66, should, since the 30th September last, be charged to the common fund. This is required by sec. 3 of 11 & 12 Vic. c. 110. It follows, therefore, as regards persons who have resided uninterruptedly in a parish for the period required by sec. 1 of 9 & 10 Vic. c. 66, that is, five years, that their relief will be chargeable upon the common fund, provided they be rendered irremovable therefrom by the provisions of that Act. It is not necessary that the parties should have received relief some time within the year preceding August, 1846, to render their relief chargeable to the common fund. The Board think it may be useful to point out, that in computing the period of five years contemplated by the statute, the time during which the party received relief must be left out of the calculation. (See the recent decision of Reg. *v.* Inhabitants of Christchurch, 3 N. S. cases.)

13*th Jan.*, 1849.

Clerk of the Cosford Union.—Stating that the guardians have considered a person to be irremovable under sec. 1 of the 9 & 10 Vic. c. 66, if he has lived five years in a parish after deducting the time during which he has received relief; and inquiring whether that view is correct.

Ans.—The Court of Queen's Bench in the case of Reg. *v.* Harrow (3 N. S. C. p. 232) has expressly decided that the course pursued by the guardians of the Cosford Union is correct. According to that decision the five years' residence need not come down to the time of the application for the warrant of removal, nor be wholly uninterrupted.

29*th Jan.*, 1849.

Clerk of the Aberayron Union—Makes the following inquiries:—Query 1st. "If *A. B.* has been resident in the parish of C. for the last twenty years, the last fifteen years of which he has received relief, is he removable or irremovable? See Reg. *v.* Harrow on the Hill." Query 2nd. "As the late decision in Reg. *v.* Christchurch has reversed the opinion of the Attorney and Solicitor-General, as to the computation of time in the receipt of relief before the 9 & 10 Vic. cap. 66, (26th August, 1846,) on which we have hitherto acted, many of our paupers will become removable who have hitherto been considered irremovable, and must be transferred or removed from one parish to another, the same pauper will consequently appear in the relief list of each parish (see General Order for Accounts, Article 17, No. 2) if such transfer should take place during this half-year, can the board of guardians resolve on such transfers not taking effect till the next half-year, or what is the proper course to take under such circumstances?" Query 3rd. "Will it be a good ground of appeal against an order of removal, that the grounds of removal do not state the length of residence of the pauper in the removing parish, otherwise it is impossible in many cases for the appellant parish to ascertain the length of such residence, or whether such pauper be removable or not until after removal, when appeal will be too late."

Ans.—1st. Under the circumstances set forth, the pauper *A. B.* is not removable from the parish of his residence. 2nd. As regards the effect of the decision of the Court of Queen's Bench in the case of Reg. *v.* Christchurch, the guardians cannot lawfully pass any resolution on the subject which will prevent the cost of relief to paupers whose cases are found to come within that decision, from being distributed according to the strict law as now determined, commencing from the time when the union accounts were last closed and audited. 3rd. It does not appear to this Board that an omission to state the length of a pauper's residence in the removing parish, will in itself be a good ground of appeal against an order of removal since the passing of the 11 & 12 Vic cap. 31.

14*th Feb.*, 1849.

Clerk of the Knighton Union—Makes the following inquiry—"Supposing a person to have lived in a parish ten years at the time of the passing of the Act 9 & 10 Vic. c. 66, and for the four last years of that time to have been an acknowledged pauper of, and in the receipt of relief from some other parish, would that person have been irremovable according to the provisions of that Act."

Ans.—The 1st sec. of the 9 & 10 Vic. c. 66, has a complete retrospective effect, and the entire period during which a pauper has resided continuously in a parish may, therefore, be taken into consideration in ascertaining whether or not he has acquired irremovability under that section. In the case suggested the pauper would be irremovable from the parish of the residence.

[*Case submitted under* 11 & 12 *Vic. c.* 110, *s.* 4.]

23*rd January,* 1849.

Clerk of the Northallerton Union—Submitting, at the request of the overseers of Ainderby Steeple, a statement of the case of a pauper named Hewson, with a view to ascertaining the opinion of the Board as to his removability from that parish.

Ans.—The Board wish to be informed whether the guardians of the Northallerton Union are aware that their interests are involved in the question now submitted to the Board in so far as it bears upon the further question, whether the relief given to the pauper should be charged to the township of Ainderby Steeple or to the common fund of the union. Seeing that this is the case, and having regard to the terms of sec. 4 of the 11 & 12 Vic. cap. 110, the Board do not think they could properly advise upon the primary question of irremovability, without knowing whether the guardians of the Northallerton Union concur in the statement of the facts of the case furnished by the overseers of Ainderby Steeple. The whole case would, indeed, be brought more regularly before the Board were they furnished with a joint statement analogous to that required by the section referred to; which should be drawn up by the clerk to the guardians and signed by the chairman on behalf of the board of guardians, and by the guardians of the particular township interested.

27*th February,* 1849.

The same—Submitting the following statement, for the opinion of the Board :—

"Case stated by the board of guardians of the Northallerton Union for the opinion of the Poor Law Board, at a meeting of the Board held on the 31st January, 1849.

In December, 1843, a person of the name of Hewson came to reside in the township of Ainderby Steeple where he did not belong, and still resides there with a wife and child. In June last they became chargeable to that township in consequence of the wife's infirmity, and have ever since continued chargeable to that township. In July last an order of removal was obtained which was abandoned as not being sustainable, and another order was applied for to remove the paupers to a township, not in Northallerton Union, as their place of legal settlement; but before the order could be obtained the paupers had resided five years in the said township, consequently the magistrates doubted whether the paupers had not become irremovable, because, as they think, the last clause of the proviso to the first sec. of the 9 & 10 Vic. cap. 66, applies only to relief given to paupers by a parish in which such person does not reside, and therefore the time during which relief was given by Ainderby Steeple to the paupers is not to be excluded in the computation of time "thereinbefore mentioned." The guardians of this union contend that by the previous clause of the proviso, relief given to paupers by any parish, no matter whether the paupers reside in such parish or not, is to be excluded in the computation of time "thereinbefore mentioned," and that the clause referred to by the magistrates is not to be coupled with the preceding one, that being a distinct clause to prevent collusion between paupers residing in parishes to which they do not belong, and the overseers, &c., of the parishes to which they do belong. There is no guardian at present for Ainderby Steeple.

Your opinion is therefore respectfully desired whether the paupers are removable to their place of legal settlement or are now irremovable. (Signed) B. WILFORD, *Chairman.*

Ans.—The Board coincide in the view entertained by the guardians of the Northallerton Union as expressed in the statement, and are of opinion that the time during which the paupers were in the receipt of relief whilst residing in the township of Ainderby Steeple should certainly be excluded from the computation of the five years' residence contemplated by the Statute. As therefore, in the present instance, it appears that a sufficient period in the whole irrespective of relief does not remain, the paupers are now removable from Ainderby Steeple.

---

2. BREACH OF RESIDENCE.

22*nd Jan.,* 1848.

Clerk of the Stow-on-the-Wold Union—Submitting the following case for the opinion of the

Board, as to the removability of the pauper:—
"Henry Bayley, aged 61, applied to the guardians on the last board day for relief, stating that he had resided in the parish of Mangersbury during the last five years, and a few weeks beside; that in that time he had occupied two houses in the parish at two different times; that in every year he and his wife had left for a few weeks in the summer to go 'hop picking,' but that he kept possession of the house at Mangersbury and the key during his absence, leaving a few articles of small value in the house, such as a few plates and dishes, &c."

Ans.—The Board are of opinion that the absence of the pauper from the parish of Mangersbury for a few weeks during the summer was not an interruption of his residence in that parish, and as the facts are stated in the letter, the pauper is now irremovable from Mangersbury, by reason of the five years' residence.

9*th May*, 1848.

Clerk of the Market Bosworth Union.—Requesting the Board's opinion as to the removability of a pauper under the following circumstances:—

"A pauper belonging to Markfield, but who has been residing in Newbold (both parishes in this union) for eleven or twelve years, but about four years ago went into the infirmary at Leicester for two or three months, and about a year afterwards went in again for about the same period, his wife and family still living at Newbold, and he being permanently ill and never likely to recover."

Ans.—The Board are disposed to consider upon the analogy of the case of Nias *v.* Davis (11 Jurist, 472) that the abiding of the pauper in the infirmary at Leicester, under the circumstances described in the letter, did not operate as a breach of his residence in Newbold, and therefore that the pauper is not removable from Newbold to Markfield.

[*Note.*—This opinion was given before the decision of *Q. v. Salford*, 3 N. S. C., 286, which may make a difference.]

16*th Feb.*, 1849.

Clerk of the Bedford Union.—Requesting the Board's opinion as to whether there has been a breach of residence in the following case:—

"John Hewitt, a poor person belonging to the parish of Renhold, has resided at Clapham upwards of five years, with the exception of a few weeks whilst he was a patient in the Bedford Infirmary, situated in another parish, but during his absence his wife remained in his house, at Clapham. Hewitt, of course, left Clapham *animo revertendi.*"

Ans.—Although the decision of the Court of Queen's Bench in the case of Reg. *v.* Salford, raises some doubt as to the view which the Court may take upon the question submitted, the Board (as at present advised) do not think that the abiding in the hospital was, in this instance, an interruption of the pauper's residence in the parish of Clapham.

21*st June*, 1848.

Clerk of the Great Boughton Union.—Stating the following case, for the opinion of the Board:

Samuel Lloyd, at present residing in the township of Tarvin, where he has lived for the last twenty years, went about three months back to his daughter, who lives in a distant township, with the intention of asking her whether she could take him to lodge with her; she said, no, she could not; he then remained with her, on a visit, as he states, for about fourteen days, and then returned to Tarvin. Samuel Lloyd did not give up his own house, or lodging, in the township of Tarvin, and he came to that township to receive his relief from the relieving officer every week during his temporary absence. The overseers of Tarvin contend, that this departure and absence break the residence of five years required by the recent statute, 9 & 10 Vic. cap. 66. sec. 1.

Ans.—The Board were of opinion that the continuity of the pauper's residence in Tarvin was not interrupted by his temporary absence under the circumstances described in this case.

23*rd Jan.*, 1849.

R. J. Elton, Esq., J. P. Chard.—Stating the circumstances under which a man, named James Norrish, and his wife, left their home and went into another parish for a short period; and inquiring whether, under those circumstances, a change of settlement was caused.

Ans.—From the facts at present before them, the Board do not understand that any question is involved as to the change of the settlement, but as to whether or not the absence of a pauper and his wife, under certain circumstances, from a parish, operated to break the continuance of the residence therein, so as to render the parties removable. It is not stated how long the pauper and his wife had resided in the parish from which they came, but from the nature of the inquiry the

Board are led to suppose that such residence must have exceeded the term of five years, required by sec. 1 of the 9 & 10 Vic. cap. 66, to create irremovability. The Board, however, collect from your statement, that the wife left her home for the purpose of attending on a sick woman in another parish, being accompanied by her husband, aged 70, who was not willing to be left alone; that they remained for a period of four or five weeks in the latter place without renting any premises there, and that afterwards they both returned to the same home they had previously occupied, and which they had not absolutely relinquished. If these be the facts of the case, the Board certainly think that the absence of Norrish for the temporary object stated, would not be held to break the continuity of the residence nor disturb the irremovability of the parties, supposing that to have existed.

30*th Jan.*, 1849.

Clerk of the Wells Union—Requesting advice as to the course to be pursued by the guardians, in reference to the decision of the Court of Queen's Bench in Reg. *v.* Hallifax.

Ans.—The Board can only state that the Court of Queen's Bench, in the case referred to, has decided that an order of removal, carried into execution by the removal of the party named therein, does in point of law interrupt the residence of such party in the parish from which the removal takes place. The Board certainly consider that such decision should be acted upon by the guardians of the Wells Union in all cases to which it may be applicable.

---

3. SCOTCH AND IRISH PAUPERS.

19*th Jan.*, 1849.

Clerk of the Okehampton Union—Stating the case of Thomas Haley, an Irishman, chargeable to the parish of Northlew, in which he has resided for the last thirty-eight years; and with reference to the decision in Reg. *v.* Christchurch, inquiring "whether an Irishman, having resided thirty-eight years in a parish, but having received relief from that parish for two years of that time, and who is now receiving relief therefrom, but which is not charged to the common fund of the union, but to the aforesaid parish, is removable to Ireland or not, no other settlement having been obtained by the aforesaid Irishman in England."

Ans.—The decision in Reg. *v.* Christchurch has no special application to the case of this pauper. The point decided in Reg. *v.* Christchurch was, that the relief given before the passing of the Act 9 & 10 Vic. cap. 66, is to be treated in like manner as relief granted subsequently; in other words, that the time during which the pauper received relief, is in all cases to be excluded from the computation of the period of residence, viz., five years, required by sec. 1. If that course be followed in the present instance, it will be found that a residence of five years and upwards in the parish of Northlew, after excluding the period of relief, will remain, rendering the pauper, on that ground, irremovable.

The fact of Thomas Haley being an Irishman, does not, as the Poor Law Board consider, make any difference with regard to the question of irremovability. The Poor Law Commissioners were advised by the Law Officers of the Crown, that the provisions of 9 & 10 Vic. cap. 66. apply equally to the removal of persons born in Scotland or Ireland, as to that of persons having settlements in England.

[*See also, Merthyr Tydvil Union, post, page* 45.]

---

4. TEMPORARY SICKNESS OR ACCIDENT.

9*th Nov.*, 1848.

Clerk of the Shepton Mallet Union.—Inquiring whether relief granted to able-bodied men (who are not irremovable) for midwifery fees and relief during the confinement of their wives, should be charged to the common fund of the union.

Ans.—As the facts are stated the paupers who receive the relief in question are irremovable, by reason of the sickness, on account of which the relief is required, not being such as will produce permanent disability; which exemption from removal, it will be seen, arises from the 4th sec. of the 9 & 10 Vic. c. 66. The cost of the relief, therefore, given in such cases, will be chargeable upon the common fund of the union, under the 3rd sec. of the 11 & 12 Vic. c. 110.

[*Case submitted under* 11 & 12 *Vic.* c. 110, *sec.* 4.]

25*th Nov.*, 1848.

Clerk of the Horncastle Union.—Stating the case of a single woman, pregnant, named Bromfield; and requesting the Board's opinion as to her irremovability.

Ans.—The Board inquired whether this pauper became chargeable by reason of general destitution, or in consequence of any peculiar sickness. They also requested a joint statement of the case as under sec. 4 of the 11 & 12 Vic. c. 110; pointing out that such statement should be drawn up by the clerk, and signed by the chairman on behalf of the board of guardians, and by the guardians of the particular parish concerned.

12*th Feb.*, 1849.

The same.—Enclosing a joint statement of the case of Susan Bromfield, in the following terms :—" Case for the opinion of the Poor Law Board. A single woman, named Susan Bromfield, residing in the parish of Belchford, but not settled in that parish, was admitted into the workhouse of this union by an order of the relieving officer prior to the 1st day of October last, and has been an inmate of the workhouse ever since, and her maintenance has been charged to the parish of Belchford. The cause of her destitution is pregnancy, which being of a nature to produce merely a temporary disability, the guardian for Belchford contends that she is irremovable under the statute of 9 & 10 Vic. c. 66, sec. 4, and therefore that her relief ought to be charged to the general fund of the union under the statute 11 & 12 Vic. c. 110, sec. 2, [§ 3 ?] and not to the parish of Belchford. The pauper did not become chargeable by reason of general destitution, but in consequence of her pregnancy only. There was no sickness or bodily ailment affecting this pauper, other than such as is usually attendant on cases of pregnancy. *The pauper was prevented by her pregnancy from working for her livelihood, and thereby she became destitute and chargeable.*

" The board of guardians of the Horncastle Union and the guardian of the parish of Belchford desire the opinion of the Poor Law Board on the case above stated, and they hereby agree to abide by and act upon such opinion

" Dated the 28th day of November, 1848.

(Signed) " JAMES DYMOKE,
" *Chairman.*
" WILLIAM WOULD,
" *Guardian of Belchford.*"

Ans.—Upon the statement now before them the Board are of opinion that the case is not within sec. 4 of the 9 & 10 Vic. c. 66, and that the pauper is removable; consequently the cost of her relief should not be charged to the common fund of the Horncastle Union.

2*nd Feb.*, 1849.

Clerk of the Stafford Union.—With reference to the combined operation of the 9 & 10 Vic. c. 66, sec. 4, and the 11 & 12 Vic. c. 111, sec. 1, inquiring whether relief made necessary to a person, in consequence of the temporary sickness or accident of his wife or child, renders such person irremovable from the parish in which he has not resided five years, and is otherwise removable to the parish of his legal settlement. And also, whether the cost of such relief should be charged to the common fund of the union, or to the parish in which he resides. And whether the costs incurred in the burial of such wife or child should be charged to the common fund of the union, or to the parish in which he resided at the time of his wife's or child's death.

Ans.—The 4th sec. of the 9 & 10 Vic. c. 66, appears to the Board to apply to every case where a person becomes chargeable in respect of relief made necessary by sickness or accident not likely to produce permanent disability, whether the sickness or accident be that of the head or of any member of the family ; and, as regards this point, the Board do not consider that the 11 & 12 Vic. c. 111, sec. 1, affects the question. In the case suggested in the letter, the cost of the relief should apparently be charged to the common fund of the union, and the same rule will apply to the expenses of the burial.

6*th Feb.*, 1849.

Clerk of the Ludlow Union.—Inquiring whether the Board consider that a pauper is irremovable under the 4th sec. of the 9 & 10 Vic. c. 66, because she is in a state of pregnancy, though she may be in good health, and well able to do her accustomed work as a servant in a farm-house, and in all other respects unquestionably removable.

Ans.—Under the 4th sec. of the statute quoted, a pauper is not necessarily rendered irremovable by the fact of pregnancy, although the chargeability of the pauper might ensue upon it. If the pregnancy simply produce general destitution, and the application for relief be the result of such destitution, it does not appear to the Board in this case that the 4th sec. would prevent the removal of the pauper. If, however, the pregnancy be accompanied with such ailments as constitute sickness, within the meaning of the above quoted section, and the relief is rendered necessary by the sickness, then undoubtedly the section would operate to restrain the removal of the party.

16*th Feb.*, 1849.

Clerk of the Stafford Union.—Inquiring whether a pauper, certified by the medical officer to be ill of consumption, is exempted by such sickness from liability to be removed to the place of her legal settlement, and whether the cost of relief and burial of such pauper should be charged to the common fund of the union or to the parish in which the pauper had resided twelve months at the time she became destitute.

Ans.—Although it is generally highly probable that consumption will end in death, the Board think that the medical officer should state whether, in his opinion, it will produce permanent disability in the particular case in question. If it will, the pauper is chargeable to the parish of the residence, and it then remains for the overseers of that parish to determine whether they will apply for an order of removal. On the other hand, if the sickness which causes the chargeability will not produce permanent disability, the removal of the pauper is restrained by sec. 4 of the 9 & 10 Vic. c. 66, and the relief given in such case would be a charge upon the common fund of the Stafford Union, under sec. 3 of the 11 & 12 Vic. c. 110. In that case, moreover, the cost of the funeral in the event of the pauper's death, would follow the charge for the relief of the pauper while living.

The Board give this general opinion upon the case submitted to them, at the same time reserving to themselves the right of deciding formally upon any question which may be specially referred to them, according to the facts of the case, under sec. 4 of the 11 & 12 Vic. c. 110.

5. SETTLEMENT AND IRREMOVABILITY.

12th Sept., 1848.

Clerk of the Loughborough Union.—Requesting the Board's advice upon the following case:—"A man gained his settlement in one of the parishes of this union by possession of an estate, and he has ever since continued to reside in the same parish; his son, who was living with him, and unemancipated at the time he gained such settlement, and who has done no act on his own part to gain a settlement, has since the passing of the 4 & 5 Wm. 4, c. 76, removed from such parish, and has hitherto resided more than ten miles from the place of his father's settlement. The son has been lately committed to prison, in another county to that in which he and his family are residing, and the question now is, whether the son's wife and family are, during his absence, legally removable. Would the 68th sec. of the above-mentioned statute affect the son's settlement under the circumstances above stated? If not, would not the latter part of the first sec. of the 9 & 10 Vic. c. 66, prevent the family from being removable, as the husband being in prison is himself irremovable?"

Ans.—The party referred to derived his settlement through his father; and even had the father lost his settlement, obtained by estate, by removal from the parish, the derivative settlement of the son would not be destroyed thereby; (see Reg. *v.* Hendon, 12 L. I. R. M. C. 3.) But in the present case, it appears that the father has not lost such settlement; assuming, therefore, that the son has not gained a settlement in any other parish he still retains his derivative settlement. In Reg. *v.* Hendon, Lord Denman observed,—"The settlement, put an end to by sec. 68, is that gained by the person himself, but not a settlement gained by derivation through him." With respect to the question of the irremovability of the son's wife and family, the Board refer the guardians of the Loughborough Union to the provisions of the recent Act, 11 & 12 Vic. c. 111, amending the 9 & 10 Vic. c. 66.

6. SETTLEMENT AND UNION CHARGEABILITY.

[*Case submitted under* 11 *&* 12 *Vic.* c. 110, sec. 4.]

12th Jan., 1849.

Clerk of the Lymington Union.—Stating the case of a pauper named Stephen Rickman, and requesting the Board's opinion as to his chargeability to the common fund of the union.

Ans.—Before the Board can entertain the question they require to be furnished with a joint statement analogous to that referred to in sec. 4 of the 11 & 12 Vic. c. 110, which should be drawn up by the clerk to the guardians, and signed by the chairman on behalf of the board of guardians, and by the guardian of the particular parish interested.

26th Jan., 1849.

Lymington Union.—"Case submitted to the Poor Law Board pursuant to the Act 11 & 12 Vic. c. 110, with a request that they will entertain and determine the question, whether the pauper, to whom it relates, is a pauper of the parish of Boldre, exempted from liability to be removed from the parish of Hordle under the provisions of the 9 & 10 Vic. c. 66.—Stephen Rickman, now residing in the parish of Hordle, about five years since became the purchaser of a small property in that parish under the following circumstances:—Elias Rickman, having purchased some land of Mr. Richard Cox, agreed to sell Stephen Rickman a portion of it for £52. 10*s.*, but the latter having no money to effect the purchase, Mr. Brown, a solicitor, agreed to advance the purchase-money for him, and also a sum of money to enable him to erect a cottage on the land. Stephen Rickman commenced building a cottage, and when it was nearly completed a conveyance was, executed to him by Elias Rickman, and a receipt for the purchase-money of £52. 10*s.* as having been paid by Stephen Rickman, was endorsed on the deed. A mortgage, bearing date the day following that of the conveyance, was immediately made to Mr. Brown to cover the purchase-money which he had advanced, his costs for preparing the conveyance and mortgage, and the money advanced to Stephen Rickman to enable him to build the cottage. The interest of Stephen Rickman in the property is, and ever has been, of little or no value, and it is extremely doubtful whether in case of a sale, the property would realize the amount of the mortgage-money charged thereon and the interest due. Stephen Rickman has become chargeable to Hordle parish on account of sickness. His original settlement is in Boldre parish, and it now becomes necessary to decide the question, whether he has acquired a new settlement by his purchase in Hordle, or otherwise, in order that the relief given to him may be charged to this parish, or to the common fund of the union.

(Signed) " THOS. E. SYMONDS,
" *Chairman of the Board of Guardians of the Lymington Union, and Guardian for the Parish of Hordle.*
" 13*th Jan.*, 1849."

Ans.—The Board having given the case their consideration are of opinion, that as a settlement appears to have been gained by the pauper in the parish of Hordle, according to the case of Reg. *v.* Tidford, B. S. C. 57, admitted in Reg. *v.* Olney, 1 M. & S. 387, the pauper is not within the provisions of the 11 & 12 Vic. c. 110, sec. 3.

---

7. PROOF OF SETTLEMENT, IN REFERENCE TO UNION CHARGEABILITY.

26*th Jan.*, 1849.

Clerk of the Liskeard Union.—Inquiring whether, before a pauper, who is irremovable under the 9 & 10 Vic. c. 66, can be considered chargeable to the common fund under the 11 & 12 Vic. c. 110, s. 3, it is indispensable, in order to satisfy the terms of the latter Act, " not being settled in the parish where he resides," that strict and legal proof be given to the guardians, that such pauper has a settlement in some other parish than that in which he resides; or whether it will be sufficient, if it be proved that he is not settled in that parish. Inquiring also, whether the guardians are not now correct in interpreting sec. 1 of the 9 & 10 Vic. c. 66, agreeably to the decision in Reg. *v.* Christchurch.

Ans.—The Board do not think it necessary to be proved that the pauper has a settlement in some other parish. It is enough that he is not settled in the parish where he resides. Upon this point the Board do not think that the guardians of the Liskeard Union can always expect strict legal proof, as it is a negative proposition which cannot always admit of such proof. With regard to the interpretation of sec. 1 of 9 & 10 Vic. c. 66, the Board consider that the guardians should certainly abide by the recent decision of the Court of Queen's Bench, in the case Reg. *v.* Christchurch, in all cases to which that decision applies.

5*th March*, 1849.

Clerk of the Merthyr Tydvil Union.—Inquiring first, whether, under the 11 & 12 Vic. c. 110, sec. 3, irremovable paupers not settled in the parish in which they are resident, but of whose settlement no evidence can be given, are chargeable to the common fund of the union, although in fact the 9 & 10 Vic. c. 66, throws no additional burden on such parish as regards the paupers in question; and secondly, whether Irish, Scotch, or foreign paupers, who have a five years' residence, but no settlement, are chargeable to the common fund.

Ans.—First, as regards the paupers referred to in the first question, the Board have only to point out to the guardians that if it can be clearly shown that such paupers are not settled in the parish of their residence, and have become irremovable by reason of long residence, they are chargeable to the common fund of the union, though their actual place of settlement cannot be ascertained. Second, The Board consider in regard to the irremovability of Scotch, Irish, and foreign paupers, that the provisions of the 9 & 10 Vic. cap. 66, are applicable to these classes; and if so, that the relief of such paupers is rightly to be charged to the common fund of the union, when the circumstances of the case fall within the 3rd sec. of the 11 & 12 Vic. cap. 110.

8*th March*, 1849.

Clerk of the Bodmin Union.—Inquiring what proofs the guardians should require, with respect to the settlement of a pauper, who is irremovable by reason of residence, before they proceed to charge his relief to the common fund of the union, under the 3rd sec. of the 11 & 12 Vic. c. 110.

Ans.—Upon the point submitted, the Board do not think that they can give the guardians any precise directions. They can only observe generally, that the guardians must ascertain by the best means which may be available in the respective cases, whether the pauper be or be not settled in the parish of the residence. The guardians will not be concluded on this point by any assertion of the overseers; neither can they require the overseers to disprove the fact of such settlement. In any case in which doubts may exist, it is probable that an examination of the pauper himself would enable the guardians to clear up the matter, and to arrive at a satisfactory conclusion.

19*th March*, 1849.

Chairman of the Eastry Union.—Requesting the Board's advice as to the proper course to be pursued, in ascertaining the legal settlement of paupers relieved in the union, with reference to the chargeability of their relief to the common fund of the union, under sec. 3 of the 11 & 12 Vic. c. 110.

Ans.—It is certainly competent for the guardians of the Eastry Union to ascertain whether a pauper be legally settled in the parish of his residence, or not, before they charge the cost of his relief upon the common fund of the union. But in doing this, it is incumbent upon them to proceed in a fair and proper manner; and where they cannot find a reasonable proof of the pauper's settlement, they should (if he be irremovable) charge the cost of his relief to the common fund. They ought not to admit, as conclusive, the mere assertion made by a pauper of his having gained a settlement in the parish of his residence, without a proper investigation as to the grounds of that assertion.

30*th March*, 1849.

The same.—Inquiring whether boards of guardians have a right to adjudicate upon previously undetermined and otherwise doubtful cases of settlement, where the overseers are satisfied that such cannot be legally proved; and if they have, then what remedy have the overseers who may feel aggrieved by their decision.

Ans.—It certainly appears to the Board to be competent to the guardians, under the 3rd sec. of the Act 11 & 12 Vic. c. 110, to ascertain for themselves whether the pauper, the chargeability of whose relief they are required to determine, be settled in the parish of his residence or not. If, after investigating the matter, the guardians decide that the pauper is settled in the parish of his residence, and direct his relief to be charged accordingly to that parish, and not to the common fund of the union, it will be open to the parish officers to appeal to the auditor, and contest the charge before him. If the auditor concur with the guardians, and confirm the charge made against the parish, the overseers or any rate-payer who may be aggrieved by the charge, may appeal to the Poor Law Board, or to the Court of Queen's Bench, under the provisions of the 7 & 8 Vic. c. 101.

---

8. Orders of Maintenance, on Relations, in Cases of Union Chargeability.

1*st Feb.*, 1849.

Clerk of the Durham Union.—Stating that an infirm old man, who is irremovable to his place of settlement in consequence of a five years' residence, has become chargeable to the union, and that he has a son who, the guardians consider, is of ability to maintain him, but refuses to do so; and inquiring whether the application to a magistrate for a summons against the son should be made by one of the overseers of the parish in which the old man resides, or by the relieving officer of the district in which such parish is situate, or by the clerk of the union.

Ans.—The application to the justices for a summons, under the circumstances herein described, should not be made by the overseers of the parish in which the infirm old man is residing, but by the guardians of the Durham Union, under the provisions of sec. 8, of 11 & 12 Vic. c. 110. And according to the instructions contained in Article 202, No. 11, of the General Consolidated Order, the clerk to the guardians is required to conduct, on their behalf, such application to the justices.

---

9. Proceedings under Vagrant Act, in Cases of Union Chargeability.

19*th March*, 1849.

Clerk of the Caxton and Arrington Union.—Inquiring whether a pauper, whose relief is charged to the common fund of the union, under the 11 & 12 Vic. c. 110, sec. 3, can be punished under the Vagrant Act for deserting his wife and family, and leaving them chargeable to that fund.

Ans.—The Board entertain so much doubt whether, having regard to the terms of the 5th Geo. 4, c. 83, a chargeability to the common fund of the union is such a chargeability as is contemplated by the statute, that they cannot recommend the guardians of the Caxton and Arrington Union to attempt to obtain a conviction at present in the case of the man alluded to as having deserted his wife and family.

10. REMOVAL AND MAINTENANCE OF LUNATICS.
18*th Dec.*, 1848.

Clerk of the Bedminster Union.—A female lunatic, whose settlement is in the parish of C., but who, with her husband, has resided for more than five years in the adjoining parish of T., and is consequently irremovable, has been sent to the Somerset County Lunatic Asylum; and the guardians wish to be informed whether her maintenance in that asylum should be paid for by the parish of C., or charged to the common fund of the union.

Ans.—The removal of a lunatic pauper to an asylum is expressly excepted by the second proviso from the operation of the enacting clause in the 1st sec. of the 9 & 10 Vic. cap 66; and consequently the female lunatic referred to was not exempted from removal by that enactment. The cost of her maintenance in the asylum, therefore, does not appear to the Board to be chargeable to the common fund of the Bedminster Union, according to the 11 & 12 Vic. cap. 110. It may be that her husband is irremovable from T. under the provisions of the 9 & 10 Vic. cap. 66; but the Board do not see anything in that circumstance to prevent the justices making an order on the parish of the settlement, to provide for the maintenance of the wife, in accordance with the provisions of the Lunatic Asylums' Act, 8 & 9 Vic. cap. 126.

3*rd March*, 1849.

Clerk of the Bakewell Union.—Inquiring whether, in consequence of a lunatic being sent to a lunatic asylum, having previously resided with his family in the parish of *B.* in this union for a period of upwards of five years continuously, and thereby become irremovable under the 9 & 10 Vic. cap. 66, sec. 1, the residence of the pauper is broken.

Ans.—In conformity with the decision of the Court of Queen's Bench in the case of Reg. *v.* Salford (17 L. I. R. n. s. M. C. 170) the Board are of opinion the court would hold that the confinement of the pauper in the lunatic asylum would be an interruption of his residence. The question, however, as to the particular parish liable for the cost of the maintenance of the lunatic pauper in such case depends upon the Lunatic Asylum Acts, and not upon the provisions of the 9 & 10 Vic. c. 66.

11. RELIEF OF WAYFARERS AND WANDERERS.
3*rd Feb.*, 1849.

Clerk of the Shepton Mallet Union.—Requesting the Board's opinion as to the chargeability of the relief of a pauper, named Thomas March, under the following circumstances:—"On the 1st of October last, Thomas March, single man, aged 39 years, suffering from an ulcerated leg, left Pylle, a parish in this union, where he had been lodging without intermission during the last two years, and went to Evercreech, an adjoining parish in the union, which he supposed to be the legal place of his settlement, where he slept at a public house, and applied to the relieving officer who resided there on the following morning for relief, but he refused to relieve him, stating that he ought to have applied to the relieving officer of the district in which Pylle is situate, and referred him to the meeting of the board of guardians on that day. Thomas March then went to the house at Pylle, where he had been lodging as above stated, and where he left his clothes, and had his leg dressed, and his breakfast, and attended the meeting of the board of guardians, where he stated the above circumstances, and also that he had given up his lodgings at Pylle, and he did not know where he was going to sleep that night. The guardians then ordered him relief in the workhouse to be charged to Pylle, considering that he had not broken his residence there."

Ans.—If the relief given to this pauper by the guardians were rendered necessary through sickness, and that sickness be not likely as it appears to produce permanent disability, the relief ought to be a charge upon the common fund of the Shepton Mallet Union. But the Board gather from the facts of the case before them that the pauper was a destitute wanderer, having no home. He had left Pylle after giving up his lodgings there; had gone to Evercreech, where also he had no abode; and returned to Pylle, in which parish he no longer possessed a home. It certainly appears to the Board therefore that the case falls within the 1st sec. of the 11 & 12 Vic. cap. 110, and consequently that the cost of the pauper's relief should be borne by the common fund.

22*nd Feb.*, 1849.

Clerk of the Clifton Union.—Requesting the

Board's opinion as to the mode of charging the relief afforded in the following case:—" *A. B.* has a son *C. D.*, who resided with his father in the parish of X. for the last seven years, excepting four days and nights as here described. *C. D.* in his examination says, I am 23 years of age, my father told me on or about the 10th of November last to go out of his house and not to come there again. In consequence of what he said to me I went into Beckett's Fields, in the parish of Y., and slept there four nights, and I never returned again to my father's house. I was sent into the workhouse on the fifth day after I left my father's house."

Ans.—It appears to the Board that the pauper at the time of his being sent into the workhouse was a destitute wanderer, and therefore that the cost of his relief is chargeable to the common fund of the union, under sec. 1 of 11 & 12 Vic. cap. 110, and not to the parish of his settlement.

---

12. Removal and relief of widows.

15*th Jan.*, 1849.

Clerk of the Holywell Union.—Inquiring as to the removability and chargeability of the widows and families of persons who may have resided five years consecutively in any parish without receiving relief.

Ans.—Widows of persons who may have resided in a parish five years consecutively without receiving relief are certainly rendered irremovable by 9 & 10 Vic. c. 66, as sec. 2 would prevent the removal for the space of one year from the death of the husband. Moreover, at the expiration of the twelve months, the widow would still be irremovable by operation of sec. 1, if she had then resided in the parish for the period of five years clear of the time during which she might have been in receipt of relief. It would make no difference as regards the irremovability that a portion of the five years' residence was in the character of wife, and the remaining portion in that of widow. The case of Reg. *v.* Glossop, 17 Law Journal Rep. n.s. m.c. 171, shows that residence as widow may be joined with residence as wife to complete the five years' residence required for irremovability.

1*st Feb.*, 1849.

Town Clerk of Welch Pool.—Stating the following case, viz.:—" *B.*, a poor person, (who has not resided for five years in parish C.,) together with his wife and child, become chargeable to that parish in consequence of the husband's illness. An order is duly obtained for their removal to parish D., as the place of their legal settlement, and the justices granting the warrant for removal, therein state that they are satisfied such sickness will produce permanent disability. By a subsequent order, made by the same justices upon the day that the removal order was granted, the execution of the latter was suspended (in consequence of its being dangerous for *B.* to travel by reason of sickness,) until it should be made to appear that the same might be safely executed without danger. Shortly afterwards *B.* dies in parish C., and under the 2nd sec. of the 9 & 10 Vic. cap. 66, his widow cannot be removed therefrom for twelve calendar months next after her husband's death. In consequence of her poverty relief is continued to the widow and her child by parish C., under the suspended order." And with reference to the foregoing case, making the following inquiries:—" 1st. Whether the relief to the widow by parish C., during the twelve months next after her husband's death, can be recovered from parish D., under the suspension of the order of removal before mentioned? 2ndly. Could not parish C., immediately upon the death of *B.*, take off the suspension of the order, and direct the expenses incurred up to that time by parish C. to be repaid by parish D., and then further suspend the execution of the order for the twelve months, until the widow would become removable, and therefore the relief given to her during that period to be reimbursed by parish D?"

Ans.—1st. The Board are of opinion that the cost of the relief administered during the first year of the widowhood is not recoverable under the suspended order, in the case described.—2nd. The death of the pauper to be removed having occurred, the costs due up to the time of the decease are recoverable at once under 35 Geo. 3, cap. 101, sec. 2, but there can be no further suspension of the order. The precise effect of the 9 & 10 Vic. cap. 66, sec. 2, upon the suspended order in this case is not very clear, but the Board would recommend that if the widow be removable at the expiration of the first twelvemonth of her widowhood, and if the overseers of the parish upon which her relief may then fall think it right to remove her and her children, a fresh order should be obtained.

London: Printed by Order of the Poor Law Board, by Blackburn & Burt, 90½, Holborn Hill, and Published by Charles Knight, 90, Fleet Street.

AN

OFFICIAL CIRCULAR

OF PUBLIC DOCUMENTS AND INFORMATION:

DIRECTED BY THE POOR LAW BOARD TO BE PRINTED, CHIEFLY FOR THE USE OF THE BOARDS OF GUARDIANS AND THEIR OFFICERS.

No. 24.] APRIL, 1849. [N.S.

CONTENTS.

I.—ACCOUNTS.

1. STATISTICAL PORTION OF RELIEF LIST.

24th July, 1848.

Clerk of Chippenham Union.—Inquiring, with reference to the General Order of Accounts, whether it is intended that Columns 1 and 2 in the In-Door Relief List, Form 22, and headed, "Males and Females, Married Couples," should include those cases in which only one married person is residing in the house, whether on account of desertion, or otherwise.

Ans.—In the form of In-Door Relief List, prescribed by the General Accounts Order, it is not intended that one married person should be entered in Columns 1 and 2, under the heading, "Married Couples;" but in Columns 9 and 10, under headings, "Other Males," and "Other Females," as the case may be.

2. OUT-DOOR RELIEF LIST.

18th Oct., 1848.

Clerks of St. Thomas's Union.—In note No. 2, to the Out-Door Relief List, Form 34, it is stated that "if the relief is given on account of the sickness of a wife, or child, or specially for a wife or child, the wife or child only, and the head of the family, are to be inserted in the list; the man in the case of such sickness in Column 3, and in any other case in Column 4, the wife or child in Column 5 or 6." According to the heading of Columns 5 and 6, the families of adult males resident with the father are to be entered in Columns 1, 2, 3, and 4. These instructions are, apparently, contradictory. If the relieving officers enumerate their paupers according to the instructions in the note, they will omit, in a family consisting of a husband, wife, and six children, in cases where relief for the sickness of one child is given, the enumeration of the wife and five children; but if they enumerate in accordance with the heading of the Columns 5 and 6, they will include all the family resident with the father. Requested instructions on the subject, in order to secure uniformity of enumeration.

Ans.—On consideration, it will be seen that the contradiction to which you refer does not actually exist. In the filling up of the statistical portion of the Out-Door Relief List, the instructions at the foot of the Form, (No. 34,) in the Schedule to the General Order of Accounts, must be observed, which explain and qualify the abbreviated headings of the columns. For instance, where a man, having a wife and six children, is relieved on account of the want of work, or his own sickness, his name should be inserted in the column headed "Name of the Pauper;" and, opposite to his name, in Column 3 or 4, should be inserted 1 for the man, in Column 5, 1 for the wife, and in Column 6, 6 for the children. But if the relief be given on account of the sickness of one of the children, the man's name should be inserted in the proper column, and in Column 3, 1 for the man himself, and in Column 6, 1 for the sick child; the wife and the other five children not being in that case noticed. The term "Families" in the heading to Columns 5 and 6, applies to such members of the family only as are required to be entered, according to the directions in the Order.

8th Nov., 1848.

Clerks of same Union.—On granting relief to an able-bodied man for the sickness of one child, he would be enumerated in Column 3 of the Out-Door Relief List, his child in Column 6; but subsequent relief is granted on account of his own sickness, which would seem to require his enumeration in Column 2, and his wife and all his children in Columns 5 and 6. Must the relieving officer alter the classification, by enumerating the wife and children; or, must the enumeration of the pauper and his family remain as originally entered for the sickness of his child?

Ans.—On the second occasion of granting relief, the case should be entered anew, and the classification of the pauper and his family should be changed, and the particulars enumerated according to the actual circumstances existing when the subsequent relief is given. If this be done, the relief granted on account of the pauper's own sickness will come into new columns, and on another line in the money portion of the account; while the entry of that which was previously given him on account of the sickness of his child will of course be discontinued from the time when the allowance ceased. The money columns will thus be filled up according to the amount of the relief actually afforded on the several occasions of his becoming chargeable. The result, as regards the statistical statement, may certainly tend to exhibit a greater number of paupers as relieved during the half-year than in fact have been relieved; though the numbers relieved in any given week, or on any given day, will be correctly stated. This appears to be all the information that can be accurately obtained in the matter, owing to the nature of the subject which is exposed to so many variations and accidents; unless, indeed, the clerk may be able to rectify the gross total of the numbers relieved, by making a deduction at the close of the half-year in respect of those paupers who may, in consequence of their falling into more than one class, have been unavoidably entered more than once. It is right to add, that no pauper (according to the instructions in Note 5, in Form No. 34) should be entered more than once in the half-year, however frequently his relief may be discontinued and renewed, if his relief be so renewed from time to time under circumstances so far similar as not to cause a change of the class.

---

3. ENTRY OF COST OF RELIEF TO IRREMOVABLE POOR IN FINANCIAL STATEMENT.

19th March, 1849.

Clerk of Melton Mowbray Union.—As the irremovable poor are now a direct charge upon the union, and the amount expended for their in-maintenance and out-relief must be transferred to the common charges, previous to apportionment amongst the several parishes, inquiring whether a statement of those sums, at the foot of the half-yearly financial statement, under the head "Particulars of Common Charges," will be sufficient; or whether the amounts must also be charged to the union in the in-maintenance and out-relief columns. If the latter course be adopted, those sums will be charged twice, and the total expenditure will appear larger than the true amount. But if the former, the correct total will be given, and the full total expended in in-maintenance and out-relief respectively can always be ascertained by referring to the foot of the financial statement.

Ans.—The Board are of opinion that, in preparing the half-yearly financial statement, the proper course will be, certainly, to include the amount of the cost of relief to the irremovable poor and vagrants in the second column, under the heading "Common Charges," No. 13; and to show the total amount, divided into two heads, namely, in-maintenance and out-relief, in the note at the foot of the financial statement.

---

4. CHARGING THE COST OF RELIEF TO IRREMOVABLE POOR.

22*nd March*, 1849.

Clerk of Andover Union.—Requesting instructions as to the mode of charging the relief of the irremovable poor to the common fund, and entering the same in the accounts.

Ans.—The relief of the class of paupers referred to will, henceforth, under the provisions of the 11 & 12 Vic. c. 110, be a charge to be made directly upon the common fund of the union, (see secs. 3 & 5,) and not, as heretofore, upon the individual parishes in the first instance, and subsequently upon the union by way of reimbursement to the parishes. It appears to the Board that, for this purpose, it will be necessary to treat the union throughout the accounts as a kind of parish of itself. The total amount of the relief should be carried to the Common Charges Account, and entered under the subdivisions of in-maintenance and out-relief. In the Financial Statement, Form 17, in the Schedule to the General Accounts Order, the total will appear in the Column No. 13, with the rest of the Common Charges; but the particulars must be entered as well in the note at the foot of the form prescribed by the Order, and subdivided as above stated. The same course will apply to the relief given to vagrants, as in the case of irremovable poor.

---

5. CHARGING FUNERAL EXPENSES—AND ADJUSTING COST OF RELIEF GIVEN TO UNSETTLED POOR SUPPOSED TO BE IRREMOVABLE—REG. *v.* CHRISTCHURH.

13*th Feb.*, 1849.

Clerk of Kingsclere Union.—Requesting the directions of the Poor Law Board in consequence of the recent decision of the Court of Queen's Bench, with respect to irremovable paupers:—M. S. has lived twenty years in Burghclere, being an acknowledged pauper of, and during nearly the whole of that period relieved by the parish of Itchingswell; both parishes are in this union. M. S. has been relieved as irremovable by Burghclere, at the charge of the common fund, since the operation of the 9 & 10 Vic. c. 66. She is now dead, and the guardians consider that the expense of the funeral should be placed to Itchingswell. There are several cases, it is feared, of paupers adjudged heretofore to be relieved where they were resident, and since placed on the common fund, who (according to the late decision of the Court of Queen's Bench) were removable, and should not have been so placed, some of whom have now become irremovable; and there are others on the Irremovable List, who, if their cases were now inquired into, would be found to be removable paupers.

Ans.—If the case comes within the 31st sec. of the 7 & 8 Vic. c 101, the funeral expenses must be charged to the parish to which the pauper herself was chargeable at the time of her death, if that parish be within the Kingsclere Union; otherwise, to the parish in which the death took place. But if the pauper at the time of her death was irremovable under some provision of the 9 & 10 Vic. c. 66, and consequently chargeable to the common fund of the union, the funeral expenses would also be chargeable to that fund, under the 3rd sec. of the 11 & 12 Vic. c. 110. In point of fact, it appears that the pauper's relief at the time of her death was entered in the union accounts as a charge upon the common fund, and not against any particular parish; but it is now contended that she was not legally irremovable, and therefore not properly chargeable to the common fund. Under the circumstances stated in your letter, this appears to be correct, having regard to the decision in Reg. *v.* Christchurch; and, consequently, the relief granted to her since the time when the union accounts were last closed and audited should now be transferred from the common fund, and charged to the parish of residence. The cost of the burial will follow the charge for the relief, and will accordingly be borne by the parish of Burghclere. The Board think it right to add, that they see no legal ground, under the circumstances of the present case, for charging the funeral expenses to the parish of Itchingswell. With reference to the concluding remarks in your letter, the Board trust that the erroneous charges which resulted from the interpretation put by the law officers of the crown upon the first proviso to the 1st sec. of the 9 & 10 Vic. c. 66, will soon be adjusted.

Clerk of same Union.—Inquiring whether, in cases in which persons belonging to other unions, who had previously to the passing of the 10 & 11 Vic. c. 66, received relief through this union, at the request of such other unions, and who, on the supposition of the correctness of the opinion of the Attorney and Solicitor-General, were afterwards relieved by this union from the common fund, the relief can be at once transferred to the unions at whose expense such persons were before relieved. Or, whether orders of removal must in all cases be resorted to.

Ans.—The relief given in the Kingsclere Union to paupers settled in other unions, but supposed (upon the interpretation given by the Attorney-General and Solicitor-General) to be irremovable from some parish in the Kingsclere Union, cannot, in consequence of the decision in Reg. *v.* Christchurch, be at once transferred to such other unions. Those unions can only be made responsible upon express contract, and, therefore, if the paupers be removable, and the cases be those in which non-resident relief can be lawfully given, regard being had to the regulations of the Poor Law Commissioners, such other unions may enter into engagements to repay relief granted by the guardians of the Kingsclere Union; but, otherwise, such paupers must either be relieved at the charge of the parishes in which they reside, or be removed by orders of justices to the places of their settlement.

2nd Jan., 1849.

6. CHARGING LOSS ARISING ON THE SALE OF BROKEN STONES.

Walsall District Auditor.—The guardians of the ——— Union, some years since, employed paupers to break stones. The stones were bought and charged to the establishment, and the broken stones sold to different parties. Those sold to the surveyors of the highways of W. & D. have not been paid for, and it is believed the guardians are now advised they cannot recover from either. They have in the accounts presented for audit charged the amount thus supposed to be lost to the parishes of W. & D., and given credit to the surveyors against whom it had been charged. As he considers the amount not to be a legal charge on the poor-rates of those parishes, requested advice how to deal with it. Must it be treated as a payment disallowed, and the parties ordering the parishes to be charged, surcharged; and if it should appear there is no order for the charge, is the clerk to be surcharged for making it?

Ans.—Under the circumstances represented in your letter, the entries you describe as having been made by the guardians to the debit of the parishes of W. & D. appear to the Board to be altogether erroneous. As the Board understand the case, it seems that the guardians have charged themselves with having received from the highway surveyors certain sums which have not in fact been paid to them, and have accounted for the deficiency thereby occasioned in the balance, by charging the amounts as payments to the abovementioned parishes. These entries are incorrect, inasmuch as they are not in accordance with the facts of the case, and the only mode of rectifying the accounts appears to be, to reject the items in question altogether. With regard to the amounts with which the highway surveyors stand charged, in respect of the goods sold to them, the Board desire to remark, that if a loss be sustained thereon, through the neglect of any particular person or persons, such person or persons might be surcharged with the amount, which may have been lost through his or their neglect, and which would thus be introduced into the accounts of the union. But it does not appear, from the present statement of the case, that there is any person who can be so charged. There certainly seems to be no authority for charging any such loss to the account of the guardians with the parishes alluded to above.

15th Feb., 1849.

Clerk of the —— Union.—In the year 1842, the Poor Law Commissioners issued to this union a Labour Test Order, bearing date the 17th of August; and under that Order a great number of persons were employed at breaking stones, and the money and food given to the paupers were duly charged in the Relief Books to the parishes they were settled or resided in. The stones, after being broken, were sold at a loss, and there remains as such loss a balance of £202. 5*s*. 8*d*., which the guardians would prefer to have apportioned amongst the only parishes in the union that set their poor so to work, (five of such parishes not having any of their poor at such work;) they would cast up the total amount of the relief given for work done for each of the other three parishes respectively, and divide the amount of the loss according to those totals, but the auditor deems that mode of sharing the loss illegal, and is of opinion that it should be divided according to the declared averages then in force.

Ans.—The Board would direct the attention of the guardians to the 28th sec. of the Poor Law Amendment Act, (4 & 5 Wm. 4, c. 76,) which provides that the cost of the utensils and materials for setting the poor to work shall be charged on the common fund of the union. The consequence of this provision is, that the cost of the granite, purchased by the guardians in the present case, must be charged to such fund, and the proceeds arising from the labour of the paupers should likewise be placed to the same account. If those proceeds exceed the expenditure, so as in fact to yield a profit, the common fund will derive the advantage; if, on the other hand, there be a loss, the same fund must bear it. The question, as to what paupers have been engaged under the Out-Door Labour Test Order, is altogether immaterial for this purpose; indeed, they are virtually union paupers.

II. APPRENTICESHIP.

1. OF A BOY WHOSE FATHER IS IRREMOVABLE.

11*th Jan.*, 1848.

Clerk of Aberayron Union.—Inquiring, whether the premium to be paid on the apprenticeship of a boy, aged fifteen, whose father has resided in a parish in the union upwards of five years, and who is consequently irremovable, but who is not at present in receipt of relief, should be charged to the common fund of the union, under the 11th & 12th Vic. c. 110.

Ans.—Assuming the apprenticeship to be duly effected, and the father to be irremovable, the amount of the premium being a mode or species of relief, should be charged under sec. 3 of the above-mentioned statute to the common fund of the union.

2. FATHER DEAD AND MOTHER A LUNATIC.

3*rd Nov.*, 1848.

Clerk of Thirsk Union.—The guardians have

arranged for the apprenticeship of a boy, an inmate of the workhouse, whose mother is a widow, and is at present confined in a lunatic asylum; inquiring whether the binding can be legally effected without the consent of the mother.

Ans.—On referring to the General Consolidated Order of the 24th July, 1847, the Board perceive that, by Art. 57, in a case where the father is dead, the consent of the mother, if alive, is required to the binding of her child an apprentice. The apprenticeship proposed in the present instance, (the mother being, it appears, unable to give her consent,) cannot, therefore, be effected so as to operate as a binding under the Order in question. It would, however, be valid in other respects as a voluntary binding between the parties, who, of course, would be bound by the terms of the covenants, although not taking place under the Order referred to, the guardians would not be authorized in incurring any expenses in respect of such apprenticeship, nor in giving any premium.

III.—AUDIT OF ACCOUNTS.—CONSTRUCTION OF 11 & 12 VIC. C. 91.

4*th Nov.*, 1848.

W. J. Patterson, Esq., District Auditor.—Requesting the opinion of the Poor Law Board on the following points, in reference to the Act 11 & 12 Vic. c. 91. 1st, Sec. 5, "Provided always, that when the sum, or aggregate of the sums, disallowed by the auditors," &c.—Is this provision intended to apply to those cases only where an officer may be continuing in office at the time of the audit, or is it intended that it should operate in all cases where the amount disallowed is less than forty shillings? For instance, in the accounts of an overseer who has quitted office, a balance is shown to be due from him at the time of the audit, which balance, admitting there were no disallowances, would be certified by the auditor, and would, therefore, be paid to the treasurer of the union. But if in those accounts there were disallowances, the amount of which was less than forty shillings, may the same "be paid over with the balance due from such officer instead of being paid to the treasurer of the union," and if so, to whom should they be paid over? In cases where the amount of surcharges is less than forty shillings, can the same "be paid over with the balance due from such officer, instead of being paid to the treasurer of the union?" 2nd, In overseers' accounts, should the names of the whole of the overseers be inserted in the Certificate Form No. 1? 3rd, If a balance be found to be due from an officer in addition to disallowances or surcharges, will it be necessary for the auditor first to certify as to the amount of surcharge or disallowance, in accordance with Form No. 1, then give a statement showing the total amount due, and then a certificate that such amount is due?

Ans.—1st, In reference to the first point raised in your communination, the Board are of opinion that the reasonable construction of sec. 5 is, that the proviso to the sec. applies to all cases in which the sum disallowed is less than forty shillings, whether the officer be continuing in office at the time when the disallowance is made or not. In the case put, of an overseer whose year of office is terminated, the sums disallowed in his accounts under forty shillings may, in accordance with the terms of the proviso, be paid over, together with any balance, to the succeeding overseers. If, however, the balance be not so paid to the succeeding overseers, but to the treasurer, then the sums disallowed, whether amounting to forty shillings or not, should accompany the balance which will be so paid to the treasurer. With respect to the course of proceeding in regard to surcharges, the proviso does not in terms apply to them, but they would reasonably follow the same rule as is applicable to disallowances. 2nd, The Certificate No. 1, given in the schedule to the statute in question, should, as the Board think, contain the names of all the overseers who actually account to the auditor. 3rd, As regards your concluding inquiry, the Board have to observe that, at the Michaelmas audit, the balance of an officer's account is not to be certified as due, but the disallowances and surcharges are to be certified in Form No. 1, above alluded to. At the same time, the auditor at such audit is still required to make and sign the statement at the foot of the overseer's account, showing the state of the balance. At the Lady-day audit, disallowances or surcharges then made should, in like manner, be certified in the Form No. 1. If there be any balance due from the accounting officer beyond such disallowances and surcharges, such balance must undoubtedly be certified to be due, but the form of certificate given by the 11 & 12 Vic. c. 91, will not suffice for the purpose. In such a case, the aggregate of the disallowances or surcharges should be certified, with the balance in one sum as due, under sec. 32 of the 7 & 8 Vic. c. 101, of course after credit has been given for any sum which may have already been paid over to the succeeding officers, pursuant to sec. 5 of 11 & 12 Vic. c. 91

IV.—BASTARDY.

1. APPROPRIATION BY GUARDIANS OF MONEY PAID UNDER AN ORDER OF AFFILIATION.

12th Jan., 1849.

Clerk of Caxton and Arrington Union.—S. W., an able-bodied woman, belonging to the parish of Great Gransden, in this union, applied to the guardians for relief. She stated, that she was twenty-two years of age, and a single woman; that she had a bastard child, which was affiliated, and that the putative father had hitherto paid 1*s.* 6*d.* per week towards its maintenance, which was insufficient to support her and the child. She was ordered into the workhouse with her child, and the guardians wish to know if they can stop the 1*s.* 6*d.* per week, which is paid by the putative father, whilst the mother is in the workhouse.

Ans.—The guardians have no direct power of preventing the woman receiving from the putative father the money which, by the order of justices, he is required to pay weekly towards the support of her child whilst she continues to be an inmate of the union workhouse By sec. 5 of 7 & 8 Vic. c. 101, it will be seen, that the money payable under any such order is due and payable to the mother of the bastard child so long as she lives, and is of sound mind. If, however, when the weekly payments have been so made to the mother, she refuse voluntarily to hand over to the guardians the money which she so receives, in order that the parish may to this extent be reimbursed the cost of her maintenance, and that of her child, it will be for the guardians to consider, whether the pauper having a partial ability to maintain herself and child, they should not discharge her in the first instance from the workhouse, and thus cause her to make a fresh application when the means so derived are exhausted. In this way the Board believe the guardians would practically attain the object which they have in view, viz., that of preventing persons who have the means or ability partially to support themselves from depending wholly upon the poor-rates for their support.

2. OBLIGATION OF HUSBAND TO MAINTAIN DECEASED WIFE'S BASTARD CHILD.

7th Feb., 1849.

Clerk of Banbury Union.—Inquiring whether the husband of a woman who has had a bastard child is bound to support such child, the mother being dead.

Ans.—The obligation created by the 57th sec. of the 4 & 5 Wm. 4, c. 76, upon the husband of the mother of the bastard child to maintain such child, ceases with the death of the mother.

V.—BONDS.—Custody of bonds given by assistant overseers.

28th June, 1848.

Clerk of Droitwich Union.—Bonds have been given by the assistant overseers, in each instance, to the overseers, under the Act of 59 Geo. 3, but it is conceived by the guardians that they have no right to claim the custody of the same in preference to the overseers.

Ans.—The Board refer the guardians to the provisions of the 7th & 8th Vic. c. 101, sec. 61, which empowers the guardians, when they see fit, to put in suit any bond or security given by any officer in pursuance of that Act, or of the Act of 59 Geo. 3, notwithstanding that such bond or security may have been originally given to the overseers of the parish, or to any other person. The Board consider that, if the securities are not made out to the guardians as actual parties, they ought, in order to make them a sufficient security under the statute, to be delivered into the custody of the guardians, who could not otherwise enforce them as the statute 7 & 8 Vic. c. 101, enables them to do.

VI.—CHAPLAIN—Attendance of, at meetings of board of guardians.

23rd March, 1849.

Clerk of ——— *Union.*—Inquiring, whether the chaplain is bound to attend a meeting of the board of guardians in case they should wish for any information from him, and request him so to do.

Ans.—Under Article 154 of the General Consolidated Order, the Board think the chaplain of the ——— Union workhouse is bound to perform such duties as are conformable to the nature of his office, which may be reasonably required of him by the guardians. Attending a meeting of the guardians for the purpose of explaining any matters connected with his functions cannot be considered as otherwise than such a duty; but though the guardians might lawfully direct the chaplain to attend their meetings when any matters upon which he, individually, could give them particular and necessary information was about to be considered, the Board do not think it would be desirable for the guardians to give any general direction to the chaplain to attend their ordinary meetings, as much of his time would thereby be taken up with probably very little, if any, adequate beneficial result.

VII.—CLERK.—Printing for the union executed at an office in which the clerk has an interest.

9th April, 1846.

Mr. R. B., ——— *Union.*—Inquiring, whether a board of guardians can legally procure any of the printing which may be required for the union to be executed at a printing office in which their clerk has an interest. Observed that the Poor Law Commissioners had advised that the clerk, if a solicitor, might be employed to do the law business of the union, without incurring any penalties under the Statute 55 Geo. 3, c. 137; and that in the case of Barber *v.* Waite, 1 A. & E. 514; 3 L. I. n. s. M. C. 101, the Judges considered the statutes apply only where goods are actually supplied for the maintenance of the poor in a workhouse.

Ans.—The provisions of 55 Geo. 3, c. 137, which prohibit overseers and other parish officers from being concerned, either directly or indirectly, in providing or supplying any goods, materials, &c., for the use of any workhouse, or otherwise, for the support or maintenance of the poor, and impose a penalty for so doing, are expressly extended, by sec. 51, Poor Law Amendment Act, to every officer appointed under the provisions of that Act. They therefore extend to the clerk to the guardians: and the question is, whether the furnishing printed documents to the guardians by the clerk, or rather by a firm in which he has a pecuniary interest, is a case within the terms of 55 Geo. 3, c. 137; because, if it be a case to which the penalty would apply, it would follow that the guardians could not lawfully procure the printing to be done at such firms. The Commissioners think the point one of considerable doubt, but, on the whole, they are disposed to think the penalty would apply. In the case of Barber *v.* Waite, to which you refer, a plasterer, painter, and glazier, undertook to repair a workhouse, and supplied glass, lead pipe, paint, whiting, and pump bores, for which, and the labour, he was paid by the parish; and it was held that this was a contract for work and labour, and not for the supply of goods and materials, and, therefore, not within the statute. It is to be observed, however, that in such case the materials were applied to property of the guardians, to their windows, cisterns, walls; and the articles to which the labour and the materials were applied, and of which, when repaired, the materials formed only a part, were not supplied to the parish by the contractor. The case you put appears to the Commissioners to be distinguishable from Barber *v.* Waite, and in this respect—the goods, to which the labour of composition and printing have been applied, are supplied to the guardians; neither the labour nor the material are applied to the property of the guardians. It is true, that the greater part of the value may be produced by labour, but this would be the case of almost all manufactured goods, and would apply in nearly equal degree to clothes and many other goods clearly within the Statute. It, therefore, appears to the Commissioners, that where persons undertake to print documents for the guardians, the contract is for the supply of goods (paper) to which labour (printing) is applied, and not for work and labour, to which the materials are incidentally applied, and on these grounds it seems to the Commissioners the penalty would be held to apply.

VIII.—EDUCATION.

1. District schools.

The following letter on the subject of District Schools has been addressed by the Poor Law Board to the guardians of the Farnham and Hartley Wintney Unions:—

Poor Law Board,
Somerset House,
8th Jan., 1849.

SIR,—The Poor Law Board have had under their consideration the subject of a proposal made to them by Lord Courtenay and Mr. Pigott, Poor Law Inspectors, for the formation under 7 & 8 Vic. c. 101, and 11 & 12 Vic. c. 82, of a school district, to be composed of the Hartley Wintney and Farnham Unions. The Reports received from those inspectors point out the several advantages which would attend such a combination, and conclude by a recommendation that this Board, in pursuance of the powers vested in them, should issue the necessary order for the formation of such district.

The Board are informed by Lord Courtenay, that at a meeting of the guardians of the Hartley Wintney Union, at the close of the last month, which he attended, in conjunction with his colleague, Mr. Pigott, the guardians unanimously adopted a resolution expressing their general approval of the proposed plan. Mr. Pigott also reports, that on the 1st ultimo he attended a Special Meeting of the guardians of the Farnham Union, when the guardians resolved that it was desirable that a district for a school to be composed of the aforesaid unions should be formed, and that the workhouse at Aldershot, in the Farnham Union, would be found available for the purposes of such a school.

The Poor Law Board, being sensible of the great importance of the object to which the attention of the guardians of both unions has been directed, must express their satisfaction that the guardians have arrived at a conclusion which is at once in accordance with the views of this Board, and appears likely to conduce to the best interests of the pauper children, and of the ratepayers of the two unions. Seeing, moreover, that the circumstances of the Hartley Wintney and Farnham Unions offer some unusual local advantages and facilities for such a combination as that proposed, the Board are quite ready to give effect to the wishes of the guardians by issuing the necessary Order, provided they are furnished with the formal consent of the guardians in the enclosed Form.

The Board think it may be useful, if, in the present communication, they advert briefly to some general points or considerations which the proposal for the formation of a district school immediately suggests, as to the constitution of the district board, the appointment of the officers, and the relations between such district board and the boards of guardians which may compose the district.

1st, With respect to the constitution of such district board, it must be observed that the statute 7 & 8 Vic. c. 101 (sections 40 to 48 inclusive) points out in detail the mode in which such a combination or union is to be effected. It may suffice, therefore, in this communication, to state that the district board will consist of members to be chosen from persons rated within the district to the relief of the poor, (the qualification of such members, the number to be chosen by each union, and the period of office being fixed by this Board) that the election of the members of the district board will devolve upon the guardians of the respective unions, and further that the district board will consist exclusively of members so to be elected, with the addition of the chairman of each of the unions combined for this purpose, who will be entitled (if they are willing) to act as ex-officio members of the board.

2nd, With regard to the paid officers to be appointed for the management of the district school, the Board apprehend that something like the following will be found necessary, viz.:—

Clerk and chief master, at an ann. sal. of,	say £30
Matron and chief mistress, at	say £25
Industrial teacher for the boys, at	say £20
Under teacher for the girls, at	say £15
Chaplain,	
Medical officer, at	say £20

The guardians will find that the appointment of a chaplain is expressly required by the statute, (sec. 43.)

The Board think it most probable that the salaries of all the officers engaged in the immediate instruction and education of the children will be defrayed from the Parliamentary Grant, applicable to the repayment of the salaries of the schoolmasters and schoolmistresses of workhouse schools, while as regards the medical officer a moiety of the salary will be borne by the Grant available for this purpose. The Board having regard to the terms of the vote, are not prepared to pledge themselves that the salary of the chaplain will be paid out of the Parliamentary Grant; still as he is an officer, whose duty it is, (in the language of the statute) " to superintend the religious instruction of the infant poor," it is not improbable that his case may hereafter be brought within the conditions by which the distribution of the Parliamentary Grant is regulated.

3rd. With regard to the relation between the district board and the respective boards of guardians of the unions composing the district, the Poor Law Board find it difficult in the present communication to point out in minute detail the precise nature of those relations, or the relative powers of the two bodies. The Board must state, however, that the district board when once established will have the entire management of the school, and the education, maintenance, and clothing of the children therein. The district board will exercise these powers subject of course to the general powers of control vested in this Board, and subject to the right of visitation reserved by the statute to any of Her Majesty's Inspectors of Schools. The Poor Law Board take this opportunity to remark, that it is their desire and intention (where district schools are established) that the instruction, and training should be of a practical nature, calculated to enable the children to become at an early age independent, and this Board would require in each case that the dietary and clothing of them should be of as plain and simple a nature as is consistent with their full health and development. But the district board will, so far as these matters are concerned, be independent of the respective boards of guardians of the unions composing the district. The latter will be under the obligation to furnish from time to time the funds or contributions which they may be formally called upon to furnish for the purposes of the district school, in like manner as overseers of parishes in an ordinary union are now required by law to raise and pay over the requisite funds to the guardians of such union. The district board, with the assistance and advice of their medical officers, will see to the dieting of the children maintained in the school, though the final adoption or use of any scale of diet may be controlled and regulated by this Board. The appointment of the various officers of the school, the general control of such officers, the payment of their salaries, (these having been previously fixed and approved by this Board,) will belong to the district board, while the period during which the children of any union would remain in the district school would rest, as the duration of other relief rests, in the discretion of the guardians of the unions to which they (the children) belong, subject of course to the regulations of the Poor Law Board. There are other points of subordinate importance which will doubtless suggest themselves to the minds of the guardians, such as the admission and discharge of children, the regulations to be observed by parents who, on themselves leaving the workhouse or otherwise, may require the withdrawal of their children from the district school, the apprenticeship of the children, the duties of the various officers of the establishment, the books of account or otherwise which should be kept. These, and various points of detail, will be properly provided for in any Orders which the Poor Law Board may hereafter find it necessary to issue, under the authority of the statute for regulating the proceedings of the district board. The Poor Law Board will not, therefore, lengthen their present communication by adverting to these points. They will only mention, in addition, that they think the period of service of the members of the district board should be three years, the full period which the statute allows, (sec. 42,) and that five members should be elected for each of the unions constituting the district. I am, sir,

Your obedient servant,

(Signed) EBRINGTON,

Secretary.

2. BOOKS FOR WORKHOUSE SCHOOLS.

3rd March, 1849.

Clerk of Rochdale Union—Transmitting a resolution of the guardians, in reference to the Poor Law Board's Circular Letter of the 25th of January last, on the subject of the supply of books for the use of workhouse schools.

Ans.—The tenor of this resolution leads the Board to infer, that the object and nature of the arrangements which they have made in regard to this matter, have been misunderstood by the guardians. The attention of the Board had frequently been called to the scanty supply of books, and the necessary apparatus in workhouse schools, as well as to the unsuitable character of some of those in use. The Board, therefore, on the list of books and maps selected by the Committee of Council on Education for the use of certain schools for the poorer classes being brought under their notice, felt that the circulation of such a list among the several unions might tend to the improvement of workhouse schools; especially if similar reductions in the prices of the books, and similar facilities for obtaining them, were secured for workhouse schools that had been secured for the other schools. The arrangements which the Committee of Council had made with the several publishers would not, however, admit of the supply of books being extended to workhouse schools on the terms agreed upon between them and the Committee of Council; and the Board, therefore, with their Lordships' concurrence, entered into communication with the several publishers, and succeeded in inducing them to place workhouse schools on the same footing as those included in their Lordships' arrangements. The Committee of Council had appointed Messrs. Longman & Co. as the agents through whom the books were to be forwarded to the schools, and who were remunerated by a per centage paid by their Lordships, the very low terms on which the books were supplied not permitting of any allowance being made to them by the publishers. Every application for books is made to the Committee of Council, accompanied by a Post-office Order for the amount, and the money is then transmitted direct to the publishers, with the order for the books. It appeared to the Board that workhouse schools could be more conveniently furnished with books through Mr. Charles Knight—who, as the authorized publisher of the Poor Law Commission from its establishment, was in frequent communication with most of the unions—than through Messrs. Longman & Co., and he has been accordingly appointed their agent in the matter. The Board were not prepared to ask the Lords of the Treasury to sanction the payment of any expenses incident to the furnishing of books for workhouse schools out of the funds of the Commission, nor were they prepared to take upon themselves the receiving or paying of money transmitted by the unions to pay for the books applied for; and they, therefore, required Mr. Knight to undertake to defray all expenses of carriage from the publishers, to pay ready money for all parcels of books ordered, and to enter the same in his quarterly accounts with the unions, charging a commission of ten per cent. to cover his outlay and remunerate him for his trouble. The guardians will see that this arrangement must necessarily have been entrusted to some one agent, as the Board could not otherwise have engaged to the publishers, as they were required to do, that the books obtained from them at prices considerably below those at which they were supplied to the trade, should be applied exclusively for the use of workhouse schools, and should not be sold for any other purpose; and, moreover, it is doubtful whether the publishers would have entered into the arrangement at all if it had not been limited to one agent, as the multiplication of agents would have involved additional trouble on the publishers, besides considerably increase the expenses of carriage, &c. I am further directed to add, that the guardians are in no way restricted to the mode of obtaining books for their workhouse school, pointed out in the Board's Circular above adverted to, nor to the books and maps specified in the list accompanying it.*

IX.—GUARDIANS.

1. Election of.

25th Jan., 1849.

Clerk of Leicester Union.—In a large number of cases, the owners claiming to vote in the election of guardians for this union are non-resident, and have no place of business within the union. Under the Election Order of the 27th January, 1841, owners who were non-resident were directed to add to their statement (Form A) "an address in the parish where their voting papers might be sent," and acting upon this suggestion, nearly the whole of such voting papers were directed to be left at the offices of the agents of the respective political parties. Although this direction was not in the Election Order of the 16th January, 1845, nor in the General Consolidated Order, the practice remained the same, as it appeared but

* See this List in the *Official Circular*, No. 22, N. S.

reasonable to allow the party claiming, to state his address in the parish where the voting papers might be sent, so that he might receive them in due course, as directed by Art. 11 of the General Consolidated Order. These questions then arise, 1st, have owners the power of appointing an address in the parish where their property is situate, to which their voting papers may be sent, and is it imperative upon the relieving officer so to send them? Or, 2nd, is the proper course to be pursued by any such owners to appoint some person resident in the parish to be his proxy? Or, 3rd, supposing the power to appoint an address does not exist, and the owner has not appointed any person his proxy, is he in obtaining his voting paper, to be restricted to the mode pointed out in Art. 19 of the General Consolidated Order?

Ans.—The words in Art. 11 of the General Consolidated Order—" The address in such parish of each ratepayer, owner, and proxy, qualified to vote therein," refer not only to the place of residence or place of business which the voter may have within the parish, but also to any place of address which he may specially appoint in the event of his having no place of business or residence therein. The Board think, therefore, that where any such place of address is appointed, a *bonâ fide* endeavour should be made to deliver or leave the voting paper there on the proper day; and when that has been done, it appears to the Board that the clerk's duty in the matter will have been fulfilled. With regard to the practice which you state has been adopted in the Leicester Union, of directing non-resident owners to give addresses within the parish, at which the voting papers may be left or delivered, the Board desire to observe, that they consider the practice to be not unreasonable in itself, nor inconsistent with the terms of Form A., appended to the General Consolidated Order.

---

2. ELECTION OF GUARDIANS.

17th March, 1849.

Thos. Dodd, Esq., Preston.—In the firm of H.M. and Co. there are now only two partners, viz.—T. M. and H. M.—They are assessed in the rate-book as H. M. and Co., at upwards of 1,600*l.* for property in different wards. Are they under such circumstances entitled to give six votes each as occupiers? The firm of T. G. and Co. consists of three partners. The name of the firm is on the rate-book—Can all the partners vote as occupiers, or only T. G.? In the firm of J. S. and Brothers, which appears in the rate-book, there are two brothers, partners, viz., J. and E. S.—Are they both entitled to vote as occupiers? A. and B. are occupiers of a mill in St. Peter's Ward, for which they have been rated for more than twelve months; they have recently taken another mill in Trinity Ward, which has not yet, but will be assessed to the poor-rate before the nomination of guardians—Can they claim to vote at the next election for Trinity Ward in respect of the mill in that ward under such circumstances? The township of Preston has recently been divided into six wards, and by the order of the Board, each ward for the purposes of the election is to be considered as a separate township. Under such circumstances, can a person entitled to vote as owner, or occupier, in one ward, nominate a guardian for another ward? Should the guardian have a qualification in the ward in which he is nominated, or will it be sufficient if he has one in any other ward? Is it necessary that an owner or occupier (without any change in the property) should renew his claim yearly? See 7 & 8 Vic. c. 101. sec. 15. If a person occupy premises in several wards, will he be entitled to vote as occupier in any other than that he resides in, unless he claims in writing to do so before the 26th day of March? See 7 & 8 Vic. c. 101. sec. 21. If a partner in a firm whose name does not appear on the rate-book (although a *bonâ fide* rate-payer as partner) be nominated, will such nomination be void? In the case of partners, occupiers, is it the duty of the clerk to send out voting papers to each partner named in the rate-book, or, should a claim be made by the partners for separate papers? If a person be rated for 15*l.* for premises which he occupies, and be also rated at 10*l.* as owner of other premises for which he also pays the rates, is this a sufficient qualification for a guardian? The firm of P. and J. C. are assessed at above 1,000*l.* for a mill at St. Peter's Ward, of which they are joint owners and occupiers—are they not each entitled to six votes as owners, and each to six as occupiers? If not, cannot they add their private property as owner and occupier, which is situate in other wards, to their joint property as owner and occupier? Twelve equal partners (both owners and occupiers) are assessed at 3,000*l.*, sufficient to give all six votes, if taken separately. In that case, if it be decided that the partnership property can only give six votes, it is clear that none of these partners could vote, as they could not give a less number than one, and it is also clear that they could not vote in the name of the firm. Under the Reform Act, as many partners may vote as there may be in a firm, if the value of the property give the qualification; and the same principle seems to be intended by the 58 Geo. 3, c. 69; and also the late statute 7 & 8 Vic. c. 101, as by the 14th sec. of the latter statute it is expressly provided, "that *every* owner of property and rate-payer shall have the same number and proportion of votes according to the following scale."

Ans.—1, The Board observe, that it is certainly not free from doubt whether such a description of the occupier in the rate-book as H. M. & Co. and T. G. & Co., is an effective rating of any person other than those whose names are expressly mentioned. But they are disposed to consider that a rate defective as to the description of the occupiers may admit of explanation so as to show what parties were intended to be charged by the entry in the rate, and that the intention of the overseers who made the rate is to be looked to in determining what is a sufficient description of the parties so as to confer the right to vote as rate-payers. In the case of an actual partnership or joint occupation, all the members of the firm being equally liable to be rated, the fair presumption arising from such an entry in the rate, as H. M. & Co., is, that it was intended by the description to render liable to the rate the several persons so jointly occupying or jointly interested in the firm. In the case of Moss, appellant, Overseers of St. Michael, Lichfield, respondent, 7 M. & G. 172, (a case relating to the parliamentary franchise, and involving the construction of 2 & 3 Wm. 4, c. 45,) it was observed in the course of the argument by Maule, Justice, "If the partners were rated by the name of the firm each party would be liable to pay, and if one were called upon to pay and did pay, such payment would enure to the benefit of all." Also by Erle, Justice, "The real question is, whether the party was intended to be rated." Assuming, therefore, the sufficiency of the rating, in the cases under consideration, and that each member of the firm is entitled (upon satisfactory proof of his interest) to be regarded as a separate rate-payer and to vote as such, it remains to be considered how many votes the parties are entitled to give. The Board think that each partner is entitled to such a number of votes in respect of his share of the joint assessment as he would derive from a separate rating equal in value to that share. The limitation in the statutes 4 & 5 Wm. 4, c. 76., 7 & 8 Vic. c. 101. sec. 14, as to the number of votes, (wherein it is provided that no inhabitant or owner shall have more than six votes,) would of course apply to each of the joint partners or rate-payers, but would not prevent the firm from giving in the whole more than six votes. 2, In the case of A. & B., occupiers of a mill in St. Peter's ward, and with respect to whose right to vote in another ward (Trinity) a question is raised, the Board observe, that as the contingency upon which the inquiry proceeds has not yet arisen, (viz., the possible assessment of the parties prior to the election in respect of a second mill) the Board must decline to express any opinion. 3, The 21st sec. of the 7 & 8 Vic. c. 101, enables a rate-payer entitled to vote, and having property in different wards, to elect in which wards he will vote upon giving previous notice of his intention. The Board think that, as the right to nominate is involved in or incident to the right to vote, a person can in like manner and subject to the same conditions nominate in more than one ward. 4, The 20th section of the statute shows, that a person need not have or derive his qualification from the ward in or for which he is nominated. Apparently, the property conferring the qualification may exist in any part of the parish or of the union. 5, It is not necessary that an owner whose property does not undergo any change should renew his claim yearly. 6, The Board understand the 21st sec. of the 7 & 8 Vic. c. 101, to prevent a person voting in any other ward than that in which he resides, unless he has given the notice therein provided for. 7, With regard to the eligibility of partners as guardians whose names do not distinctly appear upon the rate-book, the Board observe, that what has been already stated with regard to the right of persons under similar circumstances to vote as rate-payers applies here. If they can be considered as legally and effectively rated under the circumstances supposed their nomination will be good. 8, The Board think that the clerk is not in strictness bound to send a voting paper to any other person than the one whose name distinctly appears on the rate. If any partner whose name does not so appear subsequently establishes his right to vote, he can have a paper on applying to the clerk in accordance with Articles 19 & 20 of General Consolidated Order. 9, The Board observe that, whatever property a person is in fact assessed upon to the poor-rates (whether he be assessed as owner or occupier) is to be taken into consideration in determining the sufficiency of the qualification for guardian. 10, The Board can only state generally, that owners of property who are also *bonâ fide* occupiers of the same property can vote as well in respect of the ownership as of the occupations, (sec. 40, Poor Law Amendment Act.) Again, as the Board think that each joint owner and joint occupier, who is effectively rated, is to be regarded for the purposes of voting under 4 & 5 Wm. 4, c. 76, as a separate owner and a separate rate-payer, it follows that in either case the property which is in their independent occupation can be added to their share in the joint occupation in determining the number of votes to which they are respectively entitled.

3. VOTING ON THE ELECTION OF OFFICERS.

5th June, 1848.

Clerk of Wakefield Union.—In the election of any officer of the union, the mode of taking the votes has usually been, where there have been more than two candidates, to strike off the person having the lowest number of votes, and so on, until only two candidates were left. One of the guardians has called the attention of the Board to the subject, insisting that this mode is wrong, and that the election, however numerous the candidates might be, should be decided by the first voting.

Ans.—If, on the first show of hands, no one candidate has a majority of the total number of guardians present and voting, the Board believe that the course described in your letter, if adopted by the guardians, would be legal.

4. GUARDIAN FURNISHING PLANS AS AN ARCHITECT FOR THE USE OF THE UNION.

12th July, 1848.

Clerk of ——— Union.—Inquiring whether the account of Mr. P., an architect, for the preparation of the plans for the erection of a temporary fever hospital for the ——— Union, can be legally paid from the poor-rates, he being at the time a guardian of the union.

Ans.—If Mr. P. did not supply " goods, materials, or provisions," but merely professional skill and labour, he is not within terms of the enactments of the 55 Geo. 3, c. 137, sec. 6, and 4 & 5 Wm. 4, c. 76, sec. 51.

5. LIABILITY OF GUARDIANS TO PENALTIES WHEN INTERESTED IN GAS WORKS WHICH SUPPLY THE WORKHOUSE WITH GAS.

6th Feb., 1849.

Clerk to ——— Union.—Inquiring whether the guardians or officers connected with the board of guardians being shareholders, or directors, or secretary of an incorporated gas company, supplying the workhouse with gas, are as such liable to the penalties of the 59 Geo. 3, c. 12, and 4 & 5 Wm. 4, c. 76.

Ans.—The question mainly depends upon the construction of the 6th sec. of the 55 Geo. 3, c. 137, as extended by sec. 51 of the 4 & 5 Wm. 4, c. 76, to the guardians and officers appointed under that Act. If the gas come under the denomination of what is termed therein " goods," (and the Board are disposed to think that it must be so considered,) the shareholders of the company, if they be also guardians of the ——— union, appear to fall within the prohibition. If this view be correct, either the shareholders must abstain from acting as guardians, or officers of the union; or an application should be made to the justices of the district for a certificate in conformity with the latter part of the 6th sec. of the Act of Geo. 3, to license the supply of gas to the workhouse by such guardians. The Board do not perceive that the secretary of the gas company comes within the prohibition, unless his salary depends upon the supply of gas to the consumers, which probably is not the case. The directors are doubtless also shareholders, if not, the same doctrine would be applicable to them as to the secretary of the company.

X.—LUNATIC PAUPER — IN A PRIVATE ASYLUM—COST OF MAINTENANCE.

27th June, 1848.

Clerk of Darlington Union. —W. D., belonging to the township of Darlington, was sent to B—— Asylum on the 4th of May, 1847, by his wife, as a private patient, at a cost of 16*s.* per week. On the 7th of October, 1847, the wife applied to the guardians of the Darlington Union to pay the cost incurred in the maintenance of the lunatic in the asylum, she being unable to do so. The guardians were satisfied of the inability of the wife to pay such cost, and agreed to pay the same and charge the amount to the parish, but they omitted to enter the pauper's name on the Relief List, or make a special minute to that effect; in consequence of which the case came before the guardians on the 16th of February, 1848, when they passed the following resolution: " Resolved, that the sum of 12*s.* per week be paid by the township of Darlington for the maintenance of W. D., now in the B——— asylum, from the 4th of May, 1847, to the present date, and continue such payment so long as the said lunatic continues in the asylum and unable to be supported by his friends." Objections being made by some of the guardians to the payment of this charge, the subject came before the board on the 6th March, 1848, when the following minute was made:—"Ordered, that the charge for the maintenance of the said W. D. be paid by the township of Darlington up to the present date, at the weekly cost of 12s. per week, and in future the weekly cost of 8s. per week for the maintenance of the said W. D., so long as he may continue a lunatic, and not able to be supported by those who are legally bound to support him." The case has been laid before the auditor, who has advised the guardians to apply to the Poor Law Board for the necessary authority in the matter.

Ans.—The Board are compelled to state, that they cannot find any legal authority for the proceedings which have been adopted by the guardians of the Darlington Union in relation to this case. In the present position of the matter, it appears to the Board that the lunatic being in a private asylum, or licensed house, a debt has been incurred by his friends for his support; and the Board are not aware of any authority which would enable the guardians of the Darlington Union to undertake to discharge this debt out of the funds in their hands, belonging to any township within the union. The township in which the lunatic may be settled can only be made liable for the cost of his maintenance by proper proceedings to be taken under the statute 8 & 9 Vic. c. 126. It will be seen that the 48th sec. of that Act only applies to the cases of lunatics who are chargeable to some parish; and that the 49th sec. is confined to the cases of wandering lunatics, and of lunatics who, not being chargeable to any parish, are under the charge of persons who neglect them. The Board gather from your statement, that W. D. does not come within any one of these three classes. So long, in fact, as he remains in the licensed house, his case is not one in which the guardians can properly interfere; but should he become legally chargeable to any parish or township, or should he be found wandering abroad in a state of lunacy, in consequence of the refusal of the proprietor of the asylum to continue to maintain him, without security for repayment of the costs of his maintenance, he might then be dealt with under the provisions of the statute adverted to.

XI.—NUISANCES REMOVAL ACT, 1848.

28th Dec., 1848.

Clerk of Cookham Union.—"In the parish of Bray, in the Cookham Union, there are certain premises in such a state as to be unwholesome for the inhabitants; there has lately been illness in all of them; there is only one common yard to five cottages, not properly enclosed, and no privy, only open holes." The above is extracted from a notice served upon the guardians under the Nuisances Removal Act, in pursuance of which they have directed proceedings to be taken against the owners of the properties in question, and against whom a summons has been obtained. It is a well-known fact, however, that these persons are too poor to remedy the evils complained of. To cleanse the premises and remove the nuisance will be but of temporary service, as it is necessary that privies, cesspools, and such like conveniences should be made; and the guardians entertain doubts whether they are authorized by the Act (4th sec.) to construct them at the cost of the ratepayers of the parish. Requested the opinion of the Board as to the extent of the powers of the guardians under the Act with reference to the foregoing case.

Ans.—The Board apprehend that under the 1st sec. of the Act in question, if sewers, drains, or cesspools be not properly constructed, the justices can order the construction to be amended or improved; but they think it is by no means clear that the justices can order any privies, cesspools, or sewers to be constructed where none existed previously. If such an order be made, however, the Board think that the guardians can, on the default of the owner or occupier, carry it into execution at the cost of the parish in which the premises are situated. At the same time the Board cannot but feel the serious consequences which must arise if private property is to be thus improved at the cost of the poor-rate. The guardians, therefore, if they proceed under any such order, should take measures to recover the cost from the owners of the property. They will perceive that civil proceedings can be taken for the recovery of the costs, and by the process of the County Court the amount may be recovered.

XII.—OVERSEERS—NEGLECTING TO PRESENT THEIR ACCOUNTS AT THE AUDIT.

31st March, 1849.

Robert Usher, Esq., District Auditor.—The

overseers of the parish of Stannington, in the Castleward Union, refusing to make out their accounts according to the form set forth in the General Order of Accounts, he had caused them to be summoned before a meeting of the justices for the county of Northumberland, and succeeded in obtaining a conviction. The following account of the matter appeared in the *Newcastle Chronicle* of 30th March :—"The overseers of the parish of Stannington appeared to answer a summons issued against them on an information laid by Mr. Robert Usher, the auditor of the Northumberland district, on the ground that they did not present their accounts at a late audit in the form and with such particulars as were set forth in the General Order of Accounts issued by the Poor Law Board, whereby they subjected themselves to a penalty. The overseers, Mr. Frederick Turner and Mr. Edward Humble, stated that they had not received or seen the General Order respecting Accounts, and, therefore, they considered they were not bound to make them out. The bench said such a defence was insufficient, because it was the duty of the overseers to know what was required of them when they took office. It appeared they had been informed of their duty by the auditor, on their presenting their accounts, and had neglected, at an adjournment of the audit, to present them in the form required. The bench, therefore, convicted the overseers, but as the auditor stated it was not his wish to have the full penalty inflicted, his object being more to establish and make known the law, the bench merely imposed a nominal fine, with costs."

XIII.—PAUPERS.—WHETHER THOSE OF SIXTY YEARS OF AGE ARE ABLE-BODIED.

25*th Feb.*, 1848.

Clerk of Cardiff Union.—Inquired, whether poor persons above the age of sixty years are exempt, by reason of having attained such age, from the operation of the General Prohibitory Order of the Poor Law Commissioners.

Ans.—The Board do not consider that a person of sixty years of age and upwards is necessarily otherwise than an able-bodied man; and unless, therefore, such a person be suffering under some of the bodily or mental infirmities which accompany advanced years, or be otherwise disabled, his case would come within the meaning of the Prohibitory Order, and the guardians could not grant out-door relief to him, except with the sanction of the Board previously obtained, under Article 6 of the Order.

XIV.—RELIEF—

1. OF ABLE-BODIED PERSONS — WORKHOUSE ACCOMMODATION.

11*th Jan.*, 1849.

Taunton Union.—The following communication has been addressed to the Poor Law Board by Edward Gulson, Esq., Poor Law Inspector :—The clerk to the board of guardians of the Taunton Union wrote to you last week, stating that the workhouse was full, and that the guardians, at their meeting on Wednesday last, had given out-door relief to several able-bodied men, not knowing how otherwise to deal with that class of applicants. This statement induced me to attend the meeting of the Taunton board yesterday, where I found an assemblage of from 150 to 200 able-bodied persons seeking relief. It was very evident, from the bearing of the applicants, many of whom were single men of loose character, that they were aware that out-door relief had been given on the previous board day, and that they had reason to believe they could not be received into the workhouse. There was a large meeting of the guardians in anticipation of the pressure, and before we proceeded to hear any case I advised the guardians—1st, To render every spare building upon the workhouse premises available for the temporary reception of the able-bodied men. 2nd, To appoint a police officer as an assistant relieving officer, for the sole purpose of relieving vagrants. 3rd, To convert the stable into a temporary vagrant ward for his use, and to make the rooms, hitherto occupied as vagrant wards, into sleeping wards for the able-bodied; and, if necessary, to hire a vacant building in the town for the reception of the boys in the workhouse, so as to enable the guardians to use the boys' yards, day rooms, and sleeping apartments, for the able-bodied. We further arranged to give out-door relief to some aged and infirm in the house, and at once to appoint a superintendent of labour, whose services we knew we could immediately obtain, in order forthwith to employ the men at stone-breaking upon the workhouse premises. Having made these preliminary arrangements, we commenced to hear the applications, and to every able-bodied applicant an admission ticket for the workhouse was offered; and as these tickets were issued, we directed the officers either to take the applicant to the receiving ward, to be washed and well cleansed, or, if he declined to go there, to remove him from the premises, leaving the order of admission in his possession, to be afterwards available if he so desired. In this way we went through all the applications, and at seven o'clock I had explained to each and all as they came in, that no relaxation of the law could be permitted, but that they might come into the workhouse and be supported in return for a daily task of work. About 100 or 120 orders of admission to the workhouse were thus given to able-bodied applicants, all of whom we were prepared to receive if necessary, rather than break down under the pressure. On visiting the workhouse next morning, I found that only 12 of the applicants ultimately availed themselves of the orders of admission, and that two of these had given notice to leave, declaring that if they could not obtain out-door relief they would not trouble the guardians further. In some cases of large families, I advised the board of guardians to relieve the able-bodied man—the head of the family—in the workhouse, and to employ him at stone-breaking, and to give the wife and children some out-door relief, provided the man came in and performed his task of work. This course was necessary, because, under the circumstances, it was important to keep all the available room for the able-bodied men. I am not, however, aware that any one of those to whom admission to the workhouse was tendered on these terms has availed himself of the offer, and I therefore have satisfaction in stating that I anticipate no further difficulty as regards the pressure at Taunton.

In consequence of these proceedings, the clerk of the Taunton board will write for the sanction of the Poor Law Board.—1st, To the appointment of a superintendent of labour. 2nd, To the appointment of the police officer as assistant relieving officer, for the purpose of searching and relieving vagrants—to both of which appointments I beg to recommend your sanction.

2. RELIEF TO ENABLE A BLIND PERSON TO PROCEED TO A HOSPITAL.

20*th Jan.*, 1849.

Clerk of Ross Union.—A pauper, chargeable to the parish of H———, in this union, having become blind, an order for his admission into Guy's Hospital, with a view to the restoration of his sight, has been obtained. Inquiring whether the guardians can legally pay the expenses of the journey of the pauper to London, and also of a person to take care of him, and conduct him into the hospital, and charge the same to the parish of H———.

Ans.—It is competent to the guardians to send the pauper to the hospital in question; or, in other words, the case being within the 2nd Exception to Art. 3 of the General Prohibitory Order, the guardians can grant him non-resident relief; and if, as appears from your statement to be the case, he must be accompanied by an attendant, the costs of the journey of such attendant are properly chargeable with the costs otherwise incurred in the matter.

3. CHARGING RELIEF OF IRREMOVABLE POOR.

12*th Jan.*, 1849.

Clerk of Bala Union.—Inquiring whether paupers belonging to the union, whose relief is charged to the common fund, but who have not resided in their respective parishes for five years without receiving relief from some other parish, can now be transferred to their own settlement parishes in the union.

Ans.—The Board understand the inquiry to have reference to the recent decision of the Court of Queen's Bench, in the case of Reg. *v.* The Inhabitants of Christchurch, which decided that the provision in the statute 9 & 10 Vic. c. 66, s. 1, excludes from the computation of five years the time or times during which the pauper may have received relief, and applies respectively to relief granted before the passing of that Act, as well as to relief granted subsequently. Where, therefore, the relief so afforded, whether before or since the date of the above statute, diminishes the period of residence to less than five years, the cost of the relief of such pauper (provided he is not irremovable on any other ground) cannot be charged to the common fund of the union, under sec. 3 of the 11 & 12 Vic. c. 110. But the relief of a pauper which has hitherto been charged to the common fund, upon the ground of his presumed irremovability, cannot be transferred to the parish of his settlement, unless that parish admit the settlement, as well as that such pauper is removable, and consent expressly or impliedly to the charge being made to them direct. In the absence of such admission and consent, the proper course is to charge the relief to the parish in which the pauper is resident, leaving the authorities of that parish to establish not only that the pauper is settled elsewhere, but also, that he is legally removable to the place of his settlement.

London: Printed by order of the Poor Law Board, by BLACKBURN & BURT, 90½, Holborn Hill, and published by CHARLES KNIGHT, 90, Fleet Street.

AN

OFFICIAL CIRCULAR

OF PUBLIC DOCUMENTS AND INFORMATION:

DIRECTED BY THE POOR LAW BOARD TO BE PRINTED, CHIEFLY FOR THE USE OF THE BOARDS OF GUARDIANS AND THEIR OFFICERS.

No. 25.] MAY, 1849. [N.S.

CONTENTS.

I.—ACCOUNTS.

1. CHARGING RELIEF OF IRREMOVABLE POOR.

2nd Feb., 1849.

Clerk of Huntingdon Union.—J. G., who has been a resident of the parish of Godmanchester in this union for upwards of eleven years past, but whose last legal settlement appears to be in the parish of St. Ives, in the St. Ives Union, has for several months past been in receipt of relief, and such relief has been charged by the relieving officer to Godmanchester parish. The guardians being satisfied of J. G.'s irremovability, have ordered his relief to be charged to the common fund of the union, under the 3rd sec. of 11 & 12 Vic. c. 110. Inquiring whether the parish of Godmanchester is entitled to repayment from the common charges fund in respect of the relief already given to J. G. at the expense of that parish, and if so, from what period. J. G. was not one of those cases whose relief fell on the common fund under the 10 & 11 Vic. c. 110, sec. 1.

Ans.—The Board apprehend that the accounts of the Huntingdon Union for the current half-year, from the close of the last audited accounts, stand open until the end of such half-year; and that it is competent to the guardians to adjust the charges in those accounts at any time during that period, until the accounts are closed for the next audit. Probably, however, it will be found to be the more convenient course, not to adjust the charges until the time when the accounts are finally prepared for the auditor. According to this view, the charge for the relief of J. G., which has been made against the parish of Godmanchester during the current half-year, may either at once, or at the time when the accounts are prepared for audit, be transferred to the common fund of the union. As J. G. is irremovable from Godmanchester, the liability of that parish for his relief ceased on the 30th of September last, according to the provisions of the 3rd sec. of the 11 & 12 Vic. c. 110; and, consequently, that parish should not be charged with any relief afforded to him since that date.

2. CHARGING RELIEF GIVEN TO CHOLERA PATIENTS.

27th Jan., 1849.

Clerk of Carlisle Union.—In consequence of the cholera having broken out in Carlisle, the guardians have taken possession of the Fever House, for the purpose of using the same as a cholera hospital, and several patients have already been sent there. Inquiring as to what fund the expenses attending the maintenance of the cholera patients, and also the expenses of the inmates of the House of Refuge, are to be charged, whether to the common fund, or to the parish to which they are sent.

Ans.—If the cholera patients you allude to are ordinary paupers, the cost of their medical treatment, under that malady, should be charged in the same manner as their ordinary relief. If they be not paupers already in receipt of relief, it will be necessary to consider whether they are irremovable by reason of a five years' residence; for if so, the charge of their relief must be borne by the common fund of the union, provided they are not settled in the parish of their residence. In any such case, in which the pauper is not irremovable under sec. 1 of the 9 & 10 Vic. c. 66, the further question will arise, whether the sickness is such as will produce "permanent disability," within the meaning of the 4th sec. On this point the Board observe, that, although the cholera is frequently fatal, it does not usually produce any "permanent disability" where the patient recovers from the attack; and they therefore think that paupers, who are patients under such circumstances, would not be removable, and that their relief must accordingly be charged to the common fund.

II.—CONTRIBUTION—RECOVERY OF—OVERSEERS RESIDING IN A DIFFERENT COUNTY FROM THE TREASURER.

28th March, 1849.

Clerk of Carnarvon Union.—Five of the parishes in this union are situated in the county of Anglesey. The treasurer resides in Carnarvon, and, consequently, calls made for contributions from those parishes are made payable to him at Carnarvon. Inquiring, before the justices of which county the overseers of the above-mentioned parishes should be summoned for not paying their calls; and also, whether, under the 1st sec. of the 2 & 3 Vic. c. 84, it is necessary that the application therein referred to by the chairman should be signed at a meeting of the board of guardians.

Ans.—The Board are disposed to think, though the point is not free from doubt, that the offence, that is, the default, takes place in the county wherein the treasurer of the union resides, to whom the payments were directed to be made. In the present instance, that is stated to be the county of Carnarvon, and those justices, (on the foregoing supposition as to the place in which the offence is committed,) would have jurisdiction in the matter. The case of Reg. *v.* Milner, reported in 2 Carr. and K. 312, appears to be analogous to the present. There, an indictment against a bankrupt for not surrendering to the fiat in bankruptcy was held to be improperly brought in the county where the bankrupt lived, the place where he was required to surrender being situate in a different county. The Board, however, desire to remark, that, under the 2 & 3 Vic. c. 84, which gives a special remedy for the recovery of contributions in arrear, the proceedings are to be taken before the justices of the district acting for the county wherein the parish in arrear with its contribution is situated. A proceeding under this Act (which defines the jurisdiction) being, therefore, quite safe, might be properly resorted to by the guardians of the Carnarvon Union in the present instance, unless there are reasons for avoiding it which are not stated in your letter. As regards the application by the chairman of the board, referred to in sec. 1 of the 2 & 3 Vic. c. 84, it is the opinion of the Board that it ought to be signed at a meeting of the guardians.

III.—CHARGEABILITY.

1. EXTRA RELIEF ON ACCOUNT OF THE SICKNESS OF A CHILD, GIVEN TO NON-SETTLED PAUPER.

6th Feb., 1849.

Wangford Union.—S.B., an able-bodied widow, with five children under 16 years of age, resides in Beccles, in this union, from whence she is legally removable; but she belongs to Mettingham, also in this union, by which latter parish she is relieved as a regular quarterly pauper. During her residence in Beccles, one of her children was taken ill, and received medical relief from the medical officer, and the mother was allowed 1*s.* 2*d.* extra on account of such sickness of her child. The guardians entertain doubts as to how the relief should be charged. Inquiring therefore, 1, Whether the regular relief should be charged, as usual, to Mettingham, and the extra relief to Beccles, (see 2nd sec. of 10 & 11 Vic. c. 110.) 2, Or, whether the extra relief, as well the permanent relief, should be charged to Mettingham. 3, Whether, as the extra relief is rendered necessary by casual sickness, the pauper is not now irremovable; and if so, whether both the regular and the extra relief should not be charged to the union fund during the time such extra relief is necessary.

Ans.—The Board consider that the pauper in question is chargeable to the parish of Mettingham, as she was an acknowledged pauper of that parish, and received relief therefrom. Any additional relief which the guardians of the Wangford Union may order on any ground must follow the original charge; and, consequently, that parish must bear the medical and additional ordinary relief. The pauper being chargeable by reason of ordinary destitution, the 4th sec. of the 9 & 10 Vic. c. 66, does not apply to the case, as it only relates to chargeability through sickness.

2. RELIEF TO ILLEGITIMATE CHILDREN.

21st March, 1849.

Clerk of Hursley Union.—A pauper settled in this union, residing in the city of Winchester, having two illegitimate children, living with their grandmother, but maintained by their father, has recently married a soldier. She is still in service in Winchester, but is about, as it is supposed, to follow her husband, now, it is believed, in Ireland. The father of the children has, since the marriage of the mother, withdrawn the support he had been affording for their maintenance, and in consequence, the grandmother has placed them in the union workhouse. Inquiring what course the guardians ought to pursue under the circumstances.

Ans.—The mother of the children being now married, she does not seem to be legally liable for their maintenance, and as her husband is a soldier, the Board believe that he cannot be made amenable to any process for the recovery of the cost of their relief, although he is bound in law to support them.

3. RELIEF TO STEP-SON, A BOY AGED 14, LIVING IN A DIFFERENT PARISH FROM THE STEP-FATHER.

28th March, 1849.

Clerk of Stow-on-the-Wold Union.—M. J., widow of J. J., with five children born in wedlock, resided for many years in the hamlet of Mangersbury, receiving relief at the cost of the hamlet, either as an inmate of the Stow-on-the-Wold Workhouse, or as an out-door pauper being a recognized parishioner of that hamlet, her husband, J. J., having gained a settlement there. Some time since she married one J. G., then resident in Mangersbury, and soon after such marriage J. G. and his wife became chargeable to that place, and were with some of the children by the former marriage, inmates of the union workhouse. An order of removal was obtained, at the instance of the parish officers of Mangersbury, for the removal of J. G., his wife, and four children, viz., Kegeil, Sarah Ann, Priscilla, and John, from Mangersbury to Great Barrington, in the same union, which order has been consented to by the parish officers of Great Barrington, and will not be appealed against. In that order the eldest son of J. G.'s wife, by the previous husband, was not included; he being of the age of fourteen years, was employed at Mangersbury as a farm labourer, and so not a pauper. Since the order was made, this lad has become chargeable to the union, and a question has been raised whether the relief given to him should be charged to the parish of Great Barrington, or to the hamlet of Mangersbury. It is admitted that J. G., having married the widow, is liable to maintain her and her children by her former husband to the full extent of his ability, but it is alleged that such liability does not affect the settlement of the son living and working in the place of his birth settlement; and as at the period when the relief was ordered for the son, J. G. was not, nor is now, in a condition to maintain the boy, (he was then a pauper inmate of the workhouse, and is now in confinement in the house of correction as an idle and disorderly person, out-relief being given to his wife and children at the charge of Great Barrington,) the relief so given to the boy would seem to be payable by the place of his birth settlement, Mangersbury. But this being doubted on behalf of the hamlet of Mangersbury, requested the Poor Law Board to state, to which of the two places the relief should be charged under the above circumstances.

Ans.—In the opinion of the Board no authority exists for charging the relief of the boy in question to the parish of Great Barrington, the settlement of the step-father. As the Board collect from the statement before them, the boy is now residing and working in the hamlet of Mangersbury, where it appears he was still remaining at the time when he required the relief, (the clothing,) which was afforded to him, he not having been included in the order for the removal of his mother and family to Great Barrington. Under these circumstances, the Board are of opinion that the hamlet of Mangersbury is liable for the relief in question. The pauper being settled in Mangersbury, where he resides, the case does not come within the 3rd sec. of the 11 & 12 Vic. c. 110, and, therefore, the union common fund cannot properly be rendered chargeable with the relief.

4. CHARGEABILITY.

4th April, 1849.

Mr. G. P. Heyward, Egham, Windsor Union.—D. P., with two illegitimate children, and far advanced in pregnancy, applied to the parish of Egham for relief on the 3rd of March, and received an order for the union workhouse, where she still remains. The board of guardians instructed the authorities of the parish to take the necessary steps for removing the pauper to her place of settlement, Little Marlow, Bucks; and she was accordingly conveyed with that view to the petty sessions at Chertsey. The case was adjourned in consequence of an omission on the part of the master of the workhouse to furnish the certificate duly attested of her alleged chargeability to Egham. It appears that she has recently quitted the Brentford Union, and that she passed the night preceding her application for relief at Egham, in the Staines Union. She was not resident, and did not "come to inhabit" in Egham. Submitted, therefore, that no grounds of removal exist, and that the pauper should be regarded as a casual pauper, and the cost of her maintenance defrayed by the common fund. Requested the opinion of the Poor Law Board on the subject.

Clerk of Windsor Union.—(To whom the above statement was referred.) The statement, as far as the guardians are acquainted with the facts appears to be correct, except that portion which supposes it to be the duty of the master of the workhouse to furnish a certificate of chargeability. Inquired as to the removability of this pauper, and her three illegitimate children: and, if they are removable, who should take the steps, and at whose expense should they be taken. She has entirely recovered from the illness under which she laboured at the time she was admitted into the workhouse, and no longer remains there on account of illness.

Ans.—It appears to the Board, that the pauper in this case, when admitted into the workhouse of the Windsor Union, was, in fact, a destitute wanderer; and the cost of her relief, subsequent to the 28th September last, is therefore chargeable to the common fund of the union, and not to the parish of Egham. She is not a person who can be removed under an order of removal for the very reason that renders her chargeable to the common fund of the union.

5. COST OF MEDICAL AND OTHER RELIEF, GIVEN AT CHILDBIRTH.

2nd April, 1849,

Clerk of Stafford Union.—M. O., a pauper legally settled by marriage in the parish of Colwich, in the Stafford Union, resided at Great Haywood, in the parish of Stow, in the same union, with her husband, C. O., who died on the 24th day of March, 1848. About three months after the decease of her husband, she removed from the parish of Stowe to the residence of her mother at Shirleywich, in the parish of Weston-upon-Trent, also in the same union, where she has continued to reside with her mother ever since. In consequence of the destitution of the pauper and the inability of the mother to provide medical attendance, the relieving officer gave an order for the medical officer to attend the pauper during childbirth, and she was confined on the 10th of December, 1848. On the 12th of December, application was made to the relieving officer for relief, and the relieving officer administered relief on the 12th, the 19th, and 26th days of December. The relief afforded by the relieving officer, and the order given by him for the attendance of the medical officer during childbirth, were subsequently confirmed by the board of guardians, and a question having arisen with reference to charging the cost of such relief, inquiring whether the extra medical fee of 10*s.* for attendance during childbirth, and the cost of the relief administered to the pauper, amounting to 15*s.* 11½*d.*, should be charged to the common fund of the union, under the Act 11 & 12 Vic. c. 110, sec. 3, and the 9 & 10 Vic. c. 66, sec. 4; or to the parish of Weston-upon-Trent, the parish in which the pauper had her place of abode.

Ans.—As it appears that the relief was rendered necessary by the general destitution, and not merely by the sickness of the pauper in question, the Board, on the whole, are of opinion that the cost of such relief should be charged to the parish of Weston-upon-Trent, wherein the pauper resides.

28*th April*, 1849.

Clerk of same Union.—Inquiring, 1st, Whether the inability of a person to maintain herself during child-birth, (in ordinary cases,) renders such person irremovable from the parish of her residence, under the Act 9 & 10 Vic. c. 66, sec. 4. 2nd, Whether the cost of relief afforded to such person should be charged to the common fund of the union, or to the parish wherein she resides. 3rd, Whether the fee paid to the medical officer for medical attendance during child-birth in such cases, should be charged to the common fund of the union or to the parish wherein the pauper resides.

Ans.—If the [temporary] inability of a pauper to maintain herself during child-birth arises from previous destitution, such pauper would not come within the 4th sec. of the 9 & 10 Vic. c. 66, and, therefore, so far as this point is concerned, would be removable; but if such inability arises in consequence of the sickness caused by child-birth, then such pauper would come within the above-mentioned section, and, being irremovable, the cost of her relief, whatever it may be, must be charged to the common fund of the union. This is the general view the Board take of the matter.

---

6. CHARGEABILITY OF DESERTED CHILD.

2*nd May*, 1849.

Clerk of Southwell Union.—A child, about three months old, was left in a hamper at the railway station at Newark. The mother is supposed to be known, but she cannot be found. The railway station is in the parish of Kettam, one of the parishes in this union. Inquiring whether the relief of the child should be charged to that parish, or to the common fund of the union.

Ans.—The child referred to is evidently a destitute foundling, within the 1st clause of the 11 & 12 Vic. c. 110; and its relief should, therefore, be charged to the common fund of the Southwell Union.

---

7. ALTERATION OF BOUNDARIES OF PARISHES BY THE TITHE COMMISSIONERS, AS IT AFFECTS CHARGEABILITY.

24*th May*, 1849.

Clerk of Atcham Union.—The parishes of Alberbury, Ford, and Pontesbury, all in the Atcham Union, are contiguous to each other; their respective boundaries were very irregular (and in some instances imperfectly known) until the tithes were commuted, which took place about three years ago, when, under the powers vested in the Tithe Commissioners, new boundary lines were laid down, whereby irregular portions of the several parishes were transferred from their original parishes to those adjacent. Thus, Ford received a portion of the other two, and Alberbury and Westbury severally received in return other portions from Ford, and so on through several changes, whereby each of the parishes gave up to, and received from, each of the others certain portions of land, with the dwelling-houses situated thereon: since this division, the portions so transferred have been, and now are assessed to the relief of the poor in the several parishes to which by such new division they are attached, and of which they thereby form a part. J. resided continuously for twenty years in the same cottage, which was originally in the parish of Pontesbury, but by the new division was transferred to Ford; during such residence he neither received relief nor was in any gaol, lunatic asylum, or the like, but at the termination of such residence, during last year (1848) he was admitted direct, under an order of the guardians of the Atcham Union, into their workhouse, where he remains chargeable. His last legal settlement is admitted to be in the parish of Alberbury, but whether it was gained in that part of the parish which remains unaffected by the new boundary is not yet ascertained. Requesting the opinion of the Poor Law Board in the following points.—1, Did the residence, as above stated, render the pauper irremovable? 2, If not, will the alteration in the parish boundary affect the settlement in Alberbury so as to render him irremovable thereto; or will that depend in any measure upon the part of the original parish (with reference to the present boundary) in which the settlement was gained? 3, If it depends on the part of the original parish in which the settlement was gained, will the pauper be legally settled in the parish in which that particular part is now situate, and (if it is not now in Ford) removable to such parish, whether it be now in Alberbury or Pontesbury, or in either of two other adjoining parishes, which are similarly affected by the Alberbury new boundary? 4, If not so settled, and removable, can the pauper be removed to the parish in which his last previous settlement was gained? 5, Can the guardians, either with or without the consent of the overseers of either of the parishes interested, charge the maintenance of the pauper to any other parish than Ford, and if so, to which of them? 6, If the pauper cease to remain chargeable, and voluntarily go to reside in some other parish, to which he may become chargeable within five years, will he be removable, and to which particular parish?

Ans.—The Board desire, in the first place, to point out, that the guardians of the Atcham Union are interested on behalf of the union generally in the question at issue, inasmuch as the pauper, if he be removable, must, under 11 & 12 Vic. c. 110, sec. 3, be charged to the common fund of the union. With regard to the question itself, the Board observe, that it appears to them to depend upon the effect of the statute 2 & 3 Vic. c. 62, sec. 34, coupled with the terms of the award, determination, or judgment actually made by the Tithe Commissioners in the present case, under the provisions of that enactment. If the statute merely enabled the Tithe Commissioners to declare what was included in the original or ancient boundaries of the parishes adverted to, then the residence of the pauper, it would in no respect have been interrupted in point of law, as such residence must be taken to have been always in the same parish as now defined by the Tithe Commissioners. But if the statute enabled the Tithe Commissioners to make an alteration in the known boundaries of the parishes, so as to transfer the locality in question, which originally formed part of one parish to another parish; and if the Tithe Commissioners, in point of fact, adopted that course in the present case, then the Board think that there has been an interruption of the pauper's residence in the parish of Pontesbury, inasmuch as he does not now reside in that parish in which the place of his abode is stated to have been originally situated. Assuming that the Tithe Commissioners have, in fact, defined new boundaries in the present case, the Board, on the whole, have come to the conclusion that the pauper, (so far as the question of residence is concerned,) is now removable from the parish of Ford, wherein he has resided since the alteration of the boundaries, but not for a period sufficient to render him irremovable under sec. 1 of the 9 & 10 Vic. c. 66. To that parish, therefore, his relief is now chargeable in the first instance, although, if the parish of his settlement (which settlement does not appear to the Board to be affected by the alteration of the parochial boundaries) will consent to the adoption of such a course, the guardians may charge his relief thereto without an order of removal being obtained. The guardians, however, cannot properly do so in the absence of such consent.

IV.—PAUPER—OF WEAK MIND POSSESSED OF A SMALL ANNUITY—ADMISSION INTO WORKHOUSE.

4*th May*, 1849.

Clerk of Patrington Union.—M. C., who is about fifty years of age, and settled in the parish of Welwick in this union, has an annuity of £10 a year, payable out of real property. He is of weak mind and body, but able to take care of himself, and has for several years lived with his brother, to whom he has paid the annuity for maintenance. The brother now refuses to maintain him any longer, and he having no other home, and being unable to provide for himself, has applied to be admitted into the union workhouse. The guardians doubt whether they can properly admit M. C. into the workhouse; and if so, what should be done with the surplus of the annuity, it being more than would be required to defray the cost of his maintenance.

Ans.—The guardians must treat M. C. either

as being a lunatic or not. If he be a lunatic, they should obtain the requisite order for his removal to an asylum, and thereupon the trustee might, under the 7 & 8 Vic. c. 101, sec. 27, pay the cost of his maintenance, though this is optional with him. If he be not a lunatic, the guardians would certainly be justified in refusing to relieve him, considering that, with the annuity in question, he is not a destitute person. The Board, however, must leave it to the guardians to decide whether his bodily and mental weakness be such as to render him incapable of properly taking care of himself, and managing his own affairs. If this be the case, the annuity, which might suffice if well managed to support him in comfort, may be found insufficient to provide for his maintenance throughout the year. He may squander it improvidently as he receives it, and be obliged to apply to the guardians in the intervals of its payment for relief as a destitute person. Whatever view the guardians may take of the case, if they give M. C. any relief it should be granted on loan, which the Act of last session (11 & 12 Vic. c. 110) gives additional facilities for recovering, and it would be well that they should intimate to the trustee of the property the resolution at which they arrive in the case.

V.—RELIEF—

1. To the families of marines.

4th Feb., 1848.

Clerk of East Stonehouse Parish. — The operation of the Act 9 & 10 Vic. c. 66, has imposed on this parish very heavy burdens as regards the families of marines, many of whom have been acknowledged and relieved by the parishes to which they belong, but their relief is now thrown on this parish. The guardians consider they are not justified in granting out-relief to a class of persons who are able-bodied and in the employ of the government, being restricted by the Prohibitory Order. Still, in case they withhold relief, they subject themselves to penal consequences. Requesting that the Poor Law Board will adopt such measures for excepting out of the restrictions of the Prohibitory Order such marine soldiers who have numerous families, or for investing the guardians with the discretionary power of granting out-relief; and also, for requiring parishes who have acknowledged marines and their families as belonging to them, after order of justices had been made and served on them, and relieved for several years, to grant out-relief in all cases of marines having large families, or being unfit for duty from sickness or any other cause, or to accept them, if removable, without a second order.

Ans.—The guardians are under a misapprehension when they say they are restricted by the Prohibitory Order from granting out-door relief to this class of paupers, as, under the 7th Exception to Art. 1 of that Order, the guardians can, if they think fit, grant out-door relief to the wife or child of any able-bodied man who shall be in the service of Her Majesty, as a soldier, sailor, or marine. Under this Exception, it is left to the guardians to decide, upon their own discretion, and according to their views of the circumstances of each individual case, as to the mode in which relief shall be afforded to the wife or children of such a person; and the Board, though they will always be ready, as far as may be within their power, to assist the guardians in any difficulty, cannot undertake to anticipate by any general advice the exercise of the guardians' discretion in the several cases of the above description which may come before them. With respect to the suggestion of the guardians, as to the parishes in which the marines are settled being required to accept their families without a second order of removal, I am to state that the Board have no power to make any regulation of this kind. It is a question depending upon the circumstances of each case, whether the parish officers can or ought to bear the charge of the relief of a pauper not resident in their parish, although some previous order of removal may have been obtained. It is, in fact, a subject beyond the control of the guardians.

15th Aug., 1848.

———, *Esq.*, Representing the following grievance, under which the ratepayers of the parish of East Stonehouse suffer :—The parish of East Stonehouse is under a board of guardians. It lies between Plymouth and Devonport, (both under local Acts.) The Marine Barracks, from which the marines are drafted to H. M. ships, are in the parish of East Stonehouse. The wives of the marines, for the most part, reside in the parish of East Stonehouse, and and when the men are drafted off for service, a period of two or three months generally elapses before any portion of their pay becomes available for the support of their families. During this time they fall upon the parish for support; and in case of the sickness of any part of the family of a marine, East Stonehouse has also, in his absence, to bear the burden of their relief. Again, when a marine is discharged, his wife and family will, in most cases, have resided in the parish more than five years, and if they are not legally irremovable, such great difficulty is generally experienced regarding their removal to the places of their respective settlements as to render this mode of relief practically nugatory. There are at the present time 103 women, with 247 children, the families of marines, receiving £9. 16*s*. 3*d*. weekly, or at the rate of £500 per annum, from the parish of East Stonehouse. The marines, to whom these women and children belong, are absent on service, and proof of settlement is scarcely, in any case, attainable. There are, on an average, from twenty to thirty marines discharged monthly in the parish of East Stonehouse, and as their places are filled up by new recruits, who either have wives, or who marry immediately, East Stonehouse is in a fair way of being swamped by the progressively increasing demands of this class, unless some other course be adopted than that which the guardians conceive has been open to them since the passing of the Irremovable Act. Inquiring whether a discharged marine who has not gained a settlement in the parish, but whose wife and family have resided five years in East Stonehouse during his service, is, together with his wife and children, removable to his place of settlement. A doubt has been expressed whether the wife and family, having resided five years continuously in the parish, can be removed with the marine to his place of settlement on his discharge from Her Majesty's service.

Ans.—If the marine, in the case you put, has not resided in East Stonehouse for the period requisite to render him irremovable under the Act, and if he is otherwise removable to his place of settlement, his wife and children will be removable with him, although they may have resided in the parish for five years; inasmuch as, by the last proviso to the 1st sec., they are removable if he is. It may, perhaps, be a question whether the time of his service as a marine in the parish can be taken into consideration in computing the period of his residence, but the Board think that it cannot.

2. WHETHER FATHER LIABLE FOR RELIEF GIVEN TO ABLE-BODIED SON, AGED 16.

17*th May*, 1849.

Clerk of Eastbourne Union.—Inquired, whether the guardians can take any proceedings to recover the relief afforded by them to a pauper aged 16, who is now in the workhouse, and who is able to work, but can get no employment. The father is able to maintain him. The guardians understand that, as the son is able to work, they cannot compel the father, under the statute of Elizabeth, to keep his son; but they think that, in the ordinary course of law, parents are bound to maintain their children until they are of age, it is but reasonable the guardians should be able to recover in the County Court the cost of the son's maintenance.

Ans.—Relief given to the son cannot, in this instance, be considered as relief to the father, inasmuch as the son is 16 years of age; the former, therefore, is not liable for the cost of the relief in question, (see 4 & 5 Wm. 4, c. 76, sec. 56.) Neither can an order of maintenance be, in this instance, obtained against the father, inasmuch as the pauper in question being able to work, does not come within the 7th sec. of the 43rd Elizabeth, c. 2, (see Rex. *v.* Gulley,) Bott, 366. The Board have to add, that the pauper being able-bodied is within the Prohibitory Order, and, consequently, cannot be relieved out of the workhouse.

3. UNDERTAKING TO REPAY RELIEF TO NON-RESIDENT PAUPERS.

22*nd May*, 1849.

Clerk of Wincanton Union.—Transmitting the following extract from the Minute Book of this Union relative to the relief of non-resident poor, and also a copy of the form adopted by the guardians, undertaking to repay such relief:—

" *Wednesday*, 9*th May*, 1849.

" The clerk having read a letter from the clerk of the Frome Union, asking if this board will consent to repay the relief to certain paupers who were chargeable to parishes within this union, previously to the passing of the Act 9 & 10 Vic. c. 66, and transferred under the opinion of the Attorney and Solicitor-General to parishes within the Frome Union, it was resolved, that this board will give an undertaking to repay such relief after they have been furnished with an examination of the pauper, in every case showing the length of time such pauper has inhabited in his present place of residence, provided such residence does not amount to five years without the receipt of relief, and also that such pauper is not exempted from liability to be removed under any of the other clauses of the statute in question, and has done no act to gain any other settlement since the passing of such statute; and provided also, that the Frome Board, by a resolution duly entered in their Minute Book, resolve to give similar undertakings with regard to all paupers similarly situated within this union, but legally settled within the Frome Union."

Ans.—As the undertaking in question applies to paupers not chargeable upon the common fund of the Wincanton Union, but who are alleged to be settled therein, the Board conclude that it is given with the concurrence of the particular parishes of the union interested in the arrangement. The Board, however, wish to be informed, what is in fact the practice of the guardians as to obtaining the assent of the parishes of the settlement, to the guardians entering into such undertaking to repay the cost of relief given to their paupers.

5th June, 1849.

Clerk of same Union.—1, The guardians allow no non-resident relief contrary to Article 3 of the General Prohibitory Order. 2, With regard to the statute referred to in the printed form of undertaking, they require the overseers of the parish of the settlement to be furnished with a formal examination of the pauper for whom non-resident relief is desired; and if, upon such examination, it appear that the pauper is still removable from his place of residence, and the guardian representing his place of settlement moves at the board the allowance of non-resident relief, an authority in the form adopted by the board is transmitted to the clerk of the union in which the pauper resides, in every case where such pauper is entitled to non-resident relief under the Prohibitory Order; and lastly, if the pauper be not entitled to non-resident relief under that Order, the board declines to grant it until the sanction of the Poor Law Board has been obtained.

Ans.—The Board expressed their satisfaction at the judicious course of proceeding above described as being pursued by the guardians in this matter.

[*Form of Undertaking.*]

WINCANTON UNION,

IN THE COUNTIES OF SOMERSET AND DORSET.

day of 184

Re

Sir,

As it appears, upon the examination of the above party, obtained through , that the case does not fall within the operation and meaning of the 9 & 10 Vic. c. 66, and that the party stands in need of parochial relief, the guardians of the poor of the Wincanton Union do hereby authorize that relief be granted at the rate of shillings and pence per week, and the advances so made shall be repaid to you quarterly, on your sending to me an account of such relief, accompanied with a certificate, signed by the relieving officer, that the party is a fit object for the continuance of the same.

By order

Clerk.

To

WINCANTON UNION,

IN THE COUNTIES OF SOMERSET AND DORSET.

day of 184

Re

Sir,

As it appears, upon the examination of the above party, obtained through , that the case does not fall within the operation and meaning of the 9 & 10 Vic. c. 66, and that the party stands in need of parochial relief, the guardians of the poor of the Wincanton Union do hereby authorize that relief be granted at the rate of shillings and pence per week, and the advances so made shall be repaid to you quarterly, on your sending to me an account of such relief, accompanied with a certificate signed by the relieving officer, that the party is a fit object for the continuance of the same.

By order,

Clerk.

To

VI.—REMOVABILITY.

1. OF MOTHER OF AN ILLEGITIMATE CHILD.

19th Feb., 1849.

Clerk of Bedale Union.—N. M., an illegitimate child, was born in the township of Kirkby Malzeard, in the year 1836, and has resided in that township up to this time. Her mother, who had been residing for about ten years previous to the year 1839, received relief from the township of Well, in this union, (her place of settlement,) from 1839 up to the passing of the Act 9 & 10 Vic. c. 66, when the relief was discontinued.

This relief was no doubt paid on account of the child as well as the mother, but the Poor Law Amendment Act (4 & 5 Wm. 4, c. 76. sec. 71) provides, that "all relief granted to such child while under the age of sixteen, shall be considered as granted to such mother." It is contended, that in consequence of the recent decision in Reg. *v*. Christchurch, the above pauper is removable. Requesting the opinion of the Poor Law Board on the point.

Ans.—As the Board collect from the statement before them, that the mother of the pauper is irremovable from the parish of Kirkby Malzeard, the pauper herself cannot, under the 9 & 10 Vic. c. 66, sec. 3, be legally removed from her mother. Therefore, being so irremovable, the cost of her relief should be borne by the common fund of the union.

2. REMOVABILITY AND CHARGEABILITY OF WIDOW.

11th April, 1849.

Clerk of Bromsgrove Union.— Inquiring whether a parish is liable to contribute to the relief of a widow, who removes herself from such parish before the expiration of twelve months next after her husband's death, such parish being that in which she was residing with her husband at the time of his death; and also, whether, in the event of her returning to such parish after she had broken her residence, she could be removed to the place of her settlement before the expiration of the first twelve months of her widowhood.

Ans.—The parish where the widow resided at the time of her husband's death is under no obligation to relieve her when she quits it. If she return to that parish during the first twelve months of her widowhood, she will not be removable therefrom to the place of her settlement until that period has elasped, and her relief must accordingly be borne by the common fund of the union in which such parish is included.

3. REMOVABILITY OF A WIDOW.

24th April, 1849.

Clerk of Calne Union.—J. D., a widow, belonging to the parish of Bremhill, in this union, but who has resided in Calne parish from the time of her marriage, upwards of twenty years ago, has been receiving relief ever since the death of her husband, which occurred about four years ago. Inquiring whether the term of her residence at Calne must be computed from the time of her marriage, or only from the time of her husband's death; as, in the former case, she would be irremovable from Calne, no relief having been afforded whilst her husband was living, and would consequently be chargeable to the common fund of the union; but, in the latter, she would be removable, having received relief the whole of the time she has been a widow.

Ans.—The time of the pauper's residence in the parish of Calne, during the lifetime of her husband, is to be taken into consideration in computing the period of her residence, under sec. 1 of the 9 & 10 Vic. c. 66, (see Q. *v*. Glossop, 17 L. I. R., N. S. M. C. 171, and Q. *v*. Whitechapel,) and consequently the pauper, according to the statement of her case in your letter, is irremovable from Calne.

4. REMOVABILITY AND CHARGEABILITY OF ORPHAN CHILDREN.

2nd May, 1849.

Clerk of Southam Union.—J. R., a pauper belonging to Stivichall, in the Warwick Union, had for upwards of five years previous to 1846 been residing with his wife and family at Southam in this union, and at the end of July in that year he became chargeable, in consequence of illness, and the relief which was given to him by the Southam Union was repaid by the Warwick Union up to the passing of the Act 9 & 10 Vic. c. 66, when the pauper became irremovable, and the Warwick Union declined to repay any further relief. The pauper, however, still requiring relief on account of illness, the relief given to him was charged to Southam parish, until the passing of the Act 10 & 11 Vic. c. 110, and it was from that time charged to the common fund of the Southam Union up to his death, which happened on the 9th of January, 1849. At his decease, the widow required relief for herself and family, and that was also charged to the common fund of the Southam Union. The widow died on the 24th of February, 1849, and the two children, Ann, aged six, and Helen, aged four years, requiring relief, the guardians have given relief to Ann, at the charge of the common fund, and to Helen, at the charge of Southam parish. The children have resided in the parish of Southam with their father and mother since their birth. The amount given to the father, and afterwards to the widow, has been the usual relief for the family, and was rendered necessary by the sickness of the man and widow respectively, and has been given without any intermission for upwards of two years. A doubt has been expressed as to whether either or both of the two orphan children are now removable, and consequently as to the proper mode of charging the relief. Can the relief given to the father and mother be considered relief to the children? If so, the elder child, Ann, will not have resided five years without relief, and the other child, Helen, is now under five years of age. But the relief to the father and mother having been continuous, will the last proviso to sec. 1. of the Act 9 and 10 Vic. c. 66, operate to render the children irremovable now the parents are dead? The above statement is submitted by the Southam Union, and the parish of Southam, to the Poor Law Board, under the provision of 11 & 12 Vic. c. 110, sec. 4, in order to obtain their decision thereon.

Ans.—It appears to the Board that Helen, the youngest child, not having resided five years in the parish of Southam is removable therefrom. As regards the eldest child, they think that the case admits of some doubt. She has, it appears, resided for more than five years in the parish of Southam, during a portion of which time her parents were in receipt of relief; and the question arising is, whether the relief so afforded to them was relief received by this child, within the first proviso to the 1st sec. of the 9 & 10 Vic. c. 66, so that in computing the period of her residence the time during which that relief was given should be excluded. If it appear from the books of the Southam Union, or otherwise, that the relief was given to the parents with reference to the child, Ann, she must be considered as having been either actually or constructively in the receipt of such relief, and the time during which she so received relief should, therefore, be excluded from the computation. But, if on the contrary, it be ascertained that no relief was given on her account, it would then seem that she was neither actually or constructively in receipt of relief; and, if so, the time during which relief was given to the parents should not be excluded. The Board understand from the statement before them that the relief was, in fact, given for the whole family; and, therefore, the time during which it was given being excluded in the computation of the period of the residence of the elder child, she will be removable, and, consequently not chargeable to the common fund of the union.

---

5. Removability of widow who had lived apart and in a different place from her husband up to his death.

7th May, 1849.

Clerk of Newton Abbot Union.—E. B., of Bickington, widow of the late J. B., deserted her husband about twenty years ago, and cohabited, during her husband's lifetime, with another man, and resided in Bickington for about twenty years, during which time her husband resided in East Ogwell, being the parish of his settlement, where he died about two years ago. Inquiring whether a residence of the widow in Bickington, under the above circumstances for more than five years, renders her irremovable from that parish.

Ans.—Under the circumstances set out in the case of E. B., the Board consider her now to be irremovable from Beckington.

---

6. Removability and chargeability.

8th May, 1849.

The Rev. ——— *Dolgelley Union.*—1. A. T., aged 44, has resided in the parish of Llanfachreth ever since she was born. That parish is also her maiden settlement. In 1838, she gave birth to an illegitimate child, a girl, who has always up to the present time resided with her. In 1840, A.T. married her present husband, J. T., who belonged to the parish of Llanelltyd, and resided there. Upon his marriage he took a cottage in the parish of Llanfachreth, and shortly after his wife was delivered of a boy, who is still living. He resided in the latter parish for about two years, when he deserted his wife and family, and went to America, where he has been ever since. After his departure, his wife applied for the first time for relief for herself and her two children. They were maintained by the parish of Llanelltyd up to August, 1846, since which time they have been chargeable to the common fund of the union. It was only within the last few days it was discovered that the eldest of the pauper's children was illegitimate. Inquiring whether the relief given to this child is chargeable to the parish of Llanfachreth, as that of the mother's maiden settlement. And also, whether the pauper and her legitimate child be removable. 2. E. O., a pauper belonging to the parish of Llanfachreth, but until lately resident in the parish of Dolgelley, where she had resided for upwards of twenty years without relief, was delivered of a bastard child about eight years ago. The child was maintained by the former parish until August, 1846, when the relief was charged to the common fund of the union. A few months ago, E. O. left the parish of Dolgelley, and went to Liverpool, where she still remains. On her departure, the relief of her child was charged to the parish of Llanfachreth, and is still so charged. Is the child removable?

Ans.—1, In the first place, the Board think that the illegitimate child of A. T. takes the settlement of her mother, as it changes until the child arrives at the age of sixteen years; and, therefore, the cost of this child's relief is not chargeable to the parish of Llanfachreth on the ground of her settlement therein. But the whole of the family appear to be removable according to the decisions in Q. *v.* St. Ebbes, and Q. *v.* Pott Shrigley, 3 N. S. C. 2, According to the statement of the case of E. O., the time during which the child in question was maintained by a parish wherein it was not residing, being deducted in computing the term of its residence in the parish of Dolgelley, there will not remain a period of five years as contemplated by sec. 1 of the 9 & 10 Vic. c. 66, and the child will accordingly be removable.

7. IRISH AND SCOTCH PAUPERS.

12*th Jan.*, 1849.

Clerk of Blackburn Union.—Inquiring whether Irish and Scotch paupers, who have resided within a township in England for upwards of five years, without receiving relief, are removable therefrom to the place of their birth in Ireland, or Scotland, since the passing of the 9 & 10 Vic. c. 66, in such form, and by such authority as they were removable by the 8 & 9 Vic. c. 117.

Ans.—The Poor Law Commissioners were advised by the law officers of the Crown in relation to this point in the negative, and the Board see no reason to differ from that opinion.

8. COMPUTATION OF PERIOD OF RESIDENCE.

5*th Feb.*, 1849.

Clerk of Newport (Salop) Union.—G. S., aged seventy, and wife, aged seventy, have resided in the parish of Cherrington, in this union, for the last twenty years, having during the period of ten years now last past received relief from the parish of Edgmond, also in this union. Edgmond now objects to continue to bear the charge of their relief, contending, that as the paupers had lived in Cherrington upwards of five years previous to the receipt of any relief, (although for the last ten years they have received regular relief from Edgmond,) they are now irremovable, and their relief ought to be charged to the common fund.

Ans.—From the facts before them, the Board are of opinion that the paupers are irremovable, according to the decision of the Court of Queen's Bench, in the case of Reg. *v.* Harrow-on-the-Hill, 3 N. S. C. 232.

9. COMPUTATION OF PERIOD OF RESIDENCE.

8*th March*, 1849.

Clerk of Easingwold Union.—Requesting the Board's opinion as to the removability of S. S. and her children, under the following circumstances:—G. S., the husband, alleged to be settled in the parish of Haley, in this union, went to reside in the township of Leeds, in April, 1837. He continued to reside with his wife in Leeds until April, 1844, when he was committed to prison, and remained there about two months. On his discharge, he returned to his wife and family at Leeds, and resided there until the month of November, 1847, when he was again sent to prison, and was subsequently transported for seven years. The periods during which the husband and the wife have been in receipt of relief are as follow:—In the months of January and February, 1842, the husband received relief from Leeds for three or four weeks; application was made to Haley for repayment thereof, which was refused on the ground of the pauper being an able-bodied man. On his committal to prison in 1844, the wife and children became chargeable to Leeds, and received relief for about seven weeks, which was repaid by Haley. On his second imprisonment, in November, 1847, the wife and children again became chargeable, and have received relief from Leeds ever since. The township of Leeds is now attempting to remove the wife and children to Haley.

Ans.—It appears to the Board that, according to the decision of the Court of Queen's Bench in the case of the Queen *v.* Pott. Shrigley, 3 N.S. c. 317, and the terms of the statute 11 & 12 Vic. c. 111, the paupers are removable.

10. COMPUTATION OF PERIOD OF RESIDENCE.

15*th March*, 1849.

A Guardian of Newtown and Llanidloes Union.—

1, Does the Act 9 & 10 Vic. c. 66, go back more than five years from the time of its passing in regard to residence, to prevent a pauper from being removed? 2, Must the five years be industrial residence, and unbroken by any relief, or five years made up at different periods of time, without the receipt of relief? 3, Are those persons not liable to be removed to be charged to the parish in which they reside, or to the union? 4, Is the expense of the removal of paupers to be borne by the parish removing, or is it to be charged to the union?

Ans.—1, The statute 9 & 10 Vic. c. 66, is to be considered as retrospective to the extent of the whole time of a pauper's residence in a particular parish. 2, With regard to the residence of a pauper, it may be composed of five years of consecutive residence without relief, or of years not entirely consecutive, *i.e.*, made up of detached portions of time, with intervals of relief between such portions in the same parish; but if there be a residence in fact, the character or capacity in which a person resides is not material; consequently, the residence need not necessarily be industrial. 3, The cost of the relief to the persons who are rendered irremovable by the statute 9 & 10 Vic. c. 66, and who are not settled in the parish of their residence, is to be charged to the union common fund, (*vide* 3rd sec. of the 11 & 12 Vic. c. 110.) Lastly, The guardians of the union have no power to procure orders of removal. They are, indeed, only concerned with irremovable paupers, and consequently, the parish seeking to remove a pauper must bear the expenses incurred in doing so.

---

11. COMPUTATION OF PERIOD OF RESIDENCE.

27*th April*, 1849.

Clerk of Dolgelley Union.—A. D. has been regularly relieved by the parish of Mallwyd since the year 1819: about the year 1822, A. D. and Gwen her daughter left Mallwyd parish and went to Llanerfyl parish, with the view of obtaining a livelihood for Gwen, who was a sempstress. A. D. then took a house in Llanerfyl for herself and her daughter Gwen, wherein they resided until 1827. About the year 1827, Gwen took another house in the parish of Llanerfyl, paid an earnest on the taking, wherein she and her mother resided until 1839, the rent of which has been paid, Gwen being tenant. From 1839 to the present time, Gwen has resided with her mother in the parish of Llanerfyl. During the years 1845 and 1846, Gwen received relief on her own account from the parish of Mallwyd, but never received any relief previously nor since that period. Inquiring whether Gwen is now removable to Mallwyd or not.

Ans.—Upon this statement of the case, the Board think that Gwen D. is not removable by reason of the statute 9 & 10 Vic. c. 66.

---

12. COMPUTATION OF PERIOD OF RESIDENCE—PERSONS EMPLOYED AND PAID BY THE SURVEYOR OF THE HIGHWAYS.

21*st Feb.*, 1849.

Clerk of Bourn Union.—Inquiring, whether under the Act 9 & 10 Vic. c. 66, sec. 1, the time during which a person has been employed and paid by the surveyor of the highways, out of the highway-rate of the parish to which he belongs, whilst residing in another parish, is to be excluded in the computation of the period of such residence; in other words, whether this is being "wholly or in part maintained by any rate," &c., within the meaning of the first proviso to the above statute.

Ans.—The Board hesitate to express any general opinion on the question you have laid before them, inasmuch as the application of the terms of the statute must depend to a great extent upon the varying circumstances of each particular case. The first proviso to sec. 1 of the 9 & 10 Vic. c. 66, contemplates the case where a person "shall be wholly or in part maintained by any rate or subscription raised in a parish in which such person does not reside, not being a *bonâ fide* charitable gift." It appears to the Board that, while the words of the clause expressly exclude on the one hand *bonâ fide* charitable gifts, they must also, on the other hand, be held to exclude *bonâ fide* wages, or payments for work done at or about the market price of labour in the place. A man so employed on such terms cannot properly be said to have been maintained by a public rate or subscription, when it was notorious he was able to maintain himself, and did, indeed, do so, *bonâ fide* by his own industry. With regard, however, to the highway-rates, the Board cannot but call to mind the fact that, instead of being simply and exclusively devoted to their proper object—the repair of the roads—and expended accordingly in the most judicious and economical manner by paying the full price for work well done by the independent labourers of the place, the highway-rates have not unfrequently been collusively and wrongfully applied to the maintenance of persons who (if supported at all at the expense of the parish) ought to have been relieved out of the rates expressly intended for the relief of the poor. The Board, therefore, cannot give any definite answer to your inquiry, without being furnished with sufficient information to enable them to decide to which of the above-mentioned classes of payments the money given in such cases as you allude to is to be referred. If it be the payment of a fair day's wages for a fair day's work, the Board would not consider the time when the pauper received such wages to be a time of relief within the meaning of the clause; but if it be a payment of wages exceeding the value of work done the case would be different.

---

13. BREACH OF RESIDENCE.

24th May, 1849.

Clerk of Clifton Union.—G. R., who is 54 years of age, resided in St. Philip and Jacob, previous to coming into the workhouse, for the last thirteen years, excepting that he went to Barbadoes as a sailor, and was absent about seven months, his wife and children residing in the house at St. Philip and Jacob during his absence. Inquiring whether the going to Barbadoes within the last five years was a break in the residence.

Ans.—The Board are of opinion that the absence of the pauper in question from this country, caused by his voyage to Barbadoes, must be considered as an interruption of his residence in the parish of St. Philip and Jacob.

---

14. BREACH OF RESIDENCE.

17th April, 1849.

Clerk of St. Faith's Union.—In consequence of the recent decision of the Court of Queen's Bench in Reg. *v.* Forncett, St. Mary, requested the opinion of the Poor Law Board upon the following cases:—1, If a pauper, whose legal settlement is in a parish belonging to this union, has completed an entire five years' residence within the city of Norwich, (not having received any relief during such five years,) and after completing such period of residence gives up his house, disposes of his furniture, and accepts of an order of admission into this union workhouse, where he remains for a certain time, and on his discharge returns to reside in Norwich—inquired, whether the pauper committed a breach of residence by giving up his house and disposing of his furniture, under the cirnumstances stated, and thereby became removable. 2, If a pauper legally belonging to a parish in this union, but who has resided in Norwich five entire years without having received relief, and subsequent to the five years was removed by an order, which was not disputed, from Norwich to the place of his legal settlement in this union, and such pauper returns again to reside in Norwich—inquired, whether the fact of the pauper having been removed under such circumstances constitutes a breach of residence, and renders the pauper removable independently of the question whether or not he gave up the occupation of his house in Norwich and disposed of his furniture in the same.

Ans.—1, The Board consider in this case that the pauper would be removable, the residence within the city of Norwich having been interrupted, according to the statement before them. 2, The pauper in this case, also, appears to be removable, according to the decision of the Court of Queen's Bench in Queen *v.* Halifax, 3 N.S.C. The Board, however, give these answers to the questions proposed to them by the guardians of the St. Faith's Union without prejudice to any future consideration of the cases brought before them hereafter under the 4th sec. of the 11 & 12 Vic. c. 110.

---

15. BREACH OF RESIDENCE.

22nd May, 1849.

The Rev. ——— *Bridgwater Union.*—An order was made some eight years ago for the removal of a pauper, who was taken by the overseer to Overstowey, the parish of her settlement. On the same day, the pauper returned to the cottage from which she was taken, and from which none of her furniture had been removed, but was subsequently relieved by the parish to which she was removed. Inquiring whether such a removal amounts to a breach of the residence of the pauper.

Ans.—The Court of Queen's Bench has expressly decided, that an order of removal executed by the actual removal of the pauper, creates an interruption of the pauper's residence in the parish from which such removal takes place. (Reg. *v.* Halifax, and Reg. *v.* Leend, 3 N. S. Cases.) If, therefore, in the case you refer to, the pauper has been continuously in the receipt of relief in the parish of Overstowey since the date of her removal under the circumstances you describe, she will, (so far as the question of residence is concerned,) be now removable from that parish, as the time during which she has been so receiving relief is to be excluded from the computation of the period of residence, according to the 1st proviso to the 1st sec. of the 9 & 10 Vic. c. 66.

16. BREACH OF RESIDENCE. — WIFE, AND CHILDREN, DESERTED BY HER HUSBAND.

21*st March*, 1849.

Clerk of Bridgwater Union.—In December last, L. S., with three children, who was then residing in the parish of Bridgwater, and had been residing there for nine years previously without receiving relief, became destitute, and required relief in consequence of being deserted by her husband, who was supposed to be settled in the parish of Chewton Mendip, in the Wells Union. This pauper not being settled in the parish where she resided, and being rendered irremovable by the 9 & 10 Vic. c. 66, a question has arisen, whether the relief granted to her and children under the circumstances stated, should be charged to Bridgwater parish, or to the common fund of the union, under 11 & 12 Vic. c. 110. The guardians are of opinion, that before they can charge the relief to the common fund, it must be shown by more satisfactory evidence than the woman has given, that her husband's settlement is not in the parish of Bridgwater, her place of residence, and have ordered the relief granted to be charged to Bridgwater parish.

Ans.—The Board think it sufficient to point out in the case of the pauper L. S. and her family, that the decision of the guardians of the Bridgwater Union in charging her relief to the parish of her residence was correct though not upon the ground stated in your letter. According to the decision in the case of Q. *v.* St. Ebbes, (N. S. Cases,) and the provisions of the 11 & 12 Vic. c. 111, the pauper in the present case was not irremovable, inasmuch as her husband by his desertion having interrupted his continued residence in Bridgwater, was not irremovable therefrom. Consequently, the cost of the relief to the wife was not chargeable to the common fund of the union. As to the proof that may be required under sec. 3 of the 11 & 12 Vic. c. 110, with regard to the settlement of an irremovable pauper, the Board may observe generally that they do not think the guardians are justified in casting upon the parish of the pauper's residence the burthen of proving his settlement to be elsewhere. It appears to the Board, that it will be enough if reasonable evidence be given to show that the pauper is not settled in the parish of the residence.

17. BREACH OF RESIDENCE.

7*th Feb.*, 1849.

Clerk of Hastings Union.—A. B., legally settled in St. John's, came to St. Peter's, and resided there for three years; he then went to and resided in St. Andrew's for one year, and afterwards came back to and resided in St. Peter's for two years, (in no instance receiving relief,) thus making, by adding the two periods together, a full five years' residence in St. Peter's. Is he not still removable to his settlement in St. John's, by reason of the interruption of the residence in St. Peter's; in short, are not the five years to be computed from the last coming to reside in St. Peter's — the words of the Act being, "Five years next before the application for the warrant?"

Ans.—The residence of the pauper, A. B., in St. Peter's, would certainly be interrupted by his absence therefrom and residence in the parish of St. Andrew's, and the residence in St. Peter's subsequent to his return to that parish could not be coupled with the residence which took place prior to his leaving for St. Andrew's. The period of the pauper's second residence in St. Peter's being in itself short of the term required by sec. 1. of 9 & 10 Vic. c. 66, it follows that he is not rendered irremovable by reason of such residence.

18. BREACH OF RESIDENCE AND CHARGEABILITY.

24*th March*, 1849.

Clerk of Bromyard Union.—A woman, named Jones, whose legal settlement is in the parish of B., in the Union of L., has resided in the parish of A. in this union for the last forty years (except as hereafter mentioned.) From 1819 to 1836 she received relief from B., her settlement parish: on the formation of the L. Union she was refused non-resident relief, and was admitted into the workhouse of that union, she taking with her the key of her dwelling. She remained in the workhouse five days, when the guardians allowed her non-resident relief, and she returned to her own house in the parish of A., where she has resided ever since, receiving relief from B. up to the autumn of 1846, when it was discontinued, on the 9 & 10

Vic. c. 66 coming into operation. Inquiring whether the five days in the workhouse of the L. Union, under the circumstances stated, interrupted the pauper's residence in A., so as to render her removable to B. A woman, named Rowberry, who has resided in the parish of N., in this union for the last nine years, without receiving any relief, is now become chargeable to that parish, her place of settlement not being known. The guardian of N. has applied to have her relief charged to the common fund on the ground of the woman being irremovable under the 9 & 10 Vic. c. 66. But this is objected to on the ground, that as she could not have been removed if the statute above referred to had not been passed, she was not now rendered irremovable, and consequently her relief cannot be charged to the common fund as proposed under the 3rd sec. of the 11 & 12 Vic. c. 110.

Ans.—In reference to the case of the pauper, Jones, the Board are of opinion, upon the authority of Reg. *v.* Tacolustone (18 L. J. R. N. S. M. C. 44,) that she is not removable from the parish of her residence. In the second case, that of the woman Rowberry, as it is stated as a fact that her settlement is in some unknown parish, (and, therefore, that she is not, as the Board understand, settled in the parish of her residence,) they are of opinion that she comes within the provisions of the 3rd sec. of the 11 & 12 Vic. c. 110, and her relief is consequently chargeable to the union common fund.

19. RELIEF REQUIRED IN CONSEQUENCE OF CONFINEMENT IN CHILDBIRTH.

5*th March*, 1849.

Clerk of Faringdon Union.—Inquiring, whether females confined with illegitimate children in some other parish than their place of settlement, and requiring relief in consequence of such confinement, should be considered as sick persons, and irremovable, and, in consequence, chargeable to the common fund of the union until they are well enough to resume their employment; or, whether the chargeability should fall on the parish where the confinement happens, and such parish be left to its remedy of obtaining an order of removal as soon as practicable.

Ans.—If the relief of the persons in question is only required in consequence of the sickness attending their confinement, and it be not of a character to produce permanent disability, then the parties would be irremovable under sec. 4 of the 9 & 10 Vic. c. 66; and the cost of the relief would be a charge upon the common fund of the Faringdon Union; but if the relief be required and given in consequence of general destitution, independently of the sickness, then the pauper is not rendered irremovable, and the charge must be borne by the parish in which the pauper resides at the time. The Board state the above as a general principle, but they do so without prejudice to the future consideration of any specific case which may hereafter be brought before them.

20. REMOVABILITY OF A PAUPER WHO IS RUPTURED.

11*th Jan.*, 1849.

Clerk of Bedminster Union.—A pauper of the name of C. H. is legally settled in St. George; he is a single man, twenty-three years of age, was in the workhouse on account of some temporary illness, at the expense of Bedminster, and is now recovered. He has, however, a rupture, which has not prevented his working. Inquiring whether such rupture will entitle Bedminster to remove the pauper to St. George.

Ans.—It appears to the Board, that the material point which arises upon this case is, whether or not the sickness which causes the chargeability is calculated to produce permanent disability, within the meaning of the 4th sec. of the 9 & 10 Vic. c. 66. If so, the pauper is removable; but if the sickness be only temporary, he is irremovable. With regard to a pauper who has a rupture, which causes chargeability, the Board may observe, generally, that the question whether such rupture will produce a permanent disability must, the Board apprehend, depend upon the nature and extent of the rupture. A rupture in itself cannot be said, necessarily, to create a permanent disability, though, doubtless, in some cases it may do so. If it does not prevent a person from working, or gaining his own livelihood, the Board conceive that it would not create a permanent disability, within the meaning of the statute. In expressing this general opinion, the Board desire to be understood as not intending thereby to conclude the parishes interested in the particular case submitted to them, should a joint reference on this subject be hereafter made to the Board, under sec. 4 of the 11 & 12 Vic. c. 110.

London: Printed by Order of the Poor Law Board, by BLACKBURN & BURT, 90½, Holborn Hill, and Published by CHARLES KNIGHT, 90, Fleet Street.

AN

OFFICIAL CIRCULAR

OF PUBLIC DOCUMENTS AND INFORMATION:

DIRECTED BY THE POOR LAW BOARD TO BE PRINTED, CHIEFLY FOR THE USE OF THE BOARDS OF GUARDIANS AND THEIR OFFICERS.

No. 26.] JUNE, 1849. [N.S.

CONTENTS.

I.—ACCOUNTS.—STATISTICAL STATEMENT.

9th May, 1849.

Clerk of Lexden and Winstree Union.—Requesting advice in reference to the filling up of the statistical statement, (Form 16.) The Instructions of the Poor Law Commissioners state, that the number of each class of paupers actually relieved on the 1st January and on the 1st July is to be shown, and that, "by persons in the receipt of relief on these particular days is meant, not only persons to whom relief is actually given on either of these days, but persons whose allowance is for any period which includes either of these days." He understands that all persons who are actually receiving relief on these days are meant; but by some it is understood that all persons who have been relieved in the half-year which includes either of those days are meant.

Ans.—The General Order for Accounts requires those paupers to be entered in the statistical statement who are on the particular day mentioned (1st January or 1st July) in receipt of relief, that is to say, those paupers are to be entered who are actually relieved on that day, or whose relief comprises that day; but those paupers who may be relieved at any other time in the half-year, but not on or for that day, are not to be inserted.

II.—COUNTY RATE ASSESSMENT.—MONMOUTHSHIRE.

Dingestow Court, near Monmouth,
June 15th, 1849.

GENTLEMEN,—Observing that you have given publicity by your Official Circulars to the Report of the Committee appointed to revise the County

Rate in the county of Devon, I have thought fit to transmit to you the Report of the Committee appointed for the same purpose in the county of Monmouth. The mode of proceeding pursued by this Committee, as appears by our Report, was somewhat different from that pursued in Devonshire; and I have thought that you might think fit to recommend it, or make it known, as it has been attended with great success.

No notice of appeal against the assessment was entered at the sessions; and we have reason to believe it to be not only a great improvement upon the former assessments, but that it is as nearly accurate and equitable as the very various and fluctuating description of the property in this county, and the complication of details, rendered practicable.

I have the honour to be,
Your obedient Servant,
S. R. BOSANQUET,
Chairman of Quarter Sessions, and Chairman of Committee.

To the Poor Law Board.

REPORT OF THE COMMITTEE.

Names of the Committee.—Sir Charles Morgan, Bart.—Edward Harris Phillips, Esq.—Samuel Richard Bosanquet, Esq.—Samuel Homfray, Esq.— Thomas Prothero, Esq.— Ferdinand Hanbury Williams, Esq.—George Cave, Esq. —William Adams Williams, Junior, Esq.—John King, Esq.—John Russell, Esq.—Rev. William Evans.

New County Rate.—Report.—We, your Committee appointed at the Easter Sessions, 1847, to revise and re-assess the county rate, now present to you our new assessment of the property liable to assessment in the respective parishes, and our Report.

The last preceding assessment to the county rate was made in the year 1840. Upon that occasion, the assessment was raised from £293,579 to £453,751.

One principal object of the Committee on that occasion was to determine the legal principle of rating; and having determined that, at that time, under the then existing Acts, the assessment ought to be made upon the gross estimated annual value of property, that Committee obtained returns of such gross value from the respective parishes, and adopted those returns as their assessment; except in cases in which the return was lower than the then existing assessment, in which cases they retained the former assessment.

Notwithstanding that, at the time of the operations of that Committee, the Act to regulate Parochial Assessments, (6 & 7 Wm. 4, c. 96,) had passed, requiring that all property should be rated to the poor's-rate at its full value, distinguishing the gross from the net annual value, yet the returns made to the Committee appear to have been in many instances very insufficient, and much below the real value of the property.

The business to be performed by your present Committee has been greater from this circumstance, as we have had not only to estimate the improvement or decrease in value since the previous assessment, but have also, in the instances alluded to, had to bring up the property to a full estimate and assessment for the first time.

The operations of your present Committee have been performed under the provisions of the recent Act, 8 & 9 Vic. c. 111. This Act provides that the assessment shall now be made, not upon the gross value, but upon the net annual value of property; upon the same principle which is applicable to the poor's-rate, under the 6 & 7 Wm. 4, c. 96. If the property, therefore, of the county had remained at the same value, and had before been fully assessed, there would have been a decrease in the county rate assessment, to the amount of from ten to twenty per cent. But, on the contrary, there has been a very considerable increase.

Immediately upon our appointment, we issued a circular to all the overseers of parishes, giving notice that we should allow them two months to prepare a correct assessment, and that if a correct assessment was not furnished when we called for it after that time, we should appoint valuers to assess the parish, under the above Act. (See Appendix A.)

We also issued a circular to all magistrates of the county, requesting them to assist the overseers in their respective divisions. (See Appendix B.)

In order to save trouble and expense to the overseers and other persons attending, we resolved to make a circuit, and to visit the principal and most central places in the county; and accordingly we held our sittings at Abergavenny, Caerleon, Chepstow, Monmouth, Newport, Newbridge, Pontypool, and Usk; some of which places we had occasion to visit several times.

After the lapse of the two months, we proceeded to summon the overseers to attend at the places nearest to their respective parishes, and to produce their corrected assessment, together with the four previous assessments, in order to judge of the nature and amount of the alterations and corrections which they had made. (See Appendix D.)

We also summoned the churchwardens to attend and produce the tithe apportionment; and the clerks to the commissioners of the property tax to produce the property tax assessments; and we invited the magistrates in the neighbourhood, not members of the Committee, to assist our proceedings by their advice and experience. We also had before us the proceedings of the previous Committee on the county rate.

In each parish, we first received the return of the overseers, upon oath; and then compared this return with the former assessment to the county rate, with their own four previous assessments, and with the assessment to the property tax. The property tax was no very useful guide except for the purpose hereafter mentioned; because the property in one parish is by permission frequently assessed in another parish, where the owner also has property.

Having examined the overseers and others as to the manner in which the assessments they returned, whether a new or old one, had been made, and the principles of it, we proceeded to test its accuracy by the following methods :—

The tithe commutation informed us of the exact amount of the tithe rent-charge, and we observed what deduction had been made in the parish assessment.

We then inquired the rents of some principal farms, and received information as to their value, according to the quality of the land and situation. When the rents were not known to the persons present, the property tax returns frequently gave us this information; but this column of the property tax returns was sometimes omitted or imperfect. The tithe rent-charge apportionment gave us the exact acreage of each farm and holding.

We next examined into the house property, the woods, and manufacturing works, and into property of any other peculiar kind within the parish; and we compared all these with the assessments in the rate-book.

A few examples sometimes enabled us to test the justness of the rate. In other instances we were obliged to go much into detail. In some cases, such as the furnaces, forges, and other iron works, and the collieries, we were forced and enabled to make a detailed assessment of the property ourselves, in correction of the return presented to us. In this last-mentioned branch, we received the most valuable and candid information and assistance from many who were themselves deeply affected by our proceedings, and most interested to keep us in ignorance of details which it would have been both difficult and laborious for us to obtain possession of.

The accurate and extensive local knowledge of the high sheriff, E. H. Phillips, Esq., one of our Committee, has been absolutely essential to the successful conclusion to which we trust we have conducted our proceedings, in the districts to which these remarks are applicable.

By these means we arrived at our conclusion in assessing the respective parishes, with as great accuracy and certainty as seems to be attainable and requisite in a proceeding of this kind.

It is observable, that we have not found occasion to employ a valuer of our own in any one instance, and we were particularly desirous to avoid such a measure if possible. It is not the province of this Committee to assess the several properties in a parish in detail, with relative justice and accurate proportion of each to the other, though we had powers under the Act to take such a step, and an approximation to such accuracy of detail was necessary to bring us to a conclusion with respect to the real values of the parishes. But we had only to ascertain the total amount of the property in each parish, and to adjust the relative values of the parishes one with another; and while these general values may be preserved for a considerable time, the particular properties in each parish are subject to changes in a few months or weeks, which are capable of adjustment by the parishoners among themselves when each rate is made; but no such perfect accuracy of detail, if once arrived at, could be maintained even for the short period during which the Committee were necessarily occupied in their proceedings.

The Committee held their first meeting for the returns of parishes at Usk, on the 24th August, 1847; and their last meeting to make assessments was at Newport, August 15th, 1848.

After the completion of the assessment, the Act requires that it should be sent to every parish, and that an interval of a month should be allowed for objections; and then that a day should be appointed by the Committee to hear the objections.

The required notices having been given, we met on the 6th of October inst. [1848] at Usk, to hear the objections. Twenty-four parishes had given notice of objection to the assessment, of which only eleven appeared at the place and time appointed.

The Committee heard the objecting parties and their evidence, and made some alterations and adjustments in favour of some of the parishes objecting; and also some alterations for parishes not objecting, from evidence which was then before the Committee for the first time.

Your Committee now present the complete assessment, as finally corrected and approved, upon all the evidence and information before them.

The total amount of the new assessment is £532,224, being an increase of £78,573 upon the former assessment, and equal to an increase of £150,000 upon the assessment of the gross estimated rental of the county, or about 33 per cent.

During the 10 years which have elapsed between the last and the present assessments, the population of the county has increased from 134,000 to 182,000, if it has increased in the same proportion as in the ten years between the census of 1831 and the census of 1841, viz., 36 per cent.; but probably the increase has not been so great; and even allowing for the imperfection of the former assessment, the increase of property has probably equalled the increase of the population.

Two extra-parochial places, St. Arvans Grange and St. Kienmark, which were omitted from former assessments, have now been brought into charge to the county rate for the first time.

The county rate being now paid to the treasurer by the boards of guardians, and not as formerly by the high constables, we have classed the parishes by the unions, instead of by divisions, as in the former arrangements. Not having had occasion to employ any valuers, the expense of the assessment to the county is inconsiderable.*

Appendix *A.* (Circular to Overseers.)

Usk, 20th April, 1847.

To the overseers of the parish of ———.—GENTLEMEN, The Committee of Magistrates appointed by the Court of Quarter Sessions to revise the assessment to the county-rate, beg to call your attention to the following provisions of the recent Act of Parliament, 8 & 9 Vic. c. 111. The Committee beg also to inform you, that they intend to give you two months' time within which to prepare a correct assessment of your parish, and that after such two months they shall summon the overseers of every parish in succession to appear before them, and produce such a correct assessment, and give full information concerning the value of the property in their parish; and if such correct assessment and full information are not given, they shall appoint valuers to assess the property, at the expense of the parish.

By the Act of the 8 and 9 Vic. c. 111, sec. 4, the Committee may direct the overseers, constables, assessors, and collectors of public rates, to make returns of the amount of the full and fair annual value of the property liable to be rated in their parish, and the name of the surveyor by whom the valuation was made; and the overseers, &c., before they make such return shall lay it before a vestry meeting.

Section 8.—Any overseer not appearing, or not making a return, or making a false return, or refusing to be sworn and examined, is liable to a penalty of £20.

Section 9.—The Committee may, if they think fit, appoint valuers to assess every parish.

Section 11.—If overseers make any false return, or false statement of the value of the property, the parish is liable to pay the whole expenses of valuing and assessing the parish.

The Committee also draw your attention to the Act 6 & 7 Wm. 4, c. 96, by which it is required that all rates shall be made upon the net annual value of the property, and no rate made in any other way is of any force or validity.

I remain, Gentlemen,
Your obedient Servant,
A. WADDINGTON,
Clerk to the Committee.

Appendix *B.* (Circular to Magistrates.)

Usk, 20th April, 1847.

SIR,—I am directed by the Committee, appointed by the Court of Quarter Sessions to revise the assessment to the county rate, to call your attention to the annexed circular, sent to the overseers of each parish; and on the part of the Committee to request you to be so kind as to ascertain the method and equality of the assessments to the poor-rates in each of the parishes within your division of
and also to render your advice and assistance to the respective overseers, in preparing a full and just assessment, previous to the time when the Committee shall have occasion to call for it.

I remain, Sir,
Your most obedient Servant,
A. WADDINGTON,
Clerk to the Committee.

(Circular to Overseers, Appendix *A.*, was enclosed with the above.)

Appendix *C.* (Second Circular to Overseers.)

Usk, 28th June, 1847.

GENTLEMEN,—The Committee of Magistrates appointed to revise the assessments to the county rate, beg to call your attention to their circular sent to you, of the date of the 20th April last, and to remind you that they shall shortly require from you a return and assessment of the full annual value of the property in your parish, liable to be assessed to the county rate.

Notice will be given you of the time and place at which they shall require your return and attendance.

In the mean time they recommend you to proceed forthwith to correct and perfect the assessment of your parish, if not yet done, and to keep in mind that the assessment must

* The whole expense, consisting chiefly of allowances to clerks, to the Property Tax Commissioners, and payments to the clerk to the Committee, and for places of meeting and printing, amounted to £190.

be made upon the rack rent,* only deducting the amount of annual repairs and insurance, and such expenses as are necessary to maintain that rent.

They will require the assessment itself to be produced and the rate books, and they will examine you upon oath as to the correct valuation of each property.

If they find any errors or unfairness in the assessment, they will direct a fresh valuation of the property to be made, at the expense of the parish.

N.B.—The overseers and vestry meeting may amend the assessment of the parish for themselves, whenever they find occasion, but they cannot pay the expenses of a valuer without the authority of the Poor Law Commissioners.

I remain, Gentlemen,
Your obedient Servant,

———

Clerk to the Committee.

* The rack rent must be understood to mean the real value of the property and not necessarily the rent actually paid.

Appendix *D.* (Summons to Overseers.)

Usk, 1848.

To the overseers of the poor of the parish of ———, *in the county of Monmouth.*—Pursuant to the Statute 8 & 9 Vic. c. 111, you are hereby required to appear before the Committee of Magistrates appointed to revise the county rate, at in on the day of at o'clock in the forenoon precisely, and then and there to make a return of the full and fair annual value of the property within your parish, liable to be assessed to the county rate, together with the name of the person who made the valuation. And also at the same time to produce before the Committee the four last assessments to the poor-rate made in your parish, and all other documents in your power relating to the value of the property liable to be assessed to the county rate.

If you are yourselves unacquainted with the value of all the property in your parish, you are requested to bring with you some person best acquainted with the property and its value.

Before making the said return, you are required by the statute above-mentioned to lay it before a vestry meeting.

I remain, Sirs,
Your obedient Servant,

———

Clerk to the Committee.

Appendix *E.* (Summons to Churchwardens.)

To the churchwardens of the parish of ———, *in the county of Monmouth.*—Pursuant to the Statute 8 & 9 Vic. c. 111, you are hereby required to appear before the Committee of Magistrates appointed to revise the county rate, at in on the day of at o'clock and then and there to produce for the inspection of the said committee, the tithe apportionment of the said parish of and give such information respecting the same as shall be required of you, and as it may be in your power to afford.

Dated at Usk, this day of 184

By order of the Committee,

———

Clerk.

Appendix *F.* (Circular to Overseers, with new county rate.)

To the overseers of the poor of the parish of ———.

By the direction of the Committee of Magistrates appointed under the 8 & 9 Vic. c. 111, to revise the county rate of the said county, I forward you herewith a copy of the proposed new rate as prepared by the said Committee, and which the Act requires that you should submit to a vestry meeting, to be called within twenty-one days after the receipt of such rate.

Any person rated to the relief of the poor, or liable to contribute to the county rate in your parish, may at all reasonable times inspect and examine the copy of the said rate whilst the same remains in your custody, and take copies thereof or extracts therefrom, without the payment of any fee for the same.

And I hereby notify to you, that if you or any person have any objections to offer to the said proposed rate, you or they must forward such objections to the said Committee at my office in Usk, on or before the second day of October next.

And I also notify to you, that the Committee have fixed and appointed the 6th day of October next, as the day upon which they will meet to hear the said objections: and the persons making such objections must attend before the Committee, at the Town Hall, in Usk, on the said last-mentioned day at eleven o'clock in the forenoon precisely.

Dated this 21st day of August, 1848.

———

Clerk to the Committee.

III.—MEDICAL OFFICERS—DUTIES OF.

3rd April, 1849.

Medical Officer of West Derby Union.—Inquiring, 1st, Whether the relieving officer is not bound to visit every applicant for medical relief previous to an order being given for the district medical officer. Poor persons frequently apply for medical relief, expecting the district medical officer will order better food than the relieving officer, thereby causing considerable extra and unnecessary trouble to the district medical officer, in consequence of the relieving officer not having previously visited to ascertain the cause of the application. 2nd, Provided the relieving officer omits to visit the applicant for medical relief, but gives an order for the district medical officer, is it then optional on the part of the district medical officer to attend upon such an order? 3rd, Whether the district medical officer is bound to attend upon the order of any other relieving officer, besides the one belonging to the same district as the medical officer himself. 4th, Provided the relieving officer be absent from home, cannot any poor person desirous of obtaining medical relief call upon the overseer or guardian to give him an order for the district medical officer? 5th, Article 206 (General Consolidated Order) states, that by a written or printed order of the guardians, relieving officer, or overseer, the district medical officer shall attend any poor person—therefore, he concluded that it is not obligatory on the district medical officer to attend without such written or printed order. 6th, Inasmuch as the district medical officer can be compelled to attend and provide medicines for any poor person upon a written or printed order of the guardians, relieving officer, or overseer, cannot the district medical officer, on his part, compel the guardians, relieving officer, or overseer, to give him an order to attend any poor person who may wish the attendance of the district medical officer, he, the district medical officer, being willing to attend such poor person?

Ans.—1st, The relieving officer is not bound to visit a pauper before giving a medical order, although it is expedient that he should visit, and, indeed, is obligatory upon him to visit such pauper as soon as he can after application for medical relief, unless such application is refused in the first instance. 2nd, The Board consider it compulsory on the medical officer to attend to an order given by a relieving officer under the circumstances supposed in your second inquiry. 3rd, The medical officer is not legally bound to attend to a medical order given by a relieving officer of his (the medical officer's) district, except in cases of paupers belonging to townships in the relieving officer's district, but residing in the medical officer's district. 4th, A poor person requiring medical relief in a case of urgency should, in the event of the relieving officer being from home, call upon the overseers, who have authority, if the case be urgent, to give a medical order. A guardian has no such authority. 5th, A medical officer is not legally bound to attend a pauper patient, unless the order calling upon him to do so be written or printed, although, probably, he may not think it expedient to insist upon such an order in all cases that may arise. 6th, The guardians, overseers, or relieving officers, are the only competent parties to say whether a person is to have medical assistance at the expense of the poor-rates; consequently, a district medical officer has no power to compel the guardians, or the other officers referred to by you, to grant an order for medical relief under the circumstances stated in your last inquiry.

IV. — PAUPERS. — EMPLOYMENT OF UNDER OUT-DOOR LABOUR TEST ORDER.

23*rd May*, 1849.

Chairman of Chard Union.—Explaining, in reference to a communication of the Poor Law Board, addressed to the clerk of the guardians, that there was no land in the neighbourhood of the union workhouse, on which out-door paupers could be employed under the Out-Door Labour Test Order, and that the part where the scarcity of work prevailed most was at a distance from the workhouse.

Ans.—The Board do not consider the proximity to the workhouse of the spot where the labour is to be performed, under the Out-Door Labour Test Order, of much importance; indeed, in the case mentioned in your letter, the most desirable situation for it, (provided the paupers could be as efficiently superintended while working there,) would appear to be the centre of the most pauperized district of the union. It is not to the place nor to the occupation in which the guardians propose to employ these paupers, but to the principles on which they propose to dispose of their labour that the Board object. The name "Out-Door Labour Test," denotes the purpose for which the Order was framed, and the end it was intended to fulfil; namely, to provide a test of destitution, not primarily to get the largest return from the labour done. It is, doubtless, desirable that the paupers, for the independent employment of whom either capital or inclination is wanting, should, in return for their maintenance out of the rates, be made to work, with as little loss to the union as possible, at some work in which they will not directly interfere with the independent labourer. If there were a field for their profitable employment, it is natural to suppose some private individual would have found it worth while to employ them upon it, not as paupers, but as independent labourers; for it is obvious that a private individual can carry on any business or trade much more advantageously than such a body as the guardians can, since he not only can pay more attention to details of management, but has also the advantage of employing free, as distinguished from forced labour. The independent labourer is induced to work by the prospect of remuneration for his exertions; while, as the guardians must proportion the pauper's relief to his necessities, and not to his work, the pauper is altogether without this, the most powerful incentive to industry. It is obvious, therefore, that the augmentation of the proceeds of pauper labour must be of less importance to the rate-payers than the diminution of pauperism; and that the efforts of the guardians should be principally directed to the removal of any motives from masters and labourers which would tend to induce any members of either of these classes to increase it. When an individual gets any work done more cheaply by pauper labour than the independent labourer could afford to do it, he benefits at the expense of the rate-payers, for they have to pay the difference between the cost of the one kind of labour and the other. Where, as used to be the case sometimes under the old Poor Law, every occupier of land employed men in the receipt of relief from the parish, it is manifest they all gained at the expense of the remaining classes of rate-payers; the tithe-owner and shopkeeper were really, though not nominally, paying a part of the farmer's farming expenses. But besides the rate-payers, the independent labourer suffers, because paupers maintained at the public expense, with whom he, therefore, cannot compete, are employed in preference to him. Where the work done by the paupers is done for the guardians, as a body, this kind of injustice is not inflicted upon any of the rate-payers; while, if proper precautions are taken in selecting the work for the paupers, the independent labourer must be benefited by the removal of the surplus labourers from competing with him in the over-stocked labour market. The Board have already stated that they do not object to the kind of employment you propose for the paupers. Indeed, spade husbandry, on land either belonging or let to the guardians, seems to combine more advantages than almost any other kind of work, in a case such as that which you describe; for, while it is likely to be the most productive, or at all events the least losing to the guardians, the amount of free labour displaced by its adoption is really not worthy of consideration. Under any circumstances, however, and notwithstanding all precautions, great disadvantages are inherent, for reasons already mentioned, in forced labour. The absence of the best incentive to industry, and the degradation attaching to work performed on such terms, are serious evils in every way, and affect not only the value of the work, but also the character of the man who does it. Letting out a gang of paupers for hire, however, to work, not for the guardians who maintain them, but indiscriminately for whatever farmer will pay the best price for their services, appears to the Board not only to involve needless degradation to the paupers, and needless injury to their already impaired feelings of self-respect, but also to be opposed to sound principle. The Board, therefore, recommend the guardians to hire a plot of ground, if the pressure seems likely to be lasting, or to open a stone-yard, if it appears only temporary in its character, and there to employ the able-bodied paupers at task-work, under inspection, in return for the relief afforded to them and to their families. There is only one other point to which the Board deem it necessary to advert, and that is the disposal of the proceeds of pauper work; these are, under the 4th and 5th Wm. 4, c. 76, s. 28, considered to belong in all cases to the guardians, and must, therefore, be paid into the common fund.

V.—RELIGION.—AGE AT WHICH CHILDREN, INMATES OF THE WORKHOUSE, MAY BE ALLOWED TO DETERMINE FOR THEMSELVES IN THE CHOICE OF RELIGION.

24th May, 1849.

Cheadle Union.—The Poor Law Board—after taking into consideration the correspondence, and the report of their inspector, Mr. Farnall, together with the evidence taken by him, as to whether an orphan girl, aged ten years, an inmate of the Cheadle Union Workhouse, should be brought up in the Roman Catholic or the Protestant religion—addressed the following letter to the board of guardians on the subject:—

The Board have given much attention to the several communications which have been addressed to them respecting the child, Ellen Lowe, who is now an inmate of the Cheadle workhouse. The principles on which such cases are to be dealt with are found very clearly laid down in the Poor Law Amendment Act, sec. 19, the first paragraph of which distinctly recognises the rights of conscience of every inmate of a workhouse; while the next, by prescribing a particular mode of dealing with children, as clearly points out the modification of that general right, rendered necessary by the usually plastic and impressionable character of a child's mind. It appears to the Board, however, that the fitness or unfitness of any "inmate of a workhouse" to form "religious principles," and adopt a particular creed, cannot be said to depend upon age alone, (though, of course, there must be a limit of infancy, which would preclude the possibility of any distinct religious views being entertained,) but rather upon the character, capacity, and circumstances of each individual. While, therefore, on the one hand, the Poor Law Board could not maintain as a general proposition, that children of ten years old are competent to think entirely for themselves in matters of religion, and to attach themselves to whatever sect they please; on the other hand, they cannot lay down a rule that no child of that age should be considered capable of forming religious opinions, and that no regard should, therefore, be paid to any conscientious scruples entertained by any inmate of a workhouse under sixteen years of age. If it appear that a child has strong religious convictions, and can give reasons himself for the faith that he holds, the Board are of opinion that he should be considered as entitled to that right of religious freedom which the Legislature recognises in every inmate, *i.e.*, as the Board think, every inmate capable of using and of enjoying it. But if he appear, on the other hand, not yet to be capable of forming a reasonable opinion on such subjects, if he should appear to be in mind, as well as age, a child, and to belong fairly in this, as well as other points of view, to the class in which the Regulations place him in the workhouse, the question then arises as to the religious creed professed by the pauper child's parents, god-parents, or next of kin, as the case may be. The Report of the committee of guardians, transmitted on the 27th ultimo, and the letter of the Rev. Mr. Dunne, one of the guardians, bearing date the 25th ultimo, although each setting forth the facts in considerable detail, did not appear to the Board to be sufficiently conclusive on some points; and the Board, therefore, caused additional inquiries to be made by their inspector, Mr. Farnall, by whose report they are now enabled to give a definite opinion upon the case. It appears that both the parents of Ellen Lowe were Roman Catholics, as is her godmother, Phœbe Lovett, and that Ellen Lowe was baptized as a Roman Catholic by the Rev. Mr. Dunne. Of her brothers and sisters, some are Roman Catholics and some Protestants. Whatever course the Board might think it their duty to recommend upon these facts, with regard to the education of an ordinary child of ten years, they cannot but feel that the case of Ellen Lowe is one of peculiar difficulty and delicacy, for whilst her tender years might seem to unfit her for judging of religious questions, or deciding for herself as to the particular form of religion she might wish to be reared in, it is, nevertheless, impossible, looking to her general intelligence, and to the nature of her evidence before Mr. Farnall, as well as to the tenor of her former answers, not to perceive that, owing probably to her having been taken at different times by different relations to attend Roman Catholic and Protestant places of worship, some of the main points of distinction between Romanism and Protestantism have been, as it were, prematurely forced upon her consideration, that she is aware of their nature, and that her preference for the latter form of worship is at present so clear and decided, that it would amount to a breach of religious freedom, and a forcing of conscience, to compel her now to attend the services of the Romish church. Under these circumstances, and having regard to what the Board consider the spirit of the Poor Law Amendment Acts, they recommend that the utmost gentleness and forbearance should be observed towards Ellen Lowe with respect to her religious feelings; and, above all, that she should not be forced or coerced in any way, but be left to the independent workings of her own mind, in order that the direction of her maturer inclinations and convictions may be ascertained. If she should prefer, now or hereafter, to conform to the Protestant form of worship, she should be allowed to do so; if, on the contrary, she shall now or hereafter prefer the Roman Catholic ritual, no impediment should be interposed. This, the Board consider, will be the proper course under the circumstances, and this course the Board recommend the guardians to adopt.

VI.—REMOVABILITY.

1. PERMANENT DISABILITY.

20th June, 1849.

Clerk of Wellington (Salop) Union.—Requesting the opinion of the Poor Law Board on the removability of a pauper under the following circumstances:—A parishioner of Preston, on the Wildmoore, in the Wellington Union, is now living in the parish of Wellington, in which he has had a continuous residence of thirty-three years, and during that period has received parochial relief for nearly thirteen years. The cost of his relief, for the last two years and a half, has been borne by the parish of Wellington, from which parish he was deemed irremovable by virtue of the statute 9 & 10 Vic. c. 66; but being permanently disabled, a doubt has arisen as to his irremovability, and the guardians are desirous to learn whether the "permanent disability" of the pauper is of itself a sufficient ground for his removal. It is not contended that he is removable on any other ground.

Ans.—The Board are not aware of any authority for holding that a pauper, who by reason of a five years' residence without relief, has become irremovable under the provisions of the 1st sec. of the 9 & 10 Vic. c. 66, is rendered removable, because he has become permanently disabled. In the present case, the pauper is irremovable from the parish of Wellington, and the relief afforded to him is therefore chargeable to the union common fund, under sec. 3 of the 11 & 12 Vic. c. 110.

---

2. COMPUTATION OF PERIOD OF RESIDENCE.

7th May, 1849.

Clerk of Rye Union.—Inquiring whether the time during which relief is given to a man having a wife and children, all residing together, is to be excluded in the computation of the time of residence in reference to the woman after the husband's death.

Ans.—The Board think that the question submitted to them is one which must be decided entirely with reference to the particular facts of each case which may arise. So far as the general principle is concerned, the Board are disposed to take the following view of the matter,—If relief be given to the head of a family, with the express intention of thereby relieving the whole or any particular members of such family, and if the said members of such family would, under ordinary circumstances, thereby become chargeable and removable under an order of removal, in such case the Board think that the time during which relief is so given to the head of the family must, for the purposes of the 9 & 10 Vic. sec. 66, be treated as time during which relief is given to the members of such family intended to be relieved, and, consequently, must be excluded from the computation of the time of residence of such members. The Board would, however, desire to point out that the time during which a child belonging to any family may have been earning wages, and contributing those wages to the general stock of such family, should not, in ordinary cases, be considered as periods of relief to such child, and should, therefore, not be excluded from the computation of the time of that child's residence. The Board would further observe, that if relief be supplied to a man and his family by any parish, other than that in which they may be resident, such family, even if not regarded as being strictly in receipt of relief, may, at all events, be considered as being, during that time, "wholly or in part maintained" by such other parishes within the meaning of the first proviso to the 1st sec. of the 9 & 10 Vic. c. 66.

VII.—SETTLEMENT—BY ESTATE.

2nd Nov., 1848.

Clerk to the Magistrates, Mathrafal Hundred, Montgomery.—Requesting the opinion of the Poor Law Board in the following case:—E. H., the widow of M. H., is now chargeable to Llangadfan parish, and an order has been made to remove her to Llanwyddun, against which order an appeal has been entered and respited to January sessions, 1848. It is admitted that the pauper is not settled in Llangadfan, and if she did not gain a settlement in Llanfihangel, that she is settled in Llanwyddun, but a difference of opinion exists as to whether she did or did not gain a settlement in Llanfihangel. All the three parishes are in the union of Llanfyllin. The facts are as follow:—M. H., the pauper's husband, held as tenant from year to year a tenement in the parish of Llanfihangel, of the yearly value of about £20. He entered upon this holding on 1st November, 1845, and died upon it, 1st September, 1846, leaving a will in Welsh, a translation of which is as follows:—"I appoint Elizabeth Hughes my wife, she and her children, co-executors of all I possess in the house and out of the house, to receive what is due and pay in the same manner." (Signed by him, and witnessed by two parties.) The children were all infants, and the widow remained with them in possession of the tenement above-mentioned for upwards of forty days after her husband's decease: that is to say, until 1st Nov., 1846, when she agreed with another party, with the consent of the landlord, to take to the tenancy and gave it up to him. On the part of Llanwyddun it is contended, on the authority of Rex *v.* Stone, 6 T. R. 295, Rex *v.* Uttoxeter, Burr. S. C. 538, 2 Bott. 620, and Rex. *v.* Wedworthy, Andr. 4 Burr. S. C. 109, 2 Bott. 612, that the widow gained a settlement at Llanfihangel by reason of having come to an estate, as executrix, and remained upon it forty days.

Ans.—The pauper in question did, as the Board consider, gain a settlement by estate in Llanfihangel, inasmuch as she was executrix of her husband's will, and thereby became possessed of the residue of his interest in the term, and by having resided on the property for forty days. But the 4 and 5 Wm. 4, c. 76, s. 68, enacts, that no person shall be deemed to retain any settlement gained by virtue of the possession of any estate or interest in any parish, for any longer time than such person shall inhabit within ten miles thereof, that is of such parish. The Board presume that the pauper has ceased to inhabit in the parish of Llanfihangel, but it does not appear whether she has ceased to inhabit within the limited distance from it, according to the terms of the statute. If she did cease to reside within the ten miles, it is not necessary to consider whether she did acquire a settlement by the residence on her husband's tenement after his decease.

VIII.—VAGRANTS—

1. RELIEF OF.

14*th Jan.*, 1849.

Clerk of Northampton Union.—Previous to the passing of the 11 and 12 Vic. cap. 110, the municipal authorities of the Borough of Northampton relieved vagrants through their police officers, but that Act making the relief to vagrants a charge upon the union, they have discontinued such relief. The vagrants were then for a short period sent to the workhouse, but not having sufficient accommodation therein for them, the guardians applied to the municipal authorities for the assistance of their police, which was granted; and it having been found beneficial, the agreement mentioned in the following resolution was made:—"The Watch Committee of the Town of Northampton having agreed to the proposal of the guardians to take the mangement of vagrants by lodging and relieving them into their hands, through their police officers, for one year, this board repaying the relief expended, and fifty pounds per annum towards the salaries of their police officers—Resolved, that the Poor Law Board be informed thereof, and requested to sanction this arrangement, this board and the municipal authorities of the town being strongly of opinion, that this mode of treating vagrants is the best they can adopt."

Ans.—The Board desire to express their satisfaction at the attention which the guardians have given to this important subject, and especially to convey their approval of the practice of confronting the class of paupers in question with the officers of police. The Board, however, deem it right to remind the guardians, that they themselves are the parties responsible for the due relief of all wayfaring and wandering poor who may be in destitute circumstances, and apply for relief in the Northampton Union; and that, therefore the Board have not the power to sanction the agreement proposed to be entered into by the guardians with the Watch Committee of the Town of Northampton on the subject; but the Board desire to state their readiness to sanction the appointment by the guardians of one or two of the police officers of the corporation, at reasonable salaries, as assistant relieving officers for the special purpose of attending to the relief of this class of paupers.

28*th April*, 1849.

Clerk of the same Union.—The guardians have taken a separate building in this town, consisting of ten rooms, at the rent of twelve shillings per week; five being sleeping apartments for men, three for women, and two used as receiving wards; one for men, and the other for women, besides a residence for the assistant relieving officer and his wife. The entrance part is occupied by the relieving officer and his wife, so that after the wayfarers, &c., are admitted, they cannot get out to go about the town begging. The officer appointed to attend to this business is George Mead, at a salary of one guinea per week; he has been in the police of the town for several years, and has been selected out of them as the best man that could be got for the purpose. He wears a dress similar to a superintendent of police, and has been sworn as a constable. The number of applicants is gradually getting less, and the whole expense of their relief for the week ending the 14th instant was six shillings and twopence.

Ans.—The Board sanction the arrangements made by the guardians in regard to the relief of vagrants, and desire to express their satisfaction at the success which has attended the efforts of the guardians in the matter.

---

2. RELIEF OF VAGRANTS.

28*th April*, 1849.

The Overseers of Epsom.—The overseers of the parish of Epsom have received the accompanying resolution of the guardians of the Epsom Union, and feel anxious to act in concert with them, so far as the law will allow them so to do. At the same time, they are certain that to attempt to carry the resolution into effect will entail a very heavy expense on this parish, in the shape of magistrates' clerk's fees, as any person taken into custody by the police cannot be liberated without being taken before a magistrate, or a bench of magistrates, and each case will cost from ten to fifteen shillings; whereas relief granted as at present does not exceed threepence per night for each vagrant; and this expense is divided amongst the several parishes of the union. Requested the direction of the Poor Law Board, as to the course which the overseers should take in the matter.

The Resolution referred to above:—

"That from and after Wednesday, the 4th of April next, no vagrant shall be admitted into the Epsom union-house, except when the master shall be satisfied, from his own inspection, that such vagrant is unable to proceed on his or her journey, from exhaustion and hunger.

"That the relieving officers and overseers of several parishes in this union be directed not to afford relief to vagrants, except in cases of illness or extreme destitution; and that they be informed that any relief given contrary to the direction will not be repaid by the board.

"That the overseers be also recommended to give into custody all able-bodied vagrants who may be found asking alms in their respective parishes.

"That a letter be written to the Commissioners of the Metropolitan Police, requesting their co-operation in carrying into effect the Resolutions of this board, in such parts of the union as are within the Metropolitan Police district."

Ans. to the Overseers of Epsom.—The Board are glad to find from this communication that the overseers of Epsom are anxious, so far as they may be enabled by the existing law to do so, to act in concert with the board of guardians in effecting the very desirable object which the guardians have in view, in repressing so serious an evil as vagrancy. The Board, however, understand the overseers to question the policy of the Resolution, which contains a recommendation to them to give into custody all able-bodied vagrants who may be found asking alms in their respective parishes, upon the ground that the cost of the prosecution for the offence of vagrancy will be found considerably to exceed the cost of the temporary relief of such persons as at present. The Board think it not improbable that an enforcement of the laws against this particular class of offenders under the Vagrant Act, might, at the outset, be productive of an increased expense to the union; but, assuming this to be so, they confidently believe that the result would show the effect of such a course to be most salutary, even as regards directly decreasing the expenses of the union, through the discouragement of applicants for relief whose destitution is only simulated. The Board understand the recommendation of the guardians to be strictly confined to the class called able-bodied vagrants, or persons capable, if they pursued a lawful calling, of earning a maintenance for themselves without resort to aid from the poor-rates. As this discipline is obviously inapplicable to cases of illness or extreme destitution, both of these are very properly excepted. In such cases, unless the relieving officer be at hand to furnish what is necessary, it will certainly be the duty of the overseers to afford relief, by either supplying the parties with articles of absolute necessity, or by giving them an order for the workhouse. See sec. 54, Poor Law Amendment Act.

Letter to Clerk of Epsom Union.—The Poor Law Board have received a letter from the overseers of Epsom, (of which the enclosed is a copy,) accompanied by certain printed resolutions, adopted by the board of guardians, having for their object the suppression of vagrancy in the parishes of that union. The overseers, (as the guardians will perceive,) while they express their desire, as far as the law will enable them, to act in concert with the board of guardians in regard to the desirable object aimed at by the Resolutions, seem to complain of the recommendation to enforce the law against able-bodied vagrants, upon the ground of the increased expense which will thereby be occasioned to the parish of Epsom. The Board have intimated their opinion upon this point to the overseers, in an answer to their communication, a copy of which is also herewith sent. With regard to the first Resolution, which applies to the admission of vagrants into the workhouse, the Board feel it incumbent upon them to observe, that it is not to its full extent supported in law. The Resolution proposes to limit the admission of persons to cases "in which the master shall be satisfied, from his own inspection, that such vagrant is unable to proceed on his or her journey from exhaustion and hunger." Now the Regulations of the Poor Law Commissioners, (see Consolidated Order, Art. 88,) provide that admission into the workhouse may take place upon (*inter alia*) the written or printed order of an overseer or relieving officer. The Board admit that an overseer could only lawfully give such an order of admission, *i. e.*, in other words, give relief in a case which is one of emergency; and in any clear case of this kind, admission of the applicant, upon the order of the overseers, would of course be legal. The Board must, however, observe, as a general proposition, that the master is not deprived of all of his discretion by the circumstance of a person presenting an order from an overseer when applying for relief at the workhouse. In any case of this kind, the master may take upon himself the responsibility of deciding whether it be one of simulated destitution, and if satisfied that it is so, of refusing admission to the applicant. As regards the second Resolution, the Board understand that by "cases of illness or extreme destitution," are meant all those cases of "sudden and urgent necessity," in which the overseers, under the 54th sec. of the Poor Law Amendment Act, and the relieving officer, under the provisions of the General Consolidated Order, (Art. 215,) are required to give relief.

2nd *May*, 1849.

Clerk of Epsom Union.—The Resolutions of the board of guardians, which have been extensively made known by hand-bills in the neighbourhood, have been attended with the most signal success, inasmuch as a vagrant is now seldom seen in the union; whilst immediately previous to the day on which those Resolutions came into operation, the district was inundated with vagrants; and so far from any case of hardship having occurred, it is now rarely that a single application for relief is made; and similar proceedings are adopted, with a like result, at Croydon, Guildford, and Chertsey.

The number of Vagrants applying at the Workhouse for Relief in each week, for five weeks previous to the 4th April, 1849, and five weeks subsequent thereto, was as follows:—

Before 4th April.				
1st Week.	2nd Week.	3rd Week.	4th Week.	5th Week.
90	113	117	144	126
After 4th April.				
1st Week.	2nd Week.	3rd Week.	4th Week.	5th Week.
Nil.	Nil.	Nil.	Nil.	Nil.

---

3. COST OF MAINTAINING VAGRANTS IN LOCK-UP HOUSE.

22*nd Dec.*, 1848.

J. H. R., Esq., J. P.—A lock-up house has been built at Ll ———, by order of the court of quarter sessions, under the authority of the Parochial Constables' Act, to which a keeper has been appointed, whose salary is paid out of the county stock. This lock-up house is for the petty sessional district in which Ll ——— is situated, and offenders of all descriptions from the district are confined there previous to, and often subsequent to examination for trial, or summary conviction before the justices. Such offenders are of course supplied with food during their confinement. The keeper is, by virtue of his appointment, a parish constable, having the superintendence of all the parish constables within the district. At the last quarter sessions for the county, the bill for the maintenance of offenders (including vagrants) in this lock-up house, was laid before the justices for allowance and payment out of the county stock; but the justices refused to order payment of it, alleging that the case of the Queen *v.* Chelmsford, had decided that the parish was liable for all costs regarding the prosecution and maintenance of vagrants, and that generally the parish was liable for the cost of all offenders in the lock-up house, where either themselves, the prosecutor, or complainant could not be charged with such maintenance from poverty or otherwise, although it is admitted that the cost of maintaining such offenders as are committed for trial for indictable offences is chargeable upon the county stock. Requested the opinion of the Poor Law Board on the matter.

Ans.—The Board feel some difficulty in giving any general answer to your inquiry, as to whether the expense of maintaining such prisoners can be defrayed from the poor-rates, because much depends upon the circumstances and the nature of the proceedings in each particular case. It is certainly to be collected from the case of Queen *v.* Chelmsford, 5. A. & E. (N. S.) 66, that the justices can make an order upon the parish officers to reimburse a parish constable certain expenses incurred by him in the prosecution of vagrants, that is, persons charged with offences under 5th Geo. 4, c. 83. The expenses sanctioned by the court according to the report of that case were the fees paid to the clerk to the justices on the prosecution of certain vagrants. The Board are not, therefore, prepared to say, that the costs incurred by the parish constable in apprehending and keeping in his custody, until the hearing before the justices, certain persons so charged with offences against the Vagrant Act, might not be properly charged to the parish by the constable in his account, under 18 Geo. 3, c. 19. sec. 4. But it does not appear to the Board, that when a lock-up house has been established in any particular parish by the justices of the county, the superintendent of such house can charge the cost of the maintenance of the poor persons confined therein to the poor-rates of the parish. Such lock-up house must, as it seems to the Board, be considered as a prison of the county, and the inmates thereof to be treated and maintained as other county prisoners, at the cost of the county rates. The Board take occasion to point out, as regards the costs of apprehending and prosecuting certain offenders under the Vagrant Act, that the 59 sec. of 7 & 8 Vic. c. 101, makes provision for the case, and enables the guardians of the union to defray the same out of the funds in their control.

---

3. COST OF PROSECUTION OF VAGRANTS.

2nd March, 1849.

Chairman of Thirsk Union.—In the accounts of the overseers of the poor of Thirsk for the half-year ending the 29th of September last, the following items are allowed by the auditor:

	£.	s.	d.
"May 3. Magistrates' clerk's bill	3	2	0
"Sept. 27. Ditto ditto	10	7	0
	13	9	0

The bill paid May 3rd includes charges for the "conviction and commitment" of 17 vagrants, at 3*s*. each, being in the whole £2. 11*s*. The bill paid on the 27th of September includes charges for the "conviction and commitment" of 62 vagrants, which, at 3*s*. each, amounts to £9. 6*s*. These accounts are made out as follows:—"The overseers of the poor of the township of Thirsk," "To Wm. Walker, clerk to the magistrates," &c.; they include other items to which no objection is raised, but it is contended that, as the vagrants were prosecuted by the constables, the accounts for the magistrates' clerk's fees ought to have been made out to them, and submitted as expenses incurred by the constables to the inhabitants, under the 18 Geo. 3, c. 19, sec. 4; and that the overseers, not having concurred or given any orders for the prosecution of vagrants, ought to have separated the charges for such prosecution from those legally charged against them, and submitted the same to the inhabitants for their approval before discharging such accounts, and placing them to the debit of the township. As a ratepayer, he directed the attention of the auditor to this circumstance, considering that, as the overseers had no legal authority for paying these charges, he ought to disallow them until such authority was obtained. In addition to the foregoing objection, he called attention to the charges of the clerk to the magistrates: there were frequently several committals in one day and at one time, when the clerk has charged for each case separately; it is contended that he ought to have charged in such instances as for one conviction and commitment only; for instance, on the 28th March, four vagrants were committed, for which he charged 12*s*., and which, if charged as one committal, would have been 3*s*.—the charges, if this plan be the correct one, would be reduced from £2. 11*s*. to £1. 1*s*., and from £9. 6*s*. to £3. 3*s*., or, in the whole, from £11. 17*s*. to £4. 4*s*. There is yet another point on which there exists considerable dissatisfaction. It has been the practice for the constable to fill up the committals from a copy given him by the clerk to the magistrates, and it is, therefore, considered incorrect for the clerk to charge his fees for cases in which he performed no duty.

Ans.—Upon the general question raised, the Board think that overseers are not warranted in paying any charges for the prosecution or conviction of vagrants, unless the steps pointed out by 18 Geo. 3. c. 19, sec. 4, have been strictly pursued, or, assuming the case to be one falling in any way within sec. 17 of 5 & 6 Vic. c. 57, unless there has been an order of justices directing the payment by the overseers of the fees or allowances to the constable, or clerk to the justices. The case of Reg. *v.* Churchwardens of Chelmsford, 5 Adol. & Ellis (N. S.) 66, is an authority to show that the charges incurred by the constable of a parish or township in prosecuting vagrants, though not directly employed or set in motion by the overseers, are legally payable out of the poor-rates under the 4th sec. of 18 Geo. 3, c. 19, where the account of the constable is at the proper time delivered to the overseers, and confirmed or allowed by the vestry. The fees paid by the constable to the clerk to the justices on such occasions could, as the decision referred to shows, properly form part of the accounts of the constable so to be delivered in. But it is not a correct proceeding for the overseers to discharge any claim of the clerk to the justices, except as forming part of the constable's account so rendered, or except there be an order of justices under sec. 17 of 5 & 6 Vic. c. 57. On this subject the Board would further refer you to the 59th sec. of the 7 & 8 Vic. c. 101, as to the payment by the guardians of costs incurred in the prosecutions there referred to, and would observe, moreover, that the 6th sec. of the 11 & 12 Vic. c. 91, affords a complete justification to the overseers who pay any money under an order of justices. Upon the second point, viz., as to the charges which can be properly made by the clerk to the justices on the occasions adverted to in your letter, the Board do not see that they are in a position to express any opinion. The amount payable must depend, as they apprehend, upon the terms of the table of fees upon which the clerk's claim arises, as also upon the course actually pursued in the respective cases; as, for instance, whether or not there are separate convictions, and separate warrants of committal made out. The Board are by no means prepared to admit, that where several persons are charged on the same day for different acts of vagrancy, they can be properly prosecuted together, and the proceedings proceed jointly. On the contrary, they think that such a course would not be correct. Each case should be heard separately and distinctly, and as all the steps must be taken distinctly, the Board think that separate fees would be properly chargeable. They assume, however, that the clerk actually performs, as he is bound to perform, the work for which he makes the charge. The Board would add, that it is only in compliance with your wish that they have given these opinions upon the general question; but they do so, of course, without prejudice to any future consideration of the point should an actual appeal involving it be brought before them.

IX.—WORKHOUSE.

1. PROFITABLE EMPLOYMENT OF PAUPERS ON WORKHOUSE LAND.

22nd *May*, 1849.

Master of the Abingdon Union Workhouse—In reply to inquiries made of him by Grenville Pigott, Esq., Poor Law Inspector, as to the employment of paupers on land belonging to the union, states—You understood me rightly that the produce of the ten acres of land adjacent to the Abingdon workhouse had enabled me, besides supplying vegetables for the use of the inmates, to credit the guardians with £100.

The potatoe crop, although a failure in most places, has not been so to any great extent here. The soil being of a light description, and the system of planting in the autumn having been followed, conduced, in a great measure, to the preservation of this valuable crop. The quality of the potatoes was such that they were eagerly sought after, and realized an average price of 11*s*. 3*d*. per sack.

By keeping, upon an average, twelve large pigs, which we purchase in a very poor condition, (spayed sows being preferred,) we can use all our spare offal from the garden, and this description of pigs will eat it, and get half fat upon it. We obtain a large quantity of manure from them, and, with a small purchase of stable dung, are enabled to manure the ground sufficiently. The liquid obtained from the washhouses, privies, &c., is all conveyed into close cesspools in the garden, from which it is pumped, and conveyed between the rows of the crops, particularly mangold wurtzel, by which means this plant attains a weight of from 20 to 25lbs. each, and sells at 20*s*. per ton. In winter the liquid manure is pumped up and distributed over such parts of the ground as are dug in, and the ground is trenched and prepared for spring crops. A gravel pit is kept always open for the employment of those who are not otherwise employed; the gravel sold to surveyors and others produces more than sufficient to purchase manure and straw for the piggery. The seeds we grow ourselves, so that no extra charge is made upon that account in this return.

In employing paupers in the garden, or on out-door work, one thing must be particularly attended to, that is, the character of the persons so employed. Unless upon particular occasions, I do not employ young able-bodied men, or even married men with families, if I can learn that they became inmates by their own misconduct. I make it a matter of favour to employ them there; and for those who do not work well while there, some sort of employment within the house is found. The old men and boys occasionally work in the garden, which makes them cheerful and keeps them in good health. The ground is worked by the spade and a light harrow, which is drawn by the boys.

You will perceive by the return herewith sent, that the common charges are credited with £52 for vegetables consumed by the officers and paupers, which number, including children, on the average, about 200 weekly.

ABINGDON UNION.

From Union Garden, between nine and ten acres, Midsummer, 1848, *to* 22*nd May,* 1849.

Dr.

	£.	s.	d.
Straw for Piggery	5	0	0
Stable Dung	3	5	0
Other Manure, made from drainage of Workhouse, ashes, and scrapings of road.			
Balance	162	17	3
	171	2	3

Cr

	£.	s.	d.
Piggery Barley, (see below)	13	2	6
Swedes, 3 tons	3	0	0
Mangold Wurtzel, 17 tons	17	0	0
Parsnips, 1½ do	4	4	1
Carrots, 16½ do.	24	19	0
Potatoes, 89 sacks	50	6	8
Peas, 19½ bushels	6	10	0
	119	2	3
Common charges, credited with vegetables for Officers and Paupers	52	0	0
	171	2	3

PIGGERY.

Dr.

		£.	s.	d.
1848.				
16th March,	Paid for 2 Pigs	5	13	0
15th May,	Do. 2 do.	5	14	0
1st June,	Do. 2 do.	6	6	0
5th ,,	Do. 2 do.	6	0	0
13th July,	Do. 2 do.	6	6	0
21st Sept.,	Do. 3 do.	11	8	0
17th Nov.,	Do. 3 do.	4	10	0
	Common charges for Barley	13	2	6
	Do. Beans and Pollard	3	13	0
	Do. Barley and Beans	8	16	6
	Do. Barley	12	19	6
	Do. Barley and Beans	16	14	6
	Grinding	1	11	0
		102	14	0
	Balance	27	16	6¾
		£130	10	6¾

Cr.

	£.	s.	d.
Bacon, 4,019lbs. at 7*d.*	120	2	9
Lard, 399lbs. at 6½*d.*	10	7	9¾
	£130	10	6¾

(Signed) RICHD. ELLIS.

---

2. EMPLOYMENT OF PAUPERS IN WORKHOUSE.

11*th Feb.,* 1848.

Clerk of Droitwich Union.—The guardians of the Droitwich Union having heard that in several union workhouses mat-making is carried on, and there being in the union workhouse many who, though unable to do any laborious work, might still, in the opinion of the guardians, be advantageously employed at such work as that, it has been determined to introduce it here. There being, however, no one in the house at present who is fully competent to instruct in the commencement of the proposed work, requested the sanction of the Poor Law Board to the guardians engaging some person as an assistant for a short time to teach the inmates. The guardians could procure a person for a very small sum beyond his rations as an assistant in the house.

Ans.—Before deciding upon the proposition of the guardians, the Board request to be informed if there are any persons in the neighbourhood of Droitwich engaged in the manufacture of mats, with whose market the proposed employment of the inmates of the workhouse would sensibly interfere. They also wish to know in what manner it is intended to dispose of the mats that may be made by the paupers.

21*st Feb.,* 1848.

Clerk of same Union.—There are few or no mat-makers in the neighbourhood of Droitwich to whose trade the proposal of the guardians could be prejudicial, and with regard to the disposal of the mats, the guardians anticipate a ready sale in the neighbourhood of the quantity that would be made. The guardians also contemplate using a very considerable number in the workhouse, as under-mattresses, to prevent the damaging of the ticks by the iron bedsteads.

Ans.—The Poor Law Board sanction the proposal of the guardians to appoint a competent person to give instruction in making mats to such of the inmates of the union workhouse as the guardians may think proper to place at such employment.

---

3. Entry of persons allowed to leave the workhouse temporarily in search of work.

13*th March*, 1849.

Clerk of Droitwich Union. — Permission is sometimes given to pauper inmates to leave the workhouse (wearing the workhouse clothes) for one, two, or three days (as the case may be) to look for employment. The master, on the paupers leaving the house, enters their names in the Admission and Discharge Book, as being discharged by the guardians, and enters them again on their return. It is contended, that the names of paupers absent under those circumstances should not be entered in the Admission and Discharge Book at all, but should be merely deducted as absent at meal-times from the totals of the classes to which they belong, according to the heading of the Daily Provisions Book, Form 25. Requested the opinion of the Poor Law Board on the point.

Ans.—The Board may remark, that the practice adopted by the master is not in strictness correct, inasmuch as paupers quitting the workhouse temporarily on leave are not "discharged" therefrom in the proper sense of the word, neither are they on the expiration of their period of leave re-admitted upon order. There may, however, be no great objection to persons quitting the workhouse, under such circumstances, being treated as discharged, for the purpose of checking the daily consumption of provisions. So far as regards the number of classes, and number of persons in each class, partaking of any particular meal, the Admission and Discharge Book is the guide for the entry of such in the Daily Provisions Consumption Account; and it is necessary, therefore, that some authentic record of persons absent on leave, and one which admits of easy reference, should be kept, or the check upon the numbers in the workhouse on any given day, or partaking of any particular meal, would be lost—a check which the Admission and Discharge Book, as framed, is intended to afford.

---

4. Married woman repeatedly discharging herself out of the workhouse, and returning again.

30*th May*, 1849.

Clerk of the Maidstone Union.—An able-bodied pauper, with his wife and several children, some of them within the age of nurture, are admitted to the workhouse under an order of the guardians. After continuing there some time, the wife gives notice to leave, and obtains her discharge, (it being considered doubtful whether the guardians have the power to prevent her leaving the workhouse without her husband,) taking with her the children under nurture. After an absence of a few days, the wife applies for and obtains re-admission to the workhouse, and again discharges herself as before. This is frequently done, the husband remaining with the elder children, and sometimes with the younger ones also, in the workhouse, and conniving no doubt with his wife in her proceedings, instead of exercising his marital rights so as to give the guardians a clear right to detain her. Inquired what course the guardians should take under the circumstances to prevent these irregular proceedings.

Ans.—The Board, in the first place, desire to remark that the words, "any pauper," in Art. 115 of the General Consodidated Order, which the guardians are aware has reference to the discharge of paupers from the workhouse, appear to them to apply to the head of the family, and not to the wife, where an able-bodied pauper is in the workhouse with his wife and children. With regard to the mode of preventing or checking the objectionable practice to which you allude, the Board think it right to point out, that, where the husband refuses, or is unwilling to exercise his marital control, so as to prevent the guardians from restraining the departure of the wife from the workhouse, it is certainly competent for the guardians, if they think fit to do so in any such case, to discharge the husband himself, and the whole of the family, from the workhouse; and if he subsequently applies for re-admission, the regulations which are prescribed in respect of a first admission should be strictly observed. The Board may add, that it will also, in such cases, be probably found useful to take care that the husband be kept to the strict performance of the labour required from the able-bodied inmates of the workhouse.

London: Printed by Order of the Poor Law Board, by Blackburn & Burt, 90½, Holborn Hill, and Published by Charles Knight, 90, Fleet Street.

AN OFFICIAL CIRCULAR

OF PUBLIC DOCUMENTS AND INFORMATION:

DIRECTED BY THE POOR LAW BOARD TO BE PRINTED, CHIEFLY FOR THE USE OF THE BOARDS OF GUARDIANS AND THEIR OFFICERS.

No. 27.] July, 1849. [N.S.

CONTENTS.

I.—ACCOUNTS.

1. Statistical and financial statements.

4th June, 1849.

Clerk of Bedford Union.—1, Are the paupers charged to the common fund to be entered in in the *Statistical Statement* in one line under the whole of the parishes in the union, or, are they to be entered and included under those of the parishes in which they respectively reside? 2, Under the head "Principal particulars of the Common Charges," in the *Financial Statement*, is it necessary that all the expenditure should be entered, so as to show how the total of Column No. 13 is made up, and should the credits, (if any,) placed to this account also appear? 3, In the statement of increase or decrease in the financial statement, are the calculations to be made according to the altered state of the account whereby the relief to irremovable poor will not be entered under "In-maintenance" and "Out-relief," as heretofore, but included under "Common Charges?"

Ans.—In reply to your first inquiry, the Board desire to state that the paupers chargeable to the common fund of the union should be entered in the statistical statement on one line below the last of the parishes. In the note at the foot of the financial statement all the principal particulars of the common charges, the total amount of which is contained in Column 13, should be specified in detail; but it is open to you to exercise your own discretion, as to setting forth any items which may stand to the credit of the common charges account. In entering in the several columns of the financial statement, the calculation of the increase or decrease of the expenditure, it will be proper to rest the comparison on the actual data, as exhibited by the accounts which have been duly prepared in accordance with the altered state of the law. The result will be, that although there may be a decrease under the heads of "In-maintenance" and "Out-relief," this will be compensated by a corresponding increase in the "Common Charges."

2. CHARGING EXPENSES INCURRED IN CONSEQUENCE OF THE PREVALENCE OF CHOLERA.

14th July, 1849.

Clerk of Keynsham Union.—In consequence of the prevalence of cholera in the parish of Keynsham, several items of expenditure have been incurred, respecting which he felt some doubt as to the proper mode of charging them. Inquired, therefore, 1. In the event of the Poor Law Board sanctioning extra remuneration to the medical officers, must the charge be made upon the common fund, or upon the parish the epidemic in which occasions that extra remuneration? 2. The services of several nurses were procured from the Bristol Infirmary, and other places, who were engaged, not with one particular pauper, but in going about from house to house, and waiting upon as many as each could attend to. Should this be charged to the common fund, or to the particular parish? 3. Brandy, arrow-root, and chloride of lime, were placed at the disposal of the medical officer; should these be charged to the common fund, or to the particular parish? 4. In numerous cases where two and three in a family were attacked with illness, and where they had but one bed, and in cases also where the bedding was destroyed by order of the medical officer, other beds and bedding were supplied, on the emergency, from the workhouse. These were ostensibly supplied on loan, but in all probability it would not be prudent to insist upon having them restored. Should the cost of these be charged to the parish, or should no notice be taken of it, but other bedding procured as may be required, and the cost charged as usual to the common fund? 5. As regards the four last questions, will it be advisable to open a new account, called the "Kenysham Cholera Account," or by some other name, where these amounts could be all entered, and the total carried to the Keynsham parochial account, as an extra separate charge?

Ans.—1. If any gratuities be granted to the medical officers of the Keynsham Union under Art. 172 of the General Consolidated Order, they must be charged, like the salaries, to the common fund. 2. If the remuneration of the nurses you refer to was paid in the shape of salary to them as general assistants of the medical officers, and if they were not restricted in their service to attendance upon certain sick paupers, chargeable to a certain parish, then that remuneration would, in the opinion of the Board, follow the rule laid down with regard to the medical officers' gratuities: but if the case were otherwise, the Board consider that it would properly constitute a parochial charge. 3. The articles delivered to the medical officers for distribution, if their application can be discriminated, (*i. e.*, if the particular paupers to whom they are given, and the quantities so given, can be ascertained,) should be treated as relief to the respective paupers, and the cost should be charged accordingly to the same fund (parochial or common) to which any other relief afforded to the same parties is chargeable. If no discrimination can be made, the only course which the Board can suggest is, to treat the expenditure as having occurred under the Regulations of the General Board of Health, and as chargeable accordingly to the common fund of the Union. 4. The Board gather from your statement of the circumstances, that the bedding you refer to was in fact relief, whether given or lent by the guardians, and is therefore chargeable in the same manner as other relief. The fact of the bedding having been supplied to paupers who were suffering from cholera, does not appear to the Board to change the character of the proceeding as a mode of relief. 5. The Board do not see that there is any occasion to open a separate account for the expenses in question in the manner you suggest.

3. ENTRY OF A BALANCE CERTIFIED BY AUDITOR IN THE LEDGER.

19th July, 1849.

Clerk of Lymington Union.—One of the

overseers of the parish of Lymington for the past year, has paid a sum of £85 1*s.* 4½*d.* to the treasurer of the Lymington Union, on account of a balance certified by the auditor to be due from the party.—Inquiring, whether this sum should be entered to the credit of Lymington parish in the ledger, as a "contribution," or under the head of "other receipts;" and also, whether the next instalment of the contribution to become due from the parish should be paid in full, or less the sum in question.

Ans.—The Board think that the payment of the sum should be entered under the head of "other receipts," and subsequently appropriated, if the guardians so think fit, in diminution of the claim of the guardians upon the particular parish for contribution. It will not, however, be the less imperative upon the parish officers to satisfy to the full extent the order of contribution which it appears will shortly become due, if the guardians think proper to apply the balance so paid over to any other parochial purpose, but the guardians will perceive, that the 32nd sec. of the 7 & 8 Vic. c. 101, requires them to apply the money so paid to the use or benefit of the parish alone interested in it.

II.—CHARGEABILITY.

8*th June*, 1849.

Clerk of Blandford Union.—H. H. and family, supposed to be settled in the parish of Houghton, but for the past eleven years industrially resident in the parish of Stickland (both in the Blandford Union) having been refused work there, and destitute, received an order for himself and family for the union workhouse; and the cost of their relief in the house was made a union charge. The pauper's apparel and household goods were left in the parish of Stickland. The pauper's wife having been informed that other persons had been seen wearing some of her apparel, requested temporary leave of absence from the workhouse that she might ascertain the truth, which was refused her by the workhouse committee. The pauper himself then gave notice to leave the workhouse, intimating his reasons for so doing, and his intentions to return. The pauper and his family accordingly left the house on a Monday, and went to Stickland, where the pauper met the relieving officer, and told him his motive in leaving the house, and that on Tuesday morning he should want an order to go into the house again. The relieving officer told him he could have no order until Saturday, which is the board day. The pauper after two applications to see his goods on Monday, could not succeed in consequence of the door of the house in which he left them being locked, and from necessity went to Houghton. The next morning he again went to Stickland, and found his goods had been removed to an out-house; and having examined them he again returned to Houghton to sleep: part of his family slept at his father's, and part at his brother's. On Wednesday, the pauper and his family returned to the relieving officer at Stickland, who then gave him a provisional order for the workhouse, as a pauper of Houghton, from his having slept there two nights. The provisional order of the relieving officer having been brought before the board, and objected to by the guardian of Houghton, the board after a full investigation of the matter (the guardians of both parishes being present) decided by a majority that as the pauper had left the house for a special purpose, as his goods and apparel were at Stickland, as he had no intention of going to Houghton—his sleeping there being a case of necessity—and as he had moreover applied for an order for the workhouse in the parish of his former residence, the cost of maintenance should be charged to the union as before, and not to the parish of Houghton. The minority of the guardians being dissatisfied with this decision, requested the opinion of the Poor Law Board as to whether the decision of the board of guardians was correct.

Ans.—The Poor Law Board consider the decision of the guardians in this case to be correct, and that there was no interruption of the residence in the parish of Stickland.

2. DITTO.

8*th June*, 1849.

Clerk of Williton Union.—Transmitted the following statement, duly signed, under sec. 4 of the 11 & 12 Vic. c. 110:—J. G., aged 60, and Sarah, his wife, aged 70, having a legal settlement in the parish of St. Decumans, have resided more than five years last past without relief, upon a leasehold tenement, (held for a term of years determinable on the death of the survivor of three lives,) in the parish of West Quantoxhead, in this union, belonging to the husband in right of his wife, whose interest therein is valued at £1. 6*s*. 8*d*. per annum. The husband, being partially disabled, was recently sent into the union workhouse, charged to the parish of West Quantoxhead, the wife continuing to reside in the parish of West Quantoxhead, where she is receiving one shilling and one loaf of bread per week out-door relief, charged to that parish. The question arises whether the relief of the husband in the workhouse, and the out-door relief of the wife, should be charged to the parish of West Quantoxhead or to the common fund of the union.

Ans.—The Board observe that the statement referred to expressly declares that the pauper is settled in the parish of St. Decumans, which is admitted by the guardians of that parish, who have signed the statement. But the other facts mentioned in the statement appear to the Board to show that the pauper has acquired a settlement by estate in the parish of West Quantoxhead. The leasehold tenement which he possesses in right of his wife having been vested in him by operation of law, is sufficient to confer upon him a settlement by estate, according to the decisions in R. *v.* Ynyscynhaiarn, (7 B. and C., 233,) and R. *v.* North Cerney, (3 B. and Ad., 463.) If this be so, then the pauper, being settled in the parish of his residence, is not within the operation of the 9 & 10 Vic. c. 66, sec. 1, nor the 11 & 12 Vic. c. 110, sec. 3.

3. DITTO.

19*th July*, 1849.

Clerk of St. Thomas Union.—H. N. was an inmate of the Bridport parochial workhouse many years before the opening of the union workhouse, and has been an inmate of the union workhouse ever since it was opened. He last left the union workhouse at Bridport on Tuesday, the 8th May, after giving three hours' notice to the master. He slept at the Honiton Union workhouse on the night of the 11th, and arrived at his brother's, in St. Thomas, on Saturday, the 12th May, in a very destitute condition. On the following Monday he applied to the assistant overseer of St. Thomas for relief, at the time being very ill. He was relieved by the overseer, and subsequently by the relieving officer, to the extent of £1. 2*s*. 8½*d*. On the 22nd of May he died of typhus fever, and was buried in St. Thomas, at an expense of £1. 1*s*. Inquired whether, under the second sec. of the 11 & 12 Vic. c. 110, the guardians of the Bridport Union are liable for the reimbursement of the relief afforded to the pauper.

Ans.—From the statement of facts before them, the Board do not consider that the guardians of the Bridport Union are liable to reimburse the amount of relief advanced to the pauper, H. N., either under sec. 2 of the 11 and 12 Vic. c. 110, or otherwise. It is quite clear that the pauper, when he became chargeable in St. Thomas Union had no fixed place of abode in the Bridport Union.

4. DITTO—RELIEF TO WIDOWS DURING THE FIRST TWELVE MONTHS OF WIDOWHOOD.

19*th June*, 1849.

Clerk of Weymouth Union.—Inquiring whether the relief given to widows during the first twelve months of their widowhood should be charged to the common fund of the union, or to the parish of the pauper's residence, in cases where such paupers would be clearly removable at the expiration of that period.

Ans.—As widows, by operation of the 2nd sec. of the 9 & 10 Vic. c. 66, are rendered irremovable during the first twelve months of their widowhood, their relief is chargeable to the union common fund, under sec. 3 of the 11 & 12 Vic. c. 110, so long as the exemption from removal continues under the first-mentioned enactment.

III.—NUISANCES.

1. REMOVAL OF—11 & 12 VIC. C. 123.

22*nd June* 1849.

Clerk of Lancaster Union.—The guardians have received verbal notice, through their clerk, that upon the premises of the Dalton Arms Inn, in the township of Bulk, in this union, several swine are kept so as to be a nuisance to the occupiers of adjoining houses. Bulk is a small agricultural township, adjoining the town of Lancaster; it belongs almost entirely to one person, and has but very few occupiers. The houses affected by the nuisance, (a row of small cottages,) although within a few yards of the pig-styes, are in the township of Lancaster. Both the owner and the occupier of the Dalton Arms Inn have been requested to remove the nuisance, but they decline to make any alteration; and as from the peculiar nature of the case, a notice under the 1st sec. of the "Nuisances' Removal and Diseases' Prevention Act, 1848," cannot be obtained from two inhabitant householders of Bulk, (as appears to be required by that sec.,) the guardians cannot proceed to obtain an order of justices for the removal of the nuisance. The guardians, therefore, think of proceeding under the Directions and Regulations of the General Board of Health, dated 3rd November last. The medical officer has not certified as to the nuisance under these Directions and Regulations, and the abatement will probably require that the swine be removed. Submitted the following questions:—1, Have the guardians power, under the above-mentioned Directions and Regulations, by themselves or their officers, to enter upon the premises and remove the nuisance? 2, Can the guardians proceed, should they deem it advisable, against the occupier, under secs. 16 & 17 of the above-mentioned Act, as a person who wilfully violates a Direction issued by the General Board of Health?

Ans.—1, The guardians of the Lancaster Union are empowered under the Directions and Regulations of the General Board of Health to enter the premises in question and remove the nuisance. 2, It appears to the Board that the case you refer to is within the 16 sec. of the Nuisances Removal Act, (11 & 12 Vic. c. 123,) and that the party alluded to, who refuses to remove the nuisance existing on his premises, has incurred a penalty under that provision, though it is to be observed the Directions and Regulations of the General Board of Health now in force, are in strictness those contained in the Order issued, not on the 3rd November, 1848, but on the 4th of April last; though the latter was, in effect, merely a renewal of the former.

2. DITTO.

20*th July*, 1849.

Clerk of Clutton Union.—At a meeting of the medical men residing in this union, the following plans were proposed for the consideration of the board of guardians, with a view to the prevention and relief of cases of cholera:—" That measures be taken to promote general and personal cleanliness, and that ventilation in every possible way should be secured: where the windows have no casements, that they should be made capable of being opened: that whitewashing be promoted both of the day-rooms and bed-rooms, particularly the bed-rooms: that the accumulations from pigstyes, &c., be removed at least twice a week. It is further urged on the serious consideration of the board of guardians, that it would be right, in case of scarcity of water, that water-barrels should be employed for the purpose of cleansing the drains in and about the cottages. It is also considered that the present depressed physical condition of the poor should be at once attended to, and by every possibility within the means of the guardians be improved; and that where there exists in the minds of the medical men the least suspicion of cholera, they should at once have unlimited power to order whatever necessaries they may think proper, without waiting for an order from the relieving officer, not only to the paupers, but also to the club patients, whose means will not allow of their otherwise obtaining them. That an inspector be appointed in each district of the union, whose duty should be to go round every portion of the district committed to his inspection once a week, and point out every nuisance therein existing, with a view to getting the same removed, by reporting the same to the guardians."

Ans.—So far as the recommendations of the medical gentlemen are in accordance with the provisions of the Act for the removal of nuisances, and the directions and regulations of the General Board of Health, in force in the Clutton Union, there is, of course, not only no objection to the guardians adopting the recommendations, but it is very desirable that they should give effect to them. Thus, as regards the removal of nuisances, this, of course, is the immediate concern of the guardians. So likewise as relates to the cleansing or purifying of dwellings, by causing them to be whitewashed or otherwise; this is a matter which the guardians, under the authority referred to, can undertake where the occupiers of the dwellings are too poor to cleanse them, or where, from any other cause, such cleansing could not practically be effected otherwise. With regard to the alteration of windows, which is recommended, the Board do not see that the law gives the guardians any power to incur expense for this object. The Board also think that the guardians cannot confer upon the medical men the power to order necessaries as is proposed; it will be for the relieving officer to supply whatever the medical officer shall declare to be needed in the particular case. With regard to the appointment of an inspector of nuisances, the Board need only observe, that under the statute referred to, and the Regulations of the General Board of Health, the guardians possess the power (which the Poor Law Board hope they will not fail to exercise) of appointing such an officer, if they deem that the present circumstances of the union require it.

IV.—PAUPERS.

1. ORDERS OF MAINTENANCE ON RELATIONS, WHEN PAUPERS, CHARGEABLE TO THE COMMON FUND.

23*rd June*, 1849.

W. G., Esq., J. P., Depwade Union.—It occasionally happens, that poor persons are sometimes wholly, and sometimes partially, maintained by their relatives, under orders from magistrates, obtained at the instance of parish officers; which orders remain in force so long as the parties are chargeable to their respective parishes. Some of these parties are now chargeable to the common fund of unions. Inquired whether parish officers can any longer enforce these payments; and also, whether officers of unions can obtain orders against the relatives of poor persons chargeable to the common fund of such unions.

Ans.—Certainly, orders of maintenance obtained by the churchwardens and overseers of a parish, cannot be enforced when the paupers become chargeable to the common fund of the union. In that case, however, the guardians of such union are enabled, under the provisions of sec. 8 of the 11 & 12 Vic. c. 110, to obtain orders of maintenance upon the relations of the paupers.

2. DITTO.

21*st July*, 1849.

Clerk of Colchester Union—Submitting the point:—A pauper is in receipt of relief properly charged to the common fund of the union. It is thought that a relative is in a condition to maintain, and that proceedings should be taken under the statute to compel contribution. Who is to take proceedings against the relative? in other words, who is to represent the common fund of the union, and in whose name the information before the justices should be laid, and by whom supported?

Ans.—The guardians of the union may in such a case obtain an order of maintenance under the 11 & 12 Vic. c. 110, sec. 8, and for this purpose they can, in conformity with the 5 & 6 Vic. c. 57, sec. 17, direct one of their officers to make the requisite application to the justices. Article 202, No. 11, of the General Consolidated Order, requires their clerk to conduct such application before the justices. The Board apprehend that the complaint should be laid on behalf of the guardians of the union.

3. PAUPERS DESERTING THEIR FAMILIES AND GOING OVER TO THE CHANNEL ISLANDS.

9*th July*, 1849.

Clerk of Redruth Union.—Parties are frequently in the habit, in this union, of leaving their families and going over to the Channel Islands. The guardians are desirous of knowing what power they have to compel such parties to maintain their families.

Ans.—The Board fear that there is no means by which redress can be obtained in these cases, unless the 3rd sec. of the 11 & 12 Vic. c. 43, relating to convictions, which incorporates certain provisions of the 11 & 12 Vic. c. 42, and includes those provisions which enable warrants for indictable offences to be executed in the Channel Islands. The Board are disposed to consider that it does, but this point must necessarily be decided by the authorities in those islands; and it is not known what view they would take of the enactments referred to. The guardians may, however, properly make trial of the supposed remedy.

V.—PUBLIC HEALTH ACT.—CONSTRUCTION OF SEC. 50 OF 11 & 12 VIC. C. 63.

28*th July*, 1849.

Overseer of Bovey Tracey, Newton Abbot Union.—At a public meeting of the rated inhabitants of this parish, the population of which is 1,700, it was unanimously agreed that the parochial officers should take measures to improve the sanitary condition of the town. Some doubts having, however, arisen as to the construction of the 50 sec. of the Public Health Act, requested to be informed whether it is necessary that three-fifths of all the rated inhabitants should attend such meeting, or whether three-fifths of those present were competent to direct the carrying out of the provisions of the sec. adverted to; and whether in that case it is necessary that the parish officers should have any order from the Poor Law Board to sanction the payment of the expenses to be incurred on the works to be done.

Ans.—Although the 50 sec. of the Public Health Act (11 & 12 Vic. c. 63.) is not free from ambiguity, the Board are disposed to consider that it will be sufficient if three-fifths of the rated inhabitants who are present at a meeting duly summoned under that sec., give their consent to the proceedings therein contemplated. The Act requires that there should be a majority of the inhabitants assembled at a meeting duly called, and that such majority should not be less than three-fifths. It appears to the Board that the majority intended is the majority of the meeting, and not the majority of all the rated inhabitants in the parish. The meeting having been duly called, those who are absent must be presumed to acquiesce in the proceedings of those who attend. If the consent of the inhabitants be duly obtained, no order of the Poor Law Board is required to enable the overseers to execute any works provided for by the enactment. As your letter does not mention the particular works contemplated in the present case, the Board can express no opinion as to whether they would come within the statute.

VI.—RELIEF—CHARGING OF TO THE COMMON FUND.

1st May. 1849.

Clerk of Louth Union.—Transmitting a form of application by a relieving officer to have relief given to a pauper, charged to the common fund of the union, which he (the clerk) had prepared with the view of keeping the provisions of the 9 & 10 Vic. c. 66, and 11 & 12 Vic. c. 110, before the relieving officers and the guardians, and of preventing paupers being charged to the common fund without due inquiry. Transmitting, also, a form of return, which he found useful in correcting the relief districts in accordance with the decision of the Court of Queen's Bench in the Reg. *v.* Christchurch. Suggesting the printing of the forms by Mr. Charles Knight, for the use of other unions.

Ans.—The proposed form of queries appears to the Board to be very useful, and might be adopted with benefit by the unions in general. The Board think that you may very properly offer the forms to Mr. Knight for publication.*

FORMS REFERRED TO ABOVE.*

No.

LOUTH UNION.

PARISH
Application made by Relieving Officer, to have the Relief given to the undermentioned pauper, charged to the common fund of the union, under 11 & 12 Vic. cap. 110, sec. 1, 2, 3, this day of 18

PARTICULARS TO BE ATTENDED TO.

THE RELIEVING OFFICER'S REPORT.

(To be founded on the best evidence that can be obtained.)

State, opposite, the name and age of the Pauper, and supposed Parish of settlement.

CLASS UNDER SEC. 3.—IRREMOVABLE POOR, (9 & 10 Vic. cap. 66, sec. 1, 2, 3, 4.)

Sec. 1.—Has the Pauper had an unbroken residence in the Parish for five years to the time of application, bearing in mind the provisoes, as to Soldiers, Marines, and Sailors, In-Pensioners, Lunatics, Hospital Patients, and Parish Relief.

Sec. 2.—Did the Pauper (if still a widow) reside with her husband at the time of his death? and *when* did the husband die?

Sec. 3.—Is the Pauper a legitimate or illegitimate child, under sixteen years of age, residing in the Parish with his or her father or mother, step-father or step-mother, or reputed father or mother, and are the latter (as the case may be) lawfully removable from the Parish.—See also 11 & 12 Vic. cap. 111.

Sec. 4.—Has the Pauper *become* chargeable in respect of Relief made necessary by sickness or accident? and will either produce permanent disability?

CLASS UNDER SEC. 1.—WAYFARERS, &c.

State, is the Pauper a "*Wayfarer?*" *i.e.*, a person proceeding to some definite destination, or "*Wanderer,*" *i.e.*, having no definite pursuit or destination, or a "*Foundling,*" *i.e.*, a child found exposed or deserted?

CLASS UNDER SEC. 2.—CASUALTIES, &c.

State in what Parish has the Pauper a *fixed abode?*

What is the nature of the *accident, bodily casualty,* or *sudden sickness?*

In what *other* Parish did the same occur?

Has the Pauper a legal settlement in the *latter* Parish?

Was the Pauper in *receipt of Relief* at the time the accident, &c., occurred? and if so, is such Relief charged to a Parish, and what Parish, or to the Common Fund?

Order of the Board {

*Signed*________________ { *Chairman or Clerk.*

LOUTH UNION.

LIST OF PAUPERS at present charged to the Common Fund of the Louth Union; showing the effect of the recent case of Regina *v.* Christchurch upon their chargeability.

NAMES OF PAUPERS.	Residence.	Time during which they have *uninterruptedly* resided in such place.	By whom this Information has been given.	Time during which they have been relieved during such period of Residence.	Parish giving such Relief previous to August, 1846.	By whom Evidence of Relief has been given.	No. of Years' Residence without receiving Relief.	Parish or Place, and to which they are now legally chargeable according to the foregoing evidence, and the case of Regina *v.* Christchurch.	Amount of Relief since last Audit.			Observations.
Thos. Cartwright, aged 69 . .	Aby .	35 years .	Pauper	7 years.	South Thoresby	Pauper	28 years	Common Fund	..	..	..	
Sarah Smith, widow, aged 72	Beesby	20 years and upwards	Pauper	during the whole period of Residence.	Saleby . .	Pauper	None.	Saleby . . .	2	6	0	

VII.—REMOVABILITY.

1. EVIDENCE OF.

18th October, 1848.

Clerk of Honiton Union.—By the Act 11 & 12 Vic. c. 110, sec. 3, it is provided that for a limited period the relief of persons rendered irremovable by the 9 & 10 Vic. c. 66, shall be charged to the common fund of the union. Inquired, What is sufficient evidence of the irremovability under the Act last-mentioned, and whether it should be shown before charging relief to the common fund, that the parish officers have attempted to obtain an order for the removal of the pauper, and failed in consequence of the operation of that act.

Ans.—Before the guardians proceed in conformity with sec. 3 of 11 & 12 Vic. c. 110, to charge the relief of irremovable poor to the common fund of the union, it will be necessary that they should satisfy themselves of the fact of the pauper being rendered irremovable by reason of some provision of the Act 9 & 10 Vic. c. 66. The Board do not see that they can advise the guardians as to the precise evidence upon which their decisions should be founded. Where, however, in any case it may appear that the overseers of a parish have applied to the justices for an order of removal, which has been refused on the ground of the justices being of opinion that the pauper is not removable by operation of the 9 & 10 Vic. c. 66, the Board think that the guardians would do right in placing the charge of relief to the common fund; assuming that, at the time of giving the relief, the circumstances were the same as when the case came before the justices. But the Board think this is not the only evidence which may be admitted. The guardians would be justified in forming their own judgment as to the fact of irremovability from the circumstances elicited by the examination which will now be properly instituted by the guardians and their officers when the application for relief is made. It is, therefore, manifest that the guardians can determine the question for themselves in many cases without much trouble and with no expense.

2. EVIDENCE OF REMOVABILITY.

8th June, 1849.

Mr. W. Bowden, Guardian of Totnes Union.—Requesting the advice of the Poor Law Board under the following circumstances:—The guardians of the Totnes Union have declined to take the evidence of the relieving officer as to the chargeability of a pauper to the common fund, although he had visited the pauper who was ill, and took his examination in writing. The guardians require the pauper to attend personally before they will allow the relief granted to be placed on the common fund. Two cases of this kind have occurred. One of them is that of Mary Skelton, who has resided in Totnes two years; the cause of her seeking relief is illness. She is attended by the medical officer, and is incapable of appearing before the board of guardians. The illness will not produce permanent disability in the opinion of the medical officer. The other case is that of Elizabeth Shapter, who has resided in Totnes about fourteen years; she has never rented more than £2. 12*s.* 6*d.* per annum, is old, and attended by the medical officer, and is not likely to be able to appear before the board. She is considered to be irremovable.

16*th June*, 1849.

Clerk of Totnes Union.—The guardians of this union having been requested by the Poor Law Board to furnish them with observations in reference to the above communication, the clerk states:—The guardians do not require the personal attendance of poor persons before they will allow relief granted to them to be placed to the common fund of the union. All the guardians require is, proper evidence of facts which will authorise them so to charge such relief; and if such proper evidence is produced from any other party than the pauper, sufficient to satisfy the guardians, the relief is charged to the common fund of the union; in fact, several cases have been so charged without the personal attendance of the pauper.

17*th July*, 1849.

The Poor Law Board. —Requesting the clerk to inform the Board as to the proceedings adopted by the guardians in the cases of the paupers, Mary Skelton and Elizabeth Shapter, with a view to ascertain their chargeability, and what were the particulars of the two cases.

Clerk of Totnes Union.—The practice of the guardians has been to require a week's notice of motion to be given previous to any pauper being transferred from a parish to the common fund of the union; and when the guardians have been moved to charge a pauper to the common fund, they have required evidence of all the facts necessary to justify the charging of the relief to the common fund. The guardians find that the auditor required the same evidence in cases in which appeals were made to him at the last audit, and refused to receive secondary evidence where the parties capable of giving the proper evidence were unable to appear before him. It should be stated, that the majority of the cases placed on the common fund by the auditor, had never been brought under the consideration of the guardians. With regard to the case of Mary Skelton, it having been stated to the guardians that she was suffering only from temporary illness, it was determined by the guardians that the consideration of the case should stand over until she was able to attend the board, as she only could give the necessary information; and if it was found she ought to be placed to the common fund, all the past relief should be transferred accordingly. As to the other case, that of Elizabeth Shapter, the only evidence offered to the guardians was, the statement made by the pauper to the relieving officer, and taken in writing by him. The guardians thought that they ought not to be satisfied with hearsay evidence, and deemed it inexpedient to make the relieving officer the party on whom should rest the responsibility of determining on the chargeability of the paupers, especially as the statement would be taken by the relieving officer, in the absence of any one representing the guardians.

Ans. to the Clerk.—The Board quite admit that in cases of doubt the guardians, before making the charge upon the common fund, are justified in having such evidence put before them as may lead to the reasonable inference of the fact of irremovability. The Board, however, differ from the guardians as to the nature of the evidence which ought to be required. As regards persons chargeable through illness, the Board think the certificate of the medical officer as to the nature of the illness and the probability of its producing permanent disability or otherwise, ought to be almost conclusive on the guardians. As regards persons alleged to be irremovable by residence, where the personal attendance of the pauper is impossible, (as it may be in consequence of infirmity,) the Board consider that if the guardians make such attendance a condition precedent to the transferring the relief to the common fund, they will go far wholly to defeat in numerous cases, the operation of the statute.

But if the Board correctly infer that as a general rule the guardians do not insist upon personal attendance, they must add that they agree with the guardians in thinking that there may be cases in which evidence beyond that afforded by the report of the relieving officer may be necessary to determine the question of irremovability. Nevertheless, if the relieving officer finds nothing to discredit the statement made to him, and the guardians are not aware of any fact or ground for disbelieving it, the Board think that the guardians would act properly in adopting the statement.

3. COMPUTATION OF THE PERIOD OF RESIDENCE.

19*th July*, 1849.

Clerk of Whitechapel Union.—Transmitting the following statement under the 4th sec. of 11 & 12 Vic. c. 110:—A question has arisen between the guardians of the Whitechapel Union and the overseers of the hamlet of Mile End New Town, part of the union, whether a pauper named William G. should be charged to the common fund of the union under the following circumstances:—The pauper is now twenty years old, and is the lawful son of Sarah G. About sixteen years ago, Sarah G. then and still being a widow with her said son, and other children, came to reside in the above hamlet, and they have constantly resided there ever since. The place of the legal settlement of Sarah G. and her said son (the pauper) is in the parish of Barking, Essex, and Sarah G. received relief from that parish for herself and family, from the time of the commencement of her residence in Mile End New Town, until October, 1846, and during all that time the pauper formed part of his mother's family, though occasionally having employment on his own account. In the year 1847, the pauper on his individual account, and on his own application received relief from the hamlet of Mile End New Town for six weeks, in 1848 for four weeks, and in 1849 for sixteen weeks. The pauper is neither blind nor deaf and dumb. The direction of the Poor Law Board is requested as to whether the pauper, William G., should properly be charged to the common fund of the union, or is removable to his place of settlement.

Ans.—It appears that the mother of the pauper received relief for herself and her family, and as the pauper formed part of her family, the Board think he must be considered to have been maintained out of a rate raised in another parish, while his mother received the relief; and this period being deducted from the whole time of abiding in the hamlet in question, there does not remain five years of residence irrespective of relief. The Board, therefore, consider that the pauper is removable, and that consequently his relief is not chargeable to the union common fund.

4. BREACH OF RESIDENCE.

3*rd April*, 1849.

Clerk of Congleton Union—Transmitting the following statement, duly signed, under sec. 4, of 11 & 12 Vic. c. 110:—A. B., whose settlement is acknowledged to be in the parish of Brereton, in the county of Chester, resided for five years before the passing of the 9 & 10 Vic. c. 66, (1846,) in Congleton, and continued to reside there without break in the residence until 1848, when he was sent to the house of correction, at Nether Knutsford, in the said county, for a month. At the expiration of the term of imprisonment he returned to Congleton, and he continues to reside there up to the present time. Is A. B. now removable to Brereton, his place of settlement? Referred to the cases of Reg. *v.* Salford, and Reg. *v.* Christchurch, as bearing upon the point.

Ans.—The Board think the case of Reg. *v.* Salford, referred to, must be taken to decide the point involved; and that there was accordingly an interruption of the pauper's residence in the present instance.

5. BREACH OF RESIDENCE.

25*th May*, 1849.

Clerk of Clifton Union.—Transmitting the following statement, duly signed, under sec. 4 of 11 & 12 Vic. c. 110:—S. G. states, "I am the widow of G. G. My husband died two years ago next June. I was married in 1824, after our marriage we lived at Yate, then in Charles Street in St. James's, then in Orange Street, I was there nearly ten years, from Orange Street I went into Little Anne Street seven years ago last Christmas. On the 24th of February last, I was charged with felony—was sent to gaol for five or six weeks in the ancient city of Bristol, and acquitted of the felony. I do not know where my husband belonged, he was an Englishman. Before my marriage I hired myself as a yearly servant to

Mrs. S., at Tytherington, one year at £4. I remained there under that hiring for the year, and received the £4." Query:—Does the being in jail constitute a break in the residence?

Ans.—The Board regret that they are unable to express any definite opinion on the question submitted, as the facts of the case are not set forth with sufficient fulness. The name of the parish in which Little Anne Street is situated, is not mentioned; nor is it stated to what parish the pauper returned on her discharge from the jail. The Board presume that the jail is not in the same parish as Little Anne Street. If S. G., on her discharge, returned to the parish including Little Anne Street, it will then be necessary for the Board to be informed whether, on her commitment, she gave up her residence there, and on her return, took up her her abode elsewhere in the same parish; or, whether she retained her residence (house or lodgings) during her imprisonment, and went back to it after her discharge.

28th June, 1849.

Clerk of same Union.—S. G. was residing in the parish of St. Philip and Jacob, charged with felony, and sent to jail in another parish, where she remained three weeks—was acquitted by the jury and returned to the same house, which she had previously occupied in St. Philip and Jacob, and in which she had left her furniture and family. There is no doubt that when she was sent to jail there was the *animus revertendi*, but not the *protestas revertendi*; and the question is, whether the being sent to jail in another parish for three weeks, does or does not constitute a break in the residence.

Ans.—Taking your present explanation in connection with the statement of facts contained in your letter of the 7th May last, the Poor Law Board now understand, that the pauper, S. G., prior to her commitment to jail in Bristol, had resided in Little Anne Street in the parish of St. Philip and Jacob in the Clifton Union, for a sufficient period to render her irremovable therefrom under sec. 1 of 9 & 10 Vic. c. 66, unless the commitment before mentioned operated as an interruption of the residence. The Board are disposed to consider that under the circumstances stated by you, the commitment had not this effect. The pauper, it appears, was committed upon a charge of felony, which charge proved to be groundless, as it is stated she was acquitted by the jury, and immediately after returned to the same house which she had previously occupied in St. Philip and Jacob, and in which too she had left her family and furniture. The home therefore of S. G. continued to be in that parish during her temporary absence, and the Board apprehend that if the pauper could have obtained bail, the justices might have allowed her to return to that home at any time previous to the trial. The attention of the Board has been called to the case of Nias *v.* Davies, (11 Jur. 472,) which appears to establish that the imprisonment of the head of a family in one county, is not necessarily an interruption of his residence in another, wherein his usual abode or home is, in which his family continue to reside during his temporary absence, and to which he returns when he quits the prison. Upon the authority of that decision the Poor Law Board think that the commitment of the pauper S. G. did not operate to break the continuity of her residence in the parish of St. Philip and Jacob. At the same time the Board cannot express a confident opinion upon the point, as though they distinguish the present case as one of commitment for trial from that of Reg. *v.* Salford, 3 N.S.C. which was a commitment in execution, they are not sure that the Court of Queen's Bench would support such a distinction.

---

6. BREACH OF RESIDENCE.

2nd June, 1849.

Clerk of Clifton Union.—Transmitting the following statement, duly signed, under the 4th sec. of the 11 & 12 Vic. c. 110:—M. A. R., is the widow of H. R., who is supposed to have been settled in the parish of St. Philip and Jacob. They were married in 1843, and on their marriage resided in St. Philip and Jacob, where the husband had been living for about twelve months before the marriage; they at first rented a house, and subsequently lived with the mother of the widow. In July, 1847, H. R. went to Staffordshire for work, and afterwards went to Newport, in Monmouthshire, where he died in September, 1847. The question is, whether the man having left St. Philip and Jacob in July, 1847, and dying in September, 1847, in Monmouthshire, there is not a break in the residence of the widow, rendering her removable to the parish in which her husband is legally settled.

Ans.—The Board gather from the communication before them, that the woman in this case did not leave the parish of St. Philip and Jacob with her husband when he quitted it in search of work; and moreover, that she had resided in the same parish prior to her marriage, though this latter fact does not distinctly appear. The Board do not think that the departure of the husband in search of work, (even assuming it to have broken his own residence in the parish of St. Philip and Jacob,) can be taken to be an interruption of the woman's residence in that parish, in which, in point of fact, she, herself, continued to inhabit. If the husband had been now alive, she would apparently have been removable, in accordance with the provisions of the 11 & 12 Vic. c. 111; but that statute does not affect the case, under its present circumstances. Assuming that the woman has not received relief on any former occasion during her residence in St. Philip and Jacob, or, if she has, that a clear period of five years still remains, after deducting such time or times of relief, it appears to the Board that she is irremovable, and that her relief should accordingly be charged to the common fund of the Clifton Union.

7. BREACH OF RESIDENCE.

6th June, 1849.

Clerk of Stow on the Wold Union.—Transmitting the following statement, duly signed, under the 4th sec. of 11 & 12 Vic. c. 110: R.A. and his wife, have resided in the parish of Stow on the Wold for about fifty years, without any breach of residence except as hereinafter mentioned. In March, 1846, R. A. and his wife became chargeable to the parish of Stow on the Wold, and so continued chargeable; and on the 7th of May, 1846, an order of justices was obtained for their removal to the parish of Kingham as their place of legal settlement. In June, 1846, they were removed by the overseers of the parish of Stow on the Wold to the parish of Kingham under the order and delivered to the parish officers of Kingham, who accepted them and relieved them. The order of justices was not appealed against. On the same day as R. A. and his wife were removed to the parish of Kingham, the parish officers of that parish hired a person and a conveyance to convey the paupers back to the parish of Stow on the Wold, to the cottage where they had resided with their son and daughter, up to the time of their removal, and they were conveyed back accordingly on the same day they were removed to Kingham, not sleeping out of the parish of Stow a night. The paupers were relieved by the parish of Kingham whilst residing in the parish of Stow on the Wold, from the time of their removal under the said order of justices, until after the passing of the 9 & 10 Vic. c. 66, when the relief was discontinued by the parish of Kingham, and the paupers again became chargeable to Stow on the Wold, and so continue to the present time. It is alleged by the parish officers of Stow on the Wold that the paupers are removable to the parish of Kingham, the continuity of their residence having been broken by their removal under the order of justices in June, 1846, and that the parish of Stow on the Wold should not be prejudiced by the act of the parish officers of Kingham. See Lord Denman's Judgment in Reg. *v.* the Inhabitants of Seend. On the other hand it is doubted whether there was such a breach in the continuity of residence as to justify a removal from Stow on the Wold to Kingham.

Ans.—The Board apprehend the Court of Queen's Bench must be taken to have decided the point involved in the present case, in Reg. *v.* Halifax, and Reg. *v.* Seend, and in accordance with such decision the pauper, R. A., appears to be now removable from the parish of Stow on the Wold.

8. BREACH OF RESIDENCE.

20th June, 1849.

Clerk of Blything Union.—Transmitting the following statement, duly signed, under sec. 4 of the 11 & 12 Vic. c. 110:—J. R. the pauper resides in the parish of Blyford, but belongs to the parish of Westhall, such parishes forming part of the Blything Union. In the year, 1821, the pauper hired a cottage in the parish of Blyford, and resided in that parish continuously, and without receiving parochial relief of any kind till the year 1842. In the quarter ending September, 1842, the pauper being still resident in Blyford, applied to the proper authorities and obtained relief: he was relieved eight weeks in that quarter, the relief being charged to the parish of Westhall. In the quarter, ending December, 1842, he was relieved four weeks, the relief as before being charged to Westhall. During the year, 1843, he did not receive any relief, but still continued to reside at Blyford. On the 4th of January, 1844, he left his cottage at Blyford, on being admitted an inmate of the union workhouse, situate in the parish of Blythburgh, where he remained a period of ninety-six days, his maintenance being charged to the parish of Westhall. Whilst he was an inmate of the workhouse, however, he continued to keep possession of his cottage in Blyford, and on quitting the workhouse, he returned to it again, where he has continued to reside to the present time. The pauper has a wife and family, and the children are all grown up and emancipated. At the time the pauper and his wife were admitted as inmates of the workhouse on the 4th of January, 1844, he left the key of his cottage with one of his daughters, who was married, and resided in the same parish, (Blyford,) to take care of his furniture. His cottage had not been occupied by any person during his residence in the workhouse. On his leaving the workhouse in April, 1844, he was allowed by the guardians out-door relief, and has continued in the receipt of such relief from that time to the present. Up to the period of the passing of the statute 9 & 10 Vic. c. 66, such relief was regularly charged to the parish of Westhall, through the union accounts; since that period it has been charged to the parish of his residence, Blyford. The point at issue between the two parishes of Westhall and Blyford is, whether or not the pauper is removable to the parish of settlement. The parish officers of Blyford contend, that when the pauper quitted Blyford, and took up his abode in the union workhouse, in the manner above described, such workhouse being situate in another parish, that it must be considered as a breach of his continuous residence in Blyford, and that consequently, the pauper is now removable to Westhall. The guardians are, therefore, desirous of obtaining the opinion of the Poor Law Board on the point in dispute. It has been mutually agreed between the parties to abide by the opinion of the Poor Law Board, and should they be of opinion that the pauper's residence in Blyford was broken by his abode in the workhouse, so as to make him removable within the meaning of the statute, the parish officers of Westhall will consent to take the pauper, without putting the parish of Blyford to the expense of obtaining orders of removal.

Ans.—The Board having regard to the decisions of the courts in Reg. *v.* Tacolnestone, (18 L. I. R. N. S. M. C. 44,) and Nias *v.* Davies, (11 Jur. 472,) are disposed to consider that under the circumstances described in the statement of J. R.'s case, there was no interruption of the pauper's residence in Blyford, in consequence of his temporary reception into the workhouse of the Blything Union in 1844. Consequently, the pauper is now irremovable, and his relief is accordingly chargeable to the common fund of the Blything Union.

---

9. BREACH OF RESIDENCE.

4th July, 1849.

Clerk of Dolgelly Union.—Transmitting the following statement, duly signed, under sec. 4 of 11 & 12 Vic. c. 110:—M. M., widow, aged 48, has resided in the parish of Llanelltyd in this union all her life time. In 1822, she was married to one E. M., who was also a resident in the same parish, and they continued to reside in that parish until his death, which took place in September, 1834. During his life time, they received no parochial relief whatever, but upon his death, his widow applied to the overseers of Llanelltyd, and received relief from them for herself and her children. Her late husband's legal settlement was in the parish of Cemmaes in the county of Montgomery: the overseers of Llanelltyd, therefore, procured an order for the removal of the pauper and her family to the parish of Cemmaes. The latter parish appealed against the order, but did not succeed, and the order was confirmed by the Quarter Sessions, held at Dolgelley at Easter, 1835. The parish of Cemmaes then repaid to the parish of Llanelltyd, the expense of the maintenance of the pauper and her family from the date of the order until its confirmation. Before the overseers of Llanelltyd put the order into execution, by the removal of the pauper and her family into the parish of her settlement, the pauper's father went to the overseers of the latter parish, and at his earnest solicitation they agreed to allow the pauper to remain in her usual place of residence at Llanelltyd, and to supply her with relief there. This they continued to do until the Poor Removal Act of August, 1846, came into operation. Since then she has been maintained at the expense of this union. As the pauper was not actually removed out of the removing parish to the parish of her settlement, nor delivered into the custody of the overseers of the latter parish, and as no absence from the parish of her residence occurred, the question arises, whether such an execution of the order will, or will not, operate as an interruption of the residence, and consequently, whether the pauper is to be considered as removable or irremovable.

Ans.—According to the facts set forth in the statement, the order of removal was not executed by the actual removal of the pauper; the overseers of Llanelltyd also, who obtained the order consented not to act upon it. It does not appear that the pauper was, in fact, ever absent from that parish, and consequently, her continous residence there was not broken. She is, therefore, irremovable, and chargeable to the common fund of the Dolgelly Union.

10. BREACH OF RESIDENCE.

20th July, 1849.

Clerk of Kingsclere Union.—Transmitting the following statement, duly signed, under sec. 4. of 11 & 12 Vic. c. 110:— W. J., who had been generally in gentlemen's service as butler, &c., and whose settlement is in the parish of Burghclere, resided without receiving relief in the parish of East Woodhay, in the same union, during five years; but in the middle of that period he engaged himself as butler to a gentleman in the parish of Chievely, Berks, at yearly wages. He was in such service six months, and during that period he left his wife and family in East Woodhay. The parish officers of Burghclere declining to take the pauper on the ground of his service in Chievely, not being a break in a five years' residence in East Woodhay, the guardians request the opinion of the Poor Law Board, as to whether this residence of W. J. in Chievely caused such an interruption in his residence in East Woodhay, as to enable the overseers of East Woodhay to remove him to Burghclere, now that he has become chargeable to East Woodhay.

Ans.—In reply, the Board desire to state, that in their opinion the engagement and residence of the pauper in the parish of Chievely, Berks, as set forth in the statement, was such as to interrupt the residence in the parish of East Woodhay.

11. BREACH OF RESIDENCE.

30th July, 1849.

Clerk of Bromley Union.—Inquiring whether a pauper formerly removed by justices order broke the residence in the removing parish, in consequence of such order being carried into effect, although the pauper only continued three days in the parish to which she was removed, and then returned to her former lodging, of which she had not given up the key. Also requesting the particulars of a case, Reg. *v.* Halifax, decided within the last twelve months in the Queen's Bench, in which it was held that residence is broken by removal under a former order, and inquiring whether the decision in the case affects the removability of paupers to any number of years after the removal.

Ans.—The order having been executed by the actual removal of the pauper, operated in point of law as an interruption of the residence, according to the decisions in Reg. *v.* Halifax, (17 L.J.R., N.S., M.C., 158,) Reg. *v.* Seend, (12 Jur. 939,) and Reg. *v.* Barnesly, (14 Jur. 511.) With regard to the particulars of the case Reg. *v.* Halifax, the Board have to state, that it will be found fully reported in several books of authority, namely, the 3 N.S.C. 268, 12 Jur. 789, 17 L.J.R., M.C. 158. It decided that where a person had been resident in a parish for 11 years, and was then removed under an order of removal to another parish where she remained for nineteen days, and returned to her home in the former parish with the promise of non-resident relief and received it for nearly two years, and then the relief being discontinued, was removed under another order; she was not exempt from removal, as the order being executed by the removal, interrupted the residence, and five years without relief had not intervened after her return. If such an order, therefore, have been made and executed, there must be a subsequent residence for five years without relief to render the party irremovable. The Board give this opinion generally, but it must not be taken as their decision upon any particular case which may be referred to them under the 4th sec. of the 11 & 12 Vic. c. 110.

12. REMOVABILITY AND CHARGEABILITY.

12th June, 1849.

Mr. John Hall, guardian of Newtown and Llandloes Union.—1, Are children (whose parents have died recently, but who had by residence become irremovable) after the decease of their parents liable to be removed to their parents' parish. 2, Is a child who has attained his sixteenth year (his parents being unable to maintain him, and being irremovable to their parish of settlement by residence) chargeable to the union to which the father is chargeable, or is he removable to his father's parish? 3, A woman having children by a former husband, and her present husband being unable to maintain them, to what parish are these children chargeable, to that of the former husband's parish or that of the present?

Ans.—1, If the orphans you refer to in your first inquiry, have not resided in the parish for five years without relief, they will not be irremovable under sec. 1. of the 9 & 10 Vic. c. 66, but if they have so resided for that period, then they will be irremovable. 2, With reference to your second inquiry, the Board would direct your attention to the 11 & 12 Vic. c. 111, under the provisions of which, (as it seems to the Board,) the child you allude to is irremovable, if his parents are so, notwithstanding he may have attained the age of sixteen years. 3, If your third question refers to the settlement of the step-children, the Board desire to inform you that the Court of Queen's Bench has expressly decided, (in R. *v.* Walthamstow 6 A. and E. 301,) that the 57th sec. of the 4 & 5 Wm. 4, c. 76, does not change the settlement of the step-children, though it renders the step-father liable to maintain them. If, however, you had in view the question of the irremovability of such children, the Board would point out that the 3rd sec. of the 9 & 10 Vic. c. 66 provides specifically for the case of step-children under sixteen years of age, so as to render their removability dependent upon that of their step-father. But if the children in question be above that age, their removability will depend upon the particular circumstances of the case.

13. REMOVABILITY.

4th July, 1849.

Clerk of St. Columb Major Union.—Transmitting the following statement, duly signed, under sec. 4 of 11 & 12 Vic. c. 110:—M. F. is a pauper at present residing in and receiving relief from the parish of Padstow, but whom it is sought by the guardians of that parish, to throw on the common fund of the St. Columb Major Union, that being the union of which the parish of Padstow forms a part. The maiden settlement of the pauper is admitted to be in the parish of Padstow, but about seven or eight years since she married her present husband, who is a sailor, and by whom she is now deserted. The pauper is ignorant of her husband's settlement, as he always refused to give her any information on the subject: she believes he is a native of Devonshire, but she is not able to speak confidently even to the fact of his being a native of Great Britain. Under these circumstances the parish conceive that it is merely necessary for them to show the marriage of the pauper to a person not settled in their parish, to entitle them to have the pauper charged on the common fund. Whilst on the other hand the board of guardians contend that before they can be called on to take the pauper, the parish must prove their non-liability, and that the maiden settlement being in Padstow, that parish must show that the pauper has gained such a legal settlement elsewhere, as entirely to supersede the original settlement, and to which she could have been removed but for the five years' residence. Although the pauper has resided in the parish of Padstow for five years, the husband has not, he being, as stated, a sailor, and the greater part of his time at sea; unless, indeed, the fact of the wife's keeping house there, which she had done for more than five years before he deserted her, sufficiently shows the *animus revertendi* in the husband. This is stated, as it is supposed that if she gains a settlement through her husband at all, he being removable through want of five years residence, she would be also.

Ans.—According to the statement of the facts of this case, it appears to the Board that the pauper is not rendered exempt from removal by the provisions of the 9 & 10 Vic. c. 66, inasmuch as the case falls within the 11 & 12 Vic. c. 111; see also the cases of Reg. *v.* St. Ebbes, and the Reg. *v.* Pott Shrigley, 3 N.S.C. If this be so, it is not necessary to enter upon the question of the settlement, nor to consider the general proposition laid down by the guardians of the St. Columb Major Union in the case.

14. BREACH OF RESIDENCE.

9th July, 1849.

Clerk of Market Bosworth Union.—Transmitting the following statement, duly signed, under sec. 4 of 11 & 12 Vic. c. 110:—S. B., a widower, aged eighty years, whose settlement was by birth at Barton in the Beans, in this union, by which parish he was acknowledged and occasionally relieved; but having resided upwards of fifty years at Market Bosworth, he became chargeable to that parish, under the Act 9 & 10 Vic. c. 66, and afterwards, in June, 1848, to the union. He went from Bosworth to Blaby on a visit to his daughter, where he stayed about six months—another daughter residing in his house at Bosworth during his absence. Does the fact of his residence at Blaby, for the time named, render him removable to Barton?

Ans.—The Board consider that, as the pauper only went on a visit to his daughter, at Blaby, it cannot be held that he went to reside there; and consequently, his absence from Market Bosworth did not create an interruption of his residence therein.

---

15. BREACH OF RESIDENCE.

21st July, 1849.

Clerk of Epping Union.—Transmitting the following statement, duly signed, under sec. 4 of 11 & 12 Vic. c. 110:—A man, whose settlement is in the parish of Epping, in the Epping Union, upwards of ten years ago went, with his wife and family, to reside in the parish of North Weald, (another parish of the Epping Union,) at the house of his wife's father and mother. He was only a lodger, the wife's father paying the rent of the house. He has continued to reside there with his wife and family, with the following exception, to the present time. About Michaelmas, 1845, the man went to Ware, having heard of a situation as luggage porter on the railway. He continued there until the following spring, when, the work getting slack, he, with several others, was discharged, and thereupon returned to North Weald. When at Ware he hired a lodging, and paid for the same weekly. When he went to Ware it was his intention, in the event of his getting regular work, to have continued there, and to have taken his family with him. Whilst at Ware, he was in the habit of coming home to North Weald sometimes every Saturday, sometimes only once in a fortnight. When he did come home he was continually heard to say, that if he could get a house at a moderate rent he would at once hire it, and take his family to Ware, for he could earn more there than at North Weald. His wife remarked that she would never leave North Weald, when he said, that if he went she must go. The man and his family having lately become chargeable, the guardians request the opinion of the Poor Law Board, where the relief ought to be charged; whether the man's going to Ware, having left his family at North Weald, constituted a break in the residence, and thereby rendered him removable and chargeable to his parent parish, Epping; or, whether it did not constitute such break in the residence, thereby rendering it a union charge.

Ans.—The Board are disposed to consider, that in the present case, the sojourning of the pauper in question, in the parish of Ware, did constitute an interruption of his residence in the parish of North Weald, and that he is, therefore, now removable from the latter parish.

---

16. REMOVABILITY OF WIDOW.

17th March, 1849.

Clerk of Cosford Union.—A woman whose husband was settled in the parish of A., resided for ten years apart from him in the parish of B.; the husband during most of that time was roving about, but never resided in B. He died upwards of twelve months ago in his own parish of A., where he was then residing. Is the wife removable from the parish of B. to the parish of A.? Or, will her having resided more than five years in B. during which time her husband was alive, (with the exception of about thirteen months which has elapsed since his death) make her irremovable. There was no legal separation in the case.

Ans.—The Board are of opinion that under the circumstances described in your letter the woman is not removable; she has resided in the parish (as the Board presume without receiving relief) for the period required by sec. 1 of the 9 & 10 Vic. c. 66; and her husband being dead, neither the 3rd proviso to that sec. 1, nor the 11 & 12 Vic. c. 111, will apply to the case.

London: Printed by order of the Poor Law Board, by BLACKBURN & BURT, 90½, Holborn Hill, and published by CHARLES KNIGHT, 90, Fleet Street.

AN

OFFICIAL CIRCULAR

OF PUBLIC DOCUMENTS AND INFORMATION:

DIRECTED BY THE POOR LAW BOARD TO BE PRINTED, CHIEFLY FOR THE USE OF THE BOARDS OF GUARDIANS AND THEIR OFFICERS.

No. 28.] AUGUST, 1849. [N.S.

CONTENTS.

SCHOOL DISTRICTS.

The Act of 11 & 12 Vic. c. 32, having removed a legal difficulty which interposed to prevent the formation of school districts, under the 7 & 8 Vic. c. 101, the Poor Law Board have within the present year, (up to August, 1849,) formed the following districts :—

1. THE CENTRAL LONDON SCHOOL DISTRICT, comprising—

The City of London Union,
The East London Union, and
The St. Saviour's Union.

2. THE SOUTH METROPOLITAN SCHOOL DISTRICT, comprising—

The St. Olave's Union,
The Parish of St. Mary Magdalene, Bermondsey,
The Parish of St. Giles, Camberwell, and
The Parish of St. Mary, Rotherhithe.

3. THE NORTH SURREY SCHOOL DISTRICT, comprising—

The Wandsworth and Clapham Union,
The Croydon Union,
The Kingston Union,
The Lewisham Union, and
The Richmond Union.

4. THE SOUTH-EAST SHROPSHIRE SCHOOL DISTRICT, comprising—

The Seisdon Union,
The Madeley Union,
The Bridgnorth Union, and
The Cleobury Mortimer Union.

5. THE FARNHAM AND HARTLEY WINTNEY SCHOOL DISTRICT, comprising—

The Farnham Union, and
The Hartley Wintney Union.

Orders similar to the following, which relate to the *Central London School District,* have been issued by the Poor Law Board to each of the above-mentioned districts :—

1. ORDER FORMING THE CENTRAL LONDON SCHOOL DISTRICT, AND CONSTITUTING THE BOARD OF MANAGEMENT OF THE DISTRICT, &c.

To the Guardians of the Poor of the City of London Union, in the County of Middlesex ·—

To the Guardians of the Poor of the East London Union, in the County of Middlesex;—
To the Guardians of the Poor of the Saint Saviour's Union, in the County of Surrey.
To the Churchwardens and Overseers of the Poor of the several Parishes and Places comprised in the said Unions;—
To the Clerk or Clerks to the Justice or Justices of the Petty Sessions held for the Division or Divisions in which the said Unions respectively are situate;—
And to all others whom it may concern.

We, the Commissioners for administering the Laws for Relief of the Poor in England, under the powers given in and by the several Statutes in that behalf, do hereby declare as follows:

Art. I.—That the following unions, that is to say, the City of London Union, in the county of Middlesex, the East London Union, in the said county of Middlesex, and the Saint Saviour's Union, in the county of Surrey, shall be combined into a district to be termed "*The Central London School District*," for the management of the classes of infant poor, not above the age of sixteen years, being chargeable to some union in the said district respectively, or to any of the parishes therein, who may be orphans, or may be deserted by their parents, or whose parents or surviving parent, or guardians, may be consenting to the placing of such children in such school.

Art. II.—That a Board of Management shall be constituted for the said district, which shall consist of the ex-officio members entitled to act according to the provision of the Act of the eighth year of the reign of Her Majesty, intituled "*An Act for the further Amendment of the Laws relating to the Poor in England*," and of twelve other members to be elected as hereinafter prescribed; so that

For the City of London Union shall be elected six guardians;
For the East London Union shall be elected four guardians;
For the Saint Saviour's Union shall be elected two guardians.

Art. III.—That the qualification for each person to be elected as a member of the said district shall consist in the being rated within the said district upon a net annual value of not less than forty pounds.

Art. IV.—That the manner of the election of each member shall be as follows: the guardians of the several unions in the said district shall, at their first ordinary meeting after the twenty-fifth day of March instant, elect some duly qualified persons, according to the number prescribed above, to be the members of the said board, on behalf of the respective unions, the candidates being respectively nominated and seconded by guardians at such meeting, and elected by a majority of the guardians present thereat, who shall vote by a show of hands, to be counted by the presiding chairman of such meeting.

Art. V.—That the first-elected members of the board of management shall continue to serve as such, from the day of the election as aforesaid until the twenty-ninth day of September One thousand eight hundred and fifty, and that thenceforth the term for which the members of said Board shall serve shall be three years.

Art. VI.—That each board of guardians of the said unions shall, on one of the last two ordinary meetings before the twenty-ninth day of September, in the year One thousand eight hundred and fifty, and subsequently in every year, when the term aforesaid shall expire, proceed, in the manner herein-before prescribed, to elect the members for their union to serve for the term next ensuing such twenty-ninth day of September.

Given under our hands and seal of office, this sixth day of March, in the year One thousand eight hundred and forty nine.

(L.S.)
M. T. BAINES, *President.*
G. GREY.
C. WOOD.
GEO. NICHOLLS, *Secretary.*

---

2. ORDER PRESCRIBING RULES AND REGULATIONS TO BE OBSERVED BY THE BOARD OF MANAGEMENT OF THE CENTRAL LONDON SCHOOL DISTRICT, AND PROVIDING FOR THE APPOINTMENT OF CERTAIN OFFICERS OF SUCH BOARD.

To the Board of Management of the Central London School District;—
To the Churchwardens and Overseers of the Poor of the several Parishes and Places comprised in the said District;—
To the Clerk or Clerks to the Justice or Justices of the Petty Sessions held for the Division or Divisions in which the said District and Parishes respectively are situate;—
And to all others whom it may concern.

Whereas, by an order under their seal bearing date the sixth day of March last, the Commissioners for administering the Laws for Relief of the Poor in England, under the powers given in and by the several statutes in that behalf, did declare, that the following unions, that is to say, the City of London Union, in the county of Middlesex, the East London Union, in the said county of Middlesex, and the St. Saviour's Union, in the county of Surrey, should be combined into a district, to be termed "*The Central London School District,*" for the management of the classes of infant poor, not above the age of sixteen years, being chargeable to some union in the said district respectively, or to any of the parishes therein, who might be orphans, or may be deserted by their parents, or whose parents or surviving parent, or guardians, might be consenting to the placing of such children in such school.

And the said Commissioners did thereby order and declare, that a board of management should be constituted for the said district, which should consist of the ex-officio members entitled to act according to the provision of the Act of the eighth year of the reign of Her Majesty, intituled "*An Act for the further Amendment of the Laws relating to the Poor in England,*" and of twelve other members to be elected as therein-after prescribed.

And whereas it is expedient that the rules and regulations herein-after set forth should be observed by the board of management of the said district; and also that certain officers should be forthwith appointed to carry into effect the orders and directions of the said board, and to assist in the administration of the relief of the poor in the school of the said district.

Now, therefore, We, the Commissioners for administering the Laws for Relief of the Poor in England, in pursuance of the authorities vested in Us by an Act of Parliament passed in the fifth year of the reign of His late Majesty King William the Fourth, intituled "*An Act for the Amendment and better Administration of the Laws relating to the Poor in England and Wales,*" and by another Act passed in the eigthth year of the reign of Her present Majesty Queen Victoria, intituled "*An Act for the further Amendment of the Laws relating to the Poor in England,*" do hereby order and direct as follows; that is to say:—

MEETINGS OF THE BOARD OF MANAGEMENT.

Art. 1.—The first meeting of the said board of management shall be held at the *Board Room of the City of London Union, situated at No.* 35, *Cannon Street, London, on Thursday, the nineteenth day of April, instant,* and shall commence at Eleven o'clock in the forenoon, or as soon after such day or hour as may be.

Art. 2.—No manager shall act in virtue of his office, except as a member, and at a meeting of the board of management.

Art. 3.—The managers shall meet *once at the least in every month* for the execution of their duties, and shall at their first meeting, so to be held as aforesaid, determine upon some fixed day of the week and upon some fixed hour for holding such monthly meetings; and it shall be competent to the said managers, when they think fit, to change the time or place for the holding of such meetings, and notice shall forthwith be given to the said Commissioners of every such change.

Art. 4.—The managers shall, at their first meeting to be held as aforesaid, and at the first meeting after every general election of managers, elect out of the whole number of managers a chairman and a vice-chairman, who, provided they be managers at the time, shall continue respectively to act as such chairman, and vice-chairman until the next general election of managers shall take place, if they so long continue respectively to be managers.

Art. 5.—If a chairman or a vice-chairman cease to be a manager, or refuse or become incapable to act as chairman or vice-chairman, before the expiration of the term of office, the managers shall at one of the two meetings within two months next after the occurrence of the vacancy, refusal, or incapacity, elect some other manager to be chairman or vice-chairman, as the case may be.

Art. 6.—Whereas no act of any meeting of the district board will be valid unless three managers be present, and concur therein; if three managers be not present at any meeting, the clerk shall make an entry of that fact in the minute book, and the time for holding such meeting shall be deemed to have expired as soon as the said entry shall have been made; but one hour at least shall be allowed to elapse from the time fixed for the commencement of the meeting, before such entry shall be made.

Art. 7.—If three, or four, or more managers be present at any ordinary meeting, such three or the majority of such four or more managers may adjourn the same to the day of the next ordinary meeting, or to some other day previous to the next ordinary meeting.

Art. 8.—An extraordinary meeting of the managers may be summoned to be held at any time, upon the requisition of any two managers, addressed to the clerk. Every such requisition shall be made in writing, in the Form A. hereunto annexed, and no business, other than the business specified in the said requisition, shall be transacted at such extraordinary meeting.

Art. 9.—Notice of every change in the period, time, or place of holding any meeting, and notice of the adjournment of any meeting, and notice of every extraordinary meeting, shall be given in writing to the said Commissioners, and to every manager. Every such notice to a manager shall be respectively in the Forms B., C., and D., hereunto annexed, and shall be given or sent by the clerk to every manager, or left at his place of abode, two days, if practicable, before the day appointed for the meeting to which it relates.

Art. 10.—If any case of emergency arise, requiring that a meeting of the managers should immediately take place, they, or any three of them, may meet at the ordinary place of meeting, and take such case into consideration, and make an order or orders thereon.

PROCEEDINGS OF THE BOARD.

Art. 11.—At every meeting the chairman, or, in his absence, a vice-chairman shall preside; but if at the commencement of any meeting the chairman and vice-chairman be absent, the managers present shall elect one of themselves to preside at such meeting as chairman thereof, until the chairman or vice-chairman may take the chair.

Art. 12.—Every question at any meeting consisting of more than three managers shall be determined by a majority of the votes of the managers present thereat, and when there shall be an equal number of votes on any question, such question shall be deemed to have been lost.

Art. 13.—At every ordinary meeting of the managers the minutes of the last ordinary meeting, and of any other meeting of the board or of any committee which may have been held since such ordinary meeting, shall be read to the board, and be signed by the chairman presiding at the meeting at which such minutes are read; and an entry of the same having been so read shall be made in the minutes of the day when read:

All reports upon the state of the school shall be then read, and the board shall proceed to give the necessary directions respecting the same.

They shall examine all books and accounts relative to the relief of the paupers of the district in the school, and give all needful directions concerning the management and discipline of the school.

They shall make the necessary orders on the proper authorities of the several unions comprised in the said district, for providing such sums as may be lawfully required by the board on account of the district;

And they shall transact any such business applicable to their duties as may not fall within any of the above classes.

Art. 14.—No resolution agreed to or adopted by the board shall be rescinded or altered by them unless some manager shall have given to the board, at a meeting, notice of a motion to rescind or alter such resolution, which notice shall be forthwith entered on the minutes by the clerk. Provided always, that this regulation shall not extend to any resolution which immediately concerns the punishment of any child in the school, or to any resolution which the Commissioners may request the managers to re-consider or amend, or to any question of emergency.

Art. 15.—The managers may at any time appoint from themselves one or more committee or committees, consisting of not less than three nor more than five persons, which committee or committees shall have such powers and authorities as the said managers shall delegate to them.

CONTRACTS.

Art. 16.—All contracts to be entered into on behalf of the district relating to the management and relief of the children in the school, or for any other purpose connected therewith, shall be made and entered into by the managers.

Art. 17.—The managers shall require tenders to be made in some sealed paper for the supply of all provisions, fuel, clothing, furniture, or other goods or materials, the consumption or cost of which may be estimated, one month with another, to exceed ten pounds per month, and of all provisions, fuel, clothing, furniture, or other goods or materials, the cost of which may be reasonably estimated to exceed fifty pounds in a single sum, to be paid for by the managers, and shall purchase the same upon contracts to be entered into after the receipt of such tenders.

Art. 18.—Any work or repairs to be executed for the said district in any school belonging to the said district, or on the premises connected with the school, or any fixtures to be put up therein, which may respectively be reasonably estimated to exceed the cost of fifty pounds in one sum, shall be contracted for by the managers, on sealed tenders, in the manner prescribed in Articles 17 and 19.

Art. 19.—Notice of the nature and conditions of the contract to be entered into of the estimated amount of the articles required, of the last day on which the tenders will be received, and the day on which the tenders will be opened, shall be given in some newspaper circulating in the district, not less than ten days previous to the last day on which such tenders are to be received, and no tender shall be opened by the clerk, or any manager, or other person, prior to the day specified in such notice, or otherwise than at a meeting of the said managers.

Art. 20.—When any tender is accepted, the party making the tender shall, in pursuance of these regulations, enter into a contract, in writing, with the board of management, containing the terms, conditions, and stipulations mutually agreed upon, and whenever the board shall deem it advisable, the party contracting shall find one or more surety or sureties, who shall enter into a bond, in such penalty as the board shall think fit, conditioned for the due performance of the contract, or shall otherwise secure the same.

Art. 21—Provided always, that if, from the peculiar nature of any provisions, fuel, clothing, furniture, goods, materials, or fixtures to be supplied, or of any work or repairs to be executed, it shall appear to the managers desirable that a specific person or persons be employed to supply or execute the same, without requiring sealed tenders as herein-before directed, it shall be lawful for the managers, with the consent of the Commissioners first had and obtained, to enter into a contract with such person or persons, and to require such sureties and securities as are specified in Article 20.

Art. 22.—Every contract to be hereafter made by the managers shall contain a stipulation requiring the contractor to send in his bill or account of the sum due to him for goods or work, on or before some day to be named in the contract.

Art. 23.—The board shall fix some day or days, not being more than twenty-one days after the end of each quarter, for the attendance of contractors and tradesmen, or their authorised agents, and the clerk shall notify such day to every contractor or tradesmen to whom money may be due, or to his agent, or he shall, under the direction of the board, cause the same to be advertised in some newspaper.

ORDERS FOR CONTRIBUTIONS AND PAYMENTS.

Art. 24.—The managers shall from time to time make orders on the proper authorities of the several unions in the said district, for the payment to the managers of such sums as may be required by the managers for the contributions of each union to the common fund of the managers.

Art. 25.—Every such order shall be made according to the Form E. hereunto annexed, and shall be signed by the presiding chairman of the meeting, and two other managers present thereat, and shall be countersigned by the clerk.

Art. 26.—The managers shall pay every sum greater than three pounds by an order, which shall be drawn upon the treasurer of the district, and shall be signed by the presiding chairman and two other managers at a meeting of the board, and shall be countersigned by the clerk.

And with reference to the officers of the said board, we, the said Commissioners, do hereby order as follows, that is to say:

MODE OF APPOINTMENT.

Art. 27.—Every officer to be appointment by the said board, shall be appointed by a majority of the managers present at any meeting of the board, and voting upon such appointment, and every such appointment shall, as soon as the same shall have been made, be reported to the said Commissioners by the clerk.

Art. 28.—No appointment of an officer other than the first, to the office of clerk or treasurer, shall be made by the managers, unless notice that such appointment will be made shall have been given at one of the two ordinary meetings of the board next preceding the meeting at which the appointment shall be made, or unless an advertisement giving notice of such appointment shall have appeared in some public paper, by the direction of the managers, at least seven days before the day on which such appointment shall be made.

Art. 29.—The managers shall, within *forty days from their first meeting*, appoint a fit and proper person to be clerk to the board, and on the happening of any vacancy hereafter shall in like manner appoint another person to fill the said office.

Art. 30.—And the said managers shall, within the like period of *forty days from their first meeting*, and from time to time whenever the said office shall be vacant, appoint a fit person to be the treasurer of the said district.

SALARIES OF THE OFFICERS.

Art. 31.—The managers shall pay to the officers appointed by them, such salaries or remuneration as the Commissioners may from time to time direct or approve.

Provided that the managers, with the approval of the Commissioners, may pay to any officer or person employed by such managers a reasonable compensation on account of extraordinary services, or other unforeseen circumstances connected with the duties of such officer or person or the necessities of the district.

Art. 32.—The salary of every officer appointed by the said managers shall be payable up to the day on which he ceases to hold such office, and no longer.

Article 33.—An officer who may be suspended, and who may without the previous removal of such suspension be dismissed by the Commissioners, shall not be entitled to any salary from the date of such suspension. Provided that if any officer or assistant or servant be suspended from the performance of his duties because his services are not required, no salary shall be payable during the time that he shall be so suspended.

Art. 34.—The managers shall not pay to any officer bound to account, to be hereafter appointed, who may have been removed, or who may be under suspension from his office, any salary claimed by such officer until his accounts shall have been audited by the auditor.

Art. 35.—If no remuneration or salary be expressly assigned to the treasurer, the profit arising from the use of money from time to time left in his hands shall be deemed to be the payment of his services.

SECURITY.

Art. 36.—Every person appointed to the office of clerk or treasurer shall respectively give a bond with two sufficient surities, conditioned for the due and faithful performance of the duties of the office; and every such officer shall give immediate notice to the board of management of the death, insolvency, or bankruptcy of either of such sureties, and shall, when required by the managers, supply a fresh surety in the place of any such surety who may die, or become bankrupt or insolvent.

Art. 37.—Provided that the managers may, if they think fit, take the security of any society or company expressly authorized by statute to guarantee or secure the faithful discharge of the duties of such officers.

Art. 38.—Provided also, that the managers may, with the consent of the said Commissioners, dispense with such security in the case of any banking firm acting as treasurer, or in the case of a treasurer being a banker or partner of such firm.

SECURITY OF OFFICERS.

Art. 39.—The managers shall require every officer to supply forthwith a fresh surety, in place of any surety who may die, or become bankrupt, or insolvent, or be released from his obligation.

Art. 40.—The managers shall once in every year, that is to say, at the audit next after the twenty-fifth day of March, cause every person having the custody of bonds given by any officer of the district to produce such bonds to the auditor (when any such shall be) for his inspection, and the fact of such inspection, and any defects apparent in the said bonds, shall be reported by such auditor to the said managers.

CUSTODY OF BONDS.

Art. 41.—The managers shall provide for the safe custody of all bonds given in pursuance of these regulations, so always that no bond given by any person shall remain in the custody of such person himself.

CONTINUANCE IN OFFICE AND SUSPENSION OF OFFICERS—SUPPLY OF VACANCIES.

Art. 42.—Every officer appointed by the managers, shall continue to hold his office until he shall die, or resign, or be removed by the Commissioners, or be proved in a manner satisfactory to the Commissioners to be insane.

Art. 43.—Provided always, that every assistant or servant may be dismissed by the managers without the consent of the said Commissioners; but every such dismissal, and the grounds thereof, shall be reported to the said Commissioners.

Art. 44.—If any officer appointed to or holding any employment under the said managers, be at any time prevented by sickness or accident, or other sufficient reason, from the performance of his duties, the managers may appoint a fit person to act as his temporary substitute, and may pay him a reasonable compensation for his services, and every such appointment shall be reported to the said Commissioners as soon as the same shall have been made.

Art. 45.—The vice-chairman, or some manager to be appointed by the board of management, may perform any of the duties assigned to the clerk until any vacancy in the office shall have been filled, or until a substitute may be appointed in the case of the sickness, accident, or absence of the clerk.

Art. 46.—When any officer appointed by the managers may die, resign, or become legally disqualified to perform the duties of his office, the board shall, as soon as conveniently may be after such death, resignation, or disqualification, give notice thereof to the said Commissioners, and proceed to make a new appointment to the office so vacant in the manner prescribed by the above regulations.

Art. 47.—If any officer give notice of an intended resignation to take effect on a future day, the board may elect a successor to such officer, in conformity with the above regulations, at any time subsequent to such notice.

Art. 48.—In every case not otherwise provided for by this order, every officer shall perform his duties in person, and shall not entrust the same to a deputy, except with the special permission of the Commissioners on the application of the board.

DUTIES OF THE OFFICERS.

Art. 49.—And we do hereby define and specify the duties of the several officers appointed to or holding their offices under this order, and direct the execution thereof to be as follows :—

Duties of the Clerk to the Board.

Art. 50.—The following shall be the duties of the clerk to the board :—

No. 1.—To attend all meetings of the board, and to keep punctually minutes of the proceedings at every meeting, to enter the said minutes in a book, and to submit the same so entered in the said book to the presiding chairman at the succeeding meeting, to be authenticated by the signature of such chairman, as a true record of the proceedings of the board.

No. 2.—To keep, check, and examine all accounts, books of accounts, minutes, books, and other documents, as required of him by the regulations of the said Commissioners, or relating to the business of the board, and from time to time to produce all such books and documents, together with the necessary vouchers, and the bonds of any officers, with any certificates relating thereto which may be in his custody, to the auditor of the said district, at the place of audit, and at the time and in such manner as may be required by the regulations of the said Commissioners in force at the time.

No. 3.—To peruse and conduct the correspondence of the board according to their directions, and to preserve the same, as well as all Orders of the Commissioners, and letters received, together with copies of all letters sent, and all letters, books, papers, and documents relating to the board, or intrusted to him by the said board, and to make all necessary copies thereof.

No. 4.—To prepare all written contracts and agreements to be entered into by any parties with the board, and to see that the same are duly executed, and to prepare all bonds or other securities to be given by any of the officers of the district, and to see that the same are duly executed by such officers and their sureties.

No. 5.—To receive all requisitions of managers for extraordinary meetings, and to summon such meetings accordingly, and to make, sign, and send all notices required to be given to the managers, by this or any other Order of the said Commissioners.

No. 6.—To countersign all orders legally made by the said board for the payment of money, and all orders legally drawn by the board upon the treasurer of the said district.

No. 7.—To ascertain, before every ordinary meeting of the board, the balance due to or from the district, in account with the treasurer, and to enter the same in the minute book.

No. 8.—To communicate to the several officers and persons engaged in the administration of relief within the district, all orders and directions of the said Commissioners, or of the said board, and, so far as may be, to give the instructions requisite for the prompt and correct execution of all such orders and directions, and to report on any neglect or failure therein which may come to his knowledge.

No. 9.—To conduct all applications by or on behalf of the said board, to any magistrate, justice or justices, at their special, petty, or general sessions, and, if he be an attorney or solicitor, to perform and execute all legal business connected with the board or in which the board shall be engaged, except prosecutions at the assizes, actions at law, suits in equity, or parliamentary business, without charge for any thing beyond disbursements.

No. 10.—To prepare and punctually transmit to the Poor Law inspector having the superintendence of the district such statement as the said inspector shall from time to time require respecting the state of school or schools in the said district.

No. 11.—To prepare and transmit all reports, answers or returns as to any question or matter connected with or relating to the administration of the laws for the relief of the children in the school or schools of the district, or to any other business of such school or schools which the said Commissioners or any Poor Law inspector may lawfully require from him.

No. 12.—To observe and execute all lawful Orders and directions of the Board applicable to his office.

Duties of the Treasurer.

Art. 51.—The following shall be the duties of the treasurer of the Board.

No. 1.—To receive all monies tendered to be paid to the managers, and to place the same to their credit.

No. 2.—To pay, out of monies for the time being in his hands belonging to the said board, all orders for money which shall be drawn upon him in conformity with Art. 26, when the same shall be presented at the house or usual place of business of the treasurer, and within the usual hours of business.

No. 3.—To keep an account, under the proper dates, of all monies received and paid by him as such treasurer, to balance the same at Lady Day and Michaelmas in every year, and to render an account of such monies to the said board, when required by them to do so.

No. 4.—Whenever there are not funds belonging to the board in his hands as treasurer of the district to report in writing the fact of such deficiency to the said Commissioners.

No. 5.—To submit a proper account, together with the bonds of any officers which may be in his custody, to the auditor, at the place of audit, and at the time and in such manner as may be required by the regulations of the said Commissioners.

No. 6.—To receive the monies payable to him as treasurer of the board, under any Act of Parliament or other authority of law.

Art. 52.—Provided that the regulations in Articles 36 and 51, shall not be applicable to cases in which the governor and company of the Bank of England may act as treasurer of the board or bankers to the managers.

RECEIPT AND PAYMENT OF MONEY BY OFFICERS.

Art. 53.—No officer appointed to or holding any office under the board, shall, directly or indirectly, receive or bargain to receive any gratuity, per-centage, or allowance of any kind with reference to any contract with the said board, or in respect of any payment made or to be made for goods supplied or work executed according to the order of such managers or on their behalf, or in respect of any duty done, or business transacted by such officer in the discharge of his office.

Art. 54.—No clerk shall, directly or indirectly cause to be paid to himself, or shall pay away on his own account or for his own benefit, any check drawn by the Board, and made payable to any person other than himself.

Art. 55.—Every clerk receiving any cheque or money from the board on account of any other party, shall transmit the same within fourteen days to the proper persons, and shall produce the receipt or acknowledgment for the same at the next ordinary meeting after the same has come to his hands.

Art. 56.—Every officer of the managers who may receive money on behalf of the board, shall forthwith pay the same into the hands of the treasurer of the board, to the credit of the board, notwithstanding that any salary or balance may be due from the board to such officer.

EXPLANATION OF TERMS.

Art. 57. — Whenever the word "Commissioners" is used in this Order, it shall be taken to mean the commissioners for administering the laws for relief of the poor in England.

Art. 58.—Whenever in describing any person or party, matter or thing, the word importing the singular number or the masculine gender only is used in this order, the same shall be taken to include and shall be applied to several persons or parties as well as one person or party, and females as well as males, and several matters or things as well as one matter or thing, respectively, unless there be something in the subject or context repugnant to such construction.

Art. 59.—Whenever in this Order any Article is referred to by its number, the Article of this Order bearing that number shall be taken to be signified thereby.

FORMS REFERRED TO IN THE ABOVE ORDER.

FORM A.

Requisition for an Extraordinary Meeting of the Board.

To the Clerk to the Board of Management of the Central London School District.

WE, the undersigned, being two of the Managers of the Central London School District, do hereby require an Extraordinary Meeting of the Board of the said District to be summoned, to be holden at on the day of 18 , at o'clock in the forenoon, to take into consideration [*set out the motion.*]

______ } Managers.
______

FORM B.

Notice of Change of Time, or Place of Meeting.

To *A. B.* ( ) Manager of the Central London School District.

SIR,—You are hereby informed, that the next Ordinary Meeting of the Board of Management of the Central London

School District will take place at on the day of 18 , at o'clock in the forenoon, for the transaction of business; and that Meetings of the said Board will henceforth be held at the same place, on in every [*as the case may be,*] at the same hour of in the noon.

(*Signed*)____________________
Clerk to the said Board.

FORM C.

Notice of an adjourned Meeting of the Board.

To *A.B.* ( ) Manager of the Central London School District.

SIR,—This is to give you notice, that an Adjourned Meeting of the Board of Management of the Central London School District will be held at on the day of 18 , to take into consideration [*set out the motion*], which meeting you are hereby requested to attend.

(*Signed*)____________________
Clerk to the said Board.

FORM D.

Notice of an Extraordinary Meeting of the Board.

To *A.B.* ( ) Manager of the London School District.

SIR,—I am directed by *C.D.* and *E.F.* two of the Managers of the Central London School District, to summon an Extraordinary Meeting of the Board of the said District, at on the day of 18 , at o'clock in the noon, to take into consideration [*set out the motion*], which meeting you are hereby requested to attend.

(*Signed*)____________________
Clerk to the aid Board.

FORM E.

To the Guardians of the Poor of the Union, in the Central London School District.

You are hereby ordered and directed to pay to *F.G.* of on behalf of the Board of Management of the Central London School District, on the day of at the sum of Pounds Shillings and Pence, as the Contribution of the said Union or Parish to the common fund of the Board of Management, and such other expenses as are chargeable by the said Board on the said Union or Parish, and to take the Receipt of the said F.G. for the said sum of *£. s. d.*

Given under our Hands, at a Meeting of the Board of Management of the Central London School District, held on the day of 18 .

(*Signed*) X.Y. *Presiding Chairman.*
W.X. } *Managers.*
U.V. }

____
(Counter Signature of the Clerk to the said Board.)

Given under our Hand and Seal of Office, this Fourth day of April, in the year One thousand eight hundred and forty-nine.

(L.S.)

M. T. BAINES, *President.*

GEO. NICHOLLS, *Secretary.*

3. ORDER DIRECTING THE APPOINTMENT AND PRESCRIBING THE DUTIES OF THE SEVERAL OFFICERS OF THE SCHOOL OF THE CENTRAL LONDON SCHOOL DISTRICT.

To the Board of Management of the Central London District School;—

To the Churchwardens and Overseers of the Poor of the several Parishes and Places comprised in the said District;—

To the Clerk or Clerks to the Justice or Justices of the Petty Sessions held for the Division or Divisions in which the said District and Parishes respectively are situate;—

And to all others whom it may concern.

Whereas, by an Order under their Seal bearing date the fourth day of April last, the Commissioners for administering the laws for relief of the poor in England, under the powers given in and by the several statutes in that behalf, did make certain rules and regulations to be observed by the board of management of the said district; and did provide for the appointment of certain officers to carry into effect the orders and directions of the said board, and to assist in the administration of the relief of the poor in the school of the said district.

And whereas the board of management of the said district school have provided a building for the reception of the poor children belonging to such district, and it is desirable that certain other officers should be appointed by the said board of management.

Now, therefore, We, the Commissioners for administering the laws for relief of the poor in England, in pursuance of the authorities vested in Us by an Act of Parliament passed in the fifth year of the reign of His late Majesty King William the Fourth, intituled "*An Act for the Amendment and better Administration of the Laws relating to the Poor in England and Wales,*" and by another Act passed in the eighth year of the reign of Her present Majesty Queen Victoria, intituled "*An Act for the further Amendment of the Laws relating to the Poor in England,*" do hereby order and direct as follows; that is to say:—

Art. 1.—The managers shall, within forty days from the date hereof, and from time to time hereafter as vacancies shall occur, appoint so many fit persons to hold the following offices in the said school, and to perform the duties respectively assigned to them as shall appear to them to be requisite ; namely.

Superintendent,
Matron,
Medical officer,
Schoolmaster,
Schoolmistress,
Nurse,
Porter,

with such assistants as the managers shall from time to time deem necessary for the efficient performance of the duties of any of the said offices and the said Commissioners shall hereafter assent to.

Art. 2.—The said managers shall also appoint, from time to time, such servants as they shall find requisite.

Art. 3.—No person shall be appointed to any office under this Order who does not agree to give one month's notice previous to resigning the office, or to forfeit one month's amount of salary, to be deducted as liquidated damages from the amount of salary due at the time of such resignation.

Art. 4.—The officers so appointed, as well as all persons temporarily discharging the duties of such offices, shall respectively perform duties herein set forth, and such other duties as may from time to time be required of them by the rules and regulations of the said Commissioners, with all such other duties conformable with the nature of their respective offices as the said managers may lawfully require them to perform.

Art. 5.—All the provisions contained in the said herein-before recited Order which relate to the mode of appointment of officers, their salaries, their continuance in office, and the supply of vacancies shall apply tô the officers, assistants, and servants to be appointed under this Order.

Art. 6.—If any superintendent and matron be husband and wife, and one of them be dismissed by Order of the Commissioners, or otherwise vacate his or her office, or die, the other, or survivor, shall, at the expiration of the then current quarter, cease to hold his or her office of superintendent or matron, as the case may be.

Art. 7.—No officer who may be dismissed by any Order of the Commissioners shall remain in the school or enter therein for the purpose of interfering in the management thereof, unless the Commissioners have consented to his subsequent appointment to an office in such school, or to his temporary employment therein.

Art. 8.—The managers may at their discretion suspend from the dischafge of his duties any officer appointed under this Order, and shall, in case of every such suspension, forthwith report the same, together with the cause thereof, to the Commissioners ; and if the Commissioners remove the suspension of such officer by the managers, he shall forthwith resume the performance of his duties.

Art. 9.—If any officer or assistant appointed to or holding any office or employment under this Order be at any time prevented by sickness or accident, or other sufficient reason, from the performance of his duties, the managers may appoint a fit person to act as a temporary substitute, and may pay him a reasonable compensation for his services: and every such appointment shall be reported to the Commissioners as soon as the same shall have been made.

Art. 10.—When any officer may die, resign, or become legally disqualified to perform the duties of his office, the managers shall, as soon as conveniently may be after such death, resignation, or disqualification, give notice thereof to the Commissioners, and proceed to make a new appointment to the office so vacant in the manner prescribed by the regulations above referred to.

Art. 11.—If any officer give notice of an intended resignation to take effect on a future day, the managers may elect a successor to such officer in conformity with the said regulations, at any time subsequent to such notice.

Art. 12.—In the case of any medical officer who may hold his office for a specified term, the managers may provide for the continuance of such officer, or appoint his successor, within the three calendar months next before the expiration of such term.

Art. 13.—Every officer and assistant to be appointed under this Order whom the managers shall require to do so, shall give security for the due performance of the duties of his office, in like manner and subject to the like provisions as are contained in the said recited Order in regard to the security of the clerk and treasurer, and every superintendent shall be required to give such security.

Duties of the Superintendent.

Art. 14.—The following shall be the duties of the superintendent :—

No. 1.—To admit the pauper children into the school, and to cause every child, upon admission, to be examined by the medical officer.

No. 2.—To cause the boys above seven years old upon admission to be cleansed and properly clothed, and to be placed in the proper wards.

No. 3.—To enforce industry, order, punctuality, and cleanliness, and the observance of all regulations for the government of the school by the children, and by the several officers, assistants, and servants therein.

No. 4.—To read prayers to the children before breakfast and after supper every day, or cause prayers to be read.

No. 5.—To visit the sleeping wards of the children once at least in the forenoon of every day, and the school-rooms during each of the intervals between the hours set apart for the instruction of the children therein, and see that such wards and the school-rooms have been properly cleansed and aired, and are in a satisfactory state in all respects.

No. 6.—To see that the meals of the children are duly provided, dressed, and served, and to superintend the distribution of the food.

No. 7.—To superintend the industrial training and employment of the boys under such assistant officers as may be appointed for that purpose with attention and punctuality.

No. 8.—To say, or cause to be said, grace before and after meals.

No. 9.—To visit all the wards of the children before nine o'clock every night, and see that all the children are in bed, and that all fires and lights in the wards are extinguished, except so far as may be necessary for the sick.

No. 10.—To receive from the porter the keys of the school at nine o'clock every night, and to deliver them to him again at six o'clock every morning, or at such hours as shall from time to time be fixed by the managers,

No. 11.—To see that the children are properly clothed, and that their clothes are kept in proper repair.

No. 12.—To send for the medical officer in case any child is taken ill, and to take care that all sick children are duly attended by the medical officer, and are provided with such medicines and attendance, diet and other necessaries, as the medical officer or the managers direct, and in the case of dangerous sickness to send for the chaplain, and any relative or friend of the sick child, resident within a reasonable distance, whom the child may desire to see.

No. 13.—To take care that no child at the approach of death shall be left unattended either during the day or the night.

No. 14.—To give immediate information of the death of any child in the school to the medical officer, if not present at the death, and to the nearest relations of the deceased who may be known to him, and who may reside within a reasonable distance, and to the guardians of the union from which the child shall have been admitted; and if the body be not removed within a reasonable time, to provide for the interment thereof.

No. 15.—When requisite, to cause the death of every child dying in the school to be duly registered by the proper Registrar of Births and Deaths within five days after the day of such death; and also to enter such death in a register kept according to Form (A.) hereunto annexed.

No. 16.—To keep such portion of the Medical Relief Book prescribed in this Order as is assigned to him in the Form marked (B.,) and to keep all books or accounts which he may hereafter, by any order of the said Commissioners, be directed to keep, to allow the same to be constantly open to the inspection of any of the managers, and to submit the same to the managers at their ordinary meetings.

No. 17.—To give immediate notice to the clerk to the board of managers whenever the number of children should exceed the maximum number prescribed by the said Commissioners.

No. 18.—To submit to the managers, at every ordinary meeting, an estimate of such provisions and other articles as are required for the use of the school, and to receive and execute the directions of the managers thereupon.

No. 19.—To receive all provisions and other articles purchased or procured for the use of the school, and before placing them in store to examine and compare them with the bills of parcels or invoices severally relating thereto; and after having proved the accuracy of such bills or invoices, to authenticate the same with his signature, and submit them to the managers at their next ordinary meeting.

No. 20.—To receive and take charge of all provisions, clothing, linen, and other articles belonging to the school, or confided to his care by the managers, and issue the same to the matron or other officers, or to the servants, as may be required.

No. 21.—To report to the managers from time to time the names of such children as are fit to be put out to service, or other employment, and to take the necessary steps for carrying into effect the directions of the managers thereon.

No. 22.—To take care that every ward, room, larder, kitchen, and other office of the school, and all the utensils and furniture thereof, be kept clean and in good order; and as often as any defect in the same, or in the state of the school, shall occur, to report the same in writing to the managers at their next ordinary meeting.

No. 23.—To submit to the managers, at every ordinary meeting, a report of the number of the inmates in the school according to any form which may from time to time be framed by them.

No. 24.—To bring before the visiting committee or the managers any child desirous of making a complaint or application to them.

No. 25.—To keep a book, in which he shall enter all his written reports to the managers, and to lay the same before the managers at every ordinary meeting.

No. 26.—To inform the visiting committee and the managers of the state of the school in every department, and to report in writing to the managers any negligence or other misconduct on the part of any of the subordinate officers or servants of the establishment; and generally to observe and fulfil all lawful orders and directions of the managers suitable to his office.

Art. 15.—The superintendent shall not, except in case of necessity, purchase or procure any articles for the use of the school, nor order any alterations or repairs of any part of the premises, or of the furniture or other articles belonging thereto, without the authority of the managers, nor apply any articles belonging to the managers to purposes other than those authorised or approved of by them.

Duties of the Matron.

Art. 16.—The following shall be the duties of the matron:—

No. 1.—In the absence of the master, or during his inability to act, to be his substitute in the admission of children into the school, and to cause every child upon such admission to be examined by the medical officer.

No. 2.—To cause the children under the age of seven years, and the female children above that age, upon their admission, to be cleansed and properly clothed, and to be placed in their proper wards.

No. 3.—To visit the sleeping wards of the children before eleven o'clock of the forenoon every day, and to see that such wards have been all duly cleansed and are properly ventilated.

No. 4. To visit all the wards of the children every night before nine o'clock, and to ascertain that all the children in such wards are in bed, and all fires and lights not necessary for the sick therein extinguished.

No. 5.—To see that the children are clean and decent in their dress and persons.

No. 6.—To superintend and give the necessary directions for making and mending the clothing supplied to the children, and to take care that all such clothing be properly numbered and marked on the inside with the name of the Central London School District.

No. 7.—To see that every child in the school has clean linen and stockings at least once a week, and that all the beds and bedding be kept in a clean and wholesome state.

No. 8.—To take charge of the linen and stockings for the use of the children, and the other linen in use in the school, and to apply the same to such purposes as shall be authorised or approved of by the managers, and to no other.

No. 9.—To superintend and give the necessary directions concerning the washing, drying, and getting up of the linen, stockings, and blankets, and to see that the same be not dried in the sleeping wards, or in the sick wards, or in any ward inhabited by any of the children.

No. 10.—To superintend the industrial training and employment of the girls in household work, and other useful occupations, with attention and punctuality.

No. 11.—To assist the superintendent in the general management of the school, and especially in—

Enforcing the observance of good order, cleanliness, punctuality, industry, and decency of demeanour among the children;

Cleansing and ventilating the sleeping wards, the dining-hall, and all other parts of the premises;

Placing in store and taking charge of the

provisions, clothing, linen, and other articles belonging to the managers.

No. 12.—To report to the superintendent any negligence or other misconduct on the part of any of the female officers, or servants of the establishment.

No. 13.—And generally to observe and fulfil all lawful orders and directions of the managers suitable to her office.

Duties of the Medical Officer.

Art. 17.—The following shall be the duties of the medical officer :—

No. 1.—To attend duly and punctually upon the children in the school requiring medical attendance.

No. 2.—To examine the state of the children on their admission into the school, and make a record of the same, and to give the requisite directions to the superintendent for their classification and treatment.

No. 3.—To give directions from time to time as to the diet, classification, and treatment of the sick children, and to make suggestions with reference to the children in general.

No. 4.—To vaccinate such of the children as may require vaccination.

No. 5.—To report in writing to the managers any defect in the diet, drainage, ventilation, warmth, or other arrangements of the school, or any excess in the number of the inmates, whether in the school generally, or in any particular ward, which he may deem to be detrimental to the health of the inmates.

No. 6.—To report in writing to the managers any defect which he may observe in the arrangements of the infirmary, and in the performance of their duties by the nurses of the sick.

No. 7.—To make a return to the managers, at each ordinary meeting, in a book prepared according to the Form (B.) hereunto annexed, and to insert therein the particulars required by such form to be inserted by the medical officer, and to enter in such return the death of every child who shall die in the school, together with the apparent cause thereof.

No. 8.—To enter in the commencement of such book, according to the Form marked (C.) hereunto annexed, the proper dietary for the sick in the school in so many different scales as he shall deem expedient.

No. 9.—To give to the managers, when required, any reasonable information respecting the case of any pauper who is or has been under his care; to make any such written report relative to any sickness prevalent among the children under his care, as the managers or Commissioners may require of him; and to attend any meeting of the district board when requested by them to do so.

No. 10.—To give a certificate respecting children whom it is proposed to apprentice.

No. 11.—In keeping the book prescribed by this Order, to employ, so far as is practicable, the terms used or recommended in the regulations and statistical nosology issued by theRegistrar-General, and also to show when the visit or attendance made or given was made or given by any person employed by himself.

Duties of the Schoolmaster and Schoolmistress.

Art. 18.—The following shall be the duties of the schoolmaster and schoolmistress until further orders and school regulations shall be issued :—

No. 1.—To instruct the boys and girls for three hours, at least, every day, in reading, writing, arithmetic, and the principles of the Christian religion, to give them such other instruction as may fit them for service, and to train them to habits of usefulness, industry, and virtue.

No. 2.—To regulate the discipline and arrangements of the school, and the industrial and moral training of the children, subject to the directions of the managers.

No. 3.—To accompany the children when they quit the school for exercise, or for attendance at public worship, according to such directions as the managers may give.

No. 4.—To see that the children are clean in their persons, to keep them orderly and decorous in their conduct, and to assist the superintendent and matron respectively in maintaining due subordination, discipline, and propriety of behaviour in all parts of the establishment at all times.

Duties of a Nurse.

Art. 19.—The following shall be the duties of a nurse for the school :—

No. 1.—To attend upon the sick in the sick wards, and to administer to them all medicines and medical applications, according to the directions of the medical officer.

No. 2.—To inform the medical officer of any defect which may be observed in the arrangements of the sick ward.

No. 3.—To take care that a light is kept at night in the sick ward.

Duties of the Porter.

Art. 20.—The following shall be the duties of the porter :—

No. 1.—To keep the gate, and to prevent any person not being an officer of the school, or of the managers, a Poor Law Inspector, or any other person authorised by law or by the Commissioners or managers, from entering into or going out of the house without the leave of the superintendent or matron.

No. 2.—To keep a book in which he shall enter the name and business of every officer or other person who shall go into the school, and the name of every officer or other person who shall go out thereof, together with the time when such officer or other person shall go in or out.

No. 3.—To receive all children who are presented for admission, and if the superintendent and matron be both absent, to place them in the ward appropriated as a receiving ward until the superintendent or matron return.

No. 4.—To examine all parcels and goods before they are received into the school, and prevent the admission of any spirituous or fermented liquors, or other articles contrary to any of the regulations issued by the Commissioners, or otherwise contrary to law.

No. 5.—To require any person entering the school whom he may suspect of having possession of any spirits or prohibited articles, to satisfy him to the contrary before he permit such person to be admitted, and in the case of any female to cause the matron to be called for the purpose of searching her, if necessary.

No. 6.—To examine all parcels taken by any child or other person out of the premises, and to prevent the unauthorized removal of any article.

No. 7.—To lock all the outer doors, and take the keys to the superintendent at nine o'clock every night, and to receive them back from him every morning at six o'clock, or at such hours as shall from time to time be fixed by the managers.

No. 8.—To assist the superintendent and matron in preserving order, and a constant observance of the regulations.

No. 9.—To inform the superintendent of all things likely to be injurious to the security and order of the school, and to obey all lawful directions of the superintendent or matron, and of the managers, suitable to his office.

Explanation of Terms.

Art. 21. — Whenever the word "Commissioners" is used in this Order, it shall be taken to mean the Commissioners for administering the Laws for Relief of the Poor in England.

Art. 22.—Whenever in describing any person or party, matter or thing, the word importing the singular number or the masculine gender only is used in this Order, the same shall be taken to include and shall be applied to several persons or parties as well as one person or party, and females as well as males, and several matters or things as well as one matter or thing, respectively, unless there be something in the subject or context repugnant to such construction.

FORM (A.)

REGISTER OF DEATHS.

CENTRAL LONDON DISTRICT SCHOOL.

Date of Death.	Name.	Age.	From what Union Admitted.

FORM (B.)

MEDICAL RELIEF BOOK.

Central London District School.

(A.) To be filled up by the Medical Officer.

Initials of Medical Officer in attendance on every Case.	Name of the Sick Child.	When admitted to Sick Ward.	When discharged.	Nature of Disease.	Days when attended.							Males. The No.* of the Dietary on which placed.							Females. The No.* of the Dietary on which placed.							Extras.			State or Termination of the Case, and in the event of Death, the apparent Cause thereof.
					S.	M.	T.	W.	Th.	F.	Sat.	S.	M.	T.	W.	Th.	F.	Sat.	S.	M.	T.	W.	Th.	F.	Sat.	What ordered.	When ordered.	When discontinued.	
					Total No. each Day																								Total quantity consumed

(B) To be filled up by the Superintendent with the Articles actually given.

Quantity of Provisions consumed.												Extras.									Remarks.
Bread.	Meat.	Bacon.	Cheese.	Rice.	Oatmeal.	Milk.						Ale.	Porter.	Wine.	Brandy.	Gin.					
lbs.	lbs.	lbs.	lbs.	lbs.	lbs.	pts.						pts.	pts.	pts.	pts.	pts.					

* The Dietaries for the Sick are to be numbered thus:—No. 1. House Diet. No. 2. Full Diet. No. 3. Low Diet. No. 4. Fever Diet.

As regards the sick Children on Diet No. 1. (House Diet) the extras only should be entered in this Book.

The number on each description of the Dietaries according to the several Sexes is to be carried by the Superintendent, at the close of each week, to a Summary at the end of the book, to be prepared in the following form:—

WEEKLY SUMMARY.

No. of the Dietary.	Description of Classes in the Diet Table.	Number of Patients each Day. S.	M.	T.	W.	Th.	F.	Sat.	Collective Number of Days.
1	House Diet.—Males								
1	House Diet.—Females								
2	Full Diet.—Males								
2	Full Diet.—Females								
3	Low Diet.—Males								
3	Low Diet.—Females								
4	Fever Diet.—Males								
4	Fever Diet.—Females								
	Total Number of sick								

FORM (C.)

* DIETARY FOR SICK CHILDREN.

No. 1.	House Diet, being the ordinary diet for the Children.									
No. 2.		Breakfast.		Dinner.					Supper.	
2	Full Diet . . .									
		ounces	pints	ounces	pints.	ounces.	ounces.	pints.	ounces.	pints.
2	Males . . .									
2	Females . . .									
		Breakfast.		Dinner.					Supper.	
3	Low Diet . . .									
		ounces.	pints.	ounces.	pints.	ounces.	ounces.	pints.	ounces.	pints.
3	Males . . .									
3	Females . . .									
		Breakfast.		Dinner.					Supper.	
4	Fever Diet . .									
		ounces.	pints.	ounces.	pints.	ounces.	ounces.	pints.	ounces.	pints.
4	Males . . .									
4	Females . . .									

N.B.—Sugar, Arrow Root, Sago, Butter, Milk, Wine, Spirits, Porter, and Beer, are in all cases to be treated as extras, to be expressly ordered when required, and the quantity is to be then specified in the proper column of this book.

* If thought proper by the Medical Officer any additional number of dietaries may be introduced, and numbered consecutively.

Given under our Hand and Seal of Office, this Twelfth day of June, in the year One thousand eight hundred and forty-nine.

(L.S.)

M. T. BAINES,
President.

GEO. NICHOLLS,
Secretary.

London: Printed by Order of the Poor Law Board, by BLACKBURN & BURT, 90½, Holborn Hill, and Published by CHARLES KNIGHT, 90, Fleet Street.

AN

OFFICIAL CIRCULAR

OF PUBLIC DOCUMENTS AND INFORMATION:

DIRECTED BY THE POOR LAW BOARD TO BE PRINTED, CHIEFLY FOR THE USE OF THE BOARDS OF GUARDIANS AND THEIR OFFICERS.

Nos. 29 & 30.] SEPTEMBER AND OCTOBER, 1849. [N.S.

CONTENTS.

I.—STATUTES OF 12 & 13 VIC., RELATING TO THE RELIEF OF THE POOR.

1. CIRCULAR LETTER TO BOARDS OF GUARDIANS ON THE ACT 12 & 13 VIC. C. 103.

Poor Law Board, Somerset House,
20th Sept., 1849.

Sir,—The Poor Law Board desire to direct the attention of the guardians to the several provisions which have been enacted in the last session of parliament regarding the relief of the poor. They are comprised in the following statutes, viz., 12 & 13 Vic. cc. 8, 13, 14, 45, 61, 64, 65, 103, and 111.

In the present communication the Board will confine themselves to the most important of these statutes, namely, the 12 & 13 Vic. c. 103, which has a general operation in all unions, and in many parishes, and requires the careful perusal of the guardians.

The first sec. of this Act continues for a limited period the provisions of the statute of last year, (11 & 12 Vic. c. 110,) which, in a union formed under the Poor Law Amendment Act, made the expenses incurred in the relief of vagrants, and of poor persons rendered irremovable by the 9 & 10 Vic. c. 66, a charge on the common fund of such union. The guardians will remember that those provisions were in force for one year only, and would have ceased on the 30th instant. The Legislature has now, however, continued their operation until the 30th of September, 1850, and until the end of the then next session of parliament.

The Board refer to their Circular Letter of the 29th of September last, explaining the provisions of the statute 11 & 12 Vic. c. 110, and their Circular Letter of the 5th of March last, which communicated the result of the important judgment of the Court of Queen's Bench in the case of Reg. *v.* Christchurch, as bearing directly upon the duties of the guardians in carrying the present Act into execution. As the term "foundlings," which is used in the first sec. of the 11 & 12 Vic. c. 110, has not any legal signification, and in its popular signification is not of general application, the guardians have occasionally found a difficulty in determining how to charge the relief of deserted children. It is now declared (by sec. 2 of the present Act) that a destitute child, under the age of twelve years, deserted by its parents or surviving parent, and not in the care or custody of some relative, guardian, or friend, and whose settlement is not known, shall be deemed to be a *destitute foundling* within the meaning of the 11 & 12 Vic. c. 110, and, consequently, the relief of any such child will be a common charge.

The guardians are aware that several statutes contain provisions which contemplate the chargeability of poor persons to some parish. It was considered that these statutes did not apply to paupers who were chargeable to the common fund. This defect is remedied by sec. 3 of the present Act, and certain statutes, namely, the Vagrant Act, (5 Geo. 4, c. 83,) the statutes for the removal of Scotch and Irish poor, (8 & 9 Vic. c. 117; 10 & 11 Vic. c. 33,) those for the removal of lunatics to asylums, (8 & 9 Vic. c. 126, and 9 & 10 Vic. c. 84,) as well as the provisions in the Poor Law Removal Act, (9 & 10 Vic. c. 66, sec. 6,) prohibiting improper removals, are made applicable to poor persons chargeable to the common fund.

Considerable doubt has been felt, since the decision of the Court of Queen's Bench in Reg. *v.* Salford, 17 L. J. R. (N.S.) M. C. 170, as to whether the removal of a pauper to a lunatic asylum or to the union workhouse, when such asylum or workhouse was situated in a different parish from that in which he had resided, was to be deemed an interruption of his residence. It is now enacted in sec. 4, that such a removal shall not be deemed to be an interruption of the residence; but that the time spent in the asylum or workhouse shall not be computed as part of the term of residence requisite to create irremovability. Moreover, the circumstance of a pauper being in receipt of relief at the charge of the common fund is to have the same effect upon the period of residence as if he were in receipt of relief at the cost of the parish, so that the time during which there has been the receipt of relief is in both cases to be excluded in computation of the period of five years.

In regard to lunatic paupers, sec. 5 provides that the costs incurred since the 25th of March last, or hereafter to be incurred, in and about the obtaining an order of justices for the removal and maintenance of a lunatic pauper removed to an asylum, and who, if not a lunatic, would have been exempt from removal under the 9 & 10 Vic. c. 66, shall, until the expiration of the time mentioned in sec. 1 of the present Act, be borne by the common fund of the union in which the pauper was resident when removed to the asylum, though the order for the payment thereof may have been made upon the overseers of the parish of the residence or of the settlement, or on the treasurer or guardians of the union in which either parish shall be comprised.

Such are the provisions which relate to the union chargeability of paupers.

The 6th sec. disqualifies persons from being appointed overseers of a parish, who, at the time of the proposed appointment, are engaged or concerned in any contract for the supply of goods, materials, or provisions for the workhouse, or for the relief of the poor in such parish, or in the union comprising it. Any act done by such a person as overseer, is not, however, if otherwise legal, to be deemed invalid by reason only of such personal disqualification.

The 7th sec. is of much practical importance to boards of guardians, who have hitherto experienced difficulties in enforcing their orders for contributions. It has been generally considered that no proceedings could be taken with effect against any one overseer for non-payment of the contribution due from his parish, unless a copy of the order had been served upon each of his colleagues. This sec. enacts that the guardians may enforce the order against the overseer upon whom a copy has been served, as fully and effectually as if a copy had been served upon every one of the overseers.

Secs. 8, 9, and 11, relate to auditors. By sec. 8, the Poor Law Board may appoint a temporary auditor when there is a vacancy in the office, or when the ordinary auditor is unable to act. By sec. 9, a limitation of nine months is fixed, within which the auditor is to proceed to recover the amount of any disallowance or surcharge. By sec. 11, he is enabled, with the consent of the Poor Law Board, to obtain reimbursement of the costs which he may incur in proceedings taken by him to enforce the attendance of any officer, or the production of any account or voucher, at his audit.

The 10th sec. empowers justices to order the payment of all proper and reasonable costs incurred in enforcing before them the provisions of the Poor Law Amendment Act (4 & 5 Wm. 4, c. 76) or of any subsequent statute incorporated with it.

Secs. 12 and 13 have reference to the orders of the Poor Law Commissioners and the Poor Law Board. By sec. 12, it is provided, that if any order of the Poor Law Commissioners or the Poor Law Board has been or shall hereafter be acted upon, within the period of fourteen days after it has been sent, the proceeding shall not be invalid, as it would probably have been under the 4 & 5 Wm. 4, c. 76, sec. 20, which provided that any such order should not be in force until the expiration of fourteen days after copies of the order had been sent. By sec. 13, a limitation of twelve months from the passing of the Act, as respects any order heretofore made, and of twelve months from the sending thereof, as respects any future order, is imposed for the issuing of a writ of *Certiorari* to remove such order into the Court of Queen's Bench.

The 14th sec. contains a provision which will be found, under certain circumstances, useful to boards of guardians. It enables the guardians of a union or parish, with the consent of the Poor Law Board, when the workhouse of another union or parish is over-crowded—or when any epidemic or contagious disease prevails or is apprehended—or when assistance is required in the emigration of poor persons—to receive, lodge, and maintain in the workhouse of the first-mentioned union or parish, any poor person belonging to the other union or parish. Every such poor person is to be treated in like manner, and to be subject to the same regulations and liabilities as the other inmates. But the abiding of the poor person in such workhouse is to be attended with the same legal consequences as if the workhouse had been situated within the union or parish from which such poor person may have been sent.

By sec. 15, a difficulty which has sometimes arisen in the criminal prosecution of collectors of the poor-rates, appointed by guardians for a parish or township within the union, is removed. The technical description of the officer in an indictment for embezzling or purloining the monies received by him is now settled by the statute, and henceforth there need be no failure of justice from any mistake in this respect.

By sec. 16, additional powers are given to boards of guardians to obtain reimbursement of the cost of the relief which they may give to paupers, where it may be found that such paupers are in possession of money which they ought to have applied in their own maintenance. Thus it is enacted, that where any pauper shall have in his possession or belonging to him any money or valuable security for money, (which term is generally applied to a bank note, or bill of exchange or promissory note,) the guardians may reimburse themselves the cost of the relief advanced during the twelve months previous, by taking and appropriating such money, or recovering it as a debt; while, in the event of the death of any pauper having in his possession, or belonging to him, any money or property, the guardians may in like manner reimburse themselves the expenses incurred by them in the burial, and also in the maintenance of the pauper, at any time during the twelve months previous to his decease.

The guardians will observe that the first part of the sec. is confined to *money and valuable securities for money;* while the latter is more extensive, and applies to *money and property.* It will be seen that the clause is permissive only, and, consequently, it will in all cases be discretionary with the guardians as to whether they shall act upon it or not.

The Board think that the guardians will seldom find it advisable to pursue property not in the actual possession of the pauper, or within his immediate control. The amount of the relief which can be recovered will, for the most part, be too small to render it worth their while to engage in litigation to recover the property which may be alleged to belong to a pauper; but where they deem it proper to do so, they will do well to apply in the first instance to the Board, as they are advised that the 59th sec. of the 7 & 8 Vic. c. 101, would extend to such proceedings on the part of the guardians.

The guardians are enabled, by sec. 17, to pay the cost of the burial of any poor person dying out of the union, who, at the time of his death, was in the receipt of relief from them; and also to recover the cost of the burial of any poor person, in like manner as the cost of relief, if given to such poor person when living, would have been recoverable.

Sec. 18 enables the guardians or other similar officers (whatever may be their correct title) of any parish governed by a local Act, to obtain orders of the Poor Law Board for the purchase, building, or enlargement of a workhouse, without previously obtaining the consent of the ratepayers and owners of property in the parish.

The inconvenience which often occurred in the proceedings of guardians when the votes given upon any question were equal, is removed by a provision (sec. 19) that, in such case, the presiding chairman shall have a second or casting vote.

Sec. 20 empowers guardians of any parish or union to expend money to the amount of £10 upon the emigration of any poor person belonging to the parish, or to any parish in the union, without the necessity of a parochial meeting to give their consent, which was required by the 4 & 5 Wm. 4, c. 76, sec. 62. This, however, is subject to some restrictions. First, the order of the Poor Law Board must be obtained; secondly, a majority of the guardians of the parish of the settlement must express their concurrence in writing in the resolution of the board of guardians for such expenditure, and such written concurrence must be transmitted to the Poor Law Board; and lastly, the aggregate amount expended in any one year must not exceed one half the average yearly poor-rate raised in the parish for the three preceding years. This enactment will remove an obstacle which has been found frequently to interfere with advantageous offers made for the benefit of poor persons and the relief of their parishes; at the same time that care is taken to prevent any parish from being charged unduly or without its own concurrence.

Lastly, sec. 21, which is an interpretation clause, contains a provision that the Commissioners for administering the laws for relief of the poor in England, may, in all cases, act and be described by the designation of "The Poor Law Board."

The Board will shortly address a communication to the guardians in regard to the other statutes referred to in the first paragraph of this letter.

I am, your obedient Servant,

W. G. LUMLEY,

Assistant Secretary.

To the Clerk to the Board of Guardians.

---

2. CIRCULAR LETTER TO BOARDS OF GUARDIANS ON THE ACT 12 & 13 VIC. CC. 8, 13, 14, 61, 64, 65, 111.

Poor Law Board, Somerset House,
22nd October, 1849.

Sir,—I am directed by the Poor Law Board to bring under the notice of the guardians the provisions of some statutes passed in the last session of parliament, which were referred to in the Circular Letter of the Board, dated the 20th ultimo.

It will appear that several of these statutes are, from their nature, of only limited application, while others, though capable of being generally applied, will nevertheless be found in practice to be of avail in a few unions only. But some of the provisions will be universally applicable.

The 12 & 13 Vic. c. 8 and c. 64, remove the inconveniences which would have resulted from the decision of the Court of Queen's Bench, in the late case of Reg. *v.* Preston, 18 L. J. R. (N.S.) M. C. 10, by which it was determined that in cities and boroughs, by virtue of the 8th sec. of the statute 43 Eliz. c. 2, the mayor, or other chief officer therein, had the exclusive right of appointing the overseers in the several parishes comprised in such cities and boroughs. As a necessary consequence from that decision, it must have been held that the mayor, or other chief officer in any city or borough, had the exclusive right to do all the other matters authorised under the 43 Eliz. c. 2, to be done by two or more justices in any county.

The 12 & 13 Vic. c. 8, gives to the justices, having jurisdiction in cities and boroughs, the exclusive right of appointing the overseers in the parishes therein, so that henceforth the mayor, in his capacity of mayor, will have no independent authority to make such appointments exclusively, though, being necessarily a justice of the city or borough, he may join in making them with any other justice or justices having jurisdiction therein.

By the 12 & 13 Vic. c. 64, any two or more justices, who have jurisdiction within a city or borough, are empowered to act therein in all matters authorised by the statute of Elizabeth to be done by justices out of general or quarter sessions, as fully as the justices of a county may act in and for any parish in the county. This statute does not exclude the mayor from acting in those cases, but merely gives a concurrent jurisdiction to the justices. It will have an important operation in respect of the allowance of poor-rates and the recovery of arrears in the cities and boroughs to which it applies.

It will be readily seen that these statutes can have only a limited application; and the next to be mentioned, (the 12 & 13 Vic. c. 65,) is still more limited in its operation. This statute deals entirely with those parishes and places which are situated partly within and partly without a borough, being divided by the boundary line of the borough, and which are liable to contribute to the county-rate, and to the borough-rate in proportion to the respective parts severally situated in the county and borough.

The mode established by the 1 Vic. c. 81, by which the partial rates were to be collected in such places proved inconvenient, and a different arrangement has been provided by the new statute.

It enables the overseers of the parish at large to assess the county, police, or district police-rate, payable by the part of the parish upon that part which is within the county, and to collect it with the poor-rate, payable by the persons assessed to the latter. Where there is a borough-rate chargeable upon a part of the parish, it may be levied and collected as a separate rate, or as a part of, and together with, the poor-rate.

The overseers are made liable to account to the auditor exactly as in the case of the poor-rate, and to pay over the balance (if any) to their successor.

The case of the payment by the guardians of a union of the county or police-rate, in obedience to a precept from the justices of the county, issued in conformity with the 7 & 8 Vic. c. 33, is provided for where any such divided parish or place, liable to the rate, is comprised in such union.

As in such places the actual amount called for by any one precept may be very small, power is given to the overseers to postpone the making of a rate for their own reimbursement until two or three calls have been made, in which case the amount will doubtless be such as to justify the making of a rate.

The 12 & 13 Vic. c. 13, which is directed to the practice of what has been called the farming of paupers, will not practically, under the present system of poor law relief administration, be of extensive operation. Poor persons, especially children, have been, and in a few parishes, still are, lodged and maintained in establishments (not being workhouses) by persons, not poor law officers, under contracts for hire or remuneration. The purport of the statute is to place such establishments under the direct control and management of the Poor Law Board.

Accordingly, it is provided that this Board may issue rules and regulations for the management of the establishments wherein any poor person is so lodged and maintained for hire, in like manner and with the like effect as in the case of any workhouse belonging to a union. The Board may prohibit the reception or retention of any poor person, or any class of poor persons, in such establishment. They may remove any officer, or servant, or assistant from it whom they shall deem unfit, or who shall wilfully disobey their orders. They may also regulate all the contracts entered into between the proprietors or managers of such establishments and boards of guardians or overseers for the maintenance of paupers, with the same effect as in the case of other contracts entered into by guardians. Lastly, they are empowered to appoint any person, either permanently or temporarily, to inspect and report upon any such establishment; and the person so appointed is to be remunerated by the guardians or overseers of the unions or parishes having paupers therein.

The power which is preserved to justices by the Poor Law Amendment Act, of visiting and examining workhouses, is given to them in respect of these establishments. And the General Board of Health are empowered, by an order, to appoint a superintending inspector to visit and inspect any such establishment from time to time, and to report thereon to that Board. The powers conferred upon such inspector by the Public Health Act are extended to this examination.

Such are the provisions which have been enacted to place these establishments, where they still exist, under due and efficient control. But the arrangements which have been entered into in most unions and well-regulated parishes, will obviously render assistance from any such source unnecessary.

Although the other statutes which remain to be mentioned relate more peculiarly to the overseers, some of them of great importance to those officers will also deserve the notice of the guardians.

Thus, the 12 and 13 Vic. c. 14, enables the justices who grant warrants of distress for levying the poor-rate, to include in each warrant the costs incurred by the overseers in procuring the warrant as well as those incurred in its execution. So much of the statute 43 Eliz. c. 2, as required the justices to commit the defaulter to prison until the arrears were paid, a power which in effect enabled them in some cases to award perpetual imprisonment, is repealed, and a discretionary power is given where the rate and costs cannot be levied under the distress warrant, to commit the defaulter to prison for a term not exceeding three calendar months.

The statute contains some provisions, with reference to the process for the recovery of poor-rates, which will be found convenient in practice; and the schedule to the Act contains forms which may be adopted in the execution of that process.

By the 12 and 13 Vic. c. 61, the legislature has continued for another period, namely, from the 1st October, 1849, to the 1st October, 1850, and to the end of the then next session of parliament, the exemption of inhabitants of parishes from liability as such to be rated to the relief of the poor, in respect of stock in trade and other property.

The statute 12 & 13 Vic. c. 45, for the amendment of the procedure at the Quarter Sessions, and the better advancement of justice in cases within the jurisdiction of those Courts, will be found to contain various provisions of great importance to the overseers and persons engaged in parochial affairs.

It is not necessary to set forth in the present communication all the details of that measure. The guardians will remember the amendments which were introduced by the statute 11 & 12 Vic. c. 31, in the practice of the sessions, in trials of appeals regarding orders of removal, by which the delays and failures of justice in these matters, which had created so much obloquy and scandal, were removed.

Amendments of the like character and effect have been introduced into the general practice of the sessions upon the trials of all appeals. It is here, however, important to refer more particularly to provisions which, except in respect of orders in bastardy, and some other matters not relating to the guardians or the parish officers, enable questions, where notice of appeal has been given, to be submitted in the form of special cases to any of the courts of Westminster for their opinion. Such questions may now, also, be referred to arbitration, in the manner, and with the powers, and under the regulations which exist in regard to arbitrations in ordinary civil matters.

Many of the questions which, arising out of assessments to the poor-rate, settlements, or other parochial matters, have frequently come before the court of quarter sessions in a state in which that court has found the greatest difficulties, both of law and fact, may be at once placed in the most satisfactory train for obtaining a precise and sound decision.

Lastly, the statute 12 & 13 Vic. c. 111, which amends the statute of the last year (11 & 12 Vic. c. 123) for the Removal of Nuisances and Prevention of Epidemic Diseases, contains various provisions which materially affect the guardians and the overseers in respect to their proceedings under the earlier statute, and under the directions which have been issued by the General Board of Health; but, as these provisions have been fully detailed and explained in the Circular Letter from that Board, dated the 15th of August last, and addressed to the clerks of all the unions, it does not appear to this Board to be necessary here to re-state them.

The Board, therefore, have only now to express their hope and belief that the numerous legislative provisions of the last sessions of parliament will be attended with success in facilitating the administration of the laws for the relief of the poor.

I am, Sir, your obedient servant,

W. G. LUMLEY,

Assistant Secretary.

To the Clerk to the Guardians.

---

3. CIRCULAR LETTER TO DISTRICT AUDITORS ON THE ACT 12 & 13 VIC. C. 103.

Poor Law Board,
Somerset House.
29th September, 1849.

Sir,—The Poor Law Board, in directing the attention of the district auditors to those provisions of the 12 & 13 Vic. c. 103, which specially relate to them, think it desirable to bring under their notice several points which affect the discharge of their duties, as well in the conduct of the audit, as in the proceedings which follow from it.

The Board desire, in the first place, to refer to the Letter of the Poor Law Commissioners of the 2nd of July, 1847, addressed to the district auditors, as it is important that the general remarks therein contained, and especially those which relate to the mode of conducting the audit, should receive careful attention.

It will be remembered that the 7 & 8 Vic. c. 101, contained the principal provisions which, prior to the passing of the 11 & 12 Vic. c. 91, defined the powers and prescribed the duties of the district auditor. Of the duties thus prescribed, one of great importance is the recovery of monies certified by him to be due from accounting officers or from other persons. He is made, as it were, the public prosecutor in these matters, and is required to certify and recover all such monies of the union or parish as he may find to have been withheld through fraud, or improperly expended, or lost through negligence or misconduct. This duty of recovering such monies he is required to discharge without being called upon to do so by any person in the particular case; and he is also required to report to the Poor Law Board all the sums which he may certify to be due.

The legislature has provided that the auditor shall not sustain any loss in respect of these proceedings, by making the guardians liable to reimburse him whatever costs and expenses he may not recover from the parties under the process which he adopts.

The 11 & 12 Vic. c. 91, contains provisions for obviating the difficulties which had been found to arise in cases of proceedings taken by auditors under the 7 & 8 Vic. c. 101, from certain technical rules of pleading and evidence.

The Poor Law Board, on the 9th of October last, addressed to boards of guardians a letter explanatory of the provisions of the 11 & 12 Vic. c. 91, and it will be convenient here to repeat such of those observations as relate to the auditor. They are as follow:—

> "The 5th section (*i. e.* of the 11 & 12 Vic. c. 91,) describes in detail what monies the auditor is to certify to be due, and the manner in which he is to do so; and removes difficulties which have heretofore been experienced. It provides that where any overseer or officer shall be continuing in office at the time of the audit, the auditor shall certify as due, such sums only as he shall disallow or surcharge in the accounts so audited. But where the term of office shall have expired, the auditor shall ascertain the *balance then* due, together with the sums, if any, disallowed or surcharged, and shall give credit for all sums which shall be proved before him to have been paid in respect of such balance to the succeeding overseers or officers, or otherwise lawfully applied on behalf of the parish or union interested therein, and shall certify the balance remaining due after such credit shall have been given. Small sums disallowed by the auditor, amounting in the aggregate to less than 40*s*., may be paid over with the balance due, instead of being paid to the treasurer. It will be observed that forms of certificate to be used by the auditor, are given in a schedule to the Act."
>
> * * * * * * * *
>
> "Section 8 requires notice to be given by the auditor to any person (not being an accounting officer) before he shall surcharge such person in respect of any improper payment which he may have authorized, so that such person having received due notice, may appear before the auditor and defend his act.
>
> "As the auditors have found much difficulty in enforcing their certificates before justices, in consequence of the technical proof required on various points, the 9th section removes the difficulty arising from this source, and sets forth clearly the only matters which the auditors shall be required to prove before the justices, and facilitates, in some respect, the proof. This enactment dispenses with the expensive proofs heretofore required from the auditor, the costs of which frequently fell upon the union or some parish in it."

No limitation of time was imposed upon the auditor in reference to his proceeding for the recovery of sums certified. If any considerable time had been allowed to elapse before taking any proceeding, and without explanation as to the cause of the delay, the justices might, perhaps, have declined to make any order to enforce the payment of the sum sought to be recovered. The General Act (11 & 12 Vic. c. 43) which regulates the proceedings of justices out of sessions with respect to summary convictions and orders of justices, imposes a limitation of six months for the commencement of any such proceeding, and it had been suggested that this enactment extended to applications by auditors. The statute of the last session, 12 & 13 Vic. c. 103, s. 9, has now established a precise limitation of *nine* months from the disallowance or surcharge, within which period the proceedings must be commenced. If, however, there be an appeal to the Court of Queen's Bench, or to the Poor Law Board, the period of nine months will not begin to run until the determination of such appeal.

It has already been noticed that the auditor is to be reimbursed by the guardians of the union or parish such expenses as he may fail to recover from the party proceeded against. As no portion of these expenses ought to fall upon the guardians —especially where there has been fraudulent or negligent conduct on the part of the person complained of—it is obvious that he ought to be required to repay the auditor the full amount of the costs and expenses necessarily incurred in the prosecution. There was some doubt, however, as to the effect of the language of the 4 & 5 Wm. 4, c. 76, s. 99, with respect to the nature and amount of the costs which the justices could award in such proceedings; and, in many instances, they confined their order to the merely formal costs there specified. The 10th sec. of 12 & 13 Vic. c. 103, now enables the justices to direct the payment, by the defendant to the auditor, of all such costs and expenses as the justices shall think fit to allow, and shall find to have been reasonably and properly incurred.

The due attendance of parties at the audit, the production to the auditor of the proper accounts and vouchers, and the making of the requisite declaration before him in regard to those accounts, are secured by the liability to the penalties prescribed by the 7 & 8 Vic. c. 101, s. 33. Although the auditor was the only person likely to institute proceedings for enforcing such penalties, no adequate provision was made for reimbursement of the costs which he might be put to in the matter. This defect is now supplied by the 12 & 13 Vic. c. 103, ss. 10 & 11, under the former of which sections the justices will be empowered to order the payment of the auditor's costs by the defendant, while the latter section enables the auditor to be reimbursed such costs by the guardians, when not recovered from the defendant, provided the consent of the Poor Law Board be first obtained.

With regard to the sums certified to be due from officers of unions and parishes, and other persons, it would, in the opinion of the Board, be convenient if in future the following course were adopted by the auditor :—

They recommended that instead of the reports to this Board of sums certified to be due, being made as at present in various forms, they should be made according to the accompanying exemplified form, and that they should correspond therewith in the size of the paper as well as in other respects. A distinct report should be made for each union, and the particulars of the sums certified should be fully set forth in each instance in the manner exemplified in this form.

In case of the audit being adjourned, it will be advisable that the auditor should report as to the sums certified in the accounts, the audit of which is closed, and state in such report to what day it has been adjourned. On the completion of the audit, he should, if necessary, forward to the Board a supplementary report.

The persons from whom money may be certified to be due, will be included in one of the following classes; viz., (1.) Paid officers of the union or of a parish comprised therein. (2.) Overseers. (3.) Guardians and other persons.

It has been hitherto the practice of the Board, upon receiving the auditor's report, to inquire of the clerk to the guardians whether the several sums certified to be due have been paid to the treasurer of the union or parish, in conformity with the provisions of the 7 & 8 Vic. c. 101, s. 32, and upon learning that payment has not been made, to communicate directly with all the parties in default, and then to inform the auditor of the fact and result of such inquiry. In future, however, the Board intend to limit this preliminary inquiry on their part to the cases of persons included in the first and third of the before-named classes. The auditor may, perhaps generally, await the result of that inquiry before he takes proceedings for the recovery of the sum certified by him to be due from any of those persons; at the same time, however, it should be noticed that he must exercise his own discretion as to particular cases where he may have reason to believe that prompt measures are requisite. But with regard to the persons included in the second class (*i.e.*) the overseers) it will be the duty of the auditor, without waiting for any previous communication from this Board, to take such measures as he shall find requisite for securing payment to the treasurer of all sums certified to be due from them.

The Board request that the auditor will, within three months after the date of the certificate, report to them whether the sum certified has been paid to the treasurer; if it has not been paid, whether he has taken, or proposes to take any, and if so, what steps for its recovery; and if he have taken any proceedings, what has been the result.

Whenever an application by way of appeal against the decision of the auditor is made to the Board, (under the 7 & 8 Vic. c. 101, sec. 36, or the 11 & 12 Vic. c. 91, sec. 4,) they will, with as little delay as possible, communicate to the auditor the fact of such appeal having been made, as proceedings against the party should be delayed until the appeal has been decided.

It may be useful to add, that when the auditor sets out his reasons for any disallowance or surcharge, he should state fully and distinctly on the face of the account the facts of the case upon which he founds his decision. It is not sufficient for the auditor merely to allege that an item is illegal or contrary to law, or to an order of the Poor Law Commissioners, without specifying the grounds on which he arrives at that conclusion.

I am, Sir, your obedient Servant,

W. G. LUMLEY,

Assistant Secretary.

To District Auditor.

FORM OF AUDITOR'S REPORT.

____________________ *Audit District.*

____________________ *Union.*

Audit for the Half-Year ended ____________________ 18 .

Commenced ______________ Adjourned to, *or* Ended ______________

I hereby report, that at the Audit of the Accounts of this Union, and of the Parishes comprised therein, for the above-named period, I certified the several Sums set forth in the following Schedule to be due from the persons therein named, [*or*] I did not certify any Sums to be due from any person.

Date of Certificate.	Names and Description of Persons.	Particulars.				Sums Certified.		
	John Smith, Thomas Jones } late Overseers of the —— of E——	Balance admitted . .	56	2	8			
		Disallowance .	1	12	6			
		Surcharge . .	23	—	7			
						80	15	9
	A. B., C. D. } late Overseers of the —— of Z——	Disallowance .	50	2	6			
		Less Balance due to them	13	13	—			
						36	9	6
	F. G. Relieving Officer	Surcharge . .	1	10	—	1	10	—
	M. N. of —— . . . . *Guardian.*							

Signed ____________________

To *District Auditor.*

The Poor Law Board. ______ *day of* ____________ 18 .

4. AN ACT TO REMOVE DOUBTS AS TO THE APPOINTMENT OF OVERSEERS IN CITIES AND BOROUGHS—12 & 13 VIC. C. 8. *Passed 22nd March*, 1849.

43 *Eliz.* c. 2. *Justices of the Peace having Jurisdiction in certain Cities and Boroughs to have the exclusive Right of appointing Overseers.*

1. Whereas doubts have been entertained as to the proper authority for the appointment of overseers of the poor of the parishes comprised within certain cities and boroughs under the provisions of the act of the forty-third year of the reign of Queen Elizabeth, intituled *An Act for the Relief of the Poor,* and it is expedient that such doubts should be removed: Be it therefore enacted by the Queen's Most Excellent Majesty, by and with the advice and consent of the Lords Spiritual and Temporal, and Commons, in this present Parliament assembled, and by the authority of the same, that in every city, town corporate, or borough, the justices of the peace having jurisdiction therein shall have the exclusive right of appointing the overseers of the poor of the several parishes, townships, or other places separately maintaining their own poor, or of any parts thereof, within the said cities, towns corporate, and boroughs respectively, in like manner and with the same effect as the justices of any county now have in respect of the overseers of the poor of any parish within such county, and they are hereby required from time to time to make such appointments accordingly.

Repeal of Part of the 43 *Eliz.* c. 2. *s.* 10.

2. And be it enacted, that so much of the said Act as renders the mayor, alderman, and head officer of any city, town, or place corporate liable, upon the default of the nomination of overseers therein, to lose and forfeit for every such default five pounds, shall be and the same is hereby repealed.

Appointments of Overseers in Cities and Boroughs by Justices rendered valid.

3. And be it enacted, that the appointments of any overseers of the poor in such cities, towns corporate, or boroughs heretofore made by justices of the peace therein, without the concurrence of the mayor or other head officer thereof, shall be deemed and taken to be valid, and that every rate or assessment made or to be made, and every other act and thing done or to be done by any overseers so appointed, shall, if otherwise lawful, be valid for all purposes.

Saving of the City of London and Places under Local Acts.

4. Provided nevertheless, and be it enacted, that this Act shall not apply to the City of London, nor to any of the parishes comprised therein, nor to the appointment of the overseers of any parish, township, or place where such appointment is regulated by the provisions of any Local Act.

Act may be amended, &c.

5. And be it enacted, that this Act may be amended or repealed by any Act to be passed in the present session of parliament.

---

5. AN ACT TO PROVIDE A MORE EFFECTUAL REGULATION AND CONTROL OVER THE MAINTENANCE OF POOR PERSONS IN HOUSES NOT BEING THE WORKHOUSES OF ANY UNION OR PARISH—12 & 13 VIC. C. 13. *Passed 11th May*, 1849.

The Poor Law Board to issue Rules and Regulations to Houses where the Poor are maintained under Contract.

1. Whereas poor persons are sometimes lodged and maintained under contracts or agreements for certain payments in houses and establishments not being the workhouses of any union or parish, nor subject to the effective control of any guardians or overseers or other parochial authorities, and no sufficient powers are vested in any authority to regulate the houses or establishments wherein such persons are lodged and maintained, and it is expedient that such powers should be given: Be it therefore enacted by the Queen's Most Excellent Majesty, by and with the advice and consent of the Lords Spiritual and Temporal, and Commons, in this present Parliament assembled, and by the authority of the same, that it shall be lawful for the Commissioners for administering the laws for relief of the poor in England, and they are hereby required, from time to time as they shall see occasion, to make and issue all such rules, orders, and regulations for the management and government of any house or establishment wherein any poor person shall be lodged, boarded, or maintained, for hire or remuneration, under any con-

tract or agreement entered into by the proprietor, manager, or superintendent of such house or establishment, or on his behalf, with any guardians, overseers, or other persons having the ordering or management of the poor in any union or parish, or for the education of any poor children therein, in like manner and to the same extent as the said Commissioners are by law empowered to do in the case of any workhouse belonging to any union or parish; and all such rules, orders, and regulations shall have the like effect as other Rules, Orders, and Regulations of the said Commissioners, and shall be obeyed accordingly, with the like penalties on any neglect or disobedience thereof, to be enforced upon summary conviction, as penalties under the Act of the fifth year of his late Majesty King William the Fourth, intituled "An Act for the Amendment and better Administration of the laws relating to the Poor in England and Wales," may now be enforced.

Nothing herein to extend to Lunatic Asylums and Hospitals.

2. Provided nevertheless, and be it enacted, That nothing herein contained shall extend to any county lunatic asylum or hospital registered or house licensed for the reception of lunatics, nor to any hospital, infirmary, school, or other institution supported by public subscriptions, and maintained for purposes of charity only.

Rules and Regulations to be directed to the Manager or Officer of the Establishment.

3. And be it enacted, That the said Commissioners may direct their Rules, Orders, and Regulations to any person being or acting as the proprietor, manager, or superintendent, or as an officer or assistant, in any such house or establishment as aforesaid, and the same shall come into operation so soon as the said Commissioners shall therein declare, and shall be binding upon the person named therein, and, if they shall so direct, upon every person who shall afterwards succeed to him in the same capacity.

Poor Law Board may prohibit the Reception or Retention of Poor in any such House.

4. And be it enacted, That the said Commissioners shall be empowered, if at any time they shall see just cause, to prohibit, by Order under their Seal, the reception or retention of any poor person, or any class of poor persons, in any such house or establishment, and thereupon it shall not be lawful for any such proprietor, manager, or superintendent, or other officer or assistant, to receive or retain any poor person therein, contrary to the terms of such order, so long as it shall be in force, nor for any guardians, overseers, or other such persons as aforesaid to send any poor person to such house or establishment, contrary to such order, provided that no such guardians, overseers, or other such persons as aforesaid, nor any officer of any union or parish, shall incur any legal responsibility in respect of the neglect of such order, until a copy thereof shall have been sent to the guardians of the union or parish, or to the overseers of the parish, or other such persons as aforesaid, in the manner in which Orders of the said Commissioners are now sent to guardians or overseers.

Poor Law Board may remove any Officer of such House.

5. And be it enacted, That the said Commissioners may, by Order under their Seal, remove from his office or service any officer, servant, or assistant in any such house or establishment whom they shall deem unfit or incompetent to discharge the duties of his situation, or who shall at any time refuse or wilfully neglect to obey and carry into effect any of the Rules, Orders, or Regulations issued by the said Commissioners under their Seal for the regulation of such house or establishment, or of the officers or inmates thereof; and thereupon such officer, servant, or assistant shall forthwith cease to act in his office, service, or employment, and shall be entitled to claim and recover a rateable proportion of his salary, wages, or other remuneration up to the time of his being so removed, but no more, from the person liable to pay the same, subject to any defence at law which may then be open to the person from whom the same shall be claimed.

Poor Law Board may regulate Contracts.

6. And be it enacted, That the said Commissioners may from time to time issue any Order which they may deem necessary for regulating the mode in which any contract shall be entered into for the lodging, boarding, or maintenance of any poor person, with the proprietor, manager, or superintendent of such house or establishment as aforesaid, or the terms or the duration of any such contract; and if after the issuing of any such Order any contract or agree-

ment be entered into with such proprietor, manager, or superintendent, or any person on his behalf, not in accordance with such Order, the same shall be voidable, and, if the said Commissioners shall so direct, the same shall be void and of no effect; and all payments made under or in pursuance of any contract or agreement not made and entered into in conformity with such Order as aforesaid, at any time after the said Commissioners shall have declared the same to be void as aforesaid, and shall have given notice of such declaration to the guardians, overseers, or other such persons as aforesaid, shall be disallowed in the passing and auditing of their accounts, or the accounts of any of their officers by whom such payments shall have been made or charged.

Persons may be appointed to inspect Houses and the Poor maintained therein. Remuneration to such Persons.

7. And be it enacted, That the said Commissioners may, if they think fit, appoint a person either temporarily or permanently to visit any such house or establishment, and to inspect the same, and the poor persons received and maintained therein, and to make a report to such Commissioners upon any visit and inspection; and such person shall be paid by the guardians or overseers, as the case may be, of the several unions or parishes from which poor persons shall have been sent, and shall be at the time of such visitation maintained therein, such remuneration as the said Commissioners shall by Order under under their Seal direct.

Power to Justices to visit Houses—Power to General Board of Health to appoint a Superintending Inspector to visit Houses, and examine Officers, &c.

8. And be it enacted, That it shall be lawful for any justice of the peace acting in and for the jurisdiction in which such house or establishment shall be situated to visit, inspect, and examine the same, at such times as he shall think proper, for the like purpose and with the same power as any justice has now by virtue of the Act herein-before mentioned of the fifth year of his late Majesty, in respect of the workhouse of any union or parish; and it shall be lawful for the General Board of Health, where they shall think proper, by Order under the Seal of the said Board and the hands of any two or more members thereof, to authorize a superintending inspector to visit and inspect from time to time, or at such time or times as such Board shall direct, any such house or establishment, and to ascertain the state and condition of the same, and of the poor people therein, and to report thereon to the Board; and it shall be lawful for such superintending inspector accordingly so to visit and inspect, and to ascertain such state and condition, and to examine any officer, servant, assistant, or inmate of such house or establishment in relation thereto; and the powers and provisions of the "Public Health Act," 1848, in relation to the examination of persons for the purposes of an inquiry under such Act by a superintending inspector, shall extend and be applicable to the examination of such officers, servants, assistants, and inmates.

Interpretation of Act.

9. And be it enacted, That the several words used in this Act shall be construed in the same manner as in the said Act of the fifth year of his late Majesty, and the statutes explaining and amending it, and all the provisions, enactments, and regulations contained in the said Act and the said subsequent statutes shall be extended to this Act, so far as the same may be applicable, and subject to the provisions herein contained.

To apply to England and Wales only.

10. And be it enacted, That this Act shall extend only to England and Wales.

Act may be amended, &c.

11. And be it enacted, That this Act may be amended or repealed by any Act to be passed in this present session.

---

6. AN ACT TO ENABLE OVERSEERS OF THE POOR AND SURVEYORS OF THE HIGHWAYS TO RECOVER THE COSTS OF DISTRAINING FOR RATES —12 & 13 VIC. c. 14. *Passed 11th May, 1849.*

43 *Eliz.* c. 2. 5 & 6 *Wm.* 4. c. 50—*Where a Warrant of Distress is granted for a Poor Rate or Highway Rate, &c. the Costs of obtaining it may also be levied.*

1. Whereas provision is already made by law for the recovery of the sum or sums at which any person is rated or assessed to the relief of the

poor, or is rated or assessed in any rate for the highways, in England or Wales, by distress and sale of his goods and chattels, and in default of such distress by commitment to prison until the same shall be paid; but no provision is made for levying the costs and expenses incurred by the overseers of the poor or the surveyors of highways in the recovery of the same respectively: Be it therefore enacted by the Queen's Most Excellent Majesty, by and with the advice and consent of the Lords Spiritual and Temporal, and Commons, in this present Parliament assembled, and by the authority of the same, That it shall be lawful hereafter for all justices of the peace, if in their discretion they shall so think fit, in any warrant of distress they shall make and issue for the levying of any sum or sums to which any person or persons is or are now or may hereafter be rated or assessed in or by any rate or assessment for the relief of the poor or for the highways in England or Wales, or in or by any other rate or assessment which by law now or hereafter is or shall be directed to be enforced or recovered in the same manner as a poor-rate, or in any warrant for the levying of any arrears of the same, to order that sum, such as they may deem reasonable, for the costs and expenses which such overseers or surveyors, or the persons applying for such warrant, shall have incurred in obtaining the same, shall also be levied of the goods and chattels of the person or persons against whom such warrant shall be granted, together with the reasonable charges of the taking, keeping, and selling of the said distress.

Imprisonment in Default of Distress—43 *Eliz.* c. 2.—*So much of the* 43 *Eliz.* c. 2. *as relates to Commitments for Nonpayment of Rates, or for Default of Distress, repealed—Power to order Imprisonment not exceeding Three Months in default of Distress.*

2. And whereas by an Act passed in the forty-third year of the reign of Queen Elizabeth, intituled "An Act for the Relief of the Poor," it is amongst other things enacted, that in default of distress for a poor-rate it shall be lawful for two justices of the peace to commit the party against whom the distress warrant shall have issued to the common gaol of the county, there to remain without bail or mainprize until payment: And whereas it is desirable to limit the time within which a person assessed to a poor-rate, or any other of the rates or assessments aforesaid, may be imprisoned for nonpayment of the same: Be it therefore enacted, That so much of the said recited Act as relates to the commitment of any person to the county gaol for nonpayment of any poor-rate, or for default of distress whereon to levy the same, shall be and the same is hereby repealed; and every person now undergoing any such imprisonment under or by virtue of the said recited Act shall be discharged from such imprisonment so soon as he or she shall have been imprisoned three calendar months, or shall sooner pay the sum or sums with which he or she is charged; and that hereafter, when to any warrant of distress for the levying of any sum or sums to which any person or persons is or are now or may hereafter be rated or assessed in or by any rate or assessment herein-before mentioned it shall be returned by the constable or person having the execution of such warrant that he could find no goods or chattels, or no sufficient goods or chattels, whereon to levy such sum or sums, together with the costs of or occasioned by the levying of the same, it shall be lawful for any two or more justices of the peace before whom the same shall be returned, or for any two or more justices of the peace for the same county, riding, division, liberty, city, borough, or place, if in their discretion they shall so think fit, to issue their warrant of commitment against the person with relation to whom such return shall be so made as aforesaid, in the Form (D.) in the schedule to this Act annexed, or in any form to the like effect, and thereby order such person to be imprisoned in the common gaol or house of correction for any time not exceeding three calendar months, unless the sum or sums therein mentioned shall be sooner paid; and every such warrant of commitment made or issued for default of distress as aforesaid shall be made as well for the nonpayment of the costs and expences so as aforesaid incurred in obtaining such warrant of distress, if the same shall be so ordered as aforesaid, and the costs attending the said distress, and also the costs and charges of taking and conveying the party to prison, (the amount of such several costs, expenses, and charges being stated in such warrant of commitment,) as for the nonpayment of the sum or sums alleged to be due for the said rates respectively.

One Warrant may be issued against several Rate-payers; but otherwise as to a Commitment in default of Distress.

3. And be it enacted, That for the saving of

expense in the levying of any sum or sums for rate and costs as aforesaid it shall be lawful to make and issue one warrant of distress against any number of persons neglecting or refusing to pay the same, in the form in the schedule to this Act annexed; but nothing herein shall be deemed or construed to authorize justices in like manner to grant or issue one warrant of commitment against several persons in default of distress as aforesaid.

To whom Warrants of Distress or Commitment to be directed.

4. And be it enacted, That the warrants aforesaid may be directed to the churchwardens and overseers of the poor, or the overseers of the poor, or the surveyors of the highways respectively, and to the constable of the parish or township, and to any other person or persons, or to any one or more of them, as by the justices granting the same shall be deemed fit.

Summons and how served—if not obeyed, the Justices may proceed ex-parte.

5. And be it enacted, That every summons to be issued against any person for nonpayment of any sum for which he or she is or shall be so rated or assessed as aforesaid shall be directed to such person, and may be in the form (B.) in the schedule to this Act annexed, or in any form to the like effect; and the same may be served by any churchwarden or overseer of the poor, or surveyor of the highways, respectively, or constable or other person, to whom it shall be delivered for that purpose, upon the person to whom it is so directed, by delivering the same to the party personally or by leaving the same with some person for him or her at his or her last place of abode; and the person who shall serve the same in manner aforesaid shall attend at the time and place and before the justices in the said summons mentioned, to depose if necessary to the service of the said summons; and if, upon the day and at the place appointed in and by the said summons for the appearance of the party so summoned, such party shall fail to appear accordingly in obedience to such summons, then and in every such case, if it be proved upon oath or affirmation to the justices then present that such summons was duly served as aforesaid a reasonable time before the time so appointed for his or her appearance as aforesaid, it shall be lawful for such justices of the peace in their discretion, if they shall so think fit, to proceed *ex-parte*, in the same manner to all intents and purposes as if such party had personally appeared before them in obedience to the said summons.

On Payment or Tender of Rate and Costs Proceedings to cease.

6. And be it enacted, That in all cases where any proceedings have been or shall hereafter be taken to compel payment of any sum for which any such person is or shall be so rated or assessed as aforesaid, if at any time before such person shall be committed to and lodged in prison for nonpayment thereof, or for or by reason of its being returned to such warrant of distress as aforesaid that there are no goods or chattels or no sufficient goods or chattels of such person whereon the same may be levied as aforesaid, such person shall pay or tender to the churchwardens or overseers of the poor, or any of them, or to the surveyor of highways respectively, or other person authorized to collect or receive such rate, the sum so sought to be recovered, together with the amount of all costs and expenses up to that time incurred in the proceedings so taken to compel payment thereof as aforesaid, then and in every such case the person to whom such sum and costs shall be so paid or tendered shall receive the same, and thereupon no further proceedings for the recovery of the same shall be had or taken.

Costs already recovered or proceeded for deemed legal.

7. And be it enacted, That in all cases where such costs and expenses as aforesaid shall have been paid and received, or any proceedings taken or imprisonment had for nonpayment of the same, such payment and receipt, and such proceedings or imprisonment, shall be deemed legal to all intents and purposes, and no action or other proceeding shall be had or proceeded in for or in respect of the same.

Forms in Schedule valid.

8. And whereas it may be convenient, and save expense and litigation, if forms to be used for the purpose of levying the sums aforesaid should be given: Be it enacted, That the forms in the schedule to this Act contained, or forms to the same or the like effect, shall be deemed good, valid, and sufficient in law.

9. *Imprisonment for nonpayment of Church Rate limited.*

9. And whereas it is desirable to limit the time within which a person assessed to a church-rate may be imprisoned for nonpayment of the same: Be it enacted, That every person now undergoing any such imprisonment shall be discharged from such imprisonment so soon as he or she shall have been imprisoned three calendar months, or shall sooner pay the sum or sums with which he or she is charged; and that hereafter no person shall be imprisoned for the nonpayment of any church-rate for any time exceeding three calendar months.

SCHEDULE. (A. 1.)

Complaint of the Overseers or Surveyors against One Rate-payer.

To wit. } BE it remembered, That on the day of in the year of our Lord the [churchwardens and overseers of the poor, *or* the surveyors of the highways] of the parish of in the [county] of aforesaid, by *C.D.*, one of the said [overseers *or* surveyors,] complain to the undersigned, [one] of Her Majesty's justices of the peace in and for the said county, that *A.B.* of the said [parish,] being a person duly rated and assessed to [the relief of the poor, *or* the maintenance of the highways] of the said parish, in and by a rate* made on the day of in the year in the sum of hath not paid the same or any part thereof, but hath refused so to do: Wherefore the said [churchwardens and overseers *or* surveyors,] by *C.D.* aforesaid, pray that the said *A.B.* may be summoned to appear before two of Her Majesty's justices of the peace, to show cause why he hath not paid and refuses to pay the said sum.

C.D.

Made and exhibited before me
at in the county of
on this day of 1849.
E.F.

* *Or*, in and by several rates made on and on in the several sums of and of

(A. 2.)

Complaint against several Rate-payers.

To wit. } Be it remembered, That on the day of in the year of our Lord the [churchwardens and overseers of the poor, *or* the surveyors the highways] of the parish of in the [county] of aforesaid, by *C.D.*, one of the said [overseers *or* surveyors,] complain to the undersigned [one] of Her Majesty's justices of the peace in and for the said [county,] that the several persons whose names are mentioned and set out in the schedule hereunder written, being persons duly rated and assessed to [the relief of the poor, *or* the maintenance of the highways] of the said parish, in and by the rates in the said schedule mentioned, in certain sums set down opposite to their respective names in the said schedule, have not respectively paid the sums or any part thereof, but have respectively refused so to do: wherefore the said [churchwardens and overseers, *or* surveyors,] by *C.D.* aforesaid, pray that said several persons may respectively be summoned to appear before two of Her Majesty's justices of the peace, to show cause repectively why they have not paid and refuse to pay the said sums respectively.

SCHEDULE.

Names of the Rate-payers.	Residence.	Under Rate dated the 1849.	Arrears due under Rate dated the 1848.	Total Sum due.
		£ s. d.	£ s. d.	£ s. d.
A. B. - -	(here state it)	1 7 0	1 7 0	2 14 0
I. K. - - -	- - -	0 13 0	- - -	0 13 0
L. M. - -	- - -	- - -	0 18 6	0 18 6
N. P. - -	- - -	0 14 3	0 14 3	1 8 6

C.D.

Made and exhibited before me
at in the county of
on this day of 1849.
E.F.

(B.)

Summons upon the Complaint.

To *A.B.* of

Whereas complaint hath this day been made before the undersigned, [one] of Her Majesty's justices of the peace in and for the [county] of by the [churchwardens and overseers of the poor, *or* surveyors of the highways] of the parish of in the said [county,] that you, being a person duly rated and assessed to [the relief of the poor, *or* the maintenance of the highways] of the said parish, in and by a rate made on the day of 1849, in the sum of , hath not paid the same or any part thereof, but hath refused so to do: these are therefore to command you, in Her Majesty's name, to be and appear on at o'clock in the forenoon, at before such two or more justices of the peace for the said [county] as may then be there, to show cause why you have not paid and refuse to pay the same, otherwise you shall be proceeded against by default as if you had appeared, and be dealt with according to law.

Given under my hand and seal, this day of in the year of our Lord at in the [county] aforesaid.

E.F.

Take notice, that you have already incurred the undermentioned costs; viz.

	s.	d.
Clerk to the justices - - - - - -		
Overseer [*or* surveyor], for obtaining the summons - - - - - - -		
Constable, for serving ditto - - - -	1	0
Ditto, travelling expenses at three-pence per per mile - - - - - - - -		
Total -		

If the amount of these charges, together with the rate claimed, be paid to the overseer [or surveyor] before the day on which the summons is returnable, all further proceedings will be stopped.

(C. 1.)

Warrant of Distress against One Rate-payer.

To the overseers of the poor [*or* to the surveyors of the highways] of the parish of in the [county] of and to the constable of and to all other peace officers in the said [county.]

WHEREAS on last past a complaint was made before *E.F.*, one of Her Majesty's justices of the peace in and for the [county] of by the [churchwardens and overseers of the poor, *or* surveyors of the highways] of the parish of in the said [county,] that *A.B.*, being a person duly rated and assessed to the relief of the poor [*or* to the maintenance of the highways] of the said parish in and by a rate made on in the sum of had not paid the same or any part thereof, but had refused so to do; and now at this day, to wit, on at the parties aforesaid appear before us, the undersigned, two of Her Majesty's justices of the peace in and for the said county [*or* the said churchwardens and overseers, *or* surveyors, by *C.D.*, one of the said overseers, *or* surveyors, appear before us, the undersigned, two of Her Majesty's justices of the peace in and for the said county; but the said *A.B.*, although duly called, doth not appear by himself, his counsel or attorney, and it is now satisfactorily proved to us on oath that the said *A.B.* has been duly served with the summons in this behalf, which required him to be and appear here at this day before such two or more justices of the peace as should now be here, to answer the said complaint, and to be further dealt with according to Law;] and now having heard the matter of the said complaint, and it being now duly proved to us upon oath [in the presence and hearing of the said *A.B.*,] that an assessment for the [relief of the poor, *or* the maintenance of the highways] of the said parish of and for other purposes chargeable thereon according to law, dated the was duly made, allowed, and published, and that the said *A.B.* is therein and thereby assessed at the sum of aforesaid,* and that the said sum hath been duly demanded of the said *A.B.*, but that he hath not paid, and hath refused and still refuses to pay the same; and the said *A.B.* now not showing to us any sufficient cause for not paying the same, These are therefore to command you, in Her Majesty's name, forthwith to make distress of the goods and chattels of the said *A.B.*; and if within the space of [*five*] days after the making of such distress the said sum, and the sum of for the costs incurred by the said [churchwardens and overseers, *or* surveyors] in obtaining this warrant, together with the reasonable charges of taking and keeping the said distress, shall not be paid, that then you do sell the said goods and chattels so by you distrained, and out of the money arising by such sale you retain the said sums of and rendering the overplus, on demand, to the said *A.B.*, the reasonable charges of taking, keeping and selling the said distress being first deducted; and if no such distress can be found that then you certify the same unto us, to the end that such further proceedings may be had herein as to the law doth appertain.

Given under our hands and seals, this day of in the year of our Lord at in the [county] aforesaid.

E.F.
G.H.

* "And that a certain other assessment for the relief," *&c., to the asterisk, if there be arrears.*

(C. 2)

Warrant of Distress against several Rate-payers.

To the Overseers of the Poor *or* the Surveyors of the Highways of the Parish of in the County of and to the Constables of and to all other Peace Officers in the said county.

WHEREAS on last past a complaint was made before *E.F.*, one of Her Majesty's justices of the peace in and for the county of by the [churchwardens and overseers of the poor, *or* the surveyors of the highways] of the parish of in the said county, that the several persons whose names are mentioned and set forth in the Schedule hereunder written, being persons duly rated and assessed to [the relief of the poor, *or* maintenance of the highways] of the said parish, in and by the rates in the Schedule in that complaint and in this warrant underwritten, in certain sums set down opposite to their respective names in the said Schedule, had not respectively paid the said sums or any part thereof, but had respectively refused so to do; and now at this day, to wit, on at the said [churchwardens and overseers, *or* surveyors] by *C.D.*, one of the said overseers, *or* surveyors, and *A.B.*, *I.K.*, and *L.M.*, some of the said parties in the said Schedule mentioned, appear before us, the undersigned, two of Her Majesty's justices of the peace in and for the said county; but the said *N.P.*, although duly called, doth not appear by himself, his counsel or attorney, and it is now satisfactorily proved to us on oath that the said *N.P.* has been duly served with the summons in this behalf, which required him to be and appear here this day before such two or more justices of the peace as should now be here to answer the said complaint, and to be further dealt with according to law, and now having heard the matter of the said complaint against the said several parties, and it being now duly proved to us on oath, in the presence of the parties so appearing as aforesaid, that an assessment for [*the relief of the poor*] of the said parish of and for other purposes chargeable therein according to law, dated the was duly made, allowed, and published, and that the said several persons whose names are mentioned and set out in the Schedule hereunder written are therein and thereby assessed at the sums set down opposite to their respective names in the said Schedule, and that the said several sums have been duly demanded of them respectively, but they have not nor hath any of them paid the said sums or any of them, or any part thereof respectively, but they have refused and still do refuse to pay the same respectively, and have not, nor hath any of them, showed to us sufficient cause for not paying the same; these are therefore to command you, in Her Majesty's name, forthwith to make distress of the goods and chattels of the several persons whose names are mentioned and set out in the Schedule hereunder written; and if within the space of *five* days after the making of such distresses respectively the said several sums set opposite to their respective names at which they were so rated and assessed as aforesaid, and the said several sums for costs incurred by the said [churchwardens and overseers, *or* surveyors] also set opposite to their respective names, together with the reasonable charges of taking and keeping the said distress in each case, shall not be paid, that then you do sell the goods and chattels of the party so making default so by you distrained, and out of the money arising by such sales respectively you retain the sums so set opposite to the name of each party whose goods you shall have so sold, rendering to him the overplus, the reasonable charges of taking, keeping, and selling the said distress being first deducted; and if in any of the cases mentioned in the Schedule hereunder written no such distress can be found, that then you certify the same unto us, to the end that such further proceedings may be had herein as to the law doth appertain.

SCHEDULE.

Names of Rate-payers.	Residence.	Under Rate dated 1849.			Arrears due under Rate dated 1848.			Costs.			Total.		
		£	s.	d.	£	s.	d.	£	s.	d.	£	s.	d.
A. B. -	(here state it)	1	7	0	1	7	0	0	6	0	3	0	0
I. K. -	- - -	0	13	0	-	-	-	0	2	0	0	15	0
L. M. -	- - -	-	-	-	0	18	6	0	3	0	1	1	6
N. P. -	- - -	0	14	3	0	14	3	0	5	0	1	13	6

Given under our hands and seals, this day of in the year of our Lord at in the county aforesaid.

E.F.
G.H.

(D.)

Warrant of Commitment in default of Distress.

To the Overseers of the Poor [*or* the Surveyors of the Highways] of the Parish of in the [County] of and to the Constable of and to all other Peace Officers in the said [County,] and to the Keeper of the [*House of Correction*] at in the said [County.]

WHEREAS on last past a complaint was made before *E.F.*, Esquire, one of Her Majesty's justices of the peace in and for the said [county] of by the [churchwardens and overseers of the poor, *or* surveyors of the highways] of the parish of in the said [county,] that *A.B.*, being a person duly rated to the [relief of the poor, *or* maintenance of the highways] of the said parish, in and by a rate made on in the sum of had not paid the same or any part thereof, but had refused so to do; and afterwards on at the parties aforesaid appeared before *E.F.* and *G.H.*, Esquires, two of Her Majesty's justices of the peace in and for the said county [*or* the said churchwardens and overseers, *or* surveyors, by *C.D.*, one of the said overseers, or surveyors, appeared before *E.F.* and *G.H.*, Esquires, two of Her Majesty's justices of the peace in and for the said county; but the said *A.B.*, although duly called, did not appear by himself, his counsel or attorney, and it was then satisfactorily proved to the said justices that the said *A.B.* had been duly served with the summons in that behalf, which required him to be and appear there at that day before such two or more justices of the peace as should then be there, to answer the said complaint, and to be further dealt with according to law;] and then having heard the matter of the said complaint, and it being then duly proved to the said justices upon oath [in the presence and hearing of the said *A.B.*] that an assessment for the [relief of the poor, *or* the maintenance of the highways] of the said parish of dated the was duly made, allowed, and published, and that the said *A.B.* was therein and thereby assessed at the sum of aforesaid, and that the said sum had been duly demanded of the said *A.B.*, but that he had not paid, and had refused and still refused to pay the same, and the said *A.B.*, then not showing to the said *E.F.* and *G.H.* any sufficient cause for not paying the same, the said justices thereupon then issued a warrant to commanding them to levy the said sum of and the sum of for the costs incurred in obtaining that warrant, by distress and sale of the goods and chattels of the said *A.B.*: and whereas it now appears to me, the undersigned, one of Her Majesty's justices of the peace in and for the said [county,] as well by the return of the said to the said warrant of distress as otherwise, that the said hath made diligent search for the goods and chattels of the said *A.B.*, but that no sufficient distress whereon to levy the said sums above mentioned could be found: these are therefore to command you the said [churchwardens and overseers, *or* surveyors] and constable and peace officers, or some or one of you, to take the said *A.B.*, and him safely to convey to the [*House of Correction*] at aforesaid, and there deliver him to the said keeper, together with this precept: and I do hereby command you, the said keeper of the said [*House of Correction*,] to receive the said *A.B.* into your custody in the said [*House of Correction*,] there to imprison him for the space of unless the said sums of and together with the sum of for the costs attending the said distress, and the further sum of being the costs and charges of this commitment, and of taking and conveying the said *A.B.* to prison, making in the whole the sum of shall be sooner paid unto you the said keeper; and for your so doing this shall be your sufficient warrant.

Given under my hand and seal this day of in the year of our Lord at in the [county] aforesaid.

J. S. (L.S.)

---

7. AN ACT TO CONTINUE UNTIL THE FIRST DAY OF OCTOBER, ONE THOUSAND EIGHT HUNDRED AND FIFTY, AND TO THE END OF THE THEN NEXT SESSION OF PARLIAMENT, THE EXEMPTION OF INHABITANTS FROM LIABILITY TO BE RATED AS SUCH IN RESPECT OF STOCK IN TRADE OR OTHER PROPERTY TO THE RELIEF OF THE POOR—12 & 13 VIC. C. 61. *Passed 28th July*, 1849.

3 & 4 *Vic.* c. 89.—*Recited Act further Continued.*

1. Whereas an Act was passed in the fourth year of the reign of her present Majesty, intituled, "An Act to exempt until the thirty-first day of December, One thousand eight hundred and forty-one Inhabitants of Parishes, Townships, and Villages from Liability to be rated as such in respect of Stock in Trade or other Property to the Relief of the Poor:" And whereas the said Act hath been since continued by sundry Acts until the first day of October in the year One thousand eight hundred and forty-nine, and to the end of the then next Session of Parliament, and it is expedient that the said Act be further continued: Be it enacted by the Queen's Most Excellent Majesty, by and with the advice and consent of the Lords Spiritual and Temporal, and Commons, in this present Parliament assembled, and by the authority of the same, that the first-mentioned Act shall continue in force until the first day of October, in the year One thousand eight hundred and fifty, and to the end of the then next session of parliament.

Act may be Amended, &c.

2. And be it enacted, That this Act may be amended or repealed by any Act to be passed in this present session of parliament.

---

8. AN ACT TO REMOVE DOUBTS AS TO THE AUTHORITY OF JUSTICES OF THE PEACE TO ACT IN CERTAIN MATTERS RELATING TO THE POOR IN CITIES AND BOROUGHS—12 & 13 VIC. C. 64. *Passed 28th July*, 1849.

Justices of the Peace in Cities and Boroughs may act in all Matters relating to the Relief of the Poor under the 43 *Elizabeth, in such Cities and Boroughs.*

Whereas by the Act of the forty-third year of the reign of Queen Elizabeth, intituled "An Act for the Relief of the Poor," authority is given to justices of the peace for counties to act in certain matters relating to the poor, and doubts have been entertained whether the same powers extend to justices of the peace having jurisdiction within cities and boroughs, and it is expedient that such doubts should be removed: Be it therefore enacted by the Queen's Most Excellent Majesty, by and with the advice and consent of the Lords Spiritual and Temporal, and Commons, in this present Parliament assembled, and by the authority of the same, that notwithstanding anything in the said Act contained, all powers and authorities which by the said Act may be exercised out of general or quarter sessions by two or more justices of any county, may be exercised within any city or borough by any two or more justices of the peace having jurisdiction within such city or borough respectively, as fully in all respects as by the justices of the county in or for any parish of such county.

Acts of the Justices in any City or Borough confirmed.

2. And be it enacted, That nothing heretofore done in any city or borough for the purposes of the said Act by any two or more justices having jurisdiction in such city or borough shall be deemed or taken to have been illegally or insufficiently done by reason only that neither of the said last-mentioned justices was mayor, bailiff, or head officer of such city or borough, but everything so done by such two or more justices, if otherwise lawful, shall be deemed to be and to have been valid to all intents and purposes.

Act may be Amended, &c.

3. And be it enacted, That this Act may be amended or repealed by any Act to be passed in this present session of parliament.

---

9. AN ACT TO PROVIDE A MORE CONVENIENT MODE OF LEVYING AND COLLECTING COUNTY RATES, COUNTY POLICE RATES, AND DISTRICT POLICE RATES, IN PARISHES SITUATED PARTLY WITHIN AND PARTLY WITHOUT THE LIMITS OF BOROUGHS WHICH ARE NOT LIABLE TO SUCH RATES—12 & 13 VIC. C. 65. *Passed 28th July*, 1849.

The Overseers of Parishes situated partly within Boroughs and partly without to collect the County Rates, County Police Rates, and District Police Rates, levyable on the Part of the Parish not comprised within the Borough.

1. Whereas there are several parishes and places in England and Wales, parts of which are comprised in boroughs not subject to contribute to the county rate or county or district police rate, while the parts out of the borough are liable to contribute thereto: And whereas there are several parishes parts of which are comprised in boroughs which are subject to district, borough, and other rates, while the parts out of the boroughs are not liable to contribute thereto: Be it enacted by the Queen's Most Excellent Majesty, by and with the advice and consent of the Lords Spiritual and Temporal, and Commons, in this present Parliament assembled, and by the authority of the same, That where any parish or place separately maintaining its own poor shall be divided in manner herein-before stated, and any county rate, or county or district police rate, or other rate which may by law be raised in like manner as a county rate, shall be assessable upon the part of the parish or place which is comprised within the county and excluded from the borough, the overseers of such parish or place shall, on receipt of any precept or other lawful demand from the justices of the county, or other due authority in that behalf, demanding the payment of any sum of money as the contribution of the part of such parish or place out of the borough towards any such rate as aforesaid, with all convenient speed assess the sum so required upon the persons liable within such part of the parish or place to pay the poor rate therein, by means of a separate rate, to be made, allowed, and published in like manner as the poor rate, and either by themselves or by the collector of poor rates for the time being appointed for the said parish or place, shall collect the same separately or with the poor rate payable by the parties assessed thereto, and for the purposes of assessing and collecting the same shall have all such powers, authorities, privileges, protections, and incidents as belong to them in the assessing and collection of the poor rate; and all provisions of the law for enforcing the collection of the poor rate, and recovering the costs of the proceedings therein, shall be applicable to the collection of the rate or rates herein provided for.

Similar Provision for the Collection of the Borough Rate in Places similarly situated.

2. And be it enacted, That in every case in which any such parish or place shall be partly within and partly without any borough, the overseers or other persons charged with the collection of the rates made for the relief of the poor in such

parish or place, upon the receipt of any warrant from the mayor, or any justice or justices of the peace, high constable, or other officer duly authorized to act in that behalf within the borough, for the payment of money for the contribution of the part of such parish within such borough towards any district, borough, or other rate, (which warrants every such mayor, justice of the peace, high constable, and other officer shall be severally empowered to direct to them in like manner as if the whole of such parish or place were within their borough,) shall assess upon and levy from the inhabitants and occupiers of all messuages, lands, tenements, and hereditaments liable to the poor rates in that part of their parish or place which is within the borough, the amount mentioned in the warrant, either as a separate rate or rates, for which the said overseers shall have all the powers which belong to them for levying a rate for the relief of the poor, or with and as part of the poor rate to which the inhabitants and occupiers of property within that part of the parish or place may be liable in common with the inhabitants and occupiers of property within the other part thereof which is not within the borough, and out of the monies so levied and collected shall pay the amount mentioned in the warrant to the person duly authorized to receive the same, and in default thereof shall be subject to all the provisions and penalties provided by this Act, or any Act concerning the non-payment of any borough rate.

Appeal against the Rate, and Audit of the Accounts.

3. And be it enacted, That any person assessed to any rate made under the authority of this Act may appeal against the same in like manner, and with the like consequences in all respects, and subject to the same provisions and regulations, as in appeals against the poor rate; and that every overseer and collector shall account for the money levied, collected, and expended under the authority of this act, to the auditor of the district comprising such parish or place, in like manner as for the poor rate, and if any balance be found to be in his hands shall apply the same towards the next rate required for the purpose of this Act, or shall pay the same to his successor in office; and in default of his so applying the same while in office, or making payment to his successor within seven days after the balance shall have been found, such auditor shall proceed to recover the same from the person holding the same, in like manner as sums certified by him to be due from persons accounting shall from time to time be recoverable, and he shall be paid his costs and expenses, when not recovered from the defendant, by the then overseers of the parish or place, who shall be reimbursed out of the balance of such rate, or, if need be, out of the next rate.

Mode of procuring the Funds when the Precept is sent to the Guardians of the Union comprising the divided Place—7 & 8 Vic. c. 33.

4. And be it enacted, That where a precept shall be issued to the guardians of the union comprising any such parish or place, under the provisions of the Act passed in the eighth year of the reign of Her Majesty, intituled, " An Act for Facilitating the Collection of County Rates, and for Relieving High Constables from Attendance at Quarter Sessions in certain Cases, and from certain other Duties," and such precept shall contain a sum to be assessed and charged in respect of any such rate as is herein provided for upon a part of such parish or place as aforesaid, the said guardians may require the overseers of such parish or place to pay to their treasurer a sum of money sufficient to enable the said guardians to pay the sum so assessed, with the other sums mentioned in the said precept, to the treasurer of the county or other person lawfully authorized to receive it; and the said overseers shall pay the amount out of any monies in their possession belonging to the parish or place, or to the part of such parish or place respectively, and reimburse themselves, if necessary, by a rate, to be levied as herein-before described, upon the persons liable thereto, or if they have no such monies shall forthwith proceed to levy and collect the requisite amount by such rate, and pay the same over to the treasurer of the said guardians: Provided, nevertheless, that if such overseers make default and do not make the requisite payment within the appointed time, they shall be subject to be proceeded against in like manner as the overseers of a parish wholly situated within the county are subjected to under the provisions of the said Act.

Where the Amount required for the County or other Rate is small, the making of the Rate for Reimbursement may be postponed.

5. And be it enacted, That where the amount required in respect of any such county rate, police or district police rate, from any part of such parish or place as aforesaid, shall in the

judgment of such overseers be so small as to render the levying and collecting of a separate rate for it inconvenient, the overseers may postpone the reimbursement of themselves for any such advance as aforesaid, and they or their successors may afterwards, on the recurrence of the next precept or other lawful demand, or of that next but one, levy and collect such a rate as aforesaid to raise the whole amount so previously advanced and unsatisfied out of the poor rates of the parish, as well as the amount required by the then precept or demand, and shall apply the sum so collected in reimbursement of the previous payments, and the satisfaction of such precept or demand, and shall apply the balance, if any, towards the discharge of the next precept or demand.

Repeal of certain Part of 1 *Vic.* c. 81.

6. And be it enacted, That from the twenty-ninth day of September, One thousand eight hundred and forty-nine, so much of the Act passed in the first year of Her Majesty, intituled, "An Act to provide for the Levying of Rates in Boroughs and Towns having Municipal Corporations in England and Wales," as applies to the making, levying, and collecting the county rate and borough rate in divided parishes or places, shall, except in respect of rates before that time made, levied, or collected, or of any arrears of rates in course of being collected, be repealed, and all balances which may remain over the sums required by the precepts under which the rate was levied shall be applicable towards the discharge of the next county rate or borough rate assessed upon such divided parish or place, and if not so applied by the party holding the same shall be recoverable by the person entitled to receive the same, on complaint before two justices of the peace of the county having jurisdiction in that part of the parish or place, who shall make an order for the payment of the sum due, to be enforced in like manner and with the like consequences as orders of justices for the payment of money shall be then by law enforceable.

Act may be Amended, &c.

7. And be it enacted, That this Act may be amended or repealed by any Act to be passed in this session of parliament.

10.—AN ACT TO CONTINUE AN ACT OF THE LAST SESSION OF PARLIAMENT, FOR CHARGING THE MAINTENANCE OF CERTAIN POOR PERSONS IN UNIONS UPON THE COMMON FUND; AND TO MAKE CERTAIN AMENDMENTS IN THE LAWS FOR THE RELIEF OF THE POOR. 12 & 13 VIC. c. 103, *passed 1st August,* 1849.

11 & 12 *Vic.* c. 110.—*Certain Provisions of* 11 & 12 *Vic.* c. 110, *continued for a limited time.*

1. Whereas by an Act passed in the twelfth year of the reign of Her present Majesty, intituled "An Act to alter the Provisions relating to the Charges for the Relief of the Poor in Unions," Provisions were made whereby the costs of the relief and the expences of the burial of certain poor persons therein described are made chargeable upon the common fund of the union until the thirtieth day of September in the present year; and it is expedient that such term should be extended, and that various amendments should be made in the laws relating to the relief of the poor: Be it therefore enacted by the Queen's Most Excellent Majesty, by and with the advice and consent of the Lords Spiritual and Temporal, and Commons in this present Parliament assembled, and by the authority of the same, that the provisions in the said Act regarding the charge of such costs and expenses upon the common fund, which provisions would, unless continued by Parliament, expire on the thirtieth day of September next, shall be continued in full force until the thirtieth day of September, One thousand eight hundred and fifty, and to the end of the then next session of parliament.

Who may be deemed a destitute foundling within the 11 & 12 *Vic.* c. 110.

2. And be it enacted, That the term "Destitute Foundling" contained in the said Act, shall extend to any destitute child under the age of twelve years who shall be deserted by both parents or by its surviving parent, and who shall not be in the care or custody of some relative, guardian, or friend, and whose settlement shall not be known.

Persons chargeable to the Common Fund brought within the Provisions of 5 *Geo.* 4, *&c.*

3. And be it enacted, That the chargeability of any person to the common fund of a union shall have the same effect and shall be attended with the same consequences as the chargeability of any poor person to a parish in respect of proceedings

to be taken under the Act of the fifth year of the reign of his late Majesty George the Fourth, intituled "An Act for the Prevention of Vagrancy," or under the statutes for the removal from England of poor persons born in Scotland or Ireland, or in the Isle of Man, or Scilly, Jersey, or Guernsey, or under the statutes for the removal of lunatic paupers to asylums, or under any statute against unlawfully causing or procuring the removal of any poor person.

Removal of a Lunatic to an Asylum, or of a Pauper to a Workhouse of the Union, not to be deemed an interruption of the residence under 9 & 10 Vic. c. 66, but the time to be excluded from computation.

4. And be it enacted, That the removal of any lunatic pauper to an asylum, licensed house, or registered hospital, under the authority of the statutes in that behalf, or of any pauper, otherwise than under an order of removal from his place of abode in any parish of a union to the workhouse of such union, shall not be deemed to be an interruption of the residence of such pauper within the meaning of the statute of the tenth year of the reign of Her Majesty, intituled "An Act to Amend the Laws relating to the Removal of the Poor," but the time spent in such lunatic asylum, licensed house, or registered hospital or workhouse respectively, and the time during which any person shall be relieved at the charge of the common fund of the union, shall be wholly excluded from the computation of the time of residence which, according to the provisions of such statute, will exempt a poor person from being removed.

The Costs of Lunatic Poor, being irremovable, to be borne by the Common Fund.

5. And be it enacted, That all the costs and expenses incurred, or hereafter to be incurred, since the twenty-fifth day of March last, in and about the obtaining any order of justices for the removal and maintenance of a lunatic pauper who shall have been or shall be removed under any such order to any asylum, licensed house, or registered hospital, and who, if not a lunatic, would have been exempt from removal by reason of some provision in the said last-recited Act of the tenth year of the reign of Her Majesty, shall, until the time when the provisions herein-before contained shall cease, be borne by the common fund of the union comprising the parish wherein such pauper lunatic was resident at the time when such lunatic pauper was so removed to such asylum, licensed house, or registered hospital, notwithstanding the order for the payment thereof shall have been made upon the overseers of such parish, or the parish of the settlement, or upon the treasurer or guardians of the union in which either parish shall be comprised.

No Person to be appointed Overseer who is interested in certain Contracts.

6. And be it enacted, That no person shall be qualified to be appointed to be an overseer of the poor in any parish who at the time of the proposed appointment shall be engaged or directly or indirectly concerned in any contract for the supply of goods, wares, materials, or provisions for the workhouse, or for the relief of the poor in such parish or in the union comprising such parish: provided always, that no rate or assessment made, nor any other act or thing done, by such person as overseer, nor the service of any notice, demand, order, or process upon him as such, shall, if in other respects legal and sufficient, be deemed invalid by reason only of such disqualification.

Recovery of Contributions when Copy of the Order served upon One Overseer.

7. And be it enacted, That where the guardians of any union or parish shall make any order for the payment of money upon overseers or other officers of any parish upon whom they are empowered by law to make it, and a copy of such order shall be served upon any one of such overseers or other officers, it shall be lawful for the said guardians to enforce such order against the person so served as fully and as effectually as if a copy thereof had been also served upon every one of such overseers or other officers.

On Vacancy in the Office of Auditor, Poor Law Board to appoint a temporary Auditor to audit Accounts incomplete.

8. And be it enacted, That when any auditor shall die, resign, or be removed, or become incompetent to act, at any time when the audit of the accounts of the parishes or unions within his district shall not be completed, the Poor Law Board may, by Order under their seal, appoint temporarily some other person to audit the accounts of the several parishes or unions which may then be ready to be audited; and such temporary auditor shall have the same powers and authorities, and shall be subject to the same

obligations and duties, as the ordinary auditor would have possessed or would have been subject to, and shall receive such remuneration as the said Commissioners shall direct for the performance of his services herein.

Certain Limitations in 11 *&* 12 *Vic. c.* 43, *not to apply to Proceedings by Auditors.*

9. And whereas in the Act of the last Session of Parliament, intituled "An Act to Facilitate the Performance of the Duties of Justices of the Peace out of Sessions within England and Wales with respect to summary Convictions and Orders," it is enacted, that in all cases where no time had then been or should thereafter be specially limited for making the complaints, or laying the informations therein referred to, every such complaint should be made and every such information laid within six calendar months from the time when the matter of such complaint or information re-respectively arose; and doubts have been entertained whether the provision aforesaid applies to proceedings by auditors to recover sums certified by them to be due in the accounts of officers or other persons, and it is desirable to remove such doubts: Be it therefore declared and enacted, That nothing in the provision of the said Act herein recited shall be deemed to apply to any such proceeding by any auditor, but that no auditor shall commence any such proceeding after the lapse of nine calendar months from the disallowance or surcharge by such auditor, or, in the event of an application by way of appeal against the same to the Court of Queen's Bench or to the Poor Law Board, after the lapse of nine calendar months from the determination thereupon.

In Proceedings for Penalties and Forfeitures under Act 5 *Wm.* 4, *or any subsequent Statute, full Costs to be allowed.*

10. And be it enacted, That in the case of the prosecution of any information, or the proceeding for any penalty or forfeiture, or for enforcing any order under the said Statute of the fifth year of the reign of his late Majesty King William the Fourth, or of any subsequent Statute incorporated therewith, where judgment shall be given against the defendant, and the justices shall order or direct such defendant to pay the costs, such costs shall, in addition to other costs lawfully chargeable, include all such costs and expenses incurred in respect of such prosecution or the laying of such information, or the preferring of the complaint, or the making of the application, and the attendance of the party, or his counsel or attorney, and the summoning and attendance of the witnesses required to prove the case, as the justices shall think fit to allow, and find to have been reasonably and properly incurred.

Auditors may recover Costs of Proceedings to enforce due Attendance at the Audit.

11. And be it enacted, That where any auditor shall lay any information for a penalty in consequence of the default of any officer or other person to attend the audit, or the adjournment thereof, or to produce the proper account or vouchers, or to make or sign the proper declaration before him, the costs incurred by such auditor, when not recovered from the defendant in such information, shall, if the Poor Law Board consent thereto, be payable to such auditor, and be chargeable in like manner as the costs incurred by an auditor in enforcing the payment of sums certified by him to be due.

Orders of the Poor Law Commissioners or Poor Law Board may be acted upon, if the Parties think fit, within the Fourteen Days after being sent.

12. And whereas by the said Act of the fifth year of the reign of his late Majesty King William the Fourth provision is made for the sending of copies of the Rules, Orders, and Regulations of the Poor Law Commissioners to certain persons therein described; and it is also therein enacted, that no Rule, Order, or Regulation of the said Commissioners, except certain Orders therein specially excepted, shall be in force until the expiration of fourteen days after the copies thereof shall have been sent by the said Commissioners: And whereas parties to whom such Orders have been addressed have often acted in conformity therewith within the period of fourteen days, and it is often convenient that they should do so: Be it therefore enacted, That nothing in the said Act contained shall be taken to invalidate any act or proceeding heretofore or hereafter to be done or taken in conformity with any Order of the said Commissioners or of the Poor Law Board by the person or persons to whom the same shall have been or shall be addressed, although the period of fourteen days shall not have elapsed from the sending of the copies of the said Order when any such Act shall have been done or proceeding taken.

Limitation of Time upon the Issue of a Certiorari to bring up the Orders of the Poor Law Commissioners or Poor Law Board.

13. And be it enacted, That no writ of *certiorari* shall be granted, issued forth, or allowed to remove into the Court of Queen's Bench any Order, Rule, or Regulation of the Poor Law Commissioners, or of the Poor Law Board, heretofore made, unless such *certiorari* be moved or applied for within twelve months next after the passing of this Act; and in respect of any Order, Rule, or Regulation to be hereafter made, within twelve months next after the day when the copy thereof shall be sent in the manner required by the several statutes in that behalf.

Guardians of a Union or Parish may contract to receive in their Workhouses certain Poor belonging to some other Union or Parish within certain Limits.

14. And be it enacted, That where the workhouse of any union or parish shall be governed and regulated by Rules, Orders, or Regulations of the Poor Law Commissioners or of the Poor Law Board, the guardians of the union or parish to which such workhouse belongs, in case of the overcrowding of the workhouse of any other union or parish, or the prevalence or reasonable apprehension of any epidemic or contagious disease, or in and towards carrying out any legal resolution for the emigration of poor persons, may, with the consent of the Poor Law Board, receive, lodge, and maintain in the first-mentioned workhouse, upon such terms as shall be mutually agreed upon by the respective boards of guardians, any poor person belonging to such other parish or union; and such poor person so received into such first-mentioned workhouse shall while therein be treated in all respects in like manner, and be subject to the same regulations and liabilities, as the other poor persons therein, and shall be deemed to be chargeable in the first instance to the common fund of the union, or to the parish in the workhouse whereof such poor person shall be received: Provided always, that the abiding of any such poor person in such workhouse shall in all other respects be attended with the same legal consequences as if such workhouse had been situated within the union or parish from which such poor person shall have been sent.

Mode of describing Collectors of Poor Rates in Indictments for Larceny and Embezzlement.

15. And whereas the guardians of certain unions and parishes under the authority of the Orders of the Poor Law Commissioners and of the Poor Law Board are empowered to appoint Collectors of poor rates and assistant overseers for some one or more of the parishes comprised within their union or for their parish, as the case may be, who collect and receive the money and other property of the parish or parishes for which they are appointed; and in cases of embezzlement or larceny of such money or property by such collector or assistant overseer difficulty has arisen as to the proper description of his office in the indictment or other proceeding: Be it therefore enacted, That in respect of any indictment or other criminal proceeding every collector or assistant overseer appointed under the authority of any Order of the Poor Law Commissioners or the Poor Law Board shall be deemed and taken to be the servant of the inhabitants of the parish whose money or other property he shall be charged to have embezzled or stolen, and shall be so described; and it shall be sufficient to state any such money or property to belong to the inhabitants of such parish, without the names of any such inhabitants being specified.

Guardians may appropiate certain Property of Paupers.

16. And be it enacted, That where any pauper shall have in his possession or belonging to him any money or valuable security for money, the guardians of the union or parish within which such pauper is chargeable may take and appropriate so much of such money or the produce of such security, or recover the same as a debt before any local court, as will reimburse the said guardians for the amount expended by them, whether on behalf of the common fund or of any parish in the relief of such pauper, during the period of twelve months prior to such taking and appropriation, or prior to such proceeding for the recovery thereof (as the case may be;) and in the event of the death of any pauper having in his possession or belonging to him any money or property, the guardians of the union or parish wherein such pauper shall die may reimburse themselves the expenses incurred by them in and about the burial of such pauper, and in and about the maintenance of such pauper at any time during the twelve months previous to the decease.

Expenses of Burials recoverable as Loans.

17. And be it enacted, That it shall be lawful for the guardians of any union or parish to pay the costs of the burial of any poor person dying out

of the limits of such union or parish who was at the time of the death in the receipt of relief from such guardians, and that the cost of burying any poor person by or under the direction of any guardians or overeeers shall be recoverable in like manner and from the same parties as the cost of any relief (if given to such person when living) would have been recoverable.

Guardians and Vestry in Parishes under Local Acts enabled to consent to Orders of the Poor Law Board.

18. And whereas by the said recited Act of the fifth year of the reign of his late Majesty the Poor Law Board are empowered, by and with the consent in writing of a majority of the guardians of any union, or with the consent of a majority of the rate-payers and owners of property entitled to vote in any parish, by writing under their hand and seal, to make certain Orders for the building, purchasing, hiring, enlarging, or altering of a workhouse: And whereas in many parishes, not comprised in any union, the affairs relating to the relief of the poor are managed by a select vestry, or by guardians appointed or elected under the authority of some local act, and in such parishes it is difficult to obtain the opinion of the rate-payers and owners of property upon any such question: Be it therefore enacted, That in any parish where there shall be a select vestry lawfully appointed, or a board of guardians appointed under any local Act, the consent in writing of the major part of the select vestry, or of the guardians, as the case may be, shall be sufficient to enable the Poor Law Board to issue any Order, Rule, or Regulation in all such cases as are herein-before referred to, where the consent of the rate-payers and owners of property would but for this provision have been requisite: Provided that where in any parish there shall be a select vestry and also a board of guardians, the consent in writing of the major part of the vestry or guardians shall be sufficient, according as such vestry or guardians respectively shall by law be empowered to carry the directions of the said Board into execution.

In case of Equality of Votes Chairman to have casting Vote.

19. And be it enacted, That in the case of an equality of votes upon any question at a meeting of the guardians of any union or parish the presiding chairman at such meeting shall have a second, or casting vote.

Guardians may expend limited Sum for Purposes of Emigration without a previous Vestry Meeting.

20. And be it enacted, That the guardians of any union, or of any separate parish for which a board of guardians is or shall be established, may expend, with the order and subject to the Rules and Regulations of the Poor Law Board, but not otherwise, any sum of money not exceeding ten pounds for each person, in and about the emigration of poor persons having settlements in such parish, or in any parish in such union respectively, without the necessity of the rate-payers and owners of property therein meeting and giving their consent (as required by the said Act of the fifth year of King William the Fourth) to such expenditure, and such guardians shall charge the same to the parish of the settlement, in every case where such poor person resided therein or was removeable thereto at the time of the emigration: Provided always, that the guardian or (if more than one) a majority of the guardians of such last-mentioned parish shall express his or their concurrence in writing in the resolution of the board of guardians for such expenditure, and that such written concurrence shall be transmitted by the clerk of the union in communicating that resolution to the Poor Law Board: Provided also, that the aggregate amount of the monies expended in the course of any one year in and about the emigration of such poor persons shall not exceed one half the average yearly poor-rate raised in the said parish for the three preceding years.

Interpretation Clause, and incorporation of the Statutes.

21. And be it enacted, That the several words used in this Act shall be construed in the manner prescribed by the said recited Act of the fifth year of the reign of his late Majesty, and the Statutes explaining and extending it; and that the Commissioners for administering the Laws for the Relief of the Poor in England may be described in all instruments, documents, and proceedings in courts of law or otherwise, and may execute all powers and authorities from time to time vested in them, by the name of "The Poor Law Board," and by such name shall be understood in this Act; and that all the provisions of the said last-mentioned Act and of the said Statutes not repealed shall extend to this Act, except where any such provision would be inconsistent with anything herein contained.

Act to extend to England and Wales only.

22. And be it enacted, That this Act shall extend only to England and Wales.

Act may be Amended, &c.

23. And be it enacted, That this Act may be amended or repealed by any Act to be passed in this session of parliament.

---

11. AN ACT TO AMEND THE NUISANCES REMOVAL AND DISEASES PREVENTION ACT, 1848—12 & 13 VIC. C. 111. *Passed 1st August,* 1849.

11 & 12 *Vic.* c. 123—*This Act to be construed with Nuisances Removal and Diseases Prevention Act,* 1848, *as One Act.*

1. Whereas it is expedient that the Nuisances Removal and Diseases Prevention Act, 1848, should be amended, and that the powers of the General Board of Health in relation to certain of the purposes of that Act should be extended: Be it therefore enacted by the Queen's Most Excellent Majesty, by and with the advice and consent of the Lords Spiritual and Temporal, and Commons, in this present Parliament assembled, and by the authority of the same, That this Act shall be deemed to be part of the Nuisances Removal and Diseases Prevention Act, 1848, and shall be construed accordingly.

Power to Summon Witnesses, &c., in certain Cases.

2. And be it enacted, That it shall be lawful for the General Board of Health, or any two of the members thereof, from time to time as such Board shall see occasion, to require, by summons under the seal of the said Board, or if by two only of the members of such Board, then under the hands of such two members and the seal of the said Board, (according to the form in the schedule annexed to this Act, or as near thereto as the case will permit,) any person to appear before such Board to testify on oath the truth touching any matters respecting which the said board are now or may hereafter be authorized to inquire (which oath any member of the said Board is hereby empowered to administer;) and every person who, after tender of reasonable expenses in that behalf, shall not appear pursuant to such summons, or shall not assign some reasonable excuse for not so appearing, or refusing to be sworn or examined, shall, upon being convicted thereof before one of Her Majesty's justices of the peace or the sheriff for the county or place at and within which such person shall have been by such summons required to appear and give evidence shall be situate, for every such neglect or refusal forfeit a sum not exceeding twenty pounds.

Secretary of Board of Health may institute and carry on Prosecution for Violation or Neglect of Regulations.

3. And be it enacted, That the secretary of the General Board of Health may, on the Order of the said Board, sealed with the seal of such Board, and signed by any two members thereof, prosecute any person for wilful violation or neglect of any Direction or Regulation issued by such Board under the Nuisances Removal and Diseases Prevention Act, 1848; and all penalties sued for and recovered by such secretary shall, notwithstanding anything contained in the last-mentioned Act, be paid to him, and be applied in defraying the costs and expenses incurred by him in such prosecutions, and the balance (if any) shall be applied in such manner as the Lords Commissioners of Her Majesty's Treasury shall direct; and if the penalties so recovered shall be insufficient to defray such costs and expenses, the deficiency shall be defrayed out of any monies which may be from time to time provided by Parliament for that purpose.

Guardians of the Poor, &c., may direct Prosecutions in certain Cases.

4. And be it enacted, That the guardians, directors, wardens, governors, or overseers of the poor, or parochial board, or other like officers having the management of the poor, or acting under the authority of any Local Act of Parliament for the paving, cleansing, drainage, or lighting any town or parish, may from time to time direct any prosecutions or legal proceedings for or in respect of the wilful violation or neglect of any Direction or Regulation issued by the General Board of Health, or in Ireland Commissioners of Health, under the Nuisances Removal and Diseases Prevention Act, 1848, and may defray the expenses of such prosecutions or proceedings out of the funds in their hands applicable to the relief of the poor.

Ex-officio Guardians may Act as Justices.

5. And be it enacted, That justices of the peace being *ex-officio* guardians of the poor may in all cases, notwithstanding their holding the office of guardian, exercise in petty session the jurisdiction

vested in them as justices of the peace under the Nuisances Removal and Diseases Prevention Act, 1848.

Guardians of the Poor &c., may take certain Proceeding upon the Certificate of Medical or Relieving Officer.

6. And be it enacted, That guardians, directors, wardens, governors, overseers, or parochial board, or other like officers having the management of the poor, or acting under such authority as aforesaid, upon the receipt of a certificate of any medical or relieving officer of the union or parish for which any such guardians, directors, governors, overseers of the poor, or parochial board, or other officers, act, stating the existence of any of the cause or causes of complaint specified in the sections numbered I. and II. in the copies of the Nuisances Removal and Diseases Prevention Act, 1848, printed by Her Majesty's printers, or in Ireland upon the receipt of a like certificate of any such medical or relieving officer, or of any two constables of the constabulary force of the district or place or of any two constables of the Dublin police within the Dublin police district, shall take all such proceedings as by the said sections respectively are required to be taken upon the receipt of a notice in writing signed by two inhabitant householders, and in the same manner (as nearly as may be) as if such notice had been given.

Guardians of the Poor, &c., may defray certain Expenses without an order of Justices, Sheriff, or Magistrates.

7. And whereas it is enacted by the Nuisances Removal and Diseases Prevention Act, 1848, that all costs and expenses reasonably incurred in carrying into effect certain provisons therein contained, and not recovered from any owner or occupier of the premises in respect of which such expenses shall have been incurred, shall upon an order in writing, specifying the sum to be paid, under the hands and seals of two justices, or in Scotland under the hands of the sheriff or magistrate, or two justices, be retained, paid, or defrayed by the treasurer of the guardians of the poor, or parochial board, or by the overseers of the poor or other proper officers, out of the funds in their hands applicable to the relief of the poor; and it is expedient that such costs and expenses should be retained, paid, and defrayed in certain cases without an order of justices, sheriff, or magistrates: Be it therefore enacted, That whenever any such costs and expenses shall have been or shall be reasonably incurred by any guardians, directors, wardens, governors, overseers of the poor, or parochial board, or other like officers having the management of the poor, and the same shall not have been recovered from the owner or occupier of the premises in respect of which such costs and expenses shall have been incurred, such costs and expenses may, where an order shall have been made by the justices for the removal or abatement of the nuisance, or in any case where the amount shall not exceed twenty shillings, be retained, paid, and defrayed by the treasurer of such guardians, or by such directors, wardens, governors, overseers, or parochial board, or other like officers, (as the case may be,) out of the funds in their hands applicable to the relief of the poor, without the order of any justice or justices of the peace, anything in the said Act to the contrary notwithstanding, and be charged as in the said Act directed.

Guardians of Unions or Parochial Boards may charge Expenses of removing Nuisances on Parish, &c., where Premises situated.

8. And be it enacted, That where the guardians of a union, or parochial board, shall, in the execution of any Order or Regulation of the Board of Health issued under the authority of the said herein-before mentioned Act, expend any money in the removal or abatement of a nuisance from any private premises or land, or from any public place, they may, if they think fit, charge the same, where the expenses do not exceed twenty shillings, to the parish or place or electoral division in the union or combination wherein the premises shall be situated in respect whereof such expenses shall have been incurred, and where they exceed twenty shillings, and the guardians or the majority of the guardians, if more than two guardians of such parish, electoral division, or place, object in writing to the said expenses being so charged, then only upon an order in writing under the hands and seals of two justices, or in Scotland under the hands of the sheriff or magistrates, or two justices, who are hereby required to make such order, upon application on behalf of such guardians.

General Board of Health may cause Inquiry to be made into State of Burial Grounds, and may direct Measures of Precaution.

9. And be it enacted, That it shall be lawful in England or Wales for the General Board of

Health, and in Ireland for the Commissioners of Health, to cause inquiry to be made by a superintending inspector, or by such other ways and means as the General Board of Health or such Commissioners may deem fit to direct, into the state of the burial grounds in any part of England or Wales excepted from the powers of the Public Health Act, 1848, or in any populous city, town, or place in England or Wales to which for the time being the said Act has not been applied, or in any populous city, town, or place in Ireland; and if it appear to the General Board of Health or the said Commissioners that any such burial ground is in such a state as to be dangerous to the health of the persons living in the neighbourhood thereof, it shall be lawful for the said General Board of Health in England and Wales, under the seal of the said Board, and under the hands of two or more members thereof, and the said Commissioners of Health in Ireland, under the hands of two or more of them, to issue such Orders as the said Board or Commissioners respectively may think fit for the application of such disinfecting substances, and for the adoption of such other measures of precaution in relation to the premises, as may, in the opinion of the said Board or Commissioners of Health, tend to lessen or remove the danger to health; and the churchwardens and other persons having the care and control of the burial grounds to which such Orders shall relate shall do all such works and matters in relation thereto as by such Orders may be directed, and all expenses incurred in the execution of such Orders shall be defrayed out of the poor rates of the parish: Provided always, that no such Order as aforesaid shall be made after the end of the next session of parliament.

Where Churchyard is dangerous to Health Churchwardens may agree for the Burial of Parishioners in the Ground of any Cemetery Company, or in the Burial Ground of any other Parish.

10. And be it enacted, That where it appears to the General Board of Health, or the Commissioners of Health in Ireland, that the churchyard or other burial ground of any parish is dangerous to health as aforesaid, and that temporary provision for interment elsewhere is urgently required, the churchwardens of such parish with the consent of the bishop of the diocese and the approval of such General Board of Health, or Commissioners of Health in Ireland, shall if possible, either agree with any cemetery company for the burial in the ground of such company of the bodies of persons having right of burial in the churchyard or other burial ground of such parish, or agree for the burial of such bodies in the churchyard or burial ground of any other parish of which the minister and churchwardens may consent thereto, and make all proper arrangements in relation to such burials: Provided always, that where any such agreement as aforesaid shall be proposed to be made by the churchwardens of any parish, such churchwardens shall submit such proposed agreement to a meeting of the vestry, or persons having the powers of vestry, in such parish, and if the majority of persons assembled at such meeting shall disapprove such agreement the churchwardens shall not proceed therewith; and the expenses incurred by such churchwardens in relation to such agreement, and in carrying the same into effect, shall be paid out of the poor rates of their parish; Provided also, that no such agreement as aforesaid shall be made after the end of the next session of parliament.

General Board of Health may direct Inquiries, where it may be expedient to prohibit Interment.

11. And be it enacted, That whereupon any such inquiry as aforesaid it appears to the General Board of Health that the state of the burial grounds in any parish or in any parishes which may be conveniently united for the purposes herein-after mentioned, and the circumstances of such parish or parishes render it expedient for the protection of the public health that interments should be prohibited in such parish or parishes, except as after mentioned, and that a burial ground or burial grounds should be provided for such parish, or for the common use of such parishes, the General Board of Health may direct a superintending inspector to make inquiry, in the manner directed by the Public Health Act, 1848, or as near thereto as circumstances will permit, into all the circumstances connected with the parochial and other burial grounds of such parish or parishes, and as to the place or places in which any burial ground or burial grounds might be provided, either within or beyond the limits of such parish or parishes, and as to the means which might be provided for the conveyance of bodies for interment, and any other arrangements which might be practicable for facilitating the convenient interment of bodies in the burial ground or burial grounds to be so provided, and as to the rights in any burial

ground in such parish or parishes, not being a parochial burial ground, which might be affected by the prohibition of interments in such parish or parishes, and as to the proportions in which several parishes (if more than one) should contribute to the expense of providing and maintaining a common burial ground or common burial grounds for such parishes, and into such other matters as the General Board of Health may think necessary for the purpose of enabling them to judge of the propriety of framing a scheme to be submitted to parliament as herein-after mentioned, and of the provisions which should be inserted therein; and such superintending inspector shall report in writing, in such manner as the General Board of Health shall direct, the result of his inquiries in relation to the premises.

Upon Report, Board of Health may frame a Scheme for providing new Burial Grounds.

12. And be it enacted, That upon the presentation of such report the General Board of Health shall cause a copy thereof to be transmitted to the bishop of the diocese, and copies thereof to be published, in such manner as they may direct, in the parish or parishes to which such report relates, and to be deposited with the minister and with the churchwardens of such parish or each of such parishes; and the General Board of Health shall receive all such statements in relation to the matter of such report as shall be delivered within a time to be limited by the said Board in this behalf, and may, where they think fit, cause further inquiry to be made in relation to the matter of such report; and if after such inquiry and report, or further inquiry as aforesaid, it appear to the said Board expedient so to do, they may frame a scheme in which shall be set forth such provisions as to the said Board under the circumstances of each case may appear proper for providing a burial ground or burial grounds for such parish or parishes as aforesaid, either within such parish or any of such parishes, or beyond the limits thereof, as the case may appear to require, to be in law the burial ground for the parish or for each of the parishes for the common use of which the same is or are provided, and for the maintenance and due management and control of such burial ground or burial grounds; for securing to the ministers and others having rights in respect of burials in the burial grounds in which interment is to be prohibited compensation by like rights in respect of burials in the burial ground or burial grounds proposed to be provided or otherwise, and for providing and securing rights in such burial ground or burial grounds in substitution for other rights (which in the opinion of the Board may require to be compensated) in grounds in which interment is to be prohibited; for the election or appointment of persons to enter into contracts for providing such burial ground or burial grounds, and to maintain and manage the same; for facilitating the conveyance of the bodies of the dead from the place of death to such burial ground or burial grounds; for determining the proportions in which the expense of providing, maintaining, and managing such burial ground or burial grounds, where the same is or are provided for the common use of any parishes, shall be defrayed by such parishes respectively; for prohibiting, after such burial ground or burial grounds shall be provided, interment in such parish or parishes, except in such cases as it may appear to the said Board may be specified and excepted; and generally for and concerning all matters in relation to such burial ground or burial grounds as aforesaid and the arrangemements consequent upon the prohibition of interments as aforesaid: Provided always, that all provisions which shall be set forth in such scheme concerning the consecration of the burial ground or burial grounds to be provided, and concerning the burial of members of the united Church of England and Ireland, and the compensation to be provided for rights in respect of burials and other rights of ministers of the said united church which may be affected by the prohibition of interment in parochial and other burial grounds, be approved by the bishop of the diocese; Provided also, that such scheme, with the reports of the superintending inspectors in relation to the matters thereof, shall be presented to both Houses of Parliament forthwith after the framing thereof, or, if Parliament be not then sitting, within fourteen days after the next meeting thereof.

Short Title of this Act.

13. And be it enacted, That in citing this Act in any Act of Parliament, deed, instrument, or other proceeding it shall be sufficient to use the words "The Nuisances Removal and Diseases Prevention Amendment Act, 1849."

Act may be amended, &c.

14. And be it enacted, That this Act may be amended or repealed by any Act to be passed in this present session of parliament.

SCHEDULE to which this Act refers.

FORM OF SUMMONS.

We, the General Board of Health, [*or* we, whose names are hereunto set, being two of the members of the Board of Health,] do hereby summon and require you personally to appear before the General Board of Health, at in the parish of in the county of on next, the day of at the hour of in the noon of the same day, and then and there to be examined, and to testify the truth touching certain matters with respect to which the Board is authorized to inquire.

Sealed with the seal of the General Board of Health, [*or* given under our hands and seals, and the seal of the General Board of Health,] this day of in the year of our Lord one thousand eight hundred and

II.—REMOVABILITY.—MARRIED WOMAN LIVING APART FROM HER HUSBAND.

25*th June*, 1849.

Clerk of Wareham and Purbeck Union.—Transmitted the following statement, duly signed, under sec. 4 of 11 & 12 Vic. c. 110:—J. C., a pauper, now residing in West Lulworth Parish, the wife of R. C., belonging to and now resident in the parish of Winfrith Newburgh, both parishes being comprised within this union, (J. C. having resided continuously for seven years in the parish of West Lulworth, separated from her husband, without receiving relief, except for the two last years, during which she has been relieved by the parish of Winfrith, the place of her husband's settlement) now applies to the guardians of the union for relief. Inquired whether such relief should be charged to West Lulworth or Winfrith Newburgh, or the pauper should be considered as irremovable from West Lulworth by her residence therein, and her relief charged to the common fund of the union.

Ans.—The Board have carefully considered this case, which presents some peculiar features; but they see no substantial ground for distinguishing it from Reg. *v.* St. Ebbs, (3 N.S.C. 308,) and Reg. *v.* Pott Shrigley, (*ib.* 317,) which decided that the removability of a wife in the absence of her husband depends upon the question whether he would be removable, if he were with her. In Reg. *v.* St. Ebbs, Lord Denman observed, "If the husband would be removable, were he in the parish, his wife must be removable in his absence." In the present case, although the husband is irremovable from Winfrith, in which parish he is both resident and settled, he would if he came into the parish of West Lulworth, be removable therefrom; and consequently, the wife is removable from the latter parish, notwithstanding that she has resided there for more than five years without relief.

III.—REMOVAL.

1. EVIDENCE OF CHARGEABILITY.

3*rd May*, 1849.

Clerk of Chard Union.—A pauper residing in the Chard Union having received relief from the Langport Union up to the passing of the 9 & 10 Vic. c. 66, is now removable under the late decision of the Court of Queen's Bench. The Langport Union objecting to repay relief, the overseers of the parish where the pauper is residing and chargeable are desirous of obtaining an order of removal. The magistrates declined to grant an order, unless the clerk of the Langport Union be summoned before them to prove that relief has been repayed up to the passing of the above-mentioned Act. Is it indispensably necessary for the clerk of Langport Union to be summoned for this purpose, and if so, at whose expense?

Ans.—It is incumbent upon the overseers of the removing parish to satisfy the justices of their power to remove the pauper in question. If, in order to do this, it be necessary to summon the clerk or other officers of the Langport Union, this course must be adopted. Those officers are not bound to attend before the justices without such process, and it is clear that, if the pauper is to be removed, the justices must have due authority for granting the requisite order of removal. The Board may remark, however, that, if non-resident relief be the object sought in the present case, it is discretional with the guardians of the Langport Union (if the settlement be duly admitted) to grant such relief or not, as they may think proper; unless, indeed, they are restrained from doing so in this case by the General Prohibitory Order.

2. REMOVAL OF IRISH AND SCOTCH PAUPERS.

9*th July*, 1849.

Clerk of Guardians Isle of Wight.—Requested the advice of the Poor Law Board as to carrying out the provisions of the Act of 8 & 9 Vic. c. 117, for the removal of Irish paupers. 1, Paupers when taken before the justices, with a view to their removal, have refused to take an oath or sign their examinations. Secondary evidence of the statements made by the paupers on their admission to the workhouse as to their place of birth has been tendered to the justices, but they have declined to receive it, as not being in conformity with the terms required by the warrant of removal. 2, Does the Act authorize the justices to remove with their parents the children of Scotch or Irish paupers born in England? The words of the statute are, "may make and issue a warrant to remove such person," any allusion to the wife and children being altogether omitted. These questions are of importance, since the wives and children of Irish soldiers, drafted on foreign service from Albany Barracks, are left chargeable to the island, and much prefer a residence in the workhouse to a removal to Ireland.

Ans.—In reply to your first inquiry, with reference to paupers who refuse to give evidence which may lead to their removal to Ireland, the Board desire to state, that in their opinion the justices have power to compel a pauper in such a case to be examined, provided he has been summoned in the manner pointed out in the 70th sec. of the 7 & 8 Vic. c. 101. With regard to your second question, the Board consider that if the father were born in Ireland, (or Scotland,) the wife and children may be removed there with him, although the children may have been born in England.

---

3. SUSPENSION OF ORDER OF REMOVAL.

6th June, 1849.

Clerk of Kidderminster Union.—Requested the opinion of the Poor Law Board on the following case:—A female pauper, living in and becoming chargeable to the borough of Kidderminster, (not in consequence of sickness or accident,) and being removable, is put under an order of removal to her own parish, and notice of such order is given in the usual way. Before the expiration of the twenty-one days when she could be legally removed, she is seized with illness, which will, in the opinion of the medical officer, produce permanent disability. Can the original order be now suspended on account of the illness, and should a duplicate be served upon the overseers of the parish to which she belongs, or what other course should the overseers adopt?

Ans.—The Board have referred to the several statutes applicable to this subject, and consider that the suspension of an order of removal can only be made at the time when the order itself is made. Under these circumstances, the Board think that no suspension of the order can be obtained in the present case. The overseers may, however, abandon the present order and obtain another, causing the latter to be suspended, in which case they may recover the subsequent expenses of the sickness; or they may rely upon the present order, and execute it by the removal of the pauper when she can be removed. But in this latter case, the Board believe that the parish officers cannot recover any of the expenses which have arisen from the non-execution of the order.

IV.—SETTLEMENT.

1. MARRIAGE WITH DECEASED WIFE'S SISTER.

15th Feb., 1849.

Clerk of Isle of Thanet Union.—A man belonging to Ramsgate, in this union, lost his wife, and was left with three children. He shortly after was married in the parish church of St. Peter to his wife's sister, who belongs to some distant parish. He is now in the workhouse with his second wife and family, and as the legality of the marriage is doubted, the guardians wish for the opinion of the Poor Law Board, as to whether the woman be legally settled in Ramsgate by marriage; or, if she can be removed to her previous settlement.

Ans.—Presuming that the marriage was solemnized subsequently to the passing of the statute 5 & 6 Wm. 4. c. 54, *i. e.*, the 31st of August, 1835, the parties in question are not legally married, inasmuch as the statute above cited renders such marriage null and void. (See Reg. *v.* Chadwick, 17 L. J. R. N. S. M. C. 33.) If this be the case, the woman in question is not the wife of the pauper, and if she be not otherwise irremovable under the 9 & 10 Vic. c. 66, she may accordingly be removed to the parish of her own settlement.

---

2. RENTING A TENEMENT.

19th Feb., 1849.

Clerk of Bedminster Union.—A widow, whose settlement was at Flax Bourton, resided at Backwell, renting a tenement at £4 a year. After she had been in such tenement two years, she married, when her second husband went and lived with her in the tenement, in which they have resided four months since their marriage. Inquired whether the second husband has gained a settlement in Backwell parish by such marriage, and referred, as bearing on the point, to Rex. *v.* North Cerney, 3 Bar. and Ad. 463, and Rex. *v.* Ynyscynhaiarn, B. and C. 233.

Ans.—The Board are of opinion that the second husband of the woman in question has gained a settlement in the parish of Backwell.

3. SETTLEMENT BY ESTATE.

14*th April*, 1849.

Clerk of Chipping Sodbury Union.—Transmitted the following statement, duly signed, under the 11 & 12 Vic. c. 110. sec. 4:—J. G. was born at Old Sodbury, in the year 1811. He was hired by Mr. H., of West Littleton, at Michaelmas, 1829, with whom he lived two years. He was hired by Mr. T., at Dodington, Michaelmas, 1831, in whose service he remained for one year and six weeks, by which means he gained a settlement at Dodington. From that time he has resided at Old Sodbury, and worked as a day labourer for different employers. About ten years ago his mother-in-law, B. S., gave him a small piece of land, (about one perch, not exceeding one pound in value,) in the parish of Old Sodbury, which was assigned to him by a deed. On this land he has erected a small cottage, where he now resides. He borrowed the whole of the money required to build upon mortgage, a great part of which is now unpaid. He is now receiving relief from the Chipping Sodbury Union. Inquired whether such relief is to be charged to the common fund of the union, or to the parish of Old Sodbury.

Ans.—Upon the facts contained in this statement, the Board are of opinion that J. G. has acquired a settlement in Old Sodbury by estate; consequently he is not rendered irremovable by reason of the Poor Removal Act, 9 & 10 Vic. c. 66; and his relief, therefore, is not chargeable to the common fund of the Chipping Sodbury Union.

4. SETTLEMENT.

13*th July*, 1849.

Clerk of Teesdale Union.—L. C. made his last will, whereby he devised unto his four sons, John, William, George, and James, and to their heirs as tenants in common, a freehold farm in the township of Middleton, in Teesdale, subject to the payment of several legacies and certain debts therein mentioned. The will contains the following clause:—"I do hereby declare it to be my will and intention, and I expressly request and direct that my said sons, George and James C —— may be allowed to receive the whole of the rents, issues, and profits arising from the whole of my aforesaid freehold hereditaments for and during the term of five years from the time of my decease, and that after payment of the interest of the beforementioned debts, and necessary repairs and expenses, they expend and apply at their discretion the remainder of such rents, issues, and profits in the completion of the dwelling-house now standing upon my said allotment at Pikestone Brow, and in the erection of a toofall thereto, to be used as a hayhouse, back kitchen, and milkhouse, and in the fencing and improvement of my said allotment." The testator died on the 31st of October, 1840. In October, 1845, at the expiration of the five years mentioned in the clause, the four sons took actual possession of the estate, but they had been in such actual possession above a fortnight, until John C —— sold his share and conveyed it to his brothers. John had resided ever after his father's death in the township of Middleton, in Teesdale. During part of the five years beforementioned, he (John) rented some property at Middleton, in Teesdale, of his two brothers William and James, as yearly tenant, commencing his tenancy in the spring of 1844, and holding for a year. He held a house and some land, the land at £7. 10*s.* a year rental, and the house at £3. 10*s.* a year. The land belonged to his brother William, and the house to James. John resided in Middleton in Teesdale during his tenancy. He did not pay the rent in cash, but did work for his brothers to above the amount which was allowed and accepted when they settled their accounts. He was assessed to and paid the parochial rates for his holding. The township of Middleton in Teesdale hesitate to accept John C ——'s widow and family (he being now dead) on the ground that the five years' clause prevented him gaining a settlement by estate, and that the renting of the house and land of two different landlords, and not paying the rent in cash, prevent a settlement by renting a tenement. On the other hand, it is contended that the possession by George and James under the clause was the possession of all, that this was not an estate in remainder but a present interest, the property merely being subject to the management of George and James for five years for specific purposes. Also, that the renting and payment in this case are sufficient. To save the cost of litigation, the township of Middleton have consented to abide by the opinion of the Poor Law Board on the subject.

Ans.—The first question raised as to the settlement by estate in this case is not free from difficulty, as the terms of the devise are peculiar, and the Board are not prepared to express any opinion as to the settlement by estate, because they think a settlement was gained by the renting of the tenement referred to by John ——. They do not find in the statutes bearing upon this point that any difficulty is raised as to the tenement being composed of separate holdings, provided that in each case there is a hiring for a year. Neither do they find it necessary that the rent should be paid in money. If it be paid in money's worth, as, for instance, in services rendered, it seems to the Board that these statutes will be satisfied. The Board, therefore, are of opinion that, under the circumstances stated in your letter, a settlement was gained by the deceased, John C ——, in the township of Middleton.

V.—VACCINATION.

24th August, 1849.

Clerk of Wem Union.—The medical officer of one of the districts having vaccinated the children of persons who are not paupers, but who are in good circumstances, and able to pay for their children being vaccinated, inquired if such practice is to be continued. The guardians think it was never intended that such persons should have their children vaccinated at the expense of the parish. Inquired also, whether in case a child be unsuccessfully vaccinated, the medical officer must again perform the operation if the child be brought to him for that purpose.

Ans.—The statute 3 & 4 Vic. c. 29, does not confine the contracts for vaccination to persons in receipt of relief from the poor rates, and the statute 4 & 5 Vic. c. 32, expressly enacts that vaccination is not to be deemed relief, the object of the legislature being to promote vaccination generally. As the contract, which the guardians are required to make for vaccination, under the 3 & 4 Vic. c. 29, is for the vaccination "of all persons resident in the union," it is certainly open to any persons therein, whether in the condition of paupers or otherwise, to apply to the public vaccinator. The Board presume that the guardians of the Wem Union have adopted the form of contract for vaccination generally used in unions, which provides that payment shall be made only for successful cases. If every case be properly attended to there ought not to arise any question as to the vaccinator's duty in the event of any child being brought to him a second time for vaccination. But the Board apprehend that if the operation has not been in the first instance successful, the vaccinator should again vaccinate the child.

Number of Persons Vaccinated by the Public Vaccinators in England and Wales, in the Years ending 29th September, 1844, 1845, 1846, 1847, 1848, and 1849.

Years.	Number of Persons Vaccinated.	Number of Persons successfully Vaccinated.
1844	290,453	278,192
1845	362,087	347,765
1846	271,219	258,165
1847	267,895	247,762
1848	390,129	374,958
1849	345,315	333,248
Totals of the 6 years.	1,927,098	1,840,090

London: Printed by order of the Poor Law Board, by BLACKBURN & BURT, 90½, Holborn Hill, and Published by CHARLES KNIGHT, 90, Fleet Street.

AN

OFFICIAL CIRCULAR

OF PUBLIC DOCUMENTS AND INFORMATION:

DIRECTED BY THE POOR LAW BOARD TO BE PRINTED, CHIEFLY FOR THE USE OF THE BOARDS OF GUARDIANS AND THEIR OFFICERS.

No. 31.] NOVEMBER, 1849. [N.S.

CONTENTS.

I.—APPRENTICESHIP.—FARMING A BUSINESS.

16th Nov., 1849.

Clerk of Brecknock Union.—Inquiring whether farming may be regarded as a "trade" or "business" under Art. 53 of the General Consolidated Order, and if so, which of the two terms should be inserted in the indenture of a poor boy, who is proposed to be apprenticed to a farmer.

Ans.—It appears to the Board that farming, if not a trade is a business, and, therefore, they are of opinion that the guardians of the Brecknock Union may properly insert that term in the indenture.

II.—BURIAL.—LIABILITY OF WIDOW TO PAY THE EXPENSE OF HER DECEASED HUSBAND'S FUNERAL.

20th Dec., 1849.

Clerk of Royston Union.—A pauper belonging to a parish in this union has for some years been separated from his wife, by mutual agreement; and for the most part of that time has been supported at the expense of the parish. The wife has, it is believed, been for a long period receiving a good income for her services as a housekeeper, but no claim has ever been made on her for the whole or any part of the relief to her husband. He has recently died in the workhouse, destitute, and the guardians of the parish, believing that the wife has the means, are desirous of knowing whether they can legally call on her to defray the funeral expenses of her late husband.

Ans.—The Board do not in this case consider the widow to be herself chargeable with the cost of the relief given to her husband in his lifetime, or with the expenses of his burial. If, however, there is now any property in her possession which can be clearly shown to have belonged to the husband at the time of his death, that property might be made available under the 12 & 13 Vic. c. 103, sec. 16, but the Board see great difficulties in the way of such a proceeding, under the circumstances of the present case, as described in your letter, and they think its result so doubtful, that they cannot recommend the guardians to adopt it.

III.—CLERK—DUTIES OF—EXAMINATION OF TREASURER'S PASS-BOOK.

14th July, 1849.

District Auditor.—1, Is it the duty of the union clerk to check the entries in the treasurer's book by those in the union books, so as to ascertain their correspondence? 2, At the end of the half-year there will generally be a difference between the balance of the treasurer's book and the balance appearing in the union ledger—Is it in such cases the duty of the clerk to be prepared at the audit to show specifically the items which comprise such difference? 3, Is the production by the clerk to the board of guardians weekly of the treasurer's declaration as to the balance in his hands, an ascertaining of such balance within the meaning of Art. 202, No. 7, of the Consolidated General Order?

Ans.—The Board are of opinion that it is the duty of the clerk to the guardians so to compare the entries in the treasurer's pass-book, as to ascertain (as far as he may be reasonably able) their general accuracy. This is, indeed, implied by Art. 202, No. 7, of the General Consolidated Order, for the balance due to or from the union at the end of each week cannot be ascertained as therein directed, unless the entries, of which that balance is the result, are found to be correct. The Board certainly think that the mere production of the treasurer's declaration as to the balance, would not be an ascertaining of the balance within the meaning of the Article referred to. Of course, the examination of the entries in the treasurer's pass-book will necessarily be more effective with reference to the payments made or entered in such book, than as to the sums received on behalf of the union; for as regards the former, the clerk must have in his immediate possession the evidence by which their accuracy can be tested. If, at the end of the half-year, there should be a difference or discrepancy between the balance of the treasurer's book and that appearing in the union ledger, the Board think that the clerk who makes up the accounts, and produces them on behalf of the guardians, may reasonably be called upon to explain the cause.

IV.—COLLECTOR.—LAYING INFORMATIONS AGAINST DEFAULTING RATEPAYERS.

2nd August, 1849.

Collector of Poor-rates, Petersfield Union.—He finds, that by an Act of Parliament recently passed for the recovery of the costs of proceedings against defaulters in the payment of poor-rates, he has no power to summon any party, although the parish officers may direct him to do so, as the Act limits that power to the parish officers themselves, so that the overseers must demand the rates of all defaulters, and get out summonses themselves for the recovery of the same. Requested the opinion of the Poor Law Board upon the subject.

Ans.—The Poor Law Board are not prepared to say that the complaint of a collector, duly appointed, as to the non-payment of poor-rates, would not be good; but looking to the provision in the Act of the present session, c. 14, sec. 8, (providing for the recovery of the costs of distraining for rates,) and to the schedules to which that section refers, by which it appears to be contemplated that the information or complaint as to non-payment should be made by the overseers, the Board think it the more desirable, as it is the more safe course, that one of the overseers themselves should make the complaint. It will be for the justice to whom the complaint is made to determine whether he will require the personal attendance of the overseer, or will allow the summons to be granted if the complaint be brought before him by some person on behalf of the overseers.

V.—ELECTION OF GUARDIANS.

1. NOMINATION.

18th April, 1849.

Clerk of Carmarthen Union.—He has treated the nomination of guardian for the parish of A. informal, in consequence of the name of the person nominated being written "Thos. Thomas" instead of "Thomas Thomas;" and the nomination for the parish of B., in consequence of the nominator describing himself as "land owner and occupier," instead of "rate-payer." Requested the Board's opinion as to the validity of these nominations.

Ans.—The Board do not consider the abbreviation of a Christian name a necessary ground for invalidating the nomination, provided the indication of the party intended to be nominated is such as to enable you to identify him. The Board also think that where a nominator describes himself as "owner and occupier," the word "occupier" may be rejected as surplusage, if the party is qualified to vote as owner; but if he is not so qualified, then the nomination will be invalid, as the word "occupier" cannot be treated as equivalent to "rate-payer."

---

2. QUALIFICATION OF CANDIDATE: FRAUD ON THE REVENUE.

13th April, 1849.

Clerk of ——— *Union.*—A. B. has been nominated for guardian of this union for the ensuing year. He was convicted about a year ago by the justices here of a fraud on the revenue, by a breach of the excise laws, and paid the penalty attached to the offence. He was also convicted in 1842, at the assizes in Liverpool, of sedition. The qualification he has obtained is by collusion with another person, who has placed him upon the rate-book as tenant, though he does not occupy the premises, but the rating is sufficient to confer the qualification. Inquired whether fraud on the revenue comes within the proviso to the 48th sec. of the 4 & 5 Wm. 4, c. 76, and if so, whether the clerk will be justified in inserting the term "disqualified" in the voting paper against the name of A. B.

Ans.—The Board can only say, that if you are satisfied of the fact of A. B.'s having been convicted of "fraud," the proviso to the 48th sec. of the 4 & 5 Wm. 4, c. 76, applies, and you will be justified in entering the word "disqualified" against his name on the voting paper. But though in the absence of a copy of the conviction, the Board can offer no opinion as to whether the particular offence committed by A. B. is one within the above provision, they think generally that a breach of excise or revenue regulations would not be a "fraud" within the meaning of the statute. Conviction for sedition certainly does not come within the meaning of the statute, so as to disqualify the person convicted for serving the office of guardian. If you are satisfied that A. B.'s rating is not *bonâ fide*, but fraudulent, it is incumbent upon you to treat the nominated person as disqualified. A fraudulent rating will not, the Board consider, confer a qualification for the office of guardian. The Board, however, make these general observations without prejudice to any future consideration of the subject should it be brought before them hereafter on appeal.

28th April, 1849.

Clerk of same Union.—Transmitting a copy of the conviction above referred to, of which the following is an extract:—"Which said information charged that the said ——— within six months then last past, that is to say, on the Thirtieth day of November, in the year of our Lord One thousand eight hundred and forty-seven, at the parish of ———, in the borough aforesaid, did knowingly harbour, keep, and conceal, and did knowingly permit, and suffer to be harboured, kept, and concealed, divers goods, to wit, two pounds' weight of manufactured tobacco of the value of eighteen shillings and eleven pence, the same being then and there goods liable to the payment of duties of customs, which before that time had been illegally unshipped from a certain vessel without payment of the said duties, contrary to the form of the statute in that case made and provided, whereby the said ——— had forfeited for his said offence the sum of two pounds sixteen shillings and nine pence, which offence has been duly proved before us the said justices, we, the said justices, do therefore convict the said ——— of the said offence, and do adjudge that the said ——— hath forfeited for his said offence the sum of one pound one shilling and three pence."

Ans.—The offence in question, which is a violation of the excise laws, is not a fraud within the meaning of the 48th sec. of 4 & 5 Wm. 4, c. 76.

---

3. CLAIMS TO VOTE IN SEVERAL WARDS.

29th Nov., 1849.

Clerk of Stoke-upon-Trent Parish. — This parish is, by an Order bearing date the 16th of December, 1845, divided into wards, for the purpose of electing guardians for each ward; and it is therein directed, that owners of property, who shall have claimed to vote, shall be entitled to vote as such owners. Several parties are possessed of property in each of the wards, but are resident or have habitations in only one. Inquiring whether a party, who claims as owner in all the wards, is entitled to vote as owner in every ward in which he shall so claim to vote, as well as in the ward in which he shall vote as occupier.

Ans.—Subject to the limitation, as to the number of votes prescribed in the 7 & 8 Vic. c. 101, s. 21, the Board consider that an owner of property, who gives the due notice, may vote in the several wards of the parish of Stoke-upon-Trent, wherein he has property as such owner, though he votes in respect of his occupation in some one ward only.

4. VALIDITY OF NOMINATIONS.

3rd *April*, 1849.

Clerk of Pwllheli Union.—Requesting the opinion of the Poor Law Board, on the validity of the following nominations of persons to be guardians. In the nomination for the parish of Carnguwch, the character and address of the nominator are omitted; the nomination for Llanfaelrhys is signed by a marksman; for Llangwnadle two persons are nominated, although the parish is entitled to return one guardian only.

Ans.—The Board consider the omission of the statement of the character in which the nominator assumes to nominate, to be fatal to the validity of a nomination, and they also consider the omission of the nominator's address to have a like effect. A nomination containing more names than there are guardians to be elected is void from uncertainty; with regard to the signing of a nomination by a marksman it will be seen that Art. 8 of the General Consolidated Order requires the nomination to be signed, and the Board are disposed to consider that a mark is not a signature within the meaning of the Order, unless properly attested; but if it be so attested in any case, the Board think that the Art. of the Order, which requires the nomination papers to be signed by the person nominating, would be sufficiently complied with.

5. RETURN WHERE THERE HAS BEEN NO ELECTION.—GUARDIAN A CONTRACTOR.

19*th April*, 1849.

Clerk of East Ward Union.—The number of guardians to be elected for the township of Kirkby Stephen in this union are three, but no person having been nominated, the guardians elected last year, by the provision 5 & 6 Vic. c. 57, s. 10, are qualified to act as such for the year 1849-50. Two of the guardians in question have signified their willingness to act as such, but the third having become a contractor to the union for the quarter ending June 31st, declines to act at present. Inquiring whether it will be right, in making the list of guardians, to insert the names of all the three guardians in question, in the column for "guardians qualified to act where no guardian has been elected;" and also, whether the contracting guardian can act at the end of his contract without incurring the penalty named in the 4 & 5 Wm. 4, c. 76, s. 51.

Ans.—The Board think you would do right in including in the column specified of the general return the three guardians elected for Kirkby Stephen last year, there having been no nomination for that township in the present year. The Board do not consider that the particular guardian who has entered into a contract with the East Ward Union for the next three months, is thereby rendered legally incapable of serving the office of guardian, though if, while continuing in such office, he performs the contract, he will doubtless expose himself to the penalties provided by the 55 Geo. 3, c. 137, as extended by sec. 51 of the 4 & 5 Wm. 4, c. 76. It is very doubtful whether his abstaining from acting as a guardian, if he continue to hold the office, would be a defence to any action. It is, however, quite optional with the party referred to whether he will continue to act as a guardian for Kirkby Stephen; perhaps the best course will be for him to decline to do so.

VI.—GUARDIANS—MEETINGS OF—MOTIONS NOT SECONDED NEED NOT BE PUT TO THE VOTE.

18*th Oct.*, 1849.

A Guardian of Lancaster Union.—Inquiring whether at a meeting of a board of guardians any guardian who moves a proposition which is not seconded can require the chairman to put such proposition to the vote.

Ans.—There is certainly no provision in the Poor Law Statutes, nor any Regulation of the Poor Law Commissioners or of the Board upon the subject; but the Board believe the almost universal practice of the different boards of guardians, as well as of public meetings of all kinds, and for all purposes throughout the country to be, that a motion falls to the ground if it be not seconded; and the Board are of opinion that a decision to that effect, given in accordance with the bye laws, or general usage, as the case may be, of the particular board of guardians to which a motion is submitted under the circumstances, ought to be adhered to.

VII.—INQUESTS.—PERSONS DYING IN THE WORKHOUSE.

16*th August*, 1849.

Clerk of Brecknock Union.—Transmitting the following resolution, passed by the guardians:—"Ordered, that no inquests be held on the bodies of persons dying in the workhouse, unless there is reason to suspect that the person has died in consequence of neglect."

Ans.—If the resolution of the guardians only

imports that they will not require the coroner to be sent for except under the particular circumstances referred to, the Board think that it is unobjectionable. But if the resolution has any further meaning, the Board must observe, that the guardians cannot themselves prevent the coroner from exercising his own judgment, and from holding an inquest upon the body of any person who dies in the workhouse. The coroner will be responsible if he holds an inquest unnecessarily, and will be subject to the control of the quarter sessions. See Q. *v.* The Justices of Carmarthenshire, 16 L.J.R.M.C. 167.

VIII.—LUNATIC PAUPER—CHARGEABILITY.

19*th Nov.*, 1849.

Clerk of Bedale Union.—J. O., and Ellen, his wife, have resided in the township of Ripon for seventeen years last past, without having received parochial relief. In the month of May last, the wife became insane, and was removed to an asylum at Gate Helmsley, by an order of justice. On the 12th of October last, two justices adjudged the settlement of the wife to be in the parish of Kirkby Fleetham, within this union, and made an order upon the overseers of the parish and the treasurer of the union, to refund the expenses of her examination and maintenance, and to pay the weekly sum of 6*s.* in future (the husband contributing 4*s.* per week) towards her maintenance. The township of Ripon is not in union. The overseers of Kirkby Fleetham contend that they are not liable to refund the sums expended by the township of Ripon, nor to maintain the pauper; the Act 12 & 13 Vic. c. 103, secs. 4, 5, having placed irremovable pauper lunatics on the same footing as other paupers, and that they must be maintained by the parish or union wherein they have had a five years' residence. Inquiring whether or not the parish of Kirkby Fleetham, or the Bedale Union, is liable to refund the expenses incurred by the township of Ripon, for the examination, &c., of the pauper Ellen, and to maintain her in the asylum, her husband being now resident in the township of Ripon, and irremovable therefrom.

Ans.—As the township of Ripon is not included in any union, the 5th sec., 12 & 13 Vic. c. 103, does not apply to the case; and although the pauper, when sent to the lunatic asylum, may have been irremovable to the parish of her settlement, yet, according to the case of Q. *v.* Leaden Roothing, (3 N. S. C.,) the justices are not thereby prevented from making an order under the 8 & 9 Vic. c. 126, to adjudicate the settlement of the lunatic in question, and to provide for the payment of the expenses of her maintenance in the lunatic asylum.

IX.—MEDICAL OFFICER. HIS DUTIES—PAUPERS BELONGING TO CLUBS—ORDERING OF NOURISHMENT.

10*th Nov.*, 1849.

Medical Officer, Brackley Union.—Inquiring whether he is bound to attend, as paupers, those who belong to clubs, from which, during illness, they receive seven shillings a week; and also, whether he has full power to order proper nourishment in all cases where he has received orders to attend, such as wine, meat, &c.; for those things have sometimes been refused when he has been attending the wife or daughter of a labourer, being told that the husband might find them out of his weekly earnings, which he has considered impossible.

Ans.—In reply to your first inquiry, the Board desire to point out, that under Art. 206, No. 1, of the General Consolidated Order, a district medical officer is bound to attend upon any poor person within his district, "whenever he may be lawfully required to furnish such attendance, by a written or printed order of the guardians, or of a relieving officer of the union, or of an overseer." The Board, understanding your inquiry to relate to an order so given by the guardians or relieving officer, consider that, whenever the medical officer receives any such order, he is bound to attend the person to whom the order has reference, without in the first instance entering into a consideration of the question whether such person ought, in the officer's opinion, to be relieved by the guardians or not. The Board think it right to add, however, that any information which the medical officer may possess or obtain, with regard to the means and resources of the pauper, may very properly be brought by him under the notice of the guardians, whose province it is to decide as to the destitution of the applicants for relief; the Board quite admit that the guardians have no right to employ you in attending any but poor persons in the sense of the Art. above quoted. With reference to your second question, the Board feel some difficulty in laying down any general rule upon the subject; but they may remark, that it is certainly competent for the medical officer, and, indeed, incumbent upon him, to prescribe for every pauper whom he may be directed to attend whatever he may deem the condition of the patient to require. If he consider particular articles of nourishment to be necessary in any such case, he should give a certificate thereof to the relieving officer, whose duty it would be to attend to it. (See Act 215, No. 5, General Consolidated Order.)

X.—MEDICAL RELIEF.—MIDWIFERY CASES. —DUTIES OF ASSISTANT OVERSEER.

29*th Nov.*, 1849.

Medical Officer, Basford Union.—Submitting two cases that have recently occurred in the parish of Heanor, which forms a part of the district for which he is medical officer:—The union medical officers are required to attend all cases of pauper confinements, and whenever disease or illness results from a confinement, the medical officer is entitled in every such case to the same fee as if he had been actually present at the birth. He has long been aware, that the authorities in the parish of Heanor have paid old women midwives for attending the poor in their confinements, and in no case whatever have his services been required, except when these old women have been unequal to their duty, or rather undertaking, or when illness, &c., have followed a confinement, and relief been required. In the case of Ann B——, one of the cases referred to, inflammation of the breast had ended in suppuration, and the matter had found its way through the skin before the medical order could be procurred from the assistant overseer. In the other case, there had been considerable flooding, producing great weakness and dropsical effusion, not only into the cellular membrane of the legs, but also into the body, before the order for medical relief was given by the relieving officer, the assistant overseer having refused to give it.

Clerk of Basford Union.—Communicating the following resolution passed by the guardians in reference to the above cases:—" Resolved, that it is considered by this Board to be an act of neglect in the discharge of his duty, on the part of the assistant overseer of Heanor, in the cases of Ann B—— and Rebecca P——, in not having given an order for the attendance of the medical officer for five days after an application for such order had been made."

The Poor Law Board to the Medical Officer.—You have misunderstood the nature of the Board's Regulations, in supposing that medical officers are required to attend all pauper midwifery cases, and that in every such case the medical officer is entitled to a special fee, whether actually present at the birth or not. A medical officer is only legally required to attend on paupers, whether for midwifery cases or for cases of illness, when called upon to do so by a written or printed order, given by some person competent to grant relief; and if a medical officer's services are not given in accordance to such a requisition, he has no legal right to a fee, or other special remuneration from the guardians, excepting always when attendance has been given on a woman in childbirth, under circumstances of difficulty or danger, who was actually receiving relief, or whom the guardians may subsequently decide to have been at the time in a destitute condition.

The Board to the Assistant Overseer of Heanor.—The medical officer of the district comprising the parish of Heanor, having complained to the Poor Law Board that you had refused orders for his attendance on Ann B—— and Rebecca P——, the Poor Law Board have caused an inquiry to be made, and are informed that at the time you refused orders for the medical officer's attendance upon these two cases, the circumstances were clearly of a "sudden and urgent" character, and that, therefore, in these two instances, you have failed to fulfil the duties of your office. The Board wish to explain to you, that although the duty of relieving the poor of your parish is vested in the board of guardians of the Basford Union and their officers, and although you are restricted from giving any relief whatever in money, still, by the 54th sec. of the Poor Law Amendment Act, you are required, in cases of sudden and urgent necessity, to give temporary relief in articles of absolute necessity. The Board consider, that an order for the attendance of the medical officer is such relief as an assistant overseer may give, under the authority of the section referred to; but before you avail yourself of the power which it confers upon you, you will be bound to satisfy yourself that the case is really one of "sudden and urgent necessity," that is to say, of such pressing exigency as not to admit of the delay which might arise in referring to the ordinary source of relief, viz., the board of guardians or the relieving officer. Moreover, by the Regulations of the Poor Law Board, it is also your duty, whenever you have given relief or granted a medical order, forthwith to report the case in writing to the relieving officer of the district, or to the board of guardians, and specify the relief, or the fact of having given such order. The Board trust that this explanation will enable you clearly to understand the nature of your own duties in the particulars referred to, and that whilst you will carefully abstain from interfering with the proper duties of the guardians and the relieving officers, you will not fail to act promptly and effectually in your own particular department, whenever an occasion of sudden and urgent necessity shall arise.

XI.—NUISANCES REMOVAL.—APPROPRIATION OF FINES—CHARGING EXPENSES.

20th August, 1849.

Clerk of Sculcoates Union.—The 17th sec. of the Nuisances Removal Act directs that all penalties recovered under that Act shall be paid to the guardians, and shall be by them applied in aid of the rates or funds for the relief of the poor. By the 126th sec. of the 5 & 6 Wm. 4, c. 76, (the Municipal Corporations Act,) it is enacted, "That when by any Act any penalties are or shall hereafter be made recoverable in a summary way before any justice, &c., and by such Act are made payable to his Majesty, or to any body corporate, &c., the same, if adjudged before any justice of a borough in which a separate Court of Quarter Sessions of the peace shall be holden, shall, notwithstanding anything in such Act, &c., be recovered for and adjudged to be paid to the treasurer of such borough to the credit of the borough fund." The parishes of Sculcoates, Sutton, Southcoates, and Drypool, in this union, are in the borough of Kingston-upon-Hull, and the sanitary committee of this board, in proceeding for the penalties under the first-mentioned Act, are met by a claim on behalf of the borough treasurer for these penalties. Inquiring, therefore, whether the provisions of the 5 & 6 Wm. 4, c. 76, render nugatory the provisions of the Nuisances Removal Act, as to the application of penalties; or, whether the Acts referred to in the 126th sec. of the Municipal Corporations Act are only Acts relating to offences against the provisions of that Act, or the bye laws of corporations.

Ans.—The Board consider that the provisions of the statutes 11 & 12 Vic., c. 123, sec. 16, and the 12 & 13 Vic., c. 111, sec. 3, which impose penalties, and direct the mode of their application, are not overruled or controlled by the provision contained in the 5 & 6 Wm. 4, c. 76, sec. 126, to which you refer. See Boden *v.* Smith, 18 L.J.R., Common Pleas (N.S.) 121.

4th Oct., 1849.

Clerk of same Union.—Requesting advice as to the mode of charging the various expenses incurred in carrying out the proceedings under the Nuisances Removal Act, and the directions of the General Board of Health. Under the former there are two classes; those incurred before the passing of the Nuisances Removal Act, 1849, and those incurred subsequently. As to those incurred subsequently, the guardians understood that they are to charge all expenses not recovered to the respective parishes in which the nuisances exist; but they wish to be informed whether they can adopt the same course with regard to expenses incurred under the Act of 1848. The Directions of the Board of Health have occasioned the following different liabilities and expenses:—1, The remuneration to the union officers for their extra labour. 2, The salary of the inspector appointed to assist the relieving officers in the investigation of nuisances. 3, The remuneration of the surgeons appointed expressly to attend cholera cases, which was originally at 10*s.* per case, so that each case might have been charged to the parish in which it occurred, but is now £5. 5*s.* weekly. 4, The rent of land for the purpose of the deposit of soil and ashes, and the pay of persons employed in carting it away from the four town parishes, viz., Sculcoates, Southcoates, Sutton, and Drypool. 5, The printing of placards and notices. The cholera has been almost confined to the town district, although there have been cases in several of the country parishes, and the proceedings for the removal of nuisances have been carried on in every parish of the union where they were found to exist.

Ans.—With reference to your remark that the guardians understand, as regards expenses incurred subsequently to the passing of the Act of 1849, "that they are to charge all expenses not recovered to the respective parishes in which the nuisances exist," the Board think it right to point out that this view is not altogether in accordance with the statute. With respect to expenses incurred in the removal of nuisances under the provisions of the Acts, the 7th sec. of the 12 & 13 Vic., c. 111, provides that any expenses which shall have been or shall be so incurred may, (when not recovered from the owner or occupier,) be paid by the guardians without an order of justices, and be charged to the parish, (see sec. 4 of the 11 & 12 Vic., c. 123,) in two classes of cases, viz., 1, Where an order shall have been made by the justices for the removal or abatement of the nuisance; and, 2, In any case where the amount shall not exceed 20*s*. The Board think that this sec. applies to expenses incurred before the passing of the Act, and not yet dealt with under the former statute, as well as to expenses incurred since its passing. With respect, however, to expenses incurred in the removal of nuisances in execution of any Order or Regulation of the General Board of Health, the 8th sec. makes a somewhat different provision, leaving it to the discretion of the guardians of the union to charge such expenses, when under 20*s*., either to the parish or to the union, as they may think fit; and rendering it necessary, where the amount exceeds 20*s*., to obtain an order of justices, if the guardians of the parish object to such parish being charged without it. The provisions of the 8th sec. do not apply to expenses incurred before the passing of the Act. With regard to the particular items of expenditure referred to in your letter as incurred under the Directions of the General Board of Health, the 1st, 2nd, 3rd, and 5th classes are clearly to be charged to the common fund of the union, except, perhaps, the payments per case to the medical practitioners, which appear to be chargeable as ordinary relief. As respects the 4th class, the Board feel some difficulty in expressing any opinion, owing to the peculiarity of the proceeding. In principle, however, it appears to fall within the rule stated above, as to the expenses incurred in the removal of nuisances under the Directions of the General Board of Health; and it will rest with the guardians to ascertain how far that rule may apply to the case, under the particular circumstances.

XII.—RELIEF.

1. DUTIES OF RELIEVING OFFICER.

31*st July*, 1849.

Clerk of Tewkesbury Union.—[The Poor Law Board having requested the observations of the guardians on a communication which they had received on the following case, from Mr. Moore, a relieving officer of the union—] J. D. had been residing at Upton Bishop, in the Ross Union, nearly five years, and becoming chargeable to that parish from want of work, orders were obtained for his removal to Ashchurch, in this union. Ashchurch gave notice of appeal, and Upton Bishop abandoned the order; the pauper then brought his family into this union, and applied to the relieving officer for relief, who, finding that he had formerly been removed to Tredington, and the man not having told him that he had gained a subsequent settlement at Ashchurch, gave him an order for admission into the workhouse, as belonging to Tredington. The paymasters of that parish feeling themselves aggrieved, brought the matter before the board of guardians, who thought it best to adopt some general rule for the future guidance of the relieving officers in similar cases, and the following minute was made: "Mr. Moore, relieving officer, having given an order for admission into the workhouse to J. D., his wife, and six children, at the charge of the parish of Tredington, they having come from another union, and their settlement at Tredington being disputed, directions were given to the relieving officers not to give orders of admission into the workhouse in future to persons who have been residing out of the union, except they are brought with orders of removal, but to refer them to the overseers of the parish to which they claim to belong."

Ans.—The Board have to point out to the guardians that the resolution which they have passed, directing their relieving officers in future not to give orders of admission to the workhouse to non-resident paupers, but to refer them to the overseers of the parish to which they claim to belong, is at variance with the provisions of the Regulations of the Poor Law Commissioners, as prescribed in their General Consolidated Order, Art. 88 & 215, (No. 6.) It is the duty of the relieving officer, where the case requires it, to give a provisional order for the pauper's admission to the workhouse, and he would not be justified in referring the pauper to the overseers for relief. The guardians appear to have overlooked the provision in the Poor Law Amendment Act, sec. 54, which prohibits overseers from granting relief except in cases of sudden and urgent necessity. With regard to the course which the relieving officer should pursue in charging the relief afforded by him in any such case, the Board consider that he should enter the pauper as chargeable to the parish where the application for relief is made to him, unless the applicant has an abode in a parish in his district, and comes to him out of such parish for the required relief, in which case he should enter it to the parish of the pauper's residence; such charge of the relief, however, made by the relieving officer, is merely provisional, and it rests with the guardians to inquire into the facts of the case, and either confirm or alter the charge, as such facts may appear to them to require. In the particular cases referred to in the present correspondence, it appears to the Board that the paupers were destitute wanderers, and, therefore, that their relief is chargeable to the union common fund.

8*th August*, 1849.

Clerk of Tewkesbury Union.—On referring to Art. 215, (No. 6,) the guardians find that it orders the relieving officers, in every case of sudden or urgent necessity, to afford such relief to the destitute person as may be requisite; and as the 54th sec. of the Poor Law Amendment Act allows the overseers to give relief in such cases, they cannot see that their resolution is at all at variance with the provisions of the Consolidated Order of the Poor Law Commissioners. In the particular case referred to, the guardians think that the paupers cannot be considered as destitute wanderers, they having left the place of their usual abode for the last four or five years, and applied for relief the same day to the relieving officer for the parish to which they supposed they belonged; if such cases are to be sent to the workhouse at the charge of the common fund of the union, the guardians are at a loss to know how to get rid of them if they afterwards discover that they belong to some parish not within the union, as not being chargeable to any particular parish, orders could not be obtained for their removal; in the present case, Tredington has obtained orders for the removal of the paupers to Ashchurch, the overseers of which parish have given notice of appeal against the order, and if the relief was now to be charged to the common fund of the union, the order would be quashed, the paupers not having been chargeable to Tredington. The guardians wished to be informed how they could, in that case, relieve the common union fund of the burden of maintaining the family, which there is no doubt belongs to one of two parishes of the union.

Ans.—The Board desire to call the attention of the guardians to the fact, that the provision in sec. 54 of the Poor Law Amendment Act, which applies to the giving of relief by overseers, is confined to cases in which the necessity of the applicant is "sudden and urgent," whilst the provision in the General Consolidated Order, Art. 215, No. 6, which defines the duty of the relieving officer in this matter, extends to cases of "sudden or urgent necessity." The power possessed by the overseers and the relieving officer respectively in this matter, (as the difference in the language employed in the two provisions plainly shows,) is widely different. Where the necessity of a person applying for relief, although urgent, is not sudden, the overseers have no power to interfere; so if it be sudden, but not urgent, they are equally restrained from ordering relief: whereas the relieving officer, on the contrary, in accordance with his duties, as prescribed by the Art. of the General Consolidated Order above cited, is bound to act in either case if presented to him, and to give the requisite provisional relief, and this whether the overseers could lawfully deal with the case or not. The Board have therefore again to point out to the guardians that their resolution, directing the relieving officer not to relieve in the first instance paupers who may not have been residing in the union, (but who nevertheless may apply for relief within it,) but to refer them to the overseers of the parish to which such paupers claim to belong, is at variance with the law. As regards the particular case of J. D., the Board will abstain from further remark, as it appears the overseers of Tredington have admitted the liability of that parish to the charge of the relief by obtaining an order of removal.

---

2. RELIEF OF CLOTHING FOR A YOUNG PERSON IN SERVICE.

17*th Oct.*, 1849.

Clerk of Swaffham Union.—Reporting in pursuance of the provision contained in the sixth Article of the General Prohibitory Order, the particulars of the case of J. S., an able-bodied man, belonging to the parish of Saham Toney, and requesting the sanction of the Poor Law Board to an allowance of ten shillings for one week, to enable him to furnish decent clothing to his daughter M. A., in service.

Ans.—The Board regret that, under the circumstances of this case, they do not think they would be justified in sanctioning the proposed relief. Such relief is, in fact, relief in aid of wages, and places the children of persons receiving assistance of this kind from the poor rates in a better position to obtain situations than the children of independent labourers. Either the party hiring M. A. S. should raise her wages, so as to enable her to provide herself with suitable clothing, advancing a part to meet the necessary outlay at first, or he will have to obtain another servant elsewhere; and if another servant is to be obtained on the terms offered to this girl, the guardians ought not to interfere to procure a preference for her at the expense of the ratepayers.

3. RELIEF OF ABLE-BODIED PAUPERS—LABOUR TEST ORDER.

9th June, 1849.

Clerk of Ashton-under-Lyne Union.—Transmitting a list of persons relieved in this union, contrary to the Labour Test Order, during the week ended 23rd of May.

Ans.—The Board, before they sanction the relief granted in these cases, request that they may be informed of the particulars of such relief in each case.

3rd August, 1849.

Clerk of same Union.—The persons reported were working in the various mills, only doing boys' work, and, consequently, merely earning boys' wages; but, in consequence of being thus situated, their employers give them the first chance of promotion, (and some, since they were reported, have got better situations, and, no doubt, others will very soon,) the guardians considered it better to relieve these persons a few weeks, temporarily, than to deprive them altogether of an opportunity of obtaining preferment; should, however, those that have not as yet ceased to be chargeable continue chargeable for a length of time, the guardians will feel it to be their duty to relieve them according to the provision of the Labour Test Order.

Ans.—The Board observe that the persons so relieved were working in the various mills, but doing boys' work, and receiving boys' wages only, which were insufficient for their maintenance. From this statement of the circumstances of the cases, it appears that the relief afforded was in fact relief in aid of wages, a mode of relief which is extremely objectionable, and which it was one of the principal objects of the Poor Law Amendment Act to put an end to. The men employed in doing boys' work must either have displaced so many boys, who would otherwise have been employed by the mill-owners, or, if boys suitable for the work could not have been procured, the mill-owners must have obtained the services of the men at a lower rate of wages than the men would have been willing to work for if they had not had assistance from the poor-rates, and part of their wages would have been paid by the ratepayers instead of the masters who employed them. The Board, therefore, cannot approve of the course taken by the guardians in these cases; and although they will not withhold their sanction to the relief which has now been actually afforded by the guardians, they cannot hold out any expectation of their doing so in future. They request that the guardians will, in all such cases, adhere to the provision of the Out-door Labour Order, and will afford relief only on the condition of the men being in no other employment, and of their being set to work by the guardians.

4. RELIEF BY WAY OF LOAN GIVEN TO THE WIFE, IF RECOVERABLE FROM THE HUSBAND.

19th Sept., 1849.

Clerk of Crediton Union.—Fanny F. is the wife of William F., a labourer residing in the parish of Bow, in the Crediton Union, where he is irremovable. Fanny F., in consequence of the ill treatment of her husband, and his not providing her with necessary food, &c., left his house a short time since, and applied to the parish authorities of Bow for relief, who gave her an order for her admission into the union workhouse, where she went, and still remains as an irremovable pauper of that parish. Her husband, it is understood, is capable of supporting her, and is now living with another woman. The guardians being desirous that the man should be prosecuted, and compelled to maintain his wife, find some difficulty in deciding who are the proper parties to institute proceedings against him. Inquired, therefore,—1, Whether the relief to the wife might be given in the way of loan, and the man proceeded against for the recovery thereof; —or, 2, Whether the man can be prosecuted under the Vagrant Act;—or, 3, Whether the woman should have her husband bound over to keep the peace, as she alleges that she is afraid to return to her husband's house, for fear of ill treatment;—or, 4, Can any other proceedings be taken in the case, either by the guardians, or the parish officers of Bow, so as to punish the man in the way his conduct deserves?

Ans.—The Board can only advise the guardians to give all future relief to the wife (while destitute) as a loan to the husband, and to proceed to recover it under the statutes. The Board think it may be doubtful whether the case is within the Vagrant Act, as the woman appears to have left her husband of her own accord; but as this would be a question for the justices, an application might properly be made to them under that Act, and if they are satisfied that the husband, being of sufficient ability, refuses, or wilfully neglects, to provide for her maintenance, except in his own house, and at the same time, by his violent conduct, renders it impossible for her to reside there, consistently with her personal safety, the Board think that a conviction under the Vagrant Act might be sustained. For that purpose, however, it would be necessary that all these facts should be established to the satisfaction of the justices. As to binding the husband over to keep the peace, the Board think this a matter for the consideration of the woman and the magistrates, and one upon which the Board cannot properly express an opinion.

XIII.—REMOVABILITY.

4th June, 1849.

Chairman of Eastry Union.—1, H. L., a pauper belonging to the parish of Telmonstone, in this union, had resided for more than five years in the parish of Eastry, previous to the month of December last, when he gave up his house, and was admitted into the union workhouse, and the expense of his maintenance charged to the common fund of the union. On the 30th of April he took his discharge to seek for work, and since then he has been travelling about the country for that purpose; but for the last four nights he has slept at the house of a relative, in the parish of Sholden, and not being able to obtain work, he has been re-admitted into the union workhouse. Has he broken his residence in Eastry, and thereby become chargeable to Telmonstone, the parish of his settlement, or is he still irremovable, and chargeable to the common fund of the union? 2, M. G., belonging to Great Mongeham, in this union, had resided upwards of eleven years in Sutton, previous to the 2nd of April last, when he gave up his residence there, and came into the union workhouse, at the expense of the common fund. On the 13th of May, 1849, he took his discharge to seek for work, and slept that night at the house of his daughter, in the parish of Deal; the next night he slept at the house of his sister, in the parish of Guston, in the Dover Union; the third night he again slept at his daughter's, at Deal, and not being able to obtain work, was then re-admitted into the union workhouse. Has this man broken his residence in Sutton or not? 3, M. A. U. had been lodged and boarded in the parish of Ash for four months, the expense of her maintenance during that time having been paid by her father, who lived in service at Canterbury, the girl being almost an idiot. In consequence of the death of the father she has become destitute, and has been admitted a few weeks ago into the union workhouse. She has no settlement. The father was a Scotchman and a soldier, and never gained a settlement in England. The mother has been dead many years, and no one knows who she was or where she came from; and the girl was born in the White Friars, an extra-parochial place in Canterbury. Ought the expense of her maintenance to have been charged to Ash or to the common fund, under 11 & 12 Vic. c. 110, sec. 1? She has since left the house for one day and night, and been re-admitted. Ought the expense of her maintenance to be still charged to Ash, or to the parish where she last slept, or to the common fund, under the above section?

Ans.—The Board, upon the facts before them, consider that, in the cases of H. L. and M. G., the paupers are not irremovable, inasmuch as there has been an interruption of the residence in each case; but upon their re-admission to the workhouse, they appear to have been destitute wanderers, and therefore, under sec. 1 of the 11 & 12 Vic. c. 110, their relief should be charged to the union common fund. As regards the case of M. A. U., the Board, before advising on the matter, request that they may be furnished with fuller and more precise information as to the circumstances under which she left the workhouse on the occasion you refer to, the girl being, as alleged, almost an idiot.

2nd July, 1849.

Chairman of same Union.—The guardians, although the majority of them acquiesced in the opinion expressed by the Poor Law Board as to H. L. and M. G. having broken their residences, and thereby become removable, yet they are of opinion that they have not explained with sufficient distinctness that they both have settlements, and, accordingly, they have determined to charge the expense of their maintenance to the parishes where they last slept, and leave it to the overseers of those parishes to take out orders of removal. The paupers certainly come under the designation of destitute wanderers, as defined by Mr. Lumley in his Commentary on the 11 & 12 Vic. c. 110; but Mr. Archbold states that, where the settlement of such is known, an order may be obtained for their removal, and the guardians are not aware of any mode of obtaining such an order, except upon the complaint of the overseers; and if so, none could be obtained if the expense was charged upon the common fund. It appears, however, that it would be much better if boards of guardians were empowered to charge the expense in such cases upon the parish of the pauper's settlement, when it is known to be in the union, as this would save expense, and the question is a much more simple one than that of adjudicating upon undetermined and disputed cases of settlement. M. A. U. is one of those persons who, although too deficient in intellect to obtain a livelihood, are, nevertheless, possessed of a considerable amount of cunning, and are perfectly capable of taking care of themselves. She took her discharge from the house, without giving any intimation of her motive for so doing, and the first night found a lodging with a friend, but not being permitted to stay there any longer, she returned to Eastry, and applied to the relieving officer for re-admission to the house.

Ans.—1, The Board think that no order of removal can be obtained in the cases of H. L. and M. G., even assuming them to have a settlement elsewhere, for the very ground upon which such charge proceeds is, that they are wanderers, that is, persons not inhabiting or residing in any parish, and the being an inhabitant in the parish, or having come to inhabit in the parish, is a necessary condition to the obtaining of a removal order. (See the case of Q. *v.* St. Paul's, Covent Garden, 2 N.S.C. 515.) Further, there is no such specific chargeability to any particular parish which would entitle the overseers to apply for an order. The Board think that the course pursued by the guardians of charging the relief to the parish wherein the pauper had slept the night before, would be as unjust to the parish as it is at variance with the general principles of law, and the scope and intention of the late statute.—2, In the case of M. A. U., the Board understand that she was living at Ash when she was first admitted into the workhouse. There seems to be no reason why, on the first occasion, she should not have been chargeable to Ash, as any other pauper living in the parish and becoming chargeable. But when she discharged herself from the workhouse, her chargeability to that parish ceased, and upon the second admission it appears that her case fell within sec. 1. of 11 & 12 Vic. c. 110. Upon the pauper's leaving the workhouse of her own accord, the then chargeability was interrupted—a new chargeability arose afterwards—and at that time the pauper appears to have had no home, but to have been a "wayfarer."

---

2. REMOVABILITY OF WIDOW.

2nd July, 1849.

Clerk of Bodmin Union.—Transmitting the following statement, duly signed, under sec. 4 of the 11 & 12 Vic. c. 110, for the opinion of the Poor Law Board:—Susan S., the widow of James S., and her three children, are now chargeable to the parish of St. Winnow, in this union. The pauper was married to her husband on the 27th of April, 1839, in the parish church of St. Winnow. Her husband was settled in the parish of Michaelstow, in the Camelford Union, but resided in St. Winnow. On the 7th July, 1844, he applied to the relieving officer of the Bodmin Union for relief, which was granted to him, first at his residence in the parish of St. Winnow, and afterwards in the union workhouse at Bodmin; he continued in the union workhouse about twelve months, and died there, and was buried at the expense of the parish of Michaelstow. The pauper, Susan S., was also a resident in the union workhouse, at Bodmin, at the time of her husband's death, and had been so, with her infant child, for about three weeks previous to his death. The whole of the relief so granted, both in and out of the workhouse, was repaid by the parish of Michaelstow, and the widow, after her husband's death, received relief until the 12th December, 1846, on account of the said parish of Michaelstow, when she and her family became chargeable to the parish of St. Winnow, being resident there, and she still continues chargeable to that parish. Whilst the paupers were resident in the union house at Bodmin, their house at St. Winnow still continued furnished, and the widow returned there after her husband's death. Are the widow and children removable on the ground of a break of the residence by the husband having been twelve months in the union workhouse at Bodmin, part of which time the wife also lived there with him, their relief having been repaid by the parish of Michaelstow? or, does the 56th sec. of the 7 & 8 Vic. c. 101, making residence in the parish, (there being also an *animus revertendi* at the time,) render them legally chargeable to the common fund of the Bodmin Union.

Ans.—If, in this case, there was a residence of the wife in the union workhouse, it seems that, by the operation of the 56th sec. of the 7 & 8 Vic. c. 101, such residence must be taken to have been in the parish to which the pauper was chargeable, namely, St. Winnow; and in this point of view there was no interruption of the residence. The more obvious construction, however, of this case is, to hold that the abiding of the woman in the workhouse for the three weeks prior to her husband's death was not an interruption in point of fact of her residence in St. Winnow.

3. REMOVABILITY OF ORPHAN CHILDREN.

8th Nov., 1849.

Overseers of Newborough, Carnarvon Union.—In the year 1831, J. R. and Elizabeth his wife, were removed by order of justices from the parish of Newborough in this union to the parish of Bangor, in the Bangor and Beaumares Union, which order was unappealed against. Bangor agreed to allow the paupers relief in Newborough, where they returned; and in about nine months the husband died in Newborough, being relieved in Newborough from the time of the removal to the time of his death. The widow continued to reside in Newborough, receiving relief from Bangor for about five years, when she gave birth to a bastard child, and subsequently to three others, all of whom, with the mother, were supported by Bangor in Newborough, until after the passing of the Act of August, 1846, when Bangor ceased to relieve. From that period down to January last, (when the mother was imprisoned for larceny,) they have all been maintained by Newborough, and since the imprisonment of the mother, the children alone have been maintained by that parish. The mother died in gaol about three months ago, leaving the children of the respective ages of thirteen, eleven, eight, and three chargeable to Newborough, the overseers of which wish to remove them to Bangor, as being the place of settlement of the mother's late husband; but that parish refuses to receive them without an order, stating that they are irremovable by reason of having been there more than five years without receiving relief, and contending that all relief given to the children must be considered as being given to their parents. The youngest child, however, is under five years old, and it is thought there can be no objection to remove him. Inquiring whether the three eldest children, under the circumstances stated, are removable or not, and also whether the youngest child, who is under five years of age, is removable.

Ans.—If it appear, as was doubtless the case, that the relief in question was given to the mother to enable her to maintain herself and her children, then, assuming that there might possibly be some question, whether the relief was given to the children within the meaning of the first proviso to the 1st sec. of the 9 & 10 Vic. c. 66, the Board consider that they must be treated as having been wholly or in part maintained by a rate, raised in a parish in which they did not reside. Consequently, it appears to the Board, upon the statement now before them, that the paupers in this case are removable to the place of their legal settlement.

4. REMOVABILITY OF A WOMAN DESERTED BY HER HUSBAND.

6th July, 1849.

Clerk of Bellingham Union.—Transmitting for the opinion of the Poor Law Board the following statement, duly signed, under sec. 4 of the 11 & 12 Vic. c. 110:—A married woman, with a family, was deserted by her husband upwards of thirty years ago. After her desertion, she and her family left the parish in which they were then residing, in another union, and came to reside in the parish of Troughend, in this union, where she has since continued to reside for thirty years, without receiving parochial relief, and without ever having heard any certain account of her husband. In April last she became, and is now, chargeable to the parish of Troughend. Her husband's settlement is not in this union. Is she irremovable, and, therefore chargeable to the common fund of the union? or, is the fact of her desertion by her husband such a break in the residence, as will render her liable to be removed to the place of her husband's settlement? *Vide* Q. *v.* St. Ebbe, 12 Jur. 1,002, and Q. *v.* Pott Shrigley, 3 N. S. C. 317.

Ans.—If the husband be now alive, the woman in question is removable, according to the decisions in the cases of The Queen *v.* St. Ebbe, and Pott Shrigley; but if the husband be dead, she is irremovable. As in this case, it is not precisely stated whether the husband be dead or alive, the Board can only point out to the guardians that, where a party has not been heard of for seven years, the law raises the presumption (which, however, may be rebutted by evidence to the contrary) that the party is dead. If the husband has not been heard of for the last seven years, and if there is no evidence to rebut the presumption of his death, he may, according to this rule, properly be presumed to be dead, and the woman be treated as irremovable.

5. COMPUTATION OF PERIOD OF RESIDENCE.

15th Sept., 1849.

A. Howell, Esq., Welshpool.—A question has in several instances arisen, as to what constitutes being in receipt of parochial relief; in other words, what constitutes the difference between occasional and constant parochial relief, with a view to a calculation of the five years during which a pauper has not been in receipt of relief; for instance, some paupers may have been occasionally in receipt of relief, say a shilling or two at a time, and given to them at uncertain times as their necessities pressed, sometimes, perhaps, at the end of one, two, or three months. What portion of time in respect to each relief is to be excluded from the computation of the time during which the pauper has not been in receipt of relief? It is possible the question may have been judicially decided. If it has, requesting to be informed of the result.

Ans.—The Board have no reason to believe that the point to which you refer has come before the Queen's Bench for a judicial decision. They think themselves that no general rule can be laid down, but that the facts and circumstances of each case must be generally investigated. Where small sums have been given, the books of the relieving officer or of the union, or possibly some other entries, may show for what time the relief was given. Where these records are wanting, the circumstances of the case may themselves show for what length of time the relief was given. But occasional or casual sums of small amount can only be treated as relief for the particular period for which such a sum would be available, and, consequently, will have frequently no sensible effect upon a long residence. Where small sums have been given at fixed stated periods, though insufficient for the entire maintenance of the pauper, yet, if given as relief, it seems to the Board, as a general rule, proper to consider that the whole time during which the relief was regularly given under such course ought to be excluded from the computation.

---

6. EXCLUSION OF TIME DURING WHICH RELIEF WAS GIVEN AT THE CHARGE OF THE COMMON FUND OF THE UNION FROM THE PERIOD OF RESIDENCE.

14*th July*, 1849.

Clerk of Northallerton Union.—Transmitting for the opinion of the Poor Law Board the following statement, duly signed, under sec. 4. of the 11 & 12 Vic. c. 110:—Margaret W—, a pauper, aged nine and a half years, was born at Northallerton, her place of legal settlement being at Darlington. Both the pauper's parents died when she was three and a half years old; from which time the pauper was maintained by the township of Darlington for three years. The grandfather then maintained her for about five months. She was then (from March, 1847, to July, 1847) maintained by the township of Northallerton as an irremovable pauper, and as such was, from July, 1847, to January, 1849, maintained out of the common fund of the Northallerton Union; but after the decision of the case, Reg. *v.* Christchurch, she was considered removable; and, consequently, the relief advanced to her since September, 1848, has been charged to the township of Northallerton. The pauper has not resided in Northallerton five years without receiving relief, but if the time during which relief was administered out of the common fund of the union is not to be reckoned, on the ground that such relief was improperly charged to the common fund of the union, or that such relief was not in any other respect given in accordance with the proviso of the 1st sec. of the 9 & 10 Vic. c. 66, as "relief from any parish," or as being "wholly, or in part maintained by any rate or subscription raised in a parish in which such person does not reside," which the overseers of Northallerton contend was the case, then the pauper will have made a five years' residence in Northallerton without receiving relief, and is now irremovable, and that the relief advanced since September last ought to be charged to the common fund of the union. But the board of guardians contend that the time during which relief was granted out of the common fund of the union must be added to the other times during which the pauper received relief from the townships of Darlington and Northallerton, in which case the pauper will not have resided at Northallerton five years without receiving relief, and is therefore now removable; and that the relief advanced to the pauper since September last is properly charged to the township of Northallerton. Is the pauper now removable to Darlington, the place of her legal settlement, or is she now irremovable?

Ans.—The first proviso to the first sec. of the 9 & 10 Vic. c. 66, refers to relief out of the rates of a "Parish," and excludes such relief from the computation of the five years' residence alluded to in the enactment; and it may be urged, that the proviso does not in its terms apply to relief received by a pauper from a "Union." But in the present case, it appears that the relief afforded to Margaret W—— from March, 1847, to 30th September, 1848, was charged to the common fund of the Northallerton Union, under the provisions of the 10 & 11 Vic. c. 110, (Bodkin's Act;) under which the relief was required to be charged in the first instance to the particular parish, and afterwards to the union by way of reimbursement to the parish. The

Board are, therefore, of opinion, that the time from March, 1847, to 30th of September, 1848, being a period during which the pauper received relief from the township of Northallerton, must be excluded from the computation of the pauper's residence in that parish; and, consequently, the pauper is not now irremovable therefrom.

7. RESIDENCE UNDER CERTIFICATE.

1*st Sept.*, 1849.

Clerk of Machynlleth Union.—Inquiring whether a pauper whose settlement is in another parish, but who has resided in Towyn under certificate for five years without receiving relief, is now removable to the parish wherein he is settled.

Ans.—The effect of a certificate, as regards the person who was the object of it, was to prevent his removal from the parish in which he resided until actually chargeable, and as regards the parish, to prevent a settlement being acquired by the pauper during the protection of the certificate. But the 9 & 10 Vic. c. 66, does not confer or alter a settlement, (see section 5,) but merely renders a person irremovable from a parish in which he has resided a certain time, namely, five years. There is nothing, therefore, as the Board consider, to prevent the operation of this statute in cases where certificates may have been granted, under the 8 & 9 Wm. 3, and the other statutes relating thereto.

8. WHETHER RELIEF TO THE PARENT MAY BE CONSIDERED RELIEF TO THE CHILD.

18*th July*, 1849.

Clerk of Wangford Union.—Transmitting, for the opinion of the Poor Law Board, the following statement, signed under sec. 4 of the 11 & 12 Vic. c. 110:—John H—— is the legitimate son of William and Charlotte H——. He was born in the parish of St. Michael Thorn, in the city of Norwich, in the month of June, 1831—he will therefore be nineteen years of age next June. At the time of his birth, his father belonged to the parish of Beccles in this union, from which parish he, the father, frequently received relief. In or about the month of December, 1837, the father was rendered incapable of working by illness, and he applied to the parish officers of Beccles for relief, who required him to remove to that parish, which he accordingly did, and lodged there with his wife and four children, (the pauper being one of them,) for one week, and was relieved by Beccles; he and his wife and children were then admitted into the workhouse, where they remained for seven weeks chargeable to Beccles; they all then (February, 1838) removed to the parish of Bungay St. Mary, also in this union, with an allowance of two shillings and two stones of flour per week, which was charged to the parish of Beccles, and continued regularly from that time until May, 1846, when the father died; from that time an allowance was made to his widow of one shilling, and one and a half stones of flour for many months, when it was reduced to one shilling, and one stone of flour, which she now receives. When John H—— (the pauper in question) was between eleven and twelve years of age, he went to work in a silk manufactory, where he continued about two years; his first earnings were sixpence per week, which increased to one shilling per week; when about fourteen years old he worked with a shoemaker for one shilling per week, and when fifteen years old he received two shillings per week for one year. This brings the pauper into his sixteenth year. During his father's lifetime he was always lodged, fed, and clothed by his father, who received his earnings; and, after the death of his father, till he was sixteen years old, he was lodged, fed, and clothed by his mother, she receiving his wages. Since he attained sixteen, he has frequently been relieved by Beccles, whilst residing in Bungay St. Mary. The pauper has never broken his residence in that parish. From the above statement, it appears clear that the pauper has not resided five years in Bungay St. Mary without relief being granted either to his father or to his mother; but it is contended, on one side, that relief to the father, even when the pauper was under sixteen, was not relief to him, (the pauper,) and that, consequently, he has resided five years in Bungay St. Mary without relief, and is, therefore, irremovable from that parish, and that his relief ought to be charged to the common fund of the union, (see sec. 3 11 & 12 Vic. c. 110,) and such opinion is grounded on the 56 sec. of the 4 & 5 Wm. 4, c. 76, which provides that relief to the child shall be considered as relief to the parent. On the other side, it is contended, that such clause does not apply to the present case, and that relief to the father was relief to the pauper; and that he (the pauper) did not, therefore, reside in Bungay St. Mary five years without relief; and, consequently, that he is removable to Beccles, and that his relief ought to be charged to that parish. The questions to be determined are as follows: — Whether, under the circumstances above stated, the pauper is irremovable from Bungay St. Mary, and, therefore, that his relief should be charged to the common fund of the union; or, whether he is removable to Beccles, and, therefore, that his relief should be charged to that parish.

Ans.—The first proviso to sec. 1 of the 9 & 10 Vic. c. 66, requires that "the time during which any such person shall receive relief from any parish, or shall be wholly or in part maintained by any rate or subscription raised in a parish in which such person does not reside, not being a *bonâ fide* charitable gift, shall, for all purposes, be excluded in the computation, &c." In the present case, the material question is, whether John H—— was, during the period from 1838 to the present time, so long in the receipt of relief from the parish of Beccles, or maintained wholly or in part by any rate raised in that parish, as that, after making the requisite deduction, five years' residence in Bungay St. Mary will not remain. Whether a child can be held to be in receipt of relief which is in fact given to his parent, must obviously depend upon the circumstances of the case. It is clear that when, as is sometimes the case, a child's earnings are fully adequate, or more than adequate, to defray the cost of his lodging and maintenance, and these earnings are paid over by him to his parent, relief given to the parent who stood in need of it could not reasonably be considered as having been given to the child, who did not stand in need of it himself; on the other hand, when the parent receives the relief given him expressly for the child, when, as is sometimes the case, the illness of the child forms the ground on which alone relief is given to the parent, such child clearly falls within the second branch of the clause above quoted, as a person "wholly or in part maintained by a rate raised in the parish." If John H—— was so maintained by a rate raised in Beccles, he is within the proviso, for he was at the time resident elsewhere. The Board feel a difficulty in ascertaining, from the statement which accompanied your letter, whether the relief which was afforded to the parents of John H—— (to the father first, and subsequently to the mother) was given to them respectively, for the specific purpose of enabling John H——, while a child, to be wholly or in part maintained by them.

9. COST OF MAINTENANCE.

12th Sept., 1849.

Clerk of Wakefield Union.—John A. is a pauper legally settled at Warmfield Cum Heath in this union. In the early part of the year, and for some time before, he resided in the parish of Charles, Plymouth, and a removal order was obtained on the 27th of March to remove him to Warmfield. The parish of Charles did not actually remove the pauper until the 25th of July. On that day he was brought with his family to Warmfield, and a claim was made for maintenance, viz., sixteen weeks' maintenance, £6. 8*s.*; truss, 2*s.* 6*d.*; clothing, £1.; total, £7. 10*s.* 6*d.* The overseers of Warmfield refuse to pay the sum claimed, and paid only £2. 8*s.*, being the maintenance of the pauper and his family for six weeks, viz., three allowed by law for giving notice of appeal, two weeks for the further allowance after an application for copies of examinations, &c., and one week for the actual removal, taking the distance of Plymouth from Warmfield into account. The parish of Charles has again applied for the balance of their claim. Requesting the opinion of the Poor Law Board as to the legality of the demand, and whether the payment of all or any part of the balance can be enforced.

Ans.—Having communicated with the guardians of the incorporation of Plymouth on this subject, and received a statement of the case from them, the Board are of opinion, that as the removal of the pauper from the parish of Charles was suspended under the combined operations of 4 & 5 Wm. 4, c. 76, sec. 79, and 11 & 12 Vic. c. 31, sec. 9, first for the period of twenty-one days, and then (copies of the depositions being demanded) for the further period of fourteen days from the date of sending the copies, the removing parish is entitled to recover under sec. 84 of 4 & 5 Wm. 4, c. 76, the cost of the maintenance of the pauper for so long a period as the law prevented the execution of the order; *i. e.*, in the present case, for two periods of twenty-one days, and fourteen days; but as there was no suspension of the order by the justices under 35 Geo. 3, c. 101, sec. 2, the period of six weeks, for which payment has already been made, appears to the Board to cover the whole time for which there could be any legal liability to repay the cost of the maintenance.

London: Printed by Order of the Poor Law Board, by BLACKBURN & BURT, 90½, Holborn Hill, and Published by CHARLES KNIGHT, 90, Fleet Street.

AN

OFFICIAL CIRCULAR

OF PUBLIC DOCUMENTS AND INFORMATION:

DIRECTED BY THE POOR LAW BOARD TO BE PRINTED, CHIEFLY FOR THE USE OF THE BOARDS OF GUARDIANS AND THEIR OFFICERS.

No. 32.] DECEMBER, 1849. [N.S.

CONTENTS.

I.—AUDIT OF ACCOUNTS.

1. SURCHARGE AGAINST GUARDIANS—APPEAL TO THE POOR LAW BOARD.

29*th May*, 1849.

Auditor of the ——— *Audit District.*—Transmitting a copy of the following certificate of surcharge for an illegal payment out of the funds of the ——— Union, against the three guardians who signed the cheque by which the payment was made, and intimating that the disallowance would be appealed against:—"At an audit of the ——— Union, held on the day underwritten, being an adjournment from the 18th April last, so far as relates to the sum of £28. 4*s.* 4*d.*, then proposed to be charged on F. J. M., Esq., J. J., and N. N., guardians of the said union, after hearing the said F. J. M., J. J., and N. N., I do hereby certify, that in the accounts of the said ——— Union I have disallowed the sum of twenty-eight pounds four shillings and fourpence, as a payment illegally made out of the funds of such union, and I find that F. J. M., Esq., J. J., and N. N., authorized the making of such illegal payment, and I do hereby surcharge the said F. J. M., J. J., and N. N., with the said sum of twenty-eight pounds four shillings and fourpence. As witness my hand this 28th day of May, 1849.

———, Auditor of the district which comprises the above-named union.

25*th July*, 1849.

Clerk of ——— *Union.*—Setting forth the circumstances under which the sum surcharged was expended, and submitting the same for the consideration of the Board, "by way of appeal under the provisions of sec. 4 of the 11 & 12 Vic. c. 91."

The Poor Law Board to the Clerk of same Union.—In a case such as the present, the Board require that the parties immediately affected by the surcharge, and against whom it was certified, should themselves directly appeal to this Board, furnishing a copy of the auditor's reasons for the surcharge, which, by the 35th sec. of 7 & 8 Vic. c. 101, he can now be called upon to state in writing in the book of account. The Board are in possession of a copy of the auditor's certificate, which he transmitted with a report on the 29th May last, but this certificate does not disclose the reasons of the auditor for deciding that the payment which he disallowed was illegal.

25*th August*, 1849.

Clerk of same Union to the Poor Law Board.——Stating that he had applied to the auditor for his reasons for the surcharge in question, who had replied as follows:—" I have already entered in the book of account, namely, the ledger, my reasons for the surcharge, my certificate being therein and embracing the reasons; I have no other to give, and to give them a second time cannot be necessary. If the Poor Law Board, as you seem to assume, construe the 35th sec. 7 & 8 Vic. c. 101, as meaning that an auditor who surcharges an item as an illegal payment is to give in addition his reasons why he thinks so, I am sorry I cannot agree with them. The 7 & 8 Vic. is before the Act directing the form of certificate, which is 11 & 12 Vic. c. 91."

12*th Sept.*, 1849.

The Poor Law Board to the Clerk of same Union.—The Board do not consider that the 35th sec. of 7 & 8 Vic. c. 101, is satisfied by a mere statement by the auditor that the particular payment which was the subject of disallowance or surcharge was illegally made. The 11 & 12 Vic. c. 91, sec. 5, which makes the form of certificate adopted by the auditor in the present case sufficient as a certificate of disallowance, does not appear to the Board to repeal that provision of the 7 & 8 Vic. c. 101, sec. 35, which requires the auditor (on demand) to state his reasons on the face of the book of account. The jurisdiction given to the Poor Law Board by 7 & 8 Vic. c. 101, sec. 36, is to determine whether the reasons stated by the auditor in any case are lawful reasons. To state simply that a payment is illegal, without adverting to the circumstances which render it so, is to state, not a reason, but a conclusion of the auditor as to what is the law. The illegality, in any case, results from certain facts taken in connexion with the rules or principles of the law applicable to them. The Board are called upon in the present case to remit the disallowance. They have an equitable power of doing this under the 11 & 12 Vic. c. 91, sec. 4. But before they can exercise this power they must be satisfied that the disallowance or surcharge (as the case may be) has been "lawfully made." (See the Section.) This ought to appear by the auditor's reasons stated on the face of the book, as required by the 7 & 8 Vic. c. 101, sec. 35. In the present case, all that the Board have before them is a copy of the auditor's certificate, which discloses no facts from which the alleged illegality of the payment can be ascertained. It does not even appear from the certificate for what object or purpose the payment was made; it is merely stated, in effect, that a payment was illegally made out of the funds of the union by certain persons. Under these circumstances, the Board do not doubt that upon another request made to him, and upon re-consideration, the auditor will readily state his reasons in the manner which the Board consider to be required by law.

2*nd Nov.*, 1849.

The Auditor to the Poor Law Board.—Stating that he had written his reasons for the surcharge in question in the ledger over against the surcharge in the following words :—" Having been required to give my reasons for surcharging F. J. M., Esq., J. J., and N. N., at my adjourned audit, on the 28th day of May, 1849, in the sum of £28. 4*s*. 4*d*., (being a payment at fol. 186 in these words, " Establishment," " —— and ——," £28. 4*s*. 4*d*.,) I do hereby declare that I have so surcharged them as the parties who signed the cheque for the payment in question, such payment being for legal and parliamentary expenses with reference to a proposed application to Parliament for a Bill to rate small tenements throughout the Berkhampstead Union, and charged to the common fund of the union, which expenses no Act of Parliament relating to the poor, nor any Order of the late Poor Law Commissioners, or of the present Poor Law Board, have authorized the board of guardians to incur, and which, therefore, I consider as having been illegally paid.

(*Signed*) " ———, 1*st Nov.*, 1849."

17*th Nov.*, 1849.

The Poor Law Board to the Clerk of same

Union.—The Board have received from Mr. ——, district auditor, a copy of his reasons formally stated on the 1st instant, for surcharging certain guardians of the ——— Union with the sum of £28. 4*s*. 4*d*. The Board, however, are not in possession of any appeal from the parties immediately affected by the surcharge, as the Board in their letter of 25th of July last pointed out was the proper course of proceeding, if those parties thought there were grounds for appealing. If no appeal be intended, the Board think it their duty to point out that the 32nd sec. of 7 & 8 Vic. c. 101, requires that the amount certified should be paid over to the treasurer of the union.

27th Nov., 1849.

Clerk of same Union to the Poor Law Board.—Transmitting the following statement of appeal:—"The auditor of this union, having disallowed the sum of £28. 4*s*. 4*d*. in the accounts of this union, and surcharged the undersigned three guardians, who signed a cheque for payment for such sum, on the ground of its being an illegal payment, we beg to submit the circumstances under which the sum in question was expended for your consideration by way of appeal, under the provisions of sec. 4 of the 11 & 12 Vic. c. 91. In the year 1845, the guardians finding that the list of excused rates within the ——— Union amounted in the whole to the enormous sum of £400 per annum, caused a special meeting of the board to be convened on the 10th of November, 1845, at which it was unanimously resolved that application should be made to Parliament in the ensuing Session for a Bill, to rate the owners of all tenements under the annual value of £10 in the several parishes forming the union, and as no time could be lost, instructions were given to Messrs. —— & ——, as solicitors, to publish notices throughout the union of such application, a similar Act having been obtained by them for the parish of ———, a short time previous. In order to comply with the standing orders, the notices were immediately, that is, on the three following Sundays, published on the several church doors, and inserted in the Gazette, &c. On the 25th of December, 1845, after nearly all the expenses had been incurred, the solicitors received a letter from the Poor Law Commissioners on the subject, in answer to a communication made to them thereon, of which a copy was forwarded to you on the 1st of July last; upon the receipt of this letter, and after interviews with several influential persons in the parishes, it was thought advisable not to proceed with the matter, under the circumstances shown by the Copies of Minutes, also forwarded to you on the 1st of July last. Of the bill in question, £17. 12*s*. 6*d*. were for costs out of pocket, including parliamentary agent's charges, and the undersigned N. N. was not at the time the expenses were incurred a member of the board. All the proceedings were sanctioned by sixteen different guardians at the meetings as shown by the minutes. The Bill has been duly taxed, and it is submitted, that under the provisions of sec. 4 of the above Act this is a payment incurred under such circumstances as make it fair and equitable that the surcharge should be remitted. Dated this 26th day of November, 1849. (*Signed*) F. J. M., Chairman; J. J., Vice-Chairman; N. N."

18th Dec., 1849.

Ans.—The Board request that you will inform the appellants, that after carefully considering all the circumstances of the case, the Board have come to the conclusion that they would not be justified in remitting the surcharge in question. It appears to the Board that the guardians of the ——— Union could have had no ground for believing that the expenses in question would be legally chargeable upon the poor-rates, if they did not succeed in obtaining an Act of Parliament containing an express clause to that effect. Had they consulted the Poor Law Commissioners on this subject in the first instance, instead of waiting till the expenses which form the subject of this surcharge had been incurred, they would have received the information communicated in Mr. Chadwick's letter of December 24th, 1845.* In a late case before the Vice-Chancellor of England, (Attorney-General *v.* Guardians of the Poor of Southampton, 18 Jur. 669) he held that it would not be "fair and equitable" (the words used in 11 & 12 Vic. c. 91, sec. 4) to allow an appropriation of the poor-rates to the repayment of expenses incurred under circumstances of a similar description, and the Board regret that in the present case they are compelled to arrive at the same conclusion.

* In this Letter the Commissioners state, "that they know of no authority under which the expenses that may be incurred in relation to this Bill could lawfully be defrayed out of the poor-rates should the Bill not pass into an Act."

2. AUDITOR'S DUTY IN REGARD TO SUMS CERTIFIED BY HIM TO BE DUE.

14*th August*, 1849.

Auditor of ——— *Audit District*.—Referring to the following remarks in a letter which had been addressed to him by the Board :—"The auditor is required by the 7 & 8 Vic. c. 101, sec. 32, to take steps for enforcing payment of the sums certified by him to be due, if the amount has not been paid over to the treasurer within seven days ;" and stating that the amount certified to be due, with reference to overseers' accounts, is the balance, which it has been the invariable custom for the outgoing overseers to transfer to their successors, under 43 Eliz., and which is transferred, in most cases, before the audit, though it does not appear in the Receipt and Payment Book, the account therein being previously closed though not audited ; and pointing out the difficulties in the way of carrying out the requirements of the statute as construed by the Board.

Ans.—The Board apprehend that the amount "certified to be due" by the auditor, with reference to overseers' accounts, is not necessarily and in all cases "the balance." A balance may be shown as the result of the transactions in the account, which nevertheless may not be "due" in the sense of sec. 32 of 7 & 8 Vic. c. 101, and 11 & 12 Vic. c. 91, sec. 5, that is, payable by or recoverable from the officer. For instance, when the accounting officer is continuing in office at the time of the audit, as at the Michaelmas audit, only such sums are to be certified as due as are disallowed or surcharged. In regard to the account rendered by the overseers at the close of their year of office, the section last referred to expressly enables the auditor to give credit to the retiring overseers for any sums proved to have been paid by them to their successors, or lawfully applied on behalf of the parish prior to the audit ; it is the sum, or balance, remaining after credit has been so given that is to be certified as due. The Board observe with respect to this provision, that it affords in itself a strong presumption that the previous state of the law did not warrant the overseers in paying over balances to their successors, (whatever practical convenience may have attended that course,) nor the auditor in regarding such payment as a discharge of the overseers' liability in respect of the balance on the account ascertained by him at the time of audit. But whatever may be properly certified as *due* at the audit, it is perfectly clear that the law casts upon the auditor the duty of recovering such sum. The Board must repeat upon this point, that the auditor is not to wait until his assistance is called for, or until he is put in motion by any party. The duty of so proceeding is imposed upon him by the statutes in terms quite unconditional, and it is manifest that the auditor can no more decline the performance of this part of his duty, than he can neglect to audit the accounts themselves. It is sufficient on this point to refer to the concluding words of sec. 5 of 11 & 12 Vic. c. 91, which are, "and he (the auditor) shall certify, report, and recover, the balance remaining due after such credit shall have been given." The ascertaining whether a sum certified as due in any case has been paid to the treasurer as the law requires (sec. 32, 7 & 8 Vic. c. 101) may possibly impose some trouble upon the auditor, as it may involve the necessity of correspondence with the various officers and treasurers of the respective unions, but the duty cannot be declined or neglected because it is troublesome. With regard to the reference in your letter to 11 & 12 Vic. c. 43, the Board have now to direct your attention to sec. 9 of the 12 & 13 Vic. c. 103, which has laid down the strict limit within which the proceedings are to be taken for the recovery of sums certified, and they think that it cannot create any real difficulty or embarrassment, inasmuch as the period of nine months affords abundance of time for commencing the requisite proceedings.

---

3. AUDITOR'S DUTY TO INQUIRE INTO THE SETTLEMENT OF PAUPERS.

26*th Nov.*, 1849.

Clerk of Cheltenham Union.—The overseers of the parish of Cheltenham recently brought to the board of guardians a list of upwards of 150 paupers, whose relief they required should be charged to the common fund of the union, under the 3rd sec. of 11 & 12 Vic. c. 110. The board of guardians have caused these parties to be examined, and where they have been satisfied that the paupers come within the definition of a poor person not settled in the parish where he resides, and who by reason of some provision in the Act of 9 & 10 Vic. c. 66, is exempted from liability to be removed, the relief has been charged to the common fund of the union ; but where the evidence was not satisfactory to them, that the paupers came within the terms of the above definition, the relief was charged to the parish where they resided. An objection to the accounts of the guardians was made to the auditor at his recent audit, on account of the relief of the last-mentioned paupers not having been charged to the common fund, and the audit has been adjourned for further examination. Inquiring whether it is the duty of the auditor to examine into the cases complained of, and ascertain whether the paupers are irremovable, and come within the terms of the 3rd sec. of the 11 & 12 Vic. c. 110; or, indeed, whether the auditor has any power to go into the question of the settlement of the pauper at all; and submitting that the 4th sec. of the 11 & 12 Vic. c. 110, provides a remedy for settling all questions arising as to irremovability between parishes and the union, and that the auditor has no power either to entertain or decide any such questions.

Ans.—The Board consider it incumbent upon the auditor to ascertain that the expenditure by the guardians of the Cheltenham Union, in respect of relief to the poor, is properly charged in the accounts. He is, therefore, bound to see that those charges which ought to be borne by the common fund of the union, and those only, are charged to that fund; and to do this he must, if required, enter into a consideration of the question of the removability or irremovability of the several paupers. Where, however, the question is not raised before him, he must necessarily take the accounts as he finds them; but certainly, he cannot avoid deciding the point when he is expressly appealed to in any particular case.

II.—CHARGEABILITY.

1. CHILD DESERTED BY ITS MOTHER.

5th Sept., 1849.

Clerk of Wincanton Union.—The mother of H. K., a boy aged eleven years, whose father has been dead upwards of ten years, has absconded, leaving her child in the parish of Charlton Horethorne, in the Wincanton Union, and the child is now in the union workhouse, at the charge of that parish. The settlement of the family is in the parish of Penselwood, also in the Wincanton Union. The father of H. K. never resided in the parish of Charlton Horethorne, but the mother did, and but for the abandonment of her residence in that parish she would now be irremovable therefrom by residence, and so would the child too, he being under sixteen years of age, and having completed a five years' residence there without receiving relief of any kind, or his mother for him or for herself. The guardian for the parish of Charlton Horethorne contends that, as the pauper has resided in the parish of Charlton upwards of five years, within the meaning of the statute, his relief in the workhouse can legally be debited only to the common fund, and he requests to have it debited accordingly. The guardians, on the other hand, contend that as the mother of the pauper has absconded, leaving him chargeable, and as the father is dead, such absconding amounts to a legal break of residence, which will subject her to be removed to her place of settlement should she again be found in the parish of Charlton; and, if that be so, the child is, by reason of the mother's absconding, also liable now to be removed; and Charlton, to relieve itself from the expense of the child's maintenance, must place him under an order of removal to his place of settlement. To settle the point at issue between the parties, the opinion of the Poor Law Board is requested.

Ans.—The Board are of opinion, upon the statement of facts communicated to them, that the mother has broken her residence in the parish of Charlton Horethorne by the desertion. If she were to return to that parish she would be removable; and as this would be the case with the mother, so also her child is removable now, according to the 10 & 11 Vic. c. 111. (See Reg. *v.* Pott Shrigley, 18 L. J. Report, N. S. M. C. 33.) As, then, the child is removable, the cost of his relief is chargeable to the parish where he resides. The Board would observe, however, that before the guardians proceed to charge the relief to the parish, it is necessary they should clearly ascertain the fact of the settlement, otherwise the case is within the 12 & 13 Vic. c. 103, sec. 2.

---

2. CHARGEABILITY OF THE INFANT CHILD OF A WOMAN IN PRISON.

8th Sept., 1849.

H. P. Markham, Esq., Northampton.—Transmitting a letter which he had addressed to the clerk of the Northampton Union, and his reply thereto, and requesting, on behalf of the magistrates of the county, to be informed what steps they ought to take with respect to the child mentioned in the correspondence:—*Mr. Markham's Letter.*—"At the last assizes, a prisoner of the name of Ann Golaker was tried and convicted, and sentenced to be imprisoned in the county jail until March next. At the time of her conviction she had a child at the breast, which child (now about eighteen months of age) has lately been weaned. The visiting justices to the jail and house of correction had this circumstance brought before them on Saturday last, and I was then directed to write to you, and request that you would report the circumstance to the board of guardians to-morrow, and request them to be good enough to make arrangements for receiving such infant child into the workhouse. However hard it may be for them to do this, I am afraid the county have no alternative in the matter. I do not see how the justices are justified in keeping the child, now it is weaned, in jail; nor do I see if they were to do so how they can charge the ratepayers with its support."

The Clerk's Reply.—"Inasmuch as this woman has no legal settlement within any parish in this union, and was not resident within the union at the time of her commitment to prison, the guardians do not think that they can legally consent to receive this child into the workhouse. Nevertheless, if you will report the whole circumstance to the Poor Law Board, and they shall be of opinion that the guardians can legally receive this child from its mother, and place it in the workhouse at the charge of any parish in this union, they will willingly do so. The guardians do not refuse to accede to the wishes of the magistrates, but doubt the right they would have to charge any parish of this union with this child's support."

The Poor Law Board to Mr. Markham.—By the refusal of the justices to maintain this child longer in the jail, it becomes destitute in the parish in which the jail is situated, and it seems to the Board that the child ought to be taken into the workhouse, and the expense charged to that parish. The Board do not think that the relief can be charged upon the common fund of the union, under 11 & 12 Vic. c. 110. sec. 1, and 12 & 13 Vic. c. 103, sec. 2, because as it is separated from the mother by no voluntary act of hers, it cannot properly be said to be "deserted" by her. The Board are not aware that the Jail Acts contain any provisions applicable to the case, and they think, therefore, that it must be decided by the general principles of the Poor Law, and that the parish to which the child has become chargeable as casual poor, must bear the burden of maintenance, unless it can discover some other parish in which the child has a settlement, and to which the burden may be transferred, or, unless the mother on her liberation from prison shall be capable of maintaining it herself. The Board assume from the statement that the child is illegitimate, though the fact is not distinctly expressed. If legitimate, there may possibly be some relation capable of maintaining it, who might be compelled to do so under the 43 Eliz. c. 2. sec. 7.

3. CHARGEABILITY OF A FOUNDLING, NOW FOURTEEN YEARS OF AGE.

20th Oct., 1849.

Clerk of Chard Union.—About fourteen years ago, H. M., an orphan, was found at the door of a late relieving officer, residing in the borough of Chard, and was taken to the workhouse, and his relief charged to the borough of Chard, to which place the child is still chargeable. Inquiring whether the charge of the relief in this case can legally be transferred to the common fund of the union.

Ans.—The Board do not think that the 11 & 12 Vic. c. 110, sec. 1, applies to a child who must have been at least thirteen years of age when that Act was passed; and the 12 & 13 Vic. c. 103, sec. 2, is confined to children under the age of twelve years; so that it does not appear that the charge for maintenance in this case can be transferred from the borough of Chard to the common fund of the union.

---

4. CHARGEABILITY WHERE RELIEF GIVEN TO THE WIFE IN THE PARISH OF HER RESIDENCE, THE HUSBAND RESIDING PARTLY IN ANOTHER PARISH.

14th August, 1849.

Clerk of Easingwold Union.—Transmitting the following statement, duly signed, under the 11 & 12 Vic. c. 110, sec. 4, for the opinion of the Poor Law Board:—William G., with his wife Jane, and three children, came to reside at Easingwold, in the Easingwold Union, on the 7th of July, 1845, and has occupied and rented a house in Easingwold up to the present time. W. G. has usually been employed as a labourer in the parish of Raskelf, which is the reputed place of his settlement, whilst his wife and family have been living at Easingwold. He usually left Easingwold on the Monday morning, and proceeded to his work at Raskelf, returning to Easingwold to his wife and family on the Saturday night, where he remained until the Monday morning, when he again went back to Raskelf. The last time W. G. was at Easingwold was on the 6th of June last. About a week afterwards he became ill of the typhus fever, and did not return to Easingwold to his wife and family, but remained at Raskelf. On the 7th of July inst., the wife and family, whilst residing at Easingwold, became destitute, and applied to the relieving officer of the union; and on the 20th of July the case came before the guardians, who ordered the wife and family to be relieved, and the relief charged to the parish of Raskelf, as the alleged place of residence and reputed settlement of the pauper's husband. No application for relief was made on behalf of W. G., who has been maintained at his mother's house at Raskelf. Inquiring whether, under the circumstances of the case, Easingwold or Raskelf should be considered the place of residence of the husband; and whether the relief in question ought to be charged to the common fund of the union, or to the parish of Raskelf, (supposing the husband to be settled in Raskelf.) And also, whether the husband and the wife and family may not be considered to have two distinct places of residence, and in this case, whether the relief ought not to be deemed as given to the wife and family, and not to the husband on account of his sickness; in which latter case the wife and family would become chargeable to the parish of Easingwold, who could apply for an order for their removal to the husband's settlement, whether at Raskelf or elsewhere.

Ans.—It appears to the Board, that as the relief given to the wife and children was rendered necessary in consequence of the sickness of the head of the family, (and that sickness, as they understand, not being of a nature to produce permanent disability,) the wife and children of W. G., residing in Easingwold, are not removable therefrom by operation of sec. 4 of 9 & 10 Vic. c. 66, so long as his continued sickness renders such relief necessary; and being so irremovable, it follows that the cost of the relief given under those circumstances should be charged to the common fund of the Easingwold Union.

5. CHARGEABILITY OF A WAYFARER.

18*th May*, 1849.

Clerk of East Retford Union.—E. S., an Irishman, a single man, aged 26, a painter by trade, came to East Retford about three weeks ago, and was employed by Mr. Holmes, a coach painter, with whom he worked about a week, when he became ill. He remained about three weeks in a tramp lodging-house, and partially recovered, and sought to obtain further employment; but his illness returned, and he has been admitted into the workhouse. Requesting to be advised whether the man should be relieved at the expense of the common fund or that of the parish of East Retford.

Ans.—From the particulars before them, the Board do not consider the pauper in this case a wanderer or wayfarer, but an inhabitant of the parish referred to, where he had been residing for three weeks at the time of his applying for relief. He came, it appears, to abide in that parish.

6. CHARGEABILITY OF A DESTITUTE WANDERER.

7*th June*, 1849.

Clerk of Pewsey Union.—Transmitting the following statement for the opinion of the Poor Law Board:—Examinations relative to the chargeability of Elijah Davis and his wife and five children, admitted into the Pewsey Union Workhouse on the 9th of May, 1849, by an order from Mr. Akerman. *Joseph Pearce Akerman,* [relieving officer,] saith, On the 12th April, 1849, I was applied to in the parish of Wilsford by Elijah Davis, who had been residing in that parish for upwards of two years, for an order for himself and wife and five children to go into the Pewsey Union Workhouse, in consequence of having been turned out of his cottage. I gave him an order accordingly, a copy of which is hereunto annexed, and described him as of Wilsford parish. He and his wife and family went into the workhouse the same evening, and remained there, as I have been informed, until Monday the 7th day of May. On Wednesday morning, the 9th May, Elijah Davis came to my house, at Upavon, and asked me for another order to go into the workhouse; I said to him, "How came you to leave the workhouse until the question about your parish was settled?" he said, "I left the workhouse on Monday to go and see for work, and my wife came out at the same time to go and see her daughter, who was at service near Devizes." I then gave him another order for the workhouse, but sent a message to the master of the workhouse not to charge the relief to any parish until the meeting of the board on the following Monday. I was informed by Davis that he slept at the public-house at Upavon on the preceding Monday and Tuesday nights, and that his wife and children also slept in the parish of Upavon on the Tuesday night. *James Chandler* saith, I am master of the Pewsey Union Workhouse. On the 12th April last, Elijah Davis and his wife and five children, of the parish of Wilsford, were admitted into the Pewsey Union Workhouse by an order from Mr. Akerman, the relieving officer, and their relief was charged by me to Wilsford parish. On the 16th April last I was directed by the board of guardians of the Pewsey Union to allow the pauper, Elijah Davis, to leave the workhouse on the following Thursday to go to Devizes to be examined as to his parish; he went out on that day, and the following day, and as I understood, to go to Devizes to be examined as to his parish. On the 7th of May, Davis's wife wished me to see her husband, and tell him he must give notice to go out, otherwise he would be sure to lose his work. I told him what his wife said; Davis then said, "If so, we must go." Davis and his wife and their children left the workhouse that day, and as they were going out Davis's wife said, "We shall most likely be back again on Wednesday;" they came accordingly to the workhouse on the Wednesday, by an order from Mr. Akerman, but I was requested by a message from Mr. Akerman not to charge the relief to any parish until board day. Davis and his wife and children are still in the workhouse. *Elijah Davis* saith, I lived in the parish of Wilsford for upwards of two years previous to April last; I rented of the late Mr. Jacob Stratton: I am a sawyer by trade: I was ejected from my cottage on the 11th April last: I was then at work in the parish of Enford as a sawyer: my goods were turned into the street: I stayed with them that night: the next morning Mr. William Hayward, the guardian of Wilsford parish, came to me, and told me I might put my goods into his barn; I did so, and I believe the goods are there still: I then applied to Mr. Akerman for an order to go into the Pewsey Union Workhouse; I went into that workhouse on the 12th April, with my wife and five children: I went out of the workhouse on the 19th April, for the purpose of going to Devizes to be examined as to my parish: I got as far as Wilsford, but as the weather was so bad I was told by Mr. Hayward to go back to the workhouse and go to Devizes the next day: I went to the magistrates' clerk's office on the next day, and was examined by him as to my parish, which I have heard is at Winterbourne Earls; I was told I should be wanted at Devizes another day, but I was never sent for. On Monday, 7th May, I received a letter from my daughter, who is in service near Devizes, requesting either I or my wife would come and bring her some more clothes, otherwise she must leave her service: the same morning Mr. Chandler brought me a message from my wife about my going to see about my work; I gave Mr. Chandler notice, and I and my wife and children left the workhouse that morning; we intended going to Devizes, as we understood it was the magistrates' meeting, and we were anxious to have it decided about our parish, and we also wanted to see our daughter. The night before I left the workhouse I was very unwell, and on our road to Devizes I found myself so ill that I was obliged to stop a little time at Manningford; my wife left me to go on and see our daughter; as soon as I got a little better I went on to Upavon, where some of my wife's friends reside. Upavon is about half a mile from the turnpike-road to Devizes. I slept at the public-house at Upavon that night; my wife and two of my children slept at Devizes, and the other three children went on and slept at Wilsford: my wife and all the five children came to me at Upavon: on the next night my wife, myself, and one child, slept at the public-house at Upavon, and the other four children slept at the houses of two of my acquaintances there: I paid for my lodging, &c., at the public-house; the following morning, the 9th May, I again applied to Mr. Akerman, the relieving officer, who lived at Upavon, for an order to go into the workhouse, in consequence of not having any house of my own. I went into the Pewsey Union Workhouse on that day, with my wife and five children, and have since remained there: I have not been examined by my parish since the 20th April, and was never sworn to my examination: I could have plenty of work as a sawyer if I could get a house to live in. Before I went to live at Wilsford I lived for twenty years in the parish of Upavon, but I never gained my settlement there. *Query*—To which of the two parishes, Wilsford or Upavon, is the relief given to the pauper, Elijah Davis, and his wife and children, since their last entrance into the Pewsey Union Workhouse, to be charged?

Ans.—The case in question appears to the Board to be that of a destitute wanderer, as the man had no home, and was going about from parish to parish without any definite purpose. The Board, therefore, consider that the cost of the relief given to the pauper, his wife and family, should be charged to the common fund of the Pewsey Union, and not to either of the parishes specified. There certainly is no ground for charging the relief to Wilsford.

---

7. Chargeability of a destitute wanderer.

27th Nov., 1849.

Clerk of Market Bosworth Union.—Upwards of thirty years ago, there lived in the parish of Market Bosworth a person named R. G., a parishioner belonging thereto, with a wife and family: the man was convicted of burglary and other offences, and sentenced to be hung, but was reprieved, and transported for life. A few years afterwards the wife married a person belonging to Cadeby, named P. B., by whom she had a son,

S. B. After being married a few years, P. B., having been informed that the marriage was illegal, abandoned the woman and married another, by whom he has a family. The woman then removed to Leicester, where she maintained herself, but the child was taken in and kept by P. B.'s father, and brought up by him as his grandson, at Osbastone, another parish in this union. The child remained there until about two years ago, when his grandmother died: he then stole the old man's pony, went off with it, and was not heard of until a few months ago, when he returned, and he has since that time been in and out of this workhouse. He has no home or settled place of residence; consequently, the parishes of Bosworth and Cadeby, between which parishes the matter is in dispute, refuse to accept him. Requesting to be informed what steps the guardians should take as to the pauper's removal, and which parish is his legal place of settlement.

Ans.—The Board are of opinion, upon the statement now before them, that the pauper in question is a destitute wanderer, chargeable to the common fund of the Market Bosworth Union.

10*th Dec.*, 1849.

Clerk of same Union.—Inquiring whether the guardians have any power to take steps to remove the pauper, by order or otherwise, to the parish to which he belongs, as they consider it would be most unjust for him to remain chargeable on the union, which, from his inability, he might do for years, when he is legally removable.

Ans.—In the present state of the law the guardians of a union have no power to obtain any order for the removal of a pauper from the union of which they are the guardians to the parish of his settlement. With regard to the particular pauper in question, the Board desire to point out that he was not at the time of his admission into the union workhouse inhabiting in any parish, according to the meaning of the 35th Geo. 3, c. 101, so as legally to be the subject of an order of removal from any parish.

---

8. Chargeability of persons attacked with cholera.

9*th Nov.*, 1849.

Clerk of Truro Union. — Inquiring whether persons who have resided in a parish, in which they are not legally settled, for a less period than five years, who are attacked with fatal cholera, and in consequence become chargeable, ought to be charged to the establishment as sick persons not liable to be removed, or should be charged to the parish in which they happen to reside as casual paupers.

Ans.—The question raised by the guardians depends upon the construction of the 4th sec. of the 9 and 10 Vic. c. 66; and assuming the question to relate to poor persons becoming chargeable on account of cholera, not being previously in receipt of relief, it appears to the Board that cholera is a kind of sickness not calculated, in general, to produce permanent disability where the patient survives, and that consequently, a poor person becoming chargeable under the circumstances supposed, would be irremovable under the section in question, and chargeable, therefore, to the common fund of the union. The Board further consider that the fact of the cholera proving fatal in any case would not make any difference with regard to the question of the irremovability and chargeability of the deceased while living, nor would it afford any ground for altering such chargeability.

---

9. Evidence of chargeability to common fund.

3*rd Sept.*, 1849.

Clerk of Newbury Union.—Inquiring on what evidence he ought, as clerk, to sanction the placing of paupers who are considered irremovable on the common fund.

Ans.—As it rests with the guardians to make the charge to the common fund, it is undoubtedly for them to be satisfied that the case falls within sec. 3 of 11 & 12 Vic. c. 110, that is, that the pauper not being settled in the parish of the residence is also irremovable from that parish, by reason of some provision of the 9 & 10 Vic. c. 66. With regard to the evidence upon which the guardians should proceed, the Board apprehend that this must depend upon and will vary with the circumstances of the several cases which come before the guardians. The Board do not think it necessary that the guardians should, in ordinary cases, insist upon having the fact of irremovability established by strictly legal evidence. If in any case, upon reasonable investigation by the guardians or their officers, and by examination of the pauper, of which it may be very proper to keep a record, it should appear that the pauper has resided continuously in the parish five years without relief; and if, further, and upon similar investigation, the existence of a settlement in such parish is also negatived, it will be proper for the guardians to make the transfer of the relief from the parish to the common fund. With regard to the settlement, it may be observed, that the statute 11 & 12 Vic. c. 110, only requires it to be shown that the pauper is not settled where he resides; it does not render it necessary that it should be established by legal evidence in what parish the pauper is settled. Particular cases of doubt and difficulty may certainly arise, calling for more deliberation and caution upon the part of the guardians, and warranting them in having the alleged fact of irremovability supported by proof of a more formal nature than can, the Board think, be requisite in ordinary cases. The Board consider that the guardians may reasonably require in this matter the co-operation of the overseers of the parishes which seek the transfer of the relief to the common fund.

---

10. PRACTICE IN REGARD TO CHARGING RELIEF TO IRREMOVABLE POOR.

1st August, 1849.

Clerk of Abergavenny Union.—It is the practice of the guardians, before directing the charging of the relief of any poor person to the common fund, first to inquire and satisfy themselves that the pauper could be removed from the parish to which he is chargeable, if the 9 & 10 Vic. c. 66, did not exist. In other words, they first require to know the parish in which the pauper is settled, and the grounds and the proof of such settlement; and unless these appear clear and satisfactory, they consider the pauper irremovable independently of that Act, and until the contrary appears, presume him to be settled in the parish in which he resides, and properly chargeable thereto. It must appear that the pauper is non-settled and removable before he can be said to have become irremovable, and within the meaning of the 9 & 10 Vic. c. 66, which can apply only to removable persons. By the 3rd sec. of the 11 & 12 Vic. c. 110, the relief of any poor person, who, not being settled in the parish where he resides, shall, by reason of some provision of the 9 & 10 Vic. c. 66, be or become exempted from the liability to be removed from the parish where he resides, is directed to be charged to the common fund, etc.; the first inquiry, therefore, seems to be that of the settlement in, or the power of removability to another parish. If not shown to exist, these Acts do not apply; but if shown, the next inquiry is, whether, by reason of some provision of the first Act, the pauper is rendered irremovable. There is frequently a difficulty in ascertaining and determining upon the removability of a pauper, and he, the clerk, is often called upon to advise the guardians upon circumstances based on the bare statement, or the hearsay and uncertain information of some guardian, relieving officer, or pauper, and mistakes, no doubt, occasionally occur. He is given to understand that the practice adopted in the Abergavenny union, as above stated, is incorrect; and that it is the general practice in other unions to inquire merely whether the pauper is shielded by either of the provisions of the 9 & 10 Vic. c. 66, and then, unless and until it appears clearly that he is settled in the parish in which he resides, to charge him to the common fund.

Ans.—The Poor Law Board do not altogether concur in the course adopted by the guardians in this matter; they do not think it is to be presumed that, because a settlement is not shown elsewhere, the pauper is settled in the parish of the residence. The Board consider that it suffices for the purposes of the 3rd. sec. of the 11 & 12 Vic. c. 110, if it appear, after due and reasonable investigation, that the pauper is not settled in the parish of the residence. There may be numerous cases in which it will be readily apparent that the pauper is not settled in the parish of the residence, although it may be impossible to establish by legal evidence in what other parish the pauper is settled. In these cases, the parish in which the pauper may happen to reside would be manifestly deprived of the benefit contemplated by the statute referred to, if the rule on which the guardians appear to have proceeded were strictly pursued. The Board agree with the guardians that the 9 & 10 Vic. c. 66, can have no application to persons who are settled in the parish of their residence, inasmuch as no question can properly arise as to their removability.

---

11. CHARGING OF RELIEF TO IRREMOVABLE WIDOWS AND PERSONS TEMPORARILY SICK.

17th August, 1849.

Clerk of Durham Union.—Inquiring, 1st, whether widows, being, during the first year of their widowhood, irremovable from the parish in which they are resident at the time of the decease of their husbands, are, in all cases, notwithstanding they have a settlement in right of their husbands in such parish, chargeable to the common fund of the union. 2nd. Whether persons being temporarily sick, and in consequence irremovable, are chargeable to the township in which they are resident during such sickness, whether settled or not in such township.

Ans.—In reply to the first question submitted, the Board are of opinion, that where widows are settled in the parish of their residence, their relief is not chargeable on the union common fund, under sec. 3 of the 11 & 12 Vic. c. 110. To bring the case within that provision, the parties must be irremovable from some parish in which they are not settled. The same rule applies to the cases of persons who, being temporarily sick, reside in the parishes of their settlement; where, however, they reside in a parish in which they are not settled, and their chargeability is caused by temporary sickness, the relief must be charged to the common fund. The Board, however, give these opinions upon the general questions asked, and without prejudice to the consideration of any specific case that may hereafter be laid before them.

III.—REMOVABILITY.

1. RESIDENCE—SUSPENDED ORDER OF REMOVAL.

29th August, 1849.

Clerk of Dolgelley Union.—Transmitting the following statement, duly signed, under the 4th sec. of 11 & 12 Vic. c. 110, for the opinion of the Poor Law Board :—Jane E., aged 59, whose legal settlement is in the parish of Tottenham, has resided in the parish of Llanaber since the year 1825. In the year 1840 she was taken ill, and was compelled in consequence to apply, for the first time in her life, for parochial relief. This was allowed her by the board of guardians, and immediately after the parish officers applied for and obtained an order for the removal of the pauper to the parish of her settlement; and as she was not in a fit state to be removed, the order was suspended, and it still continues suspended, the pauper still continuing in an unfit state to be removed, and likely to remain so as long as she lives. The guardians wish to know whether the pauper should be deemed chargeable to the common fund of the union, as she resided in the parish of her residence for upwards of five years without relief previous to the application for the order of removal, or to the removing parish. Should the Poor Law Board be of opinion that she is irremovable, the parish officers of Llanaber wish to be informed whether the cost of the relief administered to her from the date of the suspended order until the present time can be recovered from the parish of her settlement.

Ans.—The Board think, upon the present statement, the pauper irremovable from Llanaber, she having resided in that parish continuously for five years without relief. Though an order for her removal was obtained in 1840, that order it appears was not executed at the time, nor has it yet been executed. This case is distinguishable from Reg. *v.* Halifax, (Law Jour. Rep., vol. 17, N.S. M.C., page 158,) and Reg. *v.* Seend, (Law Jour. Rep., vol. 18, N.S.M.C., page 23,) because in those cases there was an actual execution of the order, which was held to break the residence of the pauper in the parish from which the removal took place. But the Board do not think that those decisions are an authority for the position that an order of removal in itself, not executed, amounts to a disruption of residence by operation of law. As regards the inquiry as to the recovery of the relief, the Board do not think it can now be recovered under the suspended order unless the pauper should die. The 9 & 10 Vic. c. 66, sec. 1, (on the supposition of the pauper being irremovable by residence,) prevents the execution of the order, though the warrant was obtained before the passing of that Act, and the 35 Geo. 3, c. 101, sec. 2, it will be seen, only enables the costs to be recovered upon the actual removal or death of the pauper.

2. BREAK OF RESIDENCE—ORDER OF REMOVAL.

16th July, 1849.

Clerk of Camelford Union.—Inquiring whether a sufficient interruption of residence took place by the execution of an order of removal in the following manner:—A man with his wife and children was removed from Lanteglos to Michaelstow (and delivered to the overseers of that parish) in the morning, but returned in the evening of the same day to Lanteglos, the removing parish, where the paupers still continued to reside together for a few days, when the parish officers of Michaelstow took the man to their solicitor at Bodmin to have him examined, and as he was returning to Lanteglos, (being before unwell,) he was taken worse at the house of his parents in the parish of St. Tudy, where he was laid up about a month and died—his wife and family still continuing in the removing parish of Lanteglos. Is this a sufficient interruption of the residence of the pauper, so as to render the widow now removable, inasmuch as she has not since that period resided in Lanteglos a sufficient time to make up a five years' residence without having been in receipt of parochial relief from some other parish? The woman, however, never resided out of the parish of Lanteglos, either as maid, wife, or widow, and as it is believed these three periods of residence may be joined to complete the five years' residence, he, the clerk, has advised the guardians that she is now irremovable, subject to the Board's opinion as to the interruption of the residence under the order of removal.

Ans.—As the woman was mentioned in the order, and was in fact removed under it, she is still removable according to the decision of the Court of Queen's Bench in several cases, but especially in the late case of the Queen *v.* The Justices of the West Riding, 13 Jur. 513, where Justice Patteson says, "Wherever an order of removal has been made and carried into execution by the removal of the paupers under it, we must hold that there is a break of residence, however short the absence may be."

---

3. REMOVABILITY OF A WIDOW.

6th August, 1849.

Clerk of Market Bosworth Union.—A pauper named Billings resided in the Ashby-de-la-Zouch Union from July, 1840, until about two years ago, when he died, leaving a widow and two children; but he belonged to Desford in this union, and was relieved on account of that parish during such residence, excepting about two years. Inquiring whether the widow is now removable, as she never received relief from Desford, the relief having been afforded to the husband whilst living, (he being the legal recipient,) and not to the woman or children.

Ans.—The Board request that the guardians will ascertain whether the relief granted to the deceased pauper Billings was given with reference to himself alone, or on behalf of his wife and children also.

1st Sept., 1849.

Clerk of same Union.—The guardians are unable to see how the question as to whether the relief was granted to the pauper Billings alone, or on behalf of his wife and family also, can affect the case. The relief was principally given on account of the illness of the man, and of course would then be afforded to the family also, and at other times to other parts of the family; but the guardians consider relief given to any part of the family as given to the man, so long as he lives, as he is the only legal recipient of such relief; and, consequently, such relief cannot be legally construed to have been given to the widow, and render her irremovable.

Ans.—The Board differ from the view which the guardians have taken respecting the inquiry contained in the Board's letter of the 6th August, which they still deem to be material. The important point in the case is, whether the widow and children can be considered, during the residence in the Ashby-de-la-Zouch Union, from 1840 to the present time, or any portion of that time, as having received relief from any parish, or having been wholly or in part maintained by a rate raised in a parish in which they did not reside, within the meaning of sec. 1 of 9 & 10 Vic. c. 66. This will depend, in the present instance, on the precise circumstances under which the relief was granted by or on behalf of the parish of Desford, and the nature of the relief. The Board think, in the case of a man having a wife and family residing with him, all of whom are reported to the guardians, and whose relief, though granted directly to him as the head of the family, is, nevertheless, given to him to provide as well for the necessities of the wife and family as for his own wants, that the true construction of sec. 1 of 9 & 10 Vic. c. 66, is to regard such wife and family, so detailed in the report, as being maintained by a rate raised in the parish where they do not reside, so as to render it necessary to exclude the time during which such relief was supplied in the computation of the period of five years on which irremovability depends. But where the wife or family were not brought before the guardians, and the relief was given to the man without reference to the wife and family, the case will be different in regard to the chargeability of the latter. It may then be difficult to hold that the latter were maintained out of relief which was not given to them in point of fact, and which was not given with any reference to them.

---

4. REMOVABILITY OF CHILDREN DESERTED BY THEIR FATHER AND STEP-MOTHER.

10th July, 1849.

Clerk of Bromsgrove Union.—Transmitting the following statements, duly signed, under the 11 & 12 Vic. c. 110, sec. 4, for the opinion of the Poor Law Board:—On the 12th of February, 1848, Ann P. and her three children by a former husband, viz., Mary, aged 12, William, aged 10, and John, aged 7, were admitted into the union workhouse at the cost of the parish of Bromsgrove, in consequence of John P., her present husband, having deserted her. On the 10th July, 1848, the guardians placed out the child William as an apprentice, and on the 17th May last Ann P.

discharged herself from the workhouse, (and is supposed to be now residing with her father in the parish of Clent,) leaving Mary and John in the workhouse, the cost of whose maintenance the guardians have ordered to be charged to the parish of Bromsgrove, (the same having been charged to the common fund of the union since the 30th September, 1848.) Question :—Are the paupers Mary and John irremovable under statute 9 & 10 Vic. c. 66? The legal place of settlement of the paupers is undoubtedly in the parish of Upton Warren, in the Droitwich Union.

Ans.—It certainly appears to the Poor Law Board, from the statement before them, that these children are legally removable from Bromsgrove to the parish of their settlement; consequently, the cost of their relief is not chargeable to the common fund of the Bromsgrove Union.

---

5. REMOVABILITY OF A WOMAN WHO HAS BEEN DESERTED BY HER HUSBAND.

17*th May*, 1849.

Clerk of Camelford Union.—Inquiring whether a deserted woman and her family can be removed under the following circumstances:—Her husband has resided more than five years in a parish in this union, but has now deserted her and gone out of the union, and cannot be found. The husband married her about three years and a half since, and brought her from another union into this union; consequently, she has not resided here beyond the period at which she would be rendered irremovable. The husband had resided five years and upwards at the time of his desertion, but the woman and children had not. Can she be removed to her husband's settlement; and supposing her husband's settlement cannot be discovered, can she then be removed to her maiden settlement, or any settlement acquired in her own right?

Ans.—The Board are of opinion that the woman, under the circumstances detailed by you, is removable, according to the decision in Q. *v.* St. Ebbes, (3 N. S. C.;) she can, therefore, be removed to the settlement of her husband, if such settlement can be found. If not, then she can be removed to her maiden settlement. With respect to the last part of your inquiry, the Board have to state that they are not aware of any settlement which a married woman can gain independently of her husband.

---

6. REMOVABILITY OF FAMILY OF A LUNATIC PAUPER.

14*th May*, 1849.

Clerk of Wantage Union.—Henry Spicer, settled at East Hanney in the County of Berks, was, with his wife and children, by reason of a provision of the Act 9 & 10 Vic. c. 66, exempted from liability to be removed from the township of Grove, in the Wantage Union. Henry Spicer has recently become a lunatic, and is now confined in the county asylum at Littlemore, Oxon. Ann, the wife of Henry Spicer, and their four children, are destitute, and relief is administered to them under the direction of the board of guardians of the Wantage Union. The officers of the township of Grove intend applying to two justices, under the provisions of the Pauper Lunatic Asylum Act, for an order upon East Hanney to defray the expense of the maintenance of Henry Spicer in the asylum. Question:—Are the wife and children of Henry Spicer liable to be removed from the township of Grove if his settlement shall be adjudged to be elsewhere, in order that the cost of their relief may be legally charged?

Ans.—Upon the information now before them, the Poor Law Board are of opinion that the woman and her children are removable from the township of Grove.

3*rd Sept.*, 1849.

Clerk of same Union.—The Poor Law Board having advised that Ann, the wife of Henry Spicer, was, with her four children, liable to be removed from the township of Grove to the place of her husband's settlement, in consequence of the removal of the husband to a lunatic asylum at Littlemore, notwithstanding that he had resided for more than five years at Grove, the guardians directed the relief given her to be charged to that township; and thereupon the township applied for and obtained an order of justices for her removal, with her children, to East Hanney, a township also in the Wantage Union: the township of East Hanney admitted the settlement, but appealed against the order, on the ground that the paupers were irremovable. The appeal was entered at the Midsummer sessions, and without argument it was arranged that the order should be confirmed by the court, subject to a special case for the opinion of the court above, on the point whether the removal to a lunatic asylum out of the residence parish was an interruption of the residence. It was also agreed that the case should not be sent up for twelve months, in the hope that a similar case might be decided, and that whatever might be the result each party should pay their own costs. The paupers are consequently still resident at Grove. As, by the Act passed on the 1st of August, 1849, the lunatic may on his recovery return to Grove, and his wife and children would then have the privilege of residing with him, whatever may be the opinion of the Court of Queen's Bench as to the state of the law at the time the order was made, it appears questionable whether the paupers can now, under any circumstances, be removed. Inquiring whether, by the passing of the above statute, these paupers are now exempted from the liability to be removed, (notwithstanding an order having previously been made for their removal, but for the reason above stated not yet put in force,) and their relief legally chargeable to the common fund of the union.

Ans.—The Board think that by operation of the 4th sec. of this recent Act, 12 & 13 Vic. c. 103, the removal of Henry Spicer to the lunatic asylum cannot be deemed an interruption of his residence in the township of Grove, that that residence must be considered to have remained virtually unbroken, and that, as at the time he was so sent to the asylum he was exempt from removal under sec. 1 of the 9 & 10 Vic. c. 66, his family are irremovable now, (notwithstanding the order of removal which has been obtained, but not executed.) As a consequence, therefore, the cost of their relief is chargeable to the common fund of the Wantage Union. The Board would observe, that their letter of the 14th of May was prior to the alteration in the law effected by the 12 & 13 Vic. c. 103.

7. REMOVABILITY OF IRISH AND SCOTCH PAUPERS.

18*th Sept.*, 1849.

Clerk of Bolton Union.—Requesting the opinion of the Poor Law Board on the construction of the 3rd sec. of the 12 & 13 Vic. c. 103, a doubt having been expressed as to the removability of Irish and Scotch paupers.

Ans.—The Board see no ground for entertaining the doubt suggested as to the effect of the 3rd sec. of the 12 & 13 Vic. c. 103, upon the irremovability of Irish and Scotch paupers. That section merely provides that, in respect of proceedings to be taken under the statutes for the removal of Scotch paupers, "the chargeability of any person to the common fund of any union shall have the same effect, and shall be attended with the same consequences, as the chargeability of any poor person to a parish." Now, chargeability to a parish has the effect, or is attended with the consequence, of rendering a pauper liable under the statutes to be removed to Scotland or Ireland, in those cases only where such pauper is not exempted from that liability by some provision of the 9 & 10 Vic. c. 66; and consequently chargeability to a union (as its effect is not made by the Act more extensive than that of chargeability to a parish) will render a Scotch or Irish pauper removable, though subject to the same limitation.

IV.—REMOVAL.

1. CERTIFICATES OF CHARGEABILITY.

24*th August*, 1849.

J. P., Esq., Solicitor.—He is professionally employed by several parishes to obtain orders for the removal of paupers to their places of settlement, and in three cases the settlements he proposes to rely on are by acknowledgment by means of relief given to the pauper by the parishes to which he seeks to remove, while the paupers were residing out of the parishes which so gave relief. But the following difficulties have occurred:—In one case the relieving officer who paid the pauper being dead, he applied to the clerk of the board of guardians for a certificate, under 7 & 8 Vic. c. 101, sec. 69, to prove the relief having been given; but the clerk refused the certificate, stating that it was not compulsory on the guardians to grant it, and as it was sought to remove a pauper into a parish within their union from a parish belonging to another union, he should advise them not to grant the certificate; and without it the charging of the relief received by the pauper while residing in parish C., to parish B. could not be proved. In other cases, the clerks are inclined to think that these certificates are evidence only of the pauper's present chargeability, whereon to found an application for an order of removal, and not to chargeability in former years, whereby the justices may assume a settlement by relief. The words of the statute appear to be very comprehensive, and it is important that the clerks of the boards of guardians should be informed of the true construction and effect of it. If these certificates are evidence of chargeability in past years, orders of removal may be obtained without incurring the great expense of bringing relieving officers and clerks of unions to give evidence before the justices; and if these certificates are evidence, then orders may be obtained when the relieving officers have died or removed to a distance since the relief was given. Inquiring whether these certificates are evidence of past as well as present chargeability, and whether a board of guardians can refuse to give a certificate when applied for.

Ans.—The certificate of chargeability in question is evidence of the facts or statements contained therein, and as the form contained in the schedule to the 7 & 8 Vic. c. 100, states a past chargeability, the Board think that the certificate, if admitted in evidence for any purpose, is necessarily evidence for all. By the 11th sec. of the 11 & 12 Vic. c. 110, this certificate is for all purposes made sufficient evidence of the chargeability of the person named therein, unless the contrary be otherwise shown. Upon the second question submitted, the Board have to state, however, that it is discretionary, they consider, with the guardians whether they will grant the certificate or not. The Board cannot be surprised at a refusal on the part of the guardians to grant it where it is intended to be used adversely to the interests of the parish on whose behalf the relief was granted by the guardians. The same modes of proof, however, are still open to the party desiring to show the chargeability of any particular pauper, which existed prior to the passing of the 7 & 8 Vic. c. 101.

---

2. COST OF MAINTENANCE UNDER AN ORDER OF REMOVAL.

16*th August*, 1849.

Clerk of Launceston Union.—By an order of removal, dated the 3rd of October, 1848, a pauper, resident in Egloskerry, was adjudged to belong and directed to be removed to Warbstowe. On the 7th of October, notice of such order, with statement of grounds of settlement, was sent by Egloskerry to the overseers of Warbstowe. There was no notice of appeal, and at the expiration of twenty-one days the pauper was delivered by Egloskerry to Warbstowe. The parish officers of Egloskerry have since applied to the overseers of Warbstowe for the amount expended in relief and maintenance of the pauper, in the interval between the sending of the notice of the order and the actual removal, considering that, under the 84th sec. of the 4 & 5 Wm. 4, c. 76, the overseers of Warbstowe are bound to pay the amount, and are individually liable, in case of non-payment, to be proceeded against by distress on their private properties in the way pointed out by sec. 99, such overseers being a *quasi* corporation, within the interpretation clause of the Act, (Withnell *v.* Gartham, 6 Term R. 396,) and, in addition, individually liable, as persons offending by non-payment within the 99th section. The parish of Warbstowe, on the other hand, says that the overseers are not a corporation for the purposes of the particular section, (84,) nor liable, individually, for the neglect of the parish to pay the costs to which it is declared subject; that there appears no general corporation for a parish, certain statutes, (as 59 Geo. 3, c. 12, sec. 17,) having made the overseers a body corporate for specific ends only—in that instance for vesting lands in these officers—that the interpretation clause of the 4 & 5 Wm. 4, c. 76, does not in any case make the term "parish" and "overseer" convertible; that at most an overseer can only be liable as an *inhabitant*, and in such case might plead that all other inhabitants should be jointly sued; that the term "parish" is equally inconvertible into "inhabitant;" and that, as sec. 84 has omitted to designate a "person," there can be no "offender" within the 99th sec. In municipal and other corporations, in hundreds, in counties, certain persons are nominated to represent the several bodies, while here no individual is pointed at through whom the corporate property may be reached. Pending this question between the parishes new overseers have been appointed. By arrangement between the parishes, it is left to the Poor Law Board to say whether the amount of such relief is recoverable, in what specific manner, and whether from the present or the late churchwardens and overseers.

Ans.—The parish of Warbstowe is only liable for the amount expended in the relief and maintenance of the pauper in question, in the interval between the sending of the notice of chargeability and the execution of the order of removal, if the case can be brought within sec. 84 of the Poor Law Amendment Act (4 & 5 Wm. 4, c. 76.) That section, in terms, applies to a case where the "settlement of the pauper shall be in question." Although there was no appeal in this case against the order of removal, yet, as the parish of Warbstowe did not so far agree to submit to such order, by sending notice that they would receive the pauper within the twenty-one days, the period required by the Act to elapse under the circumstances before the removal can be effected, (sec. 79,) the Board think it must be taken that there was some question raised as to the settlement, and that in the result, and in the absence of any appeal against the order, the pauper was "admitted" to belong to Warbstowe. Sec. 84 provides that the cost and expense may be recovered against the parish to which such poor person shall be admitted or finally adjudged to belong. The Board allow that the term "parish" is somewhat ambiguous; but they entertain no doubt that the overseers, for the time being, represent the parish in the matter, and ought, in a case to which the 84th sec. applies, to pay the amount claimed. They think that, in strictness, an order of justices should be obtained for the payment; but such a course would only increase the expense, and the Board, therefore, do not recommend the parish of Warbstowe to insist upon its being obtained. As, therefore, an order could, as the Board are advised, be legally made upon the overseers of the parish to pay such cost and expense, the Board think that the present overseers of Warbstowe can properly pay the amount.

V.—WORKHOUSE.

1. PROSECUTION FOR ABSCONDING WITH WORKHOUSE. CLOTHES.

18*th Oct.*, 1849.

Clerk of Stroud Union.—Inquiring whether, in proceeding before magistrates against two or more persons for absconding together from the workhouse with clothes belonging to the union, it would be lawful to include the names of all the offenders in one information, or whether there should be a separate information against each offender. Referred to the 11 & 12 Vic. c. 43, sec. 10.

Ans.—The Board consider that the question must depend upon all the circumstances of the case. If the absconding with the clothes be joint, so that both offenders are acting in pursuance of one joint purpose, and one assists the other to commit the offence, the prosecution should be joint; but if they do not assist each other, and do not act in pursuance of any joint purpose, so that the offences are distinct, (and this will more frequently be the case,) the Board are of opinion that the prosecutions ought to be separate.

2. BATHING PAUPERS ON ADMISSION INTO WORKHOUSE.

31*st Oct.*, 1849.

Clerk of East Grinstead Union.—It has been the invariable practice of the guardians, through the master, to refuse admission into the workhouse to any pauper (not casual) in good health, without first being bathed in warm or cold water. Inquiring whether the guardians, in the event of any such pauper refusing to be bathed, are justified in altogether denying admission.

Ans.—It is not only quite competent to the guardians to make it a regulation of their workhouse that every inmate, on admission, shall be thoroughly bathed or cleansed, but the Board are of opinion that the guardians have, by doing so, duly carried out the intention of Art. 95 of the General Consolidated Order. The use of the bath not only tends to keep the regular inmates of the workhouse free from vermin and disease, but also to check the spread of vermin and disease over the country, when used by casual paupers who come for one night's lodging only, as it is desirable it should be whenever practicable. The Board are also of opinion, that the guardians may properly refuse admission to any person in good health applying for relief, who declines complying with the regulations of the workhouse in this respect.

VI.—WORKHOUSE MASTER.—PAUPERS IN WORKHOUSE HAVING MONEY, ETC., ON THEM —HIS POWERS.

3*rd Oct.*, 1849.

Clerk of St. Austell Union.—Inquiring whether the guardians have the power to order the master of the workhouse to take possession of any money, or money order, which he may find belonging to any pauper in the workhouse, before he has reported the same to the guardians.

Ans.—The Board do not see how the guardians of the St. Austell Union can make the necessary order for the master of the workhouse to take possession of any money, &c., found on the person of the pauper applying for relief, until he has reported the case to the guardians. If, however, it be proposed that the guardians should give a general direction, beforehand, to the master of the union workhouse to take possession of such property, the Board do not think that any such general direction would be a lawful justification to the master for so acting.

London: Printed by Order of the Poor Law Board, by BLACKBURN & BURT, 90½, Holborn Hill, and Published by CHARLES KNIGHT, 90, Fleet Street.

VOLUME IX

[1850]

VOLUME IX

AN

OFFICIAL CIRCULAR

OF PUBLIC DOCUMENTS AND INFORMATION:

DIRECTED BY THE POOR LAW BOARD TO BE PRINTED, CHIEFLY FOR THE USE OF THE BOARDS OF GUARDIANS AND THEIR OFFICERS.

No. 33.] JANUARY, 1850. [N.S.

CONTENTS.

SECOND ANNUAL REPORT

OF THE

POOR LAW BOARD—1849.

TO THE QUEEN'S MOST EXCELLENT MAJESTY.

Poor Law Board, Somerset House,
31st December, 1849.

MAY IT PLEASE YOUR MAJESTY,

We, the Poor Law Board, beg leave to lay before your Majesty, the following Report of our proceedings during the year 1849:—

Poor-rate Expenditure.

As in our preceding Report, we shall, in the first place, set forth the amount of poor's-rate expended for purposes connected with the relief of the poor; and, in the next, the number of persons in receipt of relief; or, in other words, the pauperism of the country and its pecuniary cost.

The only return which presents a complete view of the expenditure from the poor's-rate, for purposes connected with the relief of the poor, is made up annually, and comprises the period from Lady-day in one year to Lady-day in the next.*

* The Return comprises all expenses under the following heads:—In-maintenance, out-relief, salaries of officers, (except assistant overseers and collectors,) loans for building and altering workhouses and for emigration purposes repaid, together with interest thereon, maintenance of lunatics in asylums, emigration expenses, extra medical relief and fees, and the cost of the burial of paupers. *See* App., Poor-rate Return, col. 4.

The latest complete return, therefore, which can now be given, is that for the year ended at Lady-day, 1849. This return shows that the amount expended during that year was £5,792,963, being a reduction, as compared with the preceding year, of £387,802, or £6. 6*s*. per cent. It may be convenient to exhibit the comparison of the expenditure for the two years in the following tabular form:—

Years ended Lady-day.	Expended for purposes connected with the Relief of the Poor in England and Wales.	Amount of Decrease in 1849, as compared with 1848.	Decrease per cent.	Rate per Head on Population.	Decrease per Head in 1849, as compared with 1848.
	£.	£.	£. s. d.	£. s. d.	£. s. d.
1848	6,180,765	387,802	6 6 0	0 7 1¾	0 0 7½
1849	5,792,963			0 6 6¼	

The tables in the Appendix contain a detailed account of this expenditure in the several counties in England and Wales, and show the rate of increase or decrease for each county. It will be perceived that there has been an increase to some extent in five counties, namely, in Middlesex, Warwickshire, Westmoreland, the West Riding of Yorkshire, and Anglesey; but in all the others there has been a decrease.

Although the expenditure of the poor-rate for all the purposes connected with the relief of the poor cannot, as already stated, be given for a later period than the year ended at Lady-day last, we are in possession of returns showing the amount expended in relief, both in-door and out-door, for the half-year ended at Michaelmas last, in 558 unions. The accounts of the remaining unions and parishes not having as yet been audited, no such returns have been received as respects them. From the returns for the 558 unions in question, it appears that the amount expended in relief during the half-year ended Michaelmas last, was £1,653,061, being a reduction, as compared with the expenditure in the same unions for the half-year ended at Michaelmas, 1848, of £97,098, or 5½ per cent.

The following table shows this result more in detail:—

—	Expenditure for In-maintenance and Out-door Relief.		
	In-maintenance.	Out-door Relief.	Total.
Unions.	£.	£.	£.
558 { Half-year ended Michaelmas, 1848	361,409	1,388,750	1,750,159
" " 1849	329,993	1,323,068	1,653,061
Decrease	31,416	65,682	97,098 or $5\frac{5}{10}$ per cent.

Extent of Pauperism—Number of Paupers.

As regards the number of paupers relieved, it has been the practice heretofore to take the number relieved during the quarter ended at Lady-day in each year, as representing the aggregate number of paupers; and thus a quarter, ordinarily the heaviest in point of destitution, became the standard for estimating the extent of pauperism: moreover, as there is frequently an interruption in the relief, the same paupers with their families were by this course entered more than once during the quarter, and were on each occasion counted as distinct persons. Such an estimate must obviously have greatly exceeded the number actually in receipt of relief. In like manner, the number of vagrants relieved was made to appear much greater than it really was, as every individual of that class was returned by each of the several unions in which he had been relieved during the quarter.

In order to establish a more accurate mode of ascertaining the pauperism of the country, the Poor Law Commissioners, by their General Order of Accounts issued in March, 1847, prescribed that a return should be made, half-yearly, of the number of poor persons in the receipt of relief on two specified days, namely, on the 1st of January, when the amount of pauperism may be expected to be the highest, and on the 1st of July, when it may be expected to be the lowest.

This Order came into complete operation in March, 1848, and returns were obtained from 580 unions of the number of paupers relieved on the 1st of July in that year. Similar returns have been received, also, as to the 1st of January, and the 1st of July, 1849. The following table shows the number in receipt of relief in those 580 unions on the 1st of July, 1848, and also the number in receipt of relief in the same unions on the 1st of July, 1849 :—

Year and Day.	Number of Paupers Relieved, *In-door* and *Out-door*. All Classes except the Insane and Vagrants.	Insane.	Vagrants.	Total.	Decrease.
1st July, 1848	867,040	12,989	13,714	893,743	
1st July, 1849	809,369	12,888	5,662	827,919	7·4 per Cent.
Decrease . .	57,671	101	8,052	65,824	

NOTE.—Population of the 580 unions on 1st July, 1848, estimated at 14,501,000, and on 1st July, 1849, at 14,694,000.

It is satisfactory to observe that there was a reduction in the number of persons of each class relieved on the 1st of July, 1849, as compared with the number relieved on the 1st of July, 1848. In the number of the insane relieved, there was a decrease of 101, vagrants, 8,052, other classes of paupers, 57,671, in all a decrease of 65,824, or 7·4 per cent.*—(*See Tables in the Appendix.*)

* Returns of the number of persons relieved on the 1st January, 1850, having been received during the progress of printing this Report, we are able to present a comparison between the number relieved on that day and the number relieved on the corresponding day in 1849. The following Table exhibits this comparison :—

SUMMARY OF RETURNS from 602 Unions and single Parishes, under Boards of Guardians, showing the Number of Paupers of all Classes relieved on the 1st January, 1849, and the 1st January, 1850, respectively.

Year and Day.	Number of Paupers Relieved, *In-door* and *Out-door*. All Classes except the Insane and Vagrants.	Insane.	Vagrants.	Total.	Decrease.
1st Jan., 1849	966,566	13,767	7,663	987,996	
1st Jan., 1850	906,316	14,227	4,129	924,672	6·4 per Cent.
Decrease . .	60,250	...	3,534	63,324	
Increase . .	...	460	...	...	

NOTE.—Population of the 602 unions on 1st January, 1849, estimated at 15,736,000, and on 1st January, 1850, at 15,945,000.

Assuming the number of paupers relieved for the residue of the kingdom to bear the same proportion to the population as is shown in the above table, the total number relieved in England and Wales, would stand thus :—

Number *actually* relieved on the 1st July, 1848	893,743	
Number *estimated* to have been relieved on the same day, in parts of the kingdom un-returned . .	183,359	
TOTAL of paupers relieved on the 1st July, 1848 . . .		1,077,102
Number *actually* relieved on the 1st July, 1849	827,919	
Number *estimated* to be relieved on the same day, in parts of the kingdom un-returned	169,877	
TOTAL of paupers relieved on the 1st July, 1849 . . .		997,796
Decrease . . .		79,306

Assuming the number of paupers relieved for the residue of the kingdom to bear the same proportion to the population as is shown in the above Return, the total numbers relieved in England and Wales would stand thus :—

Number *actually* relieved on the 1st January, 1849	987,996	
Number *estimated* to have been relieved on the same day, in parts of the kingdom un-returned . .	116,530	
TOTAL of paupers relieved 1st January, 1849 . . .		1,104,526
Number *actually* relieved on the 1st January, 1850	924,672	
Number *estimated* to have been relieved on the same day, in parts of the kingdom un-returned . .	109,140	
TOTAL of paupers relieved 1st January, 1850 . . .		1,033,812
Decrease . . .		70,714

The same Returns enable us to exhibit the actual number of adult able-bodied paupers relieved, both in-door and out-door, on the 1st January, 1850. This is set forth in the following Table, which shows also the number relieved on the 1st Jan., 1849:—

Year and Day.	Number of Adult Able-bodied Paupers relieved, both *In-door* and *Out-door*. Widows receiving Out-door Relief.	All other Classes, In-door and Out-door.	Total.	Decrease
1st Jan., 1849	52,441	149,203	201,644	15·4 per cent.
1st Jan., 1850	53,151	117,351	170,502	
Decrease	..	31,852	31,142	
Increase	710	..	..	

The mode formerly adopted for ascertaining the number of persons in receipt of relief, although affording a means of comparing the pauperism of one year with that of another, has led to erroneous conclusions in regard to the extent of pauperism. The returns set forth in our last Report were obtained under the former mode, and show that 1,626,201 persons, out of a population of 14,453,000, were relieved during the quarter ended at Lady-day, 1848. From this it has been supposed, that one in every nine of the population was a pauper. The returns, of which the foregoing table is a summary, show, however, that the number actually in receipt of relief on the 1st of July, 1848, was 893,743, out of a population of 14,501,000, or less than one pauper in every sixteen of the population.

Reduction of the Number of Vagrants Relieved.

In our last Annual Report, we adverted to a Minute which the late President of the Board had issued in the month of August, 1848, on the subject of vagrancy. This Minute urged on boards of guardians the necessity of discriminating between real and simulated destitution, in order to stay, if possible, the rapid increase of vagrancy. The recommendations of this Minute were very generally adopted, the consequence of which was a marked decrease in the number of vagrants applying for relief. It will be noticed that the number relieved on the 1st of July, 1848, before the issuing of the Minute, was 13,714, but the number relieved on the 1st of July, 1849, was only 5,662, being a decrease of 8,052, or 58·7 per cent.

We find, by reports which we have received from our inspectors, that vagrancy still continues to decrease in the unions generally. That received from Mr. Farnall especially, shows the beneficial effects arising from the practice of subjecting all vagrants seeking to be admitted into the union workhouses to the strict regulations for cleansing and searching prescribed by the Poor Law Commissioners, under the authority of the late statutes; and, on the other hand, the unfavourable consequences which result from the want of a union workhouse, or of proper vagrant wards for the reception of this class of paupers.

Irish Vagrants.

Much of the reduction in the number of vagrants relieved is doubtless attributable to the fact, that the immigration of Irish poor, which had tended so materially to the increase of vagrancy in this country, is now reduced to its ordinary average.

Emigration.

A statement will be found in the Appendix, of the places to which we have issued orders during the year, to authorize the expenditure of money for emigration purposes, and of the amount authorized to be expended in each case. The sum authorized to be expended in 1848 was £8,456. 11*s*. It amounts in the present year to £12,301. 13*s*.

While emigration to Canada has greatly diminished during the year, that to the Australian colonies and to the Cape of Good Hope has much increased. The aid which the Government affords to emigration to the latter colonies has been the main cause of this increase, as by such aid the cost to the parishes or unions has been brought below that of emigration to Canada. Another circumstance favourable to emigration to the Cape and Australia is, that it is open during the whole year, while that to the North American colonies is limited to some months of the year only.

In our Report for 1848, reference was made to the inconvenience which resulted from certain formalities required to be observed before we could authorize the expenditure of parish funds upon emigration. This inconvenience has been removed by a provision in a statute of the last session (12 & 13 Vic. c. 103, s. 20,) which enables us to issue the requisite order upon the resolution of the guardians of the parish, or of the union comprising it, (provided in the latter case the guardians of the parish interested concur in the expenditure,) without the holding of a parish meeting, as required by the Poor Law Amendment Act. A limit of £10 per head is, however, imposed upon the expenditure, where the proceedings are under the new statute.

Another provision of the same statute (s. 12) enables persons to whom the Orders of the Board are addressed, to act upon them forthwith, instead of waiting until the expiration of fourteen days, as was previously required, and thus the cause of much delay, which in emigration cases was often attended with serious inconvenience, has been removed.

We have deemed it right to make an exception to the practice, long established, of declining to sanction the emigration of wives or children to join their husbands or fathers in the colonies, in favour of the families of convicts, to whom the Government are willing to grant a passage, either wholly or partly free. The transportation of the convict is not a voluntary desertion of the family; and when the Government promotes the sending out of the family, we consider that the expenditure of the poor-rate in furtherance of that object may properly be sanctioned.

Workhouse Schools.

The state of workhouse schools throughout the country has continued to occupy much of our attention. From the 1st of October, 1846, to the end of the last parochial year—25th of March, 1849—the salaries paid by the boards of guardians to the schoolmasters and schoolmistresses of workhouses were wholly refunded out of the grant of £30,000 annually voted for that purpose by Parliament. During the current parochial year, the distribution of this grant has been regulated, not by the stipulated salaries of the teachers, but by certificates awarded to them by the Committee of Council on Education, and founded on reports of the examination of the teachers by their Lordships' Inspectors. The following table shows the classes of certificates awarded, and the sums allowed from the grant during the current year in respect of the several divisions of each class of certificates :—

Certificate.	Division.	Master. £.	s.	d.	Mistress. £.	s.	d.
Efficiency . .	1st . . 2nd . .	50	0	0	40	0	0
		and upwards.			and upwards.		
	3rd . .	45	0	0	36	0	0
Competency.	1st . .	40	0	0	32	0	0
	2nd . .	36	0	0	28	16	0
	3rd . .	33	0	0	26	8	0
Probation . .	1st . .	30	0	0	24	0	0
	2nd . .	25	0	0	20	0	0
	3rd . .	20	0	0	16	0	0
Permission .	1st . .	15	0	0	12	0	0
	2nd . .	10	0	0	8	0	0
	3rd . .	5	0	0	4	0	0

As might be expected, the sums specified in the certificates are seldom the same as the salaries stipulated to be payable to the teachers. In some instances those sums are higher than the stipulated salaries, and in others they are lower. When the former is the case, the guardians make a corresponding advance in the payments to the teachers; but when the certificate assigns to the teacher a lower sum than the salary, the guardians continue to pay the higher sum (the whole salary) agreeably to their engagement, the difference between the salary and the amount allowed under the certificate from the grant being paid out of the poor-rates. There is little doubt, that by the appointment of teachers possessing higher qualifications, the salaries of teachers and the sums specified in the certificates awarded to them, will ultimately be so adjusted as to render any payment from the rates in respect of their salaries unnecessary.

School Books, &c.

The arrangement which we have made for supplying workhouse schools with suitable books and maps at reduced prices is found to work satisfactorily. Schools which were formerly scantily supplied, and others where books of an unsuitable character were used, are now well furnished with books and maps selected from those recommended by the Committee of Council as the best adapted for the purposes of popular education.

Accommodation for the Pauper Children of the Metropolis.

We have been much engaged during the year in making provision for the more suitable accommodation of pauper children belonging to the metropolitan parishes and unions.

Up to the close of 1848, these children were maintained under contract in the two large establishments of Mr. Aubin, at Norwood, and Mr. Drouet, at Tooting; or in the schools kept up in the country by the several parishes or unions to which the children belonged, such as that for the parish of St. George the Martyr, at Lewisham, or that for the West London Union, at Edmonton; or in workhouses apart from other inmates, as in the Unions of Stepney and Whitechapel; or in workhouses, together with other inmates, as in the Greenwich and Poplar Unions.

Jonas Hanway's Acts.

Upon the repeal of the two statutes, (2 Geo. 3, c. 22, and 7 Geo. 3, c. 39,) commonly known as Jonas Hanway's Acts, at the passing of the 7 & 8 Vic. c. 101, in 1844, it ceased to be compulsory on the metropolitan parishes to send their young children into the country for nurture and maintenance; and in place of that obligation, there was substituted a series of provisions for promoting the establishment of district schools.

Metropolitan District Schools.

When, therefore, the condition of the metropolitan children was brought under our more immediate notice, by the sudden outbreak of the cholera at Mr. Drouet's establishment at Tooting, in January last, we deemed it a fitting opportunity to make renewed efforts for the establishment of district schools. No progress had been previously made in this desirable undertaking, partly owing to legislative restrictions as to size of district and amount of expenditure, which have since been removed by the 11 & 12 Vic. c. 83, partly in consequence of a reluctance among the unions and parishes to enter into a new kind of combination, and partly, perhaps, because guardians were satisfied with the arrangements of the schools at Norwood and Tooting, where the children of no less than twenty-four parishes and unions were maintained.

In dealing with this subject, we have been anxious to carry with us the convictions and feelings of the guardians; and although we are empowered to form school districts without the assent of the guardians, we deemed it important that their cordial co-operation should be secured. No school district has, therefore, been declared without the expressed concurrence of the large majority of the guardians concerned in it being first obtained; indeed, only one union, that of St. Olave's, has been comprised in a school district without such consent, an exception which we were compelled to make, in order to secure for the poor children chargeable to that union the benefit of being well educated in a healthy situation, which otherwise there appeared no immediate prospect of their obtaining.

The course taken in the formation of school districts has been this—we have set before the guardians what we conceived to be the advantages of district schools; we have allowed the guardians the alternative of entering into a combination with other parishes and unions, or of establishing single-handed a school which would insure to the children the more prominent of those advantages, namely, salubrity of situation, separation from adult paupers, and suitable instruction properly blended with industrial training.

Our success in the establishment of district schools has not been so great as we could desire; but the efforts made have not altogether been unavailing, three very important school districts having, within the year, been formed in and near the metropolis. These are:—

1. The Central London School District, comprising the City of London Union, the East London Union, and the St. Saviour's Union. The Board of Management of this district have completed all their arrangements and hold their regular meetings. They have purchased of Mr. Aubin his premises at Norwood for the district school, retaining him in the capacity of steward or superintendent of the establishment, and have appointed an efficient staff of teachers in every department. The school is now in full activity, upon an improved footing, and nearly 800 children are maintained and educated in it.

2. The South Metropolitan School District comprised, as originally formed, the Union of St. Olave's, and the large parishes, not in union, of Bermondsey, Camberwell, and Rotherhithe. After the Board of Management was constituted, it appeared desirable that the populous and important Union of Greenwich should be added, and with the consent of all parties interested this was accordingly done. Although some delay has occurred in carrying out the necessary arrangements, we believe that a school for 1,000 children will shortly be provided in this district.

3. The North Surrey School District includes the Unions of Wandsworth and Clapham, Kingston, Croydon, Richmond, and Lewisham. The managers have purchased fifty acres of land near Norwood, and have commenced the erection of a building capable of accommodating 600 children. Another parish or union might be advantageously added to this district, and the Board are prepared to take the necessary steps for that purpose whenever the occasion may arise.

Metropolitan Union and Parish Schools.

It will thus be seen that provision has been made in and around London for the proper education and training of more than 2,000 poor children. We have, moreover, sanctioned arrangements whereby, when completed, the state of the children of other metropolitan parishes will be very materially improved.

The Guardians of the Stepney Union are preparing plans for the enlargement of their school at Limehouse, which has been for many years carefully and successfully conducted.

The Guardians of the Strand Union have purchased a house and grounds well adapted for the purposes of a school at Edmonton.

The Guardians of the parish of St. George-in-the-East, having placed their children temporarily in a hired house at Mitcham, have resolved upon buying land and building school-premises on the most approved design.

The Guardians of the parish at Lambeth are enlarging and greatly improving their school near Norwood.

The Directors of the Poor of St. Pancras are, with our assent, erecting a detached building for their children upon a portion of their extensive workhouse site within the parish.

The Directors and Guardians of St. James's, Westminster, are negotiating for land at Hanwell, which has been viewed and approved by our Inspector, whereon to build a school.

The Guardians of the parish of St. Martin's-in-the-Fields, having resolved upon buying land and building a school, have, pending their inquiries for a site, placed their children under the care of the Managers of the Central London District School.

The Trustees of Islington, and the Guardians of Clerkenwell, have temporarily lodged their children in separate premises, situated in the suburbs, until permanent schools can be established for them.

All these arrangements, which are more or less matured, have been entered upon under our guidance or with our concurrence, and under the superintendence of our Inspector, Mr. Hall, who has charge of the Metropolitan District. It cannot be doubted that from the year now ending will date a general and important amelioration of the condition and prospects of a large proportion of the pauper children of the Metropolis.

Country School Districts.

Besides these Metropolitan School Districts, three districts have been formed in the country. The first is the Farnham and Hartley Wintney School District, consisting of the two unions of Farnham and Hartley Wintney, which are situated in Surrey and Hampshire. This district was formed on the 19th of June last, and the Board of Management, who entered on their duties on the 28th of August last, have purchased a workhouse at Aldershott, belonging to the Farnham Union, as the school for the district.

The second is the South-east Shropshire School District, and comprises the Bridgnorth, Cleobury Mortimer, Seisdon, and Madely Unions, in the counties of Salop, Worcester, and Stafford. This district was formed on the 7th July, and the Board of Management met for the first time on the 23rd August last. They propose to take the premises belonging to the Bridgnorth Union, hitherto occupied by the School of that union, and known as the Quatt School.

The third is the Reading and Wokingham School District, which comprises the Farringdon and Reading Unions, in the county of Berks. This district was formed on the 28th November.

Contractors' Establishments for Farming out the Poor.

Closely connected with the question of making new provision for the pauper children of the Metropolis, was that of regulating the contractors' establishments. The mortality caused by the cholera among the children at Tooting, though not proportionally greater, it is believed, than in some other public establishments, excited in an unusual degree the interest and the alarm of the public. In the absence of any apparent cause for so sudden and rapid an exhibition of the disease, an impression was created that the children had been grossly neglected, and this led to a review of the powers vested in us for the control of establishments in which the poor were received and maintained under contract. It appeared that doubts existed as to the right of exercising any direct control over the contractors, or of issuing any regulations for the management of their establishments. Such being the state of the law, the 12 & 13 Vic. c. 13, was passed, empowering us to cause these establishments to be inspected, to issue rules for their government as if they were workhouses, to remove unfit officers and servants, and to regulate the contracts between the parochial authorities and the proprietors.

The practice of farming out the poor, as it is termed, has been very limited in its operation since the passing of the Poor Law Amendment Act in 1834, so that scarcely any contractors' establishments existed at the passing of the 12 & 13 Vic. c. 13, except in the neighbourhood of London; and those are now all extinct, with the exception of one. The school at Tooting was finally broken up in the spring, on the death of the proprietor. That at Norwood is become the school for the Central London District: the two establishments at Peckham and Bow, wherein the adult poor of the City of London Union exclusively were maintained under contract, have been abandoned by the removal of the poor to the new union workhouse. The inmates (belonging to the St. Saviour's Union) of a small establishment near Dartford have been taken away, the union workhouse being rendered by enlargement capable of containing them. The remaining establishment is at Brixton, wherein a limited number of poor persons belonging to the parish of Newington are contracted for. When it was lately proposed to us to allow this arrangement (which is only temporary) we caused the premises to be carefully examined, limited the number of persons to be received therein, and revised the arrangement in other respects. Besides this metropolitan establishment, there are two at Margate, to which paupers, chiefly children who are afflicted with scrofulous disease, are sent from London for the benefit of sea bathing. These also have been inspected, and a maximum number of inmates prescribed for each establishment in accordance with a medical certificate. The proprietor of one of them has been required to receive children only, and the proprietor of the other adults only.

Formation of new Unions.

In the course of the year, five new Unions have been formed, namely, the Bedwelty Union, in the county of Monmouth, the Samford Union, in the county of Suffolk, the Penistone and Barnsley Unions, in the West Riding of Yorkshire, and the Barton-upon-Irwell Union, in the county of Lancaster.

We expressed in our last Report an intention to separate the two parishes of Aberystruth and Bedwelty from the Abergavenny Union, and to form them into a union by themselves. This was effected by an Order, dated the 24th of February last, the new union being denominated the Bedwelty Union.

The several parishes in the Samford Union were formerly incorporated by a local Act of the 39th of Geo. 3. The constitution of the board of directors and acting guardians differed in many respects from that of the unions formed under the Poor Law Amendment Act, but especially in this particular, namely, that the elected guardians held their office for life, while a considerable number of persons were entitled to act as guardians *ex-officio*. As the parishes formed a convenient and compact district, the Poor Law Commissioners did not interfere with the constitution of the incorporation. But some dissatisfaction arising among the rate-payers and other persons interested, the requisite number of the guardians assented to the dissolution of the incorporation, and an application having been made to us to dissolve it, we issued an Order for that purpose dated the 7th of February last; and by an Order dated the 24th of February, the same parishes were formed into a union, under the Poor Law Amendment Act. The Orders which regulate the proceedings and the administration of relief in other unions were extended to this, and a board of guardians having been elected at Lady-day last, the business of the union has since been conducted with the same regularity as prevails under other boards of guardians.

The Penistone Union was formed by an Order dated the 12th of July last, and comprises 15 parishes or townships, in the West Riding of Yorkshire, 8 of which had been separated from the Wortley Union, but the remainder had not previously been in any Union. On the 30th of October last the board of guardians met for the first time, and entered on their duties.

The township of Barton-upon-Irwell, and some adjoining townships, have long formed part of the Chorlton Union; but after careful inquiry and long deliberation, we came to the conclusion that a separation was absolutely necessary for the proper administration of the law in that district. Accordingly, on the 9th October last, we issued an Order to separate the extensive and populous township of Barton-upon-Irwell, with the townships of Flixton and Urmston, from the Chorlton Union, and by an Order, dated the same day, formed those townships, together with the townships of Clifton and Worsley, which had not previously been in any union, into a distinct union, under the name of the Barton-upon-Irwell Union.

On the 28th instant, we issued an Order for the formation of the Barnsley Union, which consists of 17 parishes and townships in the West Riding of Yorkshire. None of these had previously been in any union. It will be seen that 26 parishes, not previously in union under the Poor Law Amendment Act, have been, in the course of this year, incorporated in the several new unions.

Erection of New Workhouses.

Considerable progress has been made during the year in providing workhouses for unions, where hitherto great reluctance had been felt to their erection. Thus, in the county of Lancaster, Orders have been issued, with the consent of the guardians, for the building of workhouses in the Ashton-under-Lyne and Warrington Unions, while the guardians of the Oldham Union are proceeding to complete the workhouse for which the Order was issued in the previous year. In the case of the Bradford Union, in the West Riding of Yorkshire; the Kirkby Moorside Union, in the North Riding; the Easington Union, in Durham; the Truro Union, in Cornwall; and the Merthyr Tydfil Union, in Glamorganshire, similar Orders have been issued with the like consent.

The guardians of the parish of Birmingham, though possessing a workhouse of considerable extent, have found it inadequate for the demands of that parish, and have adopted plans with our approval for building a new workhouse, suitable to so populous and extensive a parish. Similar proceedings have been taken at Leicester and Oxford.

The guardians of the poor of the city of Canterbury, a union of fourteen parishes under a local Act, have recently entered upon the occupation of their new workhouse; and so also have the guardians of the City of London Union of the new workhouse which they have built in the parish of Bow, a short distance from the boundaries of the union. This workhouse is calculated to hold 1,200 inmates.

Bristol and Hull.—Refusal to submit Accounts for Audit.

The Poor Law Commissioners, in their Thirteenth and Fourteenth Reports, detailed the proceedings which they had instituted against the guardians of the poor of Kingston-upon-Hull and Bristol, to compel them to submit their accounts to the district auditors. The guardians in both cases had made returns to the writs of *mandamus;* but the guardians of the former incorporation subsequently withdrew their opposition, and suffered judgment to be given for the Crown. They now submit their accounts to the auditor.

The case relating to the city of Bristol was argued in Trinity Term last, when, besides the general question as to the power of the Poor Law Commissioners to include the incorporation in an audit district, some technical objections were taken to the order by which the district was formed, and to the terms of the writ of *mandamus.* The Court of Queen's Bench, after taking time to consider, ultimately gave judgment for the Crown. Upon this judgment, the defendants brought a writ of error, which will be determined at the sittings after next Hilary Term.

Appeals to the Board against Decisions of Auditors.

We have been much engaged in the investigation of appeals made to us against the decisions of auditors in disallowing payments, or in surcharging for defaults. The appeals for the most part are made for our intervention to remit the disallowances or surcharges under the equitable authority conferred upon us by the 11 & 12 Vic. c. 91, sec. 4.

It appears, that the existence of this authority is of great importance. If the decisions of the auditor were final, great hardship must often ensue, as persons who have filled onerous offices without remuneration would be compelled to sustain loss on account of acts which they believed to be lawful as well as beneficial. The auditor, aware of the consequences of his disallowance or surcharge, has frequently been induced to sanction illegal payments, or to overlook cases of neglect which have caused loss to the parish or the union. There was much evil in this, as illegal payments, when sanctioned by the public officer appointed to investigate them, become more difficult to be repressed. The auditor being now aware that there is an authority which can interfere, when it is fair and equitable to do so, for the purpose of remitting any disallowance or surcharge which the law may require him to make, will not hesitate to act with proper legal strictness. When a person, against whom a disallowance has been made, has any reasonable excuse to offer for the payment, he appeals to us; and after investigating the case, we issue an Order, under seal, confirming or remitting the disallowance. We are careful, however, not to allow this power to avail for the relief of persons who have recklessly, or in disregard of advice, authorized the expenditure of money for purposes not sanctioned by the law, nor to suffer paid officers to escape from the consequences of disobeying the orders applicable to their office.

Cholera.

The severe epidemic disease which had appeared at the close of the autumn of 1848, and which had much abated during the last winter and spring, returned at the commencement of the summer, occasioning great mortality. The cholera was, however, limited in regard to the places of its attack. In many of the strictly rural unions, and even in some populous and manufacturing districts, it scarcely appeared. As far as information has reached us, the cholera does not seem to have prevailed in many of the union workhouses, although several cases of persons attacked with the disease in a state of destitution, or under other peculiar circumstances, have occurred where the patients have been removed to workhouses, and there died. But it is satisfactory to find that the ordinary inmates have generally escaped.

Regulations of General Board of Health.

The General Board of Health, in the months of April and September last, renewed the Regulations which they had issued in November, 1848, for the prevention or mitigation of this disease. These Regulations were addressed to all the Boards of Guardians throughout England and Wales. But certain special Regulations were deemed requisite for particular districts where the attack of the disease was most severe. We have reason to believe that in almost every instance the authorities to whom these Regulations were addressed zealously and earnestly executed them. In many instances these Regulations were anticipated by the guardians; and we have remarked that, where the guardians have shown reluctance to adopt the recommendations or to act upon the Orders of the Board of Health, it was generally because they had themselves put in train arrangements of a similar nature, which they considered effective before the communications of the Board of Health reached them.

We have had numerous instances brought to our knowledge of great sacrifices of time and labour being made by individual members of boards of guardians, as well as by other philanthropic persons, in promoting the objects of Sanitary Committees formed by those Boards, while the officers of the guardians generally gave the most unremitting attention to the arduous duties which the visitation devolved upon them.

Remuneration of Officers for extraordinary Services during the prevalence of Cholera.

The officers were required, by the statute, to render these services as part of their official duties, so that in strictness they had no legal claim upon the guardians for any extra remuneration. It was, however, considered that these were such extraordinary services as fell within the provision in the General Consolidated Order, which enables the guardians, with our approval, to remunerate any officer for such services by a special gratuity. Where the services of the officers have been such as to warrant it, we have found the guardians in most cases prepared to admit their claims, and have readily given our assent to the payment of the gratuities proposed by the guardians. We had no direct power, in other respects, to control the expenditure in the execution of the Regulations of the Board of Health; but we endeavoured on all occasions to prevent unnecessary outlay, and at the same time sought to enforce the adoption of all preventative or remedial measures.

Removal of Nuisances.

The expenses incurred by unions in the execution of the Regulations of the Board of Health are, under the provisions of the "Nuisances Removal and Diseases Prevention Act, 1848," made a charge upon the common fund. But the Amendment Act of last session (12 & 13 Vic. c. 111) empowers boards of guardians to charge money expended in the removal of a nuisance from any private premises, or from any public place, to the parish wherein the premises shall be situate. Where, however, the amount exceeds 20*s.*, an order of two justices may be necessary to authorize the charge.

The boards of guardians generally have taken very active steps to procure the removal of nuisances by the persons individually responsible. It has been found, in numerous instances, that the giving of the notice required by the statute was sufficient to effect the object without an order of justices.

Although, in accordance with our recommendation, a separate account has been kept in most unions of what are properly to be considered the expenses occasioned by the cholera and the removal of nuisances, we believe that there has been so great a difficulty in separating these expenses from the cost of ordinary relief, that the returns cannot be relied upon as exhibiting a correct statement of the expenditure.

Amendments of the Law.

In the last session of Parliament various amendments and alterations were made in the Poor Law, with reference for the most part to matters of detail.

By a recent decision of the Court of Queen's Bench, it appeared that in boroughs and other municipal places the mayor had, by the operation of the statute of Elizabeth, and the late Acts for the regulation of those corporations, exclusive power in several important respects in reference to the appointment of overseers, and other matters relating to the management and relief of the poor. Inconveniences of a serious nature had resulted from this decision, and it was deemed advisable, by two Acts of the session, 12 & 13 Vic. cc. 8 & 64, to provide that the justices of the peace in boroughs should have the exclusive right of appointing overseers therein, and should have concurrent authority with the mayor in other matters relating to the Poor Law.

Another enactment was passed, (12 & 13 Vic. c. 65,) affecting certain parishes which are divided by the boundary lines of boroughs and counties, wherein there had previously been some practical difficulties in the levying and collecting of county, police, and borough rates, which are only chargeable upon parts of the parishes so divided.

Facilities have been given, by the 12 & 13 Vic. c. 14, for the collection of parochial rates, by the power which is conferred upon the justices of compelling defaulters to pay the costs which the overseers or collectors incur in proceedings taken to enforce payment of the rates; and certain regulations and forms are prescribed, which will be found very convenient and useful in such proceedings. At the same time, an important mitigation of the penal consequences of default in the payment of the poor-rate has been effected by this statute, inasmuch as the indefinite imprisonment until payment, which was the penalty to be awarded by the justices under the statute of Elizabeth, is now limited to a term not exceeding three months, and it is left to the discretion of the justices whether they will award that penalty at all.

The provisions of the statute 12 & 13 Vic. c. 45, for improving the procedure of Courts of Quarter Sessions, have for their object the removal of frivolous, vexatious, and purely technical objections, which have often impeded the progress of justice, and the simplifying of the practice of those courts, as well as the introduction therein of certain convenient proceedings which have long prevailed, with much practical benefit, in the higher courts of law. So many matters arising out of the Poor Law are brought before Courts of Quarter Sessions, that any amendment of the practice must necessarily be of great importance to all persons engaged in the administration of that law.

The statute (12 & 13 Vic. c. 13) for regulating the establishments where paupers are received to be lodged and boarded for hire has been already referred to.

By the 12 & 13 Vic. c. 61, the Act for the exemption of stock in trade from assessment to the poor-rate was extended for another year, namely, until the 1st of October, 1850, and to the end of the then next session of Parliament.

The Act which rendered the cost of the relief of the poor, who were exempted from being removed to the parishes of their settlement by the statute 9 & 10 Vic. c. 66, a charge upon the common fund, would have expired on the 1st of October last. But it has been continued by the statute 12 & 13 Vic. c. 103, for another year. This statute contains various amendments of the Poor Law in matters of detail, which are calculated to remove inconveniences, and to aid guardians and other persons engaged in the administration of the law.

Soon after the termination of the session of Parliament, we communicated to all boards of guardians, in two Circular Letters, the substance of the several enactments above referred to.

Questions as to the Removability of Paupers.

We are very frequently applied to under the statute 11 & 12 Vic. c. 110, s. 4, to determine questions which arise between parishes and boards of guardians as to the removability of paupers. In these cases we require to be furnished with a statement of the facts of each case, signed by the chairman of the board of guardians on their behalf, and by the guardians of the parish interested. No expense to any party is incurred, as we discourage resort to professional aid in these applications, and find, for the most part, that there is little difficulty in obtaining a distinct statement of the facts.

Parish Property.

The disposal of property belonging to parishes in different parts of the kingdom continues to occupy our attention. Notwithstanding the sales which have taken place during the last fourteen years, there is still remaining a considerable amount of this property undisposed of. The cottages are mostly of a very inferior description, and the subject of much complaint in consequence of their wretchedly dilapidated and unhealthy condition. They are often in the occupation of paupers, or of poor persons just removed from that class, who inhabit these dwellings without the payment of rent, so that no fund is raised from the property by which it can be kept in repair, and there is no other fund applicable to such repair.

Vaccination.

The returns relating to vaccination show that due attention is bestowed upon this important subject by the boards of guardians and their medical officers. We have inserted summaries of these returns in the Appendix.

Lunatic Paupers.

The state of the lunatic paupers in the union workhouses generally has been favourably reported upon by the Commissioners in Lunacy, and no cases of serious default, in regard to the relief of those lunatics who are at large, have come under our knowledge, but complaints have been made in various quarters of the difficulties which arise from some of the enactments applicable to pauper lunatics, with reference to orders for their removal to asylums, and also to the mode by which the expenses of their maintenance are to be recovered from the parties responsible. We think it desirable that these provisions should be revised, with a view to their improvement.

All which we most humbly submit to your Majesty.

(Signed) M. T. BAINES, *President.*

APPENDIX.

SUMMARY of RETURNS, showing the Total Number of Paupers (In-door and Out-door) of all classes, in Receipt of Relief on the *1st day of July*, 1848, and the *1st day of July*, 1849, in 580 Unions and single Parishes under Boards of Guardians in England and Wales.

SUMMARY of RETURNS, showing the Total Number of Paupers (In-door and Out-door) of all classes, in receipt of Relief on the *1st day of January*, 1849, and the *1st day of January*, 1850, in 602 Unions and single Parishes, under Boards of Guardians in England and Wales.

NAMES OF COUNTIES.	Number of Unions included.	Population in 1841.	Relieved on the 1st July.		Rate per Cent. of Increase or Decrease in Number of Paupers relieved on 1st July, 1849, compared with the Number relieved on 1st July, 1848.		Number of Unions included.	Population in 1841.	Relieved on the 1st January.		Rate per Cent. of Increase or Decrease in Number of Paupers relieved on 1st January, 1850, compared with the number relieved on 1st January, 1849.		NAMES OF COUNTIES.
			1848.	1849.	In-crease.	De-crease.			1849.	1850.	In-crease.	De-crease.	
ENGLAND.													ENGLAND.
Bedford	6	112,379	8,236	7,366	...	10·6	6	112,379	8,907	7,897	...	11·3	Bedford.
Berks	12	190,367	12,586	12,369	...	1·7	12	190,367	14,629	14,042	...	4·0	Berks.
Buckingham	7	138,255	12,110	11,060	...	8·7	7	138,255	13,061	12,219	...	6·4	Buckingham.
Cambridge	9	171,848	13,519	14,496	7·2	...	9	171,848	14,669	15,134	3·2	...	Cambridge.
Chester	9	344,860	17,432	13,768	...	21·0	9	344,860	15,888	14,256	...	10·3	Chester.
Cornwall	13	340,728	19,792	21,076	6·5	...	13	340,728	20,783	19,952	...	4·0	Cornwall.
Cumberland	9	177,912	8,610	8,213	...	4·6	9	177,912	9,132	8,011	...	12·3	Cumberland.
Derby	9	242,786	8,941	8,176	...	8·6	9	242,786	8,588	7,606	...	11·4	Derby.
Devon	17	430,221	33,401	34,418	3·0	...	17	430,221	34,375	34,484	0·3	...	Devon.
Dorset	12	167,874	16,371	15,972	...	2·4	12	167,874	17,430	16,233	...	6·9	Dorset.
Durham	14	326,055	18,542	19,335	4·3	...	14	326,055	18,305	19,213	5·0	...	Durham.
Essex	17	320,818	26,165	24,268	...	7·3	17	320,818	26,710	27,234	2·0	...	Essex.
Gloucester	16	330,562	20,490	22,030	7·5	...	16	330,562	24,014	22,316	...	7·1	Gloucester.
Hereford	8	110,675	8,855	7,491	...	15·4	8	110,675	8,923	8,044	...	9·9	Hereford.
Hertford	13	176,173	12,799	12,135	...	5·2	13	176,173	13,731	12,443	...	9·4	Hertford.
Huntingdon	3	55,573	3,625	3,723	2·7	...	3	55,573	4,205	4,407	4·8	...	Huntingdon.
Kent	26	523,389	30,166	30,723	1·8	...	27	534,882	35,462	36,286	2·3	...	Kent.
Lancaster	23	1,373,231	110,536	72,685	...	34·2	27	1,719,656	121,644	93,938	...	22·8	Lancaster.
Leicester	11	220,232	18,417	14,993	...	18·6	11	220,232	17,095	14,634	...	14·4	Leicester.
Lincoln	14	356,347	19,135	18,415	...	3·8	14	356,347	18,829	20,208	7·3	...	Lincoln.
Middlesex	18	679,914	39,846	37,403	...	6·1	22	846,207	59,812	52,998	...	11·4	Middlesex.
Monmouth	5	150,222	7,377	9,133	23·8	...	6	150,222	8,352	8,251	...	1·2	Monmouth.
Norfolk	20	319,246	26,108	26,001	...	0·4	21	343,277	29,461	29,276	...	0·6	Norfolk.
Northampton	12	199,104	14,664	12,598	...	14·1	12	199,104	14,822	14,387	...	2·9	Northampton.
Northumberland	11	194,138	9,796	10,300	5·1	...	12	265,988	17,364	18,673	7·5	...	Northumberland.

Nottingham	9	270,719	14,500	9,814	...	32·3	9	270,719	14,177	12,261	...	13·5	Nottingham.
Oxford	8	143,510	11,961	11,123	...	7·0	8	143,510	12,950	12,544	...	3·1	Oxford.
Rutland	2	23,150	1,139	1,020	...	10·4	2	23,150	1,220	1,223	0·2	...	Rutland.
Salop	13	191,052	8,483	9,138	7·7	...	13	191,052	9,583	9,523	...	0·6	Salop.
Somerset	17	454,446	37,714	36,763	...	2·5	17	454,446	39,436	38,145	...	3·3	Somerset.
Southampton	23	268,989	21,033	21,961	4·4	...	23	268,989	24,004	23,078	...	3·9	Southampton.
Stafford	15	396,057	16,998	15,866	...	6·7	16	443,982	18,771	19,697	5·0	...	Stafford.
Suffolk	16	302,178	22,883	23,306	1·8	...	17	314,722	25,606	27,274	6·5	...	Suffolk.
Surrey	13	254,752	15,358	14,931	...	2·8	19	523,238	36,765	33,410	...	9·1	Surrey.
Sussex	20	223,623	17,666	17,425	...	1·4	20	223,623	20,000	19,288	...	3·6	Sussex.
Warwick	12	358,244	19,317	22,368	15·8	...	12	358,244	20,286	19,260	...	5·0	Warwick.
Westmorland	3	56,469	3,038	2,968	...	2·3	3	56,469	3,126	3,132	0·2	...	Westmorland.
Wilts	17	223,246	21,163	20,459	...	8·3	17	223,246	23,886	22,342	...	6·5	Wilts.
Worcester	13	336,108	16,864	17,256	2·3	...	13	336,108	17,936	18,096	0·9	...	Worcester.
York, East Riding	9	180,218	9,224	8,493	...	7·9	9	180,218	9,662	8,956	...	7·3	York, East Riding.
,, North Riding	15	180,643	8,927	8,645	...	3·2	15	180,643	8,823	8,870	0·5	...	,, North Riding
,, West Riding	19	817,054	61,572	46,294	...	24·8	21	886,098	57,769	44,642	...	22·7	,, West Riding
Totals of England	538	12,333,367	825,359	755,977	...	8·4	560	13,351,458	920,191	853,883	...	7·2	Totals of England.
WALES.													WALES.
Anglesey	1	38,105	4,264	3,729	...	12·5	1	38,105	4,171	4,736	13·5	...	Anglesey.
Brecon	4	55,399	3,465	3,277	...	5·4	4	55,399	3,308	3,284	...	0·7	Brecon.
Cardigan	5	75,136	5,180	5,943	14·7	...	5	75,136	5,680	5,656	...	0·4	Cardigan.
Carmarthen	5	110,404	7,283	7,256	...	0·4	5	110,404	7,233	7,336	1·4	...	Carmarthen.
Carnarvon	4	86,728	8,002	8,304	3·8	...	4	86,728	7,933	7,618	...	4·0	Carnarvon.
Denbigh	3	68,483	4,675	4,889	4·6	...	3	68,483	4,818	4,706	...	2·3	Denbigh.
Flint	2	64,355	5,453	5,504	0·9	...	2	64,355	5,188	5,266	1·5	...	Flint.
Glamorgan	5	178,041	10,153	12,500	23·1	...	5	178,041	10,415	12,660	21·6	...	Glamorgan.
Merioneth	4	50,696	4,836	4,771	...	1·3	4	50,696	4,953	4,875	...	1·6	Merioneth.
Montgomery	3	58,709	6,757	7,683	13·7	...	3	58,709	6,140	5,728	...	6·7	Montgomery.
Pembroke	3	78,563	5,187	5,300	2·2	...	3	78,563	5,231	5,479	4·7	...	Pembroke.
Radnor	3	19,554	2,041	2,017	...	1·2	3	19,554	1,903	1,940	2·0	...	Radnor.
Totals of Wales	42	884,173	67,296	71,173	5·8	...	42	884,173	66,973	69,284	3·5	...	Totals of Wales.
Totals of England and Wales	580	13,217,540	892,655	827,150	...	7·3	602	14,235,631	987,164	923,167	...	6·4	Totals of England and Wales.

NOTE.—In the above Returns the net total number is given, after deducting those persons whose relief has been transferred to the Non-settled Poor accounts.

COMPARATIVE STATEMENT, showing the Number of Adult Able-bodied Paupers (Male and Female) in Receipt of Relief on the 1st *of January*, 1849, and the 1st *of January*, 1850, respectively, in 590 Unions and Single Parishes in England and Wales, under the Provisions of the Poor Law Amendment Act, exclusive of Vagrants and Insane Persons.

NAMES OF COUNTIES.	Number of Unions in each.	Population in 1841.	Number of Adult Able-bodied Paupers relieved (Male and Female.) On 1st January, 1849.		On 1st January, 1850.		Total Number of Adult able-bodied relieved, In-door and Out-door.		Increase or Decrease on 1st January, 1850, compared with 1st January, 1849.		Increase or Decrease per Cent.		NAMES OF COUNTIES.
			In-door.	Out-door.	In-door.	Out-door.	Jan. 1, 1849.	Jan. 1, 1850.	Increase.	Decrease.	Increase.	Decrease.	
ENGLAND.													ENGLAND.
Bedford	6	112,379	342	1,438	255	1,022	1,780	1,277	...	503	...	28·3	Bedford.
Berks	12	190,367	851	2,383	713	1,979	3,234	2,692	...	542	...	16·8	Berks.
Buckingham	7	138,255	437	2,572	379	2,368	3,009	2,747	...	262	...	8·7	Buckingham.
Cambridge	9	171,848	739	3,211	753	3,033	3,950	3,786	...	164	...	4·2	Cambridge.
Chester	9	344,860	363	2,733	255	2,060	3,096	2,315	...	781	...	25·2	Chester.
Cornwall	13	340,728	521	3,386	385	2,758	3,907	3,143	...	764	...	19·6	Cornwall.
Cumberland	9	177,912	321	1,441	260	1,074	1,762	1,334	...	428	...	24·3	Cumberland.
Derby	9	242,786	134	1,231	86	935	1,365	1,021	...	344	...	25·2	Derby.
Devon	17	430,221	670	4,177	494	3,853	4,847	4,347	...	500	...	10·3	Devon.
Dorset	12	167,874	424	2,810	387	2,592	3,234	2,979	...	255	...	7·9	Dorset.
Durham	14	326,055	139	3,802	138	4,032	3,941	4,170	229	...	5·8	...	Durham.
Essex	17	320,818	1,477	4,406	1,485	4,556	5,883	6,041	158	...	2·	...	Essex.
Gloucester	16	330,562	815	3,528	626	3,059	4,343	3,685	...	658	...7	15·2	Gloucester.
Hereford	8	110,675	191	1,708	178	1,383	1,899	1,561	...	338	...	17·8	Hereford.
Hertford	13	176,173	662	2,423	623	1,906	3,085	2,529	...	556	...	18·0	Hertford.
Huntingdon	3	55,573	187	587	155	734	774	889	115	...	14·9	...	Huntingdon.
Kent	27	534,882	2,113	5,471	1,922	5,589	7,584	7,511	...	73	...	1·0	Kent.
Lancaster	26	1,496,602	1,578	26,801	957	16,865	28,379	17,822	...	10,557	...	37·2	Lancaster.
Leicester	11	220,232	484	3,791	298	2,957	4,275	3,255	...	1,020	...	23·9	Leicester.
Lincoln	14	336,347	467	2,502	563	2,726	2,969	3,289	320	...	10·8	...	Lincoln.
Middlesex	18	679,914	2,425	11,413	1,948	9,652	13,838	11,600	...	2,238	...	16·2	Middlesex.
Monmouth	6	150,222	100	1,957	94	1,351	2,057	1,445	...	612	...	29·8	Monmouth.
Norfolk	20	319,246	964	4,109	1,069	3,989	5,073	5,058	...	15	...	0·3	Norfolk.
Northampton	12	199,104	356	2,733	339	2,425	3,089	2,764	...	325	...	10·5	Northampton.
Northumberland	12	265,988	234	3,152	214	3,490	3,386	3,704	318	...	9·4	...	Northumberland.
Nottingham	9	270,719	450	2,385	259	1,850	2,835	2,109	...	726	...	25·6	Nottingham.
Oxford	8	143,510	551	2,531	416	2,217	3,082	2,633	...	449	...	14·6	Oxford.
Rutland	2	23,150	50	142	46	162	192	208	16	...	8·3	...	Rutland.
Salop	13	191,052	201	1,524	235	1,333	1,725	1,568	...	157	...	9·1	Salop.
Somerset	17	454,446	1,024	5,625	836	4,906	6,649	5,742	...	907	...	13·6	Somerset.

Southampton . .	23	268,989	962	4,643	981	4,280	5,605	5,261	...	344	...	6·1	Southampton.
Stafford	15	396,057	515	2,822	399	2,620	3,337	3,019	...	318	...	9·5	Stafford.
Suffolk	16	302,178	1,082	3,733	1,421	4,217	4,815	5,638	823	...	17·1	...	Suffolk.
Surrey	15	311,870	1,265	5,034	997	4,056	6,299	4,053	...	1,246	...	19·8	Surrey.
Sussex	20	223,623	1,148	2,972	1,017	2,764	4,120	3,781	...	339	...	8·2	Sussex.
Warwick	12	358,244	700	5,028	449	3,411	5,728	3,860	...	1,868	...	32·6	Warwick.
Westmorland . .	3	56,469	98	557	99	479	655	578	...	77	...	11·8	Westmorland.
Wilts	17	223,246	1,085	3,511	966	2,956	4,596	3,922	...	674	...	14·7	Wilts.
Worcester . . .	13	336,108	396	3,038	314	3,098	3,434	3,412	...	22	...	0·6	Worcester.
York, East Riding .	9	180,218	134	1,569	176	1,492	1,703	1,668	...	35	...	2·1	York, East Riding.
„ North Riding	15	180,643	139	1,141	127	1,106	1,280	1,233	...	47	...	3·7	„ North Riding.
„ West Riding	21	886,098	699	13,600	377	8,603	14,299	8,980	...	5,319	...	37·2	„ West Riding.
Totals of 548 Unions in England . .	548	12,666,243	27,493	163,620	23,691	135,938	191,113	159,629	1,979	33,463	...	16·5	Totals of 548 Unions in England.
Wales.													Wales.
Anglesey	1	38,105	...	781	...	768	781	768	...	13	...	1·7	Anglesey.
Brecon	4	55,399	56	221	51	221	277	272	...	5	...	1·8	Brecon.
Cardigan	5	75,136	24	724	13	718	748	731	...	17	...	2·3	Cardigan.
Carmarthen . . .	5	110,404	47	887	53	963	934	1,016	82	...	8·8	...	Carmarthen.
Carnarvon . . .	4	86,728	38	1,707	74	1,658	1,745	1,732	...	13	...	0·7	Carnarvon.
Denbigh	3	68,483	100	674	97	480	774	577	...	197	...	25·5	Denbigh.
Flint	2	64,355	78	610	49	463	688	512	...	176	...	25·6	Flint.
Glamorgan . . .	5	178,041	133	1,961	95	2,596	2,094	2,691	597	..	28·5	...	Glamorgan.
Merioneth . . .	4	50,696	19	645	9	636	664	645	...	19	...	2·9	Merioneth.
Montgomery . .	3	58,709	74	800	63	871	874	934	60	...	6·9	...	Montgomery.
Pembroke	3	78,563	47	577	39	628	624	667	43	...	6·9	...	Pembroke.
Radnor	3	19,554	14	314	10	318	328	328	...	...	...	...	Radnor.
Totals of 42 Unions in Wales . .	42	884,173	630	9,901	553	10,320	10,531	10,873	782	440	3·2	...	Totals of 42 Unions in Wales.
Totals of 590 Unions in England and Wales	590	13,550,416	28,123	173,521*	24,244	146,258†	201,644	170,502	2,761	33,903	...	15·4	Totals of 590 Unions in England and Wales.
									Decrease after deducting Increase 31,142.				

* Of this number receiving out-door relief on 1st January, 1849, 52,441 were widows.

† „ „ „ 1st January, 1850, 53,151 were widows.

COMPARATIVE STATEMENT of the EXPENDITURE for the RELIEF of the POOR in ENGLAND and WALES, for the Years ended Lady-day, 1848 and 1849.

COUNTIES.	Expended for the Relief of the Poor, Years ended at Lady-day. 1848. £.	s.	1849. £.	s.	Increase or Decrease on comparison of 1849 with 1848. Increase. £.	Decrease. £.	Increase or Decrease per Cent. Increase per Cent.	Decrease per Cent.
ENGLAND.								
Bedford	49,998	0	45,737	18	. . .	4,260	. . .	8·5
Berks	92,957	0	81,085	8	. . .	11,872	. . .	12·8
Buckingham	94,236	1	82,115	4	. . .	12,121	. . .	12·9
Cambridge	91,540	10	83,427	6	. . .	8,113	. . .	8·9
Chester	96,327	2	84,004	11	. . .	12,323	. . .	12·8
Cornwall	97,868	17	89,315	15	. . .	8,553	. . .	8·7
Cumberland	43,900	13	41,816	7	. . .	2,084	. . .	4·7
Derby	61,349	14	57,008	18	. . .	4,341	. . .	7·1
Devon	229,409	10	211,024	7	. . .	18,385	. . .	8·0
Dorset	102,355	11	92,130	3	. . .	10,225	. . .	10·0
Durham	75,869	15	73,730	0	. . .	2,140	. . .	2·8
Essex	197,649	0	175,744	9	. . .	21,905	. . .	11·1
Gloucester	175,989	8	157,525	10	. . .	18,464	. . .	10·5
Hereford	54,720	9	48,590	4	. . .	6,130	. . .	11·2
Hertford	76,598	15	69,617	2	. . .	6,982	. . .	9·1
Huntingdon	31,813	1	28,656	3	. . .	3,157	. . .	9·9
Kent	225,543	18	212,457	13	. . .	13,086	. . .	5·8
Lancaster	575,812	0	503,555	13	. . .	72,256	. . .	12·5
Leicester	104,193	0	87,015	4	. . .	17,178	. . .	16·5
Lincoln	143,219	10	128,443	16	. . .	14,776	. . .	10·3
Middlesex	608,632	3	643,746	16	35,115	. . .	5·8	. .
Monmouth	36,907	3	35,060	14	. . .	1,846	. . .	5·0
Norfolk	220,902	19	201,191	17	. . .	19,711	. . .	8·9
Northampton	106,684	16	95,479	15	. . .	11,205	. . .	10·5
Northumberland	86,032	2	81,607	11	. . .	4,425	. . .	5·1
Nottingham	86,954	18	69,847	11	. . .	17,107	. . .	19·7
Oxford	94,762	19	84,854	2	. . .	9,909	. . .	10·5
Rutland	8,582	15	7,985	7	. . .	597	. . .	7·0
Salop	62,052	13	59,805	18	. . .	2,247	. . .	3·6
Somerset	204,787	10	183,779	7	. . .	21,008	. . .	10·3
Southampton	167,087	2	161,422	12	. . .	5,665	. . .	3·4
Stafford	120,475	14	110,716	19	. . .	9,759	. . .	8·1
Suffolk	165,594	18	145,287	2	. . .	20,308	. . .	12·3
Surrey	256,742	1	253,739	1	. . .	3,003	. . .	1·2
Sussex	164,946	6	155,109	7	. . .	9,837	. . .	6·0
Warwick	127,288	7	131,957	11	4,669	. . .	3·7	. .
Westmorland	15,992	8	16,258	19	267	. . .	1·7	. .
Wilts	156,245	14	145,899	8	. . .	10,346	. . .	6·6
Worcester	83,067	2	78,134	10	. . .	4,933	. . .	5·9
York, East Riding	81,314	16	78,374	1	. . .	2,941	. . .	3·6
" North "	62,208	13	56,483	11	. . .	5,725	. . .	9·2
" West "	314,017	14	329,765	19	15,748	. . .	5·0	. .
Totals of England	5,852,632	7	5,479,509	9	. . .	373,124 after deducting Increase.	. . .	6·4
WALES.								
Anglesey	20,526	12	21,458	3	932	. . .	4·5	. .
Brecon	20,910	10	18,415	0	. . .	2,496	. . .	11·9
Cardigan	20,254	4	19,547	3	. . .	707	. . .	3·5
Carmarthen	33,222	2	31,783	3	. . .	1,439	. . .	4·3
Carnarvon	31,978	10	27,889	13	. . .	4,089	. . .	12·8
Denbigh	34,604	3	33,373	15	. . .	1,230	. . .	3·6
Flint	23,963	3	22,328	14	. . .	1,634	. . .	6·8
Glamorgan	54,355	1	53,210	16	. . .	1,144	. . .	2·1
Merioneth	16,852	14	16,341	11	. . .	511	. . .	3·0
Montgomery	29,918	7	29,857	10	. . .	61	. . .	0·2
Pembroke	29,652	12	27,658	4	. . .	1,994	. . .	6·7
Radnor	11,894	5	11,589	14	. . .	305	. . .	2·6
Totals of Wales	328,132	3	313,453	6	. . .	14,678	. . .	4·5
Totals of England and Wales	6,180,764	10	5,792,962	15	. . .	387,802 after deducting Increase.	. . .	6·3

London: Printed by Order of the Poor Law Board, by BLACKBURN & BURT, 90½, Holborn Hill, and Published by CHARLES KNIGHT, 90, Fleet Street.

AN

OFFICIAL CIRCULAR

OF PUBLIC DOCUMENTS AND INFORMATION:

DIRECTED BY THE POOR LAW BOARD TO BE PRINTED, CHIEFLY FOR THE USE OF THE BOARDS OF GUARDIANS AND THEIR OFFICERS.

No. 34.] FEBRUARY, 1850. [N.S.

CONTENTS.

I.—APPRENTICESHIP.

1. LEGALITY OF BINDING AFTER THE AGE OF TWENTY-ONE YEARS.

5*th Sept.*, 1849.

Clerk of Stourbridge Union.—Inquiring whether the guardians can bind an apprentice at the age of fifteen years, for the period of eight years, or only until he attains the age of twenty-one years. Some doubt has arisen whether the General Consolidated Order does not supersede the 18th Geo. 3, c. 47, which regulates the binding of parish apprentices only until twenty-one years.

Ans.—The Board are of opinion that the 18th Geo. 3, c. 47, has neither expressly nor by necessary implication been repealed by the provisions in sec. 12 of 7 & 8 Vic. c. 101; and that the restriction imposed by it as to the age, viz., 21 years, to which parish apprentices can be bound to serve, is still in force, and is applicable to bindings which take place by guardians under the Provisions of the General Consolidated Order. In the case stated, therefore, the Board think that the lad being now fifteen cannot be bound for eight years.

---

2. APPRENTICESHIP TO MINERS.

21st Sept., 1849.

Clerk of Kidderminster Union.—Applications have been made to the guardians to bind out apprentices to persons who are miners, and some doubt has occurred to the guardians as to whether the proposed masters are "persons carrying on trade or business on their own account." These persons agree with the owners of coal and other mines to work such mines, and to be paid so much per ton for the coal or mineral raised—the contractor undertaking to find machinery, men, horses, and all the apparatus necessary for the proper working of the mines, and running all risks. Inquiring whether the guardians can, under the existing order, legally bind apprentices to such persons.

Ans.—The Board do not think it clear that a person of the description referred to is one carrying on trade or business on his own account; and they observe that the guardians of the Kidderminster Union, (some, if not all of whom, are no doubt conversant with the nature of the employment in question,) entertain the same doubt. Under these circumstances, the Board consider that the binding ought not to take place. The restriction imposed by the 53rd Art. of the General Consolidated Order, being a remedial one for the benefit of the child, ought to have full effect given to it; and consequently, no binding should be deemed allowable, where the proposed master is not clearly and undoubtedly a person carrying on trade or business on his own account.

II.—ASSISTANT OVERSEERS.—APPOINTMENT AND SECURITIES.

1st Sept., 1849.

Clerk of ——— *Union.*—The assistant overseers of some parishes of this union were appointed several years ago. Their appointments in the vestry books did not state the time for which they were elected, but fixed a yearly salary for them on their first appointment. The persons chosen to fill the office were afterwards regularly appointed by the magistrates, and gave proper bonds for the due performance of the duties of their office. The Act of Geo. 3, enabling the parishioners to appoint assistant overseers, states that the appointment shall be good till resignation or revocation by the inhabitants in vestry. At the 25th of March following their first appointment, the parishioners in vestry passed resolutions to the effect that the then officers should continue to hold their several offices as heretofore, and declared that they were thereby reappointed, but again without stating for what period, and so on at the expiration of each successive year, but no new appointment was, or has been made by the magistrates, and no new securities were or have been given. A question has now arisen, whether the circumstance of their being reappointed at the end of each year is not virtually a termination of the previous appointment, and such a reappointment as would exonerate their sureties from all liability for defalcations occurring after the first of such reappointments. The several assistant overseers are quite ready to give fresh security, but before requiring them to do so, requested the opinion of the Board as to the necessity of these officers doing so, and also whether they should be reappointed by the magistrates.

Ans.—Had there been no reappointment of these officers by the vestry, there can be no doubt that the original appointments by vestry and by the justices, as well as the securities, would all have been in full force and operation. It may, however, admit of a doubt whether the reappointments by vestry, which are stated to have already taken place, would not be held to imply a previous revocation of the appointments originally made. The Board, therefore, having regard to this doubt, think it will be prudent to hold new vestry meetings, duly convened, for the purpose of especially revoking any existing appointments of the assistant overseers in question, and making new appointments, then to obtain the confirmation of the justices in the proper course, and to take other securities from the said newly appointed officers, under the 7 & 8 Vic. c. 101, sec. 61. The vestries, should, therefore, abstain from passing any resolution, or taking any proceeding upon the subject of such appointments, so long as it is their pleasure that the assistant overseers should continue in their several offices.

III.—BAPTISMS.—REGISTRATION OF BAPTISMS IN WORKHOUSES.

3rd Dec., 1849.

Chaplain of ——— Union Workhouse—He is in the habit, as chaplain of the union workhouse, of baptizing the sick infants of the inmates in the lying-in wards, and registering such baptisms in his own parish register. His parish is in the town of B., but the workhouse is not situated in it, but in another division of the town. The late vicar of B., in whose parish the workhouse stands, thought he (the chaplain) was correct in registering such baptisms in his own books, and, indeed, requested him to do so. The new vicar has, however, sent him an authoritative demand that the names, &c., of the infants should be sent to him (the vicar) for registration in his books. Requesting to be informed if that was necessary.

Ans.—As the question is one of ecclesiastical law, the Board cannot express a positive opinion upon it. They are, however, disposed to consider that a baptism which, in fact, takes place in the parish of B., should be registered in the registry of that parish, though the rite is performed by the minister of another parish.

IV.—BASTARDY.—POWER OF JUSTICES TO MAKE AN ORDER ON PUTATIVE FATHER, NOTWITHSTANDING A PAYMENT MADE TO THE MOTHER IN SATISFACTION OF HER CLAIM.

29th March, 1849.

———, *Esq.*—Transmitting the following statement for the opinion of the Poor Law Board:—A., having a bastard child, applied for an order of affiliation upon B., on the ground of his having paid money for its maintenance within the twelve calendar months next after its birth. At the hearing it was proved, that in the month of August, 1847, (within the twelve months,) B., with a witness and a person acting as his attorney, went to the residence of A., between 9 and 10 o'clock at night, and there paid her £5, which she accepted in full satisfaction of all claim she might have upon B. in respect of her bastard child. The advocate of B. urged that this £5, having been accepted by A. in full satisfaction, the jurisdiction of the justices to make an order was ousted, the same operating as a release. On reference to sec. 5 of the 7 & 8 Vic. c. 101, (under which Act the application is made,) it will be seen that the remedy given by law is not merely a personal benefit to the mother, as, in case of her death, lunacy, or imprisonment, before the child attains the age of thirteen years, the payments under an order of justices would ensure to the benefit of the child. The justices wish to be informed whether the acknowledgment of A., given under such circumstances, does effectually bar their jurisdiction; or whether they are not, under the provisions of the statute in question, at liberty to make an order upon B. for a weekly sum in respect of the maintenance of the child.

Ans.—It appears to the Board that the justices are not stopped from entertaining the application of the mother of the bastard child for an order of affiliation on the putative father, by the fact of such a bargain having been made as that described in this case. The Board think that the justices should not exclude the proof of such bargain, but should hear it along with all the other facts of the case; and then, under sec. 3 of the 7 & 8 Vic. c. 101, "they may, if they see fit, having regard to all the circumstances of the case, proceed to make an order on the putative father." Should the justices make such order, and the putative father be dissatisfied with their decision, he may appeal to the sessions, under sec. 4 of the statute; and it would be open to that court to take the opinion of the Court of Queen's Bench upon the effect of the agreement in question. The mother, on the other hand, has no power of appeal if an order on the putative father for the maintenance of her child be refused.

V.—BONDS.—DUTY OF CLERK IN REFERENCE TO THE EXECUTION OF OFFICERS' BONDS.

9th Oct., 1849.

Clerk of Glendale Union—Is under the impression that the concluding sentence of Art. 202, No. 4, of the General Consolidated Order, "and to see that the same [officers' bonds] are duly executed by such officers and their sureties," renders it imperative on him to be present at the execution of a bond by an officer of the union and his sureties. Requesting the opinion of the Poor Law Board on the subject.

Ans.—The Board do not construe the Regulation referred to as necessarily requiring the clerk to see or witness personally the actual execution of the bond. They think it only requires the clerk to take care that the bond is duly executed. If, therefore, it is executed away from the union, it will be necessary for the clerk to take proper means for ascertaining the genuineness of the execution.

VI.—BURIAL.

1. THE COST OF BURIAL.

1st March, 1849.

Clerk of Clifton Union.—Inquiring whether the funeral of a person coming into parish A. for one night, and dying there, is to be charged to that parish or to the union, such person receiving no relief.

Ans.—The Board are of opinion that the case you refer to must be decided by the 7 & 8 Vic. c. 101, sec. 31, and that the cost of the burial should be borne by the parish in which the death occurred. It would be different where the person, being a destitute wayfarer or wanderer, has received relief, (11 & 12 Vic. c. 110, sec. 1.)

2. BURIAL OF ROMAN CATHOLIC PAUPERS.

15th Sept., 1849.

Clerk of Newcastle-under-Lyme Union.—Inquiring whether burial fees may be paid in the following cases:—1. Is the Catholic priest entitled to fees for interment in a Catholic burial-ground, in case a pauper dying in the house requests to be buried there? 2. Is he entitled to such fees in the case of a Catholic pauper, dying in the house, who leaves no request as to place of interment, but the Catholic priest prefers a claim to the interment in the Catholic burial-ground? 3. A Catholic pauper, dying out of the workhouse, and the friends desire the interment in the Catholic burial-ground, may the fees be then paid? 4. A Catholic pauper, dying out of the workhouse, and no desire is previously expressed as to place of interment, and the friends express no such desire, may the Catholic priest claim the body for interment in the Catholic burial-ground, and may the guardians pay the ordinary fees in such case, or have they power to refuse payment?

Ans.—The provision in sec. 31 of the 7 & 8 Vic. c. 101, which renders it compulsory on the guardians to pay fees on burials under their directions, only applies to the fees which are payable by the "custom" of the place. The Board understand this to refer to a legal custom, which will not extend to payments to a Catholic priest. But if the guardians direct a pauper to be buried in the Catholic burying-ground, the Board think they would be justified in paying the usual fees. The Catholic priest cannot compel the guardians to bury any pauper in the Catholic burying-ground; but the Board think that the guardians may, in the exercise of their own discretion, do so, if they think it right under the circumstances of any particular case.

3. BURIAL OF PAUPERS DYING IN WORKHOUSE.

19th Sept., 1849.

Chairman of Rotherhithe Board of Guardians.—Cases frequently occur in which the guardians have reason to believe the relations of paupers dying in the workhouse could have maintained them during their lives, but were unwilling so to do; and other cases occur where, for the sake of some burial-fee due on the death, the relations are willing to bury; and one case has happened here lately, where the daughter of the pauper received half-a-crown a week, due to the pauper during his life, and £10 on death. Have the guardians, and has the master or any officer, a discretionary power, as to whether they will allow the body of a deceased pauper to be removed from the workhouse?

Ans.—The Board think that generally the guardians would incur a serious responsibility in refusing, or in authorizing the workhouse master to refuse to deliver up the body of a pauper to a near relative who applies for it, and undertakes to bury it, and where they have no reason to doubt that such is really the intention of the party applying. With regard to the property of deceased paupers, to which your letter also refers, the Board direct your attention to the 16th and 17th secs. of the recent Act, 12 & 13 Vic. c. 103.

VII.—COUNTY COURT. — PROCEEDINGS IN FOR RECOVERY OF COSTS.

29th Nov., 1849.

Clerks of Clutton Union.—The 11 and 12 Vic. c. 123, sec. 3, provides for the recovery of costs, &c., from owners and occupiers of premises in the county court, or before justices. The former appears to be the more speedy and efficacious way of proceeding. The 5 & 6 Vic. c. 57, sec. 17, empowers guardians, by an order in writing, under the hand of the presiding chairman, &c., to appoint any officer of such guardians to make such application or complaint, or take any proceedings before any justices, at petty, or special, or general, or quarter sessions, as effectually to all intents and purposes as if the same were made or taken by such guardians, or any of them, in person. Having regard to these two statutes, it appears to them (the clerks) doubtful as to who is the proper party to enter the plaint in the county court, and appear to support it at the hearing. Requesting to be informed in what way these objects are to be attained.

Ans.—The question submitted depends entirely upon the practice of the county court. The guardians of the Clutton Union being a corporate body, they must sue as such; and whatever is the practice of the county court, in respect of actions therein at the suit of corporate bodies, must, therefore, be pursued in the present instance. The 11 & 12 Vic. c. 110, sec. 8, contains a special provision applicable to certain proceedings of guardians in county courts, but does not extend to the case in question; nevertheless, the course there pointed out will probably be recognized and authorized generally by the judge of the county court.

VIII.—DISTRICT SCHOOL.—ELECTED MANAGER RESIGNING, AND AFTERWARDS ACTING AS AN EX-OFFICIO MANAGER.

6th Dec., 1849.

Clerk of St. Olave's Union.—The chairmen of the boards of guardians of two places comprised in the South Metropolitan School District, having been respectively elected members of the board of management of the district, resigned their appointments as managers, but continued to attend such board. Inquiring whether they could legally claim to do so.

Ans.—In the opinion of the Poor Law Board, the chairman of a board of guardians, who is an elected manager of the district school, can lawfully resign his office as such manager, and still continue to act as an *ex-officio* manager.

IX.—ELECTION OF GUARDIANS.

1. QUALIFICATION OF PERSON FROM WHOM THE GUARDIANS RENT A FIELD.

4th April, 1849.

Clerk of Newton Abbot Union.—Inquiring whether a person, from whom the guardians of this union rent a field (cultivated by the paupers in the workhouse) at a fixed yearly sum, is disqualified from acting as guardian.

Ans.—The Board, as at present advised, think that a person under such circumstances as you describe, is not disqualified for the office of guardian of the poor; they do not consider that it can be said that he receives a fixed emolument from the poor-rate, in the sense of sec. 14. of the 5 & 6 Vic. c. 57

2. REFUSAL OF PERSONS ELECTED TO SERVE.

31st March, 1849.

Clerk of Braintree Union.—There have been seven persons nominated as guardians for the parish of Braintree, which returns four guardians, four of them, A., B., C., D., have declined to act. C., at the time he gave in his paper declining to act, stated that he withdrew because there should be no polling of the parish on his account, since which D. also has declined to act, and C. thereupon intimated his willingness to take the office. Under these circumstances should he (the clerk) be justified in returning C. as a guardian?

Ans.—If there has been a legal refusal, that is, a refusal in writing to serve the office of guardian, tendered to you by any of the persons nominated, (see sec. 9 of the 5 & 6 Vic. c. 57,) then the parties so refusing cease to be candidates from the time of tendering their refusals. There can be no withdrawal of such a refusal. On the other hand, if there has been no such legal refusal to serve, the parties are now legally in nomination, and their names must be inserted in the voting papers, unless, indeed, the refusal of any to serve be tendered before the issuing of the voting papers.

3. CLERK'S DUTIES IN REFERENCE TO THE ELECTION OF GUARDIANS.

5th April, 1849.

Clerk of Ellesmere Union.—Inquiring, 1st, whether, when asked by persons wishing to nominate, whether their nomination papers are properly filled up, he is bound to give them information upon that point; and if not right, is it his duty as returning officer to tell them how to correct the papers, or to make out fresh ones; and if he is not so bound, whether he is at liberty to do so if he should think proper. 2. When an informal nomination, or a nomination of a disqualified person, be sent by any person, is it his duty to inform the nominator of its being so, so that he may afterwards, if within the proper time, and he think right, send another nomination? 3. Where a firm is rated thus, "Rodenhurst and Davies," in the rate-book, without any Christian name to either, (although he may possibly ascertain their names,) should he send a voting paper to one or both;—if to one only, to which should it be sent? 4. Where a company is rated thus, "Canal Company," in the rate-book, and have an agent or clerk living at the house or office where the business is carried on, must he send a voting paper there;—if so, in whose name, and to whom must he send it?

Ans.—1. That the Board do not know that you are bound to inform persons who nominate, and who may make personal inquiries that their nomination papers are correctly filled up, though when inquiries are put to you on this head, the Board see no objection whatever to your pointing out the defect, if any, in the paper. 2. Where nominations are sent to you, the Board think it is no part of your duty to inform the nominator of any defect in the nomination, either as to the form or as to the disqualification of the nominees. It must rest entirely in your own discretion whether you will do so. 3. The Board are disposed to consider that where there is defective description of the occupiers of property in any case in the rate-book, explanation may be admitted to show what parties were intended to be charged by the entry in the rate. In the case of an actual partnership or joint occupation, all the members of the firm being equally liable to the rate, the fair presumption from such an entry in the rate, as, for example, Williams and Co., Roberts and Co., is that it was intended by the use of the indefinite word Co., to charge the several persons composing the firm, and jointly occupying, and not the person actually named only. The Board therefore consider, that where in any case of this nature it is shown that more than one person is intended to be rated, the clerk will do right to regard each member of the firm, upon reasonable proof of his interest therein, as a separate rate-payer, and as entitled (the rates assessed on the property being duly paid) to vote as such. 4. The Board think, in the case put, that the voting paper should be sent to the person whose name (if any) actually appears upon the rate

X.—GUARDIANS.

1. VALIDITY OF NOTICE OF MOTION AT A MEETING OF.

19th August, 1848.

Guardian of ——— Union.—He gave notice on Thursday last, that he should this day move the following resolution, viz.:—"That the Poor Law Board having expressed their disapproval of the resolution for discontinuing the use of the Fever Hospital by their letter of the 26th ult., this board determines to retain the use of the said Fever Hospital until the completion of the new workhouse." This day, upon proposing the above resolution, it was objected by a guardian and ruled by the chairman that the notice was bad under Article 39 of the General Consolidated Order of the Poor Law Commissioners, the seven days not having expired since the giving of such notice. Inquiring, what is the proper construction of this Article? The meetings of this board are held weekly, and it is desirable for the future there should be no mistake as to the legality of voting upon a notice duly given in writing at one meeting for the next weekly meeting of the board; or must it stand for a fortnight before it can be entertained?

Ans.—The Board express no opinion as to the decision of the chairman in the particular case you refer to. They may observe generally, however, that, in their opinion, a notice given at one meeting for the next weekly meeting is a seven days' notice within the meaning of the Order; and, moreover, that the present motion appears to have fallen within the Exceptions to the 59th Article, as referring to a case of emergency, considering that the question referred to a matter which was on the point of being concluded, viz., the relinquishment of the hospital.

2. MEETINGS OF GUARDIANS IN CASES OF EMERGENCY.—CLERK'S ATTENDANCE.

19th Nov., 1849.

Clerk of ——— Union.—At the meeting of the guardians held this day, [6th Nov.,] as soon as the minutes of the previous meeting had been read, the chairman produced a paper purporting to be the minutes of a meeting of the guardians held a few days since, upon the subject of an enlargement or alteration of the workhouse. He, the clerk, pointed out to the board that he could not enter those minutes in the minute-book, as he had no knowledge that any such meeting had been held. The chairman rested the proceedings upon Article 36 of the Consolidated Order, contending it was a meeting of emergency, and that in such cases it was not necessary for the clerk to be present, or have any knowledge of the minutes. The meeting having been held at the house of one of the guardians instead of "at the ordinary place of meeting," was ultimately deemed by the guardians not to have been a legal meeting. Requesting, however, the opinion of the Board as to the necessity of the clerk being present at meetings of emergency.

Ans.—The Board, in the first place, desire to observe, that the meetings upon the occurrence of an emergency, referred to in Art. 36 of the Consolidated Order, are meetings which may be called upon such rare and sudden occasions as require the immediate assembling of some of the guardians, when there is not time to summon an extraordinary meeting of the whole board. Occasions of this kind would be, for example, the occurrence of a fire at the union workhouse, the sudden outbreak of an epidemic therein, or the failure of the union treasurer. At such a meeting (which, it may be observed, must, according to Art. 36, be held at the ordinary place of meeting) it is obvious that the clerk may not be able to attend, as he may not at the moment be within reach, and yet it may be necessary that the meeting should take place. The Board see nothing in the General Consolidated Order, or otherwise, which renders the presence of the clerk essential to constitute a valid meeting in such a case, although it is undoubtedly desirable that the clerk should be present to record the proceedings of the guardians whenever the circumstances allow of it. If he be not present he cannot be called upon to enter the minutes; and the correct course in that event appears to be, that the chairman of the particular meeting should report the proceedings to the board of guardians at their next ordinary meeting, and the board of guardians may then order such report to be entered on their own minutes.

XI.—LUNATIC PAUPERS.

1. COST OF MAINTENANCE, AND COST OF OBTAINING ORDERS OF JUSTICES IN THE CASES OF.

21st Sept., 1849.

Clerk of Bedale Union.—Inquiring, 1st, whether sec. 5 of the 12 & 13 Vic. c. 103, applies to lunatic paupers who were sent to an asylum prior to the 25th March last, such lunatics having previously resided five years in the parish from which they were so sent. 2nd, Whether the costs of their "maintenance" in such asylum are to be charged to the common fund of the union, as well as the costs and expenses incurred in obtaining "an order of justices for their removal and maintenance."

Ans.—1st, The Board think that the 5th sec. of the 12 & 13 Vic. c. 103, applies to the cases of lunatic paupers sent to the asylum at any time before the passing of the said Act, but that the only expenses payable under that sec. are such as have been or may be incurred subsequently to the 25th March last. 2nd, The Board are of opinion that the second question proposed in your letter must be answered in the affirmative, and that the costs of the lunatic's maintenance in the asylum, as well as the costs of obtaining the orders, are chargeable upon the common fund of the union.

2. LUNATIC PAUPER POSSESSED OF MONEY IN SAVINGS' BANK.

1st Dec., 1849.

Clerk of Altrincham Union.—Elizabeth S., a person settled in the township of Plumley, in the Altrincham Union, has been confined in the county lunatic asylum at Chester since June, 1848, as a pauper lunatic, being maintained there at the cost of the township of Plumley. It has recently been discovered that she has £30 in a savings' bank, the usual deposit-book relating to which is in the hands of a Mrs. A. D., a former mistress of the lunatic, who refuses to part with it. A sum of £18. 15*s.* 2*d.* has been expended by the inhabitants of Plumley in the maintenance of the lunatic during the year ending September last, which they wish, if possible, to get repaid out of the lunatic's money in the savings' bank. Doubts are entertained whether any action can be maintained for that purpose against Mrs. A. D. to recover the deposit-book, (that being nearly the only evidence of the debt,) or against the trustees of the savings' bank for the money. Requesting the advice of the Poor Law Board on the case.

Ans.—The case appears to be provided for by the 7 & 8 Vic. c. 101, sec. 27, under which the trustees of the savings' bank will be justified, if they think fit, in paying the cost of this lunatic's maintenance; but they cannot be compelled to do so. The Board entertain great doubt whether the 12 & 13 Vic. c. 103, sec. 16, applies to the case in question.

XII.—MARRIAGE.—NOTICE OF.

1st Sept., 1849.

The Rev. ———, *Torrington Union.*—Before the banns of marriage be published between any two parties, a clergyman may require seven days' notice.—Inquiring whether the superintendent-registrar of a district under the Poor Law may require seven days' notice previous to the publication of banns at a board of guardians.

Ans.—The Board understand, that under sec. 7 of the 6 & 7 Wm. 4, c. 85, the notice of marriage is to be read at the first meeting of the board of guardians which is held after the notice has been received by the superintendent-registrar, and also at the two succeeding weekly meetings, (three times in all.) If, however, the guardians do not meet every week, it will suffice if the notice be read at any board meeting held within twenty-one days of such notice being entered in the marriage notice book.

XIII.—MEDICAL RELIEF.—IN MIDWIFERY CASES.

15*th Dec.*, 1849.

Clerk of Linton Union.—It frequently happens that application is made to the guardians for the assistance of the medical officer at an approaching confinement; but the application is refused, the guardians considering the parties of sufficient ability to provide a doctor for themselves. Notwithstanding this, the applicant makes no provision for her confinement, but when actually in labour applies, by her husband, to the relieving officer, who grants the order, being afraid of the possible consequences should he refuse. By this means persons who ought to employ their own medical man throw this burden upon their parishes, and set the guardians at defiance. Inquiring whether the relieving officer would be justified in refusing orders in such cases; and if not, in what way should the guardians act?

Ans.—Medical assistance forms only a part of general relief, and the same rules and principles apply to it which are applicable to any other form of relief. Neither the guardians nor the relieving officers are bound to relieve, nor indeed are they justified in relieving any person whose circumstances they have ascertained to be such as not to require relief; and neither the guardians nor the relieving officer can properly discharge the duties which, in accepting their respective offices, they have undertaken to perform, if, by a fear of incurring responsibility, they be deterred from withholding relief where the position and circumstances of the applicants have satisfied them that it ought not to be granted. It appears, however, to the Board, that there is a practical mode of obviating the difficulty which the guardians feel in cases like the present, and the Board therefore recommend it for their adoption. The midwifery fee of 10*s.* is an extra one, and the Board suggest to the guardians that they should cause it to be understood that such relief, whenever the circumstances of the applicant are such as to render him a fit object, would be granted by way of loan, and that the repayment of the whole, or of such part as the guardians might determine, would be rigidly enforced by them; the relieving officer will, of course, notify the fact to every one who may apply to him for an order.

XIV.—NUISANCES' REMOVAL.

20*th March*, 1849.

Clerk of Luton Union.—In some of the highways in the town of Dunstable, not being subject to the Turnpike Acts, or any local Act, filthy water is allowed to run and accumulate along the sides of the highways, occasioning a very unpleasant nuisance. This water is conducted into the highways from private property, in some instances by means of covered drains, in others, of open gutters; and in its course, before it reaches the highway, it can scarcely be deemed an offensive nuisance, under the terms of the first sec. of the 11 & 12 Vic. c. 123. As the surveyors of the highways neglect to take proceedings under the Highways' Acts against the parties who occasion these nuisances, inquiring whether the guardians would be justified in preferring indictments against the surveyors, under the 6th sec. of the Act 11 & 12 Vic. c. 123. And if so, whether the common fund of the union, or the parish of Dunstable, would be chargeable with such of the costs incurred therein as might not be recoverable of the surveyors.

Ans.—It does not appear to the Board that the matter in question is one in respect of which the guardians have any legal authority to institute a prosecution, and they certainly have no funds out of which they can properly pay the expenses of such prosecution.

XV.—OVERSEER—CEASING TO RESIDE IN PARISH.

12*th Dec.*, 1849.

Audit of West and North Lancashire Audit District.—One of the overseers of ——— has removed out of the township, but resides within two miles from the church or chapel of the township, and within one mile from the boundary of the township. Does he by this removal cease to be an overseer; or does the principle of the 59 Geo. 3, c. 12, sec. 6, render it in any degree questionable whether he be an overseer or not? There are still two overseers residing in the township, and the justices have refused to entertain an application to appoint another in the room of the one who has removed, but without assigning any reason for such refusal. The latter maintains that he is still an overseer.

Ans.—The Board are of opinion that when an overseer, who was an inhabitant of the parish at the time of his appointment, removes out of that parish before the termination of his year of office, he ceases to be an overseer of the poor therein. In stating this opinion, however, the Board assume from the statement which you have laid before them, that there are no facts in the case like those in R. *v.* Poynden, (1 Barn. and Cress., 178,) where it was held that a person might be an overseer who occupied a house in a parish as a place of business, merely attending there daily, and his clerk living there, though he himself resided with his family out of the parish. If there is no longer any inhabitancy, either actual or constructive, (as in R. *v.* Poynden,) the Board think that the party has ceased to be an overseer. (17 Geo. 2, c. 38, sec. 3.) The 59 Geo. 3, c. 12, sec. 6, does not apply, as there has been no special nomination and request of a vestry of the parish, at least so far as the Board are informed.

XVI.—PARISH HOUSES.

8th Oct., 1849.

E. England Phillips, Esq., Chilton Super, Bridgewater Union.—Calling attention to the state of the poor and poor's-house belonging to the parish of Chilton Polden, in the Bridgewater Union. The house consists of four dwellings, with one sleeping apartment appropriated for each dwelling; they are about from ten to twelve feet square. In the 1st live R. D., his wife, and seven children; 2nd B. W., wife, and five children; 3rd R. H., wife, and seven children; and 4th J. G., wife, and two children, about the ages of twenty and twenty-two. There is but one entrance to each dwelling, and only two windows; there is no well or any other source of water, for the use of the occupants or of other persons living within a few yards of the poor's-house. If they had a near supply of water, a much greater quantity would be used. Two cases of cholera have occurred in the third house during the past week, but neither has proved fatal; the inmates still continue to be allowed to sleep all together in one room, and no arrangements have been made, either to obtain another dwelling or a supply of wholesome water.

4th Dec., 1849.

The Poor Law Board having communicated with the overseers of Chilton Polden on the subject of the above-mentioned houses, learned that no rents were received from them, and subsequently wrote to the overseers as follows:—The overseers are not justified in allowing the property to be occupied rent free, and the Board will feel bound to call the attention of the district auditor to the matter, whose duty it will be to require the overseers to account for the rents, if the property be retained by the parish. The Board think, however, that the proper mode of dealing with the property is for the parish to allow the guardians of the union to sell it, under the 5 & 6 Wm. 4, c. 69, sec. 3, and to apply the produce of the sale towards the reduction of the loans to the guardians on account of the building of the union workhouse; moreover, if sold, the property would doubtless come into the hands of some person who would keep it in tenantable repair.

31st Dec., 1849.

The District Auditor (to whom the Poor Law Board forwarded a copy of their letter to the overseers.)—There are several cases in his district in which the overseers retain the poor-houses, and permit paupers to reside in them free of rent. He invariably disallows all disbursements in respect of such premises; but he has never felt it to be his duty to surcharge the overseers with rent in respect of such premises. The Board's letter of the 4th instant, in reference to the poor-house at Chilton Polden, leads him to think that they consider that the overseers, in all such cases, should be charged with rent. Requesting, therefore, their instructions on the subject.

Ans.—The overseers are bound to account for all property of the parish which is available. In regard to the poor-house in question, the overseers are by law the owners of it, and are bound, as trustees for the parish, to see that it is rendered productive, and if they do not obtain adequate rents through their own laches, the Board consider that they are liable to be surcharged for their default in such an amount as the premises might reasonably be expected to let for. It is obvious, that to allow a poor person to live in a house belonging to the parish without payment of rent, is to grant relief to the party to the extent of the annual value of the occupation, and the overseers cannot lawfully grant relief in ordinary cases of destitution. If, indeed, the guardians of the union were to order the paupers to reside in parish poor-houses without payment of rent, a serious question would arise, upon which important observations would require to be made, but such a case is not at present before the Board. The Board have made these general observations in order to indicate to you the course which you ought to adopt in dealing with this description of cases, but they will be more ready to give their advice upon particular instances when they arise.

XVII.—PRISON.—CLAIM FOR COST OF SUBSISTENCE OF INFANTS WHOSE MOTHERS ARE IMPRISONED FOR WORKHOUSE OFFENCES.

25th January, 1850.

Clerk of Taunton Union.—On the 3rd of November last, three women, inmates of the workhouse, who had each an infant child at the breast, broke the windows of the house, and were taken before the magistrates, the children being with them, when they were committed to prison for two months. The ages of the children were four months, five months, and nine and a half months. The women are now out of prison and back in the workhouse. The governor of the Taunton prison has sent to the guardians a claim for one shilling per week for the subsistence of each child during the imprisonment of the mothers. Requesting the opinion of the Poor Law Board as to whether this claim can be legally paid by the guardians, as this is the first time such a claim has been made.

Ans.—The Board are not aware of any legal authority for the guardians being charged with the expense of such subsistence, nor, consequently, for their paying the claim made by the governor of the prison.

XVIII. — RATING. — RAILWAY — PARISHES DEFENDING APPEAL AT THEIR COMMON COST.

30th August, 1849.

Messrs. Lamb & Brooks, Basingstoke—Forwarding for the approval of the Poor Law Board copies of agreements and resolutions, entered into by the respective parishes of Basing, Bromley, and Monk Sherborne, in the Basingstoke Union, for the defence in common of an appeal which the Great Western Railway Company have signified their intention of instituting against the poor-rates of those parishes on the ground of over-assessment.

Ans.—The Board are not prepared to say that the particular arrangement proposed can be legally carried into effect. The present overseers cannot, as the Board consider, bind their successors to refund to the appellants the amount which, on appeal, it may be determined they have paid in excess in respect of the rate which is the subject of appeal. Neither can the present nor future overseers undertake to remit any part of an assessment on the company contained in rates made prior to that which is so appealed against. The 11th sec. of the 11 & 12 Vic. c. 91, under which such a proceeding as is contemplated can alone legally take effect, requires that notices of appeal should be actually given at the same time against the poor-rates of the several parishes concerned. When that is done, and the appeals so brought involve some common principle, those parishes may enter into an agreement (to be approved of by this Board) to defend such appeal at their common cost. The Board would refer you to the provision contained in the 12th sec. of the 12 & 13 Vic. c. 45, which will enable the appeal to be referred to arbitration, and in that manner the matter may be adjusted.

XIX.—RELIEF.

1. TO A PERSON OF IMBECILE MIND, TO ENABLE HER TO BE SENT TO A CONVENT—PROHIBITORY ORDER.

29th Nov., 1849.

Clerk of Darlington Union.—The guardians of this union have granted 60*s.* to an able-bodied woman, aged twenty years, chargeable to the township of Darlington, to enable her to be sent to "The Convent of the Good Shepherd," Hammersmith; every means have been used by the guardians and ratepayers to prevent her going about the street in the day-time as a common prostitute, but without any success. The pauper has been in the workhouse, vagrant ward, and house of correction, three or four times, and all remedies used in these places have failed; therefore, through the recommendation of the Rev. Dr. Hagarth, the guardians have obtained a place for her in the before-named convent, and have expended the 60*s.* in clothing and sending her to the place, and as such relief is given contrary to the Prohibitory Order of the Poor Law Commissioners, the guardians request the Board to confirm the same.

Ans.—With reference to your application for the Board's sanction to this expenditure, the Board are bound to point out, that the guardians of the Darlington Union (however desirable they may deem the proceeding in question to have been) had no legal authority to make the payment referred to, nor would they be justified in charging the same to the township of Darlington.

8th Dec., 1849.

Clerk of same Union.—Although the pauper is an able-bodied woman, still she is of imbecile mind, as will be seen from the certificate of the medical officer of the district; and the guardians will, it is presumed, be justified in ordering the relieving officer to class her according to such certificate; in that case she will come under the Exceptions in the General Prohibitory Order.

The Certificate mentioned above:—" I hereby certify that M— H—, of Darlington, spinster, is of imbecile mind, and a proper subject for such an Institution as the 'Convent of the Good Shepherd,' Hammersmith."

Ans.—If the pauper in question was at the time of her being sent to the said convent of such a state of mind as required that she should be confined under the Lunatic Asylums Act, an order of justices should have been obtained for her removal to such an establishment. With respect to the Institution referred to, the Board have no knowledge of the particular purpose or object for which it is designed; nor do they gather from your letters whether it was for the cure of bodily or mental infirmity, or for moral reformation, that the pauper was sent there. But it will rest with the auditor to determine whether the case falls within any of the Exceptions to the General Prohibitory Order. The Board desire to point out, that in your former communication to them on this subject, there was no reference made to the state of the pauper's mind, but she was merely described as an able-bodied woman of immoral conduct.

2. RELIEF TO DEFRAY COST OF CONVEYING PAUPER TO A PENITENTIARY.

20th Dec., 1849.

Clerk of the Devizes Union.—Mary Ann ——, aged twenty years, has been removed to the Penitentiary, at Salisbury, under the following circumstances, and the sum of £4. 9*s.* 9*d.* has been expended by order of the guardians in providing her with necessary clothing, and in conveying her to Salisbury. Mary Ann —— was brought up in the workhouse at Sunington; at the age of sixteen she was removed into the able-bodied women's ward, and soon afterwards left the workhouse. From that time she has led the life of a common prostitute, excepting when disease or want of clothing drove her to the workhouse. She has been committed to the house of correction at Devizes ten times, for destroying various descriptions of property at the workhouse. During the term of her last imprisonment the attention of the visiting justices was directed to her case by the governor and matron, who both described her as being an orderly well-conducted person whilst there. The governor stated that the chaplain had paid great attention to her, and that she appeared most anxious to reform her conduct, and having expressed a wish to be admitted into the Penitentiary at Salisbury, the chaplain had applied for and obtained an order for her admission accordingly, upon her being furnished with suitable clothing. Upon the recommendation of the visiting justices the guardians have removed Mary Ann —— to the Penitentiary at Salisbury. Requesting the Board's sanction to the payment of the sum of £4. 9*s.* 9*d.*, the expense incurred in her removal.

Ans.—The Board fully appreciate the motives which actuated the guardians in dealing with the case of Mary Ann —— in the manner represented in your letter, and are far from doubting the advantage of their proceedings in the matter to Mary Ann —— herself; but the Board regret to be obliged to point out, that the sending of paupers to a penitentiary, or to any place for the reception of persons with a view to their moral reformation, is not an object, however desirable in itself, to which the poor-rates can be lawfully applied by the guardians; and, therefore, in the present case, no sanction that might be given by the Poor Law Board would avail to render the payment in question lawful.

3. RELIEF TO SEMPSTRESSES IN CONSTANT WORK ON ACCOUNT OF INSUFFICIENCY OF EARNINGS.

14th January, 1850.

Clerk of Bermondsey Parish.—Bringing under the notice of the Poor Law Board the applications for relief from widows and other females, who, though in very constant work as sempstresses or shirtmakers, obtain so trifling a remuneration as to render it impossible for them therewith to maintain themselves. The guardians are aware that such parties are, under the existing regulations, entitled to assistance from the parochial funds, and they receive it; but the increase of the applications leads the guardians to desire that the Board should be made acquainted with the fact, feeling, as they do, that the pay of such individuals should be such as to prevent them becoming burthensome to the parish.

Ans.—It is a circumstance greatly to be deplored, that the earnings of these workpeople, when in full employment, should not be sufficient for their support, and it is natural, when this is the case that they should apply for assistance from the poor-rates, and that the guardians should allow such assistance; nevertheless, the Poor Law Board are persuaded that the practice of making up insufficient earnings by out-door relief, must tend to produce and perpetuate the evil. The system described is injurious to the workpeople, who are rendered paupers by it, while struggling to maintain themselves in independence. It is injurious also to the rate-payers, at whose expense the employers of these workpeople are enabled to get their work done at an unduly low rate. The evil is in many respects similar to that which prevailed in agricultural districts previously to the passing of the Poor Law Amendment Act, and which was put an end to under the provisions of that Act by the Regulations of the Poor Law Commissioners. It was, up to that time, a general practice in many counties to make up wages out of the poor-rates, whereby the fund which ought to have been applied in the payment of independent labourers was rendered inadequate, the employers being unable to meet the demand both for rates and wages; and, on the other hand, the labourers were subjected to all the distressing and demoralizing influences of pauperism. The only remedy which the administrators of the Poor Law have at their command, is to refuse relief in such cases as those to which you refer, except on the condition that the applicants become entirely dependent on the poor-rates for support, and place the whole of their labour, whatever it may be worth, at the disposal of those who support them. Although the adoption of this course might temporarily increase the cost of the relief, and might possibly even be deemed harsh by the applicants themselves, still, if generally acted on, it would ultimately be advantageous, in an economical point of view, as it has been in the case of the agricultural labourers; it would also be beneficial to the workpeople themselves, as it would lessen an unfair competition for employment, and secure to those who were employed an adequate rate of remuneration.

XX.—RELIEVING OFFICER.—PLACES FOR PAYING THE POOR IN.

14*th Dec.*, 1849.

Clerk of Crediton Union.—The overseers of several parishes in this union have for several years rented rooms for paying the poor in, and have paid rents for such rooms, charging the same in their accounts with the parishes. At the last audit the auditor gave instructions that the sums to be paid for those rooms in future were to be charged to the common fund of the union. In consequence of this direction the guardians have recently been applied to by the parish officers of Crediton for the payment of a half-year's rent of a room, rented in that parish for the above purpose. The guardians, however, are of opinion, that as the poor in the majority of the parishes in the union are paid in the vestries and other places free of expense, to compel those parishes to contribute towards providing places in other parishes would be unfair. Requesting permission to have payments of this description charged in the parish officer's accounts, as heretofore.

Ans.—The guardians of the Crediton Union, in ordering relief to paupers, direct their relieving officer to pay the money or distribute the relief to the several applicants for whom it is ordered. This may be done in two ways; the relieving officer may go to the paupers and distribute the relief ordered, or he may require the pauper to come to him at a particular place to receive it from him. If the officer adopt the former course, he will require a larger salary than that which he would otherwise receive. If he adopt the latter, he must find a proper place in which to pay the paupers, or it will have to be found for him. Should he be required to find such a place, he must be paid for it in the shape of salary; but if the guardians find the place for him, they can only properly defray the expense out of the common fund of the union, because, by making this arrangement, they remove the charge of the addition to the relieving officer's salary, which would, in the former alternative, be payable out of that fund. If the relief be distributed to the paupers in any parish of the union, in the vestry-room or other building free of charge, this would be so much gain, not to any particular parish, but to the common fund of the union. It therefore appears to the Board, that the auditor acted quite correctly in giving the instructions above alluded to, the overseers not being authorized to interfere in the administration of ordinary relief to paupers, and, consequently, not being justified in providing places for this purpose, nor in charging the sums paid for the hire of such places in their accounts with their respective parishes.

XXI.—REMOVABILITY.

1. BREACH OF RESIDENCE.

7th June, 1849.

Clerk of King's Lynn Union.—Transmitting the following statement for the opinion of the Poor Law Board:—Edward Taylor, now aged eighty-one, and his wife Margaret, aged seventy-one, belonging to Sporle with Palgrave in the Swaffham Union, have lived in West Lynn in the King's Lynn Union for thirty-four years, during the greater part of which time they had no parish relief. They have no children. On the 10th of October, 1843, Edward Taylor met with an accident at West Lynn, and was immediately removed to the West Norfolk and Lynn Hospital, situate in the parish of St. Margaret, King's Lynn, where he remained twenty-one weeks; and then returned to West Lynn, to the house in which he lived at the time of the accident, and in which his wife resided during his stay in the hospital. Taylor and his wife have ever since resided at West Lynn, and received out-door relief the whole time excepting a fortnight. *Query*—Whether Edward Taylor and his wife are removable to Sporle with Palgrave; and, if not, whether their relief must be charged to the parish of West Lynn, or to the common fund of the King's Lynn Union.

Ans.—The King's Lynn Union is certainly interested in the question raised, which lies, in fact, between the parish of West Lynn and the union at large, because, if the pauper be irremovable, the cost of his relief must be borne by the common fund. However, upon the statement which accompanied your letter, the Board are prepared to state, that they consider the pauper not to be removable from West Lynn, and that his abiding in the West Norfolk and Lynn Hospital was not, under these circumstances, an interruption of the residence in West Lynn. The Board would direct the attention of the guardians of the King's Lynn Union to the observations of Mr. Justice Erle, in the case of the Q. *v.* Leaden Roothing. See 13 *Law Times*, page 138.

12th June, 1849.

Clerk of same Union.—Transmitting the following statement, duly signed, under sec. 4 of the 11 & 12 Vic. c. 110, for the opinion of the Poor Law Board:—James Twaits, (now aged seventy-three years,) Hannah, his wife, (since deceased,) and their four children, were legally removed in July, 1831, from the parish of West Lynn to the parish of St. Margaret, King's Lynn, both which parishes are now comprised in the King's Lynn Union. They returned to West Lynn on the same day, and James Twaits has resided there ever since, excepting the intervals hereinafter mentioned. In July, 1842, James Twaits and his wife applied for relief to the guardians of the King's Lynn Union, and received an order for the union workhouse, which is situate in St. Margaret's parish. They accepted the order, and were admitted into the workhouse on the 4th of July, 1842, and discharged on the 8th of the same month. They immediately returned to West Lynn, and inhabited the same room they had previously occupied, which room they did not give up on leaving West Lynn, nor was any deduction made from the rent on account of their absence. In June, 1846, Hannah Twaits died. On 18th of September, 1848, James Twaits was again admitted into the union workhouse, and was discharged on 27th of October, 1848, when he returned to the same house in which he had resided previously to his admission into the workhouse, and no deduction was made from his rent. This house was, up to Old Michaelmas, (11th October,) 1848, occupied by James Twaits, and his son lodged with him; but at Old Michaelmas, 1848, the occupation was transferred to the son, and the father has since been a lodger. James Twaits has constantly been relieved, either in or out of the workhouse, since July, 1842. *Query*—Whether the relief now given to James Twaits ought to be charged by the guardians of the King's Lynn Union to the parish of St. Margaret, or to the common fund of the union.

Ans.—The question involved in this case is, whether the abiding of the pauper in the union workhouse in 1842 for four days, and again in September and October last year, was an interruption of the pauper's residence in the parish of West Lynn. The Board are of opinion that the case is within the principle established by the decision of the Court of Queen's Bench in Reg. *v.* Tacolnestone, (18 L. J. R. N. S. M. C. 44,) and that there was no interruption of the residence in West Lynn; consequently, the relief given to the pauper is chargeable to the common fund of the King's Lynn Union.

---

2. REMOVABILITY OF WIDOW.

21st June, 1849.

Clerk of Strand Union.—Mary Terry became a widow in the month of January last, and received out-relief from the common fund of this union, residing at the time in the parish of St. Anne, Westminster. In the month of March she gave up her residence in the last named parish, and removed to the parish of Lambeth. She has, however, recently returned again to the parish of St. Anne, Westminster, being the parish in which her husband died, and has again become chargeable. As the pauper has no settlement in any parish in the Strand Union, the guardians request to be advised whether, under the above circumstances, the pauper is removable to the place of settlement, with a view to determine whether the relief shall be charged to the parish of St. Anne, Westminster, or to the common fund of the union.

Ans.—The Board consider, that so long as the pauper is in the parish of St. Anne, and requiring relief, until the termination of the first year of her widowhood, she is irremovable, and, therefore, chargeable to the common fund of the Strand Union.

---

3. REMOVABILITY OF A PERSON WHO HAD RESIDED WITH HER FATHER.

7th July, 1849.

Clerk of Pwllheli Union.—Ellen J., spinster, who has an illegitimate child, aged ten years, has resided in the parish Llangian, in this union, for the last eight years and a half, sometimes at home with her father, and sometimes in service. She has now become an inmate of the union workhouse. Inquiring whether the pauper is to be considered as irremovable, and her relief charged to the union, on account of her having lived within the parish for more than five years, but without any residence of her own; or, whether she is still liable to be removed to her father's original parish, (Bottwnog,) on account of her having been emancipated from her father prior to his having gained irremovability at Llangian by residence, and having gained no settlement on her own account.

Ans.—According to the particulars before them, the Board consider this pauper to be irremovable if she have resided for five years in the parish of Llangian without having received relief, it being quite immaterial as to whose house she may have resided in. At the same time, the Board may remark that the irremovability of her father, acquired by reason of residence, was not a settlement, and, consequently, the fact of her emancipation from her father's control would have been of no consequence if she had not been irremovable.

XXII.—SCHOOLS.—DISCHARGE OF PAUPERS FROM WORKHOUSE WHEN THEIR CHILDREN ARE AT A DISTRICT SCHOOL.

6th Dec., 1849.

Clerk of Hartley Wintney Union.—This union has joined with the Farnham Union in the formation of a district school, at Oldershott, in the latter union, and distant about ten miles from this union, and such school district being now permanently established, it may frequently happen that parents may be inmates of the Hartley Wintney Union workhouse whose children have been sent to the district school at Oldershott. Inquiring, therefore, first, What notice should be given to the governor of the workhouse by such parents of their intention to leave the house; or, on the other hand, what notice should be given by the guardians for such persons to leave the house, in order to enable the children to be fetched from the school, and so prevent the parents from giving the three hours' notice only, which is all now required, and so leaving the house before their children could be fetched from school, perhaps absconding, and thus leaving their children to be kept and maintained at the expense of the parishes to which they respectively belong; and, secondly, whether it is the duty of the guardians to cause such children to be fetched from the district school in order to leave them with their parents.

Ans.—No specific length of notice for quitting the workhouse is required by the General Consolidated Order. It is said, in Art. 115, that a "reasonable notice" shall be given, but the reasonableness of the notice must depend upon the circumstances under which it is given. A man, whose children are in a district school, ten miles distant from the workhouse, is under circumstances different from those of one who has no child, or whose child is with him in the workhouse; and he is so, moreover, by his own consent, for his child cannot have been placed in the district school without such consent. Having regard to these considerations, the Board are of opinion, that in the case of a pauper whose child or children may be in the district school, twenty-four hours' notice of quitting the workhouse would be reasonable, and that there would be no illegality in detaining the parent for that length of time, unless his children were brought to him from the school before its expiration. The Board assume that twenty-four hours would generally be found necessary in order to make proper arrangements for bringing the children from the district school to the workhouse, so that parent and child might leave the house together. As regards the second question submitted in your letter, the Board think that the guardians are bound to provide for the children being safely restored to their parents. But the most convenient mode of effecting this with reference to local circumstances is a question for the board of managers of the school, and for the guardians of the several unions to consider.

XXIII.—SETTLEMENT.

1. BY ESTATE.

2nd Feb., 1849.

Clerk of Helston Union.—About twenty-five years since, Jose, a pauper, whose settlement was in Mawgan, obtained permission of his brother-in-law to build a cottage, and inclose a garden on part of his leasehold tenement in the parish of Wendron. The pauper, who has no lease, or the promise of a lease, has never paid any rent, and has resided in the house ever since its erection. About seven years ago the pauper's brother-in-law sold his lease, but the cottage and garden was not included in the assignment. The parish of Wendron urges the guardians to make the pauper's relief a charge on the common fund, on the ground of five years' residence, but a question has arisen as to whether the pauper has, under the circumstances, an estate in Wendron, which would prevent his removal. Requesting the opinion of the Poor Law Board on this point.

Ans.—The Board are of opinion, under the circumstances of the case before them, that the pauper is settled in the parish of Wendron by estate. Upon this view, that the pauper is so settled, and he being also resident in the parish of Wendron, the case does not fall within the 3rd sec. of the 11 & 12 Vic. c. 110, and the cost of his relief is not therefore a charge upon the common fund of the Helston Union.

2. SETTLEMENT BY HIRING A TENEMENT.

13th July, 1849.

Clerk of Garstang Union.—Submitting, for the opinion of the Poor Law Board, the following case:—A. resided in the township of Ellel, and rented a tenement for several years before and up to Candlemas, 1831, at an annual rent of £16 or £17, when he went to reside in the township of Forton, and there rented premises at an annual rent of £9 for one year; in his second year of occupation of those premises he took another tenement from another person, at the annual rent of £5. 11*s.*, and occupied it for two years; but in the latter year he paid no rent for the tenement under the second hiring. Does A. gain a settlement in Forton?

Ans.—No settlement appears to have been gained by A. in the township of Forton during the year 1831–2, as the annual rent of the premises occupied by him was under £10. The provisions of the 6 Geo. 4, c. 57, prevented the settlement from being gained in that year. During the second year, however, A. increased his annual rental in Forton to more than £10, although such increase was caused by another hiring under a different landlord. At that time the 1 Wm. 4, c. 18, was in force, but in this respect it appears to agree with the former statutes, and the Board cannot find that under them it was necessary that the taking or hiring should have been from the same lessor or landlord. Then, as the occupation was sufficient, the amount of rent adequate, and, it appears, that for one year of the second hiring that amount of rent was paid, the Board are of opinion that a settlement was gained by A. in Forton.

3. SETTLEMENT IN ENGLAND OF PERSONS BORN IN SCOTLAND.

9th Oct., 1849.

Mr. J. Morgan, Edinburgh.—Inquiring by what means natives of Scotland can acquire such a right or title in England as to entitle them to parochial relief in England in the event of their becoming paupers; and if, after acquiring a parochial settlement, can they lose it; and if so, in what way?

Ans.—A destitute person, whether a native of England or Scotland, or a foreigner, who requires relief at any place in England, must be relieved by the proper authority, in the place where he is destitute. In regard to a person born in Scotland, he may acquire a settlement in England, as a native may, by various modes, which are detailed in the treatises on the subject. When he has once acquired a settlement, he will not lose it except in one particular case, viz., when the settlement was gained by the possession of an estate, and the party goes away from it, and resides in another parish, at a distance of ten miles. But a native of Scotland may, under the late statute, relating to the removal of the poor, 9 & 10 Vic. c. 66, become irremovable from the parish where he resides, after he has resided therein for five years without receiving parochial relief, though he may not have acquired a settlement therein. That statute contains some other provisions, conferring irremovability, which may occasionally apply to natives of Scotland. If any such native be not protected by this statute, and have not acquired a settlement in any parish in England, he is liable to be removed with his children, when destitute, to Scotland, under the statute 8 & 9 Vic. c. 117.

XXIV.—SMALL POX.—A PERSON WHO HAD HAD THE SMALL POX LEAVING THE WORKHOUSE PREMATURELY.

18*th Dec.*, 1849.

Clerk of Tunbridge Union.—H. G., a pauper in the union workhouse, having just recovered from the small pox, and having given notice of her intention to leave the house to-morrow; and the medical officer having stated, that in his opinion if the pauper left under three weeks from this time the disease was likely to be spread abroad, inquired what course the guardians should adopt; whether the woman should be indicted for a misdemeanor, and if so, out of what fund the expenses should come.

Ans.—The Board do not think that the law authorizes the guardians to detain the pauper in the workhouse if she persist in her desire to leave it; neither are the Board aware of any precedent of an indictment against a person under precisely such circumstances as exist in the present case. At the same time, the guardians would do right, not only to warn the pauper of her personal danger from prematurely exposing herself to the weather, but also to point out to her the provisions of the 3 & 4 Vic. c. 29, sec. 8, for preventing the spread of small pox, to the penalties of which, by some act of her own, she may possibly render herself liable.

XXV.—WORKHOUSE—POST-MORTEM EXAMINATIONS IN.

11*th Dec.*, 1841.

T. Thursfield, Esq., Surgeon, Kidderminster.—Requesting the opinion of the Poor Law Commissioners as to the right of a medical officer to make post-mortem examinations of the bodies of paupers dying in the union workhouse.

Ans.—The question contained in your letter is one which the Commissioners thought likely to arise when they framed their Order requiring the cause of death to be certified by the medical officer, and with a view to put the subject fully before you, they wish to state that nothing further is required by them in their direction to the medical officer, "to ascertain and certify the cause of death" in the case of a pauper dying in the workhouse, than a statement of what, from *apparent* circumstances and such information as can be obtained from nurses and attendants, may be considered the probable cause of death. In no case do the Commissioners desire a post-mortem examination to take place solely for the purpose of satisfying their rule. Excepting by the direction of a coroner when holding an inquest, or the direction of the board of guardians for any especial, urgent, and peculiar reason, which they may deem of sufficient importance to render such an examination necessary, or at the request of the nearest relatives of the deceased, the Commissioners deem that the medical officer would not be justified in making a post-mortem examination. The Commissioners have further to add, that they think that the board of guardians would hardly be justified in directing in any particular case that a post-mortem examination should take place if the nearest relatives of the deceased objected clearly and decidedly to the course, and the Commissioners need hardly add, that the guardians would, so far as circumstances will permit, do well to satisfy themselves of the necessity for such an examination before they took upon themselves to authorize it.

London: Printed by Order of the Poor Law Board, by BLACKBURN & BURT, 90½, Holborn Hill, and Published by CHARLES KNIGHT, 90, Fleet Street.

AN

OFFICIAL CIRCULAR

OF PUBLIC DOCUMENTS AND INFORMATION:

DIRECTED BY THE POOR LAW BOARD TO BE PRINTED, CHIEFLY FOR THE USE OF THE BOARDS OF GUARDIANS AND THEIR OFFICERS.

No. 35.] MARCH, 1850. [N.S.

CONTENTS.

I.—AUDIT.

1. NOTICE OF.

14*th March*, 1850.

James Hunt, Esq., District Auditor.—Inquiring whether in advertising notices of the audits of the union accounts in his district, there is in the opinion of the Board any legal necessity for mentioning the names of the parishes comprised in in each union, or, whether there is any other alteration or addition to the form of advertisement he now uses, which the Board deem it desirable for him to adopt in future. The insertion of the names of all the parishes would considerably increase the cost of advertisements.

Form of Advertisement used by Mr. Hunt:—

"Oxfordshire and Warwickshire Audit District. ——— Union.—I, the undersigned James Hunt, auditor of the above-named district, do hereby give notice that I have appointed the audit of the accounts of ——— Union, and of the parishes therein, and of the officers thereof, for the half-year ending this day, to commence on Monday, the fifteenth day of October next, at ten o'clock in the forenoon, at the Board Room of the Workhouse of the ——— Union, when and where all persons who by law are bound to account at such audit are required to attend and to submit all books, documents, bills, and vouchers, containing or relating to their accounts, or to monies assessed for and applicable to the relief of the poor.—Dated this 29th day of September, 1849.

"JAMES HUNT."

Ans.—The Board do not consider it necessary to specify by name in the notices in question the particular parishes comprised in the union to which such notices may refer; and they think that the form of notice proposed by you for adoption, omitting the names of the parishes, but describing them generally as "the parishes in the

——— Union," is sufficient. The Board think it right to add, that the specific notices required by the 7 & 8 Vic. c. 101, sec. 33, must of course be given to and by the overseers of the respective parishes.

2. DUTIES OF RATEPAYERS IN REGARD TO AUDIT.

16*th April*, 1850.

J. S., Esq.—On the examination of the accounts of T. R., late overseer of the parish of R., it appears that there were in his hands the sums of 8*s.* 6½*d.*, £1. 18*s.* 2*d.*, 18*s.* 11*d.*, £1. 4*s.* 11*d.*, balances on account of four poor-rates collected by him, and that such accounts were erroneously passed by the auditor. It also appears that there is a balance of £6. 0*s.* 5½*d.* in the hands of T. R. in favour of the parish, on account of the county road rate. T. R. neglected to give notice that his accounts were about to be audited, and forged the names of one of the churchwardens and the other overseer in the book which he laid before the auditor.

Auditor of ——— District [to whom the above communication was sent.]—With respect to the balances stated to be due on the different poor-rates collected by the late overseer, he, the auditor, will be ready to reimburse to the parish any amount of loss, which may appear to have been incurred by his inadvertence in collating the rate-books, which, in many instances, is a very difficult task, from the imperfect state in which they are brought before him by the overseers of the rural parishes. The county road rate, on which a balance is stated to be due from the late overseer, must, he apprehends, have been a separate rate, collected for the purpose of meeting some demands, and which was never produced before the auditor.

Ans. to J. S., Esq.—With regard to part of the balance, £6. 0*s.* 5½*d.*, stated to be due from the overseer in question, it may be observed that no responsibility attaches to the auditor from the failure of the overseer to bring such balance to account. The Board are of opinion that no personal liability attaches to an auditor to pay over any sums which, through inadvertence or the absence of necessary information, he has not, in striking the balance, found to be due, though they in reality may be, from the overseer on rendering up his accounts. In the present instance, irrespective of the sum of £6. 0*s.* 5½*d.* above adverted to, four sums of inconsiderable amount are pointed out as not having been properly accounted for. The Board do not clearly collect from the statement of the case before them, whether or not those sums, having come to the hands of the overseer in question, he has failed to give credit for them; or whether they are simply uncollected rates, which he ought to have collected, had he used due diligence in his office. But, however this may be, the Board must take occasion to observe, that it would have been competent to the rate-payers (having previously investigated the account, as the law enabled them to do) to have attended the audit, and to have then called the attention of the auditor to any item or matter which, in their opinion, required investigation. Indeed, it is to be regretted that advantage is not more frequently taken of the opportunity so afforded for urging objections, seeing that it presents a more certain mode of correcting errors, as well as a greater security against the successful commission of frauds on the part of the officer accounting, than the unaided skill and attention of the auditor, however great these may be, can afford. Such a course of proceeding is equally due to the rate-payers interested and to the auditor, who, in the discharge of his duties, may not unreasonably expect this co-operation on the part of the rate-payers, and who is manifestly placed in an invidious position by charges being subsequently made against him, with respect to errors not patent on the face of the account, where his attention was not specially directed to them at the audit. As regards the charge, as to the forgery of your name to the books, it may be right that criminal proceedings should be taken against the overseer who was guilty of it. But the Board, in the absence of precise information as to the facts, cannot undertake to advise what course of proceeding or remedy may be open.

3. DISALLOWANCE BY AUDITOR OF SUMS UNDER FORTY SHILLINGS.

12*th Jan.*, 1850.

The Poor Law Board to ———, District Auditor.—Calling his attention to the omission to include in his report of the last Michaelmas Audit a disallowance of 6*s.* 6*d.* made by him in the accounts of the parish officers of H., and requesting his explanation in reference to such omission.

The District Auditor.—He deems it necessary to certify in the case of the quoted disallowance, for the reason, that the proviso of the 5th sec. of the 11 & 12 Vic. c. 91, inferentially, though not expressly, seems to him intended to relieve auditors from the necessity of certifying in cases where the disallowance shall not amount to 40*s*. It not unfrequently happens that justices' clerks charge more than they are entitled to by the established table of fees. In reducing such charges to the amount fixed by the table, the reduction partakes more of the character of a correction than a disallowance, and he has not felt himself called upon in such cases formally to certify. In like manner where a regulated scale of medical fees has been established, or generally adopted in a district, the reduction of a charge to that scale by a few shillings did not seem to him to impose a necessity for certifying. If he is wrong in this view of the question, and it be ruled that every reduction, correction, or disallowance, be the amount ever so small, must be certified, it will enormously increase the number of certificates, as the disallowances are mostly in such small items.

Ans.—The Board cannot acquiesce in your construction of the statute, 11 & 12 Vic. c. 91, sec. 5, to the effect, that you are not required to certify any disallowance where the sum does not exceed 40*s*. They consider that under that provision, it is incumbent upon the auditor to certify every disallowance or surcharge which he makes in the account, though it may be that by the operation of the proviso to sec. 5, the sums so disallowed, if under 40*s*., need not be paid over until the balance found against the overseer is payable; that is, until the close of his year of office. It may, doubtless, often happen that the disallowance of a small sum involves a serious question, which the accounting parties have a right to bring under proper review; and they cannot properly do so unless the disallowance is duly certified. The Board would regret if any great additional labour should be imposed upon you in this respect, but judging from their experience in regard of other auditors, who certify according to their actual disallowances, they do not anticipate that the practice will occasion you any very serious amount of additional trouble.

II.—BURIAL.

1. CHARGING EXPENSES OF.

4th March, 1850.

Clerk of Honiton Union.—Transmitting the following statement, duly signed under the 11 & 12 Vic. c. 110, sec. 4, for the opinion of the Poor Law Board:—"J. H. was, in the year 1837, removed by an order of justices from the borough of Chard, Somerset, to the parish of Ottery St. Mary, and, consequently, was not at the time of his death removable from the parish in which he resided. He has since been from time to time an inmate of the Honiton Union Workhouse, chargeable to the last named parish. During this time he has been admitted into the workhouse and discharged therefrom between thirty and forty times; and, when not in the workhouse or county jail, to which he has been frequently sent, his general residence has been Ottery St. Mary. His son, a lad about sixteen years of age, has been in the house for the last six years, and has to the present time been charged to the parish of Ottery St. Mary. The last time the deceased was admitted was on the 1st day of November last, and was discharged on Thursday the 6th day of December. He went immediately to Ottery St. Mary, and on Friday the 7th applied to the relieving officer there for an order for his readmission into the workhouse, which was given to him as on account of the parish of Ottery St. Mary. He was accidentally drowned within the parish of Honiton; his body being found in that parish on the morning of Saturday the 8th. The order of admission was found in his hat; and it is supposed that he was on his way to the workhouse at the time of his death, the place where he was drowned being about a quarter of a mile from the workhouse. The guardians ordered the expenses of his burial to be charged to Ottery St. Mary, deeming that as by the Act of 7 & 8 Vic. c. 101, sec. 56, the workhouse is to be considered as part of the parish, the pauper's going from the parish to the workhouse ought to be held as a mere removal from one part of the parish to the other. The 31st sec. of the same Act authorizes the guardians to charge the expenses of the burial of any poor person "to any parish to which such person may have been chargeable," and they consider that the charge to Ottery St. Mary in this case comes under the above section, the pauper having applied for relief and received the order for admission to the workhouse.

Ans.—The Poor Law Board do not think that the deceased could be considered as chargeable to the parish of Ottery St. Mary when he was drowned. It appears that he had simply received an order for the workhouse on account of that parish, which he might have used or not, and which order did not in itself create a chargeability. The Board therefore consider that the cost of the burial should be charged according to the 7 & 8 Vic. c. 101, sec. 31, to the parish wherein the death occurred, or wherein the dead body was found, that is, the parish of Honiton.

2. BURIAL OF PAUPERS CHARGEABLE TO THE COMMON FUND, AND DYING IN THE WORKHOUSE.

23rd March, 1850.

Clerk of Rye Union.—Referring to sec. 56 of the 7 & 8 Vic. c. 101, and the 9 & 10 Vic. c. 66, requested the opinion of the Board in reference to the burial of paupers chargeable to the common fund of the union who die in the workhouse.

Ans.—The Board consider that the case of a pauper chargeable to the common fund of the Union is not within the 7 & 8 Vic. c. 101, sec. 56, which applies only to paupers chargeable to a parish. In respect, then, of such paupers who die while in receipt of relief, their burial should take place in the parish wherein they die, if that be known, as in the case of a death in the workhouse it must necessarily be.

III.—CHARGEABILITY.

1. WIDOW OF A PERSON WHO IS NOT KNOWN.

2nd March, 1849.

Clerk of Launceston Union.—Transmitting the following statement duly signed under the 4th sec. of the 11 & 12 Vic. c. 110, for the opinion of the Poor Law Board:—E. H., a widow, has resided in the parish of St. Mary Magdalene in this union for upwards of twenty years, and for the last three years has been in the receipt of regular weekly relief from that parish. She is also a native of the parish, which is the place of her maiden settlement; but she married a person, a soldier, whose settlement is unknown, but whose settlement was not in the parish of St. Mary Magdalene, and who is since dead, and there are no available means of ascertaining where his settlement was, as he was previously unknown in this district. The guardians of St. Mary Magdalene apply to have the maintenance of the pauper charged to the common fund of the union on the ground of her being irremovable by reason of residence, and being a person resident but not settled in the parish. The guardians of the union aver that as previously to the Acts conferring irremovability, the pauper was in fact irremovable by reason of the impossibility or difficulty of ascertaining her husband's settlement, and her maiden settlement being in the parish of residence, the provisions of the 11 & 12 Vic. c. 110, do not apply to the case. There are many cases similar to the above, varying in detail, but agreeing in this principle, in which the irremovability existed in fact before the 9 & 10 Vic. c. 66, by reason of the failure to discover the settlements of pauper husbands. The determination of the Poor Law Board is requested, whether the above-named pauper, and others in similar circumstances, should be relieved at the cost of the parish of St. Mary Magdalene or of the common fund of the union.

Ans.—If a pauper be removable, so far as the length of residence, or the other provisions of the statute 9 & 10 Vic. c. 66, are concerned, but the overseers of the parish of the residence are unable to ascertain the settlement of the pauper, the charge of the relief will then remain upon the parish of the residence. Where, however, the residence has occurred for a sufficient period, namely, five years; or, where the pauper is rendered irremovable by reason of the operation of any provision of the 9 & 10 Vic. c. 66, other than sec. 1, but the settlement is not known to be in the parish of the residence, then it seems to the Board that the more correct course will be for the relief of the pauper to be charged to the union common fund. In the present case, the pauper (as is admitted) is not settled in the parish of St. Mary Magdalene, by reason of her deceased husband's settlement being elsewhere, although the precise place of his settlement cannot at present be proved. The Board, therefore, consider, upon the statement of facts as submitted to them, that the relief of the pauper E. H. should be charged to the common fund of the Launceston Union.

16th March, 1849.

Clerk of same Union.—The guardians, referring to the fact that the place of settlement of the widow's husband cannot be ascertained, and her maiden settlement is in the parish of residence, so that the pauper was in fact irremovable, independently of the legislative impediment, inquired whether the expense of maintenance ought to be charged in such cases to the common fund of the union, since in the absence of a marital settlement the pauper retains her own.

Ans.—Though the settlement of the husband cannot, as it is said, be ascertained, it was nevertheless stated, as a fact, not to be in the parish of St. Mary Magdalene. Therefore it is not possible to say with certainty that the widow is settled therein. Whatever might be the consequence, as between two conflicting parishes, by reason of the failure of the proof, the Board think that the case is within the 3rd sec. of the 11 & 12 Vic. c. 110.

---

2. ORPHAN CHILD—CONSTRUCTION OF 11 & 12 VIC. C. 110, SEC. 1, AND 12 & 13 VIC. C. 103, SEC. 2.

21*st March*, 1850.

Clerk of Worcester Union.—During the prevalence of cholera in this union, an unmarried woman, whose settlement parish was then and is now unknown, died, and also one of her two children, both being under the age of twelve years. For some time afterwards, the surviving child was taken care of and supported by her brother; but on his refusing to do so any longer, the child went into another parish, and obtained leave of a woman, who was not a relative but a stranger, to allow her to stay at her house, where she remained for about three weeks. She then applied to the relieving officer, who gave her an order for admission into the workhouse, which she accepted, and she is now charged to the parish from which she was sent, which is objected to by the guardian for that parish, who contends that the relief should be charged to the common fund of the union, the child being a "destitute foundling," within the meaning of the 2nd section of the 12th & 13th Vic. c. 103. The reasons for charging the relief to the parish are—1st, That the child was not deserted by her parents. 2nd, That she was in the care of a stranger. Requesting the opinion of the Board as to whether the relief in this case should be charged to the common fund of the union, or to the parish in which the child was found destitute.

Ans.—It does not appear to the Board that the case comes within the 12 & 13 Vic. c. 103, sec. 2, as the child is an orphan, and not a deserted child. Neither was she a foundling in the ordinary sense of that word, so as to be included within the 11 & 12 Vic. c. 110, sec. 1. Nor was she a wanderer, for she was living in the parish from which she applied for relief. The Board, therefore, consider that the guardians of the Worcester Union have acted properly in charging the relief of the pauper to the parish in which she was living when the application was made.

---

3. RELIEF GIVEN TO FATHER IN CONSEQUENCE OF SICKNESS OF CHILD.

14*th Jan.*, 1850.

Clerk of Lancaster Union.—Transmitting the following statement, duly signed, under the 11 & 12 Vic. c. 110, sec. 4, for the opinion of the Poor Law Board:—J. H., a widower, and his seven children, under the age of sixteen years, reside in the township of Lancaster in this union, but are settled in the township of Ellel, in this union. J. H. and his said children have received for several weeks, and are now receiving, relief from Ellel in consequence of his want of full employment. One of his children, a boy aged fourteen years, who earned four shillings per week by work, has, since the family became chargeable, become sick and unable to work. The sickness will not produce permanent disability. The amount of weekly out-door relief has been increased in consequence of the boy's sickness. The opinion of the Poor Law Board is requested on the following points:—1. Is the relief at present afforded to J. H. and his family, or any part of such relief, chargeable to the common fund of the Lancaster Union, under sec. 1 of 12 & 13 Vic. c. 103? or, 2nd. As J. H. and his family did not become chargeable in respect of relief made necessary by sickness, or accident, is the additional relief rendered necessary by the boy's sickness chargeable to Ellel?

Ans.—The Board, upon the information before them, consider that the pauper being chargeable to the poor-rates from destitution, and not in consequence of his child's sickness, is not exempt from removal; therefore, neither is he, nor are any of his children, chargeable to the common fund of the union.

IV.—EMIGRATION—TO PORT NATAL AND THE CAPE OF GOOD HOPE.

Letter from the Colonial Land and Emigration Commissioners to the Assistant Secretary of the Poor Law Board:—

29*th Jan.*, 1850.

"Sir,—With reference to your letter of the 10th inst., requesting to be furnished, for the guidance of the Poor Law Board, with information on the subject of emigration to Port Natal, I am instructed by the Colonial Land and Emigration Commissioners to furnish an explanatory memorandum respecting the purchase of land in that settlement, and the advantages offered to the purchasers who may undertake to send out and locate at their own expense emigrants suitable to the wants of the colony. A set of regulations, dated the 22nd inst., have been framed at this office, with a view to inform parties desirous of entering in this business of the details which have to be attended to. These Regulations, which you will find subjoined, and the Memorandum, will put you in possession of the requirements of this Board, in its approval of emigrants as eligible for this district, and as entitling the party at whose expense they may be sent out, to the drawback of £10 per adult, mentioned in the 9th Article of the Memorandum.

"In communicating to you the above information, I am to observe, that the Commissioners do not apprehend that the scheme of emigration will be available for the purposes of the Poor Law Board, and that they doubt whether as yet the arrangements connected with the landing of emigrants and their subsequent accommodation at Port Natal are sufficiently advanced to justify the Poor Law Commissioners in sanctioning emigration on a large scale to that settlement. It may, however, be interesting to the Board to know that the cost of conveyance may be estimated rather below £10 per adult, that the soil and climate are very favourably spoken of, and that there is every probability that capital will be invested in this settlement.

"I am, in conclusion, to add, that emigration to the Cape is now established under government authority, and that there is an Emigration Officer at Cape Town to superintend all local arrangements in connection with this service. The inclosed Regulations explain the terms at which government emigration to the Cape is at present carried on.

"I have, &c.,
"S. WALCOTT,
"*Secretary.*"

NATAL REGULATIONS.

22nd Jan., 1850.

MEMORANDUM RESPECTING THE DEPOSIT MONEY WITH THE COLONIAL LAND AND EMIGRATION COMMISSIONERS FOR THE PURCHASE OF LAND AT NATAL.

Colonial Office, April 16, 1849.

The general regulations on the sale of colonial lands provide, that if a person pays in this country for the purchase of such lands, he becomes entitled to nominate a definite number of emigrants; and that, if they be found eligible, according to certain established rules on the subject, the Commissioners of Emigration shall provide them with a free passage to the colony, in respect of which the money has been deposited for the purchase of land. These deposits are required to be made in sums of not less than £100 each.

The purpose of the present memorandum is to explain the terms on which a settler who is willing to pay in advance for lands at Natal, but is desirous to send out his own emigrants instead of leaving them to be sent out by the Commissioners, can be allowed to effect his object. The terms will be as follows:—

1. The money must be deposited to the credit of the Commissioners at the Bank of England in sums not less than £1000 each.

2. For each such deposit a certificate will be issued by the Commissioners, which will be considered to represent the same amount of money in any purchase of Government Land at Natal.

3. The land must be purchased in conformity with all such rules, and after being exposed to sale at such upset price as may be in force in the colony at the time when it shall be actually bought.

4. The depositor is to undertake the conveyance to Natal of agricultural labourers, mechanics, skilled labourers or small farmers accustomed to some manual labour, and intending to work for their subsistence.

5. He is to engage to furnish them with a steerage passage, and to grant them, after arrival, twenty acres of land in fee for each adult, and five acres for each child, with a right of choice out of at least double that quantity, in consideration of a payment by the emigrants of not more than £10 for each adult, computed according to the Passengers' Act.

6. If any persons who belong to the foregoing classes, and for whom therefore a drawback can be claimed of the Government in the manner to be presently stated, should proceed as intermediate passengers, there must be sufficient evidence that they had enjoyed an option of proceeding in the steerage for the maximum charge above-mentioned, and that they had preferred paying the difference of price for the superior kind of accommodation.

7. The lists of the emigrants are to be submitted to the Emigration Commissioners for revision and approval, and the emigrants themselves to be inspected by an officer of that Board previous to sailing.

8. Whenever a vessel is engaged for conveying emigrants to Natal under this arrangement, the fact must be reported to the Board of Emigra-

tion, in order that the requisite survey of her may be made by the emigration officer at the port from which she is to sail. If sent from a port at which no such officer is stationed, the expense of sending one to make the survey must devolve on the depositor who is despatching the emigrants; but there are emigration officers at all the principal ports of the kingdom.

9. For each approved emigrant (two children between one and fourteen years being counted as one emigrant) who may be introduced into the colony, there will be returned to the depositor out of the amount paid by him to the credit of the Emigration Commissioners the sum of £10, on receipt from the colony of a certificate that such emigrant had been safely landed, and appeared to have been properly treated on the voyage; and, further, had been duly put in possession of the promised quantity of land.

RULES

To be observed by Persons availing themselves of the above Regulations:—

1. When a deposit has been made at the Bank of England, the depositor should forward the receipt to the Colonial Land and Emigration Commissioners, addressed to their secretary, S. Walcott, Esq., 9, Park Street, Westminster; at the same time stating the Christian and surnames of the agent or agents at Natal, whom the depositor may authorize to make use of his land certificate.

2. The depositor will apply to the Commissioners for specimens of the requisite forms for conducting the business between their office and the depositors, and it must be understood, that he is not at liberty to make use of their names in any form or printed paper, without their previous sanction.

3. The depositor must give early notice to the Commissioners of the ship which he may purpose to charter for this service. As Port Natal is a bar-harbour, vessels drawing more than eleven feet water will be required to be furnished with suitable surf-boats for landing passengers.

4. With reference to Art. 9 of the Colonial Office Regulations, and as a necessary preliminary to the allowance of £10 on approved emigrants, the following Rules must be observed:—

(1.) The emigrants must consist principally of the following classes: Farmers of small capital, accustomed to manual labour; agricultural labourers; shepherds; herdsmen; blacksmiths; wheelwrights; masons; carpenters; female domestic and farm servants.

(2.) The emigrants must be in good health, and under forty-five years of age,—but for every child above eighteen years of age, an excess of one year will be allowed in the age of the parents. Single men and women, under eighteen years of age, are not eligible (except in special cases) unless they are emigrating under the care of their parents, or with their parents' consent, under care of some near married relative.

(3.) Families, containing more than four children under fourteen years of age, are not eligible.

(4.) Persons in the habitual receipt of parish relief cannot be approved.

(5.) No allowance will be paid on an approved married emigrant who proceeds to the colony without his wife and all his children under eighteen, until his wife and children have joined him in the colony, which fact must be authenticated by the local government.

(6.) No emigrant will be approved, unless satisfactory certificates of good character, and of efficiency in his or her professed trade or calling, can, when required, be produced.

(7.) Applications for approval must be made in the form issued by the Commissioners.

(8.) Each person above fourteen must fill up a separate form.

(9.) Should it be found that any of the signatures attached to the form are not genuine, or that any other deception is attempted, the application will be at once rejected.

(10.) One hundred statute adults will be approved for every deposit of £1,000; and no more certificates ean be signed and issued by the Commissioners than in that proportion.

5. Approved emigrants must be inspected by the emigration officer at *the port of embarkation*, and no subsequent inspection will dispense with the necessity of observing this rule.

6. The regulations under which this emigration is carried on, provide for the settlement of the emigrants on land. Means, therefore, should be taken to secure them proper food and accommodation on their own land, as well as at Port Natal.

7. Any failure in the due observance of the above rules, will be considered by the Commissioners a sufficient reason for withholding from the depositor the whole or any part of the allowance referred to in Art. 4.

By order of the Board,
S. WALCOTT, Secretary.

Colonial Land and Emigration Office,
9, Park Street, Westminster,
22nd January, 1850.

NOTICE TO PARTIES DESIROUS OF EMIGRATING TO THE CAPE OF GOOD HOPE AND NATAL.

The present Paper, showing the Terms on which the Public Lands are sold at the Cape of Good Hope and Natal, and on which labourers are selected for passages thither when there are funds applicable to Emigration, is published by direction of Her Majesty's Colonial Land and Emigration Commissioners.

By order of the Board,
S. WALCOTT,
Secretary.

9, *Park Street, Westminster,*
February, 1849.

I.—REGULATIONS RESPECTING THE SALE OF LAND.

1. The unappropriated crown lands are sold in freeholds, and by public auction only.

2. Unless it be otherwise notified, the upset price will be at the Cape two shillings (2*s.*) per acre, (one acre is about half a morgen,) and at Natal four shillings (4*s.*) per acre; but the Governor for the time being will have the power to fix such higher upset price as the locality or other circumstances may render expedient, of which due notice will always be publicly given.

3. Persons desirous of becoming purchasers will apply in writing to the Secretary to the Colonial Government respecting the land they wish to have put up for sale; stating in what division it is situated, and, as far as practicable, its position, boundaries, and probable extent.

These applications, after being recorded in the Colonial Office, will be transmitted to the Surveyor General, who, if he see no objection to the land being disposed of, will call upon the applicant to deposit with him the probable expense of the survey; which expense will be calculated upon the following tariff, and be borne by the eventual purchaser.

	£.	s.	d.
For a piece of ground, and dividing the same into small lots, or erven, for the first four lots, each . . .	0	12	0
For any beyond that number . .	0	9	0
For the measurement of any piece of land up to 10 morgen . . .	0	12	0
For every morgen above 10 up to 100, per morgen	0	0	3
For 100 morgen	1	14	6
For every morgen above 100, as far as 500, per morgen	0	0	1½
For 500 morgen	4	4	6
For every morgen above 500, per morgen	0	0	1
For 3,000 morgen . . .	14	12	10
For every morgen above the same .	0	0	1
For every diagram	0	12	0

4. Should the applicant not become the purchaser, the amount deposited by him will be refunded when paid by the eventual purchaser; but should no sale take place, no refund can be made.

5. Lands offered for sale will be advertised for two months in the *Government Gazette*, at the expiration of which time they will be sold by public auction.

6. Ten per cent. of the purchase money must be paid at the time of sale, and the balance, (with the expenses of the survey, if the purchaser did not make the deposit,) within one calendar month from the day of sale; in default of which, the ten per cent. so paid will be forfeited to the Colonial Treasury.

7. Persons will be at liberty to make payments for colonial lands in this country, for which payment or deposit they will receive an order for credit to the same amount in any purchase of land they may effect in the colony, and will have the privilege of naming a proportionate number of emigrants for a free passage, as explained in the next article. The deposits must be made in one or more sums of £100 each, at the Bank of England, to the account of the Colonial Land and Emigration Commissioners; and the depositor must state at the time the district in which the land is to be selected, and give notice to the Commissioners of the deposit. Upon production of the Bank's receipt for the money, the Commissioners will furnish the depositor with a certificate, stating the amount which he has paid, and entitling him to obtain credit for that sum in any purchase which he may effect in the colony, subject to all rules and regulations in force in the colony at the time such purchase may be made.

8. For every sum of £100 deposited as above, the depositor will be entitled, for six months from the date of payment, to name a number of properly qualified emigrants, equal to seven adults, for a free passage. Two children, between one and fourteen, are to be reckoned as equal to one adult. The emigrants are required to be chosen from the class named in the subjoined regulations on emigration, and must be going out with the intention to work for wages. They are to be subject to the approval of the Commissioners, and must in all respects fall within those regulations.

II.—REGULATIONS ON THE SELECTION OF EMIGRANTS.

The following are the regulations and conditions under which parties are selected for passages when there are funds available for the purpose. There are not at present any funds applicable to emigration to Natal.

TRADE OR CALLING.

1. The emigrants to the Cape must be chiefly agricultural labourers, shepherds, herdsmen, and female domestic, and farm servants. A *few* country blacksmiths, wheelwrights, masons, bricklayers, and carpenters, and some other handicraftsmen, will occasionally be taken.

2. All the adults must be capable of labour, and going out with the intention to work for wages. Persons intending to buy land in the colony, or to invest capital in trade there, or reduced tradesmen, or persons resident in a workhouse, or in the habitual receipt of parish relief, are not eligible for a passage.

3. Emigrants who, when there are funds available, would be eligible for a passage to Natal, are agricultural labourers, mechanics, skilled labourers, and small farmers, accustomed to some manual labour, and intending to work for their subsistence.

DESCRIPTION OF FAMILY AND AGE.

4. The emigrants must consist principally of married couples, not above forty years of age. The candidates most acceptable are young married couples without children.

5. The separation of parents from children under sixteen will in no case be allowed. Single women under eighteen are not eligible unless they are emigrating with their parents, or under the immediate care of some near married relatives.

6. No emigrants, whether adults or children, can be accepted unless they have been vaccinated, or have had the small pox.

CHARACTER.

7. No applicant will be accepted without decisive certificates of good character, and of efficiency in his professed trade or calling.

FORM OF APPLICATION.

8. Applications must be made in a Form to be obtained at the office of the Commissioners, which must be duly filled up and attested, as explained in the Form itself, and then forwarded to the office, with certificates of birth and marriage of all the applicants. It must, however, be distinctly understood, that the filling up of the Form confers no claim to a passage, and that the Commissioners do not pledge themselves to accept any candidates unless they are deemed desirable for the colony.

9. Should it be found that any of the signatures attached to the certificates are not genuine, or that any other deception is attempted, the application will be rejected; or should any emigrant, on personal examination at the port of embarkation, be discovered to have made any mis-statement whatever with regard to age, calling, health, &c., such person will not be allowed to proceed in the ship.

SUBSEQUENT PROCEEDINGS.

10. The Commissioners do not pledge themselves to accept applicants although they may come within the regulations, if they are not also deemed desirable for the colony. If approved of, the emigrants will be so informed, and will receive a passage as soon as the arrangements of the Commissioners will admit.

11. Until called on by the Secretary to pay the deposit mentioned in Art. 14, applicants must on no account withdraw from employment, or make any preparation for departure. Those who fail to attend to this warning will do so at their own risk, and will have no claim whatever on the Commissioners. Due notice will be given of the ship, and of the time and place for joining her.

12. The expense of reaching the port of embarkation must be paid by the emigrants. If, after the arrival, they are found not to be in a fit state of health to embark, or to have any mental or bodily defect likely to impair their usefulness as labourers, they will be refused admission on board the ship, or, if embarked, will be landed again, without having any claim on the Commissioners.

13. Before an embarkation order is issued, the following payments, in addition to the deposits mentioned in the next article, will be required from persons receiving assistance to emigrate to the Cape.

From adults, *i. e.*, persons above fourteen years of age—

	Between the Ages of		
	14 & 40	40 & 50	50 & upwards
From Agricultural Labourers, Shepherds, Herdsmen, and Female Domestic Servants	Nil	£4	£9
From Blacksmiths, Bricklayers, Carpenters, Masons, Coopers, Wheelwrights, Millwrights, and Bakers........	£3	£6	£9
From all other Persons of the Labouring Classes..........	£5	£7	£9

For children, *i.e.*, persons under fourteen years of age—

Two children of persons assisted to emigrate on the above terms will be conveyed free. £5 will be required for each child in excess of this number.

14. In addition to the sum payable under the preceding Article, a deposit of £1 must be paid for every person above fourteen, and 10*s.* for every child above one and under fourteen years of age, which will be retained to meet the expense of bedding and mess utensils supplied by the Commissioners, and as some security that the people will come forward to embark.

15. If any emigrants fail to attend at the appointed time and place for embarkation, they will never again be allowed a free passage, and will forfeit the deposit they may have paid, unless they give to the Commissioners timely notice and a satisfactory explanation of their inability to proceed.

16. Provisions, medical attendance, and cooking utensils, will be provided by the Commissioners; also new mattresses, bolsters, blankets, and counterpanes, canvas bags to contain linen, &c., knives and forks, spoons, metal plates, and drinking mugs, which articles may be kept by the emigrants after arrival in the colony, provided they behave well on the voyage.

17. The emigrants must bring their own clothing, which will be inspected at the port by an officer of the Commissioners; and all parties are particularly desired to observe, that they will not be allowed to embark unless they provide themselves with a sufficient supply for their health during the voyage. The lowest quantity that can be admitted for each person is as follows:—

FOR MALES.	FOR FEMALES.
Four shirts,	Six shifts,
Four pairs stockings,	One flannel petticoat,
Two ditto shoes,	Four pairs stockings,
Two complete suits of exterior clothing.	Two ditto shoes,
	Two gowns.

They must also bring their own sheets and towels, and a supply of soap. As a general rule, it may be stated, that the more abundant the stock of clothing, the better for health and comfort during the passage. The usual length of the voyage to the Cape of Good Hope is about seventy days.

18. It is desirable that emigrants should take out with them the necessary tools of their trades; bulky agricultural implements, however, cannot be admitted on account of their inconvenient size and weight; neither can furniture be received on board; mattresses and feather beds are especially prohibited.

19. The whole quantity of baggage for each adult emigrant must not measure more than twenty cubic or solid feet, nor exceed half a ton weight. It must be divided into two or three boxes, the contents of which must be closely packed, so as to save space in the ship. Large packages and extra baggage will not be taken unless paid for, and then only in case there be room in the ship.

20. Each family will be allowed to take only its own luggage. Any violation of this rule will subject the party to a forfeiture of his passage.

21. On arrival in the colony, the emigrants will be at perfect liberty to engage themselves to any one willing to employ them, and to make their own bargain for wages. No repayment in service or otherwise is required from them for the passage out. The only return expected is, a strict observance on board of the Regulations framed with a view to their health and comfort during the voyage, and general good conduct and industrious habits in the colony.

22. Letters and applications should be marked outside, "Cape Emigration," or "Natal Emigration," and addressed, post paid, to "Stephen Walcott, Esquire, Secretary to the Board of Emigration, 9, Park Street, Westminster."

V.—EMPLOYMENT—Of able-bodied men at wages on workhouse land.

15*th Feb.*, 1850.

——— *Union.*—The Poor Law Board having lately had their attention directed to the system pursued by the guardians of the —— Union, in regard to the administration of relief to able-bodied men out of employment, wrote to the guardians as follows:—It appears that the guardians have had, for some years, adjoining the workhouse, ten acres of land, on which they have been in the habit of employing, at wages somewhat below the ordinary wages of the district, men of good character, with families, when out of employment; that early in the present winter the farmers of the neighbourhood discharged a great portion of their labourers, which caused so great a pressure upon the rates, that the guardians resolved to employ such applicants as were not received into the workhouse at a corn-mill. The Board understand that four hundred and thirty-five men have been so employed, and that the amount paid to them from the poor-rates was £121. 16*s*., being an average payment of 5*s*. 6¾*d*. to each man. The Board do not find that the cases of the men so employed have been reported for their sanction under Article 6 of the General Prohibitory Order, and they desire to point out to the guardians that, unless the cases of the men came within the Exceptions to Article 1 of the Order in question, the relief which has been afforded, contrary to the Provisions of that Order, will be subject to be disallowed by the auditor, as being an unlawful charge upon the poor-rates. The Board think that the money given to the men in question cannot be considered otherwise than as relief, though it may have been given nominally as wages, for it is no part of the functions of the guardians to find work at remunerative wages for the unemployed. Their duty is simply to relieve the destitute, and, in order to prevent the ratepayers being imposed upon by the idle and improvident, to exact, in return for relief to the able-bodied, a task of work sufficient to operate as a test of their actual destitution. There is an essential distinction between relief and wages, and between work done in return for relief, and work done in return for wages. Wages are practically regulated by the market value of the labour, not by the necessities of the labourer, while relief to the pauper should always be given in proportion to his necessities, not to the quantity or value of his work; and the task of work, therefore, imposed upon him, to test his destitution, should be proportioned to his ability to perform it, not to his necessities. Such are the principles to be borne in mind in granting relief to able-bodied men in return for work, in those unions in which the Labour Test Order is in force; and although carrying them out to the full extent, in some instances, may be found difficult, the Board could not, consistently with their duty, sanction such a wide departure from sound principles as appears to have taken place in the —— Union.

VI.—JUSTICES' CLERKS' FEES.

26th March, 1850.

John Shaw, Esq., Clerk to Justices, Tamworth.—Inquired whether he is not entitled, as clerk to the justices of the Coleshill division of the county of Warwick, to certain fees. By the 6 & 7 Wm. 4, c. 96, sec. 6, the justices of every petty sessions division are four times a year to hold a special sessions for hearing appeals against the rates of the parishes in the division, and they are to cause public notice to be given of such special sessions. That this duty is to be performed appears to be clear. The clerks to the justices have therefore, four times in the year, to obtain an appointment of a special session, and to cause the notices thereof to be affixed on the church door of each parish. Now, it must be apparent that this duty cannot be performed by the clerk without considerable trouble and expense; he apprehends that it will not be contended that the magistrates must themselves take this trouble and bear the expense. It must therefore follow that it is the duty of the clerk, and it appears to him but reasonable that he should receive some fee for his trouble. In discussing the magistrates' clerks right to fees for this duty, under this Act of Parliament, it may be argued, that as the Act omits to direct that any fee shall be payable, he is not therefore entitled to one, and particularly when the Act imposes no penalty for the omission of the duty. He submits, however, that this argument is not a sound one, as a great many Acts of Parliament, directing proceedings before magistrates, for which the clerk is clearly entitled to and receives the usual fees, do not expressly enact that the clerk shall be entitled to any fee at all. He therefore considers that the question must be decided by the Act of Parliament applicable to magistrates' clerks' fees in general. The 26th Geo. 2, c. 14, is the Act to which he refers. By that Act, justices in quarter sessions are to make a table of fees to be taken by clerks to justices, and such table, when ratified by the judges, is to be valid, and clerks to justices are not to demand or receive any other fee or gratuity than what is so allowed under a penalty of twenty pounds. The revised table of fees for this county was made at the Epiphany sessions, 1848, settled at Easter sessions, 1848, and approved by Lord Denman and Mr. Justice Patteson at the assizes held for the county on the 4th of August of the same year. Under the head of "poor-rates," he finds the following, amongst other fees, allowed to be taken:—"For every notice of special sessions for appeals against poor-rates, to be paid by the overseers of each parish, 2*s*." He therefore contends, that under the 26th Geo. 2, c. 14, and this table of fees, the magistrates' clerk is entitled to this fee of 2*s*. for every notice of special sessions for appeal against poor-rates, and that the same is payable by the overseers of each parish. Mr. Simkiss, the auditor, considering, he supposes, that this fee is not legally payable, disallows it in the overseers' accounts. The overseers feel themselves aggrieved, as, although he has a remedy against them to compel payment of this fee, they have no means of charging the amount in their accounts, unless they appeal against the surcharge of the auditor. Some time ago he wrote to Mr. Simkiss on the matter, and drew his attention to the Acts of Parliament mentioned, and the table of fees, but he is unable to state the grounds on which the auditor arrives at the conclusion he does. Several overseers brought the matter before the magistrates (the Earl of Aylesford and William Charles Alston, Esquire) on Wednesday last, and they expressed their opinion that he was entitled to the fees claimed by him. If the Poor Law Board be of opinion that these fees are payable, the auditor, probably, will not in future disallow them in the overseers' accounts. The difficulty will then be got over. If the Poor Law Board be of a contrary opinion, they will consider that the magistrates' clerks must be left to take the course they may think proper.

Ans.—The opinion entertained by the Poor Law Commissioners on the point was published in the "Official Circular" for January, 1848, (No. 11, N.S., p. 165,) of which a copy is enclosed herewith for your information. The Poor Law Board desire to state that, having had occasion to consider the question themselves, they concur in the view expressed in the "Official Circular" above-mentioned, and they think it right to add, that in the case of Wray *v.* Chapman (reported in the "Law Times" of 16th Feb. last), Mr. Justice Coleridge appears to intimate a similar opinion to that of the Poor Law Commissioners, as to the power of the justices at the quarter sessions to render persons liable to the payment of fees by their directions in the table of fees.

VII.—LUNATIC PAUPERS.

1. COST OF MAINTENANCE IN ASYLUM, AND COST OF OBTAINING ORDERS.

1st Sept., 1849.

R. Tucker, Esq., District Auditor.—Calling attention to the 12 & 13 Vic. c. 103, sec. 5, and inquiring whether the relief granted to a lunatic pauper by his maintenance in the asylum since Lady-day, is chargeable to the common fund, or merely the costs of "obtaining an order" for the removal and maintenance of the lunatic. The latter costs are so trifling, as not to be worthy of an enactment charging them on the common fund.

Ans.—Some doubt existed whether the removal of a pauper lunatic to an asylum did not in itself operate as an interruption of his residence within the meaning of the 9 & 10 Vic. c. 66. What might have been the decision of the Court of Queen's Bench upon this point is not clear, (see the observations of Erle J. in Queen *v.* Leaden Roothing, 13 Jur. 534.) But in the new statute 12 & 13 Vic. c. 103, sec. 4, it is declared that such a removal shall not operate as an interruption of the residence in the parish in which the pauper had his abode. A pauper, therefore, who had acquired an irremovability by residence, will not end it by being sent to a lunatic asylum. The 11 & 12 Vic. c. 110, sec. 3, renders all the cost of the relief of an irremovable pauper a charge on the common fund; and, consequently, the cost of the maintenance of a pauper lunatic, although in an asylum, if he possesses the exemption from removal otherwise conferred upon him by the Poor Removal Act, appears to be properly a charge on this fund according to this enactment. It is probable the legislature intended to remove any doubt upon this subject by the 5th sec. of the new Act. The marginal note states generally that the costs of lunatic poor, being irremovable, are to be borne by the common fund. And though the language of the section itself is not free from ambiguity, the words are certainly capable of that construction. If, however, the clause is to be construed as confined in its operation to the costs of obtaining the order, that would appear to show the understanding of the legislature to have been, that the actual maintenance of the lunatic pauper was already provided for in the same manner, as there could be no adequate ground for making the common fund liable for the mere costs of the orders, if it was not liable to the substantial and heavy expense; namely, that of the maintenance of the pauper. The Board consider, therefore, that the costs of the maintenance and relief of lunatic paupers, who, by virtue of the operation of the 9 & 10 Vic. c. 66, had become irremovable, (except to a lunatic asylum, under the Lunatic Asylum Statute,) as well as all the costs and expenses attending the order, are to be borne by the common fund of the union.

---

2. ORDER OF MAINTENANCE OF LUNATIC PAUPERS.

18*th Oct.*, 1849.

Messrs. Hill and Williams, Clerks to Magistrates, Hallowtrow, Somerset.—They had applied to two justices under 8 & 9 Vic. c. 126, sec. 58, for an order adjudicating the settlement of a pauper lunatic confined in the county asylum, and also for an order of maintenance, under sec. 62 of the same Act. The lunatic had resided for eighteen years in the parish which sent him to the asylum, and would therefore have been irremovable to the parish of his settlement if not a lunatic. The parish sending him to the asylum and the parish of his settlement, are both in the same union. The magistrates made the order adjudicating the settlement, but they considered that they had no authority to make the order for maintenance (for there were two orders prepared) in consequence of the ambiguous language of 12 & 13 Vic. c. 103, secs. 4 & 5, and the observations in "The Justice of the Peace" upon those sections, in the No. for 25th August last, which particularly point out the difference in the wording of those sections in the Bill and in the Act as passed. Referred also to a contrary opinion in the same journal for 2nd June last, and to the case of Reg. *v.* Inhabitants of Leaden Roothing in the No. for 12th May last, and inquired whether the justices are now disabled from making an order of maintenance for a lunatic pauper who has resided more than five years in the parish sending him to the asylum, and become thereby irremovable therefrom, as well as for one who had not become irremovable. The lunatic pauper in question was sent to the County Lunatic Asylum on the 14th March last. It is presumed that in any event the maintenance for the eleven days preceding 25th March last, must be paid by the parish of which the lunatic is adjudged to be a settled inhabitant, and the costs of sending him to the asylum by the parish sending him.

Ans.—The Board have no doubt that an order can be made by the justices upon the parish of the settlement under the 8 & 9 Vic. c. 126, sec. 58, to adjudicate the fact of the settlement. They think also that an order may be made under sec. 62 for the costs incurred in the examination, removal, and conveyance of the lunatic to the asylum, and the costs of the maintenance up to the 25th March last. With regard to the subsequent period, the question turns upon the proper construction of the provision contained in 5th sec. of the late statute 12 & 13 Vic. c. 103, as to whether or not it renders the union fund chargeable with the costs of the maintenance of lunatic paupers, who were irremovable except under an order in lunacy, as well as the costs of the order therein referred to. The Board observe, that the 11 & 12 Vic. c. 110, sec. 3, renders all the cost of the relief of irremovable poor a charge to the common fund, and consequently the cost of the maintenance of a pauper lunatic, though in an asylum, if he possesses the exemption from removal otherwise conferred upon him by the Poor Removal Act, appears to be properly a charge on that fund according to this enactment, such maintenance being the species of relief suited to the circumstances of such a pauper. It is probable the legislature intended to remove any doubt upon this subject by sec. 5 of the 12 & 13 Vic. c. 103. The marginal note states generally that the costs of lunatic poor, being irremovable, are to be borne by the common fund, and though the language of the section itself is not free from ambiguity, the words are certainly capable of that construction. If, however, the clause is to be construed as confined in its operation to the costs of obtaining the order, such construction appears to show the understanding of the legislature to have been, that the actual maintenance of the lunatic pauper was already provided for in the same manner, as there could be no adequate ground for making the common fund liable for the mere costs of the orders, if it was not liable to the more substantial and heavy expense of the maintenance of the pauper. The Board consider, therefore, that all costs incurred since the 25th March last, in and about the maintenance and relief of lunatic paupers, who by virtue of the operation of the 9 & 10 Vic. c. 66, had become irremovable from the parish of the residence, (except to a lunatic asylum under the statute especially relating thereto,) or in and about the obtaining of the order itself, are to be borne by the common fund of the union. Assuming this to be the correct view of the law, the Board apprehend that no order could be legally made for those costs upon the parish of the settlement under the 62nd sec. of the statute above referred to, inasmuch as the common fund is liable and not the parish. Moreover, no reason can exist why the parish from which the pauper was sent to the asylum should obtain an order of maintenance as the charge is to be borne by the union. The Board have made these remarks upon your communication, but must observe, that the question is one which the justices must decide for themselves.

3. LUNATIC PAUPER POSSESSED OF PROPERTY.

12*th Dec.*, 1849.

W. B., Esq.—H. C., who resides in the parish of C. on his freehold, consisting of a cottage and eight acres and a half of land, and who had also a freehold at ——— in the county of ———, consisting of three dwelling-houses, value of about £14 per annum, about twelve months since became insane. He has two sons and one daughter by a woman not his wife: the youngest son received the produce of his property. It appeared to the magistrates that the sons ill-treated the man, which induced them to make an order for his removal to the ——— County Asylum; and on the 22nd of January last, they made an order of £7. 4*s.* 9*d.*, on the overseers of the parish of C., expenses incurred in the removal. The man remained in the asylum till within the last month, when he returned home to his farm, being pronounced to be sane, but a cripple. The expenses, £14. 1*s.* 2*d.*, at the asylum, also are charged to this parish, making with the £7. 4*s.* 9*d.*, £21. 5*s.* 11*d.* The ratepayers consider it hard that they should be called upon to pay this sum. It is believed H. C. cannot pay the amount, or any part of it, without a sale of some of his property, or a mortgage. Requesting the advice of the Poor Law Board on the case.

Ans.—The 7 & 8 Vic. c. 101, sec. 27, would have enabled the justices to make an order to empower the overseers of the parish to which the lunatic pauper was chargeable, to take the rents of the property, or his goods, while he remained insane, and chargeable; but the provisions of that statute appear to be no longer applicable to the case. The 8 & 9 Vic. c. 126, sec. 49, would also have authorized the making an order to a like effect, but that could only be made while the lunatic was in confinement. The Board apprehend that there is no remedy for the parish in the present state of the case.

VIII.—MEDICAL RELIEF.

1. DUTIES OF GUARDIANS AND RELIEVING OFFICERS IN REGARD TO.

22*nd March*, 1850.

Mr. ———, *District Auditor.*—Stated with reference to ——— Union:—"The relief ordered by the medical officers in case of illness is extra diet, and such other necessaries as are usually recommended by medical officers in other unions. My complaint in this union is not as to the amount, or that anything improper is given, but that the medical officers 'order,' not 'recommend,' the extra relief; and that the relieving officer is directed by the board to obey such order without its propriety being questioned or reported."

Clerk of ——— *Union.*—Transmitting the following extract from the minutes of the guardians in reference to the auditor's communication, a copy of which had been forwarded to them, and also a leaf out of the medical officer's certificate book, in the last column of which the word "ordered" is introduced:—"We have never discussed the subject of the medical officer's giving orders, but finding the word ordered in the certificate books, we took it for granted the medical officers had power to give orders. We should also feel obliged, if the Poor Law Board will apprize us whether the relieving officer can refuse to accede to the medical officer's orders in any case; or whether he must bring them under the consideration of the board of guardians, and if they have power to order them not to be complied with."

Ans.—The word "ordered," inserted in the last column of the medical officer's certificate, is not to be taken as absolutely imperative, either upon the relieving officer or the guardians, but is to be regarded as a recommendation, expressive of the medical officer's sense of what is required; and the certificate is accordingly to be attended to in such a way and to such an extent as the relieving officer or the guardians, on their own responsibility, and on their knowledge of the circumstances of the individual in favour of whom the certificate is given, may deem to be actually necessary. If the word "ordered" in the certificate were to be taken in any other sense than that now pointed out, it would have the effect of constituting the medical officer the absolute judge, not only of the kind of relief to be afforded, but also of the capacity of the patient to provide it out of his own resources, without leaving even this latter question to the guardians, in whom the discretion of giving or withholding relief of every kind is vested by law. Of course it becomes them, in the exercise of this discretion, to be very guarded, and to caution the relieving officer also to be on his guard if any case should occur in which, acting on a sense of duty, they may deem it right to disregard either wholly or in part the medical officer's certificate, as this would involve a serious responsibility, and could only be justified by a knowledge that the circumstances of the individual were really such as to make the particular relief certified as being necessary by the medical officer, improper to be given at the cost of the union. The foregoing observations will, the Board believe, afford a sufficient answer to the question as to the legal powers of the guardians and the relieving officer in the case referred to; and with respect to the last question, the Board consider that if in any instance the relieving officer should, from his knowledge of the circumstances of the parties, deem it to be his duty not to carry the directions of the medical officer into full effect, he ought with the least possible delay to report the same to the board of guardians, together with his reasons for so acting, in order that they may decide whether he has exercised a sound discretion in the matter, and give directions accordingly.

---

2. PAYMENT OF FEES TO MEDICAL OFFICER FOR ATTENDANCE ON ORDER OF OVERSEER.

15th Feb., 1848.

Clerk of ——— *Union.* — Requesting the opinion of the Board upon the best mode of dealing with the following cases, namely:—A pauper (or some of his family) meets with an accident, or his wife is in childbirth, an application is made to the overseer of the poor (in the absence of the relieving officer) who gives an order to one of the medical officers to attend the case on behalf of the union. The medical officer then sends his bill accompanied with the order to the board of guardians for payment according to the scale allowed for each particular case. Should the application for payment be made through the relieving officer, and paid by him through the board, or by the parish officers and charged in their accounts? If through the Board, what investigation are the guardians called upon to make; and what power have they of refusing to pay the medical officer's bill? If they should disallow any bill, can the medical officers proceed against the overseer upon his order, and what remedy has the overseer to recover the repayment?

Ans.—With reference to the cases in question, the Board observe, that according to the conditions of the contract, the medical officer is duly to attend all poor persons requiring medical or surgical relief, whom he shall be called upon to attend, by due requisition according to the rules, &c., of the Poor Law Commissioners, or other provisions of the laws for the relief of the poor; and (the contract proceeds) shall and will provide or cause to be provided for the same, proper medicines and medical attendance; and shall assist and take care of all such poor women in cases of midwifery as he may be required to attend by any legally authorized person. Now it is to be borne in mind that an overseer can only order relief in cases of sudden and urgent necessity; and where, in the proper exercise of the duties of his office, he does in any such case give an order for medical relief, the medical officer is bound to attend the pauper in whose favour it is given. If the case is one of midwifery, then the medical officer would be entitled to the proper fee. It is, however, incumbent upon the parties interested in claiming the remuneration, to show that the case was one in which the overseer had authority to order relief. If the overseer had no authority so to interfere, it would not come within the terms of the contract, though the medical officer might perhaps have a personal remedy against the overseer who gave him the order. The overseer would not, however, be authorized in charging in his accounts the cost of any proceedings taken by the medical officer to enforce his personal claim. As to the question of payment, it appears to the Board, that in ordinary cases there will be no difficulty. In cases of midwifery, and when operations are performed, the guardians are required to pay the prescribed fees to the medical officers. These payments should be charged direct to the parish to which the pauper is legally chargeable at the time, and without the intervention of the relieving officer; although the guardians might perhaps empower him to pay the fee and enter the amount in his account, whenever he is required to take the case into his own charge in regard to subsequent relief. In the opinion of the Board, there can be, generally, but little difficulty in ascertaining whether the circumstances connected with the case of any applicant for relief are those of sudden and urgent necessity, and it is for the guardians to ascertain these circumstances from the relieving officer, the overseer, the medical officer, or other person. If there be any doubt, the medical officer, who is one of the contracting parties, is bound to clear it up, so as to show that he is entitled to the fee claimed in each case. The overseers, also, have an interest in doing so, because, having given an order, they are apparently liable to the medical officer, if he cannot recover the fee under the contract,

---

IX.—PAUPERS.—EFFECTS OF DECEASED PAUPERS.

15*th Jan.*, 1850.

Clerk of Dolgelley Union.—A pauper, named Elizabeth P., died at Dolgelley about a fortnight back: a few weeks before she died, she, with a portion of her furniture, was removed from her own house by her son R. P. to his house. Her furniture consisted of a dresser, a feather bed and pillows, and sundry small articles. She had no money, nor any valuable security for money. Her son, R. P., (a poor man,) provided the coffin and shroud, which cost about £1. 15*s.*, and he claims all the furniture as his own property; there was no rent due by the pauper. The pauper received from 3*s.* to 3*s.* 6*d.* per week relief during the last twelve months, and during the last fortnight before her death her son, R. P., was paid 4*s.* per week relief for her maintenance. Inquiring, 1. Whether R. P. is legally entitled to possess himself of the pauper's furniture. 2. If not, whether the guardians should authorize an officer of the union to seize, and sell the furniture towards reimbursing the guardians the cost of relief advanced. 3. Whether in case of the decease of an irremovable pauper, an officer of the union must wait until the first subsequent meeting of the guardians for a special authority, or whether a general authority from the guardians, applying to all such cases, to seize and sell the property of such paupers, will answer the same purpose. 4. Whether the property of such paupers when seized, is to be sold by the union officer by what is termed Dutch auction, or whether he must employ an appraiser and auctioneer to do so.

Ans.—1. The Board cannot express any opinion as to the legal right of R. P. to retain the goods of his deceased mother. But as he was at the expense of burying her, he was justified in retaining out of her property enough to reimburse him the expense which he incurred therein. 2. The Board cannot advise the guardians in this case to authorize their officer to seize the effects to which your letter alludes. The guardians may proceed in the county court to recover the property over and above what is required to satisfy the previous demand, in respect of the funeral expenses; but they must be prepared with evidence to establish that the property was really the property of the pauper at her death. And the Board think it very probable, that in this respect the guardians would fail. 3. The Board do not think that the guardians can give any general power of the nature referred to in your third inquiry. The guardians must exercise their judgment upon each case as it arises; for it is a matter entirely within their discretion, whether they will take steps to appropriate the property, or not. 4. The Board cannot say that it is absolutely necessary for the guardians to have the property appraised by a licensed appraiser. But generally such a course should be adopted. In conclusion, the Board think it right to observe, that the power given by the 16th sec. of the 12th & 13th Vic. c. 103, requires the gravest caution in its exercise by the guardians, especially in cases where the pauper was not an inmate of the union workhouse.

X.—POOR-RATES.—SUMMONS ON COMPLAINT OF COLLECTOR.

28*th Nov.*, 1849.

Collector, Redditch and Webheath, Bromsgrove Union.—Inquiring whether his demand for the rates is sufficient, and if he has the power of summoning defaulters vested in him, as he finds a great difficulty in collecting the rates, many of the rate-payers refusing to pay until a demand has been made by the overseers or their assistant.

Ans.—The Board consider that it is quite competent for you to demand the payment of any poor-rates legally due, and that the non-payment of such rate on being demanded by you would subject the parties to be summoned; but they doubt whether the 12 & 13 Vic. c. 14, empowers any one but the overseers of the parish to lay the complaint upon which the summons is to issue.

London: Printed by Order of the Poor Law Board, by BLACKBURN & BURT, 90½, Holborn Hill, and Published by CHARLES KNIGHT, 90, Fleet Street.

AN

OFFICIAL CIRCULAR

OF PUBLIC DOCUMENTS AND INFORMATION:

DIRECTED BY THE POOR LAW BOARD TO BE PRINTED, CHIEFLY FOR THE USE OF THE BOARDS OF GUARDIANS AND THEIR OFFICERS.

No. 36.] APRIL, 1850. [N.S.

CONTENTS.

I.—CHAPLAIN.—AN EX-OFFICIO GUARDIAN APPOINTED TO THE OFFICE MUST CEASE TO ACT AS GUARDIAN.

1st. Feb., 1850.

Clerk of Guisborough Union.—The guardians of this union to-day took into consideration the appointment of a chaplain, the office being vacant, when the Rev. Henry Clark, (who is the incumbent of Guisborough,) was duly proposed and seconded as a fit person to hold the appointment at a salary of —— per annum, upon which one of the guardians took an objection to his eligibility on the ground, that he, being a magistrate acting for the North Riding of the county of York, resident within the union, and a guardian of the union *ex-officio*, was not in a position to accept the appointment with a salary. The board, however, determined to proceed with the election, and leave the point in question (the facts of which were admitted) to be decided by the Poor Law Board.

Ans.—It appears to the Board, that the Rev. Henry Clark being an *ex-officio* guardian, and not an elected one, may, if he think fit, decline to act in that capacity (4 & 5 Wm. 4, c. 76, sec. 38;) and that if he do so decline, and wholly abstain, during his chaplaincy, from acting as a guardian of the Guisborough Union, he may legally accept and hold the office of chaplain to the union workhouse. It is true that the 5 & 6 Vic. c. 57, sec. 14, disqualifies him for serving as a guardian, while he holds the office of chaplain; but he may voluntarily abstain from serving as a guardian, and if he do, there appears to the Board to be no legal objection to his filling the chaplaincy. He must remember, however, that if he accept the office of chaplain, he ceases *ipso facto* to be capable of acting in any way as a guardian of the union, so long as he continue to be chaplain.

II.—CHARGEABILITY.

1. FOUNDLINGS OR WAYFARERS.

25*th Jan.*, 1850.

Clerk of Thirsk Union.—The assistant relieving officer supplied a man, who appeared to be a travelling wayfarer, and his two children, both of whom were under seven years of age, with lodging and food for one night in Thirsk. On the following morning the father, being suspected of having stolen a pair of shoes, was pursued by the police officer, and was apprehended beyond the limits of the union, with the shoes in his possession. He was brought back to Thirsk, and committed by the magistrate (who resides in a third township) from his house to the House of Correction at Northallerton, and was taken thence, with the children, who had accompanied him, to the House of Correction. The jailer refused to receive the children, and they were brought back by the police officer to Thirsk, where they remain in the union workhouse. Inquiring whether the cost of the children's maintenance should be charged to any, and what township in the union, or to the common fund.

Ans.—The Board are of opinion that the children must be treated either as destitute foundlings, within the 11 & 12 Vic. c. 110, sec. 1, and the 12 & 13 Vic. c. 103, sec. 2, or as destitute wayfarers, within the former enactment. In either case their relief will be chargeable to the common fund of the union.

---

2. CHARGEABILITY OF DESTITUTE WANDERERS.

9*th April*, 1850.

Clerk of Whitechapel Union.—1. On the 18th of January, 1849, William Shoulds, aged twenty-six, a destitute, able-bodied, single man, was admitted into the workhouse of the Whitechapel Union, and discharged on the 24th of the same month, and has several times since been re-admitted and discharged at short intervals, up to January, 1850. On the night before his first admission, and for some weeks immediately previous thereto, the pauper had been sleeping at a nightly lodging-house in the parish of Christchurch, within the same union, paying for his lodging, except Sundays, nightly, as is the usual custom in such houses: and in consideration of such nightly payments for the six working days of the week, he was entitled to the privilege of sleeping at such lodging-house on the Sunday night free of expense, this being the usual practice. These payments also entitled the pauper to the use of a common sitting-room, or kitchen, and the fire and cooking apparatus therein, in common with the other lodgers, for the purpose of sitting therein from the time of entering such lodging-house till he went to bed, and cooking his nightly meals. On each occasion of his discharge from the workhouse, and till his re-admission, he slept at one of such nightly lodging-houses, in the same parish of Christ Church, always paying his lodging as before stated, and from the time of his discharge, on the 26th September, 1849, till his last re-admission on the 16th October, 1849, a period of nineteen days, had been constantly sleeping at a lodging-house in Keate Street, in the said parish, paying his lodging nightly for the six working nights, and sleeping there on Sunday nights without payment, according to the practice before stated. The pauper is by trade a weaver, but has not followed that employment since his chargeability, and claims to have a settlement in the parish of Bethnal Green, not in but adjoining this union, by apprenticeship. 2. On the 14th November, 1849, John Langford, aged forty-three years, who claimed to have a settlement in Hackney, Middlesex, by apprenticeship, and is by trade a shoemaker, but not following his trade at this time, was, together with his child, admitted into the same workhouse. These last named paupers had been sleeping for nine consecutive nights, immediately previous to their admission into a lodging-house, in the said parish of Christ Church, paying fourpence per night for such lodging for the six working nights, and being entitled to the same privileges as to the Sunday night, and the use of the common sitting-room or kitchen as in the former case. In both the above cases the paupers were accustomed to leave the lodging-houses early every morning, to obtain their livelihood during the day, and returning at night to sleep at the lodging-houses. The guardians of the Whitechapel Union have charged the costs of the maintenance of the above paupers, on each occasion of their admission, to the common fund of the union, as wanderers, within the first clause of the 11 and 12 Vic. c. 110. The overseers of the poor of the hamlet of Mile End New Town, in the said union, have objected to their being so charged, being of opinion that the paupers were not wanderers within the meaning of the Act, and that their maintenance should have been charged to the parish of Christ Church, as the parish wherein they had lodged, previous to and at the times of their admission to the workhouse. The foregoing facts have been agreed to, and the opinion of the Poor Law Board is requested whether the paupers were or not rightly charged to the common fund of the union.

Ans.—In neither of the cases submitted to them do the Board consider the pauper to be a destitute wanderer, or wayfarer, within the meaning of the 11 and 12 Vic. c. 110, sec. 1, so as to warrant the guardians in charging the cost of the relief to the common fund of the union.

26th April, 1850.

Clerk of same Union.—Transmitting the following resolution passed by the guardians:—"That the Poor Law Board be requested to state what is the limit of the number of nights of paupers sleeping in one or in several nightly lodging-houses in the same parish, which prevents their being charged to the common fund as wanderers; and generally what constitutes a wanderer, within the meaning of the 11 and 12 Vic. c. 110, sec. 1."

Ans.—The Board cannot specify "what is the limit of the number of nights of paupers sleeping in one or in several nightly lodging-houses in the same parish, which prevents their being charged to the common fund as wanderers;" nor do they think that they can properly undertake to define what is a "wanderer," within the meaning of the Act. Whether a person in any particular case is to be considered as a destitute wayfarer or wanderer or not, must depend upon a variety of circumstances; but, generally speaking, the question will be one not admitting of much doubt.

3. Chargeability of Irremovable Pauper—Sickness.

30th Nov., 1849.

Clerk of Seisdon Union.—1. W. M., aged 74, a non-settled pauper, resident in the parish of Bobbington, and having resided there for twenty years and upwards, belonging to the parish of Worfield, in the Bridgnorth Union, about twelve months since accidentally broke his leg, and was consequently placed on the out-door relief list as a casual pauper. The broken leg has got well, but has been succeeded by an inflamed foot, which renders the pauper unable to get his living, although he can do a little work, and walk about, and is well enough to be removed. The overseers of Bobbington apply to have the pauper placed on the common fund of the union under the 11 & 12 Vic. c. 110, sec. 3, considering that the cause for which such pauper was placed under relief has ceased; and that as the pauper can only be made exempt from removal by the 9 & 10 Vic. c. 66, sec. 4, and all paupers so exempted from removal being, by the 11 & 12 Vic. c. 110, transferred from the parish where they reside to the common fund of the union wherein such parish is situated, this pauper should be so transferred.—2. R. W., aged 83, a non-settled pauper, of Claverley parish, also in the Bridgnorth Union, resident in the parish of Bobbington, where he has resided for twenty years and upwards, about twelve months since was placed on the medical relief list, and also on the out-door relief list, in consequence of his being afflicted with paralysis, from which, on account of his great age, there is no probability of his ever recovering. The overseers of Bobbington apply to have the pauper placed on the common fund of the union for the same reasons as before stated in the case of W. M., but the guardians have some doubt whether, unless the illness can be proved to produce permanent disability, they ought to allow the pauper to be placed on the common fund. Inquiring whether the relief in these cases should be charged to the common fund or the parish of residence

Ans.—In both these cases the paupers have become irremovable by length of residence in the parish wherein they respectively reside, and are, therefore, chargeable to the union common fund. Being so irremovable, the question is immaterial whether or not their cases are within any other enactment besides the 1st sec. of the 9 & 10 Vic. c. 66.

4. INTERRUPTION OF RESIDENCE—RELIEF IN WORKHOUSE.

2nd Feb., 1850.

Clerk of Cosford Union.—Requesting to be informed whether the relief has been properly charged in the following case:—An able-bodied pauper, who belongs to the parish of Layham, in this union, but who has resided in the parish of Hadleigh for twenty years last past, has been admitted into the workhouse, and charged to the "common fund." During the twenty years he has several times been admitted into the workhouse, and on leaving, upon all occasions going direct to Hadleigh parish again. The five years' residence in Hadleigh is not disputed. The workhouse being situated in a third parish, some of the guardians consider that the pauper's admission into the workhouse has broken his residence, and, consequently, that the relief should be charged to Layham, and not to the common fund.

Ans.—As by the 12 & 13 Vic. c. 103, sec. 4, the removal of a pauper to a union workhouse is not to operate as an interruption of the residence, the Board consider that, in the case in question, the pauper is not removable, and, therefore, is chargeable to the common fund of the union.

5. PERMANENT DISABILITY, SEC. 4, 9 & 10 VIC. C. 66.

11th March, 1850.

Clerk of Tiverton Union.—Requesting to be informed whether sec. 4 of the 9 & 10 Vic. c. 66, is meant to extend indiscriminately to all sick persons; that is, that all relief given on account of sickness which may not produce permanent disability, shall be charged to the common fund of the union. To construe this to the strict letter has been found to operate most disadvantageously to parishes. The guardians will, therefore, be glad to have the opinion of the Board for their guidance, as it is considered it never could have been contemplated by the statute, (while the present law of settlement exists,) that a pauper, whose settlement is not disputed, and is able-bodied, should, with his family, when casually sick, be charged to the common fund, unless as a condition precedent that he had resided five years in the parish.

Ans.—The section above cited applies to cases of chargeability, caused by temporary accident or sickness. If there be previous chargeability, caused by general destitution, upon which sickness supervenes, the case is not within the section. But, undoubtedly, the section renders the parties who fall within its terms irremovable on that ground, and the length of their residence in the parish is, therefore, immaterial. Then the 11 & 12 Vic. c. 110, sec. 3, (continued for one year by the 12 & 13 Vic. c. 103, sec. 1,) provides that the relief of all persons rendered irremovable by any provision of the former Act, (9 & 10 Vic. c. 66,) shall be a charge upon the union common fund. The Board believe that there is no doubt as to the meaning of the language, nor of the intention of the legislature in this respect.

III.—ELECTION OF GUARDIANS.

1. STATEMENT OF OWNERS—SEC. 15 OF 7 & 8 VIC. C. 101.

28th Jan., 1850.

Clerk of St. Mary Abbott's, Kensington.—A doubt has been expressed, whether it is not necessary for an owner of property annually to renew his claim to vote in the election of guardians under the provisions of the 15th sec. of the Act 7 & 8 Vic. c. 101. The words of the clause are, "That no owner of property shall be intitled to vote as such, under the provisions of the said recited Act, either in person, or proxy, during the year following the 25th day of March in any year, unless before the 1st day of February next preceding such 25th day of March, he had given to the overseers the statement required by the said Act," &c. If, therefore, an owner sent to the overseers before the 1st day of February, 1849, the required statement, must he send a similar statement before the 1st day of February, 1850, to enable him to vote in the election of guardians for the present year. It is held that he need not do so, inasmuch as having sent in the statement before the 1st day of February next preceding the 25th day of March, 1849, it necessarily follows that the statement must have been sent in before the 1st day of February, 1850; and had the legislature intended that the owner should renew his claim annually, the words "in every year" would have been introduced after the words "25th day of March." It may, moreover, be observed, that if the owner cannot vote under the 15th sec., either in person or proxy, unless he renew his claim annually, that this construction will be repugnant to the following provisions of the same clause, which expressly allow an appointment of proxy to remain in force for two years. Inquiring, whether the owners of property must give to the overseers the statement required by the Act before the 1st day of February in every year, to enable them to vote in the election of guardians for that year.

Ans.—The Board do not think it is necessary that an owner should annually renew his claim to vote in the election of guardians, under sec. 15 of the 7 & 8 Vic. c. 101, so long as the description and statement of the property originally sent as required by that statute continued to be true. If any change takes place which makes that description or statement untrue in any respect, a new claim should be sent in.

---

2. WHEN OLD BOARD CEASES AND NEW BOARD COMMENCES TO ACT.

3rd April, 1850.

Clerk of Thirsk Union.—No greater number of persons having been nominated as guardians for any parish in this union, for the current year, than ought to be elected therein, he had, in conformity with Art. 9 and 22 of the General Consolidated Order, certified their election; under Art. 23, given notice to the guardians of their election; and under 24, he had presented the list and nomination papers to the guardians. According to Art. 29 of the Order, it is not until the first meeting after the 15th of April that the guardians are required to appoint a chairman and vice-chairman for the year. The guardians feel considerable difficulty in reconciling the various Articles with each other, and several questions arise thereon which may involve serious consequences. Inquiring whether, on the election of new guardians being certified by the clerk, the old board of guardians ceases to exist, and the guardians declared to be elected take their place as a new board; or does the old board continue its existence until the first meeting after the 15th April? If the new board displaces the old one, should the guardians of the new board at their first meeting (a position which does not appear to be provided for by the order) appoint a chairman and vice-chairman and committees intermediately, until the meeting after the 15th April? and generally as to the proper course to be pursued, so as that the acts of the board may be strictly legal.

Ans.—On the completion of the election of the guardians for any parish or parishes in the Thirsk Union, the guardians then elected immediately take the place of those who previously acted for such parish or parishes, and should accordingly be summoned to attend at the next meeting of the board of guardians after such election. Under the circumstances which you describe, the elections having been completed for all the parishes in the union, the guardians newly elected should appoint a chairman, *pro. tem.*, to act at their meeting or meetings before the 15th instant, and should make the appointments required by Art. 29 of the General Consolidated Order at their first meeting after that day.

IV.—MEDICAL RELIEF.—REPAYMENT OF.

25th Jan., 1850.

Clerk of Thirsk Union.—A charge of 12*s*. has been made by the guardians of this union against the guardians of the Northallerton Union, for medical relief granted to a pauper residing in this union, but settled in the Northallerton Union, which the guardians of the Northallerton Union refuse to pay, on the ground that it is the duty of the guardians of this union to supply all medical relief to its non-settled paupers. At the same time the guardians of the Malton Union make a claim on this union for medical relief granted under the same circumstances. Requesting the opinion of the Board whether or not medical relief should be placed on the same footing as other relief, and be repaid by the guardians of the union in which the pauper is settled.

Ans.—The validity of such claim wholly depends upon the terms of the undertaking (if any) which has been entered into by the guardians of the Northallerton Union, in reference to the allowance of non-resident relief in the case alluded to. If the undertaking applies to medical relief expressly, or to relief generally, the Thirsk guardians have the same claim to be reimbursed such medical relief as they have in regard to ordinary relief. If, however, the undertaking excludes the medical relief, either in express terms or by necessary implication, the reimbursement of such relief cannot be insisted upon. As the party receiving the relief in the Thirsk Union is stated to have been a "pauper," the Board assume that he was at the same time in receipt of ordinary relief also.

V.—OVERSEER—HIS POWER TO GIVE ORDERS OF ADMISSION INTO THE UNION WORKHOUSE.

15th Jan., 1849.

Clerk of Yeovil Union.—At the meeting of the guardians on the 28th ultimo, on reading the orders for admission of paupers during the week, for confirmation, their attention was drawn to the following, from the overseer of Yeovil: "Please admit Hannah B——— to your union house, which you dare not refuse. L——

B——, overseer." The particulars of the case, as furnished by the relieving officer, are enclosed. Inquired whether, under the circumstances stated by the relieving officer, the overseer was justified in acting in opposition to the relieving officer, and using such strong language, without having first ascertained of the relieving officer his reasons for refusal.

The Relieving Officer's Statement:—Hannah B——— is a married woman, who has been deserted by her husband for four or five years. She was confined in our union house a few months ago of an illegitimate child. She left the house with her child on the 17th October last, and has since been cohabiting with a navigator at Chetnole, in Dorsetshire. She came from thence on Friday last and made an application to me for an order of admission to the workhouse. This I refused on two grounds,—First, because if she needed relief she should have applied to the relieving officer of the parish in which she resided; and—Secondly, had she lived in our union, considering her previous character and the circumstances under which she left the house, I should not have given her an order on my own responsibility, but should have awaited the decision of the board of guardians on the Tuesday following. She left, but said she should apply personally to the board on Tuesday. She came accordingly again from Chetnole, but did not arrive until after the board had broken up. I again refused her an order on the same ground; she staid at my door for a long time, but eventually procured an order from the overseer, and came into the workhouse, as I am informed by the master, in a state of intoxication."

Ans.—The Board in the first place desire to remark, that an overseer is only entitled to give orders for admission to the workhouse in cases of sudden and urgent necessity; and such an order is only operative until the next meeting of the guardians, with whom it then rests to decide on the propriety of the pauper's continuing in the workhouse, or otherwise. (See Article 90 of the General Consolidated Order.) The Board, moreover, think it right to point out, that the workhouse is only provided for the reception of paupers. The guardians of the union, or, in their absence, the master of the workhouse, must determine what applicants for relief are paupers, (that is, persons actually destitute,) who should be admitted therein. It is true that the master is, by the effect of Article 88 of the General Consolidated Order, relieved from the consequences of improperly admitting persons who are not paupers when they produce an order from an overseer; but the Board do not think that the terms of the order conclude him, or prevent the exercise of his judgment as to the fact of the applicant being a pauper. If, therefore, the master, in the fulfilment of his duty, take upon himself the responsibility of deciding in any case of suspected or simulated destitution, the Board are of opinion that he may properly refuse admission to a person, under such circumstances, who produces an order from an overseer. Of course, in refusing to admit a person producing such an order the master must be prepared to justify his conduct, should any question afterwards arise upon it. In such a case as that of Hannah B——— appears from your statement to have been, the Board do not hesitate to express their opinion that the master would have been justified in so exercising his undoubted discretion.

VI.—OVERSEERS—LIABILITIES OF, WHERE THERE IS AN ASSISTANT OVERSEER.

27th March, 1850.

Overseer of Lostwithiel, Bodmin Union.—Where there is an assistant overseer appointed by the parish to collect the rates and do all the duties for the overseers, who is answerable, the parish or overseers, in case there should be at any time a deficiency or embezzlement of the parish money? And also, what are the duties of an overseer on going out of office where there is an assistant overseer?

Ans.—Where there is an assistant overseer in a parish, duly appointed under the 59 Geo. 3, c. 12, sec. 7, he is personally responsible for the monies which come to his hands on account of the parish; and the overseers are likewise responsible in respect of the monies which they receive. The overseers, however, will not be responsible for the monies received by the assistant overseer, unless the latter cause a loss to the parish which might have been avoided by a vigilant supervision on the part of the overseers, in which case they are liable to be surcharged by the auditor to that extent. With regard to your second question, the Board desire to state, that the duties of an overseer on going out of office are the same where there is an assistant overseer as where there is not. The duties of the assistant overseer will appear in the warrant for his appointment, and in the General Order of Accounts issued by the Poor Law Commissioners in 1847.

VII.—RATING—RAILWAY.

27th Sept., 1848.

Clerk of Wortley Union.—Under the 11 & 12 Vic. c. 110, sec. 7, the guardians of any union may, on the application of the overseers of any parish comprised in it, cause a valuation to be made at any time of any property alleged to be rateable to the relief of the poor, being part only of the rateable property of such parish, &c. The Manchester, Sheffield, and Lincolnshire Railway passes through several of the townships in this union, and such railway has for several years been rated to the poor in such townships. This railway company now consider the railway is rated at too much, and have written the overseers of the poor to that effect, and threatening to appeal against the rates unless some amicable adjustment can be had thereof. The overseers are desirous to avoid the expense of appeals, particularly as the railway company have offered to refer the valuation of the railway to the arbitration of two valuers, one to be chosen by the company and the other by the overseers; but the overseers are doubtful whether, by virtue of the above-mentioned Act, the guardians can cause a valuation of the railway to be made, and the expense thereof be charged in the overseers' accounts, without having a valuation of the whole of the property in each township, being of opinion that by the section mentioned the guardians have only the power to cause a valuation to be made of property alleged to be rateable to the relief of the poor, and which has not been previously rated to the poor. Inquiring, therefore, whether the guardians have, on the application of the overseers, the power to authorize a valuation of the railway alone in each of the townships in question; and if they have such power, whether such application should be made to the guardians in writing, and if so, if the enclosed form of application will be sufficient; and whether, on receiving such application, it will be necessary for the guardians to forward the same to the Poor Law Board to issue an order for such valuation; or will the order of the guardians alone be sufficient to authorize the valuation and the payment of the expenses thereof by the overseers.

The form of application referred to above:—To the Guardians of the Wortley Union, We, the undersigned overseers of the poor, competent to make and levy the rates for the relief of the poor of the township of ———, in the Wortley Union, are of opinion that a fair and correct estimate of the railway, railway stations, and other property in this township, belonging to the Manchester, Sheffield, and Lincolnshire Railway Company, for the purposes of the Act 6 & 7 Wm. 4, c. 96, commonly called the Parochial Assessments Act, cannot be made without a new valuation, do hereby make application to the guardians of the said Wortley Union to cause a valuation to be made of the said railway, railway stations, and other property of the said Manchester, Sheffield, and Lincolnshire Railway Company, and to charge the expenses of such valuation to us the overseers of the said township of ———, As witness our hands this day of 1848.

Ans.—The Board are not aware of any reason for limiting the application of the above-mentioned enactment to property not previously assessed to the poor-rate. It appears to them that any property whatever, which is alleged to be rateable, whether previously rated or not, comes within the provision. The Board are therefore of opinion that the guardians of the Wortley Union are empowered to cause a valuation of the railway in question to be made for the use of the overseers of the several townships interested. In apportioning the expenses, the guardians should make a separate charge against each of the townships in respect of such proportion of the property to be valued as may be situated therein. Though it may not be absolutely required by the act, it is obviously advisable that the application to the guardians should be made by the overseers in writing. The form of application enclosed in your letter seems unexceptionable. On receiving such application, the guardians can act in the matter under the authority of the statute, without any order from the Poor Law Board. With reference to the proposed course of proceeding, however, the Board would remark, that it will be the duty of the guardians to procure for the overseers a valuation of the property—an object which the appointment of two arbitrators will not necessarily effect. Moreover, in a question of this kind, which involves the interests of the railway company as well as of the ratepayers, it seems hardly fair that the entire costs should fall upon the townships.

VIII.—RELIEF.

1. CHARGING RELIEF TO IRREMOVABLE POOR.

22nd Dec., 1849.

Clerk of Wincanton Union.—Transmitting for the information of the Board the following instructions, which he had prepared for the guidance of the officers of the union in charging relief to irremovable poor :—1st. All relief to be granted, or continued to any irremovable pauper, is to be charged direct to the common fund of the union, and not to any parish as heretofore; and the relieving officers and master of the workhouse must be careful to open a separate and distinct account in their respective relief lists, headed "Common Charges," to which the name of every such pauper must be correctly posted from the Application and Report Book, and from the Admission and Discharge Book. 2nd. The relieving officers in their admissions to the workhouse must be careful to state "Common Fund," when the pauper is to be so entered by the master, and any officer continuing relief at the expense of the common fund after the pauper's exemption from removal ceases, may be called upon to repay the amount to the treasurer. 3rd. The applications of all irremovable paupers must be made to the relieving officer for the parish in which such paupers reside, and must be entered by him in his Application Book as all other applications from the parish are entered. If the applicant be decided by the guardians to be irremovable, the amount of relief ordered must be correctly posted from the Parish Application Book to the "Common Charges" relief list, and not to the relief list for the parish, as is the case with all settled and removable paupers; and the letters C. C. must be placed opposite the pauper's name in the Parish Application Book, to point out that the relief is posted to "Common Charges." 4th. If any question arise between any parishes, or between the guardians and any parish, with reference to the charging of the cost of relief, the clerk will draw up a case, to be properly signed, and transmitted to the Poor Law Board, for their opinion pursuant to the provisions of the fourth section of the Act.

Ans.—The Poor Law Board desire to thank you for the copy instructions, which they have perused with attention, but they wish to offer for your information the following remarks thereon: —They have no objection to the 1st, 3rd, and 4th articles, which appear to be judicious; but they cannot approve of the 2nd article. They do not assent to the proposition that an officer is liable to repay to the treasurer of the union the cost of relief ordered by the guardians and properly expended, because he may have entered the charge erroneously in his accounts to the common fund, or to a particular parish. It rests with the guardians in making up their accounts to charge all the expenditure correctly, notwithstanding any error in the books of their officers; and on their default in this respect the auditor should set it right. The Poor Law Board, therefore, think that on any further issue of these instructions the 2nd article should be omitted.

---

2. RELIEF TO FATHER AND DAUGHTER SEPARATELY, THEY LIVING TOGETHER.

25th Jan., 1850.

Clerk of Wirrall Union.—T. E., a pauper of two and a half years' residence in Tranmere, having several children living with him, (one of whom, Elizabeth, is twenty-three years old,) applied for relief on the ground of destitution. Finding Elizabeth a separate applicant for relief on account of sickness, which of course meant destitution also, it was contended that she was not entitled to it, as she was then living with her father, and forming a part of his family, she having obtained no settlement in her own right; therefore that the relief ought, under such circumstances, to be given to the father, on the ground of destitution and sickness of his family, who were actually living with him at the time of his application. The guardians, however, thought otherwise, and ordered relief in each case, thereby putting Tranmere to the expense of two orders of removal.

Ans.—The course which the guardians of the Wirrall Union pursued, in dealing with the case of Elizabeth E. separately from that of her father, T. E., does not appear to the Board to have been illegal or improper. Relief to a child, after such child has attained the age of sixteen, is not relief to the father, under 4 & 5 Wm. 4, c. 76, sec. 56, though the father is still under a legal obligation to support his daughter if he is of sufficient ability to do so, (43 Eliz. c. 2, sec. 7;) consequently, the destitution of the daughter in the present case being altogether distinct from the destitution of the father, the Board think that their applications for relief were properly considered by the guardians as independent applications, and that the charge of such relief should, in each of the two cases, be kept distinct from the other.

IX.—REMOVABILITY.

1. REMOVABILITY OF A SCOTCHMAN.

16th Jan., 1850.

J. Thomson, Esq., Inspector, Edinburgh.—Inquiring whether a Scotchman, who has resided in a parish in England for full five years, and during that time maintained himself and family, by the proceeds of his own industry, without having recourse to public begging, or in any other way in receipt of alms, is removable from that parish when he becomes chargeable to the funds of the parish.

Ans.—The Board are advised, and are of opinion, that under the statute 9 & 10 Vic. c. 66, sec. 1, a Scotchman who has resided for five years in a parish in England without a break of such residence, and without having been in receipt of relief during that period, is not liable to removal from the parish to Scotland.

2. REMOVABILITY OF IRISH PAUPERS.

16*th Feb.*, 1850.

Clerk of Sheffield Union.—An opinion prevails amongst the officers of the Sheffield Union, that a decision has been given in the Court of Queen's Bench as to the legality of removing to their native country poor persons born in Ireland, and having no settlement in England, although they may have had a residence of five years in a parish in England. Inquiring whether any such decision has been given.

Ans.—The Board are not aware of any such decision as is referred to in your letter. A judgment was given lately in the Court of Queen's Bench in the case of Reg. *v.* All Saints, Derby; but that case related to the children of an Irishman, and did not at all effect the construction of the 9 & 10 Vic. c. 66.

3. REMOVABILITY OF WIDOW.

21*st March*, 1850.

Clerk of Brecknock Union.—T. W. and wife went to reside in the parish of Llanfigan, in this union, on the 25th of March, 1840, their legal place of settlement was in the parish of Merthyr Cyrog, also in this union. During their residence in Llanfigan, they received the following relief from Merthyr Cyrog:—1843, Lady-day quarter, 2*s.*; 1843, Michaelmas quarter, 10*s.* to buy clothes; 1844, Lady-day quarter, 2*s.* 6*d.* provisions, £1. to buy clothes, and 2*s.* 6*d.* in money; 1846, Midsummer quarter, regular weekly relief. T. W. died on the 10th of June, 1846; the widow is still in Llanfigan, and in receipt of weekly relief from Llanfigan. Inquiring whether the widow is removable.

Ans.—Looking to the nature of the relief afforded in this case, on the occasions you specify in 1843 and 1844, it appears that such relief was only given for very short intervals of time, which cannot be reckoned at more than a week, or a fortnight at the utmost, on each occasion; and consequently there will not be more than five or ten weeks of relief to deduct from the residence of six years during the period extending from Lady-day, 1840, to Lady-day, 1846. The Board, therefore, consider that the pauper in question is irremovable from the parish of Llanfigan, and chargeable to the common fund of the Brecknock Union accordingly.

4. REMOVABILITY OF DESERTED CHILDREN.

14*th Feb.*, 1850.

Clerk of Eastbourne Union.—Transmitting the following statement, duly signed under the 4th sec. of the 11 & 12 Vic. c. 110, for the opinion of the Poor Law Board. H. H., a widower, having five children, all under sixteen years of age, is settled in Brighton, but has resided in the parish of Willingdon eleven years uninterruptedly, and without receiving parochial relief. On the 12th of January last he deserted his family, and has not been heard of since. His children are now chargeable, and in the union workhouse. Has the desertion of H. H. made a breach in his residence in the parish of Willingdon?

Ans.—According to the decision of the Queen *v.* St. Ebbs, 12 Q. B. 137, the Board consider that the children in this case are legally removable.

5. REMOVABILITY OF CHILDREN DESERTED BY THEIR FATHER.

23*rd Jan.*, 1850.

Clerk of Machynlleth Union.—Edward Rowland, whose settlement is in Pennal, had resided in Towyn without relief for more than five years previous to May last, when he deserted his family and went to America, where he still is. He left his wife and three children chargeable to Towyn, and the latter parish continued to maintain them, conceiving that they had become irremovable by residence. A few weeks back the mother died. The three children are of the respective ages of six and a half years, five years, and eight weeks. The eldest child has lived in Towyn without interruption for more than five years, and also without relief. The other children have not so resided. Inquiring whether or not the children are now removable. If the father were to come to Towyn, he would no doubt be removable, it would therefore appear probable that the children are so under 9 & 10 Vic. c. 66, sec. 1.

Ans.—If Edward Rowland (the father) be

living, all the children are removable from Towyn, according to the principle of the decision in Queen *v.* Pott Shrigley (12 Q. B. R. 143.) The Board think, moreover, that (in the absence of proof to the contrary) the father must be presumed to be still living; as the presumption of life continues, in law, for seven years after the party was last known to be alive; which, in the present case, appears to have been in May last. If, however, it be shown by proof that the father is dead, then, upon the facts stated in your letter with regard to the residence and relief of the children, the eldest child would be irremovable from Towyn, but the other children would not.

6. REMOVABILITY OF STEP CHILDREN.

25th Sept., 1849.

Clerk of Kettering Union.—T. K., an acknowledged parishioner of Broughton, in this union, who was married and had one child, was transported just previous to the passing of the Poor Law Amendment Act. His wife and child afterwards came to reside in the parish of Kettering, under relief repaid by the parish of Broughton. The wife has continued to reside in Kettering, living with a person of the name of Handley, by whom she has six illegitimate children, the eldest being fifteen years of age, and the youngest one year old. These illegitimate children have been also acknowledged and relieved by Broughton parish up to August last. About a year back, T. K. died abroad, and above a month since his widow (the mother of the six illegitimate children) married Handley, whose settlement parish is Kettering. Handley is now in jail for trespassing in pursuit of game, and under any circumstances is unable to support his wife and these children, and the parish of Broughton now contend that the children have and follow the settlement of the mother, which she has acquired by her second marriage, and, therefore, object to grant them further relief. Inquiring 1st, Whether all these six children, or those above the age of nurture, can be removed from Kettering to Broughton, the mother's undisputed settlement at the birth of each of them? And 2ndly, Should the Poor Law Board be of opinion that all or any of them are irremovable, whether the relief can be properly charged to the common fund of the union?

Ans.—Assuming the children to be illegitimate, they having been born since the passing of the 4 & 5 Wm. 4, c. 76, have and follow the settlement which the mother has acquired by her recent marriage with Handley. See sec. 71 of the Act, and Reg. *v.* St. Mary Newington, 4 Queen's Bench Reports, 581. That settlement appears to be in Kettering, in which the woman and the children in question now reside. The children, therefore, are not removable, and the charge of their relief will fall upon the parish of Kettering, as the common fund of the union is only liable for the relief of persons rendered irremovable by some provision of the 9 & 10 Vic. c. 66, and not being settled in the parish of the residence.

7. REMOVABILITY OF THE FAMILY OF AN IRISHMAN WHO HAS DESERTED THEM.

12th Dec., 1849.

Clerk of Ashley-de-la-Zouch Union.—Michael Louis, an Irishman, came to Whitwick parish, in this union, six or seven years ago, with his wife Margaret, also an Irishwoman, and two children born in Ireland. Since their residence in Whitwick they have had two other children born in that parish. Michael Louis deserted his wife and children about three months ago, and has gone, it is believed, to America. The wife and her four children are now chargeable to the parish of Whitwick. The guardians feel at a loss to know how to deal with the case, as since the recent decision of the Queen *v.* the Inhabitants of Derby, it would appear doubtful whether, as the husband having absconded, and therefore cannot be summoned before justices, as required by the 2nd sec. of 8 & 9 Vic, c. 117, the wife and children can be removed to Ireland. Inquiring whether, notwithstanding the decision above referred to, the parish officers may now summon the wife to appear before two justices, and the family be removed to Ireland. The interpretation clause in 10 & 11 Vic. c. 33, amending the 8 & 9 Vic. c. 117, would seem to favour the view, that the wife might be summoned and removed.

Ans.—With reference to the question, as to the removability of the wife and children to Ireland, the Board desire to point out that according to the decision in Reg. *v.* All Saints, Derby (14 Law Times, 152,) the children in this case, if the mother were not living, could not be removed to Ireland; and the Board think the question in the present case (in which the mother is living, and is with the children) altogether too doubtful, especially having regard to the decision just mentioned, to warrant the Board in advising that these paupers could be removed to Ireland. It appears, therefore, that the woman and her children, two of whom are settled by birth in the parish of Whitwick, must remain chargeable to that parish.

8. REMOVABILITY OF A PERSON DISABLED BY ILL HEALTH.

1st Feb., 1850.

Clerk of Lancaster Union.—R. K., aged forty-five years, has a wife and three children under sixteen years of age. He and his family reside in the township of Lancaster, in this union, but are settled in the township of Cockerham in this union. R. K. is a general labourer. He has been employed, during the last few years, in various ways; as a railway labourer, an ostler, and in attending persons engaged in surveying the sea-coast. His health has been impaired for several years, and he has not been able to work as a labourer during the last eighteen months, but has been chiefly engaged in selling fish, oranges, &c., about the streets, by which occupation he has earned about one shilling and sixpence per week. He has been in the receipt of relief occasionally for several years past. About twenty months since he became chargeable, and has been in the receipt of out-door relief ever since that time. His chargeability was caused by want of work, but he was not in such a state of health as to do the work of an able-bodied out-door labourer. About six months since he obtained employment as a railway labourer, but after working a few hours he was obliged to give up his work, in consequence of his not having sufficient health and strength to perform it. He has been examined as to his state of health by two of the union medical officers, one of whom has professionally attended him for eighteen months past. The following is a copy of their report on his case: "We are of opinion that R. K. is permanently disabled, by a scrofulous habit, to such an extent as will interfere considerably with his capacity to earn his living by work. He may, probably, by the aid of good food, domestic comforts, and warm weather, be able to work a little occasionally, but the extent of his disability is such as will most probably prevent his being able to work long together, or as an able-bodied man."

Ans.—Assuming R. K. has not resided in the township of Lancaster for five years, without relief, so as to render him irremovable under 9 & 10 Vic. c. 66, sec. 1, he appears, upon the statement submitted in your letter, to be now removable from that township, as his present chargeability seems to have arisen from ordinary destitution.

9. BREACH OF RESIDENCE.

10th Jan., 1850.

Clerk of Basingstoke Union.—J. P. has been resident in the parish of Basingstoke, in this union, for a period of six years, and during all the time, except for the five weeks after mentioned, occupying a dwelling-house in that parish. The pauper's actual and admitted settlement is in the parish of West Sherborne, in the same union. About four years since, the pauper being in want of relief, was admitted into the union workhouse, and remained there five weeks, and the cost of his relief was charged to the parish of West Sherborne. The pauper retained, during the time of such relief, in the house, possession of his dwelling-house at Basingstoke, and returned to it on his quitting the house. The pauper is now in Basingstoke, and requires further relief. *Query*—Under the circumstances stated, was there a sufficient breach of residence, so as to warrant the charging of the further relief to the parish of West Sherborne? Or, is the pauper irremovable, and chargeable to the common fund?

Ans.—According to the provisions of the 12 & 13 Vic. c. 103, sec. 4, the time referred to, during which the pauper was an inmate of the workhouse, is to be excluded from the computation of the five years' residence, but is not to be deemed an interruption of the residence in Basingstoke. It appears to the Board, from the information before them, that the pauper in this case is irremovable, and, therefore, that the cost of the relief is properly chargeable to the common fund of the union.

10. BREACH OF RESIDENCE.

12th Dec., 1849.

Clerk of Haltwhistle Union.—M. W., aged thirty-four, whose place of settlement is Haltwhistle, went to the parish of St. Cuthbert Without, Carlisle, where she resided upwards of five years. She then sold off all her furniture by auction, completely broke up her dwelling-house, came voluntarily to Haltwhistle, the place of her settlement, and applied for admission into the workhouse, which was refused her. She staid all night in Haltwhistle, and returned the next day to St. Cuthbert's Without. She was there admitted into the workhouse, where she still remains. Before coming to Haltwhistle to apply for admission into the workhouse, she had been receiving relief from the parish of St. Cuthbert, and had received her weekly allowance from that parish at the time she applied. This weekly allowance would include the night she slept at Haltwhistle, the relief being paid for a week in advance. Is the woman under these circumstances removable to Haltwhistle, the place of her settlement?

Ans.—The Board are of opinion, that inasmuch as the pauper in question broke up her establishment in the parish of St. Cuthbert Without, Carlisle, at the time when she quitted her dwelling-house there, and went to Haltwhistle, she by so doing interrupted her residence in the parish of St. Cuthbert Without, Carlisle, and consequently is now removable therefrom.

---

11. BREACH OF RESIDENCE—IMPRISONMENT OF PAUPER.

6th Dec., 1849.

Clerk of Stokesley Union.—J. P., a pauper, legally settled in the township of East Rounton, in the Stokesley Union, has resided in the township of Stockton, in the Stockton Union, more than five years (exclusive of the time he was in prison) to the present time. He was a short time in Durham Jail, which is not in the township of Stockton, nor in the township of East Rounton, nor in the Stokesley Union. His term of imprisonment has now expired, and he has since returned to Stockton. If the time during which the pauper was in jail be excluded from the computation of the period of his residence, he will still have resided for more than five years in the township of Stockton. During the time J. P. was in jail he left a house in Stockton furnished, and his wife and family resided in it till his return. Inquiring whether, in consequence of the decision of the Court of Queen's Bench, in Reg. *v.* Salford, (17 L. J. R. N. S. M. C. 170,) the pauper having been in prison will have the effect of breaking his residence, so that he can now be removed to East Rounton, his settlement parish.

Ans.—Upon the authority of the case cited by you, (namely, Reg. *v.* Salford,) the Board consider that the residence of the pauper in question was interrupted by the imprisonment abovementioned; and that he is consequently now removable from the township of Stockton.

---

12. BREACH OF RESIDENCE—HUSBAND GOING AWAY IN SEARCH OF WORK.

3rd Dec., 1849.

Clerk of Williton Union.—Transmitting the following statement, duly signed under sec. 4 of 11 & 12 Vic. c. 110, for the opinion of the Poor Law Board:—On the 17th of October last, James Orchard, an able-bodied agricultural labourer, legally settled in the parish of Silworthy, in this union, but who had resided for the last eleven years uninterruptedly in the parish of Wootton-Courtney in this union, without relief, went to Wales to procure work, leaving his wife and family of five children destitute in the parish of Wootton-Courtney. His wife delivered up the key of their cottage, and the household goods and furniture it contained, to the landlord (her father, a pauper) in discharge of the rent due, and was sent with her children to the union workhouse, upon an order from the relieving officer, chargeable to the common fund, the family being considered irremovable to the place of settlement (Silworthy) by reason of more than five years' residence in Wootton-Courtney without relief. The wife and children are still chargeable to the common fund in the workhouse. Her father retains the cottage for her until she comes out of the workhouse. Her husband has not returned. If he continued his residence in Wootton-Courtney the relief would have been chargeable to the common fund; but having gone to Wales to seek for work, and the wife and family having in consequence been sent to the union workhouse in the parish of St. Decumans, the question arises whether the husband is removable to the place of his settlement—Silworthy. Your opinion is requested on behalf of the guardians of the union and the parish of Wootton-Courtney, whether the maintenance of the wife and family in the workhouse should be charged to the common fund of the union or to the parish of Wootton-Courtney. Also, whether proceedings against the husband for leaving his wife and family should be taken by the board of guardians or by the overseers of Wootton-Courtney.

Ans.—Upon the statement submitted, it appears to the Board, that the residence of the husband in the parish of Wootton-Courtney is broken by reason of his journey to Wales in search of work; and, therefore, if he returned, he would be removable from that parish, and, consequently, his wife and family are removable under the 11 & 12 Vic. c. 111. Upon the second point, as to whether proceedings against the husband for leaving his wife and family chargeable should be taken by the board of guardians or by the overseers of Wootton-Courtney, the Board desire to point out, that the 59th sec. of the 7 & 8 Vic. c. 101, enables the guardians to pay the costs of any such prosecution as is referred to, and the Board therefore consider that the guardians, and not the overseers, should direct the prosecution in the present case if they deem it proper to do so.

13. BREACH OF RESIDENCE—AN INCOMPLETE EXECUTION OF AN ORDER OF REMOVAL.

6th August, 1849.

Clerk of Whitechapel Union.—Transmitting the following statement, duly signed under sec. 4 of 11 & 12 Vic. c. 110, for the opinion of the Poor Law Board:—By an order of removal, dated the 11th April, 1849, John Lewis, and Elizabeth his wife, residing at No. 49, Queen Ann Street, Whitechapel, were ordered to be removed from the parish of St. Mary, Whitechapel, to the hamlet of Mile End New Town, and an appeal against such order has been commenced. The appellants contend that the paupers by reason of residence in the respondent's parish have become irremovable under the 9 & 10 Vic. c. 66, and this depends upon whether a former order of removal was executed so as to break the continuity of the inhabitancy under the following circumstances:—In the month of August, 1844, the pauper John Lewis and his wife then resided at the same house as now, No. 49, Queen Ann Street, in the respondent parish of St. Mary, Whitechapel, and becoming chargeable thereto, an order of justices was obtained for their removal from that parish to the hamlet of Mile End New Town, and notice of such chargeability, and a copy of the order of removal, and of the examination on which it was founded, were duly served on the overseers of the poor of the hamlet, pursuant to the provisions of the Act of Parliament then in force. After the expiration of twenty-one days from the service of the notice of chargeability, no notice of appeal being given, the beadle of the parish of St. Mary, Whitechapel, called on the paupers to deliver them under this order, but the paupers not being at home, he delivered the order of removal only without the paupers, to the beadle of the appellant's hamlet, promising to send the paupers, it being an arrangement between the parish and the hamlet, to save the overseers trouble, that notices should be served on their respective beadles. The beadle of the appellants' hamlet subsequently, in the exercise of his discretion, procured the transfer from the account of the relieving officer of the parish of Whitechapel to the account of the relieving officer of Mile End New Town, conceiving the paupers to be settled in the hamlet, and the paupers thenceforth applied to and were relieved by the latter officer for upwards of two years, but no actual removal of the paupers nor any delivery of them under the order ever took place. There has been five years' residence in the parish of St. Mary, Whitechapel, free from relief previous to the order of removal of April, 1849, if not interrupted by the order of removal of August, 1844, and its execution as above stated, if it amounts to an execution of the order. The appellants and respondents being both parishes in the Whitechapel Union, in order to avoid the expense of litigation, have agreed to abide by the opinion of the Poor Law Board, who are requested to say whether they consider the order of 1844 was sufficiently executed so as to break the continuity of residence, and thus render the paupers removable or not.

Ans.—As it appears that in point of fact the pauper was not removed under the order of removal in August, 1844, there was no interruption of the residence, notwithstanding what passed between the officers of the parish of the residence and the parish of the settlement. Hence, as there has been a residence of five years free from relief, the pauper is irremovable from the parish of Whitechapel, and his relief is consequently chargeable upon the union common fund.

X.—REMOVAL.

1. SCOTCH AND IRISH PAUPERS.—APPOINTMENT OF CONDUCTORS.

21st Jan., 1850.

Clerk of Bromsgrove Union.—By the 8th & 9th Vic. c. 117, the justices in quarter sessions for every county are required to make regulations for the removal of poor persons to Ireland, Scotland, &c., at the expense of the parish or union. The justices of Worcestershire at the General Quarter Sessions of the Peace, held on the 5th January, 1846, made the required regulations, and appointed "conductors of all such poor persons as aforesaid, removed under any warrant of justices made in this county, in pursuance of the said statute; and that all such warrants shall be directed to one of them, and to the master of the packet or vessel to whom such conductor shall deliver the parties named therein," with a scale of allowances to the clerk to the justices, to the conductor, and for the maintenance and travelling expenses of the persons to be removed. The guardians have lately had occasion to remove an Irish family under these regulations, and the allowances, &c., to the conductor amount to a much greater sum than it would have cost the guardians if they had conveyed these poor persons direct to the port of Liverpool, from whence they embarked. Inquiring whether the guardians can lawfully, by their own officers, remove poor persons under the 8th & 9th Vic. c. 117, and the regulations of the justices, without the assistance or intervention of the conductor appointed by the justices. The justices of Cumberland, on the 6th January, 1846, (see 10th vol. of the Justice of the Peace, p. 703,) ordered "that the guardians or overseers who shall apply for any such warrant of removal shall nominate to the justices making the same, some person to be the conductor of the parties to the port of embarkation, or other place not being a port, but as near as any of the ports mentioned in the schedule to the said Act, to the place where such paupers were born, and that all such warrants shall be directed to him and to the master of the vessel to whom he shall deliver the same." Such a regulation as this would meet the views of the guardians.

Ans.—The guardians of the Bromsgrove Union cannot legally depart from the regulations prescribed by the justices of the county and approved by the Secretary of State, with respect to the removal of poor persons to Ireland and Scotland, under the 8th & 9th Vic. c. 117, so long as such regulations continue in force. If, however, they are thought to be capable of improvement, an application should be made to the justices to alter them, under sec. 4 of the above statute.

2. COPY OF DEPOSITIONS TO BE FURNISHED.
22nd Jan., 1850.

Parish Officers of Burghclere, Kingsclere Union.—The family of Charles Belsher having become destitute in consequence of his imprisonment in Winchester Jail, are about to be removed under an order of removal from the parish of Newtown to the parish of Burghclere. Inquiring whether the parish officers of Burghclere have a right to demand of the parish officers of Newtown a copy of the examination on which such order has been made. Those officers have refused to supply such copy, alleging that under a recent Act of Parliament it is not compulsory on them to do so. Inquiring also whether, in the event of the parish officers of Newtown being justified in their refusal, the clerk to the magistrates would be warranted in refusing to furnish such copy on an application being made to him for the same.

Ans.—The Board direct your attention to the provisions of the 11 & 12 Vic. c. 31, passed on the 22nd July, 1848, and intitled "An Act to Amend the Procedure in respect of Orders for the Removal of the Poor in England and Wales, and Appeals therefrom." The 3rd sec. of that Act requires the clerk to the justices, who made the order of removal, to keep the depositions, and on application to furnish a copy to the overseers of the parish to which the removal is directed to be made; but as the 9th sec. prevents any appeal being brought against the order, unless notice be given within twenty-one days after the notice of chargeability, &c., has been sent, or within the further period of fourteen days, where a copy of the depositions is applied for, no appeal can be now commenced in the present case, if such twenty-one days have expired, and it will therefore be useless to incur any expense in the matter.

XI.—SETTLEMENT.—WIDOW OF AN ENGLISHMAN WHO RESIDED IN SCOTLAND.
30th Jan., 1850.

James Stewart, Esq., Inspector, Nairn.—A native of England, (a soldier,) came to Scotland above fifteen years ago, where he married and had a family. After being discharged in Ireland, he returned to Edinburgh, where he died lately, without having acquired a settlement in Scotland, leaving his wife and family chargeable on the poor's funds. *Query*—Can the wife, (who is a Scotchwoman,) and the family be sent to her husband's birthplace in England?

Ans.—The removability or irremovability of the pauper referred to, is a question which depends upon the provisions of the law of Scotland. The Board have referred to the statute 8 & 9 Vic. c. 83, but though they find in sec. 77 of that statute a provision for the removal, under certain circumstances, of poor persons from Scotland to England, Ireland, and the Isle of Man, yet that provision does not apply to the case submitted by you, as the person proposed in the present instance to be removed was born in Scotland. The Board regret that they are unable to give you any precise information on the subject.

XII.—VAGRANCY—ITS REPRESSION.
7th March, 1850.

Vice-Chairman of East Ward Union.—Representing the increasing evils of vagrancy, and the inadequacy of the union authorities, as at present constituted, to deal with it.

Ans.—Drawing attention to the recommendations contained in the Minute of the Poor Law Board, dated 4th August, 1848, and published in the Official Circular, vol. vii., 1848, p. 269, and stating as follows:—Where these recommendations have been carefully and steadily acted upon, the effect has been materially to reduce the number of applications for relief from vagrants, and the Board do not doubt that the same result would follow in the East Ward Union from the adoption of the course recommended in the Minute. The Board have lately received a Report from their Inspector, Sir J. Walsham, on the state of vagrancy in his district; from which it appears, that in the county of Essex the number of vagrants relieved in the workhouses, which, in the year 1848, was 23,516, has been reduced, in 1849, to 2,666; and of those relieved out of the workhouses, from 1,366 to 311, being a reduction in the former class of 90, in the latter of 77 per cent.* The plan which has been pursued in most of the unions in Essex, has been to appoint police constables as assistant relieving officers for the relief of this class of poor, and the remarkable decrease which has taken place in vagrancy has been mainly due to the arrangements adopted by the very able and zealous chief constable of the Essex constabulary force, Captain McHardy, and to the support which those arrangements have received from the magistracy and guardians. The measures in question, while they have nearly destroyed professional mendicancy in Essex, have increased the number of commitments of vagrants only one per cent. in 1849 over 1848; there is an absence of complaints; the rates are greatly relieved; in Captain McHardy's opinion the decrease of vagrancy has tended generally to lessen crime.

2. WHETHER A PERSON CAN BE PUNISHED AS FOR A SECOND OFFENCE, WHEN HE DOES NOT RETURN TO AND SUPPORT HIS FAMILY AFTER HIS DISCHARGE FROM JAIL.

26th Nov., 1849.

Clerk of Midhurst Union.—William Ayling, an able-bodied pauper, inmate of the workhouse, who left the same, leaving his wife and family therein chargeable to the parish of Rogate, for which offence he was apprehended, taken before a magistrate, convicted as a rogue and vagabond under the 5th Geo. 4, c. 83, sec. 4, and committed to the House of Correction for fourteen days. At the expiration of his sentence he left the prison, and instead of returning to the workhouse, is now wandering about the country. The guardians wish to be informed whether he can be again treated as a rogue and vagabond before he has returned to his family, and again deserted them. The guardians are aware, that in the event of his being able to maintain his wife and family, he could be proceeded against under the 3rd sec. of the above statute.

Ans.—The question, whether a second proceeding upon the 4th sec. of the Act above-mentioned could be sustained under the circumstances of this case, does not appear to the Board to be so free from doubt as to justify them in advising the adoption of such a course. The guardians of the Midhurst Union are already aware that under sec. 3 of the statute the pauper in question might be convicted, if it could be shown that he was able wholly or in part to maintain his family and wilfully refused or neglected to do so; and the Board may add, that repeated convictions for that offence might take place so long as the same state of facts continued.

3. APPREHENSION OF HUSBANDS DESERTING THEIR WIVES.

6th March, 1850.

Clerk of Worcester Union.—In this union there are many men who leave their wives and children chargeable, and at intervals return to their homes, and partake of the relief allowed to the children by the guardians in the absence of the father. The guardians are anxious to punish the husbands for wilfully neglecting to support their families, but it frequently happens that no warrant has been obtained for their apprehension, and the police constables refuse to apprehend without one. Inquiring whether, in case the relieving officer directs a constable to apprehend, without a warrant, a man who wilfully refuses to support his family, such constable is liable to the penalty stated in the 6th sec. of 5 Geo. 4, c. 83, for neglect of duty, in refusing to obey the directions of the relieving officer; if not, whether he would be liable to such penalty in case the relieving officer himself apprehends the man, and the constable should then refuse to take him before some justice of the peace; and if the relieving officer can legally apprehend a person in such cases without a warrant; and also whether a certificate of the chargeability of the wife and children, placed in the hands of a constable, is

* See this Rep. at p. 134 of 2nd Ann. Rep. of the Poor Law Board.

sufficient evidence that the husband has committed an act of vagrancy, so as to justify the constable in taking him into custody without having a warrant for that purpose. It has been held, that unless a constable witnesses the commitment of an act of vagrancy, he cannot apprehend without a warrant.

Ans.—The Poor Law Board are of opinion that in cases such as are above referred to, if the constable of the parish declines to apprehend a person so offending without a warrant, in a case where a warrant may be obtained, he would hardly be liable to punishment, if acting *bonâ fide* on the belief that such warrant is requisite This, however, is a question for the justices to decide, before whom the guardians can readily take the case. Apart, however, from the question of the constable's duty in the matter, the Board desire to point out, that by the 5th Geo. 4, c. 83, sec. 6, authority is given to any person, as well as to the constable, to apprehend vagrants. It appears, therefore, to be competent for the relieving officer himself, if he is prepared to prove the act of vagrancy, to apprehend the party, and take him before a justice. But the offender must, at the time of apprehension, be found committing the offence; and this summary apprehension appears to be scarcely applicable to the particular act of vagrancy referred to. A certificate of chargeability does not of itself prove that the party has been guilty of an act of vagrancy; to establish that it must be shown either that he had deserted his family and left them chargeable, or that he had the means of maintaining them wholly, or in part, and wilfully refused or neglected the performance of that obligation.

XIII.—VALUATION—OF PROPERTY UNDER 11 & 12 VIC. C. 110, SEC. 7.

20th Feb., 1850.

Clerk of Kingston Union.—The guardians are called upon, under the 7th sec. of the 11 & 12 Vic. c. 110, to cause a valuation of a particular property to be made preparatory to an appeal against the poor's rate, but the property in question being part of a larger estate divided into lots, is not of and by itself laid down in any map within the control of the parish officers. The guardians have appointed a person to make the valuation in the terms of the Act. Inquiring whether, if the property be not found laid down in a map duly authenticated, (either a parochial or tithe map,) so as to enable the surveyor or valuer to give positive evidence on an appeal, the guardians may order the valuer to survey and measure the estate, and may pay him for the same in addition to the expenses of the valuation, so as to render his evidence valid as regards the quantities as well as value.

Ans.—The Board consider that the guardians of the Kingston Union have power to contract for a valuation of the particular property to which you refer, and therefore to contract for all that is necessary to enable that valuation to be made. Consequently, if a survey and admeasurement be necessary for that purpose, the guardians may contract for it as a part of the valuation, charging the expenses in the manner prescribed by the statute.

XIV.—WORKHOUSE.—EMPLOYMENT OF BOYS IN A FACTORY DURING THE DAY.

17th Dec., 1849.

Clerk of ——— Union.—In the union workhouse there are many boys who are able to work, and who would under ordinary circumstances be apprenticed by the guardians, but for the prohibitory apprentice order, as there is no adequate employment for them in the house, and at present their labour cannot be beneficially used in the industrial employment provided by the guardians, viz., the cultivating of a piece of land rented by them for the purpose. Inquiring whether the Board would sanction the boys going out of the workhouse at stated periods of the day to work at a particular branch of the staple trade of the town, if employment could be found for a number of them together in one factory, or warehouse, and where they would be under proper rules and supervision.

Ans.—In reference to your observation, that the boys would under ordinary circumstances be apprenticed by the guardians but for "the prohibitory apprentice order," the Board desire to state that they are not aware of any legal obstacle to the apprenticing of boys in the workhouse, who may be willing to work, if suitable masters are willing to take them. With respect to the mode of employment now proposed by the guardians, the Board have to observe, that it certainly would not be lawful for the guardians to use any compulsion towards the boys in furtherance of the proposal; and supposing that the paupers would acquiesce in the employment, the Board consider it would be so objectionable an interference with the employment of independent labourers, that they would not be prepared to sanction it.

London: Printed by Order of the Poor Law Board, by BLACKBURN & BURT, 90½, Holborn Hill, and Published by CHARLES KNIGHT, 90, Fleet Street.

AN

OFFICIAL CIRCULAR

OF PUBLIC DOCUMENTS AND INFORMATION:

DIRECTED BY THE POOR LAW BOARD TO BE PRINTED, CHIEFLY FOR THE USE OF THE BOARDS OF GUARDIANS AND THEIR OFFICERS.

No. 37.] MAY, 1850. [N.S.

CONTENTS.

I.—BURIAL.

1. OF PAUPERS DYING IN UNION WORKHOUSE.

18th Feb., 1850.

Clerk of Aylsham Union. — Seven or eight deaths have occurred in the new union workhouse, recently erected at Aylsham, since its occupation; and all the persons, excepting the last, (the illegitimate child of a young woman, an inmate of the house, having a legal settlement, and relieved at the expense of one of the parishes of this union—Guestwich) have been, at the request of the relations of the deceased, and by the directions of the guardians, removed for interment to the parishes charged with their relief. The vicar of Aylsham (from the circumstance of the crowded state of the burial-ground) has repeatedly expressed his resolution to refuse the interment of any body from the workhouse in the churchyard of Aylsham, unless upon payment of an unusual fee. The guardians, however, insist upon the right of interment in Aylsham, on payment of the customary fees only; and they are fortified in their decision by the reply of the Poor Law Commissioners in the Official Circular, vol 6, June, 1846, to the inquiry of the clerk of the Bodmin union, and the provisions of the 7 & 8 Vic. c. 101, sec. 31; and accordingly the guardians ordered that the body of the child should be taken, on the following Friday, to the burial-ground in Aylsham for interment. But previous to that day a meeting of the parishioners of Aylsham was held in vestry, when it was resolved to resist the burial, and a notice to that effect was served upon the master of the workhouse and the guardians, and means were adopted to prevent the body being taken into the churchyard there. The child was then sent to Guestwich, and there interred, contrary to the order of the guardians. It being probable that other deaths may shortly occur under similar circumstances, the guardians request the advice and instructions of the Poor Law Board in the matter. More serious difficulties will present themselves in the event of the death of an inmate of the workhouse who happens to be chargeable to the common fund, and therefore not removable, or of a casual pauper, or vagrant, whose settlement may be unknown.

The following case, submitted to Dr. Addams, on behalf of the Churchwardens of the Parish of Aylsham, and his opinion thereon, were transmitted to the Poor Law Board by the Vicar of the Parish:—

Case.—In a letter written by Messrs. Repton and Scott to their proctors, they requested them, on behalf of the vicar and churchwardens of the parish of Aylsham, to get an answer to the following query from some eminent doctor:—Whether the vicar of Aylsham is bound to bury a child belonging to another parish, dying in the union workhouse at Aylsham, such child being at the time of such death chargeable to some other parish. And adding in their letter, "The law in the case is, besides the canon, the 31st & 56th secs. of the 7 & 8 Vic. c. 101."

Opinion.—In my opinion the guardians of the union have no right (arbitrarily) to enforce upon the parishioners of Aylsham the interment of the body of this child in their churchyard, though dying in the union workhouse, locally situate in the parish of Aylsham. And I think that the minister and churchwardens may justifiably refuse to bury the body, (stating at such time their ground of refusal,) leaving it to the guardians to take such steps as they may be advised, in order (if they can) to compel them to it.

Doctors' Commons, 31st Jan., 1850. L. ADDAMS.

Ans. of the Poor Law Board to the Clerk of the Guardians.—As the Board are at present advised, the guardians of the Aylsham union cannot legally insist upon the burial in the churchyard of the parish of Aylsham of the bodies of paupers who, like the child above referred to, die in the Aylsham union workhouse, being at the time of their death chargeable to some other parish in the union. It is true that the Poor Law Commissioners (as appears from letters published in their Official Circulars, including the one addressed to the clerk of the Bodmin Union, to which you particularly refer) took a different view of the combined effect of the 31st & 56th secs. of the 7 & 8 Vic. c. 101; but the Board have recently had occasion to consult Mr. Tomlinson upon the point in question, and they are advised by him, "that in the case of a pauper dying in a union workhouse, situated in the parish of A., but chargeable to some other parish (say B.) in the same union, the guardians cannot (under sec. 31 of the 7 & 8 Vic. c. 101, or at common law) insist upon the burial taking place in the parish in which the workhouse is locally situated." The Board have been furnished by the vicar of Aylsham with a copy of the opinion lately given by Dr. Addams on the same subject, which appears to coincide with Mr. Tomlinson's as above expressed. Under these circumstances, the Board think that the guardians of the Aylsham union should in future give directions, in the class of cases now under consideration, for the burial of the body in the churchyard of the parish to which the deceased pauper was chargeable at the time of his death. On this point, Mr. Tomlinson, in giving the opinion above-mentioned, remarks:—"If for the purpose of burial, the workhouse is to be considered as situated in the parish of chargeability, then the pauper must be buried as if he had died in a workhouse situated in the parish of chargeability, and consequently must be buried in the cemetery of the parish of chargeability, and not elsewhere." The Board think it right to add, that the foregoing observations do not apply to the case of paupers dying in the union workhouse, who may at the time be chargeable to the common fund of the union. It appears to the Board that the bodies of such paupers must be buried in the churchyard of the parish in which they actually die.

---

2. CHARGING COST OF BURIAL.

9th May, 1850.

Clerk of Leigh Union.—Transmitting the following statements, and requesting the opinion of the Board as to the duties of the relieving-officers in the case to which they relate:—

1. *Statement of S. W. Lane, Relieving-officer.*—"S. B., a single man, aged 26 years, resident in Tyldesley, was on Sunday night, 7th April instant, accidentally drowned, on returning home, in the township of Atherton, and carried a distance of about three hundred yards into the township of Westleigh. The two former townships are in the Atherton district, and the latter in the Pennington district, in the Leigh union. The relieving-officer of the Atherton district, who resides about one mile and a half distance from where the dead man lay, was applied to for a coffin and funeral dues, but he refused to have anything to do with the case, inasmuch as S. B. was not then in his district. Application was subsequently made for the same purpose to the relieving-officer of the Pennington district, who resides about three miles and a half from where S. B. lay, and he, therefore, gave orders for a coffin and the payment of the funeral dues. Was it the duty of the relieving-officer of the Atherton district to attend to the case when applied to, or was he justified in refusing the application? See 11 & 12 Vic. c. 110, sec. 2.

2. *Statement of S. Park, Relieving-officer.*—S. B., about 26 years of age, a drawer in a coal pit, a native of Rochdale, or the neighbourhood, where his parents now reside, got work at Mr. Darlington's colliery, in Astley, on or about the 25th March last, and went to lodge at Tyldesley. On Sunday, the 7th April, he went to visit a friend in Westleigh; on his return he had the misfortune to fall into the water in Atherton, and was taken out supposed dead; he was removed

about two hundred yards, to a cottage in Westleigh, where medical aid was procured, but to no purpose, and the body remained in Westleigh until Tuesday, before the coffin and the dues were applied for. Westleigh is in the Pennington district, and Astley, Atherton, and Tyldesley, are in Atherton district of the Leigh union. Inquired whether it was the duty of the relieving-officer for Pennington or Atherton district to furnish the coffin and the dues under the above circumstances.

Ans.—The Board understand the question submitted to them to be, which of the two relieving-officers, under the circumstances of the case, should have interfered to give directions for the interment of the body. The Board do not know whether the circumstances of the present case were such as to allow of application being first made to the guardians at their weekly meeting; if so, having regard to the provisions of the 7 & 8 Vic. c. 101, sec. 31, that course should have been followed, and their directions in the matter taken. If, however, (as is probable,) the case required to be dealt with at once, then, assuming that no person, either as relative or friend, came forward to procure the interment of the body, the interference of one of the relieving-officers was certainly called for. The Board think, as the facts are made known to them, that the relieving-officer of the Pennington district (in which the body lay) should have given the necessary direction in the first instance, reporting the case to the guardians for their confirmation of his act; for though the death may have taken place in another district, viz., in Atherton, (which, however, is a point in dispute,) still the necessity for burial certainly existed in Pennington. The question of charging the costs was a distinct matter, and one entirely for the determination of the guardians. In determining that question, the guardians would have had to ascertain the fact, (if it could be ascertained,) in what township the death actually took place. If in Atherton, that township would, under the 7 & 8 Vic. c. 101, sec 31, have been chargeable with the costs; if in Westleigh, then Westleigh would have been liable on that ground. If, however, the question of the place of death could not be satisfactorily ascertained, then Westleigh would still be liable, but on a different ground, viz., on the ground that the body was lying dead in that township. (See the language of the 31st sec.)

II.—CHARGEABILITY.

1. OF A WIDOW AND HER TWO IDIOT CHILDREN.

1st March, 1850.

Clerk of Alnwick Union.—About thirty-seven years ago, Joseph Wilson, his wife, and their two idiot children, came to reside in the township of Shilbottle. At that time, and up to the year 1843, they received relief to the amount of 4*s.* a week, whilst residing in Shilbottle, from the parish of West Denton. In 1843, the relief was increased to 9*s.* a week, which the paupers received from West Denton, whilst residing in Shilbottle, until the passing of the 9 & 10 Vic. c. 66, when the relief was discontinued. The overseers of Shilbottle then and on the 19th of May, 1849, obtained an order of justices for the removal of Wilson, his wife, and two children, from Shilbottle to West Denton. The execution of the order was suspended on account of the illness of Wilson and his wife, and a copy of the order and of the suspension was sent by post on the 29th of May, 1849, to the overseers of West Denton. No appeal has been entered against the order. The suspension has not been taken off by reason of the continued illness of the paupers; and on the 17th of November, 1849, Joseph Wilson died. The two idiot children have since the father's death, by order of justices, been removed to a lunatic asylum at the cost of Shilbottle. The widow still remains at Shilbottle, receiving relief therefrom. A question has arisen with the board of guardians, whether the maintenance money of the two idiot children in the asylum, and the relief to the widow, should be charged to the township of Shilbottle, or to the common charges—assuming the irremovability of the widow within twelve months after the decease of her husband; and they request the opinion of the Poor Law Board on this point.

Ans.—The Poor Law Board are of opinion that the woman's relief is chargeable upon the common fund of the Alnwick Union, as she is irremovable by virtue of the 9 & 10 Vic. c. 66, sec. 2. As to the case of the children, the Board think that being idiots, although above the age of twenty-one, they must be considered as still minors, according to the principle laid down in R. *v.* Much Cowarne (2 B. and Ad. 861,) and that they may be properly deemed "children" within the meaning of the 11 & 12 Vic. c. 111.

---

2. CHARGEABILITY OF A WANDERING LUNATIC.

1st March, 1850.

Clerk of East Retford Union.—On Saturday, 9th of February, the police, accompanied by the overseers of the poor, brought one Bailey, a lunatic, before the magistrates, he having been found wandering about the streets of Tuxford in this union, and he was admitted that day into the union workhouse, as a temporary provision, and an order made by the magistrates (with medical aid, &c.) for his reception in the County Lunatic Asylum. A communication was accordingly made the same day to the asylum, to ascertain if there was room, and a negative reply was received; an application was made to the Lincoln Asylum, as the nearest out of the county, and a reply was given that there would be room there in a few days. The lunatic was placed under the care of the two ablest inmates of the workhouse; but in the interim of a vacancy occurring at either asylum, he escaped in the night-time, early in the following week, carrying with him the strait waistcoat which the medical officer had caused him to be placed in. It afterwards appeared that he made to the place of abode of his mother, a widow then staying with a relation in the parish of Wellow, in the Southwell Union, with whom he had been residing at Bathley, in the same union, previously to his being found by the police at Tuxford. A few days afterwards he was brought in a cart from Wellow, by two inhabitants of that place, to the Retford union workhouse, but was refused admission on the ground that the parish of Wellow should have sent him to their own workhouse, which is in the union wherein he had been previously resident. Requesting the opinion of the Poor Law Board, as to whether the expense incurred on account of the above lunatic be chargeable to the parish of Tuxford, where he was found wandering, or to the common fund.

Ans.—The pauper appears to the Board to have been a destitute wanderer when he was brought to the workhouse of the East Retford union, and therefore the cost of his relief should have been charged to the union common fund.

---

3. Family of a prisoner.

2nd Feb., 1850.

Guardians of the Parish of Callington, Liskeard Union.—A robbery was committed in this town, and property to a considerable amount taken away. One of the parties who committed the robbery was traced to Jersey, and brought from thence to this place. The authorities in Jersey compelled the wife and family to leave the island with the husband, and they returned with him to this place, where the man was committed to the county jail to take his trial. During the time the man was in custody, the wife applied as being destitute, and was relieved by the overseer of Callington. The husband was inquired of before the magistrate respecting his settlement, but refused to give any information respecting it. After the man's committal, the woman and family being destitute were sent to the union house at Liskeard, and the relief charged to the parish of Callington. She was examined before the board of guardians, and stated she did not know her husband's parish, but understood he came from Hampshire, and that she herself was born in the parish of Duloe; her mother is now chargeable to the common fund of the union. The man never lived in Callington, but is believed to be a wandering vagabond. If the decision of the board of guardians is to stand, the family will remain a permanent charge on the parish. Inquiring whether any power exists to compel the husband to disclose his settlement, or is such evidence as the wife has given sufficient.

Ans.—If the woman above referred to was inhabiting in the parish of Callington at the time when she became destitute, the cost of her relief must be charged to that parish. If she were a wayfarer or a wanderer at that time, the cost of her relief would be chargeable upon the common fund of the Liskeard union. Whether she can be considered to have been such or not, under the circumstances of the case, is a question which the Board have not sufficient information before them to enable them to decide. With regard to the question of settlement, the husband being a prisoner can be examined thereon while in jail by the justices, under 59 Geo. 3, c. 12; but if he will not give evidence respecting his settlement, the Board do not see that he can be compelled to do so while he remains in jail, as the punishment for refusing to give evidence thereon is committal to jail. With respect to your question, whether the guardians may not, under the circumstances, avail themselves of such evidence as the wife has given respecting the settlement of the husband, the Board desire to observe, that the statement of the wife is certainly not sufficient to justify the removal of the family in the present instance.

III.—EDUCATION.—Industrial training of pauper children in the Guiltcross union, Norfolk.

The following communication on the subject of the industrial training of workhouse children, which has been addressed to Sir John Walsham and Mr. Bowyer by the master of the Guiltcross union workhouse, is recommended to the attention of boards of guardians.

Annexed to this communication will be found a farming account of the produce of 4 A. 1 R. and 35 P. of land, hired by the Guiltcross board of guardians at Kenninghall, in Norfolk. This account shows an annual profit of £15 per acre, during the three years ended at Christmas, 1849.

Of the boys now in the school, fourteen are upon an average employed on the land; whilst others, (who, however, take their turn also on the land,) are instructed in tailoring and shoemaking, or are occupied in domestic duties. The boys labouring in the field are carefully guarded from association with the men, whenever men are employed, and are superintended by the workhouse master or the schoolmaster.

The moral and industrial training of the girls in this workhouse is equally attended to, and qualifies them successfully for service.

During school-hours, the boys and girls meet in the same room, and form one school, instructed by the schoolmaster and schoolmistress; the former of whom has charge of the higher, and the latter of the lower classes. This mixed organization, which has existed for many years in the Kenninghall Workhouse School, has been found to be highly advantageous, not only to the progress of the children's learning, but also to the formation of their minds and manners.

The course of instruction, in addition to the study of the Scriptures, and to reading, writing, and arithmetic, embraces geography, grammar, and English history, in all of which the proficiency of the children is above the average observable in workhouse schools. Nor has the result of this combination of moral and intellectual with industrial training, under the watchful superintendence of the master and matron as well as of the teachers, disappointed the expectations of the guardians, who, to their great credit, have always sought to place the education of the children in their workhouse on the most effective basis. No difficulty in procuring good situations for children so trained has been ever experienced; and after leaving the workhouse, the children generally have conducted themselves most satisfactorily—the instances to the contrary being very rare. J. W.

BURY ST. EDMUND'S,
22nd May, 1850.

The following is the communication referred to above:—

To SIR JOHN WALSHAM, BART., *Poor Law Inspector of the District, and to* H. G. BOWYER, ESQ., *one of Her Majesty's Inspectors of Schools.*

GUILTCROSS UNION WORKHOUSE LAND ACCOUNT.

GENTLEMEN,—In submitting this Account, I beg leave to make the following remarks:—

At the formation of the union the guardians purchased three acres of land, of which 1 A. 2 R. 5 P. was used as the workhouse site, and for the yards and offices connected with it, leaving 1 A. 1 R. 35 P. available for the purposes of cultivation.

At Michaelmas, 1845, the guardians, in order to extend the means of employing the boys in the workhouse school, and training them in habits of industry, procured three acres of additional land; this land, which was then in hills or holes, and useless for agricultural purposes, was levelled by the paupers, the top sward being carefully kept uppermost. In the autumn of 1846, one acre of the new land was planted with wheat, and 2 R. 23 P. of the home land; the 1 A. 1 R. 35 P., mentioned above, was also planted with wheat; making in all 1 A. 2 R. 23 P. under wheat for 1847. This land produced eighteen coombs three pecks beyond a sufficient quantity reserved for seed for the wheat crop of 1848. The remainder of the land was planted with Scotch kale, cabbages, potatoes, &c., &c., which began coming into use in March, 1847, at which time this account commences. We have now 4 A. 1 R. 35 P. in cultivation.

Two dozen spades were purchased at the outset, to commence digging the land with, and six wheelbarrows were made by a pauper who was a wheelwright; pickaxes and other tools were also made by the paupers, with the assistance of the porter, who was a blacksmith. The cost for these does not appear, as there was no produce account to charge them to, but the stock being kept up they remain as dead farming stock.

The first year's account was kept merely to satisfy the guardians; but at Lady-day, 1848, the new order of accounts came into operation, and the land account now forms an item in the union ledger and master's day-book, which is duly audited by the auditor half-yearly.

The quantity of vegetables actually consumed by the paupers according to the dietary table only is charged in the provisions' accounts. Persons acquainted with domestic management and the produce of land are aware, that where vegetables are purchased a great deal is paid for that which is useless for cooking purposes. In the present case, this refuse is carefully preserved and used for feeding pigs, which were first kept in April, 1848. This accounts for the large amount of pork fatted, as compared with the small quantity of corn and pollard used for the pigs. The leaves, &c., not eaten by the pigs, become valuable manure. If the guardians would consent to keep cows, different roots and vegetables might be grown to feed them with, and these would produce an increased quantity of manure, whilst an increased quantity of manure would afford the means of raising a larger amount of roots and green crops, and secure a more extended routine in cropping the land. This would add to the profit of the land account, and give much additional comfort to the aged people and the young children in the workhouse, as a better supply of milk and butter would be obtained than can at present be had; but the immediate profit of cow-keeping would be but a trifling advantage compared with the opportunity that would be given of training the female pauper children for dairymaids, who would thereby become doubly acceptable as farm-servants, and the boys too would gain an acquaintance with the recent improved management of cows, which could not fail to be of service to them.

For the benefit of those boards of guardians or masters of workhouses who may from this statement feel desirous of entering upon the system here pursued, I would state that in all cases I change the crops, sowing alternately wheat, potatoes, carrots, parsnips, and cabbages. I have found, by the experience of the last two years, that it is best to plant early potatoes, and to plant them very early, that is to say, in February or the beginning of March. Having plenty of labour during the winter months, the land is laid in ridges two feet and a half wide, about three inches of the top soil is pared off, which removes all weeds and seeds that may be in the land; after the wheat crops a full spade's depth is taken up, together with all the crumbs, and three inches of top-soil is then forked into the sub-soil at the bottom of the trench, which gives fresh soil for the potatoes. At the time of planting a drill about three inches is drawn, and the potatoes are put in a foot apart, the sides of the ridges being chopped down so that the potatoes are covered about six inches. As the potatoes advance in growth, I have the land levelled, and in May sow swede turnips or plant cabbage plants. The potatoes are fit to dig in August, when I transplant the swede turnips or plant more cabbage plants, first giving them a good soaking in liquid manure, for which purpose all soap-suds and night-soil are carefully preserved. Two crops are thus obtained in the year from the potatoe land.

The land appropriated for the produce of cabbages is managed as follows:—In the middle of July I sow cabbage seed of a good kind, namely, the Ham or Victoria; I sow again in the second weeks of August and September—beginning to plant if possible the latter end of September—in rows three feet apart, leaving nine inches from plant to plant. These being well established in growth and earthed up, other cabbage plants are planted between those rows, as before stated, in January or February, as the weather may suit. These are put in fifteen inches from plant to plant. In early spring I draw every other plant of those first planted, which affords a supply when most wanted, and admits air to the remaining plants. After cutting the first cabbages, the ground is cleared, and the third crop of cabbages is planted, which furnish a supply till after harvest, when the cabbages between the potatoes come into use, and the cabbage land is cleared or made fit for a wheat crop. It will be seen that an abundant supply is thus produced for pigs, and if the guardians permitted cows to be kept there would be enough for them also; but it must be borne in mind that all this planting is followed up by very liberal supplies of liquid manure.

The following is a summary of profit for labour upon 4 A. 1 R. 35 P. of land, as shown in detail in the account already referred to:—

	£	s.	d.
First year	£60	2	4¼
Second year	51	17	6
To Christmas, 1849, ¾ year	67	2	1¼
	£179	1	11½

I have thus endeavoured to give all the information I can upon the subject, disclaiming any intention of teaching the well-informed farmers; my only object in preparing this statement has been, to point out to those who have the charge of children in union workhouses, a means of training them in habits of industry and preparing them for future usefulness. The fact that there are sixty boys and girls who have been trained at this workhouse now earning their own living, is some evidence of the success of the system pursued there.

I have the honour to be, Gentlemen,

Your most obedient and faithful servant,

THOMAS RACKHAM,

Master of the Workhouse of the Guiltcross Union.

Dr. *Workhouse Land, in Account with the Guiltcross Union, for the Year ended 25th March,* 1848. Cr.

Date		£. s. d.
1846.		
Nov.	2½ Bushels of Spalding Wheat, for Seed, of Mr. Read	0 18 9
1847.		
March 26	Poor Rate from Michaelmas to Lady-day . .	0 6 0
	Guano of Mr. Bryant	1 6 0
April 3	Potatoes for Seed; Cabbage, Carrot, and Parsnip Seed; Broad Beans, &c., &c., of Mackie . .	3 3 0
	Artificial Manure, of James Fison	0 16 0
	Carting 40 Loads of Manure	1 0 0
June 12	Poor Rate	0 2 6
Sept. 14	Ditto	0 3 7
	Carting Corn	0 10 0
Oct. 12	Tithes, Rev. J. B. Wilkinson	0 11 6
	Ditto, for Home Land	0 12 0
	Rent to T. Thornhill, Esq.	3 15 0
	Ditto, for Home Land	2 5 0
1848.		
Jan. 12	Paid Poor Rate, Mr. Beales	0 2 6
Feb. 14	Ditto, Mr. Youells	0 1 9¾
	James Barnes, Thrashing 18 Coombs Wheat . .	1 7 0
To March 25	Superintendent of Labour, 6 weeks	3 0 0
		20 0 7¾
	Balance for Labour . . .	60 2 4¼
		£80 3 0

Date		Average Number of Persons to supply.	Dozens of Cabbages	Weight, Stones	Quantity of Potatoes	Weight, Stones	£. s. d.
1847. March 27 to April 24	Greens used weekly for 5 weeks, which require two-fourths more than Potatoes in weight . .	205	..	255	..	..	3 4 0
May 8 to July 10	Cabbages used weekly for 10 weeks 4 times each week . . .	218	456	1146	..	..	8 19 0
July 17 to Aug. 14	Cabbages used in 5 weeks, 3 times a week	163	134	337	..	..	2 15 6
	Scarlet Runner Beans, 38 pecks, at 1*s*.	..	..	..	..	..	1 18 0
Aug. 21 to Sept. 11	Cabbages used for 4 weeks, twice per week	137	68	182	..	..	1 6 0
	Broad Beans, 72 bushels, at 1*s*. .	..	..	..	..	..	3 12 0
Sept. 18 to Oct. 23	Cabbages used in 5 weeks, twice per week	157	80	220	..	..	1 12 0
	Potatoes 24 bushels, at 1*s*. 8*d*. .	..	..	..	bush 24	stons 84	2 0 0
„ 30	Took into Store Potatoes, at 1*s*. 7½*d*.	..	..	..	172	602	13 19 6
	Carrots, 132 bushels, at 6*d*. . . .	..	..	..	..	528	3 5 0
	Parsnips, 80 bushels, at 7*d*. . . .	..	..	..	..	320	2 6 8
	Onions, 36 pecks, at 1*s*. . . .	..	..	..	..	..	1 16 0
Nov. 7 to Dec. 25	Vegetables for Sick and Invalids, and for the Establishment . . .	..	..	..	..	..	1 5 0
1848. Feb. 14	Straw, 4 Loads, cut for the Beds .	..	..	..	..	..	10 0 0
	8½ Coombs Wheat sold to Robinson	..	..	..	..	..	9 0 0
March 22	8 Coombs, 7 pecks	..	..	..	..	..	10 10 6
	5 Bushels Small Wheat . . .	..	..	..	..	..	1 5 0
Dec. 25 to March 25	Vegetables for Establishment, and Leeks, &c., for Soups, &c., and for Invalids	..	..	..	..	..	1 8 10
							£80 3 0

Dr. *Workhouse Land, in Account with the Guiltcross Union, for the year ended 25th March,* 1849. Cr.

Dr.

Date	Particulars	£. s. d.	£. s. d.
1848.	Amount actually expended in Seed, Wheat Seed, Potatoes, &c., reserved from last year's growth, except where a new Stock was thought necessary:—		
March 26	John Coulson, Jun., 2 bushels Potatoes for Seed	0 10 0	
April 11	John Fisher, 4 Pigs	4 2 0	
	James Robinson, Pollard for Pigs . .	0 7 0	
„ 27	Ditto ditto . .	0 16 0	
May 23	Ditto ditto . .	0 8 0	
June 2	Ditto ditto . .	0 8 0	
„ 4	Richard Bryant, Corn for fatting . .	3 6 0	
„ 27	James Robinson, Barley Meal, &c. . .	1 7 8	
„ 30	Richard Bryant, Corn for fatting . .	1 12 0	
July 8	James Robinson, Pollard for Pigs . .	0 8 0	
Aug. 4	Ditto ditto . .	0 16 0	
Sept. 9	Richard Bryant, Corn for fatting . .	3 4 6	
„ 11	James Robinson, Pollard for Pigs . .	0 16 0	18 1 2
	From Master's Day Book as per New Order of Accounts.		
April 27	Richard Sage, use of Draining Tools . .	0 1 0	
May 24	Poor Rate for Land, 2 Quarters . . .	0 4 1	
June 23	Finch, for Manure	0 10 0	
Aug. 16	Thatching Stack, paid Bigsby . . .	0 2 6	
Sept. 22	Carting Corn	0 6 0	1 3 7
Oct. 24	Rent paid to T. Thornhill, Esq. . . .	. . .	3 15 0
	Carried forward . . .	. .	£22 19 9

Cr.

Date	Particulars	£. s. d.	£. s. d.
	Amount actually consumed charged in the Daily Provision Account No. 25 and 26, and transferred to the Weekly Provision Account No. 27, 28, and 29, thence to the Guiltcross Union Ledger as new form of Account:—		
	First Quarter.		
1848. June 24	Pork 24¼ stones, at 4*s.* 3*d.* per stone . .	5 5 0	
	Potatoes 36 bushels, weight 144 stones, at 1*s.* 3*d.* per bushel	2 4 1	
	Cabbages 322 stones, at 3*d.* per stone . .	4 0 6	11 9 7
	Peas, Onions, and other small kinds of Vegetables used for the Establishment and for Soups	. .	1 3 0
	Second Quarter.		
to Sept. 23	Pork 17 stones 10 lbs., at 5*s.* 10*d.*, Contract price	5 1 3	
	Potatoes 14 cwt., at 4*s.*	2 16 0	
	Cabbages 696 stones, at 2¼*d.* per stone .	6 10 6	14 7 9
	Peas, Beans, and Onions for Establishment	. .	1 6 0
	Third Quarter		
Oct. 24	Wheat sold to Mr. Davey	. .	9 2 0
	As charged in Provision Account and Ledger:—		
to Dec. 23	Pork 56 stones 4 lbs., at 5*s.* 10*d.* per stone .	16 8 4	
	Potatoes 14 cwt., at 3*s.* 1*d.* per cwt. . .	2 3 0	
	Cabbages 347 stones, at 2¼*d.* per stone .	3 5 0	21 16 4
	Carried forward . . .	. .	£59 4 8

DR. *Workhouse Land, in Account with the Guiltcross Union, for the Year ended 25th March, 1849.* CR.

Date		£. s. d.	£. s. d.
1848.	Brought forward . . .	. . .	22 19 9
Oct. 24	Rent paid for 1 A. 1 R. 35 P. Home Land .	. . .	2 5 0
	Proportion of Poor Rate for Land in Kenninghall	. . .	0 5 0
	James Robinson, Barley Meal . . .	0 18 9	
Nov. 14	Robert West, Tithe Rent-charge . . .	1 16 1	
„ 24	Richard Bryant, Corn for fatting Pigs .	3 18 3	
Dec. 23	George Tyrrell, 4 Pigs	2 5 0	
	James Barnes, Thrashing Corn . . .	0 12 0	
1849.	J. W. Ewing, Seeds for the year . . .	1 18 10	
Jan. 6	Burlingham & Sons, Pollard . . .	0 14 0	
Feb. 21	Ditto ditto . . .	0 14 0	
„ 22	Richard Bryant, Corn	3 0 0	
March 5	Ditto ditto	3 9 0	
„ 24	George Tyrrell, 8 Pigs	5 8 0	
	J. W. Ewing, Seeds, &c. . . .	1 17 4	
	Richard Bryant, Corn	3 0 0	29 11 3
1849.	*From Master's Day Book:—*		
Jan. 4	Carting Muck	0 6 0	
March 24	Poor Rate for Land	0 2 0	
	Six bushels York Regent Potatoes for Seed	0 7 6	0 15 6
	Proportion of Kenninghall Poor Rate to Lady-day	. . .	0 3 0
	Estimated value of liquid Manure, although nothing was made of it previous to occupying Land	. . .	5 0 0
			60 19 6
	Balance for Labour . .	. . .	51 17 6
			£112 17 0

Date		£. s. d.	£. s. d.
1848.	Brought forward . . .	. . .	59 4 8
Oct. 24 to Dec. 23.	Wheatmeal 15 stones, at 1*s*. 9½*d*. per stone .	1 6 10½	
	Carrots 9 cwt., at 1*s*. 4*d*. per cwt. . .	0 12 0	1 18 10½
	Savoys, Brocoli, &c., for Establishment, Onions, &c., for Soups	. . .	1 10 0
	[A small quantity of Wheat left after planting for the ensuing Year. . . .		
	Fourth Quarter.		
1849. March 24	As per Provision Account and Union Ledger:—		
	Pork, 93 stones 2 lbs., at 5*s*. 6*d*. per stone .	25 12 3	
	Potatoes, 14 cwt., at 4*s*. 7½*d*. per cwt. . .	8 9 8½	
	Carrots, 96 cwt., at 1*s*. 4*d*. per cwt. . .	6 8 0	40 9 11½
	Vegetables for Establishment . . .	. . .	0 15 6
	Onions, Leeks, &c., for Soup . . .	. . .	0 13 0
	Straw, for Beds, 3 Loads, at 55*s*. . . .	. . .	8 5 0
	[This is cut, and then put into the Beds, and is frequently reduced so small that it is useless for manure.]		
			£112 17 0

Workhouse Land, in Account with the Guiltcross Union, for the three Quarters of a year ended 25th December, 1849.

DR.

Date		£. s. d.	£. s. d.
1849.			
	Burlingham and Sons, Pollard	1 2 10	
June 21	Richard Bryant, Corn	11 3 6	
			12 6 4
July 2	Ditto ditto	2 0 0	
,, 14	Ditto ditto	0 13 0	
Aug. 13	James Calver, 7 Pigs	4 7 0	
Sept. 21	Richard Bryant, Corn	2 18 9	
	S. J. Fill, Stack Cover	1 13 4	
	John Coulson, Manure for Turnips	0 15 0	
	Chas. Kerrison	0 15 7	
			13 2 8
	From Master's Day Book:—		
April 7	Spades from John Wallis	0 16 0	
	Carting Muck	0 8 0	
June 2	Poor Rates	0 3 10½	
July 15	Onion and Cabbage Seed	0 8 0	
Aug. 8	Poor Rates	0 2 0	
Sept. 12	Carting Corn	0 7 0	
			2 4 10½
Oct. 12	Rent, T. Thornhill, Esq.	3 15 0	
	Ditto, Home Land, 1 A. 1 R. 35 P.	2 5 0	
Dec. 23	Thos. Fison, Offal for Pigs	2 5 0	
	Richard Bryant, Corn for fatting	4 19 0	
	Charles Kerrison, Poles	0 17 6	
			14 1 6
	From Master's Day Book:—		
Oct. 30	Carting Muck and Potatoes, Turnips, &c.	0 4 6	
Dec. 4	Paid Barnes, Thrashing Corn	1 6 6	
,, 7	Rent Charge, Rev. T. B. Wilkinson	0 11 6	
,, 23	Carting Muck, &c.	0 8 0	
			2 10 6
			44 5 10½
	Liquid Manure from Privies, &c.	. .	6 0 0
	Balance for Labour	. .	67 2 1½
			£117 8 0

CR.

Date		£. s. d.	£. s. d.
	As Provision Accounts and Union Ledger.		
	First Quarter.		
1849.			
June 23	Pork, 540 lbs., at 5*d.* per lb.	10 13 9	
	Cabbages, 528 stones, at 2¼*d.* per stone	4 19 0	
	Potatoes, 988 lbs., at ½*d.* per lb.	1 19 8	
			17 12 5
	Vegetables for Establishment, Beans, Peas, &c.	. .	0 18 6
	Onions, &c., for Soups, &c.	. .	0 13 0
	Second Quarter.		
Sept. 22	Pork, 686 lbs., at 5*d.* per lb.	14 5 10	
	Potatoes, 4,442 lbs., or 39 cwt. 2 qrs. 18 lbs., at 3*s.* 3*d.* per cwt.	6 8 0	
	Cabbages, 988 stones, at 2¼*d.* per stone	9 5 3	
			29 19 1
	Vegetables for Establishment	. .	0 16 0
	Onions, &c., for Soups, &c.	. .	0 12 0
	Received for Turnip Seed sold	. .	5 5 0
	Third Quarter.		
Dec. 23	Carrots, 40 cwt., at 1*s.* 2*d.* per cwt.	2 6 0	
	Parsnips, 84 cwt., at 1*s.* 6*d.* per cwt.	6 6 0	
	Potatoes, 30 cwt., at 3*s.* 4*d.* per cwt.	5 0 0	
	Pork, 63 stones, at 5*s.* per stone	15 15 0	
			29 7 0
	Vegetables for Establishment	. .	0 11 0
	Onions, Leeks, &c., for Soups	. .	0 14 0
	Sold Wheat to Mr. Robinson, reserving enough for Seed	. .	19 15 0
	Straw, 5 loads, used for Beds, at 45*s.* per load	. .	11 5 0
			£117 8 0

IV.—GUARDIANS—MINUTES OF PROCEEDINGS OF.

15*th March*, 1850.

Clerks of Wareham and Purbeck Union.—The General Consolidated Order, Art. 41, directs, "That the minutes of the last ordinary meeting and of any other meeting which may have been held since such ordinary meeting, shall be read to the guardians, and * * * shall be signed by the chairman presiding at the meeting at which such minutes are read." Suppose A. B. chairman of one meeting, happens to be absent from the following meeting when the minutes are read, and at such following meeting C. D. (a guardian not present at the meeting to which the minutes refer) fills the chair, according to the Article he must sign, as chairman, minutes to which his name is not prefixed as being present at the meeting, the business of which they record, or taking any part in such meeting as chairman or otherwise, but, from his signature being at the foot of the minutes, he may erroneously, at any future time, be supposed to have attended the meeting. As this is opposed to the general mode of transacting and authenticating business at public meetings, considerable difficulty is felt on the subject. Requesting the advice of the Poor Law Board thereon. The following is the form in which the minutes are kept in this union:—

Quarter ending Lady Day, 1850. At the eighth weekly meeting of the board of guardians, held on Tuesday, the 12th day of February, 1850,

Present

A. B. (In the chair.)

E. F., G. H., J. K., L.M.

The minutes of the weekly meeting, held on Tuesday, the 5th day of February, 1850, were read and confirmed. Then follow the money entries and all resolutions, letters read, and orders given, &c. A. B., chairman. In practice, A. B. does not sign the minutes until after they have been read at the next meeting. If signed by C. D. (not present) at the following meeting to the 12th of February, he would be chairman of the meeting at which A. B. presided.

Ans.—The practice which you state has been pursued in this matter in the Wareham and Purbeck union, does not appear to the Board to be in accordance with the directions of the Article alluded to. The Board are clearly of opinion that that Article requires the minutes of the proceedings at the previous meetings of the guardians to be signed by the chairman presiding at the meeting at which such minutes are read, and not by the chairman who presided at the meeting to which such minutes relate. With reference to your remarks upon this subject, the Board may observe, that the chairman of the meeting at which the minutes of the previous meeting are read, by signing such minutes, testifies to the fact of their having been so read, and thereupon confirmed by the guardians then present as the official record; but he does not personally authenticate such minutes otherwise than by testifying to the fact of their confirmation by the board of guardians, of which, as chairman for the day, he is officially the organ.

V.—IRREMOVABLE POOR.—FORM OF JOINT STATEMENT UNDER 11 & 12 VIC. C. 110, SEC. 4.

2*nd May*, 1850.

Mr. Charles Knight, Publisher, London—Enclosing a Form which he had had prepared, headed "Joint Statement of Case, under the 11 & 12 Vic. c. 110, sec. 4," and requesting to be informed if it meets with the approbation of the Poor Law Board.

Ans.—The Board having perused the Form enclosed in your letter, they are prepared to express their general approval of it, as it appears to them well adapted for the purposes of the enactment alluded to, and likely to prove useful and convenient in the cases to which that enactment may apply.

[*Joint Statement of Case, under* 11 & 12 *Vic. c.* 110, *s.* 4.]

________________ UNION.

Day of Meeting, ________________

____

________________ 185

Sir,—I am directed by the guardians of the Union, to transmit to you the accompanying statement of the case of a pauper named and to request that you will be good enough to lay the same before the Poor Law Board, with the view of obtaining their decision thereon.

I have the honour to be,

Sir,

Your obedient Servant,

____

Clerk to the Guardians.

To the Secretary of the Poor Law Board.

______________ UNION.

Case submitted for the decision of the Poor Law Board, under the 11 *&* 12 *Vic. c.* 110, *sec.* 4.

A question having arisen between the guardians of the Union, and the parish (*or* township) of comprised in that union, with reference to the charging of the cost of the relief of a pauper named as to whether such pauper is exempted under any provision of the Act 9 & 10 Vic. c. 66, from the liability to be removed to the place of ([a]) settlement—

We, the undersigned, being respectively the presiding chairman of the board of guardians of the said union, acting on their behalf, and the guardian ([b]) of the said parish, (*or* township,) acting on behalf of the same, hereby jointly submit such question to the Poor Law Board, in accordance with the provisions of the Act 11 & 12 Vic. c. 110, sec. 4; and we request the Poor Law Board to determine such question, upon the following statement of the facts of the case, in which statement we concur, namely:—

STATEMENT. ([c])

(*a*) "*His*," or "*her*," as the case may be.
(*b*) "*Guardians*," if more than one.
(*c*) The Statement should be carefully drawn up by the clerk; and should contain precise information as to names and dates, as well as the full particulars of the several facts in the case. It is difficult to offer any definite suggestions as to the mode of preparing this Statement, as the circumstances of the various cases differ widely; but it may be remarked generally, that all the questions will necessarily arise upon the provisions of the 9 & 10 Vic. c. 66, secs. 1, 2, 3, and 4, taken in conjunction with the Amending Act, 11 & 12 Vic. c. 111; and in drawing up the Statement, the clerk should direct his attention to the specific provisions which bear upon the particular case. These will be found noticed in detail on the last page of the present sheet.

QUESTION.

Is the above-named pauper, under the circumstances detailed in the foregoing statement, exempt, in pursuance of the 9 & 10 Vic. c. 66, from the liability to be removed to the place of such pauper's settlement?

Signed at the meeting of the board of guardians of the Union, held this day of 185 , by us,

______________ { *Presiding Chairman of the said Board of Guardians.*

______________ { *Guardian* ([a]) *of the said Parish* (or *Township of*
____

Witness,

______________ { *Clerk to the Guardians of the said Union.*

[MEMORANDUM.]

If the case falls under 9 & 10 Vic. c. 66, sec. 1, it will be necessary in preparing the Statement to take notice of the following points:—

The date when the pauper began to reside in the parish, and the date of the commencement of the present chargeability.

Any occasions on which the pauper's residence in the parish may be considered to have been interrupted; with particulars of the circumstances which took place on each occasion. (See 12 & 13 Vic. c. 103, sec. 4.)

Any periods of time which are to be excluded from the computation, under the circumstances mentioned in the first proviso to 9 & 10 Vic. c. 66, sec. 1; namely—
- imprisonment in the parish;
- service as a soldier, marine, or sailor;
- residence as an in-pensioner in Greenwich or Chelsea Hospital;
- confinement in a lunatic asylum, licensed house, or registered hospital; (see 9 & 10 Vic. c. 66, sec. 1, and 12 & 13 Vic. c. 103, sec. 4;)
- residence as a patient in a hospital;
- receipt of relief from any parish, or from the common fund of any union; (see 12 & 13 Vic. c. 103, sec. 4;)
- maintenance, wholly or in part, from any rate or subscription raised in a parish other than that of the residence, not being a *bonâ fide* charitable gift;
- and lastly, admission into the union workhouse; (see 12 & 13 Vic. c. 103, sec. 4.)

The total period of uninterrupted residence in the parish; the total period to be ex-

(*a*) "*Guardians*," if more than one.

cluded therefrom, (*i.e.*, deducted;) and the total remaining period, which forms the ground of the irremovability.

If the case falls under the 9 & 10 Vic. c. 66, sec. 2, the date and circumstances of the husband's death, and the circumstances of his own and of his wife's residence at the time of his death, will probably be the chief points for consideration.

If the case falls under the 9 & 10 Vic. c. 66, sec. 4, it will be proper to state:—

Whether the pauper *became* chargeable in respect of relief made necessary by sickness or accident.

The nature of the sickness or accident.

And whether it is probable that the justices would refuse to grant a warrant of removal on the ground that such sickness or accident will not produce permanent disability.

If the case is affected by the 9 & 10 Vic. c. 66, sec. 3, or by the 11 & 12 Vic. c. 111, it will be important to specify the precise relationship of the children towards the relative, as well as the circumstances connected with the question of the parent's irremovability, and with the residence of the children in the parish.

VI.—OFFICERS.—Superannuation Allowance to Poor Law Officers: Circular.

Poor Law Board,
Somerset House,
15th April, 1850.

Sir,—I am directed by the Poor Law Board to state, that they have had under their consideration the means of providing a Superannuation Allowance for the Officers engaged in the administration of the Laws for the Relief of the Poor.

The subject presents great difficulty when viewed with reference to the only mode of securing this provision which is likely to obtain the assent of the Legislature.

A draft of a Bill has been submitted to the Poor Law Board by parties representing many of those officers, in which the Board have made some alterations, which appeared to them to be requisite. But before they express their acquiescence in its provisions, and recommend its being presented to Parliament, they are desirous of ascertaining to what extent the proposal meets with the approval of those officers whom it concerns, throughout the whole of England.

The Board therefore transmit herewith several copies of the draft, one for yourself, and the rest to be distributed by you to the master of the workhouse, the relieving-officers, and any other officers of your union who are interested in the subject, for perusal. The Board will be ready to receive any communication from those who dissent from the measure; and at the same time will be glad to learn from yourself, at your earliest convenience, how far the same meets with approval in your union.

I am, Sir, your obedient Servant,
W. G. Lumley,
Assistant Secretary.

To
The Clerk to the Guardians.

Draft of a Bill, referred to in the above Circular, intituled an Act to authorize the Establishment of a Poor Law Officers' Superannuation Fund.

Whereas it is expedient that persons who serve in certain offices connected with the administration of the laws for the relief of the poor in parishes and unions, should be required to make provisions for securing to themselves on resigning such offices a maintenance during old age or other infirmity.

The Poor Law Board may establish a Poor Law Parish and Union Officers' Superannuation Fund.

1. Be it therefore enacted by the Queen's most excellent Majesty, by and with the advice and consent of the Lords Spiritual and Temporal in this present Parliament assembled, and by the authority of the same, That it shall be lawful for the Poor Law Board, as soon after the passing of this Act as they shall see fit, by an order under their seal, to be published in the *London Gazette*, to declare that a Poor Law Officers' Superannuation Fund shall be established accordingly, and the provisions of this Act shall thenceforth be in full force and effect.

And appoint Officers, &c., to manage same.

2. And be it enacted, That the Poor Law Board shall thereupon undertake the collection, management, and distribution of such fund, and make such rules and regulations for the same as they may from time to time see fit.

Act to extend to Officers enumerated in the Order of Commissioners, and others may be added.

3. And be it enacted, That the superannuation allowances authorized by the Act shall extend to all such officers of parishes or unions as shall be set forth and enumerated in the said order for the establishment of the fund, but no auditor, chaplain, medical officer, schoolmaster or school-

mistress, collector, or assistant overseer, shall be included therein.

Provided always, That it shall be lawful for the said Board, from time to time, by any order under their seal, to be published in the *London Gazette*, to add to the list of offices enumerated in their first said order, any other office or offices which now exist, or may hereafter be created or established, connected with the administration of the law for the relief of the poor, and not being such as are hereinbefore excepted, and to place the same, and the officers employed therein, under the provisions of this Act, and all the powers, authorities, and clauses herein contained, shall in every case apply and be put in force with respect to every office which shall be so added as aforesaid, as fully and effectually to all intents and purposes as if it had been originally specified in the said first order.

Deductions to be made from Salaries, and paid over to the Poor Law Board for the purpose of investment.

4. And be it enacted, That there shall be an annual deduction after the rate of two pounds ten shillings per cent. per annum, made in quarterly proportions from the salaries of the several officers employed in such offices as may be specified in the said first order made by the said Board, or to be specified in any addition authorized to be made thereto and not within the exceptions thereof, which sums shall be deducted, collected, and received, in such manner and by and from such persons as the said Board shall, by an order under their seal, direct, and shall be from time to time paid to the account of the said Board, and shall be invested as the said Board shall from time to time direct, and the fund so created, as well as the dividends and interest accruing thereon, shall be applicable to the purposes of this Act as the said Board shall deem proper.

Rates of Superannuation Allowances.

5. And be it enacted, That from and after the making of such order by the said Board for the establishment of such superannuation fund, the said fund shall be applied according to the regulations of the said Board; first, in payment of the costs, charges, and expenses, to be incurred as well by the said Board as otherwise, in carrying out the provisions of this Act, or in the management of the said fund, or in any way incident thereto; and, secondly, in payment of such superannuation allowance to the officers employed in the several offices mentioned in such order as are hereinafter mentioned, that is to say, to an officer or person who upon his retirement from the office shall have served, whether before or after the passing of the Act of the 4th & 5th of Wm. 4, c. 76, for a period of 15 years and upwards, and under 20 years, an annual allowance amounting to one-third of the annual salary of his office; and for a period of 20 years and upwards and under 30 years, an annual allowance of one-half of such salary; and for a period of 30 years and upwards, an annual allowance of two-thirds of such salary.

Conditions on which Allowances are to be granted as to age and infirmity.

6. Provided nevertheless, and be it enacted, That no superannuation allowance shall be granted under this Act to any officer who shall be under fifty-five years of age, nor to any officer who shall not have had abatements made from his salary under the provisions of this Act for the period of fifteen years, unless upon a certificate in writing of two medical practitioners, one of whom shall be the medical officer of the parish or union to which such officer shall be attached or belong, that he is wholly incapable from some infirmity of mind or body, not caused by his own misconduct, to discharge the duties of his office, on receipt of which certificate in respect of any such officer above the age of fifty-five years who shall not have had deductions made from his salary for the said space of fifteen years, it shall be competent for the Poor Law Board at their discretion to authorize a payment to him of a superannuation allowance of one-third part only of his annual salary.

How to be computed.

7. And be it enacted, That the superannuation allowance to be granted to any officer shall be computed upon the average annual amount of the salary received by him during the seven years next preceding the time of his resignation, and in case he shall not have received his salary for that period, such superannuation allowance shall be calculated upon the average annual amount of the salary received by him during the whole period of service.

Allowances to be paid for complete Quarters of a Year only. Receipts, by whom to be given in certain cases.

8. And be it enacted, That the allowances shall only be payable in respect of complete quarters of a year, and shall commence at some one of the

customary quarter days in the year, and shall end at the last quarter day which shall occur previous to the decease of the officer who shall have been in the receipt thereof, and where the payment due at the decease of such officer shall be under the sum of twenty pounds, or where the officer entitled to the allowance shall be through mental or bodily infirmity incapable of giving a receipt or discharge for the same, the Poor Law Board shall determine to what person the payment shall be made, and the receipt of such person shall be a sufficient discharge for every payment so made.

Contributions may be made in respect of past years' service in office.

9. And be it further enacted, That any officer holding any office named in the said first order of the said Poor Law Board or in any addition thereto, may at any time contribute to the said fund in respect of any number of years of service rendered previously to the establishment of the said fund in any office named in the said orders, an amount equal to the sum which would have been abated from his salary, in case the said superannuation fund had been in existence, and such number of years shall be computed and taken into consideration in ascertaining the claim of any such officer for a superannuation allowance.

On resignation of Officer and his re-appointment, former years of service to count.

10. And be it further enacted, That if any officer or person holding any office mentioned in the said order or in the addition thereto, shall resign his office and shall afterwards be appointed to the same or any other office named therein, the aggregate number of years of service rendered in all such offices shall be computed and taken into consideration in ascertaining the claim for a superannuation allowance.

Superannuation Allowance to cease upon appointment to paid Poor Law Office.

11. And be it enacted, That in case any person in the receipt of a superannuation allowance shall be appointed to any paid office in connection with the administration of the laws for the relief of the poor, every such allowance shall cease so long as such subsequent appointment shall be held.

If Fund shall be exhausted the Superannuation payments to be reduced pro rata.

12. And be it enacted, That in case the superannuation fund shall become so reduced as to render it in the judgment of the Poor Law Board unsafe to continue the payments in full, the respective payments to all parties entitled to superannuation allowance from the said fund shall be reduced in such manner and proportion as the said Board shall find necessary during such time as the said fund shall in the opinion of the said Board be insufficient to pay the whole of the superannuation allowances chargeable thereon in full, but the amount of such reductions shall nevertheless be a charge on the said fund, payable whenever afterwards the said fund shall be deemed by the said Board capable of paying the total amount thereof to all the parties whose allowances shall have been so reduced.

The Poor Law Board and the Public not to be responsible for the failure of the Scheme.

13. And "whereas the above scheme has been proposed on behalf of the officers concerned therein upon representations after careful calculation that the same can effect the object proposed, but experience may prove that the same is insufficient, and the public ought not to be rendered responsible in case of any failure thereof," be it therefore enacted that neither the Poor Law Board nor any officer or clerk employed by such Board in the collection, management, or distribution of such fund shall be held in any way accountable or be liable to any suit in law or equity on the ground of the deficiency or failure in the fund hereafter to be raised by reason whereof no allowance can be paid, or one of a less amount than is here provided for, shall be paid to any officer who under the provisions of this Act would be entitled to receive it.

Provided that nothing herein contained shall be taken to exempt any such officer or clerk so employed as aforesaid from the consequences of his own fraud, embezzlement, or wilful neglect or misappropriation of any monies or securities belonging to the said fund, which may at any time come into his possession by virtue of such employment.

Officers dismissed, &c., to forfeit all claim.

14. And be it enacted, That nothing herein contained shall be construed so as to prevent the removal of any paid officer, and every such officer who shall be removed by the said Poor Law Board, or shall resign upon any charge of mis-

conduct or neglect of duty made against him, shall thereupon forfeit all claim upon the said superannuation fund, unless the said Poor Law Board shall make any order to the contrary.

Interpretation Clause.

15. And be it further enacted, That in the construction of this Act, the word "parish" shall be construed to include any parish, city, borough, town, township, liberty, precinct, vill, village, hamlet, tithing, chapelry, or any other place or division, or district of a place maintaining its own poor, whether parochial or extra-parochial; the word "union" shall be construed to include any number of parishes united under the provisions of any Act, whether general or local, relating to the relief or maintenance of the poor; and wherever in this Act in describing any person or party, matter or thing, the word importing the singular number or masculine gender only is used, the same shall be understood to include and shall be applied to several persons or parties, as well as one person or party, and females as well as males, and several matters and things as well as one matter or thing respectively, unless there be something in the subject or context repugnant to such construction.

Extent of Act.

16. And be it enacted, That this Act shall extend only to England and Wales.

Act may be amended.

17. And be it enacted, That this Act may be amended or repealed by any Act to be passed in this present session of Parliament.

VII.—REMOVABILITY.—Of a woman with her children, deserted by her husband.

23rd March, 1850.

Clerk of Crediton Union.—Transmitting the following statement, duly signed under sec. 4. of the 11 & 12 Vic. c. 110, for the opinion of the Poor Law Board:—A— H——— has resided in the parish of Crediton from her birth; in the year 1828, she was married to a man who belonged to the parish of Newton Saint Cyres, in the Crediton union; she has had three children by her husband, the youngest of whom is now fourteen years of age; about thirteen years since, her husband deserted her, and has not, as it is believed, lived with her since; and it is not known where he is, or whether he is living. Since his desertion she has had five illegitimate children, four of whom are now in the Crediton union workhouse, where she was confined of the fifth on the 14th December last, having been admitted for that purpose from the parish of Crediton on the 19th of September last. She, or her legitimate or illegitimate children, have received relief in the workhouse nearly the whole time since her husband left her; viz., for many years from the parish of Newton Saint Cyres, where her husband was settled, and from Crediton as irremovable paupers. The parish officers of Crediton contend that the paupers are removable to Newton Saint Cyres, in consequence of the passing of the 11 & 12 Vic. c. 111, and the recent decisions thereon, and their having been relieved by that parish in the workhouse of the union within the last five years; whilst the parish officers of Newton Saint Cyres, on the contrary, contend that the paupers are irremovable from Crediton, in consequence of a five years' residence in that parish. Should the relief at present afforded to this woman and her four illegitimate children in the workhouse of this union be charged to the parishes of Newton Saint Cyres or Crediton, or to the common fund of the union?

Ans.—With reference to the desertion of the pauper by her husband, the Board desire to point out, that if seven years have elapsed since the husband was known to be alive, he must now, according to the ordinary rules of law, be presumed to be dead; in that case, and if the pauper A— H——— has resided for five years in the parish of Crediton without relief, she is now irremovable from that parish. If she be herself irremovable, her four illegitimate children who reside with her, being under the age of sixteen, are also irremovable, by operation of the 9 & 10 Vic. c. 66, sec. 3. If the husband be still alive the case will be different, because the pauper will then be removable from the parish of Crediton; with regard to the children, however, it may be observed, that so long as they reside with her, being illegitimate, they would be irremovable, unless the provisions of the 11 & 12 Vic. c. 111, apply to them, which is a question open to great doubt.

London: Printed by Order of the Poor Law Board, by Blackburn & Burt, 90½, Holborn Hill, and Published by Charles Knight, 90, Fleet Street.

AN

OFFICIAL CIRCULAR

OF PUBLIC DOCUMENTS AND INFORMATION:

DIRECTED BY THE POOR LAW BOARD TO BE PRINTED, CHIEFLY FOR THE USE OF THE BOARDS OF GUARDIANS AND THEIR OFFICERS.

No. 38.] JUNE, 1850. [N. S.

CONTENTS.

I.—AUDITOR—ACCOUNTING OFFICERS VERIFYING ACCOUNTS BEFORE.

1st May, 1850.

District Auditor.—Inquiring, whether, by the 7 & 8 Vic. c. 101, sec. 38, an auditor can require an officer of a union to sign a declaration with respect to his accounts, or whether that section applies to overseers only; and also, whether, by the 4 & 5 Wm. 4, c. 76, sec. 47, an auditor can require an overseer or other person accounting to verify his accounts on oath; and, lastly, whether an auditor can administer an oath under that section, or whether that section is superseded by the 7 & 8 Vic. c. 101.

Ans.—1. The auditor can require the officer of a union (as well as an overseer or other officer of a parish) to sign a declaration with respect to his accounts. The words of sec. 33 of the 7 & 8 Vic. c. 101, are, "to require any person holding or accountable for any money, books, deeds, papers, goods, or chattels, relating to the poor-rate, or the relief of the poor, to produce to such auditor his accounts and vouchers, and to make or sign a declaration with respect to such accounts." 2. The Board are disposed to think that an auditor cannot administer an oath to an overseer or other person accounting to him. They think that sec. 47 of the 4 & 5 Wm. 4, c. 76, (so far as district auditors are concerned,) is virtually superseded by the provisions as to auditing contained in the 7 & 8 Vic. c. 101; and, as the making of a false declaration is punishable as perjury under the 33rd sec. of the last-named Act, there does not appear to be any reason why the auditor should require an oath to be taken by any person accounting to him.

II.—BURIAL.—Repayment of cost of burial of a non-resident pauper.

17*th June*, 1850.

Clerk of Eastbourne Union.—Thomas Worger, aged twenty-three years, a permanently disabled cripple, belonging to Alfriston, but residing at Lewes as a non-resident pauper, died on the 4th ultimo. He had been in receipt of 2*s.* 6*d.* per week relief from Alfriston from the relieving-officer of this union. The burial expenses were paid by the Lewes Union, from whom an application has been made for repayment. Inquiring, whether the Eastbourne Union is liable to repay the Lewes Union such burial expenses under the sec. 17 of the 12 & 13 Vic. c. 103.

Ans.—Under the 12 & 13 Vic. c. 103, sec. 17, it appears to the Board to be optional with the guardians of the Eastbourne Union to pay (or not, as they may think fit) the expenses of the funeral in question, unless they had entered into any engagement or undertaking with the guardians of the Lewes Union to pay these expenses, in addition to the pauper's relief, in the event of his death taking place.

III.—CONTRIBUTION ORDERS—Service of.

27*th Feb.*, 1850.

Clerk of Wellington (Somerset) Union.—Art. 83 of the General Consolidated Order appears to require the guardians to make their order in the form [M] thereto annexed, and also that it should be signed by the chairman and two guardians, and countersigned by the clerk. The statute, 12 & 13 Vic. c. 103, sec. 7, enacts, that where a copy of any order upon overseers for the payment of money shall be served upon any one of such overseers, such order may be enforced as effectually as if a copy had been served on each overseer. If, therefore, the guardians make an order as directed by the above-mentioned article, would it be proper to make a copy of each order for service, the original being retained by the clerk, and endorsed with a note of service by the person who served and examined the copy? It has been usual in this union to serve the original order.

Ans.—Although the service of a copy of the original order upon the overseers (the original order being shown to them at the same time) might be sufficient under the 12 & 13 Vic. c. 103, sec. 7, yet the Board think that the more safe and proper course is to serve the original order itself upon the overseers. The Board, therefore, recommend that this latter course should be pursued.

IV.—CHARGEABILITY.

25*th Oct.*, 1849.

Clerk of Helston Union.—J. P., aged 24, labouring under permanent disability, and living with his parents in the parish of Breage, is become chargeable thereto. The pauper has gained no settlement in his own right. His parents are settled in the parish of Wendron, but are living on their own property in Breage, and therefore irremovable. The pauper and his parents are also protected from removal by the five years' residence Act. The parish of Breage contend that as the pauper is irremovable, by the five years' residence Act, the relief now given should be charged to the common fund. The board of guardians object to the relief being so charged because the pauper is unemancipated, and therefore protected from removal by the parents' residence on their own property in Breage.

Ans.—The Poor Law Board consider, that emancipation does not affect the question which you have submitted to them, as they are of opinion that a person over the age of 21 is not a child, within the meaning of the 11 & 12 Vic. c. 114, so as to confer his parents' irremovability upon him. The case in question appears, however, to require further elucidation. The Board request to be informed of the nature of the parents' estate at Breage, which as you allege renders them irremovable therefrom, and yet appears not to confer on them a settlement.

Clerk of same Union.—The pauper's father, about 12 years since, purchased a house and land in Breage (whereon he still resides, together with the pauper, his unemancipated son,) the purchase money of which was under £30. This is the estate referred to in the former letter. The pauper's father has an acknowledged birth settlement in Wendron. It is apprehended that the 11 & 12 Vic. c. 110, relieves parishes of burthens created by the 9 & 10 Vic. c. 66, and of such burthens only. And that the pauper's case is one of irremovability, created by a previous statute (9 Geo. 1, c. 7, sec. 5) which leaves him a burthen on Breage so long as he remains unemancipated, or his father retains his estate in that parish, and that when the pauper ceases to be protected by the 9th Geo. 1, Breage would relieve itself of the burthen of his maintenance by the statutes 9 & 10 Vic. c. 66, and 11 & 12 Vic. c. 110.

Ans.—The Board do not see from the information now before them, that the pauper in question has any legal settlement in the parish of Breage. It appears to the Board that his father, though irremovable from that parish, has not acquired any settlement therein; and consequently has no settlement therein to confer upon the son. But J. P. himself, not being settled in Breage, has nevertheless resided therein for five years it would seem, without receipt of relief, and, therefore, has become irremovable from Breage.

2. CHARGEABILITY.

4th Dec., 1849.

Clerk of Barnet Union.—Transmitting the following statement, duly signed under the 4th sec. of the 11 and 12 Vic. c. 110, for the opinion of the Poor Law Board:—In June, 1847, a poor widow, named S. W., aged 78, came to reside in the parish of Ridge in this union. A few months after, she became unable to support herself, and applied for relief, which she received, and continues to receive to this present time. She has no settlement in Ridge, and is, according to the Act 9 & 10 Vic. c. 66, removable. Her supposed settlement is in Bedfordshire, but the parochial officers of Ridge are unable to obtain sufficient evidence to procure an order of removal, and they consider the case, under the circumstances, as one which should fairly be charged to the common fund, especially as the pauper had resided for the last fifteen years, prior to her residence in Ridge, in the adjoining parish of South Mimms (also in this union,) and from which she would have been irremovable.

Ans.—The Board are of opinion that S. W. is chargeable to the parish of Ridge; inasmuch as she is not (according to the information before them) irremovable therefrom, under the 9 & 10 Vic. c. 66; though, for want of evidence, the overseers cannot at present effect the removal of the pauper.

V.—ELECTION OF GUARDIANS.—QUALIFICATION OF CANDIDATE.

24th June, 1850.

M. H., Esq., South Shields Union.—Inquiring whether a ratepayer occupying property of £25 yearly value in one, or in more than one township in a union, is qualified for the office of guardian for any township of that union.

Ans.—The legal qualification for guardian is dependent upon the order prescribing such qualification, which the Poor Law Commissioners may have issued in any case. The amount of the qualification varies in different unions. In the South Shields Union, to which the Board understand your inquiry more immediately to refer, the qualification of guardian of the poor consists in the being rated to the poor-rate of some parish or parishes in the union in respect of the annual value or rental of £25. A person, therefore, who merely occupies property in the union without being rated to the poor-rate in respect of it, will not be qualified as guardian, though the annual value of such property be £25. But a person who is rated within the union for or in respect of property or hereditaments of that amount, will be eligible to be elected guardian for any township of that union. It is not necessary that the property conferring the qualification should be situate in the particular township for which the person is elected guardian; it is sufficient if the aggregate property, though situate in two or more townships, be of the annual value of £25, and if the party nominated be assessed to the poor-rate in respect thereof.

VI.—GUARDIAN.

1. ELIGIBILITY OF A FEMALE FOR THE OFFICE OF.

8th May, 1850.

Clerk of Ludlow Union.—Inquiring if a female is eligible for the office of guardian of a union, she being in every respect fully qualified as to rating, residence, &c.

Ans.—The question submitted is one upon which the law is not perfectly clear. So far, indeed, as the 38th section of the Poor Law Amendment Act, which defines the legal qualification for guardian is concerned, it contains no words which in themselves would restrict the eligibility of persons to be elected to that office to persons who are males. As regards the somewhat analogous office of overseer, it seems to have been considered by the Court of Queen's Bench, in a case which underwent much examination, (Rex *v.* Stubbs, 2 T. R. 395,) that the appointment of a woman as overseer might be good from necessity, *i. e.*, where there are no persons in the parish (being males) qualified to serve the office.

The point now raised has never come before the courts for decision, and, in the absence of such decision, the Board can only say that they think it probable that the principle expressed in Rex *v.* Stubbs, would be held to govern the case. The objections to the appointment of a female to an office of this nature, upon grounds of public policy and convenience, are so manifest, that the Board cannot readily suppose that the question will become one of practical importance in the administration of the Poor Laws; indeed, the Board do not understand, from your letter, that the question has now arisen upon any election which has actually taken place.

2. INSOLVENCY OF GUARDIAN.

24th Sept., 1849.

Clerk of ——— Union.—Inquiring, whether an elected guardian, having taken the benefit of the Insolvent Debtors' Act, since the election in April last, is thereby become disqualified from acting as a guardian, and voting in the proceedings of the board.

Ans.—If the party to whom you refer, continues to be rated to the relief of the poor, in some parish in the union, to the required amount, the fact of his having taken the benefit of the Insolvent Debtors' Act does not disqualify him from acting as a guardian of that union.

3. GUARDIAN CONTRACTING TO VALUE A PARISH IN THE UNION.

3rd June, 1850.

Clerk of Leicester Union.—At the weekly meeting of the guardians, held yesterday, it was unanimously resolved, "That the Poor Law Board be requested to order a new election for the parish of All Saints, to fill the vacancy caused by the disqualification of Mr. James Wykes." The disqualification of Mr. Wykes was caused by his being, at the time of his nomination, under contract to value the parish of All Saints.

Ans.—The Board observe from your letter that Mr. James Wykes, guardian for All Saints, is supposed to be disqualified for the office, on the ground of his being, at the time of his nomination, under contract to value that parish. The Board, however, are of opinion that a surveyor, who contracts to survey and value a parish for a certain sum, is not disqualified, by the 5 & 6 Vic. c. 57, sec. 14, for serving the office of guardian of such parish. There is, consequently, no occasion for a new election in All Saints, so far as the supposed disqualification of Mr. Wykes on the ground in question is concerned.

4. DEMAND FOR COPIES OF MINUTES OF PROCEEDINGS OF GUARDIANS.

7th August, 1849.

The Rev. W. B.—Inquiring whether, as a ratepayer and guardian of the union, he has a right to ask for copies of any resolutions that may have been passed at the board when he was absent, on paying for the same.

Ans.—The minutes of the guardians are in the custody of their clerk, who would not be justified in giving copies, or allowing inspection of them without due authority from the guardians. At the meetings of the board of guardians, the Poor Law Board consider that any individual guardian may call upon the guardians to allow a former minute to be read, when such proceeding will not interfere with the business of the meeting; but the Board doubt much whether any means exist for compelling the reading of such minute.

VII.—JUSTICES.—THEIR POWER IN REGARD TO RELIEF. *22nd April*, 1850.

The Rev. T. S. M.—Inquiring, 1. Whether a magistrate has the power to order relief to be given by a relieving-officer to a poor person during sickness, such person not being a pauper; and if so, as to the amount and time of its continuance. 2. Whether a magistrate has the power to order additional relief to be given to a pauper during sickness, as also medical advice; and if so, as to the amount, time, and terms on which it should be continued.

Ans.—1. A justice has no legal power to make any order upon a relieving-officer for relief in respect of any person, whether a pauper or otherwise. 2. A justice may order an overseer to give relief in cases specified in the Poor Law Amendment Act, (4 & 5 Wm. 4, c. 76, sec. 54,) to which the Board would refer you, as defining the extent of the authority which justices possess, to order relief in unions and the other places therein enumerated. With regard to parishes where the poor are still maintained under the 43 Eliz. c. 2, the larger powers given to justices over overseers, by the 3 Wm. and Mary, c. 11, and the 9 Geo. 1, c. 7, still remain.

VIII.—LUNATIC PAUPER.—CHARGING EXPENSES OF MAINTENANCE IN ASYLUM.

28th Feb., 1850.

Clerk of Halstead Union.—By order of one of

the magistrates of the police courts of the metropolis, sitting at Lambeth police-court, within the metropolitan police district, acting in and for the county of Surrey, (from part of which one Mary Anne Wade, a lunatic, then chargeable to the parish of Lambeth, was sent to a certain lunatic asylum, as therein-after mentioned,) dated the 12th day of January last, the settlement of the pauper was adjudged to be in the parish of Colne Engaine; and an order was thereupon made on the treasurer of this union to pay, on behalf of the churchwardens and overseers of the parish of Colne Engaine, to the guardians of the parish of Camberwell, the sum of £4. 3*s*. 6*d*., being the expenses incurred by the guardians of Camberwell, in the examination of the lunatic, and conveying her to the asylum, and also the further sum of £1. 7*s*., paid to the treasurer of the asylum for the lodging and maintenance, &c., of the lunatic in the asylum. And it was further ordered that the treasurer of the Halstead Union should pay, on account of the parish of Colne Engaine, weekly, to the treasurer of the asylum, the sum of nine shillings, for the future lodging, maintenance, &c., of the lunatic, during so long a time as she should be confined in the asylum. The lunatic is the wife of James Wade, who is now residing in the said parish of Lambeth. Their settlement in Colne Engaine is not disputed, but, inasmuch as they are irremovable, by reason of an uninterrupted five years' residence in Lambeth, the Poor Law Board are requested to state whether or not, under the circumstances, the charges above-mentioned should not be repaid from the union fund.

Ans.—As the parish of Lambeth is not a union, the 12 and 13 Vic. c. 103, sec. 5, does not apply to it; and it has been held by the Court of Queen's Bench, in the case of the Queen *v.* the Inhabitants of Leaden Roothing, (13 Law Times, 137,) that the 9 and 10 Vic. c. 66, does not prevent the justices from making an order for maintenance in an asylum upon the parish of the lunatic's settlement, under the 8 and 9 Vic. c. 126. The Board presume that "Lambeth" is the parish in which the pauper was residing when she was sent to the asylum, although you have in some parts of your letter described it as "Camberwell," apparently through an inadvertence. The foregoing remarks, however, would be equally applicable to Camberwell.

IX.—MEDICAL RELIEF—PAYMENT OF THE COST OF WHEN GIVEN BY OTHER THAN THE MEDICAL OFFICER.

14th June, 1850.

Chairman of the Guildford Union.—Requesting the Board's instructions as to the payment of the charges of medical men in such cases as the following:—1. The medical officer of the town district of Guildford received an order to attend a poor woman in labour; having satisfied himself that his attendance would not be required for a certain time, he went away to see another patient four or five miles off; in the meantime it became imperatively necessary to call in another medical man, who attended immediately, and did everything that was needful to be done. This medical man has claimed twenty shillings for his attendance on the case, but the guardians hesitate to pay the amount. 2. A poor woman was taken very ill in the middle of the night, the husband went for the medical officer, (without an order,) but he was not at home; he then requested the medical man adverted to, to see his wife, which he did. The relieving-officer, on being applied to in the morning, refused to give an order for the payment of the medical man's charge.

Ans.—The Board, in reply, desire to direct your attention to the provisions of the 11 & 12 Vic. c. 110, sec. 2, (the Poor Law Union Charges Act, passed in 1848,) which contains the following enactment:—"And it shall be lawful for the guardians of any union, if they think proper, to pay for any medical or other assistance which shall be rendered to any poor person on the happening of any accident, bodily casualty, or sudden illness, although no order shall have been given for the same by them or any of their officers, or by the overseers; and to charge the same to some one parish in the union, or to the common fund of the union, according as such parish or union would have been liable for the ordinary relief of such poor person." It appears to the Board that the above enactment would apply to such cases as those to which your letter refers, and would enable the guardians, in the exercise of their discretion, to give such compensation to the medical attendants, as may be reasonable and proper under the circumstances. It is to be observed, however, that the clause imposes no obligation on the guardians.

X.—OVERSEERS.

1. POWERS OF ASSISTANT OVERSEERS AND CHURCHWARDENS.

13th May, 1844.

The Incumbent of Hunslet, Leeds.—Submitting

the following questions for the opinion of the Commissioners, with a view to his guidance, as chairman of vestry meetings. 1. Is an assistant overseer of equal authority with an overseer; and has he power of himself to call a vestry meeting, without stating on the notice paper that it is by order of the overseers? 2. What are the duties of his office, and can he hold it without re-appointment by the newly appointed overseers? 3. Is not a churchwarden to all intents and purposes an overseer of the poor? 4. Have the other overseers power to refuse to put to the vote any proposition moved by the churchwarden and seconded by an overseer?

Ans.—If the assistant overseer to whom you allude be appointed under the 59 Geo. 3, c. 12, sec. 7, the extent of his powers and duties will depend upon the terms of his appointment. The churchwardens under the 43 Elizabeth, c. 2, sec. 1, are overseers of the poor to all intents and purposes. There appears to be nothing in the 9 Geo. 1, c. 7, to interfere with their powers in that character. If your last question refers to vestry meetings the Commissioners would observe that the duty of putting, or refusing to put any propositions to the meeting, rests with the chairman, and not with any churchwarden or overseer, as such.

30*th Jan.*, 1850.

Same writer.—Inquiring, whether the churchwardens of Hunslet are not (according to the act of Elizabeth) overseers of the poor of Hunslet; and also, whether there is not a recognised chairman of the board of overseers, or whether one must be elected at every meeting. Hunslet is a large township maintaining its own poor, and is a separate ecclesiastical parish having no hamlets or townships within itself. Some years ago the Poor Law Commissioners answered these questions affirmatively, but the then churchwarden dying, the answer has been lost.

Ans.—The Board herewith transmit to you a copy of the letter which you addressed to the Poor Law Commissioners, in April, 1844, with a copy of their reply thereto. The Board observe that at the time that reply was written it appears to have been considered that Hunslet was a parish within the meaning of the 43 Elizabeth, c. 2. If it be a township only, as the Board would infer from your letter, the churchwardens cannot act in matters relating to the relief of the poor therein, but if the district for which the overseers are appointed be a parish, the churchwardens of that parish have in all things a joint authority with them under 43 Elizabeth, c. 2, sec. 1, unless indeed such district has been made a parish under some Act of Parliament. Upon this point, the information contained in your note is not very distinct. The 13 & 14 Charles 2, c. 12, sec. 21, directs the appointment of overseers in townships to manage the relief of the poor, but in that enactment no mention is made of churchwardens, as is the case in the statute of Elizabeth, directing the appointment of overseers in parishes. With regard to your inquiry whether there is or is not a recognised chairman of the board of overseers, the Board desire to observe that in neither of the Acts above referred to, nor in any other general Act, is any provision made for the constitution of a board of overseers, nor, consequently, for any chairman of such board. The Board believe that there is no select vestry appointed under 59 Geo. 3, c. 12, at Hunslet, and, therefore, the overseers of Hunslet have at present the sole authority and duty of managing the relief of the poor.

---

2. OVERSEERS SUPPLYING GOODS TO GUARDIANS, 55 GEO. 3, C. 137, SEC. 6.

1*st May*, 1850.

Clerk of Ludlow Union.—Inquiring whether a bookseller and stationer, in Ludlow, who supplies the board of guardians with books and stationery, and who does what printing they require, falls within the provisions of the 6th sec. of the Act 55 Geo. 3, c. 137, such tradesman being at the time of so furnishing his goods an overseer of the poor of the borough of Ludlow.

Ans.—The supply of books and stationery by such person to the guardians of the Ludlow Union appears to the Board to be within the terms of the statute; but they do not consider that those terms would include printing.

XI.—PAUPER—WHO HAS MONEY IN THE SAVINGS' BANK.

17*th Jan.*, 1850.

Clerk of Rochdale Union.—During the investigation into the affairs of the Rochdale savings' bank, it has transpired that a pauper, of the name of Martha Howorth, of Spotland-bridge, has £18 in the bank. This woman became chargeable to the union in September, 1846, and from that time up to December 13th, 1849, she has received relief to the amount of £16. 14*s*. The guardians wish the Poor Law Board to issue an order, under statute 4 & 5 Wm. 4, c. 76, sec. 58, declaring such relief to be relief on loan, in order that they may recover the same from the trustees and managers of the bank, or at least so much thereof as the funds of the bank will pay.

Ans.—The Board can issue an order, declaring the relief which the guardians of the Rochdale Union may in future order to the pauper Martha Howorth to be advanced by way of loan, but such order would not have a retrospective operation. The Board, however, refer the guardians to the provision in the 12 & 13 Vic. c. 103, sec. 16, which will enable them to recover the amount expended by them in the relief of the pauper, during twelve months prior to the time when the money shall be obtainable.

XII.—PUBLICANS.—THEIR OBLIGATION TO RECEIVE WAYFARERS INTO THEIR HOUSES.

29th June, 1850.

Clerk of Chertsey Union.—The following cases having been brought under the notice of the guardians by one of the medical officers of the union, they were desirous of knowing whether there was any remedy against a publican who refuses to receive vagrants in distress:—A policeman, finding a female on a cold night sitting on the steps of a door in the village, requested the medical officer to see her, who found her incapable of proceeding further that night; but he could not procure a lodging for her in Chobham, the publicans refusing to take her in, although they were promised to be paid for it. On the following morning, after having had a night's shelter in the cage, she was enabled to go on her way. The next case was that of a man, under very similar circumstances. The last was the case of the man Giles: he is by trade a blacksmith, sometimes working in one parish for a few days, and then, in consequence, it is believed, of his dissipated habits, obliged to seek work elsewhere. He had been working for a man named B., but having been out drinking, he laid down under a shed, in a farm-yard, and feeling it cold, went into a stable, in which was a mare and a colt, by the former of which he was kicked, and received a bad compound fracture of the leg, attended with great loss of blood. B. refused to take him in, and the publicans also refused him admission. He was not in a state to be sent to the workhouse without placing his life in danger, and had it not been for one of the inhabitants kindly offering a bed, the result might have been most serious.

Ans.—The law would appear to require every innkeeper to receive a guest, he having at the time room in his house, and either the price of the guest's entertainment being tendered to him, or such circumstances occurring as will dispense with the tender; an innkeeper who refuses to receive travellers of such a class is not only liable to damages in an action on the case, at the suit of the party aggrieved, but he may also be indicted and fined at the suit of the Queen. See Rex *v.* Ivens, 7 Carr. and Payne, p. 219. In the case of a vagrant in distress, though the expense of the mere shelter in the inn would be so small as not to create any material difficulty, it is clear that the vagrant would not be prepared to pay for the necessary refreshment. The circumstances must, however, be very unusual and special, in which it is desirable to afford this particular species of relief to which you refer through the instrumentality of an innkeeper; and when it is absolutely necessary to resort to it, the Board consider it highly expedient that it should be conferred, whenever the case admits, through the agency of the relieving-officer. In cases similar to those mentioned by the medical officer, it is very desirable that the destitute wayfarers should be provided with relief by the relieving-officer, or by the overseer of the parish, who is legally competent to give the necessary aid in cases of "sudden and urgent necessity."

XIII.—RELATIONS.—PROCEEDINGS AGAINST A SON FOR REFUSING TO MAINTAIN HIS MOTHER, WHO IS CHARGEABLE TO THE COMMON FUND.

31st May, 1850.

Clerk of Blything Union.—On the 4th March last, L. N., widow, residing at Halesworth, but belonging to Westhall, both parishes within this union, applied to the guardians for relief, and was on that day admitted an inmate of the workhouse. She is about seventy years of age, and quite incapable of work. This woman has resided for more than five years in Halseworth, and is, therefore, by virtue of the 9 & 10 Vic. c. 66, now irremovable therefrom; and the cost of her maintenance in the workhouse is charged to the common fund of the union, by virtue of the provisions of the 11 & 12 Vic. c. 110, and 12 & 13 Vic. c. 103. Since the admission of the widow into the workhouse, the guardians have received information to the effect that she has a son residing in the neighbourhood, of sufficient ability to support his mother; and on the 22nd ult., at the weekly meeting of the guardians, the clerk received directions to institute the usual proceedings before the magistrates, to obtain an order upon the son to support his mother, in accordance with the provisions of the statute 43 Eliz. c. 2. On application to the magistrates' clerk for a summons, a question was raised, whether, in the case of a pauper chargeable to the common fund of the union, the clerk to the guardians could make the necessary complaint, and what authority he should obtain from the guardians for that purpose. Also, in the event of an order being made, whether the weekly sum should be directed to be paid to the guardians generally, or to the treasurer of the union; and in the event of the order being disobeyed, in what manner and by whom the twenty shillings' penalty could be enforced, and how it should be applied. As the relief granted to the widow is charged to the common fund of the union, and not directly to either of the parishes of settlement or residence, it is presumed the overseers of these parishes cannot interfere in the matter. Requesting the advice of the Poor Law Board on these points.

Ans.—The 11 & 12 Vic. c. 110, sec. 8, enables the guardians to apply for an order of maintenance in such a case as the present. The Board think that you, as clerk to the guardians, should be appointed to make the complaint before the justices on behalf of the board of guardians, under the 5 & 6 Vic. c. 57, sec. 17, and the 7 & 8 Vic. c. 191, sec. 69. As regards the payment of the money under an order of maintenance in this case, the Board apprehend that the proper form of the order (according to the precedents in cases of parochial chargeability) would be to direct the payment to be made to the board of guardians, and not to the treasurer of the union, who is only the officer of the guardians. The Board feel a difficulty in advising as to the enforcement of the penalty referred to, but recommend that if the order of maintenance be not obeyed, the son of the pauper should be indicted for disobeying it.

XIV.—RELIEF.

1. RECOVERY OF THE COST OF RELIEF GIVEN TO A PAUPER FROM PARTIES WHO WERE THE OCCASION OF AN ACCIDENT TO SUCH PAUPER, WHICH RENDERED SUCH RELIEF NECESSARY. 13*th June*, 1850.

Clerk of Luton Union.—On the 18th March last, Thomas Facer, while at work on the highway in the parish of Houghton Regis, was run over and severely injured by a horse and cart driven by a man named Sibthorpe, who was racing with another driver of a horse and cart. The horses were both going at a full gallop. The poor man became heavily chargeable to the parish of Houghton Regis, in consequence of the injuries which he sustained. Inquiring, whether the guardians or the overseers of Houghton Regis are the proper parties to sue the persons who occasioned the accident, for the cost of Facer's relief.

Ans.—The Board are not aware of any legal authority which will enable the board of guardians of the Luton Union, or the overseers of the parish of Houghton Regis, to bring any action against the parties who occasioned the accident in question to the pauper Facer, for the recovery of the cost of his relief. The Board desire to add, that it is of course competent to the pauper himself to sue such parties in his own name.

2. OUT DOOR RELIEF TO ABLE-BODIED PAUPERS UNDER ART. 6 OF THE GENERAL PROHIBITORY ORDER. 1*st June*, 1850.

Clerk of Kingsbridge Union.—Under art. 6 of the General Prohibitory Order of the Poor Law Commissioners, the guardians have frequently relieved able-bodied out-door cases of destitution, and within the prescribed time of fifteen days have reported such cases of relief to the Poor Law Commissioners; and, until a recent case of disallowance, they have met with their sanction. Inquiring, whether the guardians have the power to grant out-door relief to able-bodied paupers under art. 6 of this order for fifteen days. It is presumed that they have, but not to continue such relief beyond fifteen days, without the sanction of the Poor Law Board. If this be not so, why permit any out-door relief to be given, seeing that the relieving-officer must bear the expense if the auditor disallows the amount?

Ans.—The Board consider that the guardians cannot grant out-door relief in the case in question for the fifteen days alluded to in the above-mentioned order, so as to be valid at all events, even though the Board should think it unjustifiable by the circumstances of the case. If the Board are not able to approve of such a departure from the rule laid down in the General Prohibitory Order, the relief so given cannot in point of law be treated as legal.

3. RELIEF TO A WOMAN, WITH HER CHILDREN, WHOSE HUSBAND HAS DESERTED HER. 7*th June*, 1850.

Clerk of Bridport Union.—A. B. has been

deserted by her husband, but it is not known whether he is beyond the seas or not. She has applied for out-door relief for her two children, aged respectively 3 and 1½ years. Have not the guardians a discretionary power as to the nature of the relief, *i. e.*, whether it shall be in or out of the workhouse, under the 8th head of the 1st art. in the Out-Relief Prohibitory Order, of 1847?

Ans.—One of the conditions necessary to bring the case within exception 8 to article 1 of the General Prohibitory Order is, that the husband "shall not reside within the union." Assuming that he does not, the discretion vested in the guardians by the exception is to be exercised "subject to the regulation contained in art. 4," which applies to every case where the husband of the woman who requires the relief is "beyond the seas." If, however, the husband in the present instance is not beyond the seas, (and the Board are not aware of any ground for presuming that he is,) then you will perceive, by the remarks contained in the instructional letter which accompanied the General Prohibitory Order, that if the woman does not require relief for herself, but only applies for relief for such of her children as are within the age of nurture, the guardians cannot insist upon her entering the union workhouse, as the condition on which alone they will grant relief to such children; and that, consequently, if she refuses to enter the workhouse, the guardians have no alternative but to give her the necessary out-door relief in respect of such children, who cannot lawfully be separated from her.

---

4. RELIEF TO ENABLE A SICK PERSON TO GO TO BRIGHTON FOR THE RECOVERY OF HIS HEALTH.

6th May, 1850.

Clerk of Blaby Union. — Inquiring, whether the guardians of this union can legally allow a man, of the name of John Hiram Vann, the sum of £4 under the following circumstances?— The man belongs to the parish of Wigston Magna, has a wife and four children, and has been ill for nearly three years, and receiving relief from the parish. The medical men are of opinion that if he goes to Brighton for six or eight weeks it will cure him. Vann will require the sum of £8 for this purpose, but he is in a sick club, and they have agreed to give him £4 if this parish will advance him the other £4.

Ans.—The Board, before giving a specific answer to your question, think it desirable briefly to lay down what they consider to be the principles by which guardians should be guided in the administration of medical relief, and to indicate the extent to which, in the Board's opinion, the funds of the ratepayers may reasonably and justly be applied to that purpose. It is the more desirable that this should be clearly understood, because it is not unfrequently said, that as regards medical attendance, appliances, and remedies, the poor are equally with the rich entitled to all that skill or money can provide towards the recovery of their health. A little consideration will, however, show that this is not only unreasonable, but impracticable, the fact being, that with regard both to the appliances for the preservation of their health while well, and of its restoration when ill, the rich and the poor must, to some extent, stand on unequal footing; as the former provide what they please at their own cost and from their own large means, whilst the latter resort either to their own limited resources or to the means provided by others. And if this be the case with regard to appliances for the preservation of health, it is much more conspicuously true with regard to the appliances for its restoration. The question, therefore, really resolves itself into this, not what is the mode or what the means by which the greatest possible number of sick paupers can be restored to the enjoyment of the best possible health, at an expense, and by appliances, which only the more wealthy of the ratepayers could afford; but what is the mode in which such prompt and skilled professional attendance and reasonable remedies can be secured for paupers in case of sickness, as are in practice found to be demanded and paid for by the less wealthy class of ratepayers in the district. Now it cannot be said that such a visit to Brighton as is here proposed to be paid for out of the money of the ratepayers, would be contemplated as practicable by the bulk of the smaller ratepayers, still less of the independent labourers of Leicestershire. For these reasons, the Board, though always reluctant to refuse compliance with any wish of the guardians, feel compelled to withhold their assent to the guardians advancing a sum in gross to John Hiram Vann, to pay his travelling expenses to Brighton, and to maintain him whilst there. In this case, however, the guardians may perhaps be able to effect their object by granting him temporary non-resident relief when at Brighton, if, as appears probable, the sum proposed to be advanced by the sick club will enable him to reach that place.

XV.—RELIEVING OFFICER—HIS DUTY IN REGARD TO NECESSARIES ORDERED BY A MEDICAL OFFICER FOR A SICK PAUPER.

22nd June, 1850.

Medical Officer, Pershore Union.—Inquiring, "whether a relieving-officer has the power of refusing to supply a sick pauper with necessaries ordered by the medical officer, the order for medical relief having been given by the relieving-officer, and the necessaries being 2lbs. of mutton and 1lb. of oatmeal?"

Ans.—A medical officer is not empowered to order, authoritatively, the supply of food or articles of diet to any sick pauper under his care, though he may certify to the relieving-officer what particular necessaries he considers the pauper to require. The relieving-officer, on receiving such a certificate, will act upon it as he may deem right. He is directed by the General Consolidated Order, (art 215, No. 25,) in every case of a poor person receiving medical relief, to supply until the next meeting of the guardians such relief (not being in money) as the case on his own view, "or on the certificate of the district medical officer," may seem to require. The opinion expressed by the medical officer, in such certificate, will be entitled to the greatest weight, both with the relieving-officer and with the board of guardians; and no doubt the relieving-officer will generally exercise a wise discretion in acting in conformity with it. If in the intervals of the guardians' meetings, he refuses to furnish the food or other necessaries so recommended by the medical officer, he will do so on his own responsibility, and he must be fully prepared to justify the refusal. The Board have made the foregoing general remarks for your information and guidance, but they do not think it advisable to say more, in reply to your inquiry, without being in possession of a complete statement of the particular facts out of which that inquiry has arisen.

XVI.—REMOVABILITY.

1. UNEMANCIPATED CHILDREN OF IRISH PARENTS.

7th May, 1850.

Clerk of Whitechapel Union.—Inquiring whether the unemancipated children above the age of sixteen years (born in England) of Irish parents can be passed to Ireland along with their parents, where such parents are removable under the provisions of the 8 & 9 Vic. c. 117.

Ans.—The Board do not find any limitation as to the age of the children of Irish parents in the statute 8 & 9 Vic. c. 117, and, therefore, they do not think that an unemancipated child, though above the age of sixteen years, if living with his parents as part of the family, and chargeable to the poor-rates, along with them, is prevented from being removed to Ireland, if the parents be legally removable thereto.

---

2. BREACH OF RESIDENCE.

17th Jan., 1849.

Clerk of Penzance Union.—Transmitting the following statement, duly signed, under sec. 4 of the 11 and 12 Vic. c. 110, for the opinion of the Poor Law Board:—A question having arisen between the board of guardians of the Penzance Union and the guardians of the town of Marazion, in the said union, with reference to the charging of the cost of the relief of James Wren, a pauper, as to whether he is exempted from the liability to be removed from the parish where he resides, by reason of some provision of the Act of 9 and 10 Vic. c. 66. The facts of the case are as follow, viz.: The pauper, James Wren, is a miner, having a settlement in the parish of Gwinear, in the Redruth Union, but residing with his wife and six children in the town of Marazion, in the Penzance Union. He has resided in Marazion for the last nineteen years, except for about six months, during which period he was absent therefrom under the following circumstances:—In the early part of January, 1847, in consequence of several mines in the neighbourhood having ceased working, by which a great number of miners were thrown out of employ, the pauper was obliged to seek work at a distance from his home. He travelled so far as Marsden, in the West Riding of Yorkshire, where he obtained employment, and resided there at lodgings for about six months; during that time he on several occasions remitted money to his wife for the maintenance of herself and family, and paid rent and rates for his house at Marazion. At the end of that period, being again out of employ, he retraced his steps to Marazion, and has lived there with his family ever since. The pauper alleges that when he left Marazion, it was only with the expectation of obtaining temporary employment elsewhere, and of again returning, as he eventually did, to Marazion.

Ans.—The Board having duly considered the facts of the case before them, are of opinion that the residence of the pauper in Marazion was interrupted by his abiding and working at Marsden; where it appears by the statement that he resided for a period of six months. Consequently, so far as this point is concerned, he and his family are removable from the town of Marazion, in the Penzance Union, to his legal place of settlement.

28*th Feb.*, 1849.

Clerk of same Union.—Referring to the above reply of the Poor Law Board, and stating as follows:—The attention of the guardians has been directed to a decision of the 17th inst., by the Court of Queen's Bench, as reported in the "Justice of the Peace," in the case of Reg. *v.* Falconestone, in which it would appear that the judges were of opinion that an absence somewhat similar in its nature to that reported in Wren's case, though not of so long duration, did not amount to a breach of residence. The guardians have therefore thought it advisable to refer the Poor Law Board to the above decision, and to inquire whether the two cases are so far analogous as to induce them to alter the opinion which they have expressed on this case. It was not, perhaps, so explicitly stated as it should have been, in the statement of Wren's case, (although it might have been inferred,) that during the whole of his absence from Marazion, his wife and family continued to reside in the same house there as they occupied at the time of his leaving, and to which house he afterwards returned.

Ans.—The Poor Law Board have perused the case to which you have referred them; but it seems to them to differ in its circumstances from the present. They cannot think that when James Wren went into Yorkshire to obtain employment, he had any certain intention of returning to his place of residence in Marazion. He obtained work in Yorkshire, and did not return until his work had ceased. If the employment had continued, he would probably have remained at Marsden until the present time. Under these circumstances, therefore, the Board abide by their opinion, as expressed in their letter to you of the 17th ultimo.

1*st June*, 1850.

Clerk of same Union.—Transmitting the following statement, duly signed, under sec. 4 of the 11 and 12 Vic. c. 110, for the opinion of the Poor Law Board:—A question having arisen between the board of guardians of the Penzance Union and the town of Marazion, in the said union, with reference to the charging of the cost of relief of Thomas Thomas, a pauper, as to whether he is exempted from the liability to be removed from the said town of Marazion, where he resides, by reason of some provision of the Act 9 and 10 Vic. c. 66. The facts of the case are disclosed in the following examination of the pauper, taken before a magistrate on an application by the town of Marazion for an order for the removal of the pauper, his wife and family, to their place of settlement, and to suspend the execution thereof, on the ground of the pauper's illness:—*Copy Examination:*—"I am about thirty-nine years of age, and I am the son of Thomas and Susannah Thomas, who both died in the Church Town of the parish of Breage, in this county, some years since. I was born, as I have heard and believe, in the Church Town of the said parish of Breage, in a house which my father rented of Mr. Fisher, then of that place, shopkeeper. My father was a settled inhabitant of the said parish of Breage; and I lived with him and formed part of his family, in the said parish of Breage, until I was about twenty-two years of age. About seventeen years ago, I married Eliza Thomas, my present wife, in the parish church of St. Hilary, in this county, by whom I have two children, viz., Susan, aged about seventeen years; and Thomas, aged about fifteen years. I have never done any act to acquire a settlement in my own right, and I am now residing in, chargeable to, and in receipt of relief from the township of Marazion in this county, and which relief has been made necessary in consequence of my illness. I have lived in the said township of Marazion for about nineteen years last, with the exception of about a year and eight months, when I went to Wales and Yorkshire, and worked about the railway there. During the time I was absent, my wife and family lived in the said township of Marazion; and when I left Marazion for Wales, I intended to return again to this place, and I did so about two years since. During my absence from Marazion, I remitted money to my wife for the maintenance of herself and children. I am unable from illness to attend the petty sessions, to be examined as to my legal place of settlement." The examination so taken was reported, as shown at the foot thereof, to another justice of the peace, but they have declined to grant an order, on the ground that the pauper is exempted from the liability to be removed, in consequence of his having resided in Marazion for five years next before the application for the order. The guardians for Marazion have therefore applied to the board of guardians to charge the maintenance of the paupers to the common fund of the union, under the 11 and 12 Vic. c. 110, sec. 3. The board of guardians, however, observing by the examination, that he was absent from the town of Marazion and was in Wales and Yorkshire, working about railways there for about a year and eight months within the last five years, considered, on referring to the decision of the Poor Law Board, in the case of James Wren, that such absence constituted a breach of residence notwithstanding the allegation of the pauper, that "when he left Marazion for Wales he intended to return thither again," as he eventually did. The overseers of Marazion, on the other hand, contend that, inasmuch as they have taken the only step which they were enabled by law to do, to obtain an order of removal, and the justices applied to having declined to grant it, on the ground before referred to, the paupers must be considered as exempted from the liability to be removed, as otherwise they will be deprived on both hands of their legal remedy against the chargeability of the paupers, who are admitted not to be settled in their town. The decision of the justices is understood to have been come to, on the ground that it is expressly stated by the pauper, that he intended when he left Marazion to return thither again, and that such an intention is supported by the fact of his having continued to maintain and provide for his family in their residence at Marazion whilst he was absent.

Ans.—The Board are not prepared to express any opinion contrary to that which they gave in a similar case, respecting a pauper named James Wren, from the same parish of Marazion. But the Board perceive that this case has been already brought before the justices who hold jurisdiction, to make an order of removal, if they came to the conclusion that such an order could be legally made. They, however, had an opportunity (which this Board cannot have) of seeing and hearing the witnesses, and they entered upon a full inquiry into the circumstances, and declined to make an order of removal, on the ground of the parties being irremovable; or, at all events, because they were not satisfied that he was removable. Under these circumstances, the Poor Law Board, bearing in mind that they have a discretion as to entertaining the question, under the 4th sec. of the 11 and 12 Vic. c. 110, think that they will best exercise that discretion in declining to do so, after the justices, acting judicially, have pronounced a decision on the subject.

XVII.—REMOVAL.

1. OF SCOTCH AND IRISH POOR—CASE, AND OPINION OF MR. PEACOCK THEREON.

13th April, 1850.

Clerk of Holborn Union.—Transmitting the following case, relating to the law affecting the removal of Scotch and Irish paupers, submitted by the guardians to Mr. Barnes Peacock, together with his opinion thereon:—

Case.—By the Act of Parliament 8 & 9 Vic. c. 117, sec. 1, certain laws before the passing of that Act, in force for the removal of poor persons born in Scotland or Ireland, or in the Islands of Man, Scilly, Jersey, or Guernsey, and not settled in England, but chargeable to parishes in England, are repealed. And by sec. 2 it is enacted, "that if any person born in Scotland or Ireland, or in the Isle of Man or Scilly, or Jersey, or Guernsey, not settled in England, become chargeable to any parish in England by reason of relief given to himself or herself, or to his wife, or to any legitimate or bastard child, such person, his wife, and any child so chargeable, shall be liable to be removed respectively to Scotland, Ireland, the Isle of Man, Scilly, Jersey, or Guernsey; and if the guardians of such parish, or of any union in which the same may be comprised, or where there are no such guardians, if the overseers of such parish complain thereof to any one justice of the peace, such justice may, if such person do not attend voluntarily, summon him to come before any two justices of the peace, at any time and place to be named in the summons, and at such time and place, or on the attendance of such person, any two justices may hear and examine into the matter of such complaint; and if it be made to appear to their satisfaction, that such person is liable to be so removed as aforesaid, and if they see fit, they may make and issue a warrant, under their hands and seals, to remove such person forthwith, at the expense of such union or parish."

By sec. 7 it is enacted, "That the said Act of the 5th year of the reign of King Wm. 4, for the amendment and better administration of the laws relating to the poor in England and Wales, and all Acts to amend and extend the same, and the present Act, (except so far as the provisions of any former Act are altered, amended, or repealed, by any subsequent Act,) shall be construed as one Act."

By the 9 & 10 Vic. c. 66, sec. 1, it is enacted, that from and after the passing of that Act, "no person shall be removed, nor shall any warrant be granted for the removal of any person from any parish in which such person shall have resided for five years next before the application for the warrant: provided always, that the time during which such person shall be a prisoner in a prison, or shall be serving Her Majesty as a soldier, marine, or sailor, or reside as an in-pensioner in Greenwich or Chelsea hospitals, or shall be confined in a lunatic asylum, or house duly licensed, or hospital registered for the reception of lunatics, or as a patient in a hospital, or during which any such person shall receive relief from any parish, or shall be wholly or in part maintained by any rate or subscription raised in a parish in which such person does not reside, not being a *bonâ fide* charitable gift, shall, for all purposes, be excluded in the computation of time hereinbefore mentioned; and that the removal of a pauper lunatic to a lunatic asylum, under the provisions of any Act relating to the maintenance and care of pauper lunatics, shall not be deemed a removal within the meaning of this Act: provided always, that whenever any person shall have a wife or children having no other settlement than his or her own, such wife and children shall be removable whenever he or she is removable, and shall not be removable when he or she is not removable."

Sec. 2 enacts, "That no woman residing in any parish with her husband at the time of his death shall be removed, nor shall any warrant be granted for her removal from such parish for twelve calendar months next after his death, if she so long continue a widow."

Sec. 3 enacts, "That no child under the age of sixteen years, whether legitimate or illegitimate, residing in any parish with his or her father or mother, stepfather or stepmother, or reputed father, shall be removed; nor shall any warrant be granted for the removal of such child from such parish in any case where such father, mother, stepfather, stepmother, or reputed father, may not lawfully be removed from such parish."

By sec. 8 it is enacted, "That an Act passed in the 5th year of the reign of King Wm. 4, for the amendment and better administration of the laws relating to the poor in England and Wales, and all Acts to amend and extend the same and the present Act, except so far as the provisions of any former Act are altered, amended, or repealed, by any subsequent Act, shall be construed as one Act; and all penalties and forfeitures imposed under this Act shall be recoverable as penalties and forfeitures under the said Act for the amendment of the laws relating to the poor."

And by sec. 9 it is enacted, that the Act shall extend only to England.

The following question arises in the construction of the 1st sec. of the last-mentioned Act, viz.:—Whether Irish and Scotch paupers who have not gained a settlement in this country, are within the meaning of it, or are still removable under the first-mentioned Act, whenever they become chargeable in England. The 8th sec. of the 9 & 10 Vic. c. 66, enacts, that the 4 & 5 Wm. 4, c. 76, and all Acts to amend and extend the same and that Act, shall be construed as one Act. And the 9th sec. enacts, that that Act shall extend only to England, whilst the language of the 1st sec. is without limitation—"that no person shall be removed," &c.

The case of the Queen *v.* Mile End Old Town, 4, Adol and Ellis, 197, seems to bear by analogy on the point submitted to your consideration. That case depended upon the construction of the 4 & 5 Wm. 4, c. 76, whether that Act, and particularly the 56th sec., (as to the age up to which the parent is to be deemed answerable for relief given to a child, viz., sixteen,) applied to Irish persons becoming chargeable in England, and the court decided that that Act did not apply, that its objects were purely and exclusively English, whilst the Act then in force for the removal of Irish paupers, viz., 3 & 4 Wm. 4, c. 40, was confined merely to making provisions for the removal of certain persons born in Ireland, &c. The judgment of the court, delivered by Mr. Justice Patteson, seems almost equally applicable to the law as it at present stands, unless the words used in the 9 & 10 Vic. c. 76, "That no person," &c., must be construed as including persons other than English, notwithstanding that the general scope of the Act would appear to be English. The language of the 56th sec. of the 4 & 5 Wm. 4, c. 76, is like that used in the 1st sec. of the 9 & 10 Vic. c. 66; without any expressed limitation to English persons, that section enacts, that relief given to the wife, or to any child, &c., shall be considered as given to the husband or father, or relief given to any child, &c., shall be considered as given to such widow, but that language was not considered as extending to Irish persons, because, in the language of Mr. Justice Patteson, "The objects and provisions of that statute are purely and exclusively English."

The 3rd sec. of the 9 & 10 Vic., which enacts, that no child under the age of sixteen shall be removed from any parish where the parent may not lawfully be removed from such parish, appears to identify that statute with the objects and purposes of the English law exclusively, inasmuch as by the English law the age of sixteen is the age of emancipation of English children.

The question is of considerable importance, and the guardians of the poor of the Holborn Union, on whose behalf your opinion is requested, are desirous to be well-advised as to the true construction of the law on this point.

Opinion.—I have given this case the best consideration in my power, and am of opinion that Irish and Scotch paupers who have not gained a settlement in this country, are within the meaning of the 9 & 10 Vic. c. 66. I think this case is very different from that of the King *v.* the Inhabitants of Mile-End Old Town, 4 Ad. and Ellis, 197.

I think the enactment in the 9th sec. does not carry the case further than if the 1st sec. had enacted that no person should be removed from any parish in England in which, &c., in which case I think it would have extended to Scotch and Irish paupers. It is also worthy of remark, that the 8 & 9 Vic. c. 117, sec. 7, incorporate the 5th Wm. 4, which is also another reason for distinguishing this case from that above cited.

I am not aware of any case in which the question has been raised, and as it is of some importance, I think it would be as well to take the opinion of the Court upon it, and to contend that the meaning of the Act was to prevent the removal from any parish in England to any other parish in England.

B. PEACOCK.

March 28*th*, 1850.

---

2. OF AN ALLEGED IRREGULAR REMOVAL OF A PAUPER.

8*th Feb.*, 1850.

Clerk of S——— Union.—Transmitting a copy of a correspondence between himself and the clerk of the A——— Union, as to an alleged irregular removal of a pauper named M. A. H.

Dec. 10*th*, 1849.

The Correspondence referred to above:—The clerk of S—— Union to the clerk of A—— Union.—A woman named M. A. H., who has for some years past resided with her husband at A and W. G. in your union, has lately intruded herself into the parish of S. P., in this union, upon the ground that the husband's settlement is there. She is there become chargeable, and is now maintained in our workhouse. She states that her husband deserted her some months since, and that she was lately admitted into your union workhouse; that she applied to the board to allow her out-door relief, and was subsequently allowed 8*s.* for the express purpose of enabling her to come to S. P. As this of course would be clearly an illegal transaction, I am directed to inquire into the correctness of her statement, and if it be true, to ascertain whether your board will take her and her family back, to prevent further steps being resorted to.

12*th Dec.*, 1849.

Clerk of A—— Union to Clerk of S—— Union.—The pauper, with her husband and family, resided in the parish of W. G., in this union, for about twelve months only, when in consequence of having been deserted by her husband, who was a policeman, she applied for relief to this board for herself and three children, and an order for their admission into the workhouse was given and accepted. She subsequently made an application for out-door relief, which was granted, for her children, to the amount of 4*s.* per week, the board of course being under the impression that she would return to W. G., and endeavour to learn some tidings of her husband.

18*th Dec.*, 1849.

Clerk of S—— to Clerk of A——Union.—This woman was had before our board on Thursday last, and your letter read to her. She still adheres to her former statement, and says that nothing was communicated to her as to her being allowed out-door relief by your board; if it had been she would most certainly have remained at W. G. She further states that ——— was in the chair, and inquired of her, 1st, whether 4*s.* would be enough to enable her to reach S. P., and being informed it would not, she, after the board broke up, received from the master of the workhouse 8*s.* for that purpose. I am therefore instructed by the board to say that unless the woman and her family are taken back, and the costs of all relief administered here be repaid, a communication will be made to the Poor Law Board on the subject.

The Poor Law Board to the Clerk of A—— Union.—The Board request that the master may be called upon for a written explanation in regard to the allegation of the pauper, and that such explanation may be forwarded for the information of the Board.

16*th Feb.*, 1850.

Workhouse Master of A—— Union.—The pauper applied to me the day previous to the meeting of the guardians, Nov. 23rd, 1849, with others, for permission to see the board, for the purpose of applying for out-relief for her children. I told her that her application should be duly entered in my book, which is my usual course. She accordingly saw the board, the result of which I was not aware of until the business of the day was over. I then found by my book that she was ordered 4*s.* per week for two weeks, and after the board had broken up, the relieving-officer gave me 8*s.* to give her on leaving the house, which was done. Since that period I have heard nothing further on the subject, neither was I aware but that she was going to return to the parish of W. G.

4*th March*, 1850.

The Poor Law Board to a relieving-officer of A—— Union.—The Board request that you will furnish them with an explanation of the circumstances under which you gave the 8*s.* to the master for the purpose stated, and with a copy of any entry which you may have made in your books with respect to the case.

8*th March*, 1850.

Relieving-officer of A—— Union.—Having understood from the master that the pauper wished to have both weeks' allowance at once, I handed it over to her. I was not, however, aware but that the pauper would return to the parish to which she was chargeable. I have entered the amount, 8*s.*, in my out-relief list as 4*s.* for two weeks, as ordered by the board.

19*th April*, 1850.

The Poor Law Board to the Clerk of A—— Union.—In the absence of any direct explanation from the guardians of the A—— Union, the Board are left to form their opinion of the transaction from the communication of the guardians of the S—— Union on the one hand, and the statements of the workhouse master and relieving-officer of the A—— Union on the other. The Board have considered the answer or explanation given by those officers respectively, but cannot say that they deem them at all satisfactory. They think the course of proceeding which appears to have been adopted with regard to the case of M. A. H., is far from being such as ought to be pursued in the administration of relief to the poor. The fact is not denied, that the pauper, who was an inmate of the workhouse, was sent away with the grant of 8*s.* in money. The statement of the pauper is, that this was given for the express purpose of enabling her to go to S. P. The clerk of the A—— union in his letter of the 12th of December last, addressed to the clerk of the S—— union, denies the correctness of this statement, and says that the relief was advanced upon the pauper's application to be allowed out-relief, under the impression, on the part of the guardians, that the pauper would return to W. G., with the view of learning tidings of her husband. But the Board must observe that even upon this view of the case there appears to have been a want of reasonable caution in the course adopted. It does not appear to have been ascertained that there was any house or home in W. G. to which the pauper and her children could go, or, indeed, that the circumstances of the case afforded any reasonable security that the pauper would not become chargeable to other parishes. Moreover, assuming the case to have been a fit one for out-door relief, still the directions of the guardians, which were that the pauper was to be allowed 4*s.* per week for two weeks, were not observed, as the two weeks' relief were given at once to the pauper. Looking at the whole of the facts, the Board cannot but express their regret that the case was dealt with as it was; for the result has undoubtedly been to entail in an irregular manner a charge upon the parish of S. P. Seeing that the law has so strictly forbidden the irregular shifting of the burden of pauper relief, the Board think it their duty to remark that those who are charged with the administration of relief cannot be too careful in avoiding any act or proceeding which is liable, as in this instance, to expose them to the imputation of being actuated by any such intention. The Board have thought it necessary to address a special communication to the relieving-officer on the subject, and they trust that the guardians will themselves take occasion to admonish that officer to be cautious as to his future proceedings.

19*th April*, 1850.

The Poor Law Board to the relieving-officer of A—— Union.—The Board gather from your communication, that although the guardians of A—— union directed you to give this pauper 4*s.* a week for two weeks, you nevertheless, upon your own responsibility, gave her 8*s.* in one sum, because she wished you to do so; and you entered the amount in your out-relief list as 4*s.* a week for two weeks, as ordered by the guardians. The Board deem it their duty to call your attention to the impropriety of such a deviation on your part from the orders of the guardians, and they think it right especially to animadvert strongly upon the mode in which you appear to have dealt with the transaction in your accounts, so as to make the entries accord with the directions of the guardians, instead of with the actual expenditure. The Board trust that you will not again be guilty of any similar proceedings. With regard to the effect of the course pursued, in rendering the pauper and her family a charge upon the S—— union, the Board, while duly observing your statement that you were not aware but that the pauper would return to the parish to which she was chargeable, cannot but point out to you, that if you had given the money to her with the view of shifting the burden of her maintenance to some other parish, you would have exposed yourself to the penalties provided by the 9 & 10 Vic. c. 66, sec. 6.

19th April, 1850.

The Poor Law Board to the Clerk of S—— Union.—The Board have been in communication with the guardians and officers of the A—— union, on the subject of this case, and have this day addressed letters to the clerk of the union, and also to the relieving-officer, copies of which are herewith forwarded for the information of the guardians of the S—— union. The Board desire to add, that looking to the facts of the case, as explained in the correspondence before them, they fear that the guardians of the S—— union have no means of redress.

XVIII.—SURETIES — OF PAID OFFICERS TERMINATING THEIR OBLIGATION.

12th June, 1850.

Clerk of the Guildford Union.—Messrs. A., B., and C., who joined Mr. D., the collector of the poor-rates for ———, in this union, in a bond for the security of the parish, have given notice to the guardians that they shall no longer consider themselves responsible for him. The first-named person gave such notice some time ago, and the two latter on the last and preceding board days. Inquiring, whether the collector should be suspended until he gives fresh sureties.

Ans.—The law does not enable a surety to withdraw from his obligation at his discretion. Therefore the notices to which you refer are of no legal avail in releasing the parties in the present case from their responsibility. But it is desirable that the guardians of the Guildford union should ascertain the precise grounds upon which the sureties have taken the course which you describe, and also that they should investigate the present state of the accounts of the officer in question.

XIX.—VALUATION—UNDER 11 & 12 VIC. c. 110, SEC. 7.

4th Feb., 1850.

Clerks of Wareham and Purbeck Unions.—Inquiring, whether it is necessary, in the case of parish officers applying to the board of guardians to provide for the partial valuation of a parish, under 11 & 12 Vic. c. 110, sec. 7, the properties requiring valuation should be specified. Or, can the board of guardians appoint a person to make such valuation of part of the property, leaving it to him and the overseers to select in the course of the valuation such properties as they may afterwards consider require revision, without in the first instance particularising to the board of guardians any properties liable to be assessed?

Ans.—The Board are of opinion that the guardians should be informed of the particular property or properties to be valued, inasmuch as they are to cause the valuation to be made of the rateable property which is sought to be valued.

XX.—WORKHOUSE MASTER.—HIS POWER IN REGARD TO REFRACTORY PAUPERS.

23rd Jan., 1850.

Clerk of Elham Union.—Inquiring whether the guardians are justified in authorising the master of the workhouse to take any refractory able-bodied pauper, who may transgress during the week, before a justice; or ought he to wait until the next sitting of the board of guardians, for the case to be heard by them in the first instance?

Ans.—The Board apprehend it is quite competent to the guardians to give to the master of the workhouse such an authority as that to which you refer; indeed, in the absence of express directions to that effect from the guardians, the master would be warranted in taking before justices any persons guilty of misbehaviour in the workhouse, particularly in any case the nature and urgency of which did not admit of delay; though, as a matter of discretion, the Board think it would be advisable that (except in cases of the kind above-mentioned) he should wait for directions of the guardians at their next sitting.

London: Printed by Order of the Poor Law Board, by BLACKBURN & BURT, 90½, Holborn Hill, and Published by CHARLES KNIGHT, 90, Fleet Street.

AN

OFFICIAL CIRCULAR

OF PUBLIC DOCUMENTS AND INFORMATION:

DIRECTED BY THE POOR LAW BOARD TO BE PRINTED, CHIEFLY FOR THE USE OF THE BOARDS OF GUARDIANS AND THEIR OFFICERS.

No. 39.] JULY, 1850. [N.S.

CONTENTS.

PAGE

I.—ACCOUNTS.

1. CHARGING SALARIES OF MEDICAL OFFICERS.

21*st Dec.*, 1849.

Clerk of ——— Union.—A distinct sum is paid to the medical officers of the ——— Union in respect of each parish, for their attendance on the poor, which sum has hitherto been debited to the parish under the head of "Other Separate Charges." This method of charging the cost of medical attendance has prevailed from the time when the medical officers were appointed annually by tender, and offered their services to the guardians at a certain sum per parish fixed by themselves. At the last audit of the accounts of this union, the auditor stated, that he considered this practice was irregular; that the salaries of the medical officers, like those of other officers, should form a common charge to be borne by the union, and apportioned according to the averages; and that the 28th sec. of the Poor Law Amendment Act appeared to direct imperatively the adoption of the latter mode of distributing the salaries in question amongst the parishes. The attention of the Poor Law Commissioners was directed to the matter in 1846, but they gave no intimation that the course pursued was improper. Requesting the instructions of the Poor Law Board as to the course to be taken for the future in distributing the salaries of the medical officers amongst the parishes of the ——— Union.

Ans.—The Board are of opinion that the objection of the auditor in this case is valid, inasmuch as the medical officers are officers of the ——— Union, in like manner as are the relieving-officers; consequently, their salaries can only in strictness be charged under the 4 & 5 Wm. 4, c. 76, sec. 28, to the common fund, to which the several parishes of the union contribute according to the averages. The Poor Law Commissioners have not issued any order to the guardians directing the appointment of medical officers specifically for any particular parish or parishes in the ——— Union, or, authorizing the overseers of such parishes to appoint them. The Board understand that the Poor Law Commissioners acquiesced in the arrangement of the guardians for the payment of the medical officers' salaries, as no objection was raised against them; but now that an objection has been made, the Board are compelled to admit its force in strictness of law, and to request that the guardians will in future adhere to the provisions of the statute in this respect.

2. MODE OF ENTERING FUNERAL EXPENSES AND COST OF CLOTHING.

4*th April*, 1850.

Clerk of Newton Abbot Union.—Ever since the formation of this union he has, in accordance with the direction of the guardians, debited in-maintenance and out-relief with every item of expense referring thereto respectively. To in-maintenance he has placed the funeral expenses of paupers dying in the workhouse, as well as the clothing given (in a half-worn state or new) to paupers admitted into the workhouse in a state of disease and almost nudity, who, after being restored to health, have been allowed to go out with such clothing. Requesting permission to continue this practice, which is objected to by the district auditor, who wishes all expenses incurred in respect of in-door paupers, except the cost of their maintenance, to be placed in future to out-door relief.

Ans.—In the case of a pauper chargeable to a parish, the funeral expenses should be charged to such parish, according to the express directions of sec. 31 of the 7 & 8 Vic. c. 101; while, in the case of a pauper chargeable to the union, they are required by the 11 & 12 Vic. c. 110, secs. 1 & 3, and 12 & 13 Vic. c. 103, sec. 1, to be charged, like the relief, to the common fund. You will perceive, therefore, that the practice which you have hitherto adopted in this matter is incorrect; as, by charging the funeral expenses to in-maintenance, the amount is distributed among all the parishes which have had paupers in the workhouse, and, consequently, each such parish has to bear its proportion of the charge, whether any of its own paupers have died or not. The Board think that the funeral expenses should be entered in a separate account, under a specific heading, and not as relief, either "in-door" or "out-door." With regard to the clothing to which you refer, the Board are of opinion that, where such clothing is given to paupers, on quitting the workhouse, the rule laid down by the auditor is correct, and the expense should be charged as out-door relief.

II.—APPRENTICESHIP.—CERTIFICATE OF JUSTICES.

24*th July*, 1850.

Clerk of Carnarvon Union.—The 12th sec. of 7 & 8 Vic. c. 101, with the observation in a work of Mr. Lumley, "that the interposition of justices in the execution of the indenture, has been rendered unnecessary," incline to the belief, that the provision of sec. 61 of the Poor Law Amendment Act, which relates to indentures executed by overseers, is done away with in the cases of binding apprentices by boards of guardians. In the indentures executed by the guardians of this union, no such certificate has been made, and a dispute having arisen between a master and his apprentice, requesting the opinion of the Board on the point.

Ans.—The Board do not consider that the certificate of the justices, as to the formality of the proceedings in the case of the apprenticeship of a pauper, is required, where the indenture is executed by the guardians of a union formed under the Poor Law Amendment Act.

III.—ASSISTANT OVERSEER.

1. SIGNING NOTICES OF VESTRY MEETINGS.

11th April, 1850.

Assistant Overseer of Darlington.—At a vestry meeting held on the 25th March, an objection was taken to the notice convening the meeting, because it was signed by one overseer only, and himself as assistant overseer, it being contended that the assistant overseer had no authority to sign notices. He conceived that the Act of 1 Vic. c. 45 did not require more than one overseer to sign notices of vestry meetings, and that, even if it had required two, the terms of his appointment, viz., to "execute and perform all the other duties of an overseer of the said township," authorized him to execute any of the duties of the ordinary overseers. Requesting the opinion of the Poor Law Board thereon.

Ans.—The Board doubt whether an assistant overseer is an overseer within the meaning of the 1 Vic. c. 45. They are, upon the whole, disposed to think he is not. The signing of the notice convening a vestry is not, generally, a duty, but rather a power, and there does not appear to be any authority given by the 59 Geo. 3, c. 12, sec. 7, to the inhabitants in vestry to assign mere powers to the assistant overseer, especially when such powers, by the statute creating them, are limited in terms to the overseers.

2. WHO SHOULD RECEIVE A BOND FROM AN ASSISTANT OVERSEER.

15th July, 1850.

Clerk of Hexham Union.—Inquiring whether in the case of an assistant overseer (who is not also a collector) who is appointed under the 59 Geo. 3, and his appointment duly confirmed by the justices, but without any interference on the part of the guardians, his bond ought to be given to the churchwardens and overseers of the parish, for which he is appointed, or to the guardians of the union. And inquiring also to whom the bond should be given, when the same person is appointed both assistant overseer and collector of rates.

Ans.—Where a person is duly appointed an assistant overseer under the provisions of the statute 59 Geo. 3, c. 12, it is still competent to the vestry of the parish, to require that the officer should give a bond to the churchwardens and overseers of such parish. At the same time, a subsequent statute (7 & 8 Vic. c. 101, sec. 61) renders it incumbent upon the assistant overseer so appointed, to give security to the guardians of the union, comprising such parish. Practically, therefore, this latter provision which should be acted upon, will render it unnecessary that the same officers should also give bonds to the overseers. The Board do not see that there is any distinction, with regard to the liability of the officer, to give security to the guardians, whether he is appointed to perform the general duties of assistant overseer, apart from the collection of the rates, or conjointly with that duty; though, in the former case, security is obviously not needed to the same amount as in the latter.

IV.—AUDIT.—INSPECTION OF BOOKS BY RATE-PAYERS.

25th April, 1850.

Clerk of Huntingdon Union.—Inquiring, 1, whether the minute book of the guardians, containing all their proceedings, is one of the books that is to be opened to the inspection of the rate-payers under Art. 34 of the General Order of Accounts, or simply the relief order book and ledger, and the half-yearly statement; and, 2, whether a person who has not paid his poor-rates, can be considered a rate-payer, so as to entitle him to inspect books, &c.

Ans.—1. The minute-book, containing the record of the proceedings of the guardians of the union, is not a book open to the inspection of the rate-payers of the several parishes of the union. 2. The Board understand Art. 34 of the Order in question to mean a person who is assessed merely to the poor-rates, and not to impose a limitation, requiring that such person should not be in arrear with the payment of his poor-rates, when he claims to avail himself of the right of inspection.

V.—AUDITOR—HIS POWER TO ORDER THE CHARGE OF A PAUPER TO BE TRANSFERRED FROM ONE PARISH TO ANOTHER.

11*th July*, 1850.

Clerk of St. Columb Major Union.—Inquiring whether the district auditor has the power from an *ex parte* statement, to order the charge of any pauper to be transferred from one parish to another, or from any parish to the common fund of the union.

Ans.—The Board consider it is incumbent upon the auditor, in auditing the accounts of a union, to ascertain that the several charges therein are not only proper in themselves, but placed to the right account; and to correct any error which he may discover in the allocation of any such charge. If, therefore, he finds that any relief or other expenditure which has been charged to one parish, ought in fact to have been charged to another parish in the union, or to the common fund, it is his duty, in either case, so to alter the accounts as to effect a legal distribution of the charge. As regards the evidence on which he is to act in such a case, the auditor will judge for himself. If a person appear on behalf of the parish and produce evidence, and no person appear on behalf of the board of guardians, the auditor will be justified in acting upon the evidence actually produced, and the guardians must abide the consequences of omitting either in person or by their officers to watch over the interests of the union at the audit. The law does not contemplate that the board of guardians will allow their accounts to be audited without the attendance of some one to represent them before the auditor.

VI.—BOND OF PAID OFFICER.—RENEWAL OF BOND ON THE TERMS OF APPOINTMENT BEING ALTERED.

2*nd July*, 1850.

Clerk of Weardale Union.—It appearing from the case of Bamford and others, *v.* Iles, recently decided in the Court of Exchequer, that on any increase being made in the salary or poundage of a union-officer, his bond should be renewed, enquired whether, when the duties, sureties, or amount of security continue unaltered, the bond should bear date from its renewal, or be antedated to the date of the original bond; and also whether the appointment should be recited as dating from the alteration of salary, or from the time when the officer was originally appointed.

Ans.—On referring to the report of the case you allude to, viz. Bamford *v.* Iles, 18 L. I. R. N. S. M. C. 49, the Board observe that there was in that case, a new appointment of the assistant-overseer; the former appointment being entirely vacated, and the liability of the sureties consequently determined. But so far as the Board are aware, it has never been decided that an increase in the salary of a paid officer of a parish or union affects his security; and they can see no principle upon which it should be held to have that effect.

VII.—BURIAL.

1. RECOVERY OF EXPENSES OF BURIAL FROM A BENEFIT SOCIETY.

8*th March*, 1849.

Clerk of Brecknock Union.—W. P. and his wife, paupers of the parish of St. John the Evangelist, in this union, were some time back admitted into the union workhouse. The husband was a member of a benefit society, and was in receipt of a weekly allowance of 2*s.* 6*d.* for life: the authorities of the club refused to pay this allowance except to the man himself or some member of his family. W. P. is now dead, and there is a sum of 30*s.* payable by the club towards his funeral; which sum is to be paid, according to the articles, to "such person or persons being his widow, child, relation, or person having the charge of his funeral, as the deceased in his lifetime shall appoint, or in default of such appointment, to his widow or next of kin, or if none, to the person who shall be at the expense of his funeral." He has left a widow, who is in the workhouse. The guardians have applied for the funeral money (the parish of St. John the Evangelist having been at the expense of his funeral) but have been refused. Can this sum be recovered under the 15 sec. of the 12 & 13 Vic. c. 103, in the county court; and if so, who should be named as plaintiff?

Ans.—The latter part of 16th sec. of the 12 & 13 Vic. c. 103, enables the guardians to reimburse themselves the cost of the funeral expenses out of any money or property which at the time of the pauper's death was in his possession and belonged to him. The statute does not, however, give them the power of suing the trustees of the society in question in the county court for the money which was not "in the possession" of the pauper at his decease, and which cannot be said to have "belonged" to him, because it was not payable to him nor to his executor, but to certain specified persons. In this respect, therefore, the money payable by the society does not appear to fall within the provisions of the clause above mentioned.

2. COST OF BURIAL, TO WHAT PARISH CHARGEABLE.

3rd July, 1850.

Guardians of Gwersyllt, Wrexham Union.—Ezra Williams, aged nineteen, a collier, came last autumn, to work in the parish of Gwersyllt, and resided with his mother until about Christmas. An explosion of fire-damp put a stop to the working of the colliery, and after that he obtained work in Staffordshire. In April last, he was unwell, and returned to reside with his mother, in Gwersyllt. On the 25th May, he again set off for Staffordshire, his brother having sent him 5*s.* to pay his expenses, and informed him there was work to be had there. He proceeded into the next parish of Stansby, and died on the road, suddenly. His body, after being removed into Broughton township, where the inquest was held, was brought to his mother's house, in Gwersyllt, and the relieving-officer of the Gwersyllt district, gave the mother a coffin. Neither of them had a settlement in Gwersyllt or Stansby. The father of the young man had deserted the mother, and his residence is unknown. Inquired whether the coffin should be charged to the township where the man died, where he was buried, or to the common fund of the union.

Clerk of Wrexham Union.—[To whom the above statement was referred.] The guardians believe the facts as stated to be true, but are divided in opinion, as to whether the cost of the coffin is to be charged to the common fund, as that of a deceased wayfarer, or to Gwersyllt.

Ans.—As Ezra Williams was not chargeable to the poor-rates in his lifetime, the expenses of his funeral cannot, as it seems to the Board, be charged to the common fund of the Wrexham Union, under the 11 & 12 Vic. c. 110, sec. 1; but must be borne by the parish in which he died, (viz. Stansby,) according to the provisions of the 7 & 8 Vic. c. 101, sec. 31.

VIII.—CHARGEABILITY.

1. OF IRREMOVABLE POOR IN THE UNION WORKHOUSE.

29th May, 1850.

Clerk of Ulverstone Union.—Inquiring whether a pauper charged to the common fund, under the 11 & 12 Vic. c. 110, sec. 3, and the 12 & 13 Vic. c. 103, sec. 1, while resident in a parish and irremovable therefrom, under the provisions of the 9 & 10 Vic. c. 66, must continue to be charged to the common fund, when removed into the workhouse, or to his settlement parish, if within the union, and known; or whether, if the settlement parish be not within the union, or be not known, the pauper should be charged to the parish in which he resided previous to his admission into the workhouse.

Ans.—The Board are of opinion that, when an out-door pauper is irremovable, and therefore chargeable to the common fund of the Ulverstone Union, it is not competent for the guardians of the union, by ordering the relief of the said pauper to be given to him in the workhouse, to release the common fund, and throw the future charge upon the parish of the pauper's previous residence, or upon the parish in which the workhouse is locally situated, or upon any other fund than the common fund of the union. The Board refer the guardians to the 12 & 13 Vic. c. 103, sec. 4, by which they will see that the residence of persons rendered irremovable by any provision of the 9 & 10 Vic. c. 66, is not broken by the fact of their going into the union workhouse.

2. CHARGEABILITY OF A PERSON RELIEVED ON ACCOUNT OF SICKNESS.

29th May, 1850

Clerk of Louth Union.—A pauper became destitute, and chargeable in and to the parish of A. B., and was duly removed by an order of justices, to the parish of C. D., the place of his settlement. He afterwards returned to the parish of A. B., and became chargeable on account of sickness. Under these circumstances, should the relief be charged to the common fund, the parish of A. B., or the parish of C. D., both parishes being in the same union? It must be understood that the overseers of A. B. and C. D. were not parties to the pauper's going back.

Ans.—Assuming that the pauper in question ceases to be chargeable, and a new chargeability arises on the happening of the sickness to him in the parish of A. B., which sickness does not produce a permanent disability, the cost of his relief, as the pauper would in that case be rendered irremovable from A. B., by operation of the 9 & 10 Vic. c. 66, sec. 4, would fall upon the common fund of the union.

3. CHARGEABILITY.

Clerk of Cheltenham Union.—Transmitting for the opinion of the Poor Law Board the following statements duly signed under the 4th sec. of the 11 & 12 Vic. c. 110 :—1. E. B., a pauper, residing at Cheltenham, is admitted to be irremovable under the 1st sec. of the 9 & 10 Vic. c. 66, unless the following circumstance renders her otherwise :—About two years ago she went to St. Helens, in Worcester, to her daughter's there, and remained with her a fortnight. At the time she went to St. Helens she had no house or lodgings in Cheltenham, but lived with her daughter in Cheltenham. She had no furniture of her own. During her absence from Cheltenham her daughter made use of the bed-room she used to occupy, for her family. One of her daughter's children always slept with the pauper. Should the cost of the relief granted to this pauper be charged to the common fund, or is she removable? 2. E. S. is irremovable from Cheltenham under the 1st sec. of 9 & 10 Vic. c. 66. Her husband, who is dead, never gained a settlement in Cheltenham, and it is not known where his settlement was. Before the pauper's marriage, she acquired a settlement in Cheltenham, by hiring and service, prior to the 14th of August, 1834. The guardians contend that the relief to this pauper is chargeable to Cheltenham, as the place of her maiden settlement, and the overseers claim to charge it upon the common fund, under the 3rd sec. of 11 & 12 Vic. c. 110. To which fund is the cost of the relief to this pauper chargeable? 3. A. B., a pauper, has resided in the parish of Cheltenham for seven or eight years continuously, except as hereinafter stated; and but for the absence presently referred to, she is admitted to be irremovable under the 1st sec. of the 9 & 10 Vic. c. 66. The pauper is a widow, and her legal place of settlement is Elkstone. She has one daughter residing in Cheltenham, and another daughter residing at Avening. She has no furniture, but has resided with her daughter in Cheltenham seven or eight years in lodgings, except for the time presently referred to, and her daughter pays the rent of the lodgings. They occupy one sittingroom and one bedroom only. The pauper is occasionally employed in Cheltenham to attend women during their confinement, as a monthly nurse. She always returns to her daughter's at Cheltenham. About two years ago, her daughter at Avening was confined, and the pauper went to her house and attended upon her at that place for about two months, at the end of which time she returned to her former residence, at her daughter's at Cheltenham. Whilst she was at Avening, her daughter in Cheltenham made use of the bedroom for herself, the same as she did when the pauper was with her. When she went to Avening it was understood by herself and both daughters that she was to return to Cheltenham. Should the cost of the relief granted to this pauper be charged to the common fund, or is she removable?

Ans.—1, As no object of a temporary nature is assigned for the removal to Worcester, the pauper, E. B., appears to the Board, upon the statement before them, to be removable; therefore the cost of the relief, in this case, is chargeable to the parish of Cheltenham. 2. The case of E. S. is not very clear, but the result upon the present statement appears to be that the pauper is settled in Cheltenham; consequently she is not within the 9 & 10 Vic. c. 66, and the cost of her relief is not a charge upon the common fund of the union. 3. The statement of the case of A.B. shows that there was not a breach of her residence in Cheltenham, but merely a temporary absence from the place of her residence, for a specific purpose, in the exercise of her ordinary calling. The cost of the relief in this case should, therefore, be charged upon the common fund of the union.

IX.—COLLECTOR—APPOINTMENT OF.

23*rd May*, 1850.

Clerk of Patrington Union.—Inquiring, with reference to the appointment of a collector of poor-rates for the parish of Roos, in this union, whether the minute of the board of guardians on the subject, and the bond subsequently executed, would, in case of any dispute, be considered a sufficient proof of such appointment, or whether it will be necessary that there should be a written appointment.

Ans.—The Board consider that, according to the cases of Frost *v.* Bolland, 5 B. & C. 611, and the Queen *v.* Grimshaw, 10 Q. B. Rep. 747, the appointment of a collector of poor-rates need not be by an instrument under seal; but the minute of the board of guardians would suffice, especially if coupled with proof of his acting in that character.

X.—CONTRIBUTION ORDERS.—DEFAULTING OVERSEER.

9*th March*, 1850.

Mr. ———, Parish of A., Pocklington Union.—One of the overseers having assigned over all his effects in trust for the benefit of his creditors, and having parish monies in his hands, inquiring what steps the parish ought to take to recover such monies.

Ans.—An application may be made to the justices, under 17 Geo. 2, c. 38, sec. 3, to appoint a new overseer in the place of the insolvent overseer; or, the parish may wait until the district auditor can audit the accounts of the parish, and then the overseer will be compellable to pay over to the treasurer of the union the balance which the auditor may find to be due from him.

2nd Aug., 1850.

Clerk of Pocklington Union.—On the 3rd of November, 1849, an order was duly signed by the board of guardians, and directed to the churchwardens and overseers of A, directing them to pay to the treasurer of the union, on the 24th November, the sum of £50, and on the 16th February, the further sum of £45. On the 4th May last, another order was duly signed by the guardians, and directed to the churchwardens and overseers of A, directing them to pay to the treasurer, on the 25th May, the sum of £25, and on the 5th August next, the further sum of £30. It appears by the treasurer's books, that only the first call of £50 has been paid to him. The board on applying to the overseers, have been informed that Mr. B , the acting overseer, in 1849, has made an assignment for the benefit of his creditors, under which all his personal property has been sold by the assignees. It also appears Mr. B. had collected from the rate-payers of A the sum of £50, but had not paid the same to the treasurer; Mr. C., the overseer, collected a rate to pay the second call, (£45,) and on attending, the treasurer was informed that the first call of £50 had not been paid: Mr. C. then paid the £50 call, instead of the £45. The parishioners now refuse to have another rate laid for the £45, but have laid a rate for the May call of £25, which has been collected and paid into the hands of their bankers. The auditor, at his audit on the 11th of June last, certified that a balance of £58. 1*s.* 9*d.* was due from Mr. B., and at the same audit a balance of 19*s.* 0¼*d.* was found to be due to Mr. C., the other overseer. The order dated the 3rd November, was sent by post to the overseers of A, and the order of the 4th May last was given to the guardian of A, who is also one of the churchwardens. Inquiring what steps the guardians are to take to compel the payment of the calls in arrear, namely, the £45 due on the 16th February last, and the £25 due on the 25th May last. Should the churchwardens and overseers of the last year be proceeded against for the £45 call, and the churchwardens and overseers of the present year for the £25 call? Or, should the churchwardens and overseers of the present year be proceeded against for both calls?

Ans.—As the officers upon whom the order of the 3rd November, 1849, was served, are not now in office, it is doubtful whether it can be enforced, so far as the payment of the balance of £45 is concerned. The Board think, having regard to the language of the 2 & 3 Vic. c. 84, that the remedy given by that Act cannot be resorted to against the late officers. It appears, indeed, as regards one of the overseers of that period, (Mr. B.,) that he has assigned over his effects for the benefit of his creditors. Then, as regards the present overseers, they are not liable for the default which has arisen in respect of an order not made during their period of office, and not served upon them. Then, with regard to the order of the 4th May, it appears it was directed to the churchwardens and overseers of A, and was given to the guardian, who also, it is stated, is one of the churchwardens of A. The Board think it very doubtful whether there has been such a service of this order as is required by sec. 7 of the 12 & 13 Vic. c. 103, A being, as the Board understand, a township in the parish of Pocklington. If so, the overseers alone are the parties who are authorized to make and levy the poor-rate, and it is to them the order of the guardians should have been addressed, and served personally on one of them. The Board, upon the whole, recommend the guardians now to make an order sufficient in amount to cover the balance due from the township, and to have such order duly addressed and served upon those who are legally responsible for the payment of the contribution.

XI.—DESERTION.—Reward for the Apprehension of a Person who had Deserted his Wife and Family.

11th May, 1850.

Clerk of Ross Union.—J. P. has left his wife and family chargeable to the parish of St. Weonards, in this union, the officers of which parish have some months past offered a reward of £1 for his apprehension, and though an accurate description of him has been given, he has not been taken. The officers now wish to increase the reward to £5, but the guardians consider it a large reward, and without the sanction of the Poor Law Board they would not give any authority. Inquiring, whether the Poor Law Board will authorise a reward of £5 to be paid for the apprehension of J. P.

Ans.—The Board refer the guardians to the provisions of the 7 & 8 Vic. c. 101, sec. 59, which enable them to pay the costs incurred in the apprehension of such offenders. It is a point entirely in the discretion of the guardians of the Ross Union, what amount of reward they shall reasonably offer in a case where such a course is justifiable, and the Board cannot give any specific opinion as to the question of amount, but they would point out to the guardians, that under the section already cited, the expenses of the apprehension of J. P. may ultimately fall upon the common fund of the union.

XII.—ELECTION OF GUARDIANS—EXPENSES OF.

16*th April*, 1850.

Clerk of ——— *Union.*—At the last election of guardians for the township of R. in the ——— union, six guardians were nominated, being three more than the number of guardians allowed for that township; and, consequently, voting papers were prepared at the last moment and got ready for distribution to the rate-payers, 1,800 in number. On the evening of the 3rd inst., two days before the delivery of the papers, three of the persons so nominated gave notice that they refused to act, and the voting papers then became useless. Is the clerk entitled to any compensation for the trouble and expense incurred in preparing the voting papers beyond a sum not exceeding £10, which may be given to him by the guardians?

Ans.—In a case of a similar kind to that which you describe, it was considered by the Poor Law Commissioners, that there was not a "contested" election, within the meaning of the Election Expenses Order, (see 3, Official Circular, 55,) and the Board are not prepared to dissent from that view. But they think, that in settling the amount to be paid to you for conducting the election of guardians for R., the guardians of the ——— union may properly take into their consideration the particular circumstances attending that election, and award you a larger amount than they might otherwise have done.

XIII.—GUARDIANS.—RESOLUTION TO DISCOURAGE THE CANVASSING OF GUARDIANS FOR THEIR VOTES.

20*th April*, 1850.

Clerk of Newtown and Llanidloes Union.—In consequence of the canvassing of guardians by candidates for appointments under the board of guardians, having on some occasion been carried out to an inconvenient extent, the board on the 3rd of December last passed the following resolution, viz.—"That in case any candidate for a paid office in this union shall either directly or indirectly canvass any guardian for his vote, the clerk shall forthwith return such candidate's testimonials, and he or she shall be deemed ineligible to be elected." On Monday last, pursuant to notice given by handbill, the guardians proceeded to elect a registrar of births and deaths for the district of Llanwnog, for which office two candidates were put in nomination. After the votes of the guardians had been taken, and the successful candidate informed by the chairman of his election, a protest against the election was made on behalf of the defeated candidate, on the ground that the resolution of the board of guardians of the 3rd of December last had not been kept. Inquiring whether, in case canvassing be proved against the officer elected, the board must proceed to a fresh election.

Ans.—Though the resolution set forth in your letter is one which proposes to enforce a very salutary regulation, and embodies a principle which should influence the minds of the guardians, the Board are not prepared to state that the non-observance of that resolution can create a legal disability, so as to render the election of the officer you refer to null and void.

XIV.—LUNATIC PAUPERS.

1. CHARGEABILITY OF.

5*th April*, 1850.

Clerk of Southmolton Union.—F. C., a man belonging as it is believed to Newry, in Ireland, travelled with a pack from place to place, selling the various articles contained therein, and happening, in the quarter ending Midsummer, 1847, to be vending his goods in and about Southmolton, was taken dangerously ill in that town, and was admitted into the union workhouse, where he remained until the 15th of May, when he became a dangerous lunatic, and was sent to the county asylum, where he has ever since remained. In January, 1849, a brother of the lunatic applied to the board of guardians for their consent that he might be permitted to take the lunatic from the asylum to be placed under the protection of his relatives in Ireland, to which application the guardians were ready to assent, but as they refused to deliver the pack and watch, and some other property of the lunatic (which were taken with him to the workhouse and still remained in store there) as a preliminary to the removal of the pauper, the purpose was abandoned. And it would seem the main object was not to remove the lunatic, but to get possession of his pack. The charges of in-maintenance, and the expenses of the asylum, have been charged to the parish of Southmolton. The latter alone up to Christmas last, amount to £81. 16*s*. And it seems that under the late statute the charges in this case ought to be carried to the union common charges' account, and not to be a parochial charge on Southmolton. Inquiring, 1. Whether the guardians are justified in availing themselves of the property belonging to the lunatic in store at the workhouse to repay the expenses which have been incurred; and how are they to proceed therein. 2. Whether any, and what portion of the expenses of in-maintenance and the expenses of the asylum should be debitted to the common charges' account.

Ans.—The Board think that an order should be obtained on the treasurer of the county, under secs. 59 & 63 of the 8 & 9 Vic. c. 126, the case being one, as the Board collect, in which the pauper has no settlement in this country; or, at least, none which can be ascertained. If the order be obtained, it will, beside providing for the future cost of maintaining the lunatic, enable the parish of Southmolton to be reimbursed the cost incurred in respect of the maintenance within twelve months previous to the date of such order. But in that case the Board do not see, having regard to the limitation contained in sec. 16 of the 12 & 13 Vic. c. 103, that the guardians could take and appropriate the property of the lunatic in repayment of the expenses. The Board do not find any circumstance stated in your letter tending to show that the common fund of the union would be liable, in the event of the county not being charged with the relief. The case does not appear to fall within sec. 5 of the 12 & 13 Vic. c. 103.

2. FEE TO MEDICAL PRACTITIONERS FOR CERTIFICATES IN REGARD TO LUNATIC PAUPERS.

11*th May*, 1850.

The Secretary of the Alleged Lunatics' Friend Society.—The attention of the committee of this society has been called by a magistrate for Somersetshire, to the mode of remunerating medical men for signing certificates in the case of pauper lunatics, who stated that a practice prevailed not to pay any fee to the medical man if the person examined proved not to be a lunatic.

Ans.—The Board are not aware of any rule of law which makes any difference as to the right of a medical practitioner called in to examine a poor person alleged to be lunatic, to be paid a proper compensation for his services, whatever may be the result of that examination.

3. LIABILITY OF SON TO CONTRIBUTE TO THE MAINTENANCE OF HIS FATHER IN A LUNATIC ASYLUM.

1*st July*, 1850.

Two Justices for Salop—Burford Petty Sessional Division—A pauper lunatic has been placed in the county asylum, at the instance of his wife and sons. A son applied to the board of guardians of the Tenbury Union, stating that the lunatic was dangerous. The officers of the township proceeded in the case under the 8 & 9 Vic. c. 126, sec. 49. A question now arises whether the sons can be compelled to contribute to their parent's support in the asylum, under 59 Geo. 3, c. 12, sec. 26, or whether the course pointed out in 8 & 9 Vic. c. 126, sec. 49, for defraying the expenses incurred on the lunatic's account, precludes the operation of 59 Geo. 3, c. 12, sec. 26, in the present instance.

Ans.—The Board presume that the case is not one in which the lunatic has an estate applicable to his maintenance, and with respect to which the justices could proceed in the manner pointed out by the latter part of sec. 49 of the 8 & 9 Vic. c. 126, or under sec. 27 of the 7 & 8 Vic. c. 101. If it is not such a case, the Board think with regard to the main question, that there is nothing in those acts which controls the operation of 43 Eliz. c. 2, as extended by the 59 Geo. 3, c. 12, sec. 26, and that the children of the lunatic (if of sufficient ability) could be compelled to contribute, assuming him to become chargeable to any parish or union.

XV.—MARRIAGE REGISTERS.—PAYMENT OF FEES FOR CERTIFIED COPIES OF.

12*th July*, 1850.

Clerk of Barton-upon-Irwell Union.—Inquiring whether under the following circumstances, the fees payable to the vicar of the parish church of Eccles, in this union, for certified copies of marriages taking place in such parish church, are properly chargeable to the common fund of the union, or to the township of Barton-upon-Irwell, in which such parish church is situate:—the parish of Eccles comprises townships in three unions, though it is probable that the greater proportion of the population of the parish is within this union. The township of Stretford is in the parish of Manchester. The townships of Urmston and Flixton, are within the parish of Flixton. At the churches of the two last-named parishes, very few marriages are solemnized. At the parish church of Eccles, a considerable number of marriages are solemnized, and frequently between persons resident within the parish of Eccles, though not within this union. The registrar-general has been communicated with on the matter, who has replied as follows:—"The registrar-general is of opinion that the fees payable under the 27th section of the 1 Vic. c. 22, to the vicar of the parish church of Eccles, should be charged to the account of the township in which that church is situate, but as the question is one which may admit of doubt, he recommends that it be referred to the Poor Law Board."

Ans.—The Board concur in the opinion which you state has been expressed by the registrar-general upon the point in question. It appears that the 1 Vic. c. 22, sec. 27, refers to the 6 & 7 Wm. 4, c. 86, sec. 29, and that the latter enactment requires the guardians, in the case of a union, to charge the several sums therein mentioned to the account of the parishes in which the births or deaths respectively shall have occurred. The Board think that the sums payable under the 1 Vic. c. 22, sec. 27, in respect of the certified copies of the marriage registers should be charged by the guardians to the several parishes in which such marriages respectively take place. In the present case, however, there is no separate poor-rate made for the parish of Eccles, as such; and it appears to the Board that the word "parishes" must be read as including townships which separately maintain their own poor; and, that consequently, the charge in question should be made to the township of Barton-upon-Irwell, in which the parish church of Eccles is situate.

XVI.—MEDICAL OFFICER—DUTIES OF.

2nd July, 1850.

Clerk of Fordingbridge Union.—Inquiring whether a medical officer having received an order from the relieving-officer to attend a pauper in sickness, is justified in entering such pauper's name in the weekly return book before having seen the case, although he might have sent medicine to such pauper; and also, whether in long standing cases of sickness of paupers under sixty years of age, the medical officer can discharge such cases as incurable, and give up visiting them.

Ans.—1. It is the duty of the medical officer to attend a pauper in sickness, at the earliest practicable time after he shall have been legally required so to do. If, however, he be unavoidably prevented from visiting the pauper at once, and being in possession of what he may deem sufficient information as to the nature of the case, he orders some medicine to be taken in the interval, previous to his intended visit, the Board think he would act rightly, in entering the pauper's name in the weekly return, although he may not have seen the pauper at the time of making such entry. In the form (P) of the district medical relief book, prescribed by the General Consolidated Order, express provision is made for entering any case, where medicine is supplied by the medical officer without seeing the pauper. The medical officer must of course be prepared to justify any delay which he may suffer to take place in making his first visit to the sick pauper. 2. The Board are of opinion, that in any long standing case of sickness, whether the pauper be above or under sixty years of age, the medical officer ought not to discontinue his visits, so long as the guardians give the pauper a ticket entitling him to permanent medical relief; as the medical officer's attendance is thereby required for the case while the ticket remains in force.

XVII.—OVERSEERS.

1. CONTRATOR FOR SUPPLYING UNION WORKHOUSE WITH GOODS APPOINTED TO THE OFFICE OF OVERSEER.

27th April, 1850.

Clerk of Guiltcross Union.—On the 18th of March last, Messrs. J. E. and J. H. tendered for and became contractors for the supply of grocery and drapery for the Guiltcross Union Workhouse, and thereupon they immediately began to supply goods pursuant to their contract, and they are bound to continue to do so till the 29th of September next. On the 27th of March last, the parishioners of E., one of the parishes comprised in the union, in vestry assembled, placed the name of the said J. H. first in the nomination list as being a substantial householder qualified to serve as an overseer for the year ensuing. Previous to the vestry meeting, J. H. informed one of the churchwardens that he was not qualified to serve as an overseer, being a contractor, and immediately after the meeting, it was more publicly intimated. This was before the nomination list was presented to the magistrates. On the 28th of March last, the magistrates, notwithstanding, appointed the said J. H. as one of the overseers for the present year, which appointment was duly served upon him on the same evening. At the time of the appointment of overseers at the petty sessions, the vice-chairman of the union was present, and informed the clerk to the justices, that J. H. was a contractor, and therefore disqualified from serving as overseer, and the clerk's reply was, "then he must give up the contract." After the appointment, J. H. waited upon one of the magistrates of the division who had signed the appointment, and called his attention to the 6th sec. of the 12th & 13th Vic. c. 103, whereupon he (the magistrate) addressed a letter to the clerk of the petty sessions, requesting him to take the necessary steps to discharge J. H. from the office of overseer. The clerk expressed his regret at his having overlooked the section alluded to, and told J. H. to make himself quite easy upon the subject, as he would have no difficulty in getting off serving as overseer. J. H. has not accepted any books nor done any act as an overseer, the duties of the office having been commenced by J. L., another person appointed by the magistrates to act in conjunction with J. H., but J. L. feeling himself aggrieved at the probability of his having to serve throughout the year, applied to one of the principal parishioners, who raised an objection that J. H. was not at present excused from serving the office of overseer, referring as his authority to Archibald's Justice of the Peace, p. 20, where it is said, "After thus appointing overseers, the justices are *functi officio*, and cannot alter their appointment, R. *v*. Great Marlow, 2 East, 244." And again, "If any person thus appointed feel himself aggrieved by the appointment, he may appeal against it to the general quarter sessions, 43 Eliz. c. 2. Inquired first, Whether it be necessary for J. H. to appeal to the general quarter sessions, he being at the time of his appointment a person disqualified from serving the office of overseer, which fact was communicated to the parishioners before the nomination list was presented to the magistrates, and the clerk of the petty sessions having also been informed that J. H. was a contractor for the union before the appointment was signed by the magistrates. Secondly,—Whether it be not necessary to appeal to the general quarter sessions, or to take any and what other steps to discharge J. H. from his appointment as overseer, there being another person appointed with him.

Ans.—As the statute 12 & 13 Vic. c. 103, sec. 6, has in this instance rendered J. H.'s appointment as overseer null and void, it is not necessary for him to take any steps in the matter. If that statute had merely granted to him a privilege or exemption from serving the office of overseer, possibly it might have been necessary for him to appeal to the general quarter sessions against the appointment, but the statute goes further, and disqualifies him altogether for holding the office. Under these circumstances it is sufficient for him to decline to act as overseer, and he ought to do so without delay.

2. OBLIGATION OF OVERSEERS AS TO THE REPAIRING OF A BRIDGE.

13*th June*, 1850.

Assistant Overseer of Middlesmoor, Pateley Bridge.—There is in this township a stone bridge, for the accommodation of the public, which at present is in a very dilapidated and dangerous state, and it will require about the sum of £10 to repair it. The township has been called upon to do so, and make it safe. It has been repaired by the township in former years, as appears by the constable's account. In 1796, £3. 6*s*. were paid for the repair of the bridge, and 5*s*. in the year 1797. The constables do not collect any rates now, as their expenses are paid by the overseers. Inquiring whether the overseers will be justified in expending £10 for the repair of the bridge. There is no surveyor's-rate in the township, as each occupier makes his own road. If the overseers cannot legally pay for the repairs, inquiring how the money is to be raised; and whether, by refusing to repair the bridge, they will render themselves liable to an indictment.

Ans.—The Board apprehend that the bridge in question forms a part of a road or highway; and whatever may be the practice adopted in the township with respect to making and repairing the roads, the only legal course which appears to be open, in order to defray the expenses in question is, that a highway-rate should be levied, and a surveyor of the highways appointed. With regard to the question of indictment, the Board desire to state that, if the township is liable to repair the bridge, (of which the former repairs are evidence,) the liability may be enforced by indictment.

XVIII.—POOR-RATE—PAYMENT OF BOROUGH EXPENSES UNDER THE 6 VIC. c. 18, OUT OF.

20*th July*, 1850.

Assistant-overseer of Ashton-under-Lyne.—The town clerk of the borough of Ashton-under-Lyne, which comprises a portion only of the parish of Ashton-under-Lyne, has brought in his account for expenses incurred by him in carrying into effect, the provisions of the 6 Vic. c. 18, duly allowed by the town council of the borough, to the churchwardens and overseers for payment, who object to pay him, stating they cannot legally do so, as the poor-rate is levied from the inhabitants of the whole parish, and that the 55 sec. of the 6 Vic. c. 18, under which the account has been made out and allowed, only provides for payment from townships "within the same city or borough." Inquiring whether the churchwardens and overseers will be justified in paying the above-mentioned account, as several of the inhabitants of the parish, not within the borough, are much opposed to its being paid from the poor-rates.

Ans.—The Poor Law Commissioners having had occasion to consult Mr. Tomlinson on the same point, were advised by him that a parish situated partly within, and partly without the boundary of a borough, can be called upon to contribute under the 6 & 7 Vic. c. 18, secs. 55 & 57, towards the expenses of the town clerk and returning-officer of such borough, and that the payments must be made out of the poor-rates of the entire parish. The Board concur in the view thus expressed by Mr. Tomlinson, and recommend the overseers. of Ashton-under-Lyne, to act upon it in the present case.

XIX.—RELIEF.—SUPPLYING BEDS, BEDDING, CLOTHES &c., TO OUT-DOOR PAUPERS.

8*th April*, 1850.

Chairman of the Board of Guardians of St. Martin-in-the Field's Parish.—Referring to the Poor Law Board's communication of the 7th of February last, to the clerk of the guardians, and requesting that the guardians might be informed for their future guidance whether they are altogether precluded by law from supplying bed, bedding, and clothes, and redeeming or purchasing tools and implements, in certain cases.

Ans.—The guardians of the poor, in administering relief, can only do what the law authorises them to do in their character of guardians of the poor. The redemption or purchase of tools and implements for poor persons, is not legal relief, and as there is no statutory provision which enables the guardians to effect such object they cannot legally afford assistance of that kind at the expense of the rate-payers. The guardians, however, may properly supply requisite clothing in cases where out-door relief may lawfully be granted; and it is possible, that in some particular cases a bed or bedding may legally be given by way of necessary relief out of the workhouse; though the Board cannot recognise the systematic supply of such articles as being a legal or proper mode of affording relief. With regard to relief by way of loan the Board think it right to remark that the guardians are not justified in lending any relief, which they are not legally authorised to give; and consider that as the power of declaring relief to be advanced on loan, should be exercised by the guardians with due consideration and always with the *bonâ fide* intention of recovering the relief, it should be resorted to only where circumstances render it desirable to stop short of giving the relief absolutely to the pauper.

XX.—REMOVABILITY.

1. BREACH OF RESIDENCE, BY BEING AN INMATE OF A HOSPITAL.

22*nd July*, 1850.

Clerk of Cuckfield Union.—Transmitting the following statement, duly signed, under sec. 4 of the 11 & 12 Vic. c. 110, for the opinion of the Poor Law Board :—The pauper, John King, is legally settled in the parish of Hurstperpoint, in this union, and is in the sixty-fourth year of his age. About seventeen years ago, he came to reside in the parish of Cuckfield, and (with the exception of the interval during which he was in Guy's Hospital, as hereafter stated,) has resided there with his wife and family ever since. In the month of March, 1843, the pauper was admitted as a patient into Guy's Hospital, with an affection of the eyes, and remained there for ten weeks, at the expiration of which he was discharged; and, pursuant to his intention when he went to the hospital, returned to Cuckfield to his wife, who, during his absence, had continued to reside in his cottage there. After his return from the hospital, he was relieved in Cuckfield, by the parish of Hurstperpoint, until the guardians for Hurstperpoint, considered him to be irremovable, when he was placed on the relief list for Cuckfield, to which parish he is now chargeable. The guardians for Cuckfield contend that the pauper and and his wife are irremovable, and claim to have the cost of their maintenance charged to the common fund; the guardians of the union contend, on the contrary, that the residence of the pauper in the hospital was a disruption of his residence in Cuckfield, and that consequently the pauper and his wife are now removable.

Ans.—The Board are of opinion that the temporary abiding of the pauper, John King, in Guy's Hospital, in 1843, under the circumstances stated, was not an interruption of his residence in the parish of Cuckfield, and that the pauper is now irremovable therefrom; and that his relief, the pauper being settled in Cuckfield, is now chargeable to the common fund of the Cuckfield Union.

---

2. REMOVABILITY OF A WIDOW RESIDING IN A PLACE WHICH HAS SEPARATELY MAINTAINED ITS OWN POOR SINCE 1831.

17th July, 1850.

Clerk of Wrexham Union.—Transmitting the following statement, duly signed under the 11 & 12 Vic. c. 110, sec. 4, for the opinion of the Poor Law Board:—Prior to the year 1831, the township of Bersham was a component part of the parish of Wrexham. Thirteen other townships were united with it. Owing to the illegal manner in which the poor were maintained in this district, the Court of King's Bench, in 1831, granted a *mandamus* which was obeyed by the justices, and in pursuance of which, two overseers of the poor were appointed for each of these townships separately, and Bersham has since that year, had its own overseers, its own rates, and has maintained its own poor. Upon an appeal brought before the Court of Queen's Bench, in November 1845, it was decided in the case Reg. *v.* Acton, that no settlement could be gained in townships thus maintaining their poor prior to the year 1831, it being admitted that the townships in Gresford parish, and those in Wrexham, were circumstanced exactly alike. Mary Jones, widow, aged forty-nine, now lives in Bersham, and is in receipt of relief, and has been so continuously, since 1835. She has resided in Bersham, since 1804, and would, but for the decision in Reg. *v.* Acton, belong to that township. She is presumed to be irremovable, having resided in Bersham upwards of five years without having received relief, and also from having no settlement, by virtue of the decision above referred to. On the other hand, it is contended that she has only resided in a place maintaining its own poor for four years, without being chargeable, namely, from 1831, when the overseers of Bersham, as a separate township, were first appointed, to 1835, when she first first applied for relief. The opinion of the Poor Law Board is requested, whether the residence of the pauper in Bersham is to be computed from 1804, when it was actually commenced, or from 1831, when that township was first established a place maintaining its own poor.

Ans.—The Board observe that the question raised by the case is, whether Mary Jones is irremovable from the township of Bersham, under the 9 & 10 Vic. c. 66, sec. 1. Now, it appears to the Board that the pauper has only resided in the township or place, with reference to which alone the question arises, since 1831; for it was in that year that Bersham first commenced maintaining its own poor, as a township. It is true, that she has resided in another district (viz. the parish of Wrexham) of which Bersham formed part, since 1804; and has, indeed, lived on the same spot from that time to the present. But the Board do not think that the pauper's residence in the larger and different district (the parish of Wrexham) can be coupled with her residence in the township of Bersham, since it has formed a distinct township separately maintaining its own poor, in computing whether the pauper has lived five years in such township, with reference to the provision of the 9 & 10 Vic. c. 66, sec. 1. The Board are therefore of opinion, upon the statement of facts laid before them, that Mary Jones is not irremovable from the township of Bersham, by reason of length of residence therein. The Board may add that according to Reg. *v.* Acton (8 Q. B. R. 108,) the settlement gained by Mary Jones, in the parish of Wrexham, prior to 1831, was extinguished by the division of that parish into independent townships.

XXI.—REMOVAL.—REPAYMENT OF COST OF MAINTENANCE UNDER SUSPENDED ORDERS OF REMOVAL.

29th July, 1850.

Clerk of Swansea Union.—Submitting the following case relating to the removal of Isaac Matthews and wife, from Llanelly, to the parish of

Portynon, and requesting to be informed what course that parish should take under the circumstances:—At the weekly meeting of the guardians of this union, held on the 1st July instant, the assistant-overseer of Llanelly, attended with the above paupers whom he had brought over under an order of removal which had been obtained on the 11th July 1846, and then suspended, but which suspension had, by an order of two justices, dated in July, 1850, been taken off, and the order of removal directed to be executed by the removal of the paupers as above stated. The guardians received the paupers, and they were permitted to return to Llanelly, the guardians agreeing to allow them 3*s.* weekly, at the charge of the parish of Portynon. The guardian of Portynon was not present, and there having been recently a change of relieving-officers for that district, all the facts of the case were not made known to the board of guardians. The parish of Portynon now contends, that although at the time the order of removal was obtained in July, 1846, it was a valid order, as the statute 9 & 10 Vic. c. 66, had not then passed, and there were no grounds of appeal at that time against it, yet, inasmuch as the execution of the order was suspended and the same was unexecuted at the passing of that statute (26th August 1846) and the paupers having resided for more than five years in Llanelly, before the date and application for the order, they have become irremovable, under the provisions of the statute, as its provisions operated on all orders then obtained, but not previously executed, whether suspended or not, and the removal of the pauper in July 1850, was illegal, and the magistrates ought not to have signed the order directing the order of removal to be executed.

Ans.—The remedy of the overseers of Portynon against the order for the payment of the costs in the present case is by appeal, as that order, according to the late decision in Reg. *v.* Chedgrave, 12 Q. B. R. 206, is invalid. The Guardians of the Swansea Union can discontinue the non-resident relief to the pauper in Llanelly, and it appears to the Board upon the statement of facts submitted, that the parish of Llanelly would not be able to obtain another order of removal.

Clerk of Llanelly Union.—On the 5th August, 1845, a pauper named Mary Davies, widow of Samuel Davies, cordwainer, residing in the town and franchise of Swansea, was placed under an order of removal (to the parish of Llanelly) and suspended the same day. The pauper continued to reside at Swansea, till March, 1849, when she died; and in the course of a few days afterwards the overseers of Swansea, made an application to the overseers of Llanelly, for payment of £64. 3*s.* 3*d.*, being the amount expended under the order. The pauper's late husband and herself had lived at Swansea, for a period of upwards of thirty years, without receiving relief from any parish whatever, and whenever he was unable to follow his trade from illness or any other cause, he was assisted by a benefit society, from which he was entitled to 10*s.* per week. The clerk of the Swansea Union had referred to a letter which he had received from the Poor Law Board, relative to the case of one Isaac Matthews and wife, paupers removed from the parish of Llanelly to the parish of Portynon, in the Swansea Union. The overseers of Llanelly have applied for the amount of relief given under the order of removal, but have not yet received it, and with a view to preventing the two unions entering into litigation, requested the opinion of the Board as to whether the parish of Llanelly is entitled to the sum expended in Matthews's case. If not, whether Llanelly can recover the sum of £64. 3*s.* 3*d.* which has been paid to the overseers of Swansea, in the case of Mary Davies, as both cases were placed under orders of removal before the passing of the Removal Act.

Ans.—There appears to the Board to be an essential distinction between the two cases in question, arising from the fact that in the one case the pauper had died before the order for the costs were obtained, while in the other case, this was not so. The 35 Geo. 3, c. 101, sec. 2, enacts that the costs incurred by the suspension of any order of removal may be recovered from the parish to which the pauper is ordered to be removed, in either of two contingencies, viz., the removal, or the death of the pauper (Reg. *v.* Chagford, 4 B. and Ald. 235.) It has recently been decided in the case of Reg. *v.* Chedgrave (12 Q. B. R. 206,) that where a pauper becomes irremovable under the 9 & 10 Vic. c. 66, during the suspension of an order for his removal, such order cannot then be executed, nor the costs of the suspension recovered. But neither that decision, nor any other that the Board are aware of, interferes with the right of recovering such costs, which is expressly given by the statute in the event of the pauper's death pending the suspension of the order. Besides, the legal liability to pay, as well as the amount ordered to be paid, could only have been questioned on appeal, which is the peculiar remedy provided by the 35 Geo. 3, c. 101, sec. 2, and no appeal having been commenced within the proper time, the order for the payment is perfectly conclusive upon all parties. In accordance with the foregoing views, the Board are of opinion, that the parish of Llanelly cannot obtain repayment of the sum of £64. 3*s*. 3*d*. which is stated to have been paid to the parish of Swansea, in the case of Mary Davies, under the circumstances mentioned in your letter; and they are further of opinion (as intimated in their communication of the 7th ultimo, to the clerk of the Swansea Union) that that parish is not entitled to recover the costs incurred in the case of Isaac Matthews.

XXII. — SCHOOLMASTER — ALLOWANCE FROM PARLIAMENTARY GRANT IN RESPECT OF THE SALARY OF.

25*th July*, 1850.

Clerk of Leighton Buzzard Union.—In the year 1848, Mr. and Mrs. W. were appointed to the situations of schoolmaster and schoolmistress of the workhouse of this union, the former at an annual salary of £25, the latter of £15, which appointments and amount of salaries were duly sanctioned by the Poor Law Board. In 1849, Mr. W. succeeded in obtaining from the Committee of Council on Education, a certificate which entitled him to be paid out of the Parliamentary grant, a salary at the rate of £30 per annum, commencing from 25th March, 1849. Mrs. W. also, at the same time, succeeded in obtaining a like certificate, entitling her to receive from the same source, a salary at the rate of £24 per annum. The respective salaries of both officers have accordingly been paid to them at the rates lastly mentioned, up to 25th March last. In consequence of the alteration in the plan of distributing the Parliamentary grant, for the ensuing year, communicated to the guardians by the Board's circular of the 6th May last, a question has arisen which has created some discussion at the board of guardians, as to the amount of salary which the guardians are now authorized in paying to those officers. Under the modifications of the arrangements for distributing the Parliamentary grant, Mr. W. would be entitled from that fund to a mininum salary of £20, with 3*s*. for each child, up to the maximum salary of £24, and the joint salaries of the two officers calculated in this manner would average about £42 per annum, being a diminution of £12 from the salary of the preceding year. 1st. Is the board authorized in paying the abovementioned officers, after the rate of £40 per annum, according to the original stipulation on their appointment, with the additional sum of 3*s*. per head, for each child? or, 2nd. Should the payments be made, calculating the respective salaries at £20, and £16, with the additional sum of 3*s*. for each child? Lastly, should the guardians continue to pay them at the rate of £30 and £24 per annum, according to the certificates from the Committee of Council?

Ans.—Where a certificate of qualification has been awarded by the Committee of Council on Education, for the year ending 25th March, 1851, the quarterly payments to the teacher should accord with the amount which the certificate may entitle the guardians to be repaid out of the Parliamentary grant. In cases when no such certificate has yet been given, the teacher should be paid at the rate of the salary sanctioned by this Board, without reference to the certificate which may have been awarded to him for the past year, until a certificate for the present year is issued, according to which, the payment to the teacher must afterwards be regulated. If it shall appear that the sum to be allowed to the union, under the new certificate, is larger than the salary which has been paid to the teacher, it will be proper for the guardians to pay the difference between such salary and the amount indicated in the certificate at the end of the first quarter after the certificate is issued.

XXIII.—STAMPED RECEIPTS—FOR PAYMENTS TO THE TREASURER UNDER CONTRIBUTION ORDERS.

20*th Nov.*, 1848.

Clerk of Blaby Union.—Inquiring whether an overseer of the poor can demand from the treasurer of the union, a stamped receipt for the payment of a contribution made in pursuance of an order of the guardians.

Ans.—The General Order of the Poor Law Commissioner of the 22nd of April, 1842, on the duties of overseers in Art. 5, No. 2, requires the overseers to pay their contributions to the persons appointed in the orders of guardians, and to take the receipt of such persons and to produce it to the auditor. If those persons give a receipt, without a stamp, when a stamp is required by the statute, they may incur penalties, but the Board do not perceive how the overseers can compel them to give a receipt on a stamp.

XXIV.—WITNESSES.—REMUNERATION TO A CLERK AND A RELIEVING-OFFICER FOR ATTENDING TO GIVE EVIDENCE IN REMOVAL CASES.

13*th July,* 1850.

Guardian of ————, Tavistock Union.—Inquiring whether the clerk of a board of guardians can legally make a separate charge for attending before the justices to give evidence of the chargeability of a pauper, in a removal case, tried in the same town in which he resides, and if so, what amount would he be entitled to; also, whether he would be entitled to charge, (and to what amount) for attending the justices in a similar case, at a distance of twelve miles from his own house. Inquiring also, whether the relieving-officer would be entitled to make a separate charge for attending under similar circumstances, at a distance of eight miles from his own house, both cases applying to paupers belonging to the union of which they are the officers.

Ans.—By the 7 & 8 Vic. c. 101, sec. 70, justices have the power of determining what is a fair and reasonable remuneration to be paid to witnesses who attend before them, in cases of the kind above-mentioned. With regard to the relieving-officer, as he is bound to give up his whole time to the service of the union, this remuneration should not be more than sufficient to cover the expenses which he may incur in the attendance, as for instance, the refreshment which he may require, and the actual cost of his travelling. But with regard to the clerk, as he is not bound to give up his whole time to the service of the union, the Board consider that he should be paid a reasonable remuneration for his attendance in the same way that other witnesses are paid. What is a reasonable remuneration, will be a question for the justices to determine, in reference to the circumstances of each case. Whether, in many cases of the kind in question, the attendance of the clerk, or the relieving-officer, may not be dispensed with altogether, is a matter which requires consideration, as by the statute 7 & 8 Vic. c. 101, sec. 69, the certificate of chargeability is rendered sufficient for the purpose of proving the chargeability; and for such certificate of the guardians, no fee is demandable.

XXV.—WORKHOUSE.—A PAUPER REFUSING TO LEAVE WORKHOUSE MAY BE COMPELLED TO DO SO.

31*st Oct.*, 1849.

Clerk of Lichfield Union.—J. C., a partially disabled man, has been receiving in-door and out-door relief from this union for several years. On the 15th September he was allowed out-relief, and remained out of the workhouse till the 13th October, when he was re-admitted by order of the relieving-officer. The guardians, at their meeting on Friday, ordered him two shillings, and four pounds of bread per week, out-relief, and his discharge from the house on the following morning. The chairman and the master of the house acquainted him with the order, and the relieving-officer told him he might have his out-relief at once, but the pauper refuses to quit, stating he will not go unless he is dragged out.

Ans.—The man cannot insist on being relieved in the workhouse if the guardians order otherwise, the nature and amount of the relief to be afforded in every case resting exclusively on their decision. If the guardians are satisfied that, with the relief proposed to be allowed to J. C., he will have sufficient means for his support, they may cause him to be put out of the workhouse; and, if necessary, may call in a constable for that purpose. The Board are not informed of the grounds on which the guardians think it desirable to grant out-door relief in this case, rather than relief in the workhouse; the latter, when the workhouse is well managed, is generally found the best mode of at once securing the necessary relief to the destitute, and of preventing imposition.

London: Printed by Order of the Poor Law Board, by BLACKBURN & BURT, 90½, Holborn Hill; and Published by CHARLES KNIGHT, 90, Fleet Street.

AN

OFFICIAL CIRCULAR

OF PUBLIC DOCUMENTS AND INFORMATION:

DIRECTED BY THE POOR LAW BOARD TO BE PRINTED, CHIEFLY FOR THE USE OF THE BOARDS OF GUARDIANS AND THEIR OFFICERS.

No. 40.] AUGUST, 1850. [N.S.

CONTENTS.

I.—BURIAL.—OF PAUPERS DYING IN WORKHOUSE, IN THE PARISHES TO WHICH THEY WERE CHARGEABLE.

8th August, 1850.

The Rural Dean of Sussex.—The President of the Poor Law Board is reported to have stated in the House of Commons, " that under the law, as it at present stood, persons dying in workhouses must, of necessity, be buried in the parishes of their chargeability; except in cases where the deceased, or his nearest of kin, had requested that the body might be buried elsewhere. The parish of chargeability might, however, be many miles off." It would appear from this statement, that the authorities of an union poor-house, cannot claim the right of burying persons dying therein in the burial-ground of the parish within which the union house may be situated, unless such persons have been also chargeable to the said parish. This statement, however, appears to be at variance with the following extracts from Burn's Ecclesiastical Law, Art. Burial, " By the custom of England, any person may be buried in the churchyard where he dies, &c.;" also, " but ordinarily, it seemeth that a person may not be buried in the churchyard of another parish than that wherein he died, without the consent of the parishioners or churchwardens, where parochial right of burial is invaded thereby; and perhaps also of the incumbent, whose soil is broken." The discrepancy between these statements and that of the President of the Board is obvious. In one case, chargeability designates the parish, and in the other, residence at the time of death. In one case, the chargeable parish must of necessity receive the body for burial, in the other, it can refuse, when the death has not taken place within it. On recently visiting the church and churchyard of the parish of Ore, in this county, in his capacity of rural dean, the rector and churchwardens pointed out to him the crowded state of the burial-ground, occasioned mainly by the burial therein of all persons dying in the Hastings Union-house, situated within Ore parish, unless by desire carried elsewhere. The ground would have afforded for a great many years (perhaps in succession for ever) sufficient accommodation for all dying within the parish, who might be chargeable to it. During a period of eleven years, after the building of the union-house within it, 101 non-parishioners were interred therein and 9 parishioners. This is felt as a grievance as entailing the necessity for the parish to obtain more ground. It has been suggested that a piece of ground which is suitable for the purpose, near the union-house (which is a considerable distance from the parish church and ground) should be obtained for the use of the union.

Ans.—The general inference which you have drawn from the remarks attributed to the President in the House of Commons, on a recent debate, to the effect that in the present state of the law, the authorities of a union cannot, in respect of poor persons dying in the union workhouse, claim the right of burying such persons in the churchyard or burial-ground of the parish in which the workhouse is locally situate, unless such persons were also, at the time of their decease, chargeable to such parish, is correct. You observe that the law as thus explained, is at variance with certain statements contained in Burn's Ecclesiastical Law, which you cite, particularly the following, "By the custom of England, any person may be buried in the churchyard of the parish where he dies." The Board think it probable that, in considering this subject, your attention may not have been directed to the enactments contained in secs. 31 & 56, of the 7 & 8 Vic. c. 101, which have special application to the case. Those sections must, the Board apprehend, be regarded as controlling the common law right of burial, so far at least as it concerns the "place" of burial of that class of persons for whose interment the guardians or overseers can give directions, and as containing the only rule on the subject. By section 31, the guardians of a union have a discretionary power to direct the burial to take place either in the parish of the chargeability, or in the place of death. If that section stood alone, there could have been no doubt that in the class of cases under consideration, the guardians could direct the burial to take place in the churchyard of the parish in which the workhouse is actually situate, notwithstanding that the pauper in his lifetime might have been chargeable to a different parish. But the 56th section, it will be seen, renders the workhouse of a union for certain purposes (*i.e.*, *inter alia* for relief, removal, and burial,) constructively situate in the parish to which the poor person to be relieved, removed, or buried, (as the case may be) is or has been chargeable. The effect of this provision is, that in construction of law, the pauper does not die in the parish in which the workhouse is locally situate, but in the parish of the chargeability. The parish of the death being thus constructively identical with the parish of the chargeability, it follows, that the discretion as to the place of burial, referred to above as given in terms by the 31st section, is, in this class of cases, virtually taken away, and the guardians can only direct the burial to take place in the parish of the chargeability. Such the Board have been advised by eminent legal authority, is the state of the law on this subject. With respect to the case of the parish of Ore, which you adduce as strongly illustrating the inconveniences which result from the present practice of burying all paupers who have died in the workhouse in the churchyard of the parish, in which that workhouse is locally situate, the Board can only say, that for the future, the evil can be prevented, by the guardians, in compliance with the law as above explained, causing the paupers to be buried in the parish of the chargeability. The Board understand you to state, that if that rule were acted upon by the guardians of the Hastings Union, no difficulty would be experienced in procuring additional burying-ground for the use of the parish of Ore, or rather for those who have the rights of parishioners there. The Board would further observe, that they apprehend upon the grounds stated in the former part of this letter, that the incumbent of the parish to which a deceased pauper was chargeable, would not be legally justified in his refusal to bury, in the burial-ground of that parish, the body of such person brought from the union workhouse for interment, provided there had been a direction to bury by the guardians or their officers, and provided that convenient notice thereof had been given according to the canon. In addition to these remarks, the Board may state, that in the bill now before Parliament, provisions are contained, which it is hoped, will materially lessen the inconveniences to which you have adverted.

II.—CHARGEABILITY.

1. DESTITUTE WANDERER.

3rd Aug., 1850.

Clerk of St. Germans Union.—About a year ago, William Goard applied to the guardians for relief, and an order for admission into the union workhouse was given to him, the relief being charged to the parish of Anthony. He belongs to the parish of Botusfleming, in this union, and an order of justices for his removal has been obtained, under which he is about to be removed. The pauper, when he applied for relief, came direct from the Plympton Workhouse, where he had been relieved sometime.

Ans.—The Board request to be informed upon what ground the guardians of the St. Germans Union charged the relief of William Goard to the parish of Anthony. It appears to the Board that, at the time of his application for relief, he was a destitute wanderer, and therefore chargeable to the union common fund.

24th Aug., 1850.

Clerk of same union.—The guardians charged the relief of the pauper Goard to the parish of Anthony upon the ground of his having come into that parish obviously to claim relief at the workhouse, in right of his being settled in the union. The guardians, therefore, considered him as not falling within the description of "a destitute wayfarer or wanderer," under the 11 & 12 Vic. c. 110. The guardians apprehend these words apply solely to persons falling within the class usually designated as "casual poor," and more especially to "vagrants," in the popular sense of the term, who, as they do not "come to inhabit," and are consequently not removable, it was not reasonable should be relieved at the cost of the parish to which they may have been induced to go, only because the workhouse, or the residence of the relieving-officer, is situate within it. But when a person applies at a union workhouse, claiming a right to relief as a settled pauper within the union, it is conceived he cannot in any respect be considered to be at that time a "wayfarer" or a "wanderer," whatever may have been his previous habits of life. The guardians think it would not be reasonable that a person having a settlement in the union, and removable to such settlement, should be placed on the common fund, whereby, as they understand, he would cease to be removable; and if a practice of this kind were adopted on the supposed authority of the statute, not only would a great injustice be often inflicted on the union at large, but a door would be opened to all kinds of collusion. It would be enough for a pauper to be turned out of his house by his landlord, or to leave the workhouse and wander about the union, to bring him within this construction of the statute, and thereby to transfer the burden of his relief from the parish to the union. For these reasons, the guardians are not able to concur in the opinion of the Board, set forth in their Official Circular, No. 23, pp. 47 & 48.

Ans.—A man may, in the opinion of the Board, be, in the words of the statute, (which were carefully framed,) "a destitute wanderer or wayfarer" in one parish in a union, though he may happen to have a settlement in another parish in that union. The possession of a settlement is a very different thing from the possession of a residence or an abode, and the parish of the settlement cannot, as a matter of course, be charged with the relief because the pauper is relieved within the union which comprises that parish. Indeed, it seems that the guardians in the present instance did not charge the relief to a parish where the pauper had a settlement, or a place of abode, but to the parish of Anthony where he had neither the one nor the other. The object of the legislature in passing the enactment in question was to relieve that particular parish in a union in which the workhouse is situated, from the charge of maintaining the poor who are relieved by admission into the workhouse, as casual or vagrant poor, or persons having no residence within the union.

2. CHARGEABILITY OF A WIFE WHO HAS LEFT HER HUSBAND, AND IS LIVING IN ADULTERY.

20th Aug., 1850.

Clerk of Wincanton Union.—Transmitting the following statement, duly signed under sec. 4 of the 11 & 12 Vic. c. 110, for the opinion of the Poor Law Board:—In September, 1841, J. Y., whose place of legal settlement is the parish of Bruton, in the Wincanton Union, was married to Emma, his present wife, at Heytesbury, in the county of Wilts, and returned with her to Bruton to reside. They resided there about three months, when his wife left him, and she has not since resided or cohabited with him in any place; but she has cohabited with another man at Heytesbury, and other places in the county of Wilts, by whom she has two children, now living. She lately threw herself and children upon the parish of Wincanton, and was placed in the union workhouse there upon the common charge. She and her children have, however, been lately transferred in the union books to the charge of the parish of Bruton. Since his wife left him, J. Y. has resided wholly with his parents in Bruton; but during the last five years and a half of the period he has worked continuously as a journeyman tailor in the town of Wincanton, also within the Wincanton Union, going from Bruton to Wincanton every Monday morning, and returning to his parents every Saturday evening. During his weekly sojourn in Wincanton, he eats, drinks, and sleeps, at the house of C. C. there, but all his wearing apparel is washed and mended in Bruton; and he has never at any period rented any other than a bedroom in Wincanton, nor has he at any period ever had any household furniture or utensils of his own there. His said wife was also about four years since in the Wincanton Union workhouse, and chargeable as a casual poor wayfarer to the parish of Wincanton. The guardian for the parish of Bruton contends that the said sojourning of J. Y. in the parish of Wincanton, he not having applied for or received any relief there, is a legal industrial residence, which renders him irremovable therefrom, and that, therefore, as his wife retains her marriage settlement with him, she too is irremovable, together with her said children, and that their maintenance in the workhouse can only legally be debited to the common fund of the union. The board of guardians contend, first, that the said sojourning of J. Y. in the parish of Wincanton is not such a residence as will render him irremovable therefrom, and that if it did the wife cannot be held to be entitled to that privilege, as she has abandoned her husband to live in open adultery with another man. Secondly, that if for the purpose of determining the question as to the removability of the man and his wife from the parish of Wincanton, the fact of the adultery is to be wholly excluded from consideration, it is contended by the guardians that they must treat all relief to the wife as relief to the husband; and as she has been maintained in the union workhouse seven months out of the period that her husband has so sojourned in the said parish of Wincanton, it is submitted that the husband cannot show such a residence within that parish as will render him irremovable therefrom. The guardians contend finally upon every point that they are correct in charging the maintenance of this woman and her children to the parish of Bruton as her husband's settlement, leaving it to that parish to punish the husband, if they can, under the Vagrant Act, for allowing his wife and her children to become chargeable.

Ans.—1st. J. Y., the husband is not liable, under the Vagrant Act, for deserting his wife, nor for allowing her to become chargeable. See R. *v.* Hinton, 2 B and Ad. 227. 2nd. He is not under any liability to maintain the children who are not his children, but are illegitimate. 3rd. Those children were residing with their mother, and, by the 3rd sec. of the 9 & 10 Vic. c. 66, if under sixteen, they cannot be removed from her. 4th. The case, as regards the irremovability of J. Y., might have been open to much question; but as it appears that his residence in Wincanton (such as it was) continued for only five years and a half—that his wife received relief from the parish of Wincanton during seven months of that period, which, in law, is relief for seven months received by him—and that consequently he has not resided five years without relief, the Board are of opinion that he cannot be considered as irremovable from Wincanton; and the wife is not therefore irremovable by virtue of the 11 & 12 Vic. c. 111. 5th. But her destitution occurred, and the relief was given to her in Wincanton, and not in Bruton; and unless the latter parish assent to being charged with the relief, the Board do not see upon what legal ground the relief is now charged to that parish.

3. CHARGEABILITY OF A PERSON POSSESSING A LEASEHOLD HOUSE.

21st Aug., 1850.

Clerk of Bedminster Union.—Transmitting the following statement, duly issued under sec. 4 of the 11 & 12 Vic. c. 110, for the opinion of the Poor Law Board:—J. L. is legally settled in the parish of Portbury in the Bedminster Union independent of the following circumstance: He has resided for eleven years upon a leasehold house and garden, which he holds under ———, originally upon a lease for three lives, one of which survives. The house is situated in the parish of Tickenham, for which he pays a rent of two shillings and sixpence per annum. Six or seven years ago the pauper was ill, and whether through ignorance or not does not appear, the pauper was his family were relieved by Portbury whilst so residing at Tickenham. The pauper is again ill and chargeable. The guardians are of opinion that he is irremovable from Tickenham, and that that parish must support him, notwithstanding the relief given by Portbury in error. The value of the house and garden is six or seven pounds per annum.

Ans.—The Board are of opinion that the facts stated in this statement show that the pauper has gained a settlement by estate in the parish of Tickenham, (see R. *v.* St. Mary, Whitechapel, Burrows sett. cases 55;) and if so they think that the cost of his relief should now be charged to that parish, notwithstanding that he was relieved by the parish of Portbury six or seven years ago, under the circumstances adverted to in such statement.

---

4. CHARGEABILITY OF THE WIDOW OF A SAILOR.

26th July, 1850.

Clerk of Ipswich Union. —Transmitting the following statement, duly signed under sec. 4 of the 11 & 12 Vic., c. 110, for the opinion of the Poor Law Board :—Charles Bell, a mariner, who, when at home, resided in the parish of St. Peter, in this union, is supposed to have been lost at sea, the vessel in which he sailed not having been seen or heard of since she left a port in Denmark about four months ago. He has left a wife, (aged 29,) and six children, of the respective ages of 8, 7, 5, 4, 1½, and an infant, born the 22nd of April last. The man's settlement is in the parish of Nacton, in the Woodbridge Union, and the family has resided five month only in the parish of St. Peter. Under the above state of facts the board of guardians, and the parish of St. Peter, desire the order of the Poor Law Board, determining whether the woman is to be treated as a widow, and her relief charged to the common fund of the union, the death of her husband being still uncertain; or, whether she is removable, and the parish of St. Peter to be charged with the relief, as (assuming the husband to be dead) she was not residing in any parish with her husband at the time of his death; or, whether she is to be considered as one who has simply become chargeable in consequence of the death of her husband, in which case the parish of St. Peter would be charged with the relief, and the family would be removable.

Ans.—In the absence of more circumstantial facts as to the proceedings of the husband, the Board think it doubtful whether his death is to be presumed. If the husband were now to return to his family in St. Peter's, he would, according to the statement now before the Board, be removable, he not having resided therein for five years. The Board, therefore, think that the wife and family are removable. If, however, the presumption be admitted that the husband is dead, still, as his wife was not residing with him at the time of his death, she would not be irremovable under the 9 & 10 Vic. c. 66, sec. 2; and consequently, in either point of view, her relief is chargeable to the parish wherein she resides.

23rd Aug., 1850.

Clerk of Woodbridge Union.—Inquiring, with reference to this case, "whether a sailor, who has a house in a parish where he ordinarily resides with his wife and family when ashore, and goes to sea, which is his occupation, and is drowned, makes any breach in his residence; and if not, whether his wife and family are not considered to be residing with him, he having no other residence but where they reside, and she is not, therefore, as a widow, removable.

Ans.—In the case of the Queen *v.* E. Stonehouse (17 L. J. R. N. S. M. C, 166) the question was brought before the Court of Queen's Bench, whether the service of a marine at sea was a residence in the parish where his wife resided; but the Court did not decide the question. The Board, however, think that a mariner who is at sea, and is drowned, cannot be said to be residing at the time of his death in the same parish with his wife, either in point of fact, or in point of law.

III.—CONTRIBUTION ORDERS.—DESCRIPTION OF CHURCHWARDENS.

30th Jan., 1850.

Clerk of Wolverhampton Union. — Inquiring whether a Contribution Order made according to Form M. of the Consolidated Order, should include the names of the churchwardens as well as the overseers, and if so, whether they should be denominated as churchwardens or included under the term overseers. Also, whether in case it should be necessary to enforce the Order, any payment on account, between the time of the application to the justices and the hearing of the complaint, will invalidate the proceedings for the recovery of the remainder.

Ans.—The Board recommend that the guardians' order for contributions should be addressed to the churchwardens by name, as well as to the overseers of the parish. The Board do not think that the payment of any part of the money so called for, will interfere with the proceedings for the recovery of the residue.

IV.—GUARDIANS.—HOLDING MEETINGS IN THE DIFFERENT PARISHES OF THE UNION TO INVESTIGATE THE CASES OF OUT-DOOR PAUPERS.

6th July, 1850.

Clerk of Carnarvon Union.—The guardians are desirous of holding meetings once a year in the several parishes of which the union is comprised, provided the authorities of any of those parishes desire it. The object the guardians have in view is, that they may see the aged and infirm poor, to whom the distance from their places of abode to the workhouse where the ordinary meetings of the board are held, render it very difficult and in some cases impossible that they should appear there to state their cases. The guardians are anxious to ascertain that all the paupers, and especially this class of poor, are regularly paid and properly treated. Requesting the Poor Law Board to authorize the guardians to hold such meetings accordingly.

Ans.—Having regard to the terms of Art. 28 of the General Consolidated Order, the Board do not think that the guardians can hold the proposed meetings in the different parishes, as "ordinary meetings;" but as the object which the guardians have in view appears to be a desirable one, the Board suggest that it is competent to the guardians under Art. 40 of the above-mentioned order, to resolve themselves into a committee for the purpose of inquiring into, and reporting to their board upon the cases of out-door paupers in any particular parish or parishes of the union.

V.—LUNATIC PAUPERS.

1. INSANE PERSONS NOT ACTUALLY CHARGEABLE.

12th August, 1850.

Clerk of West Ham Union.—1. R. C. was an assistant to a surgeon at ——— in this union, and resided with his employer, who paid him for his services. Having for several days showed symptoms of insanity, and afterwards becoming dangerous, his master sent for the relieving-officer of the West Ham district, and requested him to take charge of the lunatic, with the view of having him removed to an asylum. The relieving-officer at first declined having anything to do with the case, alleging that the lunatic was not then a pauper chargeable to the parish, or one with whom he was by law required to deal. But upon the declaration of the master that he would not take care of, or allow the lunatic to remain any longer in his house, and believing that the lunatic would be turned out, and that he had no relations or friends nearer than Devonshire to whose care he could be consigned, the relieving-officer took the case into his own hands and caused the lunatic's removal in the usual way to a licensed asylum as a pauper lunatic. Upon the case being reported to the board of guardians by the relieving-officer, they considered that he had done wrong—that the lunatic was not properly a pauper chargeable to the parish—that neither the 48, 49, nor 50, sections of the 8 & 9 Vic. c. 126, operated to compel the relieving-officer to interfere; that the case was that of a private lunatic, and that the master was bound to have procured the certificate of two medical practitioners, and then have gone before two justices to remove the lunatic as directed by the 52 sec. of that Act; and that he had no right to demand the assistance of the relieving-officer in the first instance. Inquiring, whether the relieving-officer did wrong, or whether under the circumstances stated, the lunatic's removal to an asylum was in conformity with the provisions of the statute. 2. H. K.'s wife applied to the board of guardians "to have her husband taken care of," he being as she stated a lunatic and without means of support. The guardians refused the application on the ground that the man was not a pauper entitled to parochial relief, he being then, as the wife admitted, the owner of a horse and two carts and some furniture, and that the wife with the assistance of her son, was carrying on, in a small way, the business of a poulterer. In consequence of the guardians' refusal, the wife applied to a magistrate, who required the relieving-officer to wait upon him, and the magistrate expressed his decided opinion that the guardians had done wrong; that the man was in need of relief, and was therefore a pauper, and must be dealt with as such; that the wife was in fact unable to pay for the certificate of two medical practitioners, and could not therefore procure her husband's removal to an asylum; nor was she able herself to take care of him. The relieving-officer at the desire of the magistrate took up the case, and the man was removed in the usual way to an asylum as a pauper lunatic. Inquiring, whether the view taken by the magistrate of this case was the right one. 3. C. W.'s wife applied to the board of guardians "to have her husband taken care of," he being as she stated a lunatic. It appeared that the man was in receipt of 7*s.* weekly from a club, and that one of his boys residing with him, earned 4*s.* 6*d.* a week. The guardians were of opinion that this man was not a pauper requiring relief, and therefore refused to order his removal to a lunatic asylum. Inquiring whether the guardians acted rightly in this case. The main question involved in these several cases is, whether parties who although lunatics but not actually chargeable, and who would not in ordinary circumstances be entitled to receive parochial relief, or be dealt with as destitute paupers, are persons coming within any of the provisions of the Act which render it imperative upon the relieving-officer to procure their removal to an asylum as paupers chargeable to the parish or otherwise.

Ans.—The Board are of opinion that the relieving-officer was not strictly under any legal obligation to procure the orders of justices for the removal of the lunatics to the asylum in the cases of R. C. and H. K., because the lunatics were not paupers chargeable at the time of his application for such orders. He is only required to make the application under the 8 & 9 Vic. c. 126, sec. 48, where there is a proper notice from a medical officer, and where the lunatic is a pauper "chargeable;" by which word the Board consider the Legislature meant a person in actual receipt of relief. Sec. 49, indeed, applies to lunatics not necessarily paupers, yet under such circumstances as do not appear to have existed in the present instances. But although the cases of the lunatics in question were not strictly brought within the terms of the statute, the Board are not prepared to say that the relieving-officer acted blameably in the course which he pursued. In regard to the case of R. C., (No. 1,) there was no legal obligation upon his master to retain him in his house or to send him to any asylum. He could indeed have put him outside of his house, and then the case would at once have fallen within the 49th sec., and the relieving-officer would have been bound to procure an order for the lunatic's removal to the asylum. The Board do not thing that the relieving-officer was bound to compel the master to adopt this course. As the lunatic had friends and relatives, perhaps he might have been removed to the workhouse, or some other place of custody, until they could have been written to, with the view of ascertaining whether they would take charge of him. But this was a course which might have had its objections, and the Board cannot blame the relieving-officer for not pursuing it. There is no evidence of the lunatic having any property, but if he have, it may be dealt with under the provisions of the 7 & 8 Vic. c. 101, s. 27. In regard to the case of H. K., (No. 2,) the Board, as the circumstances are reported to them, are not able to say that the guardians came to a right conclusion in respect of the necessity for the relief, though certainly it was a question for them to decide. The fact of a lunatic having a horse and cart, and some furniture, does not in itself necessarily raise the inference that he had such means as rendered him an unfit object for relief. In the case of an ordinary individual, such property might be sold, if necessary, for his maintenance; but a lunatic may require immediate attention, and his property cannot immediately be rendered available. The statute above referred to would however have been applicable, so as to reach the case of the lunatic. Then, although the wife and son may have carried on a business, it does not appear that their gains from it were such as to enable them to bear the heavy expence which the maintenance of a lunatic in an asylum necessarily causes. It appears that it was represented to the justices by the wife of the lunatic, that he could not properly be taken care of at his home, and if this representation were correct, (and the probability is that such would have been the result,) an application would have become necessary, under the 49th sec. of the 7 & 8 Vic. c. 126, and the order of removal to the asylum would then have been made. Under these circumstances the Board do not consider that the relieving-officer is open to blame for obtaining, in this case, the order upon the recommendation of the justice, which, if he had not then obtained, he would probably have been compelled soon to obtain. In regard to the case of C. W., (No. 3,) the Board do not understand that any order of justices has been obtained; but they think that the guardians will collect from the tenor of the foregoing remarks, that the Board do not acquiesce in the view which they have taken of the case. The allowance from the club will not maintain the lunatic in the asylum, and the amount earned by his son will doubtless be required for the maintenance of the latter. The 7 & 8 Vic. c. 101, s. 27, enables the trustees of the society referred to, to pay over the amount to the guardians towards the cost of the lunatic's maintenance. The Board would observe generally that the circumstances of lunatics on whose behalf applications are made for relief, are not to be viewed or treated in the same manner as those of ordinary applicants. The guardians, in dealing with applications of the former kind, should apply, or be guided by a rule different somewhat from that which would regulate their decision in ordinary cases of destitution. The guardians cannot but be aware that the mode of dealing with lunatics, under such circumstances, is such as to render it a matter of much difficulty for the relatives to take the steps which are highly expedient either to work a cure, or to provide against the serious evils which sometimes result from the unguarded exposure of lunatics. At the same time the guardians are not too readily to take upon themselves the maintenance of persons of unsound mind, whose property can be made available for this purpose, or whose relatives are in such a condition of life as to be able to bear the cost.

---

2. LUNATIC PAUPER WHO HAS MONEY IN THE SAVINGS' BANK.

22*nd May*, 1850.

Clerk of Clifton Union.—Requesting the opinion of the Poor Law Board as to the best mode of recovering the cost of the maintenance of A. M. from the savings' bank at Bath. A. M. was admitted into the workhouse of the Clifton Union on the 20th of June, 1845; she was then of unsound mind, and has so continued up to the present time. She has £43. 1*s*. 5*d*. in the Bath savings' bank, and no friend, relative, or connection, that interest themselves about her.

Ans.—The Poor Law Board direct the attention of the guardians to the 7 & 8 Vic. c. 101, sec. 27, which enables the trustees of the savings' bank to pay over to the guardians the money in question, to defray the charges incurred by them in the maintenance, clothing, &c., of such insane person. It is of course neither just nor reasonable that any one should be maintained out of the poor-rates as a destitute pauper while that person has property which can be made available for her support. The Board, therefore, entertain no doubt, that on a proper representation being made to the trustees of the Bath savings' bank, as to the facts of the case in question, they will at once act upon the powers given to them by the legislature.

---

3. LUNATIC PAUPERS NATIVES OF IRELAND, HOW TO DISPOSE OF THEM WHEN CURED.

1*st July*, 1850.

Chairman of the Visitors in Lunacy in the counties of Cumberland and Westmoreland.—A large increase has recently been found in the number of Irish pauper lunatics removed to the county asylum, which entails a heavy expense on this county. But the greatest difficulty which the justices feel in regard to this class of lunatics, is how to dispose of them when they are convalescent. It is often no easy matter to obtain correct information from an Irish pauper where his settlement is, even if he knows it. But in the case of a person discharged from a lunatic asylum this difficulty is obviously increased. The justices wish to have the advice and instruction of the Poor Law Board how they should proceed in such cases. They have no right to detain persons who are no longer insane. To turn them out without any means of support, may force them to commit crime or to suffer want. It seems to the justices that there are only two other alternatives, either to send them to Ireland as vagrants (which the justices have no authority to do) or to return them to the parishes from whence they were sent to the asylum, and leave the parishes to find out their settlement, or deal with them as casual poor.

Ans.—The Board presume that your inquiry has reference to lunatics who, though born in Ireland, have been removed to the county asylum in pursuance of the statute 8 & 9 Vic., c. 126, either under sec. 48, if chargeable to any parish previously to such removal, or under sec. 49 if not so chargeable. The point which you have raised as to the future disposal of such persons upon their being discharged by the committee of visitors as cured, is certainly one of some practical difficulty. The Board do not see any provision in the statute cited which expressly requires the authorities of unions or parishes, at whose instance the removal to the asylum took place, either themselves to remove the lunatic, or otherwise to take care of him on his discharge. But a presumption appears to the Board to arise from the 72nd sec., that the union or parish liable and charged with the maintenance ought to take upon itself this responsibility. That sec. provides that the expenses of the removal or discharge of a pauper from any asylum are to be borne by the union or parish to which the pauper shall then be deemed to belong, *i.e.*, (as the 57th sec. shews) the union or parish liable for the maintenance of the lunatic when in the asylum. The exception to this is in the case of lunatics rendered chargeable to counties in the mode provided by secs. 59 and 63—lunatics whose settlements cannot be ascertained. The Board apprehend that the class of persons to whom your inquiry applies falls within this description. In those cases, therefore, where the liability of support is fixed upon the county, there can be no ground for holding the union or parish to which the lunatic belonged, as before explained, concerned with his care or custody after the discharge from the asylum. In such cases as these there seems to be no alternative, but for the person to apply, if destitute, for relief in the ordinary manner to the authorities of the parish or union in which the destitution arises. This is, of course, assuming that the discharged lunatic has no relatives or friends who will undertake to receive him. But in other cases (if any) the authorities of the union or parish, liable for the maintenance of the lunatic, seeing that they are also liable for the expenses of the removal or discharge, may, in the event of his being destitute, be properly required to take charge of the lunatic upon his discharge from the asylum.

4. PROPOSAL FOR PLACING A GIRL, WHOSE FATHER IS NOT A PAUPER, INTO A LUNATIC ASYLUM, HE PAYING PART OF THE COST AND THE PARISH THE REMAINDER.

29*th Aug.*, 1850.

Clerk of Bridgwater Union.—Application was made to the guardians on the last board-day, on behalf of a man by the name of T. S., of C——, a gardener, whose earnings are 15*s.* per week, and who has a small income arising from some house property, to send his daughter A., aged thirteen years, to the county lunatic asylum at the expense of C—— parish, the father, however, paying part of such expense. Inquiring whether the guardians can, under the circumstances, legally accede to this application. The man's family consists of a wife and this lunatic daughter.

Ans.—The guardians cannot lawfully send the girl to the asylum unless she become chargeable on the poor-rates, which the Board do not understand to be now the case. If her father should be so far destitute as to require relief on her account, and such relief should be given, and she thereby become chargeable, then, the arrangement proposed in your letter might be carried into effect, but not otherwise.

VI.—MEDICAL OFFICER'S FEE.—CHARGEABILITY OF SICK PAUPER.

16*th Feb.*, 1849.

Clerks of Beverley Union.—A man of the name of H. C., aged fifty-five, a moulder at a foundry in this town, earning 21*s.* a week, had his leg broken on the 25th of December last, in a quarrel at a tavern in St. Mary's parish, Beverley. Immediately after the accident, (about four o'clock in the afternoon,) the man was taken to his lodgings in St. Martin's parish, another parish in the town of Beverley, and where he had lodged continuously for ten weeks. Mrs. P., the occupier of the house, sent for Mr. Boulton, a surgeon, to attend the man. Mr. Boulton was from home; his assistant, however, called, and recommended medical assistance to be applied for at the dispensary, which was done, but the case was not entertained by that institution; Mrs. P. being told that, as the man was without money and destitute, she had better apply for him to the relieving-officer of the union. This officer was applied to, and gave an order for the man's admission into the workhouse. The man could not be removed, and the relieving-officer then (about seven o'clock) gave an order to Mr. Brereton, a medical officer of the union, and of the parish (St. Mary) in which the accident happened, to attend him. Mr. Brereton attended accordingly, and reduced the fracture. Mr. Boulton, the medical officer of the parish of St. Martin in which the man was lodging, contends, that in fairness he ought to have had the order to reduce the fracture. The fee payable to the medical officer for a case of this nature is £3. Requesting the opinion of the Poor Law Board, as to which of the two medical officers, in strictness, ought to have had the order, and as to which parish the medical fee and the cost of the man's maintenance ought to be charged.

Ans.—The Board are of opinion that the relieving-officer referred to, did not act correctly in sending the order to the medical officer of the district in which the accident happened: it should have been addressed to the medical officer of that district wherein the man was at the time when the relief was required. As regards the fee for reducing the fracture, under the circumstances set forth, it is certainly not payable to the district medical officer who was not called in; neither is the medical officer who came out of his district entitled, as a matter of right, to the fee prescribed under the General Consolidated Order, although he is entitled to a reasonable compensation for the service rendered; and the Board think that the guardians of the Beverley Union would do well in fixing the amount of such compensation, to abide by the scale comprised in the General Order adverted to. The charge for the relief given to this pauper is not one which the parish wherein the accident happened is liable to bear (see 11 & 12 Vic. c. 110, sec. 2); but, whether it should be a charge upon the common fund of the union, or upon the parish of the pauper's abode, depends on the question whether the accident is of such a nature as to produce a permanent disability, or not. If it is not, the common fund of the union must bear the charge; but, if it is, the parish of the pauper's abode, namely, St. Martin.

VII.—RELIEVING-OFFICER. — CHARGE OF HAVING IMPROPERLY CAUSED THE SHIFTING OF THE BURDEN OF THE RELIEF OF A PAUPER FROM ONE UNION TO ANOTHER.

The guardians of the Ll —— Union brought under the notice of the Poor Law Board the conduct of Mr. J. M., a relieving-officer of the S—— Union, in the case of Hannah Holmes, otherwise Hannah Morris, and her child, who became chargeable to the Ll —— Union. A representation was also made to the Board in reference to the same case by Mr. M. of ———. The Board (having first called for a written explanation from the relieving-officer) thought it necessary to instruct one of their inspectors to hold an official inquiry into the circumstances of the case; this the inspector accordingly did; and the Board being in possession of the depositions of the several witnesses examined by him on the occasion, addressed the following communications to the guardians of the Ll —— Union, and J. M., the relieving-officer of the S —— Union:—

24th April, 1850.

The Poor Law Board to the Guardians of the Ll—— Union.—The Poor Law inspector reports that he attended at the Ll —— workhouse on Saturday the 30th ultimo, for the purpose of investigating a charge brought against J. M., one of the relieving-officers of the S —— Union, for causing a pauper named Hannah Morris and her child to become chargeable to the Ll —— Union contrary to the 6th sec. of the 9 & 10 Vic. c. 66, in consequence of which J. M. was convicted by two magistrates at Ll —— in a penalty of two pounds with costs, on the 12th of January last. In the absence of the woman and her child, who are now supposed to be tramping about the country, the inspector was compelled to take the particulars of the case from one of the relieving-officers of the Ll—— Union, as furnished to him by the woman herself. The facts of the case, as disclosed on the present inquiry, appear to be, that Hannah Morris and her child on Christmas day last, about three o'clock in the afternoon, applied to the relieving-officer, J. M., at his residence in ——— in the S——— Union for relief, which the relieving-officer admits he gave, both in food and money. Hannah Morris then appears to have stated before the magistrates that the relieving-officer, on being requested by her to furnish a lodging, desired a servant to show her a farmhouse near the gate, giving her at the same time a paper. It is alleged that this farmhouse was in the adjoining parish of L. in the Ll —— Union, and that the paper was an order on the overseer of that parish to receive Hannah Morris and her child. This paper was not produced before the magistrates, as on the following day it appears to have been thrown into the fire by the woman herself. According to the statement of one of the magistrates, before whom the relieving-officer was charged, there can be no doubt, (observes the inspector,) that the evidence against him was not considered satisfactory, and an adjournment of the case was offered. The relieving-officer, however, who is quite inexperienced in his situation, and who, at the date of this occurrence, had not been three months in office, seems to have preferred admitting the charge in order to save himself further trouble and expense. Had he adopted a different course, he would then have had the same opportunity as at the inquiry before the inspector of proving by two witnesses, who were in his house at the time, that the paper, supposed to be an order on the overseer of the adjoining parish of L., was in Hannah Morris's possession previous to her calling at his house, and that she herself produced it to the relieving-officer. This fact is partly confirmed by a third witness, R. L., who saw a woman and child (believed to be Hannah Morris and child) about two o'clock on the day in question, when the woman produced a piece of paper in the same way as described by the other two witnesses; the time of her doing this appears to have been previous to her calling at the relieving-officer's house, which was probably about three o'clock in the afternoon; that hour being specified by two parties, although by another witness, C. L., the hour of two is mentioned. If there had been any adjournment of the case before the magistrates, the relieving-officer might have proved besides by the servant, J. W., (who was the person referred to by Hannah Morris) that he showed her, by the relieving-officer's order, a house in the parish of L., which was a lodging-house,—that he then left Hannah Morris and her child, and that this house was the only one the relieving-officer mentioned to him. The inspector further reports that J. W. seems, after the woman had failed in procuring admission into the lodging-house, to have walked with her across the bridge which divides the S—— from the Ll—— Union; but J. W. denied to the inspector having been near the house at B—— as alleged, which is in the parish of L. in the Ll—— Union, or having seen the woman there. The relieving-officer having been convicted of this charge on the uncorroborated testimony of Hannah Morris herself, it is necessary, remarks the inspector, "to advert to the observations entered against her name by the master of the workhouse in the admission and discharge book, 'Bad, quite a worthless character,' and that it will be seen by the master's evidence, he had sufficient reason for making this entry." Under these circumstances, it is fair to observe, the relieving-officer ought now to be acquitted of the charge preferred against him before the magistrates, and on which he was evidently through his own imprudence convicted. With reference to the general conclusions thus arrived at, the Board deem it necessary to state that a perusal of the depositions of the several witnesses examined by the inspector, has impressed the Board with the conviction, that though the relieving-officer's conduct on the particular occasion was wanting in proper caution, and was such as (having regard to the result which followed) naturally exposed him to the charge of causing the pauper improperly to become chargeable to another union: still there are not sufficient grounds for inferring from those depositions, that there was any wilful intention on his part to produce such a result. The Board cannot consider it as in any way satisfactorily proved that the relieving-officer gave the pauper any paper or order as alleged, and the evidence of his servant, J. W., shows that the house which he, by his master's direction, pointed out to the pauper as a place where she would be likely to obtain the shelter she needed, was not in the parish of Ll——y, but in the parish of Ll——o, in the S—— Union; though it is true that, not being able to obtain accommodation at that house, she wandered into the adjoining parish of Ll——y, and that then occurred those circumstances which ended in the pauper's becoming chargeable to Ll——y, and being taken to the workhouse. The Board think, however, that the evidence does show that the relieving-officer was irregular in his mode of treating the case; but seeing that he was at the time inexperienced in his office, the Board do not consider it requisite to do more than caution him as to his future proceedings, and warn him carefully to avoid any step which may expose him to the imputation, either of acting harshly towards the poor, or seeking to shift irregularly any burden or obligation which the law may have cast upon the district for which he acts.

The Poor Law Board to the Relieving-Officer of Ll—— Union.—After careful consideration of the evidence placed before them, the Board (although they think there is no sufficient proof of any wilful intention on your part to shift the burden of the pauper's relief upon the parish of L., or the Ll—— Union) are clearly of opinion that your mode of dealing with the application made to you by the pauper, was both irregular and indiscreet. If Hannah Holmes applied to you for relief, it was your duty, supposing her to be then in a state of destitution, to have provided her with such food and shelter, or other relief (not in money) as might have been necessary. The Board observe from the explanation in your letter of the 2nd of February last, that you gave her 6*d.* out of your own pocket, "which you thought sufficient to take her home to her own parish," but they cannot regard such a gift as a proper proceeding on the part of a relieving-officer under circumstances similar to those which existed in the present instance. The mode in which you dealt with the case led in fact, in its ultimate consequences, to the parish of L., (or the Ll—— Union,) being burdened with the relief of the pauper; and the Board cannot but consider that, although you may not have intended to bring about that result, you did not exercise due caution in the matter. As, however, you had only been recently appointed relieving-officer at the time of the occurrence of the case in question, and were therefore inexperienced in your duties, the Board do not deem it requisite on the present occasion to do more than warn you, in future, to avoid carefully any step which may expose you to the imputation either of acting harshly towards the poor, or of seeking to shift irregularly any burden or obligation which the law may have cast upon the district for which you act.

VIII.—REMOVABILITY.—BREACH OF RESIDENCE.

23rd April, 1849.

Clerk of Bodmin Union.—Transmitting the following statement, duly signed, under sec. 4 of the 11 & 12 Vic. c. 110, for the opinion of the Poor Law Board:—G. B., a pauper residing in Bodmin, but receiving relief from Lanivet, in this union, of which parish she was an acknowledged pauper, became in August, 1837, an inmate of the union workhouse, situate in Bodmin, and so continued until October in the same year; during which period she was maintained by the parish of Lanivet. Previous to her admission she had resided at Bodmin upwards of five years without receiving relief, but from the time of her discharge to the present date she has continued to reside in Bodmin, receiving relief up to December, 1846, from Lanivet, and since that time from the borough of Bodmin. Does her admission into the workhouse, and her maintenance there by the parish of Lanivet, constitute a breach of residence, or is the pauper chargeable to the common fund of the union?

Ans.—The Board consider that as the pauper, when she went into the workhouse in August, 1837, continued in fact to reside in the parish of Bodmin, (the workhouse being situate in that parish,) the residence was not thereby interrupted, notwithstanding that the relief received during the period of her being an inmate was charged to the parish of Lanivet. The Board do not think that the circumstance of the workhouse, for the limited purpose of charging the relief being constructively in Lanivet, (sec. 56 of 7 & 8 Vic. c. 101,) interrupted a residence which existed, in point of fact, in Bodmin, even if that section has a retrospective operation, which may be doubted. The Board, therefore, are of opinion, that under the circumstances of the case before them, the pauper, G. B., is irremovable from the parish of Bodmin; and, consequently, her relief is chargeable to the common fund of the union.

IX.—SCHOOL.—RECORD OF ATTENDANCE AT WORKHOUSE SCHOOL—CIRCULAR LETTER TO THE BOARDS OF GUARDIANS.

Poor Law Board,
12th July, 1850.

SIR,

The Poor Law Board wish to call the guardians' attention to the following passage in a circular dated 6th May last, on the subject of the payments from the Parliamentary Grant on account of the salaries of teachers in workhouse schools:—"As the amount of the fees will be regulated by the average number of children in the school during the year, an accurate record of the daily attendance in the school must be kept, and the guardians are requested to give the necessary directions for effecting this object."

It appears desirable that the mode of recording the attendance of the scholars should be the same in all workhouse schools, and the Board therefore request, that the guardians will provide two books for each of the teachers, prepared according to the accompanying forms, which have been suggested by the Committee of Council on Education, and appear well adapted for the purpose. In one of the books the dates of admission and discharge of every scholar, with some other particulars, are to be recorded; and in the other the daily attendance or absence of each scholar is to be noted.

The headings of the several columns in the "*School Admission and Discharge Book*," sufficiently shew how it is to be kept; and with respect to the "*School Attendance Book*," it is only necessary to state that the space for each day of the week should be divided by a diagonal line for morning and afternoon school; a dot (.) should be inserted in each division, when the child has been in school morning and afternoon; "*a*" to denote his absence; "*w*" his being at work by order of the master; and "*s*" his being sick. The form now sent is filled up as a specimen of these several entries.

This record will not only enable the school inspector, when visiting the school, to see how long each child has been under instruction, but will also enable him readily to ascertain the average number of scholars in attendance during the year.

The Board request the guardians to direct the teachers to make the necessary entries in these books daily, and to produce the same at every meeting of the guardians for their inspection, when the books are to be signed by the presiding chairman.

By order of the Board,

EBRINGTON, *Secretary*.

To

The Clerk to the Board of Guardians.

NOTE.—Mr. Charles Knight, the Board's Publisher, has been instructed to prepare copies of the Books in question for use.

[*Exemplified Form.*]

SCHOOL ADMISSION AND DISCHARGE BOOK.

No.	NAME.	Age.	Parish to which chargeable.	Date of Admission.	Whether in Workhouse School before, and how long.	Whether in any other School before, and how long.	Date of Discharge.	Observations:—showing the conduct of the child whilst in the School; the occasion of discharge; if to enter service, the nature of the service.
1	Gregory, John	8	Cirencester	11 Jan., 1849	No	Yes, 1 year		
2	Darker, W. H.	10	Preston	1 June, 1848	No	Yes, 3 years	1 May, 1850	Conduct very indifferent—left workhouse, the father having obtained employment.
3	Poole, Wm.	9	Harnhill	2 Feb., 1849	No	No		
4	Martin, Edward	11	Union	4 March, 1849	Yes, 6 months	No		
5	Dawson, Thos.	7	Driffield	10 June, 1849	No	Yes, 3 months		
6	Savage, Thos.	8	Coates	1 Jan., 1850	No	Yes, 1 year		
7	Leach, Wm.	11	Stratton	12 Feb., 1850	No	Yes, 2 years	7 May, 1850	Conduct good, and made great progress—for short time in school—left on trial prior to apprenticeship.
8	Gibbs, Wm.	10	Union	3 March, 1850	No	No		
9	Giddy, John	9	Union	2 July, 1848	No	No		
10	Morris, George	7	Union	3 Aug., 1848	No	No		
11	Smith, James	9	Baunton	4 Sept., 1848	No	Yes, 6 months		
12	Pottle, Chas.	10	Winston	16 April, 1849	Yes, 2 years	No		
13	Stevens, Thos.	10	Barnsley	29 May, 1849	Yes, 1 year	No		
14	Featherstone, Wm.	11	Union	19 Jan., 1849	Yes, 2½ years	No		
15	Monk, Fred.	8	Syde	30 March, 1850	No	No		
16	Tindall, Thos.	7	Union	30 June, 1849	No	Yes, 2 months		
17	Branch, John	9	Fairford	19 July, 1849	No	Yes, 1 year		
18	Rushbrook, Geo	8	Kemble	30 Aug., 1849	No	Yes, 6 months		
19	Eaton, Wm.	10	Poulton	1 Sept., 1849	No	Yes, 2 years		
20	Giles, Chas.	11	Poole	1 Jan., 1850	Yes, 9 months	No	16 June, 1850	Conduct good—obtained situation with a farmer.
21	Eales, Wm.	8	Union	4 June, 1849	No	No		
22	Read, Stephen	7	Union	28 Feb., 1850	No	No		
23	Ives, Henry	9	Shorncote	7 March, 1850	No	No		
24	Fisher, Robert	11	Rendcomb	16 April, 1850	No	Yes, 2 years	16 June, 1850	Conduct bad—left to reside with relations.
25	Sprunt, John	10	Stratton	21 Dec., 1849	No	No		
26	Perry, Richard	9	Union	19 Feb., 1850	No	No		
27	Harlow, Fred.	9	Union	19 Feb., 1850	No	No		

[*Exemplified Form.*]

SCHOOL ATTENDANCE BOOK.

Week of Quarter ending ______

Reference No. in School Admission and Discharge Book.	NAMES.	M.	T.	W.	Th.	F.	S.	No. of Days attendance during the Week.†	Observations.
1	Gregory, John . .	· / ·	a / ·	· / ·	w / ·	· / ·	· / ·	6	
2	Darker, W. H. . .	a / a	a / a	a / a	· / ·	· / ·	· / ·	3	
3	Poole, William . .	· / ·	· / ·	a / ·	a / ·	w / ·	w / ·	6	
4	Martin, Edward .	· / s	s / s	s / s	s / s	s / s	s / s	1	
5	Dawson, Thomas .	· / ·	· / ·	· / ·	· / ·	· / ·	· / ·	6	
6	Savage, Thomas .	· / ·	· / ·	· / ·	· / ·	· / ·	· / ·	6	
7	Leach, William .	· / ·	· / ·	· / ·	· / ·	· / ·	· / ·	6	
8	Gibbs, William .	· / ·	· / ·	· / ·	· / ·	· / ·	· / ·	6	
9	Giddy, John .	a / a	a / a	a / a	a / a	a / a	· / ·	1	
10	Morris, George .	· / ·	· / a	· / ·	· / a	· / ·	· / a	6	
11	Smith, James . .	· / ·	· / ·	· / ·	· / ·	· / ·	· / ·	6	
12	Pottle, Charles . .	· / ·	· / ·	· / ·	· / ·	· / ·	· / ·	6	
13	Stevens, Thomas .	s / s	s / s	s / s	s / s	s / s	s / s	—	
14	Featherstone, Wm. .	· / ·	· / ·	· / ·	· / ·	· / ·	· / ·	6	
15	Monk, Frederick .	· / a	· / ·	a / ·	· / ·	· / a	· / ·	6	
16	Tindall, Thomas .	w / ·	· / ·	w / ·	· / ·	w / ·	· / ·	6	
17	Branch, John . .	· / ·	· / ·	· / ·	· / ·	· / ·	· / s	6	
18	Rushbrook, George .	· / a	· / ·	· / ·	· / ·	· / a	· / ·	6	
19	Eaton, William .	· / ·	· / ·	a / ·	· / ·	a / a	· / ·	5	
20	Gills, Charles . .	s / s	s / s	s / s	s / s	s / s	s / ·	1	
21	Eales, William . .	· / ·	· / ·	· / ·	· / ·	· / ·	· / ·	6	
22	Read, Stephen . .	· / a	· / ·	· / a	· / ·	· / a	· / ·	6	
23	Ives, Henry . .	· / ·	· / ·	· / ·	· / ·	· / ·	· / ·	6	
24	Fisher, Robert . .	· / ·	· / ·	· / ·	· / ·	· / ·	· / ·	6	
25	Sprunt, John . .	· / ·	· / ·	· / ·	· / ·	· / ·	· / ·	6	
26	Perry, Richard .	w / ·	· / ·	w / ·	· / ·	w / ·	· / ·	6	
27	Harlow, Frederick .	· / ·	· / a	· / ·	a / a	· / ·	· / a	5	
	TOTAL NUMBER of attendances during the week .							136	
	DAILY AVERAGE NUMBER of Scholars							22⅓	

Produced at the Meeting of the Board of Guardians this ____________ day of ______________________

______________________________ *Chairman.*

(·) Denotes attendance at School;—placed at the upper part of the diagonal line shows morning attendance, and at the bottom, afternoon attendance.
(a) Absent by order of Master. (w) Absent at work. (s) Absent through sickness.
† A morning or afternoon attendance is reckoned as one day's attendance.

X.—SETTLEMENT—BY HIRING AND SERVICE.

17th Aug., 1850.

Clerk of Festiniog Union.—W. W., residing in the parish of Llanfihangel y traethau, in this union, is entitled to relief from the union, unless he gained a settlement in that parish under the following circumstances: — About twenty-one years ago W. W. went to the service of Captain B., under a hiring for half a year, at the wages of £5. 5*s*. 0*d*. W. W. served the half year, and received the wages, and stayed in the same service for five years. Except the agreement for the first half year, nothing was said about time of service or wages. W. W. received the same amount of wages (£5. 5*s*. 0*d*.) half-yearly. Will a hiring for a year from the expiration of the first half-year be presumed, or will the payment of the same amount of wages half-yearly, be sufficient to rebut the presumption? W. W. was unmarried, and resided during the whole time in Llanfihangel y traethau.

Ans.—Having regard to the case of R. *v.* Long Whatton, 5 T. R 447, the Board are of opinion (assuming the statement of facts laid before them to be correct) that in the present case a yearly hiring is to be presumed from the continuance of the man in the service of Captain B—— for more than a year, after the hiring for half a year; and, therefore, that the pauper acquired a settlement by hiring and service in Llanfihangel y traethau parish. In the case of R. *v.* Long Whatton, the hiring was for part of a year only, but the pauper afterwards continued in the service for three years, and the court held those circumstances sufficient to warrant the conclusion of a hiring for a year.

XI.—TREASURER.—LOSS SUSTAINED BY THE PAYMENT OF A FORGED ORDER OF THE GUARDIANS. *6th Aug.*, 1850.

Treasurer of the St. Asaph Union.—Submitting the circumstances under which forged cheques purporting to have been drawn on him by the guardians of the St. Asaph Union, in favour of the late relieving-officer of the union, had been cashed by him; and that the loss occasioned thereby ought to fall on the union.

Ans.—As regards the legal question involved in the case, viz., as to the liability to the loss of the amount of the order which was forged, the Board have to observe, that they cannot understand upon what principle or rule of law the guardians can be made liable. The Board consider that a banker who pays a cheque drawn in the name of his customer, which is a forgery, cannot hold the latter liable, however well the deception may have been executed. Neither do the Board consider that the fact of the payment made by the banker upon such forged cheque being entered in the pass-book, to the debit of the customer, would in any respect conclude him, if he should ultimately show that the cheque was in fact a forgery. The omission on the part of the customer to notice or detect at the time the erroneous entry, might lead to a question as to the fact of the cheque being a forgery, but if this fact be established, the Board believe that no question could arise as to the banker remaining responsible. In the present case, there appears to be no doubt that the order was a forgery, and the treasurer of the guardians cannot take credit in his account for, or, in other words, with, the payment of any sum of money for which he cannot produce a legal order. The Board are not aware of any authority which would enable them to require either the guardians or the clerk to reimburse the treasurer the sum which has been paid over to the relieving-officer or his agent upon this forged order.

XII.—VAGRANTS.—APPLYING FOR LODGINGS LATE AT NIGHT.

9th May, 1849.

Clerk of Hastings Union.—In dealing with vagrants and wayfarers, who are increasing in the Hastings Union, much difficulty and inconvenience is experienced by the guardians and their officers, in consequence of night lodgers being sent to the workhouse at all hours of the night by the relieving-officer of the town district, to whom they are sent by the inspector of the Hastings police. The guardians had passed a resolution, directing that no vagrants or wayfarers should be admitted to the workhouse after seven o'clock in the evening, but this proceeding of the guardians could not restrict the relieving-officers and others from the proper discharge of their duties, and thus the evil still exists. Inquiring whether the course taken by the inspector of police is a proper and legal course, and whether it is necessary that the relieving-officer should be driven to provide lodgings at a late hour for these tramps, and that the workhouse should be open to them at all hours of the night; and if so, what course should the guardians adopt in order to check it?

Ans.—The course taken by the inspector of police in directing vagrants supposed to be destitute to the relieving-officer at all hours of the night is not actually illegal; but the Board consider that such a practice is likely to lead to great inconvenience, and to increase rather than diminish vagrancy, from the facilities which it holds out for obtaining relief. It is in the discretion of the board of guardians, with a view to the orderly conduct of the workhouse, to limit the hours during which vagrants shall be admitted; and they are not bound to provide lodgings which shall be open all night for "trampers" and that class of mendicants and wanderers who habitually resort to the rates for support. It would appear to the Board that the most effectual mode which can be suggested for checking the amount of vagrancy which unfortunately exists at Hastings, would be to appoint an active and intelligent police officer as assistant relieving-officer, for the relief of vagrants and casual poor. It has been found in practice, that such an appointment deters to a great extent such persons from applying for relief, whose habits and actual wants render them unworthy recipients of it; whilst the really destitute and proper object of charity will not fear the scrutiny of a police officer, who will be empowered to relieve his temporary wants and to refer him subsequently to the relieving-officer, if necessary, for further relief and assistance. The vagrancy laws should be enforced against all persons committing acts which bring them within their provisions, and a systematic enforcement of a full task of work from such casual paupers as are admitted into the workhouse, would also be very desirable. With respect to this, the Board refer the guardians to the provisions of the 5 & 6 Vic. c. 57, sec. 5, and suggest that the guardians pass a resolution in the enclosed form, and transmit a copy of it to the Board for their approval. The different measures above mentioned would, the Board doubt not, be found effectual in diminishing the evil complained of in your letter; they have been found successful wherever they have been tried, and the Board therefore confidently recommend them for immediate adoption at Hastings.

The Form of the Resolution referred to above:—

Task of Work.

________________ *UNION.*

ORDERED:—By the guardians of the union, at a meeting of the board, held this day of one thousand eight hundred and forty-

THAT the master of the workhouse of the union, do set every adult person not suffering under any temporary or permanent infirmity of body, being an occasional poor person who shall be relieved in the said workhouse, in return for the food and lodging afforded to such person, to perform the following task of work, that is to say.—

Here insert the *kind* and *amount*, with reference to *time* or *quantity*, of the work to be performed by the males and females respectively.

PROVIDED THAT no such person shall be detained against his or her will for the performance of such task of work, for any time exceeding four hours from the hour of breakfast, on the morning next after admission.

AND PROVIDED ALSO THAT such amount of work shall not be required from any person to whose age, strength, and capacity it shall appear not to be suited.

Signed ________________

Clerk to the Guardians.

WE, the COMMISSIONERS for administering the laws for relief of the poor in England, do consent to, and approve of, the above order of the board of guardians of the union.

(L.S.) Dated this day of One thousand eight hundred and forty-

NOTICE.

Any such person as above who shall, while in such workhouse, *refuse* or *neglect* to perform such task of work suited to the age, strength, and capacity of such person, will be deemed an *idle* and *disorderly* person, and be liable to be *imprisoned* in the house of correction, with hard labour *for one calendar month.*

XIII.—WORKHOUSE.—PUNISHMENT OF DISORDERLY WOMEN.

22nd June, 1850.

Clerk of Spalding Union.—A strong spirit of insubordination has lately manifested itself amongst the female paupers of the workhouse, having suckling children, the women taking advantage of the difficulties which their condition throws in the way of punishing them in the ordinary manner, to commit all manner of breaches of discipline, almost with impunity. Some three or four are the ringleaders; and it was proposed that the master be authorized to confine these women for a few days to a separate room in the workhouse, and there set them to picking and cleaning the cocoa-nut fibre, their children being taken from them as occasion may require. Inquiring whether this is a course which the guardians may properly adopt.

Ans.—The Board see no objection to the females referred to being placed in a separate room and required to pick cocoa-nut fibre as proposed by the guardians; but the medical officer should be consulted in the first instance, and his opinion taken as to whether this proceeding would be likely to injure the health of the women or the children; in which case it should of course not be adopted.

London: Printed by Order of the Poor Law Board, by BLACKBURN & BURT, 90½, Holborn Hill; and Published by CHARLES KNIGHT, 90, Fleet Street.

AN

OFFICIAL CIRCULAR

OF PUBLIC DOCUMENTS AND INFORMATION:

DIRECTED BY THE POOR LAW BOARD TO BE PRINTED, CHIEFLY FOR THE USE OF THE BOARDS OF GUARDIANS AND THEIR OFFICERS.

No. 41.] SEPTEMBER, 1850. [N.S.

CONTENTS.

I. — AUDIT — SURCHARGE OF RELIEVING-OFFICER IN THE AMOUNT OF ILLEGAL RELIEF.

30*th August*, 1850.

Relieving-officer of ——— *Union.*—Submitting for the consideration of the Poor Law Board the particulars of a surcharge made by Mr. Vining in his, the relieving-officer's, account at the audit, which took place on the 15th May, 1849. The amount surcharged was £3. 5*s.*, being the amount of relief advanced by him to a pauper of the name of Edmund Hunt. The ground on which this relief was disallowed was that the pauper was an able-bodied man, and that the relief so given was in contravention of the order of the Poor Law Commissioners. The facts of the case were these: Edmund Hunt, the son of a widow, who, with her family, was for some years in the workhouse, was apprenticed to a carpenter, and the sum paid him for the first few years of his apprenticeship was insufficient to support him, and the guardians granted him 2*s.* 6*d.* per week. The guardians at their periodical revision of the relief-lists, continued the same pay, and the pauper list had undergone also the revision of the vestry of the parish to which this pauper belonged. Applying to the Board to issue an order to the guardians for the repayment to him of the said sum of £3. 5*s.*

Ans.—The Board are of opinion that the course pursued by the auditor was lawful and right, as the relief in question was given in direct contravention of the Poor Law Commissioners' General Prohibitory Order; and the Board do not see that the circumstances of the case, in other respects, are such as to warrant the remission of the disallowance in question.

II.—AUDITOR.—COSTS OF PROCEEDINGS FOR THE RECOVERY OF OVERSEERS' BALANCES.

14*th Sept.*, 1850.

Clerk of ——— *Union.*—Transmitting the bill of costs of the solicitor employed by the district auditor, and incurred by him in the recovery of overseers' balances. Requesting the advice of the Board as to the liability of the guardians to pay such costs, and calling their attention particularly to the charge of 17*s.* 6*d.* six times for journey and attendance at T——— special session, making together £5. 5*s.* From the absence of dates, it would appear that there was only one attendance at the special session, and the gross amount, £5. 5*s.*, divided amongst six parishes. In the event of parties being summoned for non-payment of balances, and the magistrates, on the hearing, refuse to include in the order for payment of the costs of the attendance of the auditor's solicitor, would the costs of such attendance and the travelling expenses be thrown on the parishes?

28*th Sept.*, 1850.

District Auditor—(With whom the Poor Law Board communicated on the subject of the above letter.) His solicitor's residence is thirty-two miles from T———, and he cannot go there and back without being nine hours on the road. The solicitor and himself went there to support six applications against overseers, and of course it was a very hard day's work, for which three guineas were charged, the other two guineas were for travelling and other expenses. The five guineas were divided amongst the six cases, as he considered it would not be just towards any one parish to charge the whole amount against such parish. The guardians and magistrates labour under an impression that he has no right to employ a solicitor, and that he is bound to recover overseers' balances, and take all proceedings at his own cost and risk. When the guardians know the contrary they will, in most instances, induce the magistrates to visit the defaulting overseers with the costs.

Ans. to the Clerk of ——— *Union.*—After stating that the Board had communicated with the auditor, and transmitting an extract from his reply, the Board answered as follows:—The Board think the explanation of the auditor satisfactory. With regard to the general question raised by your letter, the Board desire to remark, that the statute (7 & 8 Vic. c. 101, sec. 32,) has cast upon the auditor, in cases where balances certified by him to be due from overseers or other parties, are not sooner paid to the union treasurer, the duty of taking proceedings for the recovery; and has expressly provided that the costs incurred by the auditor in such proceedings (to the extent to which they may not be paid by the party proceeded against) are to be repaid to the auditor by the guardians. The Board certainly think that the auditor is at liberty to employ a solicitor to conduct such proceedings, and that it is advisable on many accounts that he should do so. The 11 & 12 Vic. c. 91, sec. 9, expressly recognises such right, and the 12 & 13 Vic. c. 103, sec. 10, provides that in the case of the prosecution of any information under 4 & 5 Wm. 4, c. 76 (a proceeding for the recovery of a balance is a case of this kind) the justices in awarding the costs to be paid by the defendant, may include in their order, the costs and expenses of the complainant's counsel or attorney. Where the justices do not do this (for they have a discretion in the matter) the case, so far as the auditor is concerned, then falls within the 32 sec. of 7 & 8 Vic. c. 101, that is, an expense has been incurred by the auditor in respect of his proceeding or recovery which has not been paid by the party proceeded against, and for which, consequently, the statute gives him a claim against the guardians of the union. The Board are of opinion that the present claim of the auditor, which appears to them to be reasonable, should be paid by the guardians, and the amount charged (in the proper proportions) to the several parishes for whose protection the proceedings were taken. The Board in conclusion must state their conviction that the course adopted by the auditor has been productive of much benefit, and that it will tend to secure for the future a more general and prompt compliance on the part of parish officers with the provision which in terms requires the payment to the union treasurer of all sums which on the final audit of their accounts, the auditor may certify as "due" from them.

III.—ADULTERY—OF WIFE RELIEVES THE HUSBAND FROM THE OBLIGATION TO MAINTAIN HER.

24th Sept., 1850.

Clerk of Wycombe Union.—The guardians of this union have deemed it their duty to proceed against an able-bodied man, one G. G., for neglecting to maintain his wife and child. A warrant was taken out, and the man requested that the case might be adjourned till the then next meeting, as he should then be able to prove adultery on the part of his wife. His request was complied with. On the 7th instant the case came on, when the wife, on being examined, admitted that her husband was not the father of the child. The justices dismissed the case, on the ground of the woman's adultery. Inquiring whether, under the circumstances, the guardians are bound to receive the wife and child into the workhouse; and if so, whether they have any, and if any, what remedy against the husband.

Ans.—It was decided in Rex *v.* Flinton, 1 B. & Adol. 227, that the legal obligation to maintain, referred to in section 3 of 5 Geo. 4, c. 83, does not exist in the case of a wife who has left her husband and lives in adultery, and that the husband cannot be punished for the neglect. The Board presume that the justices were satisfied at the hearing that the fact of the adultery was established in the present case, and refused to commit the man accordingly. If so, they are of opinion that the guardians have no remedy against G. G., and that if his wife be destitute, she must be relieved in the union workhouse.

IV.—BASTARD CHILDREN.—RELIEF TO MOTHERS OF.

17th June, 1850.

Clerk of Hartismere Union.—Mothers with illegitimate children have been making a practice of obtaining orders of admission into the union workhouse, and remaining there several weeks. The mother, immediately on her discharge, applies to the putative father of the child for the amount of the order that the justices may have made upon him. What she receives is quickly made away with, and she then returns to the workhouse. The guardians, in many such instances, are unable to refuse admission, as the order of the justices is for a sum of not more than one shilling or one shilling and sixpence per week. Inquiring whether the guardians can make any claim upon the putative father when the mother and child are inmates of the workhouse.

Ans.—The Board are sensible of the evil pointed out in your letter, but see much difficulty in dealing practically with such cases so as to remedy the evil. There is no mode of attaching the monies which may be paid to the mothers by the reputed fathers after the discharge of the former from the workhouse. Under the orders of justices, made under 7 & 8 Vic. c. 101, the weekly sums are payable to the mother, and her alone. If she improperly makes away with the monies so paid to her in any case, and subsequently becomes destitute, the Board do not see that admission for herself and child can safely be refused. But all relief given under such circumstances to a woman entitled to receive periodical payments from the putative father of her child, may be declared at the time to be given upon loan, and the putative father may be communicated with as to his making his payments to the woman at such times and places as may facilitate the recovery of relief so advanced upon loan. When, for instance, the mother is not in the workhouse, and the monies paid by the putative father come into her possession, there clearly would be no difficulty in dealing with the case under sec. 16 of 12 & 13 Vic. c. 103, which empowers the guardians to take any money in the possession of, or belonging to, any pauper, and appropriate the same in reimbursements of such pauper's relief. When out of the workhouse, the enforcement of this provision would of course be much more difficult, even if safely practicable at all.

V.—BOND—OF ASSISTANT OVERSEERS, UNDER 7 & 8 VIC. C. 101, SEC. 61.

28th Sept., 1850.

Overseer of Cirencester.—Forwarding to the Poor Law Board, in pursuance of their request, the appointment of Mr. James Viner, as assistant overseer of the parish, and a copy of the bond given by him to the churchwardens and overseers (who retain the original) for the due performance of his office.

Ans.—Although Mr. Viner has given a bond to the churchwardens and overseers of Cirencester, this does not dispense with the necessity for his giving security to the guardians of the Cirencester Union, pursuant to the 7 & 8 Vic. c. 101, sec. 61. The Board require that assistant overseers, appointed under the 59 Geo. 3, c. 12, should give to the guardians a "sufficient security" for the due discharge of the duties of their office. The guardians may, perhaps, in the present instance, consider that that object will be attained by the bond already entered into by Mr. Viner being placed in their custody. If this be done, and the guardians are satisfied both with the responsibility of the sureties, and the amount of the bond, the Board will offer no objection to that course.

VI.—BURIAL-GROUND.—CONSTRUCTION OF SEC. 2 OF 13 & 14 VIC. C. 101.

25*th Sept.*, 1850.

Clerk of Wolverhampton Union.—In one of the townships of this union, the workhouse not being situate therein, the present churchyard is full to repletion, and the inhabitants are anxious to obtain an additional burial-ground. Inquired, if, by sec. 2 of 13 & 14 Vic. c. 101, the guardians, with the sanction of the Poor Law Board, could legally contribute the necessary funds for such additional burial-ground, charging the same to that particular township, and if the whole board would have authority in this decision, and not the guardians of the township in question; or if, in the section referred to, the clause relative to parishes has reference only to the "guardians of any parish" not in the union.

Ans.—The words "guardians of any parish," in sec. 2 of the 13 & 14 Vic. c. 101, apply, as the Board consider, to a parish not in union, but which is governed by a board of guardians. In a union, the contribution referred to can only be made by the guardians of that union, and must come out of the common fund.

VII.—CHARGEABILITY.

1. CHARGEABILITY OF CHILDREN LIVING WITH THEIR STEPMOTHER.

28*th Sept.*, 1850.

Clerk of Falmouth Union.—Transmitting the following statement, duly signed, under the 4th sec. of the 11 & 12 Vic. c. 110, for the opinion of the Poor Law Board:—William Chapman, labourer, died in the town of Falmouth on the 4th of July last, but he was not legally settled therein. He left a widow, Sarah Chapman, forty-six years of age, (to whom he had been but a short time married,) and Elizabeth, aged seventeen years, William fifteen, John, and Mary Ann three years, his children by a former wife him surviving. A boy, named Robert, seven years of age, a child of the widow by her first husband, also formed part of William Chapman's family at the date of his decease. The parties are now chargeable. Inquiring whether such of the deceased pauper's children by the first wife, as are under five years of age, are removable to the place of their father's settlement, or whether the widow stands in *loco parentis*, and the relief to all should be charged to the common fund.

Ans.—By 9 & 10 Vic. c. 66, sec. 3, children under the age of sixteen years, residing in any parish with their stepmother, cannot lawfully be removed; and as in the case laid before the Board, the widow of William Chapman is at present irremovable, the stepchildren under five years of age are therefore not removable; and the cost of their relief is chargeable to the common fund of the Falmouth Union.

2.—CHARGEABILITY OF DESTITUTE WANDERER.

17*th Sept.*, 1850.

Clerk of Cambridge Union.—Yesterday, Hannah Sutton, an able-bodied pauper, accompanied by three children, of the respective ages of five, and two years, and six months, entered the workhouse of this union, under the usual order for admission, issued by the assistant relieving-officer for vagrants. The workhouse master, in the performance of his ordinary duty towards this class of poor, would have discharged them from the workhouse this morning, but the pauper stating that she claimed a settlement in one of the parishes in this union, she was brought before the guardians at their meeting this morning, when, upon being questioned, she stated that she is a married woman, and, with her husband, has for the past six years, (up to about the month of June or July last,) resided at Bury St. Edmunds, in Suffolk; that in consequence of her husband leaving her, in search of work, she and her family became inmates of the workhouse there for five weeks; at the end of which time she discharged herself, and in about a fortnight afterwards, at the suggestion of her brother, who resides at Bury St. Edmunds, she and her family came by a carrier's cart into this union, her brother paying the expense attending their conveyance. The pauper states that she has not heard from her husband since his departure, and does not know where he is: that he gained a settlement by apprenticeship in Barnwell parish, (meaning in all probability the parish of St. Andrew the Less, but as two parishes extend into what is commonly termed Barnwell, she is unable otherwise to define the parochial locality,) but at what time, or with whom, or as to who has possession of the indentures of apprenticeship, she appears to be unable to afford any information. It being the opinion of the guardians that this pauper and her family became irremovable from Bury St. Edmunds, they are desirous of being informed what steps they should take as to her removal back to Bury, and in the event of their being empowered so to remove her, whether the expense attending her relief ought to be borne by the parish wherein her destitution was first discovered as a vagrant; or, whether such expense should be borne by the common fund of the union.

Ans.—The Board are not able, upon this statement, to express an opinion whether or not the pauper, had she continued in Bury St. Edmunds, would have been irremovable therefrom, in respect of the provisions of the 9 & 10 Vic. c. 66. It appears, however, that she was persuaded by a relative to abandon her residence in that place, and to proceed to Cambridge, on the ground that her legal place of settlement was supposed to be in some parish in that union. The existence of such a settlement is doubtful; but, however this may be, there appears no reason for sending her with her family back to Bury St. Edmunds, nor would the guardians be justified in doing so. As regards the fund to which the cost of the relief now given to the pauper should be charged, the Board think, upon the statement before them, that, having regard to the circumstances under which she came into the Cambridge Union, and there made application for relief, the pauper must be held to have been a destitute wayfarer, or wanderer, at the time, and that the common fund is liable for her maintenance.

VIII. — DESERTION — OF CHILDREN BY MOTHER—REFUSAL OF MAGISTRATE TO COMMIT.

26*th Aug.*, 1850.

Clerk of Sheffield Union. — S. H., a widow, aged thirty, with three children, Joseph, aged six, George, aged four, and Sarah, aged one, was in receipt of six shillings per week. The guardians stopped the allowance, and offered the woman the workhouse, as she was living under circumstances of great suspicion. She refused the workhouse, and deserted two of her children, who were found wandering in the streets and brought to the workhouse. A warrant was taken out against the mother for neglecting her children, and the case was heard by one of the borough magistrates, who discharged her, stating the guardians ought not to have stopped the relief; and he therefore refused to make an order upon her or commit her for neglect. The children still remain chargeable, and the woman is at large. Requesting the advice of the Board under the circumstances.

2*nd Sept.*, 1850.

The Poor Law Board.—Inquiring what was the specific charge brought against the woman when she was taken before the magistrate, whether it was made under the Vagrant Act, sec. 3, for neglecting to maintain her children, being able wholly or in part to do so; or, under sec. 4, for running away and leaving the children chargeable. If the former, the Board will be glad to know whether any evidence was adduced of the mother's ability to maintain the children by "work or other means."

21*st Sept.*, 1850.

Clerk of the Union. — The charge brought against S. H., when she was before the magistrate, was made under the Vagrant Act, sec. 3, for neglecting to maintain her children, being able, wholly or in part, to do so. The woman having admitted to the magistrate that she was in receipt of three shillings per week wages for services done for the master of the house in which she lived, rent free, rendered it unnecessary to adduce evidence of her ability, wholly or in part, to maintain the children by "work or other means."

27*th Sept.*, 1850.

Ans.—Upon the information at present before them, the Board certainly cannot acquiesce in the judgment of the magistrate referred to, and think that he came to a wrong conclusion on the case. At the same time the Board would remark, that as the pauper is stated to have deserted her children, if the information had been laid under sec. 4 of 5 Geo. 4, c. 83, which renders a person who runs away, leaving his or her child chargeable to the parish, punishable as a rogue and vagabond, the magistrate would most probably not have refused to convict the defendant, evidence being given of the fact of desertion.

IX.—GUARDIANS.—PROCEEDINGS OF.

26*th Sept.*, 1850.

Clerk of Worksop Union.—A difference of opinion has arisen at the board of guardians on the construction of Art. 38 of the General Consolidated Order. It is contended by some of the guardians, that unless an amendment be proposed upon any motion which may have been proposed and seconded, it is not necessary or proper for the chairman to put the motion to the vote; but that being proposed and seconded without any amendment to it, such motion must be considered as carried unanimously. Requesting the advice of the Board on the point.

Ans.—A formal motion, made and seconded at a meeting of the guardians, cannot, in the opinion of the Board, be in strictness considered as a resolution of the guardians until it has been put to the vote by the chairman, and has been agreed to or negatived by the guardians. Although no specific amendment should have been proposed, it would still be competent to the guardians if they thought fit to negative the motion.

X.—LUNATIC PAUPER.—REMOVAL OF, FROM THE ASYLUM OF ONE COUNTY TO THAT OF ANOTHER.

25*th Sept.*, 1850.

Clerk of Darlington Union.—There is a pauper lunatic at present confined in the Lunatic Asylum at Hanwell, in Middlesex, belonging to the township of Darlington. The charge for maintenance, &c., is five shillings per week more than at the Lunatic Asylum for Durham; and it is desirable that the pauper should, his health permitting it, be removed to that Institution. Inquiring whether this can be legally done, and what steps should be taken in order to effect the removal.

Ans.—When a pauper lunatic is confined in a county lunatic asylum, under an order of justices, (as it is presumed is the case with the pauper alluded to in your letter,) the Board consider that the only mode by which he can be removed would be by the visiting justices of the Asylum at Hanwell making an order for the removal of the pauper, in conformity with sec. 71 of the 8 & 9 Vic. c. 126.—The Board must, however, state that this is entirely in the discretion of the justices, who probably would not act without an application from the board of guardians.

XI.—MEDICAL RELIEF.—EXTRA ALLOWANCES ORDERED BY MEDICAL OFFICERS.

21*st. Sept.*, 1850.

Clerk of the ——— Union.—Transmitting a statement prepared by the district auditor, of the cost of extras supplied to sick paupers on the orders of the medical officers of the union in the half-year ended at Lady-day, 1850, and representing that the large and increasing amount of such extras was a source of dissatisfaction to the guardians, who requested the advice of the Board in regard to the practice of the medical officers.

Ans.—It appears to the Board that the amount of the allowances referred to in the union has been unduly great, but the Board think that the remedy for this is in the hands of the guardians themselves. The medical officers are not empowered to do more than recommend that certain extra relief (such as mutton, wine, porter, &c.,) be allowed to sick persons under their care, when they may consider that such extras would tend to restore the persons to health. When the guardians entertain any doubt as to the propriety of such an allowance in any particular case, they should require the medical officer to state explicitly in writing the ground upon which he makes his recommendation, and also require the relieving-officer to make a special inquiry and report as to the circumstances of the patient, and his means of obtaining the extra nourishment independently of the guardians. If, after having considered the case, the guardians should entertain any doubt as to the propriety of allowing the extras, either on the ground of their not being really necessary, or that the patient himself has the means of obtaining them, the most expedient course would be to order the patient into the workhouse, and place him in the infirmary under the care of the medical officer of the house.

XII.—OVERSEER—GIVING ORDER FOR THE ADMISSION OF WIFE AND CHILDREN INTO THE WORKHOUSE WITHOUT THE HUSBAND.

27*th July*, 1850.

Clerk of Cirencester Union.—An overseer of one of the parishes in this union has recently granted an order to a woman, the wife of an able-bodied man (then living with her) with six or seven children, for the admission of the family into the workhouse to the exclusion of her husband, and the woman and her family are at present therein. The guardians having ascertained that at the time the order was given, the man was in full work at the ordinary wages of the country, and that the overseer was well aware of the circumstances of the whole family, directed that the cost of the maintenance of the woman and children in the workhouse should be charged to him, and that he should be apprized thereof. Inquiring, whether the guardians have any power of fixing the overseer with such cost of maintenance; and whether the auditor would be justified in disallowing the same, or surcharging the amount against any and what person; and also whether the guardians would be authorized in discharging the woman and her children from the workhouse, delivering them to the husband or to the parish of his residence. It is feared that, under the present circumstances, the husband could not be charged with having deserted his wife and children; but could he not be proceeded against as a vagrant on their again becoming chargeable by the act of the overseer or otherwise? Would the guardians be justified (the circumstances of the case remaining unaltered) in refusing to comply with another order for the admission of the woman or children, such order omitting the husband's name? Or, what would be the best mode of dealing with what appears to be an illegal proceeding?

Ans.—The law does not invest the guardians with any power to charge the costs of the relief in this case to the overseer in question; even assuming (and there seems to be strong ground for so considering) that the interference of that officer was improper. An overseer cannot lawfully give relief even in a case of destitution, unless there be circumstances showing that the necessity is sudden and urgent. None such are alleged in the present case; indeed, there is nothing to show that the parties were destitute at all. The case is one, however, to which the attention of the auditor may very properly be directed, for should it be made to appear to him that the relief was improperly given, it would be competent to him to surcharge the overseer with so much of the cost as he can be properly held to have incurred or occasioned. Upon this point, the Board must direct the attention of the guardians to Art. 90 of the General Consolidated Order, which requires that persons admitted into the workhouse upon the order (*inter alia*) of an overseer, should be brought before the guardians at the next weekly meeting, that they may decide upon the propriety of the paupers continuing in the workhouse or otherwise. Where this Article is complied with, and the guardians direct the continuance of relief, the Board do not see that the overseer could be held responsible for it, at all events after the guardians had made an order in the case. With regard to the course now to be pursued, the guardians are undoubtedly empowered, if they see fit to do so, to discharge the woman and children from the workhouse, and cause them to be delivered to the husband. The Board do not see any sufficient ground for concluding upon the statement with which you have furnished them, that the man has deserted his family, so as to render him punishable under the 4th sec. of the Vagrant Act. Whether his conduct has been such as to amount to a neglect to maintain his family within the meaning of the 3rd sec., is a point upon which the Board are not in a position, with the information before them, to express an opinion. The Board would only add, that the practical remedy (so far as the guardians are concerned) for improper interference upon the part of overseers in giving orders for relief in the workhouse, appears to the Board to be that furnished by the Article already cited, viz., that of discontinuing the relief, and calling the attention of the auditor at the audit to the charges irregularly brought upon the ratepayers.

XIII. — OFFICERS. — REDUCTION IN THE SALARIES OF PAID OFFICERS.

5*th Sept.*, 1850.

Clerk of —— Union.—Forwarding a copy of the following Resolution, passed by the guardians on the 22nd ulto:—"Resolved, that an application be made to the Poor Law Board for permission to revise the salaries of the several officers of this union, with a view to their reduction, in consequence of the reduced prices of the principal articles of food."

Ans.—The Board consider that although the price of food may be an element in fixing salaries, it is by no means of sufficient importance to render it necessary for salaries to fluctuate with every change in the price of provisions. A universal and permanent depression of prices might furnish a reason for a reduction of salaries, but such a state of things is not shown by the resolution of the guardians to exist at present, and the Board are therefore not now prepared to concur in a revision of the salaries of the officers of the union upon the ground stated by the guardians.

XIV. — PAUPERS — REFUSING TO LEAVE WORKHOUSE ON ACCOUNT OF THE WANT OF DWELLINGS.

21st Sept., 1850.

Clerk of West Firle Union.—There are two paupers in the workhouse of this union with large families who have been there a long time. There is now great complaint in the parishes to which they belong at the heavy expenses incurred by their being in the house, as work has been offered them in their parishes; but they refuse to go out, as they say they cannot anywhere get a house to live in, which is in fact the case, there being no one in either of the parishes who will let them a cottage. The paupers do not bear a very good character, and they were considerably in arrear in their rent when they went into the house. Requesting to be informed what course the guardians should adopt under the circumstances with regard to these paupers.

Ans.—If there be in fact no houses or lodging which the men can obtain sufficiently near to the place where work can be procured, or where it has been offered to them, there would appear to be no alternative but to retain them and their families in the workhouse. If, however, the guardians are satisfied that the men can obtain work at adequate wages, and dwellings at any reasonable distance from the place at which work can be procured, the Board consider that the guardians would then be justified in refusing to allow them and their families to remain in the workhouse.

XV.—POOR-RATE.—DEMAND FOR THE PAYMENT OF.

12th Sept., 1850.

Poor-rate Collector.—1. Certain owners and occupiers of property in the several parishes for which he is collector, such as overlands, furnished lodging-houses, tithes, &c., reside some miles distant and in other parishes, and there being no *bonâ fide* occupier to be found thereon, is he compelled to make a personal demand for the rate at their respective residences, or are they not required to appoint an agent to pay the rate for them; or, is not a demand through the post sufficient? 2. When payment is not made on demand, one of the enclosed notices is left with the party, a day being named for payment. On default of payment, may he not be allowed to publish a list of such defaulters on the church doors or other public place calling upon them to pay forthwith; or, would it be more advisable to summon them before the magistrates without the additional notice?

The Notice referred to above:—

Parish of TOPSHAM, May, 1850. No.

Mr.__________ I beg to inform you that your present quarter's poor-rate, at 8*d.* in the pound, is £ *s.* *d.*

Not being paid when called for, the collector will be in attendance at the vestry room, Topsham, on Thursday, the 6th of June, from 2 to 4 o'clock, for the purpose of receiving the same.

H. SOUTHCOTT, *Collector.*

Ans.—Under the 43 Eliz. c. 2, sec. 4, the poor-rate can only be levied by distress, where there has been a refusal by the party to contribute the sum assessed upon him. To constitute a refusal in any case, the Board consider there must previously have been a demand of the rate, or that which the party assessed must have understood as a demand. The Board do not say that such demand need be personal, a written notice of the amount of the rate and of its being due left at the residence of the person assessed, so that it may fairly be presumed to have reached him, would, they apprehend, be a sufficient notice. In the class of cases to which your inquiry more especially applies, in which ratepayers reside at a considerable distance from the parish where the rate is laid, the Board think that the notice might in the first instance be sent by post or otherwise to their residence. But if payment be not made in pursuance of that notice, and it should be necessary to take proceedings for the recovery of the rate, the Board think that the overseers or the collector (as the case may be) must be in a position to prove that there was a demand of such rate, and this can only be done by applying to the party himself, or at his ordinary place of abode. The justices are to be satisfied that he had means of knowledge of the claim before they can adjudge that there has been a refusal. The Board think that the collector is not entitled to put the names of those in arrear for poor-rates on the church door.

XVI.—PRISONERS.—ALLOWANCE TO INSOLVENT DEBTORS.

20th August, 1850.

Clerk of Southampton Incorporation.—Inquiring whether it falls within the province of the guardians to pay out of the poor-rates the allowance made to debtor prisoners, or whether such allowance ought to be paid out of the borough-rate by the municipal authorities. Though the borough-rate is taken from the poor-rates, and the total sum of the disbursements by the guardians, might not be reduced to that extent, yet the amount expended for out-relief, (under which head this item has been charged,) would be so much the less were it paid by the town council instead of by the guardians.

30th August, 1850.

The Poor Law Board.—Requesting the guardians to inform the Board on what ground, or under what authority the demand in question has been made upon the guardians.

31st August, 1850.

Clerk to the Guardians.—The allowance to debtor prisoners has been paid by the guardians of the poor upon the application of the keeper of the debtors' ward at the termination of each quarter, the guardians considering that under the 52nd Geo. 3, c. 160, debtor prisoners are entitled to relief not exceeding 6*d*. per diem; but as such payment has hitherto been irregular—the provisions of the aforesaid Act not having been fully complied with, inasmuch as the demand has not been made upon the application of the prisoner, but by the keepers of the debtors' ward—the guardians have determined to make no further payments until the opinion of the Poor Law Board shall have been obtained. The demand has not been made by authority, but in consequence of its having become a custom to pay such demand every quarter, the guardians being satisfied that the debtor prisoners charged for had been in jail the time specified.

11th Sept., 1850.

Ans.—As the demand in question, is made under the 52nd Geo. 3, c. 160, the Board think it right to direct the attention of the guardians of the Southampton Incorporation to the terms of that Act. The guardians will perceive that its provisions are confined to poor persons imprisoned under mesne process for debt; and that it only enables a justice of the peace, acting for the county, riding, or division, wherein any jail, not being a county jail, is situated, to order the overseers of the parish in which the jail stands to relieve such poor persons. Having regard to the provisions of the 1 & 2 Vic. c. 100, (and the subsequent Acts relating thereto,) abolishing arrest on mesne process in civil actions, except in certain cases, it is desirable that the Board should know under what circumstances the debtors, in the present instance, were imprisoned, and, as the 54th sec. of the Poor Law Amendment Act of 1834 (4 & 5 Wm. 4, c. 76) took away from the justices the power of ordering, and from the overseers the power of giving relief, except in certain cases, the Board also wish to know in what parish and county the jail alluded to in your letter is situated, and whether it is a county jail.

16th Sept., 1850.

Clerk to the Guardians.—The debtor prisoners referred to were imprisoned by order of the judge of the county court for contempt in not paying the instalments ordered. The jail is situate within the town and county of the town of Southampton, and is a borough jail.

26th Sept., 1850.

Ans.—The Board find from the statement contained in your letter, that the parties in question now in the borough jail are not imprisoned under mesne process; and, therefore, the 52nd Geo. 3, c. 160, under which the claim upon the guardians of the Southampton Incorporation in respect of maintenance is stated to be made, does not apply to the case. Even if it did so apply, the 4 & 5 Wm. 4, c. 76, sec. 54, would appear to the Board to repeal the power given to the county justices under the former statute. Upon these grounds, the Board are of opinion that the guardians are not liable to the keeper of the jail for the amount allowed to such debtor prisoners.

XVII.—RATE-BOOKS.—CUSTODY OF CLOSED RATE-BOOKS.

27th Sept., 1850.

Clerk of Northampton Union.—By an order of the Poor Law Commissioners, dated the 1st of March, 1837, the guardians of this union were directed to appoint collectors of poor-rates: one of the prescribed duties of the collectors is, "as soon as any rate-book is closed" to hand over the same to the clerk. Collectors have been appointed for the several parishes in the town of Northampton and one of the country parishes of this union. This duty of delivering over the closed rate-books of the several parishes in the town of Northampton has not until lately been complied with, the collectors retaining them for the purpose of assisting the overseers in making out the lists and producing them at the Registration Courts; but a new collector for the parishes of Saint Giles and Saint Sepulchre having been recently appointed, he, the clerk, has obtained from all the collectors all the old closed rate-books. The newly appointed collector of Saint Giles and Saint Sepulchre has applied to him for several of these closed rate-books to be delivered to him for the above-mentioned purpose; but considering that after they had been deposited with him, the clerk, in pursuance of the above-mentioned order of the Poor Law Commissioners, he ought not to give them up out of his custody, he has declined to comply with his request. This matter has been brought before the guardians, but they considering that they had no authority to direct him, the clerk, to deliver the books up, refused to make any order therein; they, however, desired him to state, that if the Poor Law Board should see fit to direct that these books should be delivered over to the churchwardens and overseers, that that part of the order directing the collectors to hand such books to the clerk should be rescinded; and that, in lieu thereof, it should be imperative on the churchwardens and overseers to see that such books were deposited and kept in the parish chests.

Ans.—The Board apprehend that the guardians cannot legally refuse to give up such rate-books to any one appointed by the vestry of the parishes to have the custody of them. In reference to the order of the Poor Law Commissioners of the 1st March, 1837, and the passage cited therefrom in your letter, the Board have to observe, that the order certainly makes it the duty of the collector of poor-rates to deliver the closed rate-books to the clerk to the guardians, who can then hold them until the parish requires them of him; an arrangement which appears to be convenient, inasmuch as the Court of Queen's Bench in the recent case of Slater & Hodgson (New Sessions Cases, vol. 2, 488) decided that the union workhouse is not an improper place for the deposit of parochial documents; still they must be producible when the exigencies of the parish require their production.

XVIII.—RATING—General instructions.

16*th July*, 1850.

Overseer of Winterbourne, Clifton Union.—Requesting the advice of the Board upon certain points connected with the rating of property to the poor-rate.

Ans.—If the existing valuation of the parish be defective or partially incorrect, the overseers in making any new rate are undoubtedly authorized by law to alter, if need be, the amounts at which particular properties now stand assessed, so as to make those amounts correspond with the present value of those properties, that is, their value to let from year to year under the circumstances mentioned in the 1st sec. of the Parochial Assessments Act (6 & 7 Wm. 4, c. 96.) Before, however, any alteration is made in any case, great care should be taken to ascertain that the circumstances justify it. The 1st sec. of the Parochial Assessments Act requires the calculation of the rateable value to be made upon an estimate of the reasonable rent of the property or subject of rating; that is, the rent at which the same may reasonably be expected to let from year to year free of tenants' rates and taxes, and subject to certain deductions. Generally speaking, the rent which is actually paid by the tenant affords a proper criterion of the value of the occupation for the purposes of the poor-rate. Where, however, the overseers have good ground for believing that the actual rent paid either exceeds the fair annual value of the property at the time the rate is made, or is less than such value, it is competent to the overseers, as the Board consider, to lower the assessment in the one case and to increase it in the other. The rule or course of proceeding, as regards estimating the rateable value by reference to the rent is thus laid down in the case of Rex *v.* Chaplin, 1 B. & Ad. 927, by Mr. Justice Taunton:—"In ascertaining what a property is worth to let, the best criterion in general is what it actually does let for." Also, by Mr. Justice Patteson:—"Where the land is not actually let, it becomes necessary to calculate what a tenant would pay for it; where it is let, the actual rent is the criterion, unless it can be clearly shown that that is too small." The Board think that these general observations will probably assist you in dealing with the subject to which your letter applies. The Board will only add, that at whatever amount an occupier is assessed in the rate, whether it exceed the rent he pays, or be below such rent, the occupier is concluded by such assessment, and the rate calculated upon it can be enforced upon him unless upon appeal he succeed in procuring an alteration of such assessment.

XIX. — RELATIONS. — LIABILITY OF FATHER UNDER 43 ELIZ. C. 2, S. 7, TO MAINTAIN HIS DAUGHTER WITH AN ILLEGITIMATE CHILD.

7th Dec., 1850.

Clerk of Bradfield Union.—R. C., aged twenty-four years, is now in the workhouse disabled from her confinement with an illegitimate child. Her father is a widower, a carpenter in constant employment, and his supposed earnings amount to about 17*s.* or 18*s.* per week. He has no other child to maintain, but refuses to assist his daughter R. C. Inquiring, whether the 43 Eliz. c. 2, sec. 7, applies to the case.

Ans.—The Board presume that during the short period immediately preceding and succeeding the delivery of her child, a woman may be considered to be an impotent person, or one not able to work, within the meaning of the 43 Eliz. c. 2, sec. 7, so that an order might be obtained upon the parent for her maintenance during that time: but, when she recovered from the confinement consequent upon her delivery, so as to be no longer unable to work, her case would not be within the above cited statute. The father of the woman would not be liable to pay any money for the maintenance of her illegitimate child.

XX.—RELIEF.—CLOTHING, &c., TO YOUNG PERSONS GOING INTO SERVICE.

10th August, 1850.

Ex-officio Guardians of ——— Union.—Referring to a letter of the Poor Law Board addressed to the guardians of the Swaffham Union, and published in the *Official Circular*, No. 31, N. S. p. 169, regarding relief in clothing to a young person in service; and inquiring whether he is right in inferring that the practice of the guardians of the ——— Union, which is to make grants, from time to time either in money or in clothing, to assist young persons in obtaining or in retaining situations is opposed to the views of the Board as set forth in that letter.

21st August, 1850.

Ans.—The ground upon which the Board refused their saction to the proposed relief [in the Swaffham case] was that the girl was already in service, and that therefore the proposed assistance to her would practically have been relief in aid of wages, which is directly contrary to a sound administration of the law. The case of children brought up in the workhouse, and going to their first place of service, is materially different; for it is manifest that, where such children are deprived of their natural protectors, unless they be assisted by the guardians at their outset in life, they might remain for years a burden upon the rates. It has therefore been the practice of the Board to sanction small grants of clothing in such cases, when the child is going to its first place of service. The Board have also in some cases sanctioned grants of clothing to other poor children on their going to their first place of service, when the circumstances of the parents seemed to call for such a course, and the remuneration the child is to receive equals the wages usually paid to young persons of the same age. But the Board never omit to recommend that great caution should be used by the guardians in making such allowances, so as not to place the children of paupers in a better position to obtain employment, than the children of independent labourers.

24th Aug., 1850.

Same writer.—Inquiring whether either in the case of children brought up in the workhouse, or of other poor children, the Board's sanction should be obtained previously to the grants of clothing being made, or whether, after their being made, in either or both cases, a report thereof should be transmitted to the Poor Law Board.

27th August, 1850.

Ans.—Before the guardians grant relief of the nature adverted to in your previous letter, it is necessary that they should report the cases, and obtain the sanction of the Board to the relief being allowed.

13th Sept., 1850.

Same writer.—Stating that the guardians of the ——— Union did not deem it right to take official cognizance of the communications which the Board had addressed to him on the subject of granting relief in clothing to young persons, as no communication thereon had been made by the Board to the guardians themselves.

21st Sept., 1850.

The Poor Law Board to the Clerk of ——— Union.—The Board have been informed that it is the practice of the Guardians of the ——— Union to make grants, either in money or in clothing, to assist the children of poor persons in obtaining or retaining situations. The Board entertain a strong opinion as to the inexpediency of permitting an expectation to prevail that the children of independent labourers are to be clothed at the expense of the poor-rates, and are by the aid of those rates to be enabled to obtain service, to the exclusion of the children of persons of a similar class whose prudence and independence of feeling prevent their resorting to the rates for such purpose. Grants of this description to children who are actually in service, are more especially objectionable, as they cannot be regarded otherwise than as relief in aid of wages, and moreover cannot lawfully be made on the ground of destitution, the child not being really destitute. In no case can the guardians lawfully make grants of clothing to the children of able-bodied poor persons without the sanction of this Board being first obtained under Art. 6. of the General Prohibitory Order. The Board will always be ready to consider any cases in which from peculiar circumstances the guardians might deem it desirable to make such grants, on the circumstance being duly reported. But it is at all times necessary that great caution should be used in sanctioning such allowances, in order not to place the recipients in a better position than the children of the independent labourer.

27th Sept., 1850.

Clerk of same Union.—The Board must have been misinformed as to the practice of the guardians. The practice has been to give grants of clothing to children of widows, or of paupers actually in receipt of relief, and to orphans on their first going to service, but in nowise afterwards. The guardians are not aware of ever having given clothing to the child of an independent labourer or poor person. No grants of money are given, it is only an outfit in clothing to the children on obtaining their first situation.

The Poor Law Board to the District Auditor.—[The Board had previously called his attention to the practice referred to in the above correspondence, and received his explanation.] Every payment from the poor-rates for a purpose of this kind, not sanctioned by the Board, is illegal and ought therefore to be disallowed by you in the account in which the item in question appears.

XXI.—REMOVABILITY.

1. RESIDENCE—ORDER OF REMOVAL MADE AND SUSPENDED, BUT NO REMOVAL TOOK PLACE.

8th April, 1850.

Clerk of Dorking Union.—Requesting the opinion of the Board as to the removability of a pauper named Elizabeth B., under the following circumstances:—"Previous to the year 1828, she gained a settlement in the parish of Brighton by hiring and service, and in that year she left Brighton and came to reside in the parish of Dorking, within this union, and remained in the last-named parish from that time, till the year 1836, without receiving any parochial relief. In the year 1836, she was taken ill, and was relieved by the parish officers of Dorking for a considerable period, and a suspended order of removal was obtained for removing her to the parish of Brighton as the place of her last legal settlement; there was no appeal against the order, and the parish officers of Brighton repaid the parish officers of Dorking the amount of maintenance expended on her under the order, and have continued to repay the relief given to her from time to time by the guardians of the Dorking Union up to the passing of the Poor Removal Act, but no removal actually took place. The parish officers of Brighton contend that inasmuch as the pauper lived five years in Dorking parish without receiving parish relief, and was not actually removed under the suspended order, that she is by the above-mentioned Act of Parliament rendered irremovable; whilst, on the other hand, the guardians of this union contend that the repayment of the relief by the parish of Brighton under the order, and subsequently thereto, amounts virtually to a removal.

Ans.—The Board consider the view taken by the parish officers of Brighton to be correct, that there having been no interruption of the residence as contemplated by the 9 & 10 Vic. c. 66, sec. 1, in the parish of Dorking, the pauper is now irremovable, and chargeable to the common fund of the Dorking Union.

2.—BREACH OF RESIDENCE.

18th Sept., 1850.

Clerk of Hexham Union.—Transmitting the following statement, duly signed under sec. 4 of the 11 & 12 Vic. c. 110, for the opinion of the Poor Law Board:—Hannah Raine, aged 48, came with her father to reside in the township of Hexham, in the Hexham Union, upwards of thirty years ago, and has continued to reside there ever since, with two exceptions, when in the Newcastle infirmary as hereinafter mentioned. She, in 1843, became chargeable to the said township of Hexham, owing to having very bad swollen legs and a discharge from one of them.

Application was then made to the overseers of the township of the High Quarter of Hexhamshire, also in the Hexham Union, the place of her settlement (her father at that time being in receipt of relief from Hexhamshire High Quarter, whilst resident in Hexham township,) to accept Hannah Raine as one of their paupers, which they did without an order of removal, and she continued to receive relief from that period from Hexhamshire High Quarter until the present time whilst residing in Hexham township. In the year 1830, she first went to the infirmary at Newcastle-upon-Tyne, about 20 miles distant from Hexham township, and in another union, her leg being then very bad, and was absent there 12 weeks. The medical men at the infirmary at first thought of amputating her leg. However, after a residence of 12 weeks in the infirmary, her leg became so much improved that she returned again to her father's house in Hexham township, and continued to reside with her father in Hexham township until 1846, when her leg became much worse than it had ever been before, and she became exceedingly ill, when another order of admission to the Newcastle infirmary was procured for her admission a second time to the infirmary, where she again went in 1846, and remained eight weeks. After the expiration of eight weeks, she was so much better, that she left the infirmary, and returned back to Hexham township to her father's house, and resided with him until his death, which took place about two years afterwards. She then commenced keeping house herself in Hexham township, in a room of her own, and she is still residing in the same township. Her relief, from its commencement in 1843, has been charged to the township of Hexhamshire High Quarter, but the overseers and guardian of that township feel dissatisfied, and think that this relief ought to be charged to the establishment, and not to their township, upon the ground of the residence in the Newcastle infirmary under the circumstances detailed, not being a breach of her residence in Hexham township; while, on the other hand, the board of guardians, in conformity with the late Poor Law Commissioners' Circular Letter of the 20th October, 1846, wherein it is stated, that any absence "such as that caused by an imprisonment or a residence in a hospital is to be treated as an interruption of the continuous residence to which the statute 9th & 10th Vic. c. 66, applies," treated this last residence in the Newcastle infirmary as a breach of residence, and that Hannah Raine was in consequence removable, and therefore they did not feel themselves justified in taking off the relief from the place of her settlement, Hexhamshire High Quarter, and charging it to the establishment. Her illness beyond all doubt is permanent, and owing to a scrofulous habit of body. If she did recover, it was her intention to return back to Hexham township to her father's residence. Question:—Is the above-named pauper, under the circumstances detailed in the foregoing statement, exempt, in pursuance of the 9 & 10 Vic. c. 66, from the liability to be removed to the place of such pauper's settlement? Or, more properly speaking, ought the guardians to charge the relief given to Hannah Raine to the establishment or to the township of the High Quarter of Hexhamshire, her place of settlement.

Ans.—From the details of the case, as before the Board, it appears to them, that after deducting the time during which the pauper was in receipt of relief, there remains a five years continuous residence in the township of Hexham, of which residence the circumstances stated in the case do not, in the opinion of the Board, legally constitute an interruption. The Board, therefore, consider that the pauper in question is now irremovable from the township of Hexham; and, consequently, that the cost of her relief is chargeable to the common fund of the Hexham Union, under the provisions of the 11 & 12 Vic. c. 110, sec. 3, continued by the Act of last session, 13 & 14 Vic. c. 101.

XXII.—SCHOOL DISTRICT.—CONTRIBUTIONS OF UNIONS TO.

17*th Sept.*, 1850.

Clerk of West London Union.—The guardians have paid to the treasurer of the board of management of the Central London School District the sum of £590, as the amount of their first contribution. Inquiring as to the mode or principle to be adopted in apportioning this sum amongst the seven parishes comprising the union.

Ans.—It will be necessary to ascertain what portion of the payment is for the common charges of the School District, and what is for the maintenance of the pauper children sent from the West London Union. The former portion should be entered in the account of the common charges of the union; and the latter allocated among the several parishes of the

union, to which, respectively, the children are chargeable. Where, however, any children maintained in the district school are chargeable to the common fund of the union, the cost of their maintenance will then be entered in the account of the common charges.

XXIII.—SETTLEMENT.

7th August, 1850.

Overseer of Llanwnda, Haverfordwest Union.—A pauper residing in the parish of St. Nicholas has been relieved by the parish of Llanwnda for upwards of ten years, upon the mistaken supposition that her father had, as servant in husbandry, gained a settlement in the latter parish; which, however, cannot be proved. Inquiring whether the parish of St. Nicholas can legally remove the pauper to the parish of Llanwnda on the ground of that parish having relieved her so long; or is the parish of St. Nicholas bound to find out her legal settlement. If that parish can remove the pauper to Llanwnda, will that parish afterwards be able to remove her to her birth settlement, since her father's settlement cannot be ascertained?

Ans.—The fact of the non-resident relief having been given to the pauper for upwards of ten years, though not conclusive in itself, will afford strong evidence of a settlement in the parish of Llanwnda, and render it necessary for the overseers of that parish to prove a settlement elsewhere. If the order of justices for the pauper's removal from St. Nicholas be made, and either be not appealed against, or be confirmed on appeal, it will conclude the parish of Llanwnda. The Board, however, wish to be informed in what manner the non-resident relief in question was given to the pauper; whether through the board of guardians of the Haverfordwest Union, or otherwise.

24th August, 1850.

Overseer of Llanwnda.—The non-resident relief in question was given to the pauper through the board of guardians of the Haverfordwest Union. The pauper's father likewise, about thirty years ago, received non-resident relief from this parish through the then overseers of the poor; the father at that time was not removed to this parish, nor at any subsequent time, and it appears that it cannot be proved that he ever gained a settlement in this parish, though the overseers at that time, from neglect of duty in enquiring into the facts of the case, did afford such relief. It appears also, that the pauper in question has been allowed non-resident relief from this parish solely upon the ground of her father having received non-resident relief, and such being considered a conclusive proof of a settlement here. It can be proved that the pauper in question was born in Fishguard parish. Will the fact of her having been born there be sufficient to gain a legal settlement in that parish, in the absence of any proof of her father having at any time gained a legal settlement in the parish of Llanwnda or elsewhere?

2nd Sept., 1850.

Ans.—The Board do not distinctly gather from your letters, whether, in the case of the pauper alluded to, an order of justices for her removal has been actually obtained by the parish of St. Nicholas. If it has, the propriety of an appeal against it by Llanwnda will mainly depend upon the nature of the evidence which that parish can adduce to rebut the strong presumption of a settlement which so long a period of non-resident relief creates in law. If the pauper's father really had no legal settlement, she will be settled in the parish of her birth, unless she has gained any other settlement for herself.

XXIV.—SICKNESS.—PAYMENT OF EXPENSES OCCASIONED BY—CHARGEABILITY.

23rd Sept., 1850.

Clerk of Wheatenhurst Union.—On Sunday, the 25th ultimo, two brothers, Nathaniel and William B., with a party of friends residing at Gloucester, had been to Stroud with a horse and light cart, to spend the day with a friend. It appears that Nathaniel drove, and on their return home at night, an altercation took place between the brothers, in consequence of Nathaniel's driving faster down the hill than appeared to be safe; and upon the horse having fallen, William alighted, followed by the other, who took a knife from his pocket to cut the reins, as he said, to release the horse, and in the scuffle William was stabbed in three places, namely, the thigh, the hand, and the abdomen, by which his intestines protruded to a very considerable extent. This happened in passing through the parish of Haresfield, in this union. The assistance of the nearest surgeon was obtained, who lived at Painswick, and W. B. was taken to the nearest house, which happened to be in the parish of Brockthrop, also in this union, occupied by one M. M. It appears that W. B. continued there until the 5th instant, when he was, by the consent of the surgeon, removed to the residence of his friends at Gloucester, who are, as well as himself, watermen, and have no other means of supporting themselves. It appears that M. M. gave up his house entirely to W. B. and his friends, who were in attendance upon him, and found all of them food during the eleven days that they remained there, and behaved in the kindest manner possible. During this time no application was made to the relieving-officer for any kind of assistance whatever, under the impression, as they were informed, that all the expenses incurred would be allowed and repaid by the county stock on the trial of the brother Nathaniel, who stands committed to answer for the offence. M. M. has, by reason of W. B. having been brought to his house, sustained a loss of £4. 15*s.* 4*d.*, which is set out and explained in the enclosed account, and has applied to the guardians for payment, under the impression that as the parties are poor, and unable to pay, that the guardians have the power to do so; inasmuch as, if an application had been made in the first place to the surgeon of the union, and to the relieving-officer, the expenses would then have been paid. The guardians have examined the account, and they have no doubt whatever but those expenses have been incurred by M. M., and if he cannot obtain it from some other source than W. B., he must inevitably lose the whole of it. The guardians, under the circumstances, are very willing to remunerate M. M. to the full extent, or in part, provided they have the sanction of the Poor Law Board for that purpose. Should the Poor Law Board give their sanction, a question may arise as to whom the payment is to be charged; that is to say, whether to Haresfield, to Brockthorp, to the common fund of this union, or to the parish in the Gloucester Union where W. B. had a fixed place of abode at the time that the accident happened.

The Account referred to above:—Four hundredweight of coals, 4*s.*; wood, 1*s.*; candles, three pounds, 1*s.* 6*d.*; maintenance of three persons in attendance, 1*s.* per day and night each, £1. 13*s.*; damage done to the bed, 12*s.*; washing, 4*s.*; loss of time, eleven days, at 2*s.* 6*d.* per day, £1. 7*s.* 6*d.*; wife's loss of time, 8*d.* per day, 7*s.* 4*d.*; injury to under blanket, 3*s.*; loss of lodger's payment for two weeks, 1*s.* per week, 2*s.*; total, £4. 15*s.* 4*d.*

Ans.—The Board think the guardians, under the provisions of the 11 & 12 Vic. c. 110, sec. 2, might pay for the assistance rendered to W. B. by M. M., if W. B. can be regarded as a "poor person," within the meaning of the statute; and it seems to the Board, upon the statement before them, that he may be so regarded. Some of the charges, however, appear to be such as ought not to be allowed; for instance, that for the attendance of three persons daily on the sick man; indeed, the guardians ought not to pay any portion which does not appear, upon a fair and reasonable view of the case to have been necessarily incurred. As regards the fund liable for such expenses, assuming that the guardians pay the demand, or any portion of it, the Board do not see that the parish of W. B.'s abode can be called upon, because the relief would not have been given by "lawful authority." (See first part of sec. 2.) Then, as between Brockthorp, where the man lay sick, and the Wheatenhurst Union, which includes that parish, the question which arises is, Where would the cost of the ordinary relief of this man have been chargeable? And that again depends upon the fact as to whether or not the accident or sickness would have produced permanent disability. If it would, the parish will be liable; if it would not, the common fund of the union must bear the charge. The guardians will see, on referring to sec. 2 of the above-cited statute, that the payments made by the guardians, in respect of assistance afforded to persons meeting with accidents, &c., are to be charged in the accounts in the same way as relief (if given to such persons) would have been charged.

XXV.—WORKHOUSE.

1. DUTY OF MASTER UNDER AN ORDER OF ADMISSION, WHEN PART OF THOSE NAMED IN THE ORDER APPLY UNDER IT.

20th July, 1850.

Clerk of Shepton-Mallett Union.—A widow, named Susan Burr, of Ashwick, in this union, obtained an order of admission to the workhouse from the relieving-officer, for herself and five children. Four of the children were brought to the workhouse by a woman, (not by the mother, who refused to come,) and were admitted by the master. Inquiring whether the master was justified in receiving only a part of the family.

Ans.—It is the duty of the relieving-officer, under certain circumstances to give orders of admission into the workhouse, and it is the duty of the master strictly to act upon such orders when he is in a position to do so. If the whole of the persons named in the order apply to the master for admission, he is, of course, able to comply with the exact terms of the order; but if a portion only of the persons named apply to him, he cannot necessarily fully obey the terms of the order, and must therefore either act upon it in part or decline to act upon it altogether. The Board consider that, under such circumstances, the master is legally justified in treating the order as distributive, and in admitting to the workhouse any person specified in the order who produces it and applies for admission under its authority. The Board are sensible of the inconvenient and mischievous consequences which would result from the creation of the belief that the head of a family might be allowed to send his wife and children into the workhouse whilst he remained out of it; and although the master would in the case supposed be legally justified in admitting any portion or member of a family without the head of it, the Board consider that he would exercise a sound discretion in declining to do so, unless the person or persons applying to him were obviously in a state of destitution. In the present case, the fact that Susan Burr did not avail herself of the order of admission is *primâ facie* evidence that she was not destitute of the means of support; and unless her children when brought to the workhouse showed evident symptoms of want and privation, the Board think that the master, although legally authorised to pursue the course he did, might not improperly have declined to receive the children until he had specially reported the case to the guardians. The head of the family, whether man or widow, is responsible for its maintenance, and in the event of either attempting to evade an order of admission, and to throw upon the rates the maintenance of his or her children, it would be open to the guardians to prosecute such person for the abandonment of his or her children, under the legal powers vested in them for that purpose.

2. ORDERS FOR ADMISSION INTO WORKHOUSE—CONSTRUCTION OF ARTS. 88 & 89 OF THE CONSOLIDATED ORDER.

7th Sept., 1850.

Clerk of Aylesbury Union.—Art. 89 of the General Consolidated Order states, that no pauper shall be admitted under any written or printed order, as mentioned in Art. 88, if the order bears date more than six days before the pauper presents it at the workhouse. Query—Would an order given on Sunday expire on the following Friday? and if so, would the master of the workhouse be justified in refusing to admit, after the hour fixed by the guardians for the admission of paupers, (5 o'clock P.M.,) or must he continue to admit until the time fixed for receiving the keys from the porter, at 9 o'clock P.M.? The inquiry applies only to able-bodied paupers, and not to the sick, who, in urgent cases, would, as now, be admitted at all hours.

Ans.—The Board think that an order of admission to the workhouse, given on Sunday, would be available on the Friday following, but not afterwards. Such an order, if presented on the latter day, would not, in the words of the Art., bear date more than six days before the day on which it is presented. With regard to the hour at which an able-bodied pauper, having an order of admission, should be received, the Board certainly think that the master would not be justified, by the regulations now in force, in refusing admittance after 5 P.M. The Board apprehend that, in ordinary cases, the applicant must be admitted until the porter, by delivering the keys to the master, closes the house for the night; and after that hour, in cases of sickness, or peculiar urgency, though, doubtless, these will be of rare occurrence.

AN

OFFICIAL CIRCULAR

OF PUBLIC DOCUMENTS AND INFORMATION:

DIRECTED BY THE POOR LAW BOARD TO BE PRINTED, CHIEFLY FOR THE USE OF THE BOARDS OF GUARDIANS AND THEIR OFFICERS.

Nos. 42 & 43.] OCTOBER AND NOVEMBER, 1850. [N.S.

CONTENTS.

I.—STATUTES OF 13 & 14 VIC., RELATING TO THE RELIEF OF THE POOR.

1. CIRCULAR LETTER TO BOARDS OF GUARDIANS.

Poor Law Board, Somerset House.
7th November, 1850.

Sir,—I am directed by the Poor Law Board to lay before the Guardians the substance of the statutes passed in the late session of Parliament, which refer to the general administration of the relief of the poor, the duties of the guardians, and the management of certain parochial affairs.

These statutes are the 13 & 14 Vic. cc. 11, 50, 53, 57, 99, & 101. It will be most convenient to consider cc. 11 & 101, in the first place.

The 13 & 14 Vic. c. 11, contains a provision to meet an inconvenience which had arisen in determining the proper averages in school districts, according to which the respective Unions and Parishes combined therein are to contribute to the common charges of such district. By the 7 & 8 Vic. c. 101, s. 47, a mode of contribution was prescribed which refers to the last declared averages of the several Unions combined. But as these averages may have been declared at different dates, it is obvious that the reference to such declarations may operate unfairly. In the case where a parish is combined with Unions whose averages have been declared in different years, the mode wholly fails. The present statute, therefore, provides a different rule of calculation, and enables the Poor Law Board to ascertain the average annual expenditure on account of the relief of the poor in every Union or Parish forming an integral part of the district, up to the same day, and to issue their order to declare the average so ascertained. The averages which shall be declared under this provision are made applicable to all accounts not closed and audited at the time when the Act passed, which was on the 17th of May, 1850.

The Poor Law Board are also empowered, from time to time, when it shall seem requisite, to declare fresh averages, to be ascertained in the same manner.

The 13 & 14 Vic. c. 101, contains various provisions which affect the Guardians.

Sec. 1 continues the statutes 11 & 12 Vic. c. 110, and 12 & 13 Vic. c. 103, so as to render the common fund of each Union liable to the charge of the relief of the irremovable poor and destitute wayfarers and wanderers for another year, that is, until the 30th day of September, 1851, and to the end of the then next session of Parliament. The provisions of these statutes in this respect are extended to the present incorporated hundreds of Norfolk and Suffolk.

To obviate, to some extent, the inconvenience which has been felt in many Unions in regard to the burial of paupers who die in the workhouse, in consequence of the overcrowding of the burial-ground of the parish wherein it is situated, the Guardians are now authorized by sec. 2 of the statute to contribute out of their funds such sum of money as the Poor Law Board shall approve, either towards the enlargement of any churchyard or consecrated public burial-ground, in the parish where the workhouse is situate, or in any other parish in the Union, or towards the procuring one in any parish in the Union. Where any burial-ground shall have been enlarged or obtained with the aid of such contribution, the Guardians may bury the dead body of any pauper dying in the workhouse in such burial-ground, provided, however, that the request of the deceased, or his wife, or next of kin, as to the burial taking place elsewhere, be duly regarded. It is also provided, that the fees payable by the custom of the parish in cases of burial, shall be paid by the Guardians where they so direct the burial.

The 3rd sec. applies to school districts, though its operation is confined to the Metropolis and its neighbourhood. It has been found in those districts which have been formed in or near the Metropolis, that owing to the great value of property, the limit of expenditure in the procuring and erecting of the school, imposed by the 7 & 8 Vic. c. 101, s. 44, has caused some difficulty to the Boards of Management. Accordingly this clause enacts, that in addition to the sum which may be raised or borrowed under the former Act, for the purpose of providing a building, each Board of Management may raise or borrow such further sum or sums as may be necessary to purchase land as a site for the school, or for the training of the children maintained there, or for the site of any addition to the school.

Sec. 4 enables Boards of Guardians to expend money in and about the emigration of poor children under the age of sixteen, being orphans or deserted, who have no settlements, or whose settlements are unknown, and to charge the cost to the parish to which they are chargeable, or to the common fund, if they be chargeable thereto. In the former case, the consent of the Guardians of the parish to the expenditure will be necessary, and the conditions required in other emigration must be duly attended to in each.

It will be seen that the Legislature have thought it right to require that special protection should be afforded to persons of these tender years, who are deprived of their natural guardians; and it is therefore provided that the emigration of no orphan or deserted child shall take place, under any of the provisions applicable to this subject, until such child shall have consented thereto before the justices at their petty sessions, and a certificate of such consent, under the hands of two justices, shall have been transmitted to the Poor Law Board. This emigration cannot take place at the cost of the poor-rate, without the order of the Poor Law Board sanctioning and authorising such emigration being first obtained; and the Board take this opportunity of reminding the Guardians, and requesting them to make known the same to their officers, and, as far as possible, to the Overseers of the parishes in the Union, that in *no case* can the emigration of poor persons, whether in the receipt of relief or not, be conducted by them unless the order of this Board *precede* it, nor unless the conditions prescribed by their order be strictly observed. The Board feel it necessary to impress this upon the Guardians and their officers, in consequence of so many cases having lately come under the notice of the Board in which, by reason of this legal provision having been neglected, Auditors have been compelled to disallow money expended by Guardians or their officers in the emigration of poor persons.

The 5th sec. will enable the Guardians or Overseers to obtain an order of justices upon the husband of a lunatic woman confined in an asylum, for or towards the payment of the cost of her maintenance in the asylum.

The inconvenience resulting from the Master of the Workhouse or Relieving Officer being appointed to fill some parochial office, is removed by the 6th sec., which it will be seen disqualifies each of them for holding the office of Overseer, Constable, or other parochial office, though it enables the Relieving Officer, with the authority of the Poor Law Board, to hold a *paid* office in a parish.

The 7th sec. authorises the fee or remuneration settled by the justices in quarter sessions for giving notice of the special sessions for hearing appeals, under the 6 & 7 Wm. 4. c. 96, to be paid by the Overseers out of the poor-rate. By this express provision for the case, a question which has created much dissatisfaction is settled.

The Guardians are aware of the provisions of the 55 Geo. 3. c. 137, s. 2, and the 7 & 8 Vic. c. 101, s. 58, relating to the punishment of persons deserting from the workhouse, and carrying with them clothes or other goods, being the property of the Union or Parish, whereby upon conviction they may be sentenced to imprisonment for a limited period. The 8th sec. of the present statute empowers the justices to adjudge any such person to be kept to hard labour. The 9th sec. subjects persons assaulting the officers of the workhouse, or the Relieving Officers, in the discharge of their duty, to the same punishment as in the case of assaults upon peace officers, and gives power to the justices to make the like order as to the costs and expenses of the prosecution.

The 10th sec., which is the last practical enactment, applies to the collection of county, borough, or police rates in parishes which are situated partly within and partly without boroughs, and authorises the employment of the ordinary collector in the parish to collect such rates, provides for his payment, and gives some additional powers for the collection of those rates.

Adverting now to the other statutes, it is necessary to observe, that by the 13 & 14 Vic. c. 50, the Act (3 & 4 Vic. c. 89) which exempts the inhabitants of parishes from liability to be rated as such to the relief of the poor in respect of *stock in trade* and other property, is continued till the 1st October, 1851, and to the end of the then next session of Parliament.

The 13 & 14 Vic. c. 53, is the Act which provides for the taking of the Census in next year. It contains various regulations for the appointment of the Enumerators and the collection of the accounts of the numbers of persons, which do not affect the Guardians. It is, however, provided, that the allowances to the officers employed in the discharge of the duties required of them, shall be paid, in the first instance, by the Guardians of Unions and Parishes, or by the Overseers of parishes, not under Boards of Guardians, who will afterwards be reimbursed by the Treasury.

The day appointed for the numbering of the population of the kingdom is the 31st of March, and the Guardians and Overseers will not be called upon to make any payment until the following months. In the meantime some arrangements will probably be entered into as to the mode by which the repayment to the Guardians shall be effected, and the Board may have occasion to address the Guardians hereafter on the subject.

The two other statutes to be noticed do not indeed relate directly to the guardians, but they contain provisions of great importance, to which it is desirable the attention of the Guardians should be directed, and the knowledge of which should be circulated by them among the parishes within their Union, as far as their opportunities will permit.

The first is the 13 & 14 Vic. c. 57, which enables any parish, the population of which exceeds 2,000, to procure a proper place in which its Vestry meetings may be held, instead of the church or vestry-room where they are now held, and also to appoint a vestry clerk as a permanent officer, to perform, in that capacity, the business of the parish, and to pay him a salary out of the poor-rate. The Guardians will, doubtless, remember the difficulties which have often been felt in respect of both these matters. No public fund existed out of which a vestry-room could be provided, and no legal authority for charging the salary or other remuneration of a vestry clerk upon the poor-rate or other parochial rate.

The statute now referred to enables the Poor Law Board, upon the application of the Churchwardens, made pursuant to a resolution of the vestry of a parish, whose population exceeds 2,000, to order either a portion or the whole of that Act to be put in force within it. If the order of the Board apply to the former of these objects, then after the order has been issued twelve months, (so that the parish shall have had time to provide another vestry-room,) the holding of a vestry meeting in the church of the parish, and except under particular circumstances in the vestry-room attached to it, is declared to be illegal.. Authority is given to the parish officers to procure the necessary accommodation, and with the order of the Poor Law Board, and the sanction of the Vestry, to borrow money to pay the cost of the erection of the building, to be repaid by annual instalments not exceeding *ten*.

The statute also enables the parish to apply to the Poor Law Board for an order to appoint a Vestry Clerk, whose salary and the security to be given by him, when required, are to be settled by the Poor Law Board. When the order for this purpose has been issued, the Vestry are to elect the person to fill the office, which he will continue to hold until he resigns, or until the Vestry, (with the consent of the Poor Law Board,) or the Poor Law Board at their own discretion, shall remove him. So long, therefore, as the parish requires the services of such an officer, and he conducts himself well, his tenure of office will be secure. The statute contains a full enumeration of the duties to be performed by this officer, though it will be competent for the parish to dispense with some of them, and for the Poor Law Board to add others.

A legal provision having thus been made for the appointment of an officer, (whose utility in many populous parishes cannot be denied,) the Board recommend the Guardians to use their endeavours to have the irregular appointments, which have for a long time prevailed in many places, determined, and legal and valid appointments made in their place. The Board desire to inform the Guardians that they have deemed it right to direct the attention of the District Auditor to this part of the statute, with the object of enforcing this last observation.

The other Act, 13 & 14 Vic. c. 99, relates to the subject of the poor-rate. It deals with the important subject of the rating small tenements, which has been frequently brought under the attention of all parties engaged in administration of the laws for the relief of the poor. The difficulties of collecting the parochial rates from the actual occupants of such property have long been felt and acknowledged. The 59 Geo. 3, c. 12, s. 19, as the Guardians are aware, provided for rating the owners of a certain class of small tenements—namely, those the yearly rent of which was between £6 and £20. The present Act enables the Vestry, if they think proper to do so, to assess the owners instead of the occupiers of all tenements in a parish the annual value of which does not exceed £6. The adoption of the Act, however, is entirely optional with the Vestry.

If the Vestry in any parish, after due notice, agree to assess the owners of such property instead of the occupiers, and make an order accordingly, then the former are to be henceforth assessed to the poor and highway-rates so long as the order of the Vestry shall remain in force. A power is however given to a majority of two-thirds at least of a meeting of the Vestry to rescind the order after it has been in force for three years. The assessment upon the owner is to be upon a reduced scale, inasmuch as he is to be assessed upon three-fourths of the annual value of the property; but a provision is contained in the Act which will enable the owner of any particular property to make within 14 days after Lady-day, a composition for a year in respect of the premises, whether they may be occupied or not, under which composition he may have a deduction made not exceeding one-half. The like remedy is given for the recovery of the rate from the owner as exists against the occupier in ordinary cases, and the latter will be held responsible for the rate if the owner makes default. At the same time it is to be observed that the statute enables the occupier to recover from his landlord the amount of the rate paid by the former, for which the latter is rendered liable by this statute.

If the owner be assessed he may appeal against the rate, and he will have the same right of voting in the Vestry as the occupier of the tenement would have had, had the rate been imposed on him.

The statute contains some other provisions which need not be specified in this letter.

The Board have reason to believe from the information which they have received, that the Act has already been received with approbation in the country, and is in the course of being adopted in numerous parishes.

The Guardians will, doubtless, perceive that the Act will have an important effect with reference to the cases which constantly come under their notice, of the application of poor persons to be excused from the payment of their rates on the ground of poverty. Where, in any parish, such applications are numerous, the proper remedy will be afforded by this statute. The indiscriminate excusal of long lists of poor persons from the payment of rates has generally had a demoralizing effect upon the poorer classes, by habituating them to the receipt of relief, granted, in the first place, under the equivocal form of exemption from a payment which, by law, they ought to make.

The Board, in conclusion, have to state that it will probably be found necessary that the Poor Law Commissioners' General Order of Accounts, which prescribes the form in which the poor-rate is to be drawn up, should be modified to meet the provisions of this statute. The Board, therefore, have this matter at present under their consideration.

I am, Sir, your obedient Servant,

W. G. LUMLEY,

Assistant Secretary.

To

The Clerk to the Board of Guardians.

2. AN ACT TO MAKE BETTER PROVISION FOR THE CONTRIBUTIONS OF UNIONS AND PARISHES IN SCHOOL DISTRICTS TO THE COMMON FUNDS OF THE RESPECTIVE DISTRICTS—13 VIC. C. 11. *Passed 17th May*, 1850.

7 & 8 *Vic. c.* 101. 11 & 12 *Vic. c.* 82. 7 & 8 *Vic. c.* 101, *s.* 47. *Repeal of* 7 & 8 *Vic. c.* 101, *s.* 47, *in part.*

1. Whereas by an Act passed in the Eighth Year of Her Majesty, intituled *An Act for the further Amendment of the Laws relating to the Poor in* England, and by the Act passed in the Twelfth Year of the Reign of Her Majesty, intituled *An Act to amend the Law for the Formation of Districts for the Education of Infant Poor*, provisions are made for the formation of school districts for the management of certain infant poor by the combination of unions and parishes into such districts: And whereas it is by the said first-recited statute enacted, "that the expenses incurred by any district board in the purchase or hire of any building or buildings to be used as a school, or in erecting, repairing, adding to, or fitting up any building, and in the purchase of utensils and materials for the employment of the inmates of such school, or of books and other objects and things necessary for the instruction of such inmates, and the salaries of the officers and servants of the establishment, and all other expenses incurred on the common account of the parishes or unions, or parishes and unions, so united for the management of any class of infant poor, or incidental to the discharge of the duties of such district board, shall be paid by such unions in the proportion of the averages last declared for every such union, and by such parishes in the proportion of the average expenditure of every such parish for the like period and purposes as those to which the declared averages of such unions shall relate: and the said Commissioners shall from time to time, by Order under their hands and seal, ascertain and declare the proportion and rates of contribution in the above respects of every such parish and union:" And whereas such provision for the contributions of the several unions and parishes in such districts is inconvenient, and it is desirable that the same should be repealed, and other provisions should be enacted for the purpose aforesaid: Be it therefore enacted by the Queen's Most Excellent Majesty, by and with the advice and con-

sent of the Lords Spiritual and Temporal, and Commons in this present Parliament assembled, and by the authority of the same, that after the passing of this Act, so much of the said Act of the Eighth Year of Her Majesty as is herein-before recited, providing for the contribution of the unions and parishes comprised in any such school district, shall be and the same is hereby repealed.

The Mode in which the Averages of Unions and Parishes combined in School Districts shall be ascertained and declared.

2. And be it enacted, That in respect of any district heretofore formed, or hereafter to be formed, under the provisions of the statutes aforesaid, the Poor Law Board shall cause an inquiry to be made as to the average annual expense incurred by, or on account of, the relief of the poor in every union and parish forming an integral part of such district during the three years ending on the twenty-fifth day of *March* next, before the date of the formation of such district, such expense to include the cost of the relief of the poor belonging to the parish; or, in the case of a union, the cost of the relief of the poor belonging to the several parishes thereof, and of those chargeable upon the common fund thereof; and in each case the payment of the salaries of all officers engaged in the administration of the relief of the poor, and other like expenses of current and ordinary nature; and the said Board shall, by an Order, declare the respective averages so ascertained, and after the issue of such Order the several unions and parishes comprised in any such district shall contribute to the several charges set forth in the clause herein-before cited from the said first-mentioned statute according to the proportion of the averages declared in such Order until the same shall be altered by any subsequent Order of the said Board.

Provision for the Declaration of fresh Averages.

3. And be it enacted, That the said Poor Law Board, from time to time, whenever it shall seem proper to them to do so, may cause a fresh inquiry to be made in manner aforesaid, in respect of any such district, as to the expense of the unions and parishes therein for the three years ending on the Twenty-fifth day of *March* next preceding such inquiry, and declare by their Order the averages ascertained by such inquiry, and thereupon the contributions of the several unions and parishes in such district to the charges aforesaid shall be calculated according to the averages so last declared.

Provision for the Case of the Addition of a Parish or Union to an existing District.

4. And be it enacted, That when any union or parish shall be added to any previously formed district the said Board shall cause the average expense of such union or parish corresponding with the period for which the averages of such district shall have been last ascertained and declared as aforesaid.

Accounts in any such District not closed and audited, to be settled according to Provisions of this Act.

5. And be it enacted, That in respect of any District heretofore formed, all charges and expenses which shall not have been closed and audited at the passing of this Act, and to which the said clause of the said first-recited statute would have applied, shall be estimated and settled according to the proportions of the averages to be declared according to the provisions of this Act.

Interpretation of Terms.

6. And be it enacted, That the several words used in this Act shall be construed in the manner prescribed by the said recited statute of the Eighth Year of the reign of Her Majesty, and the statutes explaining and extending it; and that every provision of the said several statutes not repealed shall extend to this Act, except where any such provision would be inconsistent with anything herein contained.

Act may be amended, &c.

7. And be it enacted, That this Act may be amended or repealed by any Act to be passed in this present Session of Parliament.

---

3. AN ACT TO AMEND AN ACT OF THE FIFTH AND SIXTH YEARS OF HER PRESENT MAJESTY FOR THE APPOINTMENT AND PAYMENT OF PARISH CONSTABLES—13 VIC. C. 20. *Passed 10th June,* 1850.

5 & 6 *Vic.* c. 109. *Provision in case of Discharge of Parish Constables.*

1. Whereas an Act for the Appointment and Payment of Parish Constables was passed in the Fifth and Sixth Years of Her present Majesty, and

it is desirable to amend the same: Be it therefore enacted by the Queen's Most Excellent Majesty, by and with the advice and consent of the Lords Spiritual and Temporal, and Commons, in this present Parliament assembled, and by the authority of the same, that the provisions in the said recited Act made in case of vacancy by death or disqualification of any constable during his year of office shall be extended to the discharge of any constable which shall take place under the powers of the said recited Act.

Fees and Allowances.

2. And whereas it is by the said recited Act enacted, that certain fees and allowances, to be settled by justices in general or quarter sessions assembled, shall be paid to constables for the service of summonses and execution of warrants: Be it enacted, That the said fees and allowances so settled by the justices in general or quarter sessions, and approved by a Secretary of State, as in the said recited Act is required, shall in like manner be paid to the said constables for the execution of any order of a justice made in writing, or for the performance of any occasional duties, the same being sanctioned and allowed by justices in petty session assembled.

Justices to fill up Vacancies, in the Case of Death, Resignation, &c., of paid Constables.

3. And be it enacted, That in case of the death or resignation or dismissal for misconduct of any paid constable at any time, it shall be lawful for the justices of the division in petty sessions assembled forthwith to appoint another paid constable, from and out of the list of constables allowed by the said justices at the special sessions last holden for the appointment of constables, at the same rate of salary as has been agreed by the vestry in the manner required by the said recited Act to be given to paid constables.

Notices for holding Special Sessions for Appointment of Constables to be given by Clerks.

4. And whereas it is by the said recited Act enacted, That due notice shall be given to justices to hold special sessions for the appointment of parochial constables, but it is not stated by whom such notice shall be given: Be it enacted, That such notice shall be given by the clerk or clerks to the said justices.

All Persons employed by Post Office exempt from serving as Constables.

5. And whereas it is by the said recited Act enacted, That certain persons therein named shall be freed and exempt from serving the office of constable under the said Act: Be it enacted, That the said exemption shall extend to all postmasters and persons employed in the business of the post office.

5 & 6 Vic. c. 109, s. 23, as to Appointment of Constable to take charge of Lock-up Houses, repealed. Superintendents of Constables to be appointed. When Lock-up Houses are provided Justices to appoint Constables to take charge of the same. Notice for the appointment, &c., of Constables to be given by the Clerk.

6. And whereas it is by the said recited Act enacted, That whenever the justices shall have provided a lock-up house under this Act they shall also appoint a superintending constable to have the charge thereof, who shall have all the powers and immunities of a parish constable under this Act, and shall have the superintendence of all the parish constables appointed in such parishes as shall be ordered by the said justices, and under such regulations as they shall make, and every such superintending constable shall be entitled to hold his office until dismissed by the justices in general or quarter session assembled, and shall receive such salary out of the county-rates as the justices assembled as aforesaid shall order; and it is expedient that the said enactment should be repealed, and other provisions made in lieu thereof: Be it enacted, That the said enactment shall be repealed; and it shall be lawful for the justices of the peace of any county in general or quarter session assembled to appoint a superintending constable for each or any petty sessional division within the said county, who shall have all the powers and immunities of a parish constable under the said recited Act, and shall have the superintendence of all the parish constables appointed in such parishes as shall be ordered by the said justices, and under such regulations as they shall make, and shall perform such duties as the said justices shall require of him; and whenever the justices assembled as aforesaid shall have provided a lock-up house under the said recited Act, they shall also appoint a constable to have the charge thereof, who shall also have all the powers and immunities of a parish constable under the said recited Act; and every superintending constable, and constable so appointed to the charge of a lock-up house, shall be entitled to hold his office until dismissed by the justices in general or quarter sessions assembled, and shall receive such salary and allowances out of the

county-rates as the justices assembled as aforesaid shall order: Provided always, that notice of the day at which any business relating to the appointment or dismissal, or to the fixing or ordering of the salary and allowances, of any such constable shall begin at such general or quarter session shall be given by the clerk of the peace.

Act not to apply to the City of London, the Metropolitan Police District, or any Borough or Place within the Provisions of 5 *&* 6 *Wm.* 4, *c.* 76, *and* 3 *&* 4 *Wm.* 4, *c.* 90.

7. And be it enacted, That nothing herein contained shall be taken to prevent the appointment of special constables, or to apply to the City of *London*, or the Metropolitan Police District, or to any borough which is within the provisions of an Act passed in the Sixth Year of the Reign of His late Majesty, intituled *An Act to provide for the Regulation of Municipal Corporations in* England *and* Wales, or of any charter granted in pursuance of that Act or of any Act made for the amendment thereof, or to any parish, town, or place in which rates are or shall be levied for the payment of constables under the provisions of an Act passed in the Fourth Year of the Reign of His late Majesty, making provision for the lighting and watching of parishes in *England* and *Wales*, or of any Local Act specially applying to such Parish, town, or place; and that nothing herein-before contained shall be taken to apply to the County Palatine of *Chester*.

Exempting Metropolitan Police District from Payments under this or the recited Act.

8. And for the purposes of exempting the Metropolitan Police District as herein-before provided, be it enacted, That the justices in general or quarter sessions assembled shall in each year, at the time of making up their accounts for the year, ascertain what proportion any expenses that have been incurred during the preceding year under this or the said recited Act shall bear to the gross amount of the county-rate expended within the same period, and also what proportion of the said county-rate has been levied within the Metropolitan Police District, and shall repay to each parish within the said Metropolitan Police District such proportion of the sums so levied as they shall ascertain to be a like proportion of the sums expended under this Act out of the county-rate.

Act may be amended, &c.

9. And be it enacted, That this Act may be amended or repealed by any Act to be passed in this Session of Parliament.

---

4. AN ACT TO PREVENT THE HOLDING OF VESTRY OR OTHER MEETINGS IN CHURCHES, AND FOR REGULATING THE APPOINTMENT OF VESTRY CLERKS—13 & 14 VIC. C. 57. *Passed 5th August*, 1850.

Poor Law Commissioners, upon Application of Churchwardens, &c., of any Parish where Population exceeds 2,000, *may make an Order to put this Act in force.*

1. Whereas the holding of vestry or other parochial meetings in the parish church or chapel, or in the vestry-room attached to such church or chapel, is productive of scandal to religion and other great inconveniences: for remedy thereof be it enacted by the Queen's Most Excellent Majesty, by and with the advice and consent of the Lords Spiritual and Temporal, and Commons, in this present Parliament assembled, and by the authority of the same, That it shall be lawful for the Commissioners for administering the laws for relief of the poor in *England*, at any time or times after the passing of this Act, upon application in writing of the churchwardens, or, where there are no churchwardens, of the overseers of any parish in *England* the population whereof exceeds two thousand persons according to the then last preceding census, such application being made pursuant to a resolution of the vestry of such parish, to make an order under their seal of office that this Act or any part thereof shall be applied to and be put in force within such parish; and a copy of such order shall be published in such newspaper or gazette, or both, as the said Commissioners may direct, and shall be deposited with the churchwardens or overseers (where there are no churchwardens) of any such parish.

On Expiration of 12 *Months from the publishing of any such Order certain Meetings prohibited from being held in Churches and Chapels.*

2. And be it enacted, That from and after the expiration of twelve calendar months from the making and publishing of any such order no meeting of the inhabitants of the parish for the purpose of holding a vestry, or for any

other purpose than that of divine worship, or some ecclesiastical or charitable object, or some other purpose approved by the bishop of the diocese, shall be holden in any parish church or chapel, or other consecrated church or chapel, nor in the chancel thereof, nor, except in case of urgency, and with the previous approval of the said Commissioners, in the vestry-room attached to such church or chapel, in any parish or place named in such order, any public or private Act of Parliament to the contrary notwithstanding.

Power to provide other Places of Meeting.

3. And be it enacted, That where any vestry or other meeting, by virtue of any statute, law, or custom, has heretofore been holden in the church or chapel of any parish or place named in any such order as aforesaid, or in the vestry-room of such church or chapel, any such vestry or other meeting shall from and after the making and publishing of such order be holden in such other room or place within the parish or place as shall be provided for the holding thereof in pursuance of the provisions of this Act, and all acts done in such other room or place as aforesaid shall be as good, valid, and effectual in the law, to all intents and purposes whatsoever, as if such vestry meeting had been held in the vestry-room of such church or chapel or in the body of such church or chapel as aforesaid.

Power to purchase Lands, &c., under 8 & 9 Vic. c. 18.

4. And be it enacted, That the churchwardens and overseers, or overseers alone, as the case may require, of any parish, with the sanction of the said Commissioners and of a majority of the vestry, may by agreement hire any room, or purchase or take upon lease or exchange any lands or buildings, or sell lands belonging to such parish, and invest the proceeds of such sale in the purchase of other lands and buildings, or erect suitable buildings, for the purpose of holding of any vestry and other meeting for the transaction of any business of or relating to the parish; and the Lands Clauses Consolidation Act, 1845, except the parts and enactments of that Act with respect to the purchase and taking of lands otherwise than by agreement, and with respect to the recovery of forfeitures, penalties and costs, and with respect to lands acquired by the promoters of the undertaking, but which shall not be wanted for the purpose thereof, shall, in so far as the same is consistent with this Act, be incorporated with this Act; and for the purposes of this Act the expressions "the promoters of the undertaking," or "the secretary," whenever used in that Act, shall respectively mean the churchwardens and overseers, or overseers as aforesaid: and the expression "tolls or rates," whenever used in the said first-mentioned Act, shall mean monies to be raised for the relief of the poor mentioned in this Act; and all lands and premises which shall be so purchased or taken on lease by the churchwardens and overseers, or overseers as aforesaid, of any parish shall be conveyed, demised, and assured to such churchwardens and overseers, or overseers alone as aforesaid, and their successors, in trust for the purposes of this Act, and shall be accepted, taken, and held by them as a body corporate, and the yearly rent reserved by any lease shall be chargeable upon and paid out of the monies to be raised for the relief of the poor of any such parish, and shall be paid by the churchwardens and overseers, or overseers as aforesaid, of such parish as such rent becomes payable; and if at any time any such rent be not paid within thirty days after it so becomes payable, and after demand thereof in writing, the person to whom any such rent shall be payable may either recover the same from the said churchwardens and overseers, or overseers as aforesaid, with costs of suit, by action of debt in any court of law, or may levy the same by distress of the goods and chattels of any of the said churchwardens and overseers, or overseers as aforesaid.

Poor Law Commissioners, on Receipt of a Resolution of the Vestry, authorised to require Money to be borrowed for the Purposes of the Act.

5. And be it enacted, That it shall be lawful for the Poor Law Commissioners, by an Order under their hands and seal, upon the receipt of a copy under the hands of the said churchwardens, or, where there are no churchwardens, of the overseers of any parish, of a resolution passed at a vestry duly convened and held for the purpose, after public notice of the time and place and purpose of holding such vestry shall have been given in like manner as notices of vestry meetings are published and given, consenting to the issue of such Order, to direct the churchwardens and overseers, or, where there

are no churchwardens, the overseers, and such churchwardens and overseers, as the case may be, are hereby required, if so directed by such Order and Resolution as aforesaid, to borrow any sum of money which may be required for the purposes of this Act, and to charge the poor-rates of the said parish with the repayment of the sum borrowed for such purpose and the interest thereof, so nevertheless that the sum so borrowed shall be repaid by equal annual instalments not exceeding ten.

Churchwardens, &c., within One Month after Publication of Order to convene a Meeting for electing a Vestry Clerk. Vestry Clerk elected at such Meeting not to be removable except by resolution of Vestry and Consent of Poor Law Board, &c.

6. And whereas in parishes whereof the population exceeds two thousand persons as aforesaid various duties are by law imposed upon and required to be performed by the officers of parishes, and much business is transacted at vestry meetings, and the parish officers and vestries require the assistance of a vestry clerk in respect of such duties and business; and it is expedient that provision should be made for regulating the appointment and for the payment of such vestry clerks: Be it therefore enacted, That the churchwardens or other persons to whom it belongs to convene meetings of the vestry in any such parish shall, within the space of one calendar month from and after the making and publishing of any Order of the Commissioners so applied for, if such Order extend to the appointment of vestry clerk as aforesaid, and also, in case of any subsequent vacancy in the office of vestry clerk, within one calendar month next after such vacancy, convene a meeting of the vestry of any parish named in such Order, for the special purpose of electing a vestry clerk, to perform such of the duties hereinafter mentioned as shall be applicable to such parish, in addition to those which are or may be imposed upon vestry clerks by any Act or Acts of Parliament; and public notice of such vestry, and the place of holding the same, and the special purpose thereof, shall be given, in the usual manner in which notice of the meetings of the vestry is now given, at least seven days before the day to be appointed for holding such vestry; and at such meeting the vestry shall proceed to elect some fit and competent person to be vestry clerk; and the person so elected shall not be removable from office except by a resolution passed at a vestry to be called for that special purpose in the manner herein-before mentioned, and with the consent of the said Commissioners for administering the laws for the relief of the poor in *England*, or by an Order under the seal of the said Commissioners.

Duties of Vestry Clerk.

7. And be it enacted, That it shall be the duty of such vestry clerk, unless otherwise directed by the Poor Law Commissioners,

To give notice of and attend the meetings of vestry and committees appointed thereat:

To summon and attend meetings of the churchwardens and overseers when required, and to enter the minutes thereof respectively:

To keep the account of all charity monies which the churchwardens or overseers are authorised or accustomed to distribute:

To keep the vestry books, and the parish deeds and documents, and the rate books and accounts which are closed, and to give copies of, and extracts from, the same to any person entitled thereto, such person paying for the same at the rate of fourpence for every seventy-two words or figures, and to permit any person or persons rated to the relief of the poor of the said parish, at all reasonable times, to inspect the same, or any of them, on pain of dismissal, for neglecting to give such copies or permit such inspection:

To make out, when required by the vestry, the church rate, and procure the same to be signed and completed, and to retain the custody thereof, and, where there is no collector of poor-rates or assistant overseer, to make out the poor-rate, and procure the same to be allowed, and to make all the subsequent entries in the rate books, and to give the notices thereof required by law:

To prepare and issue the necessary process for recovering of arrears of such rates respectively before the justices, and procure the summons to be served, and to attend the justices thereon, and advise the churchwardens and overseers as to the recovery of such arrears:

To keep and make out the accounts of the churchwardens, and to present such accounts to the vestry or other legal authority, to be passed, and to examine the church-rate collector's accounts and returns of arrears:

To assist the overseers in making out their accounts, (whenever required by them,) and, subject to the Rules and Regulations of the Commissioners for administering the laws for the relief of the poor, to examine, from time to time, the accounts of the assistant overseers or collectors of poor-rates, and their returns of arrears:

To attend the Audit of Accounts of the overseers, and conduct all correspondence arising therefrom.

To assist the churchwardens and overseers in preparing and making out all other parochial assessments and accounts, and in examining the accounts of the collectors of such assessments:

To ascertain and make out the list of persons liable to serve on juries, and to cause them to be printed and duly published, and returned to the justices:

To give the notices for claims to vote for Members of Parliament, and to make out lists of voters, and get the same printed and published, and duly returned, according to law, and to attend the Court for revising them, and to prepare, make out, and publish the burgess lists and the lists of constables:

To make all returns required of the churchwardens or of the overseers by law or proper authority:

To advise the churchwardens and overseers in all the duties of their office; and also to perform such other duties and services of a like nature as the said Commissioners for administering the Laws for the Relief of the Poor in *England*, from time to time, at the request of the churchwardens or overseers of any such parish, or otherwise, shall prescribe and direct to be performed by such vestry clerk.

Salary of Vestry Clerk to be fixed by Poor Law Commissioners.

8. And be it enacted, That the amount of salary or other remuneration to be paid to the vestry clerk, as well as the days and times on which and the persons by whom the same shall be payable, shall be fixed by the said Commissioners, and altered from time to time as there shall be occasion; and such salary or remuneration shall be chargeable upon and paid out of the monies to be raised for the relief of the poor of any such parish; and, where the said Commissioners shall deem requisite, such vestry clerk shall give such security and to such persons as the said Commissioners shall by their Order, under seal, direct: Provided always, that where, under the provisions of any local Act or Acts of Parliament, any person or persons shall be paid for the performance of any of the duties of vestry clerk, or for assisting in the performance of any of the duties of churchwardens or overseers of the poor, nothing herein contained respecting the duties of the vestry clerk shall apply to, or be deemed to apply to, the performance of such duties while the same are so performed, or while payment shall be made for the performance of them as aforesaid.

Churchwardens and Overseers not to be discharged from Performance of Duty.

9. And be it enacted, That nothing herein contained shall exempt or discharge, or be construed to exempt or discharge, any churchwarden or overseer of the poor from the performance of any duty required of him by law, nor oblige him to avail himself of the assistance of any vestry clerk to be appointed as aforesaid in the performance of his duties, unless he shall think fit so to do.

Interpretation of Terms. 59 *Geo.* 3, *c.* 12. 1 & 2 *Wm.* 4, *c.* 60.

10. And be it enacted, That in this Act the following words and expressions shall have the several meanings hereby assigned to them, unless there be something in the subject or context repugnant to such construction; (that is to say,) "parish" shall mean every place having separate overseers of the poor and maintaining its own poor; and also every parish or place having a separate ecclesiastical jurisdiction, and in which a vestry shall have been heretofore constituted and held for parochial as well as ecclesiastical purposes, either separately or jointly with any other parish; "churchwarden" shall mean also chapelwardens or other persons discharging the duties of churchwardens in any parish or place as last aforesaid; "vestry" shall mean the inhabitants of the parish lawfully assembled in vestry, or for any of the purposes for

which vestries are holden, except in those parishes in which there is a select vestry, elected under an Act passed in the Fifty-ninth Year of the Reign of King *George* the Third, intituled *An Act to Amend the Laws for the Relief of the Poor*, or elected under an Act passed in the Second Year of the Reign of His late Majesty, intituled *An Act for the better Regulation of Vestries, and for the Appointment of Auditors of Accounts, in certain Parishes in* England *and* Wales, or elected under the provisions of any local Act of Parliament for the government of any parish by vestries, or under, or by virtue of any prescriptive custom or otherwise, in which parishes it shall mean select vestry; "lands" shall mean lands, tenements, and hereditaments, of whatsoever nature or tenure: words importing the masculine gender shall include the feminine; words of the plural number shall include the singular; words of the singular number shall include the plural.

Act may be amended, &c.

11. And be it enacted, That this Act may be amended or repealed by any Act to be passed in this present session of Parliament.

5. AN ACT FOR THE BETTER ASSESSING AND COLLECTING THE POOR-RATES AND HIGHWAY RATES IN RESPECT OF SMALL TENEMENTS—13 & 14 VIC. C. 99. *Passed 14th August*, 1850.

Vestries to determine whether £6 Tenements shall be rated to the Owners instead of Occupiers.

1. Whereas the collection of poor-rates and highway-rates assessed upon the occupiers of tenements of small annual value is expensive, difficult, and frequently impracticable, and it is expedient to make better provision for the rating of such tenements, and for the collection of such rates: Be it therefore enacted by the Queen's Most Excellent Majesty, by and with the advice and consent of the Lords Spiritual and Temporal, and Commons, in this present Parliament assembled, and by the authority of the same, That from and after the passing of this Act it shall be lawful for the vestry of any parish, from time to time, and at all times hereafter, to declare and order that the owners of tenements in such parish, the yearly rateable value whereof shall not exceed £6, shall be rated and assessed to the rates for the relief of the poor in respect of such tenements instead of the occupiers thereof, and the Order so made shall remain in force until rescinded in the manner herein-after authorised.

Order may be rescinded by a Majority of two-thirds of persons present at Vestry.

2. And be it enacted, That it shall be lawful for the vestry of the said parish, by a majority of two-thirds at least of the votes of the persons present at a meeting duly called for that purpose pursuant to notice, as herein-after mentioned, and competent to vote thereat, at any time after the expiration of two years from the time when any such Order shall have been so made, to order that from and after a day to be fixed by such Vestry, not being less than three years from the date of such original Order, such Order shall cease and be rescinded, in which case, from and after such last-mentioned day, the said Order shall be rescinded and no longer in force: Provided, nevertheless, that the provisions in this Act contained shall remain and continue in force for the purpose of collecting and recovering any rate which may have been previously made in pursuance of such Order: Provided also, that notice for calling every such meeting as aforesaid shall be by writing, signed by four rate-payers of the parish, affixed on the principal outer door of the parish church or chapel of the parish, or on the usual place of affixing notices relating to the affairs of the parish, at some time not less than thirty or more than forty days previous to such meeting.

Whilst Order in force the poor-rates and highway-rates to be rated to Owners.

3. And be it enacted, That whilst any such Order as firstly herein-before mentioned is in force the respective owners of such tenements shall be rated and assessed (instead of the occupiers thereof) to the rates for the relief of the poor, and to the rates for the repairs of the highways, which otherwise such occupiers might by law be rated to.

Owner to be rated on a Reduced Scale.

4. And be it enacted, That whilst such Order as firstly herein-before mentioned is in force, the owner of every tenement in every parish the yearly rateable value whereof shall not exceed £6, shall be assessed to the rates for the relief of the poor, and to the rates for the repairs of the highways, in respect of such tenement at three-fourths of the amount at

which such tenement would be liable to be rated in case this Act had not passed; and further, that whilst such Order as firstly hereinbefore mentioned is in force, if any owner of one or more such tenements shall be desirous of paying a rate for one year in respect of all such tenements in any parish, whether such tenements be occupied or unoccupied, and shall give notice in writing of such his desire to the overseers of the poor and the surveyors of the highways within one calendar month after the passing of this Act, or in any subsequent year, within fourteen days next after the twenty-fifth day of *March* in that year; then and in such case such owner shall be assessed to the rates for the relief of the poor, and to the rates for the repair of the highways, in respect of such tenement or tenements respectively, whether the same be occupied or unoccupied, from thenceforth till the twenty-fifth day of *March* following, at a sum not being less than one half of the amount at which such tenement or tenements respectively would be liable to be rated if occupied in case this Act had not passed.

Remedies for recovering of Rates.

5. And be it enacted, That the rates to be assessed as aforesaid, together with the costs and charges of levying and recovering the same, may be levied on the goods of and recovered from the respective owners of such tenements as aforesaid, by distress, action, suit, or other proceeding, in the same way as such rates, if lawfully assessed on the occupiers of such tenements, might by law be levied on the goods of, or recovered from such occupiers; and, further, the goods and chattels of the occupiers of such tenements shall be liable to be distrained and sold for payment of such of the said rates as shall accrue due during their respective occupations, in the same way as if such rates were assessed on such occupiers.

Owners possessed to have the privileges of Occupiers.

6. And be it enacted, That every such owner so rated as aforesaid shall have the same right of appeal (subject to the same conditions) against rates, and the same right to vote in vestry, as if he were an occupier duly rated in respect of the same tenement.

When Owner is rated, Occupier to be entitled to the same Municipal Privileges under 5 & 6 Wm. 4, c. 76, as if he was rated instead of the Owner.

7. And be it enacted, That where the owner of any such tenement shall be rated to the relief of the poor by virtue of this Act instead of the occupier thereof, and such owner shall have paid all money due on account of any rate or rates in respect of such tenement, such occupier shall be entitled to all municipal privileges and franchises to which, by virtue of an Act made and passed in the session of Parliament held in the Fifth and Sixth Years of the Reign of King *William* the Fourth, intituled *An Act to provide for the Regulation of Municipal Corporations in* England *and* Wales, he would have been entitled if he himself had been rated, and had paid such rate or rates; and if such owner so rated as aforesaid shall not have paid such rate or rates, it shall be lawful for such occupier to tender to the overseers of the poor, or other person authorized by law to receive the same, the amount of any rate or rates then due from such owner in respect of such tenement, and such overseer or other person so authorised as aforesaid, shall be bound to receive the same; and such occupier shall, on the payment or tender of such amount, be entitled to exercise all such privileges and franchises as hereinbefore mentioned: Provided always, that any occupier so paying any rate or rates in respect of any tenement where the owner is rated to the same shall be entitled to deduct and retain the amount so paid by him from the next payment of rent to be made by him to such owner, or to recover the same from such owner as money paid to and for the use of such owner.

Owners of Tenements held for longer Periods than from Year to Year entitled to add to Rent the Amount paid for Rates.

8. And be it enacted, That such owners paying such rates in respect of tenements continuing to be held by occupiers under now existing tenancies, for a greater term than from year to year, shall be entitled to add what they shall so pay to the rent payable in respect of such tenements, and have the same remedies for recovering the same as for rent in arrear; and that occupiers, other than such as shall continue to hold under now existing tenancies for a greater term than from year to year, may (whether paying such rates voluntarily or by compulsion) deduct the respective amount so to be answered by them as aforesaid, together

with all costs and charges they may have incurred on account thereof, from the rent payable in respect of such tenements, and such amounts shall be deemed debts due from such owners to such occupiers, and be recoverable by action.

Interpretation of Terms.

9. And be it enacted, That the word "tenement" in this Act shall be construed to include any land, house, cottage, apartment, or corporeal hereditament; the word "owner" shall be construed to mean any person receiving or claiming the rent of any such tenement for his own use, or receiving the same for the use of any corporation aggregate, or of any public company, or of any landlord or lessor who shall be a minor, under coverture, or insane, or for the use of any person who shall not be usually resident within twenty miles from the parish in which such tenement shall be situated: the word "person" shall be construed to include any corporation or public company as well as any individual; the word "parish" shall be construed to include any parish, township, vill, or place maintaining its own poor separately; the word "vestry" shall be construed to include any meeting of the inhabitants of any such parish, township, vill, or place, to be held after due notice, for carrying into execution the laws for the relief of the poor; and wherever in this Act, in describing any person, matter, or thing, the word importing the singular number or the masculine gender only is used, the same shall be understood to include and be applied to several persons as well as one person, and females as well as males, and several matters or things as well as one matter or thing respectively; unless there be something in the subject or context repugnant to such construction.

Extension of Act.

10. And be it enacted, That this Act shall extend only to *England* and *Wales*, and shall not apply to any place where owners are made liable to be rated to the relief of the poor under the provisions of any Local Act.

Act may be amended, &c.

11. And be it enacted, That this Act may be amended or repealed by any Act to be passed in this present session of Parliament.

---

6. AN ACT TO CONTINUE TWO ACTS PASSED IN THE TWELFTH AND THIRTEENTH YEARS OF THE REIGN OF HER MAJESTY, FOR CHARGING THE MAINTENANCE OF CERTAIN POOR PERSONS IN UNIONS IN ENGLAND AND WALES UPON THE COMMON FUND; AND TO MAKE CERTAIN AMENDMENTS IN THE LAWS FOR THE RELIEF OF THE POOR—13 & 14 VIC. c. 101. *Passed 14th August*, 1850.

11 & 12 *Vic. c.* 110. 12 & 13 *Vic. c.* 103. *Certain Provisions of* 11 & 12 *Vic. c.* 110, *and of* 12 & 13 *Vic. c.* 103, *continued for a limited time.*

1. Whereas by an Act passed in the Twelfth Year of the Reign of Her present Majesty, intituled *An Act to alter the Provisions relating to the Charges for the Relief of the Poor in Unions*, certain provisions were made whereby the costs of the relief and the expenses of the burial of certain poor persons therein described were made chargeable upon the common fund of the union until the thirtieth day of *September*, in the year One thousand eight hundred and forty-nine: and whereas by an Act passed in the last session of Parliament such provisions were continued in full force untii the thirtieth day of *September*, in the year One thousand eight hundred and fifty, and to the end of the then next session of Parliament; and by the said last-mentioned Act other provisions for charging upon the common fund of the union the cost of removing and maintaining certain lunatic paupers were made to continue in force for the like period; and it is expedient that all the several provisions aforesaid should be continued for a limited time: Be it therefore enacted by the Queen's Most Excellent Majesty, by and with the advice and consent of the Lords Spiritual and Temporal, and Commons, in this present Parliament assembled, and by the authority of the same, that all the said several temporary provisions in the said recited Acts above referred to, shall continue in full force until the thirtieth day of *September*, One thousand eight hundred and fifty-one, and to the end of the then next session of Parliament, and shall apply, and shall be held to have applied, to the incorporated hundred of *Forehoe*, to the incorporated hundreds of *East* and *West Flegg*, and of *Tunstead*, and *Happing*, in the county of *Norfolk*, and to the incorporated hundred of *Mutford* and *Lothingland* in the county of *Suffolk*, in like manner and to the

same extent as to the unions in the said Acts referred to.

Burials of poor Persons dying in Workhouses. Contribution to enlarge or obtain Burial-grounds.

2. And be it enacted, That it shall be lawful for the guardians of any union to contribute out of the common fund, or for the guardians of any parish to contribute out of the poor-rates of such parish, such sum of money as the Poor Law Board shall approve, towards the enlargement of any churchyard or consecrated public burial-ground in the parish wherein the workhouse shall be situated, or in any other parish of the union, or towards the obtaining of any such consecrated public burial-ground, and where any such burial-ground shall be enlarged or obtained with the aid of such contribution, it shall be lawful for them to bury therein the dead body of any poor person dying in such workhouse: Provided always, that nothing in this Act contained shall discharge or vary the obligation now imposed by law upon the guardians to bury the dead body of such poor person elsewhere, in case the deceased person, or the husband, or wife, or next of kin of such deceased person, shall have so requested: Provided also, that in all cases of burial under the direction of the guardians as aforesaid the fee or fees payable by the custom of the place where the burial may be, or under the provisions of any Act of Parliament, shall be paid by the said guardians for the burial of each such body to the person or persons who by such custom or under such Act shall be entitled to receive such fee or fees, and charged by them in like manner as the relief to the deceased when living was last chargeable.

Purchase of Site for District Schools. 7 & 8 Vic. c. 101.

3. And be it enacted, that in addition to the principal sum or sums of money which the board of management of a school district formed under the authority of the Act of the Eighth Year of the Reign of Her Majesty, intituled *An Act for the further Amendment of the Laws relating to the Poor in England,* are empowered to raise or borrow for the purpose of providing a building for the school of such district, such board may, whenever any part of such district is situated within the Metropolitan police district, with the consent and order of the Poor Law Board, also raise or borrow and charge the future poor-rates of the unions and parishes respectively combined in such district with such further or other sum or sums of money as may be or may have been necessary for the purchase of any land, or interest in land, required for the site of such school, or required for the training of the children maintained thereat, or for the site of any addition to such school.

4 & 5 *Wm.* 4, *c.* 76, *s.* 62. 12 & 13 *Vic. c.* 103, *s.* 20. *Emigration of Orphans and Deserted Children.* 11 & 12 *Vic. c.* 110, *s.* 5. 9 & 10 *Vic. c.* 66.

4. And whereas authority is given by the Act of the Fifth Year of King *William* the Fourth, intituled *An Act for the Amendment and better Administration of the Laws relating to the Poor in* England *and* Wales, for defraying, out of the poor-rates of any parish, the expenses of the emigration of poor persons having settlements in such parish, and by the before-mentioned Act of the last session, the guardians of any union or separate parish for which a board of guardians is or shall be established may, to a limited extent, exercise the same authority in and about the emigration of poor persons having settlements in such parish, or in any parish of such union respectively: and whereas poor orphans and deserted children having no settlements, or whose settlements are unknown, are frequently chargeable to parishes, and it is expedient to furnish means for the purpose of facilitating the emigration of such poor orphans and deserted children so being chargeable: Be it therefore enacted, that it shall be lawful for the guardians of any union or parish, in like manner and subject to the same regulations, limitations, and restrictions, as are contained in the said last-mentioned Act, but with the consent in writing of the guardians or the majority of the guardians of the parish of the chargeability in place of the parish of the settlement, transmitted as therein specified, to expend money in and about the emigration of any poor orphan or deserted child under the age of sixteen years having no settlement, or the place of whose settlement shall not be known, who may be chargeable to some parish in their union or to their parish respectively, and such guardians shall charge the expense so incurred

to the same parish to which such orphan or deserted child was chargeable at the time of the emigration; and where any such orphan or deserted child shall be chargeable to the common fund of any union, the guardians of such union shall have the same powers (subject to the same conditions) to procure or assist in procuring the emigration of any such last-mentioned orphan or deserted child as they have with regard to poor persons rendered irremovable by virtue of an Act of the Tenth Year of Her Majesty, intituled *An Act to amend the Laws relating to the Removal of the Poor:* Provided always, that no emigration of any such orphan or deserted child, under any of the above-mentioned powers, shall take place until such orphan or deserted child shall have consented thereto before the justices assembled in petty sessions holden in or near to the union or parish the guardians whereof propose to procure such emigration, and a certificate of such consent under the hands of two of the justices present thereat shall have been transmitted to the Poor Law Board.

An Order for paying the whole or part of the Cost of Maintenance of a lunatic married Woman maintained in any Lunatic Asylum, licensed House, or registered Hospital, and chargeable to any Union or Parish, may be made upon her husband. 11 & 12 *Vic. c.* 43.

5. And be it enacted, that where any married woman being lunatic shall be duly removed to any asylum, licensed house, or registered hospital under any of the statutes in such behalf, any two justices having jurisdiction in the place wherein the husband of such lunatic shall dwell, upon application by or on behalf of the guardians of the union or of the parish having a separate board of guardians, or the overseers of the parish, to which union or parish respectively such lunatic shall be or become chargeable, may summon such husband to appear before them to show cause why an order should not be made upon him to maintain or contribute towards the maintenance of his wife in such asylum, licensed house, or registered hospital; and upon his appearance, or in the event of his not appearing upon proof of due service of such summons upon him, such justices may (if they think fit) make an order upon him to pay such sum, weekly or otherwise, for or towards the cost of the maintenance of such lunatic, as after consideration of all the circumstances of the case shall appear to them to be proper, and determine in such order how and to whom the payments shall from time to time be made, which order shall, if the payments required by it to be made be in arrear, be enforced in the manner prescribed by the statute passed in the Twelfth Year of the Reign of Her Majesty, intituled *An Act to facilitate the Performance of the Duties of Justices of the Peace within* England *and* Wales *with respect to Summary Convictions and Orders*, for the enforcing of orders of justices requiring the payment of a sum of money.

Master of a Workhouse and Relieving Officer not to be appointed to any Parochial Office.

6. And be it enacted, that no master of a workhouse nor any relieving officer shall be henceforth qualified to be appointed to the office of overseer of the poor, constable, or any other parochial or township office, so long as he shall continue to be such master of a workhouse or relieving-officer, except where the Poor Law Board shall authorise any relieving-officer to hold a paid office in a parish: Provided always, that no rate or assessment made, nor any other act or thing done, by any such person as such parochial or township officer, nor the service of any notice, demand, order, or process upon him as such, shall, if in other respects legal and sufficient, be deemed invalid by reason only of such disqualification as aforesaid.

The Fee for giving Notices of Special Sessions under the Act 6 & 7 *Wm.* 4, *c.* 96, *s.* 6, *to be paid by the Overseers out of the Poor-rate.*

7. And whereas by the Act of the Seventh Year of His late Majesty King *William* the Fourth, intituled *An Act to regulate Parochial Assessments*, it is provided, that the justices acting in and for every petty sessions division shall hold special sessions for hearing appeals against the rates of the several parishes within their respective divisions, and shall cause public notice of the time and place of the holding of such special sessions to be given in each parish, but no provision is made for the payment of the costs incurred in preparing and giving of such notice: Be it therefore enacted, that such fee or remuneration as shall have been or shall hereafter be settled by the justices of the peace at their respective general quarter sessions, according to the statute in that behalf, to be paid to the clerks to justices

of the peace for the preparing and giving of a notice of a special sessions for this purpose, or in default thereof of a notice of any special sessions, shall be paid by the overseers of each parish comprised within the division for which the special sessions are to be held, and be charged by them upon the poor-rate.

Persons committed to Prison for Offences against 55 Geo. 3, c. 137, s. 2, and 7 & 8 Vic. c. 101, ss. 57, 58, may be kept to hard Labour.

8. And whereas by an Act passed in the Fifty-fifth year of the reign of King *George* the Third, intituled *An Act to prevent poor Persons in Workhouses from embezzling certain Property provided for their Use, to alter and amend so much of an Act of the Thirty-sixth Year of His present Majesty as restrains Justices of the Peace from ordering Relief to poor Persons in certain Cases for a longer Period than One Month at a Time, and for other Purposes herein mentioned, relating to the Poor,* and by an Act passed in the Eighth Year of Her present Majesty, intituled *An Act for the further Amendment of the Laws relating to the Poor in* England, power is given to punish by imprisonment any person or persons deserting, absconding, or running away from any workhouse or workhouses, and carrying away with him, her, or them any clothes, linen, or other goods in the said Act of the Fifty-fifth year of the reign of King *George* the Third enumerated and described: Be it enacted, that in the case of every such offence it shall be lawful for the convicting justice or justices, if he or they shall so think fit, to order and adjudge that the person or persons convicted shall, during the period of imprisonment by law authorised, be kept to hard labour.

Assaults upon Workhouse Officers or Relieving Officers in the Discharge of their Duty.

9. And be it enacted, that where any person shall be charged with and convicted of any assault upon any officer of a workhouse or relieving officer in the due execution of his duty, or upon any person acting in aid of such officer, the court may sentence the offender to the same punishment as is provided by law for an assault upon a peace officer or revenue officer in the due execution of his duty, and shall have the same power as in case of such last-mentioned assault to order payment of the costs and expenses of the prosecution.

Providing for Expense of collecting Rates. 12 & 13 Vic. c. 65.

10. And whereas by an Act passed in the last session of Parliament, intituled *An Act to provide a more convenient Mode of levying and collecting County Rates, County Police Rates, and District Police Rates in Parishes situated partly within and partly without the Limits of Boroughs which are not liable to such Rates,* provision is made to enable the overseers or other persons charged with the collection of the poor-rate, in cases where any parish or place shall be partly within and partly without a borough, to assess and levy upon the inhabitants and occupiers of all messuages, lands, and tenements liable to the poor-rates in that part of the parish or place which is within the borough, the amount of money which they shall be required to raise as a contribution towards a district, borough, or other rate upon a warrant from the mayor, justice, constable, or other officer, as therein mentioned: And whereas some difficulty has arisen in certain parishes as to the payment of the expenses of collecting the rates upon such assessments, and enforcing of the payment thereof: Be it therefore enacted, That the overseers of any such parish may employ for the collection of such rate as aforesaid, or of any jail rate assessed upon any such part thereof, the collector of the poor-rates in the said parish, or some other person to be appointed with the like authority, and subject to the same regulations as regards his term of office, his remuneration, the security to be given for the discharge of his duties, and his liability to account to the auditor and other persons, as such collector of poor-rates is or shall be subject to, and to pay such remuneration out of the sum raised by the rate assessed upon such part as aforesaid; and that the collector of poor-rates, or other person as aforesaid, shall, for the purpose of collecting the rate so assessed upon such part, have all the powers, privileges, protections, and incidents which belong to the overseers in the collection of the poor-rate, and the like remedy for the recovery of the cost of proceedings to enforce the payment of the rate aforesaid, as in the case of a poor-rate; and the said overseers, in estimating the amount of their assessment for such rate upon any part of a parish divided as aforesaid, may include such a sum as will provide for the payment of the costs of the assessment and collection, and a reasonable sum in respect of

the rates which may be excused or become irrecoverable.

Construction of Act.

11. And be it enacted, That the several words used in this Act shall be construed in the manner prescribed by the said recited Act of the Fifth Year of the Reign of His late Majesty King *William* the Fourth, and the statutes explaining and extending it; and that all the provisions of the said last-mentioned Act, and of the said statutes not repealed, shall extend to this Act, except where any such provision would be inconsistent with anything herein contained.

Act to extend only to England and Wales.

12. And be it enacted, That this Act shall extend only to *England* and *Wales.*

Act may be amended, &c.

13. And be it enacted, That this Act may be amended or repealed by any Act to be passed in this present session of Parliament.

II.—RATING OWNERS UNDER 13 & 14 VIC. c. 99.

1.—CIRCULAR LETTER ACCOMPANYING GENERAL ORDER ALTERING THE FORM OF THE RATE-BOOK.

Poor Law Board,
London, 20th Nov., 1850.

Gentlemen,—The Poor Law Board having received numerous communications on the subject of the Form of Poor-rate to be used by the overseers of parishes, the vestries of which resolve to act upon the provisions of the statute, 13 & 14 Vic. c. 99, for assessing the owners of certain tenements to the poor-rate instead of the occupiers thereof, have deemed it advisable to make an alteration in the General Order of Accounts issued by the Poor Law Commissioners in March, 1847, so far as it relates to the Rate Book.

It appeared to the Board that it would be most desirable to make as little alteration as possible in the form prescribed by that Order, and that the introduction of one additional column would suffice for the present purpose: they have accordingly made a provision to that effect in the General Order, a copy of which accompanies this letter.

In this additional column (No. 12) the overseers of any parish in which the owners are liable to be assessed under the above or any other Statute, must enter the sums which the owners are called upon to pay, (whether upon any composition or otherwise,) which sums will be calculated according to the scale of liability, established by the Act under which the owners are assessed. With reference to this point it must be remembered that, besides the Statute already mentioned, the 59 Geo. 3, c. 12, s. 19, contains a provision to a like effect, in reference to a different class of tenements, and that local Acts are in force in many parishes, whereby the liability to be assessed to the poor-rate is transferred from the occupier to the owner.

The form of rate as now prescribed will be applicable in all those cases.

As it will probably be inconvenient that the publishers of these forms should keep up a stock of two Forms of Rate Book, and as it may be expedient for parishes to be possessed of books in which can be entered at any time the assessments upon the owners, instead of the occupiers, whenever the vestry of any parish shall determine to adopt the provisions of the Act 13 & 14 Vic. c. 99, the Board have deemed it advisable to authorize the use of this new Form of Rate Book by the overseers in every parish whether the owners may or may not be liable to be assessed to the poor-rate. The overseers in making out the poor-rate in this Form must, however, be careful not to make any entry in the column No. 12 against the owners, until they shall have been rendered liable to be assessed to the rate by due legal provision.

It has been suggested that the names of the owners who are liable to be assessed, instead of the occupiers, should be all entered together in a distinct part of the rate, but the Board are not prepared to issue any express directions or rule on the subject. It may, however, be found generally convenient that, where an owner is assessed, either under a composition or otherwise in respect of several contiguous tenements, the assessment of such tenements should be entered together or in immediate succession in the Rate Book. The Board must leave this matter, however, which is entirely one of convenience, to the discretion of the overseers, or other officers who are charged with the duty of making out the rate.

The Board will remind the overseers, that in

parishes where the owners are to be rated instead of the occupiers, the only alterations in the mode of entering the particulars in the Rate Book will occur in the column No. 11, for the rate on the occupier, and in the additional column (No. 12) for the rate on the owner. Where the owner is to be rated instead of the occupier, the column (No. 11) for the amount otherwise chargeable upon the occupier should, in that particular case, be left blank, and the next column (No. 12) filled up with the amount payable by the owner, which amount must be calculated upon three-fourths, or such other proportion as shall be applicable to his case, of the amount of the rateable value set out in the column No. 10. This rateable value must be the full net annual value of the property estimated as if the occupier were the person to be assessed.

Assuming that the overseers have carefully omitted to insert in column No. 11 any sums in respect of the property for which the owners are to be assessed, and have entered the sums properly chargeable upon such owners in column No. 12, they must then add together the totals of the two columns (11 and 12) in order to enable them to make the declaration at the foot of the rate as to the amount of the whole rate.

The Board have requested Mr. Charles Knight, their publisher, to prepare Rate Books in the form now prescribed; and they understand that the same will be ready for sale forthwith. The Board think it right, however, to state that it will be open to any other publisher to publish these books.

I am, Gentlemen, your obedient Servant,

W. G. LUMLEY,
Assistant Secretary.

To the Overseers of the Poor.

2.—CIRCULAR LETTER AS TO THE ALTERATION OF THE FORM OF THE RATE-BOOK.

Poor Law Board, London,
27th November, 1850.

Gentlemen,—It has been represented to the Poor Law Board that some misapprehension may possibly arise in reference to their circular of the 20th inst., as to the cases in which it will be necessary to use rate-books in the form prescribed by the general order which accompanied that circular; and I am therefore directed to state that it will be necessary to use rate-books in that form, only in those parishes in which there may be an order of the vestry to assess the owners of tenements to the poor-rate instead of the occupiers, under the provisions of the 13 & 14 Vic. c. 99, or some other enactment. In all other parishes, the rate-books in the form prescribed by the Poor Law Commissioners in their order of the 17th of March, 1847, may continue to be used.

I am, &c.,

(Signed) W. G. LUMLEY,
Assistant Secretary.

To the Overseers of the Poor.

3.—GENERAL ORDER ALTERING THE FORM OF THE POOR-RATE.

To the Guardians of the Poor of the several Unions set forth in the First and Second Schedules hereunto annexed;—

To the Guardians of the Poor of the Parish of Great Yarmouth, in the County of Norfolk, set forth in the said Second Schedule hereunto annexed;—

To the Churchwardens and Overseers of the Poor of the several Parishes and Places comprised within the said several Unions;—

To the Churchwardens and Overseers of the Poor of the said Parish of Great Yarmouth;—

To the Clerk or Clerks to the Justices of the Petty Sessions held for the Division or Divisions in which the said several Unions and the said Parish of Great Yarmouth are respectively situate;—

And to all others whom it may concern.

Whereas the Poor Law Commissioners, by an Order bearing date the seventeenth day of March, One thousand eight hundred and forty-seven, being a general rule, addressed (amongst others) to the guardians of the poor of the several unions mentioned in the first schedule hereunto annexed, and the Poor Law Board, by divers Orders, the dates whereof are respectively set forth in the second schedule hereunto annexed, addressed to the several unions and to the parish of Great Yarmouth therein also set forth, did, among other matters, order and direct the overseers of the poor of every parish in the said respective unions, and the overseers of the poor of the said parish of Great Yarmouth, to keep, among other things, a book termed a Rate Book, according to the forms and directions in the Schedules A. to the said several orders annexed.

Form of Heading to the "Rate."

An Assessment for the Relief of the Poor of the Parish of in the County of , and for other purposes chargeable thereon, according to Law, made this day of , in the year of our Lord One thousand eight hundred and . after the rate of in the pound.

	ARREARS		RATE.									COLLECTION.						
															Uncollected at Balancing this Book.			
																Irrecoverable at Balancing this Book.		
																	Otherwise not recoverable.	
No.	Due, or if excused.	If excused, write the word "excused."	Name of Occupier.	Name of Owner.	Description of Property rated.	Name or Situation of Property.	Estimated Extent.	Gross Estimated Rental.	Rateable Value.	Rate at in the Pound.	Amount of Rate Assessed upon and payable by the Owner, instead of the Occupier, by virtue of the Statute or Statutes in that behalf.	Recoverable Arrears of former Rates.	Total Amount to be collected.	Amount actually collected.	Recoverable Arrear at balancing this Book.	Amount legally excused.	Amount.	Causes.
1.	2.	3.	4.	5.	6.	7.	8.	9.	10.	11.	12.	13.	14.	15.	16.	17.	18.	19.
	£ s. d.						A. R. P.	£ s. d.	£ s. d.	£ s. .	£ s.	£ s. d.	£ s. d.	£ s.	£ s. d.	£ s. d.	£ s. d.	

Form of Declaration at the foot of the "Rate."

We, do declare the several particulars specified in the respective columns of the above Rate to be true and correct, so far as we have been able to ascertain them, to which end we have used our best endeavours.

We do also declare that the above Rate amounts in the whole to the sum of pounds shillings and pence.

_______________, *Overseer.*

_______________, *Overseer.*

_______________, *Churchwarden.*

_______________, *Churchwarden*

And whereas in many parishes, by virtue of several statutes in that behalf, the owners of certain tenements and hereditaments in such statutes particularly described are liable to be assessed to the rates levied for the relief of the poor in the place of the occupiers of such tenements and hereditaments, and it is expedient that a form of rate should be prescribed to meet such cases.

Now, therefore, We, the Poor Law Board, in pursuance of the powers given in and by the several statutes in that behalf made and provided, do hereby order and direct, that in every parish comprised in the several unions in the schedules hereunto annexed, and in the said parish of Great Yarmouth, when, under the provision of any statute or statutes in that behalf, the owners of tenements and hereditaments liable to poor-rates in any such parish shall be assessed instead of the occupiers, the overseers of such parish shall, and in any parish wherein the owners shall not be so assessed the overseers at any time may, enter the rates to be hereafter levied for the relief of the poor in a rate-book in the following form, containing the particulars therein set forth :—*(See opposite page.)*

And we do hereby order and direct, that the said overseers shall in all other respects conform to and duly observe the orders and directions contained in the aforesaid several Orders applicable to them; and that the rules and regulations prescribed in the said several Orders for the observance of the collector and assistant overseer shall be held to apply to the Form of Rate-Book hereby directed or authorised to be kept, in like manner as if the same had been set forth in the said several Orders.

And we do further order, that the several words "overseers," "collector," "parish," and "union," herein contained, shall be construed in like manner as is directed by the said several above-mentioned Orders.

The FIRST SCHEDULE referred to in the foregoing Order.

Aberaeron
Abergavenny.
Aberystwith.
Abingdon.
Albans, St.
Alcester.
Alderbury.
Alnwick.
Alresford.
Alton.
Altrincham.
Amersham.
Amesbury.
Ampthill.
Andover
Anglesey.
Asaph, St
Ashbourne.
Ashby-de-la-Zouch.
Ashford, East.
Ashford, West.
Ashton-under-Lyne.
Aston.
Atcham.
Atherstone.
Auckland.
Austell, St.
Axbridge.
Axminster.
Aylesbury.
Aylsham.

Bakewell.
Bala.
Banbury.
Bangor and Beaumaris.
Barnet.
Barnstaple.
Barrow-on-Soar.
Basford.
Basingstoke.
Bath.
Battle.
Beaminster.
Bedale.
Bedford.
Bedminster.
Belford.
Bellingham.
Belper.
Berkhampstead.
Berwick-upon-Tweed.
Beverley.
Bicester.
Bideford.
Biggleswade.
Billericay.
Billesdon.
Bingham.
Bishop Stortford.
Blaby.
Blackburn.
Blandford.
Blean.
Blofield.
Blything
Bodmin.
Bolton.
Bootle.
Bosmere and Claydon.
Boston.
Boughton, Great.
Bourn.
Brackley.
Bradfield.
Bradford (Wilts)
Bradford (York).
Braintree.
Brampton.
Brecknock.
Brentford.
Bridge.
Bridgend & Cowbridge.
Bridgwater.
Bridgnorth
Bridlington.
Bridport.
Brixworth.
Bromley.
Bromsgrove.
Bromyard.
Buckingham.
Builth.
Buntingford.
Burnley.
Burton-upon-Trent.
Bury.

Caistor
Calne.
Cambridge.
Camelford.
Cardiff.
Cardigan.
Carlisle.
Carmarthen.
Carnarvon.
Castle Ward.
Catherington.
Caxton and Arrington.
Cerne.
Chailey.
Chapel-en-le-Frith.
Chard.
Cheadle.
Chelmsford.
Cheltenham.
Chepstow.
Chertsey.
Chesterfield.
Chester-le-Street.
Chesterton.
Chippenham.
Chipping Norton.

Chipping Sodbury.
Chorley.
Chorlton.
Christchurch.
Church Stretton.
Cirencester.
Cleobury Mortimer.
Clifton.
Clitheroe.
Clun.
Clutton.
Cockermouth.
Colchester.
Columb, St., Major.
Congleton.
Conway.
Cookham.
Corwen.
Cosford.
Cranbrook.
Crediton.
Crickhowel.
Cricklade and Wootton Bassett.
Croydon.
Cuckfield.

Darlington.
Dartford.
Daventry
Depwade.
Derby.
Devizes.
Dewsbury.
Docking.
Dolgelly.
Doncaster.
Dorchester
Dore.
Dorking.
Dover.
Downham.
Drayton.
Driffield.
Droitwich.
Droxford.
Dudley.
Dulverton.
Dunmow.
Durham.
Dursley.

Easington.
Easingwold.
Eastbourne.
East Grinstead.
Easthampstead.
East Retford.
Eastry.
East Ward.
Ecclesall Bierlow
Edmonton.
Elham.
Ellesmere.
Ely.
Epping.
Epsom.
Erpingham.
Eton.
Evesham.

Faith, St.
Falmouth.
Fareham.
Faringdon.
Farnham.
Faversham.
Festiniog
Flegg, East and West.
Foleshill.
Fordingbridge.
Forehoe.
Freebridge Lynn.
Frome.
Fulham.
Fylde.

Gainsborough.
Garstang.
Gateshead.
Germans, St.
Glanford Brigg.
Glendale.
Glossop.
Gloucester.
Godstone.
Goole.
Grantham.
Gravesend and Milton.
Greenwich.
Guildford.
Guiltcross.
Guisborough.

Hackney.
Hailsham.
Halifax.
Halstead.
Haltwhistle.
Hambledon.
Hardingstone.
Hartismere.
Hartley Wintney.
Haslingden.
Hastings.
Hatfield.
Havant.
Haverfordwest
Hay.
Hayfield.
Headington.
Helmsley Blackmoor.
Helston.
Hemel Hempstead.
Hendon.
Henley.
Henstead.
Hereford.
Hertford.
Hexham.
Highworth and Swindon.
Hinckley.
Hitchin.
Holbeach.
Holborn.
Hollingbourn.
Holsworthy.
Holywell.
Honiton.
Hoo.
Horncastle.
Horsham.
Houghton-le-Spring.
Howden.
Hoxne.
Huddersfield.
Hungerford.
Huntingdon.
Hursley.

Ipswich.
Ives, St.

Keighley.
Kendal.
Kettering.
Keynsham.
Kidderminster.
Kingsbridge.
Kingsclere.
King's Lynn.
King's Norton.
Kingston-upon-Thames
Kington.
Knighton.

Lampeter.
Lancaster.
Lanchester.
Langport.
Launceston.
Ledbury.
Leek.
Leicester.
Leigh
Leighton Buzzard.
Leominster.
Lewes.
Lewisham.
Lexden and Winstree.
Leyburn.
Lichfield.
Lincoln.
Linton.
Liskeard.
Llandilo Fawr.
Llandovery.
Llanelly.
Llanfyllin.
Llanrwst.
Loddon and Clavering.
London, City of.
London, East.
London, West.
Longtown.
Loughborough.
Louth.
Ludlow.
Luton.
Lutterworth.
Lymington.

Macclesfield.
Machynlleth.
Madeley.
Maidstone.
Maldon.
Malling.
Malmesbury.
Malton.
Mansfield.
Market Bosworth.
Market Harborough.
Marlborough.
Martley.

Medway.
Melksham.
Melton Mowbray.
Mere.
Meriden.
Merthyr Tydvil.
Midhurst.
Mildenhall.
Milton.
Mitford and Launditch.
Monmouth.
Morpeth.
Mutford & Lothingland.

Nantwich.
Narberth.
Neath.
Neot's, St.
Newark.
Newbury.
Newcastle-in-Emlyn.
Newcastle-under-Lyne.
Newcastle-upon-Tyne.
Newent.
New Forest.
Newhaven.
Newmarket.
Newport (Monmouth).
Newport (Salop).
Newport Pagnell.
Newton Abbot.
Newtown and Llanidloes
Northallerton.
Northampton.
North Aylesford.
Northleach.
Northwich.
North Witchford.
Nottingham.
Nuneaton.

Oakham.
Oakhampton.
Olave's, St.
Ongar.
Ormskirk.
Orsett.
Oundle.

Pateley Bridge.
Patrington.
Pembroke.
Penkridge.
Penrith.
Penzance.
Pershore.
Peterborough.
Petersfield.
Petworth.
Pewsey.
Pickering.
Plomesgate.
Plympton, St. Mary.
Pocklington.
Pont-y-pool.
Poole.
Poplar.
Portsea Island.
Potterspury.
Prescot.
Presteigne.
Preston.
Pwllheli.

Radford.
Reading.
Redruth.
Reeth.
Reigate.
Rhayader.
Richmond (Surrey)
Richmond (Yorkshire)
Ringwood.
Risbridge.
Rochdale.
Rochford.
Romford.
Romney Marsh.
Romsey.
Ross.
Rothbury.
Rotherham.
Royston.
Rugby.
Runcorn.
Ruthin.
Rye.

Saffron Walden.
Salford.
Saviour's, St.
Scarborough.
Sculcoates.
Sedbergh.
Sedgefield.
Seisdon.
Selby.
Settle.
Sevenoaks.
Shaftesbury.
Shardlow.
Sheffield.
Sheppey.
Shepton Mallett.
Sherborne.
Shiffnall.
Shipston-upon-Stour.
Skipton.
Skirlaugh.
Sleaford.
Solihull.
Southam.
South Molton.
South Shields.
South Stoneham.
Southwell.
Spalding.
Spilsby.
Stafford.
Staines.
Stamford.
Stepney.
Steyning.
Stockbridge.
Stockport.
Stockton.
Stokesley.
Stone.
Stourbridge.
Stow.
Stow-on-the-Wold.
Strand.
Stratford-upon-Avon.
Stratton.
Stroud.
Sturminster.
Sudbury.
Sunderland.
Swaffham.
Swansea.

Tamworth.
Taunton.
Tavistock.
Teesdale.
Tenbury.
Tendring.
Tenterden.
Tetbury.
Tewkesbury.
Thakeham.
Thame.
Thanet, Isle of.
Thetford.
Thingoe.
Thirsk.
Thomas, St.
Thornbury.
Thorne.
Thrapston.
Ticehurst.
Tisbury.
Tiverton.
Todmorden.
Tonbridge.
Torrington.
Totnes.
Towcester.
Tregaron.
Truro.
Tunstead and Happing.
Tynemouth.

Uckfield.
Ulverstone.
Uppingham.
Upton-upon-Severn.
Uttoxeter.
Uxbridge.

Wakefield.
Wallingford.
Walsal.
Walsingham
Wandsworth and Clapham.
Wangford.
Wantage.
Ware.
Wareham and Purbeck.
Warminster.
Warrington.
Warwick.
Watford.
Wayland.
Weardale.
Wellingborough.
Wellington (Salop).
Wellington (Somerset).
Wells.
Welwyn.
Wem.
Weobly.
Westbourne.
West Bromwich.

Westbury-upon-Severn.	Winchester, New.
Westbury and Whorwelsdown.	Windsor.
	Winslow.
West Derby.	Wirrall.
West Firle.	Wisbeach.
West Ham.	Witham.
West Hampnett.	Witney.
West Ward.	Woburn.
Weymouth.	Wokingham.
Wheatenhurst.	Wolstanton and Burslem.
Whitby.	
Whitchurch.	Wolverhampton.
Whitechapel.	Woodbridge.
Whitehaven.	Woodstock.
Wigan.	Worcester.
Wigton.	Worksop.
Williton.	Wortley.
Wilton.	Wrexham.
Wimborne and Cranborne.	Wycombe.
Wincanton.	Yeovil.
Winchcombe.	York.

The SECOND SCHEDULE to which the above Order refers.

Names of Unions.	Dates of Orders issued subsequently to the General Order for Accounts.
BARNSLEY	23rd April, 1850.
BARTON-UPON-IRWELL	26th January, 1850.
BEDWELLTY	28th November, 1849.
KIRKBY MOORSIDE	23rd December, 1848.
NORTH BIERLEY	14th February, 1849.
OLDHAM	20th November, 1848.
PENISTONE	22nd November, 1849.
PRESTWICH	3rd August, 1850.
SAMFORD	27th March, 1849.
Name of Parish.	
YARMOUTH, GREAT	8th March, 1850.

Given under our Hands and Seal of Office, this Eighteenth day of November, in the year One thousand eight hundred and fifty.

M. T. BAINES,
President.

G. GREY.
C. WOOD.

GEO. NICHOLLS,
Secretary.

4.—13 & 14 VIC. c. 99—MEANING OF "RATEABLE VALUE"—RATING OF OWNER IN RESPECT OF TENEMENT OCCUPIED BY HIMSELF.

12*th Sept.*, 1850.

Assistant Overseer of Fordington.—Requesting advice on the following points:—1. Does the "yearly rateable value," in sec. 1 of the 13 & 14 Vic. c. 99, mean the column in rate-book headed "Rateable Value?" 2. If an owner of several cottages (all of which are rated under £6 each) occupy one of them himself, should he be assessed on the reduced scale (sec. 4) for the cottage he occupies? 3. If an owner of a single cottage, or stable, or plot of land, (rated under £6) occupy it himself, should he be assessed on the reduced scale?

Ans.—1. The Board apprehend that the term yearly rateable value, used in sec. 1. of the Act above cited, means the rateable value as estimated in accordance with the 6 & 7 Wm. 4, cap. 96, sec. 1, and not necessarily the specific sum entered in the column for Rateable Value, in the last or any other actual rate. 2. The Board are disposed to think that an owner cannot be rated under this Act in respect of a tenement of which he is also the occupier, and, therefore, that he ought not to be rated in respect of that tenement upon the reduced scale. The Act seems to contemplate throughout, that in the cases to which it is applied, the owner and the occupier will be distinct persons. Thus, sec. 1. provides that the owners may be rated instead of the occupiers; sec. 5 allows of a distress upon the goods either of the owner or of the occupier. Sec. 6 gives the owner the same right of appeal as if he were an occupier. Sec. 7 reserves certain rights to the occupier; and sec. 9 construes the word owner to mean any person receiving, or claiming the rent of the tenement, which a man can hardly be said to do who lives in his own house. The Board are inclined to consider, therefore, that in such a case the party must be rated as occupier, and not upon the reduced scale. 3. The above remarks apply equally to this case; the Board do not think it makes any difference, whether the party only owns the house he occupies, or is the owner of other houses also in the same parish.

5.—13 & 14 VIC. c. 99—APPOINTMENT OF A PERSON TO ASSIST IN MAKING RATE UNDER.

19*th Sept.*, 1850.

Clerk of Melksham Union.—Can the overseers legally charge the parish rates with the expense they must incur in making a complete rate under the provisions of the 13 & 14 Vic. c. 99. In this parish (Melksham) the owners of at least nine hundred tenements are now liable to be rated and assessed to the rates for the relief of the poor. The occupiers of upwards of six hundred of these tenements having hitherto been excused their rates, the changes as to ownership which have taken place since 1836, when the last survey of the parish was made, have not been inquired into, so that the rate is, in this respect, very incorrect. In the parish of Trowbridge, the number of small tenements brought under the operation of the above-mentioned Act is much greater; and as the making such corrections, (to be ascertained only by going from house to house,) as well as the necessary reduction in the annual amount of each assessment, will require considerable care and attention, the appointment of some competent person, either by the board of guardians or the overseers, to undertake such duties, would be more satisfactory to the ratepayers. The provisions of the Act in question have been adopted by the parishes of Trowbridge and Melksham and the chapelry of Semington, and a vestry meeting will be held in the chapelry of Sund on Friday next, when the provisions of the same statute will, no doubt, be adopted. The overseers of Trowbridge and Melksham have applied to the guardians for assistance in making a rate, and after examination of the difficulties to be contended with, the guardians are of opinion that a competent person should be appointed in each parish for that purpose.

Ans.—The Board do not, as at present informed, see that the making a rate in the parishes mentioned, in order to give effect to the Act 13 & 14 Vic. c. 99, presents such special difficulties as to render the assistance applied for necessary. It is to be borne in mind, that the overseers are themselves bound by law to assess property liable in respect of the poor-rate, to collect the information or particulars necessary to be inserted in the columns of the rate-book, and to make out that book, and this whatever may be the amount of mere personal trouble. It is only where there are special difficulties in ascertaining the annual value of property for the purpose of the rate the law allows of a professional valuation to be made at the cost of the rate. As regards collecting information as to who the present owners of small tenements in the parishes are, the Board think that the overseers can, undoubtedly, do this, though it may involve some time and trouble. Then, as regards assessing the tenements, the Board presume that the amounts at which they are at present assessed in the rate-book represent the net annual value, as defined by the 6 & 7 Wm. 4, c. 96, sec. 1, and if so, all that is necessary is, to take a proportion of that value, namely, three-fourths, and insert that amount in the rate-book, as that on which the owners are to be assessed. (See sec. 4 of the above-cited statute.) The Board request the guardians will re-consider the subject of the representation contained in their letter of the 13th inst. with reference to the foregoing observations.

6.—13 & 14 VIC. C. 99—PROVISIONS OF THE ACT AND THE MODE OF BRINGING THEM INTO OPERATION.

21st Sept., 1850.

Clerk of Bedford Union.—Transmitting the following circular, issued by the guardians to the churchwardens and overseers of the several parishes in the union in reference to the Act of 13 & 14 Vic. c. 99:—

Bedford, 10th Sept., 1850.

Gentlemen,—I am directed by the board of guardians to call your attention to the principal provisions of an Act passed in the last session of parliament (13 & 14 Vic. c. 99) for the better assessing and collecting the poor-rates and highway-rates in respect of small tenements.

Sec. 1 enacts—That it shall be lawful for the vestry of any parish to declare and order that the owners of tenements in such parish, the yearly rateable value whereof shall not exceed six pounds, shall be rated and assessed to the rate for the relief of the poor in respect of such tenements, instead of the occupiers thereof, and the order so made shall remain in force until rescinded in the manner therein after authorised. (See sec. 2.)

Sec. 2 enacts—That after the expiration of two years from the time when any such order shall have been so made, a majority of two-thirds of the votes of the persons present at a vestry may order that from and after a day to be fixed by such vestry, not being less than three years from the date of such original order, such order shall cease and be rescinded.

Sec. 3 enacts—That whilst any such order as firstly above-mentioned is in force, the respective owners of such tenements shall be rated and assessed to the poor-rates and to the highway-rates instead of the occupiers thereof.

Sec. 4 enacts—That whilst such first-mentioned order is in force, the owners of tenements, the yearly rateable value whereof shall not exceed six pounds, shall be assessed to the poor-rates and to the highway-rates at *three-fourths* of the amount at which such tenements would have been liable to be rated if the Act had not passed, but if any owner shall be desirous of paying a rate for one year in respect of all such tenements in any parish, whether such tenements be occupied or unoccupied, and shall give notice in writing of such his desire to the overseers of the poor and to the surveyor of highways, within one calendar month after the passing of the Act, (August 14th,) or in any subsequent year within fourteen days next after the 25th of March in that year, then and in such case such owner shall be assessed to the poor-rates and to the highway-rates in respect of such tenement or tenements respectively, whether the same be occupied or unoccupied, from thenceforth until the 25th of March following, at a sum not less than *one-half* of the amount at which such tenement or tenements respectively would have been liable to be rated if occupied, in case the Act had not passed.

Sec. 5—Provides remedies for the recovery of rates from owners in the same way as rates might be recovered from occupiers, and further, makes the goods and chattels of the occupiers liable to be distrained and sold for payment of such rates as shall accrue due during their respective occupations in the same way as if the rates were assessed on the occupiers.

Sec. 6 enacts—That the owners so rated shall have the same right of appeal against rates and the same right to vote in vestry as occupiers.

Sec. 7 enacts—That when owners are rated instead of the occupiers, and shall have paid the rates, such occupiers shall be entitled to all municipal privileges to which they would have been entitled if the occupiers themselves had been rated and paid the rates.

Sec. 8 enacts—That owners paying the rates in respect of tenements continuing to be held by occupiers under existing tenancies for a greater term than from year to year, shall be entitled to add what they shall so pay to the rent, and that occupiers other than as last-mentioned, may deduct the amount so to be answered by them, (see s. 5) together with all costs and charges they may have incurred on account thereof, from the rent.

Sec. 9—Interpretation of terms.—The word "tenement" is to be construed to include any land, house, cottage, apartment, or corporeal hereditament. The word "owner" is to be construed to mean any person receiving or claiming the rent of any such tenement for his own use, or receiving the same for the use of any corporation, aggregate, or of any public company, or of any landlord or lessor, who shall be a minor under coverture or insane, or for the use of any person who shall not be usually resident within twenty miles from the parish in which such tenement shall be situated. The word "person" to include any corporation or public company as well as an individual. The word "parish" is to include any township, vill, or place maintaining its own poor separately. The word "vestry" is to include any meeting of the inhabitants of any such township, vill, or place, to be held after due notice for carrying into execution the laws for the relief of the poor.

The Guardians recommend that the subject matter of this communication should be brought under the consideration of the vestry at an early opportunity; with this view I inclose a form of notice for summoning the meeting, as also a form of resolution for adopting the provisions of the Act, should the inhabitants of your parish be desirous of so doing.

I have the honour to be, Gentlemen,

Your most obedient Servant,

S. WING, *Clerk to the Guardians.*

To the Churchwardens and Overseers of the Poor.

FORM OF NOTICE.

Parish of

Notice is hereby given, that a meeting of the inhabitants of this parish will be held at in this parish, on the day of next, at o'clock in the noon, to consider the propriety of passing a resolution to declare and order that the owners of tenements in this parish, the yearly rateable value whereof shall not exceed six pounds, shall be rated and assessed to the rates for the relief of the poor in respect of such tenements instead of the occupiers thereof, pursuant to the statute passed in the last session of Parliament, intituled "An Act for the better assessing and collecting the poor-rates and highway-rates in respect of small tenements."

Dated this day of 1850.

Signed, ____________ } Churchwardens.
____

____________ } Overseers of the Poor.
____

Note.—A vestry meeting cannot legally be held earlier than the Thursday after the Sunday on or before which the notice is given, as three clear days must intervene between the Sunday on or before which the notice is given and the day of meeting.

FORM OF RESOLUTION.

At a meeting of the inhabitants of the parish of in the county of Bedford, held at in this parish, on the day of 1850, pursuant to a notice of such meeting duly published and given on Sunday the day of 1850.

Resolved, And this vestry doth declare and order that henceforth the owners of tenements in this parish, the yearly rateable value whereof shall not exceed six pounds, shall be rated and assessed to the rates for the relief of the poor in respect of such tenements instead of the occupiers thereof, pursuant to the statute passed in the last session of Parliament, intituled "An Act for the better assessing and collecting the poor-rates and highway-rates in respect of small tenements."

Note.—This resolution should be entered on the minutes of the proceedings of the vestry, and be signed by the chairman and by such other of the inhabitants present as shall think proper to sign the same.

7.—13 & 14 VIC. C. 99—WHAT TENEMENTS THE ACT APPLIES TO.

25*th Sept.*, 1850.

Vestry Clerk, Eastbourne, Sussex.—The vestry have ordered that the Act 13 & 14 Vic. c. 99, be carried into effect in this parish, and the owners rated to tenements of the rateable value of £6, and under, instead of the occupiers. A difference of opinion exists as to the construction of the Act, some considering that those occupiers who have heretofore been rated and paid the rates, should still be rated and not the owners, as the Act was intended to cause such tenements only to be assessed to the owner as were formerly excused from payment of rates. Requesting the opinion of the Poor Law Board on the point.

Ans.—The 13 & 14 Vic. c. 99, applies to all tenements the yearly rateable value of which shall not exceed £6, and requires (where the Act is adopted by the vestry) that the owners shall in future be assessed for the same in lieu of the occupiers. It makes no difference as regards the liability of the owner, that any tenements of this class may heretofore have been rated to the occupiers.

8.—13 & 14 VIC. C 99—POWER OF OVERSEERS AS TO FIXING THE SCALE AT WHICH OWNERS SHALL BE RATED.

30*th Sept.*, 1850.

Vicar of Culmstock, Somerset.—Inquiring whether the Act 13 & 14 Vic. c. 99, being adopted by the parish, and the owner of small tenements giving the notice in writing, according to the 4th sec. of the Act, of his being desirous of paying a rate for one year in respect of all such tenements, the overseers would be compelled to receive from such owners a rate reduced to the one-half, as mentioned in the sec.; or whether they would have the option of fixing it at any sum from the one-half to the three-quarters of the rate to which such tenements would have otherwise been liable.

Ans.—With regard to the proviso contained in sec. 4 of the 13 & 14 Vic. c. 99, as to the rating of an owner upon a reduced scale, under certain circumstances, the Board think that the meaning of the proviso is certainly ambiguous, as it does not appear by whom the amount of the reduced scale is to be fixed. It is, however, evidently a matter of arrangement between the owner and the overseers, the law having simply provided that the limit of the allowance shall be one-half of the amount at which such tenement would have been liable to be rated, independent of the statute above cited.

9.—13 & 14 VIC. C. 99—ONE VESTRY MEETING HAVING DECIDED NOT TO ADOPT THE PROVISIONS OF THE ACT—POWER OF A SUBSEQUENT VESTRY MEETING.

1*st Oct.*, 1850.

Churchwarden of Framlingham.—A vestry meeting was lately held in this parish, for the purpose of determining whether or not the provisions of the statute 13 & 14 Vic. c. 99, should be adopted. The vestry decided that they should not be adopted; but it is probable that after a short time the parish officers will be requested to call another meeting for the same purpose, and that a majority of the rate-payers will then be disposed to pass a resolution that such provisions shall be adopted. Inquiring whether or not, and how soon after the late vestry, another meeting may be lawfully held for the same purpose, and whether the vote of such subsequent vestry will overrule that which has already been passed.

Ans.—The Board are not aware of anything to prevent another vestry of the parish of Framlingham being convened, at any time, for the purpose of considering whether the Act of the 13 & 14 Vic. c. 99, should be adopted therein. There is nothing in the language of the Act itself to prevent this being done. If a subsequent vestry, duly convened, agree to adopt the Act, the resolution of the former one to the contrary will not prevent the Act taking effect.

10.—13 & 14 VIC. C. 99—IN WHAT CASES THE OWNERS ARE LIABLE TO BE RATED UNDER.

5*th Oct.*, 1850.

Overseer of Sunderland.—The meaning of the Act 13 & 14 Vic. c. 99, is understood to be that all property of the rateable value of £6 and under, shall be rated at three-fourths; or, if compounded for, at one-half the amount such property would have been liable to be rated had the Act not passed. The scale fixed for reductions for repairs and insurances is one-sixth of the gross rental, therefore, the terms of the Act may be construed to include a tenement of £7. 4*s.* gross rental, as follows:—Gross rental, £7. 4*s.*; rateable value, £6; tenement's value, £4. 10*s.*; or, if compounded for, £3. Some contend, however, that the Act will not allow the landlord of property, where the gross rental exceeds £6, to be rated, and they submit the following scale:—Gross rental, £6; rateable value, £5; reduced rateable value, £3. 15*s.*; or, if compounded for, £1. 17*s.* 6*d.* value. Requesting the opinion of the Poor Law Board on this point.

Ans.—Under the provisions of the statute, 13 & 14 Vic. c. 99, no owner is to be rated, if the yearly rateable value of the property exceeds six pounds. By "yearly rateable value," the Board understand to be meant, not the gross rental, but the net annual value of the property as defined by sec. 1 of the 6 & 7 Wm. 4, c. 96, *i. e.*, the value of a property to let from year to year, deducting the average cost of repairs and insurance. According to this principle, the landlord will be liable, under the statute above cited, where the gross rental exceeds £6, provided the net rental, as above defined, does not exceed that sum.

11.—13 & 14 VIC. C. 99—ALLOWANCE FOR REPAIRS IN RATING UNDER.

5th Oct., 1850.

Churchwarden of Northam, Appledore.—Inquiring, what allowance is made on houses with lands, for repairs before rated? and whether the owners of small tenements are allowed anything extra for repairs, on account of their greater responsibility, than the owners of larger properties. 2. Whether the owners can be compelled to pay the rate in respect of tenements rented at upwards of £20 per annum, where the occupiers become unable to pay the rate.

Ans.—1. In the rating of small tenements, under the recent statute (13 & 14 Vic. c. 99) the Board are not able to say what should be the rate of allowance in respect of repairs. Indeed, they apprehend that properly there can be no uniform rate, as the allowance for repairs, &c., must depend upon the nature and condition of the properties to be assessed; which will probably be very variable. The Board think, however, that no greater reduction in respect of repairs is to be made in the case where owners are assessed under the statute above cited, than where the occupiers themselves are directly assessed. The net annual value of the property should be correctly ascertained in conformity with sec. 1 of the 6th and 7th Wm. 4, c. 96, and this will involve a deduction or allowance for repairs and insurance. When this yearly rateable value is so found, then a proportion of that value or amount (viz., three-fourths) is to be taken as the sum on which the owner, under the 13 & 14 Vic. c. 99, is to be assessed. 2. As regards the inquiry respecting the liability of owners to pay the rates of their tenants who are defaulters to the poor-rate, where the rateable value is above £20 per annum, the Board desire to state that the owners are not liable in such cases.

12.—13 & 14 VIC. C. 99—WHETHER THE WORD "TENEMENT" INCLUDES LAND.

8th Oct., 1850.

Clerk of Ongar Union.—Inquiring whether, in the 13 & 14 Vic. c. 99, the word "tenement" can be deemed to include any land situate in one parish, occupied by a farmer, not exceeding the rateable annual value of £6, and being also part of a farm, the residue whereof being of considerable extent, is situate in an adjoining parish, so as to render it necessary to rate and assess the owner of the land firstly mentioned instead of the occupier thereof.

Ans.—The statute renders the owner of every "tenement" in a parish, the yearly rateable value of which shall not exceed £6, liable to be assessed in respect of it to the poor-rate, at three quarters of the amount at which such tenement would be liable to be rated had the Act not passed. Then, the interpretation clause, sec. 9, defines "tenements" to include (*inter alia*) land. In the case put, there is a piece of land in one parish, the yearly rateable value of which does not exceed £6, and the Board think that it must be rated to the poor-rate irrespective of any other land to which it may be annexed, but which is situate in another parish. They do not find anything in the Act that renders it incumbent upon the overseers to ascertain what are the terms upon which the occupier of such piece of land holds it. Whether it forms part of a demise including the whole of his occupation, or whether it be let by itself, is a matter, as it appears to the Board, immaterial to the overseers.

13.—13 & 14 VIC. C. 99—RATING OF SEVERAL TENEMENTS IN ONE OCCUPATION, BUT BELONGING TO DIFFERENT OWNERS.

10th Oct., 1850.

Rector of Necton, Norfolk.—Inquiring, whether in the case of the occupier of two or more tenements under different owners, the tenements are to be treated separately or collectively, as, for instance, A occupies under B, the owner, 140 acres of land, assessed at £150; and under D, a house assessed at £5. Is A to be rated at £155, or at £150, and D to be rated for the house at three-fourths of £5?

Ans.—As the tenements are stated to be distinct, and held under different owners, A will be rateable for the land, and D for the house, if the yearly rateable value of the latter does not exceed £6.

14.—13 & 14 VIC. C. 99—RATING TENEMENTS WHICH HAD PREVIOUSLY BEEN RATED ON A REDUCED SCALE.

10*th Oct.*, 1850.

Vestry Clerk of Pilton, Shepton Mallett.—In this parish, small tenements have always been rated at less than three-fourths of the sum at which they have been let at. Is it the intention of the statute, 13 & 14 Vic. c. 99, that this reduced rating shall be still further reduced to three-fourths of that sum when assessed on the owners?

Ans.—On referring to the terms of the recent statute, 13 & 14 Vic. c. 99, you will perceive, that where the vestry of a parish agree to adopt it, it is enacted that the owners are to be rated at three-fourths of the amount at which the tenements would be liable to be rated if the Act had not been passed. The amount here referred to, is the rateable value of the property ascertained according to the rule laid down in sec. 1 of the 6 & 7 Wm. 4, c. 96. In the case submitted in your communication, in which small tenements have not heretofore been rated upon their proper rateable value, but upon something much less, it will not be competent to the overseers to take three-fourths of this reduced value; but it will be necessary to calculate the net annual value according to the sec. above cited, and this being ascertained, to take the proportion of that amount or value as directed in sec. 4 of 13 & 14 Vic. c. 99.

15.—13 & 14 VIC. C. 99—WHETHER THE REDUCTION SHOULD BE MADE FROM THE GROSS OR THE RATEABLE VALUE OF TENEMENTS.

24*th Oct.*, 1850.

The Churchwardens of St. Clement, Worcester.—Inquiring whether in applying the Act for rating small tenements, the one-fourth should be deducted from the gross, or the rateable value of the tenements. The words of the Act are "three-fourths of the amount at which such tenement would be liable to be rated in case this Act had not been passed," (sec. 4.) Heretofore all tenements were liable to be rated at their gross annual value. There are many tenements in this parish let to tenants at 1*s*. 9*d*. per week, (£4. 11*s*. per ann.) the poor-rates in respect of which are paid by the landlord. Ought the landlord to be rated at three-fourths of £4. 11*s*., or how otherwise?

Ans.—The Board presume the amounts at which such tenements are at present assessed in the rate-book, represent the net annual value as defined by the 6 & 7 Wm. 4, c. 96, sec. 1; and, if so, all that is necessary, is to take a proportion of that value, namely, three-fourths, and insert the amount in the rate-book as that on which the owners are to be assessed.

16.—13 & 14 VIC. C. 99—MEANING OF THE WORD "OWNER."

13*th Nov.*, 1850.

Clerk of Alresford Union.—At a vestry meeting held in the parish of Cheriton in this union, for the purpose of determining whether £6 tenements shall be rated to the owners instead of occupiers, under the Act 13 & 14 Vic. c. 99, a difference of opinion existed as to the interpretation of the word owner. It was contended on one side, that the word owner must mean the person entitled to the property in question in fee simple, and as recognized in the Parochial Assessment Act: On the other side, that the word owner may be extended to a person who, for instance, rents a farm upon which is erected a number of cottages, which are subletted by him. Requesting the opinion of the Poor Law Board on the point; and also, as to whether, on coming to any resolution in reference to the above Act, the qualification and number of votes are to be taken as set forth in the Act 58, Geo. 3, c. 69.

Ans.—The Board can only refer the guardians of the Alresford Union to the definition of the term "owner" given in the above cited statute itself; which does not appear to the Board to be confined to the owner of the fee simple. They do not find any definition of the word owner in the Parochial Assessments Act. The Board are of opinion that the votes to be taken at the vestry on the question of the adoption of the statute, should be taken according to the usual scale of voting at vestries, namely, the scale provided by the 58 Geo. 3, c. 99, and the 59 Geo. 3, c. 85.

17.—13 & 14 VIC. C. 99—WHETHER THE PROVISIONS OF THE 59 GEO. 3, C. 12, CAN STILL BE ACTED UPON AS TO CERTAIN TENANTS.

14*th Nov.*, 1850.

Clerk of Bridge Union.—A vestry meeting has been held in a parish in this union to take into consideration the propriety of rating the owners of cottages under £6 a year, instead of the occupiers, in pursuance of the Act 13 & 14 Vic. c. 99. As the owners of all the cottages in the parish of the yearly rent of £6 and upwards are at present rated for the same, under the provisions of the 59 Geo. 3, c. 12, a question arose whether such owners could be so rated if the provisions of the recent Act were adopted with regard to the cottages let under £6 a year. Inquiring whether the provisions of the 59th Geo. 3, c. 12, can still be acted upon with regard to the cottages of the rateable value of £6 and under, although let from £6 a year and upwards; and the provisions of the 13 & 14 Vic. c. 99, be at the same time carried into execution with regard to all cottages let under £6 a year.

Ans.—The 13 & 14 Vic. c. 99, applies to all tenements the rateable value of which does not exceed £6 per annum; and the 59 Geo. 3, c. 12, to premises where the rent is £6 and upwards. Some cases, therefore, in the parish may perhaps fall within both of the above statutes, inasmuch as the one refers to rent and the other to rateable value, which may differ in amount from the rent. The Board are of opinion that, wherever this is found to happen, the assessment should be in accordance with the provisions of the later statute, the 13 & 14 Vic. c. 99.

18.—13 & 14 VIC. C. 99—OCCUPIERS VOTING AT VESTRY MEETINGS.

15*th Nov.*, 1850.

J. E., Esq., Gomersal.—Inquiring, whether the rating of the owners under the Act of 13 & 14 Vic. c. 99, takes away the rights of the occupiers to vote at vestry meetings, whether such occupiers reside in corporate towns under municipal regulations or elsewhere.

Ans.—The 7th sec. of the 13 & 14 Vic. c. 99, preserves to the occupiers of tenements coming within it, the exercise of municipal privileges, and franchises, but none other. The Board are of opinion, therefore, that where the owners are rated to the poor-rates in respect of such tenements instead of the occupiers, the latter will not be legally qualified to vote at the parish vestries.

19.—13 & 14 VIC. C. 99—POSTPONEMENT OF THE ASSESSMENT OF OWNERS AFTER ORDER OF VESTRY.

16*th Nov.*, 1850.

Mr. J. F., Downton, Alderbury.—On the 17th of October last there was a vestry meeting held to decide whether the owners of small tenements should be rated instead of the occupiers, when it was decided that the owners should be rated, but it was not settled whether the alteration was to be made before Lady-day next, or when the next rate was wanted. The overseers have this week received an order from the guardians of the Alderbury Union to pay a moiety of £1,147 on the 3rd of Dec. next, and there being a great many alterations to be made in the properties, and the real owners of some of the property to be discovered, the overseers will not be able to make out a rate, so as to collect the money by the 3rd of Dec. Inquiring, therefore, whether the overseers are bound by law to rate the owners instead of occupiers, the first rate after the vestry, (that is, this rate,) or whether they could defer it till Lady-day, thus giving the owners an opportunity of compounding for their cottages, and the overseers a chance of adjusting the rates of some of the cottages, which hitherto have always been excused on account of the poverty of the tenants.

Ans.—Assuming that the vestry have duly made the order under the 1st sec. of the 13 & 14 Vic. c. 99, the enactment in the 3rd sec. renders the owners immediately liable to be assessed in respect of the tenements in question to the poor-rates instead of the occupiers, and does not authorize any postponement of such assessment.

20.—13 & 14 VIC. C. 99—ANNUAL VALUE OF TENEMENTS TO BE RATED.

31*st August*, 1850.

Assistant Overseer, Darlington.—A vestry meeting has been called in this township for the purpose of considering the expediency of putting in force the statute 13 & 14 Vic. c. 99, and a question arises whether it is competent for the vestry to rate the owners of houses at £5 rateable value and under, or whether the Act means that all tenements not exceeding £6 rateable value, must be charged to the owners; in other words, whether the vestry can fix the maximum at any sum below £6 they chose. (See sec. 4.) Requesting the opinion of the Poor Law Board on the point.

Ans.—The Board think that the vestry of any parish, in adopting the provisions of the 13 & 14 Vic. c. 99, cannot legally fix the maximum annual value of the houses to be assessed under that Act at any sum below £6, but that, looking at the terms of the 1st sec. of the Act in connection with those of sec. 4, it will be compulsory to rate the owners of "all" the tenements in the township of the yearly value of £6 and under, if the owners of "any" such tenements are assessed. The terms of the 4th sec. are "the owner of every tenement," &c.

III.—TAXATION OF BILL OF COSTS.—

CONSTRUCTION OF SEC. 8 of 11 & 12 VIC. c. 31.

9th June, 1850.

T. S., Esq., Solicitor.—The clerk of the peace for the county of——, had taxed his (the solicitor's) bill of costs in a case in which he was concerned for the appellants, in a manner which appeared to him to defeat the object of the 8th sec. of the 11 & 12 Vic. c. 31. As he read the section, "it is intended that the overseers of the appellant's township shall be paid such costs as they shall have incurred;" whereas, by the taxation in the present case, nearly all such costs are disallowed. The grounds on which the clerk of the peace has proceeded are thus stated by him:—The practice in the courts of quarter sessions has, previous to the passing of the 11 & 12 Vic. c. 31, invariably been in all cases of abandonment of an order of removal, for the appellants to appear at the sessions, and to consent to the respondents having their order quashed, not upon the merits, on the respondents paying the appellants their taxed costs, which, according to several decisions, were bound to be taxed during the sitting of the court. Although, by the 8th sec. of this statute those costs may now be taxed out of court, yet the Act does not set forth any scale of costs, and his impression is that he is bound by the scale which is laid down by the sessions' rules in all other cases of appeal.

Ans.—The Board have perused the 8th sec. of the Act referred to, which applies immediately to the present case, and observe, that it is not provided that the costs to be allowed are those between attorney and client. Undoubtedly the terms of the provision are very wide, but the Board are not prepared to say that the clerk of the peace has drawn an erroneous conclusion as to the meaning and requirements of that section, in holding, that in taxing the costs claimed under that provision by the appellant parish, upon the abandonment of the order of the removal, he, as the officer of the court of quarter sessions, is bound by the scale which is laid down by that court in all other cases of appeal. The Board think that the appellant parish cannot be put in a better condition by the abandonment of the order than they would have been in if the appeal had gone on and the order had been quashed. A different construction would, probably, operate so as to discourage parishes from abandoning their orders.

IV.—VESTRY CLERK.

1.—13 & 14 VIC. c. 57 & 99.—PAYMENT OF BOROUGH EXPENSES OUT OF THE POOR-RATE—ADOPTION OF PART ONLY OF THE VESTRIES' ACT—HOLDING VESTRIES IN TOWN-HALL—ONE VESTRY MEETING FOR THE PURPOSES OF BOTH ACTS.

8th Oct., 1850.

Overseer of Deal.—Inquiring, 1. In the event of the provisions of the Act for Rating the Owners of Small Tenements being adopted in this parish, can the borough expenses be defrayed out of the poor-rate? 2. If the parish can adopt so much only of the Vestries' Act as relates to the holding of vestry meetings in other buildings than the parish church, or must all the provisions of the Act including those relating to the appointment of a vestry clerk be adopted? 3. In boroughs where there are suitable town-halls, may such town-halls be used for holding vestry meetings; and if so, is the consent of the mayor or corporation required; and will it be necessary that such consent should be renewed annually? 4. Would it be legal to call a vestry to take into consideration the Small Tenements Rating Act and the Vestries' Act at the same time, or must there be two separate vestries for the purpose?

Ans.—1. The Board do not see that the recent Act (13 & 14 Vic. c. 99.) relating to the rating of small tenements in any way affects the payment of borough rates out of the poor-rates. The law in that respect remains as it was before the Act passed. Whether the monies required by the council for the purposes of the borough should be paid directly from the poor-rate, or raised by a separate rate, must depend upon the order which the council may make in the case (see 1 Vic. c. 81.) If the council order the payment out of the poor-rate, and the parish adopt the Act above recited, the owners of the property in question would necessarily contribute towards the borough rate. 2. The Board entertain no doubt that it is competent for the parish to adopt only such part of the 13 & 14 Vic. c. 57, as relates to the providing of a vestry room, without the other provisions of the statute; and, though the point is not quite so clear, the Board also consider that they might give their sanction to the appointment of a vestry clerk in a case where vestry rooms may not have been provided. 3. A town-hall, if it afford suitable accommodation for the purpose, can certainly be used for the holding of vestries if the corporation consent thereto; but, whether the corporation could be bound to allow the continual use of it when once granted will depend upon the terms under which they give their consent. 4. One vestry meeting can be called for the purpose of taking into consideration both the Acts in question.

2.—13 & 14 VIC. C. 57.—IF THE VESTRY CLERK MUST BE AN ATTORNEY.

21*st Sept.*, 1850.

Vestry Clerk, Boston.—Inquiring, whether the vestry clerk to be appointed under the Act 13 & 14 Vic. c. 57, must be an attorney.

Ans.—There is no provision in the 13 & 14 Vic. c. 57, which makes it necessary that a vestry clerk appointed under that Act should be an attorney.

3.—13 & 14 VIC. C. 57—COMPATIBILITY OF THE OFFICES OF VESTRY CLERK, CLERK TO GUARDIANS, AND CLERK TO MAGISTRATES.

24*th Oct.*, 1850.

Clerk of ——— *Union.*—1. Is there anything inconsistent or objectionable in his holding (if appointed) the office of vestry clerk, for the parish of ———, under the Act 13 & 14 Vic. c. 57, together with his present appointment of clerk to the union within which that parish is situate? 2. Are the duties of such vestry clerk consistent with those of clerk to the magistrates for the district within which the parish of ——— is situate, with reference more particularly to the 6th clause of the 7th section of the Vestries' Act, which prescribes that it shall be the duty of the vestry clerk, *inter alia*, "To prepare and issue the necessary process for recovering of arrears of such rates respectively before the justices, and procure the summons to be served, and to attend the justices thereon, and advise the churchwardens and overseers as to the recovery of such arrears?" It seems that the statute contemplates that the vestry clerk shall in such cases appear before the magistrates as the advocate and adviser of the churchwardens and overseers, and that this is inconsistent with the duties of clerk and legal adviser to the magistrates.

Ans.—The Board do not see anything in the duties which are prescribed by the 13 & 14 Vic. c. 57, to be performed by the vestry clerk of a parish which would be inconsistent with the office of clerk of the union including such parish. But it certainly appears to the Board that the vestry clerk cannot act as clerk to the justices in matters which may be brought before them in reference to the parish for which he is appointed vestry clerk. This consideration may not, however, render it absolutely impossible for the same person to hold both offices, because he may possibly take means to procure some person to assist the guardians when the cases which he may have to conduct as vestry clerk come before them. But there would frequently be some inconvenience in such an arrangement.

4. 13 & 14 Vic. c. 57.—IF VESTRY CLERK CAN BE A COLLECTOR OF PAROCHIAL RATES.

21*st Nov.*, 1850.

Vestry Clerk of Speldhurst, Tunbridge.—Inquiring whether that part of the Act 13 & 14 Vic. c. 57, which relates to the appointment of vestry clerks only, can be put in force in this parish without embracing the entire Act; and whether, in the event of that part of the Act being brought into operation, the appointment would allow the vestry clerk to collect or assist in collecting the rates of the parish.

Ans.—The Board are empowered by the 13 & 14 Vic. c. 57, to order that the statute, or any part of it, shall come into operation upon application being made to them in the manner prescribed by the 1st section. The Board can therefore issue an order directing the adoption in a parish of so much only of the statute as provides for the appointment of a vestry clerk. The Board do not, however, find that the statute will authorize the appointment of a vestry clerk, with the duty of collecting any parochial rate. Indeed, he is to superintend the collectors, and, therefore, his appointment as a collector would be an inconsistency.

London: Printed by Order of the Poor Law Board, by BLACKBURN & BURT, 90½, Holborn Hill, and Published by CHARLES KNIGHT, 90, Fleet Street.

AN
OFFICIAL CIRCULAR

OF PUBLIC DOCUMENTS AND INFORMATION:

DIRECTED BY THE POOR LAW BOARD TO BE PRINTED, CHIEFLY FOR THE USE OF THE BOARDS OF GUARDIANS AND THEIR OFFICERS.

No. 44.] DECEMBER, 1850. [N.S.

CONTENTS.

I.—AUDIT—OF THE ACCOUNTS OF BOROUGH RATE.

8th Nov., 1850.

Auditor of the West Yorkshire Audit District. — By the recent Act of Incorporation granted to the town of Halifax, the townships of Southowran and Northowran, are situated partly within and partly without the limits of the municipal borough. A borough-rate was laid in January last, and collected under the mayor's warrant by the overseers of the poor, pursuant to the 12 & 13 Vic. c. 65, sec. 2, and at the same time a police and watch-rate, under the same authority, was collected by special overseers appointed by the council pursuant to 1 Vic. c. 81, sec. 3. Requesting instructions in reference to his duty as auditor in the above cases, and inquiring whether the collectors are bound to account to him at the half-yearly audit.

Ans.—The Board are disposed to think that the watch-rate in question might have been collected under the 12 & 13 Vic. c. 65, sec. 2., by the overseers of the two townships; but the rate not having been collected by them, but by special overseers appointed for that purpose, the Board do not find that you have any authority to audit the account of the same. As regards the borough-rate, levied under the 12 & 13 Vic. c. 65, it is competent for you, under sec. 2 of that statute, to require the overseers or collectors to account to you in respect of it. So, also, if any rate be collected under the authority of the 13 & 14 Vic. c. 101, sec. 10, you should require the parties in like manner to account to you for it.

II. — BASTARD — LEFT IN THE WORKHOUSE BY THE MOTHER, WHO IS IN SERVICE.

10th Dec., 1850.

Clerk of Chipping Sodbury Union.—Sarah W., on the 29th of April last, was sent from the workhouse to jail for twenty-one days, for destroying the property of the guardians, leaving her child in the workhouse. When she left the prison, instead of returning to the workhouse she went to service, at wages of £5. 10*s.* per annum, leaving the child chargeable to the parish of Yate. Inquiring whether the child should be sent to the mother, or whether the mother should be punished as a vagrant.

Ans.—The guardians of the Chipping Sodbury Union would not be justified in sending the child to its mother; but the latter is liable to be proceeded against under the 7 & 8 Vic. c. 101, sec. 6, for neglecting to maintain the child, if the justices shall be of opinion that she is able wholly or in part to do so. Until, however, the mother has actually earned her wages, (supposing her to have no other means,) it will be difficult to say that she is able to maintain the child, and the Board would hesitate to advise a prosecution at present. It appears to the Board that the woman could not be convicted of deserting the child, (under the latter clause of the 7 & 8 Vic. c. 101, sec. 6,) as the child did not become chargeable in consequence of her desertion of it, and the act of quitting it was not voluntary on the part of the mother.

III.—BURIAL.—REPAYMENT OF THE EXPENSES OF BURIAL PAID BY AN OVERSEER.

23rd Nov., 1850.

Overseer of Tiverton.—As one of the overseers of this parish, he signed an undertaking in the form below, on the 7th of October last, to the treasurer of the Devon and Exeter Hospital, as to Wm. Beedell, a pauper belonging to the parish. About ten days afterwards the man died in the hospital, and he, the overseer, was called on by the secretary of the hospital to pay, and did pay, twelve shillings, the expences of the removal of the body, and threepence for a post-office order. He had applied to the relieving-officer to repay the amount, but he had failed to do so. Inquiring what steps he should take to obtain reimbursement.

Copy of the form referred to above :—

To the Governors of the Devon and Exeter Hospital.

Gentlemen,—I desire you will admit of the parish of to be a patient of the said hospital, whom I hereby recommend as a proper object of your charity.

Your obedient servant,

To the Treasurer of the said Hospital.

I do hereby promise to defray all Expenses that may attend the burial or removal of the said

Witness,

Ans.—It appears to the Board that the relieving-officer has no authority in point of law to repay you the expenses of the funeral of the deceased pauper, Wm. Beedell, or of the removal of the body; at all events, not without an order of the guardians of the Tiverton Union, which they would be authorized to give only in case the deceased was chargeable as a pauper at the time of his death. The overseer, as such, has no legal authority to give an undertaking of the description signed by you in this case for the payment of the expenses out of the poor-rates. The guardians of the union are the only parties authorized by the 7 & 8 Vic. c. 101, s. 31, to provide for the expenses of the burial of paupers.

IV.—CHAPLAIN—PAYMENT OF FEE TO THE BISHOP'S SECRETARY ON THE APPOINTMENT OF A.

19th Nov., 1850.

The Rev. ————.—On his appointment to the chaplaincy of the ———— Union, he received from the clerk of the guardians a form, which he, the chaplain, enclosed to the bishop of this diocese, and returned to the guardians, signed by his lordship. The bishop's secretary, when forwarding the document, required a fee of £1. 10*s.*, which he, the chaplain, paid. He had applied to the guardians to repay him the amount, but they had refused to do so, and he requested, therefore, the advice of the Poor Law Board upon the subject.

Ans.—The consent of the bishop to the appointment of the chaplain to a union workhouse is a requisite as much for the benefit of the clergyman seeking to obtain that office, as of the guardians requiring his services therein. When, therefore, the proposed chaplain applies for such consent, and obtains it, and a fee is thereupon demanded of him by the bishop's secretary, the Board think that, whether the latter could have lawfully insisted upon payment of the fee or not, the chaplain has no legal claim upon the guardians to be reimbursed the amount.

V.—CHARGEABILITY.

1. OF A WIDOW.

15*th Nov.*, 1850.

Clerk of Honiton Union.—Inquiring whether in the following case Ann G——— is rendered irremovable by the operation of the Acts 9 & 10 Vic. c. 66, and 11 & 12 Vic. c. 110:—The pauper, for many years as a widow and as the wife of a former husband, resided in the parish of Ottery St. Mary without receiving relief. On the second marriage her husband, who had previously lived in another parish, came to Ottery St. Mary to live with her, and since the period of her second marriage she has not lived five years without the receipt of relief. She is now again a widow, and the parish officers of Ottery St. Mary have applied to have her relief charged to the common fund of the union, on the ground of five years' residence without relief in Ottery St. Mary, her last husband's settlement being in another parish.

Ans.—The Board are of opinion that the pauper is irremovable from Ottery St. Mary by reason of length of residence. Besides which, she would also be irremovable as a widow for twelve months after her husband's death, by virtue of the 9 & 10 Vic. c. 66, s. 2.

2. CHARGEABILITY OF A WIDOW.

14*th Oct.*, 1850.

Clerk of Wilton Union. — Elizabeth P., (widow,) whose maiden settlement is in Barford St. Martin, married first, John B., (now deceased,) whose settlement was in Wilton; by him she had one child, now aged six years. She married, secondly, Herbert P., (now also deceased,) whose settlement was in Compton Chamberlayne, and who, at the time of his marriage with her was a widower with one child, now aged five years. By this second marriage she had one child, now aged one year. She is living in Barford St. Martin, but the relief given to her and the three children is charged to Compton Chamberlayne. The three parishes are in this union. Inquiring, whether the guardians have done rightly in charging the whole of the relief to Compton Chamberlayne.

The Poor Law Board.—Before the Board advise on the case of Elizabeth P., they request to be informed when her second husband died, and whether she and her family were residing with him at the time of his death, and if so, in what parish.

Clerk of same Union.—Elizabeth P.'s second husband died on 20th April, 1850, at Compton Chamberlayne. She was not living with him at his decease in consequence of domestic differences, but taking her own two children with her, she went to reside with her mother at Barford St. Martin. The husband's child, by his first marriage, remained with him at Compton till his death.

Ans.—The Board presume that Elizabeth P. is now removable to Compton Chamberlayne, so far as any provision of the 9 & 10 Vic. c. 66, is concerned. If so, there is nothing to prevent the guardians of the Wilton Union from charging the parish of Compton Chamberlayne with the cost of the relief of the woman and of the two children who are settled in that parish, (provided the overseers admit the settlements and consent to the charge.) As regards the child, however, whose settlement is in Wilton, it appears to the Board that its relief cannot be charged to that parish; but the child being within the age of nurture, would be removable with the mother to Compton Chamberlayne, though not settled there. If so removed, Compton Chamberlayne would be chargeable with the child's relief; but if the removal does not take place, the parish in which the child is now residing, namely, Barford St. Martin, will be liable.

3. CHARGEABILITY OF ORPHAN CHILDREN.

22*nd Nov.*, 1850.

Clerk of Warminster Union.—Inquiring, whether the children mentioned in the following statement are not destitute children within the meaning of the 11 & 12 Vic. c. 110, sec. 1, and 12 & 13 Vic. c. 103, sec. 2:—*Statement:*—Wm. Harding, aged seven years, and Sarah Maria Harding, aged five years, are legitimate children of parents who are both dead. Their mother's maiden name was Clift. She was born in the parish of Heytesbury, in this union, where her parents were settled. About eight years ago she married in London a man named Harding, and after living with him about four years he died, leaving her with two children. At his death she returned to Heytesbury, to her mother's house, with her children, and applied for and obtained relief at the cost of that parish. The parish officers of Heytesbury used every endeavour at that time to ascertain her husband's settlement, but wholly without avail. She then went to service, and her children were allowed relief for a considerable period, and were taken care of by their grandmother. About twelve months ago the mother came to Heytesbury, and took away the children, saying she was going to be married. Nothing more was heard of her until about ten days since, when the grandmother applied for relief for the children, stating that she had been to Worcester to see her daughter, who was ill, and that she had died whilst she was there. That her daughter, just previous to her death, had informed her that she was never married to the man with whom she was then living, and by whom she had two children. That after her daughter's death this man refused to take care of these children, but was willing to support his own. The grandmother, not knowing what to do with them, brought them to Heytesbury, and has applied for and obtained relief on their account. She is herself in the receipt of parochial relief.

Ans.—The Board do not consider that these children are deserted within the meaning of the 12 & 13 Vic. c. 103. They are, according to the statement, in the custody of a relative, and, apparently, their place of settlement is known; for, as it is not known where the father's settlement was, or, in fact, whether he had any, the mother's settlement would be theirs, and that appears to have been in the parish of Heytesbury, where she was born, and where her parents were also settled.

4. CHARGEABILITY OF A PREGNANT SINGLE WOMAN.

14*th Nov.*, 1850.

Chairman of Launceston Union, and Guardian of Boyton Parish. — Requesting the opinion of the Poor Law Board on the following case:—M. C. is a single woman, aged twenty, *sui juris*. Her legal settlement is said to be in the parish of North Petherwyn, in this union. She was in service at Devonport, became unwell from pregnancy, and came to the residence of her father in the parish of Boyton, whose legal settlement is not in Boyton, but who is irremovable from residence. She left her service, but engaged to return to it and serve out her year, and left her clothes and boxes at her master's. Her father at first refused her admission into his house, but he subsequently received her. She remained at his residence, in the parish of Boyton, for seven days, and during that time went to make application for relief to the board of guardians of the Launceston Union. On her way she met the relieving-officer, who took her application, and on the next board-day an order for the workhouse was given to her, under which she was admitted. On a board-day after her admission, it was alleged on behalf of the parish of Boyton, that she was not a settled pauper of that parish, and the chargeability was therefore transferred to the common fund. On its being reported to the board of guardians that the pauper had been confined, and was again convalescent, her chargeability was directed to be transferred to the parish of Boyton, and that parish was directed to take the requisite steps for her removal to her place of settlement. The guardians of the parish of Boyton object to the relief first given to her for one week, before the fact of her being a non-settled pauper was affirmed, being charged to their parish, on the ground that she was a wayfarer; secondly, to the relief being now transferred to Boyton, and urge the following arguments: —First, that the pauper being emancipated from her father, came to Boyton to arrange with the putative father of her child; that there could be no intention of residing in Boyton, her father refusing on her arrival permission to remain in his house, and she being under an engagement to return to her service in Devonport. She had no residence in Boyton within the meaning of the 11 & 12 and 13 & 14 Vic., and the charge of her maintenance from her first admission into the workhouse must be placed to the common fund, her chargeability arising from pregnancy. Second, that her residence in the workhouse under a chargeability to the common fund, is not a residence in the parish of Boyton, and therefore the guardians cannot transfer her chargeability to that parish, nor require the parish officers to incur the expense of an attempt to remove her, which if made, must fail, inasmuch as the pauper is neither legally resident in, nor chargeable to the parish. Her maintenance during her residence in the workhouse must be charged to the common fund, and no new chargeability can arise, except there be a change of residence, 12 & 13 Vic. c. 103, s. 4. On the other hand, the guardians contend that it is an ordinary case, in which the pauper is found destitute whilst having a fixed residence (with her father) in Boyton, is properly charged to Boyton, becomes irremovable, and on an allegation of non-settlement in Boyton, is charged to the common fund during irremovability, and on this ceasing, is properly transferred to Boyton.

Ans.—The Board are of opinion that inasmuch as the father of the pauper is irremovable from Boyton by reason of residence, the pauper herself (unless she had a settlement different from that of her father,) was, by force of the statute 11 & 12 Vic. c. 111, also irremovable, and her exemption was not affected by her removal to the workhouse of the Launceston Union, whether she had or had not a settlement different from her father's does not appear upon the statement of the case before the Board. If she had not, they think she was irremovable throughout; if she had, she was irremovable only during the actual period of her illness in the workhouse.

Vicar of Boyton.—Referring to the above correspondence, and requesting information on the following point, viz.—Is the fact of a woman having a bastard child, although delivered in the workhouse, sufficient to authorize the guardians to direct the overseers of a parish to apply for an order of removal, before the pauper shall have made application for support in consequence of having a bastard child? Or, ought not the woman, having recovered from her confinement, to be dismissed from the house? The question resolves itself into this:—Is the fact of a woman having a bastard child, absolutely "a permanent disability" and cause of removal? He apprehends not. The woman may be able to maintain her bastard child by her own exertions, although incapacitated during pregnancy: or, she may affiliate and obtain an order on the putative father. It is only after she shall have shown her inability in the first case, or have failed in the second, that she becomes chargeable to the parish of her residence, and removable. The present case illustrates the point,—the woman has affiliated her child, and obtained an order on the putative father. She has now returned to her service in Devonport, and has made no application to the guardians for relief.

Ans.—The Board think that, whether a woman delivered of an illegitimate child in the workhouse, is or is not thereby rendered irremovable to her place of settlement, must depend upon circumstances. There would doubtless be a chargeability in such case, but the question is, how far the removal would be restrained by sec. 4 of the 9 & 10 Vic. c. 66. If the pauper became chargeable through sickness caused by the pregnancy, she would not be removable if the disability be merely temporary, as in all ordinary cases of this kind. If, however, in any special case, a permanent disability arose from the pregnancy or delivery, she would be removable. Again, if she became chargeable originally, not through actual sickness, but mere destitution, though arising from advanced pregnancy, she would (in consequence of the relief given her, as supposed,) be removable. In the case which you put by way of illustration, no order of removal could now be obtained on a ground quite independent of the considerations stated above, viz.—that the pauper has ceased to be chargeable, if (as the Board believe the more general, and perhaps the better opinion to be,) an order of removal cannot be obtained upon a chargeability which has ceased.

---

5. CHARGEABILITY—RELIEF AND FUNERAL EXPENSES.—NON-SETTLED PAUPER.

24th Oct., 1850.

Clerk of Newent Union.—R. P., aged 24, a single man, was, a few weeks ago, taken ill in the parish of Dymock, in which parish he had been resident for nearly five months. He was attended by the medical officer of the union, and received medical and other relief; the overseers of Dymock received directions from the guardians to have him removed to his settlement, the medical officer having certified that he was able to be removed, and that his illness was of such a nature as to render him permanently disabled. In the mean-time, and before an order of removal could be obtained, the man died, and was buried in the church-yard of Dymock. Inquiring, whether the expenses of the relief in this case, and the funeral expenses, should be charged to the common fund of the union, or to the parish of Dymock.

Ans.—The Board see no ground, on this statement, for charging the cost of the relief, or the expenses incurred in the burial of the pauper, upon the common fund of the union. The pauper was, apparently, removable, the sickness being, in the opinion of the medical officer, of a nature to produce permanent disability; and therefore he was chargeable to the parish of Dymock, and the funeral expenses, by the operation of the 7 & 8 Vic. c. 101, sec. 31, are also chargeable to that parish.

6. CHARGEABILITY OF A NON-SETTLED PAUPER WHO HAS RETURNED FROM CONFINEMENT IN A LUNATIC ASYLUM.

28*th Nov.*, 1850.

Clerk of Runcorn Union.—S. W. came into the township of Frodsham, in this union, on the 25th August, 1849, and stayed one or two nights in the township, where she attempted to commit suicide. She was removed by the overseers of Frodsham, under the order of a magistrate, as a lunatic, to Haydock Lodge Lunatic Asylum, in the county of Lancaster, where she remained seven weeks. She was then removed to the Cheshire County Lunatic Asylum, where she remained until the 19th October, 1850, when she was discharged as cured, and brought back to Frodsham, where she now is, and is in receipt of relief. The pauper is a stranger in Frodsham, has no friends there, and, at the time of her attempting to commit suicide, was passing through Frodsham (which is a thoroughfare) from Chester to Warrington. Her settlement cannot be ascertained. Inquiring, if the relief advanced to the pauper since her removal from the asylum should be charged to the township of Frodsham, or to the common fund of the union.

Ans.—The Board request that you will inform them in what manner S. W. was discharged from the Cheshire County Lunatic Asylum: how she was brought to Frodsham, and in whose charge; how long she was in that township, after her return to it, before applying for relief, or application being made for her; and what occurred in the interval.

28*th Nov.*, 1850.

Clerk of same union.—When S. W. was deemed competent to be removed from the Cheshire County Lunatic Asylum by the physician of that institution, the secretary of this institution informed the assistant-overseer of Frodsham (by whom she was removed to the asylum,) of the same, and, in consequence of such information, he personally removed the woman from the asylum to Frodsham, and she on the same day made application to the relieving-officer for relief, and has since been in the receipt of relief from that township.

Ans.—The Board experience some difficulty in advising as to the chargeability of the relief to this pauper; but looking to all the circumstances of the case, and the fact that the assistant-overseer of Frodsham brought her back to that township, and that the pauper was there when she became chargeable, they think that her relief should be charged to that township.

7. SICKNESS PRODUCING PERMANENT DISABILITY.

16*th Dec.*, 1850.

Clerk of Ongar Union.—Transmitting the following statement, duly signed, under sec. 4 of the 11 & 12 Vic. c. 110, for the opinion of the Poor Law Board:—Frances Feast, widow, and her two lawful children, namely, John, aged fourteen years, and Emma, aged eleven years, resided in the parish of Chipping Ongar for the space of eighteen months next preceding the 2nd day of November last; and during the whole of that period they were acknowledged by the churchwarden and overseer of the parish of High Laver, as paupers belonging to their parish; and have also been relieved by the board of guardians at the expense of the parish of High Laver, with 2*s.* in money, and four loaves weekly, during the whole of the above period. On or about the 2nd day of November last, Frances Feast, whilst residing in Chipping Ongar, became sick, and being a permanent pauper, was attended by Mr. George Keane, medical officer, without an order of the board of guardians or relieving-officer; and Mr. Keane ordered nourishments for the widow to the amount of 3*s.* 4¾*d.*; and such additional relief having been reported to the board of guardians, at their weekly meeting, on the 5th of November last, the guardians thereupon also ordered 2*s.* and four loaves for the pauper weekly, and confirmed the additional relief of 3*s.* 4¾*d.* to the parish of High Laver; and at the following weekly meeting, on the 12th of November last, the board ordered the above 3*s.* 4¾*d.*, and also the weekly relief above-mentioned, to be transferred to the common charges of the above union; and they have, ever since the 12th of November last, been relieved weekly, at the same rate of relief, with nourishments as prescribed by the same medical officer. The sickness of Frances Feast is not likely to produce permanent disability, and she and her two children are still residing in the parish of Chipping Ongar. Was the relief given since the 2nd of November last, properly charged to the common charges?

Ans.—As the pauper did not become chargeable by reason of her sickness, but was already in receipt of relief, the 4th sec. of the 9 & 10 Vic. c. 66, does not apply to the case, and therefore the cost of her relief is not chargeable to the common fund of the Ongar Union.

VI.—EMPLOYMENT—OF ABLE-BODIED PAUPERS IN WORKHOUSE.

31*st Oct.*, 1850.

Clerk of Hungerford Union.—Requesting the Poor Law Board to sanction the employment of the able-bodied paupers in the workhouse, at pounding stones, by the aid of a pestle and mortar. The work at the mill shall, it is proposed, be carried on as at present, when there are sufficient paupers to work it, which is not always the case. The picking of oakum, which is the work at which the paupers have hitherto been employed is found to entail an actual loss on the guardians, as it is scarcely saleable when picked. The pounding of stones is carried on, it is believed, with very good effect, in the adjoining unions of Kingsclere and Newbury. The quantity to be pounded to vary (as in the other unions) from a half bushel, to a bushel per day, according to the substance of the stones to be pounded.

Ans.—The Board approve of the able-bodied male paupers in the workhouse of the Hungerford union, being employed in the manner proposed by the guardians, namely, in pounding stones by the aid of a pestle and mortar.

VII.—GUARDIANS.

1. NOTICES OF ORDINARY MEETINGS.

31*st Oct.*, 1850.

A Guardian of ——— Union.—Submitting for the consideration of the Poor Law Board, the propriety of the clerk to the guardians being authorized to acquaint the several guardians by circular of any special business to be brought before the board, such as the appointment and dismissal of any of the officers of the establishment, or any other matter beyond the usual routine of business. At the present time a master is required for the union. He does not deem it necessary to attend every week, as there have not been any applications for relief from the parish which he represents during the year, and he thinks it was never contemplated that forty-five guardians should attend every board day to transact the ordinary business of the week, which those guardians having cases to attend to from their own respective parishes are quite sufficient to perform.

Ans.—The Poor Law Board have not deemed it expedient to issue any general rule upon this subject. The different boards of guardians have usually dealt with the question themselves, prescribing the course of proceeding which the circumstances of their respective unions may render necessary or advisable. Special notices on occasions when business of an unusual or important character is to be brought forward are no doubt desirable; but the question manifestly involves a consideration of expense, which can be determined most properly by the guardians themselves. With regard to your remarks as to the duty of a guardian of the poor in respect of his attendance at the meetings of the board of guardians, the Poor Law Board think it right to observe, that a guardian who only attends those meetings when the particular interests of his own parish may require his attendance, does not appear to the Board to fulfil the duties of his office, so as to satisfy the intentions of the law. The law contemplates that the acts or decisions of the board of guardians, whether immediately concerning the union at large, or only a particular parish therein, will be the result of the joint deliberations of all the members of such board; and, consequently, all the members of the board should as far as possible be present at all its meetings.

2. THE ORDER OF THE PROCEEDINGS OF GUARDIANS.

19*th Nov.*, 1850.

Clerk of West Derby Union.—It has, since the formation of this union, been customary at the weekly meetings of the guardians to conduct the business in the following order:—1st, The reading of the minutes of the preceding meeting. 2nd, The relief of the out-door poor. 3rd, The examination of the master's books and the admission of new cases into the house. 4th, The business arising from the minutes of former meeting, &c. 5th, Any new matters which may occur. A notice has been given of a motion for the next meeting, having for its object the future conduct of the business in conformity with the General Consolidated Order, Art. 41. Inquiring, whether it is obligatory on the guardians to conduct their business according to such order.

Ans.—It is competent to the guardians of the West Derby Union, if they see fit, to make an arrangement as to the order in which the business coming before their board is to be transacted, different from that specified in the General Consolidated Order, Art. 41; though the course there prescribed is the one which the experience of the Poor Law Commissioners led them to believe would be found generally most convenient. In this matter, the guardians are at liberty to pursue that course which, upon the whole, may be most convenient to the majority.

3. VALIDITY OF THE VOTES OF CHAIRMAN OF BOARD OF GUARDIANS.

14*th Nov.*, 1850.

Vice-Chairman of ——— Union.—In presiding at the meeting of the guardians of this union, he stated, that in case of a division on a question then under discussion, he intended to vote, and he also argued in favour of an amendment moved on the question. A division took place, and when putting the amendment to the meeting, he omitted to vote, but after the votes were taken against the amendment, he requested the clerk to place his name for the amendment, this being the side for which he had before spoken, and afterwards gave the casting vote in favour of the amendment. This the guardians consider to be illegal, because his vote was not taken when the amendment was put. Requested the opinion of the Poor Law Board on the point for his future guidance.

Ans.—If your first vote, although not given until after all the other votes had been taken, was nevertheless given before the numbers were declared by you from the chair, such vote appears to the Board to have oeen properly included in the calculation, and the casting vote will of course be equally valid. If, however, you had declared the numbers before you gave any vote, the Board think that your votes were not entitled to count.

VIII.—INSURANCE—OF WORKHOUSE AGAINST FIRE—STAMP DUTY.

4*th Dec.*, 1850.

A. B.—Inquiring, whether workhouses are exempt from the duty which attaches upon fire insurances.

Ans.—The Board do not consider workhouses to be exempt from the duty which attaches upon fire insurances.

IX.—LUNATIC PAUPER.

1. CHARGEABILITY.

9*th Nov.*, 1850.

Assistant Overseer of Birtley, Chester-le-Street Union.—T. C., in January last, had a slight stroke of palsy while at work, (he being at the time a strong and healthy man,) which affected his mind, and he has been of unsound mind ever since. He was removed to a lunatic asylum on the 14th of August last, under a justice's order. At the time of such removal he was residing in the township of Birtley, where he had been for about six weeks, but his legal settlement is in Lamesly, both places being comprised in the Chester-le-Street Union. The man was not chargeable when he was sent to the asylum, but became chargeable in consequence of such removal. The statement of the medical attendant of the asylum, on the 17th of August, after certifying him to be a lunatic, describes him as stout and healthy in appearance, but having had a slight stroke of paralysis, which had weakened him. He is at present considerably worse, and, to all appearance, not likely to get better. Inquiring whether the man is exempted from removal to his legal settlement by the 9 & 10 Vic. c. 66, he being able-bodied at the time of becoming a lunatic; and whether the expenses and maintenance ought to be charged to Birtley, or to Lamesly, or to the common fund of the union, as enacted by 12 & 13 Vic. c. 103, s. 5.

Ans.—The Board see no ground for charging the expenses of the pauper's maintenance to the common fund of the Chester-le-Street Union; but the proper course to be pursued in the case is for an order to be obtained, under the 8 & 9 Vic. c. 126, s. 62, to charge the cost upon the parish of the settlement.

2. CHARGEABILITY OF LUNATIC PAUPER.

26th Nov., 1850.

Clerk of Bromsgrove Union.—J. E., a poor person, who has resided in the parish of Bromsgrove for the last nine months, is now insane, and has been sent to a lunatic asylum. Many years ago, he acquired a settlement in the parish of Tardibrigg, in the county of Worcester, which settlement was extinguished in the year 1840, when the parish was divided into townships, and separate overseers were appointed. Inquiring, how the costs of removing this pauper to the lunatic asylum, and his maintenance there, ought to be charged; whether to the parish of Bromsgrove, or to the common fund of the union. Or, whether an order of justices can legally be made upon the county for these expenses.

Ans.—If no order of justices has been made in the case, the 8 & 9 Vic. c. 126, sec. 57, renders the parish from which the lunatic is sent to the asylum, liable in the first place to pay the charges. See also secs. 58 & 59 of the same statute as to subsequent proceedings.

7th Dec., 1850.

Clerk of same Union.—Requesting the opinion and advice of the Board on the best course to pursue in the case of J. E., which is a peculiar one, it being a known fact, that the pauper once had a settlement, which by operation of law has been extinguished, leaving him without any settlement at all. Would the justices (having jurisdiction in the matter) be warranted in adjudicating the pauper to be chargeable to the county of Worcester, and in making an order upon the treasurer of that county for his maintenance at Duddeston Hall Lunatic Asylum, in the county of Warwick, and for payment of the expenses of conveying him there?

Ans.—The Poor Law Board consider that, in the case of J. E., an order for maintenance and costs of removal may be made upon the county; and the Board recommend that steps should accordingly be taken, under the 8 & 9 Vic. c. 126, secs. 59 & 63.

3. REMOVAL OF LUNATIC PAUPER FROM ONE ASYLUM TO ANOTHER.

9th Dec., 1850.

Clerk of Tunstead and Happing Hundreds.—D. P., a person residing in the parish of New Church, Isle of Wight, has been chargeable to that parish on account of insanity, and has been conveyed to the Carisbrook Asylum in the island. The parish officers of Bacton, in these Hundreds, have received the particulars as to his settlement from New Church, and they acknowledge his settlement to be in the parish of Bacton. The pauper is now in the Asylum at Carisbrook, at a cost of 12*s.* per week, which the guardians are of opinion is an excessive charge, especially when, if the pauper was in the Norfolk Asylum, he would cost about 5*s.* 6*d.* per week only. Inquiring, whether, under these circumstances, the pauper could be removed from Carisbrook Asylum to the Norfolk Asylum; and whether, if he has been residing at New Church more than five years, the cost of his maintenance, &c., in the asylum can be legally claimed by New Church of the parish of Bacton.

Ans.—The lunatic cannot be discharged from the asylum at Carisbrook unless by the order of two visiting justices, and this Board cannot say whether the justices would authorize such discharge. If they did, the Board apprehend that the lunatic might be removed to the Norfolk Asylum; but then, probably a fresh order of justices would be requisite to effect the removal. The fact of the pauper having resided for five years in the parish of New Church may bring the case within the 12 & 13 Vic. c. 105, sec. 5; and the Board recommend an application to be made accordingly to the guardians of the poor of the Isle of Wight Incorporation.

X.—MATRON OF WORKHOUSE.—SECURITY.

10th Dec., 1850.

Clerk of Droitwich Union. — Inquiring whether the guardians can insist upon the matron giving a bond for the due performance of the duties of her office, there being a master.

Ans.—The Board do not consider that the matron of a workhouse, where there is a master, can be compelled to find security. The terms of Art. 184 of the General Consolidated Order apply to a specific case only, namely, where there is a workhouse in which there is no master.

XI.—OVERSEERS.

1. THEIR DUTIES.

26*th Nov.*, 1850.

Clerk of Chipping Sodbury Union.—If paupers become chargeable to any parish in consequence of being deserted or neglected, is it the duty of the overseers, or the officers of the union, to take the proceedings against the persons liable to maintain the paupers, with a view of punishing them as vagrants, or recover the cost of maintenance? 2. If it is the duty of the overseers, are they liable to the penalty for disobeying the orders of the guardians if they refuse to take proceedings when directed by the guardians to do so?

Ans.—It is competent either for the guardians of the Chipping Sodbury Union, or for the overseers of the respective parishes concerned, to take proceedings against the offenders referred to in your first inquiry. (See the 7 & 8 Vic. c. 101, sec. 59.) 2. The Board do not consider that the guardians can legally order the overseers to institute any particular prosecutions, so at least as to subject the latter to a penalty if they neglect to carry out such direction.

---

2. AN ASSISTANT OVERSEER NOT ENTITLED TO ATTEND MEETINGS OF THE BOARD OF GUARDIANS.

4*th Dec.*, 1850.

Chairman of Select Vestry at ——.—Inquiring whether or not the assistant overseer of a parish has the right of being present at the meetings of the board of guardians during the hearing of applications for relief from his own parish?

Ans.—An assistant overseer of a parish has no legal right to be present at a meeting of a board of guardians or to take part in the proceedings of the guardians.

XII.—POOR-RATE.

1. POWER OF OVERSEERS IN DETERMINING THE AMOUNT AND THE TIME OF COLLECTION OF.

5*th Nov.*, 1850.

The Rev. ———, *Dover Union.*—Inquiring, whether overseers can legally make a poor-rate, exceeding in amount the sum ordered by the guardians to be paid as the half-yearly contribution of the parish; and, also, whether the guardians, having ordered the contribution to be paid to the treasurer in two instalments, an interval of three months elapsing between the first and second payment, the overseer can oblige the parishioners to pay the whole sum in one rate. These inquiries, particularly the last, arise from the fact that the object avowed by the overseer of more than one parish in this union, is to collect the whole rate at once from the larger owners of land, and to give longer time to certain farmers and other occupiers.

Ans.—It rests with the overseers of a parish, in making a poor-rate, to lay it at such an amount as they, in the exercise of their own judgment, may find to be necessary to meet the exigencies of their office, and they are not bound to confine the amount of the rate to the sum called for by the guardians of the union by way of contribution from the parish. The practice to which you allude, however, in regard to the unfair or partial manner of collecting the rate when made, is manifestly an improper one; and the Board think it right to point out, that if there be any neglect on the part of the overseers to collect the rate from any of the ratepayers, the matter should be brought under the notice of the auditor, who is empowered to surcharge the overseers with the amount of any deficiency or loss incurred by their negligence or misconduct, (see 7 & 8 Vic. c. 101, sec. 32.)

---

2. BY WHOM POOR-RATE IS TO BE MADE IN A TOWNSHIP.

20*th Nov.*, 1850.

Mr. T. Searle, Great Aycliffe, Darlington.—Inquiring, whether a poor-rate made for this township, and the declaration at the foot thereof, according to the form given in the 6 & 7 Wm. 4, c. 96, signed by only one overseer and the churchwarden, can be considered a valid rate. It is held by some parties that the Act referred to does not apply to a township, parishes only being named therein; and that the signature of the churchwarden is therefore of no effect, and consequently that the rate ought to be signed by both the overseers for a township.

Ans.—The provisions of the 6 & 7 Wm. 4, c. 96, apply to townships, for although the word "parish" is used in that statute, it is enacted by the 5 & 6 Vic. c. 57, sec. 18, that the words in the Parochial Assessments Act shall be construed as in the Poor Law Amendment Act, according to which the term parish will include a township. But, as in a township, the overseers alone make the poor-rate, and execute the other duties which in parishes must be performed by the joint body of churchwardens and overseers, the Board consider that in a township a majority of the overseers should sign the declaration at the foot of the rate. Where only two overseers are appointed for a township, both of them should sign such declaration.

XIII.—RATING.

I. Pier Dues.

17th Dec., 1850.

Overseer of Forrabury, Camelford Union.—Requesting information as to the mode in which the pier or quay dues of Botreaux Castle Harbour, in this parish, should be rated to the poor-rate. One of the several Delabole Slate Quarries belongs to the proprietor of this quay, and a part of the slate he ships are put on board at it; the larger part of his slate is shipped at Portgavern, where the other quarry proprietors at Delabole have, time out of mind, shipped the whole of theirs, because the land carriage to Portgavern is less. At Portgavern there are no dues, at Botreaux they are rather heavy. The part of the slate shipped at Botreaux Castle Pier, by the proprietor, he pays no dues on, and he would not, any more than the other quarry proprietors, ship slate there, if the pier were in the hands of a tenant. Should, then, the pier dues at Botreaux Castle, which are rateable to the poor-rate, be increased by the amount of the slate dues so shipped by the owner, or should the pier dues be taken less the amount of slate which would not go on board there were the dues in the hands of a tenant? The pier was built above one hundred years ago, is hollow, sunk in the middle, out of perpendicular, and is exposed to the very heavy seas from the whole drift of the Atlantic; fears are entertained that it may wash down, and stop the trade of the place. Some years since the proprietor was advised by two eminent engineers to erect a breakwater, to protect the pier and shipping within; he did this at his own expense, without any increase of dues; the rate of dues remaining without any change. This breakwater was an outlay to renovate the property, and continue it in a state to command the dues received. Is it therefore such a charge as should be thrown on the dues divided over many years, to reduce the gross receipts to the net rateable value? The repairs of the pier are so uncertain, that in an hour a heavy sea makes a fissure in the pier which may take hundreds to amend, and then for years the repairs are very insignificant. Would it not therefore, be proper to take the average annual repairs and expenses over a large number of years? The average annual repairs and expenses for the last thirty years, are much under £100 per annum; but for the last seven are much above that amount per annum. Should the average therefore be taken for thirty years, seven years, or any other number of years? From the hazard of this property, which one storm might destroy, it is impossible to affect an insurance upon it. How, therefore, can the risk of rebuilding (should the whole pier be washed down) be arrived at? Five or six intelligent men have been examined on the risk a tenant would run if he took it at rent to leave it in the state he found it: they concur in saying, the risk of rebuilding cannot be taken at less than £100 per annum. Should this charge, therefore, be taken as insurance; or what other method should be taken to arrive at the risk a tenant would run, independent of the casual repairs? Law charges were at one time incurred in enforcing the payment of the dues; these should also perhaps be thrown over a long period of years, for an average, as they are just as uncertain as the repairs on this property. It is presumed a reasonable charge should be made on the gross receipts, for a clerk to keep the accounts and manage the property, as well as a sum for tenant's profits; as if let to a tenant, he would consider himself entitled to a profit, and would offer the less as rent accordingly.

Ans.—The assessment of the property referred to in your letter, is a matter of some difficulty in regard to the practical application of the general principle or rule, upon which property is liable to be assessed to the poor-rate. The Board think, however, that according to that rule, an estimate may be fairly made of what ought to be the amount of the assessment of the pier or quay alluded to. The material question for the overseers to consider is, what sum a tenant would give to the owner of the pier to rent it from year to year, (see 6 & 7 Wm. 4, c. 96, sec. 1.) The amount of this rent would be calculated upon a consideration of the amount of the dues which a tenant would reasonably expect to receive from the traffic which would be carried on at the pier or quay.

If any circumstances exist which would lead such tenant to believe, (on fair and reasonable grounds,) that certain goods would not be shipped at the pier when in his hands, he would naturally exclude them from his calculation of the rent which he would be willing to pay. It seems to the Board that this same consideration must influence the overseers in making their estimate of the yearly value of the property to let, upon which estimate the rate is to be founded. As to the cost of the breakwater, the Board consider that this expense should not be deducted in estimating the present annual value of the property. It was, indeed, an expenditure of capital which either increased or preserved the dues, and is so far similar to the case where a heavy sum of money is expended in the enlargement or repair of an ordinary building. The Board are not able to suggest any precise rule by which the deduction should be made on account of the annual repairs. It would seem proper, however, having regard to the peculiar nature of this property, to take a long series of years, and ascertain the average cost of that period; the number of years should undoubtedly be such as to furnish the means of striking a fair average. This can only be determined by a reference to the property itself in its present state. Where the yearly outlay for repairs is likely to be uniform for many years, a small number of years may be taken for the purpose of the average. But where the condition of the property is likely to fluctuate extensively, so that a very considerable outlay may be needed in a particular year, while in ordinary years a small expenditure only is required, there the average cost will be most fairly calculated by including a larger number of years in the series on which the average is taken. If the property be not in fact insurable, the Board presume that no deduction can be made from the gross value in respect of that item; but the peculiar nature of the property in this and other respects must necessarily be considered, in the determination of the rent which a tenant would give for it, and which, as before observed, is the basis of its rateable value. The Board do not think that any allowance can be made on the score of law charges incurred in enforcing payment of the dues. Such may, and frequently do exist, in respect of cottage and such like property, but it is not the practice to allow deductions in respect of such charges. In estimating the rateable value, no deduction, the Board consider, can be made specifically in respect of a clerk, but in estimating the reasonable rent which a yearly tenant would give for the property, regard must be had to the peculiar modes in which the profit is to be derived from the pier, namely, by the continual collection of the dues, and the outlay which the arrangements necessary for such collection involve. In regard to the tenant's profits, the Board cannot say more than what they have already stated, namely, that the rateable value is to be deduced from the rent which a tenant would reasonably pay for the occupation of the pier, and in settling that rent he will naturally consider the benefit which he can derive from the occupation.

---

2. TITHES.

12th Oct., 1850.

The Rev. ————.—He is a tithe-owner in ————, and it has always been the custom of the place that the poor-rates on the tithe, made in the course of the year, should be paid to the collector at Christmas, when the tithe was paid to him by the farmers. The present year, the collector is demanding payment of the rate for the tithe before the time at which it has always been considered due. Inquiring, whether this demand is legal.

Ans.—The Board apprehend, that the time of payment of the poor-rate upon tithes is not dependent upon the actual receipt of them by the tithe owner; who, like every other occupier in the parish, is liable as such to be rated prospectively. Neither do they consider it the duty of the overseer to inquire before he enforces payment of the poor-rate, whether the party rated is at the time of making the demand, in full possession of the benefit or advantage derivable from the occupation of the property in respect of which he is assessed. The Board would add, that a rate is in law due as soon as it has been allowed and published.

XIV.—RATING SMALL TENEMENTS.

1. NOTICE OF MEETING TO ADOPT THE PROVISIONS OF THE 13 & 14 VIC. C. 99.

23rd Oct., 1850.

Town Clerk of Oswestry.—Inquiring, in reference to the allowance of poor-rate assessments made on the owners of £6 tenements, under the

Act of 13 & 14 Vic. c. 99, whether a vestry, convened according to the notice given "for the purpose of assessing a poor-rate and other purposes," is competent to make the order under sec. 4 of the Act, that the owners of such tenements shall be rated instead of the occupier; or whether there should not have been a notice expressly given, that at the vestry it was intended to determine whether £6 tenements should be so rated, so that all parties interested might have known the particular object of the meeting. Inquiring also, whether the notice required to be given by the proviso at the end of sec. 2 does not apply to the vestry authorised to act under sec. 1, as well as to the vestries authorized under sec. 2, to rescind orders.

Ans.—The Board think that a notice convening a vestry meeting for "the purpose of assessing a poor-rate, and other purposes," is clearly insufficient to warrant such vestry meeting in making the order under sec. 1 of the above-cited statute, that the owners of tenements of and under the yearly rateable value of £6 shall be rated to the poor-rate instead of the occupiers. The Board are of opinion that the second proviso, at the end of sec. 2 of the above statute, is confined to the vestry meetings held under that section, and does not apply to meetings held under sec. 1.

2. ALLOWANCE TO RATED OWNERS IN RATING SMALL TENEMENTS.

21*st Nov.*, 1850.

J. Liddall, Esq., Wath-upon-Dearne, Rotherham Union.—The overseers of this parish have been accustomed to allow a discount of one-third to the owners of cottages on their paying the poor-rates for such cottages. When the Act 13 & 14 Vic. c. 99, came into operation, a vestry was convened; and by such vestry it was deemed unnecessary to adopt the Act. Requesting the Board's direction as to the legality of this allowance to the owners of cottages, as a notice of another vestry meeting has been given.

Ans.—The course which is stated by you to have been pursued in the parish, in making the allowance or deduction in question, in the rate assessed upon small tenements, is certainly not authorized by law. The Board do not understand that there is any local Act in force in the parish which enabled such an arrangement to be carried into effect. Unless where owners are duly assessed under 59 Geo. 3, c. 12, sec. 19, or the recent Act 13 & 14 Vic. c. 99, or some local Act, the law requires that the rate should be assessed in full upon the occupier, and that amount obtained from him, unless the justices, upon application, and with the consent of the overseers, think fit to discharge the whole or any portion of such rate on the ground of the poverty of the person assessed. The Board think it possible that the arrangement by which an allowance or deduction of one-third has been thus made to owners, upon the condition of their paying the remainder of the rate assessed upon the occupiers of cottage property, may not, upon the whole, have been found to work disadvantageously for the parish. But be that as it may, as the law does not warrant the overseers in accepting in discharge of the rate a less sum than that originally assessed, the Board are of opinion that the practice referred to should be immediately discontinued, more especially seeing that by the adoption of the provisions of the recent Act, 13 & 14 Vic. c. 99, the same advantage can be secured to the parish in a legal manner.

XV.—RELIEF.—CLAIM OF LODGING-HOUSE KEEPER FOR LODGING A DESTITUTE WOMAN IN HER CONFINEMENT.

18*th Nov.*, 1850.

Clerk of ——— Union.—An Irishwoman lately came into ——— in an advanced state of pregnancy. She took lodgings in a common lodging-house, where there was no bed for her to lie upon. When she was about to be delivered her landlady applied to the relieving-officer for medical assistance, and also for relief. The relieving-officer, believing she was not very near her time, prepared to remove her to the workhouse; but finding her worse, the medical officer was sent for, and as the woman could not be removed, he, the relieving-officer, procured for her a bed from the Fever Hospital. The guardians ordered him to give her three shillings a week during her confinement, which he regularly did. The landlady of the house claims fourteen shillings for lodging and a nurse, which the guardians refuse to allow. A summons has since issued from the County Court against the relieving-officer to recover that sum, the plaintiff alledging that the relieving-officer was bound to pay for the room occupied by the pauper who slept upon his bed. He denies that he made any arrangement about the lodgings or the nurse; the medical officer had never applied for a nurse, and he did not engage one. Requesting the opinion and advice of the Poor Law Board on two questions. 1. Are the guardians legally bound to find lodgings and a nurse out of the workhouse, for single women in a state of pregnancy, who do not apply for relief until the last moment, when it is too late to send them to the workhouse? 2. Will the relieving-officer's supplying a bed for the pauper to lie upon, subject him to the payment for lodgings when no hiring of the room has taken place?

Ans.—If the relieving-officer did not personally contract with the lodging-house keeper to find lodgings for the pauper referred to, nor engage to pay him for the lodging and the nurse, the Board do not think that, strictly speaking, he would be legally liable to pay the amount claimed. The relieving-officer states that there was no express contract to this effect; but he may, not improbably, be contradicted by the plaintiff's witnesses upon this point. Besides, there are some peculiar circumstances in the case from which an implied contract might be inferred; and as it was the duty of the relieving-officer to take care that this woman had what was absolutely necessary in her destitute situation, (including lodging, as it was impracticable to take her into the workhouse,) the court would probably give a decision in favour of the claim. Under the 11 & 12 Vic. c. 110, sec. 2, the guardians would be at liberty to sanction the payment. In regard to the general question submitted, the Board can only state that the guardians are under obligation to relieve all destitute persons who apply for relief in their union. If the necessity, whatever it may be, prevents the pauper from being removed to the workhouse, the guardians, or their officer, must make the best arrangement under the circumstances that may be practicable.

XVI.—RELIEVING-OFFICER.—His duty as to the removal of lunatic paupers.

2nd Nov., 1850.

Clerk of Honiton Union.—Inquiring, whether a relieving-officer is bound to execute personally an order made by the justices under the 8 & 9 Vic. c. 126, for the removal of a lunatic to an asylum, or whether he may not employ some trustworthy person such as the parish constable to convey the lunatic. The performance of this duty by the relieving-officer himself frequently causes great inconvenience, as it takes him away from the discharge of his regular duties, and if it could be avoided the guardians consider it would be very desirable.

Ans.—The 8 & 9 Vic. c. 126, sec. 48 & 49, requires the relieving-officer to convey, or cause to be conveyed, the lunatic to the asylum. He may, therefore, engage some person to convey the lunatic thither, and this course should be pursued when his journey to the lunatic asylum would interfere with the discharge of the ordinary duties of his office.

XVII.—REMOVABILITY.

1. Removability of widow.

19th Dec., 1850.

Clerk of Clifton Union.—Transmitting the following statement, duly signed, under sec. 4 of the 11 & 12 Vic. c. 110, for the opinion of the Poor Law Board:—Mary Ann Anthony is now, and has been for the last eighteen months, residing in the parish of St. Philip and Jacob, in this union. Her husband died a few days ago in the Bristol Infirmary (not in this union.) He was in the Infirmary about three weeks; but until he went to the Infirmary he resided in the parish of St. Philip and Jacob with his said wife. The settlement is unknown. Inquiring whether the woman is removable or not for the first twelve months of her widowhood, under the 9 & 10 Vic. c. 66, s. 2.

Ans.—Under the circumstances of the case as submitted to the Board, they are of opinion that the pauper, Mary Ann Anthony, is entitled to the benefit of the exemption from removal given by the 9 & 10 Vic. c. 66, s. 2. The Board think that the husband of the pauper was constructively residing in the parish of St. Philip and St. Jacob at the time of his death.

2. Child-birth—sec. 4, 9 & 10 Vic., c. 66.

27th Dec., 1850.

Clerk of Hollingbourn Union.—Inquiring whether cases of midwifery may be regarded as sickness under the 4th sec. of the 9 & 10 Vic., c. 66, and thereby rendering the party irremovable.

Ans.—The application of the enactment in question to a case of midwifery appears to them to depend upon the particular circumstances of such case. With regard to pregnancy, the Board apprehend that it will not of itself constitute a sickness of the kind contemplated by the statute, as likely to produce permanent disability, but it may be accompanied by such ailments as would constitute temporary sickness within the meaning of the clause. If the woman in such a case receives relief, she will be irremovable; but if the pregnancy, without being accompanied by ailments amounting to sickness, simply produces destitution, (as by incapacitating the woman for her ordinary work,) and she receives relief in consequence of that destitution, she will not be rendered irremovable under the section referred to, which contemplates a chargeability resulting from sickness or accident, and not from general destitution. Childbirth, in ordinary cases, will be a temporary sickness within the enactment.

XVIII.—VALUATION.

1. Power of valuer to require certain particulars from overseers.

20th Nov., 1850.

Mr. ———, *Warminster Union.*—Having been appointed to make a valuation of a parish for the purposes of the poor-rates, requested to know whether he can require the overseers to furnish him with a statement of the amount of poor-rates, church-rates, highway-rates, and gas-rates, collected and expended in the parish, together with the gross and rateable value of each assessment, as well as the rate in the amount.

Ans.—The Board consider it desirable that you should have the information you mention to enable you to make your valuation, but the parish officers cannot be compelled to give it to you. If you cannot obtain it, you must supply your valuation of the property, without reference to the rates which are to be deducted; or, you must make your own estimate of what those rates ought to amount to upon each particular property.

---

2. Valuation by a committee of ratepayers.

4th Nov., 1850.

Clerk of Whittlesey Union.—A committee of inhabitants having been appointed to revise the poor-rate assessment of Whittlesey, requested the Board's sanction to the expenditure of £50 from the poor-rates, in discharge of the incidental expenses that may be incurred by such committee.

Ans.—The Board have no authority to give their consent to the proposed expenditure. All that they can do in such a matter is to authorise a survey and valuation of the rateable property in the parish to be made by a proper professional valuer, under the 6 & 7 Wm. 4, c. 96, sec. 3. The Board think it right to add, that their experience shows them that valuations made by a a committee of ratepayers are not calculated to be acquiesced in by the ratepayers generally, or, at all events, to give permanent satisfaction. But however this may be, the Board see no authority for any payment out of the poor-rates, either to the committee themselves, or in respect of their proceedings; and unless, therefore, the committee will consent to give their attendances and services gratuitously, it does not appear that the object in view can practically be effected. It is to be borne in mind, that the overseers are exclusively responsible for the accuracy of the rate.

XIX.—VESTRY.—Duties of chairman—polling votes.

7th Oct., 1850.

Clerk of ——— *Union.*—The overseers of ———, about a week ago, called a meeting of the ratepayers to decide upon the adoption of the new Rating of Tenements Act in their township. The adoption of the Act having been carried at that meeting, a poll was demanded, and the chairman fixed that the time for taking such poll should be from six till nine o'clock, p.m., each successive day, the poll to be finally closed if no voter came up to vote for the space of half an hour, without restricting the number of days for which the poll should be kept open, so that the polling may go on *ad infinitum* should a a vote be polled each half hour. Inquiring, whether the overseers will be empowered to close the poll so long as a vote be polled within the specified half hour.

Ans.—The Board do not think they can properly give advice in the case you have laid before them. The chairman who granted the poll must act upon his own responsibility in closing it, or otherwise. In the case of Reg. *v.* Hedger and others, 12 A. & E. p. 159, in which the question raised was as to the granting and conducting a poll in a matter to be decided by a parish vestry, Lord Denman, in delivering judgment, says, "A poll is then demanded; and it is demanded as of right; and the president of the meeting is the person to grant it. In the absence of other business, the poll should be taken immediately; if time does not allow of that, there must be an adjournment for the purpose. Then who is to direct the adjournment?" "We think that the person who presides at the meeting is the proper individual to decide this. It is on him that it devolves both to preserve order in the meeting, and to regulate the proceedings so as to give all persons entitled a reasonable opportunity of voting. He is to do the acts necessary for these purposes on his own responsibility, and subject to being called upon to answer for his conduct if he has done anything improperly."

XX.—WORKHOUSE.—PROSECUTION OF AN INMATE FOR NOT PERFORMING A TASK OF WORK.

24th Dec., 1850.

Clerk of Tenterden Union.—The guardians have prescribed a task of work to be done by the able-bodied paupers in the union workhouse. This task is the picking daily of three pounds of oakum, which the guardians believe, from good authority, to be anything but an excessive one. The workhouse master having reported that the task had not been performed by one of the paupers, although it was suited to his age, strength, and capacity, the guardians directed him to take such steps against the pauper before the magistrates of the borough of Tenterden, as the circumstances warranted. The master accordingly attended at the petty sessions on Monday last; but, in consequence of doubts in the minds of the magistrates present whether they had power to convict, the matter at present remains in abeyance. The statute brought to their notice as applicable to the case, is 5 & 6 Vic. c. 57, sec. 5, which seems to apply to the workhouse inmates as well as to vagrants. A note in Mr. Lumley's Manual of the Duties of the Master, p. 62, shows that this is the construction which he puts upon the section referred to. If this construction is correct, there would be no hesitation on the part of the magistrates in convicting. If, however, the statute alluded to should be thought inapplicable, requested the advice of the Board as to the proper course to be adopted. The example on the part of the pauper alluded to has since been followed by others, who previously found no difficulty in performing the prescribed task.

Ans.—The Board do not see any sufficient ground for the doubt which it seems has been expressed by the justices. There is nothing in the language of the provision 5 & 6 Vic. c. 57, sec. 5, which limits its application to the class of persons called vagrants or casual poor. The statute applies in terms to "any person relieved in any workhouse for whom a task of work may be prescribed." In the present case, the Board understand, that a task of work has been prescribed by the guardians of the Tenterden Union to be performed by the able-bodied paupers in the workhouse generally, without any restriction as to any particular classes of able-bodied. If this be so, and an ordinary inmate of the workhouse has refused to perform that task, the case appears to the Board to fall directly within the section above cited. There is, indeed, a marginal note which would show that provision to have special application to casual poor; but as the Board have already observed, there is nothing in the language of the section itself to confine it to persons temporarily or casually relieved, and the Board are decidedly of opinion that it is not so confined.

London: Printed by Order of the Poor Law Board, by BLACKBURN & BURT, 90½, Holborn Hill, and Published by CHARLES KNIGHT, 90, Fleet Street.

VOLUME X
[1851]

VOLUME X

AN

OFFICIAL CIRCULAR

OF PUBLIC DOCUMENTS AND INFORMATION:

DIRECTED BY THE POOR LAW BOARD TO BE PRINTED, CHIEFLY FOR THE USE OF THE BOARDS OF GUARDIANS AND THEIR OFFICERS.

No. 45.] JANUARY, 1851. [N.S.

THIRD ANNUAL REPORT

OF THE

POOR LAW BOARD—1850.

CONTENTS.

TO THE QUEEN'S MOST EXCELLENT MAJESTY.

Poor Law Board, Somerset House,
December 31st, 1850.

MAY IT PLEASE YOUR MAJESTY,

We, the Poor Law Board, beg leave to lay before your Majesty, the following Report of our proceedings during the year 1850:—

According to the method adopted in our former Reports, we propose in the first place to show the amount of poor-rates expended for purposes connected with the relief of the poor; and then to exhibit the number of persons in receipt of relief.

Expenditure from the Poor Rates.

A complete return ("The Poor Rate Return") of the expenditure from the poor-rates for purposes connected with the relief of the poor is made up annually, and comprises the period from Lady-day to Lady-day. This return for the year ended at Lady-day 1850, shows an expenditure of £5,395,022, being a reduction, as compared with the year ended at Lady-day 1849, of £397,941, or about £6. 18*s.* per cent. Estimating the population in the year ended at Lady-day 1849 at 17,534,000, the sum expended per head on the population in that year will be found to be 6*s.* 6½*d.*; and estimating the population in the year ended at Lady-day 1850 at 17,765,000, the sum expended per head will be found to be 6*s.* 1*d.*, being a reduction of 5½*d.* per head on the expenditure of the last year, as compared with that of the preceding year.

These results are shown in the following Table:

Years ended Lady-day.	Expended for purposes connected with the Relief of the Poor in England and Wales.	Decrease in 1850, as compared with 1849.	Decrease per Cent.	Rate per head on Population.	Decrease per head in 1850, as compared with 1849.
	£.	£.		s. d.	s. d.
1849 1850	5,792,963 5,395,022	397,941	6·9	6 6½ 6 1	0 5½

* See also p. 12.

The above Table comprises all expenses under the following heads, viz., in-maintenance, out-relief, salaries of officers (except assistant overseers and collectors,) repayment of loans for building and altering workhouses, and for emigration purposes, together with interest thereon, maintenance of lunatics in asylums, emigration, extra medical relief and fees, and the burial of paupers. These expenses include all charges incident to the relief of the poor, to which the poor-rate is subject, as well as the cost of relief itself; and it will be observed, that several of these charges are of such a nature as not to be materially affected by the increase or decrease of pauperism in any particular year.

The "Poor Rate Return," the results of which have now been shown, comprehends the expenditure for, and connected with relief in the whole of England and Wales, including Parishes not in Union, places under Local Acts, and Gilbert's Unions, as well as Unions formed under the Poor Law Amendment Act. This Return, which, as has already been stated, is made up annually for the year ending at Lady-day, is the only document that exhibits the aggregate of the sums disbursed in the whole of England and Wales, from the poor-rate, for poor law purposes.

There are, however, other returns, which are made half-yearly, at Lady-day and Michaelmas, showing the expenditure for relief alone in Unions and places to which the General Order of Accounts, dated 17th of March, 1847, was issued by the Poor Law Commissioners. The following Table contains a summary of these latter Returns from 606 unions and parishes for the years ended at Michaelmas 1849 and 1850 :—

Number of Unions.	Years.	Expenditure for In-maintenance and Out-door Relief. In-maintenance.	Out-door Relief.	Total.
		£.	£.	£.
606	Year ended at Michaelmas, 1849	845,121	3,029,200	3,874,321
	" " 1850	692,269	2,776,227	3,468,496
	Decrease in year ended Michaelmas, 1850	152,852	252,973	405,825 or 10·5 per cent.

The aggregate population of the Unions and Parishes comprehended in these Returns is 14,345,636, being nearly nine-tenths of the whole population of England and Wales (Census 1841,) and they may therefore be safely taken as affording a fair indication of the rate at which the cost of relief has decreased in the whole country during the year ended at Michaelmas 1850, as compared with the year preceding. Assuming, with respect to places not comprehended in these returns, that the same relative proportion exists between the expenditure of the two years, it will be found that while the total cost of relief in the whole of England and Wales, for the year ended at Michaelmas 1849, was £4,296,000, the cost for the year ended at Michaelmas 1850, was £3,845,000, being a reduction of £451,000 in the last year. It is satisfactory to observe that the expenditure for relief has continued to decrease up to the latest period for which returns have been received.

Having thus set forth the results of the Returns which have been made to us during the last year in reference to the *cost* of relief, and compared them with those of the year preceding, we shall now present the results of the Returns received during the same periods in regard to the number of the *recipients* of relief.

Number of Paupers Relieved.

In the month of January 1850, we received Returns showing the number of paupers of all classes who were relieved in 602 Unions, on the 1st of that month. The following Table exhibits a summary of these Returns, and a comparison with the number relieved on the corresponding day in 1849 :—

Number of Unions.	Year and Day.	Number of Paupers Relieved, In-door and Out-door. All Classes except the Insane and Vagrants.	Insane Persons.	Vagrants.	Total of all Classes.
602	1st Jan., 1849	966,566	13,767	7,663	987,996
	" " 1850	906,316	14,227	4,129	924,672
	Decrease on 1st Jan., 1850, compared with 1st Jan., 1849	60,250	..	3,534	63,324 or 6·4 percent.
	Increase do. do.	..	460	..	..

Similar Returns have been received of the number relieved on the 1st July, 1850, which enable us to present the following comparison of the number relieved on that day, with the number relieved on the 1st July, 1849 :—

Number of Unions.	Year and Day.	Number of Paupers Relieved, In-door and Out-door.			
		All Classes except the Insane and Vagrants.	Insane Persons.	Vagrants.	Total of all Classes.
605	1st July, 1849	864,056	13,674	8,007	885,737
	„ „ 1850	810,611	14,294	4,803	829,708
Decrease on 1st July, 1850, compared with 1st July, 1849 . .		53,445	..	3,204	56,029 or 6·3 per cent.
Increase do. do.		..	620	..	..

It will be seen from these tables, that on each of the days mentioned, viz., 1st January, 1850, and 1st July, 1850, a large reduction has taken place in the number of persons relieved of every class (except the insane) as compared with the number relieved on the corresponding days in 1849.

Distinguishing the adult able-bodied persons relieved on the days named, the following result appears :—

STATEMENT of the NUMBER of Adult Able-bodied Paupers, (In-door and Out-door,) relieved in 590 UNIONS and SINGLE PARISHES under Boards of Guardians in England and Wales, on 1st January, 1849, and 1st January, 1850, respectively.

Number of Unions.	Year and Day.	Number of Adult Able-bodied Paupers Relieved, both In-door and Out-door.		
		Widows receiving Out-door Relief.	All other Classes, In-door and Out-door.	Total.
590	1st January, 1849	52,441	149,203	201,644
	„ „ 1850	53,151	117,351	170,502
Decrease on 1st Jan., 1850, compared with 1st Jan., 1849 . . .		..	31,852	31,142 or 15·4 per cent.
Increase do. do. .		710	..	..

STATEMENT of the NUMBER of Adult Able-bodied Paupers, (In-door and Out-door,) relieved in 605 UNIONS and SINGLE PARISHES, under Boards of Guardians in England and Wales, on 1st July, 1849, and 1st July, 1850, respectively.

Number of Unions.	Year and Day.	Number of Adult Able-bodied Paupers Relieved, both In-door and Out-door.		
		Widows receiving Out-door Relief.	All other Classes, In-door and Out-door.	Total.
605	1st July, 1849	51,172	113,387	164,559
	„ „ 1850	50,669	87,906	138,575
Decrease on 1st July, 1850, compared with 1st July, 1849 . .		503	25,481	25,984 or 15·8 per cent.

It will be observed, from this last table, which relates to the adult able-bodied paupers relieved on the 1st July, 1850, that while the reduction in the number of paupers of all classes relieved on that day amounted to only 6·3 per cent., the reduction in the number of adult able-bodied paupers relieved on the same day amounted to 15·8 per cent.

Returns of the number of persons relieved on the 1st January, 1851, having been received during the progress of printing this Report, we are able to present a comparison between the number relieved on that day and the number relieved on the corresponding day in 1850. The following Table exhibits this comparison :—

SUMMARY of RETURNS from 606 UNIONS and SINGLE PARISHES, under Boards of Guardians, showing the Number of Paupers of all Classes relieved on the 1st January, 1850, and the 1st January, 1851, respectively.

Number of Unions.	Year and Day.	Number of Paupers Relieved, both In-door and Out-door.			
		All Classes except the Insane and Vagrants.	Insane.	Vagrants.	Total.
606	1st Jan., 1850	912,815	14,346	4,167	931,328
	„ „ 1851	844,142	14,958	3,649	862,749
Decrease on 1st Jan., 1851, compared with 1st Jan., 1850 . .		68,673	..	518	68,579 or 7·4 per cent.
Increase ditto ditto .		..	612	..	..

Distinguishing the adult able-bodied persons relieved on the 1st January, 1851, the result will be as follows :—

STATEMENT of the Number of Adult Able-bodied Paupers, (In-door and Out-door,) relieved in 606 Unions and Single Parishes, under Boards of Guardians, on the 1st January, 1850, and the 1st January, 1851, respectively.

Number of Unions.	Year and Day.	Number of Adult Able-bodied Paupers relieved, both In-door and Out-door.		
		Widows receiving Out-door Relief.	All other Classes, In-door and Out-door.	Total.
606	1st January, 1850	54,000	127,159	181,159
	" " 1851	50,600	103,925	154,525
Decrease on 1st Jan., 1851, compared with 1st Jan., 1850 . . .		3,400	23,234	26,634 or 14·7 per cent.

Vagrancy.

We have in former Reports adverted to the means which were used in 1848 to direct the attention of boards of guardians to the great increase of vagrancy in the country, and the marked success which immediately followed the more careful and discriminating mode of administering relief to vagrants then recommended. We are gratified to observe that the number of vagrants relieved is still diminishing. The number relieved on the 1st of July, 1848, in 580 unions, was 13,714; on the 1st July, 1849, the number relieved in the same unions was 5,662, being a decrease of 8,052; and on the 1st July, 1850, the number relieved in the same unions was 2,954, being a reduction of 2,708 as compared with the corresponding day in 1849, and of 10,760, or 79·5 per cent., as compared with the corresponding day in 1848.

Emigration.

The emigration of poor persons at the expense of the poor-rates, has continued during the year 1850 to a greater extent, as regards the number of persons emigrating, than in the year 1849. The increase may probably be ascribed, in considerable measure, to the greater facilities for promoting emigration, which boards of guardians derive from a recent statute (12 and 13 Vic. c. 103, s. 20.) Though the number of persons who have emigrated this year has exceeded that of the preceding year, the aggregate cost to the poor-rates has been less, owing to the aid contributed by Government. A statement given in the appendix (p. 147) shows the sum expended out of the poor-rate for this object during the year to be £9,234. 16*s.* 11*d.*, and the number who have emigrated 1,962.

A large majority of the emigrants have proceeded to the Australian colonies, and to New Zealand. Some have gone to the settlement in New Zealand founded by the Canterbury Association. Early in the year our sanction was requested for emigration to Port Natal in South Africa. So far as our information with regard to the then state of that colony extended, it appeared to be unsuitable for the particular class of persons who usually emigrate under the directions of boards of guardians; and we found that our apprehensions upon this point were shared by the Colonial Land and Emigration Commissioners. We therefore declined to give our sanction to the proposal.

Education of Pauper Children.—School Districts.

The importance of affording to the children in union workhouses such an education as may best tend to raise them from the class of paupers to that of independent labourers and artizans, is becoming more and more felt by boards of guardians. Still, little progress has been made during the year in the formation of school districts under the provisions of the 7 & 8 Vic. c. 101; and although the matter has in some instances been repeatedly brought before the guardians of the unions proposed to be included in districts, the number of those opposed to their formation has appeared to be such as to preclude the hope, at all events for the present, and especially in the rural unions, that the provisions of the law in regard to such schools can be made generally available.

Workhouse Schools.

The difficulties which are found practically to obstruct the formation of school districts, show that workhouse schools must continue for some time to be the principal means of training pauper children; and we therefore feel it to be our duty to seek, in conjunction with the Committee of Council on Education, to render these schools as efficient as possible, by raising the standard of the qualification of the teachers, and encouraging Boards of Guardians to increase the means of industrial training.

We bear willing testimony to the readiness with which the Guardians generally carry out the recommendations of the Inspectors connected with the Committee of Council, as well as of those attached to this Board, and avail themselves of successful experiments made in particular unions. Our Inspector, Mr. Doyle, reporting on the education of pauper children in his district, says:—"In some unions, the education of the pauper children has attained to great excellence. There are workhouses, like that of the Atcham Union, in which the children receive an education beyond all comparison better than is within the reach of the children of labourers in any part of the county. In the girls' school of the Ludlow Union, the children now receive an education in all respects superior to what the humbler rate-payers are able to purchase for their children. This high standard of workhouse education is fast ceasing to be exceptional. The example of one good workhouse school operates upon neighbouring unions, and I find a general disposition amongst guardians throughout the district to adopt improvements which are recommended by the experience of other unions. Thus the guardians of almost every union in this district, in which there are upon an average a sufficient number of boys of an age capable of industrial occupation, either have already provided, or have determined to provide the means for their industrial training. The unions of this district being almost exclusively agricultural, the means of industrial training for boys consists chiefly in the cultivation of a few acres of land by spade husbandry. In those unions in which this system can be said to be fairly in operation, it has already been productive of much benefit, and it will be seen, by the detailed accounts furnished from some of them, that this mode of educating the children in habits of industry, is attended with considerable profit to the Guardians. The examples of the Quatt school and of the school of the Atcham Union have given a very useful impulse to this method of industrial training."

In several parts of England the industrial training of children in workhouses, by employing them in agricultural occupations, is receiving special attention; and Boards of Guardians, in many instances within the last eighteen months, have provided land expressly for this object. Our Inspector, Mr. Farnall, reports that nineteen unions in his district have provided land, in the cultivation of which 514 boys are employed. In Sir John Walsham's district, also, some successful experiments have recently been made in the employment of pauper children in agricultural pursuits.

It is gratifying to find that the mental training of these children does not suffer by their withdrawal from the school, to engage during a portion of each day in manual labour in the field. On this point, Mr. Bowyer (Inspector of Workhouse Schools) states, "The introduction of agricultural training has been everywhere attended by a marked improvement in the appearance and bodily vigour of the boys; and their progress in their studies, so far from being retarded by it, has been generally promoted, notwithstanding the reduction in the number of hours devoted to school instruction."*

Care and Education of Pauper Children in the Metropolis.

The arrangements adopted in the metropolitan unions and parishes for the better care and education of pauper children have made progress during the past year, though no new school district has been formed since the date of our last Report.

The Central London District School continues to exhibit satisfactory results, in the healthiness of the children and their early preparation for taking situations in life. The Board of Management have increased the efficiency of the school, by many judicious regulations and by their constant supervision. They have still the advantage of Mr. Aubin's services as their resident superintendent, who employs in their behalf the talents and industry which he exercised on his own account, when he was proprietor of the establishment. The number of children at this school has been increased by the addition of the West London Union to the district, which now comprehends the whole of the city; the addition was made by the mutual desire of the guardians of the West London Union and the Board of Management. The number of children is now 960, of whom 157 are chargeable to the parish of St. Martin-in-the-Fields, the guardians of which parish adhere to the arrangement mentioned by us in our last Report, and still keep their children at this district school.

The Board of Management of the South Metropolitan School District have purchased an extensive and very suitable site, and have selected plans for their building; but a financial difficulty, not wholly removed by the remedial Act 13 & 14 Vic. c. 101, s. 3, prevents their advancing at present in the execution of their plan. The limit which (under the 7 & 8 Vic. c. 101, s. 44) restrains managers from expending on the school buildings more than one-fifth of the previous

* Minutes of the Committee of Council on the Schools of Parochial Unions 1848-49-50, page 60.

annual expenditure of the several unions and parishes of the district on the relief of the poor, leaves the Board of Management of this District without sufficient funds; and though they are desirous of going beyond the limit, still, as the law now stands, their consent to do so does not warrant the Poor Law Board in authorizing the requisite expenditure. It may probably be necessary to apply to Parliament for a further amendment of the law in this respect.

The Board of Management of the North Surrey School District have opened their school, and received about 350 children, at which number, though their building will accommodate 650, they have paused, in order to complete the internal arrangements and bring the institution into good working order in all its details, before it becomes full. In the work of organization fair progress has been made; well qualified teachers and other officers have been appointed: and there is already a perceptible improvement in the appearance, the health, and the conduct of the children. In accordance with the opinion we expressed in our last Report that it would be advantageous to add another parish or union to this district, we have, by the desire of the guardians, and with the assent of the managers, added to it the populous and important parish of St. Luke, Chelsea, a parish peculiarly susceptible of the benefits to be derived from such a connection. Overtures have been made by the guardians of the parish of Kensington, and by other Boards of Guardians, to the Board of Managers, having for their object a participation in the advantages of this district school.

The school established at Edmonton by the guardians of the Strand Union works satisfactorily, though the number of children is too small to admit of a high degree of efficiency. It is not improbable that the children of some other union or parish may be sent for board and education to this school, and to such a proposition we are prepared to give a favourable consideration.

The guardians of St. George in the East and those of the Whitechapel Union were for some time in correspondence on the subject of uniting to form a school district; finally, however, each Board determined upon establishing a school independently of the other. For each school an appropriate site has been obtained, out of town; the plans for the St. George's School are now under our consideration for approval, and we expect soon to have those for the Whitechapel Union School before us.

The schools of the Stepney Union and of Lambeth parish have been enlarged and improved, and those of the parishes of St. Pancras and St. Mary, Newington, have been completed since our last Report.

The Directors of the poor of St. James, Westminster, have obtained a site for their intended school on Battersea Common.

We feel warranted, from what we are now able to report on the subject of pauper schools in the metropolis, in repeating that a great improvement is going on in the important work of teaching and training the destitute children.

Salaries of Teachers in Workhouse Schools—Parliamentary Grant.

The payment of the salaries of workhouse school teachers out of a Parliamentary Grant, the periodical examination of the schools and teachers by the Inspectors of Schools, and the making of the payment out of the grant dependent on a certificate from the Committee of Council, have already contributed materially to the improvement of these schools, and must doubtless continue to do so.

Since the date of our last Report, we have, in concert with the Committee of Council, modified the plan regulating the distribution of the grant in aid of the salaries of teachers, in order to remove the anomaly which occurred when the amount allowed to a teacher had reference only to his qualification, without regard to the number of scholars under his charge; so that the highest rate of allowance was occasionally paid to a teacher in charge of a school having the lowest number of scholars.

The present plan is as follows:—

Schoolmasters holding certificates of *efficiency* receive from the grant £30 a year, together with 5*s.* for each of the average number of children in the school, up to the maximum payment of £60 where the certificate is No. 1; £55 where it is No. 2; and £50 where it is No. 3.

Schoolmasters holding certificates of *competency*, receive £25, together with 4*s.* for each of the average number of children in the school, up to the maximum payment of £45, where the certificate is No. 1; £40 where it is No. 2; and £35 where it is No. 3.

Schoolmasters holding certificates of *probation*, receive £20, together with 3*s.* for each of the average number of children in the school, up to the maximum payment of £30, where the certificate is No. 1; £25 where it is No. 2; where it is No. 3, the salary remains at £20.

Schoolmasters holding certificates of *permission*, No. 1, receive £15 a year; No. 2, £10 a year; and No. 3, £5 a year. Teachers holding certificates of this class are not entitled to any addition from the grant on account of the number of scholars under their care.

The payments from the grant to schoolmistresses are in the proportion of four-fifths of those allowed to schoolmasters holding corresponding certificates of qualification.

Contractors' Establishments.

In our last Report we had occasion to advert to the Contractors' Establishments in and near London, wherein paupers, whether adults or children, had during many previous years been maintained. For the regulation of these houses the 12 & 13 Vic. c. 13, had been passed, the provisions of which Act brought them under our control. We mentioned that most of these houses had been discontinued, and that there remained only one such establishment near London, and two at Margate, and we described the measures which we had thought it proper to take for their better management. The same three establishments still exist; but that at Brixton will be given up in March next, when the children, about 160 in number, now maintained there, who are all chargeable to the parish of St. Mary, Newington, will be transferred to the new school buildings erected by the guardians for their reception. The two establishments at Margate are found useful for children and other paupers of scrofulous habit, who are sent thither from London for the benefit of their health.

Incorporation of the Poor of Bristol—Refusal to submit Accounts for Audit—Mandamus.

Our last Report noticed the state of the proceedings upon the writ of *mandamus*, which had been obtained against the incorporation of the poor of the city of Bristol, requiring them to produce their accounts to the District Auditor. We then stated, that a writ of error had been sued out upon the judgment pronounced in favour of the mandamus by the Court of Queen's Bench, and that the question would be finally determined at the sittings after the approaching Hilary Term. Accordingly the argument then took place before the Court of Exchequer Chamber, and the judgment of the Court of Queen's Bench was affirmed. A peremptory writ followed, and the Guardians have since submitted their accounts to the Auditor.

Oswestry Incorporation.

The state of the Oswestry incorporation had in several respects called for the particular attention of the Poor Law Board, and we had directed our Inspector to examine into the administration of relief within that district. This incorporation is constituted and governed by a local Act, and the directors of the poor, who administer the relief under it, entertained an opinion that this Board had no legal authority to control, or in any manner to interfere with them. Accordingly they declined to allow our inspector to be present as a matter of right at their meetings. We deemed it necessary to take the necessary steps to have the authority of the Board established, and a mandamus was applied for, requiring the directors to admit the inspector to their meetings. A rule *nisi* was obtained, but before the day for showing cause arrived, the directors, having taken legal advice, acknowledged the authority of the Board, and admitted the inspector. Various orders have since been issued to the incorporation for the regulation of relief, and the appointment of officers. These have been acquiesced in and duly acted upon.

Chester Incorporation.

The corporation of the poor of the city of Chester, though included in an audit district, had declined to submit their accounts to the District Auditor, on a similar objection to that urged by the incorporation of Bristol, and it had been arranged that they would abide the result of the proceedings against the latter incorporation. When the judgment had been pronounced upon the writ of error affirming the validity of the order by which the District Auditor was appointed for the city of Bristol, the Guardians of the city of Chester raised no further difficulty, but submitted their accounts to the Auditor.

The Board finding the mode by which relief was administered in the city of Chester unsatisfactory, principally in consequence of the peculiar state of the law applicable to that city, which is governed by a local Act, have deemed it necessary to issue an order directing the appointment of a relieving-officer, and also the Prohibitory Order.

Dissolution of Manchester Union—New Unions formed.

The state of the Manchester Union, which consisted of the extensive and populous township of Manchester, and eleven contiguous townships, chiefly rural, had been for some time under the consideration of the Poor Law Board. It appeared to be very difficult to provide duly, under the then existing combination, for the interests of the component townships of the union; and the Guardians were unanimous in urging upon us its dissolution, and the substitution of entirely new arrangements. After full deliberation we thought it right to accede to the proposal. It was carried into effect by means of three Orders, which we issued in the course of the spring. By the first, the Manchester Union was dissolved; by the second, the *Prestwich Union* was formed, consisting of the eleven townships separated from Manchester; and by the third, we directed the appointment of a Board of Guardians for the township of Manchester alone.

We have formed another union in the course of the year, namely, the *Hemsworth Union*, in the West Riding of Yorkshire, consisting of twenty-three townships.

New Workhouses.

Great progress has been made during the year in providing workhouses for unions in which they have been much wanted. Thus, a large and excellent new union workhouse at Oldham has been opened for the reception of inmates, and will, no doubt, be found extremely beneficial to that important union. New union workhouses have also been built in the Kirkby Moorside, Easington, and Stockton-on-Tees Unions. In the Bradford, Wortley, Ashton-under-Lyne, Leigh, and Warrington unions, new union workhouses are in a forward state, and will be ready for occupation in the course of next spring. In the Truro and Bedwelty (Monmouth) Unions, workhouses are in the course of erection. In the Barnsley Union, (which was formed only last year,) and in the Salford, Falmouth, and Swansea Unions, the Guardians are about to erect new workhouses. The authorities in the united parishes of Kingston-upon-Hull, and the incorporation of Plymouth, are also taking steps for the same purpose. The workhouse at Liverpool has been considerably enlarged and improved. We entertain a sanguine hope that in many cases in which old and ill-arranged workhouses are still retained, the Guardians are becoming sensible of the advantages which must result from abandoning them for new establishments adapted to the improved administration of the Poor Laws.

Vaccination.

The returns received by the Board on the subject of vaccination during the year, show a slight decrease in the number vaccinated above one year old; but there is an increase in the number vaccinated under that age. The Board attach great importance to the provision which the legislature has made in reference to vaccination, and they take every fitting opportunity of urging upon the guardians the extension of its benefits as widely as possible. The Notes of the Registrars of Births and Deaths appended to the Quarterly Reports of the Registrar-General afford valuable information as to the prevalence of small-pox in particular localities, and the Board lose no opportunity of referring the guardians to those notes in order that they may adopt the necessary precautions to arrest the further progress, and prevent the future recurrence of so formidable an epidemic. The Board regret to state that in many places a prejudice against vaccination still continues to exist amongst the labouring classes. The total number vaccinated in England and Wales during the year, 334,364. A summary of the returns for the year ended 29th September, 1850, is given in the Appendix, No. 29, p. 154.

Orders issued by the Poor Law Board.

Notwithstanding the consolidation of the most important of the regulations of the Poor Law Commissioners, in 1847, in one General Order, we find it necessary to issue separate orders for a great variety of purposes, such as authorizing the sale of parish property, the appropriation of money arising from the sale of such property, the making of parochial surveys and valuations, the expenditure of money for the emigration of poor persons, the confirmation or remission of disallowances by Auditors. It will be observed, by a statement in the Appendix, (No. 34, p. 162,) that we have issued, during the year 1850, 1,076 orders of this miscellaneous character.

Paid Officers—their Appointment, Salaries, &c.

Questions affecting the appointment, salaries, and conduct of paid officers employed in the administration of the Poor Laws, have necessarily occupied much of our attention, and when it is considered that these officers number nearly 13,000, it is no matter of surprise to find several cases arising in the course of the year which require lengthened investigations by our inspectors on the spot. The following statement shows the number of the several classes of paid officers at present employed in 604 unions and parishes under boards of guardians, and 30 places under local Acts, &c., together with the total and the average amounts of the fixed salaries paid to them :—

Description of Officers.	Number.	Salaries.	Average Salary to each Officer.
		£	£
Clerks	634	69,941	110
Chaplains	466	21,695	47
Medical Officers . . .	3,156	156,494	50
Relieving Officers . . .	1,377	113,110	82
Masters and Matrons . .	1,359	50,778	37
Schoolmasters	383	11,837	31
Schoolmistresses . . .	501	10,473	21
Porters	442	7,971	18
Nurses	248	3,451	14
Superintendents of Labour .	69	2,723	39
Collectors or Assistant Overseers	3,042	72,410	24*
Treasurers	622	1,464	2*
Other Officers	505	13,200	26
Total . . .	12,804	535,547	42
District Auditors . .	49	13,143	268
Total, including Auditors .	12,853	548,690	...

* Collectors and Treasurers being in most cases paid by a poundage or commission, the amount of their remuneration in those cases is not included in the above.

Superannuation Fund for Union Officers.

The attention of the Poor Law Board was carefully directed, in the early part of the last session of Parliament, to the subject of a superannuation fund for union officers. A very natural wish for the establishment of such a fund had been expressed by the officers in all parts of the country. The Board, though fully approving the object proposed, were of opinion that it could only be effected by means of contributions or deductions from the salaries of the officers themselves, without resort either to the poor-rates or to any other fund of a public character. A plan, framed upon this principle, by a committee of union officers, was submitted to the Board, in order that it might be made the groundwork of a legislative measure. Considering, however, that such a measure would effect compulsory deductions from the salaries of all the officers to whom it applied, the Board thought it just that every officer should have the opportunity of pronouncing a judgment upon it before it was submitted to Parliament. Accordingly, the draft of a Bill was prepared, and circulated among the union officers throughout the country. The result showed that the precaution was a judicious one. Though many approved, so large a proportion of the whole number signified their disapprobation, as to make it clear that the union officers differed widely and irreconcileably among themselves as to the policy and justice of the proposed measure, and that it would probably encounter active opposition from many of those for whose benefit it was intended. The Board had been of opinion from the first, that a measure of this description, founded upon the principle of a compulsory deduction from all salaries, ought not to be pressed against the will of any considerable number of the officers, and therefore no further progress was made with the Bill.

Amendments of the Law—

In the course of the last session of Parliament, several statutes were passed of much practical importance in their connection with the subject of the poor laws.

as respects Paupers chargeable to the Common Fund.

(13 & 14 VIC. c. 101. s. 1.)

By one of these, the chargeability to the union fund of certain classes of paupers is continued for another year. It will be remembered that these classes comprehend all who were rendered irremovable under the provisions of the Poor Removal Act (9 & 10 Vic. c. 66,) besides destitute wanderers, wayfarers, and foundlings, and those lunatic paupers who are maintained in asylums and licensed houses, and who, if not lunatic, would have been exempt from removal by virtue of some provision of the Poor Removal Act.

as respects the Burial of Paupers.

(13 & 14 VIC. c. 101, s. 2.)

The burial of paupers who die in the workhouse is a subject upon which the law was by no means clear, and with regard to which, especially during the late prevalence of cholera, great practical difficulties arose. By the 7 & 8 Vic. c. 101, sec. 56, it had been enacted, that for the purpose of the burial of any inmate, the workhouse of a union should be deemed to be constructively situated in the parish to which the deceased had been chargeable in his lifetime. It followed from this provision, combined with sec. 31 of the same Act, that the guardians were bound (even though no wish to that effect might have been expressed by the deceased or by any surviving relative) to bury the body in the parish of the chargeability, which might be many miles distant from the workhouse, and where the burial-ground might possibly be already overcrowded. Nor had the guardians any legal authority (however they might wish it) to contribute out of their funds towards the purchase of any new burial-ground, or the enlargement of any burial-ground already existing. During the prevalence of the late epidemic, this state of the law had frequently been productive of great embarrassment. The Act of last session has made an important change in this respect. The guardians are now authorized to contribute towards the enlargement, or the obtaining of a public burial-ground in any parish of the union, and in every such case they are authorized to bury in it the body of any poor person dying in the workhouse, except where a wish to the contrary has been expressed by the deceased, or by the husband or wife of the deceased, or by the next of kin.

as respects the Emigration of Orphan and Deserted Children.

(13 & 14 VIC. c. 101, s. 5.)

The emigration of the poor is a subject with regard to which the legislature had made certain provisions of very limited application, in the original Poor Law Amendment Act (4 & 5 Wm. 4, c. 76, s. 62.) Under that Act, parishes were enabled to facilitate the emigration of their own settled poor, by defraying the whole or part of the attendant expenses. A subsequent Act (11 & 12 Vic. c. 110, sec. 5) empowered the guardians of any union to afford pecuniary aid, out of the common fund, for the emigration of poor persons, who had been rendered irremovable from any parish of the union under the provisions of the Poor Removal Act (9 & 10 Vic. c. 66.) A still later statute (12 & 13 Vic. c. 103, sec. 20) gave additional facilities for the emigration of the settled poor. But there remained a large, and in many respects, a highly interesting class of poor, for whose emigration, however desirable, no legal provision had been made, namely, those orphan and deserted children, who, though chargeable, were neither settled inhabitants of any parish, nor irremovable. The Act of last session enables the guardians to afford means for the emigration of this class, at the expense of the poor-rate; but, with a view to the more complete protection of the children, it is expressly provided that no such emigration shall take place, until the consent of each child has been expressed before magistrates in petty session, and certified under the hands of two of the magistrates to the Poor Law Board.

as respects the Maintenance of Married Women in Lunatic Asylums, &c.

(13 & 14 VIC. c. 101, s. 4.)

The general obligation of a husband to provide a maintenance for his wife, whenever he has the ability to do so, has long been secured by law in ordinary cases. There was one important exception, however, where the wife, having become lunatic, had been removed under legal authority to a lunatic asylum. In cases of this kind, it was at least doubtful, whether there existed any means of compelling the husband to contribute towards the expense of her maintenance in the asylum. Great hardship has been frequently occasioned to parishes, who have been burthened with the heavy expense of such maintenance, without the means of obtaining from the husband even a partial reimbursement. It is now enacted, however, that when a married woman is maintained as a lunatic patient in an asylum or licensed house at the charge of any parish or union, her husband may be compelled, by the order of two justices, to pay either the whole expense or such portion of it as the justices may think proper upon consideration of all the circumstances of the particular case.

as respects the Appointment of Workhouse Masters and Relieving Officers to Parochial Offices.

(13 & 14 VIC. c. 101, s. 6.)

The efficient and satisfactory administration of the Poor Law within any Union depends so materially upon the workhouse master and the relieving-officer, that it has long been deemed essential to require the dedication of their whole time to the performance of their duties. But notwithstanding an express stipulation to this effect on the part of the Guardians, it has sometimes happened that the object has been defeated by the appointment of those officers to parochial offices, such as those of overseer, constable, or surveyor, the duties of which, if regularly appointed, they were bound to undertake, with whatever prejudice to the proper discharge of their duties in the administration of the Poor Law. It has now, therefore, been enacted, that no workhouse master or relieving-officer shall be competent to hold any parochial or township office; with this exception, however, that the relieving-officer may hold any paid office in a parish or township with the express consent of the Poor Law Board, which of course will never be given unless it be perfectly clear that his duties (as in the case of a registrar, for example, in some particular district) may be performed without interference with the proper discharge of his paramount duties as a Poor Law officer.

as respects Persons Absconding from Workhouses with Workhouse Property: and assaults on Poor Law Officers.

(13 & 14 VIC. c. 101, s. 8.)

Former statutes (55 Geo. 3, c. 137, sec. 2, and

7 & 8 Vic. c. 101, sec. 58) had provided for the punishment, by imprisonment, of persons absconding from workhouses and carrying away with them clothes, utensils, tools, &c., belonging to the workhouse. By an oversight, however, no power had been given to add hard labour to the imprisonment. This is now done by a clause of the Act of last session.

(13 & 14 Vic. c. 101.)

Another provision of the Act has given to workhouse officers and relieving-officers the same wholesome protection as that already afforded by law to constables and revenue officers, by enacting that assaults upon them when in the due execution of their duty, shall be punishable with imprisonment and hard labour, and that the costs of the prosecution for every such offence shall be payable out of the county rate.

as respects Vestries and Vestry Clerks.

(13 & 14 Vic. c. 57, s. 1.)

Some duties of an important character are cast upon the Poor Law Board by another statute of last session, viz., the 13 & 14 Vic. c. 57, intituled "An Act to prevent the holding of vestry or other meetings in churches, and for regulating the appointment of vestry clerks." Hitherto, whenever the inhabitants of a parish have been convened for any parochial purpose, the ordinary and legal place of meeting has been the vestry of the parish church. Besides the inconvenience resulting in many cases from the smallness of the vestry room, which has often occasioned an adjournment to the body of the church itself, an inconvenience of a still more serious nature has been experienced from the angry and almost riotous contests to which parish meetings have not unfrequently given rise, sometimes calling forth the censures of the Ecclesiastical Court, and always occasioning scandal and pain on account of their incongruity with the sacred character of the church in which, or in the precincts of which, such contests have taken place. With a view of obviating these evils hereafter, it is now enacted that in any parish where the population exceeds two thousand persons, the Poor Law Board may, on an application proceeding from the churchwardens, and founded on the resolution of a vestry meeting, issue an order under seal, the effect of which will be to authorize the holding of parish meetings in some convenient building or room provided for the purpose, and to prevent such meetings for any merely secular object from being at any time afterwards held in the church, or (except under special circumstances) in the vestry room attached to it. Under other provisions of the same statute, the Poor Law Board, on receiving a similar application from any parish having a population exceeding two thousand, may order the vestry to elect a vestry clerk, who is to perform the particular duties specified in the statute, and such other duties of a like nature as the Poor Law Board may require.

So many applications have already been made to the Board for orders under this Act of Parliament, as to show that a great number of parishes are likely to avail themselves of its provisions.

as respects the rating of Small Tenements.

(13 & 14 Vic. c. 99.)

Another statute of great public importance was passed in the last session (13 & 14 Vic. c. 99) which enables any parish, by a resolution of vestry, to assess, in all rates for the relief of the poor and for the repairs of the highways, the owners, instead of the occupiers, of all tenements, the yearly rateable value of which does not exceed six pounds. The Act usually known as Mr. Sturges Bourne's Act (52 Geo. 3, c. 12) had given a similar power to rate owners instead of occupiers, in respect of tenements let at any rent between twenty pounds and six pounds. The new Act, like that of Mr. Sturges Bourne, is permissive, not imperative; any parish may adopt its provisions by the order of a vestry meeting, and may either continue to do so permanently, or may, at any time after the expiration of two years from the date of the original order, rescind that order by means of another resolution in vestry. In a great many parishes the Act has already been brought into operation. The Poor Law Board have issued an Instructional Letter upon the subject for the purpose of assisting the parish officers in the discharge of the new duties which the Act imposes; and, with the same view, have also modified the form of poor-rate prescribed in the General Order of Accounts.

All which we most humbly submit to your Majesty.

(Signed) M. T. BAINES, *President.*

NAMES OF COUNTIES.	RECEIPTS.						EXPENDITURE.											
							Amount expended for the Relief of the Poor.											
	From Poor Rates.		Receipts in aid of Poor Rates.		Total Receipts.		In-Maintenance.		Out-Relief.		Other Expenses of, or immediately connected with Relief.		Total.		Costs of Proceedings at Law or in Equity.	
ENGLAND.	£.	s.	£.	s.	£.	s.	£.	s.	£.	s.	£.	s.	£.	s.	£.	s.
Bedford	58,563	2	602	14	59,165	16	6,045	3	26,987	19	10,349	2	43,382	4	184	2
Berks	97,580	3	1,138	7	98,718	10	13,578	9	42,411	19	21,433	1	77,423	9	844	15
Buckingham	92,912	5	500	18	93,413	3	10,261	18	49,180	19	18,016	1	77,458	18	551	5
Cambridge	98,323	4	1,499	18	99,823	2	10,685	5	51,802	12	18,221	19	80,709	16	558	15
Chester	107,226	3	3,548	9	110,774	12	8,079	6	51,978	11	22,986	9	83,044	6	1,274	19
Cornwall	108,889	7	1,795	14	110,685	1	11,643	2	56,962	4	16,810	1	85,415	7	2,940	9
Cumberland	51,047	8	690	2	51,737	10	6,482	13	21,398	16	12,980	3	40,861	12	523	13
Derby	77,630	13	1,458	10	79,089	3	7,039	9	31,466	6	15,962	0	54,467	15	360	9
Devon	241,725	4	7,888	10	249,613	14	27,168	12	133,478	17	38,547	17	199,195	6	3,591	5
Dorset	96,374	18	1,549	14	97,924	12	9,738	0	56,535	11	17,544	15	83,818	6	1,154	11
Durham	103,401	0	1,782	2	105,183	2	6,564	8	55,304	1	11,560	19	73,429	8	1,209	3
Essex	211,536	18	4,507	0	216,043	18	27,458	5	91,659	8	48,479	18	167,597	11	1,619	8
Gloucester	200,702	13	5,205	12	205,908	5	29,446	0	86,946	3	40,404	5	156,796	8	2,507	7
Hereford	53,989	1	1,165	3	55,154	4	5,232	16	29,555	10	9,140	18	43,929	4	631	18
Hertford	88,717	0	1,211	1	89,928	1	13,116	19	34,276	12	19,801	19	67,195	10	511	0
Huntingdon	31,728	13	344	8	32,073	1	3,191	17	18,259	0	5,578	5	27,029	2	250	14
Kent	264,305	5	9,580	0	273,885	5	48,168	13	97,045	19	56,146	18	201,361	10	3,403	19
Lancaster	632,508	16	21,897	17	654,406	13	67,298	15	218,559	12	118,883	11	404,741	18	5,331	19
Leicester	102,346	19	1,979	5	104,326	4	8,316	13	46,790	18	18,331	3	73,438	14	669	8
Lincoln	156,150	16	2,904	6	159,055	2	17,829	18	80,585	7	23,905	17	122,322	2	2,021	14
Middlesex	961,922	5	69,839	13	1,031,761	18	204,329	19	214,538	4	196,183	3	615,051	6	5,463	19
Monmouth	46,713	2	642	14	47,355	16	3,730	17	24,919	7	7,379	0	36,029	4	597	4
Norfolk	222,648	18	4,447	3	227,096	1	25,948	1	123,629	4	41,364	19	190,942	4	1,311	4
Northampton	113,681	3	1,172	5	114,853	8	10,434	4	60,787	9	19,074	14	90,296	7	969	18
Northumberland	100,839	6	1,753	12	102,592	18	8,432	13	61,197	3	16,408	9	86,038	5	888	5
Nottingham	90,458	1	1,029	8	91,487	9	9,574	15	35,880	2	17,340	4	62,795	1	616	3
Oxford	92,877	12	954	13	93,832	5	10,665	6	50,573	16	17,708	6	78,947	8	868	12
Rutland	10,513	4	115	19	10,629	3	1,457	7	4,231	17	2,042	7	7,731	11	174	9
Salop	75,181	0	1,134	13	76,315	13	10,902	9	31,261	19	16,428	13	58,593	1	765	1
Somerset	213,947	3	3,415	17	217,363	0	21,059	1	118,157	15	38,580	3	177,796	19	2,350	14
Southampton	195,977	17	8,549	14	204,527	11	31,552	10	88,492	1	36,840	19	156,885	10	2,049	17
Stafford	161,935	14	3,675	9	165,611	3	19,103	6	61,854	3	26,116	6	107,073	15	2,074	4
Suffolk	166,540	17	3,113	6	169,654	3	19,809	17	85,001	2	30,484	11	135,295	10	1,075	7
Surrey	345,776	19	22,313	12	368,090	11	66,185	18	90,465	19	71,139	1	227,790	18	4,492	16
Sussex	178,740	2	5,123	10	183,863	12	29,087	7	82,363	4	38,166	16	149,617	7	1,903	2
Warwick	151,701	13	5,019	16	156,721	9	15,917	12	68,887	16	24,713	4	109,518	12	1,407	5
Westmoreland	19,566	0	583	9	20,149	9	2,543	13	9,872	9	3,326	17	15,742	19	377	9
Wilts	166,229	4	1,694	17	167,924	1	16,982	2	83,709	1	32,076	1	132,767	4	1,183	15
Worcester	103,295	0	2,576	11	105,871	11	10,171	17	45,073	19	18,131	18	73,377	14	1,360	9
York, E. Riding	96,587	19	3,070	15	99,658	14	9,542	16	45,381	2	17,433	11	72,359	9	1,437	3
York, N. —	73,002	10	1,546	0	74,548	10	5,531	16	38,677	8	13,686	9	57,895	13	1,358	17
York, W. —	405,578	18	13,387	14	418,966	12	26,632	5	206,311	1	48,900	19	281,844	5	9,611	13
Totals of England	6,869,373	15	226,410	0	7,095,783	15	896,941	12	2,912,452	5	1,278,612	11	5,088,006	8	72,477	19
WALES.																
Anglesey	25,369	1	116	16	25,485	17	240	2	19,269	4	2,292	19	21,802	5	182	8
Brecon	26,259	12	227	1	26,486	13	1,731	3	13,653	10	3,697	13	19,082	6	154	3
Cardigan	24,458	11	172	1	24,630	12	367	4	15,238	12	2,506	16	18,112	12	221	1
Carmarthen	47,807	2	244	3	48,051	5	1,476	19	24,254	2	4,288	14	30,019	15	683	1
Carnarvon	33,746	16	117	2	33,863	18	1,018	6	22,320	11	3,030	17	26,369	14	622	11
Denbigh	39,919	1	519	1	40,438	2	3,055	6	21,732	1	6,034	3	30,821	10	741	18
Flint	29,671	9	467	15	30,139	4	1,830	1	17,275	13	4,119	17	23,225	11	502	18
Glamorgan	75,834	12	843	9	76,678	1	3,249	6	46,917	13	9,982	19	60,149	18	619	6
Merioneth	17,943	17	138	2	18,081	19	243	6	12,152	9	1,207	9	13,603	4	202	3
Montgomery	34,384	8	490	1	34,874	9	2,027	5	20,616	9	4,458	18	27,102	12	426	1
Pembroke	31,911	7	153	4	32,064	11	1,321	5	20,991	1	3,850	13	26,162	19	452	14
Radnor	13,813	13	103	1	13,916	14	762	8	8,223	1	1,577	9	10,562	18	295	5
Totals of Wales	401,119	9	3,591	16	404,711	5	17,322	11	242,644	6	47,048	7	307,015	4	5,103	9
Totals of England and Wales	7,270,492	4	230,001	16	7,500,494	0	914,264	3	3,155,096	11	1,325,660	18	5,395.021	12	77,581	8

EXPENDITURE.

Constables' Expenses; and Cost of Proceedings before Justices.	Vaccination Fees.	Payments on Account of the Registration Act, viz: Fees to Clergymen and Registrars, Outlay for Register Offices, Books, and Forms.	Payments under the Parochial Assessments Act (for Surveys, Valuations, &c.,) and Loans repaid under the same.	Payments for or towards the County, Hundred, or Borough Rate, or Police Rate.	Expenses allowed in respect of Parliamentary or Municipal Registration; and Cost of Jury Lists.	Repairs of Parish Property where lawfully made.	Expenses under the Nuisances Removal and Diseases Prevention Acts, and also under the Regulations of the General Board of Health.	Money expended for all other purposes.	Total Expenditure.	Medical Relief.
£. s.	£. s.	£. s.	£. s.	£. s.	£. s.	£. s.	£. s.	£. s.	£. s.	£. s.
506 9	194 8	396 9	108 9	11,069 5	211 3	91 1	334 10	538 11	57,016 11	2,335 4
1,572 7	494 12	646 15	122 10	14,977 18	310 17	50 5	272 6	1,827 16	98,543 10	5,019 16
1,498 16	176 9	556 11	349 2	14,826 12	364 10	33 17	246 5	1,447 11	97,509 16	3,556 5
1,271 14	334 3	769 18	340 0	15,056 5	427 3	71 19	492 2	1,849 9	101,881 4	3,753 0
1,956 17	462 7	1,486 4	323 15	12,589 16	564 4	333 18	1,529 12	7,061 17	110,627 15	3,585 2
1,245 10	763 6	1,050 5	323 9	7,386 7	441 3	129 6	1,236 0	6,024 7	106,995 9	4,140 10
294 15	239 9	600 3	101 13	6,739 2	209 2	113 6	141 15	1,990 5	51,814 15	1,467 10
1,350 7	389 5	867 16	401 18	14,627 8	321 6	20 10	423 12	3,446 12	76,676 18	1,768 11
3,339 18	1,015 4	1,797 13	183 16	21,829 2	598 4	207 3	6,774 11	9,277 6	247,809 8	6,737 5
1,343 16	780 13	561 19	37 2	10,404 10	439 12	65 12	125 19	2,315 13	101,047 13	4,168 10
729 18	434 17	1,317 1	—	21,386 14	529 9	18 14	3,549 1	4,268 7	106,872 12	2,736 11
1,862 15	489 13	1,129 19	553 13	31,754 8	219 8	356 5	1,072 4	5,159 4	211,814 4	9,106 18
1,574 9	669 2	1,455 7	697 17	46,106 11	1,094 15	165 12	1,389 8	6,981 16	219,438 12	7,120 10
636 14	62 10	317 1	—	6,574 12	219 3	55 17	201 4	934 8	53,562 11	2,237 10
423 5	143 19	527 5	100 0	18,295 11	270 13	86 7	267 3	1,489 2	89,309 15	4,024 14
521 14	167 8	207 5	43 0	3,858 12	85 7	13 15	2 14	490 7	32,669 18	1,612 12
4,389 12	998 10	1,999 7	454 17	39,535 15	1,027 3	162 13	1,328 4	12,793 5	267,454 15	9,518 10
3,391 2	2,320 16	7,208 19	1,938 4	147,882 2	1,883 13	2,356 9	5,436 7	34,030 9	616,521 18	15,647 4
971 6	329 15	716 16	260 12	21,186 5	331 4	191 19	39 19	2,604 10	100,740 8	3,266 17
2,733 1	670 13	1,254 11	16 0	24,237 17	1,138 8	173 0	598 2	5,854 13	161,020 1	4,738 6
1,811 4	1,703 19	6,067 14	634 15	268,029 18	4,754 15	381 8	9,218 14	49,439 0	962,556 12	19,631 12
918 14	114 9	444 4	7 7	8,325 15	183 18	39 11	795 18	1,916 4	49,372 8	1,498 1
1,450 0	493 8	1,397 1	423 19	23,590 17	1,176 7	172 3	256 4	6,405 18	227,619 5	7,607 17
957 4	419 5	645 17	225 17	18,255 1	372 3	178 7	132 9	1,497 6	113,949 14	3,549 7
994 13	438 5	1,023 7	—	10,704 5	162 7	20 11	883 4	3,484 11	104,637 13	2,388 16
973 14	425 0	812 8	154 14	18,661 11	508 13	106 7	1,209 16	2,668 14	88,932 1	2,777 18
1,496 17	94 4	531 0	113 13	9,799 12	326 9	50 16	244 15	1,401 6	93,874 12	3,328 7
181 19	52 18	68 3	—	1,957 11	49 5	17 6	27 19	126 16	10,387 17	366 5
593 16	178 18	743 14	23 3	11,069 17	253 1	1 11	823 1	2,936 13	75,981 16	3,592 0
2,995 13	986 16	1,333 1	347 4	30,006 8	821 14	318 4	1,965 13	4,748 3	223,670 9	8,022 19
1,061 8	1,015 16	1,335 2	258 17	35,101 10	593 17	63 17	2,093 6	4,306 19	204,765 19	8,294 19
951 15	909 0	2,135 11	831 9	35,767 3	587 9	990 15	5,449 14	9,558 12	166,329 7	4,664 7
943 16	448 3	1,085 2	77 0	27,380 16	520 9	334 19	192 18	5,157 10	172,511 16	6,170 15
2,622 15	719 2	2,422 16	226 10	89,211 1	1,430 5	146 6	6,647 9	26,612 0	362,321 18	9,715 10
1,435 10	390 2	1,102 11	845 19	15,213 8	564 0	207 3	971 16	6,701 0	178,948 2	7,432 5
1,514 16	672 11	1,493 19	136 0	5,463 6	683 17	366 6	1,430 1	5,882 7	158,569 0	4,900 9
148 13	52 8	165 5	89 14	2,720 1	66 5	45 2	57 17	497 15	19,963 8	713 19
1,072 2	471 9	880 14	76 10	24,135 4	338 6	227 7	528 17	2,259 16	163,941 4	5,858 5
598 17	343 7	835 17	328 7	23,693 1	591 14	90 8	2,335 9	3,037 14	106,592 17	4,693 19
588 14	304 9	980 13	53 2	18,500 0	450 8	149 0	1,692 5	2,218 18	98,732 1	3,141 11
732 19	183 2	656 3	199 2	11,186 15	214 5	48 7	615 10	1,594 17	74,685 10	2,219 18
5,183 14	1,063 18	4,512 17	1,886 9	48,714 0	2,030 15	742 1	12,854 13	20,170 16	388,615 1	9,728 15
60,842 18	22,617 8	55,540 3	13,295 14	1,257,811 12	27,362 13	9,395 3	75,888 6	273,007 19	6,956,246 3	216,838 19
289 8	17 3	160 11	97 10	1,916 17	34 8	15 0	54 12	668 13	25,238 15	338 6
395 4	131 16	182 13	—	6,128 6	76 16	0 1	188 4	1,024 3	27,363 12	766 7
199 2	55 5	201 1	—	6,476 3	43 11	1 4	0 13	812 7	26,122 19	506 12
323 8	88 2	331 13	—	12,228 6	102 1	0 13	174 1	996 11	44,947 11	894 3
433 17	106 13	266 11	—	3,741 7	94 19	14 12	46 7	1,802 9	33,499 0	1,231 5
402 1	131 14	233 7	101 15	6,475 10	197 8	2 1	139 11	1,387 2	40,633 17	864 7
538 5	62 15	178 13	527 15	3,689 5	188 4	2 14	200 10	870 3	29,986 13	689 7
740 13	179 12	868 14	46 13	8,703 17	292 1	33 18	3,778 4	2,562 9	77,975 5	2,337 18
130 9	124 1	104 2	4 8	1,736 1	39 9	1 2	4 10	326 15	16,276 4	607 0
304 4	21 6	210 16	70 0	5,470 15	183 11	1 6	115 6	1,413 7	35,319 4	1,012 11
361 18	86 18	276 15	52 10	4,539 2	94 1	7 11	103 11	937 19	33,075 18	790 4
158 18	20 8	81 10	—	2,117 10	64 5	—	6 15	228 0	13,535 9	294 0
4,277 7	1,025 13	3,096 6	900 11	63,222 19	1,410 14	80 2	4,812 4	13,029 18	403,974 7	10,332 0
65,120 5	23,642 1	58,636 9	14,196 5	1,321,034 11	28,773 4	9,475 5	80,700 10	286,037 17	7,360,220 10	227,170 19

Comparative Statement of the Number of Paupers, of all Classes, in Receipt of Relief, on the 1st of January, 1849, and the 1st of January, 1850, in 590 Unions; on the 1st of July, 1849, and the 1st of July, 1850, in 593 Unions; and on the 1st of January, 1850, and the 1st of January, 1851, in 595 Unions, in England and Wales.

OUT-DOOR.	Relieved on 1st of January.		Decrease.	Increase.	Relieved on 1st of July.		Decrease.	Increase.	Relieved on 1st of January.		Decrease.	Increase.
Numbers of the several Classes of Paupers Relieved out of the Workhouse (not including Lunatics, Insane persons, and Idiots)	1849.	1850.			1849.	1850.			1850.	1851.		
ABLE-BODIED, OR THE FAMILIES OF ABLE-BODIED:—												
Adult Males (married or single) relieved in cases of sudden and urgent necessity	705	308	397	—	506	201	305	—	314	200	114	—
Adult Males (married or single) relieved in cases of their own Sickness, Accident, or Infirmity	25,794	22,650	3,144	—	22,531	18,604	3,927	—	22,900	19,799	3,101	—
Adult Males relieved on Account of Sickness, Accident, or Infirmity of any of the Family, or of a Funeral	11,047	9,071	1,976	—	8,838	6,790	2,048	—	9,179	7,489	1,690	—
Adult Males (married or single) relieved on account of want of work or other causes	17,588	9,314	8,274	—	8,832	4,440	4,392	—	9,449	5,347	4,102	—
Families of Adult Males (as above) resident with the Father—												
Wives	44,043	33,062	10,981	—	32,624	23,840	8,784	—	33,447	26,399	7,048	—
Children under 16	133,233	98,616	34,617	—	97,372	72,671	24,701	—	99,507	78,356	21,151	—
Widows	52,441	53,151	—	710	51,172	50,669	503	—	54,002	50,628	3,374	—
Children under 16 dependant on Widows	119,793	126,184	—	6,391	118,479	124,122	—	5,643	127,699	123,413	4,286	—
Single Women without Children	8,993	7,603	1,390	—	7,462	6,288	1,174	—	7,686	6,385	1,301	—
Illegitimate Children and their Mothers—												
Mothers	5,429	4,508	921	—	4,639	3,920	719	—	4,551	3,703	848	—
Children	8,013	7,055	958	—	7,187	6,152	1,035	—	7,122	5,862	1,260	—
Families relieved on account of Parent being in Jail, &c.												
Wives	2,650	2,269	381	—	2,436	2,106	330	—	2,290	1,910	380	—
Children	7,143	6,186	957	—	6,428	5,746	682	—	6,238	5,427	811	—
Families of Soldiers, Sailors, and Marines relieved—												
Wives	787	656	131	—	701	540	161	—	671	544	127	—
Children	1,543	1,281	262	—	1,468	1,079	389	—	1,313	1,124	189	—

Resident Families of other Non-resident Males relieved—												
Wives	4,053	3,741	312	—	3,863	3,425	438	—	3,805	3,359	446	—
Children	10,497	9,525	972	—	10,130	9,013	1,117	—	9,686	8,538	1,148	—
NOT ABLE-BODIED :—												
Males	98,845	100,794	—	1,949	97,504	99,459	—	1,955	101,371	102,453	—	1,082
Females	202,700	209,142	—	6,442	204,073	208,642	—	4,569	210,493	212,160	—	1,667
Children under 16 relieved with Parents	35,312	37,161	—	1,849	34,851	35,201	—	350	37,654	35,467	2,187	—
Orphans or other Children under 16 relieved without Parents	16,701	17,854	—	1,153	17,034	17,323	—	298	18,086	17,230	856	—
LUNATICS, INSANE PERSONS, AND IDIOTS :—												
Males	3,694	3,984	—	290	3,880	3,927	—	47	4,016	4,233	—	217
Females	4,300	4,651	—	351	4,260	4,629	—	369	4,697	4,827	—	130
Children under 16 . . .	260	299	—	39	298	292	6	—	300	257	43	—
Total	815,044	769,687	45,357	—	747,521	708,571	38,950	—	776,998	723,851	53,147	—
VAGRANTS RELIEVED OUT OF THE WORKHOUSE .	5,308	2,696	2,612	—	4,204	2,556	1,648	—	2,723	2,220	503	—
TOTAL RELIEVED OUT OF THE WORKHOUSE . .	820,352	772,383	47,969	—	751,725	711,127	40,598	—	779,721	726,071	53,650	—
GROSS TOTAL OF PERSONS RELIEVED BOTH IN-DOOR AND OUT-DOOR	941,683	882,711	58,972	—	847,906	798,290	49,616	—	891,373	831,430	59,943	—
Deduct Persons relieved both In-door and Out-door, and included twice in the above, also Persons whose Relief has been transferred to the Non-settled Poor Accounts	832	1,505	—	—	918	1,972	—	—	1,543	1,990	—	—
NET TOTAL OF PERSONS RELIEVED, BOTH IN-DOOR AND OUT-DOOR PAUPERS	940,851	881,206	59,645	—	846,988	796,318	50,670	—	889,830	829,440	60,390	—
SUMMARY OF OUT-DOOR PAUPERS :—												
Total Number of Adult Males	157,968	146,288	11,680	—	132,049	132,659	—	610	147,396	137,530	9,866	—
Ditto do. Females	325,689	319,434	6,255	—	321,245	303,776	17,469	—	322,293	309,708	12,585	—
Ditto do. Children under 16	331,387	303,965	27,422	—	294,227	272,136	22,091	—	307,309	276,613	30,696	—

Comparative Statement of the Number of Paupers, of all Classes, in receipt of Relief on the 1st *of January*, 1849, *and the* 1st *of January*, 1850, *in* 590 *Unions; on the* 1st *of July*, 1849, *and the* 1st *of July*, 1850, *in* 593 *Unions; and on the* 1st *of January*, 1850, *and the* 1st *of January*, 1851, *in* 595 *Unions, in England and Wales.*

IN-DOOR.	Relieved on 1st of January.		Decrease.	Increase.	Relieved on 1st of July.		Decrease.	Increase.	Relieved on 1st of January.		Decrease.	Increase.
	1849.	1850.			1849.	1850.			1850.	1851.		
Numbers of the several Classes of Paupers in the Workhouse, not including Lunatics, Insane persons, and Idiots.												
ABLE-BODIED AND THEIR CHILDREN :—												
Adults:—Married Couples—												
Males	2,391	1,690	701	—	806	512	294	—	1,699	1,396	303	—
Females	2,550	1,798	752	—	1,023	655	368	—	1,807	1,506	301	—
Other Males	8,709	8,160	549	—	3,977	3,085	892	—	8,243	6,958	1,285	—
Other Females	14,464	12,626	1,838	—	10,208	9,003	1,205	—	12,759	11,877	882	—
Children under 16, of Able-bodied Inmates—												
Illegitimate Children	8,176	7,877	299	—	6,837	6,354	483	—	7,921	7,470	451	—
Other Children	14,877	11,519	3,358	—	9,544	6,940	2,604	—	11,629	10,350	1,279	—
NOT ABLE-BODIED :—												
Adults:—Married Couples—												
Males	1,611	1,350	261	—	1,229	1,025	204	—	1,381	1,205	176	—
Females	1,428	1,178	250	—	1,093	932	161	—	1,209	1,116	93	—
Other Males	19,120	18,635	485	—	16,381	16,007	374	—	18,896	19,082	—	186
Other Females	13,874	12,941	933	—	12,924	12,250	674	—	13,208	13,261	—	53
Children under 16, of Parents not Able-bodied, being Inmates—												
Illegitimate Children	1,116	965	151	—	937	913	24	—	965	1,087	—	122
Other Children	3,108	2,280	828	—	2,173	1,704	469	—	2,293	2,071	222	—
Orphans or other Children under 16, relieved without Parents	23,208	23,596	—	388	22,736	21,973	763	—	23,878	21,812	2,066	—
LUNATICS, INSANE PERSONS, AND IDIOTS :—												
Males	2,028	1,946	82	—	2,010	2,071	—	61	1,965	2,143	—	178
Females	2,559	2,479	80	—	2,554	2,601	—	47	2,500	2,648	—	148
Children under 16	284	234	50	—	198	184	14	—	234	238	—	4
Total	119,375	109,307	10,068	—	94,531	86,352	8,179	—	110,620	104,189	6,431	—
VAGRANTS RELIEVED IN THE WORKHOUSE	1,956	1,021	935	—	1,650	811	839	—	1,032	1,170	—	138
TOTAL RELIEVED IN THE WORKHOUSE	121,331	110,328	11,003	—	96,181	87,163	9,018	—	111,652	105,359	6,293	—
Summary of In-door Paupers.												
Total number of Adults:—Males	33,734	31,780	1,954	—	24,263	22,721	1,542	—	32,183	30,756	1,427	—
Females	34,796	31,012	3,784	—	27,737	25,526	2,211	—	31,473	30,295	1,178	—
Children under 16	50,845	46,515	4,330	—	42,531	38,105	4,426	—	46,964	43,138	3,826	—

London: Printed by Order of the Poor Law Board, by BLACKBURN & BURT, 90½, Holborn Hill; and Published

AN

OFFICIAL CIRCULAR

OF PUBLIC DOCUMENTS AND INFORMATION:

DIRECTED BY THE POOR LAW BOARD TO BE PRINTED, CHIEFLY FOR THE USE OF THE BOARDS OF GUARDIANS AND THEIR OFFICERS.

No. 46.] FEBRUARY, 1851. [N.S.

CONTENTS.

I.—APPRENTICESHIP—To HUSBAND ON BEHALF OF HIS WIFE.

13*th August*, 1850.

Clerk of Hereford Union.—The guardians of this union are desirous of apprenticing a pauper girl to a dressmaker, who is a married woman; but on reference to Art. 53 of the General Consolidated Order, they find a prohibition to placing a person apprentice to a married woman. Inquiring, whether this rule is peremptory, and admits of no qualification; or, whether if the husband joins with the wife, the apprenticeship may take place.

Ans.—There is no objection to a girl being bound apprentice to the husband of the milliner you refer to. The husband can, in such case, enter into the necessary covenants on behalf of his wife.

II.—BASTARDS.—MOTHERS OF, IN THE WORKHOUSE, RECEIVING MONEY FROM THE PUTATIVE FATHER—EMPLOYMENT OF THE MOTHERS IN THE WORKHOUSE.

8th May, 1850.

Clerk of ——— Union.—Harriet G. is an inmate of the ——— Union workhouse, with two bastard children, aged seven and four years. An order was made on the putative father of the younger child for 1*s.* 6*d.* weekly. It is believed that the money is regularly paid to the pauper's sister. An application has been made to the pauper by the guardians to repay the money she receives through her sister to the parish to which she and her two children are chargeable, but she refuses to do so, or quit the house. There are at present several mothers of bastards, and a considerable number of illegitimate children in the workhouse, and the guardians are aware that money is paid either directly or indirectly by the putative fathers of some of the children to the mothers. Inquiring, how far the guardians would be justified in compelling those women to quit the house as to whom they are satisfied that money on account of their offspring has been paid them, or now remains due to them; and also in compelling them whilst inmates of the workhouse, to affiliate their children.

Ans.—If the guardians think that any of the women referred to, as mothers of illegitimate children, and at present inmates of the union workhouse, can by their own exertions, aided by the receipt of money paid by the putative fathers of their children, maintain themselves and children, the guardians would be justified in discharging such paupers from the workhouse, and in refusing to give them further relief. It is, however, competent to the guardians in any such case to advance relief on loan, and if the amount is not repaid, to take summary proceedings against the woman for the recovery of it when she is in receipt of money from the putative father or otherwise. The guardians cannot legally compel the pauper inmates in question to procure orders of maintenance upon the putative fathers of their illegitimate children, but they might probably oblige the mothers to endeavour to obtain a maintenance by refusing to give them relief. The Board wish to know whether the able-bodied women among this class of paupers are required to perform work in the union workhouse. As regards the alleged payment made by the putative father of Harriet G.'s younger child, the Board recommend that the guardians communicate with the justices on the subject of such cases, in order that they may be made aware of the practice in the ——— Union, and that when applications are made to them to enforce the orders against the putative fathers, the justices may stay proceedings until they are satisfied that the money will be duly applied.

12th June, 1850.

Clerk of same Union.—The mothers of illegitimate children in the union house are generally employed about the household work, and, as far as practicable, are constantly made to assist in the numerous domestic duties necessary for keeping the workhouse clean.

Ans.—The Board fear that the number of mothers of illegitimate children now in the workhouse may in some measure be attributed to their being permitted by the guardians to reside in the workhouse without more than the usual necessary amount of household work being exacted from them. The Board therefore recommend the guardians, if there are usually a sufficient number of female adult paupers in the house to do the household work without the assistance of the women in question, to withdraw the mothers of illegitimate children from that work, and to set them to oakum picking, or some other kind of hard work which can be done as task work. If, under this arrangement, there should be a deficiency of labour for household purposes, some of the elder girls in the school might usefully be employed in cleaning the house under the superintendence of the matron during a certain portion of each day, provided they are not set to work in company with any of the adult inmates; or, if that be impracticable, with such only as are of respectable character and conduct.

III.—BURIAL-GROUND.—CONTRIBUTION FROM THE POOR-RATES TOWARDS THE ENLARGEMENT OF A CHURCHYARD.

16th Sept., 1850.

Clerk to Ruthin Union.—Applying for permission to expend £25 from the common fund of the union towards enlarging the churchyard of Llanrhydd for the purpose of burying the paupers dying in the workhouse.

Ans.—The Board wish to be informed more fully as to the circumstances which, in the opinion of the guardians of the Ruthin Union, render it desirable to incur the expenditure of £25 towards enlarging the churchyard of Llanrhydd, for the purpose of burying the bodies of paupers dying in the workhouse; and as to the manner in which such enlargement is to be made, whether by the guardians alone, or in conjunction with any other parties.

26th Sept., 1850.

Clerk to same Union.—The parishioners of Llanrhydd intend expending from two to three hundred pounds in repairing the church and improving the churchyard, and they purpose appropriating a piece of waste land, which is not now available for burial-ground, (although on one side of the churchyard,) almost entirely to the burial of bodies from the workhouse of this union, providing the guardians will grant them £25 towards building a wall, clearing obstructions, &c. It appears that forty have been buried in the churchyard within the last four years from this workhouse, and the parishioners say, "The consequence is, that any vacant space there may be in the small burial-ground of the parish is fast filling up, and in a short time the whole will be occupied."

Ans.—Having regard to sec. 2 of 13 & 14 Vic. c. 101, (which only admits of the application of the funds in the hands of the guardians to the particular object therein named,) the Board do not feel that at present they have before them such precise information as to what is really intended in this case as to give the assent asked for. They therefore wish to know how much the parishioners of Llanrhydd propose to expend on enlarging the churchyard alone, and what are the particulars of such proposed expenditure.

15th Oct., 1850.

Curate of Llanrhydd.—The small burial-ground of the parish having become much crowded, partly in consequence of the number of bodies interred from the Ruthin Union workhouse, an enlargement of the churchyard has become necessary. The parishioners are in course of expending a sum of money, nearly equal to that voted by the guardians, in enclosing one side; and as the additional space to be gained by the improvement is almost exclusively intended for the use of the Ruthin Union, an application was made to the guardians by the churchwardens and himself (the curate) with a view to obtain a sum of money sufficient to enable them to carry out the enlargement, and thereby avoid to the union a much larger expense at a future time. Whatever is done to the church will be done at the expense of private individuals, without reference to the enlargement of the churchyard.

Ans.—The Board will be prepared to give their consent to the contribution of a sum of money towards the object in question by the guardians of the Ruthin Union; but they wish to be informed of the mode in which, and the person from whom, the land is to be acquired for the purpose. As the land in question must be ultimately consecrated, the Board believe that it must be conveyed to some duly authorised party with a proper title, and they wish therefore to know whether this point has been duly considered.

1st Nov., 1850.

Curate of Llanrhydd.—The proposed addition to the burial-ground of the parish of Llanrhydd will not require to be conveyed or consecrated, as the space of ground referred to is already within the consecrated precincts of the ancient churchyard, but is at present unavailable for the purposes of interment on account of the ancient fence being insufficient to protect it from trespass, and its being also covered with trees, stones, and other obstructions; and in order to avoid the necessity of purchasing and walling-in a new piece of ground, application was made to the Ruthin Union by the ministers and churchwardens, for a sum of money in aid of a contribution from the parish to enable them to build the wall and remove the obstructions mentioned, (the space thus to be rendered available to be appropriated to the burial of bodies from the union workhouse,) and so postpone, for an indefinite period, the necessity of the Ruthin Union being put to the greater expense that would attend the purchase and consecration of new ground. The guardians of the union unanimously acceded to the proposition of the applicants, and voted a sum of £25 for the purpose.

Ans. to the Guardians of the Union.—Having regard to the facts explained by the curate of Llanrhydd in his communications, the Board are now prepared to consent to the proposed outlay; and they accordingly sanction the expenditure of £25 by the guardians of the Ruthin Union, in aid of a contribution from the parish of Llanrhydd towards enlarging the burial-ground of that parish, in the manner described by that gentleman.

IV.—CHARGEABILITY.

1. OF WIDOWS.

19*th July*, 1850.

Clerk of Braintree Union.—Inquiring whether relief given in case of temporary illness to paupers, and to widows during the first year of their widowhood, living in parishes in which they have not acquired a legal settlement, and therefore for the time irremovable, should not be charged to the establishment or union fund.

Ans.—The Board are not able to give a positive answer to your inquiry, without some degree of qualification. They may remark generally that all poor persons who are rendered irremovable from any parish in the Braintree Union, by any of the provisions of the 9 & 10 Vic. c. 66, and relieved by the guardians of that union, are chargeable to the common fund, under the 11 & 12 Vic. c. 110, sec. 3, and 12 & 13 Vic. c. 103, sec. 1; provided they are not settled in the parish of their residence. Among the persons so rendered irremovable are widows, who come within the terms of the 9 & 10 Vic. c. 66, sec. 2, which extend to every "woman residing in any parish with her husband at the time of his death," and prevent her removal from such parish "for twelve calendar months next after his death, if she so long continue a widow." The 4th sec. of the same Act prevents the removal of any person becoming chargeable in respect of relief made necessary by sickness or accident, if such sickness or accident is not calculated to produce permanent disability.

2. CHARGEABILITY OF A WOMAN LIVING SEPARATE FROM HER HUSBAND.

10*th Jan.*, 1851.

Clerk of Stokesley Union.—R. R., about twenty years ago, was legally settled in Hutton, where he then lived with his wife and children. He soon after left his wife and children chargeable to Hutton, and was not heard of until August last, when he was found living at Gateshead with a woman to whom he is supposed to be married, and who has a daughter now of the age of fifteen years. R. R.'s children by his former wife are all either dead or emancipated. R. R. left his house and furniture in charge of his wife, who has for upwards of twenty years kept house and lived at Hutton. During that period she has been frequently chargeable, but she has been more than five years on and off during that period without relief. About thirteen years ago she had a child which was supposed to be a bastard, but it was never affiliated; and Hutton allowed it one shilling a week for its maintenance until about twelve months ago, when he went out to service. Since August last, R. R. has allowed his first wife 2*s.* a week. Inquiring, whether the wife may be removed to Gateshead, her husband having rented a house there for the last three or four years at the yearly rent of £23, and paid the rates for the same, though within the last two months he has gone to reside at Newcastle; or, whether the overseers should proceed against the husband for not maintaining his wife.

Ans.—The Board are of opinion, upon the information now before them, that the pauper is removable to the place of her settlement; but whether that be in the parish of Gateshead they cannot upon the present statement of the facts of the case undertake to say. It is for the overseers of Hutton to determine whether they will procure an order of justices for the removal of the pauper. If it be true that the woman has been guilty of adultery, and there has been no condonation of the offence upon the part of the husband, he is not legally bound to maintain her, nor liable to prosecution under the Vagrant Act for omitting to do so, (see R. *v.* Flinton, 2 B. and Adol. 227.)

3. CHARGEABILITY OF DESTITUTE WANDERERS.

4*th April*, 1850.

Clerk of Bridport Union.—Transmitting the following statement duly signed under sec. 4 of the 11 and 12 Vic. c. 110, for the opinion of the Poor Law Board:—William Quarrel and family had resided in the parish of Allington for five years and three months, when on the 18th May, 1849, they were admitted into the Bridport Union workhouse and charged on the common fund. They were, and are settled in Beaminster, in the Beaminster Union. On the 9th October, 1849, the pauper gave notice to the master of the workhouse, and on that day he, his wife and family, left it. They went to the house of one Downton, in the parish of Bothenhampton, in the Bridport Union. The pauper's wife and Downton's wife are sisters. The pauper and his family slept in Downton's house that night. They paid nothing for refreshment or lodging. On the next morning after breakfast, the pauper and his wife and family went to Beaminster, and slept there two nights. The pauper then came to Allington for an order for the workhouse, but did not get any, and returned to Beaminster the same day, and slept there two nights more. He and his family then obtained an order for the vagrant ward of the Bridport Union, and after sleeping there two nights they were admitted into the house, on the 16th October, 1849, and charged on the common fund, where they remain. The Bridport board of guardians are of opinion that the pauper and his family are now removable, from having ceased to reside in Allington, but they do not know to what parish they are chargeable, so that such parish may remove them. They desire the Poor Law Board to determine whether the cost of relief is to be charged to Allington or Bothenhampton.

Ans.—The paupers were, it appears, admitted into the workhouse in October last, as destitute wanderers, and, consequently, were properly charged to the common fund of the union, (under 11 and 12 Vic. c. 110, sec. 1.) Nothing appears to have occurred since to alter this chargeability, and, consequently, the paupers continue chargeable to the common fund of the union, and are not removable.

4. Chargeability of a person residing in East Dean.

30*th Jan.*, 1851.

Clerk of Westbury-on-Severn Union.—By the 5 & 6 Vic. c. 48, the forest of Dean was divided into two townships, by the names of East Dean and West Dean; and by the 2nd sec. of that statute it was enacted that each of the said townships should thenceforth and for ever from and after the passing of the Act maintain its own poor, and for the purposes of the Act be vested with such and the like powers, privileges, and immunities, and be subject to the same laws, authorities, and regulations, as other townships in England and Wales maintaining their own poor. John Ferris was born in that part of the Forest of Dean now called the township of East Dean, and never gained a settlement out of it; he of course never gained any settlement in the township before the passing of the Act, nor has he gained one out of it since. He has lived in the same part of the Forest the whole of his life, and has now, with his wife and family, become chargeable. Inquiring, whether, under the circumstances, the relief given to John Ferris and his family ought to be charged to the township of East Dean or to the common fund.

Ans.—It appears to the Board, upon the statement before them, that the pauper has resided for five years in the township of East Dean without having received relief, and is consequently irremovable therefrom. With regard to his settlement, the Board consider that as at the time of his birth that which is now the township of East Dean formed part of a large extra-parochial district, he did not acquire any settlement in that township by birth; and as he has gained no settlement subsequently, he is not now settled therein; under these circumstances, it appears that the cost of his relief is chargeable on the common fund of the Westbury-on-Severn Union.

5. Chargeability of sick paupers.

5*th Nov.*, 1850.

Clerk of Chard Union.—Inquiring, whether relief made necessary by sickness or accident, to persons not legally settled or having resided five years in the parish in which they reside, should be charged to the common fund or to the parishes in which they reside.

Ans.—The Board desire to direct the attention of the guardians of the Chard Union to the terms of the enactment contained in the 9 & 10 Vic. c. 66, sec. 4, which are as follow, namely, "no warrant shall be granted for the removal of any person becoming chargeable in respect of relief made necessary by sickness or accident, unless the justices granting the warrant shall state in such warrant that they are satisfied that the sickness or accident will produce permanent disability." Then, the 11 & 12 Vic. c. 110, since continued by the 12 & 13 Vic. c. 103, and the 13 & 14 Vic. c. 101, renders the relief of all paupers who are irremovable under any provision of the 9 & 10 Vic. c. 66, a charge upon the common fund of the union. On referring to the language of the 4th sec. of the last named Act, it will be seen that your inquiry is somewhat too general in its terms. Relief, rendered necessary by sickness or accident, is not chargeable upon the common fund of the union in all cases, but only in those where the sickness or accident will not produce "permanent disability." The point, therefore, to be determined by the guardians in this class of cases is, whether the disability is of a temporary or permanent character. If the former, the relief given will be charged upon the common fund; if the latter, upon the parish of the residence.

V.—CHILD-DROPPING.—REWARDS FOR THE APPREHENSION OF PARTIES GUILTY OF.

22nd April, 1850.

Clerk of Haverfordwest Union.—The guardians have passed a resolution, offering a reward of two guineas to any person or persons who shall give such information as may lead to the conviction of any party guilty of "child-dropping." Requesting the Board's approval of the resolution; and inquiring whether the parish maintaining the child or the common fund should be charged with the reward and expenses of apprehension and conviction.

Ans.—The Board entertain much doubt as to whether the guardians are justified in offering any general reward of the nature described, to be paid out of the poor-rates. They consider that the correct course for the guardians to pursue in the matter would be to offer a reward for the apprehension of any known particular offender, under the provisions of the 7 & 8 Vic. c. 101, sec. 59, and then apply to this Board for direction as to the mode of charging the expenses thus incurred.

VI.—CLOTHING.—OF A DISTINCTIVE CHARACTER FOR A CERTAIN CLASS OF WORKHOUSE INMATES.

2nd Feb., 1850.

Clerk of Wincanton Union.—In this union there are several lads of the age of sixteen years and upwards, who are in the constant habit of obtaining admissions to the workhouse upon the plea of want of work, and when admitted, of absconding with the clothing given them to wear, selling the same, and then returning and giving themselves up to be committed to prison for the offence. The same individuals have several times repeated the offence, and four have done so during the past week, notwithstanding that they had several times received all the punishment allowed by law. It is seldom that the guardians have been enabled to discover the purchasers of the clothing, so as to bring them to justice. In one or two instances they have, however, done so, and the parties have been punished; but still the offence remains unchecked. The guardians propose for the future, if the Board see no objection to it, to try the effect, upon the return of every such offender to the house, of clothing him in some distinctive dress, unlike any of the other inmates, and such as will not be likely to obtain a purchaser should he abscond with it.

Ans.—The Board think that the guardians may properly direct that the clothing supplied to paupers who act in the manner stated by you, should be made of such materials, and in such a form as not to be likely to obtain a purchaser, in case the pauper shall abscond from the house and attempt to sell the clothes with which he has been furnished. The clothes should also be marked in several places with the name of the union, but not so that the mark or stamp shall be publicly visible on the exterior of the garment; see 55 Geo. 3, c. 137, sec. 2.

VII.—GUARDIANS.

1. BYE-LAW AS TO ALTERING OR RESCINDING RESOLUTIONS.

6th Sept., 1850.

Clerk of ——— Union.—Inquiring whether Art. 39 of the General Consolidated Order, will override and supersede a bye-law of the guardians which has been in force ever since the formation of the union. The bye-law is to the effect that no resolution of the guardians shall be rescinded or altered unless a majority of at least two-thirds of the guardians present at the discussion shall concur in the proposed alteration or rescinding, &c. The inquiry has reference to the following motion, viz.: "That the guardians, in compliance with the directions of the Poor Law Board, do now proceed to elect a chaplain for the workhouse." Some of the guardians contend that this is a new motion altogether, while others insist that it is in fact a motion to rescind the one carried by a majority at a former meeting of the guardians, that is, "Not to elect a paid chaplain."

Ans.—The Board do not see that the 39th Art. of the General Consolidated Order interferes with the bye-law described in your letter as acted upon by the guardians of the ——— Union, inasmuch as they refer to entirely distinct points, the one to the "notice" for rescinding or altering a resolution; the other, to the "majority" requisite to carry the revocation or alteration. But the 38th Art. of the order does appear to the Board to override the bye-law, as it makes the decision of every question dependent upon a simple majority of the guardians present and voting.

2. GUARDIANS REPRESENTING TWO PARISHES—VOTING.

15th *August*, 1850.

Guardian of Cirencester Union.—Inquiring, whether a person who is guardian for two parishes in the same union can vote for each of such two parishes.

Ans.—If a person be returned as guardian for two or more parishes in the same union, the Board are of opinion that it is not competent for him to vote at the board of guardians for each of such parishes. The Board consider that in such a case he has but one vote.

VIII.—ELECTION OF GUARDIANS.

1. QUALIFICATION OF TREASURER FOR THE OFFICE OF GUARDIAN.

6*th May*, 1850.

Clerk of Royston Union.—Mr. H. F., the treasurer of this union, has been duly elected guardian of the parish of Royston for the ensuing year, but some doubts have arisen whether, under the 5 & 6 Vic. c. 57, sec. 14, he is eligible to act in consequence of his holding that office, although he receives no salary for it except the use of the money in his hands. The sec. referred to enacts that "no person receiving any fixed salary or emolument," &c., shall be capable of serving as guardian; and the question therefore is, does the word "fixed" apply as well to the word "emolument" as to "salary."

Ans.—Art. 174 of the General Consolidated Order, which provides that if no specific salary be paid to the treasurer of a union, the use of the money left in his hands shall be deemed to be the payment of his services; or, in other words, his salary or emolument. This provision appears to the Board to bring the treasurer within the prohibition contained in the statute 5 & 6 Vic. c. 57, sec. 14.

Clerk of same Union.—Inquiring whether Mr. H. F.'s election is void, or whether he is only considered "incapable of serving as guardian" so long as he continues to hold the office of treasurer; and in case he should resign that office, whether he would be eligible to act as guardian. Inquiring also, whether, in the event of Mr. F.'s election being considered void, the Board will issue an order for a new election.

Ans.—The Board consider that Mr. F., as being the treasurer of the Royston Union, was disqualified for the office of guardian, and that consequently the election for Royston was void. The resignation of the office of treasurer would not enable him to act as guardian upon the election which has already taken place, though he would, after such resignation, be eligible at another election, and capable of acting if elected. The Board will be prepared to issue an order for a new election of guardians for Royston (Cambridge) upon application being made to them by the guardians of the Royston Union for that purpose.

2. INSPECTION OF OWNERS' CLAIMS.

28*th Jan.*, 1851.

Clerk of Rhayader Union.—Inquired, whether in a case where the population of the parish does not exceed two thousand persons, the overseers are to allow the owners' claims, &c., which may be in their possession, to be inspected between the 5th and 10th of February, there being no register of claims.

Ans.—In cases where the population does not exceed two thousand persons, and where there is no register of claims, the overseers are not bound to allow the owners' claims which may be in their possession to be inspected between the 5th and 10th of February.

IX.—EMIGRATION.—12 & 13 VIC. c. 103.

4*th March*, 1850.

Clerk of Cranbrook Union. — Inquiring, whether the sums raised for emigration purposes under a resolution of the guardians in pursuance of the statute of 12 & 13 Vic. c. 103, can be charged on the rates of the parish, and extended over a period of five years for repayment; or, whether the amount must be paid out of the funds belonging to the guardians, and charged to the parish in the present half yearly expenditure.

Ans.—The guardians of the Cranbrook Union cannot charge the future poor-rates of the parish with sums raised for emigration purposes under the 12 & 13 Vic. c. 103. The Board would point out, however, that under the 4 & 5 Wm. 4,

c. 76, sec. 62, the power still remains to the ratepayers to meet in vestry, and resolve to borrow money for emigration purposes.

X.—EMPLOYMENT.

1. OF WORKHOUSE INMATES.

2nd Feb., 1850.

Clerk of New Forest Union.—Requesting the advice of the Board as to the best mode of employing the inmates of the workhouse who are not able to work in the garden, and who were formerly employed in picking oakum or pounding gypsum: for neither of those articles is there at present any market.

Ans.—With regard to the reason stated for discontinuing the work on which the paupers of your union were formerly employed, the Board would point out to the guardians that profitable market for the produce of pauper labour is a matter only of secondary importance—the primary object being to keep them at work in such a manner as will lead them to prefer a life of independence to one of dependence upon the ratepayers. You do not state to which class the paupers you refer to belong; but if they be adults, the Board think that they may be usefully employed in cleansing the wards and yards of their respective classes, and be afterwards set to work at stone-breaking, if the guardians decide upon abandoning the former mode of employment.

2. EMPLOYMENT OF WORKHOUSE INMATES.

23rd August, 1850.

Clerk of Bath Union.—The board of guardians, being anxious to provide a test for a class of male paupers who are constantly resorting to the workhouse, on the plea of inability to procure employment, and for whom the workhouse does not appear to be a sufficient test, are of opinion that it would be desirable to have a stone-yard attached to the workhouse, where all such persons might be placed to stone-breaking, to be paid daily according to the amount of work performed; and of course, under such circumstances, having no admission to the workhouse either for rations or lodging. Requesting the sanction of the Poor Law Board to this arrangement, and inquiring whether the expenses attendant thereon should be considered as a union or parochial charge; and if the latter, what method should be adopted for keeping the accounts.

Ans.—The Board are quite prepared to sanction stone-breaking, as a mode of employing the able-bodied who are in receipt of relief, but the Board cannot sanction relief being granted to any able-bodied man without the application of the workhouse test, so long as there is room for his reception in the workhouse. The Board recommend the guardians to require every able-bodied male pauper relieved in the workhouse to break a certain quantity of stone daily, under proper superintendence; and if the workhouse should at any time become full, the Board will then be prepared to issue the out-door-labour-test order, under the regulations provided, in which the guardians may require the performance of a certain amount of work in return for the relief afforded. Any expenses which the guardians may incur in providing work for the able-bodied paupers, must be charged to the common fund, and that fund must also be credited with any profit which may arise from the labour of the paupers.

XI.—LUNATICS—NOT IN A STATE OF DESTITUTION—DUTY OF RELIEVING-OFFICER.

8th Jan., 1851.

Clerk of Sheffield Union.—Submitting two cases of insane persons extracted from the relieving-officer's report books, with the view of obtaining the opinion of the Board as to whether they are, according to the present law, cases in which a relieving-officer can legally give an order for admission into the workhouse, require a certificate as to insanity from a medical practitioner, take the lunatic before justices, and state that from destitution the patient is chargeable to some township in the union. The following are the extracts referred to:—"Mary R., 45; insane, see medical certificate; husband, Samuel R., warehouseman, 30*s.* per week wages; keeps a retail grocer's shop; has three children, John six, Jane four, Ellen eight months." "Hannah H.; insane; husband, Joseph H., is employed as a setter-in of razors; earns from 24*s.* to 25*s.* per week; has no children; rent £8. 8*s.* per annum: has a lodger, which pays 3*s.* per week; wife sent by her husband to Dunnington House asylum, at 8*s.* per week cost, on the 8th January, 1850, from whence her husband fetched her, improved in mind, the first week of September. She is now under care of her husband and her husband's sister." The general impression of the inhabitants of the union is, that the workhouse may be claimed as an asylum for all classes, and it is therefore with great difficulty that the relieving-officers can act strictly in accordance with their own impressions of what the law is. The point on which the advice of the Board is requested is, whether destitution forms the basis of relief in cases of insanity as it does in respect of other claims for relief.

Ans.—The Board would, in the first place, refer the guardians to the duties of the relieving-officer as prescribed by Art. 215, No. 6, of the General Consolidated Order. That Article imposes upon this officer the duty, in any case of sudden or urgent necessity, of affording requisite relief either by giving an order of admission into the workhouse or otherwise. If a poor person, not previously chargeable, become suddenly insane, and be in such a state of destitution as to require relief suitable to his case, but have not the means of procuring it, the relieving-officer would be bound to provide it. If he provided it by giving an order for the workhouse, or otherwise, he might obtain an order of justices for the removal of the insane person to an asylum. But in neither case would he be justified in acting unless there be an urgent necessity. If the case would admit of delay, or if the party be not in a state of destitution, the relieving-officer should not interfere, but receive the application when made to him, and bring it before the guardians for their decision. If the party were previously chargeable, the relieving-officer may be required to obtain at once an order of justices under the 8 & 9 Vic. c. 126, sec. 48. But no difficulty arises as to such cases. The relieving-officer is therefore under no obligation, nor would he act rightly in interfering in cases of insanity simply on the ground that the parties may be insane. He must satisfy himself, before he can act without consulting the guardians, that there is destitution, and that the case is one of suddenness or urgency. It is true that insanity may cause destitution where otherwise the poor person might have continued without requiring relief, but still the officer is bound to exercise his judgment, and satisfy himself that under the circumstances there is such an amount of destitution as to render it necessary for him to interfere before he has an opportunity of reporting the case to the board of guardians. The instances mentioned by you scarcely seem to exhibit such destitution.

XII.—NUISANCES — APPOINTMENT OF INSPECTOR OF.

11th Jan., 1851.

Clerk of Haslingden Union. — Inquiring whether the guardians can appoint an inspector of nuisances at a fixed salary in the absence of directions and regulations from the Board of Health. In the event of the guardians not being empowered to appoint an inspector, inquiring whether they can, after a notice has been received by them from two householders of the existence of a nuisance, employ a person to examine into the nuisance so notified, and to execute the order of the justices; and also, whether they can pay such inspector a specific remuneration in such case.

Ans.—Upon the construction of the 11 & 12 Vic. c. 103, the Board are of opinion that the guardians of the Haslingden Union cannot now employ a person at a fixed salary as an inspector of nuisances, either in the union generally or in any particular parish. The power of the guardians to employ officers for that purpose took effect under sec. 14 of the Act; but it was limited by the duration of the directions and regulations of the General Board of Health. The Board are of opinion, however, that the guardians can, under the 1st sec. of the Act, employ a person as their agent to inspect any particular nuisance to which their attention may be called by the notice of the inhabitants under that sec., or by the certificate of the medical or relieving-officer under sec. 6 of the 12 & 13 Vic. c. 111. The Board also think that the guardians may employ such person to execute the order of the justices in the matter, if any be made, and may pay him a reasonable remuneration for his services, though such payment must be made in respect of each occasion.

XIII.—ORDERS—OF THE POOR LAW COMMISSIONERS—EVIDENCE.

16th Dec., 1850.

Clerk of Rotherham Union.—The guardians of this union have given directions for an indictment to be preferred at the next quarter sessions against an inmate of the workhouse for an assault on the porter, and it is believed that it may be necessary on the trial to produce a copy of the General Consolidated Order of the 24th July, 1847. There seems to be some doubt whether a copy of the order, printed by the Queen's printer, can be given in evidence without proof that it was so printed, as the 7 & 8 Vic. c. 101, sec. 71, does not make copies purporting to be so printed, evidence. Requesting the opinion of the Poor Law Board on this point.

Ans.—The Board consider that the production of the copy of the Poor Law Commissioners' General Consolidated Order of the 24th July, 1847, will be of itself sufficient. They apprehend that the court will give credence to the copy as having been printed by the proper authority. Besides, as the copy purports to be under the seal of the Poor Law Commissioners and signed by the Commissioners, the 8 & 9 Vic. c. 113, (to which the Board desire to refer you,) will make it admissible in evidence.

XIV.—OVERSEERS.—THEIR POWER TO COLLECT POOR-RATES, NOTWITHSTANDING THE APPOINTMENT OF ASSISTANT OVERSEERS.

12*th Nov.*, 1850.

Clerk of Birmingham Parish.—By the 46th sec. of the Local Act, (1 & 2 Wm. 4, c. 68,) relating to this parish, the guardians are empowered to appoint assistant overseers, for the purpose of collecting the rates made and assessed for the relief of the poor, and to pay them such poundage or salary as they may think fit. By the same section the guardians are also empowered to take security from them for the proper discharge of their duties; and by sec. 47, the guardians may suspend or dismiss them, as and when they may think proper, and appoint others in their room. By sec. 48, such assistant overseers are required to pay over all monies to the guardians or their treasurer. Sec. 56 enacts that the overseers may divide the parish into districts, for the more easy collection of the rates. And sec. 46 provides, that the guardians may from time to time allot to the assistant overseers such districts as they may think proper. Such assistant overseers have been duly appointed by the guardians, the districts have been formed by the overseers, and allotted by the guardians. Inquiring whether, all this having been done, the overseers of the poor, or any of them, have the power, personally, to collect the rate, or any portion of it, as though such assistant overseers had not been appointed. The 66th sec. of the Local Act, whereby it is enacted that the demand of any rate by the assistant overseers shall be deemed a valid demand, and such assistant overseers are empowered to take all necessary proceedings for the recovery of such rate. The necessity, therefore, for the overseers of the poor personally demanding a rate, or, indeed, taking any step with a view to its recovery, does not appear to arise.

Ans.—By the general statutes relating to the poor-rates, the overseers of the poor are required to collect that rate; and although the appointment of an assistant overseer may relieve the overseers from the trouble of collection, they are not (without express provision to that effect) thereby deprived of the power and right of collecting the poor-rate when they desire to do so. In the Local Act for Birmingham, the Board do not find any provision which deprives the overseers of this right; the contrary, the clauses which refer to the recovery of the rates upon distress, evidently contemplate that the overseers have an authority to collect. The 66th sec. of the Act refers to an overseer or assistant overseer having attended at the dwelling-house or place of abode of the person intended to be summoned, and having demanded of such person the rate which is in arrear.

XV.—PARISH.—SITUATE PARTLY IN ONE COUNTY AND PARTLY IN ANOTHER.

9*th August*, 1850.

Clerk of Hay Union.—The guardians of the Hay Union have been served with the following notice by the parish officers of that portion of the parish of Glasbury which is situate in the county of Radnor:—"We, the overseers and churchwardens of the parish of Glasbury, in the county of Radnor, do hereby give you notice, that from and after the 1st day of August next, we, on behalf of the ratepayers of the said parish of Glasbury, do object to all paupers (now or afterwards living or residing in that portion of the parish of Glasbury which has, by a recent decision of the Court of Queen's Bench, been decided to be a portion of the county of Brecon) being relieved or continued chargeable to the said parish of Glasbury in the county of Radnor. And we do further give notice, that each and every case of chargeability of paupers residing in that said portion of the parish of Glasbury, which, by the force and effect of the said decision, is now declared to be a portion of the said county of Brecon, which may by any decision or order of your Board be placed to the said parish of Glasbury in the county of Radnor, will be objected to by us on account of the ratepayers of our said parish of Glasbury, in the said county of Radnor, at the next audit of accounts for the Hay Union." Requested the attention of the Poor Law Board to the Acts Wm. 4, c. 64, sec. 26, schedule M., and 7 & 8 Vic. c. 61, and to the recent decision of the Court of Queen's Bench, in Reg. *v.* The Inhabitants of Brecknockshire, reported (shortly) in No. 27. vol. 14, of the Justice of the Peace, with the view of ascertaining their opinion, as to whether the detached portion of the parish of Glasbury, now by such decision declared to be a part of the county of Brecon, has ceased to be a part of the parish of Glasbury, in the county of Radnor, for parochial and poor law purposes. If their opinion be in the affirmative, by what authority are rates to be imposed on, and the poor resident in the detached district in question maintained. If in the negative, what power have the overseers of the parish of Glasbury, in the county of Radnor, to impose rates on the inhabitants of the county of Brecon, especially those for county purposes.

Ans.—It is not of importance to the guardians of the Hay Union, whether the piece of land in question be in one county or the other; it appears that the whole parish of Glasbury is partly in the county of Radnor, and partly in the county of Brecon. The result of the late decision in the Reg. *v.* Inhabitants of Brecknockshire is, that a portion of the parish which was considered to be in the county of Radnor is, by the force of the late statute 7 & 8 Vic. c. 61, now to be taken to be in the county of Brecon; the whole of the parish is, however, in the Hay Union, and there is no ground for the guardians entering into any inquiry as to the situation of the different parts of the parish with respect to the chargeability of the paupers or the levying of the rates. The 9th clause of the 43 Eliz. c. 2, provides distinctly for the case, inasmuch as though the justices are to act within their respective jurisdictions in matters which come before them, the churchwardens and overseers are required, without dividing themselves, duly to execute their office in all places within the said parish in all things to them belonging. There must be one rate for the relief of the poor over the whole parish, the payments by the overseers apply to the whole of the parish, and the chargeability of paupers in any part is a chargeability to the whole. It seems probable that there has been some inattention in this parish to this provision of the statute of Elizabeth, otherwise no such question as that now submitted could well have arisen.

XVI.—PUBLICATIONS. — PROVIDED OUT OF THE POOR-RATES.

6th Dec., 185).

Assistant Overseer of Darlington.—Inquiring whether the overseers can legally provide out of the poor-rates, for the use of the assistant overseers' office, a copy of the Poor Law Statutes, from time to time, and the *Official Circular* of the Poor Law Board.

Ans.—The Board think it competent for the overseers of Darlington to procure, for their own use, and consequently for the use of the assistant overseer, a copy of the statutes relating to their office, and of the *Official Circular*, which is issued under the authority of this Board, who have a general control in the administration of the law relating to the relief of the poor.

XVII.—RATING.

1. PLANTATIONS—BRICK YARDS—QUARRIES.

31*st Dec.*, 1850.

Mr. F. J. Turner, Congleton.—Inquiring whether plantations and woods, which have only been thinned, are liable to be rated to the poor-rate; and if so, upon what principle the rateable value should be fixed. Inquiring also, how brick-yards and quarries are to be treated.

Ans.—With regard to the rating of woods and plantations, the Board direct me to state, that the express mention of "saleable underwoods," in the 43 Eliz. c. 2, has been held to exempt, by implication, all other kinds of wood from liability to assessment for the relief of the poor. The definition of "underwood," given by Mr. Justice Bayley in the case of R. *v.* Ferrybridge, (1 B. & C., 375,) is as follows:—"Generally speaking, that term is applied to a species of wood, which grows expeditiously, and sends up many shoots from one stool, the root remaining perfect from which the shoots are cut, and producing new shoots, and so yielding a succession of profits." Whether the woods and plantations you refer to are of this character, the Board are unable to judge from the information contained in your letter. With regard to the rating of brick-yards, the Board observe, that you do not raise any specific question on the subject, and they can only refer you generally, therefore, to the decision in Reg. *v.* Westbrook, (2 N. S. C. 599, 11 Jur., 515,) the effect of which is stated in the marginal note to the report in the following terms:—"Where land containing brick-earth is let for the purpose of making bricks, the lessee paying the lessor a certain sum per acre for the land, and also a royalty on a fixed sum per thousand for all the bricks made, the proper criterion for the sessions for estimating the rateable value of such land is (taking into consideration the purposes to which such land is to be applied, and the privileges which a tenant would enjoy by reason of his occupation) the sum which a tenant from year to year may reasonably be expected to give, after making the deductions specified in the 6 & 7 Wm. 4, c. 96. The royalty is to be considered in the nature of rent, and must be taken into account in estimating the amount which a tenant would give." With respect to quarries, the rule for ascertaining the rateable value is of a like nature; namely, to estimate what they would let for, from year to year, that is, taking one year with another. This will depend upon the average annual produce.

2. RATING OF SMALL TENEMENTS UNDER 13 & 14 VIC. c. 99.

24th Dec., 1850.

Assistant Overseer, Reddish, Stockport.—Inquiring what notice should be given for calling a vestry meeting, under the 1st sec. of the 13 & 14 Vic. c. 99, and by whom the notice should be signed.

Ans.—The notice to be given in calling a vestry meeting, under the 1st sec. of the Act referred to, may be signed by any of the persons authorised to sign notices of vestry meetings, under the 1st Vic. c. 45, sec. 3; and it must be published three clear days before the meeting is held, so that the meeting cannot be held earlier than the Thursday following the Sunday on which the notice is given. The Board believe that proper forms may be obtained of Mr. C. Knight, their publisher.

XVIII.—RELATIONS.—PAYMENT OF COST OF AN ORDER OF MAINTENANCE.

7th Jan., 1851.

Clerk of Nantwich Union.—On the 20th ult., a complaint, at the instance of the guardians, was heard at the Nantwich petty sessions, against Mr. W. W., under the 43 Eliz. c. 2, sec. 7, and 59 Geo. 3, c. 12, sec. 26, calling upon him to show cause why he should not contribute to the maintenance of his three grandchildren. The justices made the order applied for, and ordered the costs of and attending the obtaining of such order (the amount being then ascertained) to be paid by the grandfather. The clerk to the petty sessions now, however, advises the magistrates that they were wrong in directing the payment of costs, as they had no power to do so, but simply to make an order of maintenance. Requesting the opinion of the Board, after perusing sec. 18 of 11 & 12 Vic. c. 43, as to whether the justices had power to grant costs against the defendant as above-stated.

Ans.—The 11 & 12 Vic. c. 43, sec. 18, to which you refer, appears to the Board to support the order for costs made by the justices in the case in question.

XIX.—RELIEF.

1. TO BUY A HORSE AND CART.

31st Dec., 1850.

Clerk of Great Broughton Union.—The guardians of the Great Broughton Union have ordered the sum of 60*s.* to R. L., a pauper belonging to Ashton, to buy a horse, so as to enable him to get his living. Requesting the approval of the Poor Law Board thereto.

Ans.—The application of the poor-rates to the purchase of a horse for a pauper would be altogether illegal, and the Board could not, by any sanction of theirs, render the proposed expenditure lawful.

2. RELIEF TO THE CHILDREN OF A WOMAN WHOSE HUSBAND IS BEYOND THE SEAS.

11th Sept., 1850.

Clerk of Droitwich Union.—A woman, whose husband is beyond the seas, having left her with several children dependent upon her, applied to the guardians a few days ago for out-door relief for her children, not for herself. The guardians were unwilling to grant out-relief to the children, unless they could compel the mother to come into the workhouse with them. Formerly it was alleged that relief to the children was not relief to the wife, and that she consequently could not be compelled to come into the workhouse with them. The 25th sec. of the 7 & 8 Vic. c. 101, subjects women whose husbands are beyond the seas to the same condition as widows; and relief to children under sixteen years of age of a widow is directed by the 56th sec. of 4 & 5 Wm. 4, c. 76, to be considered as relief to the widow. Taking therefore the two enactments together, it would appear that relief to the children of the woman deserted by her husband, would be relief to the mother, but from the tenor of Mr. Lumley's Notes on the General Orders of the Poor Law Commissioners, page 312, it would seem that he thinks otherwise.

Ans.—The present case appears to be within Art. 4 of the General Prohibitory Order, which declares that all relief given by the guardians in the cases therein specified, (whether it be for the wife, child, or children,) shall be given to the woman in the same manner, and subject to the same conditions as if she were a widow. The application of the woman in the present case, therefore, must be dealt with in the same manner as if she were a widow, which, indeed, for the purposes of relief, she must be considered to be; and it will accordingly only be necessary to ascertain whether the case is within any, and if any, what exception to the General Prohibitory Order. As far as the Board are acquainted with the circumstances of the case, it appears to fall within Art. 1, Excep. 5; and if so, there is nothing to prevent the guardians from giving out-door relief to the children without requiring the mother to enter the workhouse. The point raised in your letter as to whether relief to the children is in law relief to the mother does not appear to the Board to be of any importance in the present case, or indeed in any case arising under Art. 4 of the General Prohibitory Order.

3. RELIEF TO SINGLE WOMEN DURING PREGNANCY.

14*th Dec.*, 1850.

Clerk of Keynsham Union.—It is the habit of the guardians, when applied to for relief by single women in a state of pregnancy, to allow a small sum weekly for some few weeks previous to their confinement, in order to obviate the necessity of bringing them into the workhouse, an asylum which such persons in this union are found very earnestly to seek, for the sake of the comforts and attention which are provided in such an establishment, and which they cannot obtain at their own homes. The district auditor has informed the relieving-officers that he shall disallow such items in future, as he considers that all single females who require relief, and are able to be removed, should receive it in the workhouse only. The guardians are of opinion, that it is their duty to decide who under the Prohibitory Order are not able-bodied. Requesting the opinion of the Poor Law Board on the point.

Ans.—The fact of a woman being pregnant does not of itself take her out of the class of able-bodied, and the guardians have erred in supposing that out-door relief can lawfully be given without the previous sanction of this Board to single women solely on account of their being pregnant. Whatever the decision of the guardians may be in regard to any case, the legality or illegality of the relief is of course a matter for the consideration of the auditor, when the accounts come to be audited. The Board consider the class of persons in question should be relieved in the workhouse, the discipline of which ought to be such as not to afford an inducement to poor persons to seek relief in it, so long as they can maintain themselves.

11*th Jan.*, 1851.

Clerk of same Union.—The guardians cannot see how a pregnant woman, within a few weeks of her confinement, can be said to be able-bodied, the period mentioned being one during which many women are totally incapable of attending to their ordinary work; and the guardians are of opinion that no persons can be better judges of the fact than themselves, as they have in each case that comes before them the opportunity of either hearing the statements of such applicants, or of examining persons who can speak as to their capabilities to labour. It is not the habit of the guardians to give relief to women merely because they are pregnant; but when they do so, it is because such persons are unable, by reason of that pregnancy, to follow their ordinary avocations, and to earn their own maintenance. They think that the decision of that point is a matter entirely within their province, and that the auditor, not having the means of judging of the fact whether a person so relieved is or not able-bodied, has not the means of deciding that the relief is illegal.

Ans.—On re-perusing their letter of the 14th ult., the Board observe that it referred to the effect of pregnancy in general, rather than to the particular portion of the period of pregnancy to which the guardians of the Keynsham Union appear more especially to allude. The Board now desire me to state, that it certainly appears to them that, generally speaking, a woman in the last stage of pregnancy cannot be considered as able-bodied. She may be able-bodied during the greater part of the duration of her pregnancy, or she may be disabled during a long portion of it. In most cases, she will probably be disabled for a few weeks prior to her delivery; but as cases differ in this respect, it will be a question in each particular instance, whether the pauper is able-bodied or not. It will rest with the guardians to decide this question for themselves in the first instance, though undoubtedly the auditor may have to exercise a judgment upon it ultimately if it be brought before him at the audit of the accounts.

XX.—REMOVAL—OF SCOTCH AND IRISH POOR.

26th Nov., 1850.

Clerk of Leeds Township.—By the 8 & 9 Vic. c. 117, sec. 2, it would appear that as the relief of the poor in the township of Leeds is administered by a board of guardians, the proceedings to be taken for the removal of persons born in Scotland, Ireland, &c., who may become chargeable, can only be taken by the guardians of the township, or their officers, as they are alone authorised to complain of the chargeability, and not by the overseers or their assistant overseers. But as the 1st sec. of the 10 & 11 Vic. c. 33, enacts "that it shall be lawful for any guardian, relieving-officer, or overseer of any parish or union in England, to take and convey before two justices without summons or warrant every poor person who shall become chargeable to any parish in England under the first-cited Act," it has been contended that these words restore to the churchwardens and overseers the power to make these complaints of chargeability, which was given to them by the 3 & 4 Wm. 4, c. 40, but which Act was repealed by the 1st sec. of 8 & 9 Vic. c. 117. On the other hand, it is argued, that although the words "any guardian, relieving-officer, or overseers," in the 1st sec. of 10 & 11 Vic. c. 33, are undoubtedly very large if standing alone without reference to any other statute, yet that they must be read in connexion with the two statutes referred to in the preamble of that sec., (the 8 & 9 Vic. c. 83, sec. 77, and the 8 & 9 Vic. c. 117,) and that they can be taken only to extend to authorise the persons empowered by the statute 8 & 9 Vic. c. 117, sec. 2, to complain to the justices respecting chargeable Scotch and Irish poor, &c., to take and convey such chargeable persons before the justices without summons, and that they do not enable any other officer or person than those mentioned in the said sec. 2 (that is, in the township of Leeds, the guardians only to the exclusion of the overseers) to complain to the justices with a view to the removal of the parties chargeable. Under these circumstances, inquired, 1st. Whether the guardians alone, or the overseers alone, or the guardians or overseers indifferently, have authority within the township of Leeds to convey chargeable Scotch or Irish poor, &c., before two justices, and to make complaint to the justices of their chargeability. 2nd. In case the guardians alone have authority to convey the persons chargeable before the justices, and to complain of their chargeability, what form of authority should be given by the guardians to their officers, (relieving-officers or others) to originate and complete those proceedings and complaints, seeing that the guardians as such can act only in their corporate capacity, sitting as a board, and cannot individually convey the parties before the justices nor complain of their chargeability. 3rd. In case the Board should be of opinion that the guardians alone in the township of Leeds have authority to originate the proceedings necessary for the removal of chargeable Irish and Scotch poor, &c., how are the expenses necessarily incurred in and about the procuration and execution of the justices' warrants of removal to be defrayed—that is to say, by whose order and out of what fund. Up to Midsummer last the expenses of such removals have been usually paid by the treasurer of the borough fund by order of the court of quarter sessions; but at the last Michaelmas sessions, the recorder declined to make the customary order, as his attention had been called to the limitations in the early part of sec. 5. of 8 & 9 Vic. c. 117, which superseded the repealed Act of 3 & 4 Wm. 4, c. 40, the orders of court thitherto having been made under the supposed authority of the concluding words of sec. 2. of the last-named Act.

Ans.—The Board consider that the 10 & 11 Vic. c, 33, does nothing more than enable one of the parties therein named to take the pauper referred to before the justices without a summons or warrant. When the pauper is brought before them, the application for the warrant of removal must still be made in accordance with the 8 & 9 Vic. c. 117, sec. 2, so that in the case of paupers born in Scotland or Ireland becoming chargeable to the township of Leeds, the guardians of that township must make the complaint, and apply for the order or warrant. Then the 5 & 6 Vic. c. 57, sec. 17, and the 7 & 8 Vic. c. 101, sec. 69, provide the means by which boards of guardians can appoint officers or other persons to make applications on their behalf to justices and otherwise. Under these statutes, the guardians of the township of Leeds will be enabled to make through their officers the application or complaint to the justices which is required by 8 & 9 Vic. c. 117, sec. 2. The expenses which the guardians may incur in respect of these applications and the execution of the warrants, they must pay out of the funds in their possession, unless the population of the township is under thirty thousand, in such case the costs and charges are to be paid by the town council of the borough, under sec. 5. of the 8 & 9 Vic. c. 117.

XXI.—VALUATION — BY A COMMITTEE OF RATE-PAYERS.

23rd Dec., 1850.

Overseer of Deal.—The following resolution has been passed by the vestry of the parish of Deal:—"That the churchwardens and overseers, in connection with the following persons, Messrs. ————, be appointed as a committee to carry out the new valuation of the parish, that they be empowered to make terms with a surveyor or surveyors to assist them, and that the expenses be paid out of the poor-rates." The committee are composed of several tradesmen and private gentlemen, and before entering on their duties, they are anxious for the advice of the Poor Law Board on the following points. Has such a committee power to act and carry out a new valuation or re-adjustment of the rate? Will the expenses be allowed? If the committee complete the valuation or re-adjustment without calling in a surveyor, will the rate be good if made on a sound basis? Would the following basis be considered as just and equitable, and agreeable to law, namely, "That the gross annual value should be estimated at what a property might reasonably be expected to let at from year to year?" To make the duties of the committee less complicated, they think of adding to the basis the following, "And that an uniform reduction of twenty-five per cent. be allowed for repairs, assurances, etc., and the balance be the rateable value;" will this addition be just and in accordance to law?

Ans.—The Board do not generally approve of arrangements for the re-valuation of the rateable property of a parish by means of a committee of rate-payers. At the same time, if in any case such a committee be requested to give their aid to the overseers in the matter, and are willing to do so gratuitously, there is nothing in point of law to prevent it. But the Board must point out, that in such case no remuneration can be legally paid to such committee, nor can they charge any expenses upon the poor-rate. It should be borne in mind, moreover, that the overseers are alone responsible for making the poor-rates; and, consequently, it will rest with them to decide how far they will avail themselves of the labours or advice of the committee, who have no compulsory authority whatever in point of law. With regard to the basis of the valuation, the Board would direct your attention to the provisions of the 6 & 7 Wm. 4, c. 96, sec. 3, which contains an express enactment on the subject.

XXII.—VESTRY.—PUBLICATION OF NOTICES OF.

18th Sept., 1850.

Clerk of Ringwood Union.—By the 1 Vic. c. 45, sec. 2, notices of vestry meetings are required to be affixed on or near to the doors of all the churches and chapels within the district. In addition to the ancient parish church of Ringwood, there has been recently erected a church at Bisterne within the parish, and another church at Burley Ville parish, about 150 yards beyond or out of the parish, but which latter church comprises within its district the tithing of Burley, the whole of which is within the parish of Ringwood, The overseers affix copies of notices to Ringwood and Bisterne churches, but not upon the door of the church at Burley Ville. Is this a sufficient publication?

Ans.—The Poor Law Board consider that, according to the case of Ormerod *v.* Chadwick, 16 Meeson and Welsby 367, the publication of the notice of vestry meetings on Bisterne church is clearly correct. In strictness it may not be absolutely necessary to publish such notices on the church at Burley Ville, (that church not being locally situate within the parish, although comprising the tithing which is within the parish,) but unless some objection exists of which the Board are not aware, it would seem to be very reasonable and proper to do so.

XXIII. — WORKHOUSE. — EMPLOYMENT OF FEMALE PAUPERS IN HOUSEHOLD WORK.

27th Oct., 1850.

Clerk of Droitwich Union.—The guardians, at a meeting held the 10th of October, 1849, resolved, "That the question of employing women of notoriously bad character in the domestic affairs of the house be referred to the Poor Law Board for their opinion." In order that the Board may understand the reason of this resolution, he (the clerk) has forwarded to them the minutes of the guardians on the subject. The question was first mooted in consequence of its being discovered that great laxity of discipline prevailed in the workhouse. The advantage of keeping women of bad character as closely confined to their own ward as possible is a point on which the guardians are unanimous, but in the absence of more respectable female pauper inmates to do the work, whilst there are female inmates at all in the house capable of performing the services required, the guardians cannot agree as to the propriety or policy of relieving them therefrom, or inflicting upon them the punishment of close confinement to their own ward, as in that case the ratepayers would have to bear the expense of hiring paid servants in their place. Under these circumstances, from a wish on the part of some of the guardians to make the workhouse as irksome and uncomfortable as possible to women of abandoned character, with the view of maintaining proper discipline therein, and bringing about a settlement of the question, the above resolution was passed. [A copy of the minutes of the proceedings of the guardians in relation to this matter accompanied the clerk's communication.]

Ans.—The Board are very sensible of the evils likely to arise from women of bad character being employed in the household work of the establishment, when not placed under vigilant superintendence; but the expediency of so employing them, and the mode of their employment, must, in a great measure, depend upon local circumstances, and be left to the discretion of the master and matron of the workhouse, under the direction of the guardians and the visiting committee. The Board think, however, that in no case should persons of bad character be employed in places of trust, or such as would be likely to bring them into contact with the other inmates. The elder girls ought, for the most part, to be employed in the duties connected with their own wards, under the superintendence of the matron and schoolmistress; and if at any time the assistance of an adult female inmate is requisite, care should be taken that she is not left alone with the children, unless she be a woman of good character. If female paupers are of necessity at any time employed in the male wards, they should be superintended by the matron. As regards Sarah D., the woman whose employment as cook gave rise to the resolution of the guardians, [as shown by the copy minutes,] the Board have no hesitation in saying, that if she was known to be of bad character, she ought not to have been placed in a situation which admitted of her having intercourse with the other inmates, and more especially with such of the girls as were appointed to assist in doing the cooking or kitchen work. The Board concur with the minority of the guardians present at the meeting of the 14th of March last, in opinion, that if a suitable person from amongst the inmates of the workhouse could not be selected to act as cook, the proper course would be to engage the services of a person as cook at a fixed salary, a practice which many boards of guardians have adopted with beneficial results, even in an economical point of view. The responsibility of regulating all matters of detail in connection with the management and discipline of the workhouses, which are not provided for by the general regulations, must necessarily rest with the guardians themselves, and the Board see no reason to doubt the discretion and vigilance of the Droitwich guardians in this respect.

London. Printed by Order of the Poor Law Board, by BLACKBURN & BURT, 90½, Holborn Hill, and Published by CHARLES KNIGHT, 90, Fleet Street.

AN

OFFICIAL CIRCULAR

OF PUBLIC DOCUMENTS AND INFORMATION:

DIRECTED BY THE POOR LAW BOARD TO BE PRINTED, CHIEFLY FOR THE USE OF THE BOARDS OF GUARDIANS AND THEIR OFFICERS.

No. 47.] [N.S.

CONTENTS.

I.—ACCOUNTS.

1. ENTRY OF COST OF RELIEF TO IRREMOVABLE POOR IN THE FINANCIAL STATEMENT.

19*th April,* 1851.

The Poor Law Board to Mr. ——, *District Auditor.*—The Board transmit for your explanation the Financial Statement (Form 17) of the —— Union, for the half year ended Michaelmas, 1850, which the Board observe you have signed as correct. It appears in regard to certain of the parishes that there are entries of receipts on account of irremovable poor; whereas the charge for the relief of that class of poor ought to be entered entirely among the common charges of the union, and not form any parochial charge whatever.

25*th April,* 1851.

Mr. ——, *District Auditor.*—Forwarding the following communication which he had received on this subject from the clerk of the —— Union:—"The entries inquired about by the Poor Law Board are quite correct, and arise in the following way: Their order is, as you are aware, that on its being ascertained that a pauper is chargeable to the common fund, not only shall it have a prospective application, but also a retrospective one, so that it does not apply to pay afforded anterior to the preceding audit; hence then it follows as of course, that when a direction is given by the board of guardians to transfer a pauper, we have to go back to ascertain what amount of pay he has received from the parish to which he was chargeable, and then credit the parish and debit the general fund with the amount; the only way it is imagined of complying with the order."

Ans.—The course described by the clerk as having been pursued in the class of cases which he mentions, does not appear to the Board to be correct with regard to the Financial Statement, though it may have been perfectly proper as respects the union ledger. If the cost of the relief of any pauper be charged in the first instance to some parish in the union, and the charge be subsequently transferred by the guardians to some other parish, or to the common fund of the union, during the currency of the same half-year, the proper entries should of course be made in the parochial ledger to effect such transfer, supposing the relief to have been already charged therein to the debit of the first-mentioned parish. But although these entries must be made in the ledger to render it correct, the Board consider that in preparing the Financial Statement, a different course should be pursued, and that no notice should be taken therein, either of the original charge to the debit of the first-mentioned parish, or of the corresponding credit. The Financial Statement should simply exhibit the account as it ought to have been throughout; for if all the entries in the ledger be followed in the Statement, it is manifest that the cost of the same relief will be inserted twice, and the statement thus rendered inaccurate as regards the union generally, though there may be no error in the balance of the account with respect to the particular parish. A similar remark will apply to the preparation of the Statistical Statement, in reference to the number of paupers relieved.

2. Entry of cost of relief to irremovable poor.

15*th May*, 1851.

The Poor Law Board to ———, *District Auditor.*—By the last half-year's financial statement of the South Molton Union, it appears in regard to many of the parishes that there are entries of receipts on account of irremovable poor, whereas the charge for this class of poor should be entered entirely among the common charges of the union, and not form any parochial charge whatever. Requesting explanation.

17*th May*, 1851.

Ans. of District Auditor.—When the expenditure for this class of poor was first made a common charge, the clerks were directed by the Poor Law Board to charge it in the first instance to the parishes, and at the close of every half-year to transfer the amount to the debit of common charges' account in the ledger, and to credit the respective parishes. This mode of charging the irremovable expenditure is still practised in the Torrington and South Molton Unions, but not in other unions of the district, because, as he was informed by the clerk of the Bideford Union, a subsequent order was issued by the Poor Law Board not to make the expenditure a parochial charge, but a common charge only. This last order had never reached him. Finding the union and parochial ledgers at South Molton made up in the way the clerk was first directed to make the entries, when he last audited the union accounts, he was led to pass them as they were made up, although aware of the different mode of entering this head of expenditure in the Bideford Union, and directed the Bideford plan to be adopted for the future. The irremovable poor expenditure being charged in columns 2 and 13, it became necessary to credit the parishes in one of the columns of No. 2, with their respective amounts in order to make the totals agree. The first adopted plan shows the amount of irremovable poor expenditure in each parish, whereas the other mode of entering this class of expenditure does not show it: for it does not form a part of the out-relief, but is charged under the head of common charges only. The relieving-officers of the Torrington and South Molton Unions have not kept the irremovable poor apart from the other classes of poor in their out-relief lists, but at the close of each half-year they have abstracted them from their out-relief lists, and their statements have been submitted to the guardians for their approval; and the clerks, after they have been examined and passed by the Board, have entered them in their minute books, debiting and crediting common charges to the parishes accordingly.

25*th June*, 1851.

The Poor Law Board to the District Auditor.—The course you describe as being pursued in this respect in the South Molton and Torrington Unions is not correct. The statutes relating to the subject (11 & 12 Vic. c. 110, sec. 3, and subsequent Acts) constitute the cost of the relief of the irremovable poor a charge upon the common fund of the union direct: and it follows that there should be no separate entry in the union accounts against any parish in respect of such relief. The mode still adopted in the two unions just mentioned was the one prescribed by the Poor Law Commissioners in their circular of the 26th August, 1847,* in reference to the provisions of the 10 & 11 Vic. c. 110, (Mr. Bodkin's Act,) which contemplated that the several parishes would be charged in the first instance with the relief of the irremovable poor, and accordingly provided for their reimbursement from the common fund of the union.

* See Official Circular, Vol. VII., N.S., page 142.

But since the passing of the Act of the following year, the 11 & 12 Vic. c. 110, which makes the relief in question a direct charge upon the common fund, the position of the matter is altered.

25*th June*, 1851.

The Poor Law Board to the Clerks of South Molton and Torrington Unions.—Transmitting for the information of each, a copy of the above correspondence, and requesting that he would be careful, in future, to observe the directions contained in the Board's circular of the 23rd April, 1849.

5*th July*, 1851.

Clerk of South Molton Union.—The relief to the irremovable poor has, in the first instance, been applied for and entered in the relief lists of the parishes wherein the recipients are resident. And, at the end of the half-year, a list of these has been extracted from the relief lists, with the amount of relief administered to each. This list has been submitted to the guardians, and after having been canvassed, corrected, and finally approved by them, it has been copied into the minutes of their proceedings, with an order for the transfer of the total amount to the debit of common charges, and to the credit of each parish in the proportion in which it has been charged, and thus the provisions of the statute have been substantially complied with. This course was adopted, and has been pursued as the most convenient from the difficulty of deciding on the moment, whether the application for relief is or is not within the provisions of the statutes which place the charge of it to any other than the ordinary parochial account. To arrive at an accurate conclusion requires strict inquiry and investigation. The parish of residence is interested in spreading the charges of all their now settled poor over the union; and without considerable caution, a great majority of such poor, whether removable or not, and particularly if there be any difficulty in ascertaining, or substantiating the legal settlement, would ultimately become union charges. The relief lists and accounts have been dealt with in the same way as above-stated for the current half-year, and it would be very difficult, if not impracticable, to alter them until the end of the Michaelmas half-year. As to the financial statement (form 17) for the current half-year, there will be no difficulty in making it accord with the Board's view, by omitting any notice of the credit in column 3, and inserting in columns 1 and 2 the amount of relief in respect of each parish, minus the amount administered to non-settled irremovable poor and vagrants.

5*th Aug.*, 1851.

The Poor Law Board to the Clerk of South Molton Union.—The Board think the course hitherto pursued by the guardians of the South Molton Union in this matter is not altogether correct. The Board consider that the guardians should determine the incidence of the charge of the relief of each pauper as soon as it may be practicable to do so after the granting of the relief. Where, however, the relief in any case is charged in point of fact to the debit of any parish in the union ledger, and the charge is subsequently transferred by the guardians during the currency of the same half-year to the common fund of the union, it will of course be necessary and proper that the parish concerned should be credited, and the common fund account debited, accordingly, so as duly to effect the transfer in the ledger; but the Board think that no notice should be taken of the error and its correction in the financial statement, in which the relief should be entered solely under the head of common charges. If the error and its correction, which must necessarily appear in the union ledger, be introduced also into the financial statement, it is manifest that the same relief will be entered in the statement twice over.

II.—AUDIT.

1. HOLDING THE AUDIT OF THE PAROCHIAL AND UNION ACCOUNTS AT DIFFERENT TIMES.

5*th Sept.*, 1851.

G. Barnes, Esq., District Auditor.—Inquiring whether with reference to the several articles in the general order for accounts relative to the audit, and especially to articles 24 and 33, he is at liberty to appoint a different time for the audit of the union and parochial accounts respectively. The overseers' accounts are often ready for the audit two or three weeks before those of the clerk. During that time he could audit many parochial accounts, and could so change the direction of such early audits as to bring within them occasionally the accounts of all the assistant overseers and collectors in his district. His experience has shown him that there is little check, excepting by the auditor, upon such officers, and that an early audit of their accounts is very desirable.

Ans.—Under the general order for accounts, the Board think that the time fixed for the audit of the union accounts and those of the parishes need not necessarily be the same. If, however, different times for the audit be fixed for these separate accounts, due notice thereof must be given according to Art. 33.

2. PAYMENT OF COST OF CLEANING WORKHOUSE CLOCK—RENT OF RELIEF STATIONS.

13*th March*, 1851.

Clerk of Walsall Union.—Inquiring, 1, Whether the guardians are legally authorised to pay for the necessary repairs and cleaning of the kitchen clock of the union workhouse. 2, Whether they can legally pay for the hire of a room in each of the parishes in this union, to be used as a relief station by the relieving-officer when he is engaged in paying the paupers their weekly allowances as directed by the guardians.

Ans.—1, The Board think that the kitchen clock of the workhouse must be considered to be part of the furniture thereof, which the guardians are required by Art. 151 of the General Consolidated Order to keep in repair; therefore, if such repair be needed, the cost is a proper charge upon the common fund of the union. 2, In regard to relief stations, the Board consider it is competent for the guardians to provide them in one of the two following ways: either by fixing the salary of the relieving-officer at such an amount as would cover the cost of providing fit places or stations for distributing the relief, leaving him to carry out the necessary arrangement; or, the guardians themselves can pay the rent, or compensation for such stations. Whichever course be adopted the cost is properly chargeable to the common fund of the union.

III.—AUDITOR—ADMINISTRATION OF OATH BY.

21*st Oct.*, 1851.

William Rees, Esq., District Auditor.—Referring to section 16 of the statute 14 & 15 Vic. c. 99, and inquiring whether district auditors are thereby empowered to administer an oath to persons who may be legally required to attend an audit of accounts.

Ans.—The office of an auditor is so peculiar, and his duties bear so little resemblance to those which appear to have been chiefly contemplated by the legislature in the 14 & 15 Vic. c. 99, sec. 16, that the Board do not recommend you, in your capacity of district auditor, to act upon such provision at present, until there has been some judicial exposition of the extent of its operation. The Board, indeed, conceive that this power is the less necessary as an auditor is already authorized to require a declaration from every party accounting, and any wilful falsehood in such declaration is punishable in the same manner as perjury, (see 7 & 8 Vic. c. 101, sec. 33.)

IV.—STATUTES.

1. CIRCULAR TO BOARDS OF GUARDIANS ON THE 14 & 15 VIC. C. 11.

Poor Law Board, London, June 26th, 1851.

Sir,—I am directed by the Poor Law Board to bring under the notice of the Guardians the provisions of the statute, 14 & 15 Vic. c. 11, for the better protection of persons who are under the care and control of others as apprentices or servants.

Sec. 1 enacts that if the master or mistress of *any person*, being legally liable to provide for such person, as an apprentice or servant, necessary food, clothing, or lodging, shall wilfully and without lawful excuse refuse or neglect to provide the same, or shall unlawfully and maliciously assault such person, whereby the life of such person shall be endangered, or the health of such person shall have been or shall be likely to be permanently injured, such master or mistress shall be guilty of a misdemeanor, and be liable to be imprisoned, with or without hard labour, for any term not exceeding three years.

Sec. 2 enables the court to allow the costs of a prosecution for every such offence, to be paid in the same manner as the costs of prosecutions under the 7th Geo. 4, c. 64.

The above clauses are of a general character, but the subsequent clauses particularly affect Boards of Guardians in the discharge of their duties, providing for the registration of young persons sent from the workhouse as servants. They also provide for the visitation of such young persons and of apprentices bound out by guardians or overseers while in service.

Sec. 3 requires the guardians, and where there are no guardians, the overseers, to keep a register, wherein shall be entered the name of every young person under the age of sixteen, hired or taken as a servant from the workhouse, together with certain other particulars set out in the book, and mentioned below. The entry, when made, is to be signed by the presiding chairman of the board of guardians, or by an Overseer.

The Form of Register set forth in the Schedule is as follows:—

Name of Child	Age	Date of hiring or taking as Servant	Name of Master or Mistress	Trade or other description of Master or Mistress	Residence of Master or Mistress

The Board must observe, however, that the use of this book will not supersede that of the Register of parish apprentices, required by the 42 Geo. 3, c. 46, and the 7 & 8 Vic. c. 101.

Secs. 4 & 5 provide for the periodical visitation of young servants and apprentices.

By the former section the guardians or overseers, as the case may be, where any young person under the age of sixteen shall have been or shall be hired or taken as a servant from the workhouse, or shall have been or shall be bound as an apprentice by such guardians or overseers, are required, so long as such young person shall be under sixteen, and shall be known to them to reside as servant or apprentice *in the same service* into which such young person shall have so gone as a servant from such workhouse, or as such apprentice, within the union or parish respectively, or within five miles from any part thereof, to cause the relieving officer, or where there is no relieving officer, then some other officer duly authorized for the purpose, to visit such young person at least *twice* in every year, and to report to them in writing whether he has found reason to believe that such young person is not supplied with necessary food, or is subjected to cruel or illegal treatment in any respect.

Sec. 5 provides for the case where the residence of the master or mistress shall be more than five miles from the union or parish, from the workhouse of which the young person shall have been hired, or taken as a servant, or from which union or parish the young person shall have been bound apprentice, and requires in respect of any such hiring or binding hereafter, the guardians or overseers of such union or parish to send a written notice of the hiring, taking, or binding, specifying the name and age of the apprentice or servant, and the name, description, and residence of the master or mistress, to the guardians or overseers of the union or parish in which the master or mistress shall reside. The names of such young persons and apprentices are then to be registered in a proper book by the guardians or overseers receiving the notice, and the latter are to cause such young persons to be visited as frequently and in the same manner as young persons hired out from their own workhouse.

The guardians will perceive, that in carrying these provisions into execution they must give their directions to their officers to make the visitations at such times, and in such manner, as to enable them to obtain correct information as to the ordinary treatment of the young persons visited. At the same time, the visits must not be made at unseasonable hours, or in such a manner as to create unnecessary inconvenience or annoyance to the master or mistress of the young person; and the officers should be informed that this Board will be prepared to treat with due animadversion any impertinence, or unnecessary and offensive intrusion, on the part of those officers in the discharge of this duty.

The Board request that if any case of cruel or illegal treatment be reported to the guardians of so serious a character as to require a prosecution, the guardians will immediately communicate the same to this Board.

It is also to be observed, that the statute authorises a visit at any reasonable time, though it requires that such visits shall take place twice a year at least; so that if, on any occasion, the guardians have probable cause to believe that any such young person is subjected to ill-treatment, it will be competent for them to cause their officer forthwith to visit such person, and report upon the case to them at once.

The 6th sec. of the Act will be found to relieve the guardians from a difficulty which has not unfrequently arisen, in regard to the prosecution of persons charged with certain offences. It will be remembered, that the 7 & 8 Vic. c. 101, sec.

59, confers upon boards of guardians power to pay the costs of prosecutions in respect to various offences and misdemeanours therein specified. But in respect to other offences, it is at least doubtful how far they were legally authorized in expending their funds upon the prosecutions; and, consequently, a failure of justice may sometimes have taken place.

It is now, however, provided, that where any complaint shall be made of an offence against this Act (the nature of which appears from the 1st sec.,) or of any bodily injury inflicted upon any poor person under the age of 16 years, being an indictable offence, amounting to a felony, or an attempt to commit a felony, or an assault with intent to commit a felony, and two examining justices shall certify, that they deem it necessary for the purposes of public justice, that the prosecution shall be conducted by the guardians of the union or parish, or the overseers where there are no guardians, such guardians or overseers shall, upon personal service of the certificate, or a duplicate thereof, upon the clerk of the guardians, or upon one of the overseers, conduct the prosecution, and pay such reasonable costs as shall not be allowed to them by an order of the Court out of the common fund of the union, or out of the funds in the hands of the guardians or overseers of the parish.

Sec. 7 enables the examining justices, when they deem it necessary to certify as before mentioned, to bind over the clerk, or some other officer of the guardians, in case of a parish not under a board of guardians, one of the overseers, to prosecute such offender.

I am, your obedient servant,

W. G. LUMLEY, *Assistant Secretary.*

To the Clerk of the Guardians

---

2. AN ACT FOR THE BETTER PROTECTION OF PERSONS UNDER THE CARE AND CONTROL OF OTHERS AS APPRENTICES OR SERVANTS; AND TO ENABLE THE GUARDIANS AND OVERSEERS OF THE POOR TO INSTITUTE AND CONDUCT PROSECUTIONS IN CERTAIN CASES.—14 VIC. c. 11. *Passed 20th May*, 1851.

Whereas it is expedient to make provision for the better protection of persons who are under the care and control of others as apprentices or servants; Be it therefore enacted by the Queen's most Excellent Majesty, by and with the advice and consent of the Lords Spiritual and Temporal, and Commons, in this present Parliament assembled, and by the authority of the same.

Persons refusing or neglecting to supply necessary food to apprentices or servants, or unlawfully assaulting them, guilty of a misdemeanor.

1. That where the master or mistress of any person shall be legally liable to provide for such person, as an apprentice or as a servant, necessary food, clothing, or lodging, and shall wilfully and without lawful excuse refuse or neglect to provide the same, or where the master or mistress of any such person shall unlawfully and maliciously assault such person whereby the life of such person shall be endangered, or the health of such person shall have been or shall be likely to be permanently injured, such master or mistress shall be guilty of a misdemeanor, and being convicted thereof shall be liable to be imprisoned, with or without hard labour, in the common gaol or house of correction, for any term not exceeding three years.

Costs of prosecution.

2. That the costs and expenses of the prosecution of any such misdemeanor as aforesaid may be allowed and ordered by the court before which the indictment shall be tried, in like manner as the costs of the prosecution in certain cases of misdemeanor under the Act of the seventh year of the reign of King George the Fourth, chapter sixty-four, or may be allowed and ordered by the court of Queen's Bench, in case the indictment shall have been removed into that court, to be paid by the treasurer of the county or other officer who would have been liable to pay under the order of the court in which, but for such removal, the indictment would have been tried.

A Register to be kept of young persons hired or taken as servants from any workhouse. Not to supersede obligation to keep register as required by 42 Geo. 3, c. 46 and 7 & 8 Vic. c. 101.

3. That the guardians of every union and of every separate parish under the management of a board of guardians, and the overseers of every parish not in union or under the management of a board of guardians, shall provide and keep a book or books, and shall cause to be registered therein the name of every young person under the age of sixteen who shall hereafter be hired or taken as a servant from the workhouse of such union or parish, together with the several other particulars specified in the schedule hereunto annexed; and every such entry shall be signed by the presiding chairman of such board of guardians at an ordinary meeting thereof, or by some one of such overseers; provided that nothing herein

contained shall be taken to supersede or affect the obligation to keep such register of poor children apprenticed by overseers or guardians as is required by the statute of the forty-second year of King George the Third, chapter forty-six, and the statute of the eighth year of Queen Victoria, chapter one hundred and one.

Young persons hired from workhouses or bound out as pauper apprentices to be visited periodically by officer of guardians or overseers.

4. That where any young person under the age of sixteen shall have been or shall be hired or taken as a servant from the workhouse of any union or parish, or shall have been or shall be bound out as an apprentice by the guardians of any union, or the guardians or overseers of any parish, it shall be lawful for such guardians or overseers respectively, and they are hereby required, so long as such young person shall be under the age of sixteen, and shall be known to them to reside as servant or apprentice in the same service into which such young person shall have so gone as a servant from such workhouse or as such apprentice within such union or parish respectively, or within five miles of any part of such union or parish, to cause the relieving officer, or, where there is no relieving officer, then some other officer duly authorized for the purpose, to visit such young person at least twice in every year, and to report to them in writing whether he has found reason to believe that such young person is not supplied with necessary food, or is subjected to cruel or illegal treatment in any respect.

As to young persons hired or bound to masters residing at a distance from unions or parishes.

5. That where any young person under the age of sixteen shall hereafter be hired or taken as a servant from the workhouse of any union or parish, or shall be bound out as an apprentice by the guardians of any union, or by the guardians or overseers of any parish, and the residence of the master or mistress shall be more than five miles from any part of such union or parish, then a written notice of such hiring, taking, or binding, specifying the name and age of the apprentice or servant, and the name, description, and residence of such master or mistress, shall be forthwith sent from such guardians or overseers to the guardians or overseers of the union or parish in which such master or mistress shall reside; and thereupon it shall become the duty of such last-mentioned guardians or overseers to cause the particulars contained in such notice to be registered in some book or books, to be provided by them for the purpose, together with the name of the union or parish from which such notice shall have been received; and such last-mentioned guardians or overseers shall cause such young person to be visited as frequently and in the same manner in all respects as if such young person had been hired or taken from their own workhouse, or had been bound out as an apprentice by themselves.

Guardians and overseers authorized and required to prosecute in certain cases. Costs of prosecution.

6. That where any complaint shall be made of an offence against this Act, or of any bodily injury inflicted upon any poor person under the age of sixteen years, for which the party committing it is liable to be indicted, and the circumstances of which offence amount in point of law to a felony or an attempt to commit a felony, or an assault with intent to commit a felony, and two justices of the peace before whom the examination is taken shall certify under their hands that they deem it necessary for the purposes of public justice that the prosecution should be conducted by the guardians of the union or of the parish, or where there are no guardians by the overseers of the parish in which the offence shall have been committed, such guardians or overseers, as the case may be, shall, upon personal service of such certificate or a duplicate thereof upon the clerk of such guardians, or upon any one of such overseers, conduct the prosecution, and shall pay the costs reasonably and properly incurred by them therein, (so far as the same shall not be allowed to them under any order of the court trying the indictment, or of the court of Queen's Bench,) out of the common fund of the union, or out of the funds in the hands of the guardians or overseers (as the case may be) of such parish.

Justices empowered to bind over officer of guardians or an overseer to prosecute.

7. That in the case of a union or parish under a board of guardians the clerk or some other officer of such union or parish, and in the case of a parish not under a board of guardians one of the overseers thereof, may, if such two justices of the peace before whom the examination is taken shall deem it necessary for the purposes of public justice and shall certify as hereinbefore mentioned, be bound over to prosecute.

Interpretation of terms.

8. That the words "guardians," "union," "overseers," "justice of the peace," "officer,"

"poor," "parish," and "workhouse," used in this Act, shall be construed in like manner as in the Act of the fifth year of the reign of King William the Fourth, chapter seventy-six.

Extent of Act.

9. That this Act shall extend only to England and Wales.

SCHEDULE.

FORM OF REGISTER.

Name of Child.	Age	Date of hiring or taking as Servant.	Name of Master or Mistress.	Trade or other description of Master or Mistress.	Residence of Master or Mistress.

3. CIRCULAR TO BOARDS OF GUARDIANS.

14 & 15 VIC. CC. 39, 47, 105.

Poor Law Board, London,
30th September, 1851.

Sir,—I am directed by the Poor Law Board to call the attention of the guardians to some statutes passed in the last session of Parliament which relate to the administration of the laws for the relief of the poor.

1. The first of these, in point of importance, is the 14 & 15 Vic. c. 105.

Section 1 of this statute continues the temporary provisions which have been made by former Acts for charging the relief of certain poor persons in unions upon the common fund for another year, namely, until the 30th day of September, 1852, and to the end of the then next session of Parliament.

Section 2 removed a doubt which has frequently arisen in respect of unions or parishes divided into wards for the election of guardians. In some parishes or wards there may be no contest, and the election of guardians for such parishes or wards may be completed on the last day of nomination; whereas in others the election may be contested, and protracted for a considerable time. It has been doubted who are to constitute the board of guardians during the interval; namely, whether the whole of the guardians of the last year, or those whose election is completed, together with the guardians of the last year for the parishes where the election is not complete.

This section provides that the guardians who are elected for the several parishes in a union, or for the several wards in any parish, shall continue to act as such until the 15th day of April inclusive in each year; and after that day every guardian newly elected for any such parish or ward shall act as such guardian for the ensuing year.

If on this day the election shall not have been concluded in respect of any parish or ward, the provision in the 7 & 8 Vic. c. 101, s. 17, will, as the Board presume, come into operation, and the guardian of the previous year will continue to be entitled to act for the period of forty days after the 25th of March, or until his successor has been elected.

Sec. 3 provides a remedy for certain fraudulent and improper practices which have sometimes occurred during the election of guardians, rendering parties guilty of any of the offences therein specified liable to punishment upon summary conviction.

It enacts, that if any person, pending or after the election of any guardian, shall wilfully, fraudulently, and with intent to affect the result of such election, commit any of these acts; that is to say—

Fabricate (in whole or in part), alter, deface, destroy, abstract, or purloin any nomination or voting paper used therein;

Or personate any person entitled to vote at such election;

Or falsely assume to act in the name or on the behalf of any person so entitled to vote;

Or interrupt the distribution or collection of the voting papers;

Or distribute or collect the same under a false pretence of being lawfully authorized to do so.

Every such person so offending shall be liable, upon conviction before two justices, to be imprisoned for a period not exceeding three months, with or without hard labour.

The Board anticipate that this enactment will tend to remove the objections which have been sometimes urged against the present mode of election of guardians by voting papers delivered and collected, in consequence of the frauds to which it has been exposed.

Sec. 4 enables guardians, with the consent of the Poor Law Board, to subscribe annually towards the support and maintenance of any public hospital or infirmary for the reception of sick, diseased, disabled, or wounded persons, or of persons suffering from any permanent or natural infirmity.

It will be observed that this authority is limited to particular cases only, and requires the consent of the Poor Law Board to be given to its exercise. Those boards of guardians who may be desirous of subscribing to hospitals or infirmaries should communicate with this Board, so that no question may arise as to the legality of payments made by way of subscriptions to such establishments.

Sec. 5 supplies an authority to boards of guardians, where they think fit, to pay or reimburse any of their officers the expenses necessarily incurred in repairing or restoring property belonging to such officer, which may have been unlawfully, wilfully, and maliciously damaged, injured, or destroyed by any person applying or having applied for relief, as well as the costs which may be incurred in the prosecution of the offender, and which shall not have been allowed by the court.

Cases have not unfrequently arisen where vagrants or dissatisfied and malicious paupers have destroyed the windows or other property of the relieving officer or master of the workhouse. It has been considered that the guardians could not legally reimburse their officer for the loss which he had thus sustained, as such reimbursement was not a purpose to which the funds in the possession of the guardians were legally applicable. This section invests the guardians with a discretionary power to do this. The guardians will do doubt exercise due discrimination in availing themselves of this power, and ascertain in every case that there has been no unnecessary harshness or misconduct of any kind on the part of the officer, which may have provoked the attack upon his property. With reference to the costs of prosecuting such offenders, the Board think that the guardians should either be informed of the prosecution before it is commenced, or as soon afterwards as shall be practicable, in order that they may exercise a control over it, if they deem it necessary, before it is too late for them to interfere.

Sec. 6. The provision contained in this section is one which, though not of general application, will occasionally prove very convenient.

Where in any union or parish there shall be a workhouse or building having adequate provision for the reception, maintenance, and education of poor children, and there shall be more accommodation therein at any time than the guardians may require for the poor children of their own union or parish, such guardians may, under this section, with the consent of the Poor Law Board, contract with the guardians of any other union or parish, any part of which is not more than twenty miles *from such workhouse* or other building, for the reception, maintenance, and instruction therein of any poor children of particular classes, namely, children under the age of sixteen, being orphans or deserted by their parents, or whose parents or surviving parent shall consent.

Such last-mentioned children, while at such workhouse, are to be maintained and instructed in the same manner in all respects, and be subject to the like control and management of the guardians as the children of the union or parish to which such workhouse belongs; but the abiding of any such child in any such workhouse is to be attended with the same legal consequences as if such workhouse had been situated within the union or parish from which such child shall have been sent.

The 7 & 8 Vic. c. 101, s. 51, enables the guardians of a union or parish to send such children as are above described to a district school within a certain limit as to distance, and the 12 & 13 Vic. c. 103, s. 14, empowers the guardians of one union or parish to contract for the reception and maintenance in their workhouse of the paupers of another union or parish in the particular cases therein specified. Comparatively few school districts have yet been established; and the last-recited provision is limited to cases quite distinct from those which form the subject of the new enactment.

Sec. 7. The 5 & 6 Wm. 4, c. 69, contained in its schedule a form of security to be given in respect of money borrowed for the purposes of the Poor Law Amendment Act, but through some defect in the enacting part of the statute that form was found not to be available. A form is provided by section 7 of the present Act, which will be applicable to all cases of money borrowed under an order of the Poor Law Commissioners or Poor Law Board. As this form of security will now be sufficient, and will be less expensive than that which has heretofore been used, the Board will think it their duty to require its adoption in all cases which may come before them.

Sec. 8. The charges under suspended orders of removal not having been hitherto payable until the time when the suspension was taken off, much inconvenience has often been felt, particularly in small parishes, by the large demand suddenly made on the death or actual removal of a pauper, whose illness may have been of long duration, and whose chargeability to the parish may have been forgotten.

Provision is now made in sec. 8, by which the overseers of the parish of the settlement may pay the costs of the maintenance from time to time during the suspension of the order of removal. The Legislature have left the exercise of this power in the direction of the overseers, as it may in some cases be considered advisable not to make the payment until the removal. But the Board think that the course authorized by the statute may generally be pursued with great advantage, as it will induce a more careful and vigilant inquiry into the circumstances and condition of the pauper to whom the order applies, and obviate the inconvenience which might result from a large demand being made unexpectedly in respect of the pauper on his death or removal taking place.

Sec. 9 is one of much importance to those unions which extend into several separate jurisdictions. The treasurer of a union may reside or have his place of business in one jurisdiction, while the overseer or officer who ought to pay money to the treasurer may live in another jurisdiction; and doubts have been entertained, when it has been necessary to take legal proceedings for default of payment, as to what justices were empowered to hear the complaint and enforce the payment.

Under this sec. the justices of the county, district, or place in which the overseer or officer shall reside at the time of the default, or in which the treasurer shall reside or have his place of business, shall have jurisdiction to hear and determine the complaint.

Those justices should therefore be applied to whose jurisdiction will be most convenient for the several parties in the particular case.

Sec. 10. As copies of orders of removal and statements of the grounds of removal may be sent by post, so notices of appeal against such orders and statements of the grounds of such appeal may now be sent by post, according to this sec.

Sec. 11. Under sec. 6 of the 9 & 10 Vic. c. 66, any officer of a parish or union wrongfully causing any poor person to be removed or conveyed or to depart from a parish under the circumstances therein described, is rendered punishable upon conviction before two justices; but some difficulties have been experienced in carrying this clause into effect, and it is the object of the present sec. to remove those difficulties. In the first place it is enacted, that the word "officer" in the 9 & 10 Vic. c. 66, sec. 6, shall include an "overseer," there having been some doubt whether an overseer is within the legal construction of that clause.

Another point is also cleared up, namely, as to what justices should hear the complaint. The parish from which the pauper was sent might be in one county or jurisdiction, and that to which the pauper was removed might be in another, and it has been a question which justice ought to hear the complaint in such a case. It is now enacted that the term "justices" shall apply to "the justices of either county or jurisdiction," so that the justices of either may hear and determine the complaint. Here it will of course be a question in what jurisdiction it will be most convenient that the case should be heard, which will generally depend upon the place of abode of the witnesses who may be required to prove the case.

Lastly, provision is made in respect of the application of the penalty. The 4 & 5 Wm. 4, c. 76, sec. 99, and the 9 & 10 Vic. c. 66, sec. 6, taken together, seemed to require that the penalty should be paid to the parish where the offence was committed, and there was no doubt that the offence was always, in part at least, committed in that parish from which the pauper was sent, so that the penalty was payable to the offending parish. This sec. directs that the penalty shall be paid to the overseers of the parish to which the pauper becomes chargeable by reason of the unlawful removal.

Sec. 12 has been framed with the view of diminishing the costs which parishes incur in the litigation of questions of settlement or chargeability, and confers upon the Poor Law Board a power of deciding questions affecting the settlement, removal, or chargeability of poor persons when submitted to them by the parties interested therein by agreement in writing duly executed.

It is quite optional with the parties whether they will submit the question to the Board, or not, and it is also in the discretion of the Poor Law Board whether they will entertain the question. If they do so, and determine the question by an order, their order will be conclusive in all courts between the parties submitting the question, as to the question determined.

The Board do not propose to prescribe any particular course to be pursued by parties desirous of availing themselves of this provision. But they must state distinctly that, as a general rule, they will think it necessary to require a statement of facts, mutually agreed upon, to be laid before them, and the question or questions upon which their decision is requested, to be clearly and precisely stated.

Sec. 13 facilitates the proceedings of parishes

upon the removal of paupers, by authorizing the officers who are empowered by the 9 & 10 Vic. c. 66, sec. 7, to deliver a pauper under an order of removal at the workhouse of the parish or union to which such pauper is to be removed, at the same time to deliver a written statement of the charges for the maintenance of the pauper to the officer of the workhouse, which delivery is to be deemed to be a delivery of such statement to the overseers of the parish, and a sufficient demand in any proceedings for the recovery of such charges.

The Poor Law Commissioners, in their circular of the 17th of September, 1846, advised the guardians to give directions to the officers of the workhouse, especially the master and the porter, that when a pauper should be brought to the workhouse with a warrant of removal under the 9 & 10 Vic. c. 66, sec. 7, they should take the earliest opportunity of communicating the fact of his delivery at the workhouse to the overseers to whom the warrant was addressed.

The Board recommend the guardians to give similar directions with reference to this statement of charges, as it is the more important that this should be done as the overseers upon service of such a statement become immediately liable to proceedings for the discharge of the amount.

Secs. 14 and 15 apply only to the dissolution of the asylum districts which were formed under the 7 & 8 Vic. c. 101, in the metropolis, and they are of too limited an application to require particular notice in this letter.

Sec. 16 is also confined to the metropolis and its neighbourhood, and extends the powers of raising money conferred upon the Board of Management of a school district situated within the Metropolitan Police District.

Sec. 17. The powers of the Board of Management of any school district over the land of the district had not hitherto been well defined, and it is now provided by this section that they may, subject to the order and regulations of the Poor Law Board, deal with the land belonging to the district in like manner as the guardians of a union may deal with that belonging to the union.

The 13 & 14 Vic. c. 101, sec. 9, subjected persons assaulting the officers of a workhouse or relieving-officers in the discharge of their duty to the same punishment as in the case of assaults upon peace-officers, and gave power to the justices to make the like order as to the costs and expenses of the prosecution. By the present section this provision is extended to an assault upon any person included under the word "officer" in the 4 & 5 Wm. 4, c. 76, or upon any other person acting in his aid.

Without enumerating all the persons comprehended under that word in the 109th sec. of that statute, it may be well to remark that it applies to a *collector, vestry clerk*, and *assistant-overseer*.

II. The Board, in their circular of the 26th of June last,* communicated to the guardians an abstract of the statute 14 & 15 Vic. c. 11, relating to the protection of parish apprentices and young servants, and need not now refer further to it.

III. The Act for exempting inhabitants from liability to be rated as such to the relief of the poor in respect of stock in trade or other property is continued by the 14 & 15 Vic. c. 47, till the 1st of October, 1852, and to the end of the then next session of Parliament.

IV. By the 14 & 15 Vic. c. 39, which amends the 13 & 14 Vic. c. 99, (the small tenements rating Act,) with reference to its effect upon certain parliamentary franchises, an explanation is given of the word *tenement* as used in that Act, by which the operation of the statute is somewhat restricted. By sec. 2 it is enacted, that the word "tenement" therein shall be construed to mean any house, cottage, apartment, or building, and *land* in the same parish, held with the same parish, or any of them, *but shall not* include any other *land* or corporeal hereditament.

It will be seen, therefore, that the owners of small pieces of land occupied alone, without house or building, will not be liable to be assessed to the poor and highway rates in the place of the occupiers.

Sec. 3. removes a doubt which has been felt as to the application of the statute to owners in respect of the payment of monies out of the poor-rate to the borough, county, police, or other similar rate. It is now enacted, that the words "rates for the relief of the poor" used in the 13 & 14 Vic. c. 99, shall be construed to mean "rates for the relief of the poor and for other purposes chargeable thereon according to law." The same section also renders the owners of this class of tenements liable to be assessed to the rates levied in divided parishes under the 12 & 13 Vic. c. 65.

The Board do not think it necessary for them to bring any other enactment of the session under the special notice of the guardians at this time.

I am, sir, your obedient servant,

W. G. LUMLEY, *Assistant Secretary.*

To the Clerk of the Board of the Guardians.

* See page 36.

4.—AN ACT TO EXEMPT BURGESSES AND FREEMEN IN CERTAIN CASES FROM THE OPERATION OF AN ACT FOR THE BETTER ASSESSING AND COLLECTING THE POOR RATES AND HIGHWAY RATES IN RESPECT OF SMALL TENEMENTS.—14 & 15 VIC. C. 39. *Passed 24th July*, 1851.

2 & 3 *Wm*. 4, *c*. 45, *sec*. 32. *Sec*. 33. 13 & 14 *Vic*. *c*. 99.

Whereas by section thirty-two of the Act of the session of Parliament holden in the second and third years of King William the Fourth, chapter forty-five, it is provided, that every person who would have been entitled to vote in the election of a member or members to serve in any future Parliament for any city or borough not included in the schedule marked (A.) to that Act annexed, either as a burgess or freeman, or in the city of London, as a freeman and liveryman, if that Act had not been passed, should be entitled to vote in such election, provided such person should be duly registered according to the provisions therein-after contained; but that no person should be so registered in any year unless he should on the last day of July in that year be qualified in such manner as would entitle him then to vote if such day was the day of election, and that Act had not been passed: And whereas by section thirty-three of the said Act it is provided that any person then having a right to vote in the election for any city or borough, except as therein mentioned, in virtue of any other qualification than as a burgess or freeman or as a freeman and liveryman, or in the case of a city or town being a county of itself as a freeholder or burgage tenant as therein-before mentioned, should retain such right of voting so long as he should be qualified as an elector according to the usage and custom of such city or borough, or any law then in force subject as in the said Act mentioned: And whereas it is expedient to amend the Act of the last session of Parliament, chapter ninety-nine, so far as it may affect the rights reserved by the said several sections of the said Act of the second and third years of King William the Fourth: Be it enacted, therefore, by the Queen's most excellent Majesty, by and with the advice and consent of the Lords Spiritual and Temporal, and Commons, in this present Parliament assembled, and by the authority of the same, as follows:

Right of voting reserved by recited provisions of 2 & 3 Wm. 4, c. 45, to persons then entitled not to be affected by the change of rating under 13 & 14 Vic. c. 99.

1. Where any person to whom a right of voting was retained or reserved by the recited provisions of the said Act of the second or third years of King William the Fourth is or shall be the occupier of any such tenement as in the said Act of the last session of Parliament mentioned, and the owner of such tenement has been or shall be rated to the relief of the poor instead of the occupier thereof, and such owner shall have paid all money due on account of any rate or rates in respect of such tenement, or such occupier shall have tendered the amount thereof in the manner prescribed by such Act, such occupier shall be entitled, not only to the municipal privileges and franchises reserved to him by such Act, but also to all such right of voting at elections of a member or members to serve in Parliament for any city or borough, and all other rights and privileges, as such occupier would have been entitled to under the recited provisions of the said Act of the second and third years of King William the Fourth, and the other provisions of such Act, and any Acts amending the same, relating to the right of voting so retained or reserved, if such occupier had been himself rated in respect of such tenement, and had duly paid or tendered the rate or rates to which he was liable in consequence of such rating.

Construction of the words "tenement,"

2. That the word "tenement" in the said recited Act of the last session of Parliament shall be construed to mean any house, cottage, apartment, or building, and land in the same parish held with the same or any of them, but shall not include any other land or corporeal hereditament.

and "rates for the relief of the poor."

3. That the words "rates for the relief of the poor" in the said recited Act of the last session of Parliament shall be construed to mean rates for the relief of the poor and for other purposes chargeable thereon according to law; and that the owners of any tenements who shall be liable to be rated in respect of such tenements to any such rate by virtue of the same Act shall also be liable to be rated to any rate or rates authorized to be assessed and levied by the second section of the Act of the session of Parliament holden in the twelfth and thirteenth years of Her present Majesty, chapter sixty-five.

---

5. AN ACT TO CONTINUE AN ACT OF THE FOURTEENTH YEAR OF HER MAJESTY FOR CHARGING THE MAINTENANCE OF CERTAIN POOR PERSONS IN UNIONS IN ENGLAND AND WALES UPON THE COMMON FUND; AND TO MAKE CERTAIN

AMENDMENTS IN THE LAWS FOR THE RELIEF OF THE POOR—14 & 15 VIC. C. 105. *Passed 8th August,* 1851.

13 *&* 14 *Vic. c.* 101.

1. Whereas by an Act passed in the Fourteenth Year of Her Majesty, chapter One hundred and one, certain Provisions made by the several Acts therein mentioned, for charging upon the Common Fund of the Union the costs of the relief and the expenses of the burial of certain poor persons therein described, and the costs of removing and maintaining certain lunatic paupers, were continued until the Thirtieth Day of September in the Year One thousand eight hundred and fifty-one, and to the end of the then next Session of Parliament, and were made to apply to certain incorporated hundreds therein mentioned; and it is expedient that all the several Provisions aforesaid should be continued for a limited time, and that certain amendments should be made in the laws relating to the relief of the poor: Be it therefore enacted by the Queen's most Excellent Majesty, by and with the advice and consent of the Lords Spiritual and Temporal, and Commons, in this present Parliament assembled, and by the Authority of the same, as follows:

Certain Provisions of 13 *&* 14 *Vic. c.* 101, *continued for a limited time.*

1. All the said several temporary Provisions in the said Acts above referred to shall continue in full force until the Thirtieth Day of September, One thousand eight hundred and fifty-two, and to the end of the then next session of Parliament.

The new board of guardians to be constituted from and after the 15th April in each year.

2. The guardians elected for the several parishes in any union formed or to be formed under the Act of the Fifth Year of King William the Fourth, Chapter Seventy-six, or for the several Wards in any parish divided into wards, shall continue to act as such until the Fifteenth Day of April inclusive in each Year, notwithstanding their successors may have been elected previously to that day; and from and after the said Fifteenth Day of April every guardian newly elected for any such parish or ward shall act as such guardian for the ensuing year.

Penalties for Malpractices at the Election of Guardians.

3. If any person, pending or after the election of any guardian or guardians, shall wilfully, fraudulently, and with intent to affect the result of such election, commit any of the Acts following; that is to say, fabricate in whole or in part, alter, deface, destroy, abstract, or purloin any Nomination or Voting Paper used therein; or personate any person entitled to vote at such election; or falsely assume to act in the name or on the behalf of any person so entitled to vote; or interrupt the distribution or collection of the Voting Papers; or distribute or collect the same under a false pretence of being lawfully authorized to do so; every such person so offending shall for every such offence be liable, upon conviction thereof before any two Justices, to be imprisoned in the Common Gaol or House of Correction for any Period not exceeding Three Months, with or without hard labour.

Guardians empowered to subscribe to Hospital or Infirmary, with the consent of the Poor Law Board.

4. Whereas doubts have been entertained with regard to the legal authority of guardians to subscribe towards the funds of any hospital or infirmary: Be it enacted, That the guardians of any union or parish may, with the consent of the Poor Law Board, pay out of the Common Fund of such union, or, in the case of a parish, out of the funds in the hands of such guardians, any sum of money as an annual subscription towards the support and maintenance of any public Hospital or Infirmary for the reception of sick, diseased, disabled, or wounded persons, or of persons suffering from any permanent or natural infirmity.

Power to Guardians to reimburse for damage to the Property of their officers in certain cases.

5. The guardians may, where they think fit, pay to or reimburse any of their officers the expense necessarily incurred in repairing or restoring property belonging to such officer which may have been unlawfully, wilfully, and maliciously damaged, injured, or destroyed by any person applying or having applied for relief, and such costs and expenses incurred in the prosecution of the offender as may not be allowed by the court before which the prosecution or trial shall take place.

Certain poor children of a Union or Parish may, with consent of Poor Law Board, be sent to a Workhouse, &c., belonging to another Union or Parish (within 20 miles) where there is adequate Accommodation. Proviso.

6. Where in any union or parish there shall be a workhouse or building having adequate provision for the reception, maintenance, and education of poor children, and there shall be more accommo-

dation therein at any time than the guardians of such union or parish shall require for the poor children of their own union or parish, such guardians may, with the consent of the Poor Law Board, contract with the guardians of any other union or parish, any part of which is not more than twenty miles from such workhouse or other building, for the reception, maintenance, and instruction therein of any poor children under the age of sixteen years chargeable to such other union or parish, or to any parish in such other union, being orphans or deserted by their parents, or whose parents or surviving parent shall consent; and such last-mentioned children while at such workhouse or other building shall be maintained and instructed in the same manner in all respects as the children of the union or parish to which such workhouse or other building shall belong, and shall be subject to the control and management of the guardians of such union or parish, or their officers, in like manner as if such children were chargeable to such union or parish: Provided always, that the abiding of any such child in any such workhouse or building shall in all other respects be attended with the same legal consequences as if such workhouse or building had been situated within the union or parish from which such child shall have been sent.

Form of Security.

7. Every security for money borrowed under the authority of any Order of the Poor Law Commissioners or the Poor Law Board may be made according to the form set forth in the schedule hereunto annexed, or as near thereto as the circumstances of the case will admit.

Payments under suspended Orders of Removal.

8. Where the execution of any Order of Justices for the removal of a pauper shall have been or shall be suspended, the overseers of the parish to which the removal is thereby ordered to be made may from time to time during the continuance of the suspension, if they think fit, pay to the overseers of the parish obtaining such order the costs and expenses incurred in the maintenance and relief of the poor person mentioned in such order, either directly or through the guardians of the union comprising either or both of such parishes, and shall have credit for every such payment in the charges allowed by any order of justices subsequently made.

What Justices shall have jurisdiction to hear and determine complaints as to non-payment of money to the Treasurer of the Union.

9. Where the overseer or any other officer of any parish, or any officer of a union, shall neglect to pay in due course of law money lawfully payable by him as such overseer or officer to the treasurer of such union or parish, residing or having his place of business in a county, district, or place different from that in which such overseer or officer shall reside at the time of any such default, and by reason of such neglect such overseer or officer shall be liable to be summoned before a justice or justices, any justice or justices of either county, district, or place, shall have jurisdiction to hear and determine the complaint.

Notice of Appeal, &c., may be sent by Post.

10. It shall be lawful and sufficient to send any notice of appeal against an order of removal, or statement of grounds of appeal against such order, by Post or otherwise, in like manner as a copy of an order of removal and statement of grounds of removal may now be sent by law.

Explanation of the terms "Officer" and "Justices" in 9 & 10 Vic. c. 66, s. 6, and provision for the application of the Penalty.

11. And whereas by the Statute of the Tenth Year of Her Majesty, Chapter Sixty-six, Section Six, any officer of a parish or union wrongfully causing or procuring any poor person to be removed or conveyed or to depart from a parish under the circumstances therein described is rendered punishable upon conviction before two justices: And whereas it is expedient to remove doubts which have arisen thereon: Be it enacted, That the term "Officer" shall include any Overseer, and that the term "Justices" shall apply to the Justices of the county or other jurisdiction in which the parish may be situated from or to which such poor person shall be removed; and that the penalty imposed by the Act shall be paid to the overseers of the parish to which the poor person shall become chargeable in consequence of such unlawful removal, conveyance, or departure, to be applied in aid of the poor rate of such last-mentioned parish.

Power to refer, by mutual consent, questions of settlement, removal, or chargeability to Poor Law Board.

12. The guardians of any two unions or parishes, or the guardians of a union and the guardians of a parish, or the guardians of a union or parish and the overseers of any parish, or the overseers of any two parishes, between whom any question affecting the settlement, removal, or chargeability of any poor person shall arise, may, if they think fit so to do, by agreement in writing,

executed in respect of any guardians by sealing with their common seal, and in respect of overseers by the signatures of a majority of them, submit such question to the Poor Law Board for their decision; and the said Board may, if they see fit, entertain such question, and by an Order under their seal determine the same; and every such order shall be in all courts and for all purposes final and conclusive, between the parties submitting such question, as to the question therein determined.

As to delivery of statement of Charges for maintenance of paupers.

13. And whereas by the Statute of the Tenth Year of Her Majesty, Chapter Sixty-six, Section Seven, it is enacted, that the delivery of any pauper under any warrant of removal directed to the overseers of any parish at the workhouse of such parish, or of any union to which such parish belongs, to any officer of such workhouse, shall be deemed a delivery of such pauper to the overseers of such parish: Be it enacted, That the delivery of a written statement of the charges for the maintenance of any pauper delivered under any order or warrant of removal directed to the overseers of any parish, at the workhouse of such parish, or of any union to which such parish belongs, to any officer of such workhouse, at the time of the delivery of such pauper, shall be deemed a delivery of such statement to the overseers of such parish, and shall be deemed a sufficient demand thereof in any proceedings for the recovery of such charges.

Poor Law Board empowered to dissolve any asylum district. Provision for its property.

14. The Poor Law Board may, if they see fit, upon the application or with the consent of the acting members of the board of management, at any time, by an order under their seal, dissolve any combination of unions of parishes, or unions and parishes, formed under the Act of the Eighth Year of Her Majesty, Chapter One hundred and one, into districts for the purpose of providing and managing asylums for the temporary relief and setting to work therein of destitute houseless poor, and, prior to issuing any such order of dissolution, may empower, by their order, the board of management of such district to pay and apply any funds in their possession in discharge of any liabilities then outstanding against such board, and to sell and dispose of any land, buildings, or other property belonging to them, and to apply the produce of the same to the like purpose; and any surplus that may remain after satisfying all liabilities shall be returned to the several unions and parishes in proportion to their original contributions.

How conveyance may be executed.

15. The conveyance of such property by the acting members of the said board of management of any such district, when approved and sealed by the Poor Law Board, shall be deemed valid, notwithstanding any defect which may exist in the number required to constitute such board of management.

The limit of the expense to be incurred in school districts within the Metropolitan Police districts extended from one-fifth to one-third.

16. And whereas provision is made in the said last-mentioned Act for the combination of unions and parishes into school districts, and authority is given to the district board, subject to the Order of the Poor Law Board, to borrow or raise such sum or sums of money as may be necessary for the purpose of purchasing any site, or purchasing, hiring, or building, and of fitting up and furnishing, a building, or buildings for such school; and it is further provided that the principal sum or sums to be raised for the purpose of providing such building or buildings, and charged on any union or parish not included in a union, shall in no case exceed one-fifth of the average annual amount of the aggregate expenditure relating to the relief of the poor within any union, or of the like expenditure within any such parish, for three years ending the Twenty-fifth day of March next preceding the raising of the money. And whereas by the Act of the Fourteenth Year of Her Majesty, Chapter One hundred and one, Section Three, with reference to school districts situated within the Metropolitan Police district, the cost of the site of any such school may be borrowed over and above the amount so limited as aforesaid: And whereas it is expedient with respect to such last-mentioned school districts that the limit of expenditure fixed by the said Act of the Eighth Year of Her Majesty should be enlarged: Be it therefore enacted, That in respect of any school district situated within the said Metropolitan Police district such limit shall be enlarged from one-fifth to one-third.

Provision for disposal of School district property.

17. The board of management of any school district may in like manner, and subject to the like order, rules, and regulations of the Poor Law Board, as in the case of the guardians of a union,

exchange, demise, sell, or otherwise dispose of any land belonging to the said district, and apply the rents or produce of any such exchange, sale, or disposition for the benefit of the said district in such manner as the said Poor Law Board shall direct.

Assaults upon Poor Law officers in the execution of their duty.

18. The provision in the Act of the Fourteenth Year of Her Majesty, Chapter One hundred and one, Section Nine, relative to assaults upon certain poor law officers in the execution of their duties, or upon persons acting in their aid, shall extend to an assault upon any person included under the word "officer" in the said Act of the Fifth year of King William the Fourth, Chapter Seventy-six, or upon any other person acting in his aid.

Construction of Terms.

19. The several words used in this Act shall be construed in the manner prescribed by the Act of the Fifth Year of King William the Fourth, Chapter Seventy-six, and the Statutes explaining and extending it; and all the provisions of the said last-mentioned Act and of the said Statutes not repealed shall extend to this Act, except where any provision would be inconsistent with anything herein contained.

Extent of the Act.

20. This Act shall extend only to England and Wales.

SCHEDULE.

FORM OF SECURITY TO BE GIVEN FOR LOAN OBTAINED UNDER THE ACT OF THE FIFTH YEAR OF KING WILLIAM THE FOURTH, OR ANY ACT INCORPORATED THEREWITH.

This Deed, made the Day of in the Year One thousand eight hundred , witnesseth, That in consideration of the sum of lent and advanced to the guardians of the Poor of the union in the county of , *or* to the guardians of the poor of the parish of in the county of , *or* to the board of management of the district school, *or* to the overseers of the poor of the parish of in the county of , under the provisions of the Act [*here state the Act authorizing the loan*], and in pursuance of and upon the authority of the order of the Poor Law Board bearing Date the Day of , by [*here set out the name and description of the Public Board, Commissioners, or Company, or the person lending the money*], the receipt of which

sum is testified by the memorandum at the foot hereof by our treasurer, *or* (*in the case of the overseers*) by us, we, the said guardians, *or* we, the said board of management, *or* we, the said overseers, do hereby charge the future poor rates to be raised in the several parishes comprised in the said union, namely [*here set out the names of the parishes comprised in the union*], *or* in the several unions and parishes comprised in the said district, namely [*here set out the unions and parishes combined in the district*], *or* in the said parish, with the repayment to the said of the said sum of by [*here insert the number of yearly instalments by which the loan is to be repaid, not exceeding the number limited by the statute or statutes under which it is advanced, but including those to which the time of repayment has been extended under any statute in that behalf*] instalments, on the days in the years following; that is to say, the sum of on the day of in the year 18 , the sum of on the day of in the year 18 , the sum of on the day of in the year 18 , together with interest at the rate of pounds per centum per annum, by yearly payments on the days aforesaid, *or* by half-yearly payments on the day of and on the day of in every year, upon the principal for the time being unpaid, according to the terms of this security: Provided that nothing herein contained shall prevent the said from receiving the repayment of the whole or any part of the aforesaid sum at any time before the day of payment of the last instalment, if willing to do so.

In testimony whereof we, the guardians aforesaid, *or* we, the said board of management, have hereunto affixed our common seal, *or* we, the said overseers, have hereunto set our hands and seals.

(L.S.) (L.S.) (L.S.)

Received this day of the above-mentioned sum of from the said

A.B., Treasurer of the union, *or* parish, *or* district board.

C.D., and *E.F.*, overseers of the poor of the said parish

Registered by the Poor Law Board this day of 18 .

Seal of the Poor Law Board (L.S.)

London: Printed by Order of the Poor Law Board, by BLACKBURN & BURT, 90½, Holborn Hill, and Published by CHARLES KNIGHT, 90, Fleet Street.

AN

OFFICIAL CIRCULAR

OF PUBLIC DOCUMENTS AND INFORMATION:

DIRECTED BY THE POOR LAW BOARD TO BE PRINTED, CHIEFLY FOR THE USE OF THE BOARDS OF GUARDIANS AND THEIR OFFICERS.

No. 48.] [N.S.

CONTENTS.

I.—APPRENTICESHIP—OF CHILDREN TO MINERS.

11th March, 1851.

Clerk of West Bromwich Union.—Two notices dated the 5th February, 1851, were sent by the Bromsgrove union to the guardians of the Walsall union, being proposals to bind William Robbins and John Smith from the Bromsgrove union workhouse to one Joseph Bayley, a miner, stated to reside near the toll-gate, Darlaston, in the Walsall union. These notices were about a week afterwards forwarded by the Walsall Union to the guardians of the West Bromwich Union, the word "Darlaston" being erased, and the words, "in the parish of Wednesbury," which parish is in this union, written across. The guardians of the West Bromwich union, on the notices being laid before them, called the attention of the Bromsgrove guardians to the Official Circular for February, 1850, by which it appeared that the Poor Law Board were of opinion that the binding of poor children to miners ought not to take place, and stated that the guardians of the West Bromwich Union objected to the children named in the notices in question being bound. The guardians of the West Bromwich Union have, however, received from the Bromsgrove Union notices that these two children have been bound to Joseph Bayley by indentures bearing date the 5th of March instant. Requesting the opinion of the Poor Law Board as to whether the binding under all the circumstances can be considered legal.

26th March, 1851.

Clerk of Bromsgrove Union.—After the receipt of the letter from the West Bromwich Union adverted to by the guardians of that union, reference was made to the Official Circular of February, 1850, page 18, and as the

Poor Law Board did not give an independent opinion on the question put by the guardians of the Kidderminster Union, and as the guardians of the Bromsgrove Union are unanimous in opinion that a miner or butty-collier is undoubtedly a person carrying on trade or business on his own account, they did not consider the objection made by the guardians of the West Bromwich Union to be sufficient to prevent the binding of the boys, and the same was proceeded with. The majority of boys placed out by the guardians of the Bromsgrove Union that have been apprenticed to miners residing within the unions of Walsall and West Bromwich, all of whom, that have conducted themselves properly, have prospered and are doing well. For many years before the formation of the union, the overseers of Bromsgrove were in the habit of binding boys apprentices to miners and many of those boys have grown up men and acquired considerable property. The guardians have reason to believe that all the boys which have been apprenticed by them are well cared for, and the guardians believe they cannot dispose of boys to more advantage to themselves than by following up the practice of binding them to miners. If the guardians are not allowed to apprentice boys in this way it will lead to very serious inconvenience and difficulty.

29*th April*, 1851.

The Poor Law Board to the Clerk of Bromsgrove Union.—With reference to the letter to which you allude, published in the Official Circular for February, 1850, the Board desire to point out that they did express in that letter a strong intimation that upon the circumstances stated to them in the case therein mentioned, the binding was not (in their opinion) in conformity with the regulations prescribed by the General Consolidated Order of the Poor Law Commissioners. The Board have to add that they continue to entertain the same opinion.

2*nd Oct.*, 1851.

Clerk of Bromsgrove Union.—By article 55 of the General Consolidated Order, 1847, it is ordered, that "where any premium is given, it shall in part consist of clothes supplied to the apprentice at the commencement of the binding and in part of money, one moiety whereof shall be paid to the master at the binding and the residue at the termination of the first year of the binding." The guardians of this union rarely give a money premium; usually two suits of clothing only, without money at the time of the binding. Inquiring whether the course pursued by the guardians is the proper one. Most of the children placed out by the guardians are taken out of the workhouse, and previously to their being apprenticed, which is generally to persons residing out of the union, the children are sent on trial for a period never less than a month; and the notice required by article 66 is always as a matter of course given. If the children suit and the master be approved, the parties usually attend at a meeting of the guardians when the binding is effected. Inquiring whether under these circumstances the certificate required by article 59 from the medical officer of the workhouse is sufficient, or whether the conditions of article 62 must be conformed to. The children when they leave the workhouse are discharged from the in-door relief list, the actual place of residence at the time of binding not being within the union.

10*th Nov.*, 1851.

The Poor Law Board to the Clerk of Bromsgrove Union.—The Board consider article 55 of the General Consolidated Order is intended to apply to cases in which it is desired to give some premium other than clothing; and with regard to such cases, it provides that the premium shall not consist wholly of money. The Board think that consistently with the letter of this article, it is competent for the guardians if they deem it expedient, to give clothing without money as a premium upon the binding of an apprentice. As to your second question the Board are of opinion that under the circumstances stated by you, the certificate required by article 59 as to the child's fitness to be bound apprentice to the particular trade will be sufficient, inasmuch as when the first step towards the proposed binding was taken, the child was resident within the union.

17*th Nov.*, 1851.

The Poor Law Board to the Clerk of Bromsgrove Union.—The Board have abstained until the present time from giving a definite answer to the general question raised in the letter from the guardians of the Bromsgrove union of the 26th March last, in reference to the apprenticeship of pauper children to coal miners, styled in the district, "butties," because they have been desirous of obtaining full information upon a subject which is obviously of considerable importance in the Bromsgrove and other adjoining unions. The Board accordingly instructed their inspector, Mr. Graves, to inquire and report upon the subject, and they have now before them the result of his inquiries. The Board learn from this report that in the mining districts of Staffordshire and Worcestershire the "butties" are necessarily persons of some capital, and that in many cases they possess a considerable capital invested in houses and tools. It appears, moreover, that their connection with particular mines is often one of long duration, and that they are therefore commonly not persons who change their residence frequently from place to place. Upon the more full information thus obtained the Board are of opinion that, regarded as a class, the butty colliers of Staffordshire and Worcestershire may properly be considered as "carrying on business on their own account," and that so far as the terms of the General Consolidated Order (apprenticeship of pauper children) are concerned, there is nothing to render the apprenticeship of pauper children to such persons illegal. At the same time the Board desire to state that they have reason to believe that among the butty colliers there are not unfrequently to be found men, who, from their character—from their not having a permanent residence—or from other causes are unfit persons to be entrusted with the care of apprentices. The Board therefore must state to the guardians that it appears to them that much discrimination and careful inquiry are requisite before apprenticeship to masters following the business now under consideration can safely take place, and that they rely with confidence on the vigilance and discretion of the guardians in order to guard against the obvious evils which might otherwise occur.

II.—AUDITOR.

1. Certifying balances at the Michaelmas audit.

9th Dec., 1850.

Mr. ——, *District Auditor*—Transmitting report of sums certified at the last Michaelmas audit to be due from the officers of parishes in three unions in his district.

Ans.—The Board request that you will in future furnish them with a separate report for each union in which you certify sums to be due, either from the officers of such union or from the overseers of parishes in it. The Board perceive that you have apparently certified in some instances balances as "due" from overseers of some of the parishes in your district. As your report refers to the Michaelmas Audit, the Board request to be informed upon what ground you took this course, sec. 5 of the 11 & 12 Vic. c. 91, not appearing to them to authorize the auditor to certify a balance to be due from an overseer at the rendering of his account at Michaelmas, at which time his period of office has not expired. Whatever the auditor may disallow or surcharge in the accounts at that audit is no doubt by the terms of that provision to be then certified as "due," and recovered also, unless the amount do not exceed 40s; but the section, in the Board's opinion, clearly makes the distinction herein referred to.

Mr. ——, *District Auditor*.—No instructions having been given me to the contrary, I have certified in all the receipt and payment books (not in those only where there are disallowances or surchages) the balances that appear on the face of them at Michaelmas, and in those parishes where there are disallowances or surcharges I have certified them also, (separately,) according to the form in the Schedule of the above Act, and have reported the particulars to your Board. I do not consider that the 5th section of the Act prohibits a certificate of the balance that appears on the face of the account at Michaelmas, though as a sum due and recoverable it is surplusage; such sum being only what is certified to as a surcharge or disallowance. It is important in any district that the state of the accounts at Michaelmas should be settled as in most parishes they then change hands virtually though not legally, and unless a certificate of their state appears, there is no satisfactory evidence of it to the ratepayers, and that would soon lead to great abuses. It seems to me the form of return for Michaelmas and Lady-day should be different. The Michaelmas return containing the disallowances and surchages only. The Lady-day return, the disallowances, surchages, and balances. This would harmonize with sec. 5.

Ans.—The Board collect from your letter that you have somewhat misapprehended the purport of their communication. They did not intend to convey the notion that it was unnecessary at the Michaelmas audit to ascertain the balance of the transactions contained in the account of the Overseers or other accounting officers, and to declare the same in the form or words appended to the books of receipts and payments. There is nothing in the 11 & 12 Vic. c. 95, sec. 5, to dispense with this duty on the part of the auditor. But having so ascertained the balance, the Board do not think, for the reasons stated in their former letter, that the auditor should at the Michaelmas audit proceed to certify the balance as "due." They apprehend that at that time the balance is not due in the sense of the 7 & 8 Vic. c. 101, sec. 32, and 11 & 12 Vic. c. 91, sec. 5; but whatever is then disallowed and surcharged is "due," and should be so certified, though the proviso to sec. 5 of the last recited Act operates to prevent the payment over of the sums disallowed or surcharged if in the aggregate they do not amount to 40*s*. [Forwarded a copy of the circular addressed to district auditors on the 29th of September, 1849.]

2. DISALLOWANCES BY AUDITOR IN THE ACCOUNTS OF CONTINUING OFFICERS.

19*th March*, 1851

Poor Law Board to Mr. ——, *District Auditor.*—Inquiring whether the sum mentioned in his audit report of the 16th Dec. last as having been certified by him to be due from the overseers of the parish of Marazion, at his audit of their accounts for the half year ended at Michaelmas last, had been paid to the treasurer of the Penzance union, as required by sec. 32 of the Act 7 & 8 Vic. c. 101.

Mr. ——, *District Auditor to the Poor Law Board.*—As the same officers continued in office he allowed them to debit themselves with the sums disallowed, for which they will be accountable at the next audit. His reason for adopting this course is that in nearly every case in which such disallowances are now made it is not on account of an illegal expenditure, but simply for want of the proper receipts and vouchers being produced for monies actually and legally expended, which parish officers upon being newly appointed are not aware of the necessity of laying before the auditor, but without which the latter is of course bound to disallow the payments. This being explained to the overseers, and the receipts produced at the ensuing audit, they are then allowed to take credit for the sums which for want of those vouchers were previously disallowed; and thus any confusion with regard to accounts with the treasurer, which has hitherto been productive of so much misunderstanding between the overseers, treasurer, and auditor is altogether avoided.

Ans.—The Board apprehend it is not legally correct for the auditor to allow in the accounts of one half year, a payment which he may have disallowed in the accounts of a previous half year. When he has once disallowed a payment in the accounts of the overseers, and dealt with the case in the way contemplated by 7 & 8 Vic. c. 101, sec. 32, and 11 & 12 Vic. c. 91, sec. 5, the parties affected by the disallowance should be left to pursue the course which the law has prescribed in such cases, *i.e.*, if they do not acquiesce in the disallowance, to make their formal appeal against it. This course if strictly pursued, will be more likely to ensure a correct practice upon the part of the overseers, and to prevent the introduction into the parochial accounts of items not legally admissible, either by reason of the absence of a proper authority to incur the charge, or the proper evidence or voucher of payment.

III.—AVERAGES—ON WHICH THE COST OF RELIEF CHARGED ON THE COMMON FUND SHOULD BE CALCULATED.

2*nd Oct.*, 1851.

Clerk of Corwen Union—Transmitting the following notice which he had received from the guardian and overseers of the parish of Bettws, in the Corwen Union, viz.,—"We the undersigned guardian and overseers of the poor of the parish of Bettws gwerfil goch, do hereby give notice that we object to and protest against the expenditure incurred for the maintenance, relief, or burial of any person legally chargeable to the common or general fund of this union, being charged to the different parishes herein in any manner different from the cost of building the workhouse." They state in the letter accompanying this notice, "We rest our case upon the construction of the 10 & 11 Vic. c. 110, which, as we are advised, specifies the particular manner in which the maintenance, &c., of union paupers shall be charged to the common fund, viz., in the same manner as the cost of building and providing workhouses, &c." The facts of the case are simply the following:—At the formation of the union there were averages declared, which averages are the basis upon which the money borrowed for the building of the workhouse is apportioned to the several parishes yearly up to the present time. In November, 1843, new averages were declared, which form the basis upon which all other expences chargeable to the common fund of the union are in like manner apportioned, which also include all relief to irremovable poor, &c. These are the "current averages." The parish authorities of Bettws contend that it is not upon the "current averages," but upon the averages declared at the formation of the union that the relief to be charged to the common fund of the union should be distributed amongst the different parishes, the tenor of which would be to relieve the parish of Bettws to some extent in regard to this charge, as the first averages in respect to this parish are much below the averages declared in 1843. The parties ground their objection on the wording of the Act 10 & 11 Vic. c. 110. It is presumed that if they have any objection to make, it should be made before the auditor. Requested to be informed whether the view taken by the overseers is the correct one.

Ans.—The Board do not concur in the view taken by the parish officers of Bettws upon this subject. The parish officers of Bettws state that they rest their cause upon the construction of 10 & 11 Vic. c. 110, which they are advised has not been varied by any subsequent enactment. The Board have to point out, however, that that statute is not now in force, as it expired on the 1st of October, 1848, (see sec. 2.) The statute under which the cost of the relief and burial of certain classes of paupers is at present charged to the common fund of the union is the 11 & 12 Vic. c. 110, continued by subsequent Acts, the last of which is the 14 & 15 Vic. c. 105. The expression used in the 11 & 12 Vic. c. 110, sec. 1 and 3 is that the expense in question "shall be charged to the common fund of the union." Now, the "common fund of the union" is described in the 4 & 5 Wm. 4, c. 76, sec. 28, which directs that the several parishes in the union shall contribute and be assessed to a common fund for certain purposes in proportion to the last averages ascertained by the Poor Law Commissioners; consequently, the apportionment of the common fund relief must be made in the Corwen Union according to the averages last declared, and not according to those which were previously in force. If the parish officers of Bettws should still adhere to their own view after this communication, it will certainly be competent to them to bring their objection under the consideration of the auditor.

IV.—BURIAL.

1. OVERSEERS REMOVING THE BODY OF A POOR PERSON INTO THE WORKHOUSE BEFORE BURIAL.

6th March, 1851.

Clerk of Crediton Union.—On the 11th of February, a man applied to the overseer of Crediton, and stated that his child had just died of decline in a tent which he had recently fixed by the side of the road near Hollocombe, in that parish, and that he wanted the parish to bury the body as he was unable to do so. The workhouse of the union being situated in Crediton, and not far distant from the place where the child died, (three miles only,) and the overseer considering it would be less expensive than to have the body taken to an inn, gave instructions for conveying it to the workhouse to have the necessary arrangements made for its interment, which was done accordingly. The relieving-officer of Crediton lives in the adjoining parish of Sandford, a distance of two miles from Crediton, and at the time the man applied to the overseer of Crediton the relieving-officer was absent from home, being engaged in relieving the poor at distant parishes. Inquiring whether the overseers of Crediton, under the circumstances, acted legally in having the body of this child conveyed to the workhouse.

Ans.—According to the strict rules of law, the overseer of the parish of Crediton was not justified in pursuing the course stated. He was not required by law to interfere with the burial of the dead body; but as in so doing he doubtless acted with the best intention, it does not appear to the Board that any further step need be taken in the matter. At the same time it may be proper to suggest to the overseers, in any future cases which may occur, to advise the parties who may apply to them respecting burial, to lay their case before the relieving-officer of the district at the earliest practicable period at which that can be done.

---

2. BURIAL OF POOR PERSONS DYING IN A HOSPITAL.

4th June, 1851.

Secretary to the General Hospital, Birmingham.—The 7 & 8 Vic. c. 101, sec. 31, provides "that it shall be lawful for guardians, or where there are no guardians, for the overseers, to bury the body of any poor person which may be within their parish or union respectively, and to charge the expense thereof to any parish under their control, to which such person may have been chargeable, or in which he may have died, or otherwise in which such body may be." A poor woman, named Hollier, died in the general hospital, and consequently, within the parish of Birmingham, and the body remained there up to the period of its interment. Inquiring whether the 7 & 8 Vic. c. 101, sec. 31, did not fix the legal liability of the cost of interment upon the guardians of the poor for the parish of Birmingham. The hospital is a private charity, supported by voluntary contributions for the purpose of affording relief to the sick and lame poor, and has no funds whatever for providing for the interment of any patient dying within its walls. The guardians of the poor for the parish of Birmingham have repeatedly repudiated all legal responsibility in such cases, and have uniformly refused to bury upon the plea that the paupers have been admitted from another parish.

Ans.—Though the statute, 7 & 8 Vic. c. 101, sec. 31, confers upon the guardians of the poor of Birmingham an authority to bury the dead body of any poor person which may be within their parish, it does not render them absolutely compellable to do so. They have a discretion in the matter, which the Board presume that they will exercise properly. In regard to paupers brought from a distance, the late statute 12 & 13 Vic. c. 103, sec. 17, will render some additional assistance to the governors of the hospital. But they have no legal claim upon the guardians, or any parochial authority in respect of persons brought to them and dying in their hospital who are not paupers. According to the case of Q. *v.* Steward, (12 Ad. & E., 773) the legal obligation to bury the bodies of persons lying dead within the hospital appears to rest with the governors of the hospital.

V.—CHARGEABILITY.

1. Of paupers to the common fund.

10th March, 1851.

Clerk of Lincoln Union.—Upon an application to the guardians to place a pauper on the common charges account the practice is to ascertain by the best evidence which may be available, whether the pauper be settled in the parish of his residence or not, and if after investigating the matter they are satisfied that he is not settled therein, and irremovable, direct the relief to be charged to the common fund of the union. If afterwards such pauper ceases to be chargeable and continues so for any length of time whatever, and upon the chargeability occurring again, would the guardians be competent to place the cost of such pauper's relief upon the common fund at once without requiring the evidence to be gone through again as in the first instance; or, in other words, having once constituted a pauper's irremovability and charged the relief to the common fund, is that sufficient to warrant the guardians in charging all subsequent relief given to that account, presuming, of course that the pauper continues to reside in the same parish.

Ans.—The Board do not think they can suggest any rule which shall be universally applicable in all cases of this kind; but they may observe generally, that they consider the guardians, on the return of a pauper under the circumstances you describe, should not charge the relief again on the common fund, as a matter of course, but should make such inquiries as may be necessary in regard to the circumstances which may have occurred since his last chargeability. Where the guardians had previously ascertained the pauper to be irremovable by residence, such irremovability will no doubt be generally found to continue, where there has been no subsequent interruption of the residence. In such cases, it will not be necessary for the guardians to enter into any fresh investigation of the prior circumstances connected with the irremovability; but it will be open to enquiry whether the pauper's residence has continued unbroken since the former investigation, and whether any settlement has in the mean time been acquired in the parish of the residence. It may be added that some cases may possibly arise where a fresh investigation of the whole of the circumstances may become necessary; as. for example, where it can be shown that the guardians formed an erroneous conclusion, or were misinformed as to the facts in the first instance.

2. Evidence of chargeability.

10th March, 1851.

Clerk of Brackley Union.—The guardians at their last meeting ordered out-relief on account of sickness to a pauper named Nathaniel T——. The pauper has been living at Brackley for some years, but reputed to belong to Whitfield; but the guardians of that parish who were present at the meeting would not acknowledge his settlement. No evidence was given of his not belonging to Brackley, but the guardian of that parish proposed, that being a case of sickness, the relief should go to the common charges account, which proposal was negatived on a division, and ordered to be charged to Brackley. Requesting the Board's opinion as to what account the relief of the pauper should be charged; and requesting also that the Board would more clearly define to the guardians what evidence they should require in order to decide upon disputed questions of this kind.

Ans.—The Board desire to point out that, as the case in question is one in which the Brackley Union and a particular parish therein are jointly interested, they think it desirable that before advising on the case, they should be furnished with the joint statement for which the 11 & 12 Vic. c. 110, sec. 4, provides. This statement containing precise information as to facts, names, and dates, should be drawn up by you as the clerk to the guardians, signed by the presiding chairman on the part of the board of guardians of the particular parish interested in the matter. With regard to the inquiry contained in your letter, as to what evidence the guardians should require with respect to the pauper's settlement in cases of this kind, the Board desire me to state, that they do not think the 11 & 12 Vic. c. 110, sec. 3, renders it necessary to be proved that the pauper has a settlement in some other parish than that of his residence; it appears to them to be sufficient if it can be shown that he is not settled in the parish where he resides. Upon this point, the Board do not consider that the guardians can always expect to receive strict legal proof; though they are not prepared to give any precise advice as to the nature of the evidence on which they should act. The Board can only observe, generally, that the guardians will not be precluded from further inquiry into the matter by any assertion of the overseers; but they should be guided in their decision by the best information they may be able to obtain. Probably in any case of doubt, an examination of the pauper himself will enable the guardians to clear up the difficulty, and arrive at a satisfactory conclusion. It is to be borne in mind, that the decision of the guardians as to the mode of charging the relief in any such case is not final; but is subject to the revision of the auditor, whose decision is in its turn liable to be reviewed upon appeal to the Court of Queen's Bench, or the Poor Law Board.

---

3. CHARGEABILITY OF CHILD DESERTED BY THE FATHER.

22nd July, 1850.

Clerk of Boston Union.—R. B. deserted his wife many years since. She came to reside at Skirbeck, where she has lived ever since. About twelve months since, R. B. came back to his wife, bringing with him a child about ten years of age, which he stated to be his by a second woman, whom he had married, and who was dead. He and the child resided with the first wife about nine months, and the man then ran away, leaving the child in Skirbeck with the first wife. This woman gets her living by nursing, and after her husband's second desertion, she put her child out to a sister residing in Boston, at 2*s.* 6*d.* a week, where the child remained about six weeks. The woman then being unable to continue this payment, applied to have the child admitted into the workhouse, which was done. Inquiring whether the child so admitted ought to be charged to Boston, where it had resided six weeks before admission; to Skirbeck, where it was left by its so called father; or to "Common Charges" as a foundling.

Ans.—The Board consider the child in question is not a foundling within the meaning of the 2nd section of the 12th & 13th Vic. c. 103, inasmuch as, although deserted by its parents, they think, under the circumstances, the child cannot be said not to have been in the care or custody of its friends. Then, as the chargeability did not arise in the parish of Skirbeck, but in the parish of Boston where the child was residing at the time it was deserted, the Board, think on the statement submitted by you, that the parish of Boston is chargeable with the relief.

---

4. RELIEF RENDERED NECESSARY BY SICKNESS OF WHICH THE PAUPER DIED.

15*th Aug.*, 1851.

Clerk of Camelford Union—Transmitting the following statement, duly signed under the 10th & 11th Vic. c. 110, sec. 4, for the opinion of the Poor Law Board:—A man named John ——, residing in the parish of Forrabury in this union, whose legal settlement was in the parish of St. Gennys in the Stratton union, was taken ill with fever. The relieving officer reported his case at the meeting of the guardians held on the 4th ult. The relief given was directed to be kept in abeyance until the meeting of the guardians on the 18th ult., to discover whether he had resided five years in Forrabury parish, or whether he was removable to his legal settlement. The result of such inquiry was the discovery of a residence of three years, and before the meeting of the guardians on the 18th ult. the pauper died. His chargeability arose from sickness prior to which he was able-bodied. On the 18th ult., an application was made for his funeral expenses, and a discussion ensued as to where the relief and such expenses should be charged. The relief when first given was kept in abeyance, no opportunity was therefore afforded to Forrabury parish to prove a suspended order of removal supposing permanent disability could have been certified as likely to result from the fever. The relief having been rendered necessary by sickness, would not the common fund be liable to sustain the charge, the pauper being irremovable by reason of such sickness? Within the fortnight the pauper died from the sickness causing such chargeability, but if he had not died, permanent disability might not have resulted, and the pauper would still have been irremovable. The opinion of the Poor Law Board is requested what fund should bear the relief given to the pauper under the circumstances stated.

Ans.—As the relief afforded to the pauper was rendered necessary by sickness, and as it does not appear that the sickness was such as would probably have satisfied any justices that it would produce permanent disability, the Board think that the pauper was irremovable by virtue of the 9 & 10 Vic. c. 66, sec. 4. Consequently the cost of the both relief and the burial are cast upon the common fund by the 11 & 12 Vic. c. 110, sec. 3.

VI.—CONTRIBUTION ORDERS.—DUTIES OF OVERSEERS.

28*th May*, 1851.

Clerks of Wareham and Purbeck Unions.—Contribution Orders were made and served upon the then overseers in March, 1851, and the first instalment became payable on the 30th April, 1851, before which day new overseers were appointed. Who are the parties responsible for the payment of the money ordered, the overseers on whom the orders were served, or their successors? It unavoidably happens that the audit of some of the union accounts does not take place until some time after lady-day, and in the mean time, the old overseers, as the parties liable to account, hold all the books which they deliver over to the new ones after the audit. Whose duty is it in the interval, and after the appointment of new overseers to make and collect any rates which may be required for the purpose of meeting contribution orders?

Ans.—Generally an order for contribution served by the guardians of any union upon the overseers of any parish therein is only operative upon the individuals to whom it is addressed, and cannot be enforced against their successors in office, who are not named in the order. With regard to your second question the Board have to point out that when an overseer has quitted office, he has no further power to collect the outstanding arrears of poor-rates; but his successors in office are empowered, and indeed bound to collect such arrears.

VII.—ELECTION OF GUARDIANS.

1. REGISTER OF OWNERS AND PROXIES.

9*th April*, 1851.

Clerk of Tavistock Union.—In Tavistock there is a contest for Guardians. The population is much more than 2,000. There is in existence a register of owners and proxies made in the year 1845 or 1846, (the first year after the passing the Statute 6 & 7 Vic. c. 101,) on claims then sent in, but no revision has ever been made of it under the statute. The overseers have marked on the ordinary rate book the number of votes each rate-payer and owner is, in their opinion, entitled to, but he, the clerk, has not inserted the owners' votes in the voting papers. Inquiring whether or not he ought to allow any votes to owners and proxies under the circumstances; and if so, whether any more should be allowed than he may find in the register referred to.

Ans.—As no revision of the register of owners for Tavistock has been made in the manner contemplated by the 7 & 8 Vic. c. 101, in dealing at the present election of guardians with the question of the votes of owners and proxies, you will not be concluded by the entries in the register made at the period mentioned in your letter. It is right that you should require the production of the claims, or statements of the owners and proxies originally sent, in order to satisfy yourself that they are in accordance with the provision of the statute above cited, and contain the requisite particulars. Where this may appear, and the parties who made the claim retain the same interest in the property, you should allow the several owners the number of votes according to the scale provided by section 14 of the statute referred to. You should not rely upon the present entry in the register as to the number of votes. You should also bear in mind the limitation of time as to the duration of the appointment of the proxy. The owners are not disfranchised because there has been no revision of the register, which appears to be only necessary when there have been objections made to the claims of such owners.

2. NOMINATION OF EX-OFFICIO GUARDIANS FOR ELECTION.

13th March, 1851.

Clerk of Camelford Union.—Inquiring, whether a justice of the peace, residing in the union qualified and acting as such justice, being already an ex-officio guardian can be nominated as a guardian to be elected for any parish in the union; and supposing such justice of the peace to be nominated, and another person nominated also for the parish, and only one guardian can be elected, should the nomination of such justice be treated as invalid. It is understood that there are some duties and powers which can only be exercised by elected guardians, and that one or more guardians, as the case may be, must be elected by the rate-payers.

Ans.—The Board do not find any distinct authority which will determine the question; but, they are disposed to consider that a person legally qualified to act as an ex-officio guardian may be nominated as an elective guardian; because it is optional with him whether he will act as an ex-officio guardian, but it is not so if he be duly elected a guardian. If the Board are correct in this view, then, should another person also be nominated in a parish where only one guardian is to be elected, there must be a contested election, unless either of the two candidates should send notice of his refusal to act as an elected guardian; in which case the election as regards that person would cease. The Board desire to add that they are not aware of any matter upon which an elective guardian can vote while an ex-officio guardian cannot.

29th March, 1851.

Clerk of same Union.—Inquiring whether, under secs. 33 & 34 of the 4 & 5 Wm. 4, c. 76, the powers of agreeing for union settlements and a common rate are not vested altogether in the elected guardians and are not the ex-officio guardians excluded.

Ans.—Under secs. 33 & 34 of the 4 & 5 Wm. 4, c. 76, it is only necessary for all the elective guardians to sign the agreement mentioned therein. There is, however, nothing to prevent the ex-officio guardians also signing the agreement. In such cases, moreover, there will not necessarily be any voting, as a unanimous agreement is required to be given in writing.

3. ELECTION OF GUARDIANS IN A PARISH WHERE NO RATE HAD BEEN MADE FOR TWELVE MONTHS.

3rd April, 1851.

Clerk of Camelford Union.—There has been no legal poor-rate made in the parish of Forrabury from Lady-day, 1850, to Lady-day, 1851; consequently, no rates have been paid. In what manner, therefore, are the qualified voters to be distinguished? Are they not all disqualified under the circumstances; and if so, will this put an end to the election, because if not qualified to vote they are all, it is presumed, disqualified to nominate. Who is then to represent the parish?

Ans.—Assuming no valid poor-rate has been made during the last twelve months, the Board do not think it follows necessarily that there are no persons qualified to vote in the parish as rate-payers, within the meaning of the 4 & 5 Wm. 4, c. 76, sec. 40. The Board presume that at a former period, valid poor-rates have been made so as to be effectual and binding upon the parishioner. In the case of Bushell, App., Luckett Resp. 2 M. & G. & S. 111, it appears to have been decided that when a rate is once made, it exists until superseded by another duly made, allowed, and published; and that there is always an existing rate. Upon this view of the case, it would seem that the last valid poor-rate made for Forrabury has been the "existing rate," or the rate in force during the last twelvemonths. Persons assessed in that rate would, therefore, have satisfied the requirement in 4 & 5 Wm, 4, c. 76, sec. 40, as to the being rated to the poor-rate during the year immediately preceding the time of voting. Then, with regard to the payment of rates, what is required is, that a person should have paid all that has been assessed on him for the period of "one whole year," as well as the rates due from him at the time of voting, except those which have been made during the last six months (see the same section) where any person was duly assessed in the last valid rate, which though made more than a year ago, still continues to be the existing rate of the parish according to the decision cited before; and that rate has been paid with all previous arrears, (if any,) the Board are strongly disposed to think that such person is a rate-payer within the meaning of the 40th sec., and entitled to vote in the present election.

VIII.—ORDERS OF THE POOR LAW BOARD DETERMINING QUESTIONS AFFECTING THE SETTLEMENT, REMOVAL, OR CHARGEABILITY OF POOR PERSONS UNDER THE 14 & 15 VIC. c. 105, SEC. 12.

1. ORDER AS TO THE PARISHES OF BUCKLAND BREWER AND PARKHAM.—*Dated 4th Nov.*, 1851.

To THE GUARDIANS OF THE POOR of the Bideford Union, in the County of Devon;—

To the Churchwardens and Overseers of the Parish of Buckland Brewer, in the said County;—

To the Churchwardens and Overseers of the Parish of Parkham, in the said County;—

To the Clerk or Clerks to the Justices of the Petty Sessions held for the Division or Divisions in which the said Union is situate;—

To the Treasurer of the said Union;—

And to all others whom it may concern.

Whereas a question respecting the settlement of Emma Palmer, a poor person, now an inmate of the workhouse of the Bideford Union, in the County of Devon, has arisen between the Parish of Buckland Brewer, in the said County, and the Parish of Parkham, also in the said County: And whereas Ambrose Galsworthy and James Hamlyn, Churchwardens, and Briant Bartlett and Thomas Abbott, Overseers of the Poor of the said Parish of Buckland Brewer, and George Furse and Reuben Grigg, Churchwardens, and John Squance and Edmund Andrew, Overseers of the Poor of the said Parish of Parkham, have thought fit to submit such question to the Poor Law Board for their decision, by an agreement in writing, bearing date the Thirteenth day of October, One thousand eight hundred and fifty-one, and executed, in respect of the said Churchwardens and Overseers, by their respective signatures thereto, and by such agreement mutually agreed upon the following statement of facts relative to the said Emma Palmer and the question as to her place of legal settlement:—

"That she was born on the sixteenth day of October, One thousand eight hundred and forty-one, and is the illegitimate child of Ann Nicholls, a widow, then Ann Palmer, single woman.

"That the said Ann Nicholls, at or about Michaelmas in the year One thousand eight hundred and forty-four, married one William Nicholls, a labourer, who then was legally settled in the said Parish of Buckland Brewer; that at the birth of the said Emma Palmer, and up to the time of the marriage of the said Ann Nicholls with the said William Nicholls she, the said Ann Nicholls, was legally settled in the said Parish of Parkham; that the said William Nicholls, after his marriage with the said Ann Nicholls, did not acquire any other settlement, but remained legally settled in the said Parish of Buckland Brewer up to his death, which happened on the Twentieth of May, One thousand eight hundred and forty-five: that the said Ann Nicholls has not gained any settlement since the death of her said husband; that the said Ann Nicholls, with her said child Emma Palmer, has been chargeable to the said Parish of Buckland Brewer, with intermissions during which she has not received relief, from the death of the said William Nicholls to the present time."

And whereas the Poor Law Board have seen fit to entertain such question.

Now, therefore, We, the Poor Law Board, having duly considered the said statement of facts and the question submitted to us, do, under the authority of the Statute passed in the fifteenth year of the reign of Her Majesty, intituled "*An Act to continue an Act of the Fourteenth Year of Her Majesty, for charging the Maintenance of certain poor Persons in Unions in England and Wales upon the Common Fund, and to make Amendments in the Laws for the Relief of the Poor,*" and of the several other Statutes in that behalf, determine that the said Emma Palmer was, at the time of the execution of the said agreement, settled in the said Parish of Buckland Brewer.

Given under our Hand and Seal of Office, this Fourth day of November, in the year One thousand eight hundred and fifty-one.

M. T. BAINES, *President.*

COURTENAY, *Secretary.*

2. Order as to the Parishes of Richmond and Lewisham.—*Dated* 8*th Dec.*, 1851.

Whereas a question, respecting the removability to the Parish of Richmond, in the County of Surrey, of Charlotte Anthony and her children, poor persons, now chargeable to the Parish of Lewisham, in the County of Kent, has arisen between the said Parishes: And whereas William Chapman, Alfred Stansfield, John Greville Hiscoke, Churchwardens and Overseers of the said Parish of Richmond, and, Simon Southorn, Henry Couchman, and John Charles Covell, Churchwardens and Overseers of the said Parish of Lewisham, have thought fit to submit such question to the Poor Law Board for their decision, by an agreement in writing, bearing date the Twenty-sixth day of November last, and executed, in respect of the said Churchwardens and Overseers, by their respective signatures thereto, and by such agreement mutually agreed upon the following statement of facts, relative to the said Charlotte Anthony and children, and the question as to their removability to the said Parish of Richmond.

"Charlotte Anthony, with her husband Luis Anthony, since deceased, and such of her children named in the order of removal hereinafter referred to as were then born, came to reside in the Parish of Lewisham aforesaid, on the 28 August, 1845, and the said Charlotte Anthony has thence hitherto continued to reside with such children, and with those born subsequently to the said 28th of August, 1845, in that Parish, but her late husband, the said Luis Anthony, ceased to reside in the said Parish of Lewisham, and never returned thereto, after about the middle of the month of April in the year 1850, and was not residing with his said wife (and now widow) the said Charlotte Anthony in the said Parish of Lewisham at the time of his decease hereinafter referred to. That in or about the middle of the month of April, 1850, the said Luis Anthony, being then ill, was admitted into and received as an In-patient of St. George's Hospital, Middlesex, and thenceforth continued an In-patient thereof to the day of his death, which occurred in such hospital on the 21st of May, 1850. That shortly after that event happened, viz., on the 14th of June, 1850, the said Charlotte Anthony applied to and was relieved by the said Parish of Lewisham, and she and her said children have thence hitherto regularly received relief from that Parish. That on the 27th of September last (1851) an order was obtained by the Parish officers of Lewisham, for the removal of the said Charlotte Anthony, and her said five children, to the said Parish of Richmond, that Parish being admitted to be the place of their last legal settlement."

And whereas the Poor Law Board have seen fit to entertain such question.

Now, therefore, We, the Poor Law Board having duly considered the said statement of facts and the question submitted to Us, do, under the authority of the Statute, &c., and of the several other Stututes in that behalf, determine that the said Charlotte Anthony, and her five children, named, respectively, Annie, William, Charles, James and Emily, were, at the time of the execution of the said agreement, legally removable to the said Parish of Richmond.

---

3. Order as to the Town of Aberystwyth and Parish of Llanfihangel Ystrad.—*Dated* 9*th Dec.*, 1851.

Whereas a question respecting the removability of Elizabeth Thomas, a pauper, from the Town of Aberystwyth, in the County of Cardigan, to the Parish of Llanfihangel Ystrad, in the same County, has arisen between the said Town and Parish: And whereas John Matthews, David Lewis, and Hugh Davies, Overseers of the Poor of the said Town of Aberystwyth, and J. J. Jones, and W. S. Davies, Overseers of the Poor of the said Parish of Llanfihangel Ystrad, have thought fit to submit such question to the Poor Law Board for their decision, by an agreement in writing, bearing date the Thirtieth day of September last, and executed, in respect of the said Overseers, by their respective signatures thereto, and by such agreement mutually agreed upon the following statement of facts relative to the said Elizabeth Thomas, and the question as to her removability from the said Town of Aberystwyth to the said Parish of Llanfihangel Ystrad.

"The pauper is the widow of one David Thomas, the place of whose settlement was in Llanfihangel Ystrad, and who died about 18 years ago. The pauper was living at Aberystwyth when her husband died, and was in service at an Inn there. She was in service as cook at this Inn for 12 years in the whole. Soon after she left her service at this Inn, namely, in September, 1839, she became chargeable to Aberystwyth, and was removed therefrom by an order of Justices, dated 24th September, 1839, to Llanfihangel

Ystrad, and after residing in that Parish for two or three days after her removal, she went back again to live to Aberystwyth, and was relieved by Llanfihangel Ystrad for about six weeks. When she returned from Llanfihangel Ystrad she went to reside with a married daughter who lives in Aberystwyth, and has resided with her ever since, with the exceptions hereinafter stated. She went out occasionally for a few days as cook, during the summer seasons, at lodging-houses in Aberystwyth. She was also out occasionally for a few days at a gentleman's house out of the town of Aberystwyth during the time there were visitors there. In the month of December, 1846, the pauper became chargeable to the Aberystwyth, and being irremovable on account of a five years' residence, was relieved by Aberystwyth until the 27th April, 1850. Some time in the spring of 1850, the pauper was requested, by a gentleman residing at a place called Tan-y-bwlch, in an adjoining Parish to Aberystwyth, (whose cook had left him,) to supply the cook's place for a few days, until he could find another cook. She went to Tan-y-bwlch accordingly, and acted as cook there for about eleven weeks from the time she went there, with occasional intervals of absence for one, two, or three days. She was paid sometimes one shilling for her day's work. Sometimes, when she remained for the whole week, she had four shillings for the week, besides her board. She remained at Tan-y-bwlch for four or five weeks out of the eleven weeks at the wages of four shillings a week, without leaving at all, and slept there all that time. When she left Tan-y-bwlch at the end of the eleven weeks she returned to her daughter's at Aberystwyth, and in about six months after her return she again became chargeable to Aberystwyth, and an order for her removal to Llanfihangel Ystrad was made on the 3rd December, 1850, against which the present appeal is pending. During the absence of the pauper at Tan-y-bwlch the pauper left her clothes, with the exception of a few things she wanted for immediate use, at her daughter's house, and her daughter washed for her, and she always considered her daughter's house as her home, and intended to return to it whenever she left Tan-y-bwlch. The pauper did not rent any apartments at her daughter's house, and could not claim any as a matter of right, she being merely suffered to come and reside there when out of a situation out of charity, and she had not a single article of household furniture of her own therein, nor did she pay or agree to pay anything to her daughter for her lodgings during the time she lived with her."

And whereas the Poor Law Board have seen fit to entertain such question.

Now, therefore, We, the Poor Law Board, having duly considered the said statement of facts and the question submitted to Us, do, under the authority of the Statute, &c., and of the several other Statutes in that behalf, determine that the said Elizabeth Thomas, at the time of the execution of the said agreement, was not removable from the said Town of Aberystwyth to the said Parish of Llanfihangel Ystrad.

---

4. ORDER AS TO THE TOWNSHIPS OF HUNSLET AND HOLBECK.—*Dated 13th Dec.,* 1851.

Whereas a question respecting the removal of Joseph Rhodes, his wife and children, from the Township of Holbeck, in the Borough of Leeds, in the County of York, has arisen between the said Township and the Township of Hunslet, in the said Borough and County: And whereas William Pape, Samuel Oxley, Henry Bushby, and Richard Kilburn, Overseers of the Poor of the said Township of Holbeck, and Benjamin Mellor, George Oakes, George Taylor, and William Spong, junior, Overseers of the Poor of the said Township of Hunslet, have thought fit to submit such question to the Poor Law Board for their decision, by an agreement in writing, bearing date the Twelfth day of November last, and executed, in respect of the said Overseers, by their respective signatures thereto, and by such agreement mutually agreed upon the following statement of facts, relative to the said Joseph Rhodes, his wife and children, and the question as to their removability from the said Township of Holbeck.

"That the pauper (Joseph Rhodes) is about thirty-one years old, and has a wife and children.

"That his settlement is admitted to be in the Township of Hunslet.

"That upwards of ten years ago the said pauper went to reside in the Township of Holbeck, with his wife and family, and has ever since continued to inhabit, and still does inhabit, in that Township, except for about seven weeks, when the pauper went to and continued at Liverpool, under the following circumstances, namely,—

"That up to and in the year One thousand eight hundred and forty-seven the pauper was a housekeeper in the Township of Holbeck, residing therein, with his wife and children. He was then out of work, and on that account left Holbeck to go to Liverpool in order to seek work there. He left his wife and children in his house at Holbeck, and if he had got work at Liverpool he would have stopped there, and then sent for his wife and family, but if he did not get any work there his intention was to return to his wife and family at Holbeck, and to his house there, in which he left them residing.

"The pauper sought work in Liverpool for about four weeks and got none, and at the end of that time he fell ill, and he remained sick at his lodgings in Liverpool for about three weeks, and whilst he was so laid ill there his wife went to him with one of his children, and his other children she had left at her mother's in Holbeck.

"That without consulting the pauper, and without his knowledge, his wife gave up his house at Holbeck to the landlord, who wanted rent of him, and in order to satisfy his claim she left part of the furniture in the house for the landlord, and the rest of the things she took and left at her mother's, but of this the pauper did not know anything till his wife went to him at Liverpool.

"Whilst he was sick at Liverpool, and his wife and child were with him there, the pauper received a letter informing him that his old masters, Messieurs Taylor and Wordsworth, could give him employment at Holbeck, and, therefore, when he was better, he left Liverpool, with his wife and child, and returned to Holbeck, where he took another house, and he and they have continued to reside in Holbeck ever since that time.

"The pauper was absent at Liverpool in the whole about seven weeks, during about four of which he was seeking work but got none, and the rest of the time he was ill, and when better, he returned to Holbeck as before mentioned.

"Whilst the pauper was at Liverpool, he continued in the same intention to remain there for good, if he got employment, but if he got none his intention was certainly to return to Holbeck again, and he remained of this mind until he got the letter informing him that he might get work again at Holbeck, and so he then returned to Holbeck."

And whereas the Poor Law Board have seen fit to entertain such question.

Now, therefore, We, the Poor Law Board, having duly considered the said statement of facts and the question submitted to Us, do, under the authority of the Statute &c., and of the several other statutes in that behalf, Determine, that the said Joseph Rhodes, his wife and children, were, at the time of the execution of the said agreement, removable from the said Township of Holbeck.

5. ORDER AS TO THE PARISHES OF LLANRWST AND SAINT OSWALD.—*Dated 28th Dec.*, 1851.

Whereas a question, respecting the removability of Thomas Jones, a pauper, from the Parish of Saint Oswald, in the City and County of the City of Chester, to the Parish of Llanrwst, in the County of Denbigh, has arisen between the said Parishes: And whereas Thomas Davies and John Evans, Overseers of the Poor of the said Parish of Llanrwst, and George Downes and James Weedow, Overseers of the Poor of the said Parish of Saint Oswald, have thought fit to submit such question to the Poor Law Board for their decision, by an agreement in writing, executed, in respect of the said Overseers, by their respective signatures thereto, and by such agreement mutually agreed upon the following statement of facts, relative to the said Thomas Jones, and, the following question, that is to say, whether the said pauper, under the circumstances detailed in the said statement, is exempt, in pursuance of the 9th and 10th Vic. c. 66, from the liability to be removed to the place of such pauper's settlement.

Thomas Jones, the above-named pauper, is admitted to be settled by birth and apprenticeship in the Parish of Llanrwst. He has resided in the Parish of St. Oswald, comprised in the Chester Incorporation, for the last 27 years, and now resides there. About 5 years ago he went to the Board of Guardians of the Llanrwst Union for Parish relief, when he was allowed 5*s.* temporary relief, and 1*s.* weekly. About a month afterwards, the pauper and his wife went to Llanrwst Board for an advance in his weekly relief, which was accordingly advanced to 2*s.* per week. The pauper and his wife returned on the following day to their residence at St. Oswald aforesaid. On pauper's wife's death, which happened about two years ago, his weekly relief was discontinued, and in about three or four weeks afterwards he gave up his house, and went to lodgings in the same Parish, where he remained until he was admitted in the workhouse,—the cost of his maintenance, while there, charged to and paid by the Parish of Saint Oswald. The pauper on the 3rd day of March last voluntarily left the workhouse and went in search of work to various places; he was absent about three weeks, and during that period went to Llanrwst and several other Towns, remaining a night in each, and returned to his lodgings in St. Oswald's aforesaid. Had the pauper succeeded in finding work he would not have returned to St. Oswald's, but was determined to do so in case he should be unsuccessful. The pauper was, by order dated the Third June last, removed from St. Oswald to the Parish of Llanrwst, and the latter Parish lodged an appeal, which is now pending, notice and grounds of appeal having been duly served upon the Respondents.

And whereas, We, the said Poor Law Board have seen fit to entertain such question.

Now, therefore, We, the said Poor Law Board, having duly considered the said statement of facts, and the question submitted to Us, do, under the authority of the Statute &c., and of the several other Statutes in that behalf, determine that the said Thomas Jones at the time of the execution of the said agreement, was not legally removable to the said Parish of Llanrwst.

6. ORDER AS TO THE PARISH OF WESTWARD, PARISH AND TOWNSHIP OF ABOVE DERWENT. —*Dated* 10*th Jan.*, 1852.

Whereas, by an Order of Two of Her Majesty's Justices of the Peace in and for the County of Cumberland, bearing date the Twentieth day of August last, the Churchwardens and Overseers of the Poor of the Parish of Westward, in the said County, were required to remove Daniel Tyson, Dinah his wife, and their children, named respectively, Elizabeth and Henry, paupers, from the said Parish to the Township of Above Derwent, in the said County, but the said paupers were not removed from the said parish of Westward, and the said Daniel Tyson has, since the date of the said Order, died, leaving his widow, the said Dinah Tyson, and her said children, in the receipt of relief from the said Parish of Westward.

And whereas certain questions respecting the removability to the said Township of Above Derwent, and chargeability, of the said Dinah Tyson, and her children, have arisen between the said Township and Parish: And whereas John Dover, Thomas Bell, and John Dover, Churchwardens and Overseers of the said Township of Above Derwent, and William Graham, Matthew Magnay, John Martin, Henry Wood, and George Johnston, Churchwardens and Overseers of the said Parish of Westward, have thought fit to submit such questions to the Poor Law Board for their decision, by an agreement in writing, bearing date the First day of November last, and executed, in respect of the said Churchwardens and Overseers, by their respective signatures thereto, and by such agreement mutually agreed upon the following statement of facts relative to the said Dinah Tyson, and her said children, Elizabeth and Henry, and the questions hereinafter set forth, touching their removability to the said Township of Above Derwent, and chargeability.

The pauper, Daniel Tyson, aged 73, (the lawful son of Henry Tyson and Rebecca, his wife,) was, by reason of permanent sickness, to the satisfaction of the Justices, chargeable to the said Parish of Westward, at the time when the application for the said order was made, (the said Parish of Westward then and still being part of the Wigton Poor Law Union,) and his daughter and son were then unemancipated members of his said family.

Medical and other evidence of the said pauper's sickness, as to whether such sickness was likely to lead to the said pauper's permanent disability, was given and taken by and before the said Justices making the said order of removal, but not reduced into writing.

In or about the year 1803 the pauper's father (the said Henry Tyson), and the said pauper Daniel Tyson, jointly, rented and occupied a tenement and farm, consisting of a dwelling-house, farm buildings, and about twenty acres of land, with a right of common thereto, situate in the said Township of Above Derwent, of the annual value of twenty pounds and upwards, viz., of the value of thirty pounds a year. They farmed and occupied the same for three years, and resided and slept the whole time on the said farm, in the said Township of Above Derwent. The said tenement and farm are situate more than ten miles from the subsequent place of residence of the said pauper, Daniel Tyson, and from the said parish of Westward.

The said pauper Daniel Tyson died since the making and serving of the said order, leaving Dinah his wife, his said daughter, and his said son, him surviving.

At the date of the making of the said order,

and also at the time of the death of the said Daniel Tyson, his said wife and two children were residing with him in the said Parish of Westward, and the said widow and children are still, whether legally or not, receiving relief therefrom.

No complaint in writing was made by the said Churchwardens and Overseers of the said Parish of Westward, to the said Justices, of the chargeability of the said paupers, but a verbal complaint was made by the said Churchwardens and Overseers of Westward to the said Justices.

Under the above-mentioned circumstances, the following Questions are hereby submitted to the Poor Law Board for their decision :—

First.—Had the said Daniel Tyson, at the time of making the said order, lost his settlement in the Township of Above Derwent by reason of his having ceased to inhabit within ten miles from that Township?

Secondly.—Are the widow and children of the said Daniel Tyson irremovable from the said Parish of Westward, by reason of the death of the said Daniel Tyson since the making of the said order?

Thirdly.—Have the widow and children of the said Daniel Tyson, by reason of the death of the said Daniel Tyson since the making of the said order of removal, ceased to be chargeable to the said Parish of Westward, and have they thereby become chargeable to the said Wigton Union (wherein the said Parish of Westward is situate)?

Fourthly.—In case the said order of removal has become incapable of being executed at present, by reason of the death of the said Daniel Tyson before the removal of himself and family, will the said order of removal be capable of being executed after twelve calendar months shall have expired since the death of the said Daniel Tyson, notwithstanding the said widow and children of the said Daniel Tyson should have become chargeable to the said Wigton Union (as suggested in the question thirdly above stated)?

Fifthly.—The said Justices (making the said order) having had medical and other evidence as to the sickness of the said pauper being of such a character as to tend to render the said pauper permanently disabled, should such Justices, before making the said order, have had such medical and other evidence reduced into writing and sent to the appellants, together with the copy of the other evidence taken before them; and does the fact of the omission of taking and sending such evidence render the said order bad?

Sixthly.—Does the fact that no complaint in writing (but only a verbal one) was made by the said Churchwardens and Overseers of the said Parish of Westward to the said Justices, on the making of the said order, of the legal chargeability of the said pauper, to the said Parish of Westward, render the said order bad?

And whereas the Poor Law Board have seen fit to entertain the said several Questions, except the fourth and fifth.

Now, therefore, We, the Poor Law Board, having duly considered the said statement of facts, and the several questions submitted to Us, do, under the authority of the Statute &c., and of the several other Statutes in that behalf, determine as follows; that is to say,—

That on the day of the date of the said Order of the Justices, for the removal of the said Daniel Tyson to the said Township of Above Derwent, the said Daniel Tyson had not lost his settlement therein, by ceasing to inhabit within the distance of ten miles from the said Township.

That the said Dinah Tyson, and her children, at the time of the execution of the said agreement, were not legally removable from the said Parish of Westward, and the said Dinah Tyson, and her children, Elizabeth and Henry, at the time of the execution of such agreement, were chargeable to the Common Fund of the Wigton Union, in the said County of Cumberland, the said Parish of Westward being comprised therein.

That although no complaint was made in writing, at the time of the making of the aforesaid Order, by the said Churchwardens and Overseers, of the said Parish of Westward, to the said Justices, of the legal chargeability of the said Daniel Tyson to the said Parish of Westward, the aforesaid order of such Justices is not on that account null and void.

---

7. Order as to the Parish of Penrith and Township of Martindale.—*Dated 21st Jan., 1852.*

Whereas a question, respecting the removability of Edmund Slater, his wife and family, poor persons, from the Parish of Penrith, in the

County of Cumberland, to the Township of Martindale, in the County of Westmoreland, has arisen between the said Parish and Township: And whereas Thomas Smith, Isaac Wilson, George Foster, James Robison, and George Martindale, Churchwardens and Overseers of the said Parish of Penrith, and, Joseph Rothery, and Thomas Green, Churchwardens and Overseers of the said Township of Martindale, have thought fit to submit such question to the Poor Law Board, for their decision, by an agreement in writing, executed, in respect of the said Churchwardens and Overseers, by their respective signatures thereto, and by such agreement mutually agreed upon the following statement of facts, relative to the said Edmund Slater, his wife and family, and the question as to their removability to the said Township of Martindale.

"Edmund Slater gained a settlement by renting a farm at Sandwick, in the Township of Martindale, (in the West Ward Union, in the County of Westmoreland,) for seven years, at a rent of £25 per year, and paid all rates; his term expired at Candlemas, 1839. E. S. then came to Penrith, with his wife and family, and resided there about two years. In 1841, E. S. hired to James Pool of Patterdale, for 7*s*. per week, with board and lodging, and continued so hired for upwards of a year (his wife and family during this period continued to reside in Penrith;) the said E. S. slept the whole of this time in his master's house at Patterdale; he was a waggoner in Mr. Pool's employ, and came to Penrith three times a week with Mr. Pool's waggons; he brought his dirty clothes early in the week for his wife to wash, and took them back at the end of the week, sometimes calling at the house for them, and sometimes his wife carried them to the inn where he stopped; during the period of this hiring he never once slept at the house in Penrith where his wife and family resided. E. S. was taken ill, and in consequence obliged to leave Patterdale, and again came to Penrith, where he resided, with his wife and family, until April, 1844, when he again hired to Mr. Pool of Patterdale, at 6*s*. per week, with board and lodging, and remained so hired for upwards of a year; this hiring and service was the same in every respect, and attended with the same circumstances as the former, as to his sleeping at Patterdale, bringing his clothes to wash at Penrith, &c. In May, 1845, he was again taken ill, and obliged to leave his employ, and returned to Penrith, and resided with his wife and family. The said E. S. states that, had it not been for illness, he would not have left Mr. Pool's service, but would have remained as long as Mr. Pool had employment for him. In September, 1848, the said E. S. made an application to the Relieving Officer of the Penrith District for relief: his case was laid before the Board of Guardians of the Penrith Union, who ordered him to be relieved, and he has ever since continued to receive a weekly pension, charged to the Parish of Penrith, residing there with his wife and family.

"Since Candlemas, 1839, the pauper's wife and family have all along resided in Penrith, and have lived in several houses, the pauper sometimes taking the house, and sometimes the wife; the wife in general paid the rent, the pauper having only paid the rent in two or three cases, but during the period that the pauper was in Mr. Pool's employ the wife both took the house and paid the whole of the rent. Whilst the pauper was in the service of Mr. Pool he supplied his wife with money for the maintenance of herself and family, or for payment of rent, or for any other purpose; he was engaged to Mr. Pool by the week, and received his wages weekly, or he could not have maintained his family. They are both now residing in Penrith, the wife in one house, and the husband in another."

And whereas the Poor Law Board have seen fit to entertain such question.

Now, therefore, We, the Poor Law Board, having duly considered the said statement of facts, and the question submitted to Us, do, under the authority of the Statute passed in the Fifteenth year of the reign of Her Majesty, intituled "*An Act to continue an Act of the Fourteenth Year of Her Majesty, for charging the Maintenance of certain Poor Persons in Unions in England and Wales upon the Common Fund; and to make certain Amendments in the Laws for the Relief of the Poor*," and of the several other Statutes in that behalf, determine that the said Edmund Slater, his wife and family, were, at the time of the execution of the said agreement, legally removable to the said Township of Martindale.

London: Printed by Order of the Poor Law Board, by BLACKBURN & BURT, 90½, Holborn Hill, and Published by CHARLES KNIGHT, 90, Fleet Street.

AN

OFFICIAL CIRCULAR

OF PUBLIC DOCUMENTS AND INFORMATION:

DIRECTED BY THE POOR LAW BOARD TO BE PRINTED, CHIEFLY FOR THE USE OF THE BOARDS OF GUARDIANS AND THEIR OFFICERS.

No. 49.] [N.S.

CONTENTS.

I.—ACCOUNTS.—CHARGING COST OF RELIEF TO IRREMOVABLE POOR.

19*th April*, 1851.

The Poor Law Board to Mr. ———, *District Auditor*.—It appears in regard to certain of the parishes in the A—— Union, that there are entries in the Financial Statement for Michaelmas last, of receipts on account of irremovable poor, whereas the charge for the relief of that class of poor ought to be entered entirely among the common charges of the union, and should not form any parochial charge whatever.

22nd April, 1851.

Mr. ——, District Auditor, to the Poor Law Board.—The charges for the relief of the irremovable poor do not in fact form any parochial or township charge separately. The clerk enters the account in the union books in the form in which they are inserted in the financial statement, in order to balance his books, which he, the auditor, believes will be found to be in accordance with instructions from the Board in a letter to the union clerks, dated 26th August, 1847. Although the 11 & 12 Vic. makes the charge direct upon the unions, the guardians have continued in their books the same mode of showing the township in which those cases occur, the whole amount of the cost of the irremovable poor being carried in the union books to "common charges," and apportioned to the separate townships according to the averages, as may be seen by the abstract issued to the several townships. By reference to the finanical statement, it will be seen that the cost of the irremovable poor paid by order of the guardians by the relieving-officer of the town-ship of A., for example, was £131. 7*s.* 2*d.* The common charges account in the union ledger was therefore debited with that amount, and the township of A. in the union books got credit for it. The collective account of the irremovable poor was then apportioned to the debit of the several townships, and the A. portion, as may be seen by the half-yearly abstract, was £61. 6*s.* 3*d.* only. The cost of the irremovable poor, therefore, does not in any shape appear either in the township or parochial books, or in the half-yearly abstract delivered by the guardians to the several townships, excepting to show the separate proportion of each township under the head of common charges. In all other respects the financial statement of the A. Union is, he believes, correct, and in conformity with the directions of the Board.

9th May, 1851.

Ans.—As the statute 11 & 12 Vic. c. 110, sec. 3, (continued by subsequent statutes) constitutes the cost of the relief of irremovable poor a charge upon the common fund of the union direct, it follows that there should be no separate entry in the union accounts against any parish on account of such relief. You state indeed in reference (as the Board understand) to the A. Union that the charges for the relief of the irremovable poor do not in fact form any parochial or township charge whatever. If this be so, the Board do not see why the particular mode of entry in the union ledger described in your letter should be persevered in. The Circular of the Poor Law Commissioners of the 26th August, 1847, is mentioned as sanctioning that mode of entry. That Circular had reference to the charging of relief under 10 & 11 Vic. c. 110, (Mr. Bodkin's Act,) and in requiring that the expense which parishes might incur in the relief of a certain class of irremovable poor should be borne by the common fund of the union, the statute in effect provided for the reimbursement of the parishes, for the language of the statute implied that a charge in respect of such relief would be first incurred by them. But the case is different since the passing of 11 & 12 Vic. c 110. As already observed, the cost of the irremovable poor is thereby treated as the exclusive liability of the common fund. It is therefore no longer correct first to debit the parish with the amount of the relief, and then to credit it with the amount repaid by or transferred to common charges. If the entries in the ledger be made in the manner now pointed out as the correct mode, then as regards the Financial Statement, the only entry of the relief of irremovable poor will appear in column No. 13 among the common charges (see on this point the Board's Circular of 23rd April, 1849.)

II.—APPRENTICESHIP.—LIABILITY OF MASTER TO REPAY COST OF RELIEF GIVEN TO AN APPRENTICE.

7th June, 1851.

Clerk of Guiltcross Union.—On the 16th October, 1848, J. C., a poor boy aged fourteen years, belonging to a parish in the above-named union, was duly apprenticed by the guardians pursuant to the statute of 7 & 8 Vic. c. 112, sec. 32, to two persons as joint owners of a vessel to serve as an apprentice to the sea service till he (J. C.) should attain the age of twenty-one years. J. C., however, has come home destitute and has been admitted into the union workhouse by an order from the relieving-officer. One of the masters to whom J. C. was bound, alleges that the apprentice about eighteen months since ran away and sold all his clothes, and that he has within the last twelve months been to prison three times for theft. It appears that one of the masters is not now a shipowner. In the indenture is contained a joint covenant on the part of the masters for indemnifying the parish to which the boy belongs from all charges during the term of the apprenticeship. Inquiring whether the remaining master is bound to take the apprentice back, he having ran away; or is otherwise liable to repay to the union the expense of the boy's maintenance whilst in the union workhouse during the remainder of the term.

Ans.—As the indenture has not been cancelled nor the apprenticeship terminated (so far as the Board are informed) by any other legal means, the masters are still under obligation to provide for the apprentice, and to indemnify the parish under the last covenant of the indenture for any cost which it has been put to in the matter of the pauper's relief.

III.—ELECTION OF GUARDIANS.

1. EXPENSES—CENSUS OF 1851.

3rd Sept., 1851.

District Auditor.—Some clerks of unions in his district are of opinion that they are entitled to charge for the contested elections of guardians in April last, on the population taken on the 31st of March last, and he observed that in the Justice of the Peace, No. 27, vol. 15, page 440, an opinion was given that they are only entitled to charge upon the population of 1841, the census of 1851 not having been completed in April, which agrees with his own view of the case. Inquiring whether the charge should be made according to the population of 1841, or of that of 1851.

Ans.—The Board are of opinion that the enumeration of the census of 1851 is not available for the purpose in question, as until the returns were completely certified by the highest authority, they could not constitute a strict legal standard, and although at the time of such elections the clerks to the guardians might have been in possession of certain information, yet the Board do not consider that such information was of sufficient authority to justify them in charging the election expenses in accordance with it.

2. COMPLETION OF ELECTION OF GUARDIANS—QUALIFICATION OF CANDIDATES.

13th March, 1851.

Clerk of Newbury Union.—Requesting the opinion of the Board in reference to the election of guardians, as to when it may be said to be complete, and on or after what day the guardians should hold their first meeting. The difficulty felt will arise more particularly in cases where there is no contest in any of the parishes. In case of no contest, the election would, under Art. 9 of the General Order, be complete on the 26th March; and as by sec. 17 of 7 & 8 Vic. c. 101, the guardians for the current year continue until the election of guardians for the "succeeding year has taken place," when those for the current year will be out of office. As the guardians of this union meet weekly on Tuesdays, the first day of the new guardians' meeting should be the first of April. Now, by Art. 29 of the General Consolidated Order, the guardians shall at the first "meeting after the 15th of April elect a chairman," &c. The first meeting after the 15th will be the 22nd April. Is the board to sit without a chairman or to elect a temporary chairman, &c., for three weeks, or is it to be understood that the election, although there is no contest, is not complete until the 15th of April, and that the first day of meeting would be the 22nd. But there is a difficulty even should there be a contest. The votes would be ascertained in the course of the 9th of April, or the following day; and as soon as they are ascertained, the election, under Art. 22, is complete, and the guardians of the current year are out of office. In that case the first meeting of the new guardians should be held on the 15th; but by Art. 29, the election of a chairman cannot take place until the 22nd, being the first meeting after the 15th. Again, therefore, will it be necessary to elect on the 15th, for the day, only, a temporary chairman, or is it to be understood that the election, notwithstanding Art. 22, is not complete until the 15th. Another question will also, probably, arise in this union at the next election in reference to a candidate's qualification. A. is rated in S., as an occupier, and in N. (under the recent Act) as an owner of property; can he add the rates together to make up the qualification required? By form A to the General Consolidated Order the qualification is "being rated to any parish in the union;" by the Act 4 & 5 Wm. 4, sec. 38, the qualification is to consist in being rated to the poor rate of some parish or parishes in such union. He will be rated in more than one parish and to more than one rate.

Ans.—On the completion of the election of the guardians for any parish or parishes in the Newbury Union, the guardians then elected immediately take the place of those who previously acted for such parish or parishes, and should accordingly be summoned to attend at the next meeting of the board of guardians. If at the approaching election, there should be no contest in any parish of the union, the election for all the parishes will be completed on the 26th March; and a chairman should consequently be chosen to act *pro tem.* at the meeting or meetings of the newly-elected guardians, until the 15th April. At their first meeting after that day, the guardians should proceed to make the appointments required by Art. 29 of the General Consolidated Order. If, however, there should be a contest in any parish or parishes, that circumstance may possibly affect the course to be pursued, in regard to the appointment of a temporary chairman; but in no case are the appointments referred to in Art. 29, to be made before the first meeting after the 15th April. On the question you raise as to the qualification of a candidate under certain circumstances for the office of guardian, the Board having regard to 4 & 5 Wm. 4, c. 76, sec. 38, think it is not necessary in order to confer the legal qualification for guardian in a union, that the whole of the property in respect of which a person is assessed should be situate in the same parish. They consider that if a person be assessed to the poor-rate in two or more parishes within the union in respect of hereditaments, the aggregate annual value of which amounts to the sum fixed by the order of the Poor Law Commissioners, such person will be legally qualified. The Board think it will make no difference in this respect, though in one parish the person should be assessed as occupier, and in the other in his capacity of owner.

---

3. Refusal of Guardian to Serve.

16th April, 1852.

Clerk of South Shields Union.—In the election of guardians which has just taken place for this union, there were contests for the respective townships of South Shields and Westor, the following gentleman having been duly elected by a majority of votes, guardians for both townships, viz., J. R., J. P., B. T. W. These double returns have long been subjects of dissatisfaction to the ratepayers, inasmuch as the board of guardians is thereby weakened. None of those guardians when nominated tendered a refusal in writing or otherwise, to serve the office, nor have they done so since, but there is reason to believe that they will now formally refuse to serve for one of two townships before the clerk's return is made, if by so doing they can strengthen the board of guardians by letting in the candidates next to them on the poll. It is laid down by Mr. Lumley, in his Election Manual, 1848, p. 62, that a nominee has full power at any time to withdraw from the election, and that his refusal is available at any time until the return is made, as the Commissioners consider that to be the conclusion of the election, (3 Off. Cir. 109.) It is further laid down by Mr. Lumley, p. 63, that the refusal to serve, if given before the return is complete, has been considered by the Commissioners to have the effect of removing the party wholly from the election, and consequently that the candidate next on the poll must take the place of the person so declining to serve, (3 Off. Cir. 55, 109,) but that a refusal after the return is made is ineffectual, and does not let in the candidate next on the poll, (3 Off. Cir. 109.) The clerk, as returning officer, will withhold his return of the guardians elected until he receives the opinion of the Poor Law Board on the following points:—1. Can any of the gentlemen elected as above for the several townships of South Shields and Westor, now tender a refusal to act for one of the two townships, the clerk's return of the elected guardians of the union not having yet been made? 2. Would the effect of such partial refusal be to remove the party wholly from the election, or only partially from it, so far as regards the particular township embraced by the refusal? 3. Would the candidates next on the poll for that particular township take the place of the person so declining to serve?

Ans.—The Board are of opinion that a guardian is elected as soon as it is ascertained that he has a majority of the votes given in the election. In the cases referred to in your letter, it has been ascertained that the parties in question have a majority of votes. The Board think, therefore, that those parties cannot now tender their refusal to serve under the 5 & 6 Vic. c. 67, sec. 9, because the effect of such a refusal is to stop the election as regards the person who tenders it; whereas, according to the opinion of the Board, the election is in fact concluded in the cases adverted to, although the clerk's return, or certificate of the result, has not yet been made.

IV.—GUARDIAN.—ELIGIBILITY OF OVERSEER FOR THE OFFICE OF.

25th March, 1851.

Clerk of Stoke-upon-Trent Parish.—Inquiring whether a person who is appointed overseer of the poor can be legally a guardian of the parish if he should be elected to the office.

Ans.—The Board think that a person appointed overseer of the poor can be legally a guardian of the same parish if he be duly qualified and elected as such.

V.—GUARDIANS.

1. THE CHAIRMAN OF THE FIRST MEETING AFTER THE ANNUAL ELECTION, AND BEFORE THE APPOINTMENT OF THE CHAIRMAN FOR THE YEAR.

20th March, 1851.

Clerk of Newton Abbot Union.— Inquiring whether, after the election of the new board of guardians for the union, the clerk is not the proper person, as returning officer, to take the chair on the assembling of the new board, until they shall have elected their chairman for the ensuing year.

Ans.—The clerk (who is the officer of the guardians, and not himself a guardian or a member of the board) is not the proper person to take the chair on the occasion you refer to. The chairman and vice-chairman for the current year will continue to hold their offices respectively until the first meeting after the 15th April, unless they previously cease to be guardians by the election of other guardians in their stead, either on the 26th March, or the 9th April, as the case may be. If the chairman and vice-chairman all cease to be guardians on the 26th March, the guardians present at the next meeting should elect one of themselves to be chairman for the day, and so on, from time to time, until the first meeting after the 15th April, when the appointments for the ensuing year will be made under Art. 29 of the General Consolidated Order.

2. PRESENCE OF STRANGERS AT MEETINGS OF GUARDIANS.

19th Dec., 1851.

Clerk of Kingsbridge Union.—Inquiring whether a guardian can on application to the chairman have the board-room cleared of strangers.

Ans.—The admission of strangers to the board-room is not a matter of legal right, but is to be determined by the guardians themselves; and it is competent to any guardian to submit a motion on the subject with the view of ascertaining the opinion of the majority of the guardians as to whether any strangers who are present shall be directed to withdraw.

VI.—LUNATIC PAUPER.

1. DISPOSAL OF THE PROPERTY OF.

7th Nov., 1851.

Clerk of Great Boughton Union.—Sarah E., the wife of ——, formerly resident at Tattenhall, within this union, but now a prisoner in the jail of this county in pursuance of his sentence for felony, has become a lunatic, and been sent to the county asylum. There is a cow and some furniture belonging to the prisoner upon the premises, late in his occupation, which the lunatic's mother is about to remove. There are no children. The lunatic is in the asylum at the expense of the union, being irremovable owing to a five year's residence. Can the board of guardians make application to the justices for their interference and order to seize under 8 & 9 Vic. c. 126, s. 49?

Ans.—The property in question does not in point of law belong to the lunatic, and therefore cannot be seized under the 8 & 9 Vic. c. 126, s. 49.

2. LIABILITY OF THE PARISH OF SETTLEMENT TO PAY THE COST OF MAINTENANCE OF LUNATIC PAUPER.

25th Sept., 1851.

Clerk of York Union.—J. B., a lunatic, is settled in the parish of St. Martin, Coney Street, but was sent to a licensed house kept by Messrs. Walker & Matherson, at Heworth, in the County of York, under an order of two justices, dated July 15, 1850, and became chargeable to the parish of St. Mary, Bishophill the Elder, from which she was sent to that house. She remained there until the 2nd of April, 1851, when the guardians of the York Union having directed her to be discharged from this house, in order that she might be removed to the East and North Ridings of Yorkshire County Lunatic Asylum, an order dated the 2nd April, 1851, was obtained for her confinement in this asylum. The parish of Bishophill the Elder did not apply for an order of reimbursement upon the parish of her settlement while she was in the licensed house, but on the 4th of July, 1851, and while she was still remaining in the County Asylum, two justices of the City of York and County of the same City made an order upon the application of the former parish, which recited both the previous orders, and adjudged the settlement of the pauper to be in the parish of St. Martin, Coney Street, and ordered the overseers of the latter parish to pay, with other sums not disputed, the sum of £1. 6*s*., being the costs of the removal to the licensed house at Heworth, and the sum of £18. 13*s*., being the cost of her maintenance therein. The overseers of St. Martin, Coney Street, object to pay these sums, and contend that they are not liable because the place of confinement has been changed and the confinement itself interrupted. They rely upon the case of the R. *v.* Wolverhampton, reported in the 3 N. S. C. 683, wherein it was decided that the justices cannot make an order to adjudicate the settlement and avoid the costs in respect of a lunatic pauper, who had ceased to be in confinement.

Ans.—It appears to the Board that the order in the present case is valid. The pauper was in confinement when it was issued, and though there has been a removal of the pauper from one place of confinement to another, there has been no real interruption of the confinement itself. If the order of reimbursement may be made at all, the 62nd sec. of the 8 & 9 Vic. c. 126, authorizes the justices in making their order for the payment to the overseers of the parish from which the lunatic shall have been sent, of the expenses incurred in and about the examination and removal of the lunatic to the licensed house, together with the monies paid to the proprietor thereof and incurred within twelve calendar months previous to the date of the order. The sums now in question fall within the terms of this provision. It is not necessary to say what might have been the effect of an actual discharge of the lunatic as cured, followed at some subsequent period, owing to a recurrence of the disorder, by a perfectly new confinement under a fresh order. But to hold that the right to reimbursement of the expenses incurred within the year ceases because the pauper has been simply moved from one place of confinement to another, under a new order of justices, the actual confinement itself being really uninterrupted, would, as it appears to the Board, effect a great hardship, which the Board think the Legislature did not contemplate; and they find nothing in the statute which requires them to draw this conclusion from the language which has been used. The Board, therefore, are of opinion that the overseers of St. Martin, Coney Street, should pay the two sums set forth in the order now objected to.

VII.—POOR-RATE.—CLAIM TO BE REFUNDED A SUM PAID AS POOR-RATE.

24*th Jan*., 1851.

Mr. ——, *Tavistock.*—At Michaelmas, 1848, he took an estate situated in the parish of Tavistock, in the Barnstable Union, at the yearly rent of £380. At that time it appeared by a reference to the union and parish books, that there was a balance of about £13 standing against the parish. He continued in the occupation of his farm until Michaelmas last, when he gave it up to his landlord. On making up the Michaelmas accounts it turned out that there was a balance, on the union and parish, amounting to upwards of £300. As the whole of his rates had been duly paid up, he, of course, contributed his proportion of this large balance, such proportion being about £12; and he now feels aggrieved at having thus paid towards the expenses of the parish for a period during which he had not been in occupation. The overseers, and indeed the rate-payers generally, admit that this state of things has entailed on him much hardship, and they will gladly refund him the amount he has overpaid, provided they can legally do so.

Ans.—By law, the rates for the relief of the poor are made prospectively, and, as you were in the occupation of the premises alluded to at the time of the rates being levied, which produced the balance in favour of the parish, amounting to upwards of £300, you were liable to contribute your proportion thereof. The Board therefore do not think that the law would warrant the overseers of Tavistock in refunding any portion of such balance to you; and the Board have no power to direct them to do so. As regards persons who may remove out of, or come into the parish since the making of the last rate, the Board have to point out that the 17 Geo. 2, c. 38, sec. 12, enables the outgoing and incoming tenants, under certain circumstances, to divide the liability (so far as that particular rate is concerned) between them; but, whether the present case is one which allows of such an adjustment, the Board are not, upon the information before them, able to say.

VIII—RATING.

1. OWNERS—UNDER 13 & 14 VIC. c. 99.

3rd July, 1851.

Assistant Overseer, East Williamson, Narberth Union.—The vestry of this hamlet having adopted the provisions of the Act 13 & 14 Vic. c. 99, for assessing the owners of small tenements to the poor-rate instead of the occupiers, requested the instructions of the Board on the following points:—A tenant occupies a farm of the net rateable value of £20 under different owners, thus, under—

The owner	A	the rateable value of	£5	15	0
Do.	B	do.	6	0	0
Do.	C	do.	5	5	0
Do.	D	do.	3	0	0
		Total	£20	0	0

These several owners do not reside in the hamlet, and the tenant claims to be assessed on one-half the rateable value. Can the owners by giving the required notice claim to have the several properties separately assessed and on one-half the rateable value? 2. A tenant holds a farm of the net rateable value of £70 under one owner. This tenant occupies the greater part of the farm himself, and lets out to under tenants the remainder. Some of these under tenant have lands and some have only cottages, but neither the land nor the cottages are above £6 rateable value when taken separately. The head tenant has given notice claiming to be rated in respect of these small holdings at one-half. Can the head tenant claim the benefit of the Act in this case? As he is not the owner, how is the rate to be made out if one-half be entered against the owner, and not against the tenant? and further, can the owner himself claim to have the under tenants assessed at one-half when in fact there are no tenants direct under him, as he lets the whole to the head tenant? 3. A man bought a piece of ground and built a house thereon, in which he dwells. He is both the owner and the tenant. The rateable value is £5. 10*s*. He has no other property whatever. Can this man claim to be assessed at one-half? 4. The owner of several small tenements in this hamlet has sent notice claiming to be assessed at one-half the rateable value of the same. This owner is not resident here, and has not named a person residing in the hamlet who may be applied to for the rates. Is the assistant overseer of the hamlet to demand the rates? 5. The owner of several small tenements in this hamlet is residing in England. He has no resident agent, and has not sent any notice whatever to the overseers. It is presumed that this owner is to be rated at three-fourths of the rateable value. How are the rates to be recovered in this case? must they be demanded of the different tenants? and on their refusal to pay, must they be proceeded against by distress?

Ans.—1. If the owners of the several properties occupied as a farm at a total value of £20, give the notice required under sec. 4 of the above-cited statute, they will be severally entitled to be assessed in respect thereof upon such a sum, not exceeding three-fourths nor less than one-half of the annual rateable value, as may be agreed upon by the overseers, but if any such owner has not already given the notice he cannot give it now until next year within the fourteen days next after the 25th of March. 2. The Board consider that the head tenant (as he is called in the second case put by you) can, if he have given the notice above referred to, claim to be assessed at a sum between three-fourths and one-half for the property he has underlet in the manner described. 3 The Board are of opinion that the above Act does not apply in the case of property which is occupied by the owner himself. 4. There is much difficulty in regard to the point raised in this case as to the steps for obtaining payment of the rate, but the Board consider that you cannot distrain upon the owner's goods unless a demand for the payment of the rate has been made upon him wherever he may be residing. Whether you can distrain upon the goods of the occupier after making the demand upon him, without having made it upon the owner of the property, the Board are not prepared positively to state. 5. The owner of the tenements in this case should be assessed upon three-fourths of the rateable annual value, and as to the recovery of the rates, the Board refer you to their remarks under case 4.

---

2. RATING RAILWAY—AMENDING OF POOR-RATE AFTER THE AMOUNT HAD BEEN BROUGHT INTO AN ACCOUNT WHICH HAD BEEN CLOSED.

2nd Dec., 1851.

Secretary of the Great Western Railway Company.—In November, 1850, the overseers of Trowbridge made a poor-rate in which they assessed this company at the sum of £990 in respect of their property in the parish. The company entered an appeal against the rate at the January Quarter Sessions, which appeal was by consent adjourned till the Sessions held in July, when it was tried, and the rateable value of the company's property reduced to the sum of £140. In the meantime, and pending the appeal, the overseers made other rates, viz., one in February and one in May. The Company, believing that the subsequent rates would follow the decision of the Sessions on the rate appealed against, paid the February rate in full, the amount being £82. 10*s*. instead of £11. 13*s*. 4*d*. The May rate remained unpaid at the time of the decision on the appeal, but no appeal had been entered against it; a verbal understanding having passed between the parish officers and the officers of the company to the effect above stated. After the appeal the company claimed to have all the rates reduced, but the overseers urged that as the amount of the February rate had been carried into accounts which were closed and audited, it would be inconvenient, if not impossible, to refund the amount to the company. On this the company offered, if the overseers would reduce the May rate to the amount to which the sessions had reduced that which was the subject of the appeal, they would abandon the overpayment made on the February rate, but the overseers refused this and summoned the company for the full amount of the May rate. At the hearing on the summons, the chairman of the Petty Sessions, expressed his opinion that the overseers ought to consent to make the reduction, and to have the rate amended if it could be done. The overseers stated that they could not consent to the rate being amended, because the auditor would not allow the reduction in passing the accounts of the parish. The company contended that the parish officers might amend the rate as in the case of an error, and obtain the magistrates allowance of the correction without a formal appeal, and this being contravened by the overseers', the magistrates were requested to adjourn the case in order that the opinion of the Poor Law Board might be asked whether the auditor would be justified in refusing to pass the overseers' accounts if the May rate should be reduced to the amount fixed by the Sessions on the appeal against the November rate. The adjournment was granted, and the 3rd of December fixed for the hearing of the case. Inquiring whether the magistrates may with the consent of all parties amend the rate, and whether the auditor would be justified in passing the overseers' accounts with the reduced amount of the rate only brought to their debit; or, whether the overseers might not in fact, if they chose, write off the difference as an error in the rate, and be entitled to have their accounts passed with such reduction made.

Ans.—If an appeal had been entered at the proper sessions on behalf of the Great Western Railway Company, against the poor-rate made for the parish of Trowbridge in May last, such rate might have been then amended by the justices, as regards the assessment on the company; but the Board apprehend that neither the overseers nor the justices have any power now to amend or alter the rate in any respect. Under these circumstances, the legal obligation on the company to pay the rate, which is actually assessed upon them, and for the payment of which they have been summoned, seems to be clear and distinct. The Board would greatly regret any injustice that might result to the company from the enforcement of the rate in question, but, as at present advised, they can suggest no alternative in the case.

---

3. RATING GAS WORKS, LUNATIC ASYLUM, AND MARKET HALL.

8 *Jan.*, 1851.

Joseph Lloyd, Esq., Kilford, Denbigh.—Submitting the following questions in regard to the rating of certain properties in the parish of Denbigh:—1. Gas works established by a company, the buildings, etc., of which, although close to the town, are in an adjoining parish, about fifty yards from the boundary of the two parishes, but the pipes are laid in the town of Denbigh and all the profits of the works are derived from the inhabitants of Denbigh. To what extent can the overseers assess the portion of the works which is in the parish of Denbigh? 2. The North Wales lunatic asylum built at the joint expense of five counties, and with the assistance of some private subscriptions is in the parish of Denbigh. The private patients in the institution are divided into two classes, first and second, while the remainder are pauper lunatics. In this extensive building, erected at the cost of upwards of £30,000, are necessarily a large establishment of keepers, servants, and other officers of various denominations. How far will the overseers be justified in rating this property? 3. A new market hall and assembly room the property of the corporation of Denbigh. As to this property it is contended that the overseers are not justified in assessing it in the same ratio as other property in the parish because it is mortgaged. How should the property be rated?

Ans.—1. The gas company are rateable in the parish of Denbigh to the extent to which they are occupiers of land in that parish by reason of the pipes there laid down, see (Rex *v.* Brighton Gas Company, 5 B & C 466 and other cases.) The Board are not prepared to express any opinion as to what portion of the profits of the company may be derived from the occupation of the land in Denbigh, and, at what amount they ought to be rated in that parish in respect of that occupation. 2. The county lunatic asylum is rateable to the poor rate, but cannot be assessed on a higher value or more improved rent than the value or rent at which the lands whereon the buildings are erected were assessed at the time of their purchase, (see 8 & 9 Vic. c. 126, sec. 25.) 3. Assuming the liability of the corporation of Denbigh to be rated to the poor rate in respect of the new market hall, the Board do not think that the fact of the property being mortgaged would in itself render it rateable at a less amount, or lower ratio than other property in the parish, unless the yearly letting value were thereby reduced.

---

4. RATING—ARREARS OF OLD POOR RATES—NEW RATE.

17*th May*, 1851.

Overseers of Rowley Regis.—Before making out another rate book, the overseers are desirous of obtaining information on the following points:—Are columns No. 16 and 17 of the present rate book to have their amounts transferred to column No. 2 of the new rate, as well as the amounts of column No. 15, and if so how are the Overseers to act in the following cases? 1. Widow B. is excused payment for a house, No. 2427, and leaves the parish. C. D. enters upon the house, No. 2427, having previously occupied a house, No. 96, for which he has paid the rate. How is the amount excused in No. 2427, column 16, of the present rate book, to be transferred to column 2 of the new rate book? Is the word excused to be written against one who has paid all his rates? 2. Against house, No. 238, occupied by E. F., there appears a sum in column 17. This house is taken down. Is this sum to be transferred to column No. 2 of the new rate book? 3. Are amounts "legally excused" in the present rate, to be carried to column No. 2 of the new rate, if the same parties are assessed therein?

Ans.—1. When a new poor rate is made, the mode of dealing with the arrears due from any rate-payer in respect of former rates will depend upon the fact whether such ratepayer is assessed in the new rate or not. If he be so assessed, the arrears should be carried forward in the new rate against him, but if he be not included in such rate, some other person being assessed in his stead in respect of the same property, the arrears due from the former cannot be carried forward as against the latter. The same remark will apply to rates excused. In the case put by you, (1) rates assessed on Widow B., and duly excused, ought not to be carried forward into the next rate, in which widow B. will not be included. In the case 2, the occupier, E.F., may continue to be rated for the premises, although the house may be taken down; and if so, the arrears due on the assessment of the property in its previous state should be brought forward, and entered in column 2 in the new rate, though the rateable value of the property in that rate may be less than in former assessments. 3. The amounts of poor rate legally excused in the present rate are not to be carried forward to column No. 2 of the new rate even if the same parties are assessed in both rates in respect of the same property.

IX—RELIEF.

1. CHARGING MEDICAL RELIEF.

29*th Dec.*, 1851.

The Rev. H. W. T., Ilfracombe.—Inquiring whether the cost of medical attendance on union paupers ought to be charged to the union or to the parish in the following cases:—1. A person who had resided for more than five years in a parish to which he did not belong was taken ill and an application was made to the relieving or parish officer for a medical order which was obtained. An application was made also to the guardians for relief, who being satisfied that the pauper was chargeable to the union ordered the cost of his maintenance to be paid out of the union funds. 2. A person suffering from sickness or accident not likely to produce permanent disability had first medical attendance and then other relief.

Ans.—In both of these cases the cost of the relief should be charged in the accounts in like manner as the cost of any other relief given to the paupers, (see the 11 & 12 Vic. c. 110, sec. 3.) If the paupers in the two cases in question are irremoveable (having become chargeable through temporary sickness,) their ordinary relief is chargeable to the common fund of the union, provided they are not settled in the parishes in which they reside.

---

2. CHARGING MEDICAL RELIEF GRANTED BEFORE THE GUARDIANS HAD ASCERTAINED THAT THE PAUPER WAS CHARGEABLE TO THE COMMON FUND.

30*th May*, 1851.

Clerk of Festiniog Union.—William, aged 12, son of David Griffith, residing the parish of Llanfihangel y Traethau in this union, met with a serious accident, obtained a medical order, and had his arm amputated. The meeting of the guardians was held the next day after the arm was amputated, when David Griffith attended to be examined. He has resided constantly in Llanfihangel y Traethau during the last seventeen years, without parochial relief, and is settled elsewhere. The guardians admitted him to be irremoveable, and his relief thenceforth to be payable out of the common fund. Before admitting paupers to be relieved out of the common fund the guardians have always required the paupers to attend to be examined at the Board, or that their examinations should be taken by the clerk, and read at the board. As soon as the guardians are satisfied, the poor are thenceforth relieved out of the common fund, but the guardians have not been in the habit of reimbursing out of the common fund to the parishes any relief previously advanced. According to the practice of the Board, the fee for amputating the arm of William Griffith should be paid by the parish of residence, inasmuch as he was not at the time chargeable to the union. On behalf of the parish it is contended that under the circumstances the fee ought to be charged to the common fund. The guardians request to be informed whether, in point of law, the fee should be charged to the parish or to the common fund?

Ans.—The Board collect from your letter, that when the guardians of the Festiniog Union have ascertained that a pauper is irremoveable, they charge his future relief to the common fund of the union, but do not reimburse out of that fund any relief which may have been previously advanced and charged to a particular parish. The Board, in the first place, have to point out that the practice thus pursued by the guardians is not altogether correct. When a pauper applies for and obtains relief, he is at that time legally chargeable either to some particular parish in the union, or to the common fund. It is therefore necessary that the guardians should ascertain as soon as possible in what manner his relief ought to be charged, and when they have done so, they should charge to the same fund (whether that of the union or any parish therein,) all the relief which he may have previously received, as well as that which may be afterwards afforded to him. Where the guardians may not be able to determine the question of the pauper's chargeability immediately on his first receiving relief, the most convenient course will be to enter the relief in the relieving officer's and in the relief order book, as a charge upon the parish of the pauper's abode; but no entry need be made in the general or parochial ledger, until it has been ascertained to what fund the relief is to be charged. When this has been ascertained, the requisite entry may be made in the ledger accordingly. It may be added that if the relief be charged to a parish in the first instance, and it be afterwards ascertained that it was so charged wrongly, the error should at once be corrected, so far as regards the accounts of the current quarter, but such correction, of course, cannot extend to any accounts that have been closed and audited. With regard to the present case, the Board are of opinion upon the statement before them, that the whole of the relief afforded to David Griffith should be charged to the common fund of the Festiniog Union.

---

3. RELIEF IN CLOTHING TO A GIRL GOING INTO SERVICE—PROCEEDINGS UNDER THE VAGRANT ACT AGAINST THE FATHER.

29th Aug., 1851.

Clerk of Axminster Union.—The guardians have procured a place of service for Elizabeth G., a girl 14 years of age, who has for several years been an inmate of the workhouse. Prior to her going into service it will be necessary that she should be supplied with certain articles of clothing, the cost of which will be about 25*s*. Requesting the sanction of the Board to the guardians supplying her with such clothing accordingly. The circumstances of the case as follow:—The girl is the only child of a man named Matthew G., of Axminster, labourer, who is considered by the relieving officer an able-bodied man. This man is well known to have no constant work, but is a hanger-on at different inns in the town, and is said to earn very little wages and the greater part of what he does earn he spends in drink. He has been brought before the magistrates to show cause why he should not be compelled to maintain his child, but inasmuch as the overseers failed to prove his ability to support the child the case was dismissed. Requesting the advice of the Board as to how the guardians should deal with the man.

Ans.—The Board having regard to the circumstances of the case, sanction an outfit of clothing to the value of twenty-five shillings being supplied by the guardians to the girl Elizabeth G. on her going to a place of service. The Board observe in your letter the following statement with respect to the father of this girl:—"He has been brought before the magistrates to show cause why he should not be compelled to maintain his child; but inasmuch as the overseers failed to prove the ability of the father to support the child, the case was dismissed." The Board request to be informed more distinctly as to the nature of the proceedings which were taken before the magistrates on the occasion alluded to, whether they were taken under the 43 Eliz. c. 2, sec. 7, with a view to obtain an order upon the man requiring him to contribute towards his daughter's support, or under the 5 Geo. 4, c. 83, with a view to the infliction of the penalties imposed by that Act. If the latter were the case, the Board will be glad to know whether the man was charged under sec. 3 with neglecting or refusing to maintain his daughter, being of ability to do so; or under sec. 4, with running away and leaving her chargeable.

23rd Sept., 1851.

Clerk of same union.—Matthew G., the father of the girl Elizabeth G., was summoned before the magistrates under the vagrant Act of 5 Geo. 4, c. 83, sec. 3, on the information of the overseers, "for, that being a person able to work and maintain himself and family, did wilfully neglect so to do, whereby his daughter had become chargeable to the parish of Axminster, and was then actually chargeable thereto."

Ans.—Upon the complaint made by the overseers in the case you refer to, under the 5 Geo. 4, c. 83, sec. 3, the magistrates were bound to ascertain whether the father of the girl, Elizabeth G., had the ability to maintain his child. They appear to have decided in the negative, and the Board see no reason to suppose that the justices came to wrong conconclusion in the matter. There is nothing in the correspondence before the Board to show that Matthew G. deserted his child; but she requiring relief was admitted by the guardians into the Axminster union workhouse without her father. They might have required him to come into the workhouse at the same time, and this course would have been in accordance with the law, and the order of the Poor Law Commissioners. The Board, however, presume that the girl is now in service, and therefore no longer in receipt of relief; and under these circumstances, it does not seem necessary at present to consider the question raised by the guardians as to any further proceedings to be taken against the father.

4. RELIEF TO PERSONS POSSESSED OF FREEHOLD COTTAGES.

21st August, 1851.

Clerk of Cardigan Union.—Inquiring whether weekly allowances can be legally made to individuals on their assigning over their freehold cottages to the overseers of the poor of the parish making such allowances to them, such assignment to be made upon trust to sell the cottages on the death of the parties making the same, but the paupers to continue in possession during their lives.

Ans.—The overseers have no legal authority to make weekly allowances of relief to any poor persons; and the Board cannot acquiesce in their becoming the owners of any property of the kind in question, under the circumstances to which you refer. It rests with the guardians of the union to determine whether the parties in possession of the freehold cottages are proper objects of relief. Certainly, as a general rule persons possessed of property cannot be considered as coming within the class of destitute persons, for whose benefit the poor-rate is provided. In some cases, however, it may be that such property, from the incumbrances and charges to which it may be subject, is an actual disadvantage to the owner; in others, that the benefit derived from it is very inconsiderable. It will be necessary for the guardians to discriminate between the different cases, and to decide in each according to the circumstances, whether they will refuse relief altogether, or grant it either absolutely, or upon condition that the applicant shall dispose of his property.

---

5. RELIEF OUT OF THE WORKHOUSE UNDER SEC. 27 OF 4 & 5 WM. 4, C. 76.

16*th Jan.*, 1851.

J. R. Hogg, Esq., Brixham, Devon.—By statute 4 & 5 Wm. 4, cap. 76, sec. 27, it appears that two magistrates may direct that relief shall be given to any adult person, who shall from old age or infirmity be wholly unable to work, without requiring that such person shall reside in any workhouse, provided that one justice shall certify of his own knowledge that the person is wholly unable to work, and provided that such person shall be lawfully entitled to relief, and shall desire to receive the same out of the workhouse. Inquiring,—1. Whether the Poor Law Commissioners have issued any General Order with reference to this section. 2. Whether, if all the required provisions of the clause are complied with, the justices can order such relief in kind or quantity, as may be deemed necessary for the actual requirements of the case, that is, such relief as is *bonâ fide* sufficient for the maintenance of the pauper.

Ans.—1. Neither the Poor Law Commissioners nor the Poor Law Board have issued any Order affecting specially the class of cases to which the enactment alluded to applies. 2. The Board believe that the true construction of the section in question is, that although the justices may direct relief to be given to the pauper without requiring him to reside in the workhouse, the guardians have the legal power of determining in all other respects the kind and amount of the relief to be afforded.

6. RELIEF TO AN ABLE-BODIED WOMAN DESERTED BY HER HUSBAND.

3*rd Dec.*, 1851.

Clerk of Chesterton Union.—An able-bodied woman whose husband has deserted her and it is believed is now in America, and who has 5 children of the respective ages of 10, 6, 4, 2 years and three months, to support, applied this day to the board for relief, and the guardians ordered her out-relief to the amount of 4*s.* in money and 2*s.* 4*d.* in kind. It is clear she cannot maintain this family, but none of the exceptions in the General Prohibitory Order appear to authorize the guardians in giving out-door relief in such a case as the present. He, the clerk, had therefore informed the guardians it would be his duty to report the case to the Poor Law Board for their sanction, if they granted out-door relief to the woman. Requested the sanction of the Board to the guardians giving to the family such out-door relief as they shall from time to time deem requisite according to the circumstances of the case.

Ans.—If there is sufficient evidence of the husband being in America, the case would come within Art. 4 of the Prohibitory Order, and the guardians might give relief as in the case of a widow. If it cannot be shown that the man is beyond the seas, but he is still not residing within the union, the case would come within Exception 8 to Art. 1 of the Order, and the guardians might, if they thought fit, allow out-door relief for the children under the age of nurture.

X.—REMOVABILITY.

1. BREACH OF RESIDENCE BY GOING TO AN INFIRMARY AND AFTERWARDS TO THE SEA-SIDE FOR THE PURPOSE OF SEA-BATHING.

6*th July*, 1851.

Clerk of Amesbury Union.—Transmitting the following statement duly signed under the 11 & 12 Vic. c. 110, sec. 4, for the opinion of the Poor Law Board:—Jessie —— was born a bastard in the Westbury union workhouse, on the 27th of Sept., 1839. She was removed with her mother Amelia —— to Orcheston St. George by order of justices on the 5th of November, 1839, and both mother and daughter were on the 8th of the same month admitted into the Amesbury union workhouse where they remained until the 13th of January, 1840, the cost of their maintenance being charged to the parish of Orcheston St. George. They were readmitted into the Amesbury union workhouse on the

3rd of February, 1840, and discharged again on the 17th of the same month. They then went to reside in the parish of Shrewton, and both lived there from the 17th of February, 1840, to the 17th of January, 1849, when the mother died there. Relief was given to the mother and child for one week in the early part of November, 1845, which was charged to the parish of Orcheston St. George; and in consequence of the illness of the mother, relief was subsequently given to them in the first week of November, 1847, and continued weekly until the 17th of January, 1849, when the mother died, and such relief was charged to the parish of Shrewton where they lived. After the death of her mother, Jessie —— continued to reside in the parish of Shrewton, living with an aunt, and her relief was charged to that parish until the 17th of February, 1849, when she was admitted an in-patient of the Salisbury infirmary, which is situate in the parish of Fisherton Anger, and there she remained until the 14th of April, 1849. On her leaving the infirmary, she returned to Shrewton to her aunt, and remained there until the 27th of October, 1849, receiving relief weekly, such relief being charged from the 14th of April to the 12th of May, to the parish of Shrewton, but from that period charged to the common fund of the union. On the 27th of October, 1849, she was a second time admitted to the Salisbury infirmary, and continued an in-patient there until the 25th of May, 1850, when she was discharged and went to the parish of Mudiford in the county of Southampton, for the benefit of sea-bathing, and at the expense of the president of the infirmary. She remained at Mudiford until the 29th of September, 1850, when she returned to Shrewton, and was removed from thence to the Amesbury union workhouse on the 27th of November, 1850, where she now is, her relief having been since that time charged to the parish of Orcheston St. George, on the ground of her irremovability from Shrewton being broken by her residence upon two occasions, as has been stated, in the parish of Fisherton Anger whilst at the Salisbury infirmary, and by her residence from May to October, 1850, in the parish of Mudiford. The said Jessie —— was not sent to the infirmary by the board of guardians but admitted on the ordinary recommendation of a governor upon each occasion. Is the pauper under the circumstances detailed in the foregoing statement exempt in pursuance of the 9 & 10 Vic. c. 66 from the liability to be removed to the place of such pauper's settlement?

Ans.—The Board consider that the pauper's temporary abode in the parishes of Fisherton Anger and Mudiford, for the sole purpose of the recovery of her health at the Salisbury infirmary, and by means of sea-bathing, did not, legally speaking, operate as an interruption of her residence in the parish of Shrewton.

---

2. BREACH OF RESIDENCE BY LONG ABSENCE OCCASIONED BY SICKNESS.

3rd Dec., 1851.

Clerk of St. Columb Major Union.—Submitting the following statement duly signed under sec. 4 of the 11 & 12 Vic. c. 110, for the opinion of the Poor Law Board:—Jane Trathan, an aged pauper, states that she has lived in the parish of Newlyn about eight years, and that she never received any parochial relief until within a few weeks since. That at the time she came into the said parish of Newlyn, and from that time, until about three or four months since, she lived with her son, who about that time left and went to Australia, when the pauper went to reside with a daughter who also lived in the said parish of Newlyn. That about a year and a half since, the pauper having two daughters living at a place called Hayle, in the western part of this country, went on a visit to one of them, having as she alleges the intention to return again to her said son with whom she was then living. That whilst she was at Hayle, she was taken ill and was confined to her bed for six or seven weeks. She remained there six or seven, (or it may be more,) months, but says, "I should not have abided there so long if it had not been for my illness. I came home to my son's as soon as I got able." On leaving her son's, the pauper states that she carried away a change of clothes in a handkerchief but left her box and other clothes at her son's which she did not afterwards send for. That she had lived with her son for eight years before, and had no one else to rely on. Whilst at Hayle the pauper was maintained by her daughter's husband there. The guardians contend that the pauper having been absent from the parish of Newlyn for so long a time, and having been resident at Hayle during all that time, where she was maintained and supported by her daughters in the same manner as she had previously been at Newlyn by her son, had committed such a breach of residence as to render her removable to the place of her legal settlement. On the other hand, the parish contends that the pauper leaving her clothes &c. behind, and always intending to return again to her son's, which she in fact did, had not committed a breach of residence, although the time of her absence was a long one.

Ans.—The Board are of opinion that there was only a temporary absence in this case, and no breach of residence in point of law; and consequently that the pauper is now irremovable from the parish of Newlyn.

3. DITTO.

14th June, 1850.

Clerk of Pateley Bridge Union.—Transmitting the following statement duly signed under the 11 & 12 Vic. c. 110, s. 4, for the opinion of the Poor Law Board:—J. H., a young man nineteen years of age, is the son of W. H., and living with his parents in the township of Hartwith-cum-Winsley, in this union, where they have resided more than six years without relief. About a year ago he was attacked with illness, which rendered him incapable of labour. On the 20th day of Nov., 1849, he was sent to the General Infirmary at Leeds, where he remained until the 22nd of January following, when he was discharged and returned to his father's house. His settlement, derived from his parents, is in the township of High and Low Bishopside in this union. Inquiring whether the residence of J. H. was broken by his being at Leeds, and also whether he is now removable or not.

Ans.—It is not necessary to inquire how far the pauper's residence was interrupted by his abode in the infirmary at Leeds, because his father, with whom he now resides, is, according to the statement, irremovable from Hartwith-cum-Winsley, and if so, then, by force of the statute 11 & 12 Vic. c. 111, the pauper himself is also irremovable, and consequently the cost of his relief is chargeable to the common fund of the Pateley Bridge Union.

4. REMOVABILITY OF PAUPER CHARGEABLE TO THE COMMON FUND.

24th Jan., 1851.

Clerk of Crediton Union.—Transmitted the following resolution passed by the board of guardians:—"The clerk having laid before the board a letter from the Poor Law Board of the 10th instant, stating that the fact of the pauper William Northcote being chargeable to the common fund of the union prevented his being removable to the parish of his settlement, as an order of removal must be founded on a chargeability to some parish, and that the guardians had no authority in law to obtain orders of removal,—Ordered, that the clerk do refer the Poor Law Board to the note appended to the 1st sec. of the 11 & 12 Vic. c. 110, in Archbold's Buller's Acts of 1848, and to the 3rd sec. of the 12 & 13 Vic. c. 103," with a view to their reconsideration of the case.

Ans.—The Board are aware of the opinion expressed by Mr. Archbold in his edition of the statute in question. They are not able, however, to concur in that opinion, nor, in fact, does the same view appear to be expressed in the last edition of Mr. Archbold's Poor Law. The statute 13 & 14 Charles 2nd, and subsequent statutes, by which the removal of paupers to their place of settlement is authorized and regulated, confine the power of removal to the case where the person becomes actually chargeable to some parish or township, the order being there made upon the complaint of the churchwardens and overseers of such parish or township. In the case of destitute wayfarers and wanderers, apart from the consideration that they do not come to abide or settle in the sense of the 13 & 14 Charles 2nd, their relief is expressly made chargeable, not upon any parish or township, but on the common fund of a different district, namely, the union. The Board apprehend, therefore, that as in this class of cases no such chargeability exists as is contemplated by the statutes referred to, it would have required express statutory powers to enable the removal of a person chargeable to a union. No such power has, however, been given either to the guardians or other officers.

5. REMOVABILITY OF DESTITUTE WANDERER.

5th August, 1850.

Clerk of Newton Abbot Union.—Transmitted the following statement duly signed under the 11 & 12 Vic. c. 110, c. 4, for the opinion of the Poor Law Board:—E. A. G., a female pauper about twenty years old. When an infant about a fortnight old, she was found in the parish of St. Mary Church in this union, where she had been abandoned. Her parents were never discovered. She was maintained in the said parish of St. Mary Church until the union was formed, when she was sent into the union workhouse at the charge of the said parish, where she remained until fit for service. For the last nine or ten years she has lived in several parishes of this union as a servant. A short time since she left the union workhouse, and went into the parish of Denbury to reside as a servant, and lived with a farmer there about a fortnight; came away from thence with about 3*s*. wages into the parish of Wolborough, where she slept one night, and having lost and expended the said money in the said parish of Wolborough, she was received into the union workhouse, (situate in Wolborough) and charged to that parish. Since that, she left the workhouse, and went into the service of a farmer in the parish of Teignrace, with whom she lived and served about ten days, at the end of which time she left and again came into the parish of Wolborough with 3*s*., which she had received for wages. With this money she bought a pair of shoes and hose at shops in the said parish, and slept there one night; the next day she applied to the relieving-officer of Highweek, at his house there, who gave her an order for one night's relief as a vagrant, and told her she must apply to the board at their next meeting. She refused to accept this offer, and (as she states) walked about the streets and roads all night, and next morning applied for relief to the relieving-officer at Wolborough at his residence at Kingskerswell, who took her case down and ordered her to attend the board, (who met on the same day,) where she attended, and the board admitted her into the workhouse again at the charge of Wolborough. A few days after she left the workhouse and went to Ashburton in quest of a situation, where she slept, (paying for her bed with part of the proceeds of the sale of a pair of shoes.) She then went to Bovey Tracey, and not succeeding in procuring a place, she returned to the parish of Wolborough, where, having no means to pay for a bed, she slept in a linhay, and afterwards went to the relieving-officer at Kingskerswell, who gave her an order for the workhouse, where she now is at the charge of the parish of Wolborough. She states that her object in returning from her place of service to Wolborough was, that she might the more readily obtain admission into the union workhouse situate in that parish.

Ans.—The Board consider that in this case the pauper is a destitute wanderer, the cost of whose relief should be charged to the common fund of the Newton Abbot Union.

XI.—SMOKING IN WORKHOUSE.

29th Nov., 1851.

Clerk of —— Union.—Requesting the sanction of the Board to the use of tobacco being continued in the workhouse, the charge for which had been objected to by the district auditors, who reported to the guardians as follows:—"In the course of my examination of the books of the master, my attention was again attracted by a charge, which I may observe is a most unusual one, for tobacco. I am informed that this charge arose from, and has been continued in consequence of a recommendation (some years since) of the medical officer of your workhouse. The charge for tobacco during the half-year last past amounted to the sum of £3. 6*s*. 2*d*. I allude to this charge in consequence of perceiving that the weekly cost per head of the in-door paupers in the ——— Union is still considerably above that of other unions in my district, and I deem it right to direct your attention thereto with a view to an inquiry as to the cause."

Ans.—The Board cannot sanction the practice of smoking tobacco in the workhouse under the authority of the guardians only, since it is provided by Article 121, of the General Consolidated Order that no pauper shall smoke in any room of the workhouse except by the special direction of the medical officer. They desire to point out, however, that if the deprivation of smoking tobacco be likely to be injurious to the health of any inmate, it is open to the medical officer to direct the use of tobacco in any particular case. But such direction must be entered in the workhouse medical relief book as an extra allowance rendered necessary by the state of the pauper's health.

XII.—STAMP DUTY.—SECURITIES UNDER THE PAROCHIAL ASSESSMENT ACT.

10th March, 1851.

Clerk of Ely Union.—Inquiring whether the general exemption from stamp duty which applies to contracts and securities entered into under the Poor Law Amendment Act, extends also to securities given under the Parochial Assessments Act for the expense of a survey and valuation.

Ans.—The Board are of opinion that by force of the 5 & 6 Vic. c. 57, sec. 18, the exemption as to stamp duty in the 4 & 5 Wm. 4. 76, sec. 86 is extended to proceedings under the Parochial Assessments Act.

XIII. — VACCINATION. — RE-VACCINATION WHEN THE EFFECT OF THE FIRST VACCINATION HAS CEASED.

23rd Dec., 1851.

Clerks of Linton Union.—It being a very common opinion that the effect of vaccination ceases after seven years, have the medical officers of the union a discretionary power to vaccinate persons in their districts every seven years or oftener if they consider it necessary, and make the usual charges for the same?

Ans.—It appears to the Board somewhat doubtful whether, on a strict construction of the terms of the vaccination contracts, the vaccinators would be able to enforce their claim to remuneration for cases which they may have re-vaccinated. Having, however, regard to the object of the contracts and of the Act of Parliament under which they were framed, namely, the prevention of small-pox, the Board consider that it will not be expedient to refuse the fee on re-vaccination in cases where the guardians may be satisfied that the re-vaccination has really taken place, and has been successful.

XIV.—VALUATION.—PAYMENT OF EXPENSES INCURRED IN THE VALUATION OF PART OF A PARISH.

14th April, 1851.

Clerk of Hertford Union.—Transmitting minutes of the proceedings of the board of guardians. "11th January, 1851.—A request in writing under the hands of the churchwardens and overseers of the poor of the parish of Walkern having this day been presented to this Board, requesting the Board to sanction the appointment of E. L. for the purpose of revising a part of the old assessment in consequence of the new inclosure of part of that parish the same is approved and sanctioned accordingly." "29th March, 1851.—Resolved that a sum of £8. 17*s*. 9*d*. for expenses of a valuation made of part of the rateable property of the parish of Walkern, according to a resolution of this Board made on 11th January last be approved and paid, but as on reading the Act 11 & 12 Vic. c. 110, sec. 7, this board doubts of the proper way of paying and charging the expenses, the clerk is directed to inquire of the Poor Law Board their directions on the subject."

Ans.—The proper course of proceeding to be adopted in this matter appears to the Board to be as follows:—The guardians of the Hertford Union, having caused the valuation in question to be made, should themselves pay the valuer what is due to him under his contract, and should charge the amount of such payment to the account of the parish of Walkern in the union ledger. In order to provide the funds for this expenditure, the guardians should make an order upon the overseers of Walkern to pay the required sum to the union treasurer, as the present case appears to be one in which the overseers, who applied for the valuation, are the parties chargeable with the expenses under the provisions of the enactment alluded to.

XV.—WORKHOUSE MASTER.

10th May, 1851.

Clerk of Pembroke Union.—Inquiring what entry the master of the workhouse should make in his "Report Book" with respect to any infant which may be left at the door of the workhouse, or brought to him from elsewhere, in an exposed and deserted state, (the parentage being unknown,) whether the child should be entered as chargeable to the parish in which it was found, or whether the child should be entered on the "common charges," until the next meeting of the board after the discovery of the exposed child.

Ans.—The Board think the best course to be pursued is for the master to make no entry as to the chargeability of the child, but leave a blank in the column of the above book which is applicable to that part of the case, until it has been brought before the guardians at their next meeting, and they have decided as to the parish or the fund liable in respect of the cost of the relief.

London: Printed by Order of the Poor Law Board, by BLACKBURN & BURT, 90½, Holborn Hill, and Published by CHARLES KNIGHT, 90, Fleet Street.

AN

OFFICIAL CIRCULAR

OF PUBLIC DOCUMENTS AND INFORMATION:

DIRECTED BY THE POOR LAW BOARD TO BE PRINTED, CHIEFLY FOR THE USE OF THE BOARDS OF GUARDIANS AND THEIR OFFICERS.

No. 50.] [N.S.

CONTENTS.

I.—ACCOUNTS. — 1. AUDITOR'S DUTY IN AUDITING ACCOUNTS OF DEFAULTING OVERSEER.

31*st Jan.*, 1852.

District Auditor. — Requested the Board's advice as to the course he should pursue under the following circumstances:—C. J. was appointed overseer of the Township of Moreton in March, 1850, in conjunction with D. H. C. J.

having served the office before, and D. H. being an illiterate man, the former undertook to transact the business of the township. C. J. made a rate on the 4th of May, 1850, and obtained its allowance by two justices, having affixed the name of D. H. thereto without his knowledge. The rate amounted to £44. 19*s*. 7½*d*., and was collected in due course by C. J., with the exception of a few empty houses, and cases of excusal from payment on account of poverty. The death of the late auditor of the district prevented the Lady-day audit from taking place till the 9th September. C. J. in the mean time became insolvent, and his effects were sold by his landlord, who after deducting what was due to him for rent, handed the balance, amounting to £32. 7*s*. 7¾*d*., to the present overseers of Moreton. At the Lady-day audit, D. H. attended and stated these facts; but he, the auditor, thought it his duty nevertheless to certify the balance due from the overseers as it stands in their accounts, viz., £21. 11*s*., besides the £32. 7*s*. 7¾*d*. C. J. is now in low circumstances working for his daily bread. On the 16th December, 1851, the parish books were submitted to him, the auditor, by the assistant overseer, not made up or verified, when he required that this should be done, and that the balance of £53. 18*s*. 7*d*., due from the late overseers, C. J. and D. H. should be entered therein. On the assistant overseer laying the accounts before the present overseers, they refused to verify them, being unwilling to take upon themselves the liability to pay the sum of £21. 11*s*., which is due from the former overseers. Although a meeting of rate-payers have unanimously absolved D. H. from any loss occasioned by C. J.'s failure, yet he, the auditor, does not feel justified in taking cognizance of that fact without the sanction of the Poor Law Board. D. H. considers that under the authority of the cases R. *v*. Justices of Essex, 3 B. & Ad. 941, and R. *v*. Justices of Gloucestershire, 1 B. & Ad. 1, he cannot be made liable for the default of C. J.

Ans.—The Board think the course you took when the accounts were presented to you on the 16th December last, was not altogether correct, having regard to the 7 & 8 Vic. c. 101, sec. 33. If the account was in a shape that allowed of its being audited at all, the Board think this should have been done. Any alteration that might have been needed in the accounts in consequence of the omission of any sum, or item, which ought to have been entered as a debit, should have been made by yourself as auditor, by way of surcharge upon the party accounting. The Board presume that you adjourned the audit; and they think it will be best now to call on the overseers of the township to submit such an account as they are prepared to verify. As regards the case which has occasioned the immediate application to the Board, they feel a difficulty in advising you as to including or otherwise a particular item in the account, seeing that they may be appealed to hereafter by any party dissatisfied with your decision. They may state generally that they do not think that the overseers of one year can be debited, (that is surcharged,) with a balance certified to be due from preceding overseers, (the two sets of overseers being different persons,) such balance not having in fact been paid over or come into the possession of the first-mentioned overseers.

2. MODE OF ENTERING IN ACCOUNTS INCREASED DIET ALLOWED TO ABLE-BODIED WOMEN SUCKLING CHILDREN.

30*th July*, 1852.

Workhouse Master, Whittlesey.—The medical officer of the workhouse, in March last, recommended the guardians to adopt for the women suckling children, the diet, No. 2, form R, of the Consolidated Order, as containing a larger allowance of meat than the ordinary house diet. The guardians having sanctioned the proposed alteration, the medical officer commenced entering the names of such women in the medical relief book, (form 2,) separately from the sick, and at the end of the week, the total quantities of provisions, &c., consumed, were carried by him, the master, to the "Weekly Provisions Consumption Account," (form 26 of the Accounts Order) in the same manner as the "Sick as per Medical Relief Book," in the same form. The Poor Law Inspector objects to this manner of entering the provisions consumed by this class of paupers, stating that the number of individuals and the quantities consumed should be entered separately in "the Daily Provisions Consumption Account" (form 25). This form, however, does not contain a sufficient number of columns for the purpose. Requested the opinion of the Board as to the proper way of accounting for the consumption of provisions by the class of paupers above-mentioned.

Ans.—The Board think that the paupers referred to are certainly not to be entered among the sick, and should not appear in the Workhouse Medical Relief Book, (form 2.) The forms in the Order for Accounts issued to the united parishes of Whittlesey do not deviate from those which have been prescribed in the General Order for Accounts; and, the Board consider that the proper course to be pursued in respect of paupers of the description referred to is to enter them on the line marked thus † in the "Daily Provisions Consumption Account," in conformity with the instructions at the foot of the form (No. 25).

---

3. ACCOUNTS—FINANCIAL STATEMENT.

28th April, 1851.

District Auditor.—Referred to the Board's Circulars of the 4th April, 1851, addressed to District Auditors, and the 23rd April, 1849, and 15th of March, 1850, addressed to Boards of Guardians, relative to the mode of preparing the Financial Statement, form 17. The example given by the Board shows how to treat the credit that appears in the common charges for the amount repaid by the Paymaster General, but it does not show how, for instance, a credit that may arise from the sale of broken stones, or the profit of "garden account," &c. should be dealt with, such receipts being carried to the credit of common charges, and the parishes and townships thereby deriving benefit according to their respective averages. When any credit appears in the common charges, the same is deducted from the given amount, and the balance is divided among the several parishes and townships in the union according to the averages; consequently, unless some provision, such as that made respecting the treasury repayment, is made for such credits, there will be a difficulty in stating the "principal particulars of other common charges," so that the total of the statement and the total of column 13 shall exactly correspond. He has at former audits dealt with such credits precisely in the manner the Board intends that the treasury repayment shall be treated. Inquired whether this course is the correct one.

Ans.—The credits arising in the account of common charges, other than the amounts repaid by the treasury, being generally very small, may either be confined to the common charges account in the union ledger, and deducted from the sum to be divided; or, they may be entered in the financial statement in the same manner as the repayment made by the treasury.

---

4. ACCOUNTS.—CHARGING "EXTRA MEDICAL FEES."

18th June, 1852.

Clerk of Preston Union.—Inquired whether the extra medical fees, directed by the General Consolidated Order to be paid in particular cases, should be charged to the common fund of the union, or to the several parishes to which the paupers in respect of whom such fees are payable, belong; or, whether they should be entered in the general ledger and the financial statement as extra medical fees.

Ans.—The General Order for Accounts, specifies "extra medical fees" as one of the headings in the union ledger; and in the financial statement there is a column set apart for the entry of these payments, as "charged to the parishes." They are in fact payments made in respect of particular paupers, and can, therefore, be distinctly allocated; and they have always been regarded by the Poor Law Commissioners, as well as by the Board, as relief to the several paupers; and, consequently, chargeable to the same fund as any other relief to those paupers. They ought, therefore, to be charged to the parish or township, if the pauper be chargeable to a parish or township; and to the common fund of the union, if the pauper be irremovable under the 9 and 10 Vic. cap. 66, or otherwise chargeable to the common fund under the 11 & 12 Vic. c. 110.

II.—ASSISTANT OVERSEERS.—APPOINTED UNDER THE 59 GEO. 3, C. 12, WHETHER BOUND TO SEND MONTHLY STATEMENTS TO THE GUARDIANS.

24th June, 1852.

Clerk of St. Thomas Union:—Inquired whether the guardians can require assistant overseers, appointed under the 59 Geo. 3, c. 12, to make out and deliver to them the monthly statements, (form 9,) prescribed by the General Order for Accounts.

Ans.—The guardians cannot lawfully require assistant overseers, appointed under the 59 Geo. 3, c. 12, to make out and deliver to them the monthly statements, (form 9,) which collectors of poor-rates, whom they appoint, are bound to do according to art. 10 of the General Order for Accounts.

III.—AUDIT. — RECOVERY OF SUMS CERTIFIED TO BE DUE AT.

27th Feb., 1852.

J. J. Collins, Esq., Clerk to the Magistrates, Saffron Walden.—On the 2nd of February instant, Mr. Banks, district auditor, laid an information against J. B., late overseer of Arkesden, for the recovery of £40. 11*s*. 2*d*. which he had certified to be due from him. J. B. not having attended the summons, the case was heard in his absence, and the magistrates adjudged the money to be due from him, and directed that he should pay the sum of 9*s*. besides for costs. The proceedings were taken under 7 & 8 Vic. c. 101, sec. 32, which directs that the amounts due shall be recovered in the same manner as penalties and forfeitures may be recovered under the provisions of the first recited act, (viz. 4 & 5 Wm. 4, c. 76.) The 4 & 5 Wm. 4, c. 76, sec. 99, enacts that all penalties and forfeitures shall, upon proof and conviction of the offences before any two justices of the peace, &c., be levied, together with the costs, &c., by warrant of distress, under the hands of the justices before whom the party may have been convicted, &c. Inquiring what is the next step to be taken by the magistrates, and whether an order is to be made on J. B.; as if this be the case, it must be served, and proof of the service given, and that the money is still unpaid, before they can issue the distress warrant; also, whether the magistrates have any power to commit J. B. to prison, the 7 & 8 Vic. only applying to the recovery of the money, and not to the punishment of the defaulter; and if so, whether the term of imprisonment ought not to have been adjudged at the hearing.

Ans.—The Board are of opinion that no conviction is necessary before a distress warrant is issued, to recover a sum certified by a district auditor to be due under the 7 & 8 Vic. c. 101, sec. 32. They believe that the general practice in such cases, is for the justices to issue a distress warrant, for the recovery of the sum certified, in like manner they issue a distress warrant for the recovery of a poor rate. Sums certified under the 7 & 8 Vic. c. 101, sec. 32, are to be recovered in the same manner as penalties and forfeitures are recoverable under the 4 & 5 Wm. 4, c. 76, that is, by warrant of distress in the first instance, and by warrant of commitment afterwards, in default of sufficient distress. It is not required, however, that there should be any conviction; for, although there be a default in payment, there is no offence committed. The Board have been favoured with a copy of an opinion given by an experienced counsel, [Mr. Pashley,] upon the subject of the proceedings to be taken under the 7 & 8 Vic. c. 101, sec. 32, in connection with the 4 & 5 Wm. 4, c. 76, for the recovery of sums certified by the auditor to be due. As this opinion may perhaps be useful to you, the Board forward a copy of it herewith for your consideration.

Copy of opinion referred to.—The 7 & 8 Vic. c. 101, sec. 32, seems to me designed to give the same powers for enforcing payment in this case, as are conferred for enforcing payment of penalties under 4 & 5 Wm. 4, c. 76. Now the conviction, though essential to establish the fact of the commission of an ordinary statutory offence, is not, I think, any part of the mode of recovering the penalty to which the offence is subjected. I am entirely disposed to think, that the only instrument needed in this case is the distress warrant, and that on the fair construction of 7 & 8 Vic. c. 101, sec. 32, it is clearly to be seen that the legislature never meant the ceremony of convicting or ordering, by a separate instrument to take place. The same reasoning leads somewhat further, for it seems to follow, that an information is not requisite in such a case as the present, although the defaulter must doubtless be formally summoned. My conclusion, that the warrant need not be preceded by any formal instrument under seal, is fortified by the high authority of Baron Parke, both in Johnson *v.* Reid, 6 M. & W. 124, and in the recent case of Lindsey *v.* Leigh, in the Exchequer Chamber, 3, New Sessions, Cases 99 & 113, where it is laid down that no formal conviction different from the warrant of commitment is needed under 4 Geo. 4, c. 34, sec. 3. Secondly, It only remains to consider whether the distress warrant may be followed up by a commitment. I think it may be so followed up. The 7 & 8 Vic. c. 101, sec. 32, when coupled with 4 & 5 Wm. 4, c. 76, sec. 9, treats the nonpayment of money under circumstances like these as an *offence;* and the party who fails to pay, as an *offender*. The statute of Elizabeth, (43 Eliz. c. 2, sec. 4,) did just the same thing, in the case of nonpayment of poor-rate, for it gives expressly a distress and sale "of the *offender's* goods" (although no other conviction of the offence, except that implied in the distress warrant, has ever been deemed needful). Now the commitment in default of distress, under sec. 99, is in effect, (just like that under 43 Eliz. c. 2, sec. 4,) a mere commitment in *execution*, for a civil debt; the defaulter can obtain his liberty at any time by paying; I therefore consider the warrant of commitment, as well as the distress warrant, under 4 & 5 Wm. 4, c. 76, to be comprehended in the general words of 7 & 8 Vic. c. 101, whereby recovery of the money due from defaulting overseers is authorized to be recovered in the same manner as penalties, &c., under the former act. The recent case of Omerod *v.* Chadwick, 16 Mees. and Welsby, 367,383, is also an authority tending to the conclusions at which I arrive. The distress warrant will I think do, and may be properly dated of the day when the hearing took place. It would be as well that the justices should be together when they sign it.

IV.—AUDITOR.—PAYMENT OF BALANCES CERTIFIED BY HIM TO BE DUE FROM OVERSEERS.

22*nd Jan.*, 1852.

District Auditor—At his last audit of the accounts of the Bromyard Union, he found that the balances certified by him at his preceding Lady-day audit, to be due from the overseers of parishes comprised in that union, had been paid in by them to the treasurer of the guardians; and that the guardians had immediately given cheques to the new overseers for the respective amounts so paid in. As the course pursued in this case differs entirely from that pursued in the other unions in his district, requested the Board's instructions in regard to it. A copy of the above communication was sent to the guardians for their observations.

Clerk of Bromyard Union.—Previous to the Lady-day audit, the guardians calculated the calls to be made upon the several parishes in the union, for the quarter ending Midsummer, 1851; and issued their warrants for such calls, considering at the time that the new overseers would, as in all former years, receive from the old overseers such balances as might be found due from them at the audit, the auditor never having up to that time ordered such balances to be paid into the hands of the union treasurer. The order of the auditor, therefore, took the guardians as well as the overseers by surprise, and several of the latter, notwithstanding such order, paid over the balances to their successors, who were thereby put in a position to meet the calls made by the guardians; while those overseers who had not received such balances from their predecessors, were without funds, in consequence of their neglect to make new rates, arising from their belief that they should receive the balances. In this dilemma they represented the hardship of their case to the guardians, who, to meet the contingency in the best way they could, issued cheques to the new overseers, for the respective balances paid in by the old overseers, as stated by the auditor. The guardians were aware of the irregularity of this procedure, but while it only occasioned a little additional trouble to the clerk and the treasurer, it seemed the only mode of removing the difficulty in which the overseers were placed, without defeating the object of requiring the immediate payment of the balances due from the overseers on leaving office.

Ans.—Perhaps, strictly speaking, the course pursued by the guardians was not at variance with the provisions of the 7 & 8 Vic. c. 101, sec. 32, which require them to apply the monies paid in to the treasurer, to the use of the parish or parishes interested in the sum so paid. Hence the guardians might have applied such payments at once to the calls due from the respective parishes, or to any other purposes of those parishes, or might have directed the money to be paid to the succeeding overseers. The Board, however, think. that under ordinary circumstances the application of the money towards the payment of the calls is the preferable course, as being more clearly in accordance with the intention of the legislature.

V.—BASTARDS.—1. LIABILITY OF GRANDPARENTS TO MAINTAIN.

23*rd June*, 1852.

Clerk of Camelford Union.—Some of the guardians of the Camelford Union believe that grandfathers and grandmothers, if of sufficient ability, are liable to have an order of maintenance made upon them for the support of the illegitimate children of their sons or daughters. He has told such of the guardians as hold this opinion that it is not correct, as he believes that an order of maintenance cannot be made even on the mother of a bastard child. Requesting the Board's opinion on the point.

Ans.—The Board acquiesce in the opinion which you have expressed to the guardians, namely, that grandfathers and grandmothers, on either side, connot be compelled to maintain the bastards of their sons or daughters.

2. Receipt and application of payments for bastard child whose mother is in the workhouse.

10*th March*, 1852.

Assistant Overseer, Kentisbeare, Tiverton Union.—A woman belonging to the parish of Kentisbeare, who had an illegitimate child eight months since, applied to the magistrates, who made an order of one shilling and sixpence per week on the putative father for the maintenance of the child. The money was paid to the mother regularly every week. Five weeks ago she applied for relief, and was admitted into the workhouse with her child, where she now is. Inquired, who is empowered to receive the weekly allowance from the putative father, and in what way is the money to be applied.

Ans.—Where an order has been made, under the 7 & 8 Vic. c. 101, on the reputed father of an illegitimate child, for the support of such child, sec. 5 provides, "that all money payable under such order shall be due and payable to the mother of the bastard child, in respect of such time, and so long as she lives and is of sound mind, &c." The mother of the illegitimate child is, therefore, the person alone entitled to receive the money or payments made by the putative father, under the order, notwithstanding she and her child may be chargeable to the parish. But as it appears, in the case to which your letter refers, that the mother is now an inmate of the workhouse of the Tiverton Union, the Board wish to point out, that if money be found in her possession, whether derived from payments made by the putative father, or otherwise, it will be competent for the guardians, under the 12 & 13 Vic. c. 103, sec. 16, to take and appropriate it towards defraying the costs of her relief.

---

3. Enforcement of order of affiliation after the death of the mother.

14*th July*, 1852.

Clerk of Hinchley Union.—In the year 1851 an order of affiliation was made upon Thomas ——, for payment of 1*s.* 6*d.* per week, on account of an illegitimate child, belonging to Emma ——, of Sapcote, but he has for some time past refused to pay anything towards the child's support. Inquiring whether the guardians can now take any steps against the man, so as to ensure payment to the child after the death of the mother, who is rapidly sinking from pulmonary disease; or whether the guardians will be able to proceed against him after the mother's death for the recovery of the 1*s.* 6*d.* per week, in case the child should then become chargeable, as will most likely be the case.

Ans.—It is not lawful for the guardians now to enforce the order of affiliation, but if the mother of the child die, the justices would be empowered to appoint some person to have the custody of the child, and if it then become chargeable to the poor-rate, the guardians can, under the 7th section of the 7 & 8 Vic. c. 101, enforce the order upon the putative father.

VI.—BURIAL.—1. Expenses of the burial of a person who had been drowned.

18*th July*, 1851.

Clerk of Newton Abbot Union.—R. C., aged 21, had been living at Torquay in the parish of Tornoham about three months. On the 29th June, ultimo, he went down to Tor Abby Sands, in the same parish, for the purpose of bathing, and was drowned, his body being washed on shore in the neighbouring parish of Cockington. It was removed to Torquay for the purpose of holding an inquest, and was buried in Tornoham. Inquiring whether the expense of the burial should be charged to Tornoham, the parish where the deceased had resided, or to Cockington, where the body was found. The deceased had no settlement in either of these parishes or in the union, nor had he been in receipt of relief.

Ans.—The Board collect from your statement of the case that R. C. died in the parish of Tornoham, where also the burial took place. The 7 & 8 Vic. c. 101, sec. 31, enables the guardians to charge the expense of burying the body of any poor person to the parish to which he may have been chargeable, or in which he may have died, or otherwise in which such body may be. The deceased in the present case, not having been chargeable to the poor-rate, the Board consider that the guardians should charge the costs of the burial to the parish of Tornoham, as being that in which he died.

9*th August*, 1851.

Clerk of same Union.—It appeared by the evidence given on the inquest, held on the body of R. C., that his clothes were found at Corban Head, in the parish of Cockington, and that the body was found in deep water, and landed at the pier of Torquay, to which it was towed by its discoverers.

Ans.—The additional facts submitted to the Board in relation to R. C., do not alter their previously expressed opinion on the case. As the guardians are not in a position to prove where the death of R. C. actually occurred, and as they gave directions for the burial to take place in the parish of Tornoham where the dead body was then lying, the Board consider that the guardians are justified in charging the expenses of the burial to that parish. There is the less ground to object to this course, inasmuch as that was the parish in which the deceased had been residing previously to his death.

---

2. MODE OF CHARGING THE EXPENSES OF THE BURIALS OF PAUPERS.

23*rd Feb.*, 1852.

Clerk of Alderbury Union—Inquired to what account the funeral expenses of paupers dying in the workhouse should be charged. On reference to the Poor Law Official Circular, Nos. 14 & 15, p. 212, N. S. it appears that the expenses in question should be entered in the accounts under the head of "In Maintenance," but in the Official Circular, No. 39, N. S. it is laid down that these expenses should be entered in a separate account, under a specific heading, and not as relief either "in-door" or "out-door." Hitherto the expenses of the funeral of an in-door pauper have been paid by the relieving officer, and charged in his out-relief list to the parish to which the pauper belonged.

Ans.—The rule for determining the chargeability of the funeral expenses of paupers is laid down in the 7 & 8 Vic. c. 110, and that rule is referred to in the Official Circular, No. 39, N. S., to which your letter alludes. With regard to the entry of the charge in the accounts, the Board have to observe that where the burial occurs in the case of an out-door pauper, the relieving officer who defrays the expenses will properly enter the amount in his out-door relief list, or his receipt and expenditure book. But as regards the funeral of a pauper dying in the workhouse, the relieving officer is not concerned in the matter; and it will rest with the guardians to direct the charge to be made in the union ledger, in the manner pointed out in the Official Circular above-mentioned.

VII. — CHARGEABILITY. — 1. DESTITUTE WANDERER.

13*th August*, 1851.

Clerk of Sleaford Union.—J. H., single-woman, aged 17, left her service at Sleaford pregnant, on the 29th July last, and went from thence to her grandmother's at Osbournby, about seven miles from Sleaford. The grandmother being from home, the girl applied to the overseer for relief, who took her in for the night, and the following day she applied to the relieving-officer of the Osbournby district at Heckington for an order for admission into the workhouse, which he gave her. Her parents are both dead, and her settlement is unknown. The guardians charged Osbournby with the girl's maintenance at the workhouse. Inquiring if this course is correct, the guardian of Osbournby objecting to it.

Ans.—As the girl had no home at Osbournby it appears to the Board that she was a destitute wanderer when relieved, and is therefore properly chargeable to the common fund of the Sleaford Union, under the 11 & 12 Vic. c. 110, sec. 1, continued by subsequent Acts.

---

2. CHARGEABILITY OF WIDOW.

3*rd Dec.*, 1851.

Clerk of Selby Union.—The relief which was granted to William Buttery and his wife up to the time of his death, was charged to the parish of Brayton, (in which they were settled,) though the paupers were living at Selby; but the overseers of Brayton now desire that the relief of the widow should be charged to the common fund of the union, during the year of her widowhood, if she should so long reside in Selby. Inquired whether the relief of the widow can be so charged; or, whether it must be debited as heretofore to the parish of Brayton.

Ans.—If the widow was residing in the parish of Brayton with her husband at the time of his death, she is now irremovable therefrom, by operation of the 9 & 10 Vic. c. 66, sec. 2, and her relief for twelve months from his decease is chargeable to the common fund of the union.

---

3. CHARGEABILITY OF WIDOW.

19*th March*, 1852.

Clerk of Falmouth Union.—Elizabeth Woolcock, when about thirty years of age, married John

Winn, labourer, at the parish church of Madron in Cornwall. Immediately after the marriage they went to reside in apartments in a house in Chapel Row, in the borough of Penryn, belong-to Mr. James B. Read, at a rent of £3. 10*s*. per year. John Winn died about twelve months after the marriage, at Scilly, where his wife went to attend upon him, and where she continued seven weeks. Their furniture having been left in the house in Chapel Row, the wife, after the husband's death, returned into it, and she continued to reside therein, till after her marriage with her second husband, John Woolcock, labourer, which took place at the parish church of St. Gluvias, Cornwall, about one year after the death of her first husband. Her second husband came to reside with her, on the marriage, in the rooms in Chapel Row, where they continued for upwards of three months. The furniture in the rooms was the property of her first husband, who died intestate, and she never took out letters of administration to his effects, but considered that after his death she was the tenant of the rooms in her own right. Her second husband, John Woolcock, died on the 22nd of December last; and she has never resided out of Penryn, (except during the time she was at Scilly, as above stated,) since she came there with her first husband, being many more than five years since. Miss Read, the daughter of the landlord of the house in Chapel Row, kept the rent account, and she does not recollect hearing of the pauper's second marriage. The only person she ever knew or recognized as the tenant during the entire period of the occupation, was the original taker. The tenancy commenced about the year 1836 and terminated about the year 1838. Inquired whether Elizabeth Woolcock gained a settlement in Penryn under the above circumstances, or whether the cost of her maintenance should be charged to the common fund of the Falmouth Union, she being irremovable.

Ans.—The present case appears to the Board to be very similar in its leading circumstances to that of R. *v.* Barnard Castle, (2 A. & E., 108,) in which no judgment was given, as the court were divided in opinion. The question on which the decision of the case must turn, seems to the Board to be this:—Whether Elizabeth Woolcock, on the death of her first husband, commenced a new tenancy of the premises in her own right, or occupied them as the representative of her deceased husband, without having taken out letters of administration, though entitled to do so. Having regard to the difference of opinion which existed among the judges before whom the case of R. *v.* Barnard Castle was argued, the Board feel considerable difficulty in coming to a conclusion with reference to the present case; but on the whole, they are disposed to consider that Elizabeth Woolcock commenced a new tenancy of the premises in her own right at the death of her first husband, and that upon her subsequent marriage the estate vested in her second husband by operation of law, whereby, in connection with his residence on the spot for forty days, he acquired a settlement in the borough of Penryn, according to the principle of the decision in R. *v.* North Cerney (3 B. & Ad. 463). This settlement was of course communicated to his wife, and she is therefore now settled, as well as resident, in the borough of Penryn, and consequently chargeable thereto.

---

4. CHARGEABILITY OF THE WIDOW OF MAN WHO DIED OUT OF THE PARISH IN WHICH HIS FAMILY RESIDED.

2nd July, 1852.

Clerk of South Molton Union.—John H. an able-bodied labourer who had a wife and three children, and was legally settled in the parish of Roborough, in the Torrington Union, took a house in the parish of Burrington, in the South Molton Union, and went there to reside at Lady-day, 1851. About six weeks since he procured work on the Taw Vale line of railway, now forming, and in order to be within a convenient distance from his labour, he left his wife and children in his house at Burrington, and lodged during the working days with his wife's sister in the parish of Chawleigh, in the Crediton Union; but returned to his own house in Burrington every Saturday night, and remained with his wife and family till the following Monday morning, when he went back to his work on the railway. On Monday, the 14th of June instant, he was taken ill on the ground, and was unable to continue his work, and left it with the intention of returning to his house at Burrington; but became so weak that he could not get further than his lodging at Chawleigh. His, wife on hearing of his illness, went to Chawleigh to attend on him, and remained with him there till his death, except that she once went home to Burrington to see her children and make some arrangements for them whilst she should be absent. John H. died on the 19th June, and was buried at Chawleigh, at the charge of that parish. Grace H., the widow, returned after her husband's death to Burrington, and with her three children resides in the house taken by her husband. She has applied to the guardians of the South Molton Union for relief, and an order has been made for 4*s*. and 4 loaves per week for four weeks. Inquired whether Grace H. is removable from the parish of Burrington, and whether the relief now allowed to her, and any future relief that she may require within twelve calendar months from her husband's death, should be charged to the parish of Burrington, or, to the common fund of the union.

Ans.—The Board are of opinion that in construction of law, the husband at the time of his death is to be considered as having been resident in the parish of Burrington, in which he had his fixed abode, and in which his family lived, and from which he was absent only for a temporary purpose. The Board think it must also be considered that Grace H. was residing with him in that parish at the time of his decease. The case falls, therefore, within the 9 & 10 Vic. c. 66, sec. 2; and the pauper and her children are irremovable, and the relief which may be necessary for them dnring the first twelve months of the woman's widowhood, will be charged on the common fund of the union.

---

5. Chargeability — Maintenance of a married woman in a lunatic asylum while the husband was a prisoner, breach of residence.

25*th Feb.*, 1852.

Clerk of Great Boughton Union.—Requesting the Board's opinion as to the fund to which the cost of the maintenance of a pauper named Sarah Ellson, in the county lunatic asylum, should be charged. Sarah Ellson, the wife of John Ellson, a prisoner in Chester Castle for felony, was removed from Tattenhall, in the Great Boughton Union, (where she had been resident for many years with her husband,) to the lunatic asylum, on the 22nd of September last, at the instance of the overseers of the above-mentioned township. The pauper died on the 17th of January last, and was buried by her friends. The guardian for the townships of Tattenhall insists, that as the lunatic was irremovable from that township, in consequence of the husband's length of residence therein, the cost of her maintenance in the asylum ought to be charged to the common fund of the union: while the board of guardians urge that the imprisonment of the husband out of the township broke his residence therein, and consequently that of his wife, who thereupon became removable to the place of her husband's settlement; and being so removable, the township of Tattenhall, and not the common fund of the union, should be called upon to pay for the pauper's removal to the asylum, and maintenance while there. On the one hand the case of R. *v.* Pott Shrigley, and R. *v.* Salford are relied upon; and on the other, the recent case of the Overseers of Hartfield *v.* Overseers of Rutherford, decided by the Queen's Bench on the 21st ult., which the officers for Tattenhall contend is in every respect identical with this case.

Ans.—The Board are of opinion that, according to the decision in the case of Hartfield *v.* Rutherford, the pauper, at the time of her decease, was legally exempt from removal from the township of Tattenhall, by reason of residence therein. Consequently, the cost of the relief in question is chargeable to the common fund of the Great Boughton Union.

---

6. Chargeability of pauper from the parish in which workhouse is situated, and where she had been nurse more than five years.

6*th Dec.*, 1851.

Clerk of Honiton Union.—Transmitted the following joint statement under the 11 & 12 Vic. c. 110, sec. 4, for the opinion of the Poor Law Board:—Caroline Pyle, the widow of William Pyle, a pensioner, resided with her husband in Exeter for many years previous to his death, which happened on the 5th of August, 1843. During their residence at Exeter, they became chargeable to the corporation of the poor, and were removed under an order of justices to the parish of Awliscombe, in the Honiton Union. After the husband's death, his widow was relieved by the parish of Awliscombe until November 1843, when the guardians appointed her to the situation of nurse in the Honiton Union Workhouse. This situation she continued to fill, (residing in the union workhouse at Honiton,) until the 8th of September, 1851, when she was dismissed. Since leaving the workhouse, she has resided in the town of Honiton, and relief has been granted her and charged to that parish. The parish officers of Honiton have applied to have the relief charged to the common fund of the union, she not being settled in their parish, but in the parish of Awliscombe, and being irremovable by residence in the parish of Honiton since November, 1843, a period more than five years. Before the guardians direct the transfer of the relief to the common fund of the union, they are desirous of obtaining the opinion of the Poor Law Board, whether the residence in the union workhouse at Honiton, as nurse, is such an industrial residence in Honiton, as to render a pauper irremovable, under the 9 & 10 Vic. c. 66.

Ans.—As the pauper was an officer of the union for a period of five years, and resided during that time in the parish of Honiton, the Board are of opinion that she gained exemption from removal, under the 9 & 10 Vic. c. 66, sec. 1, by such residence, and is now chargeable upon the common fund of the union.

7. CHARGEABILITY OF PAUPER ILLEGALLY REMOVED FROM THE PARISH IN WHICH HE WAS DESTITUTE.

18*th March*, 1852.

Clerk of Great Boughton Union.—A pauper named John I., who claims to be settled in the township of Aldersey, in the Great Boughton Union, was brought (being nearly blind) by another wanderer like himself to the house of one of the overseers of that township and left there. The overseer has since been convicted by the justices in the penalty of £5 and costs for having taken the pauper into the adjoining township of Handley, and for having left him there at the house of Mr. Prince, one of the relieving officers of the union. The guardian for Handley complains of the pauper being chargeable to that township, in consequence of his illegal removal; and the board of guardians wish to know whether any means can be adopted to relieve the ratepayers of Handley from the charge of the pauper's maintenance, and to fix such charge on the township of Aldersey, which ought to have continued liable to the relief of the pauper till he was legally removed from thence.

Ans.—If the pauper, when he applied for relief, was a destitute wanderer, (as from the information laid before the Board appears to be the case,) his relief should be charged to the common fund of the union, under the 11 & 12 Vic. c. 110, and the continuing acts, and not to either of the townships of Handley or Aldersey.

Clerk of Great Boughton Union.—An objection has been raised to charging the cost of the maintenance of John I. to the common fund of the union, on the ground that as he claimed to be settled in Aldersey, it was the duty of the overseers of Handley to obtain an order from the justices to remove him to that township, and that he was not a wanderer or wayfarer within the words of the statute 11 & 12 Vic. c. 110, but a person coming to reside in the place of his alleged settlement, and illegally removed therefrom. On the other hand, the overseers of Handley contend that they ought not to be charged with the relief of the pauper, or with the costs of his removal, as he had not, within the words of the statute relating to the removal of the poor, come to "reside" and "inhabit" in their township, but was illegally brought there. Inquired whether the Board are still of opinion that the relief of the pauper should be charged to the common fund of the union, as in that case he will be deprived of his settlement in the township of Aldersey, and the overseers of that township, by their illegal removal, will have successfully relieved themselves of a burden which they are legally, as it appears to the guardians, bound to bear.

Ans.—The reasons of the Board for considering that the pauper in question is chargeable to the common fund, are, that he became destitute in Handley, and that he was not at the time an inhabitant of that parish, so that the overseers thereof could not have obtained an order of removal to the place of his settlement. It also appears from the statement contained in your first communication, that John I. had actually wandered into the township of Aldersey, and although the pauper may have claimed that township as his place of settlement, there is nothing in the correspondence which has taken place upon the subject, to show that such claim is well founded. Be that as it may, however, the destitution occurred, and the relief was granted to the pauper, in the township of Handley, where he had no home; and the Board, therefore, think that he is chargeable to the common fund, as a destitute wayfarer, or wanderer, within the meaning of the 11 & 12 Vic. c. 110, sec. 1.

8. CHARGEABILITY OF A WOMAN LIVING IN ADULTERY AWAY FROM HER HUSBAND.

9*th March*, 1852.

Clerk of Witham Union.—Transmitting the following statement duly signed under the 11 & 12 Vic. c. 110, sec. 4, for the opinion of the Poor Law Board:—Ann Harvey, the wife of

Isaac Harvey, now residing in Hatfield Peveral, in which parish he has resided about twenty years, became chargeable to the parish of Witham on the 30th January, 1852, and the relieving officer gave her an order for admission to the workhouse of the Witham Union. The application for relief was made in the parish of Witham, where she was at the time residing in lodgings, and the order given was on account of that parish. On the Monday following Ann Harvey's admission, the parish of. Wickham Bishops agreed to have her relief transferred from Witham to Wickham Bishops, subject to the opinion of the Poor Law Board, whether such relief ought to be charged to that parish, or to the common fund of the union. Isaac Harvey has a legal settlement in the parish of Wickham Bishops, but he has resided for a longer period than five years in Hatfield Peveral, and has for a considerable time been separated from his wife, allowing her for maintenance, 2*s.* 6*d.* per week. About four or five months ago this payment was discontinued, and the woman having become chargeable the husband was summoned before the magistrates, but as it was shown that she had been living in adultery, the magistrates refused to make an order upon him. The Guardians refuse to charge the cost of the relief of Ann Harvey to the common fund, on the ground that she is removable from Witham, where she has not resided five years, to Wickham Bishops, the place of her husband's settlement. The guardian of Wickham Bishops considers that Ann Harvey is not removable, that the residence of her husband Isaac Harvey should be considered her residence, as, though she has no doubt wandered away from her husband, no acknowledged or legal separation has taken place between them, and that therefore she ought to be placed on the common fund as an irremovable pauper. Question:—What is the course which should be adopted in charging the relief of Ann Harvey?

Ans.—The Board are of opinion that Ann Harvey is chargeable to the parish of Witham, and removable therefrom. It is stated that she was residing in that parish when she applied for relief, and by the statute 11 & 12 Vic. c. 111, she is removable therefrom, supposing her husband would be so if he were there. It is clear that if the husband were now in the parish of Witham, he would not, (upon the facts stated,) be exempt from removal; and, consequently, Ann Harvey is not exempt. The result is, that being now removable from Witham, her relief is chargeable to that parish while she continues therein.

---

9. CHARGEABILITY OF A WIDOW WHOSE SETTLEMENT WAS UNKNOWN.—SERVANT HIRED FROM THE WORKHOUSE, POWER OF GUARDIANS TO REMOVE HER FROM HER SITUATION.
2nd June, 1852.

The Rev. H. S., Saint Thomas Union.—1. Some time during the year 1849, W. S. came with his wife, to live in the parish of D. During their residence there, they were in lodgings. W. S. died in February, 1850. All that is known of him is, that before he came to D. he was working for some time on the South Devon Railway, in the parish of S. B., and that he had been residing for some time previously (how long unknown,) in the parish of either W. or H. His widow, (who is now in the workhouse of the Saint Thomas Union,) is of weak intellect, and is wholly unable to give any information upon the subject of her husband's former places of abode, or even where she was married. Inquired whether the cost of the maintenance of the widow is rightly charged to the parish of D., or whether the pauper should not rather be regarded as a vagrant, and her maintenance charged to the common fund of the union. 2. In February, 1852, Mr. S., of the parish of D., took a girl, aged about thirteen, from the union workhouse, and signed an agreement, which was approved by the guardians, to keep the girl for a twelvemonth, guaranteeing her attendance at public worship once every Sunday, and engaging to attend to her moral training. The guardians, however, having learnt that Mr. S. has a female servant in his house who has been delivered of a bastard child since she has been in his service, resolved to remove the girl from her situation, and Mr. S. promised to give her up to the guardians, but has since refused to do so. Inquired what course should be pursued for the removal of the girl from the service of Mr. S.

Ans.—1. According to the facts communicated the Board do not consider the case of the widow of W. S. to be that of a wanderer, or wayfarer, within the meaning of the statute. The Board will, however, communicate with the guardians of the St. Thomas Union on the subject. 2. As the girl in question is in service, the Board do not find any authority in law which will justify the guardians in taking her out of such service, and so putting an end to the contract, which, as the Board understand, exists solely between her and her master. At the same time, the Board think the circumstances which you describe as to the character of her fellow-servant are greatly to be regretted. They have also to add, that if the girl were subjected to any such ill-treatment as would bring the case within the recent Statute, (14 & 15 Vic. c.11,) the guardians, (seeing that the girl was taken as a servant from the workhouse,) would be empowered to interfere in the way for which that statute provides. But the Board do not understand that any such ill-treatment is imputed in the present instance.

A copy of the above answer was sent to the guardians of the Saint Thomas Union for their observations.

16*th June*, 1852.

Clerks of Saint Thomas Union.—The guardians are of opinion that as there has been no personal misconduct on the part of Mr. S., so as to dissolve the contract which they have entered into with him in the case of the girl referred to, they have no power to interfere in the matter. As regards the case of the widow of W. S., the guardians are of opinion that the pauper is rightly charged to D., she not being a casual pauper; and that the difficulty, (or even impossibility,) of obtaining evidence of her settlement does not make her chargeable to the common fund of the union.

The Board transmitted a copy of the above letter from the clerks of the Saint Thomas Union, to the Rev. H. S., and informed him that they had nothing to add to the remarks which they made in their previous communication to him.

---

10. CHARGEABILITY OF PAUPER RECEIVING MEDICAL RELIEF ONLY.

14*th June*, 1852.

Vice Chairman of Blandford Union.—A labouring man, residing and settled in the parish of Langton, in the Blandford Union, was accidentally injured in the parish of Shilling Okeford, in the Sturminster Union. The guardians of the latter union now claim to be paid the expenses of medical and other attendance upon the man during the time that he was unable to be removed from Shilling Okeford. Requested the Board's opinion, as to whether the expenses the Blandford Board of guardians may be disposed to allow in this case, are to be charged to the parish of Langton, or to the common fund of the union, the man not having been in the receipt of parochial relief, either at the time of the accident, or at any other time.

Ans.—The question raised in this case appears to the Board to depend on the 11 and 12 Vic. c.110, sec. 2. They consider upon the facts stated that the parish where the poor man met with the accident, and at whose charge medical and other relief have been supplied to him, is entitled, under 11 & 12 Vic. c. 110, sec. 82, to be reimbursed the cost of such relief, either by the parish of the abode, or by the union containing that parish. As to which of these be liable, the Board observe, that it is provided by the section referred to, that where the person meeting with the accident is not at the time in receipt of relief, the costs arising from the accident are to be borne or reimbursed by the parish in which the person may have his place of abode, unless, by reason of any provision of the law, he would, if otherwise chargeable, have been chargeable to the common fund of the union, in which case the payment or reimbursement is to be made by the union, at the cost of the union. As it is stated that the parish of the pauper's abode, (Langton,) is also the parish of his settlement, his relief would in no case be chargeable to the common fund of the Blandford Union, had he become chargeable there from any other cause than the present; and therefore the parish of Langton is liable, as the Board consider, to bear or reimburse the relief given under the circumstances stated.

VIII.—CHILDREN.—1. EMPLOYMENT AND APPRENTICESHIP OF PAUPER CHILDREN.

1*st March*, 1851.

Clerk of Wakefield Union.—Two applications have been made to the guardians, one for the employment of the children in the workhouse, from eight years and upwards, as pieceners in a woollen mill about five miles from Wakefield, the employer to provide the children's food and lodging from Monday morning to Saturday night, and the guardians to find the clothing, and food and lodging, in the union workhouse from Saturday evening to Monday morning. The other is for apprenticing an orphan boy, (about fourteen years old,) now in the workhouse, to a master chimney sweeper, the boy's father having been of that trade, which the boy would also like to follow. The guardians have declined to entertain either of the applications until they have been submitted to the Poor Law Board for their sanction.

Ans.—The first proposal is liable to the objection that the children, although continuing to be paupers, would, during the working days of the week, be transferred to the care of the mill owner, who is not under the control of the guardians, or of the Poor Law Board. The arrangement also involves the great practical objection of making relief supplementary to remuneration for labour, and keeping the children paupers though actively employed for six days of the week. Neither is there any provision that the children shall receive the instruction, which as inmates of the workhouse they should receive. Another difficulty attending the proposal would be the weekly admission of the children into the workhouse, as they would have to pass through the receiving wards. The Board under the circumstances consider that they would not be justified in giving their sanction to the proposed arrangement. With regard to the apprenticeship of an orphan boy of fourteen years of age to a master chimney sweeper, such an apprenticeship cannot legally be effected, as the 3 & 4 Vic. c. 85, sec. 3, prevents children under sixteen years of age from being apprenticed to chimney sweepers.

---

2. PRESENTATION OF BIBLE AND PRAYER BOOK TO CHILDREN ON LEAVING WORKHOUSE TO GO INTO SERVICE.

1st July, 1852.

Clerk of Northwich Union.—Inquiring whether the guardians would be justified in presenting to each boy or girl who may leave the workhouse to go into service, a Bible and Prayer-book, at the expense of the common fund of the union, or of the township to which such boy or girl may be chargeable at the time.

Ans.—The Board will raise no objection to the proposal of the guardians being carried into effect.

IX. — CONSTABLES' EXPENSES. — LIABILITY OF OVERSEERS TO PAY EXPENSES OF APPREHENDING A DRUNKEN MAN.

14th July, 1852.

Mr. R. G., Dodbrooke, Kingsbridge Union.—A bill has been sent in to the overseers of the parish of Dodbrooke, by the superintendent constable, for the expenses, &c. of apprehending a man for being drunk on a Saturday night, keeping him in custody till Monday morning, and then taking him before a magistrate, by whom he was fined 5*s*. Inquired whether the overseers are legally bound to pay the amount of the bill.

Ans.—The proper course will be for the overseers to lay the account in question before the vestry of the parish, pursuant to the 18 Geo. 3, c. 19, sec. 4, and it will be for the vestry to determine whether the account shall be paid. If the account be approved by the vestry, the overseers can discharge it, but if the account or any part of it be disallowed by the vestry, then it will be for the constable to apply to the justices at a petty sessions, who will be empowered to settle what is properly due to the constable; and their determination will be binding on the overseers.

X.—CONTRIBUTION ORDERS.—PERSONAL SERVICE OF, IS NECESSARY,

16th Sept., 1852.

Clerk of Ross Union.—Inquired whether it is necessary to serve the churchwardens and overseers, personally, with an order of contribution, before such order can be enforced; or whether it is sufficient to leave one order, directed to the churchwardens and overseers, at the dwelling-house of one overseer of a parish. The justices are of opinion that the latter is not the proper course.

Ans.—The Board direct your attention to the 12 & 13 Vic. c. 103, sec. 7, which provides, that where in any such case as you refer to a copy of the order shall be served upon any one of the overseers, the guardians may enforce the order against the person so served, as fully and as effectually as if a copy thereof had been also served upon every one of the overseers. The Board think that, under this enactment, personal service is necessary; and that it will not be sufficient merely to leave the order at the dwelling-house of the overseer intended to be served.

XI.—DESERTION OF FAMILY.—1. PROCEEDINGS FOR.

11th Oct., 1851.

Clerk of Narberth Union.—Inquiring 1st. Whether the guardians have the power to order proceedings to be taken against a person who has deserted his family and left them chargeable to a parish in the union; and, if so, who in such case is to prefer the complaint. 2ndly. Whether the guardians can legally order their clerk to appear at the Petty Sessions to conduct the case. And 3rdly. What remedy have the guardians against an overseer who refuses to complain against a person for deserting his wife and family.

Ans.—1st. The guardians of the Narberth Union may certainly direct proceedings to be taken against persons who are guilty of the offence of deserting their families, and leaving them chargeable to the parish, (see 7 & 8 Vic. c. 101, sec. 59.) 2nd. The guardians may make the necessary application to the justices through their officers, under sec. 68 of the above-mentioned statute, and may therefore require you as their clerk to appear at the Petty Sessions to conduct such cases for them. 3rd. The Board are of opinion that the guardians cannot compel the overseers to take proceedings in the cases in question.

---

2. LIABILITY OF A MAN, WHOSE WIFE IS LIVING IN ADULTERY, TO PUNISHMENT FOR DESERTING HIS FAMILY.

14*th March*, 1851.

Clerk to the Justices, Marlborough, Marlborough Union.—The following case has been brought before the bench of magistrates for the division of Marlborough, on which they request the opinion of the Poor Law Board.—G. R. Philpot, with his wife and four children, were some time since living at Calne. The wife formed an improper intimacy with another man, who in November last assisted her in turning her husband out of his own house; whereupon it is believed he went to London, and is now supposed to be residing there. The wife and children, with the paramour, continued to live at Philpot's house at Calne about a month after this. On the 19th December, the wife took three of the children to Averbury, in the Marlborough Union, the husband's parish, and left them in a field near the house of their grandfather. On the 20th December, the three children were taken into the Marlborough Union workhouse, and charged to the parish of Averbury. The relieving officer of the Marlborough Union has applied to the magistrates for a warrant to apprehend Philpot, either under the 5 Geo. 4, c. 83, sec. 3, for neglecting to maintain his family, or under sec. 4 of the same act for running away and leaving the children chargeable. The magistrates, not considering the circumstances sufficient to justify them in issuing a warrant, declined to do so.

Ans.—In the opinion of the Board, G. R. Philpot is not liable under the 5 Geo. 4, c. 83, in respect of the desertion of his wife, inasmuch as he is not bound to maintain a wife living in adultery. Yet he is bound to maintain his children, and in case of his neglect or refusal, (being of sufficient ability to do so, wholly or in part,) he renders himself liable to be proceeded against under sec. 3 of the Vagrant Act.

---

3. PUNISHMENT OF WOMAN FOR DESERTING HER ILLEGITIMATE CHILDREN.

22*nd June*, 1852.

Clerk of Lincoln Union.—A woman having two illegitimate children, aged four and three, deserted them, leaving them in an empty house in the Castle Dyking, an extra-parochial place in the City of Lincoln; and they have since been admitted into the Lincoln Union workhouse. The cost of their maintenance has been charged to the common fund of the union. Inquired whether the mother can be punished for deserting her children under the circumstances mentioned; and if so, in what manner, and by whom proceedings should be taken against her.

Ans.—As the children are in fact chargeable to the union, the Board consider that the mother is punishable under the 7 & 8 Vic. c. 101, sec. 6, and 12 & 13 Vic. c. 103, sec. 3; and that the guardians of the Lincoln Union may institute the proceedings under those statutes accordingly.

XII.—ELECTION OF GUARDIANS.—

1. VALIDITY OF NOMINATION.

29*th March*, 1851.

Clerk of Downham Union.—He has received two nominations of persons to be guardians for the parish of Wimbotsham within this union. The nomination of Mr. Goulder, one of the candidates, appears to be correct; but in that of Mr. Mumford, the other candidate, the name of the parish at the commencement of the document has been omitted, which he considers invalidates the nomination, as the Order of the Poor Law Board requires that the nomination shall be in the form prescribed in the schedule to the Order; and in the notices of election given by the clerk before the 15th March, it is stated that the nomination must be in the form prescribed by the Board. Requesting the opinion of the Board as to the validity of the nomination of Mr. Mumford. The following is the nomination paper referred to above :—

FORM OF NOMINATION PAPER.

Parish Downham Union } This 24th day of March, 1851.

Names of Persons Nominated to be Guardians.	Residence.	Quality or Calling of Persons Nominated.
George Mumford.	Downham.	Farmer & Merchant.

I, being (a Ratepayer) or (Owner of Property in the parish of Wimbotsham,) nominate the above to be guardian (or guardians) for the said parish.

(TIMOTHY FLANAGAN, Yeoman,) Signature and Address of Nominator.

Ans.—As the name of the parish is given in another and a material part of the nomination paper, the Board, as at present advised, think that the omission of the name at the commencement of it cannot mislead or create uncertainty, and should not in itself be regarded as invalidating the nomination. But the nomination appears to be defective in other respects, namely, 1st, The address of the nominator is omitted. 2nd, He has not expressly stated in which capacity, that is, whether as owner, or as ratepayer, he assumes to nominate.

2. VALIDITY OF NOMINATION.

1st April, 1851.

Clerk of Camelford Union.—In his notice of election of guardians for the current year he appointed the late guardian for Michaelstow as the person to receive nomination papers in the parish. Before the 26th instant, the annual vestry in the parish was held, and the late guardian was requested to act again, but he was not nominated in the proper form. On the 26th instant a nomination paper for another guardian was sent to the house of the late guardian, the person appointed to receive it, but he, having been requested by the vestry to continue in the office, refused to take it. The person thus nominated then sent the nomination paper to the relieving officer, who was not appointed to receive it, instead of sending it to him, the clerk. Consequently, he did not get it until the 28th instant. Inquired whether this nomination is void.

Ans.—It appears to the Board that the nomination for the parish of Michaelstow was sent to the person authorized to receive it, in sufficient time; and that in this respect article 8 of the General Consolidated Order of 24th July, 1847, was complied with. If, therefore, the nomination were otherwise correct, as to the form of the document, and the due qualification of the parties, the Board think it ought now to be treated as valid, although it did not, by reason of the wrongful act of the agent of the clerk, reach the hands of the latter until the 28th ultimo.

3. INSPECTION OF VOTING PAPERS.

14th April, 1851.

Clerk of Droitwich Union.—In one of the parishes of the Droitwich Union there has been a contested election for the office of guardian. The election being now over, the voting papers will be delivered to the guardians at their next meeting. The successful candidate has applied for leave to inspect and take copies of all the voting papers; which he, the clerk, has declined to grant, stating that the papers would all be delivered to the guardians at their next meeting, when any guardian would, as he presumed, be entitled to inspect them; and that, as to taking copies, he could give no opinion. Inquired how he ought to act in the matter.

Ans.—You will act rightly in delivering the voting papers, with your return of the election, to the guardians at their next meeting; and you properly declined to allow the voting papers to be inspected and copied before such delivery. It will be for the board of guardians then to determine whether the inspection requested shall be allowed; and, if so, under what conditions.

4. OWNER'S CLAIM TO VOTE IN.

11th Feb., 1852.

Mr. ——, *Guardian of Dudley Union.*—In January, 1851, L. W., residing in the parish of Rowley Regis, in the Dudley Union, delivered to the overseers of the parish a claim to vote in the election of guardians as owner of a freehold dwelling house and property then in his own occupation; and his claim being duly entered in the register of owners, he voted at the following election of guardians. At Christmas, 1851, he ceased to occupy the dwelling house and property in question, and let it to a tenant, who has continued to occupy it to the present time, L. W. himself going to reside in the parish of Hales Owen, in the Stourbridge Union. Inquired, whether in case of any objection being made to the vote of L. W., the omission by him to make a fresh claim in January, 1852, would be sufficient ground for expunging his claim from the register.

Ans.—It appears to the Board that where the address of the owner becomes, by a change of residence, substantially different from that contained in the statement previously given by him, under which he claimed to vote in respect of the property, he ought to give a fresh statement, before the first day of February next following such change. So too, if having himself previously occupied the property, he subsequently lets it to a tenant, so as to receive a rent for it, a new statement should be given, specifying that rent and the name of the tenant. The Board cannot do more than give this general answer to your question, as they do not know how far Mr. L. W. may be prepared to controvert the facts alleged in your letter. The clerk to the guardians will have full opportunity (if the objection be taken) of hearing evidence on both sides, and of forming his judgment upon that evidence.

5. QUALIFICATION OF VOTERS.

2nd April, 1851.

Clerk of Bridlington Union.—At a meeting of the inhabitants of the parish of Bridlington, held on the 20th February last, it was resolved to adopt the act 13 & 14 Vic. c. 99. No poor-rate has since been made, but the overseers of the poor have given notice of making one on the 3rd of April next. Five persons have been nominated to be guardians for the parish for the ensuing year, but as only three guardians are to be elected, it will be necessary to issue voting papers on the 5th of April. Inquired whether the occupiers of tenements, the rateable value of which do not exceed £6 each, whose names may be entered in the rate to be made on the 3rd of April, and who have been rated for the whole of the preceding year, will, if not otherwise disqualified, be entitled to vote in the election of guardians for the parish; and whether persons who came to reside in the parish on the 6th of April, 1850, and were rated to the first poor-rate made afterward, viz., on the 11th of April, 1850, and to all subsequent rates, in respect of property exceeding the rateable value of £6, will be entitled to vote at such election, provided they are assessed in the rate to be made on the 3rd of April next.

Ans.—In order to be qualified to vote as a ratepayer in the election of guardians, under 4 & 5 Wm. 4, c. 76, a person must (among other things) have been rated to the poor-rate for the year immediately preceding the day of voting. The day of voting in the present year will be the 5th of April. The Board collect from your statement that the occupiers will have satisfied that condition, as the owners, it appears, have not hitherto been assessed under the 13 & 14 Vic. c. 99, but it is presumed that they will be in a rate to be made on the 3rd of April instant. That rate, if made, will not, however, be perfected or be operative, until after allowance and publication. The latter cannot take place, at the earliest, until the 6th of April. The rate in existence on the 5th of April will therefore be the last poor-rate which was duly made, allowed, and published in the parish prior to the 3rd of April, and not the one made on that day. If the occupiers referred to are assessed in such last rate, and have satisfied the other conditions mentioned in 4 & 5 Wm. 4, c. 76, sec. 40, the Board think their votes must be admitted in the election of guardians, (see Bushell, App. Luckett Resp., 2 M. G. & S. 111.) With reference to the second question, the Board desire to point out that a rate made on the 11th of April, 1850, could not have become an operative rate until after the 14th of that month. The Board, therefore, think that a person rated for the first time in the parish in that rate will not have been rated for the year preceding the day of voting, (5th of April,) in the present year, and will not, consequently, be qualified to vote in the present election of guardians.

London: Printed by Order of the Poor Law Board, by BLACKBURN & BURT, 90½, Holborn Hill, and Published by CHARLES KNIGHT, 90, Fleet Street.

AN

OFFICIAL CIRCULAR

OF PUBLIC DOCUMENTS AND INFORMATION:

DIRECTED BY THE POOR LAW BOARD TO BE PRINTED, CHIEFLY FOR THE USE OF THE BOARDS OF GUARDIANS AND THEIR OFFICERS.

No. 51.] [N.S.

CONTENTS.

PAGE

I.—ELECTION OF GUARDIANS.—Construction of Election Expenses Order.

8th May, 1851.

Clerk of ——— *Union.*—Transmitting the following resolution of the guardians:—"Ordered that the bills of the clerk for conducting the contested elections for H. and Hors. be sent to the Poor Law Board with an inquiry whether the charges for distributing the voting papers are to be paid by the board, or by the clerk out of his allowance of one farthing and one halfpenny a head on the population under the Election Expenses Order." The following are the items objected to in these bills, namely, In the H. election bill—

	£.	s.	d.
The payment to Mr. R. L. for delivering and collecting the voting papers in the town of H. . .	1	10	0
And the payment to Mr. P. E. for delivering and collecting the voting papers in the —— allotment, distant from the town 12 miles	1	7	0
And in the Hors. election bill—			
The payment to Mr. J. C., jun. for delivering and collecting the voting papers in Hors. . .	0	15	0
Total	£3	12	0

By the Election Expenses Order of the 24th July, 1847, article 3, it is directed that the compensation to be paid to the clerk for the performance of the duties therein referred to, should include the remuneration of the persons who might have been employed to assist him in conducting and completing the election; and should in respect of the several unions named in the schedule marked B, therein referred to, (in which schedule this union is placed,) be such sum, not exceeding fifteen pounds, as the guardians should determine, and that the same should be defrayed out of the common fund of the union. Under this article the sum paid to him as clerk by the guardians during the last three years for conducting and completing the election of guardians for the 68 parishes of which the union is composed has been three pounds per annum, and there not having been a contested election during those years, and the business of the elections having been conducted by himself and his clerks without any extra assistance, he had accepted those payments without remark; but in the present year, in which there have been two contested elections, he had to pay £3. 12*s*., as stated above, to the persons employed by him in delivering and collecting the voting papers; and the annual allowance of three pounds for conducting the election being insufficient to cover these payments, the question has arisen, which is stated in the resolution of the guardians, whether they are to be borne by him out of the remuneration of one farthing and one halfpenny per head on the population under the 4th art. or the Election Expenses Order, or by the guardians; and in the latter case, another question arises, whether these payments are to be charged to the common fund of the union, or to the parishes in which the elections have taken place.

Ans.—The Election Expenses Order certainly provides that the remuneration or allowance per head derived under art. 4 of the Order shall be paid to the clerk in addition to the compensation to be awarded to him by the guardians under art. 3. The compensation under art. 3 is to include the remuneration of the several persons appointed to assist him in the conduct of the election, as for instance the persons who deliver and collect the voting papers. The object of the entire Order (though two different modes of payment are provided by it,) is to secure to the clerk a reasonable, but not an excessive remuneration for his trouble in conducting the election. Where therefore the sum received under art. 4 is small, the allowance under art. 3 should, as the Board consider, be fixed at such an amount (the clerk having to pay his assistants from that source) as will, combined with the amount receivable under art. 4, afford him a fair and reasonable remuneration. The Board must remark that the bills for printing the voting papers payable to the clerk under art. 4, are to be charged to the parishes wherein the contests occurred.

II.—LUNATIC.

1. MODE OF CHARGING EXPENSES OF APPLICATION TO JUSTICES FOR AN ORDER IN THE CASE OF A SUPPOSED LUNATIC, WHERE THEY DECLINE TO MAKE SUCH ORDER.

17th June, 1852.

Clerks of St. Thomas Union.—J. M., not settled but resident in the parish of Dunsford for about three years, having been recently taken before the magistrates, under the provisions of the statute 8 & 9 Vic. c. 126, for the purpose of obtaining an order for his admission into the county asylum, the magistrates decided that he was not insane, and declined to make any order. The expenses of the application having been charged to the parish of Dunsford, the guardian for that parish has applied to have them transferred to the common fund of the union. The Board of guardians, however, doubt, whether they can legally comply with this request, inasmuch as the 12 & 13 Vic. c. 103, sec. 5, enacts "that all the costs and expenses incurred, or hereafter to be incurred, since the 25th day of March last, [1849,] in and about obtaining any order of justices for the removal and maintenance of a lunatic pauper, who shall have been or shall be removed under any such order to any asylum, &c., and who if not a lunatic would have been exempt from removal, by reason of some provision of the 9 & 10 Vic, c. 66, shall be borne by the common fund of the union." It will be observed that no order has been obtained, consequently no removal under any order has taken place. If an order had been obtained, and a removal to the asylum effected, and the insanity had been certified to be of a temporary nature only, all the costs and expenses in and about obtaining the order, &c., and the maintenance, would have been charged to the common fund of the union. If the insanity had been certified to be of a permanent character, then the pauper would have been removable from not having resided five years in the parish of Dunsford. The pauper is now receiving relief in consequence of a temporary illness, and such relief is charged to the common fund of the union, under the statute 14 & 15 Vic. c. 105, sec. 1. It is contended on behalf of the parish of Dunsford, that there are expenses incurred "about obtaining an order," though no order was made. On the other hand, it is contended that the statute contemplates only cases in which an order is actually obtained, either for removal or maintenance; and that this may be inferred from the words, "who shall have been or shall be removed under such order," and also from the words at the end of the section, "notwithstanding the order shall be made on the overseers," &c. Requested the Board's opinion as to whether the expenses referred to, should be charged to the common fund of the union.

Ans.—The Board request that you will inform them who made the application to the justices with a view of obtaining an order for the pauper's admission into the county lunatic asylum, and under what circumstances, and by what authority such application was made. The Board do not distinctly ascertain from the statement before them, whether J. M. was, at the time of such application, or immediately previous, in the receipt of relief from the poor rate of any parish. If he was, they wish to know from what parish the relief was supplied to him.

Clerk of St. Thomas Union.—J. M. had attempted to destroy himself by hanging; and as soon as he recovered, he was taken to the union workhouse by the overseer of Dunsford, and the cost of his relief was charged to that parish. As the pauper was in a weak and excited state, the medical officer of the workhouse was immediately sent for, and he thought the pauper was, after such an attempt, an improper person to remain in the workhouse. He accordingly reported him to be so to the relieving officer of the district, who thereupon took the steps incumbent upon him under the 48th sec. of the 8 & 9 Vic. c. 126, and took the pauper before the magistrates, who declined to make an order for his admission into the asylum, as they did not consider him to be of unsound mind. The pauper then returned to the workhouse, and remained there, chargeable to the parish of Dunsford, until the 15th of March last, when he left, and has not since been chargeable. The guardians consider, J. M. was constructively, if not actually chargeable, by reason of his wife being maintained in the county lunatic asylum, as the 56th sec. of the 4 & 5 Wm. 4, c. 76, enacts, that all relief given to, or on account of the wife, &c., shall be considered as given to the husband of such wife, &c.

Ans.—The Board upon the facts communicated to them, do not consider that this case comes within the provisions of the 12 & 13 Vic. c. 103, sec. 5. They think it must be held, that the pauper J. M. was legally chargeable to the parish of Dunsford, when proceedings were taken under the 8 & 9 Vic. c. 126, sec 48, with a view to his removal to a lunatic asylum; and that he being so chargeable, the costs incurred by the relieving officer for the object contemplated, (although no order was actually made by the justices,) would properly fall upon the parish of Dunsford.

---

2. CHARGEABILITY OF LUNATIC.

17th Jan., 1852.

Clerk of Louth Union.—About fifteen months ago, John Mullheron, a dangerous lunatic found wandering in the town of Louth, was conveyed by direction of the guardians to Bethlem Hospital, London, where he has remained ever since. The guardians have been informed that it is the intention of the governor of the hospital to discharge him on Friday next; and one of the relieving officers of the union had been instructed to go to London, for the purpose of fetching the lunatic back to Louth. It is now intended to remove him on his return to Louth, to Gate Elmsley Lunatic Asylum, in the county of York, where it has been ascertained that there is a vacancy for him; and where it is intended he shall remain (if uncured) until the County Lunatic Asylum is ready for the reception of lunatics, which it is expected will be the case in the ensuing spring. The expenses of the removal of the lunatic to Bethlem Hospital have been paid from the common fund of the union; but a doubt is entertained by the guardians, whether, on the lunatic's return to Louth, he can still be considered as a wandering lunatic, and whether the justices can make an order for his removal to the Gate Elmsley Asylum, and the expenses of such an order, if obtained, and of his removal and future maintenance, be paid out of the common fund of the union. Requested the Board's advice in the matter.

Ans.—The Board are disposed to consider that on the lunatic's return to Louth, in the custody of an officer of the guardians, he could not then be viewed as a destitute wayfarer or wanderer, so as to render his subsequent relief a charge on the common fund of the union, whatever may have been his condition before his removal to Bethlem Hospital. If placed in the workhouse, (and this would probably be the course pursued,) he would be chargeable to the parish in which the workhouse stands. The proceedings for his confinement in a licensed house can then be taken under 8 & 9 Vic. c. 126, sec. 48. If the lunatic has a settlement which can be ascertained, an order for maintenance and reimbursement of expenses can be made upon the parish of the settlement (secs. 58 & 62.) If, however, the settlement cannot be ascertained, the county can be rendered liable for the maintenance, in accordance with secs. 59 & 63.

---

3. CHARGEABILITY OF IRREMOVABLE LUNATIC.

5th May, 1852.

Clerk of Blandford Union.—The wife of an able-bodied labourer having become insane, was sent, by an order of justice, to the county asylum in June 1839, her maintenance has hitherto been charged to the parish from which she was sent, under the act 8 & 9 Vic. c. 126, sec. 57. It has lately been discovered, however, that the pauper's husband is not settled in the parish from which his wife was sent to the asylum, but that he was irremovable therefrom by an industrial residence of more than five years. In August, 1849, the 12 & 13 Vic. c. 103, was passed to meet such cases, and enacts (sec. 5,) that the costs of lunatic paupers who are irremovable, shall be borne by the common fund of the union in which they reside. The guardians are, therefore, desirous of being informed if they are empowered to charge the cost of the maintenance of the lunatic referred to under the 12 & 13 Vic. c. 103, sec 5, to the common fund of the union; or whether the parish officers of the parish in which she resided, must apply to the justices, and prove the settlement of the husband and the irremovability from his present place of residence, and at the same time request to have an order on the guardians for the cost of the lunatic's maintenance at the asylum.

Ans.—The lunatic, when sent to the asylum, having been irremovable from the parish from which she was sent under 9 & 10 Vic. c. 66, it appears to the Board, that the guardians of the Blandford Union can, under the 12 & 13 Vic. c. 103, sec. 5, transfer the charge of the relief of the lunatic from the parish referred to, to the common fund of the union, without the authority of an order of justices.

---

4. MAINTENANCE OF LUNATIC, AND REMOVAL OF HIS FAMILY.

14th April, 1852.

Clerk of Carlisle Union.—John Cavannah, who is stated by his mother to have been born in the parish of St. Paul, Dublin, came with his wife and children to reside in Carlisle about twelve months ago. On the 19th ult. he became insane, and was sent by the guardians to Dunston Lodge Asylum, and his wife and children are now chargeable to the common fund of the Carlisle Union. Inquired whether the guardians can obtain an order of justices on the County of Cumberland for the cost of the man's maintenance at Dunston Lodge. It is presumed that Cavannah's wife and children cannot be removed to Ireland in his absence.

Ans.—The Board understand this to be the case of a man born in Ireland, and having no settlement in this country. If this be so, they consider that an application may be made to the justices, under the 8 & 9 Vic. c. 126, sec. 63, for an order upon the county for the maintenance of the lunatic. As regards the sending the wife of the lunatic to Ireland without her husband, the

Board think that your view of the case is corroborated by the judgment given by Mr. Justice Coleridge in the Q. *v.* St. Mary-le-bone, 4 New S. C., 476.

---

5. Destitute lunatic supposed to be possessed of property, but not chargeable on the poor rates.

5*th Jan.*, 1852.

Secretary to the Commissioners in Lunacy.—Forwarding a copy of correspondence relative to the case of Ann Aynscombe, a poor and unprotected lunatic, residing at Chiddingstone, in the county of Kent, and within the Sevenoaks Union; and requesting that they might receive any observations or suggestions upon the case, with which the Poor Law Board could furnish them.

Extracts from the correspondence referred to above:—

The Commissioners in Lunacy, to the Clerk of the Sevenoaks Union.—

25*th August*, 1851.

The Commissioners desire amongst other particulars, to know whether or not the said Ann Aynscombe be a chargeable pauper, as having received relief in any shape from her parish, or union. If such be the case, and her mental state be such as is represented, there would appear to be no difficulty or reason for delay in sending her to the county asylum, for which purpose, as the commissioners are informed, an order and medical certificate were recently obtained, but not acted upon. You will oblige this Board by communicating upon the subject with the relieving officer, of the district, or parochial authorities, and favouring the commissioners by a reply at your earliest convenience.

The Clerk of the Sevenoaks Union, to the Commissioners in Lunacy.—

28*th August*, 1851.

It appears that this party is not, nor has she ever been chargeable to any parish in the union. The relieving officer of the district states, that he went to visit her yesterday, on the receipt of a communication from me, and found her living in a house by herself, with the doors barred, and that she would not let him into her dwelling; but from the conversation he held with her through the window, she appeared to him to be insane. Under these circumstances, the guardians conceive that they have no power to interfere in the matter. The relieving officer stated that the party has a brother, a farmer, resident in the parish of Chiddingstone.

The Commissioners in Lunacy, to Dr. Baller, Penshurst.

29*th Dec.* 1851.

Much correspondence has passed between the Rev. Thomas Harvey, rector of Cowden, and this Board relative to Ann Aynscombe, a lunatic unprotected, residing at Chiddingstone; and the commissioners in lunacy have addressed repeated communications upon the subject of her neglected condition to her brother, John Aynscombe, of the Wilderness Farm, near Chiddingstone, and the guardians of the Sevenoaks Union, with a view to the lunatic being made chargeable as a pauper, and sent to the county asylum. Hitherto, the brother referred to, has not taken the necessary steps for that purpose, by applying for relief for his sister, and consequenty much difficulty, as I have fully, and more than once, explained to Mr. Harvey, exists in dealing with the case legally, inasmuch as Ann Aynscombe is neither a chargeable pauper, nor a wandering lunatic, nor a lunatic neglected, or illtreated, by any relative or other person having the charge of her, so as to bring her case within the provisions of the act 8 & 9 Vic. c. 126, sec. 49. Mr. Harvey having referred this Board to you for further information respecting her, I am directed to request, that you will favour them with such particulars as you are able, and deem material with reference to her mental and bodily condition; also as to her means of livelihood, and the circumstances under which she is now residing at Chiddingstone, in a house stated to be wholly, or partly her own property.

Dr. Baller, to the Commissioners in Lunacy.

2*nd Jan.*, 1852.

Some time since, I was requested by Mr. Harvey to visit Ann Aynscombe for the purpose of ascertaining her mental and bodily condition; which I did, and subsequently attended an investigation into her case, and signed a certificate as to her being a lunatic. At that time her brother, John Aynscombe, was present, and did not positively object to her removal to an asylum, which was thought desirable. I was, however, shortly after informed that he had opposed it, and which he continues to do; thus I presume, assuming the care and protection of his sister. I happened to meet her in the road to day, and find that her mind is in the same unsettled state. She is much wasted from the want, I believe, of a due supply of nourishment: she appears to be in a very miserable state; and I should not be at all surprised to hear of her being found dead, in her wretched habitation, from cold and inanition. It was said, but I know not on what authority, that she has some claim in a share of the cottage she occupies, which is in a very dilapidated and miserable state. As to her subsistence, no one knows whence it comes; but Mr. Harvey allows me to say that he is of opinion, it must be by some small pittance, or some credit at a shop, yielded by her brother. I beg to add, that I am fully persuaded of the necessity of doing something for the poor woman, and that Mr. Harvey has been actuated solely from humane considerations in calling the attention of the Commissioners to her present condition.

The Commissioners in Lunacy, to the Clerk of the Sevenoaks Union.

29th Dec., 1851.

You will oblige this Board by immediately informing them what, if any, further proceedings have been taken for the care and protection of Ann Aynscombe, the neglected lunatic at Chiddingstone, whose case, as the Commissioners are informed, is one of great urgency. The commissioners especially desire to know whether or not any relief has been given to her by the parish, or applied for by her brother John Aynscombe. The commissioners will further feel obliged by your furnishing them with such particulars as you are able respecting her present mental and bodily condition; also as to her means of livelihood, and the circumstances under which she is residing in the house stated to be wholly or partly her own, at Chiddingstone.

The Clerk of the Sevenoaks Union, to the Commissioners in Lunacy.

1st Jan., 1852.

No relief has been given to her by her parish, neither has she made application for relief. From the statement of the relieving officer of the district in which she resides, it appears that she is in much the same situation as when I wrote to you on the 28th August last. I regret that I am unable to furnish any information regarding her on my own personal knowledge.

Ans.—The Board cannot find that the laws for the relief of the poor supply any means of affording that aid which appears to be required in the case of Ann Aynscombe. The only power which is given to any poor law authority, is dependent upon the woman's being chargeable, or being ill-used by her relatives, or others who may have her in their charge; and both contingencies are negatived in the present case. The Board cannot recommend that the guardians of the union should assume that the person in question is chargeable, in order to enable them to obtain the requisite order of removal to an asylum, no application having been made for relief.

6. BURIAL OF LUNATICS DYING IN ASYLUMS.

3rd March, 1852.

Clerk of Marlborough Union.—Stated that he had received a communication from the County Lunatic Asylum, acquainting him of the death of a pauper belonging to the union, and stating that the formal notice would follow within the time prescribed by law, and that the object of the communication was to ascertain whether the relatives of the deceased, or the union officers, desire to remove the body for interment elsewhere, or the former to follow her remains to the grave; and it mentioned the time and place proposed for interment, unless the officers of the asylum should hear to the contrary. Inquired whether it forms part of his duty to make any arrangements in cases like the one referred to; or whether he is in any way responsible in the matter.

Ans.—Upon reference to the 8 & 9 Vic. c. 126, sec. 75, it will be seen that the notice of the death of any pauper patient in a lunatic asylum should be sent to the relieving officer of the union, or to the overseer of the parish who signed the statement accompanying the order for the admission of the lunatic into the asylum. It does not appear to the Board that the law casts any duty in respect of the notice in question upon the clerk to the board of guardians.

III.—NUISANCES.—EXTRA REMUNERATION TO RELIEVING OFFICER EMPLOYED IN OBTAINING REMOVAL OF.

17th June, 1851.

Clerk of Bromsgrove Union.—Inquired whether the guardians can legally call upon their officers, and especially the relieving officers, to look after and certify to the existence of nuisances (specified in the Nuisances Removal and Diseases Prevention Acts,) and to see to their removal without being paid extra for such service; and whether also the guardians can, under Art. 172 of the General Consolidated Order, remunerate their officers from time to time for the performance of such service.

Ans.—The law has not conferred upon the guardians any authority to cause general inspections to be made in respect of nuisances. They are to act upon express informations to be laid before them, either under the 11 & 12 Vic. c. 123, sec. 1, by the parties named therein; or under the 12 & 13 Vic. c. 111, sec. 6, by the medical or relieving officer. If under either of these sections the relieving officer should render any extraordinary services, and the guardians should wish to pay him a reasonable gratuity, under Art. 172 of the General Consolidated Order, this Board will give due consideration to the proposal; but they feel bound to point out to the guardians that great caution is necessary in acting upon the discretionary authority given by that art. of the order.

IV.—ORPHANS.—Detention in the Workhouse of Orphans under 16 Years of Age.

9th Feb., 1852.

Clerk of Worcester Union.—Two orphan children, of the respective ages of seven and five years, were, on the death of their parents, taken charge of by an uncle, who applied for out-door relief for them whilst residing with him, which the guardians refused; but offered to admit them into the workhouse, believing that the children would be better provided for there. Both the children were admitted into the workhouse, where they have remained up to the present time; but the uncle has applied to have the elder child given up to him. This application the guardians have refused to comply with, or rather deferred, until the Board's opinion upon the subject can be ascertained. The guardians are desirous of preventing the uncle from having the child, and wish to know whether they have authority to detain it in the workhouse in opposition to his request, as they are satisfied that his bad example will have a very pernicious effect upon the child.

Ans.—The Poor Law Commissioners considered that the guardians of the poor are empowered to detain in the workhouse children under the age of sixteen years, in cases where such children having no parents are in destitute circumstances, and where the guardians are fully satisfied that the real interests of the children require that they should be so detained. This opinion has not been questioned; and the Poor Law Board think that the guardians may properly act upon it in such a case as the present.

V.—RATING.—House and Field Unoccupied.

22nd August, 1851.

Messrs. ———, *Solicitors, London.*—A client of theirs is the owner of a house in Leicestershire, with the adjoining garden, orchard, and field. The field has been mown this summer, but the premises are unoccupied, and the owner has put a person in possession merely for the purpose of taking care of them. A demand has now been made upon him, not only for poor-rate but also for highway-rate, but as there has been no beneficial occupation of the property, they conceive that he is not liable for the rates in question. Requesting the opinion of the Board as to whether they consider the owner is liable for these rates, and to what extent.

Ans.—So far as the field is concerned there appears to have been an occupation of it in respect of which the owner is certainly rateable if he took the grass. As regards the house, however, it would appear to the Board upon the statement before them that the owner ought not to be assessed in respect of it; but if the assessment of the whole property be in one sum his only remedy would be by appeal to the Sessions in respect of the excess.

VI.—OVERSEERS.

1. Legality of Justices' Orders when made without Summoning the Overseers.

15th Aug., 1851.

Overseers of Yarpole, Leominster Union.—Inquired whether they were bound to pay two bills of 15*s.* and 35*s.* incurred by the parish constable in apprehending persons supposed to have committed theft, the justices having ordered the payment of the same. The overseers were not summoned to appear before the justices before the making of the orders for the payment of the bills; neither were they aware that the constable had any demand against the parish until the justices' orders were delivered to them.

Ans.—As the overseers to whom the orders in question were addressed were not summoned to attend the justices before these orders were made, the Board are of opinion that they are not valid or legal orders, or such as can be enforced against the overseers. The Board have been advised by counsel that the summoning of the overseer is an essential preliminary to the making of a lawful order upon them under the 5 & 6 Vic. c. 109, sec. 17.

---

2. POWER OF OVERSEERS TO GIVE AN ORDER FOR A COFFIN.

9th August, 1852.

Mr. H. H. Kidd, Assistant Overseer, Lostwithiel, Bodmin Union.—On the 5th of April, M. M., a miner, resident in the parish of Lostwithiel, applied to him for an order for a coffin for his child, which he and the overseer hesitated to give until enquiry had been made with regard to the man's earnings. It was found that M. M. had but fourpence in his possession, that he had been unfortunate in his work at the mine, and that his pay-day would not be due until the end of the month, when he would not receive more than 18*s*. M. M. had a wife and five children, and bears a good character for sobriety and honesty. Under these circumstances, the overseers had granted the relief applied for. At the following meeting of the board, the contractor sent in his bill for the coffin, which the guardians, who, it is believed, had been misinformed as to the amount of the man's earnings, refused to pay. Inquired whether the overseers have power to interfere in cases of emergency such as the present.

Ans.—If the guardians, or their authorised officer, did not order the burial of the body of the child to take place at the expense of the poor rates, they cannot be required to pay the expenses which you have incurred; and the Board cannot interfere with the guardians' decision in the matter.

24th August, 1852.

Mr. H. H. Kidd.—His impression is, that in the case of a poor person dying while in the receipt of relief ordered by the guardians, the overseers may, in the absence of the relieving officer, give an order for a coffin; but that if the person dying is not chargeable to the parish at the time of his or her death, the case should be referred to the guardians, or (as they only sit fortnightly), to the relieving officer. Requested to be informed as to whether his view of the matter is correct.

Ans.—The Board desire to direct your attention to the terms of the 7 & 8 Vic. c. 101, sec. 31, which enacts, that it shall be lawful for guardians, or where there are no guardians, for the overseers to bury the body of any poor person which may be within their parish or union respectively, &c. You will perceive from these terms, that the overseers of a parish in a union have no authority to provide for the burial of paupers under the above enactment; but that such authority is confined to the guardians, and (according to the language of a subsequent part of the section,) "any of their officers duly authorized."

VII.—PUNISHMENT—OF A PAUPER ON HIS RE-ADMISSION INTO THE WORKHOUSE FOR AN OFFENCE COMMITTED BEFORE HE QUITTED IT.

3rd March, 1851.

Clerk of Rye Union.—Inquired whether a pauper who has violated the regulations of the workhouse, but has quitted it before the commencement of the punishment ordered by the guardians for such violation, can be punished for the same offence after his re-admission to the workhouse, within seven days from the time of such offence. The circumstances which have induced the above inquiry are as follow: Two young men were placed in the infectious ward which communicates with the yard, or space between the back of the premises of the workhouse offices and the infirmary, and which yard or space is enclosed by a brick wall. During the night, the paupers removed a portion of the lock on the door of the ward, got over the wall, and went off the workhouse premises, but returned again over the wall after being absent for a few hours, when they were detected by the porter, who had previously discovered that the paupers were not in the ward. On the following Monday, the 10th instant, the guardians directed that the paupers should be shut up, and their diet altered, they having committed two offences, by damaging the workhouse property, and getting over the walls twice, such punishment to commence on Friday last. Before that day, however, (namely on Tuesday,) both the paupers gave the required notice to the master and quitted the workhouse. On last Friday evening one of the paupers obtained from the relieving officer an order for his re-admission into the workhouse, where he now is by virtue of such order. There are reasons for presuming that the paupers left the workhouse on Tuesday last to avoid the punishment, which they no doubt knew they were liable to for the offences they had committed.

Ans.—Having regard to Art. 133 of the General Consolidated Order, the Board think that the guardians are not now empowered to punish the pauper in question for an offence against the regulations of the union workhouse not committed since his last admission.

VIII.—PROPERTY—OF DECEASED PAUPERS.

19th Feb., 1851.

Clerk of Dolgelley Union.—Three paupers, named Lewis Jones, Ellen Morris, and Margaret Lewis, recently died in the Dolgelley Union, leaving property varying in value from £3 to £6 each, and the relations or friends of each appropriated to themselves certain portions of such property, either immediately previous or subsequent to the paupers' decease. It has, however, become difficult to ascertain what portion of the property has been so taken away, by whom it has been taken, and where it is to be found; because the parties, having concealed it, say, when it is discovered, that it had been given to them by the paupers in the presence of witnesses whom they name. Requested the opinion of the Poor Law Board, 1st. Whether it is the duty of the overseers of the parish wherein a pauper dies possessed of property, (or, if not, whose duty is it,) to secure such property on behalf of the guardians, until their next meeting. 2nd. Whether the guardians may authorize the overseers or officers, or any other persons to sell such property, and to deduct from the proceeds, the amount of the guardians' claim for relief, and the expenses of the sale, and then pay the balance to the union treasurer. 3rd. Whether the guardians are bound to direct that such property shall be sold, and the produce thereof, (the expenses incurred being first deducted,) paid to the union treasurer, to the credit of the parish or union, (as the case may be,) towards the reimbursement of the amount of the twelve months' relief, and funeral expenses, or 4th, Whether the guardians are authorized to order such property to be deposited in safe custody, for the purpose of being given by them, from time to time, at their discretion, to paupers, by way of relief in kind, or relief by way of loan; and 5th, Whether a pauper in receipt of regular parochial relief, say, for the period of two years or upwards, previous to his decease, can, within that period, give away any of his property; and whether a person receiving the same, and knowing the pauper to be at that time in receipt of regular weekly relief, is liable to a prosecution.

Ans.—1st. The Board do not find that the duty of seizing the effects of deceased paupers, on the part of the guardians, is imposed by law upon any particular officer or person. 2nd. The Board consider that the guardians may direct any one of their officers, or any other person on their behalf, to obtain possession of such property, and, as they are to be reimbursed the expenses which they have incurred, they are called upon to cause the property to be fairly sold, with a view to raising the required amount. The guardians will observe, that they are to be reimbursed the expenses of the burial; therefore assuming that the 12 & 13 Vic. c. 103, sec. 16, is generally applicable, the Board do not think that the guardians can sell the property to reimburse themselves, until the expenses of the burial have been paid. 3rd. The Board are not prepared to state that the guardians are compelled to cause the property to be sold, but, they cannot recommend the guardians to adopt any other course. The sale, fairly conducted, will alone determine the value, and show to the parties concerned that there has not been an undue appropriation of it by the guardians. 4th. The above remarks apply to the fourth question. 5th. The Board are not aware of any provision of the law which prevents a pauper from giving away his property during the time when he is in the receipt of relief, if the guardians of the union do not interfere to prevent it; and, they are clearly of opinion that there is no ground for prosecuting the party receiving it. The proper remedy against such a proceeding is the exercise of due vigilance on the part of the relieving officer and the guardians, and the abstaining from granting relief to persons possessed of property which can be rendered available to remove destitution.

IX.—POOR-RATE.

1. ASSESSMENT OF NEW PREMISES TO, AND EXCUSAL FROM PAYMENT OF, POOR-RATE.

25th March, 1852.

Overseers of Luton, Luton Union.—Inquired 1st. If premises which were formerly rateable to the poor-rate be taken down and others more valuable erected on the site, whether the overseers have the power to rate such new premises at their increased value so soon as they are fit for occupation, if a rate is being made at that time; or, whether such new premises must be actually occupied again before they can be rated; and whether, in either of the cases mentioned, the occupier can be called upon for a proportion of a rate for the occupation of such premises, during any part of the time for which such rate is made. 2nd. Whether, if from illness, poverty, or being in receipt of permanent relief, the parish officers consider that certain individuals cannot pay their rates, and a list containing the names of such persons, with the causes why they cannot pay, be drawn up and signed by the overseers and churchwardens, and presented to the magistrates, the magistrates can refuse to sign the same; and, if so, what steps are the overseers to take in order to account to the auditor for the amount so asked to be excused; and can they be allowed to carry the same to the column in the rate book prepared for irrecoverable amounts.

Ans.—1st. A poor-rate cannot lawfully be made in respect of premises under such circumstances as those described, until they are occupied. But, if after a rate has been made for the parish, the property should become occupied, a proportionate amount of such rate will be payable by the occupier, in respect of the time during which it is occupied, (see the 17 Geo. 2, c. 38, sec. 12.) This amount should, however, be calculated according to the then value of the property. 2nd. When persons who have been rated to the poor-rate in respect of premises occupied by them, are unable to pay the rates, they can themselves apply to the justices to be excused the payment; or, some party may make the application on their behalf, and the overseers of the parish can then give their assent, if they think fit, to such excusal, but it is no part of their duty, nor is it proper for them to interfere to procure the excusal of the payment of the poor-rate. Where the parties do not so apply, or where the justices decline to excuse, the overseers must take proper means to enforce payment of the rate, and can only take credit in the rate book for irrecoverable rates in cases where actual bankruptcy, insolvency, or some similar cause, has occurred to render the collection or recovery of the same impracticable. If the number of occupiers in the parish who cannot pay their rates be considerable, the Board think that the parish would do well to adopt the provisions of the statute 13 & 14 Vic. c. 99, for assessing the owners, instead of the occupiers of small tenements.

2. Recovery of arrears of poor rates.

19th March, 1851.

Clerk of Dolgelley Union.—There is an arrear of four years' poor rates for a mill occupied in a parish in the union, and the overseers entertain some doubt whether in consequence of the length of time which has elapsed, such arrear can now be recovered by them. The arrear has been carried on from one quarter to the other in the rate book from the commencement. Requested the opinion of the Poor Law Board on the point.

Ans.—The Board do not find that there is any statute which limits the time within which the arrears of poor rates are to be enforced. The 43 Eliz. c. 2, sec. 3, and the 17 Geo. 2, c. 38, sec. 11, enable subsequent overseers to recover the arrears of poor rates which should have been paid to their predecessors.

3.—Rating almshouses.

17th Jan., 1852,

Rev. P. S. Bagge, Elsworth, Caxton and Arrington Union.—Inquired whether some almshouses for aged "widows, in the parish of Elsworth, for which he, as" rector of the parish, acts as trustee, are assessed to the poor-rate; and if so, whether they may, by a resolution of a vestry meeting of the parish, be omitted from the rate.

Ans.—According to the case of Rex *v.* Munday, 1 East 584, the Board apprehend that the almshouses referred to are legally liable to be assessed to the poor-rate. The vestry of the parish have no authority to direct that any property which is legally assessable, should be omitted from the rate. Neither can the overseers do so on their own authority; indeed the omission from the rate of property liable to be assessed thereto, would render the rate open to appeal on that ground.

4. Validity of rate, the deductions from land and rent charge not being equal.

21st June, 1852.

The Rev. ——, *Camelford Union.*—At a vestry meeting, held in the parish of T———, some time since, it was determined, in assessing property therein, to deduct 20 per cent. in the case of land, and 10 per cent. in the case of the rent charge. Inquired whether such unequal deductions as those above referred to are sufficient to invalidate the poor-rate.

Ans.—The Board cannot express any positive opinion upon the question raised in your letter. They can only remark generally, that it is the duty of the overseers to make a fair and equal rate, and to this end they should take care that all the rateable property in the parish is assessed upon its actual rateable value, according to the principles laid down in the Parochial Assessments Act, 6 & 7 Wm. 4, c. 96, s. 1. The Board may remark, that whatever doubt may exist as to the value of the land, the value of the tithe rent charge is readily ascertainable by reference to the averages according to which such rent charge is calculated in the current year. With regard to the deductions to be made in computing the rateable value, the Board desire to state that a uniform reduction of 20 per cent. in the value of all the land in the parish, without reference to the different circumstances of different properties, does not appear to be a correct course of proceeding; and if such reduction be merely arbitrary, and the advantage be unfairly withheld from the tithe owner, the rate would apparently be open to appeal upon that ground.

---

5. RATING OF SMALL PROPERTIES, 13 & 14 VIC. c. 99.

20th Jan., 1852.

Overseer of Datchworth, Hertford Union.—It has been determined by the vestry of the parish of Datchworth, to rate the owners of tenements of the annual value of £6, instead of the occupiers. A person who occupies a small farm and land in the parish, of the yearly rateable value of £11. 10*s.* belonging to A. B., also occupies a cottage and garden of the yearly rateable value of £3. 10*s.* belonging to C. D. The two properties are forty yards apart, and have hitherto been separately assessed to the poor-rate. Inquired whether the tenement belonging to C. D., should be rated to the occupier, or to the owner.

Ans.—It appears to the Board, upon the information now before them, that the owner of the cottage and garden referred to in the parish of Datchworth is properly assessable to the poor-rate, under the 13 & 14 Vic. c. 99, in respect of such property.

---

6. COMMUTATION BY OWNERS OF SMALL TENEMENTS.

14th Feb., 1852.

Assistant Overseer of Collingburn, Kingston Union.—Inquired how long a commutation effected by agreement between the overseers of a parish in which the 13 & 14 Vic. c. 99, is adopted, and the owner of small tenements rated under that act, will continue in force in accordance with the provisions of the 4th sec. of that act.

Ans.—A commutation thus agreed to will be binding on both parties until the 25th day of March next, following the date of the agreement; but it will then expire, unless the agreement be renewed for another year, which may be done under the enactment referred to.

---

7. RATING SMALL TENEMENTS UNDER 13 & 14 VIC. c. 99.

3rd April, 1851.

Mr. Fleming, Downton, Alderbury Union.—1st. Inquired whether a person who rents three or four tenements of one landlord, of the aggregate rateable value of more than £6. is to be rated at the full amount as if they were one tenement; or, whether the owner is to be rated under the 13 & 14 Vic. c. 99, sec. 4, at the reduced scale of three-fourths of the rateable value. 2nd. Whose name is to appear in the rate-book as owner, and whose as occupier in a case where two or more cottages or pieces of land are rented by a person of one landlord, and sublet to two or three separate persons, so that each subletting is of the yearly rateable value of less than £6. 3rd. Whether, if any owner of one or more of such tenements, shall be desirous of paying a rate for one year, and shall give notice thereof in writing, according to the 2nd section of the above statute, the overseers are obliged to rate them at one-half the yearly rateable value only; or, whether they can rate them at three-fourths, if they think proper. 4th. Whether the notice of compounding must be renewed every year; and whether any particular form of notice must be used.

Ans.—1st. The tenements, if distinct, are to be treated as such within the above cited statute, though held together by one person, and the owner should be rated on the reduced scale accordingly. 2nd. the actual occupier of each separate tenement is to appear upon the rate as the occupier, and his immediate landlord, who receives the rent from him, is to be rated as the owner. 3rd. Where the required notice has been given, the owner is to be assessed at less than three-fourths, but not less than one-half of the yearly rateable value of his tenements. The statute leaves it uncertain who is to determine the exact amount, but this point may be settled by mutual agreement between the overseers and the owner. 4th. The notice of composition to be given by the owner, under sec. 4 of the statute, must be given every year; but there is no particular form of notice required by the act to be adopted.

X.—RELATIONS.

1. LIABILITY OF MAN TO MAINTAIN HIS WIFE'S STEP-CHILDREN.

24th April, 1851.

E. Hinxman, Jun., Esq., Guardian, Amesbury Union.—A labourer belonging to the parish of Little Darnford lately died, leaving a family of four young children, all under fourteen years of age. Shortly before his last illness he married a second wife, by whom, however, he had no children. This widow is now about to be married again. Inquired whether her future husband will become liable to keep the four children.

Ans.—The law does not cast any obligation upon the second husband to maintain the step-children of his wife. The liability cast upon the husband by the 4 & 5 Wm. 4, c. 76, sec. 57, is confined to his wife's own children.

---

2. ENFORCEMENT OF ORDER OF MAINTENANCE MADE ON GRANDFATHER OF CHILDREN DESERTED BY THEIR FATHER.

7th Feb., 1852.

Overseer of Sherford, Kingsbridge Union.—A man named Hatherly, six or seven years ago married a woman belonging to the parish of Sherford, and some time after deserted her, when she became, with her two children, chargeable to that parish. Being unable to find the husband, an application was made to the justices for an order on the children's grandfather, who owned a small portion of land in the north of Devon, and he was directed to pay 3*s*. per week towards their maintenance, which he did up to Lady-day, 1850, since which time no further payments have been made. The late overseer of Sherford made several applications by letter for the payment of the money, but in consequence of the distance, did not make a personal demand. This he, the present overseer, has done, and being refused payment, he applied to the magistrates to grant a summons, which they refused to do, on the ground that they could not enforce the payment, in consequence of the order having been made for the maintenance of the two children, whilst the relief had been entered in the name of the mother. He asked the clerk to the guardians and the relieving-officer, if the relief was granted in the usual way, and was informed by both that it was quite regular, and that it could not be given in any other way. The mother is not living with the children, but resides in the parish in respectable service. He can produce the maternal grandmother, with whom the children reside, to prove that she has received the money regularly, and expended it on them. At the last audit, the auditor insisted on his getting the money immediately. Requested the Board's advice in the matter.

Clerk of Kingsbridge Union.—[To whom a copy of the above communication was sent for the observations of the guardians.] The relief granted to the two children in question was entered in the usual way, the mother residing in the same parish as the children, and not having deserted them; and the relief granted was for the children and not for the mother.

Ans.—[To the clerk, a copy being sent to the overseer.] If the mother does not herself require relief, but relief is given (as the Board collect from your statement that it is in the present instance,) for and on account of the children only, it should, as the Board consider, be entered in the name of the latter. It may be further remarked, that, as the children are legitimate, and the mother is not a widow, nor the father beyond the seas, or in the custody of the law, or in a lunatic asylum, the relief given to the children is not, in construction of law, relief to the mother. If, therefore, the relief be entered and charged as given to the children, the Board presume that the difficulty felt by the justices will be removed, and that they will enforce the order of maintenance, made on the grandfather of the children, in favour of the parish of Sherford.

XI.—RELIEF.

1. TO NON-RESIDENT PAUPERS UNDER EXCEPTION 2, TO ARTICLE 3, OF THE GENERAL PROHIBITORY ORDER.

17th Jan., 1851.

Clerk of Pembroke Union.—The guardians having resolved to withdraw the relief given to their non-resident poor residing in the Haverford West Union, requested the opinion of the Poor Law Board as to the construction of the second exception to article 3 of the General Prohibitory Order (which declares that no relief shall be given to any person who does not reside within the union,) and more especially whether the "bodily and mental infirmities" mentioned in the 2nd exceptions, have reference to cases of merely a temporary character, or those also of a permanent nature, such as old age, blindness, &c.; also in the event of paupers under the above circumstances being legally relievable out of the union, whether the relieving officers of the union in which they reside, or the relieving officers of the union in which they are settled, should pay the relief granted.

Ans.—In order to bring the case of an infirm pauper within the exception in question, it is not material whether the infirmity be of a permanent or a temporary character; the case will be within the exception so long as the infirmity continues, whatever may be the probability as to its longer or shorter duration. Such a degree of old age as to produce a physical disability for labour would be within the exception, and so would blindness. With respect to the other inquiry contained in your letter, the Board have to point out that if the guardians of the Pembroke Union discontinue the allowance of relief to any non-resident pauper, the duty of relieving such pauper will devolve, as a matter of course, upon the guardians of the union in which he resides, who will charge the relief to the parish of his residence, or to the common fund of the union, as the case may require. If he be not exempt from removal, and the relief be consequently charged to the parish of the residence, it will then be open to the overseers of that parish, (if they think fit to do so,) to apply for an order to remove the pauper to the parish of his settlement.

---

2. PAYMENT OF ARREARS OF NON-RESIDENT RELIEF TO BASTARD AFTERWARDS ADMITTED INTO THE WORKHOUSE.

1st May, 1852.

Clerk of Falmouth Union.—John T., a boy belonging to, and an acknowledged pauper of the town of Falmouth, in the Falmouth Union, but resident within the Truro Union, was for sometime allowed the sum of 1*s.* 6*d.* per week, whilst so non-resident; but recent circumstances have shown the guardians of the Falmouth Union, that the allowance of non-resident relief was not consistent with the orders of the Poor Law Board; and they, therefore, discontinued it, and directed the pauper to be admitted into the union workhouse, where he now is. There is an arrear of 22*s.* due to the person with whom the pauper resided at Truro; and the guardians desire the sanction of the Board to the discharge of the same, as the non-payment of the money would, in their opinion, be a breach of faith on their part.

Ans.—The Board request to be informed of the age of the boy referred to, and whether he is an orphan; and if not, what are the circumstances of his parents or surviving parent, and under what circumstances the relief was allowed by the guardians whilst he resided in the Truro Union.

Clerk of Falmouth Union.—John T. is represented to be 9½ years old, and illegitimate. He was taken to Elizabeth T———, (the person to whom the money claimed is owing,) when about five months old, and continued with her at Truro up to the date of the present application. The boy was deserted by his mother several years ago, and her place of abode is not known to the guardians. The relief was first allowed because the boy had no friends. Elizabeth T———, at the last meeting of the guardians, applied for an outfit of clothing for the boy, as she has procured him a situation at Truro, in which he will learn the trade of a cordwainer, and has arranged to give him his lodgings free of cost, whilst he is learning the trade.

Ans.—If what is now claimed be the amount of the out relief which has not been paid, the guardians can pay it; but if it be the cost of the boy's maintenance after the guardians had given notice to discontinue the relief, the Board are not aware of the authority which the guardians possess for paying it, nor of the fund to which it could be charged. The Board think it very desirable that steps should be taken to bind John T—— apprentice under the regulations contained in the General Consolidated Order applicable to the case.

---

3. RELIEF TO THE CHILDREN OF A WOMAN WHOSE HUSBAND HAS BEEN TRANSPORTED.

29th May, 1852.

Clerk of Tiverton Union.—Elizabeth R., whose husband was transported some years ago, and who has since given birth to a bastard child, has applied to the guardians for relief for her three legitimate children, under 13 years of age. The guardians offered her admission into the workhouse, which she declined, but left her children there. Inquired whether she can be punished for deserting her children, and whether the guardians can refuse her any relief other than in the workhouse.

Ans.—Under Article 4 of the General Prohibitory Order, relief given to the wives and children of persons circumstanced as your letter describes, is in conformity with the 7 & 8 Vic. c. 101, s. 25, to be given in the same manner, and subject to the same conditions, as if such wives were widows. The effect of this provision is to enable the guardians to exercise a discretion as to whether they will give in or out-door relief in such cases, in like manner as they are empowered to do in the cases of widows. The guardians may, therefore, if they think fit, decline to relieve the wife and children, except in the workhouse, unless under the circumstances following:—Where the children are under the age of nurture, and relief is applied for on their account only, and the guardians are satisfied that the relief is required for them alone, and not for the parent; in which case, as the guardians cannot legally separate the children from their mothers, the Board apprehend that the guardians would be obliged to give out-door relief to the extent of the maintenance of such children. With regard to the question raised, whether Elizabeth R. would be liable to punishment for deserting her children, the Board are unable to express any certain opinion. They think it is open to considerable doubt whether the terms of the 7 & 8 Vic. c. 110, sec. 35, empowering the wife to be treated, under certain circumstances, as a widow, for the purposes of relief, subject her also to the penal consequences which, under the 5 Geo. 4, c. 83, clearly attach to the head of the family, if he neglect to maintain his children, or is otherwise guilty of deserting them.

XII.—RELIEVING OFFICER.—REPAYMENT OF EXPENSES INCURRED BY.

18th July, 1851.

Relieving Officer, Poole Union.—Inquired whether he is entitled to be reimbursed the following expenses incurred by him as relieving-officer, viz., For journeys to Wimborne to give evidence before the magistrates in matters relating to lunatic paupers, and to the removal of paupers, belonging to, or residing in any parish of the union. 2. For postage incurred in writing to the guardians, or to the overseers of any parish within his district on matters purely parochial.

Ans.—You are not bound to attend before the justices at Wimborne as a witness in the cases which you specify, unless your expenses are paid; but as to the postage of letters under the circumstances described, the Board do not think that you can make any legal claim upon the guardians of the Poole Union.

XIII.—REMOVABILITY.

1. REMOVABILITY OF MOTHER OF BASTARD CHILD.

23rd Jan., 1853.

Clerk of Holsworthy Union.—Transmitting the following statement, duly signed under sec. 4 of the 11 & 12 Vic. c. 110, for the opinion of the Poor Law Board:—Mary ——, a single woman, residing in the parish of St. Pancras Week, in the Holsworthy Union, has applied for relief for her bastard child. Mary —— was born in one of the parishes of the city of Exeter, where her parents are legally settled and now reside. At the age of four years she was taken from her parents by her grandfather, who lives in Pancras Week, and continued with him until about four years since, when she went into service in that parish. She remained in this service during the four years, when being pregnant, she left, and went to Exeter to see her parents, but left her box and clothes at Pancras Week, having no intention, as she states, of remaining in Exeter. At the expiration of three weeks she returned to the parish of Pancras Week, and stayed about a fortnight with her former master, and then returned to her grandfather, in whose house she was confined of her present bastard, and has continued to reside with him up to the time of the present application for relief. The questions submitted are:—1st. Is the woman, Mary —— removable? 2nd. Is the bastard child removable? 3rd. If not removable, is the relief to the bastard child to be charged to the common fund, or to the parish of Pancras Week?

Ans.—With reference to the terms in which the questions are stated, the Board desire to point out that the pauper in the present case is Mary —— herself, and not her child, although it may be on account of the latter that the relief is specifically needed. Upon the facts set forth in the statement, Mary —— appears to be irremovable from the parish of Pancras Week, under the 9 & 10 Vic. c. 66, sec. 1, and, consequently, her child is also irremovable, by virtue of the 3rd section of the same act. The Board are therefore of opinion that the cost of the relief afforded to Mary —— should be charged to the common fund of the Holsworthy Union.

---

2. REMOVABILITY OF WIDOW WHO LEFT HER RESIDENCE WITHIN THE FIRST YEAR OF HER WIDOWHOOD, TO GO INTO SERVICE IN ANOTHER PARISH.

1st July, 1852.

The Rev. E. R., Holsworthy Union. — Eliza H., a widow with one child, resided with her late husband in the parish of Clawton. In February last, an order was obtained for the removal of the husband, with his wife and child, from that parish to the parish of Sheepwash, his legal settlement. The order was suspended in consequence of his illness, and he died in the parish of Clawton. Some time after the death of her husband, Eliza H. gave up her residence at Clawton, and went to reside with her father in the parish of Preworthy. After a residence of some weeks in Preworthy, she hired herself as a yearly servant in the parish of Thornbury, and remained in such service for two months, and then left and returned to Clawton, in which parish she slept one night, and on the following day applied for relief on the ground of inability to support her child. Inquired whether Eliza H. is removable from the parish of Clawton under the above circumstances.

Ans.—The Board are not aware that the point raised can be said to have been expressly decided. But in the case of Reg. *v.* St. Marylebone, 20 L. J. Rep. (M. C.) 173, there was a strong expression of opinion on the part of the court, that if there was a break of the residence during the first twelvemonths of the widowhood, the privilege of the irremovability of the widow, under the 9 & 10 Vic. c. 66, sec. 2, would be gone. According to that view, it appears to the Board that in the case which you have brought under their notice, the residence in the parish of Clawton was interrupted, so that the removal of the pauper would not be restrained by that provision.

3. REMOVABILITY OF WIDOW, TEMPORARILY ABSENT IN THE PARISH OF HER HUSBAND'S SETTLEMENT DURING HIS ILLNESS.

28th May, 1852.

Clerk of Camelford Union.—Sarah Gribble, is the widow of William Gribble, late of St. Seath, in the Camelford Union, labourer. She was married to him in St. Seath church, four years and a half since. She had resided in St. Seath about twelve months before she married him. About two months since her husband, William Gribble, whose supposed legal settlement was in Frithelstock, Devon; was taken ill and returned to Frithelstock to his parents for change of air, where he died in about a week; his widow the said Sarah Gribble being with him in Frithelstock at the time of his death. Before they left St. Seath for Frithelstock, they placed one child with a sister in law, in St. Seath, to nurse during their absence, and they did not dispose of their furniture, but allowed it to remain in the dwelling they had occupied since their marriage, which consisted of separate rooms in their brother-in-law's house, for which they paid a yearly rent of two pounds. After her husband's death, Sarah Gribble returned to St. Seath, where she now resides. Inquired whether the widow is removable to the parish of her husband's settlement, inasmuch as she was residing with him there at the time of his death, and would, had she remained, have become chargeable to that parish, and could not have been removed from thence for twelve months after his death if he had not been settled there; or, whether she is now irremovable from St. Seath and chargeable to the common fund of the Camelford Union.

Ans.—The Board consider that the pauper in question was only temporarily absent with her husband in the parish of Frithelstock, where he died, and that she did not thereby interrupt her residence in the parish of St. Seath, in which, they collect, from the statements before them, she had resided for a period exceeding five years. As it is not stated that the pauper was in receipt of relief during that period, the Board are of opinion that she is now irremovable from the parish of St. Seath; and that, not being settled in that parish, the cost of her relief is chargeable to the common fund of the Camelford Union.

4. REMOVABILITY OF MEN RECEIVING RELIEF ON ACCOUNT OF SICKNESS IN THEIR FAMILIES.

July 9th, 1852.

Clerk of Leighton Buzzard Union.—1. J. G. who has resided, with his wife and children, in the parish of Leighton Buzzard during the last four years, but who is legally settled in the parish of Olney, has been allowed relief in consequence of the illness (arising from pregnancy) of his wife; and the relief has been charged to the parish of Leighton Buzzard. 2. A. B., who has resided, with his wife and children, at Cheddington for the last four years, but who is settled in the parish of Windsor, has been allowed relief in consequence of the temporary illness of one of his children, and the relief has been charged to the parish of Cheddington.

Inquired whether J. G. and A. B., who are still in the receipt of relief, are removable to the parishes in which they are respectively settled, under sec. 3 of the 11 & 12 Vic. c. 110, (subject to the suspension of the order of removal as regards the sick members;) or, whether, under 9 & 10 Vic. c. 66, they are irremovable, and the relief which they receive chargeable to the common fund of the union.

Ans.—As regards the pauper "J. G.," the Board apprehend that pregnancy of itself will not constitute a sickness of the kind contemplated by the 9 & 10 Vic. c. 66, sec. 4, as likely to produce permanent disability, but it may be accompanied by such ailments as would constitute temporary sickness, within the meaning of the clause. If the woman in such a case receives relief she will be irremovable; but if the pregnancy, without being accompanied by ailments amounting to sickness, simply produces destitution, (as by incapacitating the woman for her ordinary work,) and she receives relief in consequence of that destitution, she will not be rendered irremovable under the section referred to, which contemplates a chargeability resulting from sickness or accident, and not from general destitution. Child-birth in ordinary cases will be a temporary sickness within the enactment. As to the pauper "A. B." the statement forwarded appears to the Board to bring the case within the 3rd sec. of the 9 & 10 Vic. c. 66; and, if so, the paupers are not removable, but the cost of their relief is chargeable to the common fund of the Leighton Buzzard Union.

5. REMOVABILITY OF PERSONS BORN IN SCOTLAND, IRELAND, OR THE CHANNEL ISLANDS.

23rd June, 1852.

Clerk of Northwich Union.—Inquired whether the act 9 & 10 Vic. c. 66, extends to persons born in Ireland, Scotland, or the Channel Islands, who have not gained settlements in England, but have become chargeable to a parish therein.

Ans.—The Poor Law Commissioners in 1846 were advised by the then Attorney General and Solicitor General, that the 9 & 10 Vic. c. 66, applied to the removal as well of persons born in Scotland, Ireland, or the Channel Islands, as of persons having settlements in England, so as to over-ride, *pro tanto*, the provisions of the 8 & 9 Vic. c. 117. The Board have reason to believe that this construction of the law has been very generally concurred in; and though they are not aware of any express decision of the courts upon the point, they think it may be useful to direct your attention to the remarks of Mr. Justice Patteson in the case of Reg. *v.* Giles without, Cripplegate (L. J. R., N. S. M. C. 26.)

XIV. — REMOVAL. — RECOVERY OF RELIEF AND COSTS UNDER SUSPENDED ORDERS OF REMOVAL.

26th Feb., 1851.

Mr. H. J. Pech, Overseer of Baldock, Hitchen Union.—On the 5th March, 1849, an order was obtained for the removal of William O. from the parish of Baldock to the parish of Eaton Socon, and was suspended, and the notice of the same sent by post to the overseers of the latter parish, on the 15th of that month. The sum of £21. 13*s.* 1¾*d.* is now due to the parish of Baldock, for relief afforded to the pauper since the notice of the order was posted. A similar order was obtained and suspended on the 12th March 1849, in the case of Elizabeth H., legally settled in the parish of Walkem, and the notice to the overseers was posted on the 2nd April. In this case the sum of £12. 6*s.* 9*d.* is due for relief given to the pauper. In neither case has the suspension been taken off, or any order of justices been made for payment of the relief and costs, but applications have been made to the overseers of the parishes of Eaton Socon, and Walkem, for payment of the same, but without success. Inquired what course should be adopted to obtain payment of the money.

Ans.—It is probable, that according to a late decision of the Court of Queen's Bench, in *re* the Overseers of Chedgrave, (20 L. J. R., N. S. M. C. 23,) the statute 4 & 5 Wm. 4, c. 76, sec. 84, may be available; and that the justices may make an order for the repayment of the costs of the relief in the cases referred to, if notice of the order has been duly served within the time specified in that section, and the order for the removal of the paupers be submitted to. This is not, however, a course which has been hitherto pursued, so far as the Board are aware, and they cannot express any positive opinion as to its legality in a case where the pauper has not been removed.

London: Printed by Order of the Poor Law Board, by BLACKBURN & BURT, 90½, Holborn Hill, and Published by CHARLES KNIGHT, 90, Fleet Street.